Webster's
Spanish-English
Dictionary

Created in Cooperation with
the Editors of
MERRIAM-WEBSTER

FEDERAL
STREET
PRESS

A Division of Merriam-Webster, Incorporated
Springfield, Massachusetts

This 2009 edition published by
Federal Street Press,
A Division of Merriam-Webster, Incorporated
P.O. Box 281
Springfield, MA 01102

Federal Street Press books are available for bulk purchase for sales promotion and premium use. For
details write the manager of special sales, Federal
Street Press, P.O. Box 281, Springfield, MA 01102

ISBN 978-1-59695-062-7

Printed in the United States of America

09   10   11   12   5   4   3   2   1

Contents

Preface 4a

Conjugation of Spanish Verbs 6a

Irregular English Verbs 18a

Abbreviations Used in This Work 23a

Pronunciation Symbols 24a

Spanish-English Dictionary 1

English-Spanish Dictionary 187

Common Spanish Abbreviations 417

Spanish Numbers 422

English Numbers 424

Preface

This Spanish-English Dictionary is a concise reference to the core vocabulary of Spanish and English. Its 40,000 entries and over 50,000 translations provide up-to-date coverage of the basic vocabulary and idioms in both languages. In addition, the book includes many specifically Latin-American words and phrases.

IPA (International Phonetic Alphabet) pronunciations are given for all English words. Included as well are tables of irregular verbs in both languages and the most common Spanish and English abbreviations.

This book shares many details of presentation with larger Spanish-English Dictionaries, but for reasons of conciseness it also has a number of features uniquely its own. Users need to be familiar with the following major features of this dictionary.

Main entries follow one another in strict alphabetical order, without regard to intervening spaces or hyphens. The Spanish letter combinations *ch* and *ll* are alphabetized within the letters *C* and *L*; however, the Spanish letter *ñ* is alphabetized separately between *N* and *O*.

Homographs (words spelled the same but having different meanings or parts of speech) are run on at a single main entry if they are closely related. Run-on homograph entries are replaced in the text by a boldfaced swung dash (as **haber** . . . *v aux* . . . — ~ *nm* . . .). Homographs of distinctly different origin (as **date¹** and **date²**) are given separate entries.

Run-on entries for related words that are not homographs may also follow the main entry. Thus we have the main entry **calcular** *vt* followed by run-on entries for — **calculador, -dora** *adj* . . . — **calculadora** *nf* . . . and — **cálculo** *nm*. However, if a related word falls later in the alphabet than a following unrelated main entry, it will be entered at its own place; **ear** and its run-on — **eardrum** precede the main entry **earl** which is followed by the main entry **earlobe**.

Variant spellings appear at the main entry separated by *or* (as **judgment** *or* **judgement, paralyze** *or Brit* **paralyse,** and **cacahuate** *or* **cacahuete**).

Inflected forms of English verbs, adjectives, adverbs, and nouns are shown when they are irregular (as **wage** . . . **waged; waging; ride** . . . **rode; ridden; good** . . . **better, best;** and **fly** . . . *n, pl* **flies**) or when there might be doubt about their spelling (as **ego** . . . *n, pl* **egos**). Inflected forms of Spanish irregular verbs are shown in the section Conjugation of Spanish Verbs on page 6a; numerical references to this table are included at the main entry (as **poseer** {20} *vt*). Irregular plurals of Spanish nouns or adjectives are shown at the main entry (as **ladrón, -drona** *n, mpl* **-drones**).

Cross-references are provided to lead the user to the appropriate main entry (as **mice → mouse** and **sobrestimar → sobreestimar**).

Pronunciation information is either given explicitly or implied for all English words. Pronunciation of Spanish words is assumed to be regular and is generally omitted; it is included, however, for certain foreign borrowings (as **pizza** ['pitsa, 'pisa]). A full list of the pronunciation symbols used appears on page 24a.

The grammatical function of entry words is indicated by an italic **functional label** (as *vt, adj,* and *nm*). Italic **usage labels** may be added at the entry or sense as well (as **timbre** *nm* . . . **4** *Lat* : postage stamp, **center** *or Brit* **centre** . . . *n* . . ., or **garra** *nf* . . . **2** *fam* : hand, paw). These labels are also included in the translations (as **bag** *n* . . . **2** HANDBAG : bolso *m,* cartera *f Lat*).

Usage notes are occasionally placed before a translation to clarify meaning or use (as **que** *conj* . . . **2** (*in comparisons*) : than).

Synonyms may appear before the translation word(s) in order to provide context for the meaning of an entry word or sense (as **sitio** *nm* . . . **2** ESPACIO : room, space; or **meet** . . . *vt* . . . **2** SATISFY : satisfacer).

Bold notes are sometimes used before a translation to introduce a plural sense or a common phrase using the main entry word (as **mueble** *nm* . . . **2 ~s** *nmpl* : furniture, furnishings, or **call** . . . *vt* . . . **2 ~ off** : cancelar). Note that when an entry word is repeated in a bold note, it is replaced by a swung dash.

Conjugation of Spanish Verbs

Simple Tenses

Tense	Regular Verbs Ending in -AR hablar	
PRESENT INDICATIVE	hablo	hablamos
	hablas	habláis
	habla	hablan
PRESENT SUBJUNCTIVE	hable	hablemos
	hables	habléis
	hable	hablen
PRETERIT INDICATIVE	hablé	hablamos
	hablaste	hablasteis
	habló	hablaron
IMPERFECT INDICATIVE	hablaba	hablábamos
	hablabas	hablabais
	hablaba	hablaban
IMPERFECT SUBJUNCTIVE	hablara	habláramos
	hablaras	hablarais
	hablara	hablaran
	or	
	hablase	hablásemos
	hablases	hablaseis
	hablase	hablasen
FUTURE INDICATIVE	hablaré	hablaremos
	hablarás	hablaréis
	hablará	hablarán
FUTURE SUBJUNCTIVE	hablare	habláremos
	hablares	hablareis
	hablare	hablaren
CONDITIONAL	hablaría	hablaríamos
	hablarías	hablaríais
	hablaría	hablarían
IMPERATIVE		hablemos
	habla	hablad
	hable	hablen
PRESENT PARTICIPLE (GERUND)	hablando	
PAST PARTICIPLE	hablado	

Regular Verbs Ending in **-ER**		Regular Verbs Ending in **-IR**	
comer		vivir	
como	comemos	vivo	vivimos
comes	coméis	vives	vivís
come	comen	vive	viven
coma	comamos	viva	vivamos
comas	comáis	vivas	viváis
coma	coman	viva	vivan
comí	comimos	viví	vivimos
comiste	comisteis	viviste	vivisteis
comió	comieron	vivió	vivieron
comía	comíamos	vivía	vivíamos
comías	comíais	vivías	vivíais
comía	comían	vivía	vivían
comiera	comiéramos	viviera	viviéramos
comieras	comierais	vivieras	vivierais
comiera	comieran	viviera	vivieran
or		*or*	
comiese	comiésemos	viviese	viviésemos
comieses	comieseis	vivieses	vivieseis
comiese	comiesen	viviese	viviesen
comeré	comeremos	viviré	viviremos
comerás	comeréis	vivirás	viviréis
comerá	comerán	vivirá	vivirán
comiere	comiéremos	viviere	viviéremos
comieres	comiereis	vivieres	viviereis
comiere	comieren	viviere	vivieren
comería	comeríamos	viviría	viviríamos
comerías	comeríais	vivirías	viviríais
comería	comerían	viviría	vivirían
	comamos		vivamos
come	comed	vive	vivid
coma	coman	viva	vivan
comiendo		viviendo	
comido		vivido	

Compound Tenses

1. Perfect Tenses

The perfect tenses are formed with *haber* and the past participle:

PRESENT PERFECT
> he hablado, etc. (*indicative*);
> haya hablado, etc. (*subjunctive*)

PAST PERFECT
> había hablado, etc. (*indicative*);
> hubiera hablado, etc. (*subjunctive*)
> *or*
> hubiese hablado, etc. (*subjunctive*)

PRETERIT PERFECT
> hube hablado, etc. (*indicative*)

FUTURE PERFECT
> habré hablado, etc. (*indicative*)

CONDITIONAL PERFECT
> habría hablado, etc. (*indicative*)

2. Progressive Tenses

The progressive tenses are formed with *estar* and the present participle:

PRESENT PROGRESSIVE
> estoy llamando, etc. (*indicative*);
> esté llamando, etc. (*subjunctive*)

IMPERFECT PROGRESSIVE
> estaba llamando, etc. (*indicative*);
> estuviera llamando, etc. (*subjunctive*)
> *or*
> estuviese llamando, etc. (*subjunctive*)

PRETERIT PROGRESSIVE
> estuve llamando, etc. (*indicative*)

FUTURE PROGRESSIVE
> estaré llamando, etc. (*indicative*)

CONDITIONAL PROGRESSIVE
     estaría llamando, etc. (*indicative*)

PRESENT PERFECT PROGRESSIVE
     he estado llamando, etc. (*indicative*);
     haya estado llamando, etc. (*subjunctive*)

PAST PERFECT PROGRESSIVE
     había estado llamando, etc. (*indicative*);
     hubiera estado llamando, etc. (*subjunctive*)
     or
     hubiese estado llamando, etc. (*subjunctive*)

Irregular Verbs

The *imperfect subjunctive*, the *future subjunctive*, the *conditional*, and most forms of the *imperative* are not included in the model conjugations, but can be derived as follows:

The *imperfect subjunctive* and the *future subjunctive* are formed from the third person plural form of the preterit tense by removing the last syllable (*-ron*) and adding the appropriate suffix:

PRETERIT INDICATIVE, THIRD PERSON PLURAL (querer)	quisieron
IMPERFECT SUBJUNCTIVE (querer)	quisiera, quisieras, etc. *or* quisiese, quisieses, etc.
FUTURE SUBJUNCTIVE (querer)	quisiere, quisieres, etc.

The conditional uses the same stem as the future indicative:

FUTURE INDICATIVE (poner)	pondré, pondrás, etc.
CONDITIONAL (poner)	pondría, pondrías, etc.

The third person singular, first person plural, and third person plural forms of the *imperative* are the same as the corresponding forms of the present subjunctive.

The second person singular form of the *imperative* is generally the same as the third person singular of the present indicative. Exceptions are noted in the model conjugations list.

The second person plural (*vosotros*) form of the *imperative* is formed by removing the final -r of the infinitive form and adding a -d (ex.: *oír* → *oíd*).

Model Conjugations of Irregular Verbs

The model conjugations below include the following simple tenses: the *present indicative* (*IND*), the *present subjunctive* (*SUBJ*), the *preterit indicative* (*PRET*), the *imperfect indicative* (*IMPF*), the *future indicative* (*FUT*), the second person singular form of the *imperative* (*IMPER*) when it differs from the third person singular of the present indicative, the *gerund* or *present participle* (*PRP*), and the *past participle* (*PP*). Each set of conjugations is preceded by the corresponding infinitive form of the verb, shown in bold type. Only tenses containing irregularities are listed, and the irregular verb forms within each tense are displayed in bold type.

Each irregular verb entry in the Spanish-English section of this dictionary is cross-referenced by number to one of the following model conjugations. These cross-reference numbers are shown in curly braces { } immediately following the entry's functional label.

1 **abolir** *(defective verb)* : *IND* abolimos, abolís *(other forms not used);* *SUBJ* *(not used);* *IMPER* *(only second person plural is used)*

2 **abrir** : *PP* abierto

3 **actuar** : *IND* **actúo, actúas, actúa,** actuamos, actuáis, **actúan;** *SUBJ* **actúe, actúes, actúe,** actuemos, actuéis, **actúen;** *IMPER* **actúa**

4 **adquirir** : *IND* **adquiero, adquieres, adquiere,** adquirimos, adquirís, **adquieren;** *SUBJ* **adquiera, adquieras, adquiera,** adquiramos, adquiráis, **adquieran;** *IMPER* **adquiere**

5 **airar** : *IND* **aíro, aíras, aíra,** airamos, airáis, **aíran;** *SUBJ* **aíre, aíres, aíre,** airemos, airéis, **aíren;** *IMPER* **aíra**

6 **andar** : *PRET* **anduve, anduviste, anduvo, anduvimos, anduvisteis, anduvieron**

7 **asir** : *IND* **asgo,** ases, ase, asimos, asís, asen; *SUBJ* **asga, asgas, asga, asgamos, asgáis, asgan**

8 **aunar** : *IND* **aúno, aúnas, aúna,** aunamos, aunáis, **aúnan;** *SUBJ* **aúne, aúnes, aúne,** aunemos, aunéis, **aúnen;** *IMPER* **aúna**

9 **avergonzar** : *IND* **avergüenzo, avergüenzas, avergüenza,** avergonzamos, avergonzáis, **avergüenzan;** *SUBJ* **avergüence, avergüences, avergüence,** avergoncemos, avergoncéis, **avergüencen;** *PRET* **avergoncé;** *IMPER* **avergüenza**

10 **averiguar** : *SUBJ* **averigüe, averigües, averigüe, averigüe-mos, averigüéis, averigüen;** *PRET* **averigüé,** averiguaste, averiguó, averiguamos, averiguasteis, averiguaron

11 **bendecir** : *IND* **bendigo, bendices, bendice,** bendecimos, bendecís, **bendicen;** *SUBJ* **bendiga, bendigas, bendiga, bendigamos, bendigáis, bendigan;** *PRET* **bendije, bendijiste, bendijo, bendijimos, bendijisteis, bendijeron;** *IMPER* **bendice**

12 **caber** : *IND* **quepo,** cabes, cabe, cabemos, cabéis, caben; *SUBJ* **quepa, quepas, quepa, quepamos, quepáis, quepan;** *PRET* **cupe, cupiste, cupo, cupimos, cupisteis, cupieron;** *FUT* **cabré, cabrás, cabrá, cabremos, cabréis, cabrán**

13 **caer** : *IND* **caigo,** caes, cae, caemos, caéis, caen; *SUBJ* **caiga, caigas, caiga, caigamos, caigáis, caigan;** *PRET* **caí, caíste, cayó, caímos, caísteis, cayeron;** *PRP* **cayendo;** *PP* **caído**

14 **cocer** : *IND* **cuezo, cueces, cuece,** cocemos, cocéis, **cuecen;** *SUBJ* **cueza, cuezas, cueza, cozamos, cozáis, cuezan;** *IMPER* **cuece**

15 **coger** : *IND* **cojo,** coges, coge, cogemos, cogéis, cogen; *SUBJ* **coja, cojas, coja, cojamos, cojáis, cojan**

16 **colgar** : *IND* **cuelgo, cuelgas, cuelga,** colgamos, colgáis, **cuelgan;** *SUBJ* **cuelgue, cuelgues, cuelgue, colguemos, colguéis, cuelguen;** *PRET* **colgué,** colgaste, colgó, colgamos, colgasteis, colgaron; *IMPER* **cuelga**

17 **concernir** *(defective verb; used only in the third person singular and plural of the present indicative, present subjunctive, and imperfect subjunctive)* see 25 **discernir**

18 **conocer** : *IND* **conozco,** conoces, conoce, conocemos, conocéis, conocen; *SUBJ* **conozca, conozcas, conozca, conozcamos, conozcáis, conozcan**

19 **contar** : *IND* **cuento, cuentas, cuenta,** contamos, contáis, **cuentan;** *SUBJ* **cuente, cuentes, cuente,** contemos, contéis, **cuenten;** *IMPER* **cuenta**

20 **creer** : *PRET* **creí, creíste, creyó, creímos, creísteis, creyeron;** *PRP* **creyendo;** *PP* **creído**

21 **cruzar** : *SUBJ* **cruce, cruces, cruce, crucemos, crucéis, crucen;** *PRET* **crucé,** cruzaste, cruzó, cruzamos, cruzasteis, cruzaron

22 **dar** : *IND* **doy,** das, da, damos, **dais,** dan; *SUBJ* **dé,** des, **dé,** demos, **deis,** den; *PRET* **di, diste, dio, dimos, disteis, dieron**

23 **decir** : *IND* **digo, dices, dice,** decimos, decís, **dicen;** *SUBJ* **diga, digas, diga, digamos, digáis, digan;** *PRET* **dije, dijiste, dijo,** dijimos, dijisteis, dijeron; *FUT* **diré, dirás, dirá, diremos, diréis, dirán;** *IMPER* **di;** *PRP* **diciendo;** *PP* **dicho**

24 **delinquir** : *IND* **delinco,** delinques, delinque, delinquimos, delinquís, delinquen; *SUBJ* **delinca, delincas, delinca, delincamos, delincáis, delincan**

25 **discernir** : *IND* **discierno, disciernes, discierne,** discernimos, discernís, **disciernen;** *SUBJ* **discierna, disciernas, discierna,** discernamos, discernáis, **disciernan;** *IMPER* **discierne**

26 **distinguir** : *IND* **distingo,** distingues, distingue, distinguimos, distinguís, distinguen; *SUBJ* **distinga, distingas, distinga, distingamos, distingáis, distingan**

27 **dormir** : *IND* **duermo, duermes, duerme,** dormimos, dormís, **duermen;** *SUBJ* **duerma, duermas, duerma, durmamos, durmáis, duerman;** *PRET* dormí, dormiste, **durmió,** dormimos, dormisteis, **durmieron;** *IMPER* **duerme;** *PRP* **durmiendo**

28 **elegir** : *IND* **elijo, eliges, elige,** elegimos, elegís, **eligen;** *SUBJ* **elija, elijas, elija, elijamos, elijáis, elijan;** *PRET* elegí, elegiste, **eligió,** elegimos, elegisteis, **eligieron;** *IMPER* **elige;** *PRP* **eligiendo**

29 **empezar** : *IND* **empiezo, empiezas, empieza,** empezamos, empezáis, **empiezan;** *SUBJ* **empiece, empieces, empiece, empecemos, empecéis, empiecen;** *PRET* **empecé,** empezaste, empezó, empezamos, empezasteis, empezaron; *IMPER* **empieza**

30 **enraizar** : *IND* **enraízo, enraízas, enraíza,** enraizamos, enraizáis, **enraízan;** *SUBJ* **enraíce, enraíces, enraíce, enraicemos, enraicéis, enraícen;** *PRET* **enraicé,** enraizaste, enraizó, enraizamos, enraizasteis, enraizaron; *IMPER* **enraíza**

31 **erguir** : *IND* **irgo** *or* **yergo, irgues** *or* **yergues, irgue** *or* **yergue,** erguimos, erguís, **irguen** *or* **yerguen;** *SUBJ* **irga** *or* **yerga, irgas** *or* **yergas, irga** *or* **yerga, irgamos, irgáis, irgan** *or* **yergan;** *PRET* erguí, erguiste, **irguió,** erguimos, erguisteis, **irguieron;** *IMPER* **irgue** *or* **yergue;** *PRP* **irguiendo**

32 **errar** : *IND* **yerro, yerras, yerra,** erramos, erráis, **yerran;** *SUBJ* **yerre, yerres, yerre,** erremos, erréis, **yerren;** *IMPER* **yerra**

33 **escribir** : *PP* **escrito**

34 **estar** : *IND* **estoy, estás, está,** estamos, estáis, **están;** *SUBJ* **esté, estés, esté,** estemos, estéis, **estén;** *PRET* **estuve, estuviste, estuvo, estuvimos, estuvisteis, estuvieron;** *IMPER* **está**

35 **exigir** : *IND* **exijo,** exiges, exige, exigimos, exigís, exigen; *SUBJ* **exija, exijas, exija, exijamos, exijáis, exijan**

36 **forzar** : *IND* **fuerzo, fuerzas, fuerza,** forzamos, forzáis, **fuerzan;** *SUBJ* **fuerce, fuerces, fuerce, forcemos, forcéis, fuercen;** *PRET* **forcé,** forzaste, forzó, forzamos, forzasteis, forzaron; *IMPER* **fuerza**

37 **freír** : *IND* **frío, fríes, fríe,** freímos, freís, **fríen;** *SUBJ* **fría, frías, fría,** friamos, friáis, **frían;** *PRET* freí, **freíste, frió, freímos, freísteis,** frieron; *IMPER* **fríe;** *PRP* **friendo;** *PP* **frito**

38 **gruñir** : *PRET* gruñí, **gruñiste, gruñó,** gruñimos, gruñisteis, **gruñeron;** *PRP* **gruñendo**

39 **haber** : *IND* **he, has, ha, hemos,** habéis, **han;** *SUBJ* **haya, hayas, haya, hayamos, hayáis, hayan;** *PRET* **hube, hubiste, hubo, hubimos, hubisteis, hubieron;** *FUT* **habré, habrás, habrá, habremos, habréis, habrán;** *IMPER* **he**

40 **hacer** : *IND* **hago,** haces, hace, hacemos, hacéis, hacen; *SUBJ* **haga, hagas, haga, hagamos, hagáis, hagan;** *PRET* **hice, hiciste, hizo, hicimos, hicisteis, hicieron;** *FUT* **haré, harás, hará, haremos, haréis, harán;** *IMPER* **haz;** *PP* **hecho**

41 **huir** : *IND* **huyo, huyes, huye,** huimos, huís, **huyen;** *SUBJ* **huya, huyas, huya, huyamos, huyáis, huyan;** *PRET* **huí,** huiste, **huyó,** huimos, huisteis, **huyeron;** *IMPER* **huye;** *PRP* **huyendo**

42 **imprimir** : *PP* **impreso**

43 **ir** : *IND* **voy, vas, va, vamos, vais, van;** *SUBJ* **vaya, vayas, vaya, vayamos, vayáis, vayan;** *PRET* **fui, fuiste, fue, fuimos, fuisteis, fueron;** *IMPF* **iba, ibas, iba, íbamos, ibais, iban;** *IMPER* **ve;** *PRP* **yendo;** *PP* **ido**

44 **jugar** : *IND* **juego, juegas, juega,** jugamos, jugáis, **juegan;** *SUBJ* **juegue, juegues, juegue, juguemos, juguéis, jueguen;** *PRET* **jugué,** jugaste, jugó, jugamos, jugasteis, jugaron; *IMPER* **juega**

45 **lucir** : *IND* **luzco,** luces, luce, lucimos, lucís, lucen; *SUBJ* **luzca, luzcas, luzca, luzcamos, luzcáis, luzcan**

46 **morir** : *IND* **muero, mueres, muere,** morimos, morís,

mueren; *SUBJ* **muera, mueras, muera, muramos, muráis, mueran;** *PRET* morí, moriste, **murió,** morimos, moristeis, **murieron;** *IMPER* **muere;** *PRP* **muriendo;** *PP* **muerto**

47 **mover** : *IND* **muevo, mueves, mueve,** movemos, movéis, **mueven;** *SUBJ* **mueva, muevas, mueva,** movamos, mováis, **muevan;** *IMPER* **mueve**

48 **nacer** : *IND* **nazco,** naces, nace, nacemos, nacéis, nacen; *SUBJ* **nazca, nazcas, nazca, nazcamos, nazcáis, nazcan**

49 **negar** : *IND* **niego, niegas, niega,** negamos, negáis, **niegan;** *SUBJ* **niegue, niegues, niegue, neguemos, neguéis, nieguen;** *PRET* **negué,** negaste, negó, negamos, negasteis, negaron; *IMPER* **niega**

50 **oír** : *IND* **oigo, oyes, oye,** oímos, oís, **oyen;** *SUBJ* **oiga, oigas, oiga, oigamos, oigáis, oigan;** *PRET* oí, **oíste, oyó,** oímos, oísteis, **oyeron;** *IMPER* **oye;** *PRP* **oyendo;** *PP* **oído**

51 **oler** : *IND* **huelo, hueles, huele,** olemos, oléis, **huelen;** *SUBJ* **huela, huelas, huela,** olamos, oláis, **huelan;** *IMPER* **huele**

52 **pagar** : *SUBJ* **pague, pagues, pague, paguemos, paguéis, paguen;** *PRET* **pagué,** pagaste, pagó, pagamos, pagasteis, pagaron

53 **parecer** : *IND* **parezco,** pareces, parece, parecemos, parecéis, parecen; *SUBJ* **parezca, parezcas, parezca, parezcamos, parezcáis, parezcan**

54 **pedir** : *IND* **pido, pides, pide,** pedimos, pedís, **piden;** *SUBJ* **pida, pidas, pida, pidamos, pidáis, pidan;** *PRET* pedí, pediste, **pidió,** pedimos, pedisteis, **pidieron;** *IMPER* **pide;** *PRP* **pidiendo**

55 **pensar** : *IND* **pienso, piensas, piensa,** pensamos, pensáis, **piensan;** *SUBJ* **piense, pienses, piense,** pensemos, penséis, **piensen;** *IMPER* **piensa**

56 **perder** : *IND* **pierdo, pierdes, pierde,** perdemos, perdéis, **pierden;** *SUBJ* **pierda, pierdas, pierda,** perdamos, perdáis, **pierdan;** *IMPER* **pierde**

57 **placer** : *IND* **plazco,** places, place, placemos, placéis, placen; *SUBJ* **plazca, plazcas, plazca, plazcamos, plazcáis, plazcan;** *PRET* plací, placiste, plació *or* **plugo,** placimos, placisteis, placieron *or* **pluguieron**

58 **poder** : *IND* **puedo, puedes, puede,** podemos, podéis, **pueden;** *SUBJ* **pueda, puedas, pueda,** podamos, podáis, **puedan;** *PRET*

pude, pudiste, pudo, pudimos, pudisteis, pudieron; *FUT* **podré, podrás, podrá, podremos, podréis, podrán;** *IMPER* **puede;** *PRP* **pudiendo**

59 **podrir** *or* **pudrir : ** *PP* **podrido** (*all other forms based on* pu-drir)

60 **poner : ** *IND* **pongo,** pones, pone, ponemos, ponéis, ponen; *SUBJ* **ponga, pongas, ponga, pongamos, pongáis, pongan;** *PRET* **puse, pusiste, puso, pusimos, pusisteis, pusieron;** *FUT* **pondré, pondrás, pondrá, pondremos, pondréis, pondrán;** *IMPER* **pon;** *PP* **puesto**

61 **producir : ** *IND* **produzco,** produces, produce, producimos, producís, producen; *SUBJ* **produzca, produzcas, produzca, produzcamos, produzcáis, produzcan;** *PRET* **produje, produjiste, produjo, produjimos, produjisteis, produjeron**

62 **prohibir : ** *IND* **prohíbo, prohíbes, prohíbe,** prohibimos, prohibís, **prohíben;** *SUBJ* **prohíba, prohíbas, prohíba,** prohibamos, prohibáis, **prohíban;** *IMPER* **prohíbe**

63 **proveer : ** *PRET* **proveí, proveíste, proveyó, proveímos, proveísteis, proveyeron;** *PRP* **proveyendo;** *PP* **provisto**

64 **querer : ** *IND* **quiero, quieres, quiere,** queremos, queréis, **quieren;** *SUBJ* **quiera, quieras, quiera,** queramos, queráis, **quieran;** *PRET* **quise, quisiste, quiso, quisimos, quisisteis, quisieron;** *FUT* **querré, querrás, querrá, querremos, querréis, querrán;** *IMPER* **quiere**

65 **raer : ** *IND* **rao** *or* **raigo** *or* **rayo,** raes, rae, raemos, raéis, raen; *SUBJ* **raiga** *or* **raya, raigas** *or* **rayas, raiga** *or* **raya, raigamos** *or* **rayamos, raigáis** *or* **rayáis, raigan** *or* **rayan;** *PRET* **raí, raíste, rayó, raímos, raísteis, rayeron;** *PRP* **rayendo;** *PP* **raído**

66 **reír : ** *IND* **río, ríes, ríe, reímos,** reís, **ríen;** *SUBJ* **ría, rías, ría, riamos, riáis, rían;** *PRET* reí, **reíste, rió, reímos, reísteis, rieron;** *IMPER* **ríe;** *PRP* **riendo;** *PP* **reído**

67 **reñir : ** *IND* **riño, riñes, riñe,** reñimos, reñís, **riñen;** *SUBJ* **riña, riñas, riña, riñamos,** riñáis, **riñan;** *PRET* reñí, reñiste, **riñó,** reñimos, reñisteis, **riñeron;** *PRP* **riñendo**

68 **reunir : ** *IND* **reúno, reúnes, reúne,** reunimos, reunís, **reúnen;** *SUBJ* **reúna, reúnas, reúna,** reunamos, reunáis, **reúnan;** *IMPER* **reúne**

69 **roer : ** *IND* **roo** *or* **roigo** *or* **royo,** roes, roe, roemos, roéis, roen;

SUBJ roa *or* roiga *or* roya, roas *or* roigas *or* royas, roa *or* roiga *or* roya, roamos *or* roigamos *or* royamos, roáis *or* roigáis *or* royáis, roan *or* roigan *or* royan; *PRET* roí, roíste, royó, roímos, roísteis, royeron; *PRP* royendo; *PP* roído

70 **romper** : *PP* **roto**

71 **saber** : *IND* **sé**, sabes, sabe, sabemos, sabéis, saben; *SUBJ* **sepa, sepas, sepa, sepamos, sepáis, sepan**; *PRET* **supe, supiste, supo, supimos, supisteis, supieron**; *FUT* **sabré, sabrás, sabrá, sabremos, sabréis, sabrán**

72 **sacar** : *SUBJ* **saque, saques, saque, saquemos, saquéis, saquen**; *PRET* **saqué**, sacaste, sacó, sacamos, sacasteis, sacaron

73 **salir** : *IND* **salgo**, sales, sale, salimos, salís, salen; *SUBJ* **salga, salgas, salga, salgamos, salgáis, salgan**; *FUT* **saldré, saldrás, saldrá, saldremos, saldréis, saldrán**; *IMPER* **sal**

74 **satisfacer** : *IND* **satisfago**, satisfaces, satisface, satisfacemos, satisfacéis, satisfacen; *SUBJ* **satisfaga, satisfagas, satisfaga, satisfagamos, satisfagáis, satisfagan**; *PRET* **satisfice, satisficiste, satisfizo, satisficimos, satificisteis, satisficieron**; *FUT* **satisfaré, satisfarás, satisfará, satisfaremos, satisfaréis, satisfarán**; *IMPER* **satisfaz** *or* **satisface**; *PP* **satisfecho**

75 **seguir** : *IND* **sigo, sigues, sigue**, seguimos, seguís, **siguen**; *SUBJ* **siga, sigas, siga, sigamos, sigáis, sigan**; *PRET* seguí, seguiste, **siguió**, seguimos, seguisteis, **siguieron**; *IMPER* **sigue**; *PRP* **siguiendo**

76 **sentir** : *IND* **siento, sientes, siente**, sentimos, sentís, **sienten**; *SUBJ* **sienta, sientas, sienta, sintamos, sintáis, sientan**; *PRET* sentí, sentiste, **sintió**, sentimos, sentisteis, **sintieron**; *IMPER* **siente**; *PRP* **sintiendo**

77 **ser** : *IND* **soy, eres, es, somos, sois, son**; *SUBJ* **sea, seas, sea, seamos, seáis, sean**; *PRET* **fui, fuiste, fue, fuimos, fuisteis, fueron**; *IMPF* **era, eras, era, éramos, erais, eran**; *IMPER* **sé**; *PRP* **siendo**; *PP* **sido**

78 **soler** (*defective verb; used only in the present, preterit, and imperfect indicative, and the present and imperfect subjunctive*) *see* 47 **mover**

79 **tañer** : *PRET* **tañí**, tañiste, **tañó**, tañimos, tañisteis, **tañeron**; *PRP* **tañendo**

80 **tener** : *IND* **tengo, tienes, tiene**, tenemos, tenéis, **tienen**; *SUBJ* **tenga, tengas, tenga, tengamos, tengáis, tengan**; *PRET* **tuve**,

tuviste, tuvo, tuvimos, tuvisteis, tuvieron; *FUT* **tendré, ten-drás, tendrá, tendremos, tendréis, tendrán;** *IMPER* **ten**

81 **traer** : *IND* **traigo,** traes, trae, traemos, traéis, traen; *SUBJ* **traiga, traigas, traiga, traigamos, traigáis, traigan;** *PRET* **traje, trajiste, trajo, trajimos, trajisteis, trajeron;** *PRP* **trayendo;** *PP* **traído**

82 **trocar** : *IND* **trueco, truecas, trueca,** trocamos, trocáis, **true-can;** *SUBJ* **trueque, trueques, trueque, troquemos, troquéis, truequen;** *PRET* **troqué,** trocaste, trocó, trocamos, trocasteis, trocaron; *IMPER* **trueca**

83 **uncir** : *IND* **unzo,** unces, unce, uncimos, uncís, uncen; *SUBJ* **unza, unzas, unza, unzamos, unzáis, unzan**

84 **valer** : *IND* **valgo,** vales, vale, valemos, valéis, valen; *SUBJ* **valga, valgas, valga, valgamos, valgáis, valgan;** *FUT* **valdré, valdrás, valdrá, valdremos, valdréis, valdrán**

85 **variar** : *IND* **varío, varías, varía,** variamos, variáis, **varían;** *SUBJ* **varíe, varíes, varíe,** variemos, variéis, **varíen;** *IMPER* **varía**

86 **vencer** : *IND* **venzo,** vences, vence, vencemos, vencéis, vencen; *SUBJ* **venza, venzas, venza, venzamos, venzáis, venzan**

87 **venir** : *IND* **vengo, vienes, viene,** venimos, venís, **vienen;** *SUBJ* **venga, vengas, venga, vengamos, vengáis, vengan;** *PRET* **vine, viniste, vino, vinimos, vinisteis, vinieron;** *FUT* **vendré, vendrás, vendrá, vendremos, vendréis, vendrán;** *IMPER* **ven;** *PRP* **viniendo**

88 **ver** : *IND* **veo,** ves, ve, vemos, veis, ven; *PRET* **vi,** viste, **vio,** vimos, visteis, vieron; *IMPER* **ve;** *PRP* **viendo;** *PP* **visto**

89 **volver** : *IND* **vuelvo, vuelves, vuelve,** volvemos, volvéis, **vuel-ven;** *SUBJ* **vuelva, vuelvas, vuelva,** volvamos, volváis, **vuel-van;** *IMPER* **vuelve;** *PP* **vuelto**

90 **yacer** : *IND* **yazco** *or* **yazgo** *or* **yago,** yaces, yace, yacemos, yacéis, yacen; *SUBJ* **yazca** *or* **yazga** *or* **yaga, yazcas** *or* **yazgas** *or* **yagas, yazca** *or* **yazga** *or* **yaga, yazcamos** *or* **yazgamos** *or* **yagamos, yazcáis** *or* **yazgáis** *or* **yagáis, yazcan** *or* **yazgan** *or* **yagan;** *IMPER* **yace** *or* **yaz**

Irregular English Verbs

INFINITIVE	PAST	PAST PARTICIPLE
arise	arose	arisen
awake	awoke	awoken *or* awaked
be	was, were	been
bear	bore	borne
beat	beat	beaten *or* beat
become	became	become
befall	befell	befallen
begin	began	begun
behold	beheld	beheld
bend	bent	bent
beseech	beseeched *or* besought	beseeched *or* besought
beset	beset	beset
bet	bet	bet
bid	bade *or* bid	bidden *or* bid
bind	bound	bound
bite	bit	bitten
bleed	bled	bled
blow	blew	blown
break	broke	broken
breed	bred	bred
bring	brought	brought
build	built	built
burn	burned *or* burnt	burned *or* burnt
burst	burst	burst
buy	bought	bought
can	could	—
cast	cast	cast
catch	caught	caught
choose	chose	chosen
cling	clung	clung
come	came	come
cost	cost	cost
creep	crept	crept
cut	cut	cut
deal	dealt	dealt
dig	dug	dug
do	did	done
draw	drew	drawn

INFINITIVE	PAST	PAST PARTICIPLE
dream	dreamed or dreamt	dreamed or dreamt
drink	drank	drunk or drank
drive	drove	driven
dwell	dwelled or dwelt	dwelled or dwelt
eat	ate	eaten
fall	fell	fallen
feed	fed	fed
feel	felt	felt
fight	fought	fought
find	found	found
flee	fled	fled
fling	flung	flung
fly	flew	flown
forbid	forbade	forbidden
forecast	forecast	forecast
forego	forewent	foregone
foresee	foresaw	foreseen
foretell	foretold	foretold
forget	forgot	forgotten or forgot
forgive	forgave	forgiven
forsake	forsook	forsaken
freeze	froze	frozen
get	got	got or gotten
give	gave	given
go	went	gone
grind	ground	ground
grow	grew	grown
hang	hung	hung
have	had	had
hear	heard	heard
hide	hid	hidden or hid
hit	hit	hit
hold	held	held
hurt	hurt	hurt
keep	kept	kept
kneel	knelt or kneeled	knelt or kneeled
know	knew	known
lay	laid	laid
lead	led	led
lean	leaned	leaned
leap	leaped or leapt	leaped or leapt
learn	learned	learned

INFINITIVE	PAST	PAST PARTICIPLE
leave	left	left
lend	lent	lent
let	let	let
lie	lay	lain
light	lit *or* lighted	lit *or* lighted
lose	lost	lost
make	made	made
may	might	—
mean	meant	meant
meet	met	met
mow	mowed	mowed *or* mown
pay	paid	paid
put	put	put
quit	quit	quit
read	read	read
rend	rent	rent
rid	rid	rid
ride	rode	ridden
ring	rang	rung
rise	rose	risen
run	ran	run
saw	sawed	sawed *or* sawn
say	said	said
see	saw	seen
seek	sought	sought
sell	sold	sold
send	sent	sent
set	set	set
shake	shook	shaken
shall	should	—
shear	sheared	sheared *or* shorn
shed	shed	shed
shine	shone *or* shined	shone *or* shined
shoot	shot	shot
show	showed	shown *or* showed
shrink	shrank *or* shrunk	shrunk *or* shrunken
shut	shut	shut
sing	sang *or* sung	sung
sink	sank *or* sunk	sunk
sit	sat	sat
slay	slew	slain
sleep	slept	slept

INFINITIVE	PAST	PAST PARTICIPLE
slide	slid	slid
sling	slung	slung
smell	smelled *or* smelt	smelled *or* smelt
sow	sowed	sown *or* sowed
speak	spoke	spoken
speed	sped *or* speeded	sped *or* speeded
spell	spelled	spelled
spend	spent	spent
spill	spilled	spilled
spin	spun	spun
spit	spit *or* spat	spit *or* spat
split	split	split
spoil	spoiled	spoiled
spread	spread	spread
spring	sprang *or* sprung	sprung
stand	stood	stood
steal	stole	stolen
stick	stuck	stuck
sting	stung	stung
stink	stank *or* stunk	stunk
stride	strode	stridden
strike	struck	struck
swear	swore	sworn
sweep	swept	swept
swell	swelled	swelled *or* swollen
swim	swam	swum
swing	swung	swung
take	took	taken
teach	taught	taught
tear	tore	torn
tell	told	told
think	thought	thought
throw	threw	thrown
thrust	thrust	thrust
tread	trod	trodden *or* trod
wake	woke	woken *or* waked
waylay	waylaid	waylaid
wear	wore	worn
weave	wove *or* weaved	woven *or* weaved
wed	wedded	wedded
weep	wept	wept
will	would	—

INFINITIVE	PAST	PAST PARTICIPLE
win	won	won
wind	wound	wound
withdraw	withdrew	withdrawn
withhold	withheld	withheld
withstand	withstood	withstood
wring	wrung	wrung
write	wrote	written

Abbreviations in this Work

adj	adjective	*nmf*	masculine or feminine noun
adv	adverb		
adv	adverbial phrase	*nmfpl*	plural noun invariable for gender
algn	alguien (someone)		
art	article	*nmfs & pl*	noun invariable for both gender and number
Brit	Great Britain		
conj	conjunction	*nmpl*	masculine plural noun
conj phr	conjunctive phrase	*nms & pl*	invariable singular or plural masculine noun
esp	especially		
etc	et cetera	*npl*	plural noun
f	feminine	*ns & pl*	noun invariable for plural
fam	familiar or colloquial		
fpl	feminine plural	*pl*	plural
interj	interjection	*pp*	past participle
Lat	Latin America	*prep*	preposition
m	masculine	*prep phr*	prepositional phrase
mf	masculine or feminine	*pron*	pronoun
mpl	masculine plural	*s.o.*	someone
n	noun	*sth*	something
nf	feminine noun	*usu*	usually
nfpl	feminine plural noun	*v*	verb
nfs & pl	invariable singular or plural feminine noun	*v aux*	auxiliary verb
		vi	intransitive verb
nm	masculine noun	*v impers*	impersonal verb
		vr	reflexive verb
		vt	transitive verb

Pronunciation Symbols

VOWELS

æ	ask, bat, glad
ɑ	cot, bomb
a	*New England* aunt, *British* ask, glass, *Spanish* casa
ɛ	egg, bet, fed
ə	about, javelin, Alabama
ə	when italicized as in əl, əm, ən, indicates a syllabic pronunciation of the consonant as in bottle, prism, button
i	very, any, thirty, *Spanish* piña
i:	eat, bead, bee
ɪ	id, bid, pit
o	Ohio, yellower, potato, *Spanish* óvalo
o:	oats, own, zone, blow
ɔ	awl, maul, caught, paw
ʊ	sure, should, could
u:	boot, few, coo
ʌ	under, putt, bud
eɪ	eight, wade, bay
aɪ	ice, bite, tie
aʊ	out, gown, plow
ɔɪ	oyster, coil, boy
:	indicates that the preceding vowel is long. Long vowels are almost always diphthongs in English, but not in Spanish.

STRESS MARKS

ˈ	high stress	**pen**manship
ˌ	low stress	penman**ship**

CONSONANTS

b	baby, labor, cab
d	day, ready, kid
dʒ	just, badger, fudge
ð	then, either, bathe
f	foe, tough, buff
g	go, bigger, bag
h	hot, aha
j	yes, vineyard
k	cat, keep, lacquer, flock
l	law, hollow, boil
m	mat, hemp, hammer, rim
n	new, tent, tenor, run
ŋ	rung, hang, swinger
p	pay, lapse, top
r	rope, burn, tar
s	sad, mist, kiss
ʃ	shoe, mission, slush
t	toe, button, mat
t̬	indicates that some speakers of English pronounce this sound as a voiced alveolar flap [ɾ], as in later, catty, battle
tʃ	choose, batch
θ	thin, ether, bath
v	vat, never, cave
w	wet, software
z	zoo, easy, buzz
ʒ	azure, beige
h, k, *p, t*	when italicized indicate sounds which are present in the pronunciation of some speakers of English but absent in the pronunciation of others, so that *whence* [ˈhwɛnts] can be pronounced as [ˈhwɛns], [ˈhwɛnts], [ˈwɛnts], or [ˈwɛns]

Spanish-English
Dictionary

A

a¹ *nf* : a, first letter of the Spanish alphabet

a² *prep* **1** : to **2** ~ **las dos** : at two o'clock **3 al día siguiente** : (on) the following day **4** ~ **pied** : on foot **5 de lunes** ~ **viernes** : from Monday until Friday **6 tres veces** ~ **la semana** : three times per week **7** ~ **la** : in the manner of, like

abadía *nf* : abbey

abajo *adv* **1** : down, below, downstairs **2** ~ **de** *Lat* : under, beneath **3 de** ~ : (at the) bottom **4 hacia** ~ : downwards

abalanzarse {21} *vr* : hurl oneself, rush

abandonar *vt* **1** : abandon, leave **2** RENUNCIAR A : give up — **abandonarse** *vr* **1** : neglect oneself **2** ~ **a** : give oneself over to — **abandonado, -da** *adj* **1** : abandoned, deserted **2** DESCUIDADO : neglected **3** DESALIÑADO : slovenly — **abandono** *nm* **1** : abandonment, neglect **2 por** ~ : by default

abanico *nm* : fan — **abanicar** {72} *vt* : fan

abaratar *vt* : lower the price of — **abaratarse** *vr* : become cheaper

abarcar {72} *vt* **1** : cover, embrace **2** *Lat* : monopolize

abarrotar *vt* : pack, cram — **abarrotes** *nmpl Lat* **1** : groceries **2 tienda de** ~ : grocery store

abastecer {53} *vt* : supply, stock — **abastecimiento** *nm* : supply, provisions — **abasto** *nm* **1** : supply **2 no dar** ~ **a** : be unable to cope with

abatir *vt* **1** : knock down, shoot down **2** DEPRIMIR : depress — **abatirse** *vr* **1** : get depressed **2** ~ **sobre** : swoop down on — **abatido, -da** *adj* : dejected, depressed — **abatimiento** *nm* : depression, dejection

abdicar {72} *v* : abdicate — **abdicación** *nf, pl* **-ciones** : abdication

abdomen *nm, pl* **-dómenes** : abdomen — **abdominal** *adj* : abdominal

abecé *nm* : ABC — **abecedario** *nm* : alphabet

abedul *nm* : birch

abeja *nf* : bee — **abejorro** *nm* : bumblebee

aberración *nf, pl* **-ciones** : aberration

abertura *nf* : opening

abeto *nm* : fir (tree)

abierto, -ta *adj* : open

abigarrado, -da *adj* : multicolored

abismo *nm* : abyss, chasm — **abismal** *adj* : vast, enormous

abjurar *vi* ~ **de** : abjure

ablandar *vt* : soften (up) — **ablandarse** *vr* : soften

abnegarse {49} *vr* : deny oneself — **abnegado, -da** *adj* : self-sacrificing — **abnegación** *nf, pl* **-ciones** : self-denial

abochornar *vt* : embarrass — **abochornarse** *vr* : get embarrassed

abofetear *vt* : slap

abogado, -da *n* : lawyer — **abogacía** *nf* : legal profession — **abogar** {52} *vi* ~ **por** : plead for, defend

abolengo *nm* : lineage

abolir {1} *vt* : abolish — **abolición** *nf, pl* **-ciones** : abolition

abollar *vt* : dent — **abolladura** *nf* : dent

abominar *vt* : abominate — **abominable** *adj* : abominable — **abominación** *nf, pl* **-ciones** : abomination

abonar *vt* **1** : pay (a bill, etc.) **2** : fertilize (the soil) — **abonarse** *vr* : subscribe — **abonado, -da** *n* : subscriber — **abono** *nm* **1** : payment, installment **2** FERTILIZANTE : fertilizer **3** : season ticket (to the theater, etc.)

abordar *vt* **1** : tackle (a problem) **2** : accost, approach (a person) **3** *Lat* : board — **abordaje** *nm* : boarding

aborigen *nmf, pl* **-rígenes** : aborigine — ~ *adj* : aboriginal, native

aborrecer {53} *vt* : abhor, detest — **aborrecible** *adj* : hateful — **aborrecimiento** *nm* : loathing

abortar *vi* : have a miscarriage — *vt* : abort — **aborto** *nm* : abortion, miscarriage

abotonar *vt* : button — **abotonarse** *vr* : button up

abovedado, -da *adj* : vaulted

abrasar *vt* : burn, scorch — **abrasarse** *vr* : burn up — **abrasador, -dora** *adj* : burning

abrasivo, -va *adj* : abrasive — **abrasivo** *nm* : abrasive

abrazar {21} *vt* : hug, embrace — **abrazarse** *vr* : embrace — **abraza-**

dera *nf* : clamp — **abrazo** *nm* : hug, embrace

abrebotellas *nms & pl* : bottle opener — **abrelatas** *nms & pl* : can opener

abrevadero *nm* : watering trough

abreviar *vt* 1 : shorten, abridge 2 : abbreviate (a word) — **abreviación** *nf*, *pl* **-ciones** : shortening — **abreviatura** *nf* : abbreviation

abridor *nm* : bottle opener, can opener

abrigar {52} *vt* 1 : wrap up (in clothing) 2 ALBERGAR : cherish, harbor — **abrigarse** *vr* : dress warmly — **abrigado, -da** *adj* 1 : sheltered 2 : warm, wrapped up (of persons) — **abrigo** *nm* 1 : coat, overcoat 2 REFUGIO : shelter, refuge

abril *nm* : April

abrillantar *vt* : polish, shine

abrir {2} *vt* 1 : open 2 : unlock, undo — *vi* : open up — **abrirse** *vr* 1 : open up 2 : clear up (of weather)

abrochar *vt* : button, fasten — **abrocharse** *vr* : fasten, do up

abrogar {52} *vt* : annul, repeal

abrumar *vt* : overwhelm — **abrumador, -dora** *adj* : overwhelming, oppressive

abrupto, -ta *adj* 1 ESCARPADO : steep 2 ÁSPERO : rugged, harsh 3 REPENTINO : abrupt

absceso *nm* : abscess

absolución *nf*, *pl* **-ciones** 1 : absolution 2 : acquittal (in law)

absoluto, -ta *adj* 1 : absolute, unconditional 2 **en absoluto** : not at all — **absolutamente** *adv* : absolutely

absolver {89} *vt* 1 : absolve 2 : acquit (in law)

absorber *vt* 1 : absorb 2 : take up (time, energy, etc.) — **absorbente** *adj* 1 : absorbent 2 INTERESANTE : absorbing — **absorción** *nf*, *pl* **-ciones** : absorption — **absorto, -ta** *adj* : absorbed, engrossed

abstemio, -mia *adj* : abstemious — **∼** *n* : teetotaler

abstenerse {80} *vr* : abstain, refrain — **abstención** *nf*, *pl* **-ciones** : abstention — **abstinencia** *nf* : abstinence

abstracción *nf*, *pl* **-ciones** : abstraction — **abstracto, -ta** *adj* : abstract — **abstraer** {81} *vt* : abstract — **abstraerse** *vr* : lose oneself in thought — **abstraído, -da** *adj* : preoccupied

absurdo, -da *adj* : absurd, ridiculous — **absurdo** *nm* : absurdity

abuchear *vt* : boo, jeer — **abucheo** *nm* : booing

abuelo, -la *n* 1 : grandfather, grand-

mother 2 **abuelos** *nmpl* : grandparents

abulia *nf* : apathy, lethargy

abultar *vi* : bulge, be bulky — *vt* : enlarge, expand — **abultado, -da** *adj* : bulky

abundar *vi* : abound, be plentiful — **abundancia** *nf* : abundance — **abundante** *adj* : abundant

aburrir *vt* : bore — **aburrirse** *vr* : get bored — **aburrido, -da** *adj* 1 : bored 2 TEDIOSO : boring — **aburrimiento** *nm* : boredom

abusar *vi* 1 : go too far 2 **∼ de** : abuse — **abusivo, -va** *adj* : outrageous, excessive — **abuso** *nm* : abuse

abyecto, -ta *adj* : abject, wretched

acá *adv* : here, over here

acabar *vi* 1 : finish, end 2 **∼ de** : have just (done something) 3 **∼ con** : put an end to 4 **∼ por** : end up (doing sth) — *vt* : finish — **acabarse** *vr* : come to an end — **acabado, -da** *adj* 1 : finished, perfect 2 AGOTADO : old, wornout — **acabado** *nm* : finish

academia *nf* : academy — **académico, -ca** *adj* : academic

acaecer {53} *vi* : happen, occur

acallar *vt* : quiet, silence

acalorar *vt* : stir up, excite — **acalorarse** *vr* : get worked up — **acalorado, -da** *adj* : emotional, heated

acampar *vi* : camp — **acampada** *nf* **ir de ∼** : go camping

acanalado, -da *adj* 1 : grooved 2 : corrugated (of iron, etc.)

acantilado *nm* : cliff

acaparar *vt* 1 : hoard 2 MONOPOLIZAR : monopolize

acápite *nm Lat* : paragraph

acariciar *vt* 1 : caress 2 : cherish (hopes, ideas, etc.)

ácaro *nm* : mite

acarrear *vt* 1 : haul, carry 2 OCASIONAR : give rise to — **acarreo** *nm* : transport

acaso *adv* 1 : perhaps, maybe 2 **por si ∼** : just in case

acatar *vt* : comply with, respect — **acatamiento** *nm* : compliance, respect

acatarrarse *vr* : catch a cold

acaudalado, -da *adj* : wealthy, rich

acaudillar *vt* : lead

acceder *vi* 1 : agree 2 **∼ a** : gain access to, enter

acceso *nm* 1 : access 2 ENTRADA : entrance 3 : attack, bout (of an illness) — **accesible** *adj* : accessible

accesorio *nm* : accessory — **accesorio, -ria** *adj* : incidental

accidentado, -da *adj* **1** : eventful, turbulent **2** : rough, uneven (of land, etc.) **3** HERIDO : injured — **~** *n* : accident victim

accidental *adj* : accidental — **accidentarse** *vr* : have an accident — **accidente** *nm* **1** : accident **2** : unevenness (of land)

acción *nf, pl* **-ciones 1** : action **2** ACTO : act, deed **3** : share, stock (in finance) — **accionar** *vt* : activate — *vi* : gesticulate — **accionista** *nmf* : stockholder

acebo *nm* : holly

acechar *vt* : watch, stalk — **acecho** *nm* **estar al ~ por** : be on the lookout for

aceite *nm* : oil — **aceitar** *vt* : oil — **aceitera** *nf* **1** : oilcan **2** : cruet (in cookery) **3** *Lat* : oil refinery — **aceitoso, -sa** *adj* : oily

aceituna *nf* : olive

acelerar *v* : accelerate — **acelerarse** *vr* : hurry up — **aceleración** *nf, pl* **-ciones** : acceleration — **acelerador** *nm* : accelerator

acelga *nf* : (Swiss) chard

acentuar {3} *vt* **1** : accent **2** ENFATIZAR : emphasize, stress — **acentuarse** *vr* : stand out — **acento** *nm* **1** : accent **2** ÉNFASIS : stress, emphasis

acepción *nf, pl* **-ciones** : sense, meaning

aceptar *vt* : accept — **aceptable** *adj* : acceptable — **aceptación** *nf, pl* **-ciones 1** : acceptance **2** ÉXITO : success

acequia *nf* : irrigation ditch

acera *nf* : sidewalk

acerbo, -ba *adj* : harsh, caustic

acerca *prep* **~ de** : about, concerning

acercar {72} *vt* : bring near or closer — **acercarse** *vr* : approach, draw near

acero *nm* **1** : steel **2 ~ inoxidable** : stainless steel

acérrimo, -ma *adj* **1** : staunch, steadfast **2** : bitter (of an enemy)

acertar {55} *vt* : guess correctly — *vi* **1** ATINAR : be accurate **2 ~ a** : manage to — **acertado, -da** *adj* : correct, accurate

acertijo *nm* : riddle

acervo *nm* : heritage

acetona *nf* : acetone, nail-polish remover

achacar {72} *vt* : attribute, impute

achacoso, -sa *adj* : sickly

achaparrado, -da *adj* : squat, stocky

achaque *nm* : aches and pains

achatar *vt* : flatten

achicar {72} *vt* **1** : make smaller **2** ACOBARDAR : intimidate **3** : bail out (water) — **achicarse** *vr* : become intimidated

achicharrar *vt* : scorch, burn to a crisp

achicoria *nf* : chicory

aciago, -ga *adj* : fateful, unlucky

acicalar *vt* : dress up, adorn — **acicalarse** *vr* : get dressed up

acicate *nm* **1** : spur **2** INCENTIVO : incentive

ácido, -da *adj* : acid, sour — **acidez** *nf, pl* **-deces** : acidity — **ácido** *nm* : acid

acierto *nm* **1** : correct answer **2** HABILIDAD : skill, sound judgment

aclamar *vt* : acclaim — **aclamación** *nf, pl* **-ciones** : acclaim, applause

aclarar *vt* **1** CLARIFICAR : clarify, explain **2** : rinse (clothing) **3 ~ la voz** : clear one's throat — *vi* : clear up — **aclararse** *vr* : become clear — **aclaración** *nf, pl* **-ciones** : explanation — **aclaratorio, -ria** *adj* : explanatory

aclimatar *vt* : acclimatize — **aclimatarse** *vr* **~ a** : get used to — **aclimatación** *nf, pl* **-ciones** : acclimatization

acné *nm* : acne

acobardar *vt* : intimidate — **acobardarse** *vr* : become frightened

acodarse *vr* **~ en** : lean (one's elbows) on

acoger {15} *vt* **1** REFUGIAR : shelter **2** RECIBIR : receive, welcome — **acogerse** *vr* **1** : take refuge **2 ~ a** : resort to — **acogedor, -dora** *adj* : cozy, welcoming — **acogida** *nf* **1** : welcome **2** REFUGIO : refuge

acolchar *vt* : pad

acólito *nm* MONAGUILLO : altar boy

acometer *vt* **1** : attack **2** EMPRENDER : undertake — *vi* **~ contra** : rush against — **acometida** *nf* : attack, assault

acomodar *vt* **1** ADAPTAR : adjust **2** COLOCAR : put, make a place for — **acomodarse** *vr* **1** : settle in **2 ~ a** : adapt to — **acomodado, -da** *adj* : well-to-do — **acomodaticio, -cia** *adj* : accommodating, obliging — **acomodo** *nm* : job, position

acompañar *vt* **1** : accompany **2** ADJUNTAR : enclose — **acompañamiento** *nm* : accompaniment — **acompañante** *nmf* **1** COMPAÑERO : companion **2** : accompanist (in music)

acompasado, -da *adj* : rhythmic, measured

acondicionar *vt* : fit out, equip — **acondicionado, -da** *adj* : equipped

acongojar *vt* : distress, upset — **acongojarse** *vr* : get upset

aconsejar vt : advise — **aconsejable** adj : advisable

acontecer {53} vi : occur, happen — **acontecimiento** nm : event

acopiar vt : gather, collect — **acopio** nm : collection, stock

acoplar vt : couple, connect — **acoplarse** vr : fit together — **acoplamiento** nm : connection, coupling

acorazado, -da adj : armored — **acorazado** nm : battleship

acordar {19} vt 1 : agree (on) 2 Lat : award — **acordarse** vr : remember

acorde adj 1 : in agreement 2 ~ con : in keeping with — ~ nm : chord (in music)

acordeón nm, pl **-deones** : accordion

acordonar vt 1 : cordon off 2 : lace up (shoes)

acorralar vt : corner, corral

acortar vt : shorten, cut short — **acortarse** vr : get shorter

acosar vt : hound, harass — **acoso** nm : harassment

acostar {19} vt : put to bed — **acostarse** vr 1 : go to bed 2 TUMBARSE : lie down

acostumbrar vt : accustom — vi ~ a : be in the habit of — **acostumbrarse** vr ~ a : get used to — **acostumbrado, -da** adj 1 HABITUADO : accustomed 2 HABITUAL : usual

acotar vt 1 ANOTAR : annotate 2 DELIMITAR : mark off (land) — **acotación** nf, pl **-ciones** : marginal note — **acotado, -da** adj : enclosed

acre adj 1 : pungent 2 MORDAZ : harsh, biting

acrecentar {55} vt : increase — **acrecentamiento** nm : growth, increase

acreditar vt 1 : accredit, authorize 2 PROBAR : prove — **acreditarse** vr : prove oneself — **acreditado, -da** adj 1 : reputable 2 : accredited (in politics, etc.)

acreedor, -dora adj : worthy — ~ n : creditor

acribillar vt 1 : riddle, pepper 2 ~ a : harass with

acrílico nm : acrylic

acrimonia nf or **acritud** nf 1 : pungency 2 RESENTIMIENTO : bitterness, acrimony

acrobacia nf : acrobatics — **acróbata** nmf : acrobat — **acrobático, -ca** adj : acrobatic

acta nf 1 : certificate 2 : minutes pl (of a meeting)

actitud nf 1 : attitude 2 POSTURA : posture, position

activar vt 1 : activate 2 ESTIMULAR : stimulate, speed up — **actividad** nf : activity — **activo, -va** adj : active — **activo** nm : assets pl

acto nm 1 ACCIÓN : act, deed 2 : act (in theater) 3 en el ~ : right away

actor nm : actor — **actriz** nf, pl **-trices** : actress

actual adj : present, current — **actualidad** nf 1 : present time 2 ~es nfpl : current affairs — **actualizar** {21} vt : modernize — **actualización** nf, pl **-ciones** : modernization — **actualmente** adv : at present, nowadays

actuar {3} vi 1 : act, perform 2 ~ de : act as

acuarela nf : watercolor

acuario nm : aquarium

acuartelar vt : quarter (troops)

acuático, -ca adj : aquatic, water

acuchillar vt : knife, stab

acudir vi 1 : go, come 2 ~ a : be present at, attend 3 ~ a : turn to

acueducto nm : aqueduct

acuerdo nm 1 : agreement 2 de ~ : OK, all right 3 de ~ con : in accordance with 4 estar de ~ : agree

acumular vt : accumulate — **acumularse** vr : pile up — **acumulación** nf, pl **-ciones** : accumulation — **acumulador** nm : storage battery — **acumulativo, -va** adj : cumulative

acunar vt : rock

acuñar vt 1 : mint (money) 2 : coin (a word)

acuoso, -sa adj : watery

acupuntura nf : acupuncture

acurrucarse {72} vr : curl up, nestle

acusar vt 1 : accuse 2 MOSTRAR : reveal, show — **acusación** nf, pl **-ciones** : accusation, charge — **acusado, -da** adj : prominent, marked — ~ n : defendant

acuse nm ~ de recibo : acknowledgment of receipt

acústica nf : acoustics — **acústico, -ca** adj : acoustic

adagio nm 1 REFRÁN : adage, proverb 2 : adagio (in music)

adaptar vt 1 : adapt 2 AJUSTAR : adjust, fit — **adaptarse** vr ~ a : adapt to — **adaptable** adj : adaptable — **adaptación** nf, pl **-ciones** : adaptation — **adaptador** nm : adapter (in electricity)

adecuar {8} vt : adapt, make suitable — **adecuarse** vr ~ a : be appropriate for — **adecuado, -da** *adj* : suitable, appropriate

adelantar *vt* **1** : advance, move forward **2** PASAR : overtake **3** : pay in advance — **adelantarse** *vr* **1** : move forward, get ahead **2** : be fast (of a clock) — **adelantado, -da** *adj* **1** : advanced, ahead **2** : fast (of a clock) **3** por ~ : in advance — **adelante** *adv* **1** : ahead, forward **2** ¡~! : come in! **3** más ~ : later on, further on — **adelanto** *nm* **1** : advance **2** or ~ de dinero : advance payment

adelgazar {21} *vt* : make thin — *vi* : lose weight

ademán *nm, pl* **-manes 1** GESTO : gesture **2** ~es *nmpl* : manners **3** en ~ de : as if to

además *adv* **1** : besides, furthermore **2** ~ de : in addition to, as well as

adentro *adv* **1** : inside, within — **adentrarse** *vr* ~ en : go into, get inside of

adepto, -ta *n* : follower, supporter

aderezar {21} *vt* **1** : season, dress — **aderezo** *nm* : dressing, seasoning

adeudar *vt* **1** : debit **2** DEBER : owe — **adeudo** *nm* **1** DÉBITO : debit **2** *Lat* : debt

adherirse {76} *vr* : adhere, stick — **adherencia** *nf* : adherence — **adhesión** *nf, pl* **-siones 1** : adhesion **2** APOYO : support — **adhesivo, -va** *adj* : adhesive — **adhesivo** *nm* : adhesive

adición *nf, pl* **-ciones** : addition — **adicional** *adj* : additional

adicto, -ta *adj* : addicted — ~ *n* : addict

adiestrar *vt* : train

adinerado, -da *adj* : wealthy

adiós *nm, pl* **adioses 1** : farewell **2** ¡~! : good-bye!

aditamento *nm* : attachment, accessory

aditivo *nm* : additive

adivinar *vt* **1** : guess **2** PREDECIR : foretell — **adivinación** *nf, pl* **-ciones** : guessing, prediction — **adivinanza** *nf* : riddle — **adivino, -na** *n* : fortune-teller

adjetivo *nm* : adjective

adjudicar {72} *vt* : award — **adjudicarse** *vr* : appropriate — **adjudicación** *nf, pl* **-ciones** : awarding

adjuntar *vt* : enclose (with a letter, etc.) — **adjunto, -ta** *adj* : enclosed, attached — ~ *n* : assistant

administración *nf, pl* **-ciones 1** : administration **2** : administering (of a drug, etc.) **3** DIRECCIÓN : management — **administrador, -dora** *n* : administrator, manager — **administrar** *vt* **1** : manage, run **2** : administer (a drug, etc.) — **administrativo, -va** *adj* : administrative

admirar *vt* : admire — **admirarse** *vr* : be amazed — **admirable** *adj* : admirable — **admiración** *nf, pl* **-ciones 1** : admiration **2** ASOMBRO : amazement — **admirador, -dora** *n* : admirer

admitir *vt* **1** : admit **2** ACEPTAR : accept — **admisible** *adj* : admissible, acceptable — **admisión** *nf, pl* **-siones 1** : admission **2** ACEPTACIÓN : acceptance

ADN *nm* : DNA

adobe *nm* : adobe

adobo *nm* : marinade

adoctrinar *vt* : indoctrinate — **adoctrinamiento** *nm* : indoctrination

adolecer {53} *vi* ~ de : suffer from

adolescente *adj* & *nmf* : adolescent — **adolescencia** *nf* : adolescence

adonde *conj* : where

adónde *adv* : where

adoptar *vt* : adopt (a child), take (a decision) — **adopción** *nf, pl* **-ciones** : adoption — **adoptivo, -va** *adj* : adopted, adoptive

adoquín *nm, pl* **-quines** : cobblestone

adorar *vt* : adore, worship — **adorable** *adj* : adorable — **adoración** *nf, pl* **-ciones** : adoration, worship

adormecer {53} *vt* **1** : make sleepy **2** ENTUMECER : numb — **adormecerse** *vr* : doze off — **adormecimiento** *nm* : drowsiness — **adormilarse** *vr* : doze

adornar *vt* : decorate, adorn — **adorno** *nm* : ornament, decoration

adquirir {4} *vt* **1** : acquire **2** COMPRAR : purchase — **adquisición** *nf, pl* **-ciones 1** : acquisition **2** COMPRA : purchase

adrede *adv* : intentionally, on purpose

adscribir {33} *vt* : assign, appoint

aduana *nf* : customs (office) — **aduanero, -ra** *adj* : customs — ~ *n* : customs officer

aducir {61} *vt* : cite, put forward

adueñarse *vr* ~ de : take possession of

adular *vt* : flatter — **adulación** *nf, pl* **-ciones** : adulation, flattery — **adulador, -dora** *adj* : flattering — ~ *n* : flatterer

adulterar *vt* : adulterate

adulterio *nm* : adultery — **adúltero, -ra** *n* : adulterer

adulto, -ta *adj* & *n* : adult

adusto, -ta *adj* : stern, severe

advenedizo, -za *n* : upstart

advenimiento *nm* : advent, arrival

adverbio *nm* : adverb — **adverbial** *adj* : adverbial

adversario, -ria *n* : adversary, opponent — **adverso, -sa** *adj* : adverse — **adversidad** *nf* : adversity

advertir {76} *vt* **1** AVISAR : warn **2** NOTAR : notice — **advertencia** *nf* : warning

adviento *nm* : Advent

adyacente *adj* : adjacent

aéreo, -rea *adj* : aerial, air

aerobic *nm* : aerobics *pl*

aerodinámico, -ca *adj* : aerodynamic

aeródromo *nm* : airfield

aerolínea *nf* : airline

aeromozo, -za *n* : flight attendant, steward *m*, stewardess *f*

aeronave *nf* : aircraft

aeropuerto *nm* : airport

aerosol *nm* : aerosol, spray

afable *adj* : affable — **afabilidad** *nf* : affability

afán *nm*, *pl* **afanes 1** ANHELO : eagerness **2** EMPEÑO : effort, hard work — **afanarse** *vr* : toil — **afanosamente** *adv* : industriously, busily — **afanoso, -sa** *adj* **1** : eager **2** TRABAJOSO : arduous

afear *vt* : make ugly, disfigure

afección *nf*, *pl* **-ciones** : ailment, complaint

afectar *vt* : affect — **afectación** *nf*, *pl* **-ciones** : affectation — **afectado, -da** *adj* : affected

afectivo, -va *adj* : emotional

afecto *nm* : affection — **afecto, -ta** *adj* ~ **a** : fond of — **afectuoso, -sa** *adj* : affectionate, caring

afeitar *vt* : shave — **afeitarse** *vr* : shave — **afeitada** *nf* : shave

afeminado, -da *adj* : effeminate

aferrarse {55} *vr* : cling, hold on

afianzar {21} *vt* : secure, strengthen — **afianzarse** *vr* : become established

afiche *nm* *Lat* : poster

afición *nf*, *pl* **-ciones 1** : penchant, fondness **2** PASATIEMPO : hobby — **aficionado, -da** *n* **1** ENTUSIASTA : enthusiast, fan **2** AMATEUR : amateur — **aficionarse** *vr* ~ **a** : become interested in

afilar *vt* : sharpen — **afilado, -da** *adj* : sharp — **afilador** *nm* : sharpener

afiliarse *vr* ~ **a** : join, become a member of — **afiliación** *nf*, *pl* **-ciones** : affiliation — **afiliado, -da** *adj* : affiliated

afín *adj*, *pl* **afines** : related, similar — **afinidad** *nf* : affinity, similarity

afinar *vt* **1** : tune **2** PULIR : perfect, refine

afirmar *vt* **1** : state, affirm **2** REFORZAR : strengthen — **afirmación** *nf*, *pl* **-ciones** : statement, affirmation — **afirmativo, -va** *adj* : affirmative

afligir {35} *vt* **1** : afflict **2** APENAR : distress — **afligirse** *vr* : grieve — **aflic-** ción *nf*, *pl* **-ciones** : grief, sorrow — **afligido -da** *adj* : sorrowful, distressed

aflojar *vt* : loosen, slacken — *vi* : ease up — **aflojarse** *vr* : become loose, slacken

aflorar *vi* : come to the surface, emerge — **afloramiento** *nm* : outcrop

afluencia *nf* : influx — **afluente** *nm* : tributary

afortunado, -da *adj* : fortunate, lucky — **afortunadamente** *adv* : fortunately

afrentar *vt* : insult — **afrenta** *nf* : affront, insult

africano, -na *adj* : African

afrontar *vt* : confront, face

afuera *adv* **1** : out **2** : outside, outdoors — **afueras** *nfpl* : outskirts

agachar *vt* : lower — **agacharse** *vr* : crouch, stoop

agalla *nf* **1** BRANQUIA : gill **2 tener** ~**s** *fam* : have guts

agarrar *vt* **1** ASIR : grasp **2** *Lat* : catch — **agarrarse** *vr* : hold on, cling — **agarradera** *nf* *Lat* : handle — **agarrado, -da** *adj* *fam* : stingy — **agarre** *nm* : grip, grasp — **agarrón** *nm*, *pl* **-rones** : tug, pull

agasajar *vt* : fête, wine and dine — **agasajo** *nm* : lavish attention

agave *nm* : agave

agazaparse *vr* : crouch down

agencia *nf* : agency, office — **agente** *nmf* : agent, officer

agenda *nf* **1** : agenda **2** LIBRETA : notebook

ágil *adj* : agile — **agilidad** *nf* : agility

agitar *vt* **1** : agitate, shake **2** : wave, flap (wings, etc.) — **agitarse** *vr* **1** : toss about **2** INQUIETARSE : get upset — **agitación** *nf*, *pl* **-ciones 1** : agitation, shaking **2** INTRANQUILIDAD : restlessness — **agitado, -da** *adj* **1** : agitated, excited **2** : choppy, rough (of the sea)

aglomerar *vt* : amass — **aglomerarse** *vr* : crowd together

agnóstico, -ca *adj* & *n* : agnostic

agobiar *vt* **1** : oppress **2** ABRUMAR : overwhelm — **agobiado, -da** *adj* : weary, weighed down — **agobiante** *adj* : oppressing, oppressive

agonizar {21} *vi* : be dying — **agonía** *nf* **1** : death throes **2** PENA : agony — **agonizante** *adj* : dying

agorero, -ra *adj* : ominous

agostar *vt* : wither

agosto *nm* : August

agotar *vt* **1** : deplete, use up **2** CANSAR : exhaust, weary — **agotarse** *vr* **1**

: run out, give out 2 CANSARSE : get tired — **agotado, -da** *adj* 1 CANSADO : exhausted 2 : sold out — **agotador, -dora** *adj* : exhausting — **agotamiento** *nm* : exhaustion

agraciado, -da *adj* 1 : attractive 2 AFORTUNADO : fortunate

agradar *vi* : be pleasing — **agradable** *adj* : pleasant, agreeable — **agrado** *nm* 1 : taste, liking 2 con ~ : with pleasure

agradecer {53} *vt* : be grateful for, thank — **agradecido, -da** *adj* : grateful — **agradecimiento** *nm* : gratitude

agrandar *vt* : enlarge — **agrandarse** *vr* : grow larger

agrario, -ria *adj* : agrarian, agricultural

agravar *vt* 1 : make heavier 2 EMPEORAR : aggravate, worsen — **agravarse** *vr* : get worse

agraviar *vt* : insult — **agravio** *nm* : insult

agredir {1} *vt* : attack

agregar {52} *vt* 1 : add, attach — **agregado, -da** *n* : attaché — **agregado** *nm* : aggregate

agresión *nf, pl* **-siones** : aggression, attack — **agresividad** *nf* : aggressiveness — **agresivo, -va** *adj* : aggressive — **agresor, -sora** *n* : aggressor, attacker

agreste *adj* : rugged, wild

agriar *vt* : sour — **agriarse** *vr* 1 : turn sour (of milk, etc.) 2 : become embittered

agrícola *adj* : agricultural — **agricultura** *nf* : agriculture, farming — **agricultor, -tora** *n* : farmer

agridulce *adj* 1 : bittersweet 2 : sweet-and-sour (in cooking)

agrietar *vt* : crack — **agrietarse** *vr* 1 : crack 2 : chap

agrimensor, -sora *n* : surveyor

agrio, agria *adj* : sour

agrupar *vt* : group together — **agruparse** *vr* : form a group — **agrupación** *nf, pl* **-ciones** : group, association — **agrupamiento** *nm* : grouping

agua *nf* 1 : water 2 ~ oxigenada : hydrogen peroxide 3 ~s negras *or* ~s residuales : sewage

aguacate *nm* : avocado

aguacero *nm* : downpour

aguado, -da *adj* 1 : watery 2 *Lat fam* : soft, flabby — **aguar** {10} *vt* 1 : water down, dilute 2 ~ la fiesta *fam* : spoil the party

aguafuerte *nm* : etching

aguanieve *nf* : sleet

aguantar *vt* 1 SOPORTAR : bear, withstand 2 SOSTENER : hold — *vi* : hold out, last — **aguantarse** *vr* 1 : resign oneself 2 CONTENERSE : restrain oneself — **aguante** *nm* 1 : patience 2 RESISTENCIA : endurance

aguardar *vt* : await

aguardiente *nm* : clear brandy

aguarrás *nm* : turpentine

agudo, -da *adj* 1 : acute, sharp 2 : shrill, high-pitched (in music) — **agudeza** *nf* 1 : sharpness 2 : witticism

agüero *nm* : augury, omen

aguijón *nm, pl* **-jones** 1 : stinger (of an insect) 2 ESTÍMULO : goad, stimulus — **aguijonear** *vt* : goad

águila *nf* : eagle

aguja *nf* 1 : needle 2 : hand (of a clock) 3 : spire (of a church)

agujero *nm* : hole

agujeta *nf* 1 *Lat* : shoelace 2 ~s *nfpl* : (muscular) stiffness

aguzar {21} *vt* 1 : sharpen 2 ~ el oído : prick up one's ears

ahí *adv* 1 : there 2 por ~ : somewhere, thereabouts

ahijado, -da *n* : godchild, godson *m*, goddaughter *f*

ahínco *nm* : eagerness, zeal

ahogar {52} *vt* 1 : drown 2 ASFIXIAR : smother — **ahogarse** *vr* : drown — **ahogo** *nm* : breathlessness

ahondar *vt* : deepen — *vi* : elaborate, go into detail

ahora *adv* 1 : now 2 ~ mismo : right now

ahorcar {72} *vt* : hang, kill by hanging — **ahorcarse** *vr* : hang oneself

ahorita *adv Lat fam* : right now

ahorrar *vt* : save, spare — *vi* : save up — **ahorrarse** *vr* : spare oneself — **ahorro** *nm* : saving

ahuecar {72} *vt* 1 : hollow out 2 : cup (one's hands)

ahumar {8} *vt* : smoke, cure — **ahumado, -da** *adj* : smoked

ahuyentar *vt* : scare away, chase away

airado, -da *adj* : irate, angry

aire *nm* 1 : air 2 ~ acondicionado : air-conditioning 3 al ~ libre : in the open air, outdoors — **airear** *vt* : air, air out

aislar {5} *vt* 1 : isolate 2 : insulate (in electricity) — **aislamiento** *nm* 1 : isolation 2 : (electrical) insulation

ajar *vt* 1 : crumple, wrinkle 2 ESTROPEAR : spoil

ajedrez *nm* : chess

ajeno, -na *adj* 1 : someone else's 2 EXTRAÑO : alien 3 ~ a : foreign to

ajetreado, -da *adj* : hectic, busy —

ajetrearse vr : bustle about — **ajetreo** nm : hustle and bustle
ají nm, pl **ajíes** Lat : chili pepper
ajo nm : garlic
ajustar vt 1 : adjust, adapt 2 ACORDAR : agree on 3 SALDAR : settle — **ajustarse** vr : fit, conform — **ajustable** adj : adjustable — **ajustado, -da** adj 1 : close, tight 2 CEÑIDO : tight-fitting — **ajuste** nm : adjustment
ajusticiar vt : execute, put to death
al (contraction of **a** and **el**) → a²
ala nf 1 : wing 2 : brim (of a hat)
alabanza nf : praise — **alabar** vt : praise
alacena nf : cupboard, larder
alacrán nm, pl **-cranes** : scorpion
alado, -da adj : winged
alambre nm : wire
alameda nf 1 : poplar grove 2 : tree-lined avenue — **álamo** nm : poplar
alarde nm : show, display — **alardear** vi : boast
alargar {52} vt 1 : extend, lengthen 2 PROLONGAR : prolong — **alargarse** vr : become longer — **alargador** nm : extension cord
alarido nm : howl, shriek
alarmar vt : alarm — **alarma** nf : alarm — **alarmante** adj : alarming
alba nf : dawn
albahaca nf : basil
albañil nm : bricklayer, mason
albaricoque nm : apricot
albedrío nm libre **~** : free will
alberca nf 1 : reservoir, tank 2 Lat : swimming pool
albergar {52} vt : house, lodge — **albergue** nm 1 : lodging 2 REFUGIO : shelter 3 **~ juvenil** : youth hostel
albóndiga nf : meatball
alborear v impers : dawn — **albor** nm : dawning — **alborada** nf : dawn
alborotar vt : excite, stir up — vi : make a racket — **alborotarse** vr : get excited — **alborotado, -da** adj : excited, agitated — **alborotador, -dora** n : agitator, rioter — **alboroto** nm : ruckus
alborozar {21} vt : gladden — **alborozo** nm : joy
álbum nm : album
alcachofa nf : artichoke
alcalde, -desa n : mayor
alcance nm 1 : reach 2 ÁMBITO : range, scope
alcancía nf : money box
alcantarilla nf : sewer, drain
alcanzar {21} vt 1 : reach 2 LLEGAR A : catch up with 3 LOGRAR : achieve, at-

tain — vi 1 : suffice, be enough 2 **~ a** : manage to
alcaparra nf : caper
alcázar nm : fortress, castle
alce nm : moose, European elk
alcoba nf : bedroom
alcohol nm : alcohol — **alcohólico, -ca** adj & n : alcoholic — **alcoholismo** nm : alcoholism
aldaba nf : door knocker
aldea nf : village — **aldeano, -na** n : villager
aleación nf, pl **-ciones** : alloy
aleatorio, -ria adj : random
aleccionar vt : instruct, teach
aledaño, -ña adj : bordering — **aledaños** nmpl : outskirts
alegar {52} vt : assert, allege — vi Lat : argue — **alegato** nm 1 : allegation (in law) 2 Lat : argument
alegoría nf : allegory — **alegórico, -ca** adj : allegorical
alegrar vt : make happy, cheer up — **alegrarse** vr : be glad — **alegre** adj 1 CONTENTO : glad, happy 2 : colorful, bright — **alegremente** adv : happily — **alegría** nf : joy, cheer
alejar vt 1 : remove, move away 2 ENAJENAR : estrange — **alejarse** vr : move away, drift apart — **alejado, -da** adj : remote — **alejamiento** nm 1 : removal 2 : estrangement (of persons)
alemán, -mana adj, mpl **-manes** : German — **alemán** nm : German (language)
alentar {55} vt : encourage — **alentador, -dora** adj : encouraging
alergia nf : allergy — **alérgico, -ca** adj : allergic
alero nm : eaves pl
alertar vt : alert — **alerta** adv : on the alert — **alerta** adj & nf : alert
aleta nf 1 : fin, flipper 2 : small wing
alevosía nf : treachery — **alevoso, -sa** adj : treacherous
alfabeto nm : alphabet — **alfabético, -ca** adj : alphabetical — **alfabetismo** nm : literacy — **alfabetizar** {21} vt 1 : teach literacy 2 : alphabetize
alfalfa nf : alfalfa
alfarería nf : pottery
alféizar nm : sill, windowsill
alfil nm : bishop (in chess)
alfiler nm : pin 2 BROCHE : brooch — **alfiletero** nm : pincushion
alfombra nf : carpet, rug — **alfombrilla** nf : small rug, mat
alga nf : seaweed
álgebra nf : algebra

algo *pron* **1** : something **2** ~ **de** : some, a little — ~ *adv* : somewhat, rather

algodón *nm, pl* **-dones** : cotton

alguacil *nm* : constable, bailiff

alguien *pron* : somebody, someone

alguno, -na *adj* (**algún** *before masculine singular nouns*) **1** : some, any **2** (*in negative constructions*) : not any, not at all **3 algunas veces** : sometimes — ~ *pron* **1** : one, someone, somebody **2 algunos, -nas** *pron pl* : some, a few

alhaja *nf* : jewel

alharaca *nf* : fuss

aliado, -da *n* : ally — ~ *adj* : allied

alianza *nf* : alliance — **aliarse** {85} *vr* : form an alliance

alias *adv* & *nm* : alias

alicaído, -da *adj* : depressed

alicates *nmpl* : pliers

aliciente *nm* **1** : incentive **2** : attraction (to a place)

alienar *vt* : alienate — **alienación** *nf, pl* **-ciones** : alienation

aliento *nm* **1** : breath **2** ÁNIMO : encouragement, strength

aligerar *vt* **1** : lighten **2** APRESURAR : hasten, quicken

alimaña *nf* : pest, vermin

alimentar *vt* : feed, nourish — **alimentarse** *vr* ~ **con** : live on — **alimentación** *nf, pl* **-ciones 1** : feeding **2** NUTRICIÓN : nourishment — **alimenticio, -cia** *adj* : nourishing — **alimento** *nm* : food, nourishment

alinear *vt* : align, line up — **alinearse** *vr* ~ **con** : align oneself with — **alineación** *nf, pl* **-ciones 1** : alignment **2** : lineup (in sports)

aliño *nm* : dressing, seasoning — **aliñar** *vt* : season, dress

alisar *vt* : smooth

alistarse *vr* : join up, enlist — **alistamiento** *nm* : enlistment

aliviar *vt* : relieve, soothe — **aliviarse** *vr* : recover, get better — **alivio** *nm* : relief

aljibe *nm* : cistern, tank

allá *adv* **1** : there, over there **2 más** ~ : farther away **3 más** ~ **de** : beyond

allanar *vt* **1** : smooth, level out **2** *Spain* : break into (a house) **3** *Lat* : raid — **allanamiento** *nm* **1** *Spain* : breaking and entering **2** *Lat* : raid

allegado, -da *n* : close friend, relation

allí *adv* : there, over there

alma *nf* : soul

almacén *nm, pl* **-cenes 1** : warehouse **2** *Lat* : shop, store **3 grandes almacenes** : department store — **alma-**

cenamiento *or* **almacenaje** *nm* : storage — **almacenar** *vt* : store

almádena *nf* : sledgehammer

almanaque *nm* : almanac

almeja *nf* : clam

almendra *nf* **1** : almond **2** : kernel (of nuts, fruit, etc.)

almiar *nm* : haystack

almíbar *nm* : syrup

almidón *nm, pl* **-dones** : starch — **almidonar** *vt* : starch

almirante *nm* : admiral

almohada *nf* : pillow — **almohadilla** *nf* : small pillow, pad — **almohadón** *nm, pl* **-dones** : bolster, large cushion

almorranas *nfpl* : hemorrhoids, piles

almorzar {36} *vi* : have lunch — *vt* : have for lunch — **almuerzo** *nm* : lunch

alocado, -da *adj* : crazy, wild

áloe *or* **aloe** *nm* : aloe

alojar *vt* : house, lodge — **alojarse** *vr* : lodge, room — **alojamiento** *nm* : lodging, accommodations *pl*

alondra *nf* : lark

alpaca *nf* : alpaca

alpinismo *nm* : mountain climbing — **alpinista** *nmf* : mountain climber

alpiste *nm* : birdseed

alquilar *vt* : rent, lease — **alquilarse** *vr* : be for rent — **alquiler** *nm* : rent, rental

alquitrán *nm, pl* **-tranes** : tar

alrededor *adv* **1** : around, about **2** ~ **de** : approximately — **alrededor de** *prep phr* : around — **alrededores** *nmpl* : outskirts

alta *nf* : discharge (of a patient)

altanería *nf* : haughtiness — **altanero, -ra** *adj* : haughty

altar *nm* : altar

altavoz *nm, pl* **-voces** : loudspeaker

alterar *vt* **1** : alter, modify **2** PERTURBAR : disturb — **alterarse** *vr* : get upset — **alteración** *nf, pl* **-ciones 1** : alteration **2** ALBOROTO : disturbance — **alterado, -da** *adj* : upset

altercado *nm* : altercation, argument

alternar *vi* **1** : alternate **2** ~ **con** : socialize with — *vt* : alternate — **alternarse** *vr* : take turns — **alternativa** *nf* : alternative — **alternativo, -va** *adj* : alternating, alternative — **alterno, -na** *adj* : alternate

Alteza *nf* : Highness

altiplano *nm* : high plateau

altitud *nf* : altitude

altivez *nf, pl* **-veces** : haughtiness — **altivo, -va** *adj* : haughty

alto, -ta *adj* **1** : tall, high **2** RUIDOSO

: loud — **alto** *adv* **1** ARRIBA : high **2**
: loud, loudly — **~** *nm* **1** ALTURA
: height, elevation **2** : stop, halt — **~**
interj : halt!, stop! — **altoparlante** *nm*
Lat : loudspeaker

altruista *adj* : altruistic — **altruismo**
nm : altruism

altura *nf* **1** : height **2** ALTITUD : altitude
3 a la ~ de : near, up by

alubia *nf* : kidney bean

alucinar *vi* : hallucinate — **alucinación**
nf, pl -**ciones** : hallucination

alud *nm* : avalanche

aludir *vi* : allude, refer — **aludido, -da**
adj **darse por ~** : take it personally

alumbrar *vt* **1** : light, illuminate **2** PARIR
: give birth to — **alumbrado** *nm*
: (electric) lighting — **alumbramien-**
to *nm* : childbirth

aluminio *nm* : aluminum

alumno, -na *n* : pupil, student

alusión *nf, pl* -**siones** : allusion

aluvión *nm, pl* -**viones** : flood, barrage

alzar {21} *vt* : lift, raise — **alzarse** *vr*
: rise (up) — **alza** *nf* : rise — **alza-**
miento *nm* : uprising

ama → amo

amabilidad *nf* : kindness — **amable**
adj : kind, nice

amaestrar *vt* : train

amagar {52} *vt* **1** : show signs of **2**
AMENAZAR : threaten — *vi* **1** : be immi-
nent — **amago** *nm* **1** INDICIO : sign **2**
AMENAZA : threat

amainar *vi* : abate

amamantar *v* : breast-feed, nurse

amanecer {53}*v impers* : dawn — *vi*
: wake up — **~** *nm* : dawn, daybreak

amanerado *adj* : affected, mannered

amansar *vt* **1** : tame **2** APACIGUAR
: soothe — **amansarse** *vr* : calm down

amante *adj* **~ de** : fond of — **~** *nmf*
: lover

amañar *vt* : rig, tamper with

amapola *nf* : poppy

amar *vt* : love

amargar {52} *vt* : make bitter — **amar-**
gado, -da *adj* : embittered — **amar-**
go, -ga *adj* : bitter — **amargo** *nm*
: bitterness — **amargura** *nf* : bitterness, grief

amarillo, -lla *adj* : yellow — **amarillo**
nm : yellow

amarrar *vt* **1** : moor **2** ATAR : tie up

amasar *vt* **1** : knead **2** : amass (a fortune, etc.)

amateur *adj & nmf* : amateur

amatista *nf* : amethyst

ambages *nmpl* **sin ~** : without hesitation, straight to the point

ámbar *nm* : amber

ambición *nf, pl* -**ciones** : ambition —
ambicionar *vt* : aspire to — **ambi-**
cioso, -sa *adj* : ambitious

ambiente *nm* **1** AIRE : atmosphere **2**
MEDIO : environment, surroundings *pl*
— **ambiental** *adj* : environmental

ambigüedad *nf* : ambiguity — **am-**
biguo, -gua *adj* : ambiguous

ámbito *nm* : domain, sphere

ambos, -bas *adj & pron* : both

ambulancia *nf* : ambulance

ambulante *adj* : traveling, itinerant

ameba *nf* : amoeba

amedrentar *vt* : intimidate

amén *nm* **1** : amen **2 ~ de** : in addition
to

amenazar {21} *vt* : threaten — **ame-**
naza *nf* : threat, menace

amenizar {21} *vt* : make pleasant, enliven — **ameno, -na** *adj* : pleasant

americano, -na *adj* : American

ameritar *vt Lat* : deserve

ametralladora *nf* : machine gun

amianto *nm* : asbestos

amiba → ameba

amígdala *nf* : tonsil — **amigdalitis** *nf*
: tonsilitis

amigo, -ga *adj* : friendly, close — **~** *n*
: friend — **amigable** *adj* : friendly

amilanar *vt* : daunt — **amilanarse** *vr*
: lose heart

aminorar *vt* : diminish

amistad *nf* : friendship — **amistoso,**
-sa *adj* : friendly

amnesia *nf* : amnesia

amnistía *nf* : amnesty

amo, ama *n* **1** : master *m*, mistress *f* **2**
ama de casa : homemaker, house-
wife **3 ama de llaves** : housekeeper

amodorrado, -da *adj* : drowsy

amolar {19} *vt* **1** : grind, sharpen **2** MO-
LESTAR : annoy

amoldar *vt* : adapt, adjust —
amoldarse *vr* **~ a** : adapt to

amonestar *vt* : admonish, warn —
amonestación *nf, pl* -**ciones** : admo-
nition, warning

amoníaco *or* **amoniaco** *nm* : ammonia

amontonar *vt* : pile up — **amon-**
tonarse *vr* : pile up (of things), form a
crowd (of persons)

amor *nm* : love

amordazar {21} *vt* : gag

amorío *nm* : love affair — **amoroso,**
-sa *adj* **1** : loving **2** *Lat* : sweet, lovable

amoratado, -da *adj* : black-and-blue

amortiguar {10} *vt* : muffle, soften,
tone down — **amortiguador** *nm*
: shock absorber

amortizar {21} *vt* : pay off — **amortización** *nf* : repayment
amotinar *vt* : incite (to riot) — **amotinarse** *vr* : riot, rebel
amparar *vt* : shelter, protect — **ampararse** *vr* 1 ~ **de** : take shelter from 2 ~ **en** : have recourse to — **amparo** *nm* : refuge, protection
ampliar {85} *vt* 1 : expand 2 : enlarge (a photograph) — **ampliación** *nf, pl* **-ciones** 1 : expansion, enlargement 2 : extension (of a building)
amplificar {72} *vt* : amplify — **amplificador** *nm* : amplifier
amplio, -plia *adj* : broad, wide, ample — **amplitud** *nf* 1 : breadth, extent 2 ESPACIOSIDAD : spaciousness
ampolla *nf* 1 : blister 2 : vial, ampoule — **ampollarse** *vr* : blister
ampuloso, -sa *adj* : pompous
amputar *vt* : amputate — **amputación** *nf, pl* **-ciones** : amputation
amueblar *vt* : furnish (a house, etc.)
amurallar *vt* : wall in
anacardo *nm* : cashew nut
anaconda *nf* : anaconda
anacrónico, -ca *adj* : anachronistic — **anacronismo** *nm* : anachronism
ánade *nmf* : duck
anagrama *nm* : anagram
anales *nmpl* : annals
analfabeto, -ta *adj & n* : illiterate — **analfabetismo** *nm* : illiteracy
analgésico *nm* : painkiller, analgesic
analizar {21} *vt* : analyze — **análisis** *nm* : analysis — **analítico, -ca** *adj* : analytical, analytic
analogía *nf* : analogy — **análogo, -ga** *adj* : analogous
ananá *or* **ananás** *nm, pl* **-nás** : pineapple
anaquel *nm* : shelf
anaranjado, -da *adj* : orange-colored
anarquía *nf* : anarchy — **anarquista** *adj & nmf* : anarchist
anatomía *nf* : anatomy — **anatómico, -ca** *adj* : anatomic, anatomical
anca *nf* 1 : haunch 2 ~s **de rana** : frogs' legs
ancestral *adj* : ancestral
ancho, -cha *adj* : wide, broad, ample — **ancho** *nm* : width
anchoa *nf* : anchovy
anchura *nf* : width, breadth
anciano, -na *adj* : aged, elderly — ~ *n* : elderly person
ancla *nf* : anchor — **anclar** *v* : anchor
andadas *nfpl* 1 : tracks 2 **volver a las** ~ : go back to one's old ways
andadura *nf* : walking, journey

andaluz, -luza *adj & n, mpl* **-luces** : Andalusian
andamio *nm* : scaffold
andanada *nf* 1 : volley 2 **soltar una** ~ : reprimand
andanzas *nfpl* : adventures
andar {6} *vi* 1 CAMINAR : walk 2 IR : go, travel 3 FUNCIONAR : run, work 4 ~ **en** : rummage around in 5 ~ **por** : be approximately — *vt* : cover, travel — ~ *nm* : gait, walk
andén *nm, pl* **-denes** 1 : (train) platform 2 *Lat* : sidewalk
andino, -na *adj* : Andean
andorrano, -na *adj* : Andorran
andrajos *nmpl* : tatters — **andrajoso, -sa** *adj* : ragged
anécdota *nf* : anecdote
anegar {52} *vt* : flood — **anegarse** *vr* 1 : be flooded 2 AHOGARSE : drown
anemia *nf* : anemia — **anémico, -ca** *adj* : anemic
anestesia *nf* : anesthesia — **anestésico, -ca** *adj* : anesthetic — **anestésico** *nm* : anesthetic
anexar *vt* : annex, attach — **anexo, -xa** *adj* : attached — **anexo** *nm* : annex
anfibio, -bia *adj* : amphibious — **anfibio** *nm* : amphibian
anfiteatro *nm* : amphitheater
anfitrión, -triona *n, mpl* **-triones** : host, hostess *f*
ángel *nm* : angel — **angelical** *adj* : angelic, angelical
angloparlante *adj* : English-speaking
anglosajón, -jona *adj, mpl* **-jones** : Anglo-Saxon
angosto, -ta *adj* : narrow
anguila *nf* : eel
ángulo *nm* 1 : angle 2 ESQUINA : corner — **angular** *adj* : angular — **anguloso, -sa** *adj* : angular
angustiar *vt* 1 : anguish, distress 2 INQUIETAR : worry — **angustiarse** *vr* : get upset — **angustia** *nf* 1 : anguish 2 INQUIETUD : worry — **angustioso, -sa** *adj* 1 : anguished 2 INQUIETANTE : distressing
anhelar *vt* : yearn for, crave — **anhelante** *adj* : yearning, longing — **anhelo** *nm* : longing
anidar *vi* : nest
anillo *nm* : ring
ánima *n* : soul
animación *nf, pl* **-ciones** 1 VIVEZA : liveliness 2 BULLICIO : hustle and bustle — **animado, -da** *adj* : cheerful, animated — **animador, -dora** *n* 1 : (television) host 2 : cheerleader

animadversión *nf, pl* **-siones** : animosity

animal *nm* : animal — **~** *nmf* : brute, beast — **~** *adj* : brutish

animar *vt* 1 ALENTAR : encourage 2 ALEGAR : cheer up — **animarse** *vr* 1 : liven up 2 **~ a** : get up the nerve to

ánimo *nm* 1 : spirit, soul 2 HUMOR : mood, spirits *pl* 3 ALIENTO : encouragement

animosidad *nf* : animosity, ill will

animoso, -sa *adj* : spirited, brave

aniquilar *vt* : annihilate — **aniquilación** *n, pl* **-ciones** : annihilation

anís *nm* : anise

aniversario *nm* : anniversary

ano *nm* : anus

anoche *adv* : last night

anochecer {53} *vi* : get dark — **~** *nm* : dusk, nightfall

anodino, -na *adj* : insipid, dull

anomalía *nf* : anomaly

anonadado, -da *adj* : dumbfounded

anónimo, -ma *adj* : anonymous — **anonimato** *nm* : anonymity

anorexia *nf* : anorexia

anormal *adj* : abnormal — **anormalidad** *nf* : abnormality

anotar *vt* 1 : annotate 2 APUNTAR : jot down — **anotación** *nf, pl* **-ciones** : annotation, note

anquilosarse *vr* 1 : become paralyzed 2 ESTANCARSE : stagnate — **anquilosamiento** *nm* 1 : paralysis 2 ESTANCAMIENTO : stagnation

ansiar {85} *vt* : long for — **ansia** *nf* 1 INQUIETUD : uneasiness 2 ANGUSTIA : anguish 3 ANHELO : longing — **ansiedad** *nf* : anxiety — **ansioso, -sa** *adj* 1 : anxious 2 DESEOSO : eager

antagónico, -ca *adj* : antagonistic — **antagonismo** *nm* : antagonism — **antagonista** *nmf* : antagonist

antaño *adv* : yesteryear, long ago

antártico, -ca *adj* : antarctic

ante[1] *nm* 1 : elk, moose 2 GAMUZA : suede

ante[2] *prep* 1 : before, in front of 2 : in view of 3 **~ todo** : above all

anteanoche *adv* : the night before last

anteayer *adv* : the day before yesterday

antebrazo *nm* : forearm

anteceder *vt* : precede — **antecedente** *adj* : previous, prior — **~** *nm* : precedent — **antecesor, -sora** *n* 1 : ancestor 2 PREDECESOR : predecessor

antedicho, -cha *adj* : aforesaid

antelación *nf, pl* **-ciones** 1 : advance notice 2 **con ~** : in advance

antemano *adv* **de ~** : beforehand

antena *nf* : antenna

antenoche → **anteanoche**

anteojos *nmpl* 1 : glasses, eyeglasses 2 **~ bifocales** : bifocals

antepasado, -da *n* : ancestor

antepecho *nm* : ledge

antepenúltimo, -ma *adj* : third from last

anteponer {60} *vt* 1 : place before 2 PREFERIR : prefer

anterior *adj* 1 : previous, earlier 2 DELANTERO : front — **anterioridad** *nf* **con ~** : beforehand, in advance — **anteriormente** *adv* : previously

antes *adv* 1 : before, earlier 2 ANTERIORMENTE : previously 3 PRIMERO : first 4 MEJOR : rather 5 **~ de** : before, previous to 6 **~ que** : before

antesala *nf* : waiting room

antiaéreo, -rea *adj* : antiaircraft

antibiótico *nm* : antibiotic

anticipar *vt* 1 : move up (a date, etc.) 2 : pay in advance — **anticiparse** *vr* 1 : be early 2 ADELANTARSE : get ahead — **anticipación** *nf, pl* **-ciones** 1 : anticipation 2 **con ~** : in advance — **anticipado, -da** *adj* 1 : advance, early 2 **por ~** : in advance — **anticipo** *nm* 1 : advance (payment) 2 : foretaste

anticoncepción *nf, pl* **-ciones** : contraception — **anticonceptivo, -va** *adj* : contraceptive — **anticonceptivo** *nm* : contraceptive

anticongelante *nm* : antifreeze

anticuado, -da *adj* : antiquated, outdated

anticuario, -ria *n* : antique dealer — **anticuario** *nm* : antique shop

anticuerpo *nm* : antibody

antídoto *nm* : antidote

antier → **anteayer**

antiestético, -ca *adj* : unsightly

antifaz *nm, pl* **-faces** : mask

antífona *nf* : anthem

antigualla *nf* : relic, old thing

antiguo, -gua *adj* 1 : ancient, old 2 ANTERIOR : former 3 ANTICUADO : old-fashioned 4 **muebles antiguos** : antique furniture — **antiguamente** *adv* 1 : long ago 2 ANTES : formerly — **antigüedad** *nf* 1 : antiquity 2 : seniority (in the workplace) 3 **~es** *nfpl* : antiques

antihigiénico, -ca *adj* : unsanitary

antihistamínico *nm* : antihistamine

antiinflamatorio, -ria *adj* : anti-inflammatory

antílope *nm* : antelope

antinatural *adj* : unnatural

antipatía *nf* : aversion, dislike — **antipático, -ca** *adj* : unpleasant

antirreglamentario, -ria *adj* : unlawful

antirrobo, -ba *adj* : antitheft

antisemita *adj* : anti-Semitic — **antisemitismo** *nm* : anti-Semitism

antiséptico, -ca *adj* : antiseptic — **antiséptico** *nm* : antiseptic

antisocial *adj* : antisocial

antítesis *nf* : antithesis

antojarse *vr* 1 APETECER : crave 2 PARECER : seem, appear — **antojadizo, -za** *adj* : capricious — **antojo** *nm* : whim, craving

antología *nf* : anthology

antorcha *nf* : torch

antro *nm* : dive, den

antropófago, -ga *nmf* : cannibal

antropología *nf* : anthropology

anual *adj* : annual, yearly — **anualidad** *nf* : annuity — **anuario** *nm* : yearbook, annual

anudar *vt* : knot — **anudarse** *vr* : tie, knot

anular *vt* : annul, cancel — **anulación** *nf, pl* **-ciones** : annulment, cancellation

anunciar *vt* 1 : announce 2 : advertise (products) — **anunciante** *nmf* : advertiser — **anuncio** *nm* 1 : announcement 2 *or* **publicitario** : advertisement

anzuelo *nm* 1 : fishhook 2 **morder el** ~ : take the bait

añadir *vt* : add — **añadidura** *nf* 1 : additive, addition 2 **por** ~ : in addition, furthermore

añejo, -ja *adj* : aged, vintage

añicos *nmpl* **hacer(se)** ~ : smash to pieces

añil *adj & nm* : indigo (color)

año *nm* 1 : year 2 **Año Nuevo** : New Year

añorar *vt* : long for, miss — **añoranza** *nf* : nostalgia

añoso, -sa *adj* : aged, old

aorta *nf* : aorta

apabullar *vt* : overwhelm

apacentar {55} *vt* : pasture, graze

apachurrar *vt Lat* : crush

apacible *adj* : gentle, mild

apaciguar {10} *vt* : appease, pacify — **apaciguarse** *vr* : calm down

apadrinar *vt* 1 : be a godparent to 2 : sponsor (an artist, etc.)

apagar {52} *vt* 1 : turn or switch off 2 EXTINGUIR : extinguish, put out — **apagarse** *vr* EXTINGUIRSE : go out 1 : die down — **apagado, -da** *adj* 1 : off, out 2 : dull, subdued (of colors, sounds, etc.) — **apagador** *nm Lat*

: (light) switch — **apagón** *nm, pl* **-gones** : blackout

apalancar {72} *vt* 1 LEVANTAR : jack up 2 ABRIR : pry open — **apalancamiento** *nm* : leverage

apalear *vt* : beat up, thrash

aparador *nm* 1 : sideboard 2 *Lat* : shop window

aparato *nm* 1 : machine, appliance, apparatus 2 : system (in anatomy) 3 OSTENTACIÓN : ostentation — **aparatoso, -sa** *adj* 1 : ostentatious 2 ESPECTACULAR : spectacular

aparcar {72} *v Spain* : park — **aparcamiento** *nm Spain* 1 : parking 2 : parking lot

aparcero, -ra *n* : sharecropper

aparear *vt* : mate, pair up — **aparearse** *vr* : mate

aparecer {53} *vi* 1 : appear 2 PRESENTARSE : show up — **aparecerse** *vr* : appear

aparejar *vt* 1 : rig (a ship) 2 : harness (an animal) — **aparejado, -da** *adj* **llevar** ~ : entail — **aparejo** *nm* 1 : equipment, gear 2 : harness (for an animal) 3 : rigging (for a ship)

aparentar *vt* 1 : seem 2 FINGIR : feign — **aparente** *adj* : apparent, seeming

aparición *nf, pl* **-ciones** 1 : appearance 2 FANTASMA : apparition — **apariencia** *nf* 1 : appearance, look 2 **en** ~ : apparently

apartado *nm* 1 : section, paragraph 2 ~ **postal** : post office box

apartamento *nm* : apartment

apartar *vt* 1 ALEJAR : move away 2 SEPARAR : set aside, separate — **apartarse** *vr* 1 : move away 2 DESVIARSE : stray — **aparte** *adv* 1 : apart, separately 2 ADEMÁS : besides

apasionar *vt* : excite, fascinate — **apasionarse** *vr* : get excited — **apasionado, -da** *adj* : passionate, excited — **apasionante** *adj* : exciting

apatía *nf* : apathy — **apático, -ca** *adj* : apathetic

apearse *vr* 1 : dismount 2 : get out of or off (a vehicle)

apedrear *vt* : stone

apegarse {52} *vr* ~ **a** : become attached to, grow fond of — **apegado, -da** *adj* : devoted — **apego** *nm* : fondness

apelar *vi* 1 : appeal 2 ~ **a** : resort to — **apelación** *nf, pl* **-ciones** : appeal

apellido *nm* : last name, surname — **apellidarse** *vr* : have for a last name

apenar *vt* 1 : sadden — **apenarse** *vr* 1 : grieve 2 *Lat* : become embarrassed

apenas *adv* : hardly, scarcely — ~ *conj* : as soon as
apéndice *nm* : appendix — **apendicitis** *nf* : appendicitis
apercibir *vt* **1** : warn **2** *Lat* : notice — **apercibirse** *vr* ~ **de** : notice — **apercibimiento** *nm* : warning
aperitivo *nm* **1** : appetizer **2** : aperitif
apero *nm* : tool, implement
apertura *nf* : opening
apesadumbrar *vt* : sadden — **apesadumbrarse** *vr* : be weighed down
apestar *vi* : stink — **apestoso, -sa** *adj* : stinking, foul
apetecer {53} *vt* : crave, long for — **apetecible** *adj* : appealing
apetito *nm* : appetite — **apetitoso, -sa** *adj* : appetizing
ápice *nm* **1** : apex, summit **2** PIZCA : bit, smidgen
apilar *vt* : pile up — **apilarse** *vr* : pile up
apiñar *vt* : pack, cram — **apiñarse** *vr* : crowd together
apio *nm* : celery
apisonadora *nf* : steamroller
aplacar {72} *vt* : appease, placate — **aplacarse** *vr* : calm down
aplanar *vt* : flatten, level
aplastar *vt* : crush — **aplastante** *adj* : overwhelming
aplaudir *v* : applaud — **aplauso** *nm* **1** : applause **2** : acclaim
aplazar {21} *vt* : postpone, defer — **aplazamiento** *nm* : postponement
aplicar {72} *vt* : apply — **aplicarse** *vr* : apply oneself — **aplicable** *adj* : applicable — **aplicación** *nf, pl* -ciones : application — **aplicado, -da** *adj* : diligent
aplomo *nm* : aplomb
apocarse {72} *vr* : belittle oneself — **apocado, -da** *adj* : timid — **apocamiento** *nm* : timidity
apodar *vt* : nickname
apoderar *vt* : empower — **apoderarse** *vr* ~ **de** : seize — **apoderado, -da** *n* : agent, proxy
apodo *nm* : nickname
apogeo *nm* : peak, height
apología *nf* : defense, apology
apoplegía *nf* : stroke, apoplexy
aporrear *vt* : bang on, beat
aportar *vt* : contribute — **aportación** *nf, pl* -ciones : contribution
apostar[1] {19} *v* : bet, wager
apostar[2] *vt* : station, post
apostillar *vt* : annotate — **apostilla** *nf*
apóstol *nm* : apostle

apóstrofo *nm* : apostrophe
apostura *nf* : elegance, grace
apoyar *vt* **1** : support **2** INCLINAR : lean, rest — **apoyarse** *vr* ~ **en** : lean on, rest on — **apoyo** *nm* : support
apreciar *vt* **1** ESTIMAR : appreciate **2** EVALUAR : appraise — **apreciable** *adj* : considerable — **apreciación** *nf, pl* -ciones **1** : appreciation **2** VALORACIÓN : appraisal — **aprecio** *nm* **1** : appraisal **2** ESTIMA : esteem
aprehender *vt* : apprehend — **aprehensión** *nf, pl* -siones : apprehension, capture
apremiar *vt* : urge — *vi* : be urgent — **apremiante** *adj* : pressing, urgent — **apremio** *nm* : urgency
aprender *v* : learn — **aprenderse** *vr* : memorize
aprendiz, -diza *n, mpl* -dices : apprentice, trainee — **aprendizaje** *nm* : apprenticeship
aprensión *nf, pl* -siones : apprehension, dread — **aprensivo, -va** *adj* : apprehensive
apresar *vt* : capture, seize — **apresamiento** *nm* : seizure, capture
aprestar *vt* : make ready — **aprestarse** *vr* : get ready
apresurar *vt* : speed up — **apresurarse** *vr* : hurry — **apresuradamente** *adv* : hurriedly, hastily — **apresurado, -da** *adj* : in a rush
apretar {55} *vt* **1** : press, push (a button) **2** : tighten (a knot, etc.) **3** ESTRECHAR : squeeze — *vi* **1** : press (down) **2** : fit too tightly — **apretón** *nm, pl* -tones **1** : squeeze **2** ~ **de manos** : handshake — **apretado, -da** *adj* **1** : tight **2** *fam* : tightfisted
aprieto *nm* : predicament, jam
aprisa *adv* : quickly
aprisionar *vt* : imprison
aprobar {19} *vt* **1** : approve of **2** : pass (an exam, etc.) — *vi* : pass — **aprobación** *nf, pl* -ciones : approval
apropiarse *vr* ~ **de** : take possession of, appropriate — **apropiación** *nf, pl* -ciones : appropriation — **apropiado, -da** *adj* : appropriate
aprovechar *vt* : take advantage of, make good use of — *vi* : be of use — **aprovecharse** *vr* ~ **de** : take advantage of — **aprovechado, -da** *adj* **1** : diligent **2** OPORTUNISTA : opportunistic
aproximar *vt* : bring closer — **aproximarse** *vr* : approach — **aproximación** *nf, pl* -ciones : approximation — **aproximadamente** *adv*

: approximately — **aproximado, -da**
adj : approximate
apto, -ta *adj* **1** : suitable **2** CAPAZ : capable — **aptitud** *nf* : aptitude, capability
apuesta *nf* : bet, wager
apuesto, -ta *adj* : elegant, good-looking
apuntalar *vt* : prop up, shore up
apuntar *vt* **1** : aim, point **2** ANOTAR : jot down **3** SEÑALAR : point at **4** : prompt (in theater) — **apuntarse** *vr* **1** : sign up **2** : score, chalk up (a victory, etc.) — **apunte** *nm* : note
apuñalar *vt* : stab
apurar *vt* **1** : hurry, rush **2** AGOTAR : use up **3** PREOCUPAR : trouble — **apurarse** *vr* **1** : worry **2** *Lat* : hurry up — **apuradamente** *adv* : with difficulty — **apurado, -da** *adj* **1** : needy **2** DIFÍCIL : difficult **3** *Lat* : rushed — **apuro** *nm* **1** : predicament, jam **2** *Lat* : hurry
aquejar *vt* : afflict
aquel, aquella *adj, mpl* **aquellos** : that, those
aquél, aquélla *pron, mpl* **aquéllos 1** : that (one), those (ones) **2** : the former
aquello *pron* : that, that matter
aquí *adv* **1** : here **2** AHORA : now **3** por ~ : hereabouts
aquietar *vt* : calm — **aquietarse** *vr* : calm down
ara *nf* **1** : altar **2 en ~s de** : for the sake of
árabe *adj* : Arab, Arabic — ~ *nm* : Arabic (language)
arado *nm* : plow
arancel *nm* : tariff
arándano *nm* : blueberry
araña *nf* **1** : spider **2** LÁMPARA : chandelier
arañar *v* : scratch, claw — **arañazo** *nm* : scratch
arar *v* : plow
arbitrar *v* **1** : arbitrate **2** : referee, umpire (in sports) — **arbitraje** *nm* : arbitration — **arbitrario, -ria** *adj* : arbitrary — **arbitrio** *nm* **1** : (free) will **2** JUICIO : judgment — **árbitro, -tra** *n* **1** : arbitrator **2** : referee, umpire (in sports)
árbol *nm* : tree — **arboleda** *nf* : grove
arbusto *nm* : shrub, bush
arca *nf* **1** : ark **2** COFRE : chest
arcada *nf* **1** : arcade **2 ~s** *nfpl* : retching
arcaico, -ca *adj* : archaic
arcano, -na *adj* : arcane, secret
arce *nm* : maple tree
archipiélago *nm* : archipelago
archivar *vt* : file — **archivador** *nm* : filing cabinet — **archivo** *nm* **1** : file **2** : archives *pl*
arcilla *nf* : clay
arco *nm* **1** : arch **2** : bow (in sports, music, etc.) **3** : arc (in geometry) **4 ~ iris** : rainbow
arder *vi* : burn
ardid *nm* : scheme, ruse
ardiente *adj* **1** : burning **2** FOGOSO : ardent
ardilla *nf* **1** : squirrel **2 ~ listada** : chipmunk
ardor *nm* **1** : burning **2** ENTUSIASMO : passion, ardor
arduo, -dua *adj* : arduous
área *nf* : area
arena *nf* **1** : sand **2** PALESTRA : arena — **arenoso, -sa** *adj* : sandy, gritty
arenque *nm* : herring
arete *nm* *Lat* : earring
argamasa *nf* : mortar
argentino, -na *adj* : Argentinian, Argentine
argolla *nf* : hoop, ring
argot *nm* : slang
argüir {41} *vt* **1** : argue **2** DEMOSTRAR : prove, show — *vi* : argue
argumentar *vt* : argue, contend — **argumentación** *nf, pl* **-ciones** : (line of) argument — **argumento** *nm* **1** : argument, reasoning **2** TRAMA : plot, story line
árido, -da *adj* : dry, arid — **aridez** *nf, pl* **-deces** : aridity
arisco, -ca *adj* : surly
aristocracia *nf* : aristocracy — **aristócrata** *nmf* : aristocrat — **aristocrático, -ca** *adj* : aristocratic
aritmética *nf* : arithmetic — **aritmético, -ca** *adj* : arithmetic, arithmetical
armar *vt* **1** : arm **2** MONTAR : assemble — **arma** *nf* **1** : arm, weapon **2 ~ de fuego** : firearm — **armada** *nf* : navy — **armado, -da** *adj* : armed — **armadura** *nf* **1** : armor **2** ARMAZÓN : framework — **armamento** *nm* : armament, arms *pl*
armario *nm* **1** : (clothes) closet **2** : cupboard, cabinet
armazón *nmf, pl* **-zones** : frame, framework
armisticio *nm* : armistice
armonizar {21} *vt* **1** : harmonize **2** : reconcile (differences, etc.) — *vi* : harmonize, go together — **armonía** *nf* : harmony — **armónica** *nf* : harmonica — **armónico, -ca** *adj* : harmonic — **armonioso, -sa** *adj* : harmonious
arnés *nm, pl* **-neses** : harness

aro *nm* **1** : hoop, ring **2** *Lat* : earring

aroma *nm* : aroma, scent — **aromático, -ca** *adj* : aromatic

arpa *nf* : harp

arpón *nm*, *pl* **-pones** : harpoon

arquear *vt* : arch, bend — **arquearse** *vr* : bend, bow

arqueología *nf* : archaeology — **arqueológico, -ca** *adj* : archaeological — **arqueólogo, -ga** *n* : archaeologist

arquero, -ra *n* **1** : archer **2** PORTERO : goalkeeper, goalie

arquetipo *nm* : archetype

arquitectura *nf* : architecture — **arquitecto, -ta** *n* : architect — **arquitectónico, -ca** *adj* : architectural

arrabal *nm* **1** : slum **2** ~es *nmpl* : outskirts

arracimarse *vr* : cluster together

arraigar {52} *vi* : take root, become established — **arraigarse** *vr* : settle down — **arraigado, -da** *adj* : deeply rooted, well established — **arraigo** *nm* : roots *pl*

arrancar {72} *vt* **1** : pull out, tear off **2** : start (an engine), boot (a computer) — *vi* **1** : start an engine **2** : get going — **arranque** *nm* **1** : starter (of a car) **2** ARREBATO : outburst **3** **punto de** ~ : starting point

arrasar *vt* **1** : destroy, devastate **2** LLENAR : fill to the brim

arrastrar *vt* **1** : drag **2** ATRAER : draw, attract — *vi* : hang down, trail — **arrastrarse** *vr* **1** : crawl, creep **2** HUMILLARSE : grovel — **arrastre** *nm* **1** : dragging **2** : trawling (for fish)

arrear *vt* : urge on

arrebatar *vt* **1** : snatch, seize **2** CAUTIVAR : captivate — **arrebatarse** *vr* : get carried away — **arrebatado, -da** *adj* : hotheaded, rash — **arrebato** *nm* : outburst

arreciar *vi* : intensify, worsen

arrecife *nm* : reef

arreglar *vt* **1** COMPONER : fix **2** ORDENAR : tidy up **3** SOLUCIONAR : solve, work out — **arreglarse** *vr* **1** : get dressed (up) **2** **arreglárselas** *fam* : get by, manage — **arreglado, -da** *adj* **1** : fixed, repaired **2** ORDENADO : tidy **3** SOLUCIONADO : settled, sorted out **4** ATAVIADO : smart, dressed-up — **arreglo** *nm* **1** : arrangement **2** REPARACIÓN : repair **3** ACUERDO : agreement

arremangarse {52} *vr* : roll up one's sleeves

arremeter *vi* : attack, charge — **arremetida** *nf* : attack, onslaught

arremolinarse *vr* **1** : crowd around, mill about **2** : swirl (about)

arrendar {55} *vt* : rent, lease — **arrendador, -dora** *n* : landlord, landlady *f* — **arrendamiento** *nm* : rent, rental — **arrendatario, -ria** *n* : tenant, renter

arrepentirse {76} *vr* **1** : regret, be sorry **2** : repent (for one's sins) — **arrepentido, -da** *adj* : repentant — **arrepentimiento** *nm* : regret, repentance

arrestar *vt* : arrest, detain — **arresto** *nm* : arrest

arriar *vt* : lower

arriba *adv* **1** (*indicating position*) : above, overhead **2** (*indicating direction*) : up, upwards **3** : upstairs **4** ~ **de** : more than **5 de** ~ **abajo** : from top to bottom

arribar *vi* **1** : arrive **2** : dock, put into port — **arribista** *nmf* : parvenu, upstart — **arribo** *nm* : arrival

arriendo → **arrendimiento**

arriesgar {52} *vt* : risk, venture — **arriesgarse** *vr* : take a chance — **arriesgado, -da** *adj* : risky

arrimar *vt* : bring closer, draw near — **arrimarse** *vr* : approach

arrinconar *vt* **1** : corner, box in **2** ABANDONAR : push aside

arrobar *vt* : entrance — **arrobarse** *vr* : be enraptured — **arrobamiento** *nm* : rapture, ecstasy

arrodillarse *vr* : kneel (down)

arrogancia *nf* : arrogance — **arrogante** *adj* : arrogant

arrojar *vt* **1** : hurl, cast **2** EMITIR : give off, spew out **3** PRODUCIR : yield — **arrojarse** *vr* : throw oneself — **arrojado, -da** *adj* : daring — **arrojo** *nm* : boldness, courage

arrollar *vt* **1** : sweep away **2** DERROTAR : crush, overwhelm **3** : run over (with a vehicle) — **arrollador, -dora** *adj* : overwhelming

arropar *vt* : clothe, cover (up) — **arroparse** *vr* : wrap oneself up

arroyo *nm* **1** RIACHUELO : stream **2** : gutter (in a street)

arroz *nm*, *pl* **arroces** : rice

arrugar {52} *vt* : wrinkle, crease — **arrugarse** *vr* : get wrinkled — **arruga** *nf* : wrinkle, crease

arruinar *vt* : ruin, wreck — **arruinarse** *vr* **1** : be ruined **2** EMPOBRECERSE : go bankrupt

arrullar *vt* : lull to sleep — *vi* : coo — **arrullo** *nm* **1** : lullaby **2** : cooing (of doves)

arrumbar *vt* : lay aside

arsenal *nm* : arsenal

arsénico *nm* : arsenic

arte *nmf* (*usually m in singular, f in plural*) **1** : art **2** HABILIDAD : skill **3** ASTUCIA : cunning, cleverness **4** → **bello**

artefacto *nm* : artifact, device

arteria *nf* : artery

artesanía *nm* **1** : craftsmanship **2** : handicrafts *pl* — **artesanal** *adj* : handmade — **artesano, -na** *n* : artisan, craftsman

ártico, -ca *adj* : arctic

articular *vt* : articulate — **articulación** *nf, pl* -**ciones 1** : articulation, pronunciation **2** COYUNTURA : joint

artículo *nm* **1** : article **2** ~s de primera necesidad : essentials **3** ~s de tocador : toiletries

artífice *nmf* : artisan, craftsman

artificial *adj* : artificial

artificio *nm* **1** HABILIDAD : skill **2** APARATO : device **3** ARDID : artifice, ruse — **artificioso, -sa** *adj* : cunning, deceptive

artillería *nf* : artillery

artilugio *nm* : gadget

artimaña *nf* : ruse, trick

artista *nmf* **1** : artist **2** ACTOR : actor, actress *f* — **artístico, -ca** *adj* : artistic

artritis *nms & pl* : arthritis — **artrítico, -ca** *adj* : arthritic

arveja *nf Lat* : pea

arzobispo *nm* : archbishop

as *nm* : ace

asa *nf* : handle

asado, -da *adj* : roasted, grilled — **asado** *nm* : roast — **asador** *nm* : spit — **asaduras** *nfpl* : offal, entrails

asalariado, -da *n* : wage earner — ~ *adj* : salaried

asaltar *vt* **1** : assault **2** ROBAR : mug, rob — **asaltante** *nmf* **1** : assailant **2** ATRACADOR : mugger, robber — **asalto** *nm* **1** : assault **2** ROBO : mugging, robbery

asamblea *nf* : assembly, meeting

asar *vt* : roast, grill — **asarse** *vr fam* : roast, feel the heat

asbesto *nm* : asbestos

ascender {56} *vi* **1** : ascend, rise up **2** : be promoted (in a job) **3** ~ a : amount to — *vt* : promote — **ascendencia** *nf* : ancestry, descent — **ascendiente** *nmf* : ancestor — ~ *nm* : influence — **ascensión** *nf, pl* -**siones** : ascent — **ascenso** *nm* **1** : ascent, rise **2** : promotion (in a job) — **ascensor** *nm* : elevator

asco *nm* **1** : disgust **2** hacer ~s de : turn up one's nose at **3** me da ~ : it makes me sick

ascua *nf* **1** : ember **2** estar en ~s *fam* : be on edge

asear *vt* : clean, tidy up — **asearse** *vr* : get cleaned up — **aseado, -da** *adj* : clean, tidy

asediar *vt* **1** : besiege **2** ACOSAR : harass — **asedio** *nm* **1** : siege **2** ACOSO : harassment

asegurar *vt* **1** : assure **2** FIJAR : secure **3** : insure (a car, house, etc.) — **asegurarse** *vr* : make sure

asemejarse *vr* **1** : be similar **2** ~ a : look like, resemble

asentar {55} *vt* **1** : set down **2** INSTALAR : set up, establish **3** *Lat* : state — **asentarse** *vr* **1** : settle **2** ESTABLECERSE : settle down — **asentado, -da** *adj* : settled, established

asentir {76} *vi* : assent, agree — **asentimiento** *nm* : assent

aseo *nm* : cleanliness

asequible *adj* : accessible, attainable

aserrar {55} *vt* : saw — **aserradero** *nm* : sawmill — **aserrín** *nm, pl* -**rrines** : sawdust

asesinar *vt* **1** : murder **2** : assassinate — **asesinato** *nm* **1** : murder **2** : assassination — **asesino, -na** *n* **1** : murderer, killer **2** : assassin

asesorar *vt* : advise, counsel — **asesorarse** *vr* ~ de : consult — **asesor, -sora** *n* : advisor, consultant — **asesoramiento** *nm* : advice, counsel

asestar {55} *vt* **1** : aim (a weapon) **2** : deal (a blow)

aseverar *vt* : assert — **aseveración** *nf, pl* -**ciones** : assertion

asfalto *nm* : asphalt

asfixiar *vt* : asphyxiate, suffocate — **asfixiarse** *vr* : suffocate — **asfixia** *nf* : asphyxiation, suffocation

así *adv* **1** : like this, like that, thus **2** ~ de : so, that (much) **3** ~ que : so, therefore **4** ~ que : as soon as **5** ~ como : as well as — ~ *adj* : such, like that — ~ *conj* AUNQUE : even though

asiático, -ca *adj* : Asian, Asiatic

asidero *nm* : handle

asiduo, -dua *adj* : frequent, regular

asiento *nm* : seat

asignar *vt* **1** : assign, allocate **2** DESTINAR : appoint — **asignación** *nf, pl* -**ciones 1** : assignment **2** SUELDO : salary, pay — **asignatura** *nf* : subject, course

asilo *nm* **1** : asylum, home **2** REFUGIO : refuge, shelter — **asilado, -da** *n* : inmate

asimilar *vt* : assimilate — **asimilarse** *vr* ~ a : resemble

asimismo *adv* **1** : similarly, likewise **2** TAMBIÉN : as well, also

asir {7} *vt* : seize, grasp — **asirse** *vr* ~ **a** : cling to

asistir *vi* ~ **a** : attend, be present at — *vt* : assist — **asistencia** *nf* **1** : attendance **2** AYUDA : assistance — **asistente** *nmf* **1** : assistant **2 los** ~**s** : those present

asma *nf* : asthma — **asmático, -ca** *adj* : asthmatic

asno *nm* : ass, donkey

asociar *vt* : associate — **asociarse** *vr* **1** : form a partnership **2** ~ **a** : join, become a member of — **asociación** *nf*, *pl* **-ciones** : association — **asociado, -da** *adj* : associate, associated — ~ *n* : associate, partner

asolar {19} *vt* : devastate

asomar *vt* : show, stick out — *vi* : appear, show — **asomarse** *vr* **1** : appear **2** : stick one's head out (of a window)

asombrar *vt* : amaze, astonish — **asombrarse** *vr* : be amazed — **asombro** *nm* : amazement, astonishment — **asombroso, -sa** *adj* : amazing, astonishing

asomo *nm* **1** : hint, trace **2 ni por** ~ : by no means

aspaviento *nm* : exaggerated gestures, fuss

aspecto *nm* **1** : aspect **2** APARIENCIA : appearance, look

áspero, -ra *adj* : rough, harsh — **aspereza** *nf* : roughness, harshness

aspersión *nf*, *pl* **-siones** : sprinkling — **aspersor** *nm* : sprinkler

aspiración *nf*, *pl* **-ciones** **1** : breathing in **2** ANHELO : aspiration

aspiradora *nf* : vacuum cleaner

aspirar *vi* ~ **a** : aspire to — *vt* : inhale, breathe in — **aspirante** *nmf* : applicant, candidate

aspirina *nf* : aspirin

asquear *vt* : sicken, disgust

asquerosidad *nf* : filth, foulness — **asqueroso, -sa** *adj* : disgusting, sickening

asta *nf* **1** : flagpole **2** CUERNO : antler, horn **3** : shaft (of a spear) — **astado, -da** *adj* : horned

asterisco *nm* : asterisk

asteroide *nm* : asteroid

astigmatismo *nm* : astigmatism

astillar *vt* : splinter — **astilla** *nf* : splinter, chip

astillero *nm* : shipyard

astral *adj* : astral

astringente *adj* & *nm* : astringent

astro *nm* **1** : heavenly body **2** : star (of movies, etc.)

astrología *nf* : astrology

astronauta *nmf* : astronaut — **astronáutica** *nf* : astronautics

astronave *nf* : spaceship

astronomía *nf* : astronomy — **astronómico, -ca** *adj* : astronomical — **astrónomo, -ma** *n* : astronomer

astucia *nf* **1** : astuteness **2** ARDID : cunning, guile — **astuto, -ta** *adj* **1** : astute **2** TAIMADO : crafty

asueto *nm* : time off, break

asumir *vt* : assume — **asunción** *nf*, *pl* **-ciones** : assumption

asunto *nm* **1** : matter, affair **2** NEGOCIO : business

asustar *vt* : scare, frighten — **asustarse** *vr* ~ **de** : be frightened of — **asustadizo, -za** *adj* : jumpy, skittish — **asustado, -da** *adj* : frightened, afraid

atacar {72} *v* : attack — **atacante** *nmf* : attacker

atado *nm* : bundle

atadura *nf* : tie, bond

atajar *vt* : block, cut off — *vi* ~ **por** : take a shortcut through — **atajo** *nm* : shortcut

atañer {79} *vi* ~ **a** : concern, have to do with

ataque *nm* **1** : attack, assault **2** ACCESO : fit **3** ~ **de nervios** : nervous breakdown

atar *vt* : tie up, tie down — **atarse** *vr* : tie (up)

atardecer {53} *v impers* : get dark — ~ *nm* : late afternoon, dusk

atareado, -da *adj* : busy

atascar {72} *vt* **1** : block, clog **2** ESTORBAR : hinder — **atascarse** *vr* **1** OBSTRUIRSE : become obstructed **2** : get bogged down — **atasco** *nm* **1** : blockage **2** EMBOTELLAMIENTO : traffic jam

ataúd *nm* : coffin

ataviar {85} *vt* : dress (up) — **ataviarse** *vr* : dress up — **atavío** *nm* : attire

atemorizar {21} *vt* : frighten — **atemorizarse** *vr* : get scared

atención *nf*, *pl* **-ciones** **1** : attention **2 prestar** ~ : pay attention **3 llamar la** ~ : attract attention — ~ *interj* : attention!, watch out!

atender {56} *vt* **1** : attend to **2** CUIDAR : look after **3** : heed (advice, etc.) — *vi* : pay attention

atenerse {80} *vr* ~ **a** : abide by

atentamente *adv* **1** : attentively **2 le saluda** ~ : sincerely yours

atentar {55} vi ~ **contra** : make an attempt on — **atentado** nm : attack
atento, -ta adj 1 : attentive, mindful 2 CORTÉS : courteous
atenuar {3} vt 1 : dim (lights), tone down (colors, etc.) 2 DISMINUIR : lessen — **atenuante** nmf : extenuating circumstances
ateo, atea adj : atheistic — ~ n : atheist
aterciopelado, -da adj : velvety, downy
aterido, -da adj : frozen stiff
aterrar {55} vt : terrify — **aterrador, -dora** adj : terrifying
aterrizar {21} vi : land — **aterrizaje** nm : landing
aterrorizar {21} vt : terrify
atesorar vt : hoard, amass
atestar {55} vt 1 : crowd, pack 2 : testify to (in law) — **atestado, -da** adj : stuffed, packed
atestiguar {10} vt : testify to
atiborrar vt : stuff, cram — **atiborrarse** vr : stuff oneself
ático nm 1 : penthouse 2 DESVÁN : attic
atildado, -da adj : smart, neat
atinar vi : be on target
atípico, -ca adj : atypical
atirantar vt : tighten
atisbar vt 1 : spy on 2 VISLUMBRAR : catch a glimpse of — **atisbo** nm : sign, hint
atizar {21} vt 1 : poke (a fire) 2 : rouse, stir up (passions, etc.) — **atizador** nm : poker
atlántico, -ca adj : Atlantic
atlas nm : atlas
atleta nmf : athlete — **atlético, -ca** adj : athletic — **atletismo** nm : athletics
atmósfera nf : atmosphere — **atmosférico, -ca** adj : atmospheric
atolondrado, -da adj 1 : scatterbrained 2 ATURDIDO : bewildered, dazed
átomo nm : atom — **atómico, -ca** adj : atomic — **atomizador** nm : atomizer
atónito, -ta adj : astonished, amazed
atontar vt : stun, daze
atorar vt : block — **atorarse** vr : get stuck
atormentar vt : torment, torture — **atormentarse** vr : torment oneself, agonize — **atormentador, -dora** n : tormenter
atornillar vt : screw
atorrante nmf Lat : bum, loafer
atosigar {52} vt : harass, annoy
atracar {72} vi : dock, land — vt : hold up, mug — **atracarse** vr fam ~ de : gorge oneself with — **atracadero**

nm : dock, pier — **atracador, -dora** n : robber, mugger
atracción nf, pl **-clones** : attraction
atraco nm : holdup, robbery
atractivo, -va adj : attractive — **atractivo** nm : attraction, appeal
atraer {81} vt : attract
atragantarse vr : choke
atrancar {72} vt : block, bar — **atrancarse** vr : get blocked, get stuck
atrapar vt : trap, capture
atrás adv 1 DETRÁS : back, behind 2 ANTES : before, earlier 3 **para** ~ or **hacia** ~ : backwards
atrasar vt 1 : put back (a clock) 2 DEMORAR : delay — vi : lose time — **atrasarse** vr : fall behind — **atrasado, -da** adj 1 : late, overdue 2 : backward (of countries, etc.) 3 : slow (of a clock) — **atraso** nm 1 RETRASO : delay 2 : backwardness 3 ~**s** nmpl : arrears
atravesar {55} vt 1 CRUZAR : cross 2 TRASPASAR : pierce 3 : lay across (a road, etc.) 4 : go through (a situation) — **atravesarse** vr : be in the way
atrayente adj : attractive
atreverse vr : dare — **atrevido, -da** adj 1 : bold 2 INSOLENTE : insolent — **atrevimiento** nm 1 : boldness 2 DESCARO : insolence
atribuir {41} vt 1 : attribute 2 : confer (powers, etc.) — **atribuirse** vr : take credit for
atribular vt : afflict, trouble
atributo nm : attribute
atrincherar vt : entrench — **atrincherarse** vr : dig oneself in
atrocidad nf : atrocity
atronador, -dora adj : thunderous
atropellar vt 1 : run over 2 : violate, abuse (a person) — **atropellarse** vr : rush — **atropellado, -da** adj : hasty — **atropello** nm : abuse, outrage
atroz adj, pl **atroces** : atrocious
atuendo nm : attire
atufar vt : vex — **atufarse** vr : get angry
atún nm, pl **atunes** : tuna
aturdir vt 1 : stun, shock 2 CONFUNDIR : bewilder — **aturdido, -da** adj : dazed, bewildered
audaz adj, pl **-daces** : bold, daring — **audacia** nf : boldness, audacity
audible adj : audible
audición nf, pl **-clones** 1 : hearing 2 : audition (in theater, etc.)
audiencia nf : audience
audífono nm 1 : hearing aid 2 ~**s** nmpl Lat : headphones, earphones
audiovisual adj : audiovisual

auditar *vt* : audit — **auditor, -tora** *n* : auditor

auditorio *nm* **1** : auditorium **2** PÚBLICO : audience

auge *nm* **1** : peak **2** : (economic) boom

augurar *vt* : predict, foretell — **augurio** *nm* : omen

augusto, -ta *adj* : august

aula *nf* : classroom

aullar {8} *vi* : howl — **aullido** *nm* : howl

aumentar *vt* : increase, raise — *vi* : increase, grow — **aumento** *nm* : increase, rise

aun *adv* **1** : even **2** ~ **así** : even so

aún *adv* **1** : still, yet **2 más** ~ : furthermore

aunar {8} *vt* : join, combine — **aunarse** *vr* : unite

aunque *conj* **1** : though, although, even if **2** ~ **sea** : at least

aureola *nf* **1** : halo **2** FAMA : aura

auricular *nm* **1** : telephone receiver **2** ~**es** *nmpl* : headphones

aurora *nf* : dawn

ausentarse *vr* : leave, go away — **ausencia** *nf* : absence — **ausente** *adj* : absent — ~ *nmf* **1** : absentee **2** : missing person (in law)

auspicios *nmpl* : sponsorship, auspices

austero, -ra *adj* : austere — **austeridad** *nf* : austerity

austral *adj* : southern

australiano, -na *adj* : Australian

austríaco *or* **austriaco, -ca** *adj* : Austrian

auténtico, -ca *adj* : authentic, genuine — **autenticidad** *nf* : authenticity

auto *nm* : auto, car

autoayuda *nf* : self-help

autobiografía *nf* : autobiography — **autobiográfico, -ca** *adj* : autobiographical

autobús *nm, pl* -**buses** : bus

autocompasión *nf* : self-pity

autocontrol *nm* : self-control

autocracia *nf* : autocracy

autóctono, -na *adj* : indigenous, native

autodefensa *nf* : self-defense

autodidacta *adj* : self-taught

autodisciplina *nf* : self-discipline

autoestop → **autostop**

autografiar *vt* : autograph — **autógrafo** *nm* : autograph

autómata *nm* : automaton

automático, -ca *adj* : automatic — **automatización** *nf, pl* -**ciones** : automation — **automatizar** {21} *vt* : automate

automotor, -triz *adj, fpl* -**trices** : self-propelled

automóvil *nm* : automobile — **automovilista** *nmf* : motorist — **automovilístico, -ca** *adj* : automobile, car

autonomía *nf* : autonomy — **autónomo, -ma** *adj* : autonomous

autopista *nf* : expressway, highway

autopropulsado, -da *adj* : self-propelled

autopsia *nf* : autopsy

autor, -tora *n* **1** : author **2** : perpetrator (of a crime)

autoridad *nf* : authority — **autoritario, -ria** *adj* : authoritarian

autorizar {21} *vt* : authorize, approve — **autorización** *nf, pl* -**ciones** : authorization — **autorizado, -da** *adj* **1** PERMITIDO : authorized **2** : authoritative

autorretrato *nm* : self-portrait

autoservicio *nm* **1** : self-service restaurant **2** SUPERMERCADO : supermarket

autostop *nm* **1** : hitchhiking **2 hacer** ~ : hitchhike — **autostopista** *nmf* : hitchhiker

autosuficiente *adj* : self-sufficient

auxiliar *vt* : aid, assist — ~ *adj* : auxiliary — ~ *nmf* **1** : assistant, helper **2** ~ **de vuelo** : flight attendant — **auxilio** *nm* **1** : aid, assistance **2 primeros** ~**s** : first aid

avalancha *nf* : avalanche

avalar *vt* : guarantee, endorse — **aval** *nm* : guarantee, endorsement

avanzar {21} *v* : advance, move forward — **avance** *nm* : advance — **avanzado, -da** *adj* : advanced

avaricia *nf* : greed, avarice — **avaricioso, -sa** *adj* : avaricious, greedy — **avaro, -ra** *adj* : miserly — ~ *n* : miser

avasallar *vt* : overpower, subjugate — **avasallador, -dora** *adj* : overwhelming

ave *nf* : bird

avecinarse *vr* : approach

avecindarse *vr* : settle, take up residence

avellana *nf* : hazelnut

avena *nf* **1** : oats *pl* **2** *or* **harina de** ~ : oatmeal

avenida *nf* : avenue

avenir {87} *vt* : reconcile, harmonize — **avenirse** *vr* : agree, come to terms

aventajar *vt* : be ahead of, surpass

aventar {55} *vt* **1** : fan **2** : winnow (grain) **3** *Lat* : throw, toss

aventurar *vt* : venture, risk — **aventurarse** *vr* : take a risk — **aventura** *nf* **1** : adventure **2** RIESGO : risk **3** AMORÍO : love affair — **aventurado, -da** *adj*

: risky — **aventurero, -ra** *adj* : adventurous — **~** *n* : adventurer

avergonzar {9} *vt* : shame, embarrass — **avergonzarse** *vr* : be ashamed, be embarrassed

averiar {85} *vt* : damage — **averiarse** *vr* : break down — **avería** *nf* 1 : damage 2 : breakdown (of an automobile) — **averiado, -da** *adj* 1 : damaged, faulty 2 : broken down (of an automobile)

averiguar {10} *vt* 1 : find out 2 INVESTIGAR : investigate — **averiguación** *nf, pl* -**clones** : investigation, inquiry

aversión *nf, pl* -**slones** : aversion, dislike

avestruz *nm, pl* -**truces** : ostrich

aviación *nf, pl* -**clones** : aviation — **aviador, -dora** *n* : aviator

aviar {85} *vt* : prepare, make ready

ávido, -da *adj* : eager, avid — **avidez** *nf, pl* -**deces** : eagerness

avío *nm* 1 : preparation, provision 2 **~s** *nmpl* : gear, equipment

avión *nm, pl* **aviones** : airplane — **avioneta** *nf* : light airplane

avisar *vt* 1 : notify 2 ADVERTIR : warn — **aviso** *nm* 1 : notice 2 ADVERTENCIA : warning 3 *Lat* : advertisement, ad 4 **estar sobre ~** : be on the alert

avispa *nf* : wasp — **avispón** *nm, pl* -**pones** : hornet

avispado, -da *adj fam* : clever, sharp

avistar *vt* : catch sight of

avivar *vt* 1 : enliven, brighten 2 : arouse (desire, etc.) 3 : intensify (pain)

axila *nf* : underarm, armpit

axioma *nm* : axiom

ay *interj* 1 : oh! 2 : ouch!, ow!

ayer *adv* : yesterday — **~** *nm* : yesteryear, days gone by

ayote *nm Lat* : pumpkin

ayudar *vt* : help, assist — **ayudarse** *vr* **~ de** : make use of — **ayuda** *nf* : help, assistance — **ayudante** *nmf* : helper, assistant

ayunar *vi* : fast — **ayunas** *nfpl* **en ~** : fasting — **ayuno** *nm* : fast

ayuntamiento *nm* 1 : town hall, city hall (building) 2 : town or city council

azabache *nm* : jet

azada *nf* : hoe — **azadonar** *vt* : hoe

azafata *nf* : stewardess *f*

azafrán *nm, pl* -**franes** : saffron

azalea *nf* : azalea

azar *nm* 1 : chance 2 **al ~** : at random — **azaroso, -sa** *adj* : hazardous (of a journey, etc.), eventful (of a life)

azorar *vt* 1 : alarm 2 DESCONCERTAR : embarrass — **azorarse** *vr* : get embarrassed

azotar *vt* : beat, whip — **azote** *nm* 1 LÁTIGO : whip, lash 2 CALAMIDAD : scourge

azotea *nf* : flat or terraced roof

azteca *adj* : Aztec

azúcar *nmf* : sugar — **azucarado, -da** *adj* : sugary — **azucarera** *nf* : sugar bowl — **azucarero, -ra** *adj* : sugar

azufre *nm* : sulphur

azul *adj & nm* : blue — **azulado, -da** *adj* : bluish

azulejo *nm* 1 : ceramic tile 2 *Lat* : bluebird

azur *n* : azure, sky blue

azuzar {21} *vt* : incite, urge on

B

b *nf* : b, second letter of the Spanish alphabet

babear *vi* : drool, slobber — **baba** *nf* : saliva, drool

babel *nmf* : bedlam

babero *nm* : bib

babor *nm* : port (side)

babosa *nf* : slug — **baboso, -sa** *adj* 1 : slimy 2 *Lat fam* : silly

babucha *nf* : slipper

babuino *nm* : baboon

bacalao *nm* : cod

bache *nm* 1 : pothole, rut 2 DIFICULTADES : bad time

bachiller *nmf* : high school graduate — **bachillerato** *nm* : high school diploma

bacon *nm Spain* : bacon

bacteria *nf* : bacterium

bagaje *nm* : baggage, luggage

bagatela *nf* : trinket

bagre *nm* : catfish

bahía *nf* : bay

bailar *v* : dance — **bailarín, -rina** *n, mpl* -**rines** : dancer — **baile** *nm* 1 : dance 2 FIESTA : dance party, ball

bajar *vt* 1 : bring down, lower 2 DESCENDER : go down, come down — *vi* : descend, drop — **bajarse** *vr* **~ de** : get out of, get off — **baja** *nf* 1 : fall, drop 2 CESE : dismissal 3 PERMISO : sick leave 4 : (military) casualty — **bajada** *nf* : descent, drop 2 PENDIENTE : slope

bajeza *nf* : lowness, meanness

bajío *nm* : sandbank, shoal

bajo, -ja *adj* **1** : low, lower **2** : short (in stature) **3** : soft, faint (of sounds) **4** VIL : base, vile — **bajo** *adv* **1** : low **2 habla más ~** : speak more softly — **~** *nm* **1** : ground floor **2** DOBLADILLO : hem **3** : bass (in music) — **~** *prep* : under, below — **bajón** *nm, pl* **-jones** : sharp drop, slump

bala *nf* **1** : bullet **2** : bale (of cotton, etc.)

balada *nf* : ballad

balancear *vt* **1** : balance **2** : swing (one's arms, etc.), rock (a boat) — **balancearse** *vr* : swing, sway — **balance** *nm* **1** : balance **2** : balance sheet — **balanceo** *nm* : swaying, rocking

balancín *nm, pl* **-cines 1** : seesaw **2** MECEDORA : rocking chair

balanza *nf* : scales *pl*, balance

balar *vi* : bleat

balaustrada *nf* : balustrade, banister

balazo *nm* **1** DISPARO : shot **2** : bullet wound

balbucear *vi* **1** : stammer, stutter **2** : babble (of a baby) — **balbuceo** *nm* : stammering, muttering, babbling

balcón *nm, pl* **-cones** : balcony

balde *nm* **1** : bucket, pail **2 en ~** : in vain

baldío, -día *adj* **1** : uncultivated **2** INÚTIL : useless — **baldío** *nm* : wasteland

baldosa *nf* : floor tile

balear *vt Lat* : shoot (at) — **baleo** *nm Lat* : shot, shooting

balido *nm* : bleat

balín *nm, pl* **-lines** : pellet

balística *nf* : ballistics — **balístico, -ca** *adj* : ballistic

baliza *nf* **1** : buoy **2** : beacon (for aircraft)

ballena *nf* : whale

ballesta *nf* **1** : crossbow **2** : spring (of an automobile)

ballet *nm* : ballet

balneario *nm* : spa

balompié *nm* : soccer

balón *nm, pl* **-lones** : ball — **baloncesto** *nm* : basketball — **balonvolea** *nm* : volleyball

balsa *nf* **1** : raft **2** ESTANQUE : pond, pool

bálsamo *nm* : balsam, balm — **balsámico, -ca** *adj* : soothing

baluarte *nm* : bulwark, bastion

bambolear *vi* : sway, swing — **bambolearse** *vr* : sway, rock

bambú *nm, pl* **-búes** *or* **-bús** : bamboo

banal *adj* : banal

banana *nf Lat* : banana — **banano** *nm Lat* : banana

banca *nf* **1** : banking **2** BANCO : bench — **bancario, -ria** *adj* : bank, banking

— bancarrota *nf* : bankruptcy —

banco *nm* **1** : bank **2** BANCA : stool, bench, pew **3** : school (of fish)

banda *nf* **1** : band, strip **2** : band (in music) **3** PANDILLA : gang **4** : flock (of birds) **5 ~ sonora** : sound track — **bandada** *nf* : flock (of birds), school (of fish)

bandazo *nm* : lurch

bandeja *nf* : tray, platter

bandera *nf* : flag, banner

banderilla *nf* : banderilla

banderín *nm, pl* **-rines** : pennant, small flag

bandido, -da *n* : bandit

bando *nm* **1** : proclamation, edict **2** PARTIDO : faction, side

bandolero, -ra *n* : bandit

banjo *nm* : banjo

banquero, -ra *n* : banker

banqueta *nf* **1** : stool, footstool **2** *Lat* : sidewalk

banquete *nm* : banquet

bañar *vt* **1** : bathe, wash **2** SUMERGIR : immerse **3** CUBRIR : coat, cover — **bañarse** *vr* **1** : take a bath **2** : go swimming — **bañera** *nf* : bathtub — **bañista** *nmf* : bather — **baño** *nm* **1** : bath, swim **2** BAÑERA : bathtub **3 ¿dónde está el ~?** : where is the bathroom? **4 ~ María** : double boiler

baqueta *nf* **1** : ramrod **2 ~s** *nfpl* : drumsticks

bar *nm* : bar, tavern

barajar *vt* **1** : shuffle (cards) **2** CONSIDERAR : consider — **baraja** *nf* : deck of cards

baranda *nf* : rail, railing — **barandal** *nm* : handrail, banister

barato, -ta *adj* : cheap — **barato** *adv* : cheap, cheaply — **barata** *nf Lat* : sale, bargain — **baratija** *nf* : trinket — **baratillo** *nm* : secondhand store, flea market

barba *nf* **1** : beard, stubble **2** BARBILLA : chin

barbacoa *nf* : barbecue

barbaridad *nf* **1** : barbarity, cruelty **2 ¡qué ~!** : that's outrageous! — **barbarie** *nf* : barbarism, savagery — **bárbaro, -ra** *adj* : barbaric

barbecho *nm* : fallow land

barbero, -ra *n* : barber — **barbería** *nf* : barbershop

barbilla *nf* : chin

barbudo, -da *adj* : bearded

barca *nf* **1** : boat **2 ~ de pasaje** : ferryboat — **barcaza** *nf* : barge — **barco** *nm* : boat, ship

barítono *nm* : baritone

barman *nm* : bartender

barnizar {21} *vt* **1** : varnish **2** : glaze (ceramics) — **barniz** *nm, pl* **-nices 1** : varnish **2** : glaze (on ceramics)

barómetro *nm* : barometer

barón *nm, pl* **-rones** : baron — **baronesa** *nf* : baroness

barquero *nm* : boatman

barquillo *nm* : wafer, cone

barra *nf* **1** : bar, rod, stick **2** : counter (of a bar, etc.)

barraca *nf* **1** : hut, cabin **2** CASETA : booth, stall

barranco *nm or* **barranca** *nf* : ravine, gorge, gully

barredera *nf* : street-sweeping machine

barrenar *vt* : drill — **barrena** *nf* : drill, auger

barrer *v* : sweep

barrera *nf* : barrier

barreta *nf* : crowbar

barriada *nf* : district, quarter

barrica *nf* : cask, keg

barricada *nf* : barricade

barrido *nm* : sweep, sweeping

barriga *nf* : belly

barril *nm* **1** : barrel, keg **2 de** ~ : draft

barrio *nm* **1** : neighborhood **2** ~ **bajo** : slums *pl*

barro *nm* **1** : mud **2** ARCILLA : clay **3** GRANO : pimple, blackhead — **barroso, -sa** *adj* : muddy

barrote *nm* : bar (on a window)

barrunto *nm* **1** : suspicion **2** INDICIO : sign, indication

bártulos *nmpl* : things, belongings

barullo *nm* : racket, ruckus

basa *nf* : base, pedestal — **basar** *vt* : base — **basarse** *vr* ~ **en** : be based on

báscula *nf* : scales *pl*

base *nf* **1** : base **2** FUNDAMENTO : basis, foundation **3** ~ **de datos** : database — **básico, -ca** *adj* : basic

basquetbol *or* **básquetbol** *nm Lat* : basketball

bastar *vi* : be enough, suffice — **bastante** *adv* **1** : fairly, rather **2** SUFICIENTE : enough — ~ *adj* : enough, sufficient — ~ *pron* : enough

bastardo, -da *adj & n* : bastard

bastidor *nm* **1** : frame **2** : wing (in theater) **3 entre** ~**es** : behind the scenes, backstage

bastilla *nf* : hem

bastión *nf, pl* **-tiones** : bastion, stronghold

basto, -ta *adj* : coarse, rough

bastón *nm, pl* **-tones 1** : cane, walking stick **2** : baton (in parades)

basura *nf* : garbage, rubbish — **basurero, -ra** *n* : garbage collector

bata *nf* **1** : bathrobe, housecoat **2** : smock (of a doctor, laboratory worker, etc.)

batallar *vi* : battle, fight — **batalla** *nf* **1** : battle, fight, struggle **2 de** ~ : ordinary, everyday — **batallón** *nm, pl* **-llones** : battalion

batata *nf* : yam, sweet potato

batear *v* : bat, hit — **bate** *nm* : baseball bat — **bateador, -dora** *n* : batter, hitter

batería *nf* **1** : battery **2** : drums *pl* **3** ~ **de cocina** : kitchen utensils *pl*

batir *vt* **1** : beat, whip **2** DERRIBAR : knock down — **batirse** *vr* : fight — **batido** *nm* : milk shake — **batidor** *nm* : eggbeater, whisk — **batidora** *nf* : electric mixer

batuta *nf* : baton

baúl *nm* : trunk, chest

bautismo *nm* : baptism — **bautismal** *adj* : baptismal — **bautizar** {21} *vt* : baptize — **bautizo** *nm* : baptism, christening

baya *nf* : berry

bayeta *nf* : cleaning cloth

bayoneta *nf* : bayonet

bazar *nm* : bazaar

bazo *nm* : spleen

bazofia *nf fam* : rubbish, hogwash

beato, -ta *adj* : blessed

bebé *nm* : baby

beber *v* : drink — **bebedero** *nm* : watering trough — **bebedor, -dora** *n* : (heavy) drinker — **bebida** *nf* : drink, beverage — **bebido, -da** *adj* : drunk

beca *nf* : grant, scholarship

becerro, -rra *n* : calf

befa *nf* : jeer, taunt

beige *adj & nm* : beige

beisbol *or* **béisbol** *nm* : baseball — **beisbolista** *nmf* : baseball player

beldad *nf* : beauty

belén *nf, pl* **-lenes** : Nativity scene

belga *adj* : Belgian

beliceño, -ña *adj* : Belizean

bélico, -ca *adj* : military, war — **belicoso, -sa** *adj* : warlike

beligerancia *nf* : belligerence — **beligerante** *adj & nmf* : belligerent

belleza *nf* : beauty — **bello, -lla** *adj* **1** : beautiful **2 bellas artes** : fine arts

bellota *nf* : acorn

bemol *adj & nm* : flat (in music)

bendecir {11} *vt* **1** : bless **2** ~ **la mesa** : say grace — **bendición** *nf, pl* **-ciones** : benediction, blessing — **bendito, -ta** *adj* **1** : blessed, holy **2** DI-

CHOSO : fortunate **3 ¡bendito sea
Dios!** : thank goodness!
benefactor, -tora n : benefactor
beneficiar vt : benefit, assist — **beneficiarse** vr : benefit, profit — **beneficiario, -ria** n : beneficiary — **beneficio** nm **1** : gain, profit **2** BIEN : benefit
— **beneficioso, -sa** adj : beneficial —
benéfico, -ca adj : charitable
benemérito, -ta adj : worthy
beneplácito nm : approval, consent
benévolo, -la adj : benevolent, kind —
benevolencia nf : benevolence, kindness
bengala nf or **luz de ~** : flare
benigno, -na adj **1** : mild **2** : benign (in
medicine) — **benignidad** nf : mild-
ness, kindness
benjamín, -mina n, mpl **-mines**
: youngest child
beodo, -da adj & n : drunk
berenjena nf : eggplant
berrear vi **1** : bellow, low **2** : bawl, howl
(of a person) — **berrido** nm **1** : bellowing **2** : howl, scream (of a person)
berro nm : watercress
berza nf : cabbage
besar vt : kiss — **besarse** vr : kiss
(each other) — **beso** nm : kiss
bestia nf : beast, animal — **bestial** adj
: bestial, brutal — **bestialidad** nf
: brutality
betabel nm Lat : beet
betún nm, pl **-tunes** : shoe polish
bianual adj : biannual
biberón nm, pl **-rones** : baby's bottle
Biblia nf : Bible — **bíblico, -ca** adj
: biblical
bibliografía nf : bibliography — **bibli-
ográfico, -ca** adj : bibliographic, bib-
liographical
biblioteca nf : library — **bibliotecario,
-ria** n : librarian
bicarbonato nm **~ de soda** : baking
soda
bicentenario nm : bicentennial
bíceps nms & pl : biceps
bicho nm : small animal, bug
bicicleta nf : bicycle — **bici** nf fam : bike
bicolor adj : two-tone
bidón nm, pl **-dones** : large can, drum
bien adv **1** : well, good **2** CORRECTA-
MENTE : correctly, right **3** MUY : very,
quite **4** DE BUENA GANA : willingly **5**
~ que : although **6** **más ~** : rather
— **bien** adj **1** : all right, well **2** AGRAD-
ABLE : pleasant, nice **3** SATISFACTORIO
: satisfactory **4** CORRECTO : correct,
right — **bien** nm **1** : good **2 —es** nmpl
: property, goods

bienal adj & nf : biennial
bienaventurado, -da adj : blessed, fortunate
bienestar nm : welfare, well-being
bienhechor, -chora n : benefactor
bienintencionado, -da adj : well-
meaning
bienvenido, -da adj : welcome — **bienvenida** nf **1** : welcome **2 dar la ~ a**
: welcome (s.o.)
bife nm Lat : steak
bifocales nmpl : bifocals
bifurcarse {72} vr : fork — **bifurcación** nf, pl **-ciones** : fork, branch
bigamia nf : bigamy
bigote nm **1** : mustache **2 ~s** nmpl
: whiskers (of an animal)
bikini nm : bikini
bilingüe adj : bilingual
bilis nf : bile
billar nm : pool, billiards
billete nm **1** : bill, banknote **2** BOLETO
: ticket — **billetera** nf : billfold, wallet
billón nm, pl **-llones** : trillion
bimensual, -suale adj : twice a month
— **bimestral** adj : bimonthly
binario, -ria adj : binary
bingo nm : bingo
binoculares nmpl : binoculars
biodegradable adj : biodegradable
biofísica nf : biophysics
biografía nf : biography — **biográfico,
-ca** adj : biographical — **biógrafo, -fa**
n : biographer
biología nf : biology — **biológico, -ca**
adj : biological, biologic — **biólogo,
-ga** n : biologist
biombo nm : folding screen
biomecánica nf : biomechanics
biopsia nf : biopsy
bioquímica nf : biochemistry — **bio-
químico, -ca** adj : biochemical
biotecnología nf : biotechnology
bipartidista adj : bipartisan
bípedo nm : biped
biquini → bikini
birlar vt fam : swipe, pinch
bis adv **1** : twice (in music) **2** : A (in an
address) — **~** nm : encore
bisabuelo, -la n : great-grandfather m,
great-grandmother f
bisagra nf : hinge
bisecar {72} vt : bisect
biselar vt : bevel
bisexual adj : bisexual
bisiesto adj año **~** : leap year
bisnieto, -ta n : great-grandson m,
great-granddaughter f
bisonte nm : bison, buffalo
bisoño, -ña n fam : novice

bistec *nm* : steak
bisturí *nm* : scalpel
bisutería *nf* : costume jewelry
bit *nm* : bit (unit of information)
bizco, -ca *adj* : cross-eyed
bizcocho *nm* : sponge cake
bizquear *vi* : squint — **bizquera** *nf*
: squint
blanco, -ca *adj* : white — **blanco, -ca** *n*
: white person — **blanco, -ca** *n* 1 : white
2 DIANA : target, bull's-eye 3 : blank
(space) — **blancura** *nf* : whiteness
blandir {1} *vt* : wave, brandish
blando, -da *adj* : soft, tender 2 DÉBIL
: weak-willed 3 INDULGENTE : lenient
— **blandura** *nf* 1 : softness, tenderness 2 DEBILIDAD : weakness 3 INDUL-
GENCIA : leniency
blanquear *vt* 1 : whiten, bleach 2
: launder (money) — *vi* : turn white —
blanqueador *nm Lat* : bleach
blasfemar *vi* : blaspheme — **blasfemia**
nf : blasphemy — **blasfemo, -ma** *adj*
: blasphemous
bledo *nm* **no me importa un ~** *fam* : I
couldn't care less
blindaje *nm* : armor, armor plating —
blindado, -da *adj* : armored
bloc *nm, pl* **blocs** : (writing) pad
bloquear *vt* 1 OBSTRUIR : block, obstruct
2 : blockade — **bloque** *nm* 1 : block 2
: bloc (in politics) — **bloqueo** *nm* 1
OBSTRUCCIÓN : blockage 2 : blockade
blusa *nf* : blouse — **blusón** *nm, pl*
-sones : smock
boato *nm* : showiness
bobina *nf* : bobbin, reel
bobo, -ba *adj* : silly, stupid — ~ *n*
: fool, simpleton
boca *nf* 1 : mouth 2 ENTRADA : entrance
3 **~ arriba** : faceup 4 **~ abajo** : facedown, prone 5 **~ de riego** : hydrant
bocacalle *nf* : entrance (to a street)
bocado *nm* 1 : bite, mouthful 2 : bit (of
a bridle) — **bocadillo** *nm Spain*
: sandwich
bocajarro *nm* **a ~** : point-blank
bocallave *nf* : keyhole
bocanada *nf* 1 : swallow, swig 2 : puff,
gust (of smoke, wind, etc.)
boceto *nm* : sketch, outline
bochorno *nm* 1 VERGÜENZA : embarrassment 2 : muggy weather — **bochornoso, -sa** *adj* 1 VERGONZOSO
: embarrassing 2 : muggy, sultry
bocina *nf* 1 : horn 2 : mouthpiece (of a
telephone) — **bocinazo** *nm* : honk,
toot
boda *nf* : wedding
bodega *nf* 1 : wine cellar 2 : warehouse

3 : hold (of a ship or airplane) 4 *Lat*
: grocery store
bofetear *vt* : slap — **bofetada** *nf or*
bofetón *nm* : slap (in the face)
boga *nf* : fashion, vogue
bohemio, -mia *adj & n* : bohemian
boicotear *vt* : boycott — **boicot** *nm, pl*
-cots : boycott
boina *nf* : beret
bola *nf* 1 : ball 2 *fam* : fib
bolera *nf* : bowling alley
boleta *nf Lat* : ticket — **boletería** *nf Lat*
: ticket office
boletín *nm, pl* **-tines** 1 : bulletin 2 **~
de noticias** : news release
boleto *nm* : ticket
boliche *nm* 1 : bowling 2 BOLERA
: bowling alley
bolígrafo *nm* : ballpoint pen
bolillo *nm* : bobbin
boliviano, -na *adj* : Bolivian
bollo *nm* : bun, sweet roll
bolo *nm* 1 : bowling pin 2 **~s** *nmpl*
: bowling
bolsa *nf* 1 : bag 2 *Lat* : pocketbook,
purse 3 **la Bolsa** : the stock market —
bolsillo *nm* : pocket — **bolso** *nm*
Spain : pocketbook, handbag
bomba *nf* 1 : bomb 2 **~ de gasolina**
: gas pump
bombachos *nmpl* : baggy trousers
bombardear *vt* : bomb, bombard —
bombardeo *nm* : bombing, bombardment — **bombardero** *nm* : bomber
(airplane)
bombear *vt* : pump — **bombero, -ra** *n*
: firefighter
bombilla *nf* : lightbulb — **bombillo** *nm*
Lat : lightbulb
bombo *nm* 1 : bass drum 2 **a ~s y
platillos** : with a great fanfare
bombón *nm, pl* **-bones** : candy, chocolate
bonachón, -chona *adj, mpl* **-chones**
fam : good-natured
bonanza *nf* 1 : fair weather (at sea) 2
PROSPERIDAD : prosperity
bondad *nf* : goodness, kindness —
bondadoso, -sa *adj* : kind, good
boniato *nm* : sweet potato
bonificación *nf, pl* **-ciones** 1 : bonus,
extra 2 DESCUENTO : discount
bonito, -ta *adj* : pretty, lovely
bono *nm* 1 : bond 2 VALE : voucher
boquear *vi* : gasp — **boqueada** *nf*
: gasp
boquerón *nm, pl* **-rones** : anchovy
boquete *nm* : gap, opening
boquiabierto, -ta *adj* : open-mouthed,
speechless

boquilla *nf* : mouthpiece (of a musical instrument)

borbollar *vi* : bubble

borbotar *or* **borbotear** *vi* : boil, bubble, gurgle — **borbotón** *nm*, *pl* **-tones** 1 : spurt 2 **salir a borbotones** : gush out

bordar *v* : embroider — **bordado** *nm* : embroidery, needlework

borde *nm* 1 : border, edge 2 **al ~ de** : on the verge of — **bordear** *vt* : border — **bordillo** *nm* : curb

bordo *nm* **a ~** : aboard, on board

borla *nf* 1 : pom-pom, tassel 2 : powder puff

borracho, -cha *adj & n* : drunk — **borrachera** *nf* : drunkenness

borrar *vt* : erase, blot out — **borrador** *nm* 1 : rough draft 2 : eraser (for a blackboard)

borrascoso, -sa *adj* : stormy

borrego, -ga *n* : lamb, sheep — **borrego** *nm* *Lat* : false rumor, hoax

borrón *nm* 1 : smudge, blot 2 **~ y cuenta nueva** : let's forget about it — **borroso, -sa** *adj* 1 : blurry, smudgy 2 INDISTINTO : vague, hazy

bosque *nm* : woods, forest — **boscoso, -sa** *adj* : wooded

bosquejar *vt* : sketch (out) — **bosquejo** *nm* : outline, sketch

bostezar {21} *vi* : yawn — **bostezo** *nm* : yawn

bota *nf* : boot

botánica *nf* : botany — **botánico, -ca** *adj* : botanical

botar *vt* 1 : throw, hurl 2 *Lat* : throw away 3 : launch (a ship) — *vi* : bounce

bote *nm* 1 : small boat 2 *Spain* : can 3 TARRO : jar 4 SALTO : bounce, jump

botella *nf* : bottle

botín *nm*, *pl* **-tines** 1 : ankle boot 2 DESPOJOS : booty, plunder

botiquín *nm*, *pl* **-quines** 1 : medicine cabinet 2 : first-aid kit

botón *nm*, *pl* **-tones** 1 : button 2 YEMA : bud — **botones** *nmfs & pl* : bellhop

botulismo *nm* : botulism

boutique *nf* : boutique

bóveda *nf* : vault

boxear *vi* : box — **boxeador, -dora** *n* : boxer — **boxeo** *nm* : boxing

boya *nf* : buoy — **boyante** *adj* 1 : buoyant 2 PRÓSPERO : prosperous, thriving

bozal *nm* 1 : muzzle 2 : halter (for a horse)

bracear *vi* 1 : wave one's arms 2 NADAR : swim, crawl

bracero, -ra *n* : day laborer

bragas *nf* *Spain* : panties

bragueta *nf* : fly, pants zipper

braille *adj & nm* : braille

bramante *nm* : twine, string

bramar *vi* 1 : bellow, roar 2 : howl (of the wind) — **bramido** *nm* : bellow, roar

brandy *nm* : brandy

branquia *nf* : gill

brasa *nf* : ember

brasier *nm* *Lat* : brassiere

brasileño, -ña *adj* : Brazilian

bravata *nf* 1 : boast, bravado 2 AMENAZO : threat

bravo, -va *adj* 1 : fierce, savage 2 : rough (of the sea) 3 *Lat* : angry — **~** *interj* : bravo!, well done! — **bravura** *nf* 1 FEROCIDAD : fierceness 2 VALENTÍA : bravery

braza *nf* 1 : breaststroke 2 : fathom (measurement) — **brazada** *nf* : stroke (in swimming)

brazalete *nm* 1 : bracelet 2 : (cloth) armband

brazo *nm* 1 : arm 2 : branch (of a river, etc.) 3 **~ derecho** : right-hand man 4 **~s** *nmpl* : hands, laborers

brea *nf* : tar

brebaje *nm* : concoction

brecha *nf* : breach, gap

brécol *nm* : broccoli

bregar {52} *vi* 1 LUCHAR : struggle 2 TRABAJAR : work hard — **brega** *nf* **andar a la ~** : struggle

breña *nf* *or* **breñal** *nm* : scrubland, brush

breve *adj* 1 : brief, short 2 **en ~** : shortly, in short — **brevedad** *nf* : brevity, shortness — **brevemente** *adv* : briefly

brezal *nm* : moor, heath — **brezo** *nm* : heather

bricolaje *or* **bricolage** *nm* : do-it-yourself

brida *nf* : bridle

brigada *nf* 1 : brigade 2 EQUIPO : gang, team, squad

brillar *vi* : shine, sparkle — **brillante** *adj* 1 : brilliant, shiny — **~** *nm* : diamond — **brillantez** *nf* : brilliance — **brillo** *nm* 1 : luster, shine 2 ESPLENDOR : splendor — **brilloso, -sa** *adj* : shiny

brincar {72} *vi* : jump about, frolic — **brinco** *nm* : jump, skip

brindar *vi* : drink a toast — *vt* : offer, provide — **brindarse** *vr* : offer one's assistance — **brindis** *nm* : drink, toast

brío *nm* 1 : force, determination 2 ÁNIMO : spirit, verve — **brioso, -sa** *adj* : spirited, lively

brisa *nf* : breeze

británico, -ca *adj* : British
brizna *nf* 1 : strand, thread 2 : blade (of grass)
brocado *nm* : brocade
brocha *nf* : paintbrush
broche *nm* 1 : fastener, clasp 2 ALFILER : brooch
brocheta *nf* : skewer
brócoli *nm* : broccoli
bromear *vi* : joke, fool around — **broma** *nf* : joke, prank — **bromista** *adj* : fun-loving, joking — ~ *nmf* : joker, prankster
bronca *nf fam* : fight, row
bronce *nm* : bronze — **bronceado, -da** *adj* : suntanned — **bronceado** *nm* : tan — **broncearse** *vr* : get a suntan
bronco, -ca *adj* 1 : harsh, rough 2 : untamed, wild (of a horse)
bronquitis *nf* : bronchitis
broqueta *nf* : skewer
brotar *vi* 1 : bud, sprout 2 : stream, gush (of a river, tears, etc.) 3 : arise (of feelings, etc.) 4 : break out (in medicine) — **brote** *nm* 1 : outbreak 2 : sprout, bud, shoot (of plants)
brujería *nf* : witchcraft — **bruja** *nf* 1 : witch 2 *fam* : old hag — **brujo** *nm* : warlock, sorcerer — **brujo, -ja** *adj* : bewitching
brújula *nf* : compass
bruma *nf* : haze, mist — **brumoso, -sa** *adj* : hazy, misty
bruñir {38} *vt* : burnish, polish
brusco, -ca *adj* 1 SÚBITO : sudden, abrupt 2 TOSCO : brusque, rough — **brusquedad** *nf* : abruptness, brusqueness
brutal *adj* : brutal — **brutalidad** *nf* : brutality
bruto, -ta *adj* 1 : brutish, stupid 2 : crude (of petroleum, etc.), uncut (of diamonds) 3 **peso** ~ : gross weight — ~ *n* : brute
bucal *adj* : oral
bucear *vi* 1 : dive, swim underwater 2 ~ **en** : delve into — **buceo** *nm* : (underwater) diving
bucle *nm* : curl
budín *nm, pl* **-dines** : pudding
budismo *nm* : Buddhism — **budista** *adj & nmf* : Buddhist
buenamente *adv* 1 : easily 2 VOLUNTARIAMENTE : willingly
buenaventura *nf* 1 : good luck 2 **decir la** ~ **a uno** : tell s.o.'s fortune
bueno, -na *adj* (**buen** *before masculine singular nouns*) 1 : good 2 AMABLE : kind 3 APROPIADO : appropriate 4 SALUDABLE : well, healthy 5 : nice, fine (of weather) 6 **buenos días** : hello, good day 7 **buenas noches** : good night 8 **buenas tardes** : good afternoon, good evening — **bueno** *interj* : OK!, all right!
buey *nm* : ox, steer
búfalo *nm* : buffalo
bufanda *nf* : scarf
bufar *vi* : snort — **bufido** *nm* : snort
bufet *or* **bufé** *nm* : buffet-style meal
bufete *nm* 1 : law practice 2 MESA : writing desk
bufo, -fa *adj* : comic — **bufón, -fona** *n, mpl* **-fones** : buffoon, jester — **bufonada** *nf* : wisecrack
buhardilla *nf* : attic, garret
búho *nm* : owl
buitre *nm* : vulture
bujía *nf* : spark plug
bulbo *nm* : bulb (of a plant)
bulevar *nm* : boulevard
búlgaro, -ra *adj* : Bulgarian
bulla *nf* : uproar, racket
bulldozer *nm* : bulldozer
bullicio *nm* 1 : uproar 2 AJETREO : hustle and bustle — **bullicioso, -sa** *adj* : noisy, boisterous
bullir {38} *vi* 1 : boil 2 AJETREARSE : bustle, stir
bulto *nm* 1 : package, bundle 2 VOLUMEN : bulk, size 3 FORMA : form, shape 4 PROTUBERANCIA : lump, swelling
bumerán *nm, pl* **-ranes** : boomerang
buñuelo *nm* : fried pastry
buque *nm* : ship
burbujear *vi* : bubble — **burbuja** *nf* : bubble
burdel *nm* : brothel
burdo, -da *adj* : coarse, rough
burgués, -guesa *adj & n, mpl* **-gueses** : bourgeois — **burguesía** *nf* : bourgeoisie
burlar *vt* : trick, deceive — **burlarse** *vr* ~ **de** : make fun of — **burla** *nf* 1 MOFA : mockery, ridicule 2 BROMA : joke, trick
burlesco, -ca *adj* : comic, funny
burlón, -lona *adj, mpl* **-lones** : mocking
burocracia *nf* : bureaucracy — **burócrata** *nmf* : bureaucrat — **burocrático, -ca** *adj* : bureaucratic
burro, -rra *n* 1 : donkey 2 *fam* : dunce — ~ *adj* : stupid — **burro** *nm* 1 : sawhorse 2 *Lat* : stepladder
bus *nm* : bus
buscar {72} *vt* 1 : look for, seek 2 **ir a** ~ **a uno** : fetch s.o. — *vi* : search — **busca** *nf* : search — **búsqueda** *nf* : search

busto *nm* : bust (in sculpture)
butaca *nf* 1 : armchair 2 : (theater) seat
butano *nm* : butane

buzo *nm* : diver
buzón *nm, pl* -zones : mailbox
byte ['bait] *nm* : byte

C

c *nf* : c, third letter of the Spanish alphabet
cabal *adj* 1 : exact 2 COMPLETO : complete — **cabales** *nmpl* **no estar en sus ～** : not be in one's right mind
cabalgar {52} *vi* : ride — **cabalgata** *nf* : cavalcade
caballa *nf* : mackerel
caballería *nf* 1 : cavalry 2 CABALLO : horse, mount — **caballeriza** *nf* : stable
caballero *nm* 1 : gentleman 2 : knight (rank) — **caballerosidad** *nf* : chivalry — **caballeroso, -sa** *adj* : chivalrous
caballete *nm* 1 : ridge (of a roof) 2 : easel (for a canvas) 3 : bridge (of the nose)
caballito *nm* 1 : rocking horse 2 ～**s** *nmpl* : merry-go-round
caballo *nm* 1 : horse 2 : knight (in chess) 3 ～ **de fuerza** : horsepower
cabaña *nf* : cabin, hut
cabaret *nm, pl* -rets : nightclub, cabaret
cabecear *vi* 1 : shake one's head, nod 2 : pitch, lurch (of a boat)
cabecera *nf* 1 : head (of a bed, etc.) 2 : heading (in a text) 3 **médico de ～** : family doctor
cabecilla *nmf* : ringleader
cabello *nm* : hair — **cabelludo, -da** *adj* : hairy
caber {12} *vi* 1 : fit, go (into) 2 **no cabe duda** : there's no doubt
cabestro *nm* : halter
cabeza *nf* 1 : head 2 **de ～** : head first — **cabezada** *nf* 1 : butt (of the head) 2 **dar ～s** : nod off
cabezal *nm* : bolster, headrest
cabida *nf* 1 : room, capacity 2 **dar ～ a** : accomodate, find room for
cabina *nf* 1 : booth 2 : cab (of a truck, etc.) 3 : cabin, cockpit (of an airplane)
cabizbajo, -ja *adj* : downcast
cable *nm* : cable
cabo *nm* 1 : end, stub 2 TROZO : bit 3 : corporal (in the military) 4 : cape (in geography) 5 **al fin y al ～** : after all 6 **llevar a ～** : carry out, do
cabra *nf* : goat

cabriola *nf* 1 : leap, skip 2 **hacer ～s** : prance around
cabrito *nm* : kid (goat)
cacahuate *or* **cacahuete** *nm* : peanut
cacao *nm* 1 : cacao (tree) 2 : cocoa (drink)
cacarear *vi* : crow, cackle — *vt fam* : boast about
cacería *nf* : hunt
cacerola *nf* : pan, saucepan
cacharro *nm* 1 *fam* : thing, piece of junk 2 *fam* : jalopy 3 ～**s** *nmpl* : pots and pans
cachear *vt* : search, frisk
cachemir *nm or* **cachemira** *nf* : cashmere
cachete *nm Lat* : cheek — **cachetada** *nf Lat* : slap
cacho *nm* 1 *fam* : piece, bit 2 *Lat* : horn
cachorro, -rra *n* 1 : cub 2 PERRITO : puppy
cactus *or* **cacto** *nm* : cactus
cada *adj* 1 : each, every
cadalso *nm* : scaffold
cadáver *nm* : corpse
cadena *nf* 1 : chain 2 : (television) channel 3 ～ **de montaje** : assembly line
cadencia *nf* : cadence
cadera *nf* : hip
cadete *nmf* : cadet
caducar {72} *vi* : expire — **caducidad** *nf* : expiration
caer {13} *vi* 1 : fall, drop 2 ～ **bien a uno** : be to one's liking 3 **dejar ～** : drop 4 **me cae bien** : I like her, I like him — **caerse** *vr* : drop, fall (down)
café *nm* 1 : coffee 2 : café — ～ *adj Lat* : brown — **cafetera** *nf* : coffeepot — **cafetería** *nf* : coffee shop, cafeteria — **cafeína** *nf* : caffeine
caída *nf* 1 : fall, drop 2 PENDIENTE : slope
caimán *nm, pl* -manes : alligator
caja *nf* 1 : box, case 2 : checkout counter, cashier's desk (in a store) 3 ～ **fuerte** : safe 4 ～ **registradora** : cash register — **cajero, -ra** *n* 1 : cashier 2 : (bank) teller — **cajetilla** *nf* : pack (of cigarettes) — **cajón** *nm, pl* -jones 1

: drawer (in furniture) **2** : large box, crate

cajuela *nf Lat* : trunk (of a car)

cal *nf* : lime

cala *nf* : cove

calabaza *nf* **1** : pumpkin, squash, gourd **2 dar ~s a** *fam* : give the brush-off to — **calabacín** *nm, pl* **-cines** *or* **calabacita** *nf Lat* : zucchini

calabozo *nm* **1** : prison **2** CELDA : cell

calamar *nm* : squid

calambre *nm* **1** ESPASMO : cramp **2** : (electric) shock

calamidad *nf* : calamity

calar *vt* **1** : soak (through) **2** PERFORAR : pierce — **calarse** *vr* : get drenched

calavera *nf* : skull

calcar {72} *vt* **1** : trace **2** IMITAR : copy, imitate

calcetín *nm, pl* **-tines** : sock

calcinar *vt* : char

calcio *nm* : calcium

calcomanía *nf* : decal

calcular *vt* : calculate, estimate — **calculador, -dora** *adj* : calculating — **calculadora** *nf* : calculator — **cálculo** *nm* **1** : calculation **2** : calculus (in mathematics and medicine) **3 ~ biliar** : gallstone

caldera *nf* **1** : cauldron **2** : boiler (for heating, etc.) — **caldo** *nm* : broth, stock

calefacción *nf, pl* **-ciones** : heating, heat

calendario *nm* : calendar

calentar {55} *vt* : heat (up), warm (up) — **calentarse** *vr* : get warm, heat up — **calentador** *nm* : heater — **calentura** *nf* : temperature, fever

calibre *nm* **1** : caliber **2** DIÁMETRO : bore, diameter — **calibrar** *vt* : calibrate

calidad *nf* **1** : quality **2 en ~ de** : as, in the capacity of

cálido, -da *adj* : hot, warm

calidoscopio *nm* : kaleidoscope

caliente *adj* **1** : hot **2** ACALORADO : heated, fiery

calificar {72} *vt* **1** : qualify **2** EVALUAR : rate **3** : grade (an exam, etc.) — **calificación** *nf, pl* **-ciones** **1** : qualification **2** EVALUACIÓN : rating **3** NOTA : grade — **calificativo, -va** *adj* : qualifying — **calificativo** *nm* : qualifier, epithet

caligrafía *nf* : penmanship

calistenia *nf* : calisthenics

cáliz *nm, pl* **-lices** : chalice

caliza *nf* : limestone

callar *vi* : keep quiet, be silent — *vt* **1** : silence, hush **2** OCULTAR : keep secret — **callarse** *vr* : remain silent — **callado, -da** *adj* : quiet, silent

calle *nf* : street, road — **callejear** *vi* : wander about the streets — **callejero, -ra** *adj* **1** : street **2 perro callejero** : stray dog — **callejón** *nm, pl* **-jones** **1** : alley **2 ~ sin salida** : dead-end street

callo *nm* : callus, corn

calma *nf* : calm, quiet — **calmante** *adj* : soothing — **~** *nm* : tranquilizer — **calmar** *vt* : calm, soothe — **calmarse** *vr* : calm down — **calmo, -ma** *adj Lat* : calm — **calmoso, -sa** *adj* **1** : calm **2** LENTO : slow

calor *nm* **1** : heat, warmth **2 tener ~** : be hot — **caloría** *nf* : calorie

calumnia *nf* : slander, libel — **calumniar** *vt* : slander, libel

caluroso, -sa *adj* **1** : hot **2** : warm, enthusiastic (of applause, etc.)

calvo, -va *adj* : bald — **calvicie** *nf* : baldness

calza *nf* : wedge

calzada *nf* : roadway

calzado *nm* : footwear — **calzar** {21} *vt* **1** : wear (shoes) **2** : put shoes on (s.o.)

calzones *nmpl Lat* : panties — **calzoncillos** *nmpl* : underpants, briefs

cama *nf* : bed

camada *nf* : litter, brood

camafeo *nm* : cameo

cámara *nf* **1** : chamber **2** *or* **~ fotográfica** : camera **3** : house (in government)

camarada *nmf* : comrade — **camaradería** *nf* : camaraderie

camarero, -ra *n* **1** : waiter, waitress *f* **2** : steward *m*, stewardess *f* (on a ship, etc.) — **camarera** *nf* : chambermaid *f*

camarón *nm, pl* **-rones** : shrimp

camarote *nm* : cabin, stateroom

cambiar *vt* **1** : change **2** CANJEAR : exchange — *vi* **1** : change **2** : shift gears (of an automobile) — **cambiarse** *vr* **1** : change (clothing) **2** : move (to a new address) — **cambiable** *adj* : changeable — **cambio** *nm* **1** : change **2** CANJE : exchange **3 en ~** : on the other hand

camello *nm* : camel

camilla *nf* : stretcher — **camillero** *nm* : orderly (in a hospital)

caminar *vi* : walk — *vt* : cover (a distance) — **caminata** *nf* : hike

camino *nm* **1** : road, path **2** RUTA : way **3 a medio ~** : halfway (there) **4 ponerse en ~** : set out

camión *nm, pl* **-miones** **1** : truck **2** *Lat*

: bus — **camionero, -ra** *n* **1** : truck driver **2** *Lat* : bus driver — **camioneta** *nm* : light truck, van

camisa *nf* **1** : shirt **2** ~ **de fuerza** : straitjacket — **camiseta** *nf* : T-shirt, undershirt — **camisón** *nm, pl* **-sones** : nightshirt, nightgown

camorra *nf fam* : fight, trouble

camote *nm Lat* : sweet potato

campamento *nm* : camp

campana *nf* : bell — **campanada** *nf* : stroke (of a bell), peal — **campanario** *nm* : bell tower — **campanilla** *nf* : (small) bell

campaña *nf* **1** : countryside **2** : (military or political) campaign

campeón, -peona *n, mpl* **-peones** : champion — **campeonato** *nm* : championship

campesino, -na *n* : peasant, farm laborer — **campestre** *adj* : rural, rustic

camping *nm* **1** : campsite **2 hacer** ~ : go camping

campiña *nf* : countryside

campo *nm* **1** : field **2** CAMPIÑA : countryside, country **3** CAMPAMENTO : camp

camuflaje *nm* : camouflage — **camuflar** *vt* : camouflage

cana *nf* : gray hair

canadiense *adj* : Canadian

canal *nm* **1** : canal **2** MEDIO : channel **3** : (radio or television) channel — **canalizar** {21} *vt* : channel

canalete *nm* : paddle (of a canoe)

canalla *nf* : rabble — ~ *nmf fam* : swine, bastard

canapé *nm* **1** : canapé **2** SOFÁ : sofa, couch

canario *nm* : canary

canasta *nf* : basket — **canasto** *nm* : large basket

cancelar *vt* **1** : cancel **2** : pay off, settle (a debt) — **cancelación** *nf, pl* **-ciones** **1** : cancellation **2** : payment in full (of a debt)

cáncer *nm* : cancer — **canceroso, -sa** *adj* : cancerous

cancha *nf* : court, field (for sports)

canciller *nm* : chancellor

canción *nf, pl* **-ciones** **1** : song **2** ~ **de cuna** : lullaby — **cancionero** *nm* : songbook

candado *nm* : padlock

candela *nf* : candle — **candelabro** *nm* : candelabra — **candelero** *nm* **1** : candlestick **2 estar en el** ~ : be in the limelight

candente *adj* : red-hot

candidato, -ta *n* : candidate — **candidatura** *nf* : candidacy

cándido, -da *adj* : naïve — **candidez** *nf* **1** : simplicity **2** INGENUIDAD : naïveté

candil *nm* : oil lamp — **candilejas** *nfpl* : footlights

candor *nm* : naïveté, innocence

canela *nf* : cinnamon

cangrejo *nm* : crab

canguro *nm* : kangaroo

caníbal *nmf* : cannibal — **canibalismo** *nm* : cannibalism

canicas *nfpl* : (game of) marbles

canino, -na *adj* : canine — **canino** *nm* : canine (tooth)

canjear *vt* : exchange — **canje** *nm* : exchange, trade

cano, -na *adj* : gray, gray-haired

canoa *nf* : canoe

canon *nm, pl* **cánones** : canon

canonizar {21} *vt* : canonize

canoso, -sa *adj* : gray, gray-haired

cansar *vt* : tire (out) — *vi* : be tiring — **cansarse** *vr* : get tired — **cansado, -da** *adj* **1** : tired **2** PESADO : tiresome — **cansancio** *nm* : fatigue, weariness

cantalupo *nm* : cantaloupe

cantar *v* : sing — ~ *nm* : song — **cantante** *nmf* : singer

cántaro *nm* **1** : pitcher, jug **2 llover a** ~ **s** *fam* : rain cats and dogs

cantera *nf* : quarry (excavation)

cantidad *nf* **1** : quantity, amount **2 una** ~ **de** : lots of

cantimplora *nf* : canteen, water bottle

cantina *nf* **1** : canteen, cafeteria **2** *Lat* : tavern, bar

canto *nm* **1** : singing, song **2** BORDE, LADO : edge **3 de** ~ : on end, sideways **4** ~ **rodado** : boulder — **cantor, -tora** *adj* **1** : singing **2 pájaro** ~ : songbird — ~ *n* : singer

caña *nf* **1** : cane, reed **2** ~ **de pescar** : fishing pole

cáñamo *nm* : hemp

cañería *nf* : pipes, piping — **caño** *nm* **1** : pipe **2** : spout (of a fountain) — **cañón** *nm, pl* **-ñones** **1** : cannon **2** : barrel (of a gun) **3** : canyon (in geography)

caoba *nf* : mahogany

caos *nm* : chaos — **caótico, -ca** *adj* : chaotic

capa *nf* **1** : cape, cloak **2** : coat (of paint, etc.), coating (in cooking) **3** ESTRATO : layer, stratum **4** : (social) class

capacidad *nf* **1** : capacity **2** APTITUD : ability

capacitar *vt* : train, qualify — **capacitación** *nf, pl* **-ciones** : training

caparazón *nm, pl* **-zones** : shell
capataz *nmf, pl* **-taces** : foreman
capaz *adj, pl* **-paces 1** : capable, able **2** ESPACIOSO : spacious
capellán *nm, pl* **-llanes** : chaplain
capilla *nf* : chapel
capital *adj* **1** : capital **2** PRINCIPAL : chief, principal — ~ *nm* : capital (assets) — ~ *nf* : capital (city)
capitalismo *nm* : capitalism — **capitalista** *adj & nmf* : capitalist, capitalistic — **capitalizar** {21} *vt* : capitalize
capitán, -tana *n, mpl* **-tanes** : captain
capitolio *nm* : capitol
capitular *vi* : capitulate, surrender — **capitulación** *nf, pl* **-ciones** : surrender
capítulo *nm* : chapter
capó *nm* : hood (of a car)
capote *nm* : cloak, cape
capricho *nm* **1** : whim, caprice — **caprichoso, -sa** *adj* : whimsical, capricious
cápsula *nf* : capsule
captar *vt* **1** : grasp **2** ATRAER : gain, attract (interest, etc.) **3** : harness (waters)
capturar *vt* : capture, seize — **captura** *nf* : capture, seizure
capucha *nf* : hood (of clothing)
capullo *nm* **1** : cocoon **2** : (flower) bud
caqui *adj & nm* : khaki
cara *nf* **1** : face **2** ASPECTO : appearance **3** *fam* : nerve, gall **4** ~ **a** *or* **de** ~ **a** : facing
carabina *nf* : carbine
caracol *nm* **1** : snail **2** : conch **3** RIZO : curl
caribe *adj* : Caribbean
carácter *nm, pl* **-racteres 1** : character **2** ÍNDOLE : nature — **característica** *nf* : characteristic — **característico, -ca** *adj* : characteristic — **caracterizar** {21} *vt* : characterize
caramba *interj* : oh my!, good grief!
carámbano *nm* : icicle
caramelo *nm* **1** : caramel **2** DULCE : candy
carátula *nf* **1** CARETA : mask **2** : jacket (of a record, etc.) **3** *Lat* : face (of a watch)
caravana *nf* **1** : caravan **2** REMOLQUE : trailer
caray → **caramba**
carbohidrato *nm* : carbohydrate
carbón *nm, pl* **-bones 1** : coal **2** : charcoal (for drawing) — **carboncillo** : charcoal — **carbonero, -ra** *adj* : coal — **carbonizar** {21} *vt* : char — **carbono** *nm* : carbon — **carburador** *nm* : carburetor — **carburante** *nm* : fuel
carcajada *nf* : loud laugh, guffaw

cárcel *nf* : jail, prison — **carcelero, -ra** *n* : jailer
carcinógeno *nm* : carcinogen
carcomer *vt* : eat away at — **carcomido, -da** *adj* : worm-eaten
cardenal *nm* **1** : cardinal **2** CONTUSIÓN : bruise
cardíaco *or* **cardiaco, -ca** *adj* : cardiac, heart
cárdigan *nm, pl* **-gans** : cardigan
cardinal *adj* : cardinal
cardiólogo, -ga *n* : cardiologist
cardo *nm* : thistle
carear *vt* : bring face-to-face
carecer {53} *vi* ~ **de** : lack — **carencia** *nf* : lack, want — **carente** *adj* ~ **de** : lacking (in)
carestía *nf* **1** : high cost **2** ESCASEZ : dearth, scarcity
careta *nf* : mask
cargar {52} *vt* **1** : load **2** : charge (a battery, a purchase, etc.) **3** LLEVAR : carry **4** ~ **de** : burden with — *vi* **1** : load **2** ~ **con** : pick up, carry away — **carga** *nf* **1** : load **2** CARGAMENTO : freight, cargo **3** RESPONSABILIDAD : burden **4** : charge (in electricity, etc.) — **cargado, -da** *adj* **1** : loaded, burdened **2** PESADO : heavy, stuffy **3** : charged (of a battery) **4** FUERTE : strong, concentrated — **cargamento** *nm* : cargo, load — **cargo** *nm* **1** : charge **2** PUESTO : position, office
cariarse *vr* : decay (of teeth)
caribe *adj* : Caribbean
caricatura *nf* **1** : caricature **2** : (political) cartoon — **caricaturizar** *vt* : caricature
caricia *nf* : caress
caridad *nf* **1** : charity **2** LIMOSNA : alms *pl*
caries *nfs & pl* : cavity (in a tooth)
cariño *nm* : affection, love — **cariñoso, -sa** *adj* : affectionate, loving
carisma *nm* : charisma — **carismático, -ca** *adj* : charismatic
caritativo, -va *adj* : charitable
cariz *nm, pl* **-rices** : appearance, aspect
carmesí *adj & nm* : crimson
carmín *nm, pl* **-mines** *or* ~ **de labios** : lipstick
carnada *nf* : bait
carnal *adj* **1** : carnal **2 primo** ~ : first cousin
carnaval *nm* : carnival
carne *nf* **1** : meat **2** : flesh (of persons or fruits) **3** ~ **de cerdo** : pork **4** ~ **de gallina** : goose bumps **5** ~ **de ternera** : veal
carné *nm* → **carnet**

carnero *nm* 1 : ram, sheep 2 : mutton (in cooking)

carnet *nm* 1 ~ **de conducir** : driver's license 2 ~ **de identidad** : identification card, ID

carnicería *nf* 1 : butcher shop 2 MATANZA : slaughter — **carnicero, -ra** *n* : butcher

carnívoro, -ra *adj* : carnivorous — **carnívoro** *nm* : carnivore

carnoso, -sa *adj* : fleshy

caro, -ra *adj* 1 : expensive 2 QUERIDO : dear — **caro** *adv* : dearly

carpa *nf* 1 : carp 2 TIENDA : tent

carpeta *nf* : folder

carpintería *nf* : carpentry — **carpintero, -ra** *n* : carpenter

carraspear *vi* : clear one's throat — **carraspera** *nf* 1 : hoarseness 2 **tener** ~ : have a frog in one's throat

carrera *nf* 1 : running, run 2 COMPETICIÓN : race 3 : course (of studies) 4 PROFESIÓN : career, profession

carreta *nf* : cart, wagon

carrete *nm* : reel, spool

carretera *nf* : highway, road

carretilla *nf* : wheelbarrow

carril *nm* 1 : lane (of a road) 2 : rail (for a railroad)

carrillo *nm* : cheek

carrito *nm* : cart, trolley

carrizo *nm* : reed

carro *nm* 1 : wagon, cart 2 *Lat* : automobile, car — **carrocería** *nf* : body (of an automobile)

carroña *nf* : carrion

carroza *nf* 1 : carriage 2 : float (in a parade)

carruaje *nm* : carriage

carrusel *nm* : merry-go-round, carousel

carta *nf* 1 : letter 2 NAIPE : playing card 3 : charter (of an organization, etc.) 4 MENÚ : menu 5 MAPA : map, chart

cartel *nm* : poster, bill — **cartelera** *nf* : billboard

cartera *nf* 1 : briefcase 2 BILLETERA : wallet 3 *Lat* : pocketbook, handbag — **carterista** *nmf* : pickpocket

cartero, -ra *nm* : mail carrier, mailman *m*

cartílago *nm* : cartilage

cartilla *nf* 1 : primer, reader 2 : booklet, record (of a savings account, etc.)

cartón *nm*, *pl* **-tones** 1 : cardboard 2 : carton (of cigarettes, etc.)

cartucho *nm* : cartridge

casa *nf* 1 : house 2 HOGAR : home 3 EMPRESA : company, firm 4 ~ **flotante** : houseboat

casar *vt* : marry — *vi* : go together, match up — **casarse** *vr* 1 : get married 2 ~ **con** : marry — **casado, -da** *adj* : married — **casamiento** *nm* 1 : marriage 2 BODA : wedding

cascabel *nm* : small bell

cascada *nf* : waterfall

cascanueces *nms & pl* : nutcracker

cascar {72} *vt* : crack (a shell, etc.) — **cascarse** *vr* : crack, chip — **cáscara** *nf* : skin, peel, shell — **cascarón** *nm*, *pl* **-rones** : eggshell

casco *nm* 1 : helmet 2 : hull (of a boat) 3 : hoof (of a horse) 4 : fragment (of ceramics, etc.) 5 : center (of a town) 6 ENVASE : empty bottle

caserío *nm* 1 *Spain* : country house 2 POBLADO : hamlet

casero, -ra *adj* 1 : homemade 2 DOMÉSTICO : domestic, household — ~ *n* : landlord, landlady *f*

caseta *nf* : booth, stall

casete → cassette

casi *adv* 1 : almost, nearly 2 (*in negative phrases*) : hardly

casilla *nf* 1 : compartment, pigeonhole 2 CASETA : booth 3 : box (on a form)

casino *nm* 1 : casino 2 : (social) club

caso *nm* 1 : case 2 **en** ~ **de** : in the event of 3 **hacer** ~ : pay attention 4 **no venir al** ~ : be beside the point

caspa *nf* : dandruff

cassette *nmf* : cassette

casta *nf* 1 : lineage, descent 2 : breed (of animals) 3 : caste (in India)

castaña *nf* : chestnut

castañetear *vi* : chatter (of teeth)

castaño, -ña *adj* : chestnut (color)

castañuela *nf* : castanet

castellano *nm* : Spanish, Castilian (language)

castidad *nf* : chastity

castigar {52} *vt* 1 : punish 2 : penalize (in sports) — **castigo** *nm* 1 : punishment 2 : penalty (in sports)

castillo *nm* : castle

casto, -ta *adj* : chaste, pure — **castizo, -za** *adj* : pure, traditional (in style)

castor *nm* : beaver

castrar *vt* : castrate

castrense *adj* : military

casual *adj* : chance, accidental — **casualidad** *nf* 1 : coincidence 2 **por** ~ **or de** ~ : by chance — **casualmente** *adv* : by chance

cataclismo *nm* : cataclysm

catalán, -lana *adj*, *mpl* **-lanes** : Catalan — **catalán** *nm* : Catalan (language)

catalizador *nm* : catalyst

catalogar {52} *vt* : catalog, classify — **catálogo** *nm* : catalog

catapulta *nf* : catapult

catar *vt* : taste, sample

catarata *nf* **1** : waterfall **2** : cataract (in medicine)

catarro *nm* RESFRIADO : cold

catástrofe *nf* : catastrophe, disaster — **catastrófico, -ca** *adj* : catastrophic, disastrous

catecismo *nm* : catechism

cátedra *nf* : chair (at a university)

catedral *nf* : cathedral

catedrático, -ca *n* : professor

categoría *nf* **1** : category **2** RANGO : rank **3 de ~** : first-rate — **categórico, -ca** *adj* : categorical

catorce *adj & nm* : fourteen — **catorceavo** *nm* : fourteenth

catre *nm* : cot

cauce *nm* **1** : riverbed **2** VÍA : channel, means *pl*

caucho *nm* : rubber

caución *nf, pl* **-ciones** : security, guarantee

caudal *nm* **1** : volume of water, flow **2** RIQUEZA : wealth

caudillo *nm* : leader, commander

causar *vt* : cause, provoke — **causa** *nf* **1** : cause **2** RAZÓN : reason **3** : case (in law) **4 a ~ de** : because of

cáustico, -ca *adj* : caustic

cautela *nf* : caution — **cauteloso, -sa** *adj* : cautious — **cautelosamente** *adv* : cautiously, warily

cautivar *vt* **1** : capture **2** ENCANTAR : captivate — **cautiverio** *nm* : captivity — **cautivo, -va** *adj & n* : captive

cauto, -ta *adj* : cautious

cavar *v* : dig

caverna *nf* : cavern, cave

cavidad *nf* : cavity

cavilar *vi* : ponder

cayado *nm* : crook, staff

cazar {21} *vt* **1** : hunt **2** ATRAPAR : catch, bag — *vi* : go hunting — **caza** *nf* **1** : hunt, hunting **2** : game (animals) — **cazador, -dora** *n* : hunter

cazo *nm* **1** : saucepan **2** CUCHARÓN : ladle — **cazuela** *nf* : casserole

CD *nm* : CD, compact disc

cebada *nf* : barley

cebar *vt* **1** : bait **2** : feed, fatten (animals) **3** : prime (a firearm, etc.) — **cebo** *nm* **1** CARNADA : bait **2** : charge (of a firearm)

cebolla *nf* : onion — **cebolleta** *nf* : scallion, green onion — **cebollino** *nm* : chive

cebra *nf* : zebra

cecear *vi* : lisp — **ceceo** *nm* : lisp

cedazo *nm* : sieve

ceder *vi* **1** : yield, give way **2** DISMINUIR : diminish, abate — *vt* : cede, hand over

cedro *nm* : cedar

cédula *nf* : document, certificate

cegar {49} *vt* **1** : blind **2** TAPAR : block, stop up — *vi* : be blinded, go blind — **ceguera** *nf* : blindness

ceja *nf* : eyebrow

cejar *vi* : give in, back down

celada *nf* : trap, ambush

celador, -dora *n* : guard, warden

celda *nf* : cell (of a jail)

celebrar *vt* **1** : celebrate **2** : hold (a meeting), say (Mass) **3** ALEGRARSE DE : be happy about — **celebrarse** *vr* : take place — **celebración** *nf, pl* **-ciones** : celebration — **célebre** *adj* : famous, celebrated — **celebridad** *nf* : celebrity

celeridad *nf* : swiftness, speed

celeste *adj* **1** : celestial, heavenly **2** *or* **azul ~** : sky blue — **celestial** *adj* : celestial, heavenly

celibato *nm* : celibacy — **célibe** *adj* : celibate

celo *nm* **1** : zeal **2 en ~** : in heat **3 ~s** *nmpl* : jealousy **4 tener ~s** : be jealous

celofán *nm, pl* **-fanes** : cellophane

celoso, -sa *adj* **1** : jealous **2** DILIGENTE : zealous

célula *nf* : cell — **celular** *adj* : cellular

celulosa *nf* : cellulose

cementerio *nm* : cemetery

cemento *nm* **1** : cement **2 ~ armado** : reinforced concrete

cena *nf* : supper, dinner

cenagal *nm* : bog, quagmire — **cenagoso** *adj* : swampy

cenar *vi* : have dinner, have supper — *vt* : have for dinner or supper

cenicero *nm* : ashtray

cenit *nm* : zenith

ceniza *nf* : ash

censo *nm* : census

censurar *vt* **1** : censor **2** REPROBAR : censure, criticize — **censura** *nf* **1** : censorship **2** REPROBACIÓN : censure, criticism

centavo *nm* **1** : cent **2** : centavo (unit of currency)

centellear *vi* : sparkle, twinkle — **centella** *nf* **1** : flash **2** CHISPA : spark — **centelleo** *nm* : twinkling, sparkle

centenar *nm* : hundred — **centenario** *nm* : centennial

centeno *nm* : rye

centésimo, -ma adj : hundredth
centígrado adj : centigrade, Celsius
centigramo nm : centigram
centímetro nm : centimeter
centinela nmf : sentinel, sentry
central adj : central — ~ nf : main office, headquarters — **centralita** nf : switchboard — **centralizar** {21} vt : centralize
centrar vt : center — **centrarse** vr ~ **en** : focus on — **céntrico, -ca** adj : central — **centro** nm 1 : center 2 : downtown (of a city) 3 ~ **de mesa** : centerpiece
centroamericano, -na adj : Central American
ceñir {67} vt 1 : encircle 2 : fit (s.o.) tightly — **ceñirse** vr ~ **a** : limit oneself to — **ceñido, -da** adj : tight
ceño nm 1 : frown 2 **fruncir el** ~ : knit one's brow, frown
cepillo nm 1 : brush 2 : (carpenter's) plane 3 ~ **de dientes** : toothbrush — **cepillar** vt 1 : brush 2 : plane (wood)
cera nf 1 : wax, beeswax 2 : floor wax, furniture wax
cerámica nf 1 : ceramics pl 2 : (piece of) pottery
cerca¹ nf : fence — **cercado** nm : enclosure
cerca² adv 1 : close, near 2 ~ **de** : near, close to 3 ~ **de** : nearly, almost — **cercano, -na** adj : near, close — **cercanía** nf 1 : proximity 2 ~**s** nfpl : outskirts
cercar {72} vt 1 : fence in 2 RODEAR : surround
cerciorarse vr ~ **de** : make sure of
cerco nm 1 : circle, ring 2 ASEDIO : siege 3 Lat : fence
cerda nf : bristle
cerdo nm 1 : pig, hog 2 ~ **macho** : boar
cereal adj & nm : cereal
cerebro nm : brain — **cerebral** adj : cerebral
ceremonia nf : ceremony — **ceremonial** adj : ceremonial — **ceremonioso, -sa** adj : ceremonious
cereza nf : cherry
cerilla nf : match — **cerillo** nm Lat : match
cerner {56} or **cernir** vt : sift — **cernerse** vr 1 : hover 2 ~ **sobre** : loom over — **cernidor** nm : sieve
cero nm : zero
cerrar {55} vt 1 : close, shut 2 : turn off (a faucet, etc.) 3 : bring to an end — vi 1 : close up, lock up 2 : close down (a business, etc.) — **cerrarse** vr 1

: close, shut 2 TERMINAR : come to a close, end — **cerrado, -da** adj 1 : closed, shut, locked 2 : overcast (of weather) 3 : sharp (of a curve) 4 : thick, broad (of an accent) — **cerradura** nf : lock — **cerrajero, -ra** n : locksmith
cerro nm : hill
cerrojo nm : bolt, latch
certamen nm, pl **-támenes** : competition, contest
certero, -ra adj : accurate, precise
certeza nf : certainty — **certidumbre** nf : certainty
certificar {72} vt 1 : certify 2 : register (mail) — **certificado, -da** adj : certified, registered — **certificado** nm : certificate
cervato nm : fawn
cerveza nf 1 : beer 2 ~ **de barril** : draft beer — **cervecería** nf 1 : brewery 2 BAR : beer hall, bar
cesar vi : cease, stop — vt : dismiss, lay off — **cesación** nf, pl **-clones** : cessation, suspension — **cesante** adj 1 : laid off 2 Lat : unemployed — **cesantía** nf Lat : unemployment
cesárea nf : cesarean (section)
cese nm 1 : cessation, stop 2 DESTITUCIÓN : dismissal
césped nm : lawn, grass
cesta nf : basket — **cesto** nm 1 : (large) basket 2 ~ **de basura** : wastebasket
cetro nm : scepter
chabacano nm Lat : apricot
chabola nf Spain : shack, shanty
chacal nm : jackal
cháchara nf fam : gabbing, chatter
chacra nf Lat : (small) farm
chafar vt fam : flatten, crush
chal nm : shawl
chaleco nm : vest
chalet nm Spain : house
chalupa nf 1 : small boat 2 Lat : small stuffed tortilla
chamarra nf : jacket
chamba nf Lat fam : job
champaña or **champán** nm : champagne
champiñón nm, pl **-ñones** : mushroom
champú nm, pl **-pús** or **-púes** : shampoo
chamuscar {72} vt : scorch
chance nm Lat : chance, opportunity
chancho nm Lat : pig
chanclos nmpl : galoshes
chantaje nm : blackmail — **chantajear** vt : blackmail
chanza nf : joke, jest
chapa nf 1 : sheet, plate 2 INSIGNIA : badge — **chapado, -da** adj 1 : plated

2 **chapado a la antigua** : old-fashioned

chaparrón *nm, pl* **-rrones** : downpour

chapotear *vi* : splash

chapucero, -ra *adj* : shoddy, sloppy — **chapuza** *nf* : botched job

chapuzón *nm, pl* **-zones** : dip, short swim

chaqueta *nf* : jacket

charca *nf* : pond — **charco** *nm* : puddle

charlar *vi* : chat — **charla** *nf* : chat, talk — **charlatán, -tana** *adj, mpl* **-tanes** : talkative — ~ *n* 1 : chatterbox 2 FARSANTE : charlatan

charol *nm* 1 : patent leather 2 BARNIZ : varnish

chasco *nm* 1 : trick, joke 2 DECEPCIÓN : disappointment

chasis *nms & pl* : chassis

chasquear *vt* 1 : click (the tongue), snap (one's fingers) 2 : crack (a whip) — **chasquido** *nm* 1 : click, snap 2 : crack (of a whip)

chatarra *nf* : scrap (metal)

chato, -ta *adj* 1 : pug-nosed 2 APLANADO : flat

chauvinismo *nm* : chauvinism — **chauvinista** *adj* : chauvinist, chauvinistic

chaval, -vala *n fam* : kid, boy *m*, girl *f*

checo, -ca *adj* : Czech — **checo** *nm* : Czech (language)

chef *nm* : chef

cheque *nm* : check — **chequera** *nf* : checkbook

chequear *vt Lat* 1 : check, inspect, verify 2 : check in (baggage) — **chequeo** *nm* 1 : (medical) checkup 2 *Lat* : check, inspection

chica → **chico**

chicano, -na *adj* : Chicano, Mexican-American

chícharo *nm Lat* : pea

chicharrón *nm, pl* **-rrones** : pork rind

chichón *nm, pl* **-chones** : bump

chicle *nm* : chewing gum

chico, -ca *adj* : little, small — ~ *n* : child, boy *m*, girl *f*

chiflar *vt* : whistle at, boo — *vi Lat* : whistle — **chiflado, -da** *adj fam* : crazy, nuts — **chiflido** *nm* : whistling

chile *nm* : chili pepper

chileno, -na *adj* : Chilean

chillar *vi* 1 : shriek, scream 2 CHIRRIAR : screech, squeal — **chillido** *nm* 1 : scream 2 CHIRRIDO : screech, squeal — **chillón, -llona** *adj, mpl* **-llones** : shrill, loud

chimenea *nf* 1 : chimney 2 HOGAR : fireplace

chimpancé *nm* : chimpanzee

chinche *nf* : bedbug

chino, -na *adj* : Chinese — **chino** *nm* : Chinese (language)

chiquillo, -lla *n* : kid, child

chiquito, -ta *adj* : tiny — ~ *n* : little child, tot

chiribita *nf* : spark

chiripa *nf* 1 : fluke 2 **de** ~ : by sheer luck

chirivía *nf* : parsnip

chirriar {85} *vi* 1 : squeak, creak 2 : screech (of brakes, etc.) — **chirrido** *nm* 1 : squeak, creak 2 : screech (of brakes)

chisme *nm* : (piece of) gossip — **chismear** *vi* : gossip — **chismoso, -sa** *adj* : gossipy — ~ *n* : gossip

chispear *vi* : spark — **chispa** *nf* : spark

chisporrotear *vi* : crackle, sizzle — **chisporroteo** *nm* : crackle

chiste *nm* : joke, funny story — **chistoso, -sa** *adj* : funny, witty

chivo, -va *n* : kid, young goat

chocar {72} *vi* 1 : crash, collide 2 ENFRENTARSE : clash — **chocante** *adj* 1 : striking, shocking 2 *Lat* : unpleasant, rude

choclo *nm Lat* : ear of corn, corncob

chocolate *nm* : chocolate

chofer *or* **chófer** *nm* 1 : chauffeur 2 CONDUCTOR : driver

choque *nm* 1 : shock 2 : crash, collision (of vehicles) 3 CONFLICTO : clash

chorizo *nm* : chorizo, sausage

chorrear *vi* 1 : drip 2 BROTAR : pour out, gush — **chorro** *nm* 1 : stream, jet 2 HILO : trickle

chovinismo → **chauvinismo**

choza *nf* : hut, shack

chubasco *nm* : downpour, squall

chuchería *nf* 1 : knickknack, trinket 2 DULCE : sweet

chueco, -ca *adj Lat* : crooked

chuleta *nf* : cutlet, chop

chulo, -la *adj fam* : cute, pretty

chupar *vt* 1 : suck 2 ABSORBER : absorb 3 *fam* : guzzle — *vi* : suckle — **chupada** *nf* : suck, sucking — **chupete** *nm* 1 : pacifier 2 *Lat* : lollipop

churro *nm* 1 : fried dough 2 *fam* : botch, mess

chusco, -ca *adj* : funny

chusma *nf* : riffraff, rabble

chutar *vi* : shoot (in soccer)

cianuro *nm* : cyanide

cicatriz *nf, pl* **-trices** : scar — **cicatrizar** {21} *vi* : form a scar, heal

cíclico, -ca *adj* : cyclical

ciclismo *nm* : cycling — **ciclista** *nmf* : cyclist

ciclo *nm* : cycle

ciclón *nm*, *pl* **-clones** : cyclone

ciego, -ga *adj* : blind — **ciegamente** *adv* : blindly

cielo *nm* 1 : sky 2 : heaven (in religion)

ciempiés *nms & pl* : centipede

cien *adj* : a hundred, hundred — ∼ *nm* : one hundred

ciénaga *nf* : swamp, bog

ciencia *nf* 1 : science 2 a ∼ **cierta** : for a fact

cieno *nm* : mire, mud, silt

científico, -ca *adj* : scientific — ∼ *n* : scientist

ciento *adj* (*used in compound numbers*) : one hundred — ∼ *nm* 1 : hundred, group of a hundred 2 por ∼ : percent

cierre *nm* 1 : closing, closure 2 BROCHE : fastener, clasp

cierto, -ta *adj* 1 : true 2 SEGURO : certain 3 por ∼ : as a matter of fact

ciervo, -va *n* : deer, stag *m*, hind *f*

cifra *nf* 1 : number, figure 2 : sum (of money, etc.) 3 CLAVE : code, cipher — **cifrar** *vt* 1 : write in code 2 ∼ **la esperanza en** : pin all one's hopes on

cigarrillo *nm* : cigarrette — **cigarro** *nm* 1 : cigarette 2 PURO : cigar

cigüeña *nf* : stork

cilantro *nm* : cilantro, coriander

cilindro *nm* : cylinder — **cilíndrico, -ca** *adj* : cylindrical

cima *nf* : peak, summit

címbalo *nm* : cymbal

cimbrar *or* **cimbrear** *vt* : shake, rock — **cimbrarse** *or* **cimbrearse** *vr* : sway

cimentar {55} *vt* 1 : lay the foundation of 2 : cement, strengthen (relations, etc.) — **cimientos** *nmpl* : base, foundation(s)

cinc *nm* : zinc

cincel *nm* : chisel — **cincelar** *vt* : chisel

cinco *adj & nm* : five

cincuenta *adj & nm* : fifty — **cincuentavo, -va** *adj* : fiftieth — **cincuentavo** *nm* : fiftieth

cine *nm* : cinema, movies *pl* — **cinematográfico, -ca** *adj* : movie, film

cínico, -ca *adj* : cynical — ∼ *n* : cynic — **cinismo** *nm* : cynicism

cinta *nf* 1 : ribbon, band 2 ∼ **adhesiva** : adhesive tape 3 ∼ **métrica** : tape measure 4 ∼ **magnetofónica** : magnetic tape

cinto *nm* : belt, girdle — **cintura** *nf* : waist — **cinturón** *nm*, *pl* **-rones** 1 : belt 2 ∼ **de seguridad** : seat belt

ciprés *nm*, *pl* **-preses** : cypress

circo *nm* : circus

circuito *nm* : circuit

circulación *nf*, *pl* **-clones** 1 : circulation 2 TRÁFICO : traffic — **circular** *vi* 1 : circulate 2 : drive (a vehicle) — ∼ *adj* : circular

círculo *nm* : circle

circuncidar *vt* : circumcise — **circuncisión** *nf*, *pl* **-siones** : circumcision

circundar *vt* : surround

circunferencia *nf* : circumference

circunscribir {33} *vt* : confine, limit — **circunscribirse** *vr* ∼ **a** : limit oneself to — **circunscripción** *nf*, *pl* **-clones** : district, constituency

circunspecto, -ta *adj* : circumspect, cautious

circunstancia *nf* : circumstance — **circunstancial** *adj* : chance — **circunstante** *nmf* 1 : bystander 2 **los** ∼**s** : those present

circunvalación *nf*, *pl* **-clones** 1 : encircling 2 **carretera de** ∼ : bypass

cirio *nm* : candle

ciruela *nf* 1 : plum 2 ∼ **pasa** : prune

cirugía *nf* : surgery — **cirujano, -na** *n* : surgeon

cisma *nf* : schism

cisne *nm* : swan

cisterna *nf* : cistern

cita *nf* 1 : appointment, date 2 REFERENCIA : quote, quotation — **citación** *nf*, *pl* **-clones** : summons — **citar** *vt* 1 : quote, cite 2 CONVOCAR : make an appointment with 3 : summon (in law) — **citarse** *vr* ∼ **con** : arrange to meet

cítrico *nm* : citrus (fruit)

ciudad *nf* : city, town — **ciudadano, -na** *n* 1 : citizen 2 HABITANTE : resident — **ciudadanía** *nf* : citizenship

cívico, -ca *adj* : civic

civil *adj* : civil — ∼ *nmf* : civilian — **civilidad** *nf* : civility — **civilización** *nf*, *pl* **-clones** : civilization — **civilizar** {21} *vt* : civilize

cizaña *nf* : discord, rift

clamar *vi* : clamor, cry out — **clamor** *nm* : clamor, outcry — **clamoroso, -sa** *adj* : clamorous, loud

clan *nm* : clan

clandestino, -na *adj* : clandestine, secret

clara *nf* : egg white

claraboya *nf* : skylight

claramente *adv* : clearly

clarear *v impers* 1 : dawn 2 ACLARAR : clear up — *vi* : be transparent

claridad *nf* 1 : clarity, clearness 2 LUZ : light

clarificar {72} *vt* : clarify — **clarificación** *nf*, *pl* **-clones** : clarification

clarín *nm*, *pl* **-rines** : bugle

clarinete *nm* : clarinet

clarividente *adj* **1** : clairvoyant **2** PER-
SPICAZ : perspicacious — **clarividen-
cia** *nf* **1** : clairvoyance **2** PERSPICACIA
: farsightedness

claro *adv* **1** : clearly **2** POR SUPUESTO : of
course, surely — **~** *nm* **1** : clearing,
glade **2** **~** **de luna** : moonlight —
claro, -ra *adj* **1** : clear, bright **2** : light
(of colors) **3** EVIDENTE : clear, evident

clase *nf* **1** : class **2** TIPO : sort, kind

clásico, -ca *adj* : classic, classical —
clásico *nm* : classic

clasificar {72} *vt* **1** : classify, sort out **2**
: rate, rank (a hotel, a team, etc.) —
clasificarse *vr* : qualify (in competi-
tions) — **clasificación** *nf, pl* **-ciones**
1 : classification **2** : league (in sports)

claudicar {72} *vi* : back down

claustro *nm* : cloister

claustrofobia *nf* : claustrophobia —
claustrofóbico, -ca *adj* : claustropho-
bic

cláusula *nf* : clause

clausurar *vt* : close (down) — **clausu-
ra** *nf* : closure, closing

clavado *nm Lat* : dive

clavar *vt* **1** : nail, hammer **2** HINCAR
: drive in, plunge

clave *nf* **1** CIFRA : code **2** SOLUCIÓN : key
3 : clef (in music) — **~** *adj* : key

clavel *nm* : carnation

clavicémbalo *nm* : harpsichord

clavícula *nf* : collarbone

clavija *nf* **1** : peg, pin **2** : (electric) plug

clavo *nm* **1** : nail **2** : clove (spice)

claxon *nm, pl* **cláxones** : horn (of an
automobile)

clemencia *nf* : clemency, mercy —
clemente *adj* : merciful

clerical *adj* : clerical — **clérigo, -ga**
n : clergyman, cleric — **clero** *nm*
: clergy

cliché *nm* **1** : cliché **2** : negative (of a
photograph)

cliente, -ta *n* : customer, client — **clientela** *nf* : clientele, customers *pl*

clima *nm* **1** : climate **2** AMBIENTE : atmosphere — **climático, -ca** *adj* : cli-
matic

climatizar {21} *vt* : air-condition —
climatizado, -da *adj* : air-conditioned

clímax *nm* : climax

clínica *nf* : clinic — **clínico, -ca** *adj*
: clinical

clip *nm, pl* **clips** : (paper) clip

cloaca *nf* : sewer

cloquear *vi* : cluck — **cloqueo** *nm*
: cluck, clucking

cloro *nm* : chlorine

clóset *nm Lat, pl* **clósets** : (built-in)
closet, cupboard

club *nm* : club

coacción *nf, pl* **-ciones** : coercion —
coaccionar *vt* : coerce

coagular *v* : clot, coagulate — **coagularse** *vr* : coagulate — **coágulo** *nm*
: clot

coalición *nf, pl* **-ciones** : coalition

coartada *nf* : alibi

coartar *vt* : restrict, limit

cobarde *nmf* : coward — **~** *adj* : cowardly — **cobardía** *nf* : cowardice

cobaya *nf* : guinea pig

cobertizo *nm* : shelter, shed

cobertor *nm* : bedspread

cobertura *nf* **1** : cover **2** : coverage (of
news, etc.)

cobijar *vt* : shelter — **cobijarse** *vr*
: take shelter — **cobija** *nf Lat* : blanket
— **cobijo** *nm* : shelter

cobra *nf* : cobra

cobrar *vt* **1** : charge, collect **2** : earn (a
salary, etc.) **3** ADQUIRIR : acquire, gain
4 : cash (a check) — *vi* : be paid —
cobrador, -dora *n* **1** : collector **2**
: conductor (of a bus, etc.)

cobre *nm* : copper

cobro *nm* : collection (of money), cash-
ing (of a check)

cocaína *nf* : cocaine

cocción *nf, pl* **-ciones** : cooking

cocear *vi* : kick

cocer {14} *vt* **1** : cook **2** HERVIR : boil

coche *nm* **1** : car, automobile **2** : coach
(of a train) **3** *or* **~** **de caballos** : carriage **4** **~** **fúnebre** : hearse — **cochecito** *nm* : baby carriage, stroller
— **cochera** *nf* : garage, carport

cochino, -na *n* : pig, hog — **~** *adj*
fam : dirty, filthy — **cochinada** *nf*
fam : dirty thing — **cochinillo** *nm*
: piglet

cocido, -da *adj* **1** : boiled, cooked **2**
bien **~** : well-done — **cocido** *nm*
: stew

cociente *nm* : quotient

cocina *nf* **1** : kitchen **2** : (kitchen) stove
3 : (art of) cooking, cuisine — **cocinar** *v* : cook — **cocinero, -ra** *n* : cook,
chef

coco *nm* : coconut

cocodrilo *nm* : crocodile

coctel *or* **cóctel** *nm* **1** : cocktail **2** FIES-
TA : cocktail party

codazo *nm* **1** : nudge **2** **dar un** **~** **a**
: elbow, nudge

codicia *nf* : greed — **codiciar** *vt* : covet
— **codicioso, -sa** *adj* : covetous,
greedy

código *nm* 1 : code 2 ~ **postal** : zip code 3 ~ **morse** : Morse code

codo *nm* : elbow

codorniz *nf, pl* **-nices** : quail

coexistir *vi* : coexist

cofre *nm* : chest, coffer

coger {15} *vt* 1 : take (hold of) 2 ATRA-PAR : catch 3 : pick up (from the ground) 4 : pick (fruit, etc.) — **cogerse** *vr* : hold on

cohechar *vt* : bribe — **cohecho** *nm* : bribe, bribery

coherencia *nf* : coherence — **coherente** *adj* : coherent — **cohesión** *nf, pl* **-siones** : cohesion

cohete *nm* : rocket

cohibir {62} *vt* 1 : restrict 2 : inhibit (a person) — **cohibirse** *vr* : feel inhibited — **cohibido, -da** *adj* : inhibited, shy

coincidir *vi* 1 : coincide 2 ~ **con** : agree with — **coincidencia** *nf* : coincidence

cojear *vi* 1 : limp 2 : wobble (of furniture, etc.) — **cojera** *nf* : limp

cojín *nm, pl* **-jines** : cushion — **cojinete** *nm* 1 : pad, cushion 2 : bearing (of a machine)

cojo, -ja *adj* 1 : lame 2 : wobbly (of furniture) — ~ *n* : lame person

col *nf* 1 : cabbage 2 ~ **de Bruselas** : Brussels sprout

cola *nf* 1 : tail 2 FILA : line (of people) 3 : end (of a line) 4 PEGAMENTO : glue 5 ~ **de caballo** : ponytail

colaborar *vi* : collaborate — **colaboración** *nf, pl* **-ciones** : collaboration — **colaborador, -dora** *n* 1 : collaborator 2 : contributor (to a periodical)

colada *nf Spain* 1 : laundry 2 **hacer la** ~ : do the washing

colador *nm* : colander, strainer

colapso *nm* : collapse

colar {19} *vt* : strain, filter — **colarse** *vr* : sneak in, gate-crash

colcha *nf* : bedspread, quilt — **colchón** *nm, pl* **-chones** : mattress — **colchoneta** *nf* : mat

colear *vi* : wag its tail

colección *nf, pl* **-ciones** : collection — **coleccionar** *vt* : collect — **coleccionista** *nmf* : collector — **colecta** *nf* : collection (of donations)

colectividad *nf* : community — **colectivo, -va** *adj* : collective — **colectivo** *nm* 1 : collective 2 *Lat* : city bus

colector *nm* : sewer

colega *nmf* : colleague

colegio *nm* 1 : school 2 : (professional) college — **colegial, -giala** *n* : schoolboy *m*, schoolgirl *f*

colegir {28} *vt* : gather

cólera *nm* : cholera — ~ *nf* : anger, rage — **colérico, -ca** *adj* 1 : bad-tempered 2 FURIOSO : angry

colesterol *nm* : cholesterol

coleta *nf* : pigtail

colgar {16} *vt* 1 : hang 2 : hang up (a telephone) 3 : hang out (laundry) — *vi* : hang up — **colgante** *adj* : hanging — ~ *nm* : pendant

colibrí *nm* : hummingbird

cólico *nm* : colic

coliflor *nf* : cauliflower

colilla *nf* : (cigarette) butt

colina *nf* : hill

colindar *vi* ~ **con** : be adjacent to — **colindante** *adj* : adjacent

coliseo *nm* : coliseum

colisión *nf, pl* **-siones** : collision — **colisionar** *vi* ~ **contra** : collide with

collar *nm* 1 : necklace 2 : collar (for pets)

colmar *vt* 1 : fill to the brim 2 : fulfill (a wish, etc.) 3 ~ **de** : shower with — **colmado, -da** *adj* : heaping

colmena *nf* : beehive

colmillo *nm* 1 : canine (tooth) 2 : fang (of a dog, etc.), tusk (of an elephant)

colmo *nm* 1 : height, limit 2 **¡eso es el** ~ ! : that's the last straw!

colocar {72} *vt* 1 PONER : place, put 2 : find a job for — **colocarse** *vr* 1 SITUARSE : position oneself 2 : get a job — **colocación** *nf, pl* **-ciones** 1 : placement, placing 2 EMPLEO : position, job

colombiano, -na *adj* : Colombian

colon *nm* : (intestinal) colon

colonia *nf* 1 : colony 2 PERFUME : cologne 3 *Lat* : residential area — **colonial** *adj* : colonial — **colonizar** {21} *vt* : colonize — **colonización** *nf, pl* **-ciones** : colonization — **colono, -na** *n* : settler, colonist

coloquial *adj* : colloquial — **coloquio** *nm* 1 : talk, discussion 2 CONGRESO : conference

color *nm* : color — **colorado, -da** *adj* : red — **colorear** *vt* : color — **colorete** *nm* : rouge — **colorido** *nm* : colors *pl*, coloring

colosal *adj* : colossal

columna *nf* 1 : column 2 ~ **vertebral** : spine, backbone — **columnista** *nmf* : columnist

columpiar *vt* : push (on a swing) — **columpiarse** *vr* : swing — **columpio** *nm* : swing

coma[1] *nm* : coma

coma[2] *nf* : comma

comadre *nf* 1 : godmother of one's child, mother of one's godchild 2 *fam*

: (female) friend — **comadrear** *vi fam*
: gossip
comadreja *nf* : weasel
comadrona *nf* : midwife
comandancia *nf* : command headquarters, command — **comandante** *nmf* 1
: commander 2 : major (in the military) — **comando** *nm* 1 : commando
2 *Lat* : command
comarca *nf* : region, area
combar *vt* : bend, curve
combatir *vt* : combat, fight against — *vi*
: fight — **combate** *nm* 1 : combat 2
: fight (in boxing) — **combatiente**
nmf : combatant, fighter
combinar *vt* 1 : combine 2 : put together, match (colors, etc.) — **combinarse** *vr* : get together — **combinación**
nf, pl **-ciones** 1 : combination 2 : connection (in travel)
combustible *nm* : fuel — ~ *adj* : combustible — **combustión** *nf, pl* **-tiones**
: combustion
comedia *nf* : comedy
comedido, -da *adj* : moderate
comedor *nm* : dining room
comensal *nmf* : diner, dinner guest
comentar *vt* 1 : comment on, discuss 2
MENCIONAR : mention — **comentario**
nm 1 : comment, remark 2 ANÁLISIS
: commentary — **comentarista** *nmf*
: commentator
comenzar {29} *v* : begin, start
comer *vt* 1 : eat 2 *fam* : eat up, eat into
— *vi* 1 : eat 2 CENAR : have a meal 3
: dar de ~ : feed — **comerse** *vr* : eat
up
comercio *nm* 1 : commerce, trade 2 NEGOCIO : business — **comercial** *adj*
: commercial — **comercializar** {21}
vt : market — **comerciante** *nmf* : merchant, dealer — **comerciar** *vi* : do
business, trade
comestible *adj* : edible — **comestibles** *nmpl* : groceries, food
cometa *nm* : comet — ~ *nf* : kite
cometer *vt* 1 : commit 2 : un error
: make a mistake — **cometido** *nm*
: assignment, task
comezón *nf, pl* **-zones** : itchiness, itching
comicios *nmpl* : elections
cómico, -ca *adj* : comic, comical — ~
n : comic, comedian
comida *nf* 1 ALIMENTO : food 2 *Spain*
: lunch 3 *Lat* : dinner 4 tres ~s al día
: three meals a day
comienzo *nm* : beginning
comillas *nfpl* : quotation marks
comino *nm* : cumin

comisario, -ria *n* : commissioner —
comisaría *nf* : police station
comisión *nf, pl* **-siones** 1 : commission
2 COMITÉ : committee
comité *nm* : committee
como *conj* 1 : as, since 2 sí : if — ~
prep 1 : like, as 2 así : as well as —
~ *adv* 1 : as 2 APROXIMADAMENTE
: around, about
cómo *adv* 1 : how 2 ~ **no** : by all
means 3 ¿~ te llamas? : what's your
name?
cómoda *nf* : chest of drawers
comodidad *nf* : comfort, convenience
comodín *nm, pl* **-dines** : joker (in playing cards)
cómodo, -da *adj* 1 : comfortable 2 ÚTIL
: handy, convenient
comoquiera *adv* 1 : in any way 2 ~
que : however
compacto, -ta *adj* : compact
compadecer {53} *vt* : feel sorry for —
compadecerse *vr* ~ **de** : take pity on
compadre *nm* 1 : godfather of one's
child, father of one's godchild 2 *fam*
: buddy
compañero, -ra *n* : companion, partner
— **compañerismo** *nm* : companionship
compañía *nf* : company
comparar *vt* : compare — **comparable**
adj : comparable — **comparación** *nf,
pl* **-ciones** : comparison — **comparativo, -va** *adj* : comparative
comparecer *vt* : appear (before a court,
etc.)
compartimiento *or* **compartimento**
nm : compartment
compartir *vt* : share
compás *nm, pl* **-pases** 1 : compass 2
: rhythm, time (in music)
compasión *nf, pl* **-siones** : compassion, pity — **compasivo, -va** *adj*
: compassionate
compatible *adj* : compatible — **compatibilidad** *nf* : compatibility
compatriota *nmf* : compatriot, fellow
countryman
compeler *vt* : compel
compendiar *vt* : summarize — **compendio** *nm* : summary
compensar *vt* : compensate for —
compensación *nf, pl* **-ciones** : compensation
competir {54} *vi* : compete — **competencia** *nf* 1 : competition, rivalry 2 CAPACIDAD : competence — **competente**
adj : competent — **competición** *nf, pl*
-ciones : competition — **competidor,
-dora** *n* : competitor

compilar *vt* : compile

compinche *nmf fam* : friend, chum

complacer {57} *vt* : please — **complacerse** *vr* ~ **en** : take pleasure in — **complaciente** *adj* : obliging, helpful

complejidad *nf* : complexity — **complejo, -ja** *adj* : complex — **complejo** *nm* : complex

complementar *vt* : complement — **complementario, -ria** *adj* : complementary — **complemento** *nm* 1 : complement 2 : object (in grammar)

completar *vt* : complete — **completo, -ta** *adj* 1 : complete 2 PERFECTO : perfect 3 LLENO : full — **completamente** *adv* : completely

complexión *nf, pl* **-xiones** : constitution, build

complicar {72} *vt* 1 : complicate 2 IMPLICAR : involve — **complicación** *nf, pl* **-ciones** : complication — **complicado, -da** *adj* : complicated, complex

cómplice *nmf* : accomplice — ~ *adj* : conspiratorial, knowing

complot *nm, pl* **-plots** : conspiracy, plot

componer {60} *vt* 1 : make up, compose 2 : compose, write (a song) 3 ARREGLAR : fix, repair — **componerse** *vr* ~ **de** : consist of — **componente** *adj & nm* : component, constituent

comportarse *vr* : behave — **comportamiento** *nm* : behavior

composición *nf, pl* **-ciones** : composition — **compositor, -tora** *n* : composer, songwriter

compostura *nf* 1 : composure 2 REPARACIÓN : repair

comprar *vt* : buy, purchase — **compra** *nf* 1 : purchase 2 **ir de ~s** : go shopping — **comprador, -dora** *n* : buyer, shopper

comprender *vt* 1 : comprehend, understand 2 ABARCAR : cover, include — **comprensible** *adj* : understandable — **comprensión** *nf, pl* **-siones** : understanding — **comprensivo, -va** *adj* : understanding

compresa *nf* 1 : compress 2 *or* ~ **higiénica** : sanitary napkin

compresión *nf, pl* **-siones** : compression — **comprimido** *nm* : pill, tablet — **comprimir** *vt* : compress

comprobar {19} *vt* 1 VERIFICAR : check 2 DEMOSTRAR : prove — **comprobación** *nf, pl* **-ciones** : verification, check — **comprobante** *nm* 1 : proof 2 RECIBO : receipt, voucher

comprometer *vt* 1 : compromise 2 ARRIESGAR : jeopardize 3 OBLIGAR : commit, put under obligation — **comprometerse** *vr* 1 : commit oneself 2 ~ **con** : get engaged to — **comprometedor, -dora** *adj* : compromising — **comprometido, -da** *adj* 1 : compromising, awkward 2 : engaged (to be married) — **compromiso** *nm* 1 : obligation, commitment 2 : (marriage) engagement 3 ACUERDO : agreement 4 APURO : awkward situation

compuesto, -ta *adj* 1 : compound 2 ~ **de** : made up of, consisting of — **compuesto** *nm* : compound

compulsivo, -va *adj* : compelling, urgent

computar *vt* : compute, calculate — **computadora** *nf or* **computador** *nm* 1 : computer 2 ~ **portátil** : laptop computer — **cómputo** *nm* : calculation

comulgar {52} *vi* : receive Communion

común *adj, pl* **-munes** 1 : common 2 ~ **y corriente** : ordinary 3 **por lo** ~ : generally

comuna *nf* : commune — **comunal** *adj* : communal

comunicar {72} *vt* : communicate — **comunicarse** *vr* 1 : communicate 2 ~ **con** : get in touch with — **comunicación** *nf, pl* **-ciones** : communication — **comunicado** *nm* : communiqué — **comunicativo, -va** *adj* : communicative

comunidad *nf* : community

comunión *nf, pl* **-niones** : communion, Communion

comunismo *nm* : Communism — **comunista** *adj & nmf* : Communist

con *prep* 1 : with 2 A PESAR DE : in spite of 3 *(before an infinitive)* : by 4 ~ **(tal) que** : so long as

cóncavo, -va *adj* : concave

concebir {54} *v* : conceive — **concebible** *adj* : conceivable

conceder *vt* 1 : grant, bestow 2 ADMITIR : concede

concejal, -jala *n* : councilman, alderman

concentrar *vt* : concentrate — **concentrarse** *vr* : concentrate — **concentración** *nf, pl* **-ciones** : concentration

concepción *nf, pl* **-ciones** : conception — **concepto** *nm* 1 : concept 2 OPINIÓN : opinion

concernir {17} *vi* ~ **a** : concern — **concerniente** *adj* ~ **a** : concerning

concertar {55} *vt* 1 : arrange, coordinate 2 *(used before an infinitive)* : agree 3 : harmonize (in music) — *vi* : be in harmony

concesión *nf, pl* **-siones 1** : concession **2** : awarding (of prizes, etc.)

concha *nf* : shell

conciencia *nf* **1** : conscience **2** CONOCIMIENTO : consciousness, awareness — **concientizar** {21} *vt Lat* : make aware — **concientizarse** *vr Lat* ~ de : realize

concienzudo, -da *adj* : conscientious

concierto *nm* **1** : concert **2** : concerto (musical composition)

conciliar *vt* : reconcile — **conciliación** *nf, pl* **-ciones** : reconciliation

concilio *nm* : council

conciso, -sa *adj* : concise

conciudadano, -na *n* : fellow citizen

concluir {41} *vt* : conclude — *vi* : come to an end — **conclusión** *nf, pl* **-siones** : conclusion — **concluyente** *adj* : conclusive

concordar {19} *vi* : agree — *vt* : reconcile — **concordancia** *nf* : agreement — **concordia** *nf* : harmony, concord

concretar *vt* : make concrete, specify — **concretarse** *vr* : become definite, take shape — **concreto, -ta** *adj* **1** : concrete **2** DETERMINADO : specific **3** en ~ : specifically — **concreto** *nm* *Lat* : concrete

concurrir *vi* **1** : come together, meet **2** ~ a : take part in — **concurrencia** *nf* : audience, turnout — **concurrido, -da** *adj* : busy, crowded

concursar *vi* : compete, participate — **concursante** *nmf* : competitor — **concurso** *nm* **1** : competition **2** CONCURRENCIA : gathering **3** AYUDA : help, cooperation

condado *nm* : county

conde, -desa *n* : count *m*, countess *f*

condenar *vt* **1** : condemn, damn **2** : sentence (a criminal) — **condena** *nf* **1** : condemnation **2** SENTENCIA : sentence — **condenación** *nf, pl* **-ciones** : condemnation, damnation

condensar *vt* : condense — **condensación** *nf, pl* **-ciones** : condensation

condesa *nf* → **conde**

condescender {56} *vi* **1** : acquiesce, agree **2** ~ a : condescend to — **condescendiente** *adj* : condescending

condición *nf, pl* **-ciones 1** : condition, state **2** CALIDAD : capacity, position — **condicional** *adj* : conditional

condimento *nm* : condiment, seasoning

condolerse {47} *vr* : sympathize — **condolencia** *nf* : condolence

condominio *nm* **1** : joint ownership **2** *Lat* : condominium

condón *nm, pl* **-dones** : condom

conducir {61} *vt* **1** DIRIGIR : direct, lead **2** MANEJAR : drive — *vi* **1** : drive **2** ~ a : lead to — **conducirse** *vr* : behave

conducta *nf* : behavior, conduct

conducto *nm* : conduit, duct

conductor, -tora *n* : driver

conectar *vt* **1** : connect **2** ENCHUFAR : plug in — *vi* : connect

conejo, -ja *n* : rabbit — **conejera** *nf* : (rabbit) hutch

conexión *nf, pl* **-xiones** : connection — **conexo, -xa** *adj* : connected

confabularse *vr* : conspire, plot

confeccionar *vt* : make (up), prepare — **confección** *nf, pl* **-ciones 1** : making, preparation **2** : tailoring, dressmaking

confederación *nf, pl* **-ciones** : confederation

conferencia *nf* **1** : lecture **2** REUNIÓN : conference

conferir {76} *vt* : confer, bestow

confesar {55} *v* : confess — **confesarse** *vr* : go to confession — **confesión** *nf, pl* **-siones 1** : confession **2** CREDO : religion, creed

confeti *nm* : confetti

confiar {85} *vi* : trust — *vt* : entrust — **confiable** *adj* : trustworthy, reliable — **confiado, -da** *adj* **1** : confident **2** CRÉDULO : trusting — **confianza** *nf* **1** : trust **2** : confidence (in oneself)

confidencia *nf* : confidence, secret — **confidencial** *adj* : confidential — **confidencialidad** *f* : confidentiality — **confidente** *nmf* **1** : confidant, confidante *f* **2** : (police) informer

configuración *nf, pl* **-ciones** : configuration, shape

confín *nm, pl* **-fines** : boundary, limit — **confinar** *vt* **1** : confine **2** DESTERRAR : exile

confirmar *vt* : confirm — **confirmación** *nf, pl* **-ciones** : confirmation

confiscar {72} *vt* : confiscate

confitería *nm* : candy store

confitura *nf* : jam

conflagración *nf, pl* **-ciones 1** : war, conflict **2** INCENDIO : fire

conflicto *nm* : conflict

confluencia *nf* : junction, confluence

conformar *vt* : shape, make up — **conformarse** *vr* **1** RESIGNARSE : resign oneself **2** ~ con : content oneself with — **conforme** *adj* **1** : content, satisfied **2** ~ a : in accordance with — ~ *conj* : as — **conformidad** *nf* **1** : agreement **2** RESIGNACIÓN : resignation

confortar *vt* : comfort — **confortable** *adj* : comfortable

confrontar *vt* **1** : confront **2** COMPARAR : compare — *vi* : border — **confrontarse** *vr* ~ **con** : face up to — **confrontación** *nf, pl* **-ciones** : confrontation

confundir *vt* : confuse, mix up — **confundirse** *vr* : make a mistake, be confused — **confusión** *nf, pl* **-siones** : confusion — **confuso, -sa** *adj* **1** : confused **2** INDISTINTO : hazy, indistinct — **congelar** *vt* : freeze — **congelarse** *vr* : freeze — **congelación** *nf, pl* **-ciones** : freezing — **congelado, -da** *adj* : frozen — **congelador** *nm* : freezer

congeniar *vi* : get along

congestión *nf, pl* **-tiones** : congestion — **congestionado, -da** *adj* : congested

congoja *nf* : anguish, grief

congraciarse *vr* : ingratiate oneself

congratular *vt* : congratulate

congregar {52} *vt* : bring together — **congregarse** *vr* : congregate — **congregación** *nf, pl* **-ciones** : congregation, gathering

congreso *nm* : congress — **congresista** *nmf* : member of congress

conjeturar *vt* : guess, conjecture — **conjetura** *nf* : guess, conjecture

conjugar {52} *vt* : conjugate — **conjugación** *nf, pl* **-ciones** : conjugation

conjunción *nf, pl* **-ciones** : conjunction

conjunto, -ta *adj* : joint — **conjunto** *nm* **1** : collection **2** : outfit (of clothing) **3** GRUPO : band **4 en** ~ : as a whole

conjurar *vt* : ward off — *vi* : conspire, plot

conllevar *vt* : entail

conmemorar *vt* : commemorate — **conmemoración** *nf, pl* **-ciones** : commemoration — **conmemorativo, -va** *adj* : commemorative

conmigo *pron* : with me

conminar *vt* : threaten

conmiseración *nf, pl* **-ciones** : pity, commiseration

conmocionar *vt* : shock — **conmoción** *nf, pl* **-ciones 1** : shock, upheaval **2** *or* ~ **cerebral** : concussion

conmover {47} *vt* **1** : move, touch **2** SACUDIR : shake (up) — **conmoverse** *vr* : be moved — **conmovedor, -dora** *adj* : moving, touching

conmutador *nm* **1** : (electric) switch **2** *Lat* : switchboard

cono *nm* : cone

conocer {18} *vt* **1** : know **2** : meet (a person), get to know (a city, etc.) **3** RECONOCER : recognize — **conocerse** *vr* **1** : meet, get to know each other **2** : know oneself — **conocedor, -dora** *adj* & *n* : expert — **conocido, -da** *adj* : well-known — ~ *n* : acquaintance — **conocimiento** *nm* **1** : knowledge **2** SENTIDO : consciousness

conque *conj* : so

conquistar *vt* : conquer — **conquista** *nf* : conquest — **conquistador, -dora** *adj* : conquering — **conquistador** *nm* : conqueror

consabido, -da *adj* **1** : well-known **2** HABITUEL : usual

consagrar *vt* **1** : consecrate **2** DEDICAR : devote — **consagración** *nf, pl* **-ciones** : consecration

consciencia *nf* → **conciencia** — **consciente** *adj* : conscious, aware

consecución *nf, pl* **-ciones** : attainment

consecuencia *nf* **1** : consequence **2 en** ~ : accordingly — **consecuente** *adj* : consistent

consecutivo, -va *adj* : consecutive

conseguir {75} *vt* **1** : get, obtain **2** ~ **hacer algo** : manage to do sth

consejo *nm* **1** : advice, counsel **2** : council (assembly) — **consejero, -ra** *n* : adviser, counselor

consenso *nm* : consensus

consentir {76} *vt* **1** : allow, permit **2** MIMAR : pamper, spoil — *vi* : consent — **consentimiento** *nm* : consent, permission

conserje *nmf* : caretaker, janitor

conservar *vt* **1** : preserve **2** GUARDAR : keep, conserve — **conservarse** *vr* : keep — **conserva** *nf* **1** : preserve(s) **2** ~**s** *nfpl* : canned goods — **conservación** *nf, pl* **-ciones** : conservation, preservation — **conservador, -dora** *adj* & *n* : conservative — **conservatorio** *nm* : conservatory

considerar *vt* **1** : consider **2** RESPETAR : respect — **considerable** *adj* : considerable — **consideración** *nf, pl* **-ciones 1** : consideration **2** RESPETO : respect — **considerado, -da** *adj* **1** : considerate **2** RESPETADO : respected

consigna *nf* **1** ESLOGAN : slogan **2** ORDEN : orders **3** : checkroom (for baggage)

consigo *pron* : with her, with him, with you, with oneself

consiguiente *adj* **1** : consequent **2 por** ~ : consequently

consistir *vi* ~ **en 1** : consist of **2** : lie in, consist in — **consistencia** *nf* : consistency — **consistente** *adj* **1** : firm, solid **2** ~ **en** : consisting of

consolar {19} *vt* : console, comfort — **consolarse** *vr* : console oneself — **consolación** *nf, pl* **-ciones** : consolation

consolidar *vt* : consolidate — **consolidación** *nf, pl* **-ciones** : consolidation

consomé *nm* : consommé

consonante *adj* : consonant, harmonious — ~ *nf* : consonant

consorcio *nm* : consortium

conspirar *vi* : conspire, plot — **conspiración** *nf, pl* **-ciones** : conspiracy — **conspirador, -dora** *n* : conspirator

constancia *nf* **1** : record, evidence **2** PERSEVERANCIA : perseverance — **constante** *adj* : constant — **constantemente** *adv* : constantly, continually

constar *vi* **1** : be evident, be clear **2** ~ **de** : consist of

constatar *vt* **1** : verify **2** AFIRMAR : state, affirm

constelación *nf, pl* **-ciones** : constellation

consternación *nf, pl* **-ciones** : consternation

constipado, -da *adj* estar ~ : have a cold — **constipado** *nm* : cold — **constiparse** *vr* : catch a cold

constituir {41} *vt* **1** FORMAR : constitute, form **2** FUNDAR : establish, set up — **constituirse** *vr* ~ **en** : set oneself up as — **constitución** *nf, pl* **-ciones** : constitution — **constitucional** *adj* : constitutional — **constitutivo, -va** *adj* : constituent — **constituyente** *adj & nm* : constituent

constreñir {67} *vt* **1** : force, compel **2** RESTRINGIR : restrict, limit

construir {41} *vt* : build, construct — **construcción** *nf, pl* **-ciones** : construction, building — **constructivo, -va** *adj* : constructive — **constructor, -tora** *n* : builder

consuelo *nm* : consolation, comfort

consuetudinario, -ria *adj* : customary

cónsul *nmf* : consul — **consulado** *nm* : consulate

consultar *vt* : consult — **consulta** *nf* : consultation — **consultor, -tora** *n* : consultant — **consultorio** *nm* : office (of a doctor or dentist)

consumar *vt* **1** : consummate, complete **2** : commit (a crime)

consumir *vt* : consume — **consumirse** *vr* : waste away — **consumición** *nf, pl* **-ciones 1** : consumption **2** : drink (in a restaurant) — **consumido, -da** *adj* : thin, emaciated — **consumidor, -dora** *n* : consumer — **consumo** *nm* : consumption

contabilidad *nf* **1** : accounting, bookkeeping **2** : accountancy (profession) — **contable** *nmf Spain* : accountant, bookkeeper

contactar *vi* ~ **con** : get in touch with, contact — **contacto** *nm* : contact

contado, -da *adj* : numbered, few — **contado** *nm* al ~ : (in) cash

contador, -dora *n Lat* : accountant — **contador** *nm* : meter

contagiar *vt* **1** : infect **2** : transmit (a disease) — **contagiarse** *vr* **1** : be contagious **2** : become infected (with a disease) — **contagio** *nm* : contagion, infection — **contagioso, -sa** *adj* : contagious, infectious

contaminar *vt* : contaminate, pollute — **contaminación** *nf, pl* **-ciones** : contamination, pollution

contar {19} *vt* **1** : count **2** NARRAR : tell — *vi* **1** : count **2** ~ **con** : rely on, count on

contemplar *vt* **1** MIRAR : look at, behold **2** CONSIDERAR : contemplate — **contemplación** *nf, pl* **-ciones** : contemplation

contemporáneo, -nea *adj & n* : contemporary

contender {56} *vi* : contend, compete — **contendiente** *nmf* : competitor

contener {80} *vt* **1** : contain **2** RESTRINGIR : restrain, hold back — **contenerse** *vr* : restrain oneself — **contenedor** *nm* : container — **contenido, -da** *adj* : restrained — **contenido** *nm* : contents *pl*

contentar *vt* : please, make happy — **contentarse** *vr* ~ **con** : be satisfied with — **contento, -ta** *adj* : glad, happy, contented

contestar *vt* : answer — *vi* : reply, answer back — **contestación** *nf, pl* **-ciones** : answer, reply

contexto *nm* : context

contienda *nf* **1** COMBATE : dispute, fight **2** COMPETICIÓN : contest

contigo *pron* : with you

contiguo, -gua *adj* : adjacent

continente *nm* : continent — **continental** *adj* : continental

contingencia *nf* : contingency — **contingente** *adj & nm* : contingent

continuar {3} *v* : continue — **continuación** *nf, pl* **-ciones 1** : continuation **2** a ~ : next, then — **continuidad** *nf* : continuity — **continuo, -nua** *adj* **1**

: continuous, steady **2** FRECUENTE
: continual
contorno *nm* **1** : outline **2** ~**s** *nmpl*
: surrounding area
contorsión *nf*, *pl* **-siones** : contortion
contra *prep* **1** : against **2 en** ~ : against
— ~ *nm* **los pros y los** ~**s** : the pros
and cons
contraatacar {72} *v* : counterattack —
contraataque *nm* : counterattack
contrabajo *nm* : double bass
contrabalancear *vt* : counterbalance
contrabandista *nmf* : smuggler —
contrabando *nm* **1** : smuggling **2**
: contraband (goods)
contracción *nf*, *pl* **-ciones** : contraction
contrachapado *nm* : plywood
contradecir {11} *vt* : contradict —
contradicción *nf*, *pl* **-ciones** : contradiction — **contradictorio, -ria** *adj*
: contradictory
contraer {81} *vt* **1** : contract **2** ~ **matrimonio** : get married — **contraerse**
vr : contract, tighten up
contrafuerte *nm* : buttress
contragolpe *nm* : backlash
contralto *nmf* : contralto
contrapartida *nf* : compensation
contrapelo: a ~ *adv phr* : the wrong
way
contrapeso *nm* : counterbalance
contraponer {60} *vt* **1** : counter, oppose **2** COMPARAR : compare
contraproducente *adj* : counterproductive
contrariar {85} *vt* **1** : oppose **2** MO-
LESTAR : vex, annoy — **contrariedad**
nf **1** : obstacle **2** DISGUSTO : annoyance
— **contrario, -ria** *adj* **1** OPUESTO : opposite **2 al contrario** : on the contrary
3 ser ~ **a** : be opposed to
contrarrestar *vt* : counteract
contrasentido *nm* : contradiction (in
terms)
contraseña *nf* : password
contrastar *vt* **1** : check, verify **2** RESIS-
TIR : resist — *vi* : contrast — **contraste** *nm* : contrast
contratar *vt* **1** : contract for **2** : hire, engage (workers)
contratiempo *nm* **1** : mishap **2** DIFICUL-
TAD : setback
contrato *nm* : contract — **contratista**
nmf : contractor
contraventana *nf* : shutter
contribuir {41} *vt* **1** : contribute **2** : pay
taxes — **contribución** *nf*, *pl* **-ciones 1**
: contribution **2** IMPUESTO : tax — **contribuyente** *nmf* **1** : contributor **2** : taxpayer

contrincante *nmf* : opponent
contrito, -ta *adj* : contrite
controlar *vt* **1** : control **2** COMPROBAR
: monitor, check — **control** *nm* **1**
: control **2** VERIFICACIÓN : inspection,
check — **controlador, -dora** *n* : con-
troller
controversia *nf* : controversy
contundente *adj* **1** : blunt **2** : forceful,
convincing (of arguments, etc.)
contusión *nf*, *pl* **-siones** : bruise
convalecencia *nf* : convalescence —
convaleciente *adj & nmf* : convalescent
convencer {86} *vt* : convince, persuade — **convencerse** *vr* : be convinced — **convencimiento** *nm* : conviction, belief
convención *nf*, *pl* **-ciones** : convention
— **convencional** *adj* : conventional
convenir {87} *vi* **1** : be suitable, be advisable **2** ~ **en** : agree on — **conveniencia** *nf* **1** : convenience **2** : suitability (of an action, etc.) — **conveniente**
adj **1** : convenient **2** ACONSEJABLE
: suitable, advisable **3** PROVECHOSO
: useful — **convenio** *nm* : agreement,
pact
convento *nm* : convent, monastery
converger {15} *or* **convergir** *vi* : converge
conversar *vi* : converse, talk — **conversación** *nf*, *pl* **-ciones** : conversation
conversión *nf*, *pl* **-siones** : conversion
— **converso, -sa** *n* : convert
convertir {76} *vt* : convert — **convertirse** *vr* ~ **en** : turn into — **convertible** *adj & nm* : convertible
convexo, -xa *adj* : convex
convicción *nf*, *pl* **-ciones** : conviction
— **convicto, -ta** *adj* : convicted
convidar *vt* : invite — **convidado, -da**
n : guest
convincente *adj* : convincing
convite *nm* **1** : invitation **2** : banquet
convivir *vi* : live together — **conviven-
cia** *nf* : coexistence, living together
convocar {72} *vt* : convoke, call together
convulsión *nf*, *pl* **-siones 1** : convulsion **2** TRASTORNO : upheaval — **convulsivo, -va** *adj* : convulsive
conyugal *adj* : conjugal — **cónyuge**
nmf : spouse, partner
coñac *nm* : cognac, brandy
cooperar *vi* : cooperate — **cooperación** *nf*, *pl* **-ciones** : cooperation
— **cooperativa** *nf* : cooperative, coop — **cooperativo, -va** *adj* : cooperative

coordenada *nf* : coordinate
coordinar *vt* : coordinate — **coordinación** *nf*, *pl* -**ciones** : coordination — **coordinador, -dora** *n* : coordinator
copa *nf* 1 : glass, goblet 2 : cup (in sports) 3 **tomar una ~** : have a drink
copia *nf* : copy — **copiar** *vt* : copy
copioso, -sa *adj* : copious, abundant
copla *nf* 1 : (popular) song 2 ESTROFA : verse, stanza
copo *nm* 1 : flake 2 *or* **~ de nieve** : snowflake
coquetear *vi* : flirt — **coqueteo** *nm* : flirting, flirtation — **coqueto, -ta** *adj* : flirtatious — **~ nf** : flirt
coraje *nm* 1 : valor, courage 2 IRA : anger
coral[1] *nm* : coral
coral[2] *adj* : choral — **~ nf** : choir, chorale
Corán *nm* **el ~** : the Koran
coraza *nf* 1 : armor plating 2 : shell
corazón *nm*, *pl* -**zones** 1 : heart 2 : core (of fruit) 3 **mi ~** : my darling — **corazonada** *nf* 1 : hunch 2 IMPULSO : impulse
corbata *nf* : tie, necktie
corchete *nm* 1 : hook and eye, clasp 2 : square bracket (punctuation mark)
corcho *nm* : cork
cordel *nm* : cord, string
cordero *nm* : lamb
cordial *adj* : cordial — **cordialidad** *nf* : cordiality
cordillera *nf* : mountain range
córdoba *nf* : córdoba (Nicaraguan unit of currency)
cordón *nm*, *pl* -**dones** 1 : cord 2 **~ policial** : (police) cordon 3 **cordones** *nmpl* : shoelaces
cordura *nf* : sanity
corear *vt* : chant
coreografía *nf* : choreography
cornamenta *nf* : antlers *pl*
corneta *nf* : bugle
coro *nm* 1 : chorus 2 : (church) choir
corona *nf* 1 : crown 2 : wreath, garland (of flowers) — **coronación** *nf*, *pl* -**ciones** : coronation — **coronar** *vt* : crown
coronel *nm* : colonel
coronilla *nf* 1 : crown (of the head) 2 **estar hasta la ~** : be fed up
corporación *nf*, *pl* -**ciones** : corporation
corporal *adj* : corporal, bodily
corporativo, -va *adj* : corporate
corpulento, -ta *adj* : stout
corral *nm* 1 : farmyard 2 : pen, corral (for animals) 3 *or* **corralito** : playpen

correa *nf* 1 : strap, belt 2 : leash (for a dog, etc.)
corrección *nf*, *pl* -**ciones** 1 : correction 2 : correctness, propriety (of manners) — **correccional** *nm* : reformatory — **correctivo, -va** *adj* : corrective — **correcto, -ta** *adj* 1 : correct, right 2 CORTÉS : polite
corredizo, -za *adj* : sliding
corredor, -dora *n* 1 : runner, racer 2 AGENTE : agent, broker — **corredor** *nm* : corridor, hallway
corregir {28} *vt* : correct — **corregirse** *vr* : mend one's ways
correlación *nf*, *pl* -**ciones** : correlation
correo *nm* 1 : mail 2 **~ aéreo** : airmail
correr *vi* 1 : run, race 2 : flow (of a river, etc.) 3 : pass (of time) — *vt* 1 : run RECORRER : travel over, cover 3 : draw (curtains) — **correrse** *vr* 1 : move along 2 : run (of colors)
corresponder *vi* 1 : correspond 2 PERTENECER : belong 3 ENCAJAR : fit 4 **~ a** : reciprocate, repay — **corresponderse** *vr* : write to each other — **correspondencia** *nf* 1 : correspondence 2 : connection (of a train, etc.) — **correspondiente** *adj* : corresponding, respective — **corresponsal** *nmf* : correspondent
corretear *vi* : run about, scamper
corrida *nf* 1 : run 2 *or* **~ de toros** : bullfight — **corrido, -da** *adj* 1 : straight, continuous 2 *fam* : worldly
corriente *adj* 1 : current 2 NORMAL : common, ordinary 3 : running (of water, etc.) — **~ nf** 1 : current (of water, electricity, etc.), draft (of air) 2 TENDENCIA : tendency, trend — **~ nm al ~** 1 : up-to-date 2 ENTERADO : aware, informed
corrillo *nm* : clique, circle — **corro** *nm* : ring, circle (of people)
corroborar *vt* : corroborate
corroer {69} *vt* 1 : corrode (of metals) 2 : erode, wear away — **corroerse** *vr* : corrode
corromper *vt* 1 : corrupt 2 PUDRIR : rot — **corrompido, -da** *adj* : corrupt
corrosión *nf*, *pl* -**siones** : corrosion — **corrosivo, -va** *adj* : corrosive
corrupción *nf*, *pl* -**ciones** 1 : corruption 2 DESCOMPOSICIÓN : decay, rot — **corrupto, -ta** *adj* : corrupt
corsé *nm* : corset
cortar *vt* 1 : cut 2 RECORTAR : cut out 3 QUITAR : cut off — *vi* : cut — **cortarse** *vr* 1 : cut oneself 2 : be cut off (on the telephone) 3 : curdle (of milk) 4 **~ el pelo** : have one's hair cut — **cortada**

nf Lat : cut — **cortante** *adj* : cutting, sharp

cortauñas *nms & pl* : nail clippers

corte[1] *nm* **1** : cutting **2** ESTILO : cut, style **3** ~ **de pelo** : haircut

corte[2] *nf* **1** : court **2 hacer la** ~ **a** : court, woo — **cortejar** *vt* : court, woo

cortejo *nm* **1** : entourage **2** NOVIAZGO : courtship **3** ~ **fúnebre** : funeral procession

cortés *adj* : courteous, polite — **cortesía** *nf* : courtesy, politeness

corteza *nf* **1** : bark **2** : crust (of bread) **3** : rind, peel (of fruit)

cortina *nm* : curtain

corto, -ta *adj* **1** : short **2** ESCASO : scarce **3** *fam* : timid, shy **4** ~ **de vista** : nearsighted — **cortocircuito** *nm* : short circuit

corvo, -va *adj* : curved, bent

cosa *nf* **1** : thing **2** ASUNTO : matter, affair **3** ~ **de** : about **4 poca** ~ : nothing much

cosechar *v* : harvest, reap — **cosecha** *nf* **1** : harvest, crop **2** : vintage (of wine)

coser *v* : sew

cosmético, -ca *adj* : cosmetic — **cosmético** *nm* : cosmetic

cósmico, -ca *adj* : cosmic

cosmopolita *adj* : cosmopolitan

cosmos *nm* : cosmos

cosquillas *nfpl* **1** : tickling **2 hacer** ~ : tickle — **cosquilleo** *nm* : tickling sensation, tingle

costa *nf* **1** : coast, shore **2 a toda** ~ : at any cost

costado *nm* **1** : side **2 al** ~ : alongside

costar {19} *v* : cost

costarricense *or* **costarriqueño, -ña** *adj* : Costa Rican

coste *nm* → **costo** — **costear** *vt* : pay for

costero, -ra *adj* : coastal

costilla *nf* **1** : rib **2** CHULETA : chop, cutlet

costo *nm* : cost, price — **costoso, -sa** *adj* : costly

costra *nf* : scab

costumbre *nf* **1** : custom, habit **2 de** ~ : usual

costura *nf* **1** : sewing, dressmaking **2** PUNTADAS : seam — **costurera** *nf* : dressmaker

cotejar *vt* : compare

cotidiano, -na *adj* : daily

cotizar {21} *vt* : quote, set a price on — **cotización** *nf, pl* -**ciones** : quotation, price — **cotizado, -da** *adj* : in demand

coto *nm* : enclosure, reserve

cotorra *nf* **1** : small parrot **2** *fam* : chatterbox — **cotorrear** *vi fam* : chatter, gab

coyote *nm* : coyote

coyuntura *nf* **1** : joint **2** SITUACIÓN : situation, moment

coz *nm, pl* **coces** : kick (of an animal)

cráneo *nf* : cranium, skull

cráter *nm* : crater

crear *vt* : create — **creación** *nf, pl* -**ciones** : creation — **creativo, -va** *adj* : creative — **creador, -dora** *n* : creator

crecer {53} *vi* **1** : grow **2** AUMENTAR : increase — **crecido, -da** *adj* **1** : full-grown **2** : large (of numbers) — **creciente** *adj* **1** : growing, increasing **2** : crescent (of the moon) — **crecimiento** *nm* **1** : growth **2** AUMENTO : increase

credenciales *nfpl* : credentials

credibilidad *nf* : credibility

crédito *nm* : credit

credo *nm* : creed

crédulo, -la *adj* : credulous, gullible

creer {20} *v* **1** : believe **2** SUPONER : suppose, think — **creerse** *vr* : regard oneself as — **creencia** *nf* : belief — **creíble** *adj* : believable, credible — **creído, -da** *adj fam* : conceited

crema *nf* : cream

cremación *nf, pl* -**ciones** : cremation

cremallera *nf* : zipper

cremoso, -sa *adj* : creamy

crepe *nmf* : crepe, pancake

crepitar *vi* : crackle

crepúsculo *nm* : twilight, dusk

crespo, -pa *adj* : curly, frizzy

crespón *nm, pl* -**pones** : crepe (fabric)

cresta *nf* **1** : crest **2** : comb (of a rooster)

cretino, -na *n* : cretin

creyente *nmf* : believer

criar {85} *vt* **1** : nurse (a baby) **2** EDUCAR : bring up, rear **3** : raise, breed (animals) — **cría** *nf* **1** : breeding, rearing **2** : young animal — **criadero** *nm* : farm, hatchery — **criado, -da** *n* : servant, maid *f* — **criador, -dora** *n* : breeder — **crianza** *nf* : upbringing, rearing

criatura *nf* **1** : creature **2** NIÑO : baby, child

crimen *nm, pl* **crímenes** : crime — **criminal** *adj & nmf* : criminal

críquet *nm* : cricket (game)

crin *nf* : mane

criollo, -lla *adj & n* : Creole

cripta *nf* : crypt

crisantemo *nm* : chrysanthemum

crisis *nf* **1** : crisis **2 ~ nerviosa** : nervous breakdown

crispar *vt* **1** : tense (muscles), clench (one's fist) **2** IRRITAR : irritate, set on edge — **crisparse** *vr* : tense up

cristal *nm* **1** : crystal **2** VIDRIO : glass, piece of glass — **cristalería** *nf* : glassware — **cristalino, -na** *adj* : crystalline — **cristalino** *nm* : lens (of the eye) — **cristalizar** {21} *vi* : crystallize

cristiano, -na *adj & n* : Christian — **cristianismo** *nm* : Christianity — **Cristo** *nm* : Christ

criterio *nm* **1** : criterion **2** JUICIO : judgment, opinion

criticar {72} *vt* : criticize — **crítica** *nf* **1** : criticism **2** RESEÑA : review, critique — **crítico, -ca** *adj* : critical — **~** *n* : critic, reviewer

croar *vi* : croak

cromo *nm* : chromium, chrome

cromosoma *nm* : chromosome

crónica *nf* **1** : chronicle **2** : (news) report

crónico, -ca *adj* : chronic

cronista *nmf* : reporter, newscaster

cronología *nf* : chronology — **cronológico, -ca** *adj* : chronological

cronometrar *vt* : time, clock — **cronómetro** *nm* : chronometer, stopwatch

croqueta *nf* : croquette

croquis *nms & pl* : (rough) sketch

cruce *nm* **1** : crossing **2** : crossroads, intersection **3 ~ peatonal** : crosswalk

crucero *nm* **1** : cruise **2** : cruiser (ship)

crucial *adj* : crucial

crucificar {72} *vt* : crucify — **crucifijo** *nm* : crucifix — **crucifixión** *nf, pl* **-fixiones** : crucifixion

crucigrama *nm* : crossword puzzle

crudo, -da *adj* **1** : harsh, crude **2** : raw (of food) — **crudo** *nm* : crude oil

cruel *adj* : cruel — **crueldad** *nf* : cruelty

crujir *vi* : rustle, creak, crackle, crunch — **crujido** *nm* : rustle, creak, crackle, crunch — **crujiente** *adj* : crunchy, crisp

cruzar {21} *vt* **1** : cross **2** : exchange (words) — **cruzarse** *vr* **1** : intersect **2** : pass each other — **cruz** *nf, pl* **cruces** : cross — **cruzada** *nf* : crusade — **cruzado, -da** *adj* : crossed — **cruzado** *nm* : crusader

cuaderno *nm* : notebook

cuadra *nf* **1** : stable **2** *Lat* : (city) block

cuadrado, -da *adj* : square — **cuadrado** *nm* : square

cuadragésimo, -ma *adj* : fortieth, forty- — **~** *n* : fortieth, forty- (in a series)

cuadrar *vi* **1** : conform, agree **2** : add up, tally (numbers) — *vt* : square — **cuadrarse** *vr* : stand at attention

cuadrilátero *nm* **1** : quadrilateral **2** : ring (in sports)

cuadrilla *nf* : gang, group

cuadro *nm* **1** : square **2** PINTURA : painting **3** DESCRIPCIÓN : picture, description **4** : staff, management (of an organization) **5** CUADRADO : check, square **6** : (baseball) diamond

cuadrúpedo *nm* : quadruped

cuádruple *adj* : quadruple — **cuadruplicar** {72} *vt* : quadruple

cuajar *vi* **1** : curdle **2** COAGULAR : clot, coagulate **3** : set (of pudding, etc.) **4** AFIANZARSE : catch on — *vt* **1** : curdle **2 ~ de** : fill with

cual *pron* **1 el ~, la ~, los ~es, las ~es** : who, whom, which **2 lo ~** : which **3 cada ~** : everyone, everybody — **~** *prep* : like, as

cuál *pron* : which (one), what (one) — **~** *adj* : which, what

cualidad *nf* : quality, trait

cualquiera (**cualquier** *before nouns*) *adj, pl* **cualesquiera** : any, whatever — **~** *pron, pl* **cualesquiera** : anyone, whatever

cuán *adv* : how

cuando *conj* **1** : when **2** SI : since, if **3 ~ más** : at the most **4 de vez en ~** : from time to time — **~** *prep* : during, at the time of

cuándo *adv* **1** : when **2 ¿desde ~?** : since when?

cuantía *nf* **1** : quantity, extent **2** IMPORTANCIA : importance — **cuantioso, -sa** *adj* : abundant, considerable

cuanto *adv* **1** : as much as **2 ~ antes** : as soon as possible **3 en ~** : as soon as **4 en ~ a** : as for, as regards — **cuanto, -ta** *adj* : as many, whatever — **~** *pron* **1** : as much as, all that, everything **2 unos cuantos, unas cuantas** : a few

cuánto *adv* : how much, how many — **cuánto, -ta** *adj* : how much, how many — **~** *pron* : how much, how many

cuarenta *adj & nm* : forty — **cuarentavo, -va** *adj* : fortieth — **cuarentavo** *nm* : fortieth

cuarentena *nf* : quarantine

Cuaresma *nf* : Lent

cuartear *vt* : quarter, divide up — **cuartearse** *vr* : crack, split

cuartel *nm* **1** : barracks *pl* **2 ~ general** : headquarters **3 no dar ~** : show no mercy

cuarteto *nm* : quartet
cuarto, -ta *adj* : fourth — ~ *n* : fourth (in a series) — **cuarto** *nm* **1** : quarter, fourth **2** HABITACIÓN : room
cuarzo *nm* : quartz
cuatro *adj & nm* : four — **cuatrocientos, -tas** *adj* : four hundred — **cuatrocientos** *nms & pl* : four hundred
cuba *nf* : cask, barrel
cubano, -na *adj* : Cuban
cubeta *nf* **1** : keg, cask **2** *Lat* : pail, bucket
cúbico, -ca *adj* : cubic, cubed — **cubículo** *nm* : cubicle
cubierta *nf* **1** : cover, covering **2** : (automobile) tire **3** : deck (of a ship) — **cubierto** *nm* **1** : cutlery, place setting **2 a** ~ : under cover
cubo *nm* **1** : cube **2** *Spain* : pail, bucket **3** : hub (of a wheel)
cubrecama *nm* : bedspread
cubrir {2} *vt* : cover — **cubrirse** *vr* **1** : cover oneself **2** : cloud over
cucaracha *nf* : cockroach
cuchara *nf* : spoon — **cucharada** *nf* : spoonful — **cucharilla** *or* **cucharita** *nf* : teaspoon — **cucharón** *nm, pl* -**rones** : ladle
cuchichear *vi* : whisper — **cuchicheo** *nm* : whisper
cuchilla *nf* **1** : (kitchen) knife **2** ~ **de afeitar** : razor blade — **cuchillada** *nf* : stab, knife wound — **cuchillo** *nm* : knife
cuclillas *nfpl* **en** ~ : squatting, crouching
cuco *nm* : cuckoo — **cuco, -ca** *adj fam* : pretty, cute
cucurucho *nm* : ice-cream cone
cuello *nm* **1** : neck **2** : collar (of clothing)
cuenca *nf* **1** : river basin **2** : (eye) socket — **cuenco** *nm* **1** : bowl **2** CONCAVIDAD : hollow
cuenta *nf* **1** : calculation, count **2** : (bank) account **3** FACTURA : check, bill **4** : bead (for a necklace, etc.) **5 darse** ~ : realize **6 tener en** ~ : bear in mind
cuento *nm* **1** : story, tale **2** ~ **de hadas** : fairy tale
cuerda *nf* **1** : cord, rope, string **2** ~**s vocales** : vocal cords **3 dar** ~ **a** : wind up
cuerdo, -da *adj* : sane, sensible
cuerno *nm* **1** : horn **2** : antlers *pl* (of a deer)
cuero *nm* **1** : leather, hide **2** ~ **cabelludo** : scalp
cuerpo *nm* **1** : body **2** : corps (in the military, etc.)

cuervo *nm* : crow
cuesta *nf* **1** : slope **2 a** ~**s** : on one's back **3** ~ **abajo** : downhill **4** ~ **arriba** : uphill
cuestión *nf, pl* -**tiones** : matter, affair — **cuestionar** *vt* : question — **cuestionario** *nm* **1** : questionnaire **2** : quiz (in school)
cueva *nf* : cave
cuidar *vt* **1** : take care of, look after **2** : pay attention to (details, etc.) — *vi* **1** ~ **de** : look after **2** ~ **de que** : make sure that — **cuidarse** *vr* : take care of oneself — **cuidado** *nm* **1** : care **2** PREOCUPACIÓN : worry, concern **3 tener** ~ : be careful **4 ¡cuidado!** : watch out!, careful! — **cuidadoso, -sa** *adj* : careful — **cuidadosamente** *adv* : carefully
culata *nf* : butt (of a gun) — **culatazo** *nf* : kick, recoil
culebra *nf* : snake
culinario, -ria *adj* : culinary
culminar *vi* : culminate — **culminación** *nf, pl* -**ciones** : culmination
culo *nm fam* : backside, bottom
culpa *nf* **1** : fault, blame **2** PECADO : sin **3 echar la** ~ **a** : blame **4 tener la** ~ : be at fault — **culpabilidad** *nf* : guilt — **culpable** *adj* : guilty — ~ *nmf* : culprit, guilty party — **culpar** *vt* : blame
cultivar *vt* : cultivate — **cultivo** *nm* **1** : farming, cultivation **2** ~**s** : crops
culto, -ta *adj* : cultured, educated — **culto** *nm* **1** : worship **2** : (religious) cult — **cultura** *nf* : culture — **cultural** *adj* : cultural
cumbre *nf* : summit, top
cumpleaños *nms & pl* : birthday
cumplido, -da *adj* **1** : complete, full **2** CORTÉS : courteous — **cumplido** *nm* : compliment, courtesy
cumplimentar *vt* **1** : congratulate **2** CUMPLIR : carry out — **cumplimiento** *nm* : carrying out, performance
cumplir *vt* **1** : accomplish, carry out **2** : keep (a promise), observe (a law, etc.) **3** : reach (a given age) — *vi* **1** : expire, fall due **2** ~ **con el deber** : do one's duty — **cumplirse** *vr* **1** : expire **2** REALIZARSE : come true
cúmulo *nm* **1** : heap, pile **2** : cumulus (cloud)
cuna *nf* **1** : cradle **2** ORIGEN : birthplace
cundir *vi* **1** PROPAGARSE : spread, propagate **2** : go a long way
cuneta *nf* : ditch (in a road), gutter (in a street)
cuña *nf* : wedge

cuñado, -da n : brother-in-law m, sister-in-law f
cuota nf 1 : fee, dues 2 CUPO : quota 3 Lat : installment, payment
cupo nm 1 : quota, share 2 Lat : capacity, room
cupón nm, pl **-pones** : coupon
cúpula nf : dome, cupola
cura nf : cure, treatment — ~ nm : priest — **curación** nf, pl **-ciones** : healing — **curar** vt 1 : cure 2 : dress (a wound) 3 CURTIR : tan (hides) — **curarse** vr : get well
curiosear vi 1 : snoop, pry 2 : browse (in a store) — vt : look over — **curiosidad** nf : curiosity — **curioso, -sa** adj 1 : curious, inquisitive 2 RARO : unusual, strange
currículum nm, pl **-lums** or **currículo** nm : résumé, curriculum vitae

cursar vt 1 : take (a course), study 2 ENVIAR : send, pass on
cursi adj fam : affected, pretentious
cursiva nf : italics pl
curso nm 1 : course 2 : (school) year 3 en ~ : under way 4 en ~ : current
curtir vt 1 : tan 2 : harden (skin, features, etc.) — **curtiduría** nf : tannery
curva nf 1 : curve, bend 2 ~ de nivel : contour — **curvo, -va** adj : curved, bent
cúspide nf : apex, peak
custodia nf : custody — **custodiar** vt : guard, look after — **custodio, -dia** n : guardian
cutáneo, -nea adj : skin
cutícula nf : cuticle
cutis nms & pl : skin, complexion
cuyo, -ya adj 1 : whose, of whom, of which 2 en cuyo caso : in which case

D

d nf : d, fourth letter of the Spanish alphabet
dádiva nf : gift, handout — **dadivoso, -sa** adj : generous
dado, -da adj 1 : given 2 dado que : provided that, since — **dados** nmpl : dice
daga nf : dagger
daltónico, -ca adj : color-blind
dama nf 1 : lady 2 ~s nfpl : checkers
damnificar {72} vt : damage, injure
danés, -nesa adj : Danish — **danés** nm : Danish (language)
danzar {21} v : dance — **danza** nf : dance, dancing
dañar vt : damage, harm — **dañarse** vr 1 : be damaged 2 : hurt oneself — **dañino, -na** adj : harmful — **daño** nm 1 : damage, harm 2 ~s y perjuicios : damages
dar {22} vt 1 : give 2 PRODUCIR : yield, produce 3 : strike (the hour) 4 MOSTRAR : show — vi 1 ~ como : consider, regard as 2 ~ con : run into, meet 3 ~ contra : knock against 4 ~ para : be enough for — **darse** vr 1 : happen 2 ~ contra : bump into 3 ~ por : consider oneself 4 dárselas de : pose as
dardo nm : dart
dársena nf : dock
datar vt : date — vi ~ de : date from
dátil nm : date (fruit)
dato nm 1 : fact 2 ~s nmpl : data

de prep 1 : of 2 ~ Managua : from Managua 3 ~ niño : as a child 4 ~ noche : at night 5 las tres ~ la mañana : three o'clock in the morning 6 más ~ 10 : more than 10
deambular vi : wander about, stroll
debajo adv 1 : underneath 2 ~ de : under, underneath 3 por ~ : below, beneath
debatir vt : debate — **debatirse** vr : struggle — **debate** nm : debate
deber vt : owe — v aux 1 : have to, should 2 (expressing probability) : must — **deberse** vr ~ a : be due to — ~ nm 1 : duty 2 ~es nmpl : homework — **debido, -da** adj ~ a : due to, owing to
débil adj : weak, feeble — **debilidad** nf : weakness — **debilitar** vt : weaken — **debilitarse** vr : get weak — **débilmente** adv : weakly, faintly
débito nm 1 : debit 2 DEUDA : debt
debutar vi : debut — **debut** nm, pl ~s : debut — **debutante** nf : debutante f
década nf : decade
decadencia nf : decadence — **decadente** adj : decadent
decaer {13} vi : decline, weaken
decano, -na n : dean
decapitar vt : behead
decena nf : ten, about ten
decencia nf : decency
decenio nm : decade
decente adj : decent

decepcionar *vt* : disappoint — **decepción** *nf, pl* **-ciones** : disappointment
decibelio *or* **decibel** *nm* : decibel
decidir *vt* : decide, determine — *vi* : decide — **decidirse** *vr* : make up one's mind — **decididamente** *adv* : definitely, decidedly — **decidido, -da** *adj* : determined, resolute
decimal *adj* : decimal
décimo, -ma *adj & n* : tenth
decimoctavo, -va *adj* : eighteenth — ~ *n* : eighteenth (in a series)
decimocuarto, -ta *adj* : fourteenth — ~ *n* : fourteenth (in a series)
decimonoveno, -na *or* **decimonono, -na** *adj* : nineteenth — ~ *n* : nineteenth (in a series)
decimoquinto, -ta *adj* : fifteenth — ~ *n* : fifteenth (in a series)
decimoséptimo, -ma *adj* : seventeenth — ~ *n* : seventeenth (in a series)
decimosexto, -ta *adj* : sixteenth — ~ *n* : sixteenth (in a series)
decimotercero, -ra *adj* : thirteenth — ~ *n* : thirteenth (in a series)
decir {23} *vt* **1** : say **2** CONTAR : tell **3 es** ~ : that is to say **4 querer** ~ : mean — **decirse** *vr* **1** : tell oneself **2 ¿cómo se dice...en español?** : how do you say...in Spanish? — ~ *nm* : saying, expression
decisión *nf, pl* **-siones** : decision — **decisivo, -va** *adj* : decisive
declarar *vt* : declare — *vi* : testify — **declararse** *vr* **1** : declare oneself **2 . break out** (of a fire, an epidemic, etc.) — **declaración** *nf, pl* **-ciones** : statement
declinar *v* : decline
declive *nm* **1** : decline **2** PENDIENTE : slope
decolorar *vt* : bleach — **decolorarse** *vr* : fade
decoración *nf, pl* **-ciones** : decoration — **decorado** *nm* : stage set — **decorar** *vt* : decorate — **decorativo, -va** *adj* : decorative
decoro *nm* : decency, decorum — **decoroso, -sa** *adj* : decent, proper
decrecer {53} *vi* : decrease
decrépito, -ta *adj* : decrepit
decretar *vt* : decree — **decreto** *nm* : decree
dedal *nm* : thimble
dedicar {72} *vt* : dedicate — **dedicarse** *vr* ~ **a** : devote oneself to — **dedicación** *nf, pl* **-ciones** : dedication — **dedicatoria** *nf* : dedication, inscription
dedo *nm* **1** : finger **2** ~ **del pie** : toe

deducir {61} *vt* **1** INFERIR : deduce **2** DESCONTAR : deduct — **deducción** *nf, pl* **-ciones** : deduction
defecar {72} *vi* : defecate
defecto *nm* : defect — **defectuoso, -sa** *adj* : defective, faulty
defender {56} *vt* : defend — **defenderse** *vr* : defend oneself — **defensa** *nf* : defense — **defensiva** *nf* : defensive — **defensivo, -va** *adj* : defensive — **defensor, -sora** *n* **1** : defender **2** *or* **abogado defensor** : defense counsel
deferencia *nf* : deference — **deferente** *adj* : deferential
deficiencia *nf* : deficiency — **deficiente** *adj* : deficient
déficit *nm, pl* **-cits** : deficit
definir *vt* : define — **definición** *nf, pl* **-ciones** : definition — **definitivo, -va** *adj* **1** : definitive **2 en definitiva** : in short
deformar *vt* **1** : deform **2** : distort (the truth, etc.) — **deformación** *nf, pl* **-ciones** : distortion — **deforme** *adj* : deformed — **deformidad** *nf* : deformity
defraudar *vt* **1** : defraud **2** DECEPCIONAR : disappoint
degenerar *vi* : degenerate — **degenerado, -da** *adj* : degenerate
degradar *vt* **1** : degrade **2** : demote (in the military)
degustar *vt* : taste
dehesa *nf* : pasture
deidad *nf* : deity
dejar *vt* **1** : leave **2** ABANDONAR : abandon **3** PERMITIR : allow — *vi* ~ **de** : quit — **dejado, -da** *adj* : slovenly, careless
dejo *nm* **1** : aftertaste **2** : (regional) accent
delantal *nm* : apron
delante *adv* **1** : ahead **2** ~ **de** : in front of
delantera *nf* **1** : front **2 tomar la** ~ : take the lead — **delantero, -ra** *adj* : front, forward — ~ *n* : forward (in sports)
delatar *vt* : denounce, inform against
delegar {52} *vt* : delegate — **delegación** *nf, pl* **-ciones** : delegation — **delegado, -da** *n* : delegate, representative
deleitar *vt* : delight, please — **deleite** *nm* : delight
deletrear *vi* : spell (out)
delfín *nm, pl* **-fines** : dolphin
delgado, -da *adj* : thin
deliberar *vi* : deliberate — **deliberación** *nf, pl* **-ciones** : deliberation

— **deliberado, -da** *adj* : deliberate, intentional

delicadeza *nf* **1** : delicacy, daintiness **2** SUAVIDAD : gentleness **3** TACTO : tact — **delicado, -da** *adj* **1** : delicate **2** SENSIBLE : sensible **3** DISCRETO : tactful

delicia *nf* : delight — **delicioso, -sa** *adj* **1** : delightful **2** RICO : delicious

delictivo, -va *adj* : criminal

delimitar *vt* : define, set the boundaries of

delincuencia *nf* : delinquency, crime — **delincuente** *adj & nmf* : delinquent, criminal — **delinquir** {24} *vi* : break the law

delirante *adj* : delirious — **delirar** *vi* **1** : be delirious **2** ~ **por** *fam* : rave about — **delirio** *nm* **1** : delirium **2** ~ **de grandeza** : delusions of grandeur

delito *nm* : crime

delta *nm* : delta

demacrado, -da *adj* : emaciated

demandar *vt* **1** : sue **2** PEDIR : demand **3** *Lat* : request — **demanda** *nf* **1** : lawsuit **2** PETICIÓN : request **3 la oferta y la** ~ : supply and demand — **demandante** *nmf* : plaintiff

demás *adj* : rest of the, other — ~ *pron* **1 lo (la, los, las)** ~ : the rest, others **2 por** ~ : extremely **3 por lo** ~ : otherwise **4 y** ~ : and so on

demasiado *adv* **1** : too **2** : too much — ~ *adj* : too much, too many

demencia *nf* : madness — **demente** *adj* : insane, mad

democracia *nf* : democracy — **demócrata** *nmf* : democrat — **democrático, -ca** *adj* : democratic

demoler {47} *vt* : demolish — **demolición** *nf, pl* **-ciones** : demolition

demonio *nm* : devil, demon

demorar *v* : delay — **demorarse** *vr* : take a long time — **demora** *nf* : delay

demostrar {19} *vt* **1** : demonstrate **2** MOSTRAR : show — **demostración** *nf, pl* **-ciones** : demonstration

demudar *vt* : change, alter

denegar {49} *vt* : deny, refuse — **denegación** *nf, pl* **-ciones** : denial, refusal

denigrar *vt* **1** : denigrate **2** INJURIAR : insult

denominador *nm* : denominator

denotar *vt* : denote, show

densidad *nf* : density — **denso, -sa** *adj* : dense

dental *adj* : dental — **dentado, -da** *adj* : toothed, notched — **dentadura** *nf* ~ **postiza** : dentures *pl* — **dentífrico** *nm* : toothpaste — **dentista** *nmf* : dentist

dentro *adv* **1** : in, inside **2** ~ **de poco** : soon, shortly **3 por** ~ : inside

denuedo *nm* : courage

denunciar *vt* **1** : denounce **2** : report (a crime) — **denuncia** *nf* **1** : accusation **2** : (police) report

departamento *nm* **1** : department **2** *Lat* : apartment

depender *vi* **1** : depend **2** ~ **de** : depend on — **dependencia** *nf* **1** : dependence, dependency **2** SUCURSAL : branch office — **dependiente** *adj* : dependent — **dependiente, -ta** *n* : clerk, salesperson

deplorar *vt* : deplore, regret

deponer {60} *vt* : remove from office, depose

deportar *vt* : deport — **deportación** *nf, pl* **-ciones** : deportation

deporte *nm* : sport, sports *pl* — **deportista** *nmf* : sportsman *m*, sportswoman *f* — **deportivo, -va** *adj* **1** : sporty **2 artículos deportivos** : sporting goods

depositar *vt* **1** : put, place **2** : deposit (in a bank, etc.) — **depósito** *nm* **1** : deposit **2** ALMACÉN : warehouse

depravado, -da *adj* : depraved

depreciarse *vr* : depreciate — **depreciación** *nf* : depreciation

depredador *nm* : predator

deprimir *vt* : depress — **deprimirse** *vr* : get depressed — **depresión** *nf, pl* **-siones** : depression

derecha *nf* **1** : right side **2** : right wing (in politics) — **derechista** *adj* : rightwing — **derecho** *nm* **1** : right **2** LEY : law — ~ *adv* : straight — **derecho, -cha** *adj* **1** : right, right-hand **2** VERTICAL : upright **3** RECTO : straight

deriva *nf* **1** : drift **2 a la** ~ : adrift — **derivación** *nf, pl* **-ciones** : derivation — **derivar** *vi* **1** : drift **2** ~ **de** : derive from

derramamiento *nm* ~ **de sangre** : bloodshed

derramar *vt* **1** : spill **2** : shed (tears, blood) — **derramarse** *vr* : overflow — **derrame** *nm* **1** : spilling **2** : discharge, hemorrhage

derrapar *vi* : skid — **derrape** *nm* : skid

derretir {54} *vt* : melt, thaw — **derretirse** *vr* **1** : melt, thaw **2** ~ **por** *fam* : be crazy about

derribar *vt* **1** : demolish **2** : bring down (a plane, a tree, etc.) **3** : overthrow (a government, etc.)

derrocar {72} *vt* : overthrow

derrochar *vt* : waste, squander — **der-**

rochador, -dora n : spendthrift — **derroche** nm : extravagance, waste

derrotar vt : defeat — **derrota** nf : defeat

derruir {41} vt : demolish, tear down

derrumbar vt : demolish, knock down — **derrumbarse** vr : collapse, break down — **derrumbamiento** nm : collapse — **derrumbe** nm : collapse

desabotonar vt : unbutton, undo

desabrido, -da adj : bland

desabrochar vt : unbutton, undo — **desabrocharse** vr : come undone

desacato nm 1 : disrespect 2 : contempt (of court) — **desacatar** vt : defy, disobey

desacertado, -da adj : mistaken, wrong — **desacertar** {55} vi : be mistaken — **desacierto** nm : mistake, error

desaconsejar vt : advise against — **desaconsejable** adj : inadvisable

desacreditar vt : discredit

desactivar vt : deactivate

desacuerdo nm : disagreement

desafiar {85} vt : defy, challenge — **desafiante** adj : defiant

desafilado, -da adj : blunt

desafinado, -da adj : out-of-tune, off-key

desafío nm : challenge, defiance

desafortunado, -da adj : unfortunate — **desafortunadamente** adv : unfortunately

desagradar vt : displease — **desagradable** adj : disagreeable, unpleasant

desagradecido, -da adj : ungrateful

desagrado nm 1 : displeasure 2 con ～ : reluctantly

desagravio nm : amends, reparation

desagregarse {52} vr : disintegrate

desaguar {10} vi : drain, empty — **desagüe** nm 1 : drainage 2 : drain (of a sink, etc.)

desahogar {52} vt 1 : relieve 2 : give vent to (anger, etc.) — **desahogarse** vr : let off steam, unburden oneself — **desahogado, -da** adj 1 : roomy 2 ADINERADO : comfortable, well-off — **desahogo** nm 1 : relief 2 con ～ : comfortably

desahuciar vt 1 : deprive of hope 2 DESALOJAR : evict — **desahucio** nm : eviction

desaire nm : snub, rebuff — **desairar** vt : snub, slight

desalentar {55} vt : discourage — **desaliento** nm : discouragement

desaliñado, -da adj : slovenly

desalmado, -da adj : heartless, cruel

desalojar vt 1 : evacuate 2 DESAHUCIAR : evict

desamparar vt : abandon — **desamparo** nm : abandonment, desertion

desamueblado, -da adj : unfurnished

desangrarse vr : lose blood, bleed to death

desanimar vt : discourage — **desanimarse** vr : get discouraged — **desanimado, -da** adj : downhearted, despondent — **desánimo** nm : discouragement

desanudar vt : untie

desaparecer {53} vi : disappear — **desaparecido, -da** n : missing person — **desaparición** nf, pl **-ciones** : disappearance

desapasionado, -da adj : dispassionate

desapego nm : indifference

desapercibido, -da adj : unnoticed

desaprobar {19} vt : disapprove of — **desaprobación** nf, pl **-ciones** : disapproval

desaprovechar vt : waste

desarmar vt 1 : disarm 2 DESMONTAR : dismantle, take apart — **desarme** nm : disarmament

desarraigar {52} vt : uproot, root out

desarreglar vt 1 : mess up 2 : disrupt (plans, etc.) — **desarreglado, -da** adj : disorganized — **desarreglo** nm : untidiness, disorder

desarrollar vt : develop — **desarrollarse** vr : take place — **desarrollo** nm : development

desarticular vt 1 : break up, dismantle 2 : dislocate (a bone)

desaseado, -da adj 1 : dirty 2 DESORDENADO : messy

desastre nm : disaster — **desastroso, -sa** adj : disastrous

desatar vt 1 : undo, untie 2 : unleash (passions) — **desatarse** vr 1 : come undone 2 DESENCADENARSE : break out, erupt

desatascar {72} vt : unclog

desatender {56} vt 1 : disregard 2 : neglect (an obligation, etc.) — **desatento, -ta** adj : inattentive

desatinado, -da adj : foolish, silly

desautorizado, -da adj : unauthorized

desavenencia nf : disagreement

desayunar vi : have breakfast — vt : have for breakfast — **desayuno** nm : breakfast

desbancar {72} vt : oust

desbarajuste nm : disorder, confusion

desbaratar vt : ruin, destroy — **desbaratarse** vr : fall apart

desbocarse {72} *vr* : run away, bolt
desbordar *vt* 1 : overflow 2 : exceed (limits) — **desbordarse** *vr* : overflow — **desbordamiento** *nm* : overflow
descabellado, -da *adj* : crazy
descafeinado, -da *adj* : decaffeinated
descalabrar *vt* : hit on the head — **descalabro** *nm* : misfortune, setback
descalificar {72} *vt* : disqualify — **descalificación** *nf, pl* **-ciones** : disqualification
descalzarse {21} *vr* : take off one's shoes — **descalzo, -za** *adj* : barefoot
descaminar *vt* : mislead, lead astray
descansar *v* : rest — **descanso** *nm* 1 : rest 2 : landing (of a staircase) 3 : intermission (in theater), halftime (in sports)
descapotable *adj & nm* : convertible
descarado, -da *adj* : insolent, shameless
descargar {52} *vt* 1 : unload 2 : discharge (a firearm, etc.) — **descarga** *nf* 1 : unloading 2 : discharge (of a firearm, of electricity, etc.) — **descargo** *nm* 1 : unloading 2 : discharge (of a duty, etc.) 3 : defense (in law)
descarnado, -da *adj* : scrawny, gaunt
descaro *nm* : insolence, nerve
descarrilar *vi* : derail — **descarrilarse** *vr* : be derailed
descartar *vt* : reject — **descartarse** *vr* : discard
descascarar *vt* : peel, shell, husk
descender {56} *vt* 1 : go down 2 BAJAR : lower — *vi* 1 : descend 2 ~ **de** : be descended from — **descendencia** *nf* 1 : descendants *pl* 2 LINAJE : lineage, descent — **descendiente** *nmf* : descendant — **descenso** *nm* 1 : descent 2 : drop, fall (in level, in temperature, etc.)
descifrar *vt* : decipher, decode
descolgar {16} *vt* 1 : take down 2 : pick up, answer (the telephone)
descolorarse *vr* : fade — **descolorido, -da** *adj* : faded, discolored
descomponer {60} *vt* : break down — **descomponerse** *vr* 1 : rot, decompose 2 *Lat* : break down — **descompuesto, -ta** *adj Lat* : out of order
descomunal *adj* : enormous
desconcertar {55} *vt* : disconcert, confuse — **desconcertante** *adj* : confusing — **desconcierto** *nm* : confusion, bewilderment
desconectar *vt* : disconnect
desconfiar {85} *vi* ~ **de** : distrust — **desconfiado, -da** *adj* : distrustful — **desconfianza** *nf* : distrust

descongelar *vt* 1 : thaw, defrost 2 : unfreeze (assets)
descongestionante *nm* : decongestant
desconocer {18} *vt* : not know, fail to recognize — **desconocido, -da** *adj* : unknown — ~ *n* : stranger
desconsiderado, -da *adj* : inconsiderate
desconsolar *vt* : distress — **desconsolado, -da** *adj* : heartbroken — **desconsuelo** *nm* : grief, sorrow
descontar {19} *vt* : discount
descontento, -ta *adj* : dissatisfied — **descontento** *nm* : discontent
descontinuar *vt* : discontinue
descorazonado, -da *adj* : discouraged
descorrer *vt* : draw back
descortés *adj, pl* **-teses** : rude — **descortesía** *nf* : discourtesy, rudeness
descoyuntar *vt* : dislocate
descrédito {19} *nm* : discredit
descremado, -da *adj* : nonfat, skim
describir {33} *vt* : describe — **descripción** *nf, pl* **-ciones** : description — **descriptivo, -va** *adj* : descriptive
descubierto, -ta *adj* 1 : exposed, uncovered 2 **al descubierto** : in the open — **descubierto** *nm* : deficit, overdraft
descubrir {2} *vt* 1 : discover 2 REVELAR : reveal — **descubrimiento** *nm* : discovery
descuento *nm* : discount
descuidar *vt* : neglect — **descuidarse** *vr* 1 : be careless 2 ABANDONARSE : let oneself go — **descuidado, -da** *adj* 1 : careless, sloppy 2 DESATENDIDO : neglected — **descuido** *nm* : neglect, carelessness
desde *prep* 1 : from (a place), since (a time) 2 ~ **luego** : of course
desdén *nm* : scorn, disdain — **desdeñar** *vt* : scorn — **desdeñoso, -sa** *adj* : disdainful
desdicha *nf* 1 : misery 2 DESGRACIA : misfortune — **desdichado, -da** *adj* : unfortunate, unhappy
desear *vt* : wish, want — **deseable** *adj* : desirable
desecar *vt* : dry up
desechar *vt* 1 : throw away 2 RECHAZAR : reject — **desechable** *adj* : disposable — **desechos** *nmpl* : rubbish
desembarazarse {21} *vr* ~ **de** : get rid of
desembarcar {72} *vi* : disembark — *vt* : unload — **desembarcadero** *nm* : jetty, landing pier — **desembarco** *nm* : landing
desembocar {72} *vi* ~ **en** 1 : flow

into **2** : lead to (a result) — **desembocadura** *nf* **1** : mouth (of a river) **2** : opening, end (of a street)
desembolsar *vt* : pay out — **desembolso** *nm* : payment, outlay
desembragar *vi* : disengage the clutch
desempacar {72} *v Lat* : unpack
desempate *nm* : tiebreaker
desempeñar *vt* **1** : play (a role) **2** : redeem (from a pawnshop) — **desempeñarse** *vr* : get out of debt
desempleo *nm* : unemployment — **desempleado, -da** *adj* : unemployed
desempolvar *vt* : dust
desencadenar *vt* **1** : unchain **2** : trigger, unleash (protests, crises, etc.) — **desencadenarse** *vr* : break loose
desencajar *vt* **1** : dislocate **2** DESCONECTAR : disconnect
desencanto *nm* : disillusionment
desenchufar *vt* : disconnect, unplug
desenfadado, -da *adj* : carefree, confident — **desenfado** *nm* : confidence, ease
desenfrenado, -da *adj* : unrestrained — **desenfreno** *nm* : abandon, lack of restraint
desenganchar *vt* : unhook
desengañar *vt* : disillusion — **desengaño** *nm* : disappointment
desenlace *nm* : ending, outcome
desenmarañar *vt* : disentangle
desenmascarar *vt* : unmask
desenredar *vt* : untangle — **desenredarse** *vr* ~ **de** : extricate oneself from
desenrollar *vt* : unroll, unwind
desentenderse {56} *vr* ~ **de** : want nothing to do with
desenterrar {55} *vt* : dig up, disinter
desentonar *vi* **1** : be out of tune **2** : clash (of colors, etc.)
desenvoltura *nf* : confidence, ease
desenvolver {89} *vt* : unfold, unwrap — **desenvolverse** *vr* : unfold, develop
desenvuelto, -ta *adj* : confident, self-assured
deseo *nm* : desire — **deseoso, -sa** *adj* : eager, anxious
desequilibrar *vt* : throw off balance — **desequilibrado, -da** *adj* : unbalanced — **desequilibrio** *nm* : imbalance
desertar *vt* : desert — **deserción** *nf, pl* **-ciones** : desertion — **desertor, -tora** *n* : deserter
desesperar *vt* : exasperate — *vi* : despair — **desesperarse** *vr* : become exasperated — **desesperación** *nf, pl* **-ciones** : desperation, despair — **de-**

sesperado, -da *adj* : desperate, hopeless
desestimar *vt* : reject
desfalcar {72} *vt* **1** : embezzle — **desfalco** *nm* : embezzlement
desfallecer {53} *vi* **1** : weaken **2** DESMAYARSE : faint
desfavorable *adj* : unfavorable
desfigurar *vt* **1** : disfigure, mar **2** : distort (the truth)
desfiladero *nm* : mountain pass, gorge
desfilar *vi* : march, parade — **desfile** *nm* : parade, procession
desfogar {52} *vt* : vent — **desfogarse** *vr* : let off steam
desgajar *vt* : tear off, break apart — **desgajarse** *vr* : come off
desgana *nf* **1** : lack of appetite **2** : lack of enthusiasm, reluctance
desgarbado, -da *adj* : gawky, ungainly
desgarrar *vt* : tear, rip — **desgarrador, -dora** *adj* : heartbreaking — **desgarro** *nm* : tear
desgastar *vt* : wear away, wear down — **desgaste** *nm* : deterioration, wear and tear
desgracia *nf* **1** : misfortune **2 caer en** ~ : fall into disgrace **3 por** ~ : unfortunately — **desgraciadamente** *adv* : unfortunately — **desgraciado, -da** *adj* : unfortunate
deshabitado, -da *adj* : uninhabited
deshacer {40} *vt* **1** : undo **2** DESTRUIR : destroy, ruin **3** DISOLVER : dissolve **4** : break (an agreement), cancel (plans, etc.) — **deshacerse** *vr* **1** : come undone **2** ~ **de** : get rid of **3** ~ **en** : lavish, heap (praise, etc.) — **deshecho, -cha** *adj* **1** : undone **2** DESTROZADO : destroyed, ruined
desheredar *vt* : disinherit
deshidratar *vt* : dehydrate
deshielo *nm* : thaw
deshilachar *vt* : unravel — **deshilacharse** *vr* : fray
deshonesto, -ta *adj* : dishonest
deshonrar *vt* : dishonor, disgrace — **deshonra** *nf* : dishonor — **deshonroso, -sa** *adj* : dishonorable
deshuesar *vt* **1** : pit (a fruit) **2** : bone, debone (meat)
desidia *nf* **1** : indolence **2** DESASEO : sloppiness
desierto, -ta *adj* : deserted, uninhabited — **desierto** *nm* : desert
designar *vt* : appoint — **designación** *nf, pl* **-ciones** : appointment (to an office, etc.)
designio *nm* : plan
desigual *adj* **1** : unequal **2** DISPAREJO

: uneven — **desigualdad** *nf* : inequality

desilusionar *vt* : disappoint, disillusion — **desilusión** *nf, pl* **-siones** : disappointment, disillusionment

desinfectar *vt* : disinfect — **desinfectante** *adj & nm* : disinfectant

desinflar *vt* : deflate — **desinflarse** *vr* : deflate, go flat

desinhibido, -da *adj* : uninhibited

desintegrar *vt* : disintegrate — **desintegrarse** *vr* : disintegrate — **desintegración** *nf, pl* **-ciones** : disintegration

desinteresado, -da *adj* : unselfish, generous — **desinterés** *nm* : unselfishness

desistir *vi* ~ **de** : give up

desleal *adj* : disloyal — **deslealtad** *nf* : disloyalty

desleír {66} *vt* : dilute, dissolve

desligar {52} *vt* 1 : untie 2 SEPARAR : separate — **desligarse** *vr* : extricate oneself

desliz *nm, pl* **-lices** : slip, mistake — **deslizar** {21} *vt* : slide, slip — **deslizarse** *vr* : slide, glide

deslucido, -da *adj* : dingy, tarnished

deslumbrar *vt* : dazzle — **deslumbrante** *adj* : dazzling, blinding

deslustrar *vt* : tarnish, dull

desmán *nm, pl* **-manes** : outrage, excess

desmandarse *vr* : get out of hand

desmantelar *vt* : dismantle

desmañado, -da *adj* : clumsy

desmayar *vt* : lose heart — **desmayarse** *vr* : faint — **desmayo** *nm* : faint

desmedido, -da *adj* : excessive

desmejorar *vt* : impair — *vi* : deteriorate

desmemoriado, -da *adj* : forgetful

desmentir {76} *vt* : deny — **desmentido** *nm* : denial

desmenuzar {21} *vt* 1 : crumble 2 EXAMINAR : scrutinize — **desmenuzarse** *vr* : crumble

desmerecer {53} *vt* : be unworthy of — *vi* : decline in value

desmesurado, -da *adj* : excessive

desmigajar *vt* : crumble

desmontar *vt* 1 : dismantle, take apart 2 ALLANAR : level — *vi* : dismount

desmoralizar {21} *vt* : demoralize

desmoronarse *vr* : crumble

desnivel *nm* : unevenness

desnudar *vt* : undress, strip — **desnudarse** *vr* : get undressed — **desnudez** *nf, pl* **-deces** : nudity, nakedness — **desnudo, -da** *adj* : nude, naked — **desnudo** *nm* : nude

desnutrición *nf, pl* **-ciones** : malnutrition

desobedecer {53} *v* : disobey — **desobediencia** *nf* : disobedience — **desobediente** *adj* : disobedient

desocupar *vt* : empty, vacate — **desocupado, -da** *adj* 1 : vacant 2 DESEMPLEADO : unemployed

desodorante *adj & nm* : deodorant

desolado, -da *adj* 1 : desolate 2 DESCONSOLADO : devastated, distressed — **desolación** *nf, pl* **-ciones** : desolation

desorden *nm, pl* **desórdenes** : disorder, mess — **desordenado, -da** *adj* : untidy — **desordenadamente** *adv* : in a disorderly way

desorganizar {21} *vt* : disorganize — **desorganización** *nf, pl* **-ciones** : disorganization

desorientar *vt* : disorient, confuse — **desorientarse** *vr* : lose one's way

desovar *vi* : spawn

despachar *vt* 1 : deal with (a task, etc.) 2 ENVIAR : dispatch, send 3 : wait on, serve (customers) — **despacho** *nm* 1 : dispatch, shipment 2 OFICINA : office

despacio *adv* : slowly

desparramar *vt* : spill, scatter, spread

despavorido, -da *adj* : terrified

despecho *nm* 1 : spite 2 **a** ~ **de** : despite, in spite of

despectivo, -va *adj* 1 : pejorative 2 DESPRECIATIVO : contemptuous

despedazar {21} *vt* : tear apart

despedir {54} *vt* 1 : see off 2 DESTITUIR : dismiss, fire 3 DESPRENDER : emit — **despedirse** *vr* : say good-bye — **despedida** *nf* : farewell, good-bye

despegar {52} *vt* : detach, unstick — *vi* : take off — **despegado, -da** *adj* : cold, distant — **despegue** *nm* : take-off

despeinar *vt* : ruffle (hair) — **despeinado, -da** *adj* : disheveled, unkempt

despejar *vt* : clear, free — *vi* : clear up — **despejado, -da** *adj* 1 : clear, fair 2 LÚCIDO : clear-headed

despellejar *vt* : skin (an animal)

despensa *nf* : pantry, larder

despeñadero *nm* : precipice

desperdiciar *vt* : waste — **desperdicio** *nm* 1 : waste 2 ~**s** *nmpl* : scraps

desperfecto *nm* : flaw, defect

despertar {55} *vi* : awaken, wake up — *vt* : wake, rouse — **despertador** *nm* : alarm clock

despiadado, -da *adj* : pitiless, merciless

despido *nm* : dismissal, layoff
despierto, -ta *adj* : awake
despilfarrar *vt* : squander — **despilfarrador, -dora** *n* : spendthrift — **despilfarro** *nm* : extravagance, wastefulness
despistar *vt* : throw off the track, confuse — **despistarse** *vr* : lose one's way — **despistado, -da** *adj* 1 : absentminded 2 DESORIENTADO : confused — **despiste** *nm* 1 : absentmindedness 2 ERROR : mistake
desplazar {21} *vt* : displace — **desplazarse** *vr* : travel
desplegar {49} *vt* : unfold, spread out — **despliegue** *nm* : display
desplomarse *vr* : collapse
desplumar *vt* 1 : pluck 2 *fam* : fleece
despoblado, -da *adj* : uninhabited, deserted — **despoblado** *nm* : deserted area
despojar *vt* : strip, deprive — **despojos** *nmpl* 1 : plunder 2 RESTOS : remains, scraps
desportillar *vt* : chip — **desportillarse** *vr* : chip — **desportilladura** *nf* : chip, nick
despota *nmf* : despot
despotricar *vi* : rant (and rave)
despreciar *vt* : despise, scorn — **despreciable** *adj* 1 : despicable 2 **una cantidad ~** : a negligible amount — **desprecio** *nm* : disdain, scorn
desprender *vt* 1 : detach, remove 2 EMITIR : give off — **desprenderse** *vr* 1 : come off 2 DEDUCIRSE : be inferred, follow — **desprendimiento** *nm* **~ de tierras** : landslide
despreocupado, -da *adj* : carefree, unconcerned
desprestigiar *vt* : discredit — **desprestigiarse** *vr* : lose face
desprevenido, -da *adj* : unprepared
desproporcionado, -da : out of proportion
despropósito *nm* : (piece of) nonsense, absurdity
desprovisto, -ta *adj* **~ de** : lacking in
después *adv* 1 : afterward 2 ENTONCES : then, next 3 **~ de** : after 4 **después (de) que** : after 5 **~ de todo** : after all
despuntado, -da *adj* : blunt, dull
desquiciar *vt* : drive crazy
desquitarse *vr* 1 : retaliate 2 **~ con** : take it out on, get back at — **desquite** *nm* : revenge
destacar {72} *vt* : emphasize — *vi* : stand out — **destacado, -da** *adj* : outstanding
destapar *vt* : open, uncover — **destapador** *nm Lat* : bottle opener

destartalado, -da *adj* : dilapidated
destellar *vi* : flash, sparkle — **destello** *nm* : sparkle, twinkle, flash
destemplado, -da *adj* 1 : out of tune 2 MAL : out of sorts 3 : unpleasant (of weather)
desteñir {67} *vt* : fade, bleach — *vi* : run, fade — **desteñirse** *vr* : fade
desterrar {55} *vt* : banish, exile — **desterrado, -da** *n* : exile
destetar *vt* : wean
destiempo *adv* **a ~** : at the wrong time
destierro *nm* : exile
destilar *vt* : distill — **destilería** *nf* : distillery
destinar *vt* 1 : assign, allocate 2 NOMBRAR : appoint — **destinado, -da** *adj* : destined — **destinatario, -ria** *n* : addressee — **destino** *nm* 1 : destiny 2 RUMBO : destination
destituir {41} *vt* : dismiss — **destitución** *nf, pl* **-ciones** : dismissal
destornillar *vt* : unscrew — **destornillador** *nm* : screwdriver
destreza *nf* : skill, dexterity
destrozar {21} *vt* : destroy, wreck — **destrozos** *nmpl* : damage, destruction
destrucción *nf, pl* **-ciones** : destruction — **destructivo, -va** *adj* : destructive — **destruir** {41} *vt* : destroy
desunir *vt* : split, divide
desusado, -da *adj* 1 : obsolete 2 INSÓLITO : unusual — **desuso** *nm* **caer en ~** : fall into disuse
desvaído, -da *adj* 1 : pale, washed-out 2 BORROSO : vague, blurred
desvalido, -da *adj* : destitute, needy
desvalijar *vt* : rob
desván *nm, pl* **-vanes** : attic
desvanecer {53} *vt* : make disappear — **desvanecerse** *vr* 1 : vanish 2 DESMAYARSE : faint
desvariar {85} *vi* : be delirious — **desvarío** *nm* : delirium
desvelar *vt* : keep awake — **desvelarse** *vr* : stay awake — **desvelo** *nm* 1 : sleeplessness 2 **~s** *nmpl* : efforts
desvencijado, -da *adj* : dilapidated, rickety
desventaja *nf* : disadvantage
desventura *nf* : misfortune
desvergonzado, -da *adj* : shameless — **desvergüenza** *nf* : shamelessness
desvestir {54} *vt* : undress — **desvestirse** *vr* : get undressed
desviación *nf, pl* **-ciones** 1 : deviation 2 : detour (in a road) — **desviar** {85} *vt* : divert, deflect — **desviarse** *vr* 1 : branch off 2 APARTARSE : stray — **desvío** *nm* : diversion, detour

detallar *vt* : detail — **detallado, -da** *adj* : detailed, thorough — **detalle** *nm* **1** : detail **2 al ~** : retail — **detallista** *adj* : retail — *nmf* : retailer

detectar *vt* : detect — **detective** *nmf* : detective

detener {80} *vt* **1** : arrest, detain **2** PARAR : stop **3** RETRASAR : delay — **detenerse** *vr* **1** : stop **2** DEMORARSE : linger — **detención** *nf, pl* **-ciones** : arrest, detention

detergente *nm* : detergent

deteriorar *vt* : damage — **deteriorarse** *vr* : wear out, deteriorate — **deteriorado, -da** *adj* : damaged, worn — **deterioro** *nm* : deterioration, damage

determinar *vt* **1** : determine **2** MOTIVAR : bring about **3** DECIDIR : decide — **determinarse** *vr* : decide — **determinación** *nf, pl* **-ciones 1** : determination **2 tomar una ~** : make a decision — **determinado, -da** *adj* **1** : determined **2** ESPECÍFICO : specific

detestar *vt* : detest

detonar *vi* : explode, detonate — **detonación** *nf, pl* **-ciones** : detonation

detrás *adv* **1** : behind **2 ~ de** : in back of **3 por ~** : from behind

detrimento *nm* **en ~ de** : to the detriment of

deuda *nf* : debt — **deudor, -dora** *n* : debtor

devaluar {3} *vt* : devalue — **devaluarse** *vr* : depreciate

devastar *vt* : devastate — **devastador, -dora** *adj* : devastating

devenir {87} *vi* **1** : come about **2 ~ en** : become, turn into

devoción *nf, pl* **-ciones** : devotion

devolución *nf, pl* **-ciones** : return

devolver {89} *vt* **1** RESTITUIR : give back **2** : refund, pay back — *vi* : vomit — **devolverse** *vr Lat* : return, come back

devorar *vt* : devour

devoto, -ta *adj* : devout — **~** *n* : devotee

día *nm* **1** : day **2** : daytime **3 al ~** : up-to-date **4 en pleno ~** : in broad daylight

diabetes *nf* : diabetes — **diabético, -ca** *adj & n* : diabetic

diablo *nm* : devil — **diablillo** *nm* : imp, rascal — **diablura** *nf* : prank — **diabólico, -ca** *adj* : diabolic, diabolical

diafragma *nm* : diaphragm

diagnosticar {72} *vt* : diagnose — **diagnóstico, -ca** *adj* : diagnostic — **diagnóstico** *nm* : diagnosis

diagonal *adj & nf* : diagonal

diagrama *nm* : diagram

dial *nm* : dial (of a radio, etc.)

dialecto *nm* : dialect

dialogar {52} *vi* : have a talk — **diálogo** *nm* : dialogue

diamante *nm* : diamond

diámetro *nm* : diameter

diana *nf* **1** : reveille **2** BLANCO : target, bull's-eye

diario, -ria *adj* : daily — **diario** *nm* **1** : diary **2** PERIÓDICO : newspaper — **diariamente** *adv* : daily

diarrea *nf* : diarrhea

dibujar *vt* **1** : draw **2** DESCRIBIR : portray — **dibujante** *nmf* : draftsman *m*, draftswoman *f* — **dibujo** *nm* **1** : drawing **2 ~s animados** : (animated) cartoons

diccionario *nm* : dictionary

dicha *nf* **1** ALEGRÍA : happiness **2** SUERTE : good luck — **dicho** *nm* : saying, proverb — **dichoso, -sa** *adj* **1** : happy **2** AFORTUNADO : lucky

diciembre *nm* : December

dictar *vt* **1** : dictate **2** : pronounce (a sentence), deliver (a speech) — **dictado** *nm* : dictation — **dictador, -dora** *n* : dictator — **dictadura** *nf* : dictatorship

diecinueve *adj & nm* : nineteen — **diecinueveavo, -va** *adj* : nineteenth

dieciocho *adj & nm* : eighteen — **dieciochoavo, -va** *or* **dieciochavo, -va** *adj* : eighteenth

dieciséis *adj & nm* : sixteen — **dieciseisavo, -va** *adj* : sixteenth

diecisiete *adj & nm* : seventeen — **diecisieteavo, -va** *adj* : seventeenth

diente *nm* **1** : tooth **2** : prong, tine (of a fork, etc.) **3 ~ de ajo** : clove of garlic **4 ~ de león** : dandelion

diesel ['disel] *adj & nm* : diesel

diestra *nf* : right hand — **diestro, -tra** *adj* **1** : right **2** HÁBIL : skillful

dieta *nf* : diet — **dietético, -ca** *adj* : dietetic, dietary

diez *adj & nm, pl* **dieces** : ten

difamar *vt* : slander, libel — **difamación** *nf, pl* **-ciones** : slander, libel

diferencia *nf* : difference — **diferenciar** *vt* : distinguish between — **diferenciarse** *vr* : differ — **diferente** *adj* : different

diferir {76} *vt* : postpone — *vi* : differ

difícil *adj* : difficult — **dificultad** *nf* : difficulty — **dificultar** *vt* : hinder, obstruct

difteria *nf* : diphtheria

difundir *vt* **1** : spread (out) **2** : broadcast (television, etc.)

difunto, -ta *adj & n* : deceased
difusión *nf, pl* **-siones** : spreading
digerir {76} *vt* : digest — **digerible** *adj* : digestible — **digestión** *nf, pl* **-tiones** : digestion — **digestivo, -va** *adj* : digestive
dígito *nm* : digit — **digital** *adj* : digital
dignarse *vr* ~ **a** : deign to
dignatario, -ria *n* : dignitary — **dignidad** *nf* : dignity — **digno, -na** *adj* : worthy
digresión *nf, pl* **-ciones** : digression
dilapidar *vt* : waste, squander
dilatar *vt* **1** : expand, dilate **2** PROLONGAR : prolong **3** POSPONER : postpone
dilema *nm* : dilemma
diligencia *nf* **1** : diligence **2** TRÁMITE : procedure, task — **diligente** *adj* : diligent
diluir {41} *vt* : dilute
diluvio *nm* **1** : flood **2** LLUVIA : downpour
dimensión *nf, pl* **-siones** : dimension
diminuto, -ta *adj* : minute, tiny
dimitir *vi* : resign — **dimisión** *nf, pl* **-siones** : resignation
dinámico, -ca *adj* : dynamic
dinamita *nf* : dynamite
dínamo *or* **dinamo** *nmf* : dynamo
dinastía *nf* : dynasty
dineral *nm* : large sum, fortune
dinero *nm* : money
dinosaurio *nm* : dinosaur
diócesis *nfs & pl* : diocese
dios, diosa *n* : god, goddess *f* — **Dios** *nm* : God
diploma *nm* : diploma — **diplomado, -da** *adj* : qualified, trained
diplomacia *nf* : diplomacy — **diplomático, -ca** *adj* : diplomatic — ~ *n* : diplomat
diputación *nf, pl* **-ciones** : delegation — **diputado, -da** *n* : delegate
dique *nm* : dike
dirección *nf, pl* **-ciones** **1** : address **2** SENTIDO : direction **3** GESTIÓN : management **4** : steering (of an automobile) — **direccional** *nf Lat* : turn signal, blinker — **directa** *nf* : high gear — **directiva** *nf* : board of directors — **directivo, -va** *adj* : managerial — ~ *n* : manager, director — **directo, -ta** *adj* **1** DIRECTO : direct **2** DERECHO : straight — **director, -tora** *n* **1** : director, manager **2** : conductor (of an orchestra) — **directorio** *nm* : directory — **directriz** *nf, pl* **-trices** : guideline
dirigencia *nf* : leaders *pl*, leadership — **dirigente** *nmf* : director, leader
dirigible *nm* : dirigible, blimp

dirigir {35} *vt* **1** : direct, lead **2** : address (a letter, etc.) **3** ENCAMINAR : aim **4** : conduct (music) — **dirigirse** *vr* **1** ~ **a** : go towards **2** ~ **a algn** : speak to s.o., write to s.o.
discernir {25} *vt* : discern, distinguish — **discernimiento** *nm* : discernment
disciplinar *vt* : discipline — **disciplina** *nf* : discipline
discípulo, -la *n* : disciple, follower
disco *nm* **1** : disc, disk **2** : discus (in sports) **3** ~ **compacto** : compact disc
discordante *adj* : discordant — **discordia** *nf* : discord
discoteca *nf* : disco, discotheque
discreción *nf, pl* **-ciones** : discretion
discrepancia *nf* **1** : discrepancy **2** DESACUERDO : disagreement — **discrepar** *vi* : differ, disagree
discreto, -ta *adj* : discreet
discriminar *vt* **1** : discriminate against **2** DISTINGUIR : distinguish — **discriminación** *nf, pl* **-ciones** : discrimination
disculpar *vt* : excuse, pardon — **disculparse** *vr* : apologize — **disculpa** *nf* **1** : apology **2** EXCUSA : excuse
discurrir *vi* **1** : pass, go by **2** REFLEXIONAR : ponder, reflect
discurso *nm* : speech, discourse
discutir *vt* **1** : discuss **2** CUESTIONAR : dispute — *vi* : argue — **discusión** *nf, pl* **-siones** **1** : discussion **2** DISPUTA : argument — **discutible** *adj* : debatable
disecar {72} *vt* : dissect — **disección** *nf, pl* **-ciones** : dissection
diseminar *vt* : disseminate, spread
disentería *nf* : dysentery
disentir {76} *vi* ~ **de** : disagree with — **disentimiento** *nm* : disagreement, dissent
diseñar *vt* : design — **diseñador, -dora** *n* : designer — **diseño** *nm* : design
disertación *nf, pl* **-ciones** **1** : lecture **2** : (written) dissertation
disfrazar {21} *vt* : disguise — **disfrazarse** *vr* ~ **de** : disguise oneself as — **disfraz** *nm, pl* **-fraces** **1** : disguise **2** : costume (for a party, etc.)
disfrutar *vt* : enjoy — *vi* : enjoy oneself
disgustar *vt* : upset, annoy — **disgustarse** *vr* **1** : get annoyed **2** ENEMISTARSE : fall out (with s.o.) — **disgusto** *nm* **1** : annoyance, displeasure **2** RIÑA : quarrel
disidente *adj & nmf* : dissident
disimular *vt* : conceal, hide — *vi* : pretend — **disimulo** *nm* : pretense
disipar *vt* **1** : dispel **2** DERROCHAR : squander

diskette [di'sket] *nm* : floppy disk, diskette

dislexia *nf* : dyslexia — **disléxico, -ca** *adj* : dyslexic

dislocar {72} *vt* : dislocate — **dislocarse** *vr* : become dislocated

disminuir {41} *vt* : reduce — *vi* : decrease, drop — **disminución** *nf, pl* **-ciones** : decrease

disociar *vt* : dissociate

disolver {89} *vt* : dissolve — **disolverse** *vr* : dissolve

disparar *vi* : shoot, fire — *vt* : shoot — **dispararse** *vr* : shoot up, skyrocket

disparatado, -da *adj* : absurd — **disparate** *nm* : nonsense, silly thing

disparejo, -ja *adj* : uneven — **disparidad** *nf* : difference, disparity

disparo *nm* : shot

dispensar *vt* 1 : dispense, distribute 2 DISCULPAR : excuse

dispersar *vt* : disperse, scatter — **dispersarse** *vr* : disperse — **dispersión** *nf, pl* **-siones** : scattering

disponer {60} *vt* 1 : arrange, lay out 2 ORDENAR : decide, stipulate — *vi* ~ de : have at one's disposal — **disponerse** *vr* ~ a : be ready to — **disponibilidad** *nf* : availability — **disponible** *adj* : available

disposición *nf, pl* **-ciones** 1 : arrangement 2 APTITUD : aptitude 3 : order, provision (in law) 4 a ~ de : at the disposal of

dispositivo *nm* : device, mechanism

dispuesto, -ta *adj* : prepared, ready

disputar *vi* 1 : argue 2 COMPETIR : compete — *vt* : dispute — **disputa** *nf* : dispute, argument

disquete → **diskette**

distanciar *vt* : space out — **distanciarse** *vr* : grow apart — **distancia** *nf* : distance — **distante** *adj* : distant

distinguir {26} *vt* : distinguish — **distinguirse** *vr* : distinguish oneself, stand out — **distinción** *nf, pl* **-ciones** : distinction — **distintivo, -va** *adj* : distinctive — **distinto, -ta** *adj* 1 : different 2 CLARO : distinct, clear

distorsión *nf, pl* **-ciones** : distortion

distraer {81} *vt* 1 : distract 2 DIVERTIR : entertain — **distraerse** *vr* 1 : get distracted 2 ENTRETENERSE : amuse oneself — **distracción** *nf, pl* **-ciones** 1 : amusement 2 DESPISTE : absentmindedness — **distraído, -da** *adj* : distracted, absentminded

distribuir {41} *vt* : distribute — **distribución** *nf, pl* **-ciones** : distribution — **distribuidor, -dora** *n* : distributor

distrito *nm* : district

disturbio *nm* : disturbance

disuadir *vt* : dissuade, discourage — **disuasivo, -va** *adj* : deterrent

diurno, -na *adj* : day, daytime

divagar {52} *vi* : digress

diván *nm, pl* **-vanes** : divan, couch

divergir {35} *vi* 1 : diverge 2 ~ en : differ on

diversidad *nf* : diversity

diversificar {72} *vt* : diversify

diversión *nf, pl* **-siones** : fun, entertainment

diverso, -sa *adj* : diverse

divertir {76} *vt* : entertain — **divertirse** *vr* : enjoy oneself, have fun — **divertido, -da** *adj* : entertaining

dividendo *nm* : dividend

dividir *vt* 1 : divide 2 REPARTIR : distribute

divinidad *nf* : divinity — **divino, -na** *adj* : divine

divisa *nf* 1 : currency 2 EMBLEMA : emblem

divisar *vt* : discern, make out

división *nf, pl* **-siones** : division — **divisor** *nm* : denominator

divorciar *vt* : divorce — **divorciarse** *vr* : get a divorce — **divorciado, -da** *n* : divorcé *m*, divorcée *f* — **divorcio** *nm* : divorce

divulgar {52} *vt* 1 : divulge, reveal 2 PROPAGAR : spread, circulate

dizque *adv Lat* : supposedly, apparently

doblar *vt* 1 : double 2 PLEGAR : fold 3 : turn (a corner) 4 : dub (a film) — *vi* 1 : turn — **doblarse** *vr* 1 : double over 2 ~ a : give in to — **dobladillo** *nm* : hem — **doble** *adj & nm* : double — ~ *nmf* : stand-in, double — **doblemente** *adv* : doubly — **doblegar** {52} *vt* : force to yield — **doblegarse** *vr* : give in — **doblez** *nm, pl* **-bleces** : fold, crease

doce *adj & nm* : twelve — **doceavo, -va** *adj* : twelfth — **docena** *nf* : dozen

docente *adj* : teaching

dócil *adj* : docile

doctor, -tora *n* : doctor — **doctorado** *nm* : doctorate

doctrina *nf* : doctrine

documentar *vt* : document — **documentación** *nf, pl* **-ciones** : documentation — **documental** *adj & nm* : documentary — **documento** *nm* : document

dogma *nm* : dogma — **dogmático, -ca** *adj* : dogmatic

dólar *nm* : dollar

doler {47} *vi* **1** : hurt **2 me duelen los pies** : my feet hurt — **dolerse** *vr* ~ **de** : complain about — **dolor** *nm* **1** : pain **2** PENA : grief **3** ~ **de cabeza** : headache **4** ~ **de estómago** : stomachache — **dolorido, -da** **1** : sore **2** AFLIGIDO : hurt — **doloroso, -sa** *adj* : painful

domar *vt* : tame, break in

domesticar {72} *vt* : domesticate, tame — **doméstico, -ca** *adj* : domestic

domicilio *nm* : home, residence

dominar *vt* **1** : dominate, control **2** : master (a subject, a language, etc.) — **dominarse** *vr* : control oneself — **dominación** *nf, pl* **-ciones** : domination — **dominante** *adj* : dominant

domingo *nm* : Sunday — **dominical** *adj* **periódico** ~ : Sunday newspaper

dominio *nm* **1** : authority **2** : mastery (of a subject) **3** TERRITORIO : domain

dominó *nm, pl* **-nós** : dominoes *pl* (game)

don[1] *nm* : courtesy title preceding a man's first name

don[2] *nm* **1** : gift **2** TALENTO : talent — **donación** *nf, pl* **-ciones** : donation — **donador, -dora** *n* : donor

donaire *nm* : grace, charm

donar *vt* : donate — **donante** *nmf* : donor — **donativo** *nm* : donation

donde *conj* : where — ~ *prep Lat* : over by

dónde *adv* **1** : where **2 ¿de** ~ **eres?** : where are you from? **3 ¿por** ~**?** : whereabouts?

dondequiera *adv* **1** : anywhere **2** ~ **que** : wherever, everywhere

doña *nf* : courtesy title preceding a woman's first name

doquier *adv por* ~ : everywhere

dorar *vt* **1** : gild **2** : brown (food) — **dorado, -da** *adj* : gold, golden

dormir {27} *vt* : put to sleep — *vi* : sleep — **dormirse** *vr* : fall asleep — **dormido, -da** *adj* **1** : asleep **2** ENTUMECIDO : numb — **dormilón, -lona** *n* : sleepyhead, late riser — **dormitar** *vi* : doze — **dormitorio** *nm* **1** : bedroom **2** : dormitory (in a college)

dorso *nm* : back

dos *adj & nm* : two — **doscientos, -tas** *adj* : two hundred — **doscientos** *nms & pl* : two hundred

dosel *nm* : canopy

dosis *nfs & pl* : dose, dosage

dotar *vt* **1** : provide, equip **2** ~ **de** : endow with — **dotación** *nf, pl* **-ciones** **1** : endowment, funding **2** PERSONAL : personnel — **dote** *nf* **1** : dowry **2** ~**s** *nfpl* : gift, talent

dragar {52} *vt* : dredge — **draga** *nf* : dredge

dragón *nm, pl* **-gones** : dragon

drama *nm* : drama — **dramático, -ca** *adj* : dramatic — **dramatizar** {21} *vt* : dramatize — **dramaturgo, -ga** *n* : dramatist, playwright

drástico, -ca *adj* : drastic

drenar *vt* : drain — **drenaje** *nm* : drainage

droga *nf* : drug — **drogadicto, -ta** *n* : drug addict — **drogar** {52} *vt* : drug — **drogarse** *vr* : take drugs — **droguería** *nf* : drugstore

dromedario *nm* : dromedary

dual *adj* : dual

ducha *nf* : shower — **ducharse** *vr* : take a shower

ducho, -cha *adj* : experienced, skilled

duda *nf* : doubt — **dudar** *vt* : doubt — *vi* ~ **en** : hesitate to — **dudoso, -sa** *adj* **1** : doubtful **2** SOSPECHOSO : questionable

duelo *nm* **1** : duel **2** LUTO : mourning

duende *nm* : elf, imp

dueño, -na *n* **1** : owner **2** : landlord, landlady *f*

dulce *adj* **1** : sweet **2** : fresh (of water) **3** SUAVE : mild, gentle — ~ *nm* : candy, sweet — **dulzura** *nf* : sweetness

duna *nf* : dune

dúo *nm* : duo, duet

duodécimo, -ma *adj* : twelfth — ~ *n* : twelfth (in a series)

dúplex *nms & pl* : duplex (apartment)

duplicar {72} *vt* **1** : double **2** : duplicate, copy (a document, etc.) — **duplicado, -da** *adj* : duplicate — **duplicado** *nm* : copy

duque *nm* : duke — **duquesa** *nf* : duchess

durabilidad *nf* : durability

duración *nf, pl* **-ciones** : duration, length

duradero, -ra *adj* : durable, lasting

durante *prep* **1** : during **2** ~ **una hora** : for an hour

durar *vi* : endure, last

durazno *nm Lat* : peach

duro *adv* : hard — **duro, -ra** *adj* **1** : hard **2** SEVERO : harsh — **dureza** *nf* **1** : hardness **2** SEVERIDAD : harshness

E

e¹ *nf* : e, fifth letter of the Spanish alphabet

e² *conj* (*used instead of* **y** *before words beginning with i or hi*) : and

ebanista *nmf* : cabinetmaker

ébano *nm* : ebony

ebrio, -bria *adj* : drunk

ebullición *nf, pl* **-ciones** : boiling

echar *vt* **1** : throw, cast **2** EXPULSAR : expel, dismiss **3** : give off, emit (smoke, sparks, etc.) **4** BROTAR : sprout **5** PONER : put (on) **6** ~ **a perder** : spoil, ruin **7** ~ **de menos** : miss — **echarse** *vr* **1** : throw oneself **2** ACOSTARSE : lie down **3** ~ **a** : start (to)

eclesiástico, -ca *adj* : ecclesiastic — ~ *nm* : clergyman

eclipse *nm* : eclipse — **eclipsar** *vt* : eclipse

eco *nm* : echo

ecología *nf* : ecology — **ecológico, -ca** *adj* : ecological — **ecologista** *nmf* : ecologist

economía *nf* **1** : economy **2** : economics (science) — **economico, -ca** *adj* **1** : economic, economical **2** BARATO : inexpensive — **economista** *nmf* : economist — **economizar** {21} *v* : save

ecosistema *nm* : ecosystem

ecuación *nf, pl* **-ciones** : equation

ecuador *nm* : equator

ecuánime *adj* **1** : even-tempered **2** : impartial (in law)

ecuatoriano, -na *adj* : Ecuadorian, Ecuadorean, Ecuadoran

ecuestre *adj* : equestrian

edad *nf* **1** : age **2** Edad Media : Middle Ages *pl* **3** ¿qué ~ tienes? : how old are you?

edición *nf, pl* **-ciones** **1** : publishing, publication **2** : edition (of a book, etc.)

edicto *nm* : edict

edificar {72} *vt* : build — **edificio** *nm* : building

editar *vt* **1** : publish **2** : edit (a film, a text, etc.) — **editor, -tora** *n* **1** : publisher **2** : editor — **editorial** *adj* : publishing — ~ *nm* : editorial — ~ *nf* : publishing house

edredón *nm, pl* **-dones** : (down) comforter, duvet

educar {72} *vt* **1** : educate **2** CRIAR : bring up, raise **3** : train (the body, the voice, etc.) — **educación** *nf, pl* **-ciones** **1** : education **2** MODALES : (good) manners *pl* — **educado, -da** *adj* : polite — **educador, -dora** *n* : educator — **educativo, -va** *adj* : educational

efectivo, -va *adj* **1** : effective **2** REAL : real — **efectivo** *nm* : cash — **efectivamente** *adv* **1** : really **2** POR SUPUESTO : yes, indeed — **efecto** *nm* **1** : effect **2** en ~ : in fact **3** ~s *nmpl* : goods, property — **efectuar** {3} *vt* : bring about, carry out

efervescente *adj* : effervescent — **efervescencia** *nf* : effervescence

eficaz *adj, pl* **-caces** **1** : effective **2** EFICIENTE : efficient — **eficacia** *nf* **1** : effectiveness **2** EFICIENCIA : efficiency

eficiente *adj* : efficient — **eficiencia** *nf* : efficiency

efímero, -ra *adj* : ephemeral

efusivo, -va *adj* : effusive

egipcio, -cia *adj* : Egyptian

ego *nm* : ego — **egocéntrico, -ca** *adj* : egocentric — **egoísmo** *nm* : egoism — **egoísta** *adj* : egoistic — ~ *nmf* : egoist

egresar *vi* : graduate — **egresado, -da** *n* : graduate — **egreso** *nm* : graduation, commencement

eje *nm* **1** : axis **2** : axle (of a wheel, etc.)

ejecutar *vt* **1** : execute, put to death **2** REALIZAR : carry out — **ejecución** *nf, pl* **-ciones** : execution

ejecutivo, -va *adj & n* : executive

ejemplar *adj* : exemplary — ~ *nm* **1** : copy, issue **2** EJEMPLO : example — **ejemplificar** {72} *vt* : exemplify — **ejemplo** *nm* **1** : example **2** por ~ : for example

ejercer {86} *vt* **1** : practice (a profession) **2** : exercise (a right, etc.) — *vi* ~ **de** : practice as, work as — **ejercicio** *nm* **1** : exercise **2** : practice (of a profession, etc.)

ejército *nm* : army

el, la *art, pl* **los, las** : the — **el** *pron* (*referring to masculine nouns*) **1** : the one **2** ~ **que** : he who, whoever, the one that

él *pron* : he, him

elaborar *vt* **1** : manufacture, produce **2** : draw up (a plan, etc.)

elástico, -ca *adj* : elastic — **elástico** *nm* : elastic — **elasticidad** *nf* : elasticity

elección *nf, pl* **-ciones 1** : election **2** SELECCIÓN : choice — **elector, -tora** *n* : voter — **electorado** *nm* : electorate — **electoral** *adj* : electoral

electricidad *nf* : electricity — **eléctrico, -ca** *adj* : electric, electrical — **electricista** *nmf* : electrician — **electrificar** {72} *vt* : electrify — **electrizar** {21} *vt* : electrify, thrill — **electrocutar** *vt* : electrocute

electrodo *nm* : electrode

electrodoméstico *nm* : electric appliance

electromagnético, -ca *adj* : electromagnetic

electrón *nm, pl* **-trones** : electron — **electrónico, -ca** *adj* : electronic — **electrónica** *nf* : electronics

elefante, -ta *n* : elephant

elegante *adj* : elegant — **elegancia** *nf* : elegance

elegía *nf* : elegy

elegir {28} *vt* **1** : elect **2** ESCOGER : choose, select — **elegible** *adj* : eligible

elemento *nm* : element — **elemental** *adj* **1** : elementary, basic **2** ESENCIAL : fundamental

elenco *nm* : cast (of actors)

elevar *vt* **1** : raise, lift **2** ASCENDER : elevate (in a hierarchy), promote — **elevarse** *vr* : rise — **elevación** *nf, pl* **-ciones** : elevation — **elevador** *nm* **1** : hoist **2** *Lat* : elevator

eliminar *vt* : eliminate — **eliminación** *nf, pl* **-ciones** : elimination

elipse *nf* : ellipse — **elíptico, -ca** *adj* : elliptical, elliptic

elite *or* **élite** *nf* : elite

elixir *or* **elíxir** *nm* : elixir

ella *pron* : she, her — **ello** *pron* : it — **ellos, ellas** *pron pl* **1** : they, them **2 de ellos, de ellas** : theirs

elocuente *adj* : eloquent — **elocuencia** *nf* : eloquence

elogiar *vt* : praise — **elogio** *nm* : praise

eludir *vt* : avoid, elude

emanar *vi* ~ **de** : emanate from

emancipar *vt* : emancipate — **emanciparse** *vr* : free oneself — **emancipación** *nf, pl* **-ciones** : emancipation

embadurnar *vt* : smear, daub

embajada *nf* : embassy — **embajador, -dora** *n* : ambassador

embalar *vt* : wrap up, pack — **embalaje** *nm* : packing

embaldosar *vt* : pave with tiles

embalsamar *vt* : embalm

embalse *nm* : dam, reservoir

embarazar {21} *vt* **1** : make pregnant **2** IMPEDIR : restrict, hamper — **embarazada** *adj* : pregnant — **embarazo** *nm* **1** : pregnancy **2** IMPEDIMENTO : hindrance, obstacle — **embarazoso, -sa** *adj* : embarrassing

embarcar {72} *vt* : load — **embarcarse** *vr* : embark, board — **embarcación** *nf, pl* **-ciones** : boat, craft — **embarcadero** *nm* : pier, jetty — **embarco** *nm* : embarkation

embargar {52} *vt* **1** : seize, impound **2** : overwhelm (with emotion, etc.) — **embargo** *nm* **1** : embargo **2** : seizure (in law) **3 sin** ~ : nevertheless

embarque *nm* : loading (of goods), boarding (of passengers)

embarrancar {72} *vi* : run aground

embarullarse *vr fam* : get mixed up

embaucar {72} *vt* : trick, swindle — **embaucador, -dora** *n* : swindler

embeber *vt* : absorb — *vi* : shrink — **embeberse** *vr* : become absorbed

embelesar *vt* : enchant, delight — **embelesado, -da** *adj* : spellbound

embellecer {53} *vt* : embellish, beautify

embestir {54} *vt* : attack, charge at — *vi* : charge, attack — **embestida** *nf* **1** : attack **2** : charge (of a bull)

emblema *nm* : emblem

embobar *vt* : amaze, fascinate

embocadura *nf* **1** : mouth (of a river, etc.) **2** : mouthpiece (of an instrument)

émbolo *nm* : piston

embolsarse *vr* : put in one's pocket

emborracharse *vr* : get drunk

emborronar *vt* **1** : smudge, blot **2** GARABATEAR : scribble

emboscar {72} *vt* : ambush — **emboscada** *nf* : ambush

embotar *vt* : dull, blunt

embotellar *vt* : bottle (up) — **embotellamiento** *nm* : traffic jam

embrague *nm* : clutch — **embragar** {52} *vi* : engage the clutch

embriagarse {52} *vr* : get drunk — **embriagado, -da** *adj* : intoxicated, drunk — **embriagador, -dora** *adj* : intoxicating — **embriaguez** *nf* : drunkenness

embrión *nm, pl* **-briones** : embryo

embrollo *nm* : tangle, confusion

embrujar *vt* : bewitch — **embrujo** *nm* : spell, curse

embrutecer *vt* : brutalize

embudo *nm* : funnel

embuste *nm* : lie — **embustero, -ra** *adj*
: lying — **~** *n* : liar, cheat
embutir *vt* : stuff — **embutido** *nm*
: sausage, cold meat
emergencia *nf* : emergency
emerger {15} *vi* : emerge, appear
emigrar *vi* 1 : emigrate 2 : migrate (of
animals) — **emigración** *nf, pl*
-ciones 1 : emigration 2 : migration
(of animals) — **emigrante** *adj & nmf*
: emigrant
eminente *adj* : eminent — **eminencia**
nf : eminence
emitir *vt* 1 : emit EXPRESAR : express
(an opinion, etc.) 3 : broadcast (on
radio or television) 4 : issue (money,
stamps, etc.) — **emisión** *nf, pl* **-siones**
1 : emission 2 : broadcast (on radio or
television) 3 : issue (of money, etc.) —
emisora *nf* : radio station
emoción *nf, pl* **-ciones** : emotion —
emocional *adj* : emotional — **emocionante** *adj* 1 : moving, touching 2
APASIONANTE : exciting, thrilling —
emocionar *vt* 1 : move, touch 2 APA-
SIONAR : excite, thrill — **emocionarse**
vr 1 : be moved 2 APASIONARSE : get
excited — **emotivo, -va** *adj* 1 : emotional 2 CONMOVEDOR : moving
empacar {72} *vt Lat* : pack
empachar *vt* : give indigestion to —
empacharse *vr* : get indigestion —
empacho *nm* : indigestion
empadronarse *vr* : register to vote
empalagoso, -sa *adj* : excessively
sweet, cloying
empalizada *nf* : palisade (fence)
empalmar *vt* : connect, link — *vi*
: meet, converge — **empalme** *nm* 1
: connection, link 2 : junction (of a
railroad, etc.)
empanada *nf* : pie, turnover — **em-
panadilla** *nf* : meat or seafood pie
empanar *vt* : bread (in cooking)
empantanar *vt* : flood — **empantanarse** *vr* 1 : become flooded 2 : get
bogged down
empañar *vt* 1 : steam (up) 2 : tarnish
(one's reputation, etc.) — **empañarse**
vr : fog up
empapar *vt* : soak — **empaparse** *vr*
: get soaking wet
empapelar *vt* : wallpaper
empaquetar *vt* : pack, package
emparedado, -da *adj* : walled in, con-
fined — **emparedado** *nm* : sandwich
emparejar *vt* : match up, pair — **em-
parejarse** *vr* : pair off
emparentado, -da *adj* : related, kin-
dred

empastar *vt* : fill (a tooth) — **empaste**
nm : filling
empatar *vi* : result in a draw, be tied —
empate *nm* : draw, tie
empedernido, -da *adj* : inveterate,
hardened
empedrar {55} *vt* : pave (with stones)
— **empedrado** *nm* : paving, pavement
empeine *nm* : instep
empeñar *vt* : pawn — **empeñarse** *vr* 1
: insist, persist 2 ENDEUDARSE : go into
debt 3 **~ en** : make an effort to —
empeñado, -da *adj* 1 : determined,
committed 2 ENDEUDADO : in debt —
empeño *nm* 1 : determination, effort
2 **casa de ~s** : pawnshop
empeorar *vi* : get worse — *vt* : make
worse
empequeñecer {53} *vt* : diminish,
make smaller
emperador *nm* : emperor — **emperatriz** *nf, pl* **-trices** : empress
empezar {29} *v* : start, begin
empinar *vt* : raise — **empinarse** *vr*
: stand on tiptoe — **empinado, -da** *adj*
: steep
empírico, -ca *adj* : empirical
emplasto *nm* : poultice
emplazar {21} *vt* 1 : summon, subpoena 2 SITUAR : place, locate — **em-
plazamiento** *nm* 1 : location, site 2
CITACIÓN : summons, subpoena
emplear *vt* 1 : employ 2 USAR : use —
emplearse *vr* 1 : get a job 2 USARSE
: be used — **empleado, -da** *n* : employee — **empleador, -dora** *n* : employer — **empleo** *nm* 1 : occupation,
job 2 USO : use
empobrecer {53} *vt* : impoverish —
empobrecerse *vr* : become poor
empollar *vi* : brood (eggs) — *vt* : incubate
empolvarse *vr* : powder one's face
empotrar *vt* : fit, build into — **empotrado, -da** *adj* : built-in
emprender *vt* : undertake, begin —
emprendedor, -dora *adj* : enterprising
empresa *nf* 1 COMPAÑÍA : company,
firm 2 TAREA : undertaking — **empre-
sarial** *adj* : business, managerial —
empresario, -ria *n* 1 : businessman *m*,
businesswoman *f* 2 : impresario (in
theater), promoter (in sports)
empujar *v* : push — **empuje** *nm* : impetus, drive — **empujón** *nm, pl* **-jones**
: push, shove
empuñar *vt* : grasp, take hold of
emular *vt* : emulate
en *prep* 1 : in 2 DENTRO DE : into, inside

(of) **3** SOBRE : on **4** ~ **avión** : by plane **5** ~ **casa** : at home

enajenar *vt* : alienate — **enajenación** *nf, pl* **-ciones** : alienation

enagua *nf* : slip, petticoat

enaltecer {53} *vt* : praise, extol

enamorar *vt* : win the love of — **enamorarse** *vr* : fall in love — **enamorado, -da** *adj* : in love — ~ *n* : lover, sweetheart

enano, -na *adj & n* : dwarf

enarbolar *vt* **1** : hoist, raise **2** : brandish (arms, etc.)

enardecer {53} *vt* : stir up, excite

encabezar {21} *vt* **1** : head, lead **2** : put a heading on (an article, a list, etc.) — **encabezamiento** *nm* **1** : heading **2** : headline (in a newspaper)

encabritarse *vr* : rear up

encadenar *vt* **1** : chain, tie (up) **2** ENLAZAR : connect, link

encajar *vt* : fit (together) — *vi* **1** : fit **2** CUADRAR : conform, tally — **encaje** *nm* : lace

encalar *vt* : whitewash

encallar *vi* : run aground

encaminar *vt* : direct, aim — **encaminarse** *vr* ~ **a** : head for — **encaminado, -da** *adj* ~ **a** : aimed at, designed to

encandilar *vt* : dazzle

encanecer {53} *vi* : turn gray

encantar *vt* : enchant, bewitch — *vi* **me encanta esta canción** : I love this song — **encantado, -da** *adj* **1** : delighted **2** HECHIZADO : bewitched — **encantador, -dora** *adj* : charming, delightful — **encantamiento** *nm* : enchantment, spell — **encanto** *nm* **1** : charm, fascination **2** HECHIZO : spell

encapotarse *vr* : cloud over — **encapotado, -da** *adj* : overcast

encapricharse *vr* ~ **con** : be infatuated with

encapuchado, -da *adj* : hooded

encaramar *vt* : lift up — **encaramarse** *vr* ~ **a** : climb up on

encarar *vt* : face, confront

encarcelar *vt* : imprison — **encarcelamiento** *nm* : imprisonment

encarecer {53} *vt* : increase, raise (price, value, etc.) — **encarecerse** *vr* : become more expensive

encargar {52} *vt* **1** : put in charge of **2** PEDIR : order — **encargarse** *vr* ~ **de** : take charge of — **encargado, -da** *adj* : in charge — ~ *n* : manager, person in charge — **encargo** *nm* **1** : errand **2** TAREA : assignment, task **3** PEDIDO : order

encariñarse *vr* ~ **con** : become fond of

encarnar *vt* : embody — **encarnación** *nf, pl* **-ciones** : embodiment — **encarnado, -da** *adj* **1** : incarnate **2** ROJO : red

encarnizarse {21} *vr* ~ **con** : attack viciously — **encarnizado, -da** *adj* : bitter, bloody

encarrilar *vt* : put on the right track

encasillar *vt* : pigeonhole

encauzar {21} *vt* : channel

encender {56} *vt* **1** : light, set fire to **2** PRENDER : switch on, start **3** AVIVAR : arouse (passions, etc.) — **encenderse** *vr* **1** : get excited **2** RUBORIZARSE : blush — **encendedor** *nm* : lighter — **encendido, -da** *adj* : lit, on — **encendido** *nm* : ignition (switch)

encerar *vt* : wax, polish — **encerado, -da** *adj* : waxed — **encerado** *nm* : blackboard

encerrar {55} *vt* **1** : lock up, shut away **2** CONTENER : contain

encestar *vi* : score (in basketball)

enchilada *nf* : enchilada

enchufar *vt* **1** : plug in, connect — **enchufe** *nm* : plug, socket

encía *nf* : gum (tissue)

encíclica *nf* : encyclical

enciclopedia *nf* : encyclopedia — **enciclopédico, -ca** *adj* : encyclopedic

encierro *nm* **1** : confinement **2** : sit-in (at a university, etc.)

encima *adv* **1** : on top **2** ADEMÁS : as well, besides **3** ~ **de** : on, over, on top of **4** **por** ~ **de** : above, beyond

encinta *adj* : pregnant

enclenque *adj* : weak, sickly

encoger {15} *v* : shrink — **encogerse** *vr* **1** : shrink **2** : cower, cringe **3** ~ **de hombros** : shrug (one's shoulders) — **encogido, -da** *adj* **1** : shrunken **2** TÍMIDO : shy

encolar *vt* : glue, stick

encolerizar {21} *vt* : enrage, infuriate — **encolerizarse** *vr* : get angry

encomendar {55} *vt* : entrust

encomienda *nf* **1** : charge, mission **2** *Lat* : parcel

encono *nm* : rancor, animosity

encontrar {19} *vt* **1** : find **2** : meet, encounter (difficulties, etc.) — **encontrarse** *vr* **1** : meet **2** HALLARSE : find oneself, be — **encontrado, -da** *adj* : contrary, opposing

encorvar *vt* : bend, curve — **encorvarse** *vr* : bend over, stoop

encrespar *vt* **1** : curl **2** IRRITAR : irritate — **encresparse** *vr* **1** : curl one's hair

2 IRRITARSE : get annoyed **3** : become choppy (of the sea)

encrucijada nf : crossroads

encuadernar vt **1** : bind (a book) — **encuadernación** nf, pl **-ciones** : bookbinding

encuadrar vt **1** : frame **2** ENCAJAR : fit **3** COMPRENDER : contain, include

encubrir {2} vt : conceal, cover (up) — **encubierto, -ta** adj : covert — **encubrimiento** nm : cover-up

encuentro nm : meeting, encounter

encuestar vt : poll, take a survey of — **encuesta** nf **1** : investigation, inquiry **2** SONDEO : survey — **encuestador, -dora** n : pollster

encumbrado, -da adj : eminent, distinguished

encurtir vt : pickle

endeble adj : weak, feeble — **endeblez** nf : weakness, frailty

endemoniado, -da adj : wicked

enderezar {21} vt **1** : straighten (out) **2** : put upright, stand on end

endeudarse vr : go into debt — **endeudado, -da** adj : indebted, in debt — **endeudamiento** nm : debt

endiablado, -da adj **1** : wicked, diabolical **2** : complicated, difficult

endibia or **endivia** nf : endive

endosar vt : endorse — **endoso** nm : endorsement

endulzar {21} vt **1** : sweeten **2** : soften, mellow (a tone, a response, etc.) — **endulzante** nm : sweetener

endurecer {53} vt : harden — **endurecerse** vr : become hardened

enema nm : enema

enemigo, -ga adj : hostile — ~ n : enemy — **enemistad** nf : enmity — **enemistar** vt : make enemies of — **enemistarse** vr ~ **con** : fall out with

energía nf : energy — **enérgico, -ca** adj : energetic, vigorous, forceful

enero nm : January

enervar vt **1** : enervate, weaken **2** fam : get on one's nerves

enésimo, -ma adj **por enésima vez** : for the umpteenth time

enfadar vt : annoy, make angry — **enfadarse** vr : get annoyed — **enfado** nm : anger, annoyance — **enfadoso, -sa** adj : annoying

enfatizar {21} vt : emphasize — **énfasis** nms & pl : emphasis — **enfático, -ca** adj : emphatic

enfermar vt : make sick — vi : get sick — **enfermedad** nf : sickness, disease — **enfermería** nf : infirmary — **enfermero, -ra** n : nurse — **enfermizo, -za**

adj : sickly — **enfermo, -ma** adj : sick — ~ n : sick person, patient

enflaquecer {53} vi : lose weight

enfocar {72} vt **1** : focus (on) **2** : consider (a problem, etc.) — **enfoque** nm : focus

enfrascarse {72} vr ~ **en** : immerse oneself in, get caught up in

enfrentar vt **1** : confront, face **2** : bring face to face — **enfrentarse** vr ~ **con** : confront, clash with — **enfrente** adv **1** : opposite **2** ~ **de** : in front of

enfriar {85} vt : chill, cool — **enfriarse** vr **1** : get cold **2** RESFRIARSE : catch a cold — **enfriamiento** nm **1** : cooling off **2** CATARRO : cold

enfurecer {53} vt : infuriate — **enfurecerse** vr : fly into a rage

enfurruñarse vr fam : sulk

engalanar vt : decorate — **engalanarse** vr : dress up

enganchar vt : hook, snag, catch — **engancharse** vr **1** : get caught **2** ALISTARSE : enlist

engañar vt **1** EMBAUCAR : trick, deceive **2** : cheat on, be unfaithful to — **engañarse** vr **1** : deceive oneself **2** EQUIVOCARSE : be mistaken — **engaño** nm : deception, deceit — **engañoso, -sa** adj : deceptive, deceitful

engatusar vt : coax, cajole

engendrar vt **1** : beget **2** : engender, give rise to (suspicions, etc.)

englobar vt : include, embrace

engomar vt : glue

engordar vt : fatten — vi : gain weight

engorroso, -sa adj : bothersome

engranar v : mesh, engage — **engranaje** nm : gears pl

engrandecer {53} vt **1** : enlarge **2** ENALTECER : exalt

engrapar vt Lat : staple — **engrapadora** nf Lat : stapler

engrasar vt : lubricate, grease — **engrase** nm : lubrication

engreído, -da adj : conceited

engrosar {19} vt : swell — vi : gain weight

engrudo nm : paste

engullir {38} vt : gulp down, gobble up

enhebrar vt : thread

enhorabuena nf : congratulations pl

enigma nm : enigma — **enigmático, -ca** adj : enigmatic

enjabonar vt : soap (up), lather

enjaezar {21} vt : harness

enjalbegar {52} vt : whitewash

enjambrar vi : swarm — **enjambre** nm : swarm

enjaular vt **1** : cage **2** fam : jail

enjuagar {52} *vt* : rinse — **enjuague** *nm* 1 : rinse 2 ~ **bucal** : mouthwash

enjugar {52} *vt* 1 : wipe away (tears) 2 : wipe out (debt)

enjuiciar *vt* 1 : prosecute JUZGAR : try

enjuto, -ta *adj* : gaunt, lean

enlace *nm* 1 : bond, link 2 : junction (of a highway, etc.)

enlatar *vt* : can

enlazar {21} *vt* : join, link — *vi* ~ **con** : link up with

enlistarse *vr Lat* : enlist

enlodar *vt* : cover with mud

enloquecer {53} *vt* : drive crazy — **enloquecerse** *vr* 1 : go crazy

enlosar *vt* : pave, tile

enlutarse *vr* : go into mourning

enmarañar *vt* 1 : tangle 2 COMPLICAR : complicate 3 CONFUNDIR : confuse — **enmarañarse** *vr* 1 : get tangled up 2 CONFUNDIRSE : become confused

enmarcar {72} *vt* : frame

enmascarar *vt* : mask

enmendar {55} *vt* 1 : amend 2 CORREGIR : emend, correct — **enmendarse** *vr* : mend one's ways — **enmienda** *nf* 1 : amendment 2 CORRECCIÓN : correction

enmohecerse {53} *vr* 1 : become moldy 2 OXIDARSE : rust

enmudecer {53} *vt* : silence — *vi* : fall silent

ennegrecer {53} *vt* : blacken

ennoblecer {53} *vt* : ennoble, dignify

enojar *vt* 1 : anger 2 MOLESTAR : annoy — **enojarse** *vr* ~ **con** : get upset with — **enojo** *nm* 1 : anger 2 MOLESTIA : annoyance — **enojoso, -sa** *adj* : annoying

enorgullecer {53} *vt* : make proud — **enorgullecerse** *vr* ~ **de** : pride oneself on

enorme *adj* : enormous — **enormemente** *adv* : enormously, extremely — **enormidad** *nf* : enormity

enraizar {30} *vi* : take root

enredadera *nf* : climbing plant, vine

enredar *vt* 1 : tangle up, entangle 2 CONFUNDIR : confuse 3 IMPLICAR : involve — **enredarse** *vr* 1 : become entangled 2 ~ **en** : get mixed up in — **enredo** *nm* 1 : tangle 2 EMBROLLO : confusion, mess — **enredoso, -sa** *adj* : tangled up, complicated

enrejado *nm* 1 : railing 2 REJILLA : grating, grille 3 : trellis (for plants)

enrevesado, -da *adj* : complicated

enriquecer {53} *vt* : enrich — **enriquecerse** *vr* : get rich

enrojecer {53} *vt* : redden — **enrojecerse** *vr* : blush

enrolar *vt* : enlist — **enrolarse** *vr* ~ **en** : enlist in

enrollar *vt* : roll up, coil

enroscar {72} *vt* 1 : roll up 2 ATORNILLAR : screw in

ensalada *nf* : salad

ensalzar {21} *vt* : praise

ensamblar *vt* : assemble, fit together

ensanchar *vt* 1 : widen 2 AMPLIAR : expand — **ensanche** *nm* 1 : widening 2 : (urban) expansion, development

ensangrentado, -da *adj* : bloody, bloodstained

ensañarse *vr* : act cruelly

ensartar *vt* : string, thread

ensayar *vi* : rehearse — *vt* : try out, test — **ensayo** *nm* 1 : essay 2 PRUEBA : trial, test 3 : rehearsal (in theater, etc.)

enseguida *adv* : right away, immediately

ensenada *nf* : inlet, cove

enseñar *vt* 1 : teach 2 MOSTRAR : show — **enseñanza** *nf* 1 EDUCACIÓN : education 2 INSTRUCCIÓN : teaching

enseres *nmpl* 1 : equipment 2 ~ **domésticos** : household goods

ensillar *vt* : saddle (up)

ensimismarse *vr* : lose oneself in thought

ensombrecer {53} *vt* : cast a shadow over, darken

ensoñación *nf, pl* **-ciones** : fantasy, daydream

ensordecer {53} *vt* : deafen — *vi* : go deaf — **ensordecedor, -dora** *adj* : deafening

ensortijar *vt* : curl

ensuciar *vt* : soil — **ensuciarse** *vr* : get dirty

ensueño *nm* : daydream, fantasy

entablar *vt* : initiate, start

entallar *vt* : tailor, fit (clothing) — *vi* : fit

entarimado *nm* : floorboards, flooring

ente *nm* 1 : being 2 ORGANISMO : body, organization

entender {56} *vt* 1 : understand 2 OPINAR : think, believe — *vi* 1 : understand 2 ~ **de** : know about, be good at — **entenderse** *vr* 1 : understand each other 2 LLEVARSE BIEN : get along well — ~ *nm* **a mi** ~ : in my opinion — **entendido, -da** *adj* 1 : understood 2 **eso se da por** ~ : that goes without saying 3 **tener** ~ : be under the impression — **entendimiento** *nm* 1 : understanding 2 INTELIGENCIA : intellect

enterar vt : inform — **enterarse** vr : find out, learn — **enterado, -da** adj : well-informed

entereza nf 1 HONRADEZ : integrity 2 FORTALEZA : fortitude 3 FIRMEZA : resolve

enternecer {53} vt : move, touch

entero, -ra adj 1 : whole 2 TOTAL : absolute, total 3 INTACTO : intact — **entero** nm : integer, whole number

enterrar {55} vt : bury

entibiar vt : cool (down) — **entibiarse** vr : become lukewarm

entidad nf 1 : entity 2 ORGANIZACIÓN : body, organization

entierro nm 1 : burial 2 : funeral (ceremony)

entomología nf : entomology — **entomólogo, -ga** n : entomologist

entonar vt : sing, intone — vi : be in tune

entonces adv 1 : then 2 desde ~ : since then

entornado, -da adj : half-closed, ajar

entorno nm : surroundings pl, environment

entorpecer {53} vt 1 : hinder, obstruct 2 : numb, dull (wits, reactions, etc.)

entrada nf 1 : entrance, entry 2 BILLETE : ticket 3 COMIENZO : beginning 4 : inning (in baseball) 5 ~s nfpl : income 6 tener ~s : have a receding hairline

entraña nf 1 : core, heart 2 ~s nfpl VÍSCERAS : entrails, innards — **entrañable** adj : close, intimate — **entrañar** vt : involve

entrar vi 1 : enter 2 EMPEZAR : begin — vt : introduce, bring in

entre prep 1 : between 2 : among

entreabrir {2} vt : leave ajar — **entreabierto, -ta** adj : half-open, ajar

entreacto nm : intermission

entrecejo nm fruncir el ~ : knit one's brows, frown

entrecortado, -da adj : faltering (of the voice), labored (of breathing)

entrecruzar {21} vi : intertwine

entredicho nm : doubt, question

entregar {52} vt : deliver, hand over — **entregarse** vr : surrender — **entrega** nf 1 : delivery 2 DEDICACIÓN : dedication, devotion 3 ~ inicial : down payment

entrelazar {21} vt : intertwine — **entrelazarse** vr : become intertwined

entremés nm, pl -meses 1 : hors d'oeuvre 2 : short play (in theater)

entremeterse → entrometerse

entremezclar vt : mix (up)

entrenar vt : train, drill — **entrenarse** vr : train — **entrenador, -dora** n : trainer, coach — **entranamiento** nm : training

entrepierna nf : crotch

entresacar {72} vt : pick out, select

entresuelo nm : mezzanine

entretanto adv : meanwhile — ~ nm en el ~ : in the meantime

entretener {80} vt 1 : entertain 2 DESPISTAR : distract 3 RETRASAR : delay, hold up — **entretenerse** vr 1 : amuse oneself 2 DEMORARSE : dawdle — **entretenido, -da** adj : entertaining — **entretenimiento** nm 1 : entertainment, amusement 2 PASATIEMPO : pastime

entrever {88} vt : catch a glimpse of, make out

entrevistar vt : interview — **entrevista** nf : interview — **entrevistador, -dora** n : interviewer

entristecer {53} vt : sadden

entrometerse vr : interfere — **entrometido, -da** adj : meddling, nosy — n : meddler

entroncar {72} vi : be related, be connected

entumecer {53} vt : make numb — **entumecerse** vr : go numb — **entumecido, -da** adj 1 : numb 2 : stiff (of muscles, etc.)

enturbiar vt : cloud — **enturbiarse** vr : become cloudy

entusiasmar vt : fill with enthusiasm — **entusiasmarse** vr : get excited — **entusiasmo** nm : enthusiasm — **entusiasta** adj : enthusiastic — ~ nmf : enthusiast

enumerar vt : enumerate, list — **enumeración** nf, pl -ciones : enumeration, count

enunciar vt : enunciate — **enunciación** nf, pl -ciones : enunciation

envalentonar vt : make bold, encourage — **envalentonarse** vr : be brave

envanecerse {53} vr : become vain

envasar vt 1 : package 2 : bottle, can — **envase** nm 1 : packaging 2 RECIPIENTE : container 3 : jar, bottle, can

envejecer {53} v : age — **envejecido, -da** adj : aged, old — **envejecimiento** nm : aging

envenenar vt : poison — **envenenamiento** nm : poisoning

envergadura nf 1 ALCANCE : scope 2 : span (of wings, etc.)

envés nm, pl -veses : reverse side

enviar {85} vt : send — **enviado, -da** n : envoy, correspondent

envidiar vt : envy — **envidia** nf : envy,

jealousy — **envidioso, -sa** *adj* : jealous, envious

envilecer {53} *vt* : degrade, debase — **envilecimiento** *nm* : degradation

envío *nm* **1** : sending, shipment **2** : remittance (of funds)

enviudar *vi* : be widowed

envolver {89} *vt* **1** : wrap **2** RODEAR : surround **3** IMPLICAR : involve — **envoltorio** *nm* or **envoltura** *nf* : wrapping, wrapper

enyesar *vt* **1** : plaster **2** ESCAYOLAR : put in a plaster cast

enzima *nf* : enzyme

épico, -ca *adj* : epic — **épica** *nf* : epic

epidemia *nf* : epidemic — **epidémico, -ca** *adj* : epidemic

epilepsia *nf* : epilepsy — **epiléptico, -ca** *adj & n* : epileptic

epílogo *nm* : epilogue

episodio *nm* : episode

epitafio *nm* : epitaph

epíteto *nm* : epithet

época *nf* **1** : epoch, period **2** ESTACIÓN : season

epopeya *nf* : epic poem

equidad *nf* : equity, justice

equilátero, -ra *adj* : equilateral

equilibrar *vt* : balance — **equilibrado, -da** *adj* : well-balanced — **equilibrio** *nm* **1** : balance, equilibrium **2** JUICIO : good sense

equinoccio *nm* : equinox

equipaje *nm* : baggage, luggage

equipar *vt* : equip

equiparar *vt* **1** IGUALAR : make equal **2** COMPARAR : compare — **equiparable** *adj* : comparable

equipo *nm* **1** : equipment **2** : team, crew (in sports, etc.)

equitación *nf, pl* **-ciones** : horseback riding

equitativo, -va *adj* : equitable, fair, just

equivaler {84} *vi* : be equivalent — **equivalencia** *nf* : equivalence — **equivalente** *adj & nm* : equivalent

equivocar {72} *vt* : mistake, confuse — **equivocarse** *vr* : make a mistake — **equivocación** *nf, pl* **-ciones** : error, mistake — **equivocado, -da** *adj* : mistaken, wrong

equívoco, -ca *adj* : ambiguous — **equívoco** *nm* : misunderstanding

era *nf* : era

erario *nm* : public treasury, funds *pl*

erección *nf, pl* **-ciones** : erection

erguir {31} *vt* : raise, lift — **erguirse** *vr* : rise (up) — **erguido, -da** *adj* : erect, upright

erigir {35} *vt* : build, erect — **erigirse** *vr* ~ **en** : set oneself up as

erizarse {21} *vr* : bristle, stand on end — **erizado, -da** *adj* : bristly

erizo *nm* **1** : hedgehog **2** ~ **de mar** : sea urchin

ermitaño, -ña *n* : hermit

erosionar *vt* : erode — **erosión** *nf, pl* **-siones** : erosion

erótico, -ca *adj* : erotic

erradicar {72} *vt* : eradicate

errar {32} *vt* : miss — *vi* **1** : be wrong, be mistaken **2** VAGAR : wander — **errado, -da** *adj Lat* : wrong, mistaken

errata *nf* : misprint

errático, -ca *adj* : erratic

error *nm* : error — **erróneo, -nea** *adj* : erroneous, mistaken

eructar *vi* : belch, burp — **eructo** *nm* : belch, burp

erudito, -ta *adj* : erudite, learned

erupción *nf, pl* **-ciones 1** : eruption **2** SARPULLIDO : rash

esa, ésa → **ese, ése**

esbelto, -ta *adj* : slender, slim

esbozar {21} *vt* : sketch, outline — **esbozo** *nm* : sketch, outline

escabechar *vt* : pickle — **escabeche** *nm* : brine (for pickling)

escabel *nm* : footstool

escabroso, -sa *adj* **1** : rugged, rough **2** ESPINOSO : thorny, difficult **3** ATREVIDO : shocking, risqué

escabullirse {38} *vr* : slip away, escape

escalar *vt* : climb, scale — *vi* : escalate — **escala** *nf* **1** : scale **2** ESCALERA : ladder **3** : stopover (of an airplane, etc.) — **escalada** *nf* : ascent, climb — **escalador, -dora** *n* ALPINISTA : mountain climber

escaldar *vt* : scald

escalera *nf* **1** : stairs *pl*, staircase **2** ESCALA : ladder **3** ~ **mecánica** : escalator

escalfar *vt* : poach

escalinata *nf* : flight of stairs

escalofrío *nm* : shiver, chill — **escalofriante** *adj* : chilling, horrifying

escalonar *vt* **1** : stagger, spread out **2** : terrace (land) — **escalón** *nm, pl* **-lones** : step, rung

escama *nf* **1** : scale (of fish or reptiles) **2** : flake (of skin) — **escamoso, -sa** *adj* : scaly

escamotear *vt* **1** : conceal **2** ~ **algo a algn** : rob s.o. of sth

escandalizar {21} *vt* : scandalize — **escandalizarse** *vr* : be shocked — **escándalo** *nm* **1** : scandal **2** ALBOROTO : scene, commotion — **escandaloso,**

-sa *adj* **1** : shocking, scandalous **2** RUI-
DOSO : noisy

escandinavo, -va *adj* : Scandinavian

escáner *nm* : scanner

escaño *nm* **1** : seat (in a legislative
body) **2** BANCO : bench

escapar *vi* : escape, run away — **escaparse** *vr* **1** : escape **2** : leak out (of
gas, water, etc.) — **escapada** *nf* : escape

escaparate *nm* : store window

escapatoria *nf* : loophole, way out

escape *nm* **1** : leak (of gas, water, etc.)
2 : exhaust (from a vehicle)

escarabajo *nm* : beetle

escarbar *vt* **1** : dig, scratch, poke **2** ~
en : pry into

escarcha *nf* : frost (on a surface)

escarlata *adj* & *nf* : scarlet — **escarlatina** *nf* : scarlet fever

escarmentar {55} *vi* : learn one's lesson — **escarmiento** *nm* : lesson, punishment

escarnecer {53} *vt* : ridicule, mock —
escarnio *nm* : ridicule, mockery

escarola *nf* : escarole, endive

escarpa *nf* : steep slope — **escarpado,
-da** *adj* : steep

escasear *vi* : be scarce — **escasez** *nf,
pl* **-seces** : shortage, scarcity — **escaso, -sa** *adj* **1** : scarce **2** ~ **de** : short of

escatimar *vt* : be sparing with, skimp
on

escayolar *vt* : put in a plaster cast —
escayola *nf* **1** : plaster (for casts) **2**
: plaster cast

escena *nf* **1** : scene **2** ESCENARIO : stage
— **escenario** *nm* **1** : setting, scene **2**
ESCENA : stage — **escénico, -ca** *adj*
: scenic

escepticismo *nm* : skepticism — **escéptico, -ca** *adj* : skeptical — ~ *n*
: skeptic

esclarecer {53} *vt* : shed light on, clarify

esclavo, -va *n* : slave — **esclavitud** *nf*
: slavery — **esclavizar** {21} *vt* : enslave

esclerosis *nf* ~ **múltiple** : multiple
sclerosis

esclusa *nf* : floodgate, lock (of a canal)

escoba *nf* : broom

escocer {14} *vi* : sting

escocés, -cesa *adj, mpl* **-ceses 1**
: Scottish **2** : tartan, plaid — **escocés**
nm, pl **-ceses** : Scotch (whiskey)

escoger {15} *vt* : choose — **escogido,
-da** *adj* : choice, select

escolar *adj* : school — ~ *nmf* : student, pupil

escolta *nmf* : escort — **escoltar** *vt* : escort, accompany

escombros *nmpl* : ruins, rubble

esconder *vt* : hide, conceal — **esconderse** *vr* : hide — **escondidas** *nfpl* **1**
Lat : hide-and-seek **2 a** ~ : secretly,
in secret — **escondite** *nm* **1** : hiding
place **2** : hide-and-seek (game) — **es-
condrijo** *nm* : hiding place

escopeta *nf* : shotgun

escoplo *nm* : chisel

escoria *nf* **1** : slag **2** : dregs *pl* (of society, etc.)

escorpión *nm, pl* **-piones** : scorpion

escote *nm* **1** : (low) neckline **2 pagar a**
~ : go Dutch

escotilla *nf* : hatchway

escribir {33} *v* : write — **escribirse** *vr*
1 : write to one another, correspond **2**
: be spelled — **escribiente** *nmf* : clerk
— **escrito, -ta** *adj* : written — **escritos** *nmpl* : writings — **escritor,
-tora** *n* : writer — **escritorio** *nm*
: desk — **escritura** *nf* **1** : handwriting
2 : deed (in law)

escroto *nm* : scrotum

escrúpulo *nm* : scruple — **escrupuloso, -sa** *adj* : scrupulous

escrutar *vt* **1** : scrutinize **2** : count
(votes) — **escrutinio** *nm* **1** : scrutiny **2**
: count (of votes)

escuadra *nf* **1** : square (instrument) **2**
: fleet (of ships), squad (in the military) — **escuadrón** *nm, pl* **-drones**
: squadron

escuálido, -da *adj* **1** : skinny **2** SUCIO
: squalid

escuchar *vt* **1** : listen to **2** *Lat* : hear —
vi : listen

escudo *nm* **1** : shield **2** *or* ~ **de armas**
: coat of arms

escudriñar *vt* : scrutinize, examine

escuela *nf* : school

escueto, -ta *adj* : plain, simple

esculpir *v* : sculpt — **escultor, -tora** *n*
: sculptor — **escultura** *nf* : sculpture

escupir *v* : spit

escurrir *vt* **1** : drain **2** : wring out
(clothes) — *vi* **1** : drain **2** : drip-dry (of
clothes) — **escurrirse** *vr* **1** : drain **2**
fam : slip away — **escurridizo, -da**
adj : slippery, evasive — **escurridor**
nm **1** : dish drainer **2** COLADOR : colander

ese, esa *adj, mpl* **esos** : that, those

ése, ésa *pron, mpl* **ésos** : that one,
those ones *pl*

esencia *nf* : essence — **esencial** *adj*
: essential

esfera *nf* **1** : sphere **2** : dial (of a watch) — **esférico, -ca** *adj* : spherical

esfinge *nf* : sphinx

esforzar {36} *vt* : strain — **esforzarse** *vr* : make an effort — **esfuerzo** *nm* : effort

esfumarse *vr* : fade away, vanish

esgrimir *vt* **1** : brandish, wield **2** : make use of (an argument, etc.) — **esgrima** *nf* **1** : fencing **2 hacer ~** : fence

esguince *nm* : sprain, strain

eslabonar *vt* : link, connect — **eslabón** *nm, pl* **-bones** : link

eslavo, -va *adj* : Slavic

eslogan *nm, pl* **-óganes** : slogan

esmaltar *vt* : enamel — **esmalte** *nm* **1** : enamel **2 ~ de uñas** : nail polish

esmerado, -da *adj* : careful

esmeralda *nf* : emerald

esmerarse *vr* : take great care

esmeril *nm* : emery

esmoquin *nm, pl* **-móquines** : tuxedo

esnob *nmf, pl* **esnobs** : snob — **~** *adj* : snobbish

eso *pron (neuter)* **1** : that **2 ¡~ es!** : that's it!, that's right! **3 en ~** : at that point, then

esófago *nm* : esophagus

esos, ésos → **ese, ése**

espabilarse *vr* **1** : wake up **2 DARSE PRISA** : get moving — **espabilado, -da** *adj* **1** : awake **2 LISTO** : bright, clever

espaciar *vt* : space out, spread out — **espacial** *adj* : space — **espacio** *nm* **1** : space **2 ~ exterior** : outer space — **espacioso, -sa** *adj* : spacious

espada *nf* **1** : sword **2 ~s** *nfpl* : spades (in playing cards)

espagueti *nm or* **espaguetis** *nmpl* : spaghetti

espalda *nf* **1** : back **2 ~ s** *nfpl* : shoulders, back

espantar *vt* : scare, frighten — **espantarse** *vr* : become frightened — **espantajo** *nm or* **espantapájaros** *nms & pl* : scarecrow — **espanto** *nm* **1** : fright, fear — **espantoso, -sa** *adj* **1** : frightening, horrific **2 TERRIBLE** : awful, terrible

español, -ñola *adj* **1** : Spanish — **español** *nm* : Spanish (language)

esparadrapo *nm* : adhesive bandage

esparcir {83} *vt* : scatter, spread — **esparcirse** *vr* **1** : be scattered, spread out **2 DIVERTIRSE** : enjoy oneself

espárrago *nm* : asparagus

espasmo *nm* : spasm — **espasmódico, -ca** *adj* : spasmodic

espátula *nf* : spatula

especia *nf* : spice

especial *adj & nm* : special — **especialidad** *nf* : specialty — **especialista** *nmf* : specialist — **especializarse** {21} *vr* **~ en** : specialize in — **especialmente** *adv* : especially

especie *nf* **1** : species **2 CLASE** : type, kind

especificar {72} *vt* : specify — **especificación** *nf, pl* **-ciones** : specification — **específico, -ca** *adj* : specific

espécimen *nm, pl* **especímenes** : specimen

espectáculo *nm* **1** : show, performance **2 VISIÓN** : spectacle, view — **espectacular** *adj* : spectacular — **espectador, -dora** *n* : spectator

espectro *nm* **1** : spectrum **2 FANTASMA** : ghost

especulación *nf, pl* **-ciones** : speculation

espejo *nm* : mirror — **espejismo** *nm* **1** : mirage **2 ILUSIÓN** : illusion

espeluznante *adj* : terrifying, hair-raising

esperar *vt* **1** : wait for **2 CONTAR CON** : expect **3 ~ que** : hope (that) — *vi* **1** : wait — **espera** *nf* : wait — **esperanza** *nf* : hope, expectation — **esperanzado, -da** *adj* : hopeful — **esperanzar** {21} *vt* : give hope to

esperma *nmf* **1** : sperm **2 ~ de ballena** : blubber

esperpento *nm* : (grotesque) sight, fright

espesar *vt* : thicken — **espesarse** *vr* : thicken — **espeso, -sa** *adj* : thick, heavy — **espesor** *nm* : thickness, density — **espesura** *nf* **1 ESPESOR** : thickness **2** : thicket

espetar *vt* : blurt (out)

espiar {85} *vt* : spy on — *vi* : spy — **espía** *nmf* : spy

espiga *nf* : ear (of wheat, etc.)

espina *nf* **1** : thorn **2** : (fish) bone **3 ~ dorsal** : spine, backbone

espinaca *nf* **1** : spinach (plant) **2 ~s** *nfpl* : spinach (food)

espinazo *nm* : spine, backbone

espinilla *nf* **1** : shin **2 GRANO** : blackhead, pimple

espino, -sa *adj* **1** : prickly **2** : bony (of fish) **3** : difficult, thorny (of problems, etc.)

espionaje *nm* : espionage

espiral *adj & nf* : spiral

espirar *v* : breathe out, exhale

espíritu *nm* **1** : spirit **2 Espíritu Santo** : Holy Spirit — **espiritual** *adj* : spiritual — **espiritualidad** *nf* : spirituality

espita *nf* : spigot, faucet

espléndido, -da *adj* **1** : splendid **2 GE-**

NEROSO : lavish — **esplendor** *nm*
: splendor
espliego *nm* : lavender
espolear *vt* : spur on
espoleta *nf* : fuse
espolvorear *vt* : sprinkle, dust
esponja *nf* 1 : sponge 2 **tirar la ∼**
: throw in the towel — **esponjoso,
-sa** *adj* : spongy
espontaneidad *nf* : spontaneity —
espontáneo, -nea *adj* : spontaneous
espora *nf* : spore
esporádico, -ca *adj* : sporadic
esposo, -sa *n* : spouse, wife *f*, husband
m — **esposar** *vt* : handcuff — **esposas** *nfpl* : handcuffs
esprintar *vi* : sprint (in sports) — **esprint** *nm* : sprint
espuela *nf* : spur
espumar *vt* : skim — **espuma** *nf* 1
: foam, froth 2 : (soap) lather 3 : head
(on beer) — **espumoso, -sa** *adj* 1
: foamy, frothy 2 : sparkling (of wine)
esqueleto *nm* : skeleton
esquema *nf* : outline, sketch
esquí *nm* 1 : ski 2 : skiing (sport) 3 **∼
acuático** : waterskiing — **esquiador,
-dora** *n* : skier — **esquiar** {85} *vi* : ski
esquilar *vt* : shear
esquimal *adj* : Eskimo
esquina *nf* : corner
esquirol *nm* : strikebreaker, scab
esquivar *vt* 1 : evade, dodge (a blow) 2
EVITAR : avoid — **esquivo, -va** *adj*
: shy, elusive
esquizofrenia *nf* : schizophrenia — **esquizofrénico, -ca** *adj* & *n* : schizophrenic
esta, ésta → **este**[1], **éste**
estable *adj* : stable — **estabilidad** *nf*
: stability — **estabilizar** {21} *vt* : stabilize
establecer {53} *vt* : establish — **establecerse** *vr* : establish oneself, settle —
establecimiento *nm* : establishment
establo *nm* : stable
estaca *nf* : stake — **estacada** *nf* 1
: (picket) fence 2 **dejar en la ∼**
: leave in a lurch
estación *nf, pl* **-ciones** 1 : season 2 **∼
de servicio** : gas station — **estacionar** *v* : park — **estacionamiento**
nm : parking — **estacionario, -ria** *adj*
: stationary
estadía *nf Lat* : stay
estadio *nm* 1 : stadium 2 FASE : phase,
stage
estadista *nmf* : statesman
estadística *nf* : statistics — **estadístico, -ca** *adj* : statistical

estado *nm* 1 : state 2 **∼ civil** : marital
status
estadounidense *adj* & *nmf* : American
(from the United States)
estafar *vt* : swindle, defraud — **estafa**
nf : swindle, fraud — **estafador,
-dora** *n* : cheat, swindler
estallar *vi* 1 : explode 2 : break out (of
war, an epidemic, etc.) 3 **∼ en llamas** : burst into flames — **estallido**
nm 1 : explosion 2 : report (of a gun) 3
: outbreak (of war, etc.)
estampar *vt* : stamp, print — **estampa**
nf 1 : print, illustration 2 ASPECTO : appearance — **estampado, -da** *adj*
: printed
estampida *nf* : stampede
estampilla *nf* : stamp
estancarse {72} *vr* 1 : stagnate 2
: come to a halt — **estancado, -da** *adj*
: stagnant
estancia *nf* 1 : stay 2 HABITACIÓN
: (large) room 3 *Lat* : (cattle) ranch
estanco, -ca *adj* : watertight
estándar *adj* & *nm* : standard — **estandarizar** {21} *vt* : standardize
estandarte *nm* : standard, banner
estanque *nm* 1 : pool, pond 2 : reservoir (for irrigation)
estante *nm* : shelf — **estantería** *nf*
: shelves *pl*, bookcase
estaño *nm* : tin
estar {34} *v aux* : be — *vi* 1 : be 2 : be
at home 3 QUEDARSE : stay, remain
4**¿cómo estás?** : how are you? 5 **∼
a** : cost 6 **∼ bien (mal)** : be well
(sick) 7 **∼ para** : be in the mood for 8
∼ por : be in favor of 9 **∼ por** : be
about to — **estarse** *vr* : stay, remain
estarcir {83} *vt* : stencil
estárter *nm* : choke (of an automobile)
estatal *adj* : state, national
estático, -ca *adj* 1 : static 2 INMÓVIL
: unmoving, still — **estática** *nf* : static
estatua *nf* : statue
estatura *nf* : height
estatus *nm* : status, prestige
estatuto *nm* : statute — **estatutario,
-ria** *adj* : statutory
este[1], **esta** *adj, mpl* **estos** : this, these
este[2] *adj* : eastern, east — **este** *nm* 1
: east 2 : east wind 3 **el Este** : the Orient
éste, ésta *pron, mpl* **éstos** 1 : this one,
these ones *pl* 2 : the latter
estela *nf* 1 : wake (of a ship) 2 : trail (of
smoke, etc.)
estera *nf* : mat
estéreo *adj* & *nm* : stereo — **estere-
ofónico, -ca** *adj* : stereophonic

estereotipo *nm* : stereotype

estéril *adj* **1** : sterile **2** : infertile — **esterilidad** *nf* **1** : sterility **2** : stylist — **esterilizar** {21} *vt* : sterilize

estética *nf* : aesthetics — **estético, -ca** *adj* : aesthetic

estiércol *nm* : dung, manure

estigma *nm* : stigma — **estigmatizar** {21} *vt* : stigmatize

estilarse {21} *vr* : be in fashion

estilo *nm* **1** : style **2** MANERA : fashion, manner — **estilista** *nmf* : stylist

estima *nf* : esteem, regard — **estimación** *nf*, *pl* **-ciones 1** : esteem **2** VALORACIÓN : estimate — **estimado, -da** *adj* **Estimado señor** : Dear Sir — **estimar** *vt* **1** : esteem, respect **2** VALORAR : value, estimate **3** CONSIDERAR : consider

estimular *vt* **1** : stimulate **2** ALENTAR : encourage — **estimulante** *adj* : stimulating — ~ *nm* : stimulant — **estímulo** *nm* : stimulus

estío *nm* : summertime

estipular *vt* : stipulate

estirar *vt* : stretch (out), extend — **estirado, -da** *adj* **1** : stretched, extended **2** ALTANERO : stuck-up, haughty — **estiramiento** *nm* ~ **facial** : face-lift — **estirón** *nm*, *pl* **-rones** : pull, tug

estirpe *nf* : lineage, stock

estival *adj* : summer

esto *pron* (*neuter*) **1** : this **2** en ~ : at this point **3** por ~ : for this reason

estofa *nf* **1** : class, quality **2** de baja ~ : low-class

estofar *vt* : stew — **estofado** *nm* : stew

estoicismo *nm* : stoicism — **estoico, -ca** *adj* : stoic, stoical — ~ *n* : stoic

estómago *nm* : stomach — **estomacal** *adj* : stomach

estorbar *vt* : obstruct — *vi* : get in the way — **estorbo** *nm* **1** : obstacle **2** MOLESTIA : nuisance

estornino *nm* : starling

estornudar *vi* : sneeze — **estornudo** *nm* : sneeze

estos, éstos → **este, éste**

estrabismo *nm* : squint

estrado *nm* : platform, stage

estrafalario, -ria *adj* : eccentric, bizarre

estragar {52} *vt* : devastate — **estragos** *nmpl* **1** : ravages **2** hacer ~ en *or* causar ~ entre : wreak havoc with

estragón *nm* : tarragon

estrangular *vt* : strangle — **estrangulación** *nf* : strangulation

estratagema *nf* : stratagem

estrategia *nf* : strategy — **estratégico, -ca** *adj* : strategic

estrato *nm* : stratum

estratosfera *nf* : stratosphere

estrechar *vt* **1** : narrow **2** : strengthen (a bond) **3** ABRAZAR : embrace **4** ~ la mano a uno : shake s.o.'s hand — **estrecharse** *vr* : narrow — **estrechez** *nf*, *pl* **-checes 1** : narrowness **2** estrecheces *nfpl* : financial problems — **estrecho, -cha** *adj* **1** : tight, narrow **2** ÍNTIMO : close — **estrecho** *nm* : strait

estrella *nf* **1** : star **2** DESTINO : destiny **3** ~ de mar : starfish — **estrellado, -da** *adj* **1** : starry **2** : star-shaped

estrellar *v* : crash — **estrellarse** *vr* ~ contre : smash into

estremecer {53} *vt* : cause to shudder — *vi* : tremble, shake — **estremecerse** *vr* : shudder, shiver (with emotion) — **estremecimiento** *nm* : shaking, shivering

estrenar *vt* **1** : use for the first time **2** : premiere, open (a film, etc.) — **estrenarse** *vr* : make one's debut — **estreno** *nm* : debut, premiere

estreñirse {67} *vr* : be constipated — **estreñimiento** *nm* : constipation

estrépito *nm* : clamor, din — **estrepitoso, -sa** *adj* : noisy, clamorous

estrés *nm*, *pl* **estreses** : stress — **estresante** *adj* : stressful — **estresar** *vt* : stress (out)

estría *nf* : groove

estribaciones *nfpl* : foothills

estribar *vi* ~ en : stem from, lie in

estribillo *nm* : refrain, chorus

estribo *nm* **1** : stirrup **2** : running board (of a vehicle) **3** CONTRAFUERTE : buttress **4** perder los ~s : lose one's temper

estribor *nm* : starboard

estricto, -ta *adj* : strict

estridente *adj* : strident, shrill

estrofa *nf* : stanza, verse

estropajo *nm* : scouring pad

estropear *vt* **1** : ruin, spoil **2** DAÑAR : damage — **estropearse** *vr* **1** : go bad **2** AVERIARSE : break down — **estropicio** *nm* : damage, havoc

estructura *nf* : structure — **estructural** *adj* : structural

estruendo *nm* : din, roar — **estruendoso, -sa** *adj* : thunderous

estrujar *vt* : squeeze

estuario *nm* : estuary

estuche *nm* : kit, case

estuco *nm* : stucco

estudiar *v* : study — **estudiante** *nmf* : student — **estudiantil** *adj* : student — **estudio** *nm* **1** : study **2** OFICINA

: studio, office **3 ~s** *nmpl* : studies, education — **estudioso, -sa** *adj* : studious

estufa *nf* : stove, heater

estupefaciente *adj & nm* : narcotic — **estupefacto, -ta** *adj* : astonished

estupendo, -da *adj* : stupendous, marvelous

estúpido, -da *adj* : stupid — **estupidez** *nf, pl* **-deces** : stupidity

estupor *nm* **1** : stupor **2** ASOMBRO : amazement

etapa *nf* : stage, phase

etcétera : et cetera, and so on

éter *nm* : ether

etéreo, -rea *adj* : ethereal

eterno, -na *adj* : eternal — **eternidad** *nf* : eternity — **eternizarse** {21} *vr* : take forever

ética *nf* : ethics — **ético, -ca** *adj* : ethical

etimología *nf* : etymology

etíope *adj* : Ethiopian

etiqueta *nf* **1** : tag, label **2** PROTOCOLO : etiquette **3 de ~** : formal, dressy — **etiquetar** *vt* : label

étnico, -ca *adj* : ethnic

eucalipto *nm* : eucalyptus

Eucaristía *nf* : Eucharist, communion

eufemismo *nm* : euphemism — **eufemístico, -ca** *adj* : euphemistic

euforia *nf* : euphoria — **eufórico, -ca** *adj* : euphoric

europeo, -pea *adj* : European

eutanasia *nf* : euthanasia

evacuar *vt* : evacuate, vacate — *vi* : have a bowel movement — **evacuación** *nf, pl* **-ciones** : evacuation

evadir *vt* : evade, avoid — **evadirse** *vr* : escape

evaluar {3} *vt* : evaluate — **evaluación** *nf, pl* **-ciones** : evaluation

evangelio *nm* : gospel — **evangélico, -ca** *adj* : evangelical — **evangelismo** *nm* : evangelism

evaporar *vt* : evaporate — **evaporarse** *vr* : evaporate, disappear — **evaporación** *nf, pl* **-ciones** : evaporation

evasión *nf, pl* **-siones 1** : evasion **2** FUGA : escape — **evasiva** *nf* : excuse, pretext — **evasivo, -va** *adj* : evasive

evento *nm* : event

eventual *adj* **1** : temporary **2** POSIBLE : possible — **eventualidad** *nf* : possibility, eventuality

evidencia *nf* **1** : evidence, proof **2 poner en ~** : demonstrate — **evidenciar** *vt* : demonstrate, show — **evidente** *adj* : evident — **evidentemente** *adj* : evidently, apparently

evitar *vt* **1** : avoid **2** IMPEDIR : prevent — **evitable** *adj* : avoidable

evocar {72} *vt* : evoke

evolución *nf, pl* **-ciones** : evolution — **evolucionar** *vi* : evolve

exacerbar *vt* **1** : exacerbate **2** IRRITAR : irritate

exacto, -ta *adj* : precise, exact — **exactamente** *adv* : exactly — **exactitud** *nf* : precision, accuracy

exagerar *v* : exaggerate — **exageración** *nf, pl* **-ciones** : exaggeration — **exagerado, -da** *adj* : exaggerated

exaltar *vt* **1** : exalt, extol **2** EXCITAR : excite, arouse — **exaltarse** *vr* : get worked-up — **exaltado, -da** *adj* : worked up, hotheaded

examen *nm, pl* **exámenes 1** : examination, test **2** ANÁLISIS : investigation — **examinar** *vt* **1** : examine **2** ESTUDIAR : study, inspect — **examinarse** *vr* : take an exam

exánime *adj* : lifeless

exasperar *vt* : exasperate, irritate — **exasperación** *nf, pl* **-ciones** : exasperation

excavar *v* : excavate — **excavación** *nf, pl* **-ciones** : excavation

exceder *vt* : exceed, surpass — **excederse** *vr* : go too far — **excedente** *adj & nm* : surplus, excess

excelente *adj* : excellent — **excelencia** *nf* **1** : excellence **2 Su Excelencia** : His/Her Excellency

excéntrico, -ca *adj & n* : eccentric — **excentricidad** *nf* : eccentricity

excepción *nf, pl* **-ciones** : exception — **excepcional** *adj* : exceptional

excepto *prep* : except (for) — **exceptuar** {3} *vt* : exclude, except

exceso *nm* **1** : excess **2 ~ de velocidad** : speeding — **excesivo, -va** *adj* : excessive

excitar *vt* : excite, arouse — **excitarse** *vr* : get excited — **excitable** *adj* : excitable — **excitación** *nf, pl* **-ciones** : excitement, agitation, arousal — **excitante** *adj* : exciting

exclamar *v* : exclaim — **exclamación** *nf, pl* **-ciones** : exclamation

excluir {41} *vt* : exclude — **exclusión** *nf, pl* **-siones** : exclusion — **exclusivo, -va** *adj* : exclusive

excomulgar {52} *vt* : excommunicate — **excomunión** *nf, pl* **-niones** : excommunication

excremento *nm* : excrement

exculpar *vt* : exonerate

excursión *nf, pl* **-siones** : excursion —

excursionista *nmf* **1** : tourist, sight-seer **2** : hiker

excusar *vt* **1** : excuse **2** EXIMIR : exempt — **excusarse** *vr* : apologize — **excusa** *nf* **1** : excuse **2** DISCULPA : apology

exento, -ta *adj* : exempt

exequias *nfpl* : funeral rites

exhalar *vt* **1** : exhale **2** : give off (an odor, etc.)

exhaustivo, -va *adj* : exhaustive — **exhausto, -ta** *adj* : exhausted, worn-out

exhibir *vt* : exhibit, show — **exhibición** *nf, pl* **-ciones** : exhibition

exhortar *vt* : exhort, admonish

exigir {35} *vt* : demand, require — **exigencia** *nf* : demand, requirement — **exigente** *adj* : demanding

exiguo, -gua *adj* : meager

exiliar *vt* : exile — **exiliarse** *vr* : go into exile — **exiliado, -da** *adj* : exiled, in exile — **~** *n* : exile — **exilio** *nm* : exile

eximir *vt* : exempt

existir *vi* : exist — **existencia** *nf* **1** : existence **2 ~s** *nfpl* MERCANCÍA : goods, stock — **existente** *adj* : existing

éxito *nm* **1** : success, hit **2 tener ~** : be successful — **exitoso, -sa** *adj Lat* : successful

éxodo *nm* : exodus

exorbitante *adj* : exorbitant

exorcizar {21} *vt* : exorcize — **exorcismo** *nm* : exorcism

exótico, -ca *adj* : exotic

expandir *vt* : expand — **expandirse** *vr* : spread — **expansión** *nf, pl* **-siones** : expansion — **expansivo, -va** *adj* : expansive

expatriarse {85} *vr* **1** : emigrate **2** EXILIARSE : go into exile — **expatriado, -da** *adj & n* : expatriate

expectativa *nf* **1** : expectation, hope **2 ~s** *nfpl* : prospects

expedición *nf, pl* **-ciones** : expedition

expediente *nm* **1** : expedient **2** DOCUMENTOS : file, record **3** INVESTIGACIÓN : inquiry, proceedings

expedir {54} *vt* **1** : issue **2** ENVIAR : dispatch — **expedito, -ta** *adj* : free, clear

expeler *vt* : expel, eject

expendedor, -dora *n* : dealer, seller

expensas *nfpl* **1** : expenses **2 a ~ de** : at the expense of

experiencia *nf* : experience

experimentar *vi* : experiment — *vt* **1** : experiment with, test out **2** SENTIR : experience, feel — **experimentado, -da** *adj* : experienced — **experimental** *adj* : experimental — **experimento** *nm* : experiment

experto, -ta *adj & n* : expert

expiar {85} *vt* : atone for

expirar *vi* **1** : expire **2** MORIR : die

explayar *vt* : extend — **explayarse** *vr* **1** : spread out **2** HABLAR : speak at length

explicar {72} *vt* **1** : explain — **explicarse** *vr* : understand — **explicación** *nf, pl* **-ciones** : explanation — **explicativo, -va** *adj* : explanatory

explícito, -ta *adj* : explicit

explorar *vt* : explore — **exploración** *nf, pl* **-ciones** : exploration — **explorador, -dora** *n* : explorer, scout — **exploratorio, -ria** *adj* : exploratory

explosión *nf, pl* **-siones** **1** : explosion **2** : outburst (of anger, laughter, etc.) — **explosivo, -va** *adj* : explosive — **explosivo** *nm* : explosive

explotar *vt* **1** : exploit **2** : operate, run (a factory, etc.), work (a mine) — *vi* : explode — **explotación** *nf, pl* **-ciones** **1** : exploitation **2** : running (of a business), working (of a mine)

exponer {60} *vt* **1** : expose **2** : explain, set out (ideas, theories, etc.) **3** EXHIBIR : exhibit, display — *vi* : exhibit — **exponerse** *vr* **~ a** : expose oneself to

exportar *vt* : export — **exportaciones** *nfpl* : exports — **exportador, -dora** *n* : exporter

exposición *nf, pl* **-ciones** **1** : exposure **2** : exhibition (of objects, art, etc.) **3** : exposition, setting out (of ideas, etc.) — **expositor, -tora** *n* **1** : exhibitor **2** : exponent (of a theory, etc.)

exprés *nms & pl* **1** : express (train) **2** *or* **café ~** : espresso

expresamente *adv* : expressly, on purpose

expresar *vt* : express — **expresarse** *vr* : express oneself — **expresión** *nf, pl* **-siones** : expression — **expresivo, -va** *adj* **1** : expressive **2** CARIÑOSO : affectionate

expreso, -sa *adj* : express — **expreso** *nm* : express train, express

exprimir *vt* **1** : squeeze **2** EXPLOTAR : exploit — **exprimidor** *nm* : squeezer, juicer

expuesto, -ta *adj* **1** : exposed **2** PELIGROSO : risky, dangerous

expulsar *vt* : expel, eject — **expulsión** *nf, pl* **-siones** : expulsion

exquisito, -ta *adj* **1** : exquisite **2** RICO : delicious — **exquisitez** *nf* **1** : exquisiteness **2** : delicacy, special dish

éxtasis *nms & pl* : ecstasy — **extático, -ta** *adj* : ecstatic

extender {56} *vt* **1** : spread out **2** : draw up (a document), write out (a check)

— **extenderse** vr 1 : extend, spread 2 DURAR : last — **extendido, -da** adj 1 : widespread 2 : outstretched (of arms, wings, etc.)
extensamente adv : extensively
extensión nf, pl -siones 1 : extension 2 AMPLITUD : expanse 3 ALCANCE : range, extent — **extenso, -sa** adj : extensive
extenuar {3} vt : exhaust, tire out
exterior adj 1 : exterior, external 2 EXTRANJERO : foreign — ~ nm 1 : outside 2 en el ~ : abroad — **exteriorizar** {21} vt : show, reveal — **exteriormente** adv : outwardly, externally
exterminar vt : exterminate — **exterminación** nf, pl -ciones : extermination — **exterminio** nm : extermination
externo, -na adj : external
extinguir {26} vt 1 : extinguish (a fire) 2 : put an end to, wipe out — **extinguirse** vr 1 : go out (of fire, light, etc.) 2 : become extinct — **extinción** nf, pl -ciones : extinction — **extinguidor** nm Lat : fire extinguisher — **extinto, -ta** adj : extinct — **extintor** nm : fire extinguisher
extirpar vt : remove, eradicate
extorsión nf, pl -siones 1 : extortion 2 MOLESTIA : trouble
extra adv : extra — ~ adj 1 ADICIONAL : additional 2 : top-quality — ~ nmf : extra (in movies) — ~ nm : extra (expense)
extraditar vt : extradite
extraer {81} vt : extract — **extracción** nf, pl -ciones : extraction — **extracto** nm 1 : extract 2 RESUMEN : abstract, summary

extranjero, -ra adj : foreign — ~ n : foreigner — **extranjero** nm : foreign countries pl
extrañar vt : miss (someone) — **extrañarse** vr : be surprised — **extrañeza** nf : surprise — **extraño, -ña** adj 1 : foreign 2 RARO : strange, odd — ~ n : stranger
extraoficial adj : unofficial
extraordinario, -ria adj : extraordinary
extrasensorial adj : extrasensory
extraterrestre adj & nmf : extraterrestrial
extravagante adj : extravagant, outrageous — **extravagancia** nf : extravagance, outlandishness
extraviar {85} vt : lose, misplace — **extraviarse** vr : get lost — **extravío** nm : loss
extremar vt : carry to extremes — **extremarse** vr : do one's utmost — **extremadamente** adv : extremely — **extremado, -da** adj : extreme — **extremidad** nf 1 : tip, end 2 ~es nfpl : extremities — **extremista** adj & nmf : extremist — **extremo, -ma** adj 1 : extreme 2 en caso ~ : as a last resort — **extremo** nm 1 : end 2 en ~ : in the extreme, extremely 3 en ultimo ~ : as a last resort
extrovertido -da adj : extroverted — ~ n : extrovert
exuberante adj : exuberant — **exuberancia** nf : exuberance
exudar vt : exude
eyacular vi : ejaculate — **eyaculación** nf, pl -ciones : ejaculation

F

f nf : f, sixth letter of the Spanish alphabet
fabricar {72} vt 1 : manufacture 2 CONSTRUIR : build, construct 3 INVENTAR : fabricate — **fábrica** nf : factory — **fabricación** nf, pl -ciones : manufacture — **fabricante** nmf : manufacturer
fábula nf 1 : fable 2 MENTIRA : story, lie
fabuloso, -sa adj : fabulous
facción nf, pl -ciones 1 : faction 2 ~es nfpl RASGOS : features
faceta nf : facet
facha nf : appearance, look
fachada nf : façade
facial adj : facial
fácil adj 1 : easy 2 PROBABLE : likely — **facilmente** adv : easily, readily —

facilidad nf 1 : facility, ease 2 ~es nfpl : facilities, services — **facilitar** vt 1 : facilitate 2 PROPORCIONAR : provide, supply
facsímil or **facsímile** nm 1 COPIA : facsimile, copy 2 : fax
factible adj : feasible
factor nm : factor
factoría nf : factory
factura nf 1 : bill, invoice 2 HECHURA : making, manufacture — **facturar** vt 1 : bill for 2 : check in (baggage, etc.)
facultad nf 1 : faculty, ability 2 AUTORIDAD : authority 3 : school (of a university) — **facultativo, -va** adj : optional
faena nf 1 : task, job 2 ~s domésticas : housework

fagot *nm* : bassoon
faisán *nm, pl* **-sanes** : pheasant
faja *nf* **1** : sash **2** : girdle, corset **3** : strip (of land)
fajo *nm* : bundle, sheaf
falda *nf* **1** : skirt **2** : side, slope (of a mountain)
falible *adj* : fallible
fálico, -ca *adj* : phallic
fallar *vi* : fail, go wrong — *vt* **1** : pronounce judgment on **2** ERRAR : miss — **falla** *nf* **1** : flaw, defect **2** : (geological) fault
fallecer {53} *vi* : pass away, die — **fallecimiento** *nm* : demise, death
fallido, -da *adj* : failed, unsuccessful
fallo *nm* **1** : error **2** SENTENCIA : sentence, verdict
falo *nm* : phallus, penis
falsear *vt* : falsify, distort — **falsedad** *nf* **1** : falseness **2** MENTIRA : falsehood, lie — **falsificación** *nf, pl* **-ciones** : forgery, fake — **falsificador, -dora** *n* : forger — **falsificar** {72} *vt* **1** : counterfeit, forge **2** ALTERAR : falsify — **falso, -sa** *adj* **1** : false, untrue **2** FALSIFICADO : counterfeit, forged
falta *nf* **1** CARENCIA : lack **2** DEFECTO : defect, fault, error **3** AUSENCIA : absence **4** : offense, misdemeanor (in law) **5** : foul (in sports) **6 hacer ~** : be lacking, be needed **7 sin ~** : without fail — **faltar** *vi* **1** : be lacking, be needed **2** : be missing **3** QUEDAR : remain, be left **4 ¡no faltaba más!** : don't mention it! — **falto, -ta** *adj* **~ de** : lacking (in)
fama *nf* **1** : fame **2** REPUTACIÓN : reputation
famélico, -ca *adj* : starving
familia *nf* : family — **familiar** *adj* **1** : familial, family **2** CONOCIDO : familiar **3** : informal (of language, etc.) — **~** *nmf* : relation, relative — **familiaridad** *nf* : familiarity — **familiarizarse** {21} *vr* **~ con** : familiarize oneself with
famoso, -sa *adj* : famous
fanático, -ca *adj* : fanatic, fanatical — **~** *n* : fanatic — **fanatismo** *nm* : fanaticism
fanfarria *nf* : fanfare
fanfarrón, -rrona *adj, mpl* **-rrones** *fam* : boastful — **~** *n fam* : braggart — **fanfarronear** *vi* : boast, brag
fango *nm* : mud, mire — **fangoso, -sa** *adj* : muddy
fantasear *vi* : fantasize, daydream — **fantasía** *nf* **1** : fantasy **2** IMAGINACIÓN : imagination
fantasma *nm* : ghost, phantom — **fantasmal** *adj* : ghostly

fantástico, -ca *adj* : fantastic
fardo *nm* : bundle
farfullar *v* : jabber, gabble
farmacéutico, -ca *adj* : pharmaceutical — **~** *n* : pharmacist — **farmacia** *nf* : drugstore, pharmacy
faro *nm* **1** : lighthouse **2** : headlight (of an automobile) — **farol** *nm* **1** LINTERNA : lantern **2** FAROLA : streetlight — **farola** *nf* **1** : lamppost **2** FAROL : streetlight
farsa *nf* : farce — **farsante** *nmf* : charlatan, fraud
fascículo *nm* : installment, part (of a publication)
fascinar *vt* : fascinate — **fascinación** *nf, pl* **-ciones** : fascination — **fascinante** *adj* : fascinating
fascismo *nm* : fascism — **fascista** *adj & nmf* : fascist
fase *nf* : phase
fastidiar *vt* : annoy, bother — *vi* : be annoying or bothersome — **fastidio** *nm* : annoyance — **fastidioso, -sa** *adj* : annoying, bothersome
fatal *adj* **1** : fateful **2** MORTAL : fatal **3** *fam* : awful, terrible — **fatalidad** *nf* **1** : fate, destiny **2** DESGRACIA : misfortune
fatídico, -ca *adj* : fateful, momentous
fatiga *nf* : fatigue — **fatigado, -da** *adj* : weary, tired — **fatigar** {52} *vt* : tire — **fatigarse** *vr* : get tired — **fatigoso, -sa** *adj* : fatiguing, tiring
fatuo, -tua *adj* **1** : fatuous **2** PRESUMIDO : conceited
fauna *nf* : fauna
favor *nm* **1** : favor **2 a ~ de** : in favor of **3 por ~** : please — **favorable** *adj* **1** : favorable **2 ser ~ a** : be in favor of — **favorecedor, -dora** *adj* : flattering — **favorecer** {53} *vt* **1** : favor **2** : look well on, suit — **favoritismo** *nm* : favoritism — **favorito, -ta** *adj & n* : favorite
fax *nm* : fax — **faxear** *vt* : fax
faz *nf, pl* **faces** : face, countenance
fe *nf* **1** : faith **2 dar ~ de** : bear witness to **3 de buena ~** : in good faith
fealdad *nf* : ugliness
febrero *nm* : February
febril *adj* : feverish
fecha *nf* **1** : date **2 ~ de caducidad** or **~ de vencimiento** : expiration date **3 ~ límite** : deadline — **fechar** *vt* : date, put a date on
fechoría *nf* : misdeed
fécula *nf* : starch (in food)
fecundar *vt* **1** : fertilize (an egg) **2** : make fertile — **fecundo, -da** *adj* : fertile

federación *nf, pl* **-ciones** : federation — **federal** *adj* : federal

felicidad *nf* 1 : happiness 2 ¡**~es!** : best wishes!, congratulations!, happy birthday! — **felicitación** *nf, pl* **-ciones** : congratulation — **felicitar** *vt* : congratulate — **felicitarse** *vr* **~ de** : be glad about

feligrés, -gresa *n, mpl* **-greses** : parishioner

felino, -na *adj & n* : feline

feliz *adj, pl* **-lices** 1 : happy 2 AFORTUNADO : fortunate 3 **Feliz Navidad** : Merry Christmas

felpa *nf* 1 : plush 2 : terry cloth (for towels, etc.)

felpudo *nm* : doormat

femenino, -na *adj* 1 : feminine 2 : female (in biology) — **femenino** *nm* : feminine (in grammar) — **feminidad** *nf* : femininity — **feminismo** *nm* : feminism — **feminista** *adj & nmf* : feminist

fenómeno *nm* : phenomenon — **fenomenal** *adj* 1 : phenomenal 2 *fam* : fantastic, terrific

feo, fea *adj* 1 : ugly 2 DESAGRADABLE : unpleasant, nasty

féretro *nm* : coffin

feria *nf* 1 : fair, market 2 FIESTA : festival, holiday 3 *Lat fam* : small change — **feriado, -da** *adj* **día feriado** : public holiday

fermentar *v* : ferment — **fermentación** *nf, pl* **-ciones** : fermentation — **fermento** *nm* : ferment

feroz *adj, pl* **-roces** : ferocious, fierce — **ferocidad** *nf* : ferocity, fierceness

férreo, -rrea *adj* 1 : iron 2 **vía férrea** : railroad track

ferretería *nf* : hardware store

ferrocarril *nm* : railroad, railway — **ferroviario, -ria** *adj* : rail, railroad

ferry *nm, pl* **ferrys** : ferry

fértil *adj* : fertile, fruitful — **fertilidad** *nf* : fertility — **fertilizante** *nm* : fertilizer — **fertilizar** *vt* : fertilize

fervor *nm* : fervor, zeal — **ferviente** *adj* : fervent

festejar *vt* 1 : celebrate 2 AGASAJAR : entertain, wine and dine — **festejo** *nm* : celebration, festivity

festín *nm, pl* **-tines** : banquet, feast

festival *nm* : festival — **festividad** *nf* : festivity — **festivo, -va** *adj* 1 : festive 2 **día festivo** : holiday

fetiche *nm* : fetish

fétido, -da *adj* : foul-smelling, fetid

feto *nm* : fetus — **fetal** *adj* : fetal

feudal *adj* : feudal

fiable *adj* : reliable — **fiabilidad** *nf* : reliability

fiado, -da *adj* : on credit — **fiador, -dora** *n* : bondsman, guarantor

fiambres *nfpl* : cold cuts

fianza *nf* 1 : bail, bond 2 **dar ~** : pay a deposit

fiar {85} *vt* 1 : guarantee 2 : sell on credit — *vi* **ser de ~** : be trustworthy — **fiarse** *vr* **~ de** : place trust in

fiasco *nm* : fiasco

fibra *nf* 1 : fiber 2 **~ de vidrio** : fiberglass

ficción *nf, pl* **-ciones** : fiction

ficha *nf* 1 : token 2 TARJETA : index card 3 : counter, chip (in games) — **fichar** *vt* : file, index — **fichero** *nm* 1 : card file 2 : filing cabinet

ficticio, -cia *adj* : fictitious

fidedigno, -na *adj* : reliable, trustworthy

fidelidad *nf* : fidelity, faithfulness

fideo *nm* : noodle

fiebre *nf* 1 : fever 2 **~ del heno** : hay fever 3 **~ palúdica** : malaria

fiel *adj* 1 : faithful, loyal 2 PRECISO : accurate, reliable — **~** *nm* 1 : pointer (of a scale) 2 **los ~es** : the faithful — **fielmente** *adv* : faithfully

fieltro *nm* : felt

fiero, -ra *adj* : fierce, ferocious — **fiera** *nf* : wild animal, beast

fierro *nm Lat* : iron (bar)

fiesta *nf* 1 : party 2 DÍA FESTIVO : holiday, feast day

figura *nf* 1 : figure 2 FORMA : shape, form — **figurar** *vi* 1 : figure (in), be included (among) 2 DESTACAR : stand out — *vt* : represent — **figurarse** *vr* : imagine

fijar *vt* 1 : fasten, affix 2 CONCRETAR : set, fix — **fijarse** *vr* 1 : settle 2 **~ en** : notice, pay attention to — **fijo, -ja** *adj* 1 : fixed, firm 2 PERMANENTE : permanent

fila *nf* 1 : line, file, row 2 **ponerse en ~** : line up

filantropía *nf* : philanthropy — **filantrópico, -ca** *adj* : philanthropic — **filántropo, -pa** *n* : philanthropist

filatelia *nf* : philately, stamp collecting

filete *nm* : fillet

filial *adj* : filial — **~** *nf* : affiliate, subsidiary

filigrana *nf* 1 : filigree 2 : watermark (on paper)

filipino, -na *adj* : Filipino

filmar *vt* : film, shoot — **filme** *or* **film** *nm* : film, movie

filo *nm* 1 : edge 2 **dar ~ a** : sharpen

filón *nm, pl* **-lones** 1 : vein (of minerals) 2 *fam* : gold mine

filoso, -sa *adj Lat* : sharp

filosofía *nf* : philosophy — **filosófico, -ca** *adj* : philosophical — **filósofo, -fa** *n* : philosopher

filtrar *v* : filter — **filtrarse** *vr* : leak out, seep through — **filtro** *nm* : filter

fin *nm* 1 : end 2 OBJETIVO : purpose, aim 3 **en** ~ : well, in short 4 ~ **de semana** : weekend 5 **por** ~ : finally, at last

final *adj* : final — ~ *nm* : end, conclusion — ~ *nf* : final (in sports) — **finalidad** *nf* : purpose, aim — **finalista** *nmf* : finalist — **finalizar** {21} *v* : finish, end — **finalmente** *adv* : finally

financiar *vt* : finance, fund — **financiero, -ra** *adj* : financial — ~ *n* : financier — **finanzas** *nfpl* : finance

finca *nf* 1 : farm, ranch 2 *Lat* : country house

fingir {35} *v* : feign, pretend — **fingido, -da** *adj* : false, feigned

finito, -ta *adj* : finite

finlandés, -desa *adj* : Finnish

fino, -na *adj* 1 : fine 2 DELGADO : slender 3 REFINADO : refined 4 AGUDO : sharp, keen — **finura** *nf* 1 : fineness 2 REFINAMIENTO : refinement

firma *nf* 1 : signature 2 : (act of) signing 3 EMPRESA : firm, company

firmamento *nm* : firmament, sky

firmar *v* : sign

firme *adj* 1 : firm, resolute 2 ESTABLE : steady, stable — **firmeza** *nf* 1 : strength, resolve 2 ESTABILIDAD : firmness, stability

fiscal *adj* : fiscal — ~ *nmf* : district attorney — **fisco** *nm* : (national) treasury

fisgar {52} *vt* : pry into — *vi* : pry — **fisgón, -gona** *n*, *mpl* **-gones** : snoop, busybody

física *nf* 1 : physics — **físico, -ca** *adj* : physical — ~ *n* : physicist — **físico** *nm* : physique

fisiología *nf* : physiology — **fisiológico, -ca** *adj* : physiological — **fisiólogo, -ga** *n* : physiologist

fisioterapia *nf* : physical therapy — **fisioterapeuta** *nmf* : physical therapist

fisonomía *nf* : features *pl*, appearance

fisura *nf* : fissure

fláccido, -da *or* **flácido, -da** *adj* : flaccid, flabby

flaco, -ca *adj* 1 : thin, skinny 2 DÉBIL : weak

flagrante *adj* : flagrant

flamante *adj* 1 : bright, brilliant 2 NUEVO : brand-new

flamenco, -ca *adj* 1 : flamenco (of music or dance) 2 : Flemish — **fla-**

menco *nm* 1 : flamingo 2 : flamenco (music or dance)

flaquear *vi* : weaken, flag — **flaqueza** *nf* 1 : thinness 2 DEBILIDAD : weakness

flash *nm* : flash

flatulencia *nf* : flatulence

flauta *nf* 1 : flute 2 ~ **dulce** : recorder — **flautín** *nm*, *pl* **-tines** : piccolo — **flautista** *nmf* : flutist

flecha *nf* : arrow

fleco *nm* 1 : fringe 2 *Lat* : bangs *pl*

flema *nf* : phlegm — **flemático, -ca** *adj* : phlegmatic

flequillo *nm* : bangs *pl*

fletar *vt* 1 : charter, rent 2 *Lat* : transport — **flete** *nm* 1 : charter 2 : shipping (charges) 3 *Lat* : transport, freight

flexible *adj* : flexible — **flexibilidad** *nf* : flexibility

flirtear *vi* : flirt

flojo, -ja *adj* 1 SUELTO : loose, slack 2 DÉBIL : weak 3 PEREZOSO : lazy — **flojera** *nf fam* : lethargy

flor *nf* : flower — **flora** *nf* : flora — **floral** *adj* : floral — **floreado, -da** *adj* : flowered — **florear** *vi Lat* : flower, bloom — **florecer** {53} *vi* 1 : bloom, blossom 2 PROSPERAR : flourish — **floreciente** *adj* : flourishing — **florero** *nm* : vase — **florido, -da** *adj* : flowery — **florista** *nmf* : florist — **floritura** *nf* : frill, flourish

flota *nf* : fleet

flotar *vi* : float — **flotador** *nm* 1 : float 2 : life preserver (for a swimmer) — **flotante** *adj* : floating, buoyant — **flote: a** ~ *adv phr* : afloat

flotilla *nf* : flotilla, fleet

fluctuar {3} *vi* : fluctuate — **fluctuación** *nf*, *pl* **-clones** : fluctuation

fluir {41} *vi* : flow — **fluidez** *nf* 1 : fluidity 2 : fluency (of language, etc.) — **fluido, -da** *adj* 1 : fluid 2 : fluent (of language) — **fluido** *nm* : fluid — **flujo** *nm* : flow

fluorescente *adj* : fluorescent

fluoruro *nm* : fluoride

fluvial *adj* : river

fobia *nf* : phobia

foca *nf* : seal (animal)

foco *nm* 1 : focus 2 : spotlight, floodlight (in theater, etc.) 3 *Lat* : lightbulb

fofo, -fa *adj* : flabby

fogata *nf* : bonfire

fogón *nm*, *pl* **-gones** : burner

fogoso, -sa *adj* : ardent

folklore *nm* : folklore — **folklórico, -ca** *adj* : folk, traditional

follaje *nm* : foliage

folleto *nm* : pamphlet, leaflet

fomentar *vt* : promote, encourage — **fomento** *nm* : promotion, encouragement

fonda *nf* : boarding house

fondear *vt* : sound out, examine — *vi* : anchor

fondillos *nmpl* : seat (of pants, etc.)

fondo *nm* **1** : bottom **2** : rear, back, end **3** PROFUNDIDAD : depth **4** : background (of a painting, etc.) **5** *Lat* : slip, petticoat **6** ~s *nmpl* : funds, resources **7** a ~ : thoroughly, in depth **8** en el ~ : deep down

fonético, -ca *adj* : phonetic — **fonética** *nf* : phonetics

fontanería *nf Spain* : plumbing — **fontanero, -ra** *n Spain* : plumber

footing ['fuˌtɪŋ] *nm* **1** : jogging **2** hacer ~ : jog

forajido, -da *n* : bandit, outlaw

foráneo, -nea *adj* : foreign, strange

forastero, -ra *n* : stranger, outsider

forcejear *vi* : struggle — **forcejeo** *nm* : struggle

forense *adj* : forensic

forja *nf* : forge — **forjar** *vt* **1** : forge **2** CREAR, FORMAR : build up, create

forma *nf* **1** : form, shape **2** MANERA : manner, way **3** en ~ : fit, healthy **4** ~s *nfpl* : appearances, conventions — **formación** *nf*, *pl* **-ciones** **1** : formation **2** EDUCACIÓN : training

formal *adj* **1** : formal **2** SERIO : serious **3** FIABLE : dependable, reliable — **formalidad** *nf* **1** : formality **2** SERIEDAD : seriousness **3** FIABILIDAD : reliability

formar *vt* **1** : form, shape **2** CONSTITUIR : constitute **3** EDUCAR : train, educate — **formarse** *vr* **1** DESARROLLARSE : develop, take shape **2** EDUCARSE : be educated

formato *nm* : format

formidable *adj* **1** : tremendous **2** *fam* : fantastic, terrific

fórmula *nf* : formula

formular *vt* **1** : formulate, draw up **2** : make, lodge (a complaint, etc.)

formulario *nm* : form

fornido, -da *adj* : well-built, burly

foro *nm* : forum

forraje *nm* : forage, fodder — **forrajear** *vi* : forage

forrar *vt* **1** : line (a garment) **2** : cover (a book) — **forro** *nm* **1** : lining **2** CUBIERTA : book cover

fortalecer {53} *vt* : strengthen — **fortaleza** *nf* **1** : fortress **2** FUERZA : strength **3** : (moral) fortitude

fortificar {72} *vt* : fortify — **fortificación** *nf*, *pl* **-ciones** : fortification

fortuito, -ta *adj* : fortuitous, chance

fortuna *nf* **1** SUERTE : fortune, luck **2** RIQUEZA : wealth, fortune **3** por ~ : fortunately

forzar {36} *vt* **1** : force **2** : strain (one's eyes) — **forzosamente** *adv* : necessarily — **forzoso, -sa** *adj* : necessary, inevitable

fosa *nf* **1** : pit, ditch **2** TUMBA : grave **3** ~s nasales : nostrils

fósforo *nm* **1** : phosphorus **2** CERILLA : match — **fosforescente** *adj* : phosphorescent

fósil *nm* : fossil

foso *nm* **1** : ditch **2** : pit (of a theater) **3** : moat (of a castle)

foto *nf* : photo

fotocopia *nf* : photocopy — **fotocopiadora** *nf* : photocopier — **fotocopiar** *vt* : photocopy

fotogénico, -ca *adj* : photogenic

fotografía *nf* **1** : photography **2** : photograph, picture — **fotografiar** {85} *vt* : photograph — **fotográfico, -ca** *adj* : photographic — **fotógrafo, -fa** *n* : photographer

fotosíntesis *nf* : photosynthesis

fracasar *vi* : fail — **fracaso** *nm* : failure

fracción *nf*, *pl* **-ciones** **1** : fraction **2** : faction (in politics) — **fraccionamiento** *nm Lat* : housing development

fractura *nf* : fracture — **fracturarse** *vr* : fracture, break (a bone)

fragancia *nf* : fragrance, scent — **fragante** *adj* : fragrant

fragata *nf* : frigate

frágil *adj* **1** : fragile **2** DÉBIL : frail, delicate — **fragilidad** *nf* **1** : fragility **2** DEBILIDAD : frailty

fragmento *nm* : fragment

fragor *nm* : clamor, din

fragoso, -sa *adj* : rough, rugged

fragua *nf* : forge — **fraguar** {10} *vt* **1** : forge **2** IDEAR : concoct — *vi* : harden, solidify

fraile *nm* : friar, monk

frambuesa *nf* : raspberry

francés, -cesa *adj*, *mpl* **-ceses** : French — **francés** *nm* : French (language)

franco, -ca *adj* **1** : frank, candid **2** : free (in commerce) — **franco** *nm* : franc

francotirador, -dora *n* : sniper

franela *nf* : flannel

franja *nf* **1** : stripe, band **2** FLECO : fringe

franquear *vt* **1** : clear (a path, etc.) **2** : cross over (a doorstep, etc.) **3** : pay postage on (mail) — **franqueo** *nm* : postage

franqueza *nf* : frankness
frasco *nm* : small bottle, vial, flask
frase *nf* 1 : phrase 2 ORACIÓN : sentence
fraternal *adj* : brotherly, fraternal — **fraternidad** *nf* : brotherhood, fraternity — **fraternizar** {21} *vi* : fraternize — **fraterno, -na** *adj* : brotherly, fraternal
fraude *nm* : fraud — **fraudulento, -ta** *adj* : fraudulent
fray *nm* (*used in titles*) : brother, friar
frazada *nf Lat* : blanket
frecuencia *nf* 1 : frequency 2 con ~ : often, frequently — **frecuentar** *vt* : frequent, haunt — **frecuente** *adj* : frequent
fregadero *nm* : kitchen sink
fregar {49} *vt* 1 : scrub, wash 2 *Lat fam* : annoy — *vi Lat fam* : be a pest
freír {37} *vt* : fry
fregona *nf Spain* : mop
frenar *vt* 1 : brake 2 RESTRINGIR : curb, check
frenesí *nm* : frenzy — **frenético, -ca** *adj* : frantic, frenzied
freno *nm* 1 : brake 2 : bit (of a bridle) 3 CONTROL : check, restraint
frente *nm* 1 : front 2 : facade (of a building) 3 al ~ de : at the head of 4 ~ a : opposite 5 de ~ : (facing) forward 6 hacer ~ a : face up to, brave — ~ *nf* : forehead
fresa *nf* : strawberry
fresco, -ca *adj* 1 : fresh 2 FRÍO : cool 3 *fam* : insolent, nervy — **fresco** *nm* 1 : fresh air 2 FRESCOR : coolness 3 : fresco (art or painting) — **frescor** *nm* : coolness, cool air — **frescura** *nf* 1 : freshness 2 FRÍO : coolness 3 *fam* : nerve, insolence
fresno *nm* : ash (tree)
frialdad *nf* 1 : coldness 2 INDIFERENCIA : indifference
fricción *nf, pl* -**ciones** 1 : friction 2 MASAJE : rubbing, massage — **friccionar** *vt* : rub
frigidez *nf* : frigidity
frigorífico *nm Spain* : refrigerator
frijol *nm Lat* : bean
frío, fría *adj* 1 : cold 2 INDIFERENTE : cool, indifferent — **frío** *nm* 1 : cold 2 INDIFERENCIA : coldness, indifference 3 hacer ~ : be cold (outside) 4 tener ~ : be cold, feel cold
frito, -ta *adj* 1 : fried 2 *fam* : fed up
frívolo, -la *adj* : frivolous — **frivolidad** *nf* : frivolity
fronda *nf* 1 : frond 2 or ~s *nfpl* : foliage — **frondoso, -sa** *adj* : leafy
frontera *nf* : border, frontier — **fronterizo, -za** *adj* : border, on the border — **frontero, -ra** *adj* : facing, opposite
frotar *vt* : rub — **frotarse** *vr* ~ las manos : rub one's hands
fructífero, -ra *adj* : fruitful
frugal *adj* : frugal, thrifty — **frugalidad** *adj* : frugality
fruncir {83} *vt* 1 : gather (in pleats) 2 ~ el ceño : frown 3 ~ la boca : purse one's lips
frustrar *vt* : frustrate — **frustrarse** *vr* : fail — **frustración** *nf, pl* -**ciones** : frustration — **frustrado, -da** *adj* 1 : frustrated 2 FRACASADO : failed, unsuccessful — **frustrante** *adj* : frustrating
fruta *nf* : fruit — **frutilla** *nf Lat* : strawberry — **fruto** *nm* 1 : fruit 2 RESULTADO : result, consequence
fucsia *adj & nm* : fuchsia
fuego *nm* 1 : fire 2 : flame, burner (on a stove) 3 ~s artificiales *nmpl* : fireworks 4 ¿tienes fuego? : have you got a light?
fuelle *nm* : bellows
fuente *nf* 1 : fountain 2 MANANTIAL : spring 3 ORIGEN : source 4 PLATO : platter, serving dish
fuera *adv* 1 : outside, out 2 : abroad, away 3 ~ de : outside of, beyond 4 ~ de : aside from, in addition to
fuerte *adj* 1 : strong 2 : bright (of colors), loud (of sounds) 3 EXTREMO : intense 4 DURO : hard — ~ *adv* 1 : strongly, hard 2 : loudly 3 MUCHO : abundantly, a lot — ~ *nm* 1 : fort 2 ESPECIALIDAD : strong point
fuerza *nf* 1 : strength 2 VIOLENCIA : force 3 PODER : power, might 4 ~s armadas *nfpl* : armed forces 5 a ~ de : by dint of 6 a la ~ : necessarily
fuga *nf* 1 : flight, escape 2 : fugue (in music) 3 ESCAPE : leak — **fugarse** {52} *vr* : flee, run away — **fugaz** *adj, pl* -**gaces** : fleeting — **fugitivo, -va** *adj & n* : fugitive
fulano, -na *n* : so-and-so, what's-his-name, what's-her-name
fulgor *nm* : brilliance, splendor
fulminar *vt* 1 : strike with lightning 2 : strike down (with an illness, etc.) — **fulminante** *adj* : devastating
fumar *v* : smoke — **fumarse** *vr* 1 : smoke 2 *fam* : squander — **fumador, -dora** *n* : smoker
funámbulo, -la *n* : tightrope walker
función *nf, pl* -**ciones** 1 : function 2 TRABAJOS : duties *pl* 3 : performance, show (in theater) — **funcional** *adj* : functional — **funcionamiento** *nm* 1

: functioning **2 en ~** : in operation —
funcionar *vi* **1** : function, run, work
2 no funciona : out of order —
funcionario, -ria *n* : civil servant, official
funda *nf* **1** : cover, sheath **2** *or* **~ de almohada** : pillowcase
fundar *vt* **1** ESTABLECER : found, establish **2** BASAR : base — **fundarse** *vr* **~
en** : be based on — **fundación** *nf, pl*
-ciones : foundation — **fundador,
-dora** *n* : founder — **fundamental** *adj*
: fundamental, basic — **fundamentalmente** *adv* : basically — **fundamentar** *vt* **1** : lay the foundations for **2**
BASAR : base — **fundamento** *nm* **1**
: foundation **2 ~s** *nmpl* : fundamentals
fundir *vt* **1** : melt down, smelt **2** FUSIO-
NAR : fuse, merge — **fundirse** *vr* **1**
: blend, merge **2** DERRETIRSE : melt **3**
: burn out (of a lightbulb) — **fundi-
ción** *nf, pl* **-ciones** **1** : smelting **2**
: foundry
fúnebre *adj* **1** : funeral **2** LÚGUBRE
: gloomy
funeral *adj* : funeral, funerary — **~** *nm*
1 : funeral **2 ~es** *nmpl* EXEQUIAS : funeral (rites) — **funeraria** *nf* : funeral
home
funesto, ta *adj* : terrible, disastrous
fungir {35} *vi* *Lat* : act, function
furgón *nm, pl* **-gones** **1** : van, truck **2**
: freight car (of a train) **3 ~ de cola**
: caboose — **furgoneta** *nf* : van
furia *nf* **1** CÓLERA : fury, rage **2** VIOLEN-
CIA : violence — **furibundo, -da** *adj*
: furious — **furioso, -sa** *adj* **1** : furious, irate **2** INTENSO : intense, violent
— **furor** *nm* : fury
furtivo, -va *adj* : furtive
furúnculo *nm* : boil
fuselaje *nm* : fuselage
fusible *nm* : fuse
fusil *nm* : rifle — **fusilar** *vt* : shoot (by
firing squad)
fusión *nf, pl* **-siones** **1** : fusion **2** UNIÓN
: union, merger — **fusionar** *vt* **1** : fuse
2 UNIR : merge — **fusionarse** *vr*
: merge
futbol *or* **fútbol** *nm* **1** : soccer **2 ~
americano** : football — **futbolista**
nmf : soccer player, football player
fútil *adj* : trifling, trivial
futuro, -ra *adj* : future — **futuro** *nm*
: future

G

g *nf* : g, seventh letter of the Spanish alphabet
gabán *nm, pl* **-banes** : topcoat, overcoat
gabardina *nf* **1** : trench coat, raincoat **2**
: gabardine (fabric)
gabinete *nm* **1** : cabinet (in government) **2** : (professional) office
gacela *nf* : gazelle
gaceta *nf* : gazette
gachas *nfpl* : porridge
gacho, -cha *adj* : drooping
gaélico, -ca *adj* : Gaelic
gafas *nfpl* **1** : eyeglasses **2 ~ de sol**
: sunglasses
gaita *nf* : bagpipes *pl*
gajo *nm* : segment (of fruit)
gala *nf* **1** : gala **2 de ~** : formal **3 hacer
~ de** : display, show off **4 ~s** *nfpl*
: finery
galáctico, -ca *adj* : galactic
galán *nm, pl* **-lanes** **1** : leading man (in
theater) **2** *fam* : boyfriend
galante *adj* : gallant — **galantear** *vt*
: court, woo — **galantería** *nf* **1** : gal-
lantry **2** CUMPLIDO : compliment
galápago *nm* : (aquatic) turtle
galardón *nm, pl* **-dones** : reward
galaxia *nf* : galaxy
galera *nf* : galley
galería *nf* **1** : corridor **2** : gallery, balcony (in a theater)
galés, -lesa *adj, mpl* **-leses** : Welsh
galgo *nm* : greyhound
galimatías *nms & pl* : gibberish
gallardía *nf* **1** : bravery **2** ELEGAN-
CIA : elegance — **gallardo, -da** *adj* **1**
: brave **2** APUESTO : elegant, good-
looking
gallego, -ga *adj* : Galician
galleta *nf* **1** : (sweet) cookie **2** : (salted)
cracker
gallina *nf* **1** : hen **2 ~ de Guinea**
: guinea fowl — **gallinero** *nm* : hen-
house, (chicken) coop — **gallo** *nm*
: rooster, cock
galón *nm, pl* **-lones** **1** : gallon **2** : stripe
(military insignia)
galopar *vi* : gallop — **galope** *nm* : gallop
galvanizar {21} *vt* : galvanize
gama *nf* **1** : range, spectrum **2** : scale (in
music)
gamba *nf* : large shrimp, prawn

gamuza *nf* 1 : chamois (animal) 2 : chamois (leather), suede

gana *nf* 1 : desire, wish 2 APETITO : appetite 3 **de buena ~** : willingly, heartily 4 **de mala ~** : unwillingly 5 **no me da la ~** : I don't feel like it 6 **tener ~s de** : feel like, be in the mood for

ganado *nm* 1 : cattle *pl*, livestock 2 **~ ovino** : sheep *pl* 3 **~ porcino** : swine *pl* — **ganadería** *nf* 1 : cattle raising 2 GANADO : livestock

ganador, -dora *adj* : winning — **~** *n* : winner

ganancia *nf* : profit

ganar *vt* 1 : earn 2 : win (in games, etc.) 3 CONSEGUIR : gain 4 ADQUERIR : get, obtain 5 **~ a algn** : win over s.o., beat s.o. — *vi* : win — **ganarse** *vr* 1 : win, gain 2 **~ la vida** : make a living

gancho *nm* 1 : hook 2 HORQUILLA : hairpin 3 *Lat* : (clothes) hanger

gandul, -dula *adj & n fam* : good-for-nothing — **gandul** *nm Lat* : pigeon pea

ganga *nf* : bargain

gangrena *nf* : gangrene

gángster *nmf* : gangster

ganso, -sa *n* : goose, gander *m* — **gansada** *nf* : silly thing, nonsense

gañir {38} *vi* : yelp — **gañido** *nm* : yelp

garabatear *v* : scribble — **garabato** *nm* : scribble

garaje *nm* : garage

garantizar {21} *vt* : guarantee — **garante** *nmf* : guarantor — **garantía** *nf* 1 : guarantee, warranty 2 FIANZA : surety

garapiñar *vt* : candy (fruits, etc.)

garbanzo *nm* : chickpea, garbanzo

garbo *nm* : grace, elegance — **garboso, -sa** *adj* : graceful, elegant

gardenia *nf* : gardenia

garfio *nm* : hook, gaff

garganta *nf* 1 : throat 2 CUELLO : neck 3 DESFILADERO : ravine, gorge — **gargantilla** *nf* : necklace

gárgara *nf* 1 : gargling, gargle 2 **hacer ~s** : gargle

gárgola *nf* : gargoyle

garita *nf* 1 : sentry box 2 CABAÑA : cabin, hut

garito *nm* : gambling den

garra *nf* 1 : claw, talon 2 *fam* : hand, paw

garrafa *nf* : decanter, carafe — **garrafón** *nm*, *pl* **-fones** : large decanter or bottle

garrapata *nf* : tick

garrocha *nf* 1 : lance, pike 2 *Lat* : pole (in sports)

garrote *nm* : club, cudgel

garúa *nf Lat* : drizzle

garza *nf* : heron

gas *nm* 1 : gas 2 **~ lacrimógeno** : tear gas

gasa *nf* : gauze

gaseosa *nf* : soda, soft drink

gasolina *nf* : gasoline, gas — **gasoil** *or* **gasóleo** *nm* : diesel fuel — **gasolinera** *nf* : gas station, service station

gastar *vt* 1 : spend 2 CONSUMIR : consume, use up 3 DESPERDICIAR : squander, waste — **gastarse** *vr* 1 : spend 2 DETERIORARSE : wear out — **gastado, -da** *adj* 1 : spent 2 : worn-out (of clothing, etc.) — **gastador, -dora** *n* : spendthrift — **gasto** *nm* 1 : expense, expenditure 2 **~s generales** : overhead

gástrico, -ca *adj* : gastric

gastronomía *nf* : gastronomy — **gastrónomo, -ma** *n* : gourmet

gatas: a ~ *adv phr* : on all fours

gatear *vi* : crawl, creep

gatillo *nm* : trigger — **gatillero** *nm Mex* : gunman

gato, -ta *n* : cat — **gatito, -ta** *n* : kitten — **gato** *nm* : jack (for an automobile)

gaucho *nm* : gaucho

gaveta *nf* : drawer

gavilla *nf* 1 : sheaf 2 PANDILLA : gang

gaviota *nf* : gull, seagull

gay ['ge, 'gai] *adj* : gay (homosexual)

gaza *nf* : loop

gazpacho *nm* : gazpacho

géiser *nm* : geyser

gelatina *nf* : gelatin

gema *nf* : gem

gemelo, -la *adj & n* : twin — **gemelo** *nm* 1 : cuff link 2 **~s** *nmpl* : binoculars

gemir {54} *vi* : moan, groan, whine — **gemido** *nm* : moan, groan, whine

gen *or* **gene** *nm* : gene

genealogía *nf* : genealogy — **genealógico, -ca** *adj* : genealogical

generación *nf*, *pl* **-ciones** : generation

generador *nm* : generator

general *adj* 1 : general 2 **en ~** *or* **por lo ~** : in general, generally — **~** *nmf* : general — **generalidad** *nf* 1 : generalization 2 MAYORÍA : majority — **generalizar** {21} *vi* : generalize — *vt* : spread (out) — **generalizarse** *vr* : become widespread — **generalmente** *adv* : usually, generally

generar *vt* : generate

género *nm* 1 : kind, sort 2 : gender (in

grammar) **3 ~ humano** : human race
— **genérico, -ca** adj : generic
generoso, -sa adj **1** : generous, unselfish **2** : ample (in quantity) — **generosidad** nf : generosity
génesis nfs & pl : genesis
genética nf : genetics — **genético, -ca**
adj : genetic
genial adj **1** : brilliant **2** ESTUPENDO
: great, terrific
genio nm **1** : genius **2** CARÁCTER : temper, disposition **3** : genie (in mythology)
genital adj : genital — **genitales** nmpl
: genitals
genocidio nm : genocide
gente nf **1** : people **2** fam : relatives pl,
folks pl **3 ser buena ~** : be nice, be
kind
gentil adj **1** AMABLE : kind **2** : gentile
(in religion) — **gentileza** nf : kindness, courtesy
gentío nm : crowd, mob
gentuza nf : riffraff, rabble
genuflexión nf, pl **-xiones** : genuflec-
tion
genuino, -na adj : genuine
geografía nf : geography — **geográfico, -ca** adj : geographic, geographical
geología nf : geology — **geológico,
-ca** adj : geologic, geological
geometría nf : geometry — **geométrico, -ca** adj : geometric, geometrical
geranio nm : geranium
gerencia nf : management — **gerente**
nmf : manager
geriatría nf : geriatrics — **geriátrico,
-ca** adj : geriatric
germen nm, pl **gérmenes** : germ
germinar vi : germinate, sprout
gestación nf, pl **-ciones** : gestation
gesticular vi : gesticulate, gesture —
gesticulación nf, pl **-ciones** : gestic-
ulation
gestión nf, pl **-tiones 1** : procedure, step
2 ADMINISTRACIÓN : management —
gestionar vt **1** : negotiate, work towards **2** ADMINISTRAR : manage, handle
gesto nm **1** : gesture **2** : (facial) expression **3** MUECA : grimace
gigante adj & nm : giant — **gigantesco, -ca** adj : gigantic
gimnasia nf : gymnastics — **gimnasio**
nm : gymnasium, gym — **gimnasta**
nmf : gymnast
gimotear vi : whine, whimper
ginebra nf : gin
ginecología nf : gynecology — **gine-
cólogo, -ga** n : gynecologist
gira nf : tour

girar vi : turn (around), revolve — vt **1**
: turn, twist, rotate **2** : draft (checks) **3**
: transfer (funds)
girasol nm : sunflower
giratorio, -ria adj : revolving
giro nm **1** : turn, rotation **2** LOCUCIÓN
: expression **3 ~ bancario** : bank
draft **4 ~ postal** : money order
giroscopio nm : gyroscope
gis nm Lat : chalk
gitano, -na adj & n : Gypsy
glaciar nm : glacier — **glacial** adj : glacial, icy
gladiador nm : gladiator
glándula nf : gland
glasear vt : glaze, ice (cake, etc.) —
glaseado nf : icing
glicerina nf : glycerin
globo nm **1** : globe **2** : balloon **3 ~ ocular** : eyeball — **global** adj **1** : global
2 TOTAL : total, overall
glóbulo nm : blood cell, corpuscle
gloria nf : glory
glorieta nf **1** : bower, arbor **2** Spain : rotary, traffic circle
glorificar {72} vt : glorify
glorioso, -sa adj : glorious
glosario nm : glossary
glotón, -tona adj, mpl **-tones** : gluttonous — ~ n : glutton — **glotonería** nf
: gluttony
glucosa nf : glucose
gnomo ['nomo] nm : gnome
gobernar {55} v **1** : govern, rule **2** DIRI-
GIR : direct, manage **3** : steer (a boat,
etc.) — **gobernación** nf, pl **-ciones**
: governing, government — **gobernador, -dora** n : governor — **gobernante** adj : ruling, governing — ~ n
: ruler, leader — **gobierno** nm : government
goce nm : enjoyment
gol nm : goal (in sports)
golf nm : golf — **golfista** nmf : golfer
golfo nm : gulf
golondrina nf **1** : swallow **2 ~ de mar**
: tern
golosina nf : sweet, candy — **goloso,
-sa** adj : fond of sweets
golpe nm **1** : blow **2** PUÑETAZO : punch
3 : knock (on a door, etc.) **4 de ~**
: suddenly **5 de un ~** : all at once **6
~ de estado** : coup d'etat — **gol-
pear** vt **1** : hit, punch **2** : slam, bang (a
door, etc.) — vi : knock (at a door)
goma nf **1** CAUCHO : rubber **2** PEGAMEN-
TO : glue **3** or **~ elástica** : rubber
band **4 ~ de mascar** : chewing gum
5 ~ de borrar : eraser
gong nm : gong

gordo, -da adj **1** : fat, plump **2** GRUESO : thick **3** : fatty (of meat) **4** fam : big, serious — **~** n : fat person — **gorda** nf Lat : thick corn tortilla — **gordo** nm **1** GRASA : fat **2** : jackpot (in a lottery) — **gordura** nf : fatness, flab

gorgotear vi : gurgle, bubble

gorila nm : gorilla

gorjear vi **1** : chirp, tweet **2** : gurgle (of a baby) — **gorjeo** nm : chirping

gorra nf **1** : cap, bonnet **2 de ~** fam : for free

gorrear vt fam : bum, scrounge

gorrión nm, pl **-rriones** : sparrow

gorro nm **1** : cap, bonnet **2 de ~** fam : for free

gota nf **1** : drop **2** : gout (in medicine) — **gotear** vi : drip, leak — **goteo** nm : drip, dripping — **gotera** nf : leak

gótico, -ca adj : Gothic

gozar {21} vi **1** : enjoy oneself **2 ~ de algo** : enjoy sth

gozne nm : hinge

gozo nm **1** : joy **2** PLACER : enjoyment, pleasure — **gozoso, -sa** adj : joyful, glad

grabar vt **1** : engrave **2** : record, tape — **grabación** nf, pl **-ciones** : recording — **grabado** nm : engraving — **grabadora** nf : tape recorder

gracia nf **1** : grace **2** FAVOR : favor, kindness **3** HUMOR : humor, wit **4 ~s** nfpl : thanks **5 ¡(muchas) ~s!** : thank you (very much)! — **gracioso, -sa** adj : funny, amusing

grada nf **1** : step, stair **2** : row (in a theater, etc.) **3 ~s** nfpl : bleachers, grandstand — **gradación** nf, pl **-ciones** : gradation, scale — **gradería** nf : rows of seats, stands pl — **grado** nm **1** : degree **2** : grade (in school) **3 de buen ~** : willingly

graduar {3} vt **1** : regulate, adjust **2** MARCAR : calibrate **3** : confer a degree on (in education) — **graduarse** vr : graduate (from a school) — **graduación** nf, pl **-ciones** : graduation **2** : alcohol content, proof — **graduado, -da** n : graduate — **gradual** adj : gradual — **gradualmente** adv : little by little, gradually

gráfico, -ca adj : graphic — **gráfica** nf : graph — **gráfico** nm **1** : graph **2** : graphic (in computers)

gragea nf : pill, tablet

grajo nm : rook (bird)

gramática nf : grammar — **gramatical** adj : grammatical

gramo nm : gram

gran → grande

grana nf : scarlet

granada nf **1** : pomegranate **2** : grenade (in the military)

granate nm : garnet

grande adj (**gran** before singular nouns) **1** : large, big **2** ALTO : tall **3** : great (in quality, intensity, etc.) **4** Lat : grown-up — **grandeza** nf **1** : greatness **2** NOBLEZA : nobility — **grandiosidad** nf : grandeur — **grandioso, -sa** adj : grand, magnificent

granel: a ~ adv phr **1** : in bulk **2** : in abundance

granero nm : barn, granary

granito nm : granite

granizar {21} v impers : hail — **granizada** nf : hailstorm — **granizado** nm : iced drink — **granizo** nm : hail

granja nf : farm — **granjero, -ra** n : farmer

grano nm **1** : grain **2** SEMILLA : seed **3** : (coffee) bean **4** BARRO : pimple

granuja nmf : rascal

grapa nf : staple — **grapadora** nf : stapler — **grapar** vt : staple

grasa nf **1** : grease **2** : fat (in cooking, etc.) — **grasiento, -ta** adj : greasy, oily — **graso, -sa** adj : fatty, greasy, oily — **grasoso, -sa** adj Lat : greasy, oily

gratificar {72} vt **1** : give a tip or bonus to **2** SATISFACER : gratify, satisfy — **gratificación** nf, pl **-ciones 1** : bonus, tip, reward **2** SATISFACCIÓN : gratification

gratis adv & adj : free

gratitud nf : gratitude

grato, -ta adj : pleasant, agreeable

gratuito, -ta adj **1** : gratuitous, unwarranted **2** GRATIS : free

grava nf : gravel

gravar vt **1** : tax **2** CARGAR : burden — **gravamen** nm, pl **-vámenes 1** : burden, obligation **2** IMPUESTO : tax

grave adj **1** : grave, serious **2** : deep, low (of a voice, etc.) — **gravedad** nf : gravity

gravilla nf : gravel

gravitar vi **1** : gravitate **2 ~ sobre** : weigh on — **gravitación** nf, pl **-ciones** : gravitation

gravoso, -sa adj : costly, burdensome

graznar vi : caw, quack, honk — **graznido** nm : caw, squawk, honk

gregario, -ria adj : gregarious

gremio nm : guild, (trade) union

greñas nfpl : shaggy hair, mop

griego, -ga adj : Greek — **griego** nm : Greek (language)

grieta nf : crack, crevice

grifo nm Spain : faucet, tap
grillete nm : shackle
grillo nm 1 : cricket 2 ~s nmpl : fetters, shackles
grima nf **dar** ~ : annoy, irritate
gringo, -ga adj & n Lat fam : Yankee, gringo
gripe nf or **gripa** nf Lat : flu, influenza
gris adj & nm : gray
gritar v : shout, scream, cry — **grito** nm 1 : shout, scream, cry 2 **dar** ~s : shout
grosella nf : currant
grosería nf 1 : vulgar remark 2 DESCORTESÍA : rudeness — **grosero, -ra** adj 1 : coarse, vulgar 2 DESCORTÉS : rude
grosor nm : thickness
grotesco, -ca adj : grotesque, hideous
grúa nf : crane, derrick
grueso, -sa adj 1 : thick 2 CORPULENTO : stout, heavy — **gruesa** nf : gross — **grueso** nm 1 GROSOR : thickness 2 : main body, mass 3 **en** ~ : wholesale
grulla nf : crane (bird)
grumo nm : lump, clot — **grumoso, -sa** adj : lumpy
gruñir {38} vi 1 : growl, grunt 2 fam : grumble — **gruñido** nm 1 : growl, grunt 2 fam : grumble — **gruñón, -ñona** adj, mpl **-ñones** fam : grumpy, grouchy — ~ n fam : grouch
grupa nf : rump, hindquarters pl
grupo nm : group
gruta nf : grotto
guacamayo nm or **guacamaya** nf Lat : macaw
guacamole nm : guacamole
guadaña nf : scythe
guagua nf Lat 1 : baby 2 AUTOBÚS : bus
guajolote, -ta or **guajolote, -ta** n Lat : turkey
guante nm : glove
guapo, -pa adj : handsome, good-looking
guaraní nm : Guarani (language of Paraguay)
guarda nmf 1 : keeper, custodian 2 GUARDIÁN : security guard — **guardabarros** nms & pl : fender — **guardabosque** nmf : forest ranger — **guardacostas** nmfs & pl : coast guard vessel — **guardaespaldas** nmfs & pl : bodyguard — **guardameta** nmf : goalkeeper — **guardapolvo** nm : overalls pl — **guardar** vt 1 : keep 2 PROTEGER : guard, protect 3 RESERVAR : save — **guardarse** vr ~ **de** 1 : refrain from 2 : guard against — **guardarropa** nm 1

: cloakroom, checkroom 2 ARMARIO : wardrobe
guardería nf : nursery, day-care center
guardia nf 1 : guard, vigilence 2 TURNO : duty, watch — ~ nmf 1 : guard 2 or ~ **municipal** : police officer — **guardián, -diana** n, mpl **-dianes** 1 : guardian, keeper 2 GUARDA : security guard
guarecer {53} vt : shelter, protect — **guarecerse** vr : take shelter
guarida nf 1 : den, lair (of animals) 2 : hideout (of persons)
guarnecer {53} vt 1 : adorn, garnish 2 : garrison (an area) — **guarnición** nf, pl **-ciones** 1 : garnish, trimming 2 : (military) garrison
guasa nf fam 1 : joke 2 **de** ~ : in jest — **guasón, -sona** adj, mpl **-sones** fam : joking, witty — ~ n fam : joker
guatemalteco, -ca adj : Guatemalan
guayaba nf : guava
gubernamental or **gubernativo, -va** adj : governmental
guepardo nm : cheetah
güero, -ra adj Lat : blond, fair
guerra nf 1 : war, warfare 2 LUCHA : conflict, struggle — **guerrear** vi : wage war — **guerrero, -ra** adj 1 : war, fighting 2 BELICOSO : warlike — ~ n : warrior — **guerrilla** nf : guerrilla warfare — **guerrillero, -ra** adj & n : guerrilla
gueto nm : ghetto
guiar {85} vt 1 : guide, lead 2 ACONSEJAR : advise — **guiarse** vr : be guided by, go by — **guía** nf 1 : guidebook 2 ORIENTACIÓN : guidance — ~ nmf : guide, leader
guijarro nm : pebble
guillotina nf : guillotine
guinda nf : morello (cherry)
guiñar vi : wink — **guiño** nm : wink
guión nm, pl **guiones** 1 : script, screenplay 2 : hyphen, dash (in punctuation) — **guionista** nmf : scriptwriter, screenwriter
guirnalda nf : garland
guisa nf 1 : manner, fashion 2 **a** ~ **de** : by way of 3 **de tal** ~ : in such a way
guisado nm : stew
guisante nm : pea
guisar vt : cook — **guiso** nm : stew, casserole
guitarra nf : guitar — **guitarrista** nmf : guitarist
gula nf : gluttony
gusano nm 1 : worm 2 : maggot (larva)
gustar vt 1 : taste 2 Lat : like — vi 1 : be pleasing 2 **como guste** : as you like 3

me gustan los dulces : I like sweets
— **gusto** *nm* 1 : taste 2 PLACER : pleasure, liking 3 a ~ : comfortable, at ease 4 al ~ : to taste 5 **mucho** ~

: pleased to meet you — **gustoso, -sa** *adj* 1 : tasty 2 AGRADABLE : pleasant 3 **hacer algo** ~ : do sth willingly
gutural *adj* : guttural

H

h *nf* : h, eighth letter of the Spanish alphabet
haba *nf* : broad bean
habanero, -ra *adj* : Havanan — **habano** *nm* : Havana cigar
haber {39} *v aux* 1 : have, has 2 ~ de : must — *v impers* 1 **hay** : there is, there are 2 **hay que** : it is necessary (to) 3 **¿qué hay?** *or* **¿qué hubo?** : how's it going? — ~ *nm* 1 : assets *pl* 2 : credit side (in accounting) 3 ~es *nmpl* : income, earnings
habichuela *nf* 1 : bean 2 ~ **verde** : string bean
hábil *adj* 1 : able, skillful 2 LISTO : clever 3 **horas** ~es : business hours — **habilidad** *nf* : ability, skill
habilitar *vt* 1 : equip, furnish 2 AUTORIZAR : authorize
habitar *vt* : inhabit — *vi* : reside, dwell — **habitable** *adj* : habitable, inhabitable — **habitación** *nf, pl* **-ciones** 1 : room, bedroom 2 MORADA : dwelling, abode 3 : habitat (in biology) — **habitante** *nmf* : inhabitant, resident — **hábitat** *nm* : habitat
hábito *nm* : habit — **habitual** *adj* : habitual, usual — **habituar** {3} *vt* : accustom, habituate — **habituarse** *vr* ~ **a** : get used to
hablar *vi* 1 : speak, talk 2 ~ **de** : mention, talk about 3 ~ **con** : talk to, speak with — *vt* 1 : speak (a language) 2 DISCUTIR : discuss — **hablarse** *vr* 1 : speak to each other 2 **se habla inglés** : English spoken — **habla** *nf* 1 : speech 2 IDIOMA : language, dialect 3 **de** ~ **inglesa** : English-speaking — **hablador, -dora** *adj* : talkative — ~ *n* : chatterbox — **habladuría** *nf* 1 : rumor 2 ~s *nfpl* : gossip — **hablante** *nmf* : speaker
hacedor, -dora *n* : creator, maker
hacendado, -da *n* : landowner, rancher
hacer {40} *vt* 1 : do, perform 2 CONSTRUIR, CREAR : make 3 OBLIGAR : force, oblige — *vi* : act — *v impers* 1 ~ **calor/viento** : be hot/be windy 2 ~ **falta** : be necessary 3 **hace mucho tiempo** : a long time ago 4 **no lo hace** : it doesn't matter — **hacerse** *vr* 1

VOLVERSE : become 2 : pretend (to be) 3 ~ **a** : get used to 4 **se hace tarde** : it's getting late
hacha *nf* 1 : hatchet, ax 2 ANTORCHA : torch
hachís *nm* : hashish
hacia *prep* 1 : toward, towards 2 CERCA DE : near, around, about 3 ~ **abajo** : downward 4 ~ **adelante** : forward
hacienda *nf* 1 : estate, ranch 2 BIENES : property 3 *Lat* : livestock 4 **Hacienda** : department of revenue
hacinar *vt* : stack
hada *nf* : fairy
hado *nm* : fate
halagar {52} *vt* : flatter — **halagador, -dora** *adj* : flattering — **halago** *nm* : flattery — **halagüeño, -ña** *adj* 1 : flattering 2 PROMETEDOR : promising
halcón *nm, pl* **-cones** : hawk, falcon
halibut *nm, pl* **-buts** : halibut
hálito *nm* : breath
hallar *vt* 1 : find 2 DESCUBRIR : discover, find out — **hallarse** *vr* : be, find oneself — **hallazgo** *nm* : discovery, find
halo *nm* : halo
hamaca *nf* : hammock
hambre *nf* 1 : hunger 2 INANICIÓN : starvation, famine 3 **tener** ~ : be hungry — **hambriento, -ta** *adj* : hungry, starving — **hambruna** *nf* : famine
hamburguesa *nf* : hamburger
hampa *nf* : underworld — **hampón, -pona** *n, mpl* **-pones** : criminal, thug
hámster *nm* : hamster
hándicap *nm* : handicap (in sports)
hangar *nm* : hangar
haragán, -gana *adj, mpl* **-ganes** : lazy, idle — ~ *n* : slacker, idler — **haraganear** : be lazy, loaf
harapiento, -ta *adj* : ragged, in rags — **harapos** *nmpl* : rags, tatters
harina *nf* : flour
hartar *vt* 1 : glut, satiate 2 FASTIDIAR : annoy — **hartarse** *vr* 1 : gorge oneself 2 CANSARSE : get fed up — **harto, -ta** *adj* 1 : full, satiated 2 CANSADO : tired, fed up — **harto** *adv* : extremely, very — **hartura** *nf* 1 : surfeit 2 ABUNDANCIA : abundance, plenty
hasta *prep* 1 : until, up until (in time) 2

: as far as, up to (in space) **3** ¡~
luego! : see you later! **4** ~ **que** : until
— ~ *adv* : even

hastiar {85} *vt* **1** : make weary, bore **2**
ASQUEAR : sicken — **hastiarse** *vr* —
de : get tired of — **hastío** *nm* **1** : weariness, tedium **2** REPUGNANCIA : disgust

hato *nm* **1** : flock, herd **2** : bundle (of
possessions)

haya *nf* : beech

haz *nm*, *pl* **haces** **1** : bundle, sheaf **2**
: beam (of light)

hazaña *nf* : feat, exploit

hazmerreír *nm fam* : laughingstock

he {39} *v impers* ~ **aquí** : here is, here
are, behold

hebilla *nf* : buckle

hebra *nf* : strand, thread

hebreo, -brea *adj* : Hebrew — **hebreo**
nm : Hebrew (language)

hecatombe *nm* : disaster

hechizo *nm* **1** : spell **2** ENCANTO : charm,
fascination — **hechicería** *nf* : sorcery,
witchcraft — **hechicero, -ra** *n* : sorcerer, sorceress *f* — **hechizar** {21} *vt* **1**
: bewitch **2** CAUTIVAR : charm

hecho, -cha *adj* **1** : made, done **2**
: ready-to-wear (of clothing) **3** ~ **y**
derecho : full-fledged, mature —
hecho *nm* **1** : fact **2** SUCESO : event **3**
ACTO : act, deed **4** **de** ~ : in fact —
hechura *nf* **1** : making, creation **2**
FORMA : shape, form **3** : build (of the
body) **4** ARTESANÍA : workmanship

heder {56} *vi* : stink, reek — **hedion-
dez** *nf*, *pl* **-deces** : stench — **hedion-
do, -da** *adj* : stinking — **hedor** *nm*
: stench

helar {55} *v* : freeze — **helarse** *vr*
: freeze up, freeze over — **helado, -da**
adj **1** : freezing cold **2** CONGELADO
: frozen — **helada** *nf* : frost —
heladería *nf* : ice-cream parlor —
helado *nm* : ice cream — **heladora** *nf*
: freezer

helecho *nm* : fern

hélice *nf* **1** : propeller **2** ESPIRAL : spiral,
helix

helicóptero *nm* : helicopter

helio *nm* : helium

hembra *nf* **1** : female **2** MUJER : woman

hemisferio *nm* : hemisphere

hemorragia *nf* **1** : hemorrhage **2** ~
nasal : nosebleed

hemorroides *nfpl* : hemorrhoids, piles

henchir {54} *vt* : stuff, fill

hender {56} *vt* : cleave, split — **hendidura** *nf* : crevice, fissure

henequén *nm*, *pl* **-quenes** : sisal

heno *nm* : hay

hepatitis *nf* : hepatitis

heraldo *nm* : herald

herbolario, -ria *n* : herbalist

heredar *vt* : inherit — **heredad** *nm*
: rural property, estate — **heredero,
-ra** *n* : heir, heiress *f* — **hereditario,
-ria** *adj* : hereditary

hereje *nmf* : heretic — **herejía** *nf*
: heresy

herencia *nf* **1** : inheritance **2** : heredity
(in biology)

herir {76} *vt* **1** : injure, wound **2** : hurt
(feelings, pride, etc.) — **herida** *nf* : injury, wound — **herido, -da** *adj* **1** : injured, wounded **2** : hurt (of feelings,
pride, etc.) — ~ *n* : injured person,
casualty

hermano, -na *n* : brother *m*, sister *f* —
hermanastro, -tra *n* : half brother *m*,
half sister *f* — **hermandad** *nf* : brotherhood

hermético, -ca *adj* : hermetic, watertight

hermoso, -sa *adj* : beautiful, lovely —
hermosura *nf* : beauty

hernia *nf* : hernia

héroe *nm* : hero — **heroico, -ca** *adj*
: heroic — **heroína** *nf* **1** : heroine **2**
: heroin (narcotic) — **heroísmo** *nm*
: heroism

herradura *nf* : horseshoe

herramienta *nf* : tool

herrero, -ra *n* : blacksmith

herrumbre *nf* : rust

hervir {76} *v* : boil — **hervidero** *nm* **1**
: mass, swarm **2** : hotbed (of intrigue,
etc.) — **hervidor** *nm* : kettle — **hervor**
nm **1** : boiling **2** ENTUSIASMO : fervor,
ardor

heterogéneo, -nea *adj* : heterogeneous

heterosexual *adj* & *nmf* : heterosexual

hexágono *nm* : hexagon — **hexagonal**
adj : hexagonal

hez *nf*, *pl* **heces** : dregs *pl*, scum

hiato *nm* : hiatus

hibernar *vi* : hibernate — **hibernación**
nf, *pl* **-ciones** : hibernation

híbrido, -da *adj* : hybrid — **híbrido** *nm*
: hybrid

hidalgo, -ga *n* : nobleman *m*, noble-
woman *f*

hidratante *adj* : moisturizing

hidrato *nm* ~ **de carbono** : carbohydrate

hidráulico, -ca *adj* : hydraulic

hidroavión *nm*, *pl* **-aviones** : seaplane

hidroeléctrico, -ca *adj* : hydroelectric

hidrofobia *nf* : rabies

hidrógeno *nm* : hydrogen

hidroplano *nm* : hydroplane

hiedra *nf* 1 : ivy 2 ~ **venenosa** : poison ivy
hiel *nm* 1 : bile 2 AMARGURA : bitterness
hielo *nm* 1 : ice 2 FRIALDAD : coldness 3 **romper el** ~ : break the ice
hiena *nf* : hyena
hierba *nf* 1 : herb 2 CÉSPED : grass 3 **mala** ~ : weed — **hierbabuena** *nf* : mint
hierro *nm* 1 : iron 2 ~ **fundido** : cast iron
hígado *nm* : liver
higiene *nf* : hygiene — **higiénico, -ca** *adj* ; hygienic
higo *nm* : fig
hijo, -ja *n* 1 : son *m*, daughter *f* 2 **hijos** *nmpl* : children, offspring — **hijastro, -tra** *n* : stepson *m*, stepdaughter *f*
hilar *v* 1 : spin 2 ~ **delgado** : split hairs — **hilado** *nm* : yarn, thread
hilaridad *nf* : hilarity
hilera *nf* : file, row
hilo *nm* 1 : thread 2 LINO : linen 3 ALAMBRE : wire 4 : trickle (of water, etc.) 5 ~ **dental** : dental floss
hilvanar *vt* 1 : baste, tack 2 : put together (ideas, etc.)
himno *nm* 1 : hymn 2 ~ **nacional** : national anthem
hincapié *nm* **hacer** ~ **en** : emphasize, stress
hincar {72} *vt* : drive in, plunge — **hincarse** *vr* ~ **de rodillas** : kneel (down)
hinchar *vt Spain* : inflate, blow up — **hincharse** *vr* 1 : swell (up) 2 *Spain fam* : stuff oneself — **hinchado, -da** *adj* 1 : swollen 2 POMPOSO : pompous — **hinchazón** *nf, pl* **-zones** : swelling
hindú *adj & nmf* : Hindu — **hinduismo** *nm* : Hinduism
hinojo *nm* : fennel
hiperactivo, -va *adj* : hyperactive
hipersensible *adj* : oversensitive
hipertensión *nf, pl* **-siones** : hypertension, high blood pressure
hípico, -ca *adj* : equestrian, horse
hipil → **huipil**
hipnosis *nfs & pl* : hypnosis — **hipnótico, -ca** *adj* : hypnotic — **hipnotismo** *nm* : hypnotism — **hipnotizador, -dora** *n* : hypnotist — **hipnotizar** {21} *vt* : hypnotize
hipo *nm* 1 : hiccup, hiccups *pl* 2 **tener** ~ : have hiccups
hipocondríaco, -ca *adj* : hypochondriacal — ~ *n* : hypochondriac
hipocresía *nf* : hypocrisy — **hipócrita** *adj* : hypocritical — ~ *nmf* : hypocrite

hipodérmico, -ca *adj* : hypodermic
hipódromo *nm* : racetrack
hipopótamo *nm* : hippopotamus
hipoteca *nf* : mortgage — **hipotecar** {72} *vt* : mortgage
hipótesis *nfs & pl* : hypothesis — **hipotético, -ca** *adj* : hypothetical
hiriente *adj* : hurtful, offensive
hirsuto, -ta *adj* 1 : hairy 2 : bristly, wiry (of hair)
hirviente *adj* : boiling
hispano, -na *or* **hispánico, -ca** *adj & n* : Hispanic — **hispanoamericano, -na** *adj* : Latin-American — ~ *n* : Latin American — **hispanohablante** *or* **hispanoparlante** *adj* : Spanish-speaking
histeria *nf* : hysteria — **histérico, -ca** *adj* : hysterical — **histerismo** *nm* : hysteria
historia *nf* 1 : history 2 CUENTO : story — **historiador, -dora** *n* : historian — **historial** *nm* : record, background — **histórico, -ca** *adj* 1 : historical 2 IMPORTANTE : historic, important — **historieta** *nf* : comic strip
hito *nm* : milestone, landmark
hocico *nm* : snout, muzzle
hockey ['hoke, -ki] *nm* : hockey
hogar *nm* 1 : home 2 CHIMENEA : hearth, fireplace — **hogareño, -ña** *adj* 1 : home-loving 2 DOMÉSTICO : home, domestic
hoguera *nf* : bonfire
hoja *nf* 1 : leaf 2 : sheet (of paper) 3 ~ **de afeitar** : razor blade — **hojalata** *nf* : tinplate — **hojaldre** *nm* : puff pastry — **hojear** *vt* : leaf through — **hojuela** *nf Lat* : flake
hola *interj* : hello!, hi!
holandés, -desa *adj, mpl* **-deses** : Dutch
holgado, -da *adj* 1 : loose, baggy 2 : comfortable (of an economic situation, a victory, etc.) — **holgazán, -zana** *adj, mpl* **-zanes** : lazy — ~ *n* : slacker, idler — **holgazanear** *vi* : laze about, loaf — **holgura** *nf* 1 : looseness 2 BIENESTAR : comfort, ease
hollín *nm, pl* **-llines** : soot
holocausto *nm* : holocaust
hombre *nm* 1 : man 2 **el** ~ : mankind 3 ~ **de estado** : statesman 4 ~ **de negocios** : businessman
hombrera *nf* 1 : shoulder pad 2 : epaulet (of a uniform)
hombría *nf* : manliness
hombro *nm* : shoulder
hombruno, -na *adj* : mannish

homenaje *nm* **1** : homage **2 rendir ~ a** : pay tribute to
homeopatía *nf* : homeopathy
homicidio *nm* : homicide, murder — **homicida** *adj* : homicidal, murderous — **~** *nmf* : murderer
homogéneo, -nea *adj* : homogeneous
homólogo, -ga *adj* : equivalent — **~** *n* : counterpart
homosexual *adj & nmf* : homosexual — **homosexualidad** *nf* : homosexuality
hondo, -da *adj* : deep — **hondo** *adv* : deeply — **hondonada** *nf* : hollow — **hondura** *nf* : depth
hondureño, -ña *adj* : Honduran
honesto, -ta *adj* : decent, honorable — **honestidad** *nf* : honesty, integrity
hongo *nm* **1** : mushroom **2** : fungus (in botany and medicine)
honor *nm* : honor — **honorable** *adj* : honorable — **honorario, -ria** *adj* : honorary — **honorarios** *nmpl* : payment, fee — **honra** *nf* : honor — **honradez** *nf, pl* **-deces** : honesty, integrity — **honrado, -da** *adj* : honest, upright — **honrar** *vt* : honor — **honrarse** *vr* : be honored — **honroso, -sa** *adj* : honorable
hora *nf* **1** : hour **2** : (specific) time **3** CITA : appointment **4 a la última ~** : at the last minute **5 ~ punta** : rush hour **6 media ~** : half an hour **7 ¿qué ~ es?** : what time is it? **8 ~s de oficina** : office hours **9 ~s extraordinarias** : overtime
horario *nm* : schedule, timetable
horca *nf* **1** : gallows *pl* **2** : pitchfork (in agriculture)
horcajadas : a ~ *adv phr* : astride
horda *nf* : horde
horizonte *nm* : horizon — **horizontal** *adj* : horizontal
horma *nf* **1** : form, mold, last **2** : shoe tree
hormiga *nf* : ant
hormigón *nm, pl* **-gones** : concrete
hormigueo *nm* : tingling, pins and needles
hormiguero *nm* **1** : anthill **2** : swarm (of people)
hormona *nf* : hormone
horno *nm* **1** : oven (for cooking) **2** : small furnace, kiln — **hornada** *nf* : batch — **hornear** *vt* : bake — **hornillo** *nf* : portable stove
horóscopo *nm* : horoscope
horquilla *nf* **1** : hairpin, bobby pin **2** HORCA : pitchfork
horrendo, -da *adj* : horrendous, awful

— horrible *adj* : horrible — **horripilante** *adj* : horrifying — **horror** *nm* **1** : horror, dread **2** ATROCIDAD : atrocity — **horrorizar** {21} *vt* : horrify, terrify — **horrorizarse** *vr* : be horrified — **horroroso, -sa** *adj* : horrifying, dreadful
hortaliza *nf* : (garden) vegetable — **hortelano, -na** *n* : truck farmer — **horticultura** *nf* : horticulture
hosco, -ca *adj* : sullen, gloomy
hospedar *vt* : put up, lodge — **hospedarse** *vr* : stay, lodge — **hospedaje** *nm* : lodging
hospital *nm* : hospital — **hospitalario, -ria** *adj* : hospitable — **hospitalidad** *nf* : hospitality — **hospitalizar** {21} *vt* : hospitalize
hostería *nf* : small hotel, inn
hostia *nf* : host (in religion)
hostigar {52} *vt* **1** : whip **2** ACOSAR : harass, pester
hostil *adj* : hostile — **hostilidad** *nf* : hostility
hotel *nm* : hotel — **hotelero, -ra** *adj* : hotel — **~** *n* : hotel manager, hotelier
hoy *adv* **1** : today **2 de ~ en adelante** : from now on **3 ~ (en) día** : nowadays **4 ~ mismo** : this very day
hoyo *nm* : hole — **hoyuelo** *nm* : dimple
hoz *nf, pl* **hoces** : sickle
huarache *nm* : huarache (sandal)
hueco, -ca *adj* **1** : hollow, empty **2** ESPONJOSO : soft, spongy **3** RESONANTE : resonant — **hueco** *nm* **1** : hollow, cavity **2** : recess (in a wall, etc.) **3 ~ de escalera** : stairwell
huelga *nf* **1** : strike **2 declararse en ~** : go on strike — **huelguista** *nmf* : striker
huella *nf* **1** : footprint **2** VESTIGIO : track, mark **3 ~ digital** *or* **~ dactilar** : fingerprint
huérfano, -na *n* : orphan — **~** *adj* : orphaned
huerta *nf* : truck farm — **huerto** *nm* **1** : vegetable garden **2** : (fruit) orchard
hueso *nm* **1** : bone **2** : pit, stone (of a fruit)
huésped, -peda *n* : guest — **huésped** *nm* : host (organism)
huesudo, -da *adj* : bony
huevo *nm* **1** : egg **2 ~s estrellados** : fried eggs **3 ~s revueltos** : scrambled eggs — **hueva** *nf* : roe
huida *nf* : flight, escape — **huidizo, -za** *adj* **1** : shy **2** FUGAZ : fleeting
huipil *nm Lat* : traditional embroidered blouse or dress

huir {41} *vi* **1** : escape, flee **2** ~ **de** : shun, avoid

hule *nm* **1** : oilcloth **2** *Lat* : rubber

humano, -na *adj* **1** : human **2** COMPASIVO : humane — **humano** *nm* : human (being) — **humanidad** *nf* **1** : humanity, mankind **2** BENEVOLENCIA : humaneness **3** ~es *nfpl* : humanities — **humanismo** *nm* : humanism — **humanista** *nmf* : humanist — **humanitario, -ria** *adj & n* : humanitarian

humear *vi* : smoke, steam — **humareda** *nf* : cloud of smoke

humedad *nf* **1** : dampness **2** : humidity (in meteorology) — **humedecer** {53} *vt* : moisten, dampen — **humedecerse** *vr* : become moist — **húmedo, -da** *adj* **1** : moist, damp **2** : humid (in meteorology)

humildad *nf* : humility — **humilde** *adj* : humble — **humillación** *nf, pl* **-ciones** : humiliation — **humillante** *adj* : humiliating — **humillar** *vt* : humiliate — **humillarse** *vr* : humble oneself

humo *nm* **1** : smoke, steam, fumes **2** ~s *nmpl* : airs, conceit

humor *nm* **1** : mood, temper **2** GRACIA : humor **3 de buen** ~ : in a good mood — **humorismo** *nm* : humor, wit — **humorista** *nmf* : humorist, comedian — **humorístico, -ca** *adj* : humorous

hundir *vt* **1** : sink **2** : destroy, ruin (a building, plans, etc.) — **hundirse** *vr* **1** : sink **2** DERRUMBARSE : collapse — **hundido, -da** *adj* : sunken — **hundimiento** *nm* **1** : sinking **2** DERRUMBE : collapse

húngaro, -ra *adj* : Hungarian

huracán *nm, pl* **-canes** : hurricane

huraño, -ña *adj* : unsociable

hurgar {52} *vi* ~ **en** : rummage around in

hurón *nm, pl* **-rones** : ferret

hurra *interj* : hurrah!, hooray!

hurtadillas: a ~ *adv phr* : stealthily, on the sly

hurtar *vt* : steal — **hurto** *nm* **1** ROBO : theft **2** : stolen property

husmear *vt* : sniff out, pry into — *vi* : nose around

huy *interj* : ow!, ouch!

I

i *nf* : i, ninth letter of the Spanish alphabet

ibérico, -ca *adj* : Iberian — **ibero, -ra** *or* **íbero, -ra** *adj* : Iberian

iceberg *nm, pl* **-bergs** : iceberg

icono *nm* : icon

ictericia *nf* : jaundice

ida *nf* **1** : outward journey **2** ~ **y vuelta** : round-trip **3** ~s **y venidas** : comings and goings

idea *nf* **1** : idea **2** OPINIÓN : opinion

ideal *adj & nm* : ideal — **idealismo** *nm* : idealism — **idealista** *adj* : idealistic — ~ *nmf* : idealist — **idealizar** {21} *vt* : idealize

idear *vt* : devise, think up

ídem *nm* : the same, ditto

identidad *nf* : identity — **idéntico, -ca** *adj* : identical — **identificar** {72} *vt* : identify — **identificarse** *vr* **1** : identify oneself **2** ~ **con** : identify with — **identificación** *nf, pl* **-ciones** : identification

ideología *nf* : ideology — **ideológico, -ca** *adj* : ideological

idílico, -ca *adj* : idyllic

idioma *nm* : language — **idiomático, -ca** *adj* : idiomatic

idiosincrasia *nf* : idiosyncrasy — **idiosincrásico, -ca** *adj* : idiosyncratic

idiota *adj* : idiotic — ~ *nmf* : idiot — **idiotez** *nf* : idiocy

ídolo *nm* : idol — **idolatrar** *vt* : idolize — **idolatría** *nf* : idolatry

idóneo, -nea *adj* : suitable, fitting — **idoneidad** *nf* : fitness, suitability

iglesia *nf* : church

iglú *nm* : igloo

ignición *nf, pl* **-ciones** : ignition

ignífugo, -ga *adj* : fire-resistant, fireproof

ignorar *vt* **1** : ignore **2** DESCONOCER : be unaware of — **ignorancia** *nf* : ignorance — **ignorante** *adj* : ignorant — ~ *nmf* : ignorant person

igual *adv* **1** : in the same way **2 por** ~ : equally — ~ *adj* **1** : equal **2** IDÉNTICO : the same **3** LISO : smooth, even **4** SEMEJANTE : similar — ~ *nmf* : equal, peer — **igualar** *vt* **1** : make equal **2** : be equal to **3** NIVELAR : level (off) — **igualdad** *nf* **1** : equality **2** UNIFORMI-

DAD : uniformity — **igualmente** *adv* : likewise

iguana *nf* : iguana

ijada *nf* : flank

ilegal *adj* : illegal

ilegible *adj* : illegible

ilegítimo, -ma *adj* : illegitimate — **ilegitimidad** *nf* : illegitimacy

ileso, -sa *adj* : unharmed

ilícito, -ta *adj* : illicit

ilimitado, -da *adj* : unlimited

ilógico, -ca *adj* : illogical

iluminar *vt* : illuminate — **iluminarse** *vr* : light up — **iluminación** *nf, pl* -**ciones** 1 : illumination 2 ALUMBRADO : lighting

ilusionar *vt* : excite — **ilusionarse** *vr* : get one's hopes up — **ilusión** *nf, pl* -**siones** 1 : illusion 2 ESPERANZA : hope — **ilusionado, -da** *adj* : excited

iluso, -sa *adj* : naïve, gullible — ~ *n* : dreamer, visionary — **ilusorio, -ria** *adj* : illusory

ilustrar *vt* 1 : illustrate 2 ACLARAR : explain — **ilustración** *nf, pl* -**ciones** 1 : illustration 2 SABER : learning 3 **la Ilustración** : the Enlightenment — **ilustrado, -da** *adj* 1 : illustrated 2 ERUDITO : learned — **ilustrador, -dora** *n* : illustrator

ilustre *adj* : illustrious

imagen *nf, pl* **imágenes** : image, picture

imaginar *vt* : imagine — **imaginarse** *vr* : imagine — **imaginación** *nf, pl* -**ciones** : imagination — **imaginario, -ria** *adj* : imaginary — **imaginativo, -va** *adj* : imaginative

imán *nm, pl* **imanes** : magnet — **imantar** *vt* : magnetize

imbécil *adj* : stupid, idiotic — ~ *nmf* : idiot

imborrable *adj* : indelible

imbuir {41} *vt* ~ **de** : imbue with

imitar *vt* 1 COPIAR : imitate, copy 2 : impersonate — **imitación** *nf, pl* -**ciones** 1 COPIA : imitation, copy 2 : impersonation — **imitador, -dora** *n* : impersonator

impaciencia *nf* : impatience — **impacientar** *vt* : make impatient, exasperate —**impacientarse** *vr* : grow impatient — **impaciente** *adj* : impatient

impacto *nm* : impact

impar *adj* : odd — ~ *nm* : odd number

imparcial *adj* : impartial — **imparcialidad** *nf* : impartiality

impartir *vt* : impart, give

impasible *adj* : impassive

impasse *nm* : impasse

impávido, -da *adj* : fearless

impecable *adj* : impeccable, spotless

impedir {54} *vt* 1 : prevent 2 DIFICULTAR : impede, hinder — **impedido, -da** *adj* : disabled — **impedimento** *nm* : obstacle, impediment

impeler *vt* : drive, propel

impenetrable *adj* : impenetrable

impenitente *adj* : unrepentant

impensable *adj* : unthinkable — **impensado, -da** *adj* : unexpected

imperar *vi* 1 : reign, rule 2 PREDOMINAR : prevail — **imperante** *adj* : prevailing

imperativo, -va *adj* : imperative — **imperativo** *nm* : imperative

imperceptible *adj* : imperceptible

imperdible *nm* : safety pin

imperdonable *adj* : unforgivable

imperfección *nf, pl* -**ciones** : imperfection — **imperfecto, -ta** *adj* : imperfect — **imperfecto** *nm* : imperfect (tense)

imperial *adj* : imperial — **imperialismo** *nm* : imperialism — **imperialista** *adj & nmf* : imperialist

impericia *nf* : lack of skill

imperio *nm* 1 : empire 2 DOMINIO : rule — **imperioso, -sa** *adj* 1 : imperious 2 URGENTE : pressing, urgent

impermeable *adj* 1 : waterproof 2 ~ **a** : impervious to — ~ *nm* : raincoat

impersonal *adj* : impersonal

impertinente *adj* : impertinent — **impertinencia** *nf* : impertinence

ímpetu *nm* 1 : impetus 2 ENERGÍA : energy, vigor 3 VIOLENCIA : force — **impetuoso, -sa** *adj* : impetuous — **impetuosidad** *nf* : impetuosity

impío, -pía *adj* : impious, ungodly

implacable *adj* : implacable

implantar *vt* 1 : implant 2 ESTABLECER : establish, introduce

implemento *nm* *Lat* : implement, tool

implicar {72} *vt* 1 : involve, implicate 2 SIGNIFICAR : imply — **implicación** *nf, pl* -**ciones** : implication

implícito, -ta *adj* : implicit

implorar *vt* : implore

imponer {60} *vt* 1 : impose 2 : command (respect, etc.) — *vi* : be imposing — **imponerse** *vr* 1 : assert oneself, command respect 2 PREVALECER : prevail — **imponente** *adj* : imposing, impressive — **imponible** *adj* : taxable

impopular *adj* : unpopular — **impopularidad** *nf* : unpopularity

importación *nf, pl* -**ciones** 1 : importation 2 **importaciones** *nfpl* : imports — **importado, -da** *adj* : imported — **importador, -dora** *adj* : importing — ~ *n* : importer

importancia *nf* : importance — **importante** *adj* : important — **importar** *vi* 1 : matter, be important 2 **no me importa** : I don't care — *vt* 1 : import 2 ASCENDER A : amount to, cost

importe *nm* 1 : price 2 CANTIDAD : sum, amount

importunar *vt* : bother — **importuno, -na** *adj* 1 : inopportune 2 MOLESTO : bothersome

imposible *adj* : impossible — **imposibilidad** *nf* : impossibility

imposición *nf*, *pl* **-ciones** 1 : imposition 2 IMPUESTO : tax

impostor, -tora *n* : impostor

impotente *adj* : powerless, impotent — **impotencia** *nf* : impotence

impracticable *adj* 1 : impracticable 2 INTRANSITABLE : impassable

impreciso, -sa *adj* : vague, imprecise — **imprecisión** *nf*, *pl* **-siones** 1 : vagueness 2 ERROR : inaccuracy

impredecible *adj* : unpredictable

impregnar *vt* : impregnate

imprenta *nf* 1 : printing 2 : printing shop, press

imprescindible *adj* : essential, indispensable

impresión *nf*, *pl* **-siones** 1 : impression 2 IMPRENTA : printing — **impresionable** *adj* : impressionable — **impresionante** *adj* : impressive — **impresionar** *vt* 1 : impress 2 CONMOVER : affect, move — *vi* : make an impression — **impresionarse** *vr* 1 : be impressed 2 CONMOVERSE : be affected

impreso, -sa *adj* : printed — **impreso** *nm* 1 FORMULARIO : form 2 **~s** *nmpl* : printed matter — **impresor, -sora** *n* : printer — **impresora** *nf* : (computer) printer

imprevisible *adj* : unforeseeable — **imprevisto, -ta** *adj* : unexpected, unforeseen

imprimir {42} *vt* 1 : print 2 DAR : impart, give

improbable *adj* : improbable — **improbabilidad** *nf* : improbability

improcedente *adj* : inappropriate

improductivo, -va *adj* : unproductive

improperio *nm* : insult

impropio, -pia *adj* 1 : inappropriate 2 INCORRECTO : incorrect

improvisar *v* : improvise — **improvisado, -da** *adj* : improvised, impromptu — **improvisación** *nf*, *pl* **-ciones** : improvisation — **improviso: de ~** *adv phr* : suddenly

imprudente *adj* : imprudent, rash —

imprudencia *nf* : imprudence, carelessness

impúdico, -ca *adj* : shameless, indecent

impuesto *nm* 1 : tax 2 **~ sobre la renta** : income tax

impugnar *vt* : challenge, contest

impulsar *vt* : propel, drive — **impulsividad** *nf* : impulsiveness — **impulsivo, -va** *adj* : impulsive — **impulso** *nm* 1 : drive, thrust 2 MOTIVACIÓN : impulse

impune *adj* : unpunished — **impunidad** *nf* : impunity

impuro, -ra *adj* : impure — **impureza** *nf* : impurity

imputar *vt* : impute, attribute

inacabable *adj* : interminable, endless

inaccesible *adj* : inaccessible

inaceptable *adj* : unacceptable

inactivo, -va *adj* : inactive — **inactividad** *nf* : inactivity

inadaptado, -da *adj* : maladjusted — **~** *n* : misfit

inadecuado, -da *adj* 1 : inadequate 2 INAPROPIADO : inappropriate

inadmisible *adj* : inadmissible

inadvertido, -da *adj* 1 : unnoticed 2 DISTRAÍDO : distracted — **inadvertencia** *nf* : oversight

inagotable *adj* : inexhaustible

inaguantable *adj* : unbearable

inalámbrico, -ca *adj* : wireless, cordless

inalcanzable *adj* : unreachable, unattainable

inalterable *adj* 1 : unchangeable 2 : impassive (of character) 3 : fast (of colors)

inanición *nf*, *pl* **-ciones** : starvation, famine

inanimado, -da *adj* : inanimate

inaplicable *adj* : inapplicable

inapreciable *adj* : imperceptible

inapropiado, -da *adj* : inappropriate

inarticulado, -da *adj* : inarticulate

inasequible *adj* : unattainable

inaudito, -ta *adj* : unheard-of, unprecedented

inaugurar *vt* : inaugurate — **inauguración** *nf*, *pl* **-ciones** : inauguration — **inaugural** *adj* : inaugural

inca *adj* : Inca, Incan

incalculable *adj* : incalculable

incandescencia *nf* : incandescence — **incandescente** *adj* : incandescent

incansable *adj* : tireless

incapacitar *vt* : incapacitate, disable — **incapacidad** *nf* : incapacity, inability — **incapaz** *adj*, *pl* **-paces** : incapable

incautar *vt* : confiscate, seize

incendiar *vt* : set fire to, burn (down) — **incendiarse** *vr* : catch fire — **incendiario, -ria** *adj* : incendiary — ~ *n* : arsonist — **incendio** *nm* 1 : fire 2 ~ **premeditado** : arson

incentivo *nm* : incentive

incertidumbre *nf* : uncertainty

incesante *adj* : incessant

incesto *nm* : incest — **incestuoso, -sa** *adj* : incestuous

incidencia *nf* 1 : impact 2 SUCESO : incident — **incidental** *adj* : incidental — **incidente** *nm* : incident

incidir *vi* ~ **en** 1 : fall into (a habit, mistake, etc.) 2 INFLUIR EN : affect, influence

incienso *nm* : incense

incierto, -ta *adj* : uncertain

incinerar *vt* 1 : incinerate 2 : cremate (a corpse) — **incineración** *nf, pl* **-ciones** 1 : incineration 2 : cremation (of a corpse) — **incinerador** *nm* : incinerator

incipiente *adj* : incipient

incisión *nf, pl* **-siones** : incision

incisivo, -va *adj* : incisive — **incisivo** *nm* : incisor

incitar *vt* : incite, rouse

incivilizado, -da *adj* : uncivilized

inclinar *vt* : tilt, lean — **inclinarse** *vr* 1 : lean (over) 2 ~ **a** : be inclined to — **inclinación** *nf, pl* **-ciones** 1 : inclination 2 LADEAR : incline, tilt

incluir {41} *vt* 1 : include 2 ADJUNTAR : enclose — **inclusión** *nf, pl* **-siones** : inclusion — **inclusive** *adv* : up to and including — **inclusivo, -va** *adj* : inclusive — **incluso** *adv* : even, in fact — **incluso, -sa** *adj* : enclosed

incógnito, -ta *adj* 1 : unknown 2 **de** ~ : incognito

incoherente *adj* : incoherent — **incoherencia** *nf* : incoherence

incoloro, -ra *adj* : colorless

incombustible *adj* : fireproof

incomible *adj* : inedible

incomodar *vt* 1 : inconvenience 2 ENFADAR : bother, annoy — **incomodarse** *vr* 1 : take the trouble 2 ENFADARSE : get annoyed — **incomodidad** *nf* : discomfort — **incómodo, -da** *adj* 1 : uncomfortable 2 INCONVENIENTE : inconvenient, awkward

incomparable *adj* : incomparable

incompatible *adj* : incompatible — **incompatibilidad** *nf* : incompatibility

incompetente *adj* : incompetent — **incompetencia** *nf* : incompetence

incompleto, -ta *adj* : incomplete

incomprendido, -da *adj* : misunderstood — **incomprensible** *adj* : incomprehensible — **incomprensión** *nf, pl* **-siones** : lack of understanding

incomunicado, -da *adj* 1 : isolated 2 : in solitary confinement

inconcebible *adj* : inconceivable

inconcluso, -sa *adj* : unfinished

incondicional *adj* : unconditional

inconformista *adj & nmf* : nonconformist

inconfundible *adj* : unmistakable

incongruente *adj* : incongruous

inconmensurable *adj* : vast, immeasurable

inconsciente *adj* 1 : unconscious, unaware 2 IRREFLEXIVO : reckless — ~ *nm* **el** ~ : the unconscious — **inconsciencia** *nf* 1 : unconsciousness 2 INSENSATEZ : thoughtlessness

inconsecuente *adj* : inconsistent — **inconsecuencia** *nf* : inconsistency

inconsiderado, -da *adj* : inconsiderate

inconsistente *adj* 1 : flimsy 2 : watery (of a sauce, etc.) 3 : inconsistent (of an argument) — **inconsistencia** *nf* : inconsistency

inconsolable *adj* : inconsolable

inconstante *adj* : changeable, unreliable — **inconstancia** *nf* : inconstancy

inconstitucional *adj* : unconstitutional

incontable *adj* : countless

incontenible *adj* : irrepressible

incontestable *adj* : indisputable

incontinente *adj* : incontinent — **incontinencia** *nf* : incontinence

inconveniente *adj* 1 : inconvenient 2 INAPROPIADO : inappropriate — ~ *nm* : obstacle, problem — **inconveniencia** *nf* 1 : inconvenience 2 : tactless remark

incorporar *vt* 1 AGREGAR : incorporate, add 2 : mix (in cooking) — **incorporarse** *vr* 1 : sit up 2 ~ **a** : join — **incorporación** *nf, pl* **-ciones** : incorporation

incorrecto, -ta *adj* 1 : incorrect 2 DESCORTÉS : impolite

incorregible *adj* : incorrigible

incrédulo, -la *adj* : incredulous — **incredulidad** *nf* : incredulity, disbelief

increíble *adj* : incredible, unbelievable

incrementar *vt* : increase — **incremento** *nm* : increase

incriminar *vt* 1 : incriminate 2 ACUSAR : accuse

incrustar *vt* : set, inlay — **incrustarse** *vr* : become embedded

incubar *vt* : incubate — **incubadora** *nf* : incubator

incuestionable *adj* : unquestionable
inculcar {72} *vt* : instill
inculpar *vt* : accuse, charge
inculto, -ta *adj* 1 : uneducated 2 : uncultivated (of land)
incumplimiento *nm* 1 : noncompliance
2 ~ **de contrato** : breach of contract
incurable *adj* : incurable
incurrir *vi* ~ **en** 1 : incur (expenses,
etc.) 2 : fall into, commit (crimes)
incursión *nf, pl* **-siones** : raid
indagar {52} *vt* : investigate — **inda-
gación** *nf, pl* **-ciones** : investigation
indebido, -da *adj* : undue
indecente *adj* : indecent, obscene —
indecencia *nf* : indecency, obscenity
indecible *adj* : inexpressible
indecisión *nf, pl* **-siones** : indecision
— **indeciso, -sa** *adj* 1 : undecided 2
IRRESOLUTO : indecisive
indefenso, -sa *adj* : defenseless, helpless
indefinido, -da *adj* : indefinite — **indefinidamente** *adv* : indefinitely
indeleble *adj* : indelible
indemnizar {21} *vt* : indemnify, compensate — **indemnización** *nf, pl*
-ciones : compensation
independiente *adj* : independent — **independencia** *nf*: independence — **in-
dependizarse** {21} *vr* : become independent
indescifrable *adj* : indecipherable
indescriptible *adj* : indescribable
indeseable *adj* : undesirable
indestructible *adj* : indestructible
indeterminado, -da *adj* : indeterminate
indicar {72} *vt* 1 : indicate 2 MOSTRAR
: show — **indicación** *nf, pl* **-ciones** 1
: sign, indication 2 **indicaciones** *nfpl*
: directions — **indicador** *nm* 1 : sign,
signal 2 : gauge, dial, meter — **indicativo, -va** *adj* : indicative — **indicativo**
nm : indicative (mood)
índice *nm* 1 : indication 2 : index (of a
book, etc.) 3 : index finger 4 ~ **de
natalidad** : birth rate
indicio *nm* : indication, sign
indiferente *adj* 1 : indifferent 2 **me es**
~ : it doesn't matter to me — **indiferencia** *nf* : indifference
indígena *adj* : indigenous, native — ~
nmf : native
indigente *adj & nmf* : indigent — **indi-
gencia** *nf* : poverty
indigestión *nf, pl* **-tiones** : indigestion
— **indigesto, -ta** *adj* : indigestible
indignar *vt* : outrage, infuriate — **indig-
narse** *vr* : become indignant — **indignación** *nf, pl* **-ciones** : indignation

— **indignado, -da** *adj* : indignant —
indignidad *nf* : indignity — **indigno,
-na** *adj* : unworthy
indio, -dia *adj* 1 : American Indian 2
: Indian (from India)
indirecta *nf* 1 : hint 2 **lanzar una** ~
: drop a hint — **indirecto, -ta** *adj* : indirect
indisciplina *nf* : lack of discipline —
indisciplinado, -da *adj* : undisci-
plined
indiscreto, -ta *adj* : indiscreet — **indiscreción** *nf, pl* **-ciones** 1 : indiscretion
2 : tactless remark
indiscriminado, -da *adj* : indiscriminate
indiscutible *adj* : indisputable
indispensable *adj* : indispensable
indisponer {60} *vt* 1 : upset, make ill 2
ENEMISTAR : set against, set at odds —
indisponerse *vr* 1 : become ill 2 ~
con : fall out with — **indisposición**
nf, pl **-ciones** : indisposition, illness
— **indispuesto, -ta** *adj* : unwell, in-
disposed
indistinto, -ta *adj* : indistinct
individual *adj* : individual — **individualidad** *nf* : individuality — **individu-
alizar** {21} *vt* : individualize — **individuo** *nm* : individual
indivisible *adj* : indivisible
índole *nf* 1 : nature, character 2 TIPO
: type, kind
indolente *adj* : indolent, lazy — **indo-
lencia** *nf* : indolence, laziness
indoloro, -ra *adj* : painless
indómito, -ta *adj* : indomitable
indonesio, -sia *adj* : Indonesian
inducir {61} *vt* 1 : induce 2 DEDUCIR
: infer
indudable *adj* : beyond doubt — **in-
dudablemente** *adv* : undoubtedly
indulgente *adj* : indulgent — **indulgencia** *nf* : indulgence
indultar *vt* : pardon, reprieve — **indulto**
nm : pardon, reprieve
industria *nf* : industry — **industrial** *adj*
: industrial — ~ *nmf* : industrialist,
manufacturer — **industrialización** *nf,
pl* **-ciones** : industrialization — **industrializar** {21} *vt* : industrialize —
industrioso, -sa *adj* : industrious
inédito, -ta *adj* : unpublished
inefable *adj* : inexpressible
ineficaz *adj, pl* **-caces** 1 : ineffective 2
INEFICIENTE : inefficient
ineficiente *adj* : inefficient — **ineficiencia** *nf* : inefficiency
inelegible *adj* : ineligible

ineludible *adj* : unavoidable, inescapable

inepto, -ta *adj* : inept — **ineptitud** *nf* : ineptitude

inequívoco, -ca *adj* : unequivocal

inercia *nf* : inertia

inerme *adj* : unarmed, defenseless

inerte *adj* : inert

inesperado, -da *adj* : unexpected

inestable *adj* : unstable — **inestabilidad** *nf* : instability

inevitable *adj* : inevitable

inexacto, -ta *adj* 1 : inexact 2 INCORRECTO : incorrect, wrong

inexistente *adj* : nonexistent

inexorable *adj* : inexorable

inexperiencia *nf* : inexperience — **inexperto, -ta** *adj* : inexperienced, unskilled

inexplicable *adj* : inexplicable

infalible *adj* : infallible

infame *adj* 1 : infamous, vile 2 *fam* : horrible — **infamia** *nf* : infamy, disgrace

infancia *nf* : infancy — **infanta** *nf* : infanta, princess — **infante** *nm* 1 : infante, prince 2 : infantryman (in the military) — **infantería** *nf* : infantry — **infantil** *adj* 1 : child's, children's 2 INMADURO : childish

infarto *nm* : heart attack

infatigable *adj* : tireless

infectar *vt* : infect — **infectarse** *vr* : become infected — **infección** *nf, pl* -ciones : infection — **infeccioso, -sa** *adj* : infectious — **infecto, -ta** *adj* 1 : infected 2 : foul, sickening

infecundo, -da *adj* : infertile

infeliz *adj, pl* -lices : unhappy — **infelicidad** *nf* : unhappiness

inferior *adj & nmf* : inferior — **inferioridad** *nf* : inferiority

inferir {76} *vt* 1 DEDUCIR : infer 2 : cause (harm or injury)

infernal *adj* : infernal, hellish

infestar *vt* : infest

infiel *adj* : unfaithful — **infidelidad** *nf* : infidelity

infierno *nm* 1 : hell 2 **el quinto ~** *fam* : the middle of nowhere

infiltrar *vt* : infiltrate — **infiltrarse** *vr* : infiltrate

infinidad *nf* 1 : infinity 2 **una ~ de** : countless — **infinitivo** *nm* : infinitive — **infinito, -ta** *adj* : infinite — **infinito** *nm* : infinity

inflación *nf, pl* -ciones : inflation — **inflacionario, -ria** *or* **inflacionista** *adj* : inflationary

inflamar *vt* : inflame — **inflamable** *adj* : flammable, inflammable — **inflamación** *nf, pl* -ciones : inflammation — **inflamatorio, -ria** *adj* : inflammatory

inflar *vt* 1 : inflate 2 EXAGERAR : exaggerate — **inflarse** *vr* **~ de** : swell (up) with

inflexible *adj* : inflexible — **inflexión** *nf, pl* -xiones : inflection

infligir {35} *vt* : inflict

influencia *nf* : influence — **influenciar** → **influir**

influenza *nf* : influenza

influir {41} *vt* : influence — *vi* **~ en** *or* **~ sobre** : have an influence on — **influjo** *nm* : influence — **influyente** *adj* : influential

información *nf, pl* -ciones 1 : information 2 NOTICIAS : news 3 : directory assistance (on the telephone)

informal *adj* 1 : informal 2 IRRESPONSABLE : unreliable

informar *v* : inform — **informarse** *vr* : get information, find out — **informante** *nmf* : informant — **informática** *nf* : information technology — **informativo, -va** *adj* : informative — **informatizar** {21} *vt* : computerize

informe *adj* 1 : shapeless — **~ nm** 1 : report 2 **~s** *nmpl* : information, data 3 **~s** *nmpl* : references (for employment)

infortunado, -da *adj* : unfortunate — **infortunio** *nm* : misfortune

infracción *nf, pl* -ciones : violation, infraction

infraestructura *nf* : infrastructure

infrahumano, -na *adj* : subhuman

infranqueable *adj* 1 : impassable 2 INSUPERABLE : insurmountable

infrarrojo, -ja *adj* : infrared

infrecuente *adj* : infrequent

infringir {35} *vt* : infringe

infructuoso, -sa *adj* : fruitless

infundado, -da *adj* : unfounded, baseless

infundir *vt* : instill, infuse — **infusión** *nf, pl* -siones : infusion

ingeniar *vt* : invent, think up

ingeniería *nf* : engineering — **ingeniero, -ra** *n* : engineer

ingenio *nm* 1 : ingenuity 2 AGUDEZA : wit 3 MÁQUINA : device, apparatus 4 **~ azucarero** *Lat* : sugar refinery — **ingenioso, -sa** *adj* 1 : ingenious 2 AGUDO : clever, witty — **ingeniosamente** *adv* : cleverly

ingenuidad *nf* : naïveté, ingenuousness — **ingenuo, -nua** *adj* : naive

ingerir {76} *vt* : ingest, consume

ingle *nf* : groin

inglés, -glesa *adj, mpl* **-gleses** : English — **inglés** *nm* : English (language)

ingrato, -ta *adj* **1** : ungrateful **2 un trabajo ingrato** : a thankless task — **ingratitud** *nf* : ingratitude

ingrediente *nm* : ingredient

ingresar *vt* : deposit — *vi* ~ **en** : enter, be admitted into, join — **ingreso** *nm* **1** : entrance, entry **2** : admission (into a hospital, etc.) **3** ~**s** *nmpl* : income, earnings

inhábil *adj* **1** : unskillful, clumsy **2** ~ **para** : unsuited for — **inhabilidad** *nf* : unskillfulness

inhabitable *adj* : uninhabitable — **inhabitado, -da** *adj* : uninhabited

inhalar *vt* : inhale — **inhalación** *nf* : inhalation

inherente *adj* : inherent

inhibir *vt* : inhibit — **inhibición** *nf, pl* **-ciones** : inhibition

inhóspito, -ta *adj* : inhospitable

inhumano, -na *adj* : inhuman, inhumane — **inhumanidad** *nf* : inhumanity

iniciar *vt* : initiate, begin — **iniciación** *nf, pl* **-ciones 1** : initiation **2** COMIENZO : beginning — **inicial** *adj & nf* : initial — **iniciativa** *nf* : initiative — **inicio** *nm* : start, beginning

inigualado, -da *adj* : unequaled

ininterrumpido, -da *adj* : uninterrupted

injerirse {76} *vr* : interfere — **injerencia** *nf* : interference

injertar *vt* : graft — **injerto** *nm* : graft

injuriar *vt* : insult — **injuria** *nf* : insult — **injurioso, -sa** *adj* : insulting, abusive

injusticia *nf* : injustice, unfairness — **injusto, -ta** *adj* : unfair, unjust

inmaculado, -da *adj* : immaculate

inmaduro, -ra *adj* **1** : immature **2** : unripe (of fruit) — **inmadurez** *nf* : immaturity

inmediaciones *nfpl* : surrounding area

inmediato, -ta *adj* **1** : immediate **2** CONTIGUO : adjoining **3 de** ~ : immediately, right away **4** ~ **a** : next to, close to — **inmediatamente** *adv* : immediately

inmejorable *adj* : excellent

inmenso, -sa *adj* : immense, vast — **inmensidad** *nf* : immensity

inmerecido, -da *adj* : undeserved

inmersión *nf, pl* **-siones** : immersion

inmigrar *vi* : immigrate — **inmigración** *nf, pl* **-ciones** : immigration — **inmigrante** *adj & nmf* : immigrant

inminente *adj* : imminent, impending — **inminencia** *nf* : imminence

inmiscuirse {41} *vr* : interfere

inmobiliario, -ria *adj* : real estate, property

inmodesto, -ta *adj* : immodest

inmoral *adj* : immoral — **inmoralidad** *nf* : immorality

inmortal *adj & nmf* : immortal — **inmortalidad** *nf* : immortality

inmóvil *adj* : motionless, still — **inmovilizar** {21} *vt* : immobilize

inmueble *nm* : building, property

inmundicia *nf* : filth, trash — **inmundo, -da** *adj* : dirty, filthy

inmunizar {21} *vt* : immunize — **inmune** *adj* : immune — **inmunidad** *nf* : immunity — **inmunización** *nf, pl* **-ciones** : immunization

inmutable *adj* : unchangeable

innato, -ta *adj* : innate

innecesario, -ria *adj* : unnecessary, needless

innegable *adj* : undeniable

innoble *adj* : ignoble

innovar *vt* : introduce — *vi* : innovate — **innovación** *nf, pl* **-ciones** : innovation — **innovador, -dora** *adj* : innovative — ~ *n* : innovator

innumerable *adj* : innumerable

inocencia *nf* : innocence — **inocente** *adj & nmf* : innocent — **inocentón, -tona** *adj, mpl* **-tones** : naive — ~ *n* : simpleton, dupe

inocular *vt* : inoculate — **inoculación** *nf, pl* **-ciones** : inoculation

inocuo, -cua *adj* : innocuous

inodoro, -ra *adj* : odorless — **inodoro** *nm* : toilet

inofensivo, -va *adj* : inoffensive, harmless

inolvidable *adj* : unforgettable

inoperable *adj* : inoperable

inoperante *adj* : ineffective

inopinado, -da *adj* : unexpected

inoportuno, -na *adj* : untimely, inopportune

inorgánico, -ca *adj* : inorganic

inoxidable *adj* **1** : rustproof **2 acero** ~ : stainless steel

inquebrantable *adj* : unwavering

inquietar *vt* : disturb, worry — **inquietarse** *vr* : worry — **inquietante** *adj* : disturbing, worrisome — **inquieto, -ta** *adj* : anxious, worried — **inquietud** *nf* : anxiety, worry

inquilino, -na *n* : tenant

inquirir {4} *vi* : make inquiries — *vt* : investigate

insaciable *adj* : insatiable

insalubre *adj* : unhealthy

insatisfecho, -cha *adj* **1** : unsatisfied **2** DESCONTENTO : dissatisfied

inscribir {33} *vt* **1** : enroll, register **2** GRABAR : inscribe, engrave — **inscribirse** *vr* : register — **inscripción** *nf, pl* **-ciones 1** : inscription **2** REGISTRO : registration

insecto *nm* : insect — **insecticida** *nm* : insecticide

inseguro, -ra *adj* **1** : insecure **2** PELIGROSO : unsafe **3** DUDOSO : uncertain — **inseguridad** *nf* **1** : insecurity **2** PELIGRO : lack of safety **3** DUDA : uncertainty

inseminar *vt* : inseminate — **inseminación** *nf, pl* **-ciones** : insemination

insensato, -ta *adj* : senseless, foolish — **insensatez** *nf* : foolishness, thoughtlessness

insensible *adj* **1** : insensitive, unfeeling **2** : numb (in medicine) **3** IMPERCEPTIBLE : imperceptible — **insensibilidad** *nf* : insensitivity

inseparable *adj* : inseparable

insertar *vt* : insert

insidia *nf* : snare, trap — **insidioso, -sa** *adj* : insidious

insigne *adj* : noted, famous

insignia *nf* **1** : insignia, badge **2** BANDERA : flag

insignificante *adj* : insignificant, negligible

insincero, -ra *adj* : insincere

insinuar {3} *vt* : insinuate — **insinuarse** *vr* **en** : worm one's way into — **insinuación** *nf, pl* **-ciones** : insinuation — **insinuante** *adj* : insinuating, suggestive

insípido, -da *adj* : insipid

insistir *v* : insist — **insistencia** *nf* : insistence — **insistente** *adj* : insistent

insociable *adj* : unsociable

insolación *nf, pl* **-ciones** : sunstroke

insolencia *nf* : insolence — **insolente** *adj* : insolent

insólito, -ta *adj* : rare, unusual

insoluble *adj* : insoluble

insolvencia *nf* : insolvency, bankruptcy — **insolvente** *adj* : insolvent, bankrupt

insomnio *nm* : insomnia — **insomne** *nmf* : insomniac

insondable *adj* : unfathomable

insonorizado, -da *adj* : soundproof

insoportable *adj* : unbearable

insospechado, -da *adj* : unexpected

insostenible *adj* : untenable

inspeccionar *vt* : inspect — **inspección** *nf, pl* **-ciones** : inspection — **inspector, -tora** *n* : inspector

inspirar *vt* : inspire — *vi* : inhale — **inspirarse** *vr* : be inspired — **inspiración** *nf, pl* **-ciones 1** : inspiration **2** RESPIRACIÓN : inhalation — **inspirador, -dora** *adj* : inspirational

instalar *vt* : install — **instalarse** *vr* : settle — **instalación** *nf, pl* **-ciones** : installation

instancia *nf* **1** : request **2 en última ~** : ultimately, as a last resort

instantáneo, -nea *adj* : instantaneous, instant — **instantánea** *nf* : snapshot — **instante** *nm* **1** : instant **2 a cada ~** : frequently, all the time **3 al ~** : immediately

instar *vt* : urge, press

instaurar *vt* : establish — **instauración** *nf, pl* **-ciones** : establishment

instigar {52} *vt* : incite, instigate — **instigador, -dora** *n* : instigator

instinto *nm* : instinct — **instintivo, -va** *adj* : instinctive

institución *nf, pl* **-ciones** : institution — **institucional** *adj* : institutional — **institucionalizar** {21} *vt* : institutionalize — **instituir** {41} *vt* : institute, establish — **instituto** *nm* : institute — **institutriz** *nf, pl* **-trices** : governess

instruir {41} *vt* : instruct — **instrucción** *nf, pl* **-ciones 1** : instruction **2 instrucciones** *nfpl* : instructions, directions — **instructivo, -va** *adj* : structive — **instructor, -tora** *n* : instructor

instrumento *nm* : instrument — **instrumental** *adj* : instrumental

insubordinarse *vr* : rebel — **insubordinado, -da** *adj* : insubordinate — **insubordinación** *nf, pl* **-ciones** : insubordination

insuficiente *adj* : insufficient, inadequate — **insuficiencia** *nf* **1** : insufficiency, inadequacy **2 ~ cardíaca** : heart failure

insufrible *adj* : insufferable

insular *adj* : insular, island

insulina *nf* : insulin

insulso, -sa *adj* **1** : insipid, bland **2** SOSO : dull

insultar *vt* : insult — **insultante** *adj* : insulting — **insulto** *nm* : insult

insuperable *adj* : insurmountable

insurgente *adj & nmf* : insurgent

insurrección *nf, pl* **-ciones** : insurrection, uprising

intachable *adj* : irreproachable

intacto, -ta *adj* : intact

intangible *adj* : intangible

integrar *vt* : integrate — **integrarse** *vr* : become integrated — **integración**

nf, pl **-ciones** : integration — **integral** *adj* 1 : integral 2 pan ~ : whole grain bread — **íntegro, -gra** *adj* 1 : honest, upright 2 ENTERO : whole, complete — **integridad** *nf* 1 RECTITUD : integrity 2 TOTALIDAD : wholeness

intelecto *nm* : intellect — **intelectual** *adj* & *nmf* : intellectual

inteligencia *nf* : intelligence — **inteligente** *adj* : intelligent — **inteligible** *adj* : intelligible

intemperie *nf* a la ~ : in the open air, outside

intempestivo, -va *adj* : untimely, inopportune

intención *nf, pl* **-ciones** : intention, intent — **intencionado, -da** *adj* 1 : intended 2 bien ~ : well-meaning 3 mal ~ : malicious — **intencional** *adj* : intentional

intensidad *nf* : intensity — **intensificar** {72} *vt* : intensify — **intensificarse** *vr* : intensify — **intensivo, -va** *adj* : intensive — **intenso, -sa** *adj* : intense

intentar *vt* : attempt, try — **intento** *nm* 1 : intention 2 TENTATIVA : attempt

interactuar {3} *vi* : interact — **interacción** *nf, pl* **-ciones** : interaction — **interactivo, -va** *adj* : interactive

intercalar *vt* : insert, intersperse

intercambio *nm* : exchange — **intercambiable** *adj* : interchangeable — **intercambiar** *vt* : exchange, trade

interceder *vi* : intercede

interceptar *vt* : intercept — **intercepción** *nf, pl* **-ciones** : interception

intercesión *nf, pl* **-siones** : intercession

interés *nm, pl* **-reses** : interest — **interesado, -da** *adj* 1 : interested 2 EGOISTA : selfish — **interesante** *adj* : interesting — **interesar** *vt* : interest — *vi* : be of interest — **interesarse** *vr* : take an interest

interfaz *nf, pl* **-faces** : interface

interferir {76} *vi* : interfere — *vt* : interfere with — **interferencia** *nf* : interference

interino, -na *adj* : temporary, interim — **interiormente** *adv* : inwardly

interior *adj* : interior, inner — ~ *nm* : interior, inside — **interiormente** *adv* : inwardly

interjección *nf, pl* **-ciones** : interjection

interlocutor, -tora *n* : speaker

intermediario, -ria *adj & n* : intermediary

intermedio, -dia *adj* : intermediate — **intermedio** *nm* : intermission

interminable *adj* : interminable, endless

intermisión *nf, pl* **-siones** : intermission, pause

intermitente *adj* : intermittent — ~ *nm* : blinker, turn signal

internacional *adj* : international

internar *vt* : commit, confine — **internarse** *vr* : penetrate — **internado** *nm* : boarding school — **interno, -na** *adj* : internal — ~ *n* 1 : boarder 2 : inmate (in a jail, etc.)

interponer {60} *vt* : interpose — **interponerse** *vr* : intervene

interpretar *vt* 1 : interpret 2 : play, perform (in theater, etc.) — **interpretación** *nf, pl* **-ciones** : interpretation — **intérprete** *nmf* TRADUCTOR : interpreter 2 : performer (of music)

interrogar {52} *vt* : interrogate, question — **interrogación** *nf, pl* **-ciones** 1 : interrogation 2 signo de ~ : question mark — **interrogativo, -va** *adj* : interrogative — **interrogatorio** *nm* : interrogation, questioning

interrumpir *v* : interrupt — **interrupción** *nf, pl* **-ciones** : interruption — **interruptor** *nm* : (electrical) switch

intersección *nf, pl* **-ciones** : intersection

intervalo *nm* : interval

intervenir {87} *vi* 1 : take part 2 MEDIAR : intervene — *vt* 1 : tap (a telephone) 2 INSPECCIONAR : audit 3 OPERAR : operate on — **intervención** *nf, pl* **-ciones** 1 : intervention 2 : audit (in business) 3 or ~ quirúrgica : operation — **interventor, -tora** *n* : inspector, auditor

intestino *nm* : intestine — **intestinal** *adj* : intestinal

intimar *vi* ~ con : become friendly with — **intimidad** *nf* 1 : private life 2 AMISTAD : intimacy

intimidar *vt* : intimidate

íntimo, -ma *adj* 1 : intimate, close 2 PRIVADO : private

intolerable *adj* : intolerable — **intolerancia** *nf* : intolerance — **intolerante** *adj* : intolerant

intoxicar {72} *vt* : poison — **intoxicación** *nf, pl* **-ciones** : poisoning

intranquilizar {21} *vt* : make uneasy — **intranquilizarse** *vr* : be anxious — **intranquilidad** *nf* : uneasiness, anxiety — **intranquilo, -la** *adj* : uneasy, worried

intransigente *adj* : unyielding, intransigent

intransitable *adj* : impassable

intransitivo, -va *adj* : intransitive
intrascendente *adj* : unimportant, insignificant
intravenoso, -sa *adj* : intravenous
intrépido, -da *adj* : intrepid, fearless
intrigar {52} *v* : intrigue — **intriga** *nf* : intrigue — **intrigante** *adj* : intriguing
intrincado, -da *adj* : intricate, involved
intrínseco, -ca *adj* : intrinsic — **intrínsecament** *adv* : intrinsically, inherently
introducción *nf, pl* **-ciones** : introduction — **introducir** {61} *vt* 1 : introduce 2 METER : insert — **introducirse** *vr* ~ **en** : penetrate, get into — **introductorio, -ria** *adj* : introductory
intromisión *nf, pl* **-siones** : interference
introvertido, -da *adj* : introverted — ~ *n* : introvert
intrusión *nf, pl* **-siones** : intrusion — **intruso, -sa** *adj* : intrusive — ~ *n* : intruder
intuir {41} *vt* : sense — **intuición** *nf, pl* **-ciones** : intuition — **intuitivo, -va** *adj* : intuitive
inundar *vt* : flood — **inundarse** *vr* ~ **de** : be inundated with — **inundación** *nf, pl* **-ciones** : flood
inusitado, -da *adj* : unusual, uncommon
inútil *adj* 1 : useless 2 INVÁLIDO : disabled — **inutilidad** *nf* : uselessness — **inutilizar** {21} *vt* 1 : make useless 2 INCAPACITAR : disable
invadir *vt* : invade
invalidez *nf, pl* **-deces** 1 : invalidity 2 : disability (in medicine) — **inválido, -da** *adj & n* : invalid
invalorable *adj Lat* : invaluable
invariable *adj* : invariable
invasión *nf, pl* **-siones** : invasion — **invasor, -sora** *adj* : invading — ~ *n* : invader
invencible *adj* : invincible
inventar *vt* 1 : invent 2 : fabricate, make up (a word, an excuse, etc.) — **invención** *nf, pl* **-ciones** 1 : invention 2 MENTIRA : lie, fabrication
inventario *nm* : inventory
inventiva *nf* : inventiveness — **inventivo, -va** *adj* : inventive — **inventor, -tora** *n* : inventor
invernadero *nm* : greenhouse
invernal *adj* : winter
inverosímil *adj* : unlikely
inversión *nf, pl* **-siones** 1 : inversion, reversal 2 : investment (of money, time, etc.)

inverso, -sa *adj* 1 : inverse 2 CONTRARIO : opposite 3 **a la inversa** : the other way around, inversely
inversor, -sora *n* : investor
invertebrado, -da *adj* : invertebrate — **invertebrado** *nm* : invertebrate
invertir {76} *vt* 1 : invert, reverse 2 : invest (money, time, etc.) — *vi* : make an investment
investidura *nf* : investiture
investigar {52} *vt* 1 : investigate 2 ESTUDIAR : research — *vi* ~ **sobre** : do research into — **investigación** *nf, pl* **-ciones** 1 : investigation 2 ESTUDIO : research — **investigador, -dora** *n* : investigator, researcher
investir {54} *vt* : invest
inveterado, -da *adj* : deep-seated, inveterate
invicto, -ta *adj* : undefeated
invierno *nm* : winter
invisible *adj* : invisible — **invisibilidad** *nf* : invisibility
invitar *vt* : invite — **invitación** *nf, pl* **-ciones** : invitation — **invitado, -da** *n* : guest
invocar {72} *vt* : invoke — **invocación** *nf, pl* **-ciones** : invocation
involuntario, -ria *adj* : involuntary
invulnerable *adj* : invulnerable
inyectar *vt* : inject — **inyección** *nf, pl* **-ciones** : injection, shot — **inyectado, -da** *adj* **ojos inyectados** : bloodshot eyes
ion *nm* : ion — **ionizar** {21} *vt* : ionize
ir {43} *vi* 1 : go 2 FUNCIONAR : work, function 3 CONVENIR : suit 4 **¿cómo te va?** : how are you? 5 ~ **con prisa** : be in a hurry 6 ~ **por** : follow, go along 7 **vamos** : let's go — *v aux* 1 ~ **a** : be going to, be about to 2 ~ **caminando** : take a walk 3 **vamos a ver** : we shall see — **irse** *vr* : go away, be gone
ira *nf* : rage, anger — **iracundo, -da** *adj* : irate, angry
iraní *adj* : Iranian
iraquí *adj* : Iraqi
iris *nms & pl* 1 : iris (of the eye) 2 **arco** ~ : rainbow
irlandés, -desa *adj, mpl* **-deses** : Irish
ironía *nf* : irony — **irónico, -ca** *adj* : ironic, ironical
irracional *adj* : irrational
irradiar *vt* : radiate, irradiate
irrazonable *adj* : unreasonable
irreal *adj* : unreal
irreconciliable *adj* : irreconcilable
irreconocible *adj* : unrecognizable
irrecuperable *adj* : irretrievable

irreductible *adj* : unyielding
irreemplazable *adj* : irreplaceable
irreflexivo, -va *adj* : rash, unthinking
irrefutable *adj* : irrefutable
irregular *adj* : irregular — **irregularidad** *nf* : irregularity
irrelevante *adj* : irrelevant
irreparable *adj* : irreparable
irreprimible *adj* : irrepressible
irreprochable *adj* : irreproachable
irresistible *adj* : irresistible
irresoluto, -ta *adj* : indecisive, irresolute
irrespetuoso, -sa *adj* : disrespectful
irresponsable *adj* : irresponsible — **irresponsabilidad** *nf* : irresponsibility
irreverente *adj* : irreverent
irreversible *adj* : irreversible
irrevocable *adj* : irrevocable
irrigar {52} *vt* : irrigate — **irrigación** *nf, pl* -**ciones** : irrigation

irrisorio, -ria *adj* : laughable, ridiculous
irritar *vt* : irritate — **irritarse** *vr* : get annoyed — **irritable** *adj* : irritable — **irritación** *nf, pl* -**ciones** : irritation — **irritante** *adj* : irritating
irrompible *adj* : unbreakable
irrumpir *vi* ~ **en** : burst into
isla *nf* : island
islámico, -ca *adj* : Islamic, Muslim
islandés, -desa *adj, mpl* -**deses** : Icelandic
isleño, -ña *n* : islander
israelí *adj* : Israeli
istmo *nm* : isthmus
italiano, -na *adj* : Italian — **italiano** *nm* : Italian (language)
itinerario *nm* : itinerary
izar {21} *vt* : hoist, raise
izquierda *nf* : left — **izquierdista** *adj & nmf* : leftist — **izquierdo, -da** *adj* : left

J

j *nf* : j, tenth letter of the Spanish alphabet
jabalí *nm, pl* -**líes** : wild boar
jabalina *nf* : javelin
jabón *nm, pl* -**bones** : soap — **jabonar** *vt* : soap (up) — **jabonera** *nf* : soap dish — **jabonoso, -sa** *adj* : soapy
jaca *nf* : pony
jacinto *nm* : hyacinth
jactarse *vr* : boast, brag — **jactancia** *nf* : boastfulness, bragging — **jactancioso, -sa** *adj* : boastful
jadear *vi* : pant, gasp — **jadeante** *adj* : panting, breathless — **jadeo** *nm* : gasp, panting
jaez *nm, pl* **jaeces** 1 : harness 2 **jaeces** *nmpl* : trappings
jaguar *nm* : jaguar
jaiba *nf Lat* : crab
jalapeño *nm Lat* : jalapeño pepper
jalar *v Lat* : pull, tug
jalea *nf* : jelly
jaleo *nm fam* 1 : uproar, racket 2 **armar un** ~ : raise a ruckus
jalón *nm, pl* -**lones** *Lat* : pull, tug
jamaicano, -na *or* **jamaiquino, -na** *adj* : Jamaican
jamás *adv* 1 : never 2 **para siempre** ~ : for ever and ever
jamelgo *nm* : nag (horse)
jamón *nm, pl* -**mones** 1 : ham 2 ~ **serrano** : cured ham
Januká *nmf* : Hanukkah

japonés, -nesa *adj, mpl* -**neses** : Japanese — **japonés** *nm* : Japanese (language)
jaque *nm* 1 : check (in chess) 2 ~ **mate** : checkmate
jaqueca *nf* : headache, migraine
jarabe *nm* : syrup
jardín *nm, pl* -**dines** 1 : garden 2 ~ **infantil** *or* ~ **de niños** *Lat* : kindergarten — **jardinería** *nf* : gardening — **jardinero, -ra** *n* : gardener
jarra *nf* : pitcher, jug — **jarro** *nm* : pitcher — **jarrón** *nm, pl* -**rrones** : vase
jaula *nf* : cage
jauría *nf* : pack of hounds
jazmín *nm, pl* -**mines** : jasmine
jazz ['jins, 'dʒas] *nm* : jazz
jeans ['jins, 'dʒins] *nmpl* : jeans
jefe, -fa *n* 1 : chief, leader 2 **PATRÓN** : boss 3 ~ **de cocina** : chef — **jefatura** *nf* 1 : leadership 2 **SEDE** : headquarters
jengibre *nm* : ginger
jeque *nm* : sheikh, sheik
jerarquía *nf* 1 : hierarchy 2 **RANGO** : rank — **jerárquico, -ca** *adj* : hierarchical
jerez *nm, pl* -**reces** : sherry
jerga *nf* 1 : coarse cloth 2 **ARGOT** : jargon, slang
jerigonza *nf* 1 : jargon 2 **GALIMATÍAS** : gibberish

jeringa *or* **jeringuilla** *nf* : syringe — **jeringar** {52} *vt fam* : annoy, pester

jeroglífico *nm* : hieroglyphic

jersey *nm, pl* **-seys** : jersey

jesuita *adj & nm* : Jesuit

Jesús *nm* : Jesus

jilguero *nm* : goldfinch

jinete *nmf* : horseman, horsewoman *f,* rider

jirafa *nf* : giraffe

jirón *nm, pl* **-rones** : shred, tatter

jitomate *nm Lat* : tomato

jockey ['joki, 'dʒo-] *nmf, pl* **-keys** [-kis] : jockey

jocoso, -sa *adj* : humorous, jocular

jofaina *nf* : washbowl

jolgorio *nm* : merrymaking

jornada *nf* 1 : day's journey 2 : working day — **jornal** *nm* : day's pay — **jornalero, -ra** *n* : day laborer

joroba *nf* : hump — **jorobado, -da** *adj* : hunchbacked, humpbacked — ~ *n* : hunchback — **jorobar** *vt fam* : annoy

jota *nf* 1 : iota, jot 2 **no veo ni** ~ : I can't see a thing

joven *adj, pl* **jóvenes** : young — ~ *nmf* : young man *m,* young woman *f,* youth

jovial *adj* : jovial, cheerful

joya *nf* : jewel — **joyería** *nf* : jewelry store — **joyero, -ra** *n* : jeweler — **joyero** *nm* : jewelry box

juanete *nm* : bunion

jubilación *nf, pl* **-ciones** : retirement — **jubilado, -da** *adj* : retired — ~ *nmf* : retiree — **jubilar** *vt* : retire, pension off — **jubilarse** *vr* : retire — **jubileo** *nm* : jubilee

júbilo *nm* : joy, jubilation — **jubiloso, -sa** *adj* : joyous, jubilant

judaísmo *nm* : Judaism

judía *nf* 1 : bean 2 *or* ~ **verde** : green bean, string bean

judicial *adj* : judicial

judío, -día *adj* : Jewish — ~ *n* : Jew

judo ['juðo, 'dʒu-] *nm* : judo

juego *nm* 1 : game 2 : playing (of children, etc.) 3 *or* ~**s de azar** : gambling 4 CONJUNTO : set 5 **estar en** ~ : be at stake 6 **fuera de** ~ : offside (in sports) 7 **hacer** ~ : go together, match 8 ~ **de manos** : conjuring trick 9 **poner en** ~ : bring into play

juerga *nf fam* : spree, binge

jueves *nms & pl* : Thursday

juez *nmf, pl* **jueces** 1 : judge 2 ÁRBITRO : umpire, referee

jugar {44} *vi* 1 : play 2 : gamble (in a casino, etc.) 3 APOSTAR : bet 4 ~ **(al) tenis** : play tennis — *vt* : play — **jugarse** *vr* : risk, gamble (away) — **jugada** *nf* 1 : play, move 2 TRETA : (dirty) trick — **jugador, -dora** *n* 1 : player 2 : gambler

juglar *nm* : minstrel

jugo *nm* 1 : juice 2 SUSTANCIA : substance, essence — **jugoso, -sa** *adj* 1 : juicy 2 SUSTANCIAL : substantial, important

juguete *nm* : toy — **juguetear** *vi* : play — **juguetería** *nf* : toy store — **juguetón, -tona** *adj, mpl* **-tones** : playful

juicio *nm* 1 : judgment 2 RAZÓN : reason, sense 3 **a mi** ~ : in my opinion — **juicioso, -sa** *adj* : wise, sensible

julio *nm* : July

junco *nm* : reed, rush

jungla *nf* : jungle

junio *nm* : June

juntar *vt* 1 UNIR : join, unite 2 REUNIR : collect — **juntarse** *vr* 1 : join (together) 2 REUNIRSE : meet, get together — **junta** *nf* 1 : board, committee 2 REUNIÓN : meeting 3 : (political) junta 4 : joint, gasket — **junto, -ta** *adj* 1 : joined 2 PRÓXIMO : close, adjacent 3 (*used adverbially*) : together 4 ~ **a** : next to 5 ~ **con** : together with — **juntura** *nf* : joint

Júpiter *nm* : Jupiter

jurar *v* 1 : swear 2 ~ **en falso** : commit perjury — **jurado** *nm* 1 : jury 2 : juror, member of a jury — **juramento** *nm* : oath

jurídico, -ca *adj* : legal

jurisdicción *nf, pl* **-ciones** : jurisdiction

jurisprudencia *nf* : jurisprudence

justamente *adv* 1 : fairly, justly 2 PRECISAMENTE : precisely, exactly

justicia *nf* : justice, fairness

justificar {72} *vt* 1 : justify 2 DISCULPAR : excuse, vindicate — **justificación** *nf, pl* **-ciones** : justification

justo, -ta *adj* 1 : just, fair 2 EXACTO : exact 3 APRETADO : tight — **justo** *adv* 1 : just, exactly 2 ~ **a tiempo** : just in time

juvenil *adj* : youthful — **juventud** *nf* 1 : youth 2 JÓVENES : young people

juzgar {52} *vt* 1 : try (a case in court) 2 ESTIMAR : judge, consider 3 **a** ~ **por** : judging by — **juzgado** *nm* : court, tribunal

K

k *nf* : k, eleventh letter of the Spanish alphabet
kaki → **caqui**
karate *or* **kárate** *nm* : karate
kilo *nm* : kilo — **kilogramo** *nm* : kilogram

kilómetro *nm* : kilometer — **kilometraje** *nm* : distance in kilometers, mileage — **kilométrico, -ca** *adj fam* : endless
kilovatio *nm* : kilowatt
kiosco *nm* → **quiosco**

L

l *nf* : l, twelfth letter of the Spanish alphabet
la *pron* **1** : her, it **2** (*formal*) : you **3 ~ que** : the one who — **~** *art* → **el**
laberinto *nm* : labyrinth, maze
labia *nf fam* : gift of gab
labio *nm* : lip
labor *nf* **1** : work, labor **2** TAREA : task **3 ~es domésticas** : housework — **laborable** *adj* **día ~** : business day — **laborar** *vi* : work — **laboratorio** *nm* : laboratory, lab — **laborioso, -sa** *adj* : laborious
labrar *vt* **1** : cultivate, till **2** : work (metals), carve (stone, wood) **3** CAUSAR : cause, bring about — **labrado, -da** *adj* **1** : cultivated, tilled **2** : carved, wrought — **labrador, -dora** *n* : farmer — **labranza** *nf* : farming
laca *nf* **1** : lacquer **2** : hair spray
lacayo *nm* : lackey
lacerar *vt* : lacerate
lacio, -cia *adj* **1** : limp **2** : straight (of hair)
lacónico, -ca *adj* : laconic
lacra *nf* : scar
lacrar *vt* : seal — **lacre** *nm* : sealing wax
lacrimógeno, -na *adj* **gas lacrimógeno** : tear gas — **lacrimoso, -sa** *adj* : tearful
lácteo, -tea *adj* **1** : dairy **2 Vía Láctea** : Milky Way
ladear *vt* : tilt — **ladearse** *vr* : lean
ladera *nf* : slope, hillside
ladino, -na *adj* : crafty
lado *nm* **1** : side **2 al ~** : next door, nearby **3 al ~ de** : beside, next to **4 de ~** : sideways **5 por otro ~** : on the other hand **6 por todos ~s** : everywhere, all around
ladrar *vi* : bark — **ladrido** *nm* : bark
ladrillo *nm* : brick

ladrón, -drona *n, mpl* **-drones** : thief
lagarto *nm* : lizard — **lagartija** *nf* : (small) lizard
lago *nm* : lake
lágrima *nf* : tear
laguna *nf* **1** : lagoon **2** VACÍO : gap
laico, -ca *adj* : lay, secular — **~** *n* : layman *m*, layperson
lamentar *vt* **1** : regret, be sorry about **2 lo lamento** : I'm sorry — **lamentarse** *vr* : lament — **lamentable** *adj* **1** : deplorable **2** TRISTE : sad, pitiful — **lamento** *nm* : lament, moan
lamer *vt* **1** : lick **2** : lap (against) — **lamida** *nf* : lick
lámina *nf* **1** PLANCHA : sheet **2** DIBUJO : plate, illustration — **laminar** *vt* : laminate
lámpara *nf* : lamp
lampiño, -ña *adj* : beardless, hairless
lana *nf* **1** : wool **2 de ~** : woolen
lance *nm* **1** : event, incident **2** : throw (of dice, etc.) **3** RIÑA : quarrel
lanceta *nf* : lancet
lancha *nf* **1** : boat, launch **2 ~ motora** : motorboat
langosta *nf* **1** : lobster **2** : locust (insect) — **langostino** *nm* : prawn, crayfish
languidecer {53} *vi* : languish — **languidez** *nf, pl* **-deces** : languor — **lánguido, -da** *adj* : languid, listless
lanilla *nf* : nap (of fabric)
lanudo, -da *adj* : woolly
lanza *nf* : spear, lance
lanzar {21} *vt* **1** : throw **2** : shoot (a glance), give (a sigh, etc.) **3** : launch (a missile, a project) — **lanzarse** *vr* : throw oneself — **lanzamiento** *nm* : throwing, launching
lapicero *nm* : (mechanical) pencil
lápida *nf* : tombstone

lapidar vt : stone
lápiz nm, pl **-pices 1** : pencil **2 ～ de
labios** : lipstick
lapso nm : lapse (of time) — **lapsus**
nms & pl : lapse, slip (of the tongue)
largar {52} vt **1** AFLOJAR : loosen,
slacken **2** fam : give — **largarse** vr
fam : go away, beat it — **largo, -ga** adj
1 : long **2 a la larga** : in the long run **3
a lo largo** : lengthwise **4 a lo largo de**
: along — **largo** nm : length —
largometraje nm : feature film —
largueza nf : generosity
laringe nf : larynx — **laringitis** nfs & pl
: laryngitis
larva nf : larva
las → **el**
lascivo, -va adj : lascivious, lewd
láser nm : laser
lastimar vt : hurt — **lastimarse** vr : hurt
oneself — **lástima** nf **1** : pity **2 dar ～**
: be pitiful **3 me dan ～** : I feel sorry
for them **4 ¡qué ～!** : what a shame! —
lastimero, -ra adj : pitiful, wretched
— **lastimoso, -sa** adj : pitiful, terrible
lastre nm : ballast
lata nf **1** : tinplate **2** : (tin) can **3** fam
: nuisance, bore **4 dar (la) lata a** fam
: bother, annoy
latente adj : latent
lateral adj : side, lateral
latido nm **1** : beat, throb **2 ～ del
corazón** : heartbeat
latifundio nm : large estate
látigo nm : whip — **latigazo** nm : lash
latín nm : Latin (language)
latino, -na adj **1** : Latin **2** : Latin-American — **～** n : Latin American —
latinoamericano, -na adj : Latin-
American — **～** n : Latin American
latir vi : beat, throb
latitud nf : latitude
latón nm, pl **-tones** : brass
latoso, -sa adj fam : annoying
laúd nm : lute
laudable adj : laudable
laureado, -da adj : prize-winning
laurel nm **1** : laurel **2** : bay leaf (in
cooking)
lava nf : lava
lavar vt : wash — **lavarse** vr **1** : wash
oneself **2 ～ las manos** : wash one's
hands — **lavable** adj : washable —
lavabo nm **1** : sink **2** RETRETE : lavatory, toilet — **lavadero** nm : laundry
room — **lavado** nm : wash, washing
— **lavadora** nf : washing machine —
lavamanos nms & pl : washbowl —
lavandería nf : laundry (service) —
lavaplatos nms & pl **1** : dishwasher **2**

Lat : kitchen sink — **lavativa** nf
: enema — **lavatorio** nm : lavatory,
washroom — **lavavajillas** nms & pl
: dishwasher
laxante adj & nm : laxative — **laxo, -xa**
adj : loose
lazo nm **1** VÍNCULO : link, bond **2** LAZA-
DA : bow **3** : lasso, lariat — **lazada** nf
: bow, loop
le pron **1** : (to) her, (to) him, (to) it **2**
(formal) : (to) you **3** (as direct object)
: him, you
leal adj : loyal, faithful — **lealtad** nf
: loyalty, allegiance
lebrel nm : hound
lección nf, pl **-ciones 1** : lesson **2** : lecture (in a classroom)
leche nf **1** : milk **2 ～ descremada** or
～ desnatada : skim milk **3 ～ en
polvo** : powdered milk — **lechera** nf
: milk jug — **lechería** nf : dairy store
— **lechero, -ra** adj : dairy — **～** n
: milkman m, milk dealer
lecho nm : bed
lechón, -chona n, mpl **-chones** : suck-
ling pig
lechoso, -sa adj : milky
lechuga nf : lettuce
lechuza nf : owl
lector, -tora n : reader — **lectura** nf **1**
: reading **2** ESCRITOS : reading matter
leer {20} v : read
legación nf, pl **-ciones** : legation
legado nm **1** : legacy **2** ENVIADO
: legate, emissary
legajo nm : dossier, file
legal adj : legal — **legalidad** nf : legali-
ty — **legalizar** {21} vt : legalize — **le-
galización** nf, pl **-ciones** : legalization
legar {52} vt : bequeath
legendario, -ria adj : legendary
legible adj : legible
legión nf, pl **-giones** : legion — **legio-
nario, -ria** n : legionnaire
legislar vi : legislate — **legislación** nf,
pl **-ciones** : legislation — **legislador,
-dora** n : legislator — **legislatura** nf
: legislature
legítimo, -ma adj **1** : legitimate **2** GEN-
UINO : authentic — **legitimidad** nf : le-
gitimacy
lego, -ga adj **1** : secular, lay **2** IGNO-
RANTE : ignorant — **～** n : layman m,
layperson
legua nf : league
legumbre nf : vegetable
leído, -da adj : well-read
lejano, -na adj : distant, far away —
lejanía nf : distance
lejía nf : bleach

lejos *adv* 1 : far (away) 2 **a lo ~** : in the distance 3 **de ~** *or* **desde ~** : from afar 4 **~ de** : far from

lelo, -la *adj* : silly, stupid

lema *nm* : motto

lencería *nf* 1 : linen 2 : (women's) lingerie

lengua *nf* 1 : tongue 2 IDIOMA : language 3 **morderse la ~** : hold one's tongue

lenguado *nm* : sole, flounder

lenguaje *nm* : language

lengüeta *nf* 1 : tongue (of a shoe) 2 : reed (of a musical instrument)

lengüetada *nf* **beber a ~s** : lap (up)

lente *nmf* 1 : lens 2 **~s** *nmpl* : eyeglasses 3 **~s de contacto** : contact lenses

lenteja *nf* : lentil — **lentejuela** *nf* : sequin

lento, -ta *adj* : slow — **lento** *adv* : slowly — **lentitud** *nf* : slowness

leña *nf* : firewood — **leñador, -dora** *n* : lumberjack, woodcutter — **leño** *nm* : log

león, -ona *n, mpl* **leones** : lion, lioness *f*

leopardo *nm* : leopard

leotardo *nm* : leotard, tights *pl*

lepra *nf* : leprosy — **leproso, -sa** *n* : leper

lerdo, -da *adj* 1 TORPE : clumsy 2 TONTO : slow-witted

les *pron* 1 : (to) them, (to) you 2 (*as direct object*) : them, you

lesbiano, -na *adj* : lesbian — **lesbiana** *nf* : lesbian — **lesbianismo** *nm* : lesbianism

lesión *nf, pl* **-siones** : lesion, wound — **lesionado, -da** *adj* : injured, wounded — **lesionar** *vt* 1 : injure, wound 2 DAÑAR : damage

letal *adj* : lethal

letanía *nf* : litany

letárgico, -ca *adj* : lethargic — **letargo** *nm* : lethargy

letra *nf* 1 : letter 2 ESCRITURA : handwriting 3 : lyrics *pl* (of a song) 4 **~ de cambio** : bill of exchange 5 **~s** *nfpl* : arts — **letrado, -da** *adj* : learned — **letrero** *nm* : sign, notice

letrina *nf* : latrine

leucemia *nf* : leukemia

levadizo, -za *adj* **puente levadizo** : drawbridge

levadura *nf* 1 : yeast 2 **~ en polvo** : baking powder

levantar *vt* 1 : lift, raise 2 RECOGER : pick up 3 CONSTRUIR : erect, put up 4 ENCENDER : rouse, stir up 5 **~ la mesa** *Lat* : clear the table — **levan-**

tarse *vr* 1 : rise, stand up 2 : get out of bed 3 SUBLEVARSE : rise up — **levantamiento** *nm* 1 : raising, lifting 2 SUBLEVACIÓN : uprising

levante *nm* 1 : east 2 : east wind

levar *vt* **~ anclas** : weigh anchor

leve *adj* 1 : light, slight 2 : minor, trivial (of wounds, sins, etc.) — **levedad** *nf* : lightness — **levemente** *adv* : lightly, slightly

léxico *nm* : vocabulary, lexicon

ley *nf* 1 : law 2 **de (buena) ~** : genuine, pure (of metals)

leyenda *nf* 1 : legend 2 : caption (of an illustration, etc.)

liar {85} *vt* 1 : bind, tie (up) 2 : roll (a cigarette) 3 CONFUNDIR : confuse, muddle — **liarse** *vr* : get mixed up

libanés, -nesa *adj, mpl* **-neses** : Lebanese

libelo *nm* 1 : libel 2 : petition (in court)

libélula *nf* : dragonfly

liberación *nf, pl* **-ciones** : liberation, deliverance

liberal *adj & nmf* : liberal — **liberalidad** *nf* : generosity, liberality

liberar *vt* : liberate, free — **libertad** *nf* 1 : freedom, liberty 2 **~ bajo fianza** : bail 3 **~ condicional** : parole 4 **en ~** : free — **libertar** *vt* : set free

libertinaje *nm* : licentiousness — **libertino, -na** *n* : libertine

libido *nf* : libido

libio, -bia *adj* : Libyan

libra *nf* 1 : pound 2 **~ esterlina** : pound sterling

librar *vt* 1 : free, save 2 : wage, fight (a battle) 3 : draw, issue (a check, etc.) — **librarse** *vr* **~ de** : free oneself from, get rid of

libre *adj* 1 : free 2 : unoccupied (of space), spare (of time) 3 **al aire ~** : in the open air 4 **~ de impuestos** : tax-free

librea *nf* : livery

libro *nm* 1 : book 2 **~ de bolsillo** : paperback — **librería** *nf* : bookstore — **librero, -ra** *n* : bookseller — **librero** *nm Lat* : bookcase — **libreta** *nf* : notebook

licencia *nf* 1 : license, permit 2 PERMISO : permission 3 : (military) leave — **licenciado, -da** *n* 1 : graduate 2 *Lat* : lawyer — **licenciar** *vt* : dismiss, discharge — **licenciarse** *vr* : graduate — **licenciatura** *nf* : degree

licencioso, -sa *adj* : licentious

liceo *nm* : high school

licitar *vt* : bid for

lícito, -ta *adj* **1** : lawful, legal **2** JUSTO : just, fair

licor *nm* **1** : liquor **2** : liqueur — **licorera** *nf* : decanter

licuadora *nf* : blender — **licuado** *nm* : milk shake — **licuar** {3} *vt* : liquefy

lid *nf* **1** : fight **2** en buena ∼ : fair and square

líder *adj* : leading — ∼ *nmf* : leader — **liderato** *or* **liderazgo** *nm* : leadership

lidia *nf* : bullfight — **lidiar** *v* : fight

liebre *nf* : hare

lienzo *nm* **1** : cotton or linen cloth **2** : canvas (for a painting) **3** PARED : wall

liga *nf* **1** : league **2** *Lat* : rubber band **3** : garter (for stockings) — **ligadura** *nf* **1** ATADURA : tie, bond **2** : ligature (in medicine or music) — **ligamento** *nm* : ligament — **ligar** {52} *vt* : bind, tie (up)

ligero, -ra *adj* **1** : light, lightweight **2** LEVE : slight **3** ÁGIL : agile **4** FRÍVOLO : lighthearted, superficial — **ligeramente** *adv* : lightly, slightly — **ligereza** *nf* **1** : lightness **2** : flippancy (of character), thoughtlessness (of actions) **3** AGILIDAD : agility

lija *nf* : sandpaper — **lijar** *vt* : sand

lila *nf* : lilac

lima *nf* **1** : file **2** : lime (fruit) **3** ∼ para uñas : nail file — **limar** *vt* : file

limbo *nm* : limbo

limitar *vt* : limit — *vi* ∼ con : border on — **limitación** *nf, pl* -**ciones** : limitation, limit — **límite** *nm* **1** : limit **2** CONFÍN : boundary, border **3** ∼ de velocidad : speed limit **4** fecha ∼ : deadline — **limítrofe** *adj* : bordering

limo *nm* : slime, mud

limón *nm, pl* -**mones** **1** : lemon **2** ∼ verde *Lat* : lime — **limonada** *nf* : lemonade

limosna *nf* **1** : alms **2** pedir ∼ : beg — **limosnero, -ra** *n* : beggar

limpiabotas *nmfs & pl* : bootblack

limpiaparabrisas *nms & pl* : windshield wiper

limpiar *vt* **1** : clean, wipe (away) **2** ∼ en seco : dry-clean — **limpieza** *nf* **1** : cleanliness **2** : (act of) cleaning — **limpio** *adv* : cleanly, fairly — **limpio, -pia** *adj* **1** : clean, neat **2** HONRADO : honest **3** NETO : net, clear

limusina *nf* : limousine

linaje *nm* : lineage, ancestry

linaza *nf* : linseed

lince *nm* : lynx

linchar *vt* : lynch

lindar *vi* ∼ con : border on — **lindante** *adj* : bordering — **linde** *nmf or* **lindero** *nm* : boundary

lindo, -da *adj* **1** : pretty, lovely **2** de lo lindo *fam* : a lot

línea *nf* **1** : line **2** ∼ de conducta : course of action **3** en ∼ : on-line **4** guardar la ∼ : watch one's figure — **lineal** *adj* : linear

lingote *nm* : ingot

lingüista *nmf* : linguist — **lingüística** *nf* : linguistics — **lingüístico, -ca** *adj* : linguistic

linimento *nm* : liniment

lino *nm* **1** : flax (plant) **2** : linen (fabric)

linóleo *nm* : linoleum

linterna *nf* **1** FAROL : lantern **2** : flashlight

lío *nm* **1** : bundle **2** *fam* : mess, trouble **3** *fam* : (love) affair

liofilizar {21} *vt* : freeze-dry

liquen *nm* : lichen

liquidar *vt* **1** : liquefy **2** : liquidate (merchandise, etc.) **3** : settle, pay off (a debt, etc.) — **liquidación** *nf, pl* -**ciones** **1** : liquidation **2** REBAJA : clearance sale — **líquido, -da** *adj* **1** : liquid **2** NETO : net — **líquido** *nm* : liquid

lira *nf* : lyre

lírico, -ca *adj* : lyric, lyrical — **lírica** *nf* : lyric poetry

lirio *nm* : iris

lisiado, -da *adj* : disabled — ∼ *n* : disabled person — **lisiar** *vt* : disable, cripple

liso, -sa *adj* **1** : smooth **2** PLANO : flat **3** SENCILLO : plain **4** pelo ∼ : straight hair

lisonjear *vt* : flatter — **lisonja** *nf* : flattery

lista *nf* **1** : stripe **2** ENUMERACIÓN : list **3** : menu (in a restaurant) — **listado, -da** *adj* : striped

listo, -ta *adj* **1** : clever, smart **2** PREPARADO : ready

listón *nm, pl* -**tones** **1** : ribbon **2** : strip (of wood)

lisura *nf* : smoothness

litera *nf* : bunk bed, berth

literal *adj* : literal

literatura *nf* : literature — **literario, -ria** *adj* : literary

litigar {52} *vi* : litigate — **litigio** *nm* **1** : litigation **2** en ∼ : in dispute

litografía *nf* **1** : lithography **2** : lithograph (picture)

litoral *adj* : coastal — ∼ *nm* : shore, seaboard

litro *nm* : liter

liturgia *nf* : liturgy — **litúrgico, -ca** *adj* : liturgical

liviano, -na *adj* **1** LIGERO : light **2** INCONSTANTE : fickle

lívido, -da *adj* : livid

llaga *nf* : sore, wound

llama *nf* **1** : flame **2** : llama (animal)

llamar *vt* **1** : call **2** : call up (on the telephone) — *vi* **1** : phone, call **2** : knock, ring (at the door) — **llamarse** *vr* **1** : be called **2** ¿**cómo te llamas?** : what's your name? — **llamada** *nf* : call — **llamado, -da** *adj* : named, called — **llamamiento** *nm* : call, appeal

llamarada *nf* **1** : blaze **2** : flushing (of the face)

llamativo, -va *adj* : flashy, showy

llamear *vi* : flame, blaze

llano, -na *adj* **1** : flat **2** : straightforward (of a person, a message, etc.) **3** SENCILLO : plain, simple — **llano** *nm* : plain — **llaneza** *nf* : simplicity

llanta *nf* **1** : rim (of a wheel) **2** *Lat* : tire

llanto *nm* : crying, weeping

llanura *nf* : plain

llave *nf* **1** : key **2** *Lat* : faucet **3** INTERRUPTOR : switch **4** **cerrar con ~** : lock **5** **~ inglesa** : monkey wrench — **llavero** *nm* : key chain

llegar {52} *vi* **1** : arrive, come **2** ALCANZAR : reach **3** BASTAR : be enough **4** **~ a** : manage to **5** **~ a ser** : become — **llegada** *nf* : arrival

llenar *vt* **1** : fill (up), fill in — **lleno, -na** *adj* **1** : full **2** **de lleno** : completely — **lleno** *nm* : full house

llevar *vt* **1** : take, carry **2** CONDUCIR : lead **3** : wear (clothing, etc.) **4** TENER : have **5** **llevo una hora aquí** : I've been here for an hour — **llevarse** *vr* **1** : take (away) **2** **~ bien** : get along well — **llevadero, -ra** *adj* : bearable

llorar *vi* : cry, weep — **lloriquear** *vi* : whimper, whine — **lloro** *nm* : crying — **llorón, -rona** *n, mpl* **-rones** : crybaby, whiner — **lloroso, -sa** *adj* : tearful

llover {47} *v impers* : rain — **llovizna** *nf* : drizzle — **lloviznar** *v impers* : drizzle

lluvia *nf* : rain — **lluvioso, -sa** *adj* : rainy

lo *pron* **1** : him, it **2** (*formal, masculine*) : you **3** **~ que** : what, that which — **~** *art* **1** : the **2** **~ mejor** : the best (part) **3** **sé ~ bueno que eres** : I know how good you are

loa *nf* : praise — **loable** *adj* : praiseworthy — **loar** *vt* : praise

lobo, -ba *n* : wolf

lóbrego, -ga *adj* : gloomy

lóbulo *nm* : lobe

local *adj* : local — **~** *nm* : premises *pl* — **localidad** *nf* : town, locality — **localizar** {21} *vt* **1** : localize **2** ENCONTRAR : locate — **localizarse** *vr* : be located

loción *nf, pl* **-ciones** : lotion

loco, -ca *adj* **1** : crazy, insane **2** **a lo loco** : wildly, recklessly **3** **volverse ~** : go mad — **~** *n* **1** : crazy person, lunatic **2** **hacerse el loco** : act the fool

locomoción *nf, pl* **-ciones** : locomotion — **locomotora** *nf* : engine, locomotive

locuaz *adj, pl* **-cuaces** : talkative, loquacious

locución *nf, pl* **-ciones** : expression, phrase

locura *nf* **1** : insanity, madness **2** INSENSATEZ : crazy act, folly

locutor, -tora *n* : announcer

locutorio *nm* : phone booth

lodo *nm* : mud — **lodazal** *nm* : quagmire

logaritmo *nm* : logarithm

lógica *nf* : logic — **lógico, -ca** *adj* : logical — **logística** *nf* : logistics *pl*

logotipo *nm* : logo

lograr *vt* **1** : achieve, attain **2** CONSEGUIR : get, obtain **3** **~ hacer** : manage to do — **logro** *nm* : achievement, success

loma *nf* : hill, hillock

lombriz *nf, pl* **-brices** : worm

lomo *nm* **1** : back (of an animal) **2** : spine (of a book) **3** **~ de cerdo** : pork loin

lona *nf* : canvas

loncha *nf* : slice (of bacon, etc.)

lonche *nm Lat* : lunch — **lonchería** *nf Lat* : luncheonette

longaniza *nf* : sausage

longevidad *nf* : longevity — **longevo, -va** *adj* : long-lived

longitud *nf* **1** : longitude **2** LARGO : length

lonja → **loncha**

loro *nm* : parrot

los, las *pron* **1** : them **2** : you **3** **los que, las que** : those who, the ones who — **los** *art* → **el**

losa *nf* **1** : flagstone **2** *or* **~ sepulcral** : tombstone

lote *nm* **1** : batch, lot **2** *Lat* : plot of land

lotería *nf* : lottery

loto *nm* : lotus

loza *nf* : crockery, earthenware

lozano, -na *adj* **1** : healthy-looking, vigorous **2** : luxuriant (of plants) — **lozanía** *nf* **1** : (youthful) vigor **2** : luxuriance (of plants)

lubricar {72} *vt* : lubricate — **lubri-**

cante *adj* : lubricating — **~** *nm* : lubricant
lucero *nm* : bright star
luchar *vi* **1** : fight, struggle **2** : wrestle (in sports) — **lucha** *nf* **1** : struggle, fight **2** : wrestling (sport) — **luchador, -dora** *n* : fighter, wrestler
lucidez *nf, pl* **-deces** : lucidity — **lúcido, -da** *adj* : lucid
lucido, -da *adj* : magnificent, splendid
luciérnaga *nf* : firefly, glowworm
lucir {45} *vi* **1** : shine **2** *Lat* : appear, seem — *vt* **1** : wear, sport **2** OSTENTAR : show off — **lucirse** *vr* **1** : shine, excel **2** PRESUMIR : show off — **lucimiento** *nm* **1** : brilliance **2** ÉXITO : brilliant performance, success
lucrativo, -va *adj* : lucrative — **lucro** *nm* : profit
luego *adv* **1** : then **2** : later (on) **3 desde ~** : of course **4 ¡hasta ~!** : see you later! **5 ~ que** : as soon as — **~** *conj* : therefore
lugar *nm* **1** : place **2** ESPACIO : space, room **3 dar ~ a** : give rise to **4 en ~ de** : instead of **5 tener ~** : take place

lugarteniente *nmf* : deputy
lúgubre *adj* : gloomy
lujo *nm* **1** : luxury **2 de ~** : deluxe — **lujoso, -sa** *adj* : luxurious
lujuria *nf* : lust
lumbre *nf* **1** : fire **2 poner en la ~** : put on the stove
luminoso, -sa *adj* : shining, luminous
luna *nf* **1** : moon **2** : (window) glass **3** ESPEJO : mirror **4 ~ de miel** : honeymoon — **lunar** *adj* : lunar — **~** *nm* : mole, beauty spot
lunes *nms & pl* : Monday
lupa *nf* : magnifying glass
lúpulo *nm* : hops
lustrar *vt* : shine, polish — **lustre** *nm* **1** BRILLO : luster, shine **2** ESPLENDOR : glory — **lustroso, -sa** *adj* : lustrous, shiny
luto *nm* **1** : mourning **2 estar de ~** : be in mourning
luxación *nf, pl* **-ciones** : dislocation
luz *nf, pl* **luces 1** : light **2** : lighting (in a room, etc.) **3** *fam* : electricity **4 a la ~ de** : in light of **5 dar a ~** : give birth **6 sacar a la ~** : bring to light

M

m *nf* : m, 13th letter of the Spanish alphabet
macabro, -bra *adj* : macabre
macarrón *nm, pl* **-rrones 1** : macaroon **2 macarrones** *nmpl* : macaroni
maceta *nf* : flowerpot
machacar {72} *vt* : crush, grind — *vi* **~ sobre** : go on about — **machacón, -cona** *adj, mpl* **-cones** : tiresome, boring
machete *nm* : machete — **machetear** *vt* : hack with a machete
macho *adj* **1** : male **2** *fam* : macho — **~** *nm* **1** : male **2** *fam* : he-man — **machista** *nm* : male chauvinist
machucar {72} *vt* **1** : beat, crush **2** : bruise (fruit)
macizo, -za *adj* : solid — **macizo** *nm* **~ de flores** : flower bed
mácula *nf* : stain
madeja *nf* : skein, hank
madera *nf* **1** : wood **2** : lumber (for construction) **3 ~ dura** : hardwood — **madero** *nm* : piece of lumber, plank
madre *nf* **1** : mother **2 ~ política** : mother-in-law — **madrastra** *nf* : stepmother
madreselva *nf* : honeysuckle

madriguera *nf* : burrow, den
madrileño, -ña *adj* : of or from Madrid
madrina *nf* **1** : godmother **2** : bridesmaid (at a wedding)
madrugada *nf* : dawn, daybreak — **madrugador, -dora** *n* : early riser
madurar *v* **1** : mature **2** : ripen (of fruit) — **madurez** *nf, pl* **-reces 1** : maturity **2** : ripeness (of fruit) — **maduro, -ra** *adj* **1** : mature **2** : ripe (of fruit)
maestría *nf* : mastery, skill — **maestro, -tra** *adj* : masterly, skilled — **~** *n* **1** : teacher (in grammar school) **2** EXPERTO : expert, master
Mafia *nf* : Mafia
magia *nf* : magic — **mágico, -ca** *adj* : magic, magical
magisterio *nm* : teachers *pl*, teaching profession
magistrado, -da *n* : magistrate, judge
magistral *adj* **1** : masterful **2** : magisterial (of an attitude, etc.)
magnánimo, -ma *adj* : magnanimous — **magnanimidad** *nf* : magnanimity
magnate *nmf* : magnate, tycoon
magnesia *nf* : magnesia — **magnesio** *nm* : magnesium
magnético, -ca *adj* : magnetic — **mag-**

netismo *nm* : magnetism — **magneti-zar** {21} *vt* : magnetize
magnetófono *nm* : tape recorder
magnificencia *nf* : magnificence — **magnífico, -ca** *adj* : magnificent
magnitud *nf* : magnitude
magnolia *nf* : magnolia
mago, -ga *n* 1 : magician 2 **los Reyes Magos** : the Magi
magro, -gra *adj* 1 : lean 2 MEZQUINO : poor, meager
magullar *vt* : bruise — **magulladura** *nf* : bruise
mahometano, -na *adj* : Islamic, Muslim — **~** *n* : Muslim
maicena *nf* : cornstarch
maíz *nm* : corn
maja *nf* : pestle
majadero, -ra *adj* : foolish, silly — **~** *n* : fool
majar *vt* : crush
majestad *nf* 1 : majesty 2 **Su Majestad** : His/Her Majesty — **majestuoso, -sa** *adj* : majestic
majo, -ja *adj* 1 : nice 2 GUAPO : good-looking
mal *adv* 1 : badly, poorly 2 INCORRECTA-MENTE : incorrectly 3 DIFÍCILMENTE : with difficulty, hardly 4 **de ~ en peor** : from bad to worse 5 **menos ~** : it's just as well — **~** *nm* 1 : evil 2 DAÑO : harm, damage 3 ENFERMEDAD : illness — **~** *adj* → **malo**
malabarismo *nm* : juggling — **malabarista** *nmf* : juggler
malacostumbrar *vt* : spoil, pamper — **malacostumbrado, -da** *adj* : spoiled
malaria *nf* : malaria
malasio, -sia *adj* : Malaysian
malaventura *nf* : misfortune — **malaventurado, -da** *adj* : unfortunate
malayo, -ya *adj* : Malay, Malayan
malcriado, -da *adj* : bad-mannered, spoiled
maldad *nf* 1 : evil 2 : evil deed
maldecir {11} *vt* : curse, damn — *vi* 1 : curse, swear 2 **~ de** : speak ill of — **maldición** *nf, pl* **-ciones** : curse — **maldito, -ta** *adj fam* : damned
maleable *adj* : malleable
maleante *nmf* : crook
malecón *nm, pl* **-cones** : jetty
maleducado, -da *adj* : rude
maleficio *nm* : curse — **maléfico, -ca** *adj* : evil, harmful
malentendido *nm* : misunderstanding
malestar *nm* 1 : discomfort 2 INQUI-ETUD : uneasiness
maleta *nf* 1 : suitcase 2 **hacer la ~** : pack one's bags — **maletero, -ra** *n*

: porter — **maletero** *nm* : trunk (of an automobile) — **maletín** *nm, pl* **-tines** 1 PORTAFOLIO : briefcase 2 : overnight bag
malévolo, -la *adj* : malevolent — **malevolencia** *nf* : malevolence
maleza *nf* 1 : underbrush 2 MALAS HIER-BAS : weeds *pl*
malgastar *vt* : waste, squander
malhablado, -da *adj* : foul-mouthed
malhechor, -chora *n* : criminal, delinquent
malhumorado, -da *adj* : bad-tempered, cross
malicia *nf* : malice — **malicioso, -sa** *adj* : malicious
maligno, -na *adj* 1 : malignant 2 PERNI-CIOSO : harmful, evil
malla *nf* 1 : mesh 2 **~s** *nfpl* : tights
malo, -la *adj* (**mal** *before masculine singular nouns*) 1 : bad 2 : poor (in quality) 3 ENFERMO : unwell 4 **estar de malas** : be in a bad mood — **~** *n* : villain, bad guy (in movies, etc.)
malograr *vt* : waste — **malograrse** *vr* 1 FRACASAR : fail 2 : die young — **malogro** *nm* : failure
maloliente *adj* : smelly
malpensado, -da *adj* : malicious, nasty
malsano, -na *adj* : unhealthy
malsonante *adj* : rude
malta *nf* : malt
maltratar *vt* : mistreat
maltrecho, -cha *adj* : battered
malvado, -da *adj* : evil, wicked
malvavisco *nm* : marshmallow
malversar *vt* : embezzle — **malversación** *nf, pl* **-ciones** : embezzlement
mama *nf* : teat (of an animal), breast (of a woman)
mamá *nf fam* : mom, mama
mamar *vi* : suckle 2 **dar de ~ a** : breast-feed — *vt* 1 : suckle, nurse 2 : learn from childhood, grow up with — **mamario, -ria** *adj* : mammary
mamarracho *nm fam* : mess, sight
mambo *nm* : mambo
mamífero, -ra *adj* : mammalian — **mamífero** *nm* : mammal
mamografía *nf* : mammogram
mampara *nf* : screen, room divider
mampostería *nf* : masonry
manada *nf* 1 : flock, herd, pack 2 **en ~** : in droves
manar *vi* 1 : flow 2 **~ en** : be rich in — **manantial** *nm* 1 : spring 2 ORIGEN : source
manchar *vt* 1 : stain, spot, mark 2 : tarnish (a reputation, etc.) — **mancharse** *vr* : get dirty — **mancha** *nf* : stain

mancillar *vt* : sully, stain

manco, -ca *adj* : one-armed, one-handed

mancomunar *vt* : combine, join — **mancomunarse** *vr* : unite — **mancomunidad** *nf* : union

mandar *vt* 1 : command, order 2 ENVIAR : send 3 *Lat* : hurl, throw — *vi* 1 : be in charge 2 ¿mande? *Lat* : yes?, pardon? — **mandadero, -ra** *nm* : messenger — **mandado** *nm* : errand — **mandamiento** *nm* 1 : order, warrant 2 : commandment (in religion)

mandarina *nf* : mandarin orange, tangerine

mandate *nm* 1 : term of office 2 ORDEN : mandate — **mandatario, -ria** *n* 1 : leader (in politics) 2 : agent (in law)

mandíbula *nf* : jaw, jawbone

mandil *nm* : apron

mando *nm* 1 : command, leadership 2 al ~ de : in charge of 3 ~ a distancia : remote control

mandolina *nf* : mandolin

mandón, -dona *adj, mpl* **-dones** : bossy

manecilla *nf* : hand (of a clock), pointer

manejar *vt* 1 : handle, operate 2 : manage (a business, etc.) 3 : manipulate (a person) 4 *Lat* : drive (a car) — **manejarse** *vr* 1 : manage, get by 2 *Lat* : behave — **manejo** *nm* 1 : handling, use 2 : management (of a business, etc.)

manera *nf* 1 : way, manner 2 de ~ que : so that 3 de ninguna ~ : by no means 4 de todas ~s : anyway

manga *nf* 1 : sleeve 2 MANGUERA : hose

mango *nm* 1 : hilt, handle 2 : mango (fruit)

mangonear *vt fam* : boss around — *vi* 1 : be bossy 2 HOLGAZANEAR : loaf, fool around

manguera *nf* : hose

maní *nm, pl* **-níes** *Lat* : peanut

manía *nf* 1 : mania, obsession 2 MODA PASAJERA : craze, fad 3 ANTIPATÍA : dislike — **maníaco, -ca** *adj* : maniacal — ~ *n* : maniac

maniatar *vt* : tie the hands of

maniático, -ca *adj* : obsessive, fussy — ~ *n* : fussy person, fanatic

manicomio *nm* : insane asylum

manicura *nf* : manicure — **manicuro, -ra** *n* : manicurist

manido, -da *adj* : stale, hackneyed

manifestar {55} *vt* 1 : demonstrate, show 2 DECLARAR : express, declare — **manifestarse** *vr* 1 : become evident 2 : demonstrate (in politics) — **mani-**

festación *nf, pl* **-ciones** 1 : manifestation, sign 2 : demonstration (in politics) — **manifestante** *nmf* : protester, demonstrator — **manifiesto, -ta** *adj* : manifest, evident — **manifiesto** *nm* : manifesto

manija *nf* : handle

manillar *nm* : handlebars *pl*

maniobra *nf* : maneuver — **maniobrar** *v* : maneuver

manipular *vt* 1 : manipulate 2 MANEJAR : handle — **manipulación** *nf, pl* **-ciones** : manipulation

maniquí *nmf, pl* **-quíes** : mannequin, model — ~ *nm* : mannequin, dummy

manirroto, -ta *adj* : extravagant — ~ *n* : spendthrift

manivela *nf* : crank

manjar *nm* : delicacy, special dish

mano *nf* 1 : hand 2 : coat (of paint, etc.) 3 a ~ or a la ~ : at hand, nearby 4 dar la ~ : shake hands 5 de segunda ~ : secondhand 6 ~ de obra : labor, manpower

manojo *nm* : bunch

manopla *nf* : mitten

manosear *vt* 1 : handle excessively 2 : fondle (a person)

manotazo *nm* : slap

mansalva: a ~ *adv phr* : at close range, without risk

mansarda *nf* : attic

mansedumbre *nf* 1 : gentleness 2 : tameness (of an animal)

mansión *nf, pl* **-siones** : mansion

manso, -sa *adj* 1 : gentle 2 : tame (of an animal)

manta *nf* 1 : blanket 2 *Lat* : poncho

manteca *nf* : lard, fat — **mantecoso, -sa** *adj* : greasy

mantel *nm* : tablecloth — **mantelería** *n,* : table linen

mantener {80} *vt* 1 : support 2 CONSERVAR : preserve 3 : keep up, maintain (relations, correspondence, etc.) 4 AFIRMAR : affirm — **mantenerse** *vr* 1 : support oneself 2 ~ firme : hold one's ground — **mantenimiento** *nm* 1 : maintenance 2 SUSTENTO : sustenance

mantequilla *nf* : butter — **mantequera** *nf* : churn — **mantequería** *nf* : dairy

mantilla *nf* : mantilla

manto *nm* : cloak

mantón *nm, pl* **-tones** : shawl

manual *adj* : manual — ~ *nm* : manual, handbook

manubrio *nm* 1 : handle, crank 2 *Lat* : handlebars *pl*

manufactura *nf* 1 : manufacture 2
FÁBRICA : factory
manuscrito *nm* : manuscript — **manuscrito, -ta** *adj* : handwritten
manutención *nf*, *pl* **-ciones** : maintenance
manzana *nf* 1 : apple 2 : (city) block —
manzanar *nm* : apple orchard —
manzano *nm* : apple tree
maña *nf* 1 : skill 2 ASTUCIA : cunning,
guile
mañana *adv* : tomorrow — ~ *nm* el ~
: the future — ~ *nf* : morning
mañoso, -sa *adj* 1 : skillful 2 *Lat*
: finicky
mapa *nm* : map — **mapamundi** *nm*
: map of the world
mapache *nm* : raccoon
maqueta *nf* : model, mock-up
maquillaje *nm* : makeup — **maquillarse** *vr* : put on makeup
máquina *nf* 1 : machine 2 LOCOMOTORA
: locomotive 3 a toda ~ : at full
speed 4 ~ de escribir : typewriter —
maquinación *nf*, *pl* **-ciones** : machination — **maquinal** *adj* : mechanical
— **maquinaria** *nf* 1 : machinery 2
: mechanism, works *pl* (of a watch,
etc.) — **maquinilla** *nf* : small machine
— **maquinista** *nmf* 1 : machinist 2
: (railroad) engineer
mar *nmf* 1 : sea 2 alta ~ : high seas *pl*
maraca *nf* : maraca
maraña *nf* 1 : thicket 2 ENREDO : tangle,
mess
maratón *nm*, *pl* **-tones** : marathon
maravilla *nf* 1 : wonder, marvel 2
: marigold (flower) — **maravillar** *vt*
: astonish — **maravillarse** *vr* : be
amazed — **maravilloso, -sa** *adj* : marvelous
marca *nf* 1 : mark 2 : brand (on livestock) 3 or ~ de fábrica : trademark
4 : record (in sports) — **marcado, -da**
adj : marked — **marcador** *nm* 1
: scoreboard 2 *Lat* : marker, felt-
tipped pen
marcapasos *nms* & *pl* : pacemaker
marcar {72} *vt* 1 : mark 2 : brand (livestock) 3 INDICAR : indicate, show 4
: dial (a telephone, etc.) 5 : score (in
sports) — *vi* 1 : score 2 : dial (on the
telephone, etc.)
marchar *vi* 1 : go 2 CAMINAR : walk 3
FUNCIONAR : work, run — **marcharse**
vr : leave, go — **marcha** *nf* 1 : march 2
PASO : pace, speed 3 : gear (of an automobile) 4 poner en ~ : put in motion
marchitarse *vr* : wither, wilt — **marchito, -ta** *adj* : withered

marcial *adj* : martial, military
marco *nm* 1 : frame 2 : goalposts *pl* (in
sports) 3 ENTORNO : setting, framework
marea *nf* : tide — **marear** *vt* 1 : make
nauseous or dizzy 2 CONFUNDIR : confuse — **marearse** *vr* 1 : become nauseated or dizzy 2 CONFUNDIRSE : get
confused — **mareado, -da** *adj* 1 : sick,
nauseous 2 ATURDIDO : dazed, dizzy
maremoto *nm* : tidal wave
mareo *nm* 1 : nausea, seasickness 2
VÉRTIGO : dizziness
marfil *nm* : ivory
margarina *nf* : margarine
margarita *nf* : daisy
margen *nm*, *pl* **márgenes** 1 : edge,
border 2 : margin (of a page, etc.) —
marginado, -da *adj* 1 : alienated 2
clases marginadas : underclass —
~ *n* : outcast — **marginal** *adj* : marginal — **marginar** *vt* : ostracize, exclude
mariachi *nm* : mariachi musician or
band
maridaje *nm* : marriage, union — **marido** *nm* : husband
marihuana *or* **mariguana** *or* **marijuana** *nf* : marijuana
marimba *nf* : marimba
marina *nf* 1 : coast 2 *or* ~ de guerra
: navy, fleet
marinada *nf* : marinade — **marinar** *vt*
: marinate
marinero, -ra *adj* 1 : sea, marine 2
: seaworthy (of a ship) — **marinero**
nm : sailor — **marino, -na** *adj* : marine — **marino** *nm* : seaman, sailor
marioneta *nf* : puppet, marionette
mariposa *nf* 1 : butterfly 2 ~ nocturna : moth
mariquita *nf* : ladybug
marisco *nm* 1 : shellfish 2 ~s *nmpl*
: seafood
marisma *nf* : salt marsh
marítimo, -ma *adj* : maritime, shipping
mármol *nm* : marble
marmota *nf* ~ de América : groundhog
marquesina *nf* : marquee, (glass)
canopy
marrano, -na *n* 1 : pig, hog 2 *fam* : slob
marrar *vt* : miss (a target) — *vi* : fail
marrón *adj* & *nm*, *pl* **-rrones** : brown
marroquí *adj* : Moroccan
marsopa *nf* : porpoise
marsupial *nm* : marsupial
Marte *nm* : Mars
martes *nms* & *pl* : Tuesday
martillo *nm* 1 : hammer 2 ~ neumáti-

co : jackhammer — **martillar** or **martillear** v : hammer

mártir nmf : martyr — **martirio** nm 1 : martyrdom — **martirizar** {21} vt 1 : martyr 2 ATORMENTAR : torment

marxismo nm : Marxism — **marxista** adj & nmf : Marxist

marzo nm : March

mas conj : but

más adv 1 : more 2 el/la/lo ~ : (the) most 3 (in negative constructions) : (any) longer 4 ¡qué día ~ bonito! : what a beautiful day! — ~ adj 1 : more 2 : most 3 ¿quién ~? : who else? — ~ prep : plus — ~ pron 1 a lo ~ : at most 2 de ~ : extra, spare 3 ~ o menos : more or less 4 ¿tienes ~? : do you have more?

masa nf 1 : mass, volume 2 : dough (in cooking) 3 ~s nfpl : people, masses

masacre nf : massacre

masaje nm : massage — **masajear** vt : massage

mascar {72} v : chew

máscara nf : mask — **mascarada** nf : masquerade — **mascarilla** nf : mask (in medecine, etc.)

mascota nf : mascot

masculino, -na adj 1 : masculine, male 2 VARONIL : manly 3 : masculine (in grammar) — **masculinidad** nf : masculinity

mascullar v : mumble

masilla nf : putty

masivo, -va adj : mass, large-scale

masón nm, pl -sones : Mason, Freemason — **masónico, -ca** adj : Masonic

masoquismo nm : masochism — **masoquista** adj : masochistic — ~ nmf : masochist

masticar {72} v : chew

mástil nm 1 : mast 2 ASTA : flagpole 3 : neck (of a stringed instrument)

mastín nm, pl -tines : mastiff

masturbarse vr : masturbate — **masturbación** nf, pl -ciones : masturbation

mata nf : bush, shrub

matadero nm : slaughterhouse

matador nm : matador, bullfighter

matamoscas nms & pl : flyswatter

matar vt 1 : kill 2 : slaughter (animals) — **matarse** vr 1 : be killed 2 SUICIDARSE : commit suicide — **matanza** nf : slaughter, killing

matasanos nms & pl fam : quack

matasellos nms & pl : postmark

mate adj : matte, dull — ~ nm 1 : maté 2 jaque ~ : checkmate

matemáticas nfpl : mathematics — **matemático, -ca** adj : mathematical — ~ n : mathematician

materia nf 1 ASUNTO : matter 2 MATERIAL : material — **material** adj 1 : material 2 daños ~es : property damage — ~ nm 1 : material 2 EQUIPO : equipment, gear — **materialismo** nm : materialism — **materialista** adj : materialistic — **materializar** {21} vt : bring to fruition — **materializarse** vr : materialize — **materialmente** adv : absolutely

maternal adj : maternal — **maternidad** nf 1 : motherhood 2 : maternity hospital — **materno, -na** adj 1 : maternal 2 **lengua materna** : mother tongue

matinal adj : morning

matinée or **matiné** nf : matinee

matiz nm, pl -tices 1 : nuance 2 : hue, shade (of colors) — **matizar** {21} vt 1 : blend (colors) 2 : qualify (a statement, etc.) 3 ~ de : tinge with

matón nm, pl -tones 1 : bully 2 CRIMINAL : gangster, hoodlum

matorral nm : thicket

matraca nf 1 : rattle, noisemaker 2 **dar la ~ a** : pester

matriarcado nm : matriarchy

matrícula nf 1 : list, roll, register 2 INSCRIPCIÓN : registration 3 : license plate (of an automobile) — **matricular** vt : register — **matricularse** vr : register, matriculate

matrimonio nm 1 : marriage 2 PAREJA : (married) couple — **matrimonial** adj : marital

matriz nf, pl -trices 1 : matrix 2 : uterus, womb (in anatomy)

matrona nf : matron

matutino, -na adj : morning

maullar {8} vi : meow — **maullido** nm : meow

maxilar nm : jaw, jawbone

máxima nf : maxim

máxime adv : especially

máximo, -ma adj : maximum, highest — **máximo** nm 1 : maximum 2 **al ~** : to the full

maya adj : Mayan

mayo nm : May

mayonesa nf : mayonnaise

mayor adj 1 (comparative of **grande**) : bigger, larger, greater, older 2 (superlative of **grande**) : biggest, largest, greatest, oldest 3 **al por ~** : wholesale 4 ~ **de edad** : of (legal) age — ~ nmf 1 : major (in the military) 2 ADULTO : adult 3 ~es nmfpl : grown-ups — **mayoral** nm : foreman

mayordomo *nm* : butler
mayoreo *nm Lat* : wholesale
mayoría *nf* : majority
mayorista *adj* : wholesale — ~ *nmf* : wholesaler
mayormente *adv* : primarily
mayúscula *nf* : capital letter — **mayúsculo, -la** *adj* 1 : capital, uppercase 2 **un fallo mayúsculo** : a terrible mistake
maza *nf* : mace (weapon)
mazapán *nm, pl* **-panes** : marzipan
mazmorra *nf* : dungeon
mazo *nm* 1 : mallet 2 MAJA : pestle
mazorca *nf* ~ **de maíz** : corncob
me *pron* 1 (*direct object*) : me 2 (*indirect object*) : to me, for me, from me 3 (*reflexive*) : myself, to myself, for myself, from myself
mecánica *nf* : mechanics — **mecánico, -ca** *adj* : mechanical — ~ *n* : mechanic
mecanismo *nm* : mechanism — **mecanización** *nf, pl* **-ciones** : mechanization — **mecanizar** {21} *vt* : mechanize
mecanografiar {85} *vt* : type — **mecanografía** *nf* : typing — **mecanógrafo, -fa** *n* : typist
mecate *nm Lat* : rope
mecedora *nf* : rocking chair
mecenas *nmfs & pl* : patron, sponsor — **mecenazgo** *nm* : patronage, sponsorship
mecer {86} *vt* 1 : rock 2 : push (on a swing) — **mecerse** *vr* : rock, swing
mecha *nf* 1 : fuse (of a bomb, etc.) 2 : wick (of a candle)
mechero *nm* 1 : burner 2 *Spain* : cigarette lighter
mechón *nm, pl* **-chones** : lock (of hair)
medalla *nf* : medal — **medallón** *nm, pl* **-llones** 1 : medallion 2 : locket (jewelry)
media *nf* 1 : average 2 ~**s** *nfpl* : stockings 3 **a** ~**s** : by halves, halfway
mediación *nf, pl* **-ciones** : mediation
mediado, -da *adj* 1 : half full, half empty, half over 2 : halfway through — **mediados** *nmpl* **a** ~ **de** : halfway through, in the middle of
mediador, -dora *n* : mediator
medialuna *nf* 1 : crescent 2 : croissant (pastry)
medianamente *adv* : fairly
medianero, -ra *adj* **pared medianera** : dividing wall
mediano, -na *adj* 1 : medium, average 2 MEDIOCRE : mediocre
medianoche *nf* : midnight
mediante *prep* : through, by means of

mediar *vi* 1 : be in the middle 2 INTERVENIR : mediate 3 ~ **entre** : be between
medicación *nf, pl* **-ciones** : medication — **medicamento** *nm* : medicine — **medicar** {72} *vt* : medicate — **medicarse** *vr* : take medicine — **medicina** *nf* : medicine — **medicinal** *adj* : medicinal
medición *nf, pl* **-ciones** : measurement
médico, -ca *adj* : medical — ~ *n* : doctor, physician
medida *nf* 1 : measurement, measure 2 MODERACIÓN : moderation 3 GRADO : extent, degree 4 **tomar** ~**s** : take steps — **medidor** *nm Lat* : meter, gauge
medieval *adj* : medieval
medio, -dia *adj* 1 : half 2 MEDIANO : average 3 **una media hora** : half an hour 4 **la clase media** : the middle class — **medio** *adv* : half — ~ *nm* 1 : half 2 MANERA : means *pl*, way 3 **en** ~ **de** : in the middle of 4 ~ **ambiente** : environment 5 ~**s** *nmpl* : means, resources
mediocre *adj* : mediocre, average — **mediocridad** *nf* : mediocrity
mediodía *nm* : noon, midday
medioevo *nm* : Middle Ages
medir {54} *vt* 1 : measure 2 CONSIDERAR : weigh, consider — **medirse** *vr* : be moderate
meditar *vi* : meditate, contemplate — *vt* 1 : think over, consider 2 PLANEAR : plan, work out — **meditación** *nf, pl* **-ciones** : meditation
mediterráneo, -nea *adj* : Mediterranean
medrar *vt* : flourish, thrive
medroso, -sa *adj* : fearful
médula *nf* 1 : marrow 2 ~ **espinal** : spinal cord
medusa *nf* : jellyfish
megabyte *nm* : megabyte
megáfono *nm* : megaphone
mejicano → **mexicano**
mejilla *nf* : cheek
mejillón *nm, pl* **-llones** : mussel
mejor *adv* 1 (*comparative*) : better 2 (*superlative*) : best 3 **a lo** ~ : maybe, perhaps — ~ *adj* 1 (*comparative of* **bueno** *or* **bien**) : better 2 (*superlative of* **bueno** *or* **bien**) : best 3 **lo** ~ : the best thing 4 **tanto** ~ : so much the better — **mejora** *nf* : improvement
mejorana *nf* : marjoram
mejorar *vt* : improve — *vi* : improve, get better
mejunje *nm* : concoction, brew

melancolía *nf* : melancholy — **melancólico, -ca** *adj* : melancholic, melancholy

melaza *nf* : molasses

melena *nf* 1 : long hair 2 : mane (of a lion)

melindroso, -sa *adj* 1 : affected 2 *Lat* : finicky

mella *nf* : chip, nick — **mellado, -da** *adj* : chipped, jagged

mellizo, -za *adj & n* : twin

melocotón *nm, pl* **-tones** : peach

melodía *nf* : melody — **melódico, -ca** *adj* : melodic

melodrama *nm* : melodrama — **melodramático, -ca** *adj* : melodramatic

melón *nm, pl* **-lones** : melon

meloso, -sa *adj* 1 : sweet, honeyed 2 EMPALAGOSO : cloying

membrana *nf* : membrane

membrete *nm* : letterhead, heading

membrillo *nm* : quince

membrudo, -da *adj* : muscular, burly

memorable *adj* : memorable

memorándum *or* **memorando** *nm, pl* **-dums** *or* **-dos** 1 : memorandum 2 AGENDA : notebook

memoria *nf* 1 : memory 2 RECUERDO : remembrance 3 INFORME : report 4 **de** ~ : by heart 5 ~**s** *nfpl* : memoirs — **memorizar** {21} *vt* : memorize

mena *nf* : ore

menaje *nm* : household goods *pl*, furnishings *pl*

mencionar *vt* : mention, refer to — **mención** *nf, pl* **-ciones** : mention

mendaz *adj, pl* **-daces** : lying

mendigar {52} *vi* : beg — *vt* : beg for — **mendicidad** *nf* : begging — **mendigo, -ga** *n* : beggar

mendrugo *nm* : crust of bread

menear *vt* 1 : move, shake 2 : sway (one's hips) 3 : wag (a tail) — **menearse** *vr* 1 : sway, shake, move 2 *fam* : hurry up

menester *nm* **ser** ~ : be necessary — **menesteroso, -sa** *adj* : needy

menguar *vt* : diminish, lessen — *vi* 1 : decline, decrease 2 : wane (of the moon) — **mengua** *nf* : decrease, decline

menopausia *nf* : menopause

menor *adj* 1 (*comparative of* **pequeño**) : smaller, lesser, younger 2 (*superlative of* **pequeño**) : smallest, least, youngest 3 : minor (in music) 4 **al por** ~ : retail — ~ *nmf* : minor, juvenile

menos *adv* 1 (*comparative*) : less 2 (*superlative*) : least 3 ~ **de** : fewer than — ~ *adj* 1 (*comparative*) : less, fewer

2 (*superlative*) : least, fewest — ~ *prep* 1 : minus 2 EXCEPTO : except — ~ *pron* 1 : less, fewer 2 **al** ~ *or* **por lo** ~ : at least 3 **a** ~ **que** : unless —

menoscabar *vt* 1 : lessen 2 ESTROPEAR : harm, damage — **menospreciar** *vt* 1 DESPRECIAR : scorn 2 SUBESTIMAR : undervalue — **menosprecio** *nm* : contempt

mensaje *nm* : message — **mensajero, -ra** *n* : messenger

menso, -sa *adj Lat fam* : foolish, stupid

menstruar {3} *vi* : menstruate — **menstruación** *nf* : menstruation

mensual *adj* : monthly — **mensualidad** *nf* 1 : monthly payment 2 : monthly salary

mensurable *adj* : measurable

menta *nf* 1 : mint, peppermint 2 ~ **verde** : spearmint

mental *adj* : mental — **mentalidad** *nf* : mentality

mentar {55} *vt* : mention, name

mente *nf* : mind

mentir {76} *vi* : lie — **mentira** *nf* : lie — **mentirilla** *nf* : fib — **mentiroso, -sa** *adj* : lying — ~ *n* : liar

mentís *nms & pl* : denial

mentol *nm* : menthol

mentón *nm, pl* **-tones** : chin

menú *nm, pl* **-nús** : menu

menudear *vi* : occur frequently — **menudeo** *nm Lat* : retail, retailing

menudillos *nmpl* : giblets

menudo, -da *adj* 1 : small, insignificant 2 **a** ~ : often

meñique *nm or* **dedo** ~ : little finger, pinkie

meollo *nm* 1 : marrow 2 ESENCIA : essence, core

mercado *nm* 1 : market 2 ~ **de valores** : stock market — **mercadería** *nf* : merchandise, goods *pl*

mercancía *nf* : merchandise, goods *pl* — **mercante** *nmf* : merchant, dealer — **mercantil** *adj* : commercial

mercenario, -ria *adj & n* : mercenary

mercería *nf* : notions store

mercurio *nm* : mercury

Mercurio *nm* : Mercury (planet)

merecer {53} *vt* : deserve — *vi* : be worthy — **merecedor, -dora** *adj* : deserving, worthy — **merecido** *nm* **recibir su** ~ : get one's just deserts

merendar {55} *vi* : have an afternoon snack — *vt* : have as an afternoon snack — **merendero** *nm* 1 : snack bar 2 : picnic area

merengue *nm* 1 : meringue 2 : merengue (dance)

meridiano, -na *adj* 1 : midday 2 CLARO : crystal-clear — **meridiano** *nm* : meridian — **meridional** *adj* : southern

merienda *nf* : afternoon snack, tea

mérito *nm* : merit, worth — **meritorio, -ria** *adj* : deserving — ~ *n* : intern, trainee

mermar *vi* : decrease — *vt* : reduce, cut down — **merma** *nf* : decrease

mermelada *nf* : marmalade, jam

mero, -ra *adj* 1 : mere, simple 2 *Lat fam* (*used as an intensifier*) : very, real — **mero** *adv Lat fam* 1 : nearly, almost 2 **aquí** ~ : right here

merodear *vi* 1 : maraud 2 ~ **por** : prowl about (a place)

mes *nm* : month

mesa *nf* 1 : table 2 COMITÉ : committee, board

mesarse *vr* ~ **los cabellos** : tear one's hair

meseta *nf* : plateau

Mesías *nm* : Messiah

mesilla *nf* : small table

mesón *nm, pl* **-sones** : inn — **mesonero, -ra** *nm* : innkeeper

mestizo, -za *adj* 1 : of mixed ancestry 2 HÍBRIDO : hybrid — ~ *n* : person of mixed ancestry

mesura *nf* : moderation — **mesurado, -da** *adj* : moderate, restrained

meta *nf* : goal, objective

metabolismo *nm* : metabolism

metafísica *nf* : metaphysics — **metafísico, -ca** *adj* : metaphysical

metáfora *nf* : metaphor — **metafórico, -ca** *adj* : metaphoric, metaphorical

metal *nm* 1 : metal 2 : brass section (in an orchestra) — **metálico, -ca** *adj* : metallic, metal — **metalurgia** *nf* : metallurgy

metamorfosis *nfs & pl* : metamorphosis

metano *nm* : methane

metedura *nf* ~ **de pata** *fam* : blunder

meteoro *nm* : meteor — **meteórico, -ca** *adj* : meteoric — **meteorito** *nm* : meteorite — **meteorología** *nf* : meteorology — **meteorólogo, -ga** *adj* : meteorological, meteorologic — ~ *n* : meteorologist

meter *vt* 1 : put (in) 2 : place (in a job, etc.) 3 ENREDAR : involve 4 CAUSAR : make, cause 5 : spread (a rumor) 6 *Lat* : strike (a blow) — **meterse** *vr* 1 : get in, enter 2 ~ **en** : get involved in, meddle in 3 ~ **con** *fam* : pick a fight with

meticuloso, -sa *adj* : meticulous

método *nm* : method — **metódico, -ca** *adj* : methodical — **metodología** *nf* : methodology

metomentodo *nmf fam* : busybody

metralla *nf* : shrapnel — **metralleta** *nf* : submachine gun

métrico, -ca *adj* : metric, metrical

metro *nm* 1 : meter 2 : subway (train)

metrópoli *nf or* **metrópolis** *nfs & pl* : metropolis — **metropolitano, -na** *adj* : metropolitan

mexicano, -na *adj* : Mexican — **mexicoamericano, -na** *adj* : Mexican-American

mezcla *nf* 1 : mixture 2 ARGAMASA : mortar — **mezclar** *vt* 1 : mix, blend 2 CONFUNDIR : mix up, muddle 3 INVOLUCRAR : involve — **mezclarse** *vr* 1 : get mixed up 2 : mingle (socially) — **mezcolanza** *nf* : mixture

mezclilla *nf Lat* : denim

mezquino, -na *adj* 1 : mean, petty 2 ESCASO : meager — **mezquindad** *nf* : meanness, stinginess

mezquita *nf* : mosque

mezquite *nm* : mesquite

mi *adj* : my

mí *pron* 1 : me 2 *or* ~ **mismo, ~ misma** : myself 3 **a** ~ **no me importa** : it doesn't matter to me

miajas → **migajas**

miau *nm* : meow

mica *nf* : mica

mico *nm* : (long-tailed) monkey

microbio *nm* : microbe, germ — **microbiología** *nf* : microbiology

microbús *nm, pl* **-buses** : minibus

microcosmos *nms & pl* : microcosm

microfilm *nm, pl* **-films** : microfilm

micrófono *nm* : microphone

microondas *nms & pl* : microwave (oven)

microorganismo *nm* : microorganism

microscopio *nm* : microscope — **microscópico, -ca** *adj* : microscopic

miedo *nm* 1 : fear 2 **dar** ~ : be frightening — **miedoso, -sa** *adj* : fearful

miel *nf* : honey

miembro *nm* 1 : member 2 EXTREMIDAD : limb, extremity

mientras *adv or* ~ **tanto** : meanwhile, in the meantime — ~ *conj* 1 : while, as 2 ~ **que** : while, whereas 3 ~ **viva** : as long as I live

miércoles *nms & pl* : Wednesday

mies *nf* : (ripe) corn, grain

miga *nf* : crumb — **migajas** *nfpl* 1 : breadcrumbs 2 SOBRAS : leftovers

migración *nf, pl* **-ciones** : migration

migraña *nf* : migraine

migrar *vi* : migrate

mijo *nm* : millet

mil *adj & nm* : thousand

milagro *nm* : miracle — **milagroso, -sa** *adj* : miraculous

milenio *nm* : millennium

milésimo, -ma *adj* : thousandth

milicia *nf* 1 : militia 2 : military (service)

miligramo *nm* : milligram

mililitro *nm* : milliliter

milímetro *nm* : millimeter

militante *adj & nmf* : militant

militar *adj* : military — ~ *nmf* : soldier — **militarizar** {21} *vt* : militarize

milla *nf* : mile

millar *nm* : thousand

millón *nm, pl* **-llones** 1 : million 2 **mil millones** : billion — **millonario, -ria** *n* : millionaire — **millonésimo, -ma** *adj* : millionth

mimar *vt* : pamper, spoil

mimbre *nm* : wicker

mímica *nf* 1 : mime, sign language 2 IMITACIÓN : mimicry

mimo *nm* : pampering — ~ *nmf* : mime

mina *nf* 1 : mine 2 : lead (for pencils) — **minar** *vt* 1 : mine 2 DEBILITAR : undermine

mineral *adj* : mineral — ~ *nm* 1 : mineral 2 : ore (of a metal)

minería *nf* : mining — **minero, -ra** *adj* : mining — ~ *n* : miner

miniatura *nf* : miniature

minifalda *nf* : miniskirt

minifundio *nm* : small farm

minimizar {21} *vt* : minimize

mínimo, -ma *adj* 1 : minimum 2 MINÚSCULO : minute 3 **en lo más** ~ : in the slightest — **mínimo** *nm* : minimum

minino, -na *n fam* : pussycat

ministerio *nm* : ministry — **ministro, -tra** *n* 1 : minister, secretary 2 **primer ministro** : prime minister

minoría *nf* : minority

minorista *adj* : retail — ~ *nmf* : retailer

minoritario, -ria *adj* : minority

minucia *nf* : trifle, small detail — **minucioso, -sa** *adj* 1 : detailed 2 METICULOSO : thorough

minué *nm* : minuet

minúsculo, -la *adj* : minuscule, tiny

minusvalía *nf* : handicap, disability — **minusválido, -da** *adj* : disabled

minuta *nf* 1 : bill, fee 2 BORRADOR : rough draft

minuto *nm* : minute — **minutero** *nm* : minute hand

mío, mía *adj* 1 : mine 2 **una amiga mía** : a friend of mine — ~ *pron* **el mío, la mía** : mine, my own

miope *adj* : nearsighted

mirar *vt* 1 : look at 2 OBSERVAR : watch 3 CONSIDERAR : consider — *vi* 1 : look 2 ~ **a** : face, overlook 3 ~ **por** : look after — **mirarse** *vr* 1 : look at oneself 2 : look at each other — **mira** *nf* 1 : sight (of a firearm or instrument) 2 INTENCIÓN : aim, objective — **mirada** *nf* : look — **mirado, -da** *adj* 1 : careful 2 CONSIDERADO : considerate 3 **bien** ~ : well thought of — **mirador** *nm* 1 BALCÓN : balcony 2 : lookout, vantage point — **miramiento** *nm* : consideration

mirlo *nm* : blackbird

misa *nf* : Mass

miscelánea *nf* : miscellany

miserable *adj* 1 : poor 2 LASTIMOSO : miserable, wretched — **miseria** *nf* 1 : poverty 2 DESGRACIA : misfortune, misery

misericordia *nf* : mercy — **misericordioso, -sa** *adj* : merciful

mísero, -ra *adj* : wretched, miserable

misil *nm* : missile

misión *nf, pl* **-siones** : mission — **misionero, -ra** *adj & n* : missionary

mismo *adv (used for emphasis)* : right, exactly — **mismo, -ma** *adj* 1 : same 2 *(used for emphasis)* : very 3 : -self 4 **por lo** ~ : for that reason

misoginia *nf* : misogyny — **misógino** *nm* : misogynist

misterio *nm* : mystery — **misterioso, -sa** *adj* : mysterious

mística *nf* : mysticism — **místico, -ca** *adj* : mystic, mystical — ~ *n* : mystic

mitad *nf* 1 : half 2 MEDIO : middle

mítico, -ca *adj* : mythical, mythic

mitigar {52} *vt* : mitigate

mitin *nm, pl* **mítines** : (political) meeting

mito *nm* : myth — **mitología** *nm* : mythology — **mitológico, -ca** *adj* : mythological

mixto, -ta *adj* 1 : mixed, joint 2 : coeducational (of a school)

mnemónico, -ca *adj* : mnemonic

mobiliario *nm* : furniture

mocasín *nm, pl* **-sines** : moccasin

mochila *nf* : backpack, knapsack

moción *nf, pl* **-ciones** : motion

moco *nm* 1 : mucus 2 **limpiarse los** ~**s** : wipe one's nose — **mocoso, -sa** *n fam* : kid, brat

moda *nf* 1 : fashion, style 2 **a la** ~ **or de** ~ : in style, fashionable 3 ~ **pasajera** : fad — **modal** *adj* : modal — **modales** *nmpl* : manners — **modalidad** *nf* : type, kind

modelar *vt* : model, mold — **modelo**
adj : model — **~** *nm* : model, pattern
— **~** *nmf* : model, mannequin
módem *or* **modem** ['moðɛm] *nm* : modem
moderar *vt* **1** : moderate **2** : reduce
(speed, etc.) **3** PRESIDIR : chair (a
meeting) — **moderarse** *vr* : restrain
oneself — **moderación** *nf, pl* **-ciones**
: moderation — **moderado, -da** *adj &*
n : moderate — **moderador, -dora** *n*
: moderator, chairperson
moderno, -na *adj* : modern — **mod-
ernismo** *nm* : modernism — **modern-
izar** {21} *vt* : modernize
modesto, -ta *adj* : modest — **modestia**
nf : modesty
modificar {72} *vt* : modify, alter —
modificación *nf, pl* **-ciones** : alteration
modismo *nm* : idiom
modista *nmf* **1** : dressmaker **2** : (fashion) designer
modo *nm* **1** : way, manner **2** : mood (in
grammar) **3** : mode (in music) **4 a ~**
de : by way of **5 de ~ que** : so (that)
6 de todos ~s : in any case, anyway
modorra *nf* : drowsiness
modular *vt* : modulate — **modulación**
nf, pl **-ciones** : modulation
módulo *nm* : module, unit
mofa *nf* : ridicule, mockery — **mofarse**
vr **~ de** : make fun of
mofeta *nf* : skunk
moflete *nm fam* : fat cheek — **mofletu-
do, -da** *adj fam* : fat-cheeked, chubby
mohín *nm, pl* **-hines** : grimace — **mo-
hino, -na** *adj* : sulky
moho *nm* **1** : mold, mildew **2** ÓXIDO
: rust — **mohoso, -sa** *adj* **1** : moldy **2**
OXIDADO : rusty
moisés *nm, pl* **-seses** : bassinet, cradle
mojar *vt* **1** : wet, moisten **2** : dunk
(food) — **mojarse** *vr* : get wet — **mojado, -da** *adj* : wet, damp
mojigato, -ta *adj* : prudish — **~** *n*
: prude
mojón *nm, pl* **-jones** : boundary stone,
marker
molar *nm* : molar
moldear *vt* : mold, shape — **molde** *nm*
: mold, form — **moldura** *nf* : molding
mole¹ *nf* : mass, bulk
mole² *nm* **1** : Mexican chili sauce **2**
: meat served with mole
molécula *nf* : molecule — **molecular**
adj : molecular
moler {47} *vt* : grind, crush
molestar *vt* **1** : annoy, bother **2 no ~**
: do not disturb — *vi* : be a nuisance —
molestarse *vr* **1** : bother **2** OFENDERSE

: take offense — **molestia** *nf* **1** : annoyance, nuisance **2** MALESTAR : discomfort — **molesto, -ta** *adj* **1** : annoyed **2** FASTIDIOSO : annoying **3**
INCÓMODO : in discomfort — **mo-
lestoso, -sa** *adj* : bothersome, annoying
molido, -da *adj* **1** : ground (of meat,
etc.) **2** *fam* : worn out, exhausted
molino *nm* **1** : mill **2 ~ de viento**
: windmill — **molinero, -ra** *n* : miller
— **molinillo** *nm* : grinder, mill
mollera *nf* **1** : crown (of the head) **2** *fam*
: brains *pl*
molusco *nm* : mollusk
momento *nm* **1** : moment, instant **2**
: (period of) time **3** : momentum (in
physics) **4 de ~** : for the moment **5**
de un ~ a otro : any time now —
momentáneamente *adv* : momentar-
ily — **momentáneo, -nea** *adj* **1** : mo-
mentary **2** PASAJERO : temporary
momia *nf* : mummy
monaguillo *nm* : altar boy
monarca *nmf* : monarch — **monarquía**
nf : monarchy
monasterio *nm* : monastery — **monás-
tico, -ca** *adj* : monastic
mondadientes *nms & pl* : toothpick
mondar *vt* : peel
mondongo *nm* : innards *pl*, guts *pl*
moneda *nf* **1** : coin **2** : currency (of a
country) — **monedero** *nm* : change
purse
monetario, -ria *adj* : monetary
monitor *nm* : monitor
monja *nf* : nun — **monje** *nm* : monk
mono, -na *n* : monkey — **~** *adj fam*
: lovely, cute
monogamia *nf* : monogamy —
monógamo -ma *adj* : monogamous
monografía *nf* : monograph
monograma *nm* : monogram
monolingüe *adj* : monolingual
monólogo *nm* : monologue
monopatín *nm, pl* **-tines** : scooter,
skateboard
monopolio *nm* : monopoly — **monopolizar** {21} *vt* : monopolize
monosílabo *nm* : monosyllable —
monosilábico, -ca *adj* : monosyllabic
monoteísmo *nm* : monotheism —
monoteísta *adj* : monotheistic
monotonía *nf* : monotony — **monótono, -na** *adj* : monotonous
monóxido *nm* **~ de carbono** : carbon
monoxide
monstruo *nm* : monster — **monstruosidad** *nf* : monstrosity — **monstru-
oso, -sa** *adj* : monstrous

monta *nf* : importance, value
montaje *nm* **1** : assembly **2** : staging (in theater), editing (of films)
montaña *nf* **1** : mountain **2** ~ **rusa** : roller coaster — **montañero, -ra** *n* : mountain climber — **montañoso, -sa** *adj* : mountainous
montar *vt* **1** : mount **2** ESTABLECER : establish **3** ENSAMBLAR : assemble, put together **4** : stage (a performance) **5** : cock (a gun) — *vi* **1** ~ **a caballo** : ride horseback **2** ~ **en bicicleta** : get on a bicycle
monte *nm* **1** : mountain **2** BOSQUE : woodland **3** *or* ~ **bajo** : scrubland **4** ~ **de piedad** : pawnshop
montés *adj, pl* **-teses** : wild (of animals or plants)
montículo *nm* : mound, hillock
montón *nm, pl* **-tones 1** : heap, pile **2** **un** ~ **de** *fam* : lots of
montura *nf* **1** : mount (horse) **2** SILLA : saddle **3** : frame (of glasses)
monumento *nm* : monument — **monumental** *adj fam* : monumental, huge
monzón *nm, pl* **-zones** : monsoon
moño *nm* **1** : bun (of hair) **2** *Lat* : bow (knot)
mora *nf* **1** : mulberry **2** ZARZAMORA : blackberry
morada *nf* : residence, dwelling
morado, -da *adj* : purple — **morado** *nm* : purple
moral *adj* : moral — ~ *nf* **1** : ethics, morals *pl* **2** ÁNIMO : morale — **moraleja** *nf* : moral (of a story) — **moralidad** *nf* : morality — **moralista** *adj* : moralistic — ~ *nmf* : moralist
morar *vi* : live, reside
morboso, -sa *adj* : morbid
mordaz *adj* : caustic, scathing — **mordacidad** *nf* : bite, sharpness
mordaza *nf* : gag
morder {47} *v* : bite — **mordedura** *nf* : bite (of an animal)
mordisquear *vt* : nibble (on) — **mordisco** *nm* : nibble, bite
moreno, -na *adj* **1** : dark-haired, brunette **2** : dark-skinned — ~ *n* **1** : brunette **2** : dark-skinned person
moretón *nm, pl* **-tones** : bruise
morfina *nf* : morphine
morir {46} *vi* **1** : die **2** APAGARSE : die out, go out — **morirse** *vr* **1** ~ **de** : die of **2** ~ **por** : be dying for — **moribundo, -da** *adj* : moribund, dying
moro, -ra *adj* : Moorish — ~ *n* : Moor
moroso, -sa *adj* : delinquent, in arrears — **morosidad** *nf* : delinquency (in payment)

morral *nm* : backpack
morriña *nf* : homesickness
morro *nm* : snout
morsa *nf* : walrus
morse *nm* : Morse code
mortaja *nf* : shroud
mortal *adj* **1** : mortal **2** : deadly (of a wound, an enemy, etc.) — ~ *nmf* : mortal — **mortalidad** *nf* : mortality — **mortandad** *nf* : death toll
mortero *nm* : mortar
mortífero, -ra *adj* : deadly, lethal
mortificar {72} *vt* **1** : mortify **2** ATORMENTAR : torment — **mortificarse** *vr* : be distressed
mosaico *nm* : mosaic
mosca *nf* : fly
moscada *adj* → **nuez**
mosquearse *vr fam* **1** : become suspicious **2** ENFADARSE : get annoyed
mosquito *nm* : mosquito — **mosquitero** *nm* **1** : (window) screen **2** : mosquito net
mostachón *nm, pl* **-chones** : macaroon
mostaza *nf* : mustard
mostrador *nm* : counter (in a store)
mostrar {19} *vt* : show — **mostrarse** *vr* : show oneself, appear
mota *nf* : spot, speck — **moteado, -da** *adj* : speckled, spotted
mote *nm* : nickname
motel *nm* : motel
motín *nm, pl* **-tines 1** : riot, uprising **2** : mutiny (of troops)
motivo *nm* **1** : motive, cause **2** : motif (in art, music, etc.) — **motivación** *nf, pl* **-ciones** : motivation — **motivar** *vt* **1** : cause **2** IMPULSAR : motivate
moto *nf* : motorcycle, motorbike — **motocicleta** *nf* : motorcycle — **motociclista** *nmf* : motorcyclist
motor, -triz *or* **-tora** *adj* : motor — **motor** *nm* : motor, engine — **motorista** *nmf* **1** : motorcyclist **2** *Lat* : motorist
mover {47} *vt* **1** : move, shift **2** : shake (the head) **3** PROVOCAR : provoke — **moverse** *vr* **1** : move (over) **2** APRESURARSE : get a move on — **movedizo, -za** *adj* : movable, shifting — **movible** *adj* : movable
móvil *adj* : mobile — ~ *nm* **1** MOTIVO : motive **2** : mobile — **movilidad** *nf* : mobility — **movilizar** {21} *vt* : mobilize
movimiento *nm* **1** : movement, motion **2** ~ **sindicalista** : labor movement
mozo, -za *adj* : young — ~ *n* **1** : young man *m*, young woman *f* **2** *Lat* : waiter *m*, waitress *f*

muchacho, -cha *n* : kid, boy *m*, girl *f*
muchedumbre *nf* : crowd
mucho *adv* **1** : very much, a lot **2** : long, a long time — **mucho, -cha** *adj* **1** : a lot of, many, much **2 muchas veces** : often — **~** *pron* : a lot, many, much
mucosidad *nf* : mucus
muda *nf* **1** : molting (of animals) **2** : change (of clothing) — **mudanza** *nf* **1** : change **2** TRASLADO : move, change of residence — **mudar** *v* **1** : molt, shed **2** CAMBIAR : change — **mudarse** *vr* **1** : change (one's clothes) **2** TRASLA-DARSE : move (one's residence)
mudo, -da *adj* **1** : mute **2** SILENCIOSO : silent
mueble *nm* : piece of furniture **2 ~s** *nmpl* : furniture, furnishings
mueca *nf* **1** : grimace, face **2 hacer ~s** : makes faces
muela *nf* **1** : tooth, molar **2 ~ de juicio** : wisdom tooth
muelle *adj* : soft — **~** *nm* **1** : wharf, jetty **2** RESORTE : spring
muérdago *nm* : mistletoe
muerte *nf* : death — **muerto, -ta** *adj* **1** : dead **2** : dull (of colors, etc.) — **~** *nm* : dead person, deceased
muesca *nf* : nick, notch
muestra *nf* **1** : sample **2** SEÑAL : sign, show
mugir {35} *vi* : moo, bellow — **mugido** *nm* : mooing, bellowing
mugre *nf* : grime, filth — **mugriento, -ta** *adj* : filthy, grimy
muguete *nm* : lily of the valley
mujer *nf* **1** : woman **2** ESPOSA : wife **3 ~ de negocios** : businesswoman
mulato, -ta *adj & n* : mulatto
muleta *nf* **1** : crutch **2** APOYO : prop, support
mullido, -da *adj* : soft, spongy
mulo, -la *n* : mule
multa *nf* : fine — **multar** *vt* : fine
multicolor *adj* : multicolored
multicultural *adj* : multicultural
multimedia *adj* : multimedia
multinacional *adj* : multinational
multiplicar {72} *v* : multiply — **multi-plicarse** *vr* : multiply, reproduce — **múltiple** *adj* : multiple — **multipli-**

cación *nf, pl* **-ciones** : multiplication — **múltiplo** *nm* : multiple
multitud *nf* : crowd, multitude
mundo *nm* **1** : world **2 todo el ~** : everyone, everybody — **mundanal** *adj* : worldly — **mundano, -na** *adj* **1** : worldly, earthly **2 la vida mundana** : high society — **mundial** *adj* : world, worldwide
municiones *nfpl* : ammunition
municipal *adj* : municipal — **munici-pio** *nm* **1** : municipality **2** AYUN-TAMIENTO : town council
muñeca *nf* **1** : doll **2** : wrist (in anato-my) — **muñeco** *nm* **1** : boy doll **2** MANIQUÍ : dummy, puppet
muñón *nm, pl* **-ñones** : stump (of an arm or leg)
mural *adj & nm* : mural — **muralla** *nf* : wall, rampart
murciélago *nm* : bat (animal)
murmullo *nm* **1** : murmur, murmuring **2** : rustling (of leaves, etc.)
murmurar *vi* **1** : murmur, whisper **2** CRITICAR : gossip
muro *nm* : wall
musa *nf* : muse
musaraña *nf* : shrew
músculo *nm* : muscle — **muscular** *adj* : muscular — **musculatura** *nf* : mus-cles *pl* — **musculoso, -sa** *adj* : mus-cular
muselina *nf* : muslin
museo *nm* : museum
musgo *nm* : moss — **musgoso, -sa** *adj* : mossy
música *nf* : music — **musical** *adj* : mu-sical — **músico, -ca** *adj* : musical — **~** *n* : musician
musitar *vt* : mumble
muslo *nm* : thigh
musulmán, -mana *adj & n, mpl* **-manes** : Muslim
mutar *v* : mutate — **mutación** *nf, pl* **-ciones** : mutation — **mutante** *adj & nmf* : mutant
mutilar *vt* : mutilate — **mutilación** *nf, pl* **-ciones** : mutilation
mutuo, -tua *adj* : mutual
muy *adv* **1** : very, quite **2** DEMASIADO : too

N

n *nf* : n, 14th letter of the Spanish alphabet

nabo *nm* : turnip

nácar *nm* : mother-of-pearl

nacer {48} *vi* **1** : be born **2** : hatch (of an egg), sprout (of a plant) **3** SURGIR : arise, spring up — **nacido, -da** *adj & n* **recién** ~ : newborn — **naciente** *adj* **1** : new, growing **2** : rising (of the sun) — **nacimiento** *nm* **1** : birth **2** : source (of a river) **3** ORIGEN : beginning **4** BELÉN : Nativity scene

nación *nf, pl* **-ciones** : nation, country — **nacional** *adj* : national — ~ *nmf* : national, citizen — **nacionalidad** *nf* : nationality — **nacionalismo** *nm* : nationalism — **nacionalista** *adj & nmf* : nationalist — **nacionalizar** {21} *vt* **1** : nationalize **2** : naturalize (as a citizen) — **nacionalizarse** *vr* : become naturalized

nada *pron* **1** : nothing **2 de** ~ : you're welcome **3** ~ **más** : nothing else, nothing more — ~ *adv* : not at all — ~ *nf* **la** ~ : nothingness

nadar *v* : swim — **nadador, -dora** *n* : swimmer

nadería *nf* : small thing, trifle

nadie *pron* : nobody, no one

nado: a ~ *adv phr* : swimming

nafta *nf Lat* : gasoline

naipe *nm* : playing card

nalgas *nfpl* : buttocks, bottom

nana *nf* : lullaby

naranja *adj & nm* : orange (color) — ~ *nf* : orange (fruit) — **naranjal** *nm* : orange grove — **naranjo** *nm* : orange tree

narciso *nm* : narcissus, daffodil

narcótico, -ca *adj* : narcotic — **narcótico** *nm* : narcotic — **narcotizar** {21} *vt* : drug — **narcotraficante** *nmf* : drug trafficker — **narcotráfico** *nm* : drug trafficking

nariz *nf, pl* **-rices 1** : nose **2** OLFATO : sense of smell **3 narices** *nfpl* : nostrils

narrar *vt* : narrate, tell — **narración** *nf, pl* **-ciones** : narration — **narrador, -dora** *n* : narrator — **narrativa** *nf* : narrative, storytelling

nasal *adj* : nasal

nata *nf Spain* : cream

natación *nf, pl* **-ciones** : swimming

natal *adj* : native, birth — **natalicio** *nm* : birthday — **natalidad** *nf* : birthrate

natillas *nfpl* : custard

natividad *nf* : birth, nativity

nativo, -va *adj & n* : native

natural *adj* **1** : natural **2** NORMAL : normal **3** ~ **de** : native of, from — ~ *nm* **1** : temperament **2** NATIVO : native — **naturaleza** *nf* : nature — **naturalidad** *nf* : naturalness — **naturalista** *adj* : naturalistic — **naturalización** *nf, pl* **-ciones** : naturalization — **naturalizar** {21} *vt* : naturalize — **naturalizarse** *vr* : become naturalized — **naturalmente** *adv* **1** : naturally **2** POR SUPUESTO : of course

naufragar {52} *vi* **1** : be shipwrecked **2** FRACASAR : fail — **naufragio** *nm* : shipwreck — **náufrago, -ga** *adj* : shipwrecked — ~ *n* : castaway

náusea *nf* **1** : nausea **2 dar** ~**s** : nauseate **3** ~**s matutinas** : morning sickness — **nauseabundo, -da** *adj* : nauseating

náutico, -ca *adj* : nautical

navaja *nf* : pocketknife, penknife

naval *adj* : naval

nave *nf* **1** : ship **2** : nave (of a church) **3** ~ **espacial** : spaceship

navegar {52} *v* : navigate, sail — **navegable** *adj* : navigable — **navegación** *nf, pl* **-ciones** : navigation — **navegante** *adj* : sailing, seafaring — ~ *nmf* : navigator

Navidad *nf* **1** : Christmas **2 feliz** ~ : Merry Christmas — **navideño, -ña** *adj* : Christmas

naviero, -ra *adj* : shipping

nazi *adj & nmf* : Nazi — **nazismo** *nm* : Nazism

neblina *nf* : mist

nebuloso, -sa *adj* **1** : hazy, misty, foggy **2** VAGO : vague, nebulous

necedad *nf* **1** : stupidity **2 decir** ~**es** : talk nonsense

necesario, -ria *adj* : necessary — **necesariamente** *adv* : necessarily — **necesidad** *nf* **1** : need, necessity **2** POBREZA : poverty **3** ~**es** *nfpl* : hardships — **necesitado, -da** *adj* : needy — **necesitar** *vt* : need — *vi* ~ **de** : have need of

necio, -cia adj : silly, dumb
necrología nf : obituary
néctar nm : nectar
nectarina nf : nectarine
neerlandés, -desa adj, mpl **-deses** : Dutch — **neerlandés** nm : Dutch (language)
nefasto, -ta adj 1 : ill-fated 2 fam : terrible, awful
negar {49} vt 1 : deny 2 REHUSAR : refuse 3 : disown (a person) — **negarse** vr : refuse — **negación** nf, pl **-ciones** 1 : denial 2 : negative (in grammar) — **negativa** nf 1 : denial 2 RECHAZO : refusal — **negativo, -va** adj : negative — **negativo** nm : negative (of a photograph)
negligente adj : negligent — **negligencia** nf : negligence
negociar vt : negotiate — vi : deal, do business — **negociable** adj : negotiable — **negociación** nf, pl **-ciones** : negotiation — **negociante** nmf : businessman m, businesswoman f — **negocio** nm 1 : business 2 TRANSACCIÓN : deal 3 **~s** : business, commerce
negro, -gra adj : black, dark — **~** n : dark-skinned person — **negro** nm : black (color) — **negrura** nf : blackness — **negruzco, -ca** adj : blackish
nene, -na n fam : baby, small child
nenúfar nm : water lily
neón nm : neon
neoyorquino, -na adj : of or from New York
nepotismo nm : nepotism
Neptuno nm : Neptune
nervio nm 1 : nerve 2 : sinew (in meat) 3 VIGOR : vigor, energy 4 **tener ~s** : be nervous — **nerviosismo** nf : nervousness — **nervioso, -sa** adj 1 : nervous, anxious 2 **sistema nervioso** : nervous system
nervudo, -da adj : sinewy
neto, -ta adj 1 : clear, distinct 2 : net (of weight, salaries, etc.)
neumático nm : tire
neumonía nf : pneumonia
neurología nf : neurology — **neurológico, -ca** adj : neurological, neurologic — **neurólogo, -ga** n : neurologist
neurosis nfs & pl : neurosis — **neurótico, -ca** adj & n : neurotic
neutral adj : neutral — **neutralidad** nf : neutrality — **neutralizar** {21} vt : neutralize — **neutro, -tra** adj 1 : neutral 2 : neuter (in biology and grammar)
neutrón nm, pl **-trones** : neutron
nevar {55} v impers : snow — **nevada**

nf : snowfall — **nevado, -da** adj 1 : snow-covered, snowy 2 : snow-white — **nevasca** nf : snowstorm
nevera nf : refrigerator
nevisca nf : light snowfall, flurry
nexo nm : link, connection
ni conj 1 : neither, nor 2 **~ que** : as if 3 **~ siquiera** : not even
nicaragüense adj : Nicaraguan
nicho nm : niche
nicotina nf : nicotine
nidada nf : brood (of chicks, etc.)
nido nm 1 : nest 2 GUARIDA : hiding place, den
niebla nf : fog, mist
nieto, -ta n 1 : grandson m, granddaughter f 2 **nietos** nmpl : grandchildren
nieve nf : snow
nigeriano, -na adj : Nigerian
nilón or nilon nm, pl **-lones** : nylon
nimio, -mia adj : insignificant, trivial — **nimiedad** nf 1 : trifle 2 INSIGNIFICANCIA : triviality
ninfa nf : nymph
ninguno, -na (**ningún** before masculine singular nouns) adj : no, not any — **~** pron 1 : neither, none 2 : no one, nobody
niña nf 1 : pupil (of the eye) 2 **la ~ de los ojos** : the apple of one's eye
niño, -ña n : child, boy m, girl f — **~** adj 1 : young 2 INFANTIL : immature, childish — **niñero, -ra** n : baby-sitter, nanny — **niñez** nf, pl **-ñeces** : childhood
nipón, -pona adj : Japanese
níquel nm : nickel
nítido, -da adj : clear, sharp — **nitidez** nf, pl **-deces** : clarity, sharpness
nitrato nm : nitrate
nitrógeno nm : nitrogen
nivel nm 1 : level, height 2 **~ de vida** : standard of living — **nivelar** vt : level (out)
no adv 1 : not 2 (in answer to a question) : no 3 **¡como ~!** : of course! 4 **~ bien** : as soon as 5 **~ fumador** : non-smoker — **~** nm : no
noble adj & nmf : noble — **nobleza** nf : nobility
noche nf 1 : night, evening 2 **buenas ~s** : good evening, good night 3 **de ~ or por la ~** : at night 4 **hacerse de ~** : get dark — **Nochebuena** nf : Christmas Eve — **nochecita** nf : dusk — **Nochevieja** nf : New Year's Eve
noción nf, pl **-ciones** 1 : notion, concept 2 **nociones** nfpl : rudiments
nocivo, -va adj : harmful, noxious

nocturno, -na *adj* **1** : night **2** : nocturnal (of animals, etc.) — **nocturno** *nm* : nocturne

nogal *nm* **1** : walnut tree **2** ~ **americano** : hickory

nómada *nmf* : nomad — ~ *adj* : nomadic

nomás *adv Lat* : only, just

nombrar *vt* **1** : appoint **2** CITAR : mention — **nombrado, -da** *adj* : famous, well-known — **nombramiento** *nm* : appointment, nomination — **nombre** *nm* **1** : name **2** SUSTANTIVO : noun **3** FAMA : fame, renown **4** ~ **de pila** : first name

nómina *nf* : payroll

nominal *adj* : nominal

nominar *vt* : nominate — **nominación** *nf, pl* **-ciones** : nomination

nomo *nm* : gnome

non *adj* : odd, not even — ~ *nm* : odd number

nonagésimo, -ma *adj & n* : ninetieth

nopal *nm* : nopal, prickly pear

nordeste *or* **noreste** *adj* **1** : northeastern **2** : northeasterly (of wind, etc.) — ~ *nm* : northeast

nórdico, -ca *adj* : Scandinavian

noreste → nordeste

noria *nf* **1** : waterwheel **2** : Ferris wheel (at a fair, etc.)

norma *nf* : rule, norm, standard — **normal** *adj* **1** : normal **2 escuela** ~ : teacher-training college — **normalidad** *nf* : normality — **normalizar** {21} *vt* **1** : normalize **2** ESTANDARIZAR : standardize — **normalizarse** *vr* : return to normal — **normalmente** *adv* : ordinarily, generally

noroeste *adj* **1** : northwestern **2** : northwesterly (of wind, etc.) — ~ *nm* : northwest

norte *adj* : north, northern — ~ *nm* **1** : north **2** : north wind

norteamericano, -na *adj* : North American

norteño, -ña *adj* : northern

noruego, -ga *adj* : Norwegian — **noruego** *nm* : Norwegian (language)

nos *pron* **1** (*direct object*) : us **2** (*indirect object*) : to us, for us, from us **3** (*reflexive*) : ourselves **4** : each other, one another

nosotros, -tras *pron* **1** (*subject*) : we **2** (*object*) : us **3** *or* ~ **mismos** : ourselves

nostalgia *nf* **1** : nostalgia **2 sentir** ~ **por** : be homesick for — **nostálgico, -ca** *adj* : nostalgic

nota *nf* **1** : note **2** : grade, mark (in school) **3** CUENTA : bill, check — **notable** *adj* : noteworthy, notable —

notar *vt* : notice — **notarse** *vr* : be evident, seem

notario, -ria *n* : notary (public)

noticia *nf* **1** : news item, piece of news **2** ~**s** *nfpl* : news — **noticiario** *nm* : newscast — **noticiero** *nm Lat* : newscast

notificar {72} *vt* : notify — **notificación** *nf, pl* **-ciones** : notification

notorio, -ria *adj* **1** : obvious **2** CONOCIDO : well-known — **notoriedad** *nf* : fame, notoriety

novato, -ta *adj* : inexperienced — ~ *n* : beginner, novice

novecientos, -tas *adj* : nine hundred — **novecientos** *nms & pl* : nine hundred

novedad *nf* **1** : newness, innovation **2** NOTICIAS : news **3** ~**es** : novelties, latest news — **novedoso, -sa** *adj* : original, novel

novela *nf* **1** : novel **2** : soap opera (on television) — **novelesco, -ca** *adj* **1** : fictional **2** FANTÁSTICO : fabulous — **novelista** *nmf* : novelist

noveno, -na *adj* : ninth — **noveno** *nm* : ninth

noventa *adj & nm* : ninety — **noventavo, -va** *adj* : ninetieth — **noventavo** *nm* : ninetieth

novia → novio

noviazgo *nm* : engagement

novicio, -cia *n* : novice

noviembre *nm* : November

novillo, -lla *n* : young bull *m*, heifer *f*

novio, -via *n* **1** : boyfriend *m*, girlfriend *f* **2** PROMETIDO : fiancé *m*, fiancée *f* **3** : bridegroom *m*, bride *f* (at a wedding)

novocaína *nf* : novocaine

nube *nf* : cloud — **nubarrón** *nm, pl* **-rrones** : storm cloud — **nublado, -da** *adj* **1** : cloudy **2** ENTURBIADO : clouded, dim — **nublado** *nm* : storm cloud — **nublar** *vt* **1** : cloud **2** OSCURECER : obscure — **nublarse** *vr* : get cloudy — **nuboso, -sa** *adj* : cloudy

nuca *nf* : nape, back of the neck

núcleo *nm* **1** : nucleus **2** CENTRO : center, core — **nuclear** *adj* : nuclear

nudillo *nm* : knuckle

nudismo *nm* : nudism — **nudista** *adj & nmf* : nudist

nudo *nm* **1** : knot **2** : crux, heart (of a problem, etc.) — **nudoso, -sa** *adj* : knotty, gnarled

nuera *nf* : daughter-in-law

nuestro, -tra *adj* : our — ~ *pron* (*with definite article*) : ours, our own

nuevamente *adv* : again, anew

nueve *adj & nm* : nine
nuevo, -va *adj* **1** : new **2 de nuevo** : again, once more
nuez *nf, pl* **nueces 1** : nut **2** *or* ∼ **de nogal** : walnut **3** ∼ **de Adán** : Adam's apple **4** ∼ **moscada** : nutmeg
nulo, -la *adj* **1** *or* ∼ **y sin efecto** : null and void **2** INCAPAZ : useless, inept — **nulidad** *nf* **1** : nullity **2 es una** ∼ *fam* : he's a total loss
numerar *vt* : number — **numeración** *nf, pl* **-ciones 1** : numbering **2** NÚMEROS : numbers *pl*, numerals *pl* — **numeral** *adj* : numeral — **número** *nm* **1** : number, numeral **2** : issue (of a

publication) **3 sin** ∼ : countless —
numérico, -ca *adj* : numerical — **numeroso, -sa** *adj* : numerous
nunca *adv* **1** : never, ever **2** ∼ **más** : never again **3** ∼ **jamás** : never ever
nupcial *adj* : nuptial, wedding — **nupcias** *nfpl* : nuptials, wedding
nutria *nf* : otter
nutrir *vt* **1** ALIMENTAR : feed, nourish **2** FOMENTAR : fuel, foster — **nutrición** *nf, pl* **-ciones** : nutrition — **nutrido, -da** *adj* **1** : nourished **2** ABUNDANTE : considerable, abundant — **nutriente** *nm* : nutrient — **nutritivo, -va** *adj* : nourishing, nutritious

O

o¹ *nf* : o, 16th letter of the Spanish alphabet
o² *conj* (**u** *before words beginning with* o- *or* ho-) **1** : or, either **2** ∼ **sea** : in other words
oasis *nms & pl* : oasis
obcecar {72} *vt* : blind (by emotions) — **obcecarse** *vr* : become stubborn
obedecer {53} *vt* : obey — *vi* **1** : obey **2** ∼ **a** : respond to **3** ∼ **a** : be due to — **obediencia** *nf* : obedience — **obediente** *adj* : obedient
obertura *nf* : overture
obeso, -sa *adj* : obese — **obesidad** *nf* : obesity
obispo *nm* : bishop
objetar *v* : object — **objeción** *nf, pl* **-ciones** : objection
objeto *nm* : object — **objetivo, -va** *adj* : objective — **objetivo** *nm* **1** : objective, goal **2** : lens (in photography, etc.)
objetor, -tora *n* ∼ **de conciencia** : conscientious objector
oblicuo, -cua *adj* : oblique
obligar {52} *vt* : require, oblige — **obligarse** *vr* : commit oneself (to do something) — **obligación** *nf, pl* **-ciones** : obligation — **obligado, -da** *adj* **1** : obliged **2** FORZOSO : obligatory — **obligatorio, -ria** *adj* : mandatory
oblongo, -ga *adj* : oblong
oboe *nm* : oboe — ∼ *nmf* : oboist
obra *nf* **1** : work, deed **2** : work (of art, literature, etc.) **3** CONSTRUCCIÓN : construction work **4** ∼ **maestra** : masterpiece **5** ∼**s públicas** : public works — **obrar** *vt* : work, produce — *vi* : act, behave — **obrero, -ra** *adj* **la clase obrera** : the working class — ∼ *n* : worker, laborer

obsceno, -na *adj* : obscene — **obscenidad** *nf* : obscenity
obsequiar *vt* : give, present — **obsequio** *nm* : gift, present
observar *vt* **1** : observe, watch **2** ADVERTIR : notice **3** ACATAR : observe, obey **4** COMENTAR : remark — **observación** *nf, pl* **-ciones** : observation — **observador, -dora** *adj* : observant — ∼ *n* : observer — **observancia** *nf* : observance — **observatorio** *nm* : observatory
obsesionar *vt* : obsess — **obsesionarse** *vr* : be obsessed — **obsesión** *nf, pl* **-siones** : obsession — **obsesivo, -va** *adj* : obsessive — **obseso, -sa** *adj* : obsessed
obsoleto, -ta *adj* : obsolete
obstaculizar {21} *vt* : hinder — **obstáculo** *nm* : obstacle
obstante: no ∼ *conj phr* : nevertheless, however — ∼ *prep phr* : in spite of, despite
obstar {21} *vi* ∼ **a** *or* ∼ **para** : stop, prevent
obstetricia *nf* : obstetrics — **obstetra** *nmf* : obstetrician
obstinarse *vr* : be stubborn — **obstinado, -da** *adj* **1** : obstinate, stubborn **2** TENAZ : persistent
obstruir {41} *vt* : obstruct — **obstrucción** *nf, pl* **-ciones** : obstruction
obtener {80} *vt* : obtain, get
obtuso, -sa *adj* : obtuse
obviar *vt* : get around, avoid
obvio, -via *adj* : obvious — **obviamente** *adv* : obviously, clearly
oca *nf* : goose
ocasión *nf, pl* **-siones 1** : occasion **2** OPORTUNIDAD : opportunity **3** GANGA

: bargain — **ocasional** adj 1 : occasional 2 ACCIDENTAL : accidental, chance — **ocasionar** vt : cause

ocaso nm 1 : sunset 2 DECADENCIA : decline

occidente nm 1 : west 2 el **Occidente** : the West — **occidental** adj : western, Western

océano nm : ocean — **oceanografía** nf : oceanography

ochenta adj & nm : eighty

ocho adj & nm : eight — **ochocientos, -tas** adj : eight hundred — **ochocientos** nms & pl : eight hundred

ocio nm 1 : free time, leisure 2 INACTIVIDAD : idleness — **ociosidad** nf : idleness, inactivity — **ocioso, -sa** adj 1 : idle, inactive 2 INÚTIL : useless

ocre adj & nm : ocher

octágono nm : octagon — **octagonal** adj : octagonal

octava nf : octave

octavo, -va adj & n : eighth

octeto nm : byte

octogésimo, -ma adj & n : eightieth

octubre nm : October

ocular adj : ocular, eye — **oculista** nmf : ophthalmologist

ocultar vt : conceal, hide — **ocultarse** vr : hide — **oculto, -ta** adj : hidden, occult

ocupar vt 1 : occupy 2 : hold (a position, etc.) 3 : provide work for — **ocuparse** vr 1 ~ **de** : concern oneself with 2 ~ **de** : take care of (children, etc.) — **ocupación** nf, pl -**ciones** 1 : occupation 2 EMPLEO : job — **ocupado, -da** adj 1 : busy 2 : occupied (of a place) 3 **señal de ocupado** : busy signal — **ocupante** nmf : occupant

ocurrir vi : occur, happen — **ocurrirse** vr ~ **a** : occur to — **ocurrencia** nf 1 : occurrence, event 2 SALIDA : witty remark, quip

oda nf : ode

odiar vt : hate — **odio** nm : hatred — **odioso, -sa** adj : hateful

odisea nf : odyssey

odontología nf : dentistry, dental surgery — **odontólogo, -ga** n : dentist, dental surgeon

oeste adj : west, western — ~ nm 1 : west 2 el **Oeste** : the West

ofender v : offend — **ofenderse** vr : take offense — **ofensa** nf : offense, insult — **ofensiva** nf : offensive — **ofensivo, -va** adj : offensive

oferta nf 1 : offer 2 **de** ~ : on sale 3 ~ **y demanda** : supply and demand

oficial adj : official — ~ nmf 1 : skilled worker 2 : officer (in the military)

oficina nf : office — **oficinista** nmf : office worker

oficio nm : trade, profession — **oficioso, -sa** adj : unofficial

ofrecer {53} vt 1 : offer 2 : provide, present (an opportunity, etc.) — **ofrecerse** vr : volunteer — **ofrecimiento** nm : offer

ofrenda nf : offering

oftalmología nf : ophthalmology — **oftalmólogo, -ga** n : ophthalmologist

ofuscar {72} vt 1 : blind, dazzle 2 CONFUNDIR : confuse — **ofuscarse** vr ~ **con** : be blinded by — **ofuscación** nf, pl -**clones** 1 : blindness 2 CONFUSIÓN : confusion

ogro nm : ogre

oír {50} vi 1 : hear — vt 1 : hear 2 ESCUCHAR : listen to 3 **¡oiga!** or **¡oye!** : excuse me!, listen! — **oídas: de** ~ adv phr : by hearsay — **oído** nm 1 : ear 2 : (sense of) hearing 3 **duro de** ~ : hard of hearing

ojal nm : buttonhole

ojalá interj : I hope so!, if only!

ojear vt : eye, look at — **ojeada** nf : glimpse, glance

ojeriza nf 1 : ill will 2 **tener** ~ **a** : have a grudge against

ojo nm 1 : eye 2 PERSPICACIA : shrewdness 3 : span (of a bridge) 4 **¡**~**!** : look out!, pay attention!

ola nf : wave — **oleada** nf : wave, surge — **oleaje** nm : swell (of the sea)

olé interj : bravo!

oleada nf : wave, swell — **oleaje** nm : waves, surf

óleo nm 1 : oil 2 CUADRO : oil painting — **oleoducto** nm : oil pipeline

oler {51} vt : smell — vi 1 : smell 2 ~ **a** : smell of — **olerse** vr fam : have a hunch about

olfatear vt 1 : sniff 2 OLER : sense, sniff out — **olfato** nm 1 : sense of smell 2 PERSPICACIA : nose, instinct

Olimpíada or **Olimpiada** nf : Olympics pl, Olympic Games pl — **olímpico, -ca** adj : Olympic

oliva nf : olive — **olivo** nm : olive tree

olla nf 1 : pot 2 ~ **podrida** : (Spanish) stew

olmo nm : elm

olor nm : smell — **oloroso, -sa** adj : fragrant

olvidar vt 1 : forget 2 DEJAR : leave (behind) — **olvidarse** vr : forget — **olvidadizo, -za** adj : forgetful — **olvido** nm 1 : forgetfulness 2 DESCUIDO : oversight

ombligo nm : navel

omelette nmf Lat : omelet

ominoso, -sa *adj* : ominous

omitir *vt* : omit — **omisión** *nf, pl* **-siones** : omission

ómnibus *nm, pl* **-bus** *or* **-buses** : bus

omnipotente *adj* : omnipotent

omóplato *or* **omoplato** *nm* : shoulder blade

once *adj & nm* : eleven — **onceavo, -va** *adj & n* : eleventh

onda *nf* : wave — **ondear** *vi* : ripple — **ondulación** *nf, pl* **-ciones** : undulation — **ondulado, -da** *adj* : wavy — **ondular** *vt* : wave (hair) — *vi* : undulate, ripple

ónice *nmf or* **ónix** *nm* : onyx

onza *nf* : ounce

opaco, -ca *adj* 1 : opaque 2 DESLUSTRADO : dull

ópalo *nm* : opal

opción *nf, pl* **-ciones** : option — **opcional** *adj* : optional

ópera *nf* : opera

operar *vt* 1 : operate on 2 *Lat* : operate, run (a machine) — *vi* 1 : operate 2 NEGOCIAR : deal, do business — **operarse** *vr* 1 : have an operation 2 OCURRIR : take place — **operación** *nf, pl* **-ciones** 1 : operation 2 TRANSACCIÓN : transaction, deal — **operacional** *adj* : operational — **operador, -dora** *n* 1 : operator 2 : cameraman (for television, etc.)

opereta *nf* : operetta

opinar *vt* : think — *vi* : express an opinion — **opinión** *nf, pl* **-niones** : opinion

opio *nm* : opium

oponer {60} *vt* 1 : raise, put forward (arguments, etc.) 2 ~ **resistencia** : put up a fight — **oponerse** *vr* ~ **a** : oppose, be against — **oponente** *nmf* : opponent

oporto *nm* : port (wine)

oportunidad *nf* : opportunity — **oportunista** *nmf* : opportunist — **oportuno, -na** *adj* 1 : opportune, timely 2 APROPIADO : suitable

opositor, -tora *n* 1 : opponent 2 : candidate (for a position) — **oposición** *nf, pl* **-ciones** : opposition

oprimir *vt* 1 : press, squeeze 2 TIRANIZAR : oppress — **opresión** *nf, pl* **-siones** 1 : oppression 2 ~ **de pecho** : tightness in the chest — **opresivo, -va** *adj* : oppressive — **opresor, -sora** *n* : oppressor

optar *vi* 1 ~ **a** : apply for 2 ~ **por** : choose, opt for

óptica *nf* 1 : optics 2 : optician's (shop) — **óptico, -ca** *adj* : optical — ~ *n* : optician

optimismo *nm* : optimism — **optimista** *adj* : optimistic — ~ *nmf* : optimist

optometría *nf* : optometry — **optometrista** *nmf* : optometrist

opuesto *adj* 1 : opposite 2 CONTRADICTORIO : opposed, conflicting

opulencia *nf* : opulence — **opulento, -ta** *adj* : opulent

oración *nf, pl* **-ciones** 1 : prayer 2 FRASE : sentence, clause

oráculo *nm* : oracle

orador, -dora *n* : speaker

oral *adj* : oral

orar *vi* : pray

órbita *nf* 1 : orbit (in astronomy) 2 : eye socket — **orbitar** *vi* : orbit

orden *nm, pl* **órdenes** 1 : order 2 ~ **del día** : agenda (at a meeting) 3 ~ **público** : law and order — ~ *nf, pl* **órdenes** 1 : order (of food) 2 ~ **religiosa** : religious order 3 ~ **de compra** : purchase order

ordenador *nm Spain* : computer

ordenar *vt* 1 : order, command 2 ARREGLAR : put in order 3 : ordain (a priest) — **ordenanza** *nm* : orderly (in the armed forces) — ~ *nf* : ordinance, regulation

ordeñar *vt* : milk

ordinal *adj & nm* : ordinal

ordinario, -ria *adj* 1 : ordinary 2 GROSERO : common, vulgar

orear *vt* : air

orégano *nm* : oregano

oreja *nf* : ear

orfanato *or* **orfelinato** *nm* : orphanage

orfebre *nmf* : goldsmith, silversmith

orgánico, -ca *adj* : organic

organigrama *nm* : flowchart

organismo *nm* 1 : organism 2 ORGANIZACIÓN : agency, organization

organista *nmf* : organist

organizar {21} *vt* : organize — **organizarse** *vr* : get organized — **organización** *nf, pl* **-ciones** : organization — **organizador, -dora** *n* : organizer

órgano *nm* : organ

orgasmo *nm* : orgasm

orgía *nf* : orgy

orgullo *nm* : pride — **orgulloso, -sa** *adj* : proud

orientación *nf, pl* **-ciones** 1 : orientation 2 DIRECCIÓN : direction 3 CONSEJO : guidance

oriental *adj* 1 : eastern 2 : oriental — ~ *nmf* : Oriental

orientar *vt* 1 : orient, position 2 GUIAR : guide, direct — **orientarse** *vr* 1 : orient oneself 2 ~ **hacia** : turn towards

oriente *nm* 1 : east, East 2 **el Oriente** : the Orient
orificio *nm* : orifice, opening
origen *nm, pl* **orígenes** : origin — **original** *adj & nm* : original — **originalidad** *nf* : originality — **originar** *vt* : give rise to — **originarse** *vr* : originate, arise — **originario, -ria** *adj* ~ **de** : native of
orilla *nf* 1 : border, edge 2 : bank (of a river), shore (of the sea)
orinar *vi* : urinate — **orina** *nf* : urine
oriol *nm* : oriole
oriundo, -da *adj* ~ **de** : native of
orla *nf* : border
ornamental *adj* : ornamental — **ornamento** *nm* : ornament
ornar *vt* : adorn
ornitología *nf* : ornithology
oro *nm* : gold
orquesta *nf* : orchestra — **orquestar** *vt* : orchestrate
orquídea *nf* : orchid
ortiga *nf* : nettle
ortodoxia *nf* : orthodoxy — **ortodoxo, -xa** *adj* : orthodox
ortografía *nf* : spelling
ortopedia *nf* : orthopedics — **ortopédico, -ca** *adj* : orthopedic
oruga *nf* : caterpillar
orzuelo *nm* : sty (in the eye)
os *pron pl Spain* 1 (*direct or indirect object*) : you, to you 2 (*reflexive*) : yourselves, to yourselves 3 : each other, to each other
osado, -da *adj* : bold, daring — **osadía** *nf* 1 : boldness, daring 2 DESCARO : audacity, nerve
osamenta *nf* : skeleton
osar *vi* : dare
oscilar *vi* 1 : swing, sway FLUCTUAR : fluctuate — **oscilación** *nf, pl* **-ciones** 1 : swinging 2 FLUCTUACIÓN : fluctuation
oscuro, -ra *adj* 1 : dark 2 : obscure (of ideas, persons, etc.) 3 **a oscuras** : in the dark — **oscurecer** {53} *vt* 1 : darken 2 : confuse, cloud (the mind)

3 **al** ~ : at nightfall — *v impers* : get dark — **oscurecerse** *vr* : grow dark — **oscuridad** *nf* 1 : darkness 2 : obscurity (of ideas, persons, etc.)
óseo, ósea *adj* : skeletal, bony
oso, osa *n* 1 : bear 2 ~ **de peluche** *or* ~ **de felpa** : teddy bear
ostensible *adj* : evident, obvious
ostentar *vt* 1 : flaunt, display 2 POSEER : have, hold — **ostentación** *nf, pl* **-ciones** : ostentation — **ostentoso, -sa** *adj* : ostentatious, showy
osteopatía *n* : osteopathy — **osteópata** *nmf* : osteopath
osteoporosis *nf* : osteoporosis
ostra *nf* : oyster
ostracismo *nm* : ostracism
otear *vt* : scan, survey
otoño *nm* : autumn, fall — **otoñal** *adj* : autumn, fall
otorgar {52} *vt* 1 : grant, award 2 : draw up (a legal document)
otro, otra *adj* 1 : another, other 2 **otra vez** : again — ~ *pron* 1 : another (one), other (one) 2 **los otros, las otras** : the others, the rest
ovación *nf, pl* **-ciones** : ovation
óvalo *nm* : oval — **oval** *or* **ovalado, -da** *adj* : oval
ovario *nm* : ovary
oveja *nf* 1 : sheep, ewe 2 ~ **negra** : black sheep
overol *nm Lat* : overalls *pl*
ovillo *nm* 1 : ball (of yarn) 2 **hacerse un** ~ : curl up (into a ball)
ovni *or* **OVNI** *nm* (*objeto volador no identificado*) : UFO
ovular *vi* : ovulate — **ovulación** *nf, pl* **-ciones** : ovulation
oxidar *vi* : rust — **oxidarse** *vr* : get rusty — **oxidación** *nf, pl* **-ciones** : rusting — **oxidado, -da** *adj* : rusty — **óxido** *nm* : rust
oxígeno *nm* : oxygen
oye → **oír**
oyente *nmf* 1 : listener 2 : auditor (student)
ozono *nm* : ozone

P

p *nf* : p, 17th letter of the Spanish alphabet
pabellón *nm, pl* **-llones** 1 : pavilion 2 : block, building (in a hospital complex, etc.) 3 : summerhouse (in a garden, etc.) 4 BANDERA : flag

pabilo *nm* : wick
pacer {48} *v* : graze
paces → **paz**
paciencia *nf* : patience — **paciente** *adj & nmf* : patient
pacificar {72} *vt* : pacify, calm — **paci-**

ficarse *vr* : calm down — **pacífico, -ca** *adj* : peaceful, pacific — **pacifismo** *nm* : pacifism — **pacifista** *adj & nmf* : pacifist

pacotilla *nf* **de ~** : second-rate, trashy

pacto *nm* : pact, agreement — **pactar** *vt* : agree on — *vi* : come to an agreement

padecer {53} *vt* : suffer, endure — *vi* **~ de** : suffer from — **padecimiento** *nm* : suffering

padre *nm* 1 : father 2 **~s** *nmpl* : parents — **~** *adj Lat fam* : great, fantastic — **padrastro** *nm* : stepfather — **padrino** *nm* 1 : godfather 2 : best man (at a wedding)

padrón *nm, pl* **-drones** : register, roll

paella *nf* : paella

paga *nf* : pay, wages *pl* — **pagadero, -ra** *adj* : payable

pagano, -na *adj & n* : pagan, heathen

pagar {52} *vt* : pay, pay for — *vi* : pay — **pagaré** *nm* : IOU

página *nf* : page

pago *nm* : payment

país *nm* 1 : country, nation 2 REGIÓN : region, land — **paisaje** *nm* : scenery, landscape — **paisano, -na** *n* : compatriot

paja *nf* 1 : straw 2 *fam* : nonsense

pájaro *nm* 1 : bird 2 **~ carpintero** : woodpecker — **pajarera** *nf* : aviary

pajita *nf* : (drinking) straw

pala *nf* 1 : shovel, spade 2 : blade (of an oar or a rotor) 3 : paddle, racket (in sports)

palabra *nf* 1 : word 2 HABLA : speech 3 **tener la ~** : have the floor — **palabrota** *nf* : swearword

palacio *nm* 1 : palace, mansion 2 **~ de justicia** : courthouse

paladar *nm* : palate — **paladear** *vt* : savor

palanca *nf* 1 : lever, crowbar 2 *fam* : leverage, influence 3 **~ de cambio** *or* **~ de velocidades** : gearshift

palangana *nf* : washbowl

palco *nm* : box (in a theater)

palestino, -na *adj* : Palestinian

paleta *nf* 1 : small shovel, trowel 2 : palette (in art) 3 : paddle (in sports, etc.)

paletilla *nf* : shoulder blade

paliar *vt* : alleviate, ease — **paliativo, -va** *adj* : palliative

pálido, -da *adj* : pale — **palidecer** {53} *vi* : turn pale — **palidez** *nf, pl* **-deces** : paleness, pallor

palillo *nm* 1 : small stick 2 *or* **~ de dientes** : toothpick

paliza *nf* : beating

palma *nf* 1 : palm (of the hand) 2 : palm (tree or leaf) 3 **batir ~s** : clap, applaud — **palmada** *nf* 1 : pat, slap 2 **~s** *nfpl* : clapping

palmera *nf* : palm tree

palmo *nm* 1 : span, small amount 2 **~ a ~** : bit by bit

palmotear *vi* : applaud — **palmoteo** *nm* : clapping, applause

palo *nm* 1 : stick 2 MANGO : shaft, handle 3 MÁSTIL : mast 4 POSTE : pole 5 GOLPE : blow 6 : suit (of cards)

paloma *nf* : pigeon, dove — **palomilla** *nf* : moth — **palomitas** *nfpl* : popcorn

palpar *vt* : feel, touch — **palpable** *adj* : palpable

palpitar *vi* : palpitate, throb — **palpitación** *nf, pl* **-ciones** : palpitation

palta *nf Lat* : avocado

paludismo *nm* : malaria

pampa *nf* : pampa

pan *nm* 1 : bread 2 : loaf (of bread, etc.) 3 **~ tostado** : toast

pana *nf* : corduroy

panacea *nf* : panacea

panadería *nf* : bakery, bread shop — **panadero, -ra** *n* : baker

panal *nm* : honeycomb

panameño, -ña *adj* : Panamanian

pancarta *nf* : placard, banner

pancito *nm Lat* : (bread) roll

páncreas *nms & pl* : pancreas

panda *nmf* : panda

pandemonio *nm* : pandemonium

pandero *nm* : tambourine — **pandereta** *nf* : (small) tambourine

pandilla *nf* : gang

panecillo *nm Spain* : (bread) roll

panel *nm* : panel

panfleto *nm* : pamphlet

pánico *nm* : panic

panorama *nm* : panorama — **panorámico, -ca** *adj* : panoramic

panqueque *nm Lat* : pancake

pantaletas *nfpl Lat* : panties

pantalla *nf* 1 : screen 2 : lampshade

pantalón *nm, pl* **-lones** 1 *or* **pantalones** *nmpl* : pants *pl*, trousers *pl* 2 **pantalones vaqueros** : jeans

pantano *nm* 1 : swamp, marsh 2 EMBALSE : reservoir — **pantanoso, -sa** *adj* : marshy, swampy

pantera *nf* : panther

pantimedias *nfpl Lat* : panty hose

pantomima *nf* : pantomime

pantorrilla *nf* : calf (of the leg)

pantufla *nf* : slipper

panza *nf* : belly, paunch — **panzón, -zona** *adj, mpl* **-zones** : potbellied

pañal *nm* : diaper

paño *nm* **1** : cloth **2** TRAPO : rag, dust cloth **3** ~ **de cocina** : dishcloth **4** ~ **higiénico** : sanitary napkin **5** ~**s menores** : underwear

pañuelo *nm* **1** : handkerchief **2** : scarf, kerchief

papa[1] *nm* : pope

papa[2] *nf Lat* **1** : potato **2** ~**s fritas** : potato chips, french fries

papá *nm fam* **1** : dad, pop **2** ~**s** *nmpl* : parents, folks

papada *nf* : double chin

papagayo *nm* : parrot

papal *adj* : papal

papalote *nm Lat* : kite

papanatas *nmfs & pl fam* : simpleton

papaya *nf* : papaya

papel *nm* **1** : paper, sheet of paper **2** : role, part (in theater, etc.) **3** ~ **de aluminio** : aluminum foil **4** ~ **higiénico** : toilet paper **5** ~ **de lija** : sandpaper **6** ~ **pintado** : wallpaper — **papeleo** *nm* : paperwork, red tape — **papelera** *nf* : wastebasket — **papelería** *nf* : stationery store — **papeleta** *nf* **1** : ticket, slip **2** : ballot (paper)

paperas *nfpl* : mumps

papilla *nf* **1** : baby food, pap **2 hacer** ~ : smash to bits

paquete *nm* **1** : package, parcel **2** : pack (of cigarettes, etc.)

paquistaní *adj* : Pakistani

par *nm* **1** : pair, couple **2** : par (in golf) **3** NOBLE : peer **4 abierto de** ~ **en** ~ : wide open **5 sin** ~ : without equal — ~ *adj* : even (in number) — ~ *nf* **1** : par **2 a la** ~ **que** : at the same time as

para *prep* **1** : for **2** HACIA : towards **3** : (in order) to **4** : around, by (a time) **5** ~ **adelante** : forwards **6** ~ **atrás** : backwards **7** ~ **que** : so (that), in order that

parabienes *nmpl* : congratulations

parábola *nf* : parable

parabrisas *nms & pl* : windshield

paracaídas *nms & pl* : parachute — **paracaidista** *nmf* **1** : parachutist **2** : paratrooper (in the military)

parachoques *nms & pl* : bumper

parada *nf* **1** : stop **2** : (act of) stopping **3** DESFILE : parade — **paradero** *nm* **1** : whereabouts **2** *Lat* : bus stop — **parado, -da** *adj* **1** : idle, stopped **2** *Lat* : standing (up) **3 bien (mal) parado** : in good (bad) shape

paradoja *nf* : paradox

parafernalia *nf* : paraphernalia

parafina *nf* : paraffin

parafrasear *vt* : paraphrase — **paráfrasis** *nfs & pl* : paraphrase

paraguas *nms & pl* : umbrella

paraguayo, -ya *adj* : Paraguayan

paraíso *nm* : paradise

paralelo, -la *adj* : parallel — **paralelo** *nm* : parallel — **paralelismo** *nm* : similarity

parálisis *nfs & pl* : paralysis — **paralítico, -ca** *adj* : paralytic — **paralizar** {21} *vt* : paralyze

parámetro *nm* : parameter

páramo *nm* : barren plateau

parangón *nm, pl* **-gones 1** : comparison **2 sin** ~ : matchless

paraninfo *nm* : auditorium, hall

paranoia *nf* : paranoia — **paranoico, -ca** *adj & n* : paranoid

parapeto *nm* : parapet, rampart

parapléjico, -ca *adj & n* : paraplegic

parar *vt* : stop **2** *Lat* : stand, prop — *vi* **1** : stop **2 ir a** ~ : end up, wind up — **pararse** *vr* **1** : stop **2** *Lat* : stand up

pararrayos *nms & pl* : lightning rod

parásito, -ta *adj* : parasitic — **parásito** *nm* : parasite

parasol *nm* : parasol

parcela *nf* : parcel, tract (of land) — **parcelar** *vt* : parcel (up)

parche *nm* : patch

parcial *adj* **1** : partial **2 a tiempo** ~ : part-time — **parcialidad** *nf* : partiality, bias

parco, -ca *adj* : sparing, frugal

pardo, -da *adj* : brownish grey

parear *vt* : pair (up)

parecer {53} *vi* **1** : seem, look **2** ASEMEJARSE A : look like, seem like **3 me parece que** : I think that, in my opinion **4 ¿qué te parece?** : what do you think? **5 según parece** : apparently — **parecerse** *vr* ~ **a** : resemble — ~ *nm* **1** : opinion **2** ASPECTO : appearance **3 al** ~ : apparently — **parecido, -da** *adj* **1** : similar **2 bien parecido** : good-looking — **parecido** *nm* : resemblance, similarity

pared *nf* : wall

parejo, -ja *adj* **1** : even, smooth **2** SEMEJANTE : similar — **pareja** *nf* **1** : couple, pair **2** : partner (person)

parentela *nf* : relatives *pl*, kin — **parentesco** *nm* : relationship, kinship

paréntesis *nms & pl* **1** : parenthesis **2** DIGRESIÓN : digression **3 entre** ~ : by the way

paria *nmf* : outcast

paridad *nf* : equality

pariente *nmf* : relative, relation

parir vi : give birth, have a baby — vt : give birth to
parking nm : parking lot
parlamentar vi : discuss — **parlamentario, -ria** adj : parliamentary — ~ n : member of parliament — **parlamento** nm : parliament
parlanchín, -china adj, mpl **-chines** : talkative, chatty — ~ n : chatterbox
parlotear vi fam : chatter — **parloteo** nm fam : chatter
paro nm 1 : stoppage, shutdown 2 DESEMPLEO : unemployment 3 Lat : strike 4 ~ **cardíaco** : cardiac arrest
parodia nf : parody — **parodiar** vt : parody
párpado nm : eyelid — **parpadear** vi 1 : blink 2 : flicker (of light), twinkle (of stars) — **parpadeo** nm 1 : blink 2 : flicker (of light), twinkling (of stars)
parque nm 1 : park 2 ~ **de atracciones** : amusement park
parqué nm : parquet
parquear vt Lat : park
parquedad nf : frugality, moderation
parquímetro nm : parking meter
parra nf : grapevine
párrafo nm : paragraph
parranda nf fam : party, spree
parrilla nf 1 : broiler, grill 2 : grate (of a chimney, etc.) — **parrillada** nf : barbecue
párroco nm : parish priest — **parroquia** nf 1 : parish 2 : parish church — **parroquial** adj : parochial — **parroquiano, -na** n 1 : parishioner 2 CLIENTE : customer
parsimonia nf 1 : calm 2 FRUGALIDAD : thrift — **parsimonioso, -sa** adj 1 : calm, unhurried 2 FRUGAL : thrifty
parte nf 1 : part 2 PORCIÓN : share 3 LADO : side 4 : part (in negotiations, etc.) 5 **de** ~ **de** : on behalf of 6 ¿**de** ~ **de quién?** : who is speaking? 7 **en alguna** ~ : somewhere 8 **en todas** ~**s** : everywhere 9 **tomar** ~ : take part — ~ nm 1 : report 2 ~ **meteorológico** : weather forecast
partero, -ra n : midwife
partición nf, pl **-ciones** : division, sharing
participar vi 1 : participate, take part 2 ~ **en** : have a share in — vt : notify — **participación** nf, pl **-ciones** 1 : participation 2 : share, interest (in a fund, etc.) 3 NOTICIA : notice — **participante** adj : participating — ~ nmf : participant — **participe** nmf : participant
participio nm : participle

partícula nf : particle
particular adj 1 : particular 2 PRIVADO : private — ~ nm 1 : matter 2 PERSONA : individual — **particularidad** nf : peculiarity — **particularizar** {21} vt : distinguish, characterize — vi : go into details
partir vt 1 : split, divide 2 ROMPER : break, crack 3 REPARTIR : share (out) — vi 1 : depart 2 ~ **de** : start from 3 **a** ~ **de** : as of, from — **partirse** vr 1 : split (open) 2 RAJARSE : crack — **partida** nf 1 : departure 2 : entry, item (in a register, etc.) 3 JUEGO : game 4 : group (of persons) 5 **mala** ~ : dirty trick 6 ~ **de nacimiento** : birth certificate — **partidario, -ria** n : follower, supporter — **partido** nm 1 : (political) party 2 : game, match (in sports) 3 PARTIDARIOS : following 4 **sacar** ~ **de** : make the most of
partitura nf : (musical) score
parto nm 1 : childbirth 2 **estar de** ~ : be in labor
parvulario nm : nursery school
párvulo, -la — see PÁRVULO
pasa nf 1 : raisin 2 ~ **de Corinto** : currant
pasable adj : passable
pasada nf 1 : pass, wipe, coat (of paint, etc.) 2 **de** ~ : in passing 3 **mala** ~ : dirty trick — **pasadizo** nm : corridor — **pasado, -da** adj 1 : past 2 PODRIDO : bad, spoiled 3 ANTICUADO : out-of-date 4 **el año pasado** : last year — **pasado** nm : past
pasador nm 1 CERROJO : bolt 2 : barrette (for the hair)
pasaje nm 1 : passage 2 BILLETE : ticket, fare 3 PASILLO : passageway 4 PASAJEROS : passengers — **pasajero, -ra** adj : passing — ~ n : passenger
pasamanos nms & pl : handrail, banister
pasaporte nm : passport
pasar vi 1 : pass, go (by) 2 ENTRAR : come in 3 SUCEDER : happen 4 TERMINARSE : be over, end 5 ~ **de** : exceed 6 ¿**qué pasa?** : what's the matter? — vt 1 : pass 2 : spend (time) 3 CRUZAR : cross 4 TOLERAR : tolerate 5 SUFRIR : go through, suffer 6 : show (a movie, etc.) 7 **pasarlo bien** : have a good time 8 ~ **por alto** : overlook, omit — **pasarse** vr 1 : pass, go away 2 ESTROPEARSE : spoil, go bad 3 OLVIDARSE : slip one's mind 4 EXCEDERSE : go too far
pasarela nf 1 : footbridge 2 : gangway (on a ship)

pasatiempo *nm* : pastime, hobby

Pascua *nf* 1 : Easter (Christian feast) 2 : Passover (Jewish feast) 3 NAVIDAD : Christmas

pase *nm* : pass

pasear *vi* : take a walk, go for a ride — *vt* 1 : take for a walk 2 EXHIBIR : parade, show off — **pasearse** *vr* : go for a walk, go for a ride — **paseo** *nm* 1 : walk, ride 2 *Lat* : outing

pasillo *nm* : passage, corridor

pasión *nf*, *pl* **-siones** : passion

pasivo, -va *adj* : passive — **pasivo** *nm* : liabilities *pl*

pasmar *vt* : astonish, amaze — **pasmarse** *vr* : be astonished — **pasmado, -da** *adj* : stunned, flabbergasted — **pasmo** *nm* : astonishment — **pasmoso, -sa** *adj* : astonishing

paso[1], **-sa** *adj* : dried (of fruit)

paso[2] *nm* 1 : step 2 HUELLA : footprint 3 RITMO : pace 4 CRUCE : crossing 5 PASAJE : passage, way through 6 : (mountain) pass 7 **de ~** : in passing

pasta *nf* 1 : paste 2 MASA : dough 3 *or* **~s** : pasta 4 **~ de dientes** *or* **~ dentífrica** : toothpaste

pastar *v* : graze

pastel *nm* 1 : cake 2 EMPANADA : pie 3 : pastel (crayon) — **pastelería** *nf* : pastry shop

pasteurizar {21} *vt* : pasteurize

pastilla *nf* 1 : pill, tablet 2 : bar (of chocolate, soap, etc.) 3 **~ para la tos** : lozenge, cough drop

pasto *nm* 1 : pasture 2 *Lat* : grass, lawn — **pastor, -tora** *n* 1 : shepherd 2 : pastor (in religion) — **pastoral** *adj* : pastoral

pata *nf* 1 : paw, leg (of an animal) 2 : foot, leg (of furniture) 3 **meter la ~** *fam* : put one's foot in it — **patada** *nf* 1 : kick 2 : stamp (of the foot) — **patalear** *vi* 1 : kick 2 : stamp (one's feet)

patata *nf Spain* : potato

patear *vt* : kick — *vi* 1 : kick 2 : stamp (one's feet)

patentar *vt* : patent — **patente** *adj* : obvious, patent — **~** *nf* : patent

paternal *adj* : fatherly, paternal — **paternidad** *nf* 1 : fatherhood 2 : paternity (in law) — **paterno, -na** *adj* : paternal

patético, -ca *adj* : pathetic, moving

patillas *nfpl* : sideburns

patinar *vi* 1 : skate 2 RESBALAR : slip, slide — **patín** *nm*, *pl* **-tines** : skate — **patinador, -dora** *n* : skater — **patinaje** *nm* : skating — **patinazo** *nm* 1 : skid 2 *fam* : blunder — **patinete** *nm* : scooter

patio *nm* 1 : courtyard, patio 2 *or* **~ de recreo** : playground

pato, -ta *n* 1 : duck 2 **pagar el pato** *fam* : take the blame — **patito, -ta** *n* : duckling

patología *nf* : pathology — **patológico, -ca** *adj* : pathological

pataña *nf* : hoax

patria *nf* : native land

patriarca *nm* : patriarch

patrimonio *nm* 1 : inheritance 2 : (historical or cultural) heritage

patriota *adj* : patriotic — **~** *nmf* : patriot — **patriótico, -ca** *adj* : patriotic — **patriotismo** *nm* : patriotism

patrocinador, -dora *n* : sponsor — **patrocinar** *vt* : sponsor — **patrocinio** *nm* : sponsorship

patrón, -trona *n*, *mpl* **-trones** 1 : patron 2 JEFE : boss 3 : landlord, landlady *f* (of a boarding house, etc.) — **patrón** *nm*, *pl* **-trones** : pattern (in sewing) — **patronato** *nm* 1 : patronage 2 FUNDACIÓN : foundation, trust

patrulla *nf* 1 : patrol 2 : (police) cruiser — **patrullar** *v* : patrol

paulatino, -na *adj* : gradual

pausa *nf* : pause, break — **pausado, -da** *adj* : slow, deliberate

pauta *nf* : guideline

pavimento *nm* : pavement — **pavimentar** *vt* : pave

pavo, -va *n* 1 : turkey 2 **pavo real** : peacock

pavonearse *vr* : strut, swagger

pavor *nm* : dread, terror — **pavoroso, -sa** *adj* : terrifying

payaso, -sa *n* : clown — **payasada** *nf* : antic, buffoonery — **payasear** *vi Lat fam* : clown (around)

paz *nf*, *pl* **paces** 1 : peace 2 **dejar en ~** : leave alone 3 **hacer las paces** : make up, reconcile

peaje *nm* : toll

peatón *nm*, *pl* **-tones** : pedestrian

peca *nf* : freckle

pecado *nm* : sin — **pecador, -dora** *adj* : sinful — **~** *n* : sinner — **pecaminoso, -sa** *adj* : sinful — **pecar** {72} *vi* : sin

pecera *nf* : fishbowl, fish tank

pecho *nm* 1 : chest 2 MAMA : breast 3 CORAZÓN : heart 4 **dar el ~** : breast-feed 5 **tomar a ~** : take to heart — **pechuga** *nf* : breast (of fowl)

pecoso, -sa *adj* : freckled

pectoral *adj* : pectoral

peculiar *adj* 1 : particular 2 RARO : peculiar, odd — **peculiaridad** *nf* : peculiarity

pedagogía *nf* : education, pedagogy — **pedagogo, -ga** *n* : educator, teacher

pedal *nm* : pedal — **pedalear** *vi* : pedal

pedante *adj* : pedantic, pompous

pedazo *nm* 1 : piece, bit 2 **hacerse ~s** : fall to pieces

pedernal *nm* : flint

pedestal *nm* : pedestal

pediatra *nmf* : pediatrician

pedigrí *nm* : pedigree

pedir {54} *vt* 1 : ask for, request 2 : order (food, merchandise, etc.) — *vi* 1 : ask 2 **~ prestado** : borrow — **pedido** *nm* 1 : order 2 **hacer un ~** : place an order

pedregoso, -sa *adj* : rocky, stony

pedrería *nf* : precious stones *pl*

pegar {52} *vt* 1 : stick, glue, paste 2 : sew on (a button, etc.) 3 JUNTAR : bring together 4 GOLPEAR : hit, strike 5 PROPINAR : deal (a blow, etc.) 6 : transmit (an illness) 7 **~ un grito** : let out a scream — *vi* 1 : adhere, stick 2 GOLPEAR : hit — **pegarse** *vr* 1 : hit oneself, hit each other 2 ADHERIRSE : stick, adhere 3 CONTAGIARSE : be transmitted — **pegadizo, -za** *adj* 1 : catchy 2 CONTAGIOSO : contagious — **pegajoso, -sa** *adj* 1 : sticky 2 *Lat* : catchy — **pegamento** *nm* : glue

peinar *vt* : comb — **peinarse** *vr* : comb one's hair — **peinado** *nm* : hairstyle, hairdo — **peine** *nm* : comb — **peineta** *nf* : ornamental comb

pelado, -da *adj* 1 : shorn, hairless 2 : peeled (of fruit, etc.) 3 *fam* : bare 4 *fam* : broke, penniless

pelaje *nm* : coat (of an animal), fur

pelar *vt* 1 : cut the hair of (a person) 2 MONDAR : peel (fruit) 3 : pluck (a chicken, etc.), skin (an animal) — **pelarse** *vr* 1 : peel 2 *fam* : get a haircut

peldaño *nm* 1 : step (of stairs) 2 : rung (of a ladder)

pelear *vi* 1 : fight 2 DISCUTIR : quarrel — **pelearse** *vr* : have a fight — **pelea** *nf* 1 : fight 2 DISCUSIÓN : quarrel

peletería *nf* : fur shop

peliagudo, -da *adj* : tricky, difficult

pelícano *nm* : pelican

película *nf* : movie, film

peligro *nm* 1 : danger 2 RIESGO : risk — **peligroso, -sa** *adj* : dangerous

pelirrojo, -ja *adj* : red-haired — *n* : redhead

pellejo *nm* : skin, hide

pellizcar {72} *vt* : pinch — **pellizco** *nm* : pinch

pelo *nm* 1 : hair 2 : coat, fur (of an animal) 3 : pile, nap (of fabric) 4 **con ~s**

y señales : in great detail 5 **no tener ~ en la lengua** *fam* : not to mince words 6 **tomar el ~ a algn** *fam* : pull someone's leg — **pelón, -lona** *adj fam, mpl* **-lones** : bald

pelota *nf* : ball

pelotón *nm, pl* **-tones** : squad, detachment

peltre *nm* : pewter

peluca *nf* : wig

peluche *nm* 1 : plush 2 **oso de ~** : teddy bear

peludo, -da *adj* : hairy, furry

peluquería *nf* : hairdresser's, barber shop — **peluquero, -ra** *n* : barber, hairdresser

pelusa *nf* : fuzz, lint

pelvis *nfs & pl* : pelvis

pena *nf* 1 : penalty 2 TRISTEZA : sorrow 3 DOLOR : suffering, pain 4 *Lat* : embarrassment 5 **a duras ~s** : with great difficulty 6 **¡qué ~!** : what a shame! 7 **valer la ~** : be worthwhile

penacho *nm* 1 : crest, tuft 2 : plume (ornament)

penal *adj* : penal — **~** *nm* : prison, penitentiary — **penalidad** *nf* 1 : hardship 2 : penalty (in law) — **penalizar** {21} *vt* : penalize

penalty *nm* : penalty (in sports)

penar *vt* : punish — *vi* : suffer

pendenciero, -ra *adj* : quarrelsome

pender *vi* : hang — **pendiente** *adj* 1 : pending 2 **estar ~ de** : be watching out for — **~** *nf* : slope — **~** *nm Spain* : earring

pendón *nm, pl* **-dones** : banner

péndulo *nm* : pendulum

pene *nm* : penis

penetrar *vi* 1 : penetrate 2 **~ en** : go into — *vt* 1 : penetrate 2 : pierce (one's heart, etc.) 3 ENTENDER : fathom, grasp — **penetración** *nf, pl* **-ciones** 1 : penetration 2 PERSPICACIA : insight — **penetrante** *adj* 1 : penetrating 2 : sharp (of odors, etc.), piercing (of sounds) 3 : deep (of a wound, etc.)

penicilina *nf* : penicillin

península *nf* : peninsula — **peninsular** *adj* : peninsular

penitencia *nf* 1 : penitence 2 CASTIGO : penance — **penitenciaría** *nf* : penitentiary — **penitente** *adj & nmf* : penitent

penoso, -sa *adj* 1 : painful, distressing 2 TRABAJOSO : hard 3 *Lat* : shy

pensar {55} *vi* 1 : think 2 **~ en** : think about — *vt* 1 : think 2 CONSIDERAR : think about 3 **~ hacer algo** : intend to do sth — **pensador, -dora** *n*

: thinker — **pensamiento** *nm* 1
: thought 2 : pansy (flower) — **pensativo, -va** *adj* : pensive, thoughtful
pensión *nf, pl* **-siones** 1 : boarding
house 2 : (retirement) pension 3 ∼ **alimenticia** : alimony — **pensionista**
nmf 1 : lodger 2 JUBILADO : retiree
pentágono *nm* : pentagon
pentagrama *nm* : staff (in music)
penúltimo, -ma *adj* : next to last, penul-
timate
penumbra *nf* : half-light
penuria *nf* : dearth, shortage
peña *nf* : rock, crag — **peñasco** *nm*
: crag, large rock — **peñón** *nm, pl*
-ñones : craggy rock
peón *nm, pl* **peones** 1 : laborer, peon 2
: pawn (in chess)
peonía *nf* : peony
peor *adv* 1 (*comparative of* **mal**)
: worse 2 (*superlative of* **mal**) : worst
— ∼ *adj* 1 (*comparative of* **malo**)
: worse 2 (*superlative of* **malo**) : worst
pepino *nm* : cucumber — **pepinillo** *nm*
: pickle, gherkin
pepita *nf* 1 : seed, pip 2 : nugget (of
gold, etc.)
pequeño, -ña *adj* : small, little — **pe-
queñez** *nf, pl* **-ñeces** 1 : smallness 2
NIMIEDAD : trifle
pera *nf* : pear — **peral** *nm* : pear tree
percance *nm* : mishap, setback
percatarse *vr* ∼ **de** : notice
percepción *nf, pl* **-ciones** : perception
— **perceptible** *adj* : perceptible
percha *nf* 1 : perch (for birds) 2 : (coat)
hanger 3 : coatrack (on a wall)
percibir *vt* 1 : perceive 2 : receive (a
salary, etc.)
percusión *nf, pl* **-siones** : percussion
perder {56} *vt* 1 : lose 2 : miss (an opportunity, etc.) 3 DESPERDICIAR : waste
(time) — *vi* : lose — **perderse** *vr* 1
: get lost 2 DESAPARECER : disappear 3
DESPERDICIARSE : be wasted — **perde-
dor, -dora** *n* : loser — **pérdida** *nf* 1
: loss 2 ESCAPE : leak 3 ∼ **de tiempo**
: waste of time — **perdido, -da** *adj* 1
: lost 2 **un caso perdido** *fam* : a hopeless case
perdigón *nm, pl* **-gones** : shot, pellet
perdiz *nf, pl* **-dices** : partridge
perdón *nm, pl* **-dones** : forgiveness,
pardon — **perdón** *interj* : sorry! —
perdonar *vt* 1 DISCULPAR : forgive 2
: pardon (in law)
perdurar *vi* : last, endure — **per-
durable** *adj* : lasting
perecer {53} *vi* : perish, die — **perecedero, -ra** *adj* : perishable

peregrinación *nf, pl* **-ciones** *or* **pere-
grinaje** *nm* : pilgrimage — **peregrino, -na** *adj* 1 : migratory 2 RARO : unusual, odd — ∼ *n* : pilgrim
perejil *nm* : parsley
perenne *adj & nm* : perennial
pereza *nf* : laziness — **perezoso, -sa**
adj : lazy
perfección *nf, pl* **-ciones** : perfection
— **perfeccionar** *vt* 1 : perfect 2 MEJO-
RAR : improve — **perfeccionista** *nmf*
: perfectionist — **perfecto, -ta** *adj*
: perfect
perfidia *nf* : treachery — **pérfido, -da**
adj : treacherous
perfil *nm* 1 : profile 2 CONTORNO : outline 3 ∼ **es** *nmpl* RASGOS : features —
perfilar *vt* : outline — **perfilarse** *vr* 1
: be outlined 2 CONCRETARSE : take
shape
perforar *vt* 1 : perforate 2 : drill, bore (a
hole) — **perforación** *nf, pl* **-ciones**
: perforation — **perforadora** *nf*
: (paper) punch
perfume *nm* : perfume, scent — **per-
fumar** *vt* : perfume — **perfumarse** *vr*
: put perfume on
pergamino *nm* : parchment
pericia *nf* : skill
periferia *nf* : periphery, outskirts (of a
city, etc.) — **periférico, -ca** *adj* : peripheral
perilla *nf* 1 : goatee 2 *Lat* : knob 3 **venir
de** ∼**s** *fam* : come in handy
perímetro *nm* : perimeter
periódico, -ca *adj* : periodic — **periódico** *nm* : newspaper — **periodismo** *nm* : journalism — **periodista** *nmf*
: journalist
período *or* **periodo** *nm* : period
periquito *nm* : parakeet
periscopio *nm* : periscope
perito, -ta *adj & n* : expert
perjudicar {72} *vt* : harm, damage —
perjudicial *adj* : harmful — **perjuicio**
nm 1 : harm, damage 2 **en** ∼ **de** : to
the detriment of
perjurar *vi* : perjure oneself — **perjurio**
nm : perjury
perla *nf* 1 : pearl 2 **de** ∼**s** *fam* : great,
just fine
permanecer {53} *vi* : remain — **permanencia** *nf* 1 : permanence 2 : stay,
staying (in a place) — **permanente**
adj : permanent — ∼ *nf* : permanent
(wave)
permeable *adj* : permeable
permitir *vt* 1 : permit, allow 2 **¿me per-
mite?** : may I? — **permitirse** *vr*
: allow oneself — **permisible** *adj*

: permissible, allowable — **permisivo, -va** *adj* : permissive — **permiso** *nm* **1** : permission **2** : permit, license (document) **3** : leave (in the military) **4 con ~** : excuse me
permuta *nf* : exchange
pernicioso, -sa *adj* : pernicious, destructive
pero *conj* : but — **~** *nm* **1** : fault **2** REPARO : objection
perorar *vi* : make a speech — **perorata** *nf* : (long-winded) speech
perpendicular *adj & nf* : perpendicular
perpetrar *vt* : perpetrate
perpetuar {3} *vt* : perpetuate — **perpetuo, -tua** *adj* : perpetual
perplejo, -ja *adj* : perplexed — **perplejidad** *nf* : perplexity
perro, -rra *n* **1** : dog, bitch *f* **2 perro caliente** : hot dog — **perrera** *nf* : kennel
perseguir {75} *vt* **1** : pursue, chase **2** ACOSAR : persecute — **persecución** *nf, pl* **-ciones** **1** : pursuit, chase **2** ACOSO : persecution
perseverar *vi* : persevere — **perseverancia** *nf* : perseverance
persiana *nf* : (venetian) blind
persistir *vi* : persist — **persistencia** *nf* : persistence — **persistente** *adj* : persistent
persona *nf* : person — **personaje** *nm* **1** : character (in literature, etc.) **2** : important person, celebrity — **personal** *adj* : personal — **~** *nm* : personnel, staff — **personalidad** *nf* : personality — **personificar** {72} *vi* : personify
perspectiva *nf* **1** : perspective **2** VISTA : view **3** POSIBILIDAD : prospect, outlook
perspicacia *nf* : shrewdness, insight — **perspicaz** *adj, pl* **-caces** : shrewd, discerning
persuadir *vt* : persuade — **persuadirse** *vr* : become convinced — **persuasión** *nf, pl* **-siones** : persuasion — **persuasivo, -va** *adj* : persuasive
pertenecer {53} *vi* **~ a** : belong to — **perteneciente** *adj* **~ a** : belonging to — **pertenencia** *nf* **1** : ownership **2** **~s** *nfpl* : belongings
pertinaz *adj, pl* **-naces** **1** OBSTINADO : obstinate **2** PERSISTENTE : persistent
pertinente *adj* : pertinent, relevant — **pertinencia** *nf* : relevance
perturbar *vt* : disturb — **perturbación** *nf, pl* **-ciones** : disturbance
peruano, -na *adj* : Peruvian
pervertir {76} *vt* : pervert — **perversión** *nf, pl* **-siones** : perversion —

perverso, -sa *adj* : perverse — **pervertido, -da** *adj* : perverted, depraved — **~** *n* : pervert
pesa *nf* **1** : weight **2 ~s** : weights (in sports) — **pesadez** *nf, pl* **-deces** **1** : heaviness **2** *fam* : tediousness, drag
pesadilla *nf* : nightmare
pesado, -da *adj* **1** : heavy **2** LENTO : sluggish **3** MOLESTO : annoying **4** ABURRIDO : tedious **5** DURO : tough, difficult — **~** *n fam* : bore, pest — **pesadumbre** *nf* : grief, sorrow
pésame *nm* : condolences *pl*
pesar *vt* : weigh — *vi* **1** : weigh, be heavy **2** INFLUIR : carry weight **3 pese a** : despite — **~** *nm* **1** : sorrow, grief **2** REMORDIMIENTO : remorse **3 a ~ de** : in spite of
pescado *nm* : fish — **pesca** *nf* **1** : fishing **2** PECES : fish *pl*, catch **3 ir de ~** : go fishing — **pescadería** *nf* : fish market — **pescador, -dora** *n, mpl* **-dores** : fisherman — **pescar** {72} *vt* **1** : fish for **2** *fam* : catch (a cold, etc.) **3** *fam* : catch hold of, nab — *vi* : fish
pescuezo *nm* : neck (of an animal)
pese → pesar
pesebre *nm* : manger
pesero *nm* Lat : minibus
peseta *nf* : peseta
pesimismo *nm* : pessimism — **pesimista** *adj* : pessimistic — **~** *nmf* : pessimist
pésimo, -ma *adj* : awful
peso *nm* **1** : weight **2** CARGA : burden **3** : peso (currency) **4 ~ pesado** : heavyweight
pesquero, -ra *adj* : fishing
pesquisa *nf* : inquiry
pestaña *nf* : eyelash — **pestañear** *vi* : blink — **pestañeo** *nm* : blink
peste *nm* **1** : plague **2** *fam* : stench, stink **3** Lat *fam* : cold, bug — **pesticida** *nm* : pesticide — **pestilencia** *nf* **1** : stench **2** PLAGA : pestilence
pestillo *nm* : bolt, latch
petaca *nf* Lat : suitcase
pétalo *nm* : petal
petardo *nm* : firecracker
petición *nf, pl* **-ciones** : petition, request
petirrojo *nm* : robin
petrificar {72} *vt* : petrify
petróleo *nm* : oil, petroleum — **petrolero, -ra** *adj* : oil — **petrolero** *nm* : oil tanker
petulante *adj* : insolent, arrogant
peyorativo, -va *adj* : pejorative
pez *nm, pl* **peces** **1** : fish **2 ~ de col-**

ores : goldfish 3 ~ **espada** : swordfish 4 ~ **gordo** *fam* : big shot
pezón *nm, pl* **-zones** : nipple
pezuña *nf* : hoof
piadoso, -sa *adj* 1 : compassionate 2
DEVOTO : pious, devout
piano *nm* : piano — **pianista** *nmf* : pianist, piano player
piar {85} *vi* : chirp, tweet
pibe, -ba *n Lat fam* : kid, child
pica *nf* 1 : pike, lance 2 : spade (in playing cards)
picado, -da *adj* 1 : perforated 2
: minced, chopped (of meat, etc.) 3
: decayed (of teeth) 4 : choppy (of the
sea) 5 *fam* : annoyed — **picada** *nf* 1
: bite, sting 2 *Lat* : sharp descent —
picadillo *nm* : minced meat — **picadura** *nf* 1 : sting, bite 2 : (moth) hole
picante *adj* : hot, spicy
picaporte *nm* 1 : door handle 2 ALDABA
: door knocker 3 PESTILLO : latch
picar {72} *vt* 1 : sting, bite 2 : peck at,
nibble on (food) 3 PERFORAR : prick,
puncture 4 TRITURAR : chop, mince —
vi 1 : bite, take the bait 2 ESCOCER
: sting, itch 3 COMER : nibble 4 : be
spicy (of food) — **picarse** *vr* 1 : get a
cavity 2 ENFADARSE : take offense
picardía *nf* 1 : craftiness 2 TRAVESURA
: prank — **picaresco, -ca** *adj* 1 : pica-
resque 2 TRAVIESO : roguish — **pícaro,
-ra** *adj* 1 : mischievous 2 MALICIOSO
: villainous — ~ *n* : rascal, scoundrel
picazón *nf, pl* **-zones** : itch
pichón, -chona *n, mpl* **-chones**
: (young) pigeon
picnic *nm, pl* **-nics** : picnic
pico *nm* 1 : beak 2 CIMA : peak 3 PUNTA
: (sharp) point 4 : pick, pickax (tool) 5
las siete y ~ : a little after seven —
picotazo *nm* : peck — **picotear** *vt*
: peck — *vi fam* : nibble, pick — **picu-
do, -da** *adj* : pointy
pie *nm* 1 : foot (in anatomy) 2 : base,
bottom, stem 3 **al ~ de la letra**
: word for word 4 **dar ~ a** : give rise
to 5 **de ~** : standing (up) 6 **de ~s a
cabeza** : from top to bottom
piedad *nf* 1 : pity, mercy 2 DEVOCIÓN
: piety
piedra *nf* 1 : stone 2 : flint (of a lighter)
3 GRANIZO : hailstone 4 ~ **angular**
: cornerstone 5 → **pómez**
piel *nf* 1 : skin 2 CUERO : leather 3 PELO
: fur, pelt
pienso *nm* : feed, fodder
pierna *nf* : leg
pieza *nf* 1 : piece, part 2 *or* ~ **de teatro**
: play 3 HABITACIÓN : room

pigmento *nm* : pigment — **pig-
mentación** *nf, pl* **-ciones** : pigmenta-
tion
pigmeo, -mea *adj* : pygmy
pijama *nm* : pajamas *pl*
pila *nf* 1 : battery 2 MONTÓN : pile 3 FRE-
GADERO : sink 4 : basin (of a fountain,
etc.)
pilar *nm* : pillar
píldora *nf* : pill
pillar *vt* 1 : catch 2 : get (a joke, etc.) —
pillaje *nm* : pillage — **pillo, -lla** *adj*
: crafty — ~ *n* : rascal, scoundrel
piloto *nmf* : pilot — **pilotar** *vt* : pilot
pimienta *nf* : pepper (condiment) —
pimiento *nm* : pepper (fruit) — **pimentero** *nm* : pepper shaker — **pi-
mentón** *nm, pl* **-tones** 1 : paprika 2
: cayenne pepper
pináculo *nm* : pinnacle
pincel *nm* : paintbrush
pinchar *vt* 1 : pierce, prick 2 : puncture
(a tire, etc.) 3 INCITAR : goad — **pinchazo** *nm* 1 : prick 2 : puncture (of a
tire, etc.)
pingüino *nm* : penguin
pino *nm* : pine (tree)
pintar *v* : paint — **pintarse** *vr* : put on
makeup — **pinta** *nf* 1 : spot 2 : pint
(measure) 3 *fam* : appearance — **pin-
tada** *nf* : graffiti — **pinto, -ta** *adj*
: speckled, spotted — **pintor, -tora** *n,
mpl* **-tores** : painter — **pintoresco,
-ca** *adj* : picturesque, quaint — **pintura** *nf* 1 : paint 2 CUADRO : painting
pinza *nf* 1 : clothespin 2 : claw, pincer
(of a crab, etc.) 3 ~ **s** *nfpl* : tweezers
pinzón *nm, pl* **-zones** : finch
piña *nf* 1 : pine cone 2 ANANÁS : pineapple
piñata *nf* : piñata
piñón *nm, pl* **-ñones** : pine nut
pío¹, pía *adj* 1 : pious 2 : piebald (of a
horse)
pío² *nm* : peep, chirp
piojo *nm* : louse
pionero, -ra *n* : pioneer
pipa *nf* 1 : pipe (for smoking) 2 *Spain*
: seed, pip
pique *nm* 1 : grudge 2 RIVALIDAD : rivalry 3 **irse a ~** : sink, founder
piqueta *nf* : pickax
piquete *nm* : picket (line) — **piquetear**
v : picket
piragua *nf* : canoe
pirámide *nf* : pyramid
piraña *nf* : piranha
pirata *adj* : bootleg, pirated — ~ *nmf*
: pirate — **piratear** *vt* 1 : bootleg, pirate 2 : hack into (a computer)

piropo nm : (flirtatious) compliment
pirueta nf : pirouette
pirulí nm : (cone-shaped) lollipop
pisada nf 1 : footstep 2 HUELLA : foot-print
pisapapeles nms & pl : paperweight
pisar vt 1 : step on 2 HUMILLAR : walk all over, abuse — vi : step, tread
piscina nf 1 : swimming pool 2 : (fish) pond
piso nm 1 : floor, story 2 Lat : floor (of a room) 3 Spain : apartment
pisotear vt : trample (on)
pista nf 1 : trail, track 2 INDICIO : clue 3 ~ **de aterrizaje** : runway, airstrip 4 ~ **de baile** : dance floor 5 ~ **de hielo** : ice-skating rink
pistacho nm : pistachio
pistola nf 1 : pistol, gun 2 PULVER-IZADOR : spray gun — **pistolera** nf : holster — **pistolero** nm : gunman
pistón nm, pl -**tones** : piston
pito nm 1 SILBATO : whistle 2 CLAXON : horn — **pitar** vi 1 : blow a whistle 2 : beep, honk (of a horn) — vt : whistle at — **pitido** nm 1 : whistle, whistling 2 : beep (of a horn) — **pitillo** nm fam : cigarette
pitón nm, pl -**tones** nm : python
pitorro nm : spout
pivote nm : pivot
piyama nmf Lat : pajamas pl
pizarra nf 1 : slate 2 ENCERADO : black-board — **pizarrón** nm, pl -**rrones** Lat : blackboard
pizca nf 1 : pinch (of salt) 2 ÁPICE : speck, tiny bit 3 Lat : harvest
pizza ['pitsa, 'pisa] nf : pizza — **pizzería** nf : pizzeria
placa nf 1 : sheet, plate 2 INSCRIPCIÓN : plaque 3 : (police) badge
placenta nf : placenta
placer {57} vt : please — ~ nm : pleas-ure — **placentero, -ra** adj : pleasant, agreeable
plácido, -da adj : placid, calm
plaga nf 1 : plague 2 CALAMIDAD : di-saster — **plagar** {52} vt : plague, infest
plagiar vt : plagiarize — **plagio** nm : plagiarism
plan nm 1 : plan 2 en ~ de : as 3 no te pongas en ese ~ fam : don't be that way
plana nf 1 : page 2 en primera ~ : on the front page
plancha nf 1 : iron (for ironing) 2 : grill (for cooking) 3 LÁMINA : sheet, plate — **planchar** v : iron — **planchado** nm : ironing

planear vt : plan — vi : glide — **planeador** nm : glider
planeta nm : planet
planicie nf : plain
planificar {72} vt : plan — **planifica-ción** nf, pl -**ciones** : planning
planilla nf Lat : list, roster
plano, -na adj : flat — **plano** nm 1 : map, plan 2 : plane (surface) 3 NIVEL : level 4 de ~ : flatly, outright 5 **primer** ~ : foreground, close-up (in photography)
planta nf 1 : plant 2 PISO : floor, story 3 : sole (of the foot) — **plantación** nf, pl -**ciones** 1 : plantation 2 : (action of) planting — **plantar** vt 1 : plant 2 fam : deal, land — **plantarse** vr : stand firm
plantear vt 1 : expound, set forth 2 : raise (a question) 3 CAUSAR : create, pose (a problem) — **plantearse** vr : think about, consider
plantel nm 1 : staff, team 2 Lat : educa-tional institution
plantilla nf 1 : insole 2 PATRÓN : pattern, template 3 : staff (of a business, etc.)
plasma nm : plasma
plástico, -ca adj : plastic — **plástico** nm : plastic
plata nf 1 : silver 2 Lat fam : money 3 ~ **de ley** : sterling silver
plataforma nf 1 : platform 2 ~ **petrolífera** : oil rig 3 ~ **de lanza-miento** : launching pad
plátano nm 1 : banana 2 : plantain
platea nf : orchestra, pit (in a theater)
plateado, -da adj 1 : silver, silvery (color) 2 : silver-plated
platicar {72} vi : talk, chat — **plática** nf : chat, conversation
platija nf : flatfish, flounder
platillo nm 1 : saucer 2 CÍMBALO : cym-bal 3 Lat : dish, course
platino nm : platinum
plato nm 1 : plate, dish 2 : course (of a meal) 3 ~ **principal** : entrée
platónico, -ca adj : platonic
playa nf 1 : beach, seashore 2 ~ **de estacionamiento** Lat : parking lot
plaza nf 1 : square, plaza 2 : seat (in transportation) 3 PUESTO : post, posi-tion 4 MERCADO : market, marketplace 5 ~ **de toros** : bullring
plazo nm 1 : period, term 2 PAGO : in-stallment 3 a **largo** ~ : long-term
plazoleta or **plazuela** nf : small square
pleamar nf : high tide
plebe nf : common people — **plebeyo, -ya** adj & nm : plebeian
plegar {49} vt : fold, bend — **plegarse** vr 1 : give in, yield 2 : jackknife (of a

truck) — **plegable** or **plegadizo, -za**
adj : folding, collapsible
plegaria *nf* : prayer
pleito *nm* 1 : lawsuit 2 *Lat* : dispute, fight
plenilunio *nm* : full moon
pleno, -na *adj* 1 : full, complete 2 **en plena forma** : in top form 3 **en pleno día** : in broad daylight — **plenitud** *nf* : fullness, abundance
pleuresía *nf* : pleurisy
pliego *nm* : sheet (of paper) — **pliegue** *nm* 1 : crease, fold 2 : pleat (in fabric)
plisar *vt* : pleat
plomería *nf Lat* : plumbing — **plomero, -ra** *n Lat* : plumber
plomo *nm* 1 : lead 2 FUSIBLE : fuse
pluma *nf* 1 : feather 2 : (fountain) pen — **plumaje** *nm* : plumage — **plumero** *nm* : feather duster — **plumilla** *nf, pl* — **plumón** *nm, pl* **-mones** : down
plural *adj & nm* : plural — **pluralidad** *nf* : plurality
pluriempleo *nm* **hacer ~** : have more than one job
plus *nm* : bonus
plusvalía *nf* : appreciation, capital gain
plutocracia *nf* : plutocracy
Plutón *nm* : Pluto
plutonio *nm* : plutonium
pluvial *adj* : rain
poblar {19} *vt* 1 : settle, colonize 2 HABITAR : inhabit — **poblarse** *vr* : become crowded — **población** *nf, pl* **-ciones** 1 : city, town, village 2 HABITANTES : population — **poblado, -da** *adj* 1 : populated 2 : thick, bushy (of a beard, eyebrows, etc.) — **poblado** *nm* : village
pobre *adj* 1 : poor 2 **¡~ de mí!** : poor me! — **~** *nmf* 1 : poor person 2 **los ~s** : the poor 3 **¡pobre!** : poor thing! — **pobreza** *nf* : poverty
pocilga *nf* : pigsty
poción *nf, pl* **-ciones** or **pócima** *nf* : potion
poco, -ca *adj* 1 : little, not much, (a) few 2 **pocas veces** : rarely — **~** *pron* 1 : little, few 2 **hace poco** : not long ago 3 **poco a poco** : bit by bit, gradually 4 **por poco** : nearly, just about 5 **un poco** : a little, a bit — **poco** *adv* : little, not much
podar *vt* : prune
poder {58} *v aux* 1 : be able to, can 2 (*expressing possibility*) : might, may 3 (*expressing permission*) : can, may 4 **¿cómo puede ser?** : how can it be? 5 **¿puedo pasar?** : may I come in? — *vi* 1 : be possible 2 **~ con** : cope with, manage 3 **no puedo más** : I've

had enough — **~** *nm* 1 : power 2 POSESIÓN : possession — **poderío** *nm* : power — **poderoso, -sa** *adj* : powerful
podólogo, -ga *n* : chiropodist
podrido, -da *adj* : rotten
poema *nm* : poem — **poesía** *nf* 1 : poetry 2 POEMA : poem — **poeta** *nmf* : poet — **poético, -ca** *adj* : poetic
póker *nm* → **póquer**
polaco, -ca *adj* : Polish
polar *adj* : polar — **polarizar** {21} *vt* : polarize
polea *nf* : pulley
polémica *nf* : controversy — **polémico, -ca** *adj* : controversial — **polemizar** *vt* : argue
polen *nm, pl* **pólenes** : pollen
policía *nf* : police — **~** *nmf* : police officer, policeman *m*, policewoman *f* — **policíaco, -ca** *adj* 1 : police 2 **novela policíaca** : detective story
poliéster *nm* : polyester
poligamia *nf* : polygamy — **polígamo, -ma** *n* : polygamist
polígono *nm* : polygon
polilla *nf* : moth
polio or **poliomielitis** *nf* : polio, poliomyelitis
politécnico, -ca *adj* : polytechnic
política *nf* 1 : politics 2 POSTURA : policy — **político, -ca** *adj* 1 : political 2 **hermano político** : brother-in-law — **~** *n* : politician
póliza *nf* or **~ de seguros** : insurance policy
polizón *nm, pl* **-zones** : stowaway
pollo, -lla *n* 1 : chicken, chick 2 : chicken (for cooking) — **pollera** *nf Lat* : skirt — **pollería** *nf* : poultry shop — **pollito, -ta** *n* : chick
polo *nm* 1 : pole 2 : polo (sport) 3 **~ norte** : North Pole
poltrona *nf* : easy chair
polución *nf, pl* **-ciones** : pollution
polvo *nm* 1 : powder 2 SUCIEDAD : dust 3 **~s** *nmpl* : face powder 4 **hacer ~** *fam* : crush, shatter — **polvareda** *nf* : cloud of dust — **polvera** *nf* : compact (for powder) — **pólvora** *nf* : gunpowder — **polvoriento, -ta** *adj* : dusty
pomada *nf* : ointment
pomelo *nm* : grapefruit
pómez *nm* or **piedra ~** *nf* : pumice
pomo *nm* : knob, doorknob
pompa *nf* 1 : (soap) bubble 2 ESPLENDOR : pomp 3 **~s fúnebres** : funeral — **pomposo, -sa** *adj* 1 : pompous 2 ESPLÉNDIDO : splendid
pómulo *nm* : cheekbone

ponchar *vt Lat* : puncture — **poncha-dura** *nf Lat* : puncture
ponche *nm* : punch (drink)
poncho *nm* : poncho
ponderar *vt* 1 : consider 2 ALABAR : speak highly of
poner {60} *vt* 1 : put 2 AGREGAR : add 3 CONTRIBUIR : contribute 4 SUPONER : suppose 5 DISPONER : arrange, set out 6 : give (a name), call 7 ENCENDER : turn on 8 ESTABLECER : set up, establish 9 : lay (eggs) — *vi* : lay eggs — **ponerse** *vr* 1 : move (into a position) 2 : put on (clothing, etc.) 3 : set (of the sun) 4 ~ **furioso** : become angry
poniente *nm* 1 OCCIDENTE : west 2 : west wind
pontífice *nm* : pontiff
pontón *nm*, *pl* -tones : pontoon
ponzoña *nf* : poison, venom
popa *nf* 1 : stern 2 a ~ : astern
popelín *nm*, *pl* -lines : poplin
popote *nm Lat* : (drinking) straw
populacho *nm* : rabble, masses *pl*
popular *adj* 1 : popular 2 : colloquial (of language) — **popularidad** *nf* : popularity — **popularizar** {21} *vt* : popularize — **populoso, -sa** *adj* : populous
póquer *nm* : poker (card game)
por *prep* 1 : for 2 (*indicating an approximate time*) : around, during 3 (*indicating an approximate place*) : around, about 4 A TRAVÉS DE : through, along 5 A CAUSA DE : because of 6 (*indicating rate or ratio*) : per 7 *or* ~ **medio de** : by means of 8 : times (in mathematics) 9 SEGÚN : as for, according to 10 estar ~ : be about to 11 ~ **ciento** : percent 12 ~ **favor** : please 13 ~ **lo tanto** : therefore 14 ¿por qué? : why?
porcelana *nf* : porcelain, china
porcentaje *nm* : percentage
porción *nf*, *pl* -ciones : portion, piece
pordiosero, -ra *n* : beggar
porfiar {85} *vi* : insist — **porfiado, -da** *adj* : obstinate, persistent
pormenor *nm* : detail
pornografía *nf* : pornography — **pornográfico, -ca** *adj* : pornographic
poro *nm* : pore — **poroso, -sa** *adj* : porous
poroto *nm Lat* : bean
porque *conj* 1 : because 2 *or* por que : in order that — **porqué** *nm* : reason
porquería *nf* 1 SUCIEDAD : filth 2 : shoddy thing, junk
porra *nf* : nightstick, club — **porrazo** *nm* : blow, whack

portaaviones *nms & pl* : aircraft carrier
portada *nf* 1 : facade 2 : title page (of a book), cover (of a magazine)
portador, -dora *n* : bearer
portaequipajes *nms & pl* : luggage rack
portafolio *or* portafolios *nm*, *pl* -lios 1 : portfolio 2 MALETÍN : briefcase
portal *nm* 1 : doorway 2 VESTÍBULO : hall, vestibule
portamonedas *nms & pl* : purse
portar *vt* : carry, bear — **portarse** *vr* : behave
portátil *adj* : portable
portaviones *nms* → portaaviones
portavoz *nmf*, *pl* -voces : spokesperson, spokesman *m*, spokeswoman *f*
portazo *nm* dar un ~ : slam the door
porte *nm* 1 : transport, freight 2 ASPECTO : bearing, appearance 3 ~ **pagado** : postage paid
portento *nm* : marvel, wonder — **portentoso, -sa** *adj* : marvelous
porteño, -ña *adj* : of or from Buenos Aires
portería *nf* 1 : superintendent's office 2 : goal, goalposts *pl* (in sports) — **portero, -ra** *n* 1 : goalkeeper, goalie 2 CONSERJE : janitor, superintendent
portezuela *nf* : door (of an automobile)
pórtico *nm* : portico
portilla *nf* : porthole
portugués, -guesa *adj*, *mpl* -gueses : Portuguese — **portugués** *nm* : Portuguese (language)
porvenir *nm* : future
pos: en ~ de *adv phr* : in pursuit of
posada *nf* : inn
posaderas *nfpl fam* : backside, bottom
posar *vi* : pose — *vt* : place, lay — **posarse** *vr* : settle, rest
posavasos *nms & pl* : coaster
posdata *nf* : postscript
pose *nf* : pose
poseer {20} *vt* : possess, own — **poseedor, -dora** *n* : possessor, owner — **poseído, -da** *adj* : possessed — **posesión** *nf*, *pl* -siones : possession — **posesionarse** *vr* ~ **de** : take possession of, take over — **posesivo, -va** *adj* : possessive
posguerra *nf* : postwar period
posibilidad *nf* : possibility — **posibilitar** *vt* : make possible — **posible** *adj* 1 : possible 2 de ser ~ : if possible
posición *nf*, *pl* -ciones : position — **posicionar** *vt* : position — **posicionarse** *vr* : take a stand
positivo, -va *adj* : positive
poso *nm* : sediment, (coffee) grounds

posponer {60} vt 1 : postpone 2 RELEGAR : put behind, subordinate

postal adj : postal — ~ nf : postcard

postdata → **posdata**

poste nm : post, pole

póster nm, pl **-ters** : poster

postergar {52} vt 1 : pass over 2 APLAZAR : postpone

posteridad nf : posterity — **posterior** adj 1 : later, subsequent 2 TRASERO : back, rear — **posteriormente** adv : subsequently, later

postigo nm 1 : small door 2 CONTRAVENTANA : shutter

postizo, -za adj : artificial, false

postrarse vr : prostrate oneself — **postrado, -da** adj : prostrate

postre nm : dessert

postular vt 1 : advance, propose 2 Lat : nominate — **postulado** nm : postulate

póstumo, -ma adj : posthumous

postura nf : position, stance

potable adj : drinkable, potable

potaje nm : thick vegetable soup

potasio nm : potassium

pote nm : jar

potencia nf : power — **potencial** adj & nm : potential — **potente** adj : powerful

potro, -tra n : colt m, filly f — **potro** nm : horse (in gymnastics)

pozo nm 1 : well 2 : shaft (in a mine)

práctica nf 1 : practice 2 **en la ~** : in practice — **practicable** adj : practicable, feasible — **practicante** adj : practicing — ~ nmf : practitioner — **practicar** {72} vt 1 : practice 2 REALIZAR : perform, carry out — vi : practice — **práctico, -ca** adj : practical

pradera nf : grassland, prairie — **prado** nm : meadow

pragmático, -ca adj : pragmatic

preámbulo nm : preamble

precario, -ria adj : precarious

precaución nf, pl **-ciones** 1 : precaution 2 PRUDENCIA : caution, care 3 **con ~** : cautiously

precaver vt : guard against — **precavido, -da** adj : prudent, cautious

preceder v : precede — **precedencia** nf : precedence, priority — **precedente** adj : preceding, previous — ~ nm : precedent

precepto nm : precept

preciado, -da adj : prized, valuable — **preciarse** vr ~ **de** : pride oneself on, boast about

precinto nm : seal

precio nm : price, cost — **preciosidad** nf 1 VALOR : value 2 : beautiful thing — **precioso, -sa** adj 1 HERMOSO : beautiful 2 VALIOSO : precious

precipicio nm : precipice

precipitar vt 1 : hasten, speed up 2 ARROJAR : hurl — **precipitarse** vr 1 APRESURARSE : rush 2 : act rashly 3 ARROJARSE : throw oneself — **precipitación** nf, pl **-ciones** 1 : precipitation 2 PRISA : haste — **precipitadamente** adv : in a rush, hastily — **precipitado, -da** adj : hasty

preciso, -sa adj 1 : precise 2 NECESARIO : necessary — **precisamente** adv : precisely, exactly — **precisar** vt 1 : specify, determine 2 NECESITAR : require — **precisión** nf, pl **-siones** 1 : precision 2 NECESIDAD : necessity

preconcebido adj : preconceived

precoz adj, pl **-coces** 1 : early 2 : precocious (of children)

precursor, -sora n : forerunner

predecesor, -sora n : predecessor

predecir {11} vt : foretell, predict

predestinado, -da adj : predestined

predeterminar vt : predetermine

prédica nf : sermon

predicado nm : predicate

predicar {72} v : preach — **predicador, -dora** n : preacher

predicción nf, pl **-ciones** 1 : prediction 2 PRONÓSTICO : forecast

predilección nf, pl **-ciones** : preference — **predilecto, -ta** adj : favorite

predisponer {60} vt : predispose — **predisposición** nf, pl **-ciones** : predisposition

predominar vi : predominate — **predominante** adj : predominant, prevailing — **predominio** nm : predominance

preeminente adj : preeminent

prefabricado, -da adj : prefabricated

prefacio nm : preface

preferir {76} vt : prefer — **preferencia** nf 1 : preference 2 **de ~** : preferably — **preferente** adj : preferential — **preferible** adj : preferable — **preferido, -da** adj : favorite

prefijo nm 1 : prefix 2 Spain : area code

pregonar vt : proclaim, announce

pregunta nf 1 : question 2 **hacer ~s** : ask questions — **preguntar** v : ask — **preguntarse** vr : wonder

prehistórico, -ca adj : prehistoric

prejuicio nm : prejudice

preliminar adj & nm : preliminary

preludio nm : prelude

prematrimonial adj : premarital

prematuro, -ra *adj* : premature
premeditar *vt* : premeditate — **premeditación** *nf, pl* **-ciones** : premeditation
premenstrual *adj* : premenstrual
premio *nm* **1** : prize **2** RECOMPENSA : reward **3** ~ **gordo** : jackpot — **premiado, -da** *adj* : prizewinning — **premiar** *vt* **1** : award a prize to **2** RECOMPENSAR : reward
premisa *nf* : premise
premonición *nf, pl* **-ciones** : premonition
premura *nf* : haste, urgency
prenatal *adj* : prenatal
prenda *nf* **1** : piece of clothing **2** GARANTÍA : pledge **3** : forfeit (in a game) — **prendar** *vt* : captivate — **prendarse** *vr* ~ **de** : fall in love with
prender *vt* **1** SUJETAR : pin, fasten **2** APRESAR : capture **3** : light (a match, etc.) **4** *Lat* : turn on (a light, etc.) — *vi* **1** : take root **2** ARDER : catch, burn (of fire) — **prenderse** *vr* : catch fire — **prendedor** *nm Lat* : brooch, pin
prensa *nf* : press — **prensar** *vt* : press
preñado, -da *adj* **1** : pregnant **2** ~ **de** : filled with
preocupar *vt* : worry — **preocuparse** *vr* **1** : worry **2** ~ **de** : take care of — **preocupación** *nf, pl* **-ciones** : worry
preparar *vt* : prepare — **prepararse** *vr* : get ready — **preparación** *nf, pl* **-ciones** : preparation — **preparado, -da** *adj* : prepared, ready — **preparado** *nm* : preparation — **preparativo, -va** *adj* : preparatory, preliminary — **preparativos** *nmpl* : preparations — **preparatorio, -ria** *adj* : preparatory
preposición *nf, pl* **-ciones** : preposition
prepotente *adj* : arrogant, domineering
prerrogativa *nf* : prerogative
presa *nf* **1** : catch, prey **2** DIQUE : dam **3** **hacer** ~ **en** : seize
presagiar *vt* : presage, forebode — **presagio** *nm* **1** : omen **2** PREMONICIÓN : premonition
presbítero *nm* : presbyter, priest
prescindir *vi* ~ **de 1** : do without **2** OMITIR : dispense with
prescribir {33} *vt* : prescribe — **prescripción** *nf, pl* **-ciones** : prescription
presencia *nf* **1** : presence **2** ASPECTO : appearance — **presenciar** *vt* : be present at, witness
presentar *vt* **1** : present **2** OFRECER : offer, give **3** MOSTRAR : show **4** : introduce (persons) — **presentarse** *vr* **1** : show up **2** : arise, come up (of a

problem, etc.) **3** : introduce oneself — **presentación** *nf, pl* **-ciones 1** : presentation **2** : introduction (of persons) **3** ASPECTO : appearance — **presentador, -dora** *n* : presenter, host (of a television program, etc.)
presente *adj* **1** : present **2 tener** ~ : keep in mind — ~ *nm* **1** : present **2 entre los** ~**s** : among those present
presentir {76} *vt* : have a presentiment of — **presentimiento** *nm* : premonition
preservar *vt* : preserve, protect — **preservación** *nf, pl* **-ciones** : preservation — **preservativo** *nm* : condom
presidente, -ta *n* **1** : president **2** : chair, chairperson (of a meeting) — **presidencia** *nf* **1** : presidency **2** : chairmanship (of a meeting) — **presidencial** *adj* : presidential
presidio *nm* : prison — **presidiario, -ria** *n* : convict
presidir *vt* **1** : preside over, chair **2** PREDOMINAR : dominate
presión *nf, pl* **-siones 1** : pressure **2** ~ **arterial** : blood pressure **3 hacer** ~ : press — **presionar** *vt* **1** : press **2** COACCIONAR : put pressure on
preso, -sa *adj* : imprisoned — ~ *n* : prisoner
prestar *vt* **1** : lend, loan **2** : give (aid) **3** ~ **atención** : pay attention — **prestado, -da** *adj* **1** : borrowed, on loan **2 pedir** ~ : borrow — **prestamista** *nmf* : moneylender — **préstamo** *nm* : loan
prestidigitación *nf, pl* **-ciones** : sleight of hand — **prestidigitador, -dora** *n* : magician
prestigio *nm* : prestige — **prestigioso, -sa** *adj* : prestigious
presto, -ta *adj* : prompt, ready — **presto** *adv* : promptly, right away
presumir *vt* : presume — *vi* : boast, show off — **presumido, -da** *adj* : conceited, vain — **presunción** *nf, pl* **-ciones 1** : presumption **2** VANIDAD : vanity — **presunto, -ta** *adj* : presumed, alleged — **presuntuoso, -sa** *adj* : conceited
presuponer {60} *vt* : presuppose — **presupuesto** *nm* **1** : budget, estimate **2** SUPUESTO : assumption
presuroso, -sa *adj* : hasty, quick
pretender *vt* **1** : try to **2** AFIRMAR : claim **3** CORTEJAR : court, woo **4** ~ **que** : expect — **pretencioso, -sa** *adj* : pretentious — **pretendido** *adj* : supposed — **pretendiente** *nmf* **1** : candidate **2** : pretender (to a throne) — ~

nm : suitor — **pretensión** *nf, pl*
-siones 1 INTENCIÓN : intention, aspiration **2** : claim (to a throne, etc.) **3**
pretensiones *nfpl* : pretensions
pretérito *nm* : past (in grammar)
pretexto *nm* : pretext, excuse
prevalecer {53} *vi* : prevail — **prevale-
ciente** *adj* : prevailing, prevalent
prevenir {87} *vt* **1** : prevent **2** AVISAR
: warn — **prevenirse** {87} *vr* ~ **contra** *or* ~ **de** : take precautions against
— **prevención** *nf, pl* **-ciones 1** : prevention **2** PRECAUCIÓN : precaution **3**
PREJUICIO : prejudice — **prevenido,
-da** *adj* **1** : prepared, ready **2** PRECAVI-
DO : cautious — **preventivo, -va** *adj*
: preventive
prever {88} *vt* **1** : foresee **2** PLANEAR
: plan
previo, -via *adj* : previous, prior
previsible *adj* : foreseeable — **previsión** *nf, pl* **-siones 1** : foresight **2**
PREDICCIÓN : prediction, forecast —
previsor, -sora *adj* : farsighted, prudent
prieto, -ta *adj* **1** CEÑIDO : tight **2** *Lat fam*
: dark-skinned
prima *nf* **1** : bonus **2** : (insurance) premium **3** → **primo**
primario, -ria *adj* **1** : primary **2 escuela
primaria** : elementary school
primate *nm* : primate
primavera *nf* **1** : spring (season) **2**
: primrose (flower) — **primaveral** *adj*
: spring
primero, -ra *adj* (**primer** *before masculine singular nouns*) **1** : first **2** MEJOR
: top, leading **3** PRINCIPAL : main, basic
4 de primera : first-rate — ~ *n* : first
(person or thing) — **primero** *adv* **1**
: first **2** MÁS BIEN : rather, sooner
primitivo, -va *adj* : primitive
primo, -ma *n* : cousin
primogénito, -ta *adj & n* : firstborn
primor *nm* : beautiful thing
primordial *adj* : basic, fundamental
primoroso, -sa *adj* **1** : exquisite, fine **2**
HÁBIL : skillful
princesa *nf* : princess
principado *nm* : principality
principal *adj* : main, principal
príncipe *nm* : prince
principio *nm* **1** : principle **2** COMIENZO
: beginning, start **3** ORIGEN : origin **4 al**
~ : at first **5 a** ~**s de** : at the beginning of — **principiante** *nmf* : beginner
pringar {52} *vt* : spatter (with grease)
— **pringoso, -sa** *adj* : greasy
prioridad *nf* : priority
prisa *nf* **1** : hurry, rush **2 a** ~ *or* **de** ~

: quickly **3 a toda** ~ : as fast as possible **4 darse** ~ : hurry **5 tener** ~
: be in a hurry
prisión *nf, pl* **-siones 1** : prison **2** EN-
CARCELAMIENTO : imprisonment —
prisionero, -ra *n* : prisoner
prisma *nm* : prism — **prismáticos**
nmpl : binoculars
privar *vt* **1** : deprive **2** PROHIBIR : forbid
3 *Lat* : knock out — **privarse** *vr* : deprive oneself — **privación** *nf, pl*
-ciones : deprivation — **privado, -da**
adj : private — **privativo, -va** *adj* : exclusive
privilegio *nm* : privilege — **privilegiado, -da** *adj* : privileged
pro *prep* : for, in favor of — ~ *nm* **1**
: pro, advantage **2 en** ~ **de** : for, in
support of **3 los pros y los contras**
: the pros and cons
proa *nf* : bow, prow
probabilidad *nf* : probability — **probable** *adj* : probable, likely — **probablemente** *adv* : probably
probar {19} *vt* **1** : try, test **2** : try on
(clothing) **3** DEMOSTRAR : prove **4** DE-
GUSTAR : taste — *vi* : try — **probarse**
vr : try on (clothing) — **probeta** *nf*
: test tube
problema *nm* : problem — **problemáti-
co, -ca** *adj* : problematic
proceder *vi* **1** : proceed, act **2** : be appropriate **3** ~ **de** : come from —
procedencia *nf* : origin — **proce-
dente** *adj* ~ **de** : coming from, orig-
inating in — **procedimiento** *nm* **1**
: procedure, method **2** : proceedings *pl*
(in law)
procesar *vt* **1** : prosecute **2** : process
(data) — **procesador** *nm* ~ **de textos** : word processor — **procesamiento** *nm* : processing — **proce-
sión** *nf, pl* **-siones** : procession —
proceso *nm* **1** : process **2** : trial, proceedings *pl* (in law)
proclamar *vt* : proclaim — **proclama** *nf*
: proclamation — **proclamación** *nf, pl*
-ciones : proclamation
procrear *vi* : procreate — **procreación**
nf, pl **-ciones** : procreation
procurar *vt* **1** : try, endeavor **2** CON-
SEGUIR : obtain, procure — **procu-
rador, -dora** *n* : attorney
prodigar {52} *vt* : lavish — **prodigio**
nm : wonder, prodigy — **prodigioso,
-sa** *adj* : prodigious
pródigo, -ga *adj* : extravagant, prodigal
producir {61} *vt* **1** : produce **2** CAUSAR
: cause **3** : yield, bear (interest, fruit,
etc.) — **producirse** *vr* : take place —

producción *nf, pl* **-ciones** : production — **productividad** *nf* : productivity — **productivo, -va** *adj* : productive — **producto** *nm* : product — **productor, -tora** *n* : producer
proeza *nf* : exploit
profanar *vt* : profane, desecrate — **profanación** *nf, pl* **-ciones** : desecration — **profano, -na** *adj* : profane
profecía *nf* : prophecy
proferir {76} *vt* 1 : utter 2 : hurl (insults)
profesar *vt* 1 : profess 2 : practice (a profession, etc.) — **profesión** *nf, pl* **-siones** : profession — **profesional** *adj & nmf* : professional — **profesor, -sora** *n* 1 : teacher 2 : professor (at a university, etc.) — **profesorado** *nm* 1 : teaching profession 2 PROFESORES : faculty
profeta *nm* : prophet — **profético, -ca** *adj* : prophetic — **profetista** *nf* : (female) prophet — **profetizar** {21} *vt* : prophesy
prófugo, -ga *adj & n* : fugitive
profundo, -da *adj* 1 HONDO : deep 2 : profound (of thoughts, etc.) — **profundamente** *adv* : deeply, profoundly — **profundidad** *nf* : depth — **profundizar** {21} *vt* : study in depth
profuso, -sa *adj* : profuse — **profusión** *nf, pl* **-siones** : profusion
progenie *nf* : progeny, offspring
programa *nm* 1 : program 2 : curriculum (in education) — **programación** *nf, pl* **-ciones** : programming — **programador, -dora** *n* : programmer — **programar** *vt* 1 : schedule 2 : program (a computer, etc.)
progreso *nm* : progress — **progresar** *vi* 1 : (make) progress — **progresión** *nf, pl* **-ciones** : progression — **progresista** *adj & nmf* : progressive — **progresivo, -va** *adj* : progressive, gradual
prohibir {62} *vt* : prohibit, forbid — **prohibición** *nf, pl* **-ciones** : ban, prohibition — **prohibido, -da** *adj* : forbidden — **prohibitivo, -va** *adj* : prohibitive
prójimo *nm* : neighbor, fellow man
prole *nf* : offspring
proletariado *nm* : proletariat — **proletario, -ria** *adj & n* : proletarian
proliferar *vi* : proliferate — **proliferación** *nf, pl* **-ciones** : proliferation — **prolífico, -ca** *adj* : prolific
prolijo, -ja *adj* : wordy, long-winded
prólogo *nm* : prologue, foreword
prolongar {52} *vt* 1 : prolong 2 ALARGAR : lengthen — **prolongarse** *vr* : last, continue — **prolongación** *nf, pl* **-ciones** : extension

promedio *nm* : average
promesa *nf* : promise — **prometedor, -dora** *adj* : promising, hopeful — **prometer** *vt* : promise — *vi* : show promise — **prometerse** *vr* : get engaged — **prometido, -da** *adj* : engaged — *~ n* : fiancé *m*, fiancée *f*
prominente *adj* : prominent — **prominencia** *nf* : prominence
promiscuo, -cua *adj* : promiscuous — **promiscuidad** *nf* : promiscuity
promocionar *vt* : promote — **promoción** *nf, pl* **-ciones** : promotion
promontorio *nm* : promontory
promover {47} *vt* 1 : promote 2 CAUSAR : cause — **promotor, -tora** *n* : promoter
promulgar {52} *vt* 1 : proclaim 2 : enact (a law)
pronombre *nm* : pronoun
pronosticar {72} *vt* : predict, forecast — **pronóstico** *nm* 1 : prediction, forecast 2 : (medical) prognosis
pronto, -ta *adj* 1 : quick, prompt 2 PREPARADO : ready — **pronto** *adv* 1 : soon 2 RAPIDAMENTE : quickly, promptly 3 **de ~** : suddenly 4 **por lo ~** : for the time being 5 **tan ~ como** : as soon as
pronunciar *vt* 1 : pronounce 2 : give, deliver (a speech) — **pronunciarse** *vr* 1 : declare oneself 2 SUBLEVARSE : revolt — **pronunciación** *nf, pl* **-ciones** : pronunciation
propagación *nf, pl* **-ciones** : propagation
propaganda *nf* 1 : propaganda 2 PUBLICIDAD : advertising
propagar {52} *vt* : propagate, spread — **propagarse** *vr* : propagate
propano *nm* : propane
propasarse *vr* : go too far
propensión *nf, pl* **-siones** : inclination, propensity — **propenso, -sa** *adj* : prone, inclined
propiamente *adv* : exactly
propicio, -cia *adj* : favorable, propitious
propiedad *nf* 1 : property 2 PERTINENCIA : ownership, possession — **propietario, -ria** *n* : owner, proprietor
propina *nf* : tip
propinar *vt* : give, deal (a blow, etc.)
propio, -pia *adj* 1 : own 2 APROPIADO : proper, appropriate 3 CARACTERÍSTICO : characteristic, typical 4 MISMO : himself, herself, oneself
proponer {60} *vt* 1 : propose 2 : nominate (a person) — **proponerse** *vr* : propose, intend

proporción *nf, pl* **-ciones** : proportion — **proporcionado, -da** *adj* : proportionate — **proporcional** *adj* : proportional — **proporcionar** *vt* **1** : provide **2** AJUSTAR : adapt, proportion

proposición *nf, pl* **-ciones** : proposal, proposition

propósito *nm* **1** : purpose, intention **2** a ~ : incidentally, by the way **3** a ~ : on purpose, intentionally

propuesta *nf* **1** : proposal **2** : offer (of employment, etc.)

propulsar *vt* **1** : propel, drive **2** PROMOVER : promote — **propulsión** *nf, pl* **-siones** : propulsion

prorrogar {52} *vt* **1** : extend **2** APLAZAR : postpone — **prórroga** *nf* **1** : extension, deferment **2** : overtime (in sports)

prorrumpir *vi* : burst forth, break out

prosa *nf* : prose

proscribir {33} *vt* **1** : prohibit, ban **2** DESTERRAR : exile — **proscripción** *nf, pl* **-ciones** **1** : ban **2** DESTIERRO : banishment — **proscrito, -ta** *adj* : banned — ~ *n* : exile, outlaw

proseguir {75} *v* : continue — **prosecución** *nf, pl* **-ciones** : continuation

prospección *nf, pl* **-ciones** : prospecting, exploration

prospecto *nm* : prospectus

prosperar *vi* : prosper, thrive — **prosperidad** *nf* : prosperity — **próspero, -ra** *adj* : prosperous, flourishing

prostituir {41} *vt* : prostitute — **prostitución** *nf, pl* **-ciones** : prostitution — **prostituta** *nf* : prostitute

protagonista *nmf* : protagonist — **protagonizar** *vt* : star in

proteger {15} *vt* : protect — **protegerse** *vr* : protect oneself — **protección** *nf, pl* **-ciones** : protection — **protector, -tora** *adj* : protective — ~ *n* : protector — **protegido, -da** *n* : protégé

proteína *nf* : protein

protestar *v* : protest — **protesta** *nf* : protest — **protestante** *adj & nmf* : Protestant

protocolo *nm* : protocol

prototipo *nm* : prototype

protuberancia *nf* : protuberance — **protuberante** *adj* : protuberant

provecho *nm* **1** : benefit, advantage **2** ¡buen ~! : enjoy your meal! — **provechoso, -sa** *adj* : profitable, beneficial

proveer {63} *vt* : provide, supply — **proveedor, -dora** *n* : supplier

provenir {87} *vi* ~ **de** : come from

proverbio *nm* : proverb — **proverbial** *adj* : proverbial

providencia *nf* **1** : providence **2** PRECAUCIÓN : precaution — **providencial** *adj* : providential

provincia *nf* : province — **provincial** *adj* : provincial — **provinciano, -na** *adj* : provincial, parochial

provisión *nf, pl* **-siones** : provision — **provisional** *adj* : provisional

provocar {72} *vt* **1** : provoke, cause **2** IRRITAR : irritate — **provocación** *nf, pl* **-ciones** : provocation — **provocativo, -va** *adj* : provocative

próximo, -ma *adj* **1** CERCANO : near **2** SIGUIENTE : next — **próximamente** *adv* : shortly, soon — **proximidad** *nf* **1** : proximity **2** ~es *nfpl* : vicinity

proyectar *vt* **1** : plan **2** LANZAR : throw, hurl **3** : cast (light) **4** : show (a film) — **proyección** *nf, pl* **-ciones** : projection — **proyectil** *nm* : missile — **proyecto** *nm* : plan, project — **proyector** *nm* : projector

prudencia *nf* : prudence, care — **prudente** *adj* : prudent, sensible

prueba *nf* **1** : proof, evidence **2** : test (in education, medicine, etc.) **3** : event (in sports) **4** a ~ **de agua** : waterproof

psicoanálisis *nm* : psychoanalysis — **psicoanalista** *nmf* : psychoanalyst — **psicoanalizar** {21} *vt* : psychoanalyze

psicología *nf* : psychology — **psicológico, -ca** *adj* : psychological — **psicólogo, -ga** *n* : psychologist

psicópata *nmf* : psychopath

psicosis *nfs & pl* : psychosis

psicoterapia *nf* : psychotherapy — **psicoterapeuta** *nmf* : psychotherapist

psicótico, -ca *adj & n* : psychotic

psiquiatría *nf* : psychiatry — **psiquiatra** *nmf* : psychiatrist — **psiquiátrico, -ca** *adj* : psychiatric

psíquico, -ca *adj* : psychic

púa *nf* **1** : sharp point **2** : tooth (of a comb) **3** : thorn (of a plant), quill (of a porcupine, etc.) **4** : (guitar) pick

pubertad *nf* : puberty

publicar {72} *vt* **1** : publish **2** DIVULGAR : divulge, disclose — **publicación** *nf, pl* **-ciones** : publication

publicidad *nf* **1** : publicity **2** : advertising (in marketing) — **publicista** *nmf* : publicist — **publicitar** *vt* **1** : publicize **2** : advertise (a product, etc.) — **publicitario, -ria** *adj* : advertising

público, -ca *adj* : public — **público** *nm* **1** : public **2** : audience (of theater, etc.), spectators *pl* (of sports)

puchero *nm* **1** : (cooking) pot **2** GUISADO : stew **3** hacer ~s : pout

púdico, -ca *adj* : modest

pudiente *adj* : wealthy

pudín *nm, pl* **-dines** : pudding

pudor *nm* : modesty — **pudoroso, -sa** *adj* : modest

pudrir {59} *vt* 1 : rot 2 *fam* : annoy — **pudrirse** *vr* : rot

pueblo *nm* 1 : town, village 2 NACIÓN : people, nation

puente *nm* 1 : bridge 2 **hacer** ~ : have a long weekend 3 ~ **levadizo** : drawbridge

puerco, -ca *n* 1 : pig 2 **puerco espín** : porcupine — ~ *adj* : dirty, filthy

pueril *adj* : childish

puerro *nm* : leek

puerta *nf* 1 : door, gate 2 **a** ~ **cerrada** : behind closed doors

puerto *nm* 1 : port 2 : (mountain) pass 3 REFUGIO : haven

puertorriqueño, -ña *adj* : Puerto Rican

pues *conj* 1 : since, because 2 POR LO TANTO : so, therefore 3 (*used interjectionally*) : well, then

puesta *nf* 1 ~ **a punto** : tune-up 2 ~ **de sol** : sunset 3 ~ **en marcha** : starting up — **puesto, -ta** *adj* 1 : put, set 2 VESTIDO : dressed — **puesto** *nm* 1 : place 2 EMPLEO : position, job 3 : stand, stall (in a market) 4 ~ **avanzado** : outpost — ~ **que** *conj* : since, given that

púgil *nm* : boxer

pugnar *vi* : fight — **pugna** *nf* : fight, battle

pulcro, -cra *adj* : tidy, neat

pulga *nf* 1 : flea 2 **tener malas** ~**s** : have a bad temper

pulgada *nf* : inch — **pulgar** *nm* 1 : thumb 2 : big toe

pulir *vt* 1 : polish 2 REFINAR : touch up, perfect

pulla *nf* : cutting remark, gibe

pulmón *nm, pl* **-mones** : lung — **pulmonar** *adj* : pulmonary — **pulmonía** *nf* : pneumonia

pulpa *nf* : pulp

pulpería *nf Lat* : grocery store

púlpito *nm* : pulpit

pulpo *nm* : octopus

pulsar *vt* 1 : press (a button), strike (a key) 2 : play (music) — **pulsación** *nf, pl* **-ciones** 1 : beat, throb 2 : keystroke (on a typewriter, etc.)

pulsera *nf* : bracelet

pulso *nm* 1 : pulse 2 : steadiness (of hand)

pulular *vi* : swarm

pulverizar {21} *vt* 1 : pulverize, crush 2 : spray (a liquid) — **pulverizador** *nm* : atomizer, spray

puma *nf* : puma

punitivo, -va *adj* : punitive

punta *nf* 1 : tip, end 2 : point (of a needle, etc.) 3 ~ **del dedo** : fingertip 4 **sacar** ~ **a** : sharpen

puntada *nf* 1 : stitch 2 ~**s** *nfpl* : seam

puntal *nm* : prop, support

puntapié *nm* : kick

puntear *vt* : pluck (a guitar)

puntería *nf* : aim, marksmanship

puntiagudo, -da *adj* : sharp, pointed

puntilla *nf* 1 : lace edging 2 **de** ~**s** : on tiptoe

punto *nm* 1 : dot, point 2 : period (in punctuation) 3 ASUNTO : item, question 4 LUGAR : spot, place 5 MOMENTO : moment 6 : point (in a score) 7 PUNTADA : stitch 8 **a las dos en** ~ : at two o'clock sharp 9 **dos** ~**s** : colon 10 **hasta cierto** ~ : up to a point 11 ~ **de partida** : starting point 12 ~ **muerto** : deadlock 13 ~ **y coma** : semicolon

puntuación *nf, pl* **-ciones** 1 : punctuation 2 : scoring, score (in sports)

puntual *adj* 1 : prompt, punctual 2 EXACTO : accurate, detailed — **puntualidad** *nf* 1 : punctuality 2 EXACTITUD : accuracy

puntuar {3} *vt* : punctuate — *vi* : score (in sports)

punzar {21} *vt* : prick, puncture — **punzada** *nf* 1 PINCHAZO : prick 2 : sharp pain — **punzante** *adj* 1 : sharp 2 MORDAZ : biting, caustic

puñado *nm* 1 : handful 2 **a** ~**s** : by the handful

puñal *nm* : dagger — **puñalada** *nf* : stab

puño *nm* 1 : fist 2 : cuff (of a shirt) 3 : handle, hilt (of a sword, etc.) — **puñetazo** *nm* : punch (with the fist)

pupila *nf* : pupil (of the eye)

pupitre *nm* : desk

puré *nm* 1 : purée 2 ~ **de papas** *or* ~ **de patatas** *Spain* : mashed potatoes

pureza *nf* : purity

purga *nf* : purge — **purgar** {52} *vt* : purge — **purgatorio** *nm* : purgatory

purificar {72} *vt* : purify — **purificación** *nf, pl* **-ciones** : purification

puritano, -na *adj* : puritanical — ~ *n* : puritan

puro, -ra *adj* 1 : pure 2 SIMPLE : plain, simple 3 *Lat fam* : only, just — **puro** *nm* : cigar

púrpura *nf* : purple — **purpúreo, -rea** *adj* : purple

pus *nm* : pus

pusilánime *adj* : cowardly

puta *nf* : whore

putrefacción *nf, pl* **-ciones** : putrefaction, rot — **pútrido, -da** *adj* : putrid, rotten

Q

q *nf* 1 : q, 18th letter of the Spanish alphabet

que *conj* 1 : that 2 (*in comparisons*) : than 3 (*introducing a reason or cause*) : so that, or else 4 es ~ : the thing is that 5 yo — ~ tú : if I were you — ~ *pron* 1 (*referring to persons*) : who, whom 2 (*referring to things*) : that, which 3 el (la, lo, las, los) ~ : he (she, it, they) who, whoever, the one(s) that

qué *adv* 1 : how, what 2 ¡~ lindo! : how lovely! — ~ *adj* : what, which — ~ *pron* 1 : what 2 ¿~ crees? : what do you think?

quebrar {55} *vt* : break — *vi* : go bankrupt — **quebrarse** *vr* : break — **quebrada** *nf* 1 : ravine, gorge — **quebradizo, -za** *adj* : breakable, fragile — **quebrado, -da** *adj* 1 : bankrupt 2 : rough, uneven (of land, etc.) 3 ROTO : broken — **quebrado** *nm* : fraction — **quebradura** *nf* : crack, fissure — **quebrantar** *vt* 1 : break 2 DEBILITAR : weaken — **quebranto** *nm* 1 : harm, damage 2 AFLICCIÓN : grief, pain

queda *nf* → **toque**

quedar *vi* 1 PERMANECER : remain, stay 2 ESTAR : be 3 FALTAR : be left 4 : fit, look (of clothing, etc.) 5 no queda lejos : it's not far 6 ~ en : agree to, agree on — **quedarse** *vr* 1 : stay 2 ~ con : keep

quedo, -da *adj* : quiet, still — **quedo** *adv* : softly, quietly

quehacer *nm* 1 : task 2 ~es *nmpl* : chores

queja *nf* : complaint — **quejarse** *vr* 1 : complain 2 GEMIR : moan, groan — **quejido** *nm* : moan, whimper — **quejoso, -sa** *adj* : complaining, whining

quemar *vt* 1 : burn 2 MALGASTAR : squander — *vi* : burn — **quemarse** *vr* 1 : burn oneself 2 : burn (up) 3 : get sunburned — **quemado, -da** *adj* 1 : burned 2 AGOTADO : burned-out 3 estar ~ : be fed up — **quemador** *nm* : burner — **quemadura** *nf* : burn — **quemarropa: a ~** *adj & adv phr* : point-blank

querella *nf* 1 : dispute, quarrel 2 : charge (in law)

querer {64} *vt* 1 : want 2 AMAR : love 3 ~ decir : mean 4 ¿quieres pasarme la leche? : please pass the milk 5 sin ~ : unintentionally — *nm* : love — **querido, -da** *adj* : dear, beloved — ~ *n* 1 : darling 2 AMANTE : lover

queroseno *nm* : kerosene

querubín *nm, pl* -bines : cherub

queso *nm* : cheese — **quesadilla** *nf Lat* : quesadilla

quicio *nm* 1 estar fuera de ~ : be beside oneself 2 sacar de ~ : drive crazy

quiebra *nf* 1 : break 2 BANCARROTA : bankruptcy

quien *pron, pl* quienes 1 (*subject*) : who 2 (*object*) : whom 3 (*indefinite*) : whoever, anyone, some people

quién *pron, pl* quiénes 1 (*subject*) : who 2 (*object*) : whom 3 ¿de ~ es este lápiz? : whose pencil is this?

quienquiera *pron, pl* quienesquiera : whoever, whomever

quieto, -ta *adj* 1 : calm, quiet 2 INMÓVIL : still — **quietud** *nf* : stillness

quijada *nf* : jaw, jawbone (of an animal)

quilate *nm* : carat, karat

quilla *nf* : keel

quimera *nf* : illusion — **quimérico, -ca** *adj* : fanciful

química *nf* : chemistry — **químico, -ca** *adj* : chemical — ~ *n* : chemist

quince *adj & nm* : fifteen — **quinceañero, -ra** *n* : fifteen-year-old, teenager — **quincena** *nf* : two-week period, fortnight — **quincenal** *adj* : semimonthly, twice a month

quincuagésimo, -ma *adj & n* : fiftieth

quinientos, -tas *adj* : five hundred — **quinientos** *nms & pl* : five hundred

quinina *nf* : quinine

quinqué *nm* : oil lamp

quinta *nf* : country house, villa

quintaesencia *nf* : quintessence

quinteto *nm* : quintet

quinto, -ta *adj & n* : fifth — **quinto** *nm* : fifth

quiosco *nm* : kiosk, newsstand

quiropráctico, -ca *n* : chiropractor

quirúrgico, -ca *adj* : surgical

quisquilloso, -sa *adj* : fastidious, fussy

quiste *nm* : cyst

quitar *vt* 1 : remove, take away 2 : take off (clothes) 3 : get rid of, relieve (pain, etc.) — **quitarse** *vr* 1 : withdraw, leave 2 : take off (one's clothes) 3 ~ **de** : give up (a habit) 4 ~ **de encima** : get rid of — **quitaesmalte** *nm* : nail-polish remover — **quita-**

manchas *nms & pl* : stain remover — **quitanleves** *nm* : snowplow — **quitasol** *nm* : parasol
quizá *or* **quizás** *adv* : maybe, perhaps

R

r *nf* : r, 19th letter of the Spanish alphabet
rábano *nm* **1** : radish **2** ~ **picante** : horseradish
rabí *nmf, pl* **-bíes** : rabbi
rabia *nf* **1** : rage, anger **2** : rabies (disease) — **rabiar** *vi* **1** : be furious **2** : be in great pain **3** ~ **por** : be dying for — **rabioso, -sa** *adj* **1** : enraged, furious **2** : rabid, having rabies
rabino, -na *n* : rabbi
rabo *nm* **1** : tail **2 el** ~ **del ojo** : the corner of one's eye
racha *nf* **1** : gust of wind **2** SERIE : series, string — **racheado, -da** *adj* : gusty
racial *adj* : racial
racimo *nm* : bunch, cluster
raciocinio *nm* : reason, reasoning
ración *nf, pl* **-ciones 1** : share, ration **2** : helping (of food)
racional *adj* : rational — **racionalizar** {21} *vt* : rationalize
racionar *vt* : ration — **racionamiento** *nm* : rationing
racismo *nm* : racism — **racista** *adj & nmf* : racist
radar *nm* : radar
radiación *nf, pl* **-ciones** : radiation
radiactivo, -va *adj* : radioactive — **radiactividad** *nf* : radioactivity
radiador *nm* : radiator
radiante *adj* : radiant
radical *adj & nmf* : radical
radicar {72} *vi* ~ **en** : lie in, be rooted in
radio *nm* **1** : radius **2** : spoke (of a wheel) **3** : radium (element) — ~ *nmf* : radio
radioactivo, -va *adj* : radioactive — **radioactividad** *nf* : radioactivity
radiodifusión *nf, pl* **-siones** : broadcasting — **radioemisora** *nf* : radio station — **radioescucha** *nmf* : listener — **radiofónico, -ca** *adj* : radio
radiografía *nf* : X ray — **radiografiar** {85} *vt* : x-ray
radiología *nf* : radiology — **radiólogo, -ga** *n* : radiologist
raer {65} *vt* : scrape off
ráfaga *nf* **1** : gust (of wind) **2** : flash (of light)

raído, -da *adj* : worn, shabby
raíz *nf, pl* **raíces 1** : root **2** ORIGEN : origin, source **3 echar raíces** : take root
raja *nf* **1** : crack, slit **2** RODAJA : slice — **rajar** *vt* : crack, split — **rajarse** *vr* **1** : crack, split open **2** *fam* : back out
rajatabla: a ~ *adv phr* : strictly, to the letter
ralea *nf* : sort, kind
ralentí *nm* : neutral (gear)
rallar *vt* : grate — **rallador** *nm* : grater
rama *nf* : branch — **ramaje** *nm* : branches *pl* — **ramal** *nm* **1** : branch (of a railroad, etc.) — **ramificarse** {72} *vr* : branch (off) — **ramillete** *nm* **1** : bouquet **2** GRUPO : cluster, bunch — **ramo** *nm* **1** : branch **2** RAMILLETE : bouquet
rampa *nf* : ramp, incline
rana *nf* **1** : frog **2** ~ **toro** : bullfrog
rancho *nm* : ranch, farm — **ranchero, -ra** *n* : rancher, farmer
rancio, -cia *adj* **1** : rancid **2** : aged (of wine)
rango *nm* **1** : rank **2** : (social) standing
ranúnculo *nm* : buttercup
ranura *nf* : groove, slot
rapar *vt* **1** : shave **2** : crop (hair)
rapaz *adj, pl* **-paces** : rapacious, predatory
rápido, -da *adj* : rapid, quick — **rápidamente** *adv* : rapidly, fast — **rapidez** *nf* : speed — **rápido** *adv* : quickly, fast — ~ *nm* **1** : express train **2** ~**s** *nmpl* : rapids
rapiña *nf* **1** : plunder **2 ave de** ~ : bird of prey
rapsodia *nf* : rhapsody
raptar *vt* : kidnap — **rapto** *nm* : kidnapping — **raptor, -tora** *n* : kidnapper
raqueta *nf* : racket (in sports)
raro, -ra *adj* **1** : rare **2** EXTRAÑO : odd, strange — **raramente** *adv* : rarely, infrequently — **rareza** *nf* : rarity
ras *nm* **a** ~ **de** : level with
rascacielos *nms & pl* : skyscraper
rascar {72} *vt* **1** : scratch **2** RASPAR : scrape — **rascarse** *vr* : scratch oneself
rasgar {52} *vt* : rip, tear — **rasgarse** *vr* : rip

rasgo *nm* **1** : stroke (of a pen) **2** CARAC-
TERÍSTICA : trait, characteristic **3** ~**s**
nmpl FACCIONES : features

rasguear *vt* : strum

rasguñar *vt* : scratch — **rasguño** *nm*
: scratch

raso, -sa *adj* **1** : level, flat **2** : low (of a
flight) **3 soldado raso** : private (in the
army) — **raso** *nm* : satin

raspar *vt* : scrape **2** LIMAR : file down,
smooth — *vi* : be rough — **raspadura**
nf **1** : scratch **2** ~**s** *nfpl* : scrapings

rastra *nf* : rake **2 a** ~**s** : unwillingly
— **rastrear** *vt* : track, trace — **ras-
trero, -ra** *adj* **1** : creeping **2** DESPRE-
CIABLE : despicable — **rastrillar** *vt*
: rake — **rastrillo** *nm* : rake — **rastro**
nm **1** : trail, track **2** SEÑAL : sign

rasurar *vt Lat* : shave — **rasurarse** *vr*
Lat : shave

rata *nf* : rat

ratear *vt* : steal — **ratero, -ra** *n* : thief

ratificar {72} *vt* : ratify — **ratificación**
nf, pl -**ciones** : ratification

rato *nm* **1** : while **2 al poco** ~ : shortly after **3 pasar el** ~ : pass the time

ratón *nm, pl* -**tones** : mouse — **raton-
era** *nf* : mousetrap

raudal *nm* **1** : torrent **2 a** ~**es** : in
abundance — **raudo, -da** *adj* : swift

raya *nf* **1** : line **2** LISTA : stripe **3** : part
(in the hair) — **rayar** *vt* : scratch — *vi*
1 al ~ **el día** : at daybreak **2** ~ **en**
: border on — **rayarse** *vr* : get
scratched

rayo *nm* **1** : ray, beam **2** : bolt of lightning **3** ~**s X** : X rays

rayón *nm* : rayon

raza *nf* **1** : (human) race **2** : breed (of
animals) **3 de** ~ : thoroughbred,
pedigreed

razón *nf, pl* -**zones 1** : reason **2 dar** ~
: inform **3 en** ~ **de** : because of **4
tener** ~ : be right — **razonable** *adj*
: reasonable — **razonamiento** *nm*
: reasoning — **razonar** *v* : reason,
think

reacción *nf, pl* -**ciones** : reaction —
reaccionar *vi* : react — **reaccionario,
-ria** *adj & n* : reactionary

reacio, -cia *adj* : resistant, stubborn

reactivar *vt* : reactivate, revive

reactor *nm* **1** : jet (airplane) **2** ~ **nuclear** : nuclear reactor

reajustar *vt* : readjust — **reajuste** *nm*
: readjustment

real *adj* **1** : royal **2** VERDADERO : real,
true

realce *nm* **1** : relief **2 dar** ~ : highlight

realeza *nf* : royalty

realidad *nf* **1** : reality **2 en** ~ : actually, in fact

realismo *nm* : realism — **realista** *adj*
: realistic — *nmf* : realist

realizar {21} *vt* **1** : carry out **2** : achieve
(a goal) **3** : produce (a film or play) **4**
: realize (a profit) — **realizarse** *vr* **1**
: fulfill oneself **2** : come true (of a
dream, etc.) — **realización** *nf, pl*
-**ciones** : execution, realization

realmente *adv* : really, actually

realzar {21} *vt* : highlight, enhance

reanimar *vt* : revive

reanudar *vt* : resume, renew — **reanudarse** *vr* : resume

reaparecer {53} *vi* : reappear — **rea-
parición** *nf, pl* -**ciones** : reappearance

reavivar *vt* : revive

rebajar *vt* **1** : lower, reduce **2** HUMILLAR
: humiliate — **rebajarse** *vr* **1** : humble
oneself **2** ~ **a** : stoop to — **rebaja** *nf*
1 : reduction **2** DESCUENTO : discount **3**
~**s** *nfpl* : sales

rebanada *nf* : slice

rebaño *nm* **1** : herd **2** : flock (of sheep)

rebasar *vt* : surpass, exceed

rebatir *vt* : refute

rebelarse *vr* : rebel — **rebelde** *adj* : rebellious — ~ *nmf* : rebel — **rebeldía**
nf : rebelliousness — **rebelión** *nf, pl*
-**liones** : rebellion

reblandecer *vt* : soften

rebobinar *vt* : rewind

rebosar *vi* **1** : overflow **2** ~ **de** : be
bursting with — *vt* : overflow with

rebotar *vi* : bounce, rebound — **rebote**
nm **1** : bounce **2 de** ~ : on the rebound

rebozar {21} *vt* : coat in batter

rebuscado, -da *adj* : pretentious

rebuznar *vi* : bray

recabar *vt* **1** : obtain, collect **2** ~ **fondos** : raise money

recado *nm* **1** MENSAJE : message **2**
Spain : errand

recaer {13} *vi* **1** : relapse **2** ~ **sobre**
: fall on — **recaída** *nf* : relapse

recalcar {72} *vt* : emphasize, stress

recalcitrante *adj* : recalcitrant

recalentar {55} *vt* **1** : overheat **2** : re-
heat, warm up (food) — **recalentarse**
vr : overheat

recámara *nf* **1** : chamber (of a firearm)
2 *Lat* : bedroom

recambio *nm* **1** : spare part **2** : refill (for
a pen, etc.)

recapitular *vt* : recapitulate, sum up —
recapitulación *nf, pl* -**ciones** : reca-
pitulation

recargar {52} *vt* **1** : overload **2**

: recharge (a battery), reload (a firearm, etc.) — **recargado, -da** *adj* : overly elaborate — **recargo** *nm* : surcharge

recato *nm* : modesty — **recatado, -da** *adj* : modest, demure

recaudar *vt* : collect — **recaudación** *nf, pl* **-ciones** : collection — **recaudador, -dora** *n* ∼ **de impuestos** : tax collector

recelar *vt* : distrust, fear — **recelo** *nm* : distrust, suspicion — **receloso, -sa** *adj* : distrustful, suspicious

recepción *nf, pl* **-ciones** : reception — **recepcionista** *nmf* : receptionist

receptáculo *nm* : receptacle

receptivo, -va *adj* : receptive — **receptor, -tora** *n* : recipient — **receptor** *nm* : receiver (of a radio, etc.)

recesión *nf, pl* **-siones** : recession

receso *nm Lat* : recess, adjournment

receta *nf* **1** : recipe **2** : prescription (in medicine)

rechazar {21} *vt* **1** : reject, refuse **2** REPELER : repel **3** : reflect (light) — **rechazo** *nm* : rejection

rechinar *vi* **1** : squeak, creak **2** : grind, gnash (one's teeth)

rechoncho, -cha *adj fam* : chubby

recibir *vt* **1** : receive **2** ACOGER : welcome — *vi* : receive visitors — **recibidor** *nm* : vestibule, entrance hall — **recibimiento** *nm* : reception, welcome — **recibo** *nm* : receipt

reciclar *vt* **1** : recycle **2** : retrain (workers) — **reciclaje** *nm* : recycling

recién *adv* **1** : newly, recently **2** ∼ **casados** : newlyweds — **reciente** *adj* : recent — **recientemente** *adv* : recently

recinto *nm* **1** : enclosure **2** ÁREA : area, site

recio, -cia *adj* : tough, strong

recipiente *nm* : container, receptacle — ∼ *nmf* : recipient

recíproco, -ca *adj* : reciprocal, mutual

recitar *vt* : recite — **recital** *nm* : recital

reclamar *vt* : demand, ask for — *vi* : complain — **reclamación** *nf, pl* **-ciones** : claim, demand **2** QUEJA : complaint — **reclamo** *nm* **1** : lure (in hunting) **2** *Lat* : inducement, attraction

reclinar *vt* : rest, lean — **reclinarse** *vr* : recline, lean back

recluir {41} *vt* : confine, lock up — **recluirse** *vr* : shut oneself away — **reclusión** *nf, pl* **-siones** : imprisonment — **recluso, -sa** *n* : prisoner

recluta *nmf* : recruit — **reclutamiento**

nm : recruitment — **reclutar** *vt* : recruit, enlist

recobrar *vt* : recover, regain — **recobrarse** *vr* ∼ **de** : recover from

recodo *nm* : bend

recoger {15} *vt* **1** : collect, gather **2** COGER : pick up **3** LIMPIAR, ORDENAR : clean up, tidy (up) — **recogerse** *vr* : retire, withdraw — **recogedor** *nm* : dustpan — **recogido, -da** *adj* : quiet, secluded

recolección *nf, pl* **-ciones** **1** : collection **2** COSECHA : harvest

recomendar {55} *vt* : recommend — **recomendación** *nf, pl* **-ciones** : recommendation

recompensar *vt* : reward — **recompensa** *nf* : reward

reconciliar *vt* : reconcile — **reconciliarse** *vr* : be reconciled — **reconciliación** *nf, pl* **-ciones** : reconciliation

recóndito, -ta *adj* : hidden

reconfortar *vt* : comfort

reconocer {18} *vt* **1** : recognize **2** ADMITIR : admit **3** EXAMINAR : examine — **reconocible** *adj* : recognizable — **reconocido, -da** *adj* **1** : recognized, accepted **2** AGRADECIDO : grateful — **reconocimiento** *nm* **1** : recognition **2** AGRADECIMIENTO : gratitude **3** : (medical) examination

reconsiderar *vt* : reconsider

reconstruir {41} *vt* : reconstruct — **reconstrucción** *nf, pl* **-ciones** : reconstruction

recopilar *vt* **1** RECOGER : collect, gather **2** : compile — **recopilación** *nf, pl* **-ciones** : collection, compilation

récord *nm, pl* **-cords** : record

recordar {19} *vt* **1** ACORDARSE DE : remember **2** : remind — *vi* : remember — **recordatorio** *nm* : reminder

recorrer *vt* **1** : travel through **2** : cover (a distance) — **recorrido** *nm* **1** : journey, trip **2** TRAYECTO : route, course

recortar *vt* **1** : reduce **2** CORTAR : cut (out) **3** : trim (hair) — **recortarse** *vr* : stand out — **recorte** *nm* **1** : cut, cutting **2** ∼ **s de periódicos** : newspaper clippings

recostar {19} *vt* : lean, rest — **recostarse** *vr* : lie down

recoveco *nm* **1** : bend **2** RINCÓN : nook, corner

recrear *vt* **1** : recreate **2** ENTRETENER : entertain — **recrearse** *vr* : to enjoy oneself — **recreativo, -va** *adj* : recreational — **recreo** *nm* **1** : recreation, amusement **2** : recess, break (at school)

recriminar *vt* : reproach

recrudecer {53} *vi* : worsen — **recrudecerse** *vr* : intensify, get worse

rectángulo *nm* : rectangle — **rectangular** *adj* : rectangular

rectificar {72} *vt* **1** : rectify, correct **2** AJUSTAR : straighten (out) — **rectitud** *nf* **1** : straightness **2** : (moral) rectitude — **recto, -ta** *adj* **1** : straight **2** ÍNTEGRO : upright, honorable — **recto** *nm* : rectum

rector, -tora *adj* : governing, managing — ~ *n* : rector — **rectoría** *nf* : rectory

recubrir {2} *vt* : cover, coat

recuento *nm* : count, recount

recuerdo *nm* **1** : memory **2** : souvenir, remembrance (of a journey, etc.) **3** ~s *nmpl* SALUDOS : regards

recuperar *vt* **1** : recover, retrieve **2** ~ el tiempo perdido : make up for lost time — **recuperarse** *vr* ~ de : recover from — **recuperación** *nf, pl* -**ciones 1** : recovery **2** ~ de datos : data retrieval

recurrir *vi* ~ a : turn to (a person), resort to (force, etc.) — **recurso** *nm* **1** : recourse, resort **2** : appeal (in law) **3** ~s *nmpl* : resources

red *nf* **1** : net **2** SISTEMA : network, system **3** la Red : the Internet

redactar *vt* : write (up), draft — **redacción** *nf, pl* -**ciones 1** : writing, drafting **2** : editing (of a newspaper, etc.) — **redactor, -tora** *n* : editor

redada *nf* **1** : (police) raid **2** : catch (in fishing)

redescubrir {2} *vt* : rediscover

redención *nf, pl* -**ciones** : redemption — **redentor, -tora** *adj* : redeeming

redil *nm* : fold, pen

rédito *nm* : interest, yield

redoblar *vt* : redouble

redomado, -da *adj* : out-and-out

redondear *vt* **1** : make round **2** : round off (a number, etc.) — **redonda** *nf* **1** : whole note (in music) **2** a la ~ : in the surrounding area — **redondel** *nm* **1** : ring, circle **2** : bullring — **redondo, -da** *adj* **1** : round **2** PERFECTO : excellent

reducir {61} *vt* : reduce — **reducirse** *vr* ~ a : come down to, amount to — **reducción** *nf, pl* -**ciones** : reduction — **reducido, -da** *adj* **1** : reduced, limited **2** PEQUEÑO : small

redundante *adj* : redundant — **redundancia** *nf* : redundancy

reedición *nf, pl* -**ciones** : reprint

reembolsar *vt* : refund, reimburse,

repay — **reembolso** *nm* : refund, reimbursement

reemplazar {21} *vt* : replace — **reemplazo** *nm* : replacement

reencarnación *nf, pl* -**ciones** : reincarnation

reencuentro *nm* : reunion

reestructurar *vt* : restructure

refaccionar *vt Lat* : repair, renovate — **refacciones** *nfpl Lat* : repairs, renovations

referir {76} *vt* **1** : tell **2** REMITIR : refer — **referirse** *vr* ~ a : refer to — **referencia** *nf* **1** : reference **2** hacer ~ a : refer to — **referéndum** *nm, pl* -**dums** : referendum — **referente** *adj* ~ a : concerning

refinar *vt* : refine — **refinado, -da** *adj* : refined — **refinamiento** *nm* : refinement — **refinería** *nf* : refinery

reflector *nm* **1** : reflector **2** : spotlight, searchlight, floodlight

reflejar *vt* : reflect — **reflejarse** *vr* : be reflected — **reflejo** *nm* **1** : reflection **2** : (physical) reflex **3** ~s *nmpl* : highlights (in hair)

reflexionar *vi* : reflect, think — **reflexión** *nf, pl* -**xiones** : reflection, thought — **reflexivo, -va** *adj* **1** : reflective, thoughtful **2** : reflexive (in grammar)

reflujo *nm* : ebb (tide)

reforma *nf* **1** : reform **2** ~s *nfpl* : renovations — **reformador, -dora** *n* : reformer — **reformar** *vt* **1** : reform **2** : renovate, repair (a house, etc.) — **reformarse** *vr* : mend one's ways — **reformatorio** *nm* : reformatory

reforzar {36} *vt* : reinforce

refrán *nm, pl* -**franes** : proverb, saying

refregar {49} *vt* : scrub

refrenar *vt* **1** : rein in (a horse) **2** CONTENER : restrain — **refrenarse** *vr* : restrain oneself

refrendar *vt* : approve, endorse

refrescar {72} *vt* **1** : refresh, cool **2** : brush up on (knowledge) — *vi* : turn cooler — **refrescante** *adj* : refreshing — **refresco** *nm* : soft drink

refriega *nf* : scuffle, skirmish

refrigerar *vt* **1** : refrigerate **2** CLIMATIZAR : air-condition — **refrigeración** *nf, pl* -**ciones 1** : refrigeration **2** AIRE ACONDICIONADO : air-conditioning — **refrigerador** *nmf Lat* : refrigerator — **refrigerio** *nm* : refreshments *pl*

refrito, -ta *adj* : refried — **refrito** *nm* : rehash

refuerzo *nm* : reinforcement

refugiar *vt* : shelter — **refugiarse** *vr* : take refuge — **refugiado, -da** *n*

: refugee — **refugio** *nm* : refuge, shelter
refulgir {35} *vi* : shine brightly
refunfuñar *vi* : grumble, groan
refutar *vt* : refute
regadera *nf* 1 : watering can 2 *Lat* : shower head, shower
regalar *vt* : give (as a gift) — **regalarse** *vr* ~ **con** : treat oneself to
regaliz *nm, pl* -**lices** : licorice
regalo *nm* 1 : gift, present 2 PLACER : pleasure, delight
regañadientes : a ~ *adv phr* : reluctantly, unwillingly
regañar *vt* : scold — *vi* 1 QUEJARSE : grumble 2 *Spain* : quarrel — **regañón, -ñona** *adj, mpl* -**ñones** *fam* : grumpy, irritable
regar {49} *vt* 1 : irrigate, water 2 ESPARCIR : scatter
regatear *vt* 1 : haggle over 2 ESCATIMAR : skimp on — *vi* : bargain, haggle
regazo *nm* : lap (of a person)
regenerar *vt* : regenerate
regentar *vt* : run, manage
régimen *nm, pl* **regímenes** 1 : regime 2 DIETA : diet 3 ~ **de vida** : lifestyle
regimiento *nm* : regiment
regio, -gia *adj* : royal, regal
región *nf, pl* -**giones** : region, area — **regional** *adj* : regional
regir {28} *vt* 1 : rule 2 ADMINISTRAR : manage, run 3 DETERMINAR : govern, determine — *vi* : apply, be in force — **regirse** *vr* ~ **por** : be guided by
registrar *vt* 1 : register 2 GRABAR : record, tape 3 : search (a house, etc.), frisk (a person) — **registrarse** *vr* 1 : register 2 : be recorded (of temperatures, etc.) — **registrador, -dora** *adj* **caja registradora** : cash register — ~ *n* : registrar — **registro** *nm* 1 : registration 2 : register (book) 3 : registry (office) 4 : range (of a voice, etc.) 5 INSPECCIÓN : search
regla *nf* 1 : rule, regulation 2 : ruler (for measuring) 3 MENSTRUACIÓN : period — **reglamentación** *nf, pl* -**ciones** 1 : regulation 2 REGLAS : rules *pl* — **reglamentar** *vt* : regulate — **reglamentario, -ria** *adj* : regulation, official — **reglamento** *nm* : regulations *pl*, rules *pl*
regocijar *vt* : gladden, delight — **regocijarse** *vr* : rejoice — **regocijo** *nm* : delight, rejoicing
regodearse *vr* : be delighted — **regodeo** *nm* : delight
regordete *adj fam* : chubby
regresar *vi* : return, come back, go

back — *vt Lat* : give back — **regresión** *nf, pl* -**siones** : regression — **regresivo, -va** *adj* : regressive — **regreso** *nm* 1 : return 2 **estar de** ~ : be back, be home early
reguero *nm* 1 : irrigation ditch 2 SEÑAL : trail, trace 3 **correr como un** ~ **de pólvora** : spread like wildfire
regular *adj* 1 : regular 2 MEDIANO : medium, average 3 **por lo** ~ : in general — ~ *vt* : regulate, control — **regulación** *nf, pl* -**ciones** : regulation, control — **regularidad** *nf* : regularity — **regularizar** {21} *vt* : normalize, make regular
rehabilitar *vt* 1 : rehabilitate 2 : reinstate (s.o. in a position) 3 : renovate (a building, etc.) — **rehabilitación** *nf* 1 : rehabilitation 2 : reinstatement (in a position) 3 : renovation (of a building, etc.)
rehacer {40} *vt* 1 : redo 2 REPARAR : repair — **rehacerse** *vr* 1 : recover 2 ~ **de** : get over
rehén *nm, pl* -**henes** : hostage
rehuir {41} *vt* : avoid, shun
rehusar {8} *v* : refuse
reimprimir *vt* : reprint — **reimpresión** *nf, pl* -**siones** : reprinting, reprint
reina *nf* : queen — **reinado** *nm* : reign — **reinante** *adj* : reigning — **reinar** *vi* 1 : reign 2 PREVALECER : prevail
reincidir *vi* : backslide, relapse
reino *nm* : kingdom, realm
reintegrar *vt* 1 : reinstate 2 : refund (money), reimburse (expenses, etc.) — **reintegrarse** *vr* ~ **a** : return to — **reintegro** *nm* : reimbursement
reír {66} *vi* : laugh — *vt* : laugh at — **reírse** *vr* : laugh
reiterar *vt* : repeat, reiterate
reivindicar {72} *vt* 1 : claim 2 RESTAURAR : restore
reja *nf* : grille, grating — **rejilla** *nf* : grille, grate, screen
rejuvenecer {53} *vt* : rejuvenate — **rejuvenecerse** *vr* : be rejuvenated
relación *nf, pl* -**ciones** 1 : relation, connection 2 COMUNICACIÓN : relationship, relations *pl* 3 RELATO : account 4 LISTA : list 5 **con** ~ **a** *or* **en** ~ **a** : in relation to — **relacionar** *vt* : relate, connect — **relacionarse** *vr* ~ **con** : be connected to, interact with
relajar *vt* : relax — **relajarse** *vr* : relax — **relajación** *nf, pl* -**ciones** : relaxation — **relajado, -da** *adj* 1 : relaxed 2 : dissolute, lax (in behavior)
relamerse *vr* : smack one's lips, lick its chops

relámpago *nm* : flash of lightning — **relampaguear** *vi* : flash

relatar *vt* : relate, tell

relativo, -va *adj* 1 : relative 2 **en lo relativo a** : with regard to — **relatividad** *nf* : relativity

relato *nm* 1 : account, report 2 CUENTO : story, tale

releer {20} *vt* : reread

relegar {52} *vt* : relegate

relevante *adj* : outstanding, important

relevar *vt* 1 : relieve, take over from 2 ~ **de** : exempt from — **relevo** *nm* 1 : relief, replacement 2 **carrera de** ~**s** : relay race

relieve *nm* 1 : relief (in art, etc.) 2 IMPORTANCIA : prominence, importance 3 **poner en** ~ : emphasize

religión *nf, pl* **-giones** : religion — **religioso, -sa** *adj* : religious — ~ *n* : monk *m*, nun *f*

relinchar *vi* : neigh, whinny — **relincho** *nm* : neigh, whinny

reliquia *nf* 1 : relic 2 ~ **de familia** : family heirloom

rellenar *vt* 1 : refill 2 : stuff, fill (in cooking) — **relleno, -na** *adj* : stuffed, filled — **relleno** *nm* : stuffing, filling

reloj *nm* 1 : clock 2 *or* ~ **de pulsera** : wristwatch 3 ~ **de arena** : hourglass 4 **como un** ~ : like clockwork

relucir {45} *vi* 1 : glitter, shine 2 **sacar a** ~ : bring up, mention — **reluciente** *adj* : brilliant, shining

relumbrar *vi* : shine brightly

remachar *vt* 1 : rivet 2 RECALCAR : stress, drive home — **remache** *nm* : rivet

remanente *nm* : remainder, surplus

remanso *nm* : pool

remar *vi* : row

rematar *vt* 1 : conclude, finish up 2 MATAR : finish off 3 LIQUIDAR : sell off cheaply 4 *Lat* : auction — *vi* 1 : shoot (in sports) 2 TERMINAR : end — **rematado, -da** *adj* : utter, complete — **remate** *nm* 1 : shot (in sports) 2 FIN : end

remedar *vt* : imitate, mimic

remediar *vt* 1 : remedy, repair 2 : solve (a problem) 3 EVITAR : avoid — **remedio** *nm* 1 : remedy, cure 2 SOLUCIÓN : solution 3 **sin** ~ : hopeless

rememorar *vi* : recall

remendar {55} *vt* : mend

remesa *nf* 1 : remittance 2 : shipment (of merchandise)

remezón *nm, pl* **-zones** *Lat* : mild earthquake, tremor

remiendo *nm* : mend, patch

remilgado, -da *adj* 1 : prudish 2 AFEC-TADO : affected — **remilgo** *nm* : primness, affectation

reminiscencia *nf* : reminiscence

remisión *nf, pl* **-siones** : remission

remiso, -sa *adj* 1 : reluctant 2 NEGLIGENTE : remiss

remitir *vt* 1 : send, remit 2 ~ **a** : refer to, direct to — *vi* : subside, let up — **remite** *nm* : return address — **remitente** *nmf* : sender (of a letter, etc.)

remo *nm* : paddle, oar

remodelar *vt* 1 : remodel 2 : restructure (an organization)

remojar *vt* : soak, steep — **remojo** *nm* **poner en** ~ : soak

remolacha *nf* : beet

remolcar {72} *vt* : tow, tug — **remolcador** *nm* : tugboat

remolino *nm* 1 : whirlwind, whirlpool 2 : crowd (of people) 3 : cowlick (of hair)

remolque *nm* 1 : towing, tow 2 : trailer (vehicle)

remontar *vt* 1 : overcome 2 SUBIR : go up — **remontarse** *vr* 1 : soar 2 ~ **a** : date from, go back to

rémora *nf* : hindrance

remorder {47} *vt* : trouble, worry — **remordimiento** *nm* : remorse

remoto, -ta *adj* : remote — **remotamente** *adv* : remotely, slightly

remover {47} *vt* 1 : stir 2 : move around, turn over (earth, embers, etc.) 3 REAVIVAR : bring up again 4 DESPEDIR : fire, dismiss

remunerar *vt* : remunerate

renacer {48} *vi* : be reborn, revive — **renacimiento** *nm* 1 : rebirth, revival 2 **el Renacimiento** : the Renaissance

renacuajo *nm* : tadpole, pollywog

rencilla *nf* : quarrel

renco, -ca *adj Lat* : lame

rencor *nm* 1 : rancor, hostility 2 **guardar** ~ : hold a grudge — **rencoroso, -sa** *adj* : resentful

rendición *nf, pl* **-ciones** : surrender — **rendido, -da** *adj* 1 : submissive 2 AGOTADO : exhausted

rendija *nf* : crack, split

rendir {54} *vt* 1 : render, give 2 PRODUCIR : yield, produce 3 CANSAR : exhaust — *vi* : make progress, go a long way — **rendirse** *vr* : surrender, give up — **rendimiento** *nm* 1 : performance 2 : yield, return (in finance, etc.)

renegar {49} *vt* : deny — *vi* 1 QUEJARSE : grumble 2 ~ **de** ABJURAR : renounce, disown — **renegado, -da** *n* : renegade

renglón nm, pl **-glones 1** : line (of writing) **2** Lat : line (of products)
reno nm : reindeer
renombre nm : renown — **renombrado, -da** adj : famous, renowned
renovar {19} vt **1** : renew, restore **2** : renovate (a building, etc.) — **renovación** nf, pl **-ciones 1** : renewal **2** : renovation (of a building, etc.)
renquear vi : limp, hobble
rentar vt **1** : produce, yield **2** Lat : rent — **renta** nf **1** : income **2** ALQUILER : rent **3 impuesto sobre la ~** : income tax — **rentable** adj : profitable
renunciar vt **1** : resign **2 ~ a** : renounce, relinquish — **renuncia** nf **1** : renunciation **2** DIMISIÓN : resignation
reñir {67} vi **~ con** : argue with, fall out with — vt **1** : scold **2** DISPUTAR : fight — **reñido, -da** adj **1** : hardfought **2 ~ con** : on bad terms with
reo, rea n **1** : accused, defendant **2** CULPABLE : culprit
reojo mirar de ~ : out of the corner of one's eye
reorganizar {21} vt : reorganize
repantigarse {52} vr : sprawl out
reparar vt **1** : repair, fix **2** : make amends for (an offense, etc.) — vi **1 ~ en** ADVERTIR : take notice of **2 ~ en** CONSIDERAR : consider — **reparación** nf, pl **-ciones 1** : reparation, amends **2** ARREGLO : repair — **reparo** nm **1** : reservation, objection **2 poner ~s a** : object to
repartir vt **1** : allocate **2** DISTRIBUIR : distribute **3** ESPARCIR : spread — **repartición** nf, pl **-ciones** : distribution — **repartidor, -dora** n : delivery person, distributor — **reparto** nm **1** : allocation **2** DISTRIBUCIÓN : delivery **3** : cast (of characters)
repasar vt **1** : review, go over **2** ZURCIR : mend — **repaso** nm **1** : review **2** : mending (of clothes)
repeler vt **1** : repel **2** REPUGNAR : disgust — **repelente** adj : repellent, repulsive
repente nm **1** : fit, outburst **2 de ~** : suddenly — **repentino, -na** adj : sudden
repercutir vi **1** : reverberate **2 ~ en** : have repercussions on — **repercusión** nf, pl **-siones** : repercussion
repertorio nm : repertoire
repetir {54} vt **1** : repeat **2** : have a second helping of (food) — **repetirse** vr **1** : repeat oneself **2** : recur (an event, etc.) — **repetición** nf, pl **-ciones 1** : repetition **2** : rerun, repeat (of a program, etc.) — **repetido, -da**

adj **1** : repeated **2 repetidas veces** : repeatedly, time and again — **repetitivo, -va** adj : repetitive, repetitious
repicar {72} vt : ring — vi : ring out, peal — **repique** nm : ringing, pealing
repisa nf **1** : shelf, ledge **2 ~ de ventana** : windowsill
replegar {49} vt : fold — **replegarse** vr : retreat, withdraw
repleto, -ta adj **1** : replete, full **2 ~ de** : packed with
replicar {72} vt : reply, retort — vi : answer back — **réplica** nf **1** RESPUESTA : reply **2** COPIA : replica, reproduction
repliegue nm **1** : fold **2** : (military) withdrawal
repollo nm : cabbage
reponer {60} vt **1** : replace **2** REPLICAR : reply — **reponerse** vr : recover
reportar vt **1** : yield, bring **2** Lat : report — **reportaje** nm : article, (news) report — **reporte** nm Lat : report — **reportero, -ra** n : reporter
reposar vi **1** DESCANSAR : rest **2** : stand, settle (of liquids, dough, etc.) — **reposado, -da** adj : calm, relaxed — **reposición** nf, pl **-ciones 1** : replacement **2** : rerun, repeat (of a program, etc.) — **reposo** nm : rest
repostar vi **1** : stock up on **2** : refuel (an airplane, etc.) — vi : fill up, refuel
reprender vt : reprimand, scold — **reprensible** adj : reprehensible
represalia nf **1** : reprisal **2 tomar ~s** : retaliate
represar vt : dam
representar vt **1** : represent **2** : perform (a play, etc.) **3** APARENTAR : look, appear as — **representación** nf, pl **-ciones 1** : representation **2** : performance (of a play, etc.) **3 en ~ de** : on behalf of — **representante** nmf **1** : representative **2** ACTOR : performer — **representativo, -va** adj : representative
represión nf, pl **-siones** : repression
reprimenda nf : reprimand
reprimir vt **1** : repress **2** : suppress (a rebellion, etc.)
reprobar {19} vt **1** : reprove, condemn **2** Lat : fail (an exam, etc.)
reprochar vt : reproach — **reprocharse** vr : reproach oneself — **reproche** nm : reproach
reproducir {61} vt : reproduce — **reproducirse** vr **1** : breed, reproduce **2** : recur (of an event, etc.) — **reproducción** nf, pl **-ciones** : reproduction — **reproductor, -tora** adj : reproductive
reptil nm : reptile

república nf : republic — **republicano, -na** adj & n : republican

repudiar vt : repudiate

repuesto nm : spare (auto) part

repugnar vt : disgust — **repugnancia** nf : disgust — **repugnante** adj : disgusting

repujar vt : emboss

repulsivo, -va adj : repulsive

reputar vt : consider, deem — **reputación** nf, pl **-ciones** : reputation

requerir {76} vt 1 : require 2 : summon, send for (a person)

requesón nm, pl **-sones** : cottage cheese

réquiem nm : requiem

requisito nm 1 : requirement 2 ~ **previo** : prerequisite

res nf 1 : beast, animal 2 Lat or **carne de** ~ : beef

resabio nm 1 VICIO : bad habit, vice 2 DEJO : aftertaste

resaca nf 1 : undertow 2 **tener** ~ : have a hangover

resaltar vi 1 : stand out 2 **hacer** ~ : bring out, highlight — vt : emphasize

resarcir {83} vt : compensate, repay — **resarcirse** vr ~ **de** : make up for

resbalar vi 1 : slip, slide 2 : skid (of an automobile) — **resbalarse** vr : slip, skid — **resbaladizo, -za** adj : slippery — **resbalón** nm, pl **-lones** : slip — **resbaloso, -sa** adj Lat : slippery

rescatar vt 1 : rescue, ransom 2 RECUPERAR : recover, get back — **rescate** nm 1 : rescue 2 : ransom (money) 3 RECUPERACIÓN : recovery

rescindir vt : cancel — **rescisión** nf, pl **-siones** : cancellation

rescoldo nm : embers pl

resecar {72} vt : dry (out) — **resecarse** vr : dry up — **reseco, -ca** adj : dry, dried-up

resentirse {76} vr 1 : suffer, be weakened 2 OFENDERSE : be offended 3 ~ **de** : feel the effects of — **resentido, -da** adj : resentful — **resentimiento** nm : resentment

reseñar vt 1 : review 2 DESCRIBIR : describe — **reseña** nf 1 : review, report 2 DESCRIPCIÓN : description

reservar vt 1 : reserve 2 GUARDAR : keep, save — **reservarse** vr 1 : save oneself 2 : keep for oneself — **reserva** nf 1 : reservation 2 PROVISIÓN : reserve 3 **de** ~ : spare, in reserve — **reservación** nf, pl **-ciones** : reservation — **reservado, -da** adj 1 : reserved 2 : confidential (of a document, etc.)

resfriar {85} vt : cool — **resfriarse** vr 1 : cool off 2 CONSTIPARSE : catch a cold — **resfriado** nm CATARRO : cold — **resfrío** nm Lat : cold

resguardar vt : protect — **resguardarse** vr : protect oneself — **resguardo** nm 1 : protection 2 RECIBO : receipt

residir vi 1 : reside, live 2 ~ **en** : lie in — **residencia** nf 1 : residence 2 or ~ **universitaria** : dormitory — **residencial** adj : residential — **residente** adj & nmf : resident

residuo nm 1 : residue 2 ~ **s** nmpl : waste — **residual** adj : residual

resignar vt : resign — **resignarse** vr ~ **a** : resign oneself to — **resignación** nf, pl **-ciones** : resignation

resina nf 1 : resin 2 ~ **epoxídica** : epoxy

resistir vt 1 AGUANTAR : stand, bear 2 : withstand (temptation, etc.) — vi : resist — **resistirse** vr ~ **a** : be resistant to — **resistencia** nf 1 : resistance 2 AGUANTE : endurance, stamina — **resistente** adj : resistant, strong, tough

resma nf : ream

resollar {19} vi : breathe heavily, pant

resolver {89} vt 1 : resolve 2 DECIDIR : decide — **resolverse** vr : make up one's mind — **resolución** nf, pl **-ciones** : resolution 2 DECISIÓN : decision 3 FIRMEZA : determination, resolve

resonar {19} vi : resound — **resonancia** nf 1 : resonance 2 CONSECUENCIAS : impact, repercussions pl — **resonante** adj : resonant, resounding

resoplar vi 1 : puff, pant 2 : snort (with annoyance)

resorte nm 1 MUELLE : spring 2 **tocar** ~ **s** : pull strings

respaldar vt : back, endorse — **respaldarse** vr : lean back — **respaldo** nm 1 : back (of a chair, etc.) 2 APOYO : support, backing

respectar vt : concern, relate to — **respectivo, -va** adj : respective — **respecto** nm 1 **al** ~ : in this respect 2 ~ **a** : in regard to, concerning

respetar vt : respect — **respetable** adj : respectable — **respeto** nm 1 : respect 2 **presentar sus** ~ **s** : pay one's respects — **respetuoso, -sa** adj : respectful

respingo nm : start, jump

respirar v : breathe — **respiración** nf, pl **-ciones** : respiration, breathing — **respiratorio, -ria** adj : respiratory — **respiro** nm 1 : breath 2 DESCANSO : respite, break

resplandecer {53} *vi* : shine — **resplandeciente** *adj* : shining, gleaming — **resplandor** *nm* **1** : brilliance, gleam **2** : flash (of lightning, etc.)

responder *vt* : answer, reply — *vi* **1** : answer **2** REPLICAR : answer back **3** ~ **a** : respond to **4** ~ **de** : answer for (something)

responsable *adj* : responsible — **responsabilidad** *nf* : responsibility

respuesta *nf* **1** : answer, reply **2** REACCIÓN : response

resquebrajar *vt* : split, crack — **resquebrajarse** *vr* : crack

resquicio *nm* **1** : crack, crevice **2** VESTIGIO : trace, glimmer

resta *nf* : subtraction

restablecer {53} *vt* : reestablish, restore — **restablecerse** *vr* : recover — **restablecimiento** *nm* : restoration, recovery

restallar *vi* : crack, crackle

restar *vt* **1** : deduct, subtract **2** DISMINUIR : minimize — *vi* : be left — **restante** *adj* **1** : remaining **2** **lo** ~ : the rest

restauración *nf, pl* **-ciones** : restoration

restaurante *nm* : restaurant

restaurar *vt* : restore

restituir {41} *vt* : return, restore — **restitución** *nf, pl* **-ciones** : restitution

resto *nm* **1** : rest, remainder **2** ~**s** *nmpl* : leftovers **3** *or* ~**s mortales** : mortal remains

restregar {49} *vt* : rub, scrub — **restregarse** *vr* : rub

restringir {35} *vt* : restrict, limit — **restricción** *nf, pl* **-ciones** : restriction, limitation — **restrictivo, -va** *adj* : restrictive

resucitar *vt* : resuscitate, revive — *vi* : come back to life

resuelto, -ta *adj* : determined, resolved

resuello *nm* : heavy breathing, panting

resultar *vi* **1** : succeed, work out **2** SALIR : turn out (to be) **3** ~ **de** : be the result of **4** ~ **en** : result in — **resultado** *nm* : result, outcome

resumir *v* : summarize, sum up — **resumen** *nm, pl* **-súmenes 1** : summary **2 en** ~ : in short

resurgir {35} *vi* : reappear, revive — **resurgimiento** *nm* : resurgence — **resurrección** *nf, pl* **-ciones** : resurrection

retahíla *nf* : string, series

retal *nm* : remnant

retardar *vt* **1** RETRASAR : delay **2** POSPONER : postpone

retazo *nm* **1** : remnant, scrap **2** : fragment (of a text, etc.)

retener {80} *vt* **1** : retain, keep **2** : withhold (funds, etc.) **3** DETENER : detain — **retención** *nf, pl* **-ciones 1** : retention **2** : deduction, withholding (of funds)

reticente *adj* : reluctant — **reticencia** *nf* : reluctance

retina *nf* : retina

retintín *nm, pl* **-tines 1** : tinkling, jingle **2 con** ~ : sarcastically

retirar *vt* **1** : remove, take away **2** : withdraw (funds, statements, etc.) — **retirarse** *vr* **1** : retreat, withdraw **2** JUBILARSE : retire — **retirada** *nf* **1** : withdrawal **2 batirse en** ~ : beat a retreat — **retirado, -da** *adj* **1** : remote, secluded **2** JUBILADO : retired — **retiro** *nm* **1** : retreat **2** JUBILACIÓN : retirement **3** *Lat* : withdrawal

reto *nm* : challenge, dare

retocar {72} *vt* : touch up

retoño *nm* : sprout, shoot

retoque *nm* **1** : retouching **2 el último** ~ : the finishing touch

retorcer {14} *vt* **1** : twist, contort **2** : wring out (clothes, etc.) — **retorcerse** *vr* **1** : get twisted up **2** : squirm, writhe (in pain) — **retorción** *nm, pl* **-jones** : cramp, spasm — **retorcimiento** *nm* : twisting, wringing out

retórica *nf* : rhetoric — **retórico, -ca** *adj* : rhetorical

retornar *v* : return — **retorno** *nm* : return

retozar {21} *vi* : frolic, romp — **retozón, -zona** *adj* : playful, frisky

retractarse *vr* **1** : withdraw, back down **2** ~ **de** : take back, retract

retraer {81} *vt* : retract — **retraerse** *vr* : withdraw — **retraído, -da** *adj* : withdrawn, shy

retrasar *vt* **1** : delay, hold up **2** APLAZAR : postpone **3** : set back (a clock) — **retrasarse** *vr* **1** : be late **2** : fall behind (in work, etc.) — **retrasado, -da** *adj* **1** : retarded **2** : in arrears (of payments) **3** : backward (of a country) **4** : slow (of a clock) — **retraso** *nm* **1** : delay **2** SUBDESARROLLO : backwardness **3** ~ **mental** : mental retardation

retratar *vt* **1** : portray **2** FOTOGRAFIAR : photograph **3** DIBUJAR : paint a portrait of — **retrato** *nm* **1** : portrayal **2** DIBUJO : portrait **3** FOTOGRAFÍA : photograph

retrete *nm* : restroom, toilet

retribuir {41} *vt* **1** : pay **2** RECOMPENSAR : reward — **retribución** *nf, pl*

-ciones 1 : payment **2** RECOMPENSA : reward

retroactivo, -va *adj* : retroactive

retroceder *vi* **1** : go back, turn back **2** CEDER : back down — **retroceso** *nm* **1** : backward movement **2** : backing down

retrógrado, -da *adj & nmf* : reactionary

retrospectiva *nf* : hindsight — **retrospectivo, -va** *adj* : retrospective

retrovisor *nm* : rearview mirror

retumbar *vi* : resound, reverberate, rumble

reumatismo *nm* : rheumatism

reunir {68} *vt* **1** : unite, join **2** TENER : have, possess **3** RECOGER : gather, collect — **reunirse** *vr* : meet, gather — **reunión** *nf, pl* **-niones 1** : meeting **2** : (social) gathering, reunion

revalidar *vt* : confirm, ratify

revancha *nf* **1** : revenge **2** : rematch (in sports)

revelar *vt* **1** : reveal, disclose **2** : develop (film) — **revelación** *nf, pl* **-ciones** : revelation — **revelado** *nm* : developing (of film) — **revelador, -dora** *adj* : revealing

reventar {55} *v* **1** : burst, blow up — **reventarse** *vr* : burst — **reventón** *nm, pl* **-tones** : blowout, flat tire

reverberar *vi* : reverberate — **reverberación** *nf, pl* **-ciones** : reverberation

reverenciar *vt* : revere — **reverencia** *nf* **1** : bow, curtsy **2** VENERACIÓN : reverence — **reverendo, -da** *adj & nmf* : reverend — **reverente** *adj* : reverent

reversa *nf Lat* : reverse (gear)

reverso *nm* **1** : back, reverse **2 el ~ de la medalla** : the complete opposite — **reversible** *adj* : reversible

revertir {76} *vi* **1** : revert **2 ~ en** : result in

revés *nm, pl* **-veses 1** : back, wrong side **2** CONTRATIEMPO : setback **3** BOFETADA : slap **4** : backhand (in sports) **5 al ~** : the other way around, upside down, inside out

revestir {54} *vt* **1** : coat, cover **2** ASUMIR : take on, assume — **revestimiento** *nm* : covering, coating

revisar *vt* **1** : examine, inspect **2** : check over, overhaul (machinery, etc.) **3** MODIFICAR : revise — **revisión** *nf, pl* **-siones 1** : revision **2** INSPECCIÓN : inspection, check — **revisor, -sora** *n* : inspector

revistar *vt* : review, inspect (troops, etc.) — **revista** *nf* **1** : magazine, jour-

nal **2** : revue (in theater) **3 pasar ~** : review, inspect

revivir *vi* : revive, come alive again — *vt* : relive

revocar {72} *vt* : revoke

revolcar {82} *vt* : knock over, knock down — **revolcarse** *vr* : roll around

revolotear *vi* : flutter, flit — **revoloteo** *nm* : fluttering, flitting

revoltijo *nm* : mess, jumble

revoltoso, -sa *adj* : rebellious

revolución *nf, pl* **-ciones** : revolution — **revolucionar** *vt* : revolutionize — **revolucionario, -ria** *adj & n* : revolutionary

revolver {89} *vt* **1** : mix, stir **2** : upset (one's stomach) **3** DESORGANIZAR : mess up — **revolverse** *vr* **1** : toss and turn **2** VOLVERSE : turn around

revólver *nm* : revolver

revuelo *nm* : commotion

revuelta *nf* : uprising, revolt — **revuelto, -ta** *adj* **1** : choppy, rough **2** DESORDENADO : messed up **3 huevos revueltos** : scrambled eggs

rey *nm* : king

reyerta *nf* : brawl, fight

rezagarse {52} *vr* : fall behind, lag

rezar {21} *vi* **1** : pray **2** DECIR : say — *vt* : say, recite — **rezo** *nm* : prayer

rezongar {52} *vi* : gripe, grumble

rezumar *v* : ooze

ría *nf* : estuary

riachuelo *nm* : brook, stream

riada *nf* : flood

ribera *nf* : bank, shore

ribetear *vt* : border, trim — **ribete** *nm* **1** : border, trim **2** : embellishment

rico, -ca *adj* **1** : rich, wealthy **2** ABUNDANTE : abundant **3** SABROSO : rich, tasty — **~** *n* : rich person

ridiculizar {21} *vt* : ridicule — **ridículo, -la** *adj* : ridiculous — **ridículo** *nm* **1 hacer el ~** : make a fool of oneself **2 poner en ~** : ridicule

riego *nm* : irrigation

riel *nm* : rail

rienda *nf* **1** : rein **2 dar ~ suelta a** : give free rein to

riesgo *nm* : risk

rifa *nf* : raffle — **rifar** *vt* : raffle (off) — **rifarse** *vr fam* : fight over

rifle *nm* : rifle

rígido, -da *adj* **1** : rigid, stiff **2** SEVERO : harsh, strict — **rigidez** *nf, pl* **-deces 1** : rigidity, stiffness **2** SEVERIDAD : harshness, strictness

rigor *nm* **1** : rigor, harshness **2** EXACTITUD : precision **3 de ~** : essential, obligatory — **riguroso, -sa** *adj* : rigorous

rima *nf* 1 : rhyme 2 ~s *nfpl* : verse, poetry — **rimar** *vi* : rhyme

rimbombante *adj* : showy, pompous

rímel *nm* : mascara

rincón *nm, pl* **-cones** : corner, nook

rinoceronte *nm* : rhinoceros

riña *nf* 1 : fight, brawl 2 DISPUTA : dispute, quarrel

riñón *nm, pl* **-ñones** : kidney

río *nm* 1 : river 2 TORRENTE : torrent, stream

riqueza *nf* 1 : wealth 2 ABUNDANCIA : richness 3 ~s **naturales** : natural resources

risa *nf* 1 : laughter, laugh 2 **dar** ~ **a algn** : make s.o. laugh 3 **morirse de la** ~ *fam* : die laughing

risco *nm* : crag, cliff

risible *adj* : laughable

ristra *nf* : string, series

risueño, -ña *adj* : cheerful, smiling

ritmo *nm* 1 : rhythm 2 VELOCIDAD : pace, speed — **rítmico, -ca** *adj* : rhythmical

rito *nm* : rite, ritual — **ritual** *adj & nm* : ritual

rival *adj & nmf* : rival — **rivalidad** *nf* : rivalry, competition — **rivalizar** {21} *vi* ~ **con** : rival, compete with

rizar {21} *vt* 1 : curl 2 : ripple (a surface) — **rizarse** *vr* : curl — **rizado, -da** *adj* 1 : curly 2 : choppy (of water) — **rizo** *nm* 1 : curl 2 : ripple (in water) 3 : loop (in aviation)

róbalo *nm* : bass (fish)

robar *vt* 1 : steal 2 : burglarize (a house, etc.) 3 SECUESTRAR : kidnap — **robo** *nm* : robbery, theft

roble *nm* : oak

robot *nm, pl* **-bots** : robot — **robótica** *nf* : robotics

robustecer {53} *vt* : make stronger, strengthen — **robusto, -ta** *adj* : robust, sturdy

roca *nf* : rock, boulder

roce *nm* 1 : rubbing, chafing 2 RASGUÑO : graze, scratch 3 **tener un** ~ **con** : have a brush with

rociar {85} *vt* : spray, sprinkle — **rocío** *nm* : dew

rocoso, -sa *adj* : rocky

rodaja *nf* : slice

rodar {19} *vi* 1 : roll, roll down, roll along 2 GIRAR : turn, go around 3 : travel (of a vehicle) 4 : film (of movies, etc.) — *vt* 1 : film, shoot 2 : break in (a vehicle) — **rodaje** *nm* 1 : filming, shooting 2 : breaking in (of a vehicle)

rodear *vt* 1 : surround, encircle 2 *Lat* : round up (cattle) — **rodearse** *vr* ~ **de** : surround oneself with — **rodeo** *nm* 1 : rodeo, roundup 2 DESVÍO : detour 3 **andar con** ~s : beat around the bush

rodilla *nf* : knee

rodillo *nm* 1 : roller 2 : rolling pin (for pastry)

roer {69} *vt* 1 : gnaw 2 ATORMENTAR : eat away at, torment — **roedor** *nm* : rodent

rogar {16} *vt* : beg, request — *vi* : pray

rojo, -ja *adj* 1 : red 2 **ponerse** ~ : blush — **rojo** *nm* : red — **rojez** *nf* : redness — **rojizo, -za** *adj* : reddish

rollizo, -za *adj* : plump, chubby

rollo *nm* 1 : roll, coil 2 *fam* : boring speech, lecture

romance *nm* 1 : romance 2 : Romance (language)

romano, -na *adj & n* : Roman

romántico, -ca *adj* : romantic — **romanticismo** *nm* : romanticism

romería *nf* : pilgrimage, procession

romero *nm* : rosemary

romo, -ma *adj* : blunt, dull

rompecabezas *nms & pl* : puzzle

romper {70} *vt* 1 : break 2 RASGAR : rip, tear 3 : break off (relations), break (a contract) — *vi* 1 : break (of the day, waves, etc.) 2 ~ **a** : begin to, burst out with 3 ~ **con** : break off with — **romperse** *vr* : break

ron *nm* : rum

roncar {72} *vi* : snore — **ronco, -ca** *adj* : hoarse

ronda *nf* 1 : rounds *pl*, patrol 2 : round (of drinks, etc.) — **rondar** *vt* 1 : patrol 2 : hang around (a place) 3 : be approximately (an age, a number, etc.) — *vi* 1 : be on patrol 2 MERODEAR : prowl about

ronquera *nf* : hoarseness

ronquido *nm* : snore

ronronear *vi* : purr — **ronroneo** *nm* : purr, purring

ronzar {21} *vt* : munch, crunch

roña *nf* 1 : mange 2 SUCIEDAD : dirt, filth — **roñoso, -sa** *adj* 1 : mangy 2 SUCIO : dirty 3 *fam* : stingy

ropa *nf* 1 : clothes *pl*, clothing 2 ~ **interior** : underwear — **ropaje** *nm* : robes *pl*, regalia — **ropero** *nm* : wardrobe, closet

rosa *nf* : rose (flower) — ~ *adj* : rose-colored — ~ *nm* : rose (color) — **rosado, -da** *adj* 1 : pink 2 **vino rosado** : rosé — **rosado** *nm* : pink (color) — **rosal** *nm* : rosebush

rosario *nm* : rosary
rosbif *nm* : roast beef
rosca *nf* 1 : thread (of a screw) 2 ESPIRAL : ring, coil
roseta *nf* : rosette
rosquilla *nf* : doughnut
rostro *nm* : face
rotación *nf*, *pl* **-ciones** : rotation — **rotativo, -va** *adj* : rotary, revolving
roto, -ta *adj* : broken, torn
rotonda *nf* : traffic circle, rotary
rótula *nf* : kneecap
rótulo *nm* 1 : heading, title 2 ETIQUETA : label, sign
rotundo, -da *adj* : categorical, absolute
rotura *nf* : break, tear, fracture
rozar {21} *vt* 1 : graze, touch lightly 2 APROXIMARSE DE : touch on, border on — *vi* : scrape, rub — **rozarse** *vr* 1 : rub, chafe 2 ~ **con** *fam* : rub elbows with — **rozadura** *nf* : scratch
rubí *nm*, *pl* **rubíes** : ruby
rubicundo, -da *adj* : ruddy
rubio, -bia *adj* & *n* : blond
rubor *nm* : flush, blush — **ruborizarse** {21} *vr* : blush
rúbrica *nf* 1 : flourish (in writing) 2 TÍTULO : title, heading
rudeza *nf* : roughness, coarseness
rudimentos *nmpl* : rudiments, basics — **rudimentario, -ria** *adj* : rudimentary
rudo, -da *adj* 1 : rough, harsh 2 GROSERO : coarse, unpolished
rueda *nf* 1 : wheel 2 CORRO : circle, ring 3 RODAJA : (round) slice 4 **ir sobre** ~**s** : go smoothly — **ruedo** *nm* : bullring

ruego *nm* : request
rugir {35} *vi* : roar — **rugido** *nm* : roar
rugoso, -sa *adj* 1 : rough 2 ARRUGADO : wrinkled
ruibarbo *nm* : rhubarb
ruido *nm* : noise — **ruidoso, -sa** *adj* : loud, noisy
ruina *nf* 1 : ruin, destruction 2 COLAPSO : collapse 3 ~**s** *nfpl* : ruins, remains — **ruinoso, -sa** *adj* : run-down, dilapidated
ruiseñor *nm* : nightingale
ruleta *nf* : roulette
rulo *nm* : curler, roller
rumano, -na *adj* : Romanian, Rumanian
rumba *nf* : rumba
rumbo *nm* 1 : direction, course 2 ESPLENDIDEZ : lavishness 3 **con** ~ **a** : bound for, heading for 4 **perder el** ~ : go off course
rumiar *vt* : mull over — *vi* : chew the cud — **rumiante** *adj* & *nm* : ruminant
rumor *nm* 1 : rumor 2 MURMULLO : murmur — **rumorearse** *or* **rumorarse** *vr* : be rumored — **rumoroso, -sa** *adj* : murmuring, babbling
ruptura *nf* 1 : break, rupture 2 : breach (of a contract) 3 : breaking off (of relations)
rural *adj* : rural
ruso, -sa *adj* : Russian — **ruso** *nm* : Russian (language)
rústico, -ca *adj* 1 : rural, rustic 2 **en rústica** : in paperback
ruta *nf* : route
rutina *nf* : routine — **rutinario, -ria** *adj* : routine

S

s *nf* : s, 20th letter of the Spanish alphabet
sábado *nm* : Saturday
sábana *nf* : sheet
sabandija *nf* : bug
saber {71} *vt* 1 : know 2 SER CAPAZ DE : know how to, be able to 3 ENTERARSE : learn, find out 4 **a** ~ : namely — *vi* 1 : taste 2 ~ **de** : know about — ~ *nm* : knowledge — **sabelotodo** *nmf fam* : know-it-all — **sabido, -da** *adj* : well-known — **sabiduría** *nf* 1 : wisdom 2 CONOCIMIENTO : learning, knowledge — **sabiendas: a** ~ *adv phr* : knowingly — **sabio, -bia** *adj* 1 : learned 2 PRUDENTE : wise, sensible

sabor *nm* : flavor, taste — **saborear** *vt* : savor
sabotaje *nm* : sabotage — **saboteador, -dora** *n* : saboteur — **sabotear** *vt* : sabotage
sabroso, -sa *adj* : delicious, tasty
sabueso *nm* 1 : bloodhound 2 *fam* : sleuth
sacacorchos *nms* & *pl* : corkscrew
sacapuntas *nms* & *pl* : pencil sharpener
sacar {72} *vt* 1 : take out 2 OBTENER : get, obtain 3 EXTRAER : extract, withdraw 4 : bring out (a book, a product, etc.) 5 : take (photos), make (copies) 6 QUITAR : remove 7 ~ **adelante** : bring up (children), carry out (a project,

etc.) 8 ~ **la lengua** : stick out one's
tongue — *vi* : serve (in sports)
sacarina *nf* : saccharin
sacerdote, -tisa *n* : priest *m*, priestess *f*
— **sacerdocio** *nm* : priesthood —
sacerdotal *adj* : priestly
saclar *vt* : satisfy
saco *nm* 1 : bag, sack 2 : sac (in anatomy) 3 *Lat* : jacket
sacramento *nm* : sacrament — **sacramental** *adj* : sacramental
sacrificar {72} *vt* : sacrifice — **sacrifi-
carse** *vr* : sacrifice oneself — **sacrificio** *nm* : sacrifice
sacrilegio *nm* : sacrilege — **sacrílego,
-ga** *adj* : sacrilegious
sacro, -cra *adj* : sacred — **sacrosanto,
-ta** *adj* : sacrosanct
sacudir *vt* 1 : shake GOLPEAR : beat 3
CONMOVER : shake up, shock — **sacu-
dirse** *vr* : shake off — **sacudida** *nf* 1
: shaking 2 : jolt (of a train, etc.),
tremor (of an earthquake) 3 : (emotional) shock
sádico, -ca *adj* : sadistic — ~ *n*
: sadist — **sadismo** *nm* : sadism
saeta *nf* : arrow
safari *nm* : safari
sagaz *adj, pl* **-gaces** : shrewd, saga-
cious — **sagacidad** *nf* : shrewdness
sagrado, -da *adj* : sacred, holy
sal *nf* : salt
sala *nf* 1 : room, hall 2 : living room (of a
house) 3 ~ **de espera** : waiting room
salar *vt* : salt — **salado, -da** *adj* 1
: salty 2 GRACIOSO : witty 3 **agua salada** : salt water
salario *nm* : salary, wage
salchicha *nf* : sausage — **salchichón**
nf, pl **-chones** : salami-like cold cut
saldar *vt* 1 : settle, pay off 2 VENDER
: sell off — **saldo** *nm* 1 : balance (of
an account) 2 ~s *nmpl* : remainders,
sale items
salero *nm* : saltshaker
salir {73} *vi* 1 : go out, come out 2 PAR-
TIR : leave 3 APARECER : appear 4 RE-
SULTAR : turn out 5 : rise (of the sun) 6
~ **adelante** : get by 7 ~ **con** : go out
with, date 8 ~ **de** : come from —
salirse *vr* 1 : leave ESCAPARSE : leak
out, escape 3 SOLTARSE : come off 4 ~
con la suya : get one's own way —
salida *nf* 1 : exit 2 : (action of) leaving,
departure 3 SOLUCIÓN : way out 4 : leak
(of gas, liquid, etc.) 5 OCURRENCIA
: witty remark 6 ~ **de emergencia**
: emergency exit 7 ~ **del sol** : sunrise
— **saliente** *adj* 1 : departing, outgoing
2 DESTACADO : outstanding

saliva *nf* : saliva
salmo *nm* : psalm
salmón *nm, pl* **-mones** : salmon
salmuera *nf* : brine
salón *nm, pl* **-lones** 1 : lounge, sitting
room 2 ~ **de belleza** : beauty salon 3
~ **de clase** : classroom
salpicar {72} *vt* 1 : splash, spatter 2 ~
de : pepper with — **salpicadera** *nf*
Lat : fender — **salpicadura** *nf* : splash
salsa *nf* 1 : sauce 2 : (meat) gravy 3
: salsa (music)
saltamontes *nms & pl* : grasshopper
saltar *vi* 1 : jump, leap 2 REBOTAR
: bounce 3 : come off (of a button, etc.)
4 ROMPERSE : shatter 5 ESTALLAR : explode, blow up — *vt* 1 : jump (over) 2
OMITIR : skip, miss — **saltarse** *vr* 1
: come off 2 OMITIR : skip, miss
saltear *vt* : sauté
saltimbanqui *nmf* : acrobat
salto *nm* 1 : jump, leap 2 : dive (into
water) 3 ~ **de agua** : waterfall —
saltón, -tona *adj, mpl* **-tones** : bulging, protruding
salud *nf* 1 : health 2 ¡**salud!** : here's to
your health! 3 ¡**salud!** *Lat* : bless you!
(when someone sneezes) — **saludable** *adj* : healthy
saludar *vt* 1 : greet, say hello to 2
: salute (in the military) — **saludo** *nm*
1 : greeting 2 : (military) salute 3 ~s
: best wishes, regards
salva *nf* ~ **de aplausos** : round of applause
salvación *nf, pl* **-ciones** : salvation
salvado *nm* : bran
salvador, -dora *n* : savior, rescuer
salvadoreño, -ña *adj* : (El) Salvadoran
salvaguardar *vt* : safeguard
salvaje *adj* 1 : wild 2 PRIMITIVO : savage, primitive — ~ *nmf* : savage
salvar *vt* 1 : save, rescue 2 RECORRER
: cover, travel 3 SUPERAR : overcome
— **salvarse** *vr* : save oneself — **sal-
vavidas** *nms & pl* 1 : life preserver —
bote ~ : lifeboat
salvia *nf* : sage (plant)
salvo, -va *adj* : safe — **salvo** *prep* 1
: except (for), save 2 ~ **que** : unless
samba *nf* : samba
San → **santo**
sanar *vt* : heal, cure — *vi* : recover —
sanatorio *nm* 1 : sanatorium 2 HOSPI-
TAL : clinic, hospital
sanción *nf, pl* **-ciones** : sanction —
sancionar *vt* : sanction
sandalia *nf* : sandal
sándalo *nm* : sandalwood
sandía *nf* : watermelon

sandwich ['sandwitʃ, 'saŋgwitʃ] *nm, pl* **-wiches** [-dwitʃes, -gwi-] : sandwich
saneamiento *nm* : sanitation
sangrar *vt* **1** : bleed **2** : indent (a paragraph) — *vi* : bleed — **sangrante** *adj* : bleeding — **sangre** *nf* **1** : blood **2 a ~ fría** : in cold blood — **sangriento, -ta** *adj* : bloody
sanguijuela *nf* : leech
sanguinario, -ria *adj* : bloodthirsty — **sanguíneo, -nea** *adj* : blood
sano, -na *adj* **1** : healthy **2** : (morally) wholesome **3** ENTERO : intact **4 sano y salvo** : safe and sound — **sanidad** *nf* **1** : health **2** : public health, sanitation — **sanitario, -ria** *adj* : sanitary, health — **sanitario** *nm Lat* : toilet
santiamén *nm* **en un ~** : in no time at all
santo, -ta *adj* **1** : holy **2 Santo, Santa** (**San** *before masculine names except those beginning with D or T*) : Saint — **~** *n* : saint — **santo** *nm* **1** : saint's day **2** *Lat* : birthday — **santidad** *nf* : holiness, sanctity — **santiguarse** {10} *vr* : cross oneself — **santuario** *nm* : sanctuary
saña *nf* **1** : fury **2** BRUTALIDAD : viciousness
sapo *nm* : toad
saque *nm* : serve (in tennis, etc.), throw-in (in soccer)
saquear *vt* : sack, loot — **saqueador, -dora** *n* : looter — **saqueo** *nm* : sacking, looting
sarampión *nm* : measles *pl*
sarape *nm Lat* : serape
sarcasmo *nm* : sarcasm — **sarcástico, -ca** *adj* : sarcastic
sardina *nf* : sardine
sardónico, -ca *adj* : sardonic
sargento *nmf* : sergeant
sarpullido *nm* : rash
sartén *nmf, pl* **-tenes** : frying pan
sastre, -tra *n* : tailor — **sastrería** *nf* **1** : tailoring **2** : tailor's shop
Satanás *nm* : Satan — **satánico, -ca** *adj* : satanic
satélite *nm* : satellite
sátira *nf* : satire — **satírico, -ca** *adj* : satirical
satisfacer {74} *vt* **1** : satisfy **2** CUMPLIR : fulfill, meet **3** PAGAR : pay — **satisfacerse** *vr* **1** : be satisfied **2** VENGARSE : take revenge — **satisfacción** *nf, pl* **-ciones** : satisfaction — **satisfactorio, -ria** *adj* : satisfactory — **satisfecho, -cha** *adj* : satisfied
saturar *vt* : saturate — **saturación** *nf, pl* **-ciones** : saturation

Saturno *nm* : Saturn
sauce *nm* : willow
sauna *nmf* : sauna
savia *nf* : sap
saxofón *nm, pl* **-fones** : saxophone
sazón *nf, pl* **-zones** **1** : seasoning **2** MADUREZ : ripeness **3 a la ~** : at that time, then **4 en ~** : ripe, in season — **sazonar** *vt* : season
se *pron* **1** (*reflexive*) : himself, herself, itself, oneself, yourself, yourselves, themselves **2** (*indirect object*) : (to) him, (to) her, (to) you, (to) them **3** : each other, one another **4 ~ dice que** : it is said that **5 ~ habla inglés** : English spoken
sebo *nm* **1** : fat **2** : tallow (for candles, etc.) **3** : suet (for cooking)
secar {72} *v* : dry — **secarse** *vr* : dry (up) — **secador** *nm* : hair dryer — **secadora** *nf* : (clothes) dryer
sección *nf, pl* **-ciones** : section
seco, -ca *adj* **1** : dry **2** : dried (of fruits, etc.) **3** TAJANTE : sharp, brusque **4** *fam* : thin, skinny **5 a secas** : simply, just **6 en seco** : suddenly
secretar *vt* : secrete — **secreción** *nf, pl* **-ciones** : secretion
secretario, -ria *n* : secretary — **secretaría** *nf* : secretariat
secreto, -ta *adj* : secret — **secreto** *nm* **1** : secret **2 en ~** : in confidence
secta *nf* : sect
sector *nm* : sector
secuaz *nmf, pl* **-cuaces** : follower, henchman
secuela *nf* : consequence
secuencia *nf* : sequence
secuestrar *vt* **1** : kidnap **2** : hijack (an airplane, etc.) **3** EMBARGAR : confiscate, seize — **secuestrador, -dora** *n* **1** : kidnapper **2** : hijacker (of an airplane, etc.) — **secuestro** *nm* **1** : kidnapping **2** : hijacking (of an airplane, etc.) **3** : seizure (of goods)
secular *adj* : secular
secundar *vt* : support, second — **secundario, -ria** *adj* : secondary
sed *nf* **1** : thirst **2 tener ~** : be thirsty
seda *nf* : silk
sedal *nm* : fishing line
sedar *vt* : sedate — **sedante** *adj & nm* : sedative
sede *nf* **1** : seat, headquarters **2 Santa Sede** : Holy See
sedentario, -ria *adj* : sedentary
sedición *nf, pl* **-ciones** : sedition — **sedicioso, -sa** *adj* : seditious
sediento, -ta *adj* : thirsty
sedimento *nm* : sediment

sedoso, -sa *adj* : silky, silken
seducir {61} *vt* **1** : seduce **2** ATRAER : captivate, charm — **seducción** *nf, pl* **-clones** : seduction — **seductor, -tora** *adj* **1** : seductive **2** ENCANTADOR : charming — ~ *n* : seducer
segar {49} *vt* : reap — **segador, -dora** *n* : reaper, harvester
seglar *adj* : lay, secular — ~ *nm* : layperson, layman *m*, laywoman *f*
segmento *nm* : segment
segregar {52} *vt* : segregate — **segregación** *nf, pl* **-clones** : segregation
seguir {75} *vt* : follow — *vi* : go on, continue — **seguida: en ~** *adv phr* : right away — **seguido** *adv* **1** : straight (ahead) **2** *Lat* : often — **seguido, -da** *adj* **1** : continuous **2** CONSECUTIVO : consecutive — **seguidor, -dora** *n* : follower
según *prep* : according to — ~ *adv* : it depends — ~ *conj* : as, just as
segundo, -da *adj* : second — ~ *n* : second (one) — **segundo** *nm* : second (unit of time)
seguro, -ra *adj* **1** : safe **2** FIRME : secure **3** CIERTO : sure, certain **4** FIABLE : reliable — **seguramente** *adv* : for sure, surely — **seguridad** *nf* **1** : safety **2** GARANTÍA : security **3** CERTEZA : certainty **4** CONFIANZA : confidence — **seguro** *adv* : certainly — ~ *nm* **1** : insurance **2** : safety (device)
seis *adj & nm* : six — **seiscientos, -tas** *adj* : six hundred — **seiscientos** *nms & pl* : six hundred
seísmo *nm* : earthquake
selección *nf, pl* **-clones** : selection — **seleccionar** *vt* : select, choose — **selectivo, -va** *adj* : selective — **selecto, -ta** *adj* : choice, select
sellar *vt* **1** : seal **2** TIMBRAR : stamp — **sello** *nm* **1** : seal **2** TIMBRE : stamp **3** *or* ~ **distintivo** : hallmark
selva *nf* **1** : jungle **2** BOSQUE : forest
semáforo *nm* : traffic light
semana *nf* : week — **semanal** *adj* : weekly — **semanario** *nm* : weekly
semántica *nf* : semantics — **semántico, -ca** *adj* : semantic
semblante *nm* **1** : countenance, face **2** APARIENCIA : look
sembrar {55} *vt* **1** : sow **2** ~ **de** : strew with
semejar *vi* : resemble — **semejarse** *vr* : look alike — **semejante** *adj* **1** : similar **2** TAL : such — ~ *nm* : fellowman — **semejanza** *nf* : similarity
semen *nm* : semen — **semental** *nm* **1** : stud **2 caballo** ~ : stallion

semestre *nm* : semester
semiconductor *nm* : semiconductor
semifinal *nf* : semifinal
semilla *nf* : seed — **semillero** *nm* **1** : nursery (for plants) **2** HERVIDERO : hotbed, breeding ground
seminario *nm* **1** : seminary **2** CURSO : seminar, course
sémola *nf* : semolina
senado *nm* : senate — **senador, -dora** *n* : senator
sencillo, -lla *adj* **1** : simple **2** ÚNICO : single — **sencillez** *nf* : simplicity
senda *nf or* **sendero** *nm* : path, way
sendos, -das *adj pl* : each, both
senil *adj* : senile
seno *nm* **1** : breast, bosom **2** : sinus (in anatomy) **3** ~ **materno** : womb
sensación *nf, pl* **-clones** : feeling, sensation — **sensacional** *adj* : sensational — **sensacionalista** *adj* : sensationalistic, lurid
sensato, -ta *adj* : sensible — **sensatez** *nf* : good sense
sensible *adj* **1** : sensitive **2** APRECIABLE : considerable, significant — **sensibilidad** *nf* : sensitivity — **sensitivo, -va** *or* **sensorial** *adj* : sense, sensory
sensual *adj* : sensual, sensuous — **sensualidad** *nf* : sensuality
sentar {55} *vt* **1** : seat, sit **2** ESTABLECER : establish, set — *vi* **1** : suit **2** ~ **bien a** : agree with (of food or drink) — **sentarse** *vr* : sit (down) — **sentado, -da** *adj* **1** : sitting, seated **2 dar por sentado** : take for granted
sentencia *nf* **1** FALLO : sentence, judgment **2** MÁXIMA : saying — **sentenciar** *vt* : sentence
sentido, -da *adj* **1** : heartfelt, sincere **2** SENSIBLE : touchy, sensitive — **sentido** *nm* **1** : sense **2** CONOCIMIENTO : consciousness **3** DIRECCIÓN : direction **4 doble** ~ : double entendre **5** ~ **común** : common sense **6** ~ **del humor** : sense of humor **7** ~ **único** : one-way
sentimiento *nm* **1** : feeling, emotion **2** PESAR : regret — **sentimental** *adj* : sentimental — **sentimentalismo** *nm* : sentimentality
sentir {76} *vt* **1** : feel **2** OÍR : hear **3** LAMENTAR : be sorry for **4 lo siento** : I'm sorry — *vi* : feel — **sentirse** *vr* : feel
seña *nf* **1** : sign **2** ~ **s** *nfpl* DIRECCIÓN : address **3** ~ **s particulares** : distinguishing marks
señal *nf* **1** : signal **2** AVISO, INDICIO : sign **3** DEPÓSITO : deposit **4 dar ~es**

de : show signs of **5 en ~ de** : as a token of — **señalado, -da** *adj* : notable — **señalar** *vt* **1** INDICAR : indicate, point out **2** MARCAR : mark **3** FIJAR : fix, set — **señalarse** *vr* : distinguish oneself

señor, -ñora *n* **1** : gentleman *m*, man *m*, lady *f*, woman *f* **2** : Sir *m*, Madam *f* **3** : Mr. *m*, Mrs. *f* **4 señora** : wife *f* **5 el Señor** : the Lord — **señorial** *adj* : stately — **señorita** *nf* **1** : young lady, young woman **2** : Miss

señuelo *nm* **1** : decoy **2** TRAMPA : bait, lure

separar *vt* **1** : separate **2** QUITAR : detach, remove **3** APARTAR : move away **4** DESTITUIR : dismiss — **separarse** *vr* **1** APARTARSE : separate **2** : part company — **separación** *nf, pl* **-ciones** : separation — **separado, -da** *adj* **1** : separate **2** : separated (of persons) **3 por separado** : separately

septentrional *adj* : northern

séptico, -ca *adj* : septic

septiembre *nm* : September

séptimo, -ma *adj* : seventh — **~** *n* : seventh

sepulcro *nm* : tomb, sepulchre — **sepultar** *vt* : bury — **sepultura** *nf* **1** : burial **2** TUMBA : grave

sequedad *nf* : dryness — **sequía** *nf* : drought

séquito *nm* : retinue, entourage

ser {77} *vi* **1** : be **2 a no ~ que** : unless **3 ¿cuánto es?** : how much is it? **4 es más** : what's more **5 ~ de** : belong to **6 ~ de** : come from **7 son las diez** : it's ten o'clock — **~** *nm* **1** ENTE : being **2 ~ humano** : human being

serbio, -bia *adj* : Serb, Serbian

serenar *vt* : calm — **serenarse** *vr* : calm down — **serenata** *nf* : serenade — **serenidad** *nf* : serenity — **sereno, -na** *adj* **1** : serene, calm **2** : fair, clear (of weather) — **sereno** *nm* : night watchman

serie *nf* **1** : series **2 fabricación en ~** : mass production **3 fuera de ~** : extraordinary — **serial** *nm* : serial

serio, -ria *adj* **1** : serious **2** RESPONSABLE : reliable **3 en serio** : seriously — **seriedad** *nf* : seriousness

sermón *nm, pl* **-mones** : sermon — **sermonear** *vt* : lecture, reprimand

serpentear *vi* : twist, wind — **serpiente** *nf* **1** : serpent, snake **2 ~ de cascabel** : rattlesnake

serrado, -da *adj* : serrated

serrano, -na *adj* **1** : mountain **2 jamón serrano** : cured ham

serrar {55} *vt* : saw — **serrín** *nm, pl* **-rrines** : sawdust — **serrucho** *nm* : saw, handsaw

servicio *nm* **1** : service **2 ~s** *nmpl* : restroom — **servicial** *adj* : obliging, helpful — **servidor, -dora** *n* **1** : servant **2 su seguro servidor** : yours truly — **servidumbre** *nf* **1** : servitude **2** CRIADOS : help, servants *pl* — **servil** *adj* : servile

servilleta *nf* : napkin

servir {54} *vt* : serve — *vi* **1** : work, function **2** VALER : be of use — **servirse** *vr* **1** : help oneself **2 sírvase sentarse** : please have a seat

sesenta *adj & nm* : sixty

sesgo *nm* : bias, slant

sesión *nf, pl* **-siones 1** : session **2** : showing (of a film), performance (of a play)

seso *nm* : brain — **sesudo, -da** *adj* **1** : sensible **2** *fam* : brainy

seta *nf* : mushroom

setecientos, -tas *adj* : seven hundred — **setecientos** *nms & pl* : seven hundred

setenta *adj & nm* : seventy

setiembre *nm* → **septiembre**

seto *nm* **1** : fence **2 ~ vivo** : hedge

seudónimo *nm* : pseudonym

severo, -ra *adj* **1** : harsh, severe **2** : strict (of a teacher, etc.) — **severidad** *nf* : severity

sexagésimo, -ma *adj & n* : sixtieth

sexo *nm* : sex — **sexismo** *nm* : sexism — **sexista** *adj & nmf* : sexist

sexteto *nm* : sextet

sexto, -ta *adj & n* : sixth

sexual *adj* : sexual — **sexualidad** *nf* : sexuality

sexy *adj, pl* **sexy** *or* **sexys** : sexy

si *conj* **1** : if **2** (*in indirect questions*) : whether **3 ~ bien** : although **4 ~ no** : otherwise, or else

sí¹ *adv* **1** : yes **2 creo que ~** : I think so **3 porque ~** *fam* : (just) because — **~** *nm* : consent

sí² *pron* **1 de por ~** *or* **en ~** : by itself, in itself, per se **2 fuera de ~** : beside oneself **3 para ~** (**mismo**) : to himself, to herself, for himself, for herself **4 entre ~** : among themselves

sico- → **psico-**

SIDA *or* **sida** *nm* : AIDS

siderurgia *nf* : iron and steel industry

sidra *nf* : (hard) cider

siega *nf* **1** : harvesting **2** : harvest (time)

siembra *nf* **1** : sowing **2** : sowing season

siempre *adv* 1 : always 2 *Lat* : still 3 **para ~** : forever, for good 4 **~ que** : whenever, every time 5 **~ que** *or* **~ y cuando** : provided that

sien *nf* : temple

sierra *nf* 1 : saw 2 CORDILLERA : mountain range 3 **la ~** : the mountains *pl*

siervo, -va *n* : slave

siesta *nf* : nap, siesta

siete *adj & nm* : seven

sífilis *nf* : syphilis

sifón *nm, pl* **-fones** : siphon

sigilo *nm* : secrecy

sigla *nf* : acronym, abbreviation

siglo *nm* 1 : century 2 **hace ~s** : for ages

significar {72} *vt* 1 : mean, signify 2 EXPRESAR : express — **significación** *nf, pl* **-ciones** 1 : significance, importance 2 : meaning (of a word, etc.) — **significado, -da** *adj* : well-known — **significado** *nm* : meaning — **significativo, -va** *adj* : significant

signo *nm* 1 : sign 2 **~ de admiración** : exclamation point 3 **~ de interrogación** : question mark

siguiente *adj* : next, following

sílaba *nf* : syllable

silbar *v* 1 : whistle 2 ABUCHEAR : hiss, boo — **silbato** *nm* : whistle — **silbido** *nm* 1 : whistle, whistling 2 ABUCHEO : hiss, booing

silenciar *vt* : silence — **silenciador** *nm* : muffler — **silencio** *nm* : silence — **silencioso, -sa** *adj* : silent, quiet

silicio *nm* : silicon

silla *nf* 1 : chair 2 *or* **~ de montar** : saddle 3 **~ de ruedas** : wheelchair — **sillón** *nm, pl* **-llones** : armchair, easy chair

silo *nm* : silo

silueta *nf* 1 : silhouette 2 CONTORNO : outline, shape

silvestre *adj* : wild

silvicultura *nf* : forestry

símbolo *nm* : symbol — **simbólico, -ca** *adj* : symbolic — **simbolismo** *nm* : symbolism — **simbolizar** {21} *vt* : symbolize

simetría *nf* : symmetry — **simétrico, -ca** *adj* : symmetrical, symmetric

simiente *nf* : seed

símil *nm* 1 : simile 2 COMPARACIÓN : comparison — **similar** *adj* : similar, alike

simio *nm* : ape

simpatía *nf* 1 : liking, affection 2 AMABILIDAD : friendliness — **simpático, -ca** *adj* 1 : nice, likeable 2 AMABLE : pleasant, kind — **simpatizante** *nmf*

: sympathizer — **simpatizar** {21} *vi* 1 : get along, hit it off 2 **~ con** : sympathize with

simple *adj* 1 SENCILLO : simple 2 MERO : pure, sheer 3 TONTO : simpleminded — **~** *n* : fool, simpleton — **simpleza** *nf* 1 : simpleness 2 TONTERÍA : silly thing — **simplicidad** *nf* : simplicity — **simplificar** {72} *vt* : simplify

simposio *or* **simposium** *nm* : symposium

simular *vt* 1 : simulate 2 FINGIR : feign — **simulacro** *nm* : simulation, drill

simultáneo, -nea *adj* : simultaneous

sin *prep* 1 : without 2 **~ que** : without

sinagoga *nf* : synagogue

sincero, -ra *adj* : sincere — **sinceramente** *adv* : sincerely — **sinceridad** *nf* : sincerity

síncopa *nf* : syncopation

sincronizar {21} *vt* : synchronize

sindicato *nm* : (labor) union — **sindical** *adj* : union, labor

síndrome *nm* : syndrome

sinfín *nm* 1 : endless number 2 **un ~ de** : no end of

sinfonía *nf* : symphony — **sinfónico, -ca** *adj* : symphonic

singular *adj* 1 : exceptional, outstanding 2 PECULIAR : peculiar 3 : singular (in grammar) — **~** *nm* : singular — **singularizar** {21} *vt* : single out — **singularizarse** *vr* : stand out

siniestro, -tra *adj* 1 : sinister 2 IZQUIERDO : left — **siniestro** *nm* : disaster

sinnúmero *nm* → **sinfín**

sino *conj* 1 : but, rather 2 EXCEPTO : except, save

sinónimo, -ma *adj* : synonymous — **sinónimo** *nm* : synonym

sinopsis *nfs & pl* : synopsis

sinrazón *nf, pl* **-zones** : wrong

sintaxis *nfs & pl* : syntax

síntesis *nfs & pl* : synthesis — **sintético, -ca** *adj* : synthetic — **sintetizar** {21} *vt* 1 : synthesize 2 RESUMIR : summarize

síntoma *nm* : symptom — **sintomático, -ca** *adj* : symptomatic

sintonía *nf* 1 : tuning in (of a radio) 2 **en ~ con** : in tune with — **sintonizar** {21} *vt* : tune (in) to

sinuoso, -sa *adj* : winding

sinvergüenza *nmf* : scoundrel

sionismo *nm* : Zionism

siquiera *adv* 1 : at least 2 **ni ~** : not even — **~** *conj* : even if

sirena *nf* 1 : mermaid 2 : siren (of an ambulance, etc.)

sirio, -ria *adj* : Syrian

sirviente, -ta n : servant, maid f
sisear vi : hiss — **siseo** nm : hiss
sismo nm : earthquake — **sísmico, -ca** adj : seismic
sistema nm 1 : system 2 **por ~** : systematically — **sistemático, -ca** adj : systematic
sitiar vt : besiege
sitio nm 1 : place, site 2 ESPACIO : room, space 3 CERCO : siege 4 **en cualquier ~** : anywhere
situar {3} vt : situate, place — **situarse** vr 1 : be located 2 ESTABLECERSE : get oneself established — **situación** nf, pl **-ciones** : situation, position — **situado, -da** adj : situated, placed
slip nm : briefs pl, underpants pl
smoking nm : tuxedo
so prep : under
sobaco nm : armpit
sobar vt 1 : finger, handle 2 : knead (dough) — **sobado, -da** adj : worn, shabby
soberanía nf : sovereignty — **soberano, -na** adj & n : sovereign
soberbia nf : pride, arrogance — **soberbio, -bia** adj : proud, arrogant
sobornar vt : bribe — **soborno** nm 1 : bribe 2 : (action of) bribery
sobrar vi 1 : be more than enough 2 RESTAR : be left over — **sobra** nf 1 : surplus 2 **de ~** : to spare 3 **~s** nfpl : leftovers — **sobrado, -da** adj : more than enough — **sobrante** adj : remaining
sobre[1] nm : envelope
sobre[2] prep 1 : on, on top of 2 POR ENCIMA DE : over, above 3 ACERCA DE : about 4 **~ todo** : especially, above all
sobrecama nmf Lat : bedspread
sobrecargar {52} vt : overload, overburden
sobrecoger {15} vt : startle — **sobrecogerse** vr : be startled
sobrecubierta nf : dust jacket
sobredosis nfs & pl : overdose
sobreentender {56} vt : infer, understand — **sobreentenderse** vr : be understood
sobreestimar vt : overestimate
sobregiro nm : overdraft
sobrellevar vt : endure, bear
sobremesa nf **de ~** : after-dinner
sobrenatural adj : supernatural
sobrenombre nm : nickname
sobrentender → **sobreentender**
sobrepasar vt : exceed
sobreponer {60} vt 1 : superimpose 2 ANTEPONER : put before — **sobreponerse** vr **~ a** : overcome

sobresalir {73} vi 1 : protrude 2 DESTACARSE : stand out — **sobresaliente** adj : outstanding
sobresaltar vt : startle — **sobresaltarse** vr : start, jump up — **sobresalto** nm : fright
sobrestimar → **sobreestimar**
sobretodo nm : overcoat
sobrevenir {87} vi : happen, ensue
sobrevivencia nf → **supervivencia**
sobreviviente adj & nmf → **superviviente**
sobrevivir vi : survive — vt : outlive
sobrevolar {19} vt : fly over
sobriedad nf 1 : sobriety 2 MODERACIÓN : restraint
sobrino, -na n : nephew m, niece f
sobrio, -bria adj : sober
socarrón, -rrona adj, mpl **-rrones** : sarcastic
socavar vt : undermine
sociable adj : sociable — **social** adj : social — **socialismo** nm : socialism — **socialista** adj & nmf : socialist — **sociedad** nf 1 : society 2 EMPRESA : company 3 **~ anónima** : incorporated company — **socio, -cia** n 1 : partner 2 MIEMBRO : member — **sociología** nf : sociology — **sociólogo, -ga** n : sociologist
socorrer vt : help — **socorrista** nmf : lifeguard — **socorro** nm : help
soda nf : soda (water)
sodio nf : sodium
sofá nm : couch, sofa
sofisticación nf, pl **-ciones** : sophistication — **sofisticado, -da** adj : sophisticated
sofocar {72} vt 1 : suffocate, smother 2 : put out (a fire), stifle (a rebellion, etc.) — **sofocarse** vr 1 : suffocate 2 fam : get upset — **sofocante** adj : suffocating, stifling
sofreír {66} vt : sauté
soga nf : rope
soja nf → **soya**
sojuzgar vt : subdue, subjugate
sol nm 1 : sun 2 **hacer ~** : be sunny
solamente adv : only, just
solapa nf 1 : lapel (of a jacket) 2 : flap (of an envelope) — **solapado, -da** adj : secret, underhanded
solar[1] adj : solar, sun
solar[2] nm : lot, site
solariego, -ga adj : ancestral
solaz nm, pl **-laces** : solace 2 DESCANSO : relaxation — **solazarse** {21} vr : relax
soldado nm 1 : soldier 2 **~ raso** : private
soldar {19} vt : weld, solder — **solda-**

dor *nm* : soldering iron — **soldador,
-dora** *n* : welder
soleado, -da *adj* : sunny
soledad *nf* : loneliness, solitude
solemne *adj* : solemn — **solemnidad**
nf : solemnity
soler {78} *vi* 1 : be in the habit of 2
suele llegar tarde : he usually arrives
late
solicitar *vt* 1 : request, solicit 2 : apply
for (a job, etc.) — **solicitante** *nmf*
: applicant — **solícito, -ta** *adj* : solici-
tous, obliging — **solicitud** *nf* 1 : concern 2 PETICIÓN : request 3 : application (for a job, etc.)
solidaridad *nf* : solidarity
sólido, -da *adj* 1 : solid 2 : sound (of an
argument, etc.) — **sólido** *nm* : solid —
solidez *nf* : solidity — **solidificar**
{72} *vt* : solidify — **solidificarse** *vr*
: solidify, harden
soliloquio *nm* : soliloquy
solista *nmf* : soloist
solitario, -ria *adj* 1 : solitary 2 AISLADO
: lonely, deserted — ~ *n* : recluse —
solitaria *nf* : tapeworm — **solitario**
nm : solitaire
sollozar {21} *vi* : sob — **sollozo** *nm*
: sob
solo, -la *adj* 1 : alone 2 AISLADO : lonely 3 **a solas** : alone, by oneself —
solo *nm* : solo
sólo *adv* : just, only
solomillo *nm* : sirloin
solsticio *nm* : solstice
soltar {19} *vt* 1 : release 2 DEJAR CAER
: let go of, drop 3 DESATAR : unfasten,
undo — **soltarse** *vr* 1 : break free 2
DESATARSE : come undone
soltero, -ra *adj* : single, unmarried —
~ *n* 1 : bachelor *m*, single woman *f* 2
apellido de soltera : maiden name
soltura *nf* 1 : looseness 2 : fluency (in
language) 3 AGILIDAD : agility, ease
soluble *adj* : soluble
solución *nf*, *pl* **-ciones** : solution —
solucionar *vt* : solve, resolve
solventar *vt* 1 : settle, pay 2 RESOLVER
: resolve — **solvente** *adj & nm* : solvent
sombra *nf* 1 : shadow 2 : shade (of a
tree, etc.) 3 ~**s** *nfpl* : darkness, shad-
ows — **sombreado, -da** *adj* : shady
sombrero *nm* : hat
sombrilla *nf* : parasol, umbrella
sombrío, -bría *adj* : dark, somber,
gloomy
somero, -ra *adj* : superficial
someter *vt* 1 : subjugate 2 SUBORDINAR
: subordinate 3 : subject (to treatment,

etc.) 4 PRESENTAR : submit, present —
someterse *vr* 1 : submit, yield 2 ~ **a**
: undergo
somnífero, -ra *adj* : soporific — **somnífero** *nm* : sleeping pill — **somnoliento, -ta** *adj* : drowsy, sleepy
somos → **ser**
son[1] → **ser**
son[2] *nm* 1 : sound 2 **en ~ de** : as, in
the manner of
sonajero *nm* : (baby's) rattle
sonámbulo, -la *n* : sleepwalker
sonar {19} *vi* 1 : sound 2 : ring (as a
bell) 3 : look or sound familiar 4 ~ **a**
: sound like — **sonarse** *vr or* ~ **las
narices** : blow one's nose
sonata *nf* : sonata
sondear *vt* 1 : sound, probe 2 : survey,
sound out (opinions, etc.) — **sondeo**
nm 1 : sounding, probing 2 ENCUESTA
: survey, poll
soneto *nm* : sonnet
sónico, -ca *adj* : sonic
sonido *nm* : sound
sonoro, -ra *adj* 1 : resonant, sonorous 2
RUIDOSO : loud
sonreír {66} *vi* : smile — **sonreírse** *vr*
: smile — **sonriente** *adj* : smiling —
sonrisa *nf* : smile
sonrojar *vt* : cause to blush — **sonrojarse** *vr* : blush — **sonrojo** *nm* : blush
sonrosado, -da *adj* : rosy, pink
sonsacar {72} *vt* : wheedle (out)
soñar {19} *v* 1 : dream 2 ~ **con**
: dream about 3 ~ **despierto** : daydream — **soñador, -dora** *adj*
: dreamy — ~ *n* : dreamer — **soñoliento, -ta** *adj* : sleepy, drowsy
sopa *nf* : soup
sopesar *vt* : weigh, consider
soplar *vi* : blow — *vt* : blow out, blow
off, blow up — **soplete** *nm* : blow-
torch — **soplo** *nm* : puff, gust
soplón, -plona *n*, *pl* **-plones** *fam*
: sneak
sopor *nm* : drowsiness — **soporífero,
-ra** *adj* : soporific
soportar *vt* 1 SOSTENER : support 2
AGUANTAR : bear — **soporte** *nm* : support
soprano *nmf* : soprano
sor *nf* : Sister (in religion)
sorber *vt* 1 : sip 2 ABSORBER : absorb 3
CHUPAR : suck up — **sorbete** *nm*
: sherbet — **sorbo** *nm* 1 : sip, swallow
2 **beber a ~s** : sip
sordera *nf* : deafness
sórdido, -da *adj* : sordid, squalid
sordo, -da *adj* 1 : deaf 2 : muted (of a

sound) — **sordomudo, -da** *n* : deaf-mute

sorna *nf* : sarcasm

sorprender *vt* : surprise — **sorprenderse** *vr* : be surprised — **sorprendente** *adj* : surprising — **sorpresa** *nf* : surprise

sortear *vt* **1** : raffle off, draw lots for **2** ESQUIVAR : dodge — **sorteo** *nm* : drawing, raffle

sortija *nf* **1** : ring **2** : ringlet (of hair)

sortilegio *nm* **1** HECHIZO : spell **2** HECHICERÍA : sorcery

sosegar {49} *vt* : calm, pacify — **sosegarse** *vr* : calm down — **sosegado, -da** *adj* : calm, tranquil — **sosiego** *nm* : calm

soslayo: de ~ *adv phr* : obliquely, sideways

soso, -sa *adj* **1** : insipid, tasteless **2** ABURRIDO : dull

sospechar *vt* : suspect — **sospecha** *nf* : suspicion — **sospechoso, -sa** *adj* : suspicious — **~** *n* : suspect

sostener {80} *vt* **1** : support **2** SUJETAR : hold **3** MANTENER : sustain, maintain — **sostenerse** *vr* **1** : stand (up) **2** CONTINUAR : remain **3** SUSTENTARSE : support oneself — **sostén** *nm, pl* **-tenes 1** APOYO : support **2** SUSTENTO : sustenance **3** : brassiere, bra — **sostenido, -da** *adj* **1** : sustained **2** : sharp (in music) — **sostenido** *nm* : sharp

sótano *nm* : basement

soterrar {55} *vt* **1** : bury **2** ESCONDER : hide

soto *nm* : grove

soviético, -ca *adj* : Soviet

soy → ser

soya *nf* : soy

Sr. *nm* : Mr. — **Sra.** *nf* : Mrs., Ms. — **Srta.** *or* **Srita.** *nf* : Miss, Ms.

su *adj* **1** : his, her, its, their, one's **2** (*formal*) : your

suave *adj* **1** : soft **2** LISO : smooth **3** APACIBLE : gentle, mild — **suavidad** *nf* **1** : softness, smoothness **2** APACIBILIDAD : mildness, gentleness — **suavizar** {21} *vt* : soften, smooth

subalimentado, -da *adj* : undernourished, underfed

subalterno, -na *adj* **1** SUBORDINADO : subordinate **2** SECUNDARIO : secondary — **~** *n* : subordinate

subarrendar {55} *vt* : sublet

subasta *nf* : auction — **subastar** *vt* : auction (off)

subcampeón, -peona *n, mpl* **-peones** : runner-up

subcomité *nm* : subcommittee

subconsciente *adj* & *nm* : subconscious

subdesarrollado, -da *adj* : underdeveloped

subdirector, -tora *n* : assistant manager

súbdito, -ta *n* : subject

subdividir *vt* : subdivide — **subdivisión** *nf, pl* **-siones** : subdivision

subestimar *vt* : underestimate

subir *vt* **1** : climb, go up **2** LLEVAR : bring up, take up **3** AUMENTAR : raise — *vi* **1** : go up, come up **2** ~ **a** : get in (a car), get on (a bus, etc.) — **subirse** *vr* **1** : climb (up) **2** ~ **a** : get in (a car), get on (a bus, etc.) **3** ~ **a la cabeza** : go to one's head — **subida** *nf* **1** : ascent, climb **2** AUMENTO : rise **3** PENDIENTE : slope — **subido, -da** *adj* **1** : bright, strong **2** ~ **de tono** : risqué

súbito, -ta *adj* **1** : sudden **2 de súbito** : all of a sudden, suddenly

subjetivo, -va *adj* : subjective

subjuntivo, -va *adj* : subjunctive — **subjuntivo** *nm* : subjunctive (case)

sublevar *vt* : stir up, incite to rebellion — **sublevarse** *vr* : rebel — **sublevación** *nf, pl* **-ciones** : uprising, rebellion

sublime *adj* : sublime

submarino, -na *adj* : underwater — **submarino** *nm* : submarine — **submarinismo** *nm* : scuba diving

subordinar *vt* : subordinate — **subordinado, -da** *adj* & *n* : subordinate

subproducto *nm* : by-product

subrayar *vt* **1** : underline **2** ENFATIZAR : emphasize, stress

subrepticio, -cia *adj* : surreptitious

subsanar *vt* **1** : rectify, correct **2** : make up for (a deficiency), overcome (an obstacle)

subscribir → suscribir

subsidio *nm* : subsidy, benefit

subsiguiente *adj* : subsequent

subsistir *vi* **1** : live, subsist **2** SOBREVIVIR : survive — **subsistencia** *nf* : subsistence

substancia *nf* → **sustancia**

subterfugio *nm* : subterfuge

subterráneo, -nea *adj* : underground, subterranean — **subterráneo** *nm* : underground passage

subtítulo *nm* : subtitle

suburbio *nm* **1** : suburb **2** : slum (outside a city) — **suburbano, -na** *adj* : suburban

subvencionar *vt* : subsidize — **sub-**

vención *nf, pl* **-ciones** : subsidy, grant

subvertir {76} *vt* : subvert — **subversión** *nf, pl* **-siones** : subversion — **subversivo, -va** *adj & n* : subversive

subyacente *adj* : underlying

subyugar {52} *vt* : subjugate, subdue

succión *nf, pl* **-ciones** : suction — **succionar** *vt* : suck up, draw in

sucedáneo *nm* : substitute

suceder *vi* 1 : happen, occur 2 ~ **a** : follow 3 **suceda lo que suceda** : come what may — **sucesión** *nf, pl* **-siones** : succession — **sucesivo, -va** *adj* : successive — **suceso** *nm* 1 : event 2 INCIDENTE : incident — **sucesor, -sora** *n* : successor

suciedad *nf* 1 : dirtiness 2 MUGRE : dirt, filth

sucinto, -ta *adj* : succinct, concise

sucio, -cia *adj* : dirty, filthy

suculento, -ta *adj* : succulent

sucumbir *vi* : succumb

sucursal *nf* : branch (of a business)

sudadera *nf* : sweatshirt — **sudado, -da** *adj* : sweaty

sudafricano, -na *adj* : South African

sudamericano, -na *adj* : South American

sudar *vi* : sweat

sudeste → sureste

sudoeste → suroeste

sudor *nm* : sweat — **sudoroso, -sa** *adj* : sweaty

sueco, -ca *adj* : Swedish — **sueco** *nm* : Swedish (language)

suegro, -gra *n* 1 : father-in-law *m*, mother-in-law *f* 2 **suegros** *nmpl* : in-laws

suela *nf* : sole (of a shoe)

sueldo *nm* : salary, wage

suelo *nm* 1 : ground 2 : floor (in a house) 3 TIERRA : soil, land

suelto, -ta *adj* : loose, free — **suelto** *nm* : loose change

sueño *nm* 1 : dream 2 **coger el** ~ : get to sleep 3 **tener** ~ : be sleepy

suero *nm* 1 : whey 2 : serum (in medicine)

suerte *nf* 1 : luck, fortune 2 AZAR : chance 3 DESTINO : fate 4 CLASE : sort, kind 5 **por** ~ : luckily 6 **tener** ~ : be lucky

suéter *nm* : sweater

suficiencia *nf* 1 CAPACIDAD : competence, proficiency 2 PRESUNCIÓN : smugness — **suficiente** *adj* 1 : enough, sufficient 2 PRESUNTUOSO : smug — **suficientemente** *adv* : enough

sufijo *nm* : suffix

sufragio *nm* : suffrage, vote

sufrir *vt* 1 : suffer 2 SOPORTAR : bear, stand — *vi* : suffer — **sufrido, -da** *adj* 1 : long-suffering 2 : sturdy, serviceable (of clothing) — **sufrimiento** *nm* : suffering

sugerir {76} *vt* : suggest — **sugerencia** *nf* : suggestion — **sugestión** *nf, pl* **-tiones** : suggestion — **sugestionable** *adj* : impressionable — **sugestionar** *vt* : influence — **sugestivo, -va** *adj* 1 : suggestive 2 ESTIMULANTE : interesting, stimulating

suicidio *nm* : suicide — **suicida** *adj* : suicidal — *nmf* : suicide (victim) — **suicidarse** *vr* : commit suicide

suite *nf* : suite

suizo, -za *adj* : Swiss

sujetar *vt* 1 : hold (on to) 2 FIJAR : fasten 3 DOMINAR : subdue — **sujetarse** *vr* 1 ~ **a** : hold on to, cling to 2 ~ **a** : abide by — **sujeción** *nf, pl* **-ciones** 1 : fastening 2 DOMINACIÓN : subjection — **sujetador** *nm Spain* : brassiere, bra — **sujetapapeles** *nms & pl* : paper clip — **sujeto, -ta** *adj* 1 : fastened 2 ~ **a** : subject to — **sujeto** *nm* 1 : individual 2 : subject (in grammar)

sulfuro *nm* : sulfur — **sulfúrico, -ca** *adj* : sulfuric

sultán *nm, pl* **-tanes** : sultan

suma *nf* 1 : sum, total 2 : addition (in mathematics) 3 **en** ~ : in short — **sumamente** *adv* : extremely — **sumar** *vt* 1 : add (up) 2 TOTALIZAR : add up to, total — *vi* : add up — **sumarse** *vr* ~ **a** : join

sumario, -ria *adj* : concise — **sumario** *nm* 1 : summary 2 : indictment (in law)

sumergir {35} *vt* : submerge, plunge — **sumergirse** *vr* : be submerged — **sumergible** *adj* : waterproof (of a watch, etc.)

sumidero *nm* : drain

suministrar *vt* : supply, provide — **suministro** *nm* : supply, provision

sumir *vt* : plunge, immerse — **sumirse** *vr* ~ **en** : sink into

sumisión *nf, pl* **-siones** : submission — **sumiso, -sa** *adj* : submissive

sumo, -ma *adj* 1 : highest, supreme 2 **de suma importancia** : of great importance

suntuoso, -sa *adj* : sumptuous, lavish

super *or* **súper** *nm fam* : supermarket

superabundancia *nf* : overabundance

superar *vt* 1 : surpass, outdo 2 VENCER : overcome — **superarse** *vr* : improve oneself

superávit *nm* : surplus
superestructura *nf* : superstructure
superficie *nf* 1 : surface 2 ÁREA : area — **superficial** *adj* : superficial
superfluo, -flua *adj* : superfluous
superintendente *nmf* : supervisor, superintendent
superior *adj* 1 : superior 2 : upper (of a floor, etc.) 3 ~ **a** : above, higher than — ~ *nm* : superior — **superioridad** *nf* : superiority
superlativo, -va *adj* : superlative — **superlativo** *nm* : superlative
supermercado *nm* : supermarket
superpoblado, -da *adj* : overpopulated
supersónico, -ca *adj* : supersonic
superstición *nf, pl* **-ciones** : superstition — **supersticioso, -sa** *adj* : superstitious
supervisar *vt* : supervise, oversee — **supervisión** *nf, pl* **-siones** : supervision — **supervisor, -sora** *n* : supervisor
supervivencia *nf* : survival — **superviviente** *adj* : surviving — ~ *nmf* : survivor
suplantar *vt* : supplant, replace
suplemento *nm* : supplement — **suplementario, -ria** *adj* : supplementary
suplente *adj & nmf* : substitute
suplicar {72} *vt* : beg, entreat — **súplica** *nf* : plea, entreaty
suplicio *nm* : ordeal, torture
suplir *vt* 1 : make up for 2 REEMPLAZAR : replace
supo, etc. → saber
suponer {60} *vt* 1 : suppose, assume 2 SIGNIFICAR : mean 3 IMPLICAR : involve, entail — **suposición** *nf, pl* **-ciones** : supposition
supositorio *nm* : suppository
supremo, -ma *adj* : supreme — **supremacía** *nf* : supremacy
suprimir *vt* 1 : suppress, eliminate 2 : delete (text) — **supresión** *nf, pl* **-siones** 1 : suppression, elimination 2 : deletion (of text)
supuesto, -ta *adj* 1 : supposed, alleged 2 **por supuesto** : of course — **supuesto** *nm* : assumption — **supuestamente** *adv* : allegedly
sur *nm* 1 : south, South 2 : south wind 3 **del** ~ : south, southerly
surafricano, -na → sudafricano
suramericano, -na → sudamericano
surcar {72} *vt* 1 : plow (earth) 2 : cut through (air, water, etc.) — **surco** *nm* : groove, furrow, rut
sureño, -ña *adj* : southern, Southern — ~ *n* : Southerner

sureste *adj* 1 : southeast, southeastern 2 : southeasterly (of wind, etc.) — ~ *nm* : southeast, Southeast
surf *or* **surfing** *nm* : surfing
surgir {35} *vi* 1 : arise 2 APARECER : appear — **surgimiento** *nm* : rise, emergence
suroeste *adj* 1 : southwest, southwestern 2 : southwesterly (of wind, etc.) — ~ *nm* : southwest, Southwest
surtir *vt* 1 : supply, provide 2 ~ **efecto** : have an effect — **surtirse** *vr* ~ **de** : stock up on — **surtido, -da** *adj* 1 : assorted, varied 2 : stocked (with merchandise) — **surtido** *nm* : assortment, selection — **surtidor** *nm* : gas pump
susceptible *adj* 1 : susceptible, sensitive 2 ~ **de** : capable of — **susceptibilidad** *nf* : sensitivity
suscitar *vt* : provoke, arouse
suscribir {33} *vt* 1 : sign (a formal document) 2 RATIFICAR : endorse — **suscribirse** *vr* ~ **a** : subscribe to — **suscripción** *nf, pl* **-ciones** : subscription — **suscriptor, -tora** *n* : subscriber
susodicho, -cha *adj* : aforementioned
suspender *vt* 1 : suspend 2 COLGAR : hang 3 *Spain* : fail (an exam, etc.) — **suspensión** *nf, pl* **-siones** : suspension — **suspenso** *nm* 1 *Spain* : failure (in an exam, etc.) 2 *Lat* : suspense
suspicaz *adj, pl* **-caces** : suspicious
suspirar *vi* : sigh — **suspiro** *nm* : sigh
sustancia *nf* 1 : substance 2 **sin** ~ : shallow, lacking substance — **sustancial** *adj* : substantial, significant — **sustancioso, -sa** *adj* : substantial, solid
sustantivo *nm* : noun
sustentar *vt* 1 : support 2 ALIMENTAR : sustain, nourish 3 MANTENER : maintain — **sustentarse** *vr* : support oneself — **sustentación** *nf, pl* **-ciones** : support — **sustento** *nm* 1 : means of support, livelihood 2 ALIMENTO : sustenance
sustituir {41} *vt* : replace, substitute — **sustitución** *nf, pl* **-ciones** : replacement, substitution — **sustituto, -ta** *n* : substitute
susto *nm* : fright, scare
sustraer {81} *vt* 1 : remove, take away 2 : subtract (in mathematics) — **sustraerse** *vr* ~ **a** : avoid, evade — **sustracción** *nf, pl* **-ciones** : subtraction
susurrar *vi* 1 : whisper 2 : murmur (of water) 3 : rustle (of leaves, etc.) — *vt* : whisper — **susurro** *nm* 1 : whisper 2

: murmur (of water) **3** : rustle, rustling (of leaves, etc.)

sutil *adj* **1** : delicate, fine **2** : subtle (of fragrances, differences, etc.) — **sutileza** *nf* : subtlety

sutura *nf* : suture

suyo, -ya *adj* **1** : his, her, its, one's, theirs **2** (*formal*) : yours **3 un primo suyo** : a cousin of his/hers — ~ *pron* **1** : his, hers, its (own), one's own, theirs **2** (*formal*) : yours

switch *nm Lat* : switch

T

t *nf* : t, 21st letter of the Spanish alphabet

taba *nf* : anklebone

tabaco *nm* : tobacco — **tabacalero, -ra** *adj* : tobacco

tábano *nm* : horsefly

taberna *nf* : tavern

tabicar {72} *vt* : wall up — **tabique** *nm* : thin wall, partition

tabla *nf* **1** : board, plank **2** LISTA : table, list **3** ~ **de planchar** : ironing board **4** ~**s** *nfpl* : stage, boards *pl* — **tablado** *nm* **1** : flooring **2** PLATAFORMA : platform **3** : (theater) stage — **tablero** *nm* **1** : bulletin board **2** : board (in games) **3** PIZARRA : blackboard **4** ~ **de instrumentos** : dashboard, instrument panel

tableta *nf* **1** : tablet, pill **2** : bar (of chocolate)

tablilla *nf* : slat — **tablón** *nm, pl* **-lones** **1** : plank, beam **2** ~ **de anuncios** : bulletin board

tabú *adj* : taboo — **tabú** *nm, pl* **-búes** or **-bús** : taboo

tabular *vt* : tabulate

taburete *nm* : stool

tacaño, -na *adj* : stingy, miserly

tacha *nf* **1** : flaw, defect **2 sin** ~ : flawless

tachar *vt* **1** : cross out, delete **2** ~ **de** : accuse of, label as

tachón *nm, pl* **-chones** : stud, hobnail — **tachuela** *nf* : tack, hobnail

tácito, -ta *adj* : tacit

taciturno, -na *adj* : taciturn

taco *nm* **1** : heel (of the foot) **2** : stub (of a check) — **talonario** *nm* : checkbook

taco *nm* **1** : stopper, plug **2** *Lat* : heel (of a shoe) **3** : cue (in billiards) **4** : taco (in cooking)

tacón *nm, pl* **-cones** **1** : heel (of a shoe) **2 de** ~ **alto** : high-heeled

táctica *nf* : tactic, tactics *pl* — **táctico, -ca** *adj* : tactical

tacto *nm* **1** : (sense of) touch, feel **2** DELICADEZA : tact

tafetán *nm, pl* **-tanes** : taffeta

tailandés, -desa *adj* : Thai

taimado, -da *adj* : crafty, sly

tajar *vt* : cut, slice — **tajada** *nf* **1** : slice **2 sacar** ~ *fam* : get one's share — **tajante** *adj* : categorical — **tajo** *nm* **1** : cut, gash ESCARPA : steep cliff

tal *adv* **1** : so, in such a way **2 con** ~ **que** : provided that, as long as **3 ¿qué** ~**?** : how are you?, how's it going? — ~ *adj* **1** : such, such a **2** ~ **vez** : maybe, perhaps — ~ *pron* **1** : such a one, such a thing **2** ~ **para cual** : two of a kind

taladrar *vt* : drill — **taladro** *nm* : drill

talante *nm* **1** HUMOR : mood **2** VOLUNTAD : willingness

talar *vt* : cut down, fell

talco *nm* : talcum powder

talego *nm* : sack

talento *nm* : talent — **talentoso, -sa** *adj* : talented

talismán *nm, pl* **-manes** : talisman, charm

talla *nf* **1** : sculpture, carving **2** ESTATURA : height **3** : size (in clothing) — **tallar** *vt* **1** : sculpt, carve **2** : measure (someone's height)

tallarín *nf, pl* **-rines** : noodle

talle *nm* **1** : waist, waistline **2** FIGURA : figure **3** : measurements *pl* (of clothing)

taller *nm* **1** : workshop **2** : studio (of an artist)

tallo *nm* : stalk, stem

talón *nm, pl* **-lones** **1** : heel (of the foot) **2** : stub (of a check) — **talonario** *nm* : checkbook

taltuza *nf* : gopher

tamal *nm* : tamale

tamaño, -ña *adj* : such a, such a big — **tamaño** *nm* **1** : size **2 de** ~ **natural** : life-size

tambalearse *vr* **1** : teeter, wobble **2** : stagger, totter (of persons)

también *adv* : too, as well, also

tambor *nm* : drum — **tamborilear** *vi* : drum

tamiz *nm* : sieve — **tamizar** {21} *vt* : sift

tampoco *adv* : neither, not either

tampón *nm, pl* **-pones** **1** : tampon **2** : ink pad (for stamping)

tan *adv* **1** : so, so very **2** ~ **pronto como** : as soon as **3** ~ **sólo** : only, merely

tanda *nf* **1** TURNO : turn, shift **2** GRUPO : batch, lot, series
tangente *nf* : tangent
tangible *adj* : tangible
tango *nm* : tango
tanque *nm* : tank
tantear *vt* **1** : feel, grope **2** SOPESAR : size up, weigh — *vi* : feel one's way — **tanteador** *nm* : scoreboard — **tanteo** *nm* **1** : weighing, sizing up **2** PUNTUACIÓN : scoring (in sports)
tanto *adv* **1** : so much **2** (*in expressions of time*) : so long — ~ *nm* **1** : certain amount **2** : goal, point (in sports) **3** un ~ : somewhat, rather — **tanto, -ta** *adj* **1** : so much, so many **2** (*in comparisons*) : as much, as many **3** *fam* : however many — ~ *pron* **1** : so much, so many **2** entre ~ : meanwhile **3** por lo ~ : therefore
tañer {79} *vt* **1** : ring (a bell) **2** : play (a musical instrument)
tapa *nf* **1** : cover, top, lid **2** *Spain* : snack
tapacubos *nms & pl* : hubcap
tapar *vt* **1** : cover, put a lid on **2** OCULTAR : block out **3** ENCUBRIR : cover up — **tapadera** *nf* **1** : cover, lid **2** : front (to hide a deception)
tapete *nm* **1** : small rug, mat **2** : cover (for a table)
tapia *nf* : (adobe) wall, garden wall — **tapiar** *vt* **1** : wall in **2** : block off (a door, etc.)
tapicería *nf* **1** : upholstery **2** TAPIZ : tapestry — **tapicero, -ra** *n* : upholsterer
tapioca *nf* : tapioca
tapiz *nm, pl* **-pices** : tapestry — **tapizar** {21} *vt* : upholster
tapón *nm, pl* **-pones** **1** : cork **2** : cap (for a bottle, etc.) **3** : plug, stopper (for a sink)
tapujo *nm* sin ~s : openly, outright
taquigrafía *nf* : stenography, shorthand — **taquígrafo, -fa** *n* : stenographer
taquilla *nf* **1** : box office **2** RECAUDACIÓN : earnings *pl*, take — **taquillero, -ra** *adj* un éxito taquillero : a box-office hit
tarántula *nf* : tarantula
tararear *vt* : hum
tardar *vi* **1** : take a long time, be late **2** a más ~ : at the latest — *vt* : take (time) — **tardanza** *nf* : lateness, delay — **tarde** *adv* **1** : late **2** ~ o temprano : sooner or later — ~ *nf* **1** : afternoon, evening **2** ¡buenas ~s! : good afternoon!, good evening! **3** en la ~ *or* por la ~ : in the afternoon, in the evening — **tardío, -día** *adj* : late, tardy — **tardo, -da** *adj* : slow

tarea *nf* **1** : task, job **2** : homework (in education)
tarifa *nf* **1** : fare, rate **2** LISTA : price list **3** ARANCEL : duty, tariff
tarima *nf* : platform, stage
tarjeta *nf* **1** : card **2** ~ de crédito : credit card **3** ~ postal : postcard
tarro *nm* : jar, pot
tarta *nf* **1** : cake **2** TORTA : tart
tartamudear *vi* : stammer, stutter — **tartamudeo** *nm* : stutter, stammer
tartán *nm, pl* **-tanes** : tartan, plaid
tártaro *nm* : tartar
tarugo *nm* **1** : block (of wood) **2** *fam* : blockhead, dunce
tasa *nf* **1** : rate **2** IMPUESTO : tax **3** VALORACIÓN : appraisal — **tasación** *nf, pl* **-ciones** : appraisal — **tasar** *vt* **1** : set the price of **2** VALORAR : appraise, value
tasca *nf* : cheap bar, dive
tatuar {3} *vt* : tattoo — **tatuaje** *nm* : tattoo, tattooing
taurino, -na *adj* : bull, bullfighting — **tauromaquia** *nf* : (art of) bullfighting
taxi *nm, pl* **taxis** : taxi, taxicab — **taxista** *nmf* : taxi driver
taza *nf* **1** : cup **2** : (toilet) bowl — **tazón** *nm, pl* **-zones** : bowl
te *pron* **1** (*direct object*) : you **2** (*indirect object*) : for you, to you, from you **3** (*reflexive*) : yourself, for yourself, to yourself, from yourself
té *nm* : tea
teatro *nm* : theater — **teatral** *adj* : theatrical
techo *nm* **1** : roof **2** : ceiling (of a room) **3** LÍMITE : upper limit, ceiling — **techumbre** *nf* : roofing
tecla *nf* : key (of a musical instrument or a machine) — **teclado** *nm* : keyboard — **teclear** *vt* : type in, enter
técnica *nf* **1** : technique, skill **2** TECNOLOGÍA : technology — **técnico, -ca** *adj* : technical — ~ *n* : technician
tecnología *nf* : technology — **tecnológico, -ca** *adj* : technological
tecolote *nm Lat* : owl
tedio *nm* : boredom — **tedioso, -sa** *adj* : tedious, boring
teja *nf* : tile — **tejado** *nm* : roof
tejer *v* **1** : knit, crochet **2** : weave (on a loom)
tejido *nm* **1** : fabric, cloth **2** : tissue (of the body)
tejón *nm, pl* **-jones** : badger
tela *nf* **1** : fabric, material **2** ~ de araña : spiderweb — **telar** *nm* : loom — **telaraña** *nf* : spiderweb, cobweb
tele *nf fam* : TV, television

telecomunicación *nf, pl* -ciones : telecommunication

teledifusión *nf, pl* -siones : television broadcasting

teledirigido, -da *adj* : remote-controlled

telefonear *v* : telephone, call — telefónico, -ca *adj* : telephone — telefonista *nmf* : telephone operator — teléfono *nm* 1 : telephone 2 llamar por ~ : make a phone call

telegrafiar {85} *v* : telegraph — telegráfico, -ca *adj* : telegraphic — telégrafo *nm* : telegaph

telegrama *nm* : telegram

telenovela *nf* : soap opera

telepatía *nf* : telepathy — telepático, -ca *adj* : telepathic

telescopio *nm* : telescope — telescópico, -ca *adj* : telescopic

telespectador, -dora *n* : (television) viewer

telesquí *nm, pl* -squís : ski lift

televidente *nmf* : (television) viewer

televisión *nf, pl* -siones : television, TV — televisar *vt* : televise — televisor *nm* : television set

telón *nm, pl* -lones 1 : curtain (in theater) 2 ~ de fondo : backdrop, background

tema *nm* : theme

temblar {55} *vi* 1 : tremble, shiver 2 : shake (of a building, the ground, etc.) — temblor *nm* 1 : shaking, trembling 2 *or* ~ de tierra : tremor, earthquake — tembloroso, -sa *adj* : trembling, shaky

temer *vt* : fear, dread — *vi* : be afraid — temerario, -ria *adj* : reckless — temeridad *nf* 1 : recklessness 2 : rash act — temeroso, -sa *adj* : fearful — temor *nm* : fear, dread

temperamento *nm* : temperament — temperamental *adj* : temperamental

temperatura *nf* : temperature

tempestad *nf* : storm — tempestuoso, -sa *adj* : stormy

templar *vt* 1 : temper (steel) 2 : moderate (temperature) 3 : tune (a musical instrument) — templarse *vr* : warm up, cool down — templado, -da *adj* 1 : temperate, mild 2 TIBIO : lukewarm 3 VALIENTE : courageous — templanza *nf* 1 : moderation 2 : mildness (of weather)

templo *nm* : temple, synagogue

tempo *nm* : tempo

temporada *nf* 1 : season, time 2 PERÍODO : period, spell — temporal *adj* 1 : temporal 2 PROVISIONAL : temporary — ~ *nm* : storm — temporero, -ra *n* : temporary or seasonal worker

temporizador *nm* : timer

temprano, -na *adj* : early — temprano *adv* : early

tenaz *adj, pl* -naces : tenacious — tenaza *nf or* tenazas *nfpl* 1 : pliers 2 : tongs (for the fireplace, etc.) 3 : claw (of a crustacean)

tendedero *nm* : clothesline

tendencia *nf* : tendency, trend

tender {56} *vt* 1 : spread out, stretch out 2 : hang out (clothes) 3 : lay (cables, etc.) 4 : set (a trap) — *vi* ~ a : have a tendency towards — tenderse *vr* : stretch out, lie down

tendero, -ra *n* : shopkeeper

tendido *nm* 1 : laying (of cables, etc.) 2 : seats *pl*, stand (at a bullfight)

tendón *nm, pl* -dones : tendon

tenebroso, -sa *adj* 1 : gloomy, dark 2 SINIESTRO : sinister

tenedor, -dora *n* 1 : holder 2 ~ de libros : bookkeeper — tenedor *nm* 1 : table fork — teneduría *nf* ~ de libros : bookkeeping

tener {80} *vt* 1 : have, possess 2 SUJETAR : hold 3 TOMAR : take 4 ~ frío (hambre, *etc.*) : be cold (hungry, etc.) 5 — ... años : be ... years old 6 ~ por : think, consider — *v aux* ~ que : have to, ought to 2 tenía pensado escribirte : I've been thinking of writing to you — tenerse *vr* 1 : stand up 2 ~ por : consider oneself

tenería *nf* : tannery

tengo → tener

tenia *nf* : tapeworm

teniente *nmf* : lieutenant

tenis *nms & pl* 1 : tennis 2 ~ *nmpl* : sneakers — tenista *nmf* : tennis player

tenor *nm* 1 : tenor 2 : tone, sense (in style)

tensar *vt* 1 : tense, make taut 2 : draw (a bow) — tensarse *vr* : become tense — tensión *nf, pl* -siones 1 : tension 2 ~ arterial : blood pressure — tenso, -sa *adj* : tense

tentación *nf, pl* -clones : temptation

tentáculo *nm* : tentacle

tentar {55} *vt* 1 : feel, touch 2 ATRAER : tempt — tentador, -dora *adj* : tempting

tentativa *nf* : attempt

tentempié *nm fam* : snack

tenue *adj* 1 : tenuous 2 : faint, weak (of sounds) 3 : light, fine (of thread, rain, etc.)

teñir {67} *vt* 1 : dye 2 ~ de : tinge with

teología *nf* : theology — teólogo, -ga *n* : theologian

teorema *nm* : theorem

teoría *nf* : theory — **teórico, -ca** *adj* : theoretical

tequila *nm* : tequila

terapia *nf* 1 : therapy 2 ~ **ocupacional** : occupational therapy — **terapeuta** *nmf* : therapist — **terapéutico, -ca** *adj* : therapeutic

tercermundista *adj* : third-world

tercero, -ra *adj* (tercer *before masculine singular nouns*) 1 : third 2 **el Tercer Mundo** : the Third World — ~ *n* : third (in a series)

terciar *vt* : sling (sth over one's shoulders), tilt (a hat) — *vi* 1 : intervene 2 ~ **en** : take part in

tercio *nm* : third

terciopelo *nm* : velvet

terco, -ca *adj* : obstinate, stubborn

tergiversar *vt* : distort, twist

termal *adj* : thermal, hot — **termas** *nfpl* : hot springs

terminar *vt* : conclude, finish — *vi* 1 : finish 2 ACABARSE : come to an end — **terminarse** *vr* 1 : run out 2 ACABARSE : come to an end — **terminación** *nf, pl* -**ciones** : termination, conclusion — **terminal** *adj* : terminal, final — ~ *nm* (*in some regions f*) : (electric or electronic) terminal — ~ *nf* (*in some regions m*) : terminal, station — **término** *nm* 1 : end 2 PLAZO : period, term 3 ~ **medio** : happy medium 4 ~**s** *nmpl* : terms — **terminología** *nf* : terminology

termita *nf* : termite

termo *nm* : thermos

termómetro *nm* : thermometer

termostato *nm* : thermostat

ternero, -ra *n* : calf — **ternera** *nf* : veal

ternura *nf* : tenderness

terquedad *nf* : obstinacy, stubbornness

terracota *nf* : terra-cotta

terraplén *nm, pl* -**plenes** : embankment

terráqueo, -quea *adj* : earth, terrestrial

terrateniente *nmf* : landowner

terraza *nf* 1 : terrace 2 BALCÓN : balcony

terremoto *nm* : earthquake

terreno *nm* 1 : terrain 2 SUELO : earth, ground 3 SOLAR : plot, tract of land — **terreno, -na** *adj* : earthly — **terrestre** *adj* : terrestrial

terrible *adj* : terrible

terrier *nmf* : terrier

territorio *nm* : territory — **territorial** *adj* : territorial

terrón *nm, pl* -**rones** 1 : clod (of earth) 2 ~ **de azúcar** : lump of sugar

terror *nm* : terror — **terrorífico, -ca** *adj* : terrifying — **terrorismo** *nm* : terrorism — **terrorista** *adj & nmf* : terrorist

terroso, -sa *adj* : earthy

terso, -sa *adj* 1 : smooth 2 : polished, flowing (of a style) — **tersura** *nf* : smoothness

tertulia *nf* : gathering, group

tesis *nfs & pl* : thesis

tesón *nm* : persistence, tenacity

tesoro *nm* 1 : treasure 2 : thesaurus (book) 3 **el Tesoro** : the Treasury — **tesorero, -ra** *n* : treasurer

testaferro *nm* : figurehead

testamento *nm* : testament, will — **testamentario, -ria** *n* : executor, executrix *f* — **testar** *vi* : draw up a will

testarudo, -da *adj* : stubborn

testículo *nm* : testicle

testificar {72} *v* : testify — **testigo** *nmf* 1 : witness 2 ~ **ocular** : eyewitness — **testimoniar** *vi* : testify — **testimonio** *nm* : testimony

tétano *or* **tétanos** *nm* : tetanus

tetera *nf* : teapot

tetilla *nf* 1 : teat, nipple (of a man) 2 : nipple (of a baby bottle) — **tetina** *nf* : nipple (of a baby bottle)

tétrico, -ca *adj* : somber, gloomy

textil *adj & nm* : textile

texto *nm* : text — **textual** *adj* 1 : textual 2 EXACTO : literal, exact

textura *nf* : texture

tez *nf, pl* **teces** : complexion

ti *pron* 1 : you 2 ~ **mismo,** ~ **misma** : yourself

tía → tío

tianguis *nms & pl Lat* : open-air market

tibio, -bia *adj* : lukewarm

tiburón *nm, pl* -**rones** : shark

tic *nm* : tic

tiempo *nm* 1 : time 2 ÉPOCA : age, period 3 : weather (in meteorology) 4 : halftime (in sports) 5 : tempo (in music) 6 : tense (in grammar)

tienda *nf* 1 : store, shop 2 *or* ~ **de campaña** : tent

tiene → tener

tienta *nf* **andar a** ~**s** : feel one's way, grope around

tierno, -na *adj* 1 : tender, fresh, young 2 CARIÑOSO : affectionate

tierra *nf* 1 : land 2 SUELO : ground, earth 3 *or* ~ **natal** : native land 4 **la Tierra** : the Earth 5 **por** ~ : overland 6 ~ **adentro** : inland

tieso, -sa *adj* 1 : stiff, rigid 2 ERGUIDO : erect 3 ENGREÍDO : haughty

tiesto *nm* : flowerpot

tifoideo, -dea *adj* **fiebre tifoidea** : typhoid fever

tifón *nm, pl* **-fones** : typhoon
tifus *nm* : typhus
tigre, -gresa *n* 1 : tiger, tigress *f* 2 *Lat* : jaguar
tijera *nf or* **tijeras** *nfpl* : scissors — **tijeretada** *nf* : cut, snip
tildar *vt* ~ **de** : brand as, call
tilde *nf* 1 : tilde 2 ACENTO : accent mark
tilo *nm* : linden (tree)
timar *vt* : swindle, cheat
timbre *nm* 1 : bell 2 : tone, timbre (of a voice, etc.) 3 SELLO : seal, stamp 4 *Lat* : postage stamp — **timbrar** *vt* : stamp
tímido, -da *adj* : timid, shy — **timidez** *nf* : timidity, shyness
timo *nm fam* : swindle, hoax
timón *nm, pl* **-mones** 1 : rudder 2 **coger el** ~ : take the helm, take charge
tímpano *nm* 1 : eardrum 2 ~s *nmpl* : timpani, kettledrums
tina *nf* 1 : vat 2 BAÑERA : bathtub
tinieblas *nfpl* 1 : darkness 2 **estar en** ~ **sobre** : be in the dark about
tino *nm* 1 : good judgment, sense 2 TACTO : tact
tinta *nf* 1 : ink 2 **saberlo de buena** ~ : have it on good authority — **tinte** *nm* 1 : dye, coloring 2 MATIZ : overtone — **tintero** *nm* : inkwell
tintinear *vi* : jingle, tinkle, clink — **tintineo** *nm* : jingle, tinkle, clink
tinto, -ta *adj* 1 : dyed, stained 2 : red (of wine)
tintorería *nf* : dry cleaner (service)
tintura *nf* 1 : dye, tint 2 ~ **de yodo** : tincture of iodine
tiña *nf* : ringworm
tío, tía *n* : uncle *m*, aunt *f*
tiovivo *nm* : merry-go-round
típico, -ca *adj* : typical
tiple *nm* : soprano
tipo *nm* 1 : type, kind 2 FIGURA : figure (of a woman), build (of a man) 3 : rate (of interest, etc.) 4 : (printing) type, typeface — **tipo, -pa** *n fam* : guy *m*, gal *f*
tipografía *nf* : typography, printing — **tipográfico, -ca** *adj* : typographical — **tipógrafo, -fa** *n* : printer
tique *or* **tíquet** *nm* : ticket — **tiquete** *nm Lat* : ticket
tira *nf* 1 : strip, strap 2 ~ **cómica** : comic strip
tirabuzón *nf, pl* **-zones** 1 : corkscrew 2 RIZO : curl, coil
tirada *nf* 1 : throw 2 DISTANCIA : distance 3 IMPRESIÓN : printing, issue — **tirador** *nm* : handle, knob — **tirador, -dora** *n* : marksman *m*, markswoman *f*

tiranía *nf* : tyranny — **tiránico, -ca** *adj* : tyrannical — **tiranizar** {21} *vt* : tyrannize — **tirano, -na** *adj* : tyrannical — ~ *n* : tyrant
tirante *adj* 1 : taut, tight 2 : tense (of a situation, etc.) — ~ *nm* 1 : (shoulder) strap 2 ~s *nmpl* : suspenders
tirar *vt* 1 : throw 2 DESECHAR : throw away 3 DERRIBAR : knock down 4 DISPARAR : shoot, fire 5 IMPRIMIR : print — *vi* 1 : pull 2 DISPARAR : shoot 3 ATRAER : attract 4 *fam* : get by, manage 5 ~ **a** : tend towards — **tirarse** *vr* 1 : throw oneself 2 *fam* : spend (time)
tiritar *vi* : shiver
tiro *nm* 1 : shot, gunshot 2 : shot, kick (in sports) 3 : team (of horses, etc.) 4 **a** ~ : within range
tiroides *nmf* : thyroid (gland)
tirón *nm, pl* **-rones** 1 : pull, yank 2 **de un** ~ : in one go
tirotear *vt* : shoot at — **tiroteo** *nm* : shooting
tisis *nfs & pl* : tuberculosis
títere *nm* : puppet
titilar *vi* : flicker
titiritero, -ra *n* 1 : puppeteer 2 ACRÓBATA : acrobat
titubear *vi* 1 : hesitate 2 BALBUCEAR : stutter, stammer — **titubeante** *adj* : hesitant, faltering — **titubeo** *nm* : hesitation
titular *vt* : title, call — **titularse** *vr* 1 : be called, be titled 2 LICENCIARSE : receive a degree — ~ *adj* : titular, official — ~ *nm* : headline — ~ *nmf* : holder, incumbent — **título** *nm* 1 : title 2 : degree, qualification (in education)
tiza *nf* : chalk
tiznar *vt* : blacken (with soot, etc.) — **tizne** *nm* : soot
toalla *nf* : towel — **toallero** *nm* : towel rack
tobillo *nm* : ankle
tobogán *nm, pl* **-ganes** 1 : toboggan, sled 2 : slide (in a playground, etc.)
tocadiscos *nms & pl* : record player
tocado, -da *adj fam* : touched, not all there — **tocado** *nm* : headgear, headdress
tocador *nm* : dressing table
tocar {72} *vt* 1 : touch, feel 2 MENCIONAR : touch on, refer to 3 : play (a musical instrument) — *vi* 1 : knock, ring 2 ~ **en** : touch on, border on
tocayo, -ya *n* : namesake
tocino *nm* 1 : bacon 2 : salt pork (for cooking) — **tocineta** *nf Lat* : bacon
tocólogo, -ga *n* : obstetrician
tocón *nm, pl* **-cones** : stump (of a tree)

todavía adv 1 AÚN : still 2 (in comparisons) : even 3 ~ no : not yet

todo, -da adj 1 : all 2 CADA, CUALQUIER : every, each 3 a toda velocidad : at top speed 4 todo el mundo : everyone, everybody — ~ pron 1 : everything, all 2 todos, -das pl : everybody, everyone, all — **todo** nm : whole — **todopoderoso, -sa** adj : almighty, all-powerful

toga nf 1 : toga 2 : gown, robe (of a judge, etc.)

toldo nm : awning, canopy

tolerar vt : tolerate — **tolerancia** nf : tolerance — **tolerante** adj : tolerant

toma nf 1 : capture 2 DOSIS : dose 3 : take (in film) 4 ~ de corriente : wall socket, outlet 5 ~ y daca : give-and-take — **tomar** vt 1 : take 2 : have (food or drink) 3 CAPTURAR : capture, seize 4 ~ el sol : sunbathe 5 ~ tierra : land — vi : drink (alcohol) — **tomarse** vr 1 : take (time, etc.) 2 : drink, eat, have (food, drink)

tomate nm : tomato

tomillo nm : thyme

tomo nm : volume

ton nm sin ~ ni son : without rhyme or reason

tonada nf : tune

tonel nm : barrel, cask

tonelada nf : ton — **tonelaje** nm : tonnage

tónica nf 1 : tonic (water) 2 TENDENCIA : trend, tone — **tónico, -ca** adj : tonic — **tónico** nm : tonic (in medicine)

tono nm 1 : tone 2 : shade (of colors) 3 : key (in music)

tontería nf 1 : silly thing or remark 2 ESTUPIDEZ : foolishness 3 decir ~s : talk nonsense — **tonto, -ta** adj 1 : stupid, silly 2 a tontas y a locas : haphazardly — ~ n : fool, idiot

topacio nm : topaz

toparse vr ~ con : run into, come across

tope nm 1 : limit, end 2 or ~ de puerta : doorstop 3 Lat : bump — ~ adj : maximum

tópico, -ca adj 1 : topical, external 2 MANIDO : trite — **tópico** nm : cliché

topo nm : mole (animal)

toque nm 1 : (light) touch 2 : ringing, peal (of a bell) 3 ~ de queda : curfew 4 ~ de diana : reveille — **toquetear** vt : finger, handle

tórax nms & pl : thorax

torbellino nm : whirlwind

torcer {14} vt 1 : twist, bend 2 : turn (a corner) 3 : wring (out) — vi : turn —

torcerse vr 1 : twist, sprain 2 FRUSTRARSE : go wrong 3 DESVIARSE : go astray — **torcedura** nf 1 : twisting 2 ESGUINCE : sprain — **torcido, -da** adj : twisted, crooked

tordo, -da adj : dappled — **tordo** nm : thrush (bird)

torear vt 1 : fight (bulls) 2 ELUDIR : dodge, sidestep — vi : fight bulls — **toreo** nm : bullfighting — **torero, -ra** n : bullfighter

tormenta nf : storm — **tormento** nm 1 : torture 2 ANGUSTIA : torment, anguish — **tormentoso, -sa** adj : stormy

tornado nm : tornado

tornar vt CONVERTIR : render, turn — vi : go back, return — **tornarse** vr : become, turn into

torneo nm : tournament

tornillo nm : screw

torniquete nm 1 : turnstile 2 : tourniquet (in medicine)

torno nm 1 : winch 2 : (carpenter's) lathe 3 ~ de alfarero : (potter's) wheel 4 ~ de banco : vise 5 en ~ a : around, about

toro nm 1 : bull 2 ~s nmpl : bullfight

toronja nf : grapefruit

torpe adj 1 : clumsy, awkward 2 ESTÚPIDO : stupid, dull

torpedear vt : torpedo — **torpedo** nm : torpedo

torpeza nf 1 : clumsiness, awkwardness 2 ESTUPIDEZ : slowness, stupidity

torre nf 1 : tower 2 : turret (on a ship, etc.) 3 : rook, castle (in chess)

torrente nm 1 : torrent 2 ~ sanguíneo : bloodstream — **torrencial** adj : torrential

tórrido, -da adj : torrid

torsión nf, pl -siones : twisting

torta nf 1 : torte, cake 2 Lat : sandwich

tortazo nm fam : blow, wallop

tortícolis nfs & pl : stiff neck

tortilla nf 1 : tortilla 2 or ~ de huevo : omelet

tórtola nf : turtledove

tortuga nf 1 : turtle, tortoise 2 ~ de agua dulce : terrapin

tortuoso, -sa adj : tortuous, winding

tortura nf : torture — **torturar** vt : torture

tos nf 1 : cough 2 ~ ferina : whooping cough

tosco, -ca adj : rough, coarse

toser vi : cough

tosquedad nf : coarseness

tostar {19} vt 1 : toast 2 BRONCEAR : tan — **tostarse** vr : get a tan — **tostada**

nf **1** : piece of toast **2** *Lat* : tostada —
tostador *nm* : toaster
tostón *nm, pl* **-tones** *Lat* : fried plantain chip
total *adj & nm* : total — ~ *adv* : so,
after all — **totalidad** *nf* : whole — **to-**
talitario, -ria *adj & n* : totalitarian —
totalitarismo *nm* : totalitarianism —
totalizar {21} *vt* : total, add up to
tóxico, -ca *adj* : toxic, poisonous —
tóxico *nm* : poison — **toxicomanía** *nf*
: drug addiction — **toxicómano, -na** *n*
: drug addict — **toxina** *nf* : toxin
tozudo, -da *adj* : stubborn
traba *nf* : obstacle, hindrance
trabajar *vi* **1** : work **2** : act, perform (in
theater, etc.) — *vt* **1** : work (metal) **2**
: knead (dough) **3** MEJORAR : work on,
work at — **trabajador, -dora** *adj*
: hard-working — ~ *n* : worker —
trabajo *nm* **1** : work **2** EMPLEO : job **3**
TAREA : task **4** ESFUERZO : effort **5**
costar ~ : be difficult **6** ~ **en**
equipo : teamwork **7** ~**s** *nmpl*
: hardships, difficulties — **trabajoso,**
-sa *adj* : hard, laborious
trabalenguas *nms & pl* : tongue twister
trabar *vt* **1** : join, connect **2** OBSTAC-
ULIZAR : impede **3** : strike up (a conversation, etc.) **4** : thicken (sauces) —
trabarse *vr* **1** : jam ENREDARSE : become entangled **3 se le traba la**
lengua : he gets tongue-tied
trabucar {72} *vt* : mix up
tracción *nf* : traction
tractor *nm* : tractor
tradición *nf, pl* **-ciones** : tradition —
tradicional *adj* : traditional
traducir {61} *vt* : translate — **traduc-**
ción *nf, pl* **-ciones** : translation — **tra-**
ductor, -tora *n* : translator
traer {81} *vt* **1** : bring **2** CAUSAR : cause,
bring about **3** CONTENER : carry, have **4**
LLEVAR : wear — **traerse** *vr* **1** : bring
along **2 traérselas** : be difficult
traficar {72} *vi* ~ **en** : traffic in —
traficante *nmf* : dealer, trafficker —
tráfico *nm* **1** : trade (of merchandise)
2 : traffic (of vehicles)
tragaluz *nf, pl* **-luces** : skylight
tragar {52} *vt* **1** : swallow **2** *fam* : put up
with — *vi* : swallow — **tragarse** *vr* **1**
: swallow **2** ABSORBER : absorb, swallow up
tragedia *nf* : tragedy — **trágico, -ca** *adj*
: tragic
trago *nm* **1** : swallow, swig **2** *fam*
: drink, liquor — **tragón, -gona** *adj*
fam : greedy — ~ *nmf fam* : glutton
traicionar *vt* : betray — **traición** *nf, pl*

-ciones 1 : betrayal **2** : treason (in
law) — **traidor, -dora** *adj* : traitorous,
treacherous — ~ *n* : traitor
tráiler *nm* : trailer
traje *nm* **1** : dress, costume **2** : (man's)
suit **3** ~ **de baño** : bathing suit
trajinar *vi fam* : rush around — **trajín**
nm, pl **-jines** *fam* : hustle and bustle
trama *nf* **1** : plot **2** : weave, weft (of fabric) — **tramar** *vt* **1** : plot, plan **2**
: weave (fabric)
tramitar *vt* : negotiate — **trámite** *nm*
: procedure, step
tramo *nm* **1** : stretch, section **2** : flight
(of stairs)
trampa *nf* **1** : trap **2 hacer** ~**s** : cheat
— **trampear** *vt* : cheat
trampilla *nf* : trapdoor
trampolín *nm, pl* **-lines 1** : diving board
2 : trampoline (in a gymnasium, etc.)
tramposo, -sa *adj* : crooked, cheating
— ~ *n* : cheat, swindler
tranca *nf* **1** : cudgel, club **2** : bar (for a
door or window)
trance *nm* **1** : critical juncture **2** : (hypnotic) trance **3 en** ~ **de** : in the
process of
tranquilo, -la *adj* : calm, tranquil —
tranquilidad *nf* : tranquility, peace —
tranquilizante *nm* : tranquilizer —
tranquilizar {21} *vt* : calm, soothe —
tranquilizarse *vr* : calm down
trans- *see also* **tras-**
transacción *nf, pl* **-ciones** : transaction
transatlántico, -ca *adj* : transatlantic
— **transatlántico** *nm* : ocean liner
transbordador *nm* **1** : ferry **2** ~ **espa-**
cial : space shuttle — **transbordar** *vt*
: transfer — *vi* : change (of trains, etc.)
— **transbordo** *nm* **hacer** ~ : change
(trains, etc.)
transcribir {33} *vt* : transcribe —
transcripción *nf, pl* **-ciones** : tran-
scription
transcurrir *vi* : elapse, pass — **trans-**
curso *nm* : course, progression
transeúnte *nmf* : passerby
transferir {76} *vt* : transfer — **transfe-**
rencia *nf* : transfer, transference
transformar *vt* **1** : transform, change **2**
CONVERTIR : convert — **transfor-**
marse *vr* : be transformed — **trans-**
formación *nf, pl* **-ciones** : transfor-
mation — **transformador** *nm*
: transformer
transfusión *nf, pl* **-siones** : transfusion
transgredir {1} *vt* : transgress —
transgresión *nf* : transgression
transición *nf, pl* **-ciones** : transition
transido, -da *adj* : overcome, stricken

transigir {35} *vi* : give in, compromise
transistor *nm* : transistor
transitar *vi* : go, travel — **transitable** *adj* : passable
transitivo, -va *adj* : transitive
tránsito *nm* 1 : transit 2 TRÁFICO : traffic 3 **hora de máximo ~** : rush hour — **transitorio, -ria** *adj* : transitory
transmitir *vt* 1 : transmit 2 : broadcast (radio, TV, etc.) 3 CEDER : pass on — **transmisión** *nf, pl* **-siones** 1 : broadcast 2 TRANSFERENCIA : transfer 3 : transmission (of an automobile) — **transmisor** *nm* : transmitter
transparentarse *vr* : be transparent — **transparente** *adj* : transparent
transpirar *vi* : perspire, sweat — **transpiración** *nf, pl* **-ciones** : perspiration, sweat
transponer {60} *vt* : transpose, move — **transponerse** *vr* 1 : set (of the sun, etc.) 2 DORMITAR : doze off
transportar *vt* : transport, carry — **transportarse** *vr* : get carried away — **transporte** *nm* : transport, transportation
transversal *adj* **corte ~** : cross section
tranvía *nm* : streetcar, trolley
trapear *vt Lat* : mop
trapecio *nm* : trapeze
trapisonda *nf* : scheme, plot
trapo *nm* 1 : cloth, rag 2 **~s** *nmpl fam* : clothes
tráquea *nf* : trachea, windpipe
traquetear *vi* : rattle around, shake — **traqueteo** *nm* : rattling
tras *prep* 1 DESPUÉS DE : after 2 DETRÁS DE : behind
tras- *see also* **trans-**
trascender {56} *vi* 1 : leak out, become known 2 EXTENDERSE : spread 3 **~ de** : transcend — **trascendencia** *nf* : importance — **trascendental** *adj* 1 : transcendental 2 IMPORTANTE : important
trasegar *vt* : move around
trasero, -ra *adj* : rear, back — **trasero** *nm* : buttocks *pl*
trasfondo *nm* 1 : background 2 : undercurrent (of suspicion, etc.)
trasladar *vt* 1 : transfer, move 2 POSPONER : postpone — **trasladarse** *vr* : move, relocate — **traslado** *nm* 1 : transfer, move 2 COPIA : copy
traslapar *vt* : overlap — **traslaparse** *vr* : overlap
traslucirse {45} *vr* 1 : be translucent 2 REVELARSE : be revealed — **traslúcido, -da** : translucent

trasnochar *vi* : stay up all night
traspasar *vt* 1 : pierce, go through 2 EXCEDER : go beyond 3 ATRAVESAR : cross, go across 4 : transfer (a business, etc.) — **traspaso** *nm* : transfer, sale
traspié *nm* 1 : stumble, trip 2 ERROR : blunder
trasplantar *vt* : transplant — **trasplante** *nm* : transplant
trasquilar *vt* : shear
traste *nm* 1 : fret (on a guitar, etc.) 2 *Lat* : (kitchen) utensil 3 **dar al ~ con** : ruin 4 **irse al ~** : fall through
trastos *nmpl fam* : pieces of junk, stuff
trastornar *vt* 1 : disturb, disrupt 2 VOLVER LOCO : drive crazy — **trastornarse** *vr* : go crazy — **trastornado, -da** *adj* : disturbed, deranged — **trastorno** *nm* 1 : disturbance, disruption 2 : (medical or psychological) disorder
trastrocar *vt* : change, switch around
tratable *adj* : friendly, sociable
tratar *vi* 1 **~ con** : deal with 2 **~ de** : try to 3 **~ de** *or* **~ sobre** : be about, concern 4 **~ en** : deal in — *vt* 1 : treat 2 MANEJAR : deal with, handle — **tratarse** *vr* **~ de** : be about, concern — **tratado** *nm* 1 : treatise 2 CONVENIO : treaty — **tratamiento** *nm* : treatment — **trato** *nm* 1 : treatment 2 ACUERDO : deal, agreement 3 **~s** *nmpl* : dealings
trauma *nm* : trauma — **traumático, -ca** *adj* : traumatic
través *nm* 1 **a ~ de** : across, through 2 **de ~** : sideways
travesaño *nm* : crosspiece
travesía *nf* : voyage, crossing (of the sea)
travesura *nf* 1 : prank 2 **~s** *nfpl* : mischief — **travieso, -sa** *adj* : mischievous, naughty
trayecto *nm* 1 : trajectory, path 2 VIAJE : journey 3 RUTA : route — **trayectoria** *nf* : path, trajectory
traza *nf* 1 : design, plan 2 ASPECTO : appearance — **trazado** *nm* 1 : outline, sketch 2 DISEÑO : plan, layout — **trazar** {21} *vt* 1 : trace, outline 2 : draw up (a plan, etc.) — **trazo** *nm* : stroke, line
trébol *nm* 1 : clover, shamrock 2 **~es** *nmpl* : clubs (in playing cards)
trece *adj & nm* : thirteen — **treceavo, -va** *adj* : thirteenth — **treceavo** *nm* : thirteenth (fraction)
trecho *nm* 1 : stretch, period 2 DISTANCIA : distance 3 **de ~ a ~** : at intervals

tregua *nf* **1** : truce **2 sin** ~ : without respite

treinta *adj & nm* : thirty — **treintavo, -va** *adj* : thirtieth — **treintavo** *nm* : thirtieth (fraction)

tremendo, -da *adj* : tremendous, enormous

trementina *nf* : turpentine

trémulo, -la *adj* : trembling, flickering

tren *nm* **1** : train **2** ~ **de aterrizaje** : landing gear

trenza *nf* : braid, pigtail — **trenzar** {21} *vt* : braid — **trenzarse** *vr Lat* : get involved

trepar *vi* **1** : climb **2** : creep, spread (of a plant) — **treparse** *vr* : climb (up) — **trepador, -dora** *adj* : climbing — **trepadora** *nf* **1** : climbing plant **2** *fam* : social climber

trepidar *vi* : shake, vibrate

tres *adj & nm* : three — **trescientos, -tas** *adj* : three hundred — **trescientos** *nms & pl* : three hundred

treta *nf* : trick

triángulo *nm* : triangle — **triangular** *adj* : triangular

tribu *nf* : tribe — **tribal** *adj* : tribal

tribulación *nf, pl* **-ciones** : tribulation

tribuna *nf* **1** : dais, platform **2** : grandstand, bleachers *pl* (in a stadium)

tribunal *nm* : court, tribunal

tributar *vt* : pay, render — *vi* : pay taxes — **tributo** *nm* **1** : tribute **2** IMPUESTO : tax

triciclo *nm* : tricycle

tricolor *adj* : tricolored

tridimensional *adj* : three-dimensional

trigésimo, -ma *adj & n* : thirtieth

trigo *nm* : wheat

trigonometría *nf* : trigonometry

trillado, -da *adj* : trite

trillar *vt* : thresh — **trilladora** *nf* : threshing machine

trillizo, -za *n* : triplet

trilogía *nf* : trilogy

trimestral *adj* : quarterly

trinar *vi* : warble

trinchar *vt* : carve

trinchera *nf* **1** : trench, ditch **2** IMPERMEABLE : trench coat

trineo *nm* : sled, sleigh

trinidad *nf* : trinity

trino *nm* : trill, warble

trío *nm* : trio

tripa *nf* **1** : gut, intestine **2** ~**s** *nfpl fam* : belly, tummy

triple *adj & nm* : triple — **triplicar** {72} *vt* : triple

trípode *nm* : tripod

tripular *vt* : man — **tripulación** *nf, pl* **-ciones** : crew — **tripulante** *nmf* : crew member

tris *nm* **estar en un** ~ **de** : be within an inch of

triste *adj* **1** : sad **2** SOMBRÍO : dismal, gloomy **3** MISERABLE : sorry, miserable — **tristeza** *nf* : sadness, grief

tritón *nm, pl* **-tones** : newt

triturar *vt* : crush, grind

triunfar *vi* : triumph, win — **triunfal** *adj* : triumphal — **triunfante** *adj* : triumphant — **triunfo** *nm* : triumph, victory

trivial *adj* : trivial

triza *nf* **1** : shred, bit **2 hacer** ~**s** : smash to pieces

trocar {82} *vt* **1** CONVERTIR : change **2** INTERCAMBIAR : exchange

trocha *nf* : path, trail

trofeo *nm* : trophy

trombón *nm, pl* **-bones 1** : trombone **2** : trombonist (musician)

trombosis *nf* : thrombosis

trompa *nf* **1** : trunk (of an elephant), snout **2** : horn (musical instrument) **3** : tube (in anatomy)

trompeta *nf* : trumpet — **trompetista** *nmf* : trumpet player

trompo *nm* : top (toy)

tronada *nf* : thunderstorm — **tronar** {19} *vi* **1** : thunder, rage — *vt Lat fam* : shoot — *v impers* : thunder

tronchar *vt* **1** : snap **2** TRUNCAR : cut short

tronco *nm* **1** : trunk (of a tree) **2** : torso (of a person) **3 dormir como un** ~ : sleep like a log

trono *nm* : throne

tropa *nf* : troops *pl*, soldiers *pl*

tropel *nm* : mob

tropezar {29} *vi* **1** : trip, stumble **2** ~ **con** : come up against, run into — **tropezón** *nm, pl* **-zones 1** : stumble **2** EQUIVOCACIÓN : mistake, slip

trópico *nm* : tropic — **tropical** *adj* : tropical

tropiezo *nm* **1** CONTRATIEMPO : snag, setback **2** EQUIVOCACIÓN : mistake, slip

trotar *vi* **1** : trot **2** *fam* : rush about — **trote** *nm* **1** : trot **2** *fam* : rush, bustle **3 al** ~ : at a trot, quickly

trozo *nm* : piece, bit, chunk

trucha *nf* : trout

truco *nm* **1** : knack **2** ARDID : trick

trueno *nm* : thunder

trueque *nm* : barter, exchange

trufa *nf* : truffle

truncar {72} *vt* **1** : cut short **2** : thwart, spoil (plans, etc.)

tu *adj* : your
tú *pron* : you
tuba *nf* : tuba
tuberculosis *nf* : tuberculosis
tubo *nm* 1 : tube, pipe 2 ~ **de escape** : exhaust pipe (of a vehicle) 3 ~ **de desagüe** : drainpipe — **tubería** *nf* : pipes *pl*, tubing
tuerca *nf* : nut (for a screw)
tuerto, -ta *adj* : one-eyed, blind in one eye
tuétano *nm* : marrow
tufo *nm* 1 : vapor 2 *fam* : stench, stink
tugurio *nm* : hovel
tulipán *nm, pl* **-panes** : tulip
tullido, -da *adj* : crippled, paralyzed
tumba *nf* : tomb, grave
tumbar *vt* : knock down, knock over — **tumbarse** *vr* : lie down — **tumbo** *nm* **dar ~s** : jolt, bump around
tumor *nm* : tumor
tumulto *nm* 1 : commotion, tumult 2 MOTÍN : riot — **tumultuoso, -sa** *adj* : tumultuous
tuna *nf* : prickly pear
túnel *nm* : tunnel
túnica *nf* : tunic
tupé *nm* : toupee
tupido, -da *adj* : dense, thick
turba *nf* 1 : peat 2 MUCHEDUMBRE : mob, throng

turbación *nf, pl* **-ciones** 1 : disturbance 2 CONFUSIÓN : confusion
turbante *nm* : turban
turbar *vt* 1 : disturb, upset 2 CONFUNDIR : confuse, bewilder
turbina *nf* : turbine
turbio, -bia *adj* 1 : cloudy, murky 2 : blurred (of vision, etc.) — **turbión** *nm, pl* **-biones** : squall
turbulencia *nf* : turbulence — **turbulento, -ta** *adj* : turbulent
turco, -ca *adj* : Turkish — **turco** *nm* : Turkish (language)
turista *nmf* : tourist — **turismo** *nm* : tourism, tourist industry — **turístico, -ca** *adj* : tourist, travel
turnarse *vr* : take turns, alternate — **turno** *nm* 1 : turn 2 ~ **de noche** : night shift
turquesa *nf* : turquoise
turrón *nm, pl* **-rrones** : nougat
tutear *vt* : address as *tú*
tutela *nf* 1 : guardianship (in law) 2 **bajo la ~ de** : under the protection of
tuteo *nm* : addressing as *tú*
tutor, -tora *n* 1 : guardian 2 : tutor (in education)
tuyo, -ya *adj* : yours, of yours — ~ *pron* 1 **el tuyo, la tuya, lo tuyo, los tuyos, las tuyas** : yours 2 **los tuyos** : your family, your friends

U

u¹ *nf* : u, 22d letter of the Spanish alphabet
u² *conj* (*used before words beginning with o- or ho-*) : or
uapití *nm* : American elk, wapiti
ubicar {72} *vt Lat* 1 COLOCAR : place, position 2 LOCALIZAR : find — **ubicarse** *vr* : be located
ubre *nf* : udder
Ud., Uds. → **usted**
ufanarse *vr* ~ **de** : boast about — **ufano, -na** *adj* 1 : proud 2 ENGREÍDO : self-satisfied
ujier *nm* : usher
úlcera *nf* : ulcer
ulterior *adj* : later, subsequent — **ulteriormente** *adv* : subsequently
últimamente *adv* : lately, recently
ultimar *vt* 1 : complete, finish 2 *Lat* : kill — **ultimátum** *nm, pl* **-tums** : ultimatum
último, -ma *adj* 1 : last 2 : latest, most

recent (in time) 3 : farthest (in space) 4 **por último** : finally
ultrajar *vt* : outrage, insult — **ultraje** *nm* : outrage, insult
ultramar *nm* **de ~** *or* **en ~** : overseas — **ultramarino, -na** *adj* : overseas — **ultramarinos** *nmpl* **tienda de ~** : grocery store
ultranza: a ~ *adv phr* : to the extreme — **a ~** *adj phr* : out-and-out, complete
ultrasonido *nm* : ultrasound
ultravioleta *adj* : ultraviolet
ulular *vi* 1 : hoot (of an owl) 2 : howl (of a wolf, the wind, etc.) — **ululato** *nm* : hoot (of an owl)
umbilical *adj* : umbilical
umbral *nm* : threshold
un, una *art, mpl* **unos** 1 : a, an 2 **unos** *or* **unas** *pl* : some, a few 3 **unos** *or* **unas** *pl* : about, approximately — **un** *adj* → **uno**

unánime *adj* : unanimous — **unanimidad** *nf* : unanimity
uncir {83} *vt* : yoke
undécimo, -ma *adj & n* : eleventh
ungir {35} *vt* : anoint — **ungüento** *nm* : ointment
único, -ca *adj* **1** : only, sole **2** EXCEPCIONAL : unique — **~** *n* : only one — **únicamente** *adv* : only
unicornio *nm* : unicorn
unidad *nf* **1** : unit **2** ARMONÍA : unity — **unido, -da** *adj* **1** : united **2** : close (of friends, etc.)
unificar {72} *vt* : unify — **unificación** *nf, pl* **-ciones** : unification
uniformar *vt* **1** : standardize **2** : put into uniform — **uniformado, -da** *adj* : uniformed — **uniforme** *adj & nm* : uniform — **uniformidad** *nf* : uniformity
unilateral *adj* : unilateral
unir *vt* **1** : unite, join **2** COMBINAR : combine, mix together — **unirse** *vr* **1** : join together **2** ~ **a** : join — **unión** *nf, pl* **uniones 1** : union **2** JUNTURA : joint, coupling
unísono *nm* **al ~** : in unison
unitario, -ria *adj* : unitary
universal *adj* : universal
universidad *nf* : university, college — **universitario, -ria** *adj* : university, college
universo *nm* : universe
uno, una (**un** *before masculine singular nouns*) *adj* : one — **~** *pron* **1** : one **2 unos, unas** *pl* : some **3 uno(s) a otro(s)** : one another, each other **4 uno y otro** : both — **uno** *nm* : one (number)
untar *vt* **1** : smear, grease **2** *fam* : bribe — **untuoso, -sa** *adj* : greasy, sticky
uña *nf* **1** : nail, fingernail **2** : claw (of a cat, etc.), hoof (of a horse, etc.)
uranio *nm* : uranium

Urano *nm* : Uranus
urbano, -na *adj* : urban, city — **urbanidad** *nf* : politeness, courtesy — **urbanización** *nf, pl* **-ciones** : housing development — **urbanizar** *vt* : develop, urbanize — **urbe** *nf* : large city
urdir *vt* **1** : warp **2** PLANEAR : plot — **urdimbre** *nf* : warp (of a fabric)
urgir {35} *v impers* : be urgent, be pressing — **urgencia** *nf* **1** : urgency **2** EMERGENCIA : emergency — **urgente** *adj* : urgent
urinario, -ria *adj* : urinary — **urinario** *nm* : urinal (place)
urna *nf* **1** : urn **2** : ballot box (for voting)
urraca *nf* : magpie
uruguayo, -ya *adj* : Uruguayan
usar *vt* **1** : use **2** LLEVAR : wear — **usarse 1** EMPLEARSE : be used **2** : be worn, be in fashion — **usado, -da** *adj* **1** : used **2** GASTADO : worn, worn-out — **usanza** *nf* : custom, usage — **uso** *nm* **1** : use **2** DESGASTE : wear and tear **3** USANZA : custom, usage
usted *pron* **1** (*used in formal address; often written as* **Ud.** *or* **Vd.**) : you **2** ~**es** *pl* (*often written as* **Uds.** *or* **Vds.**) : you (all)
usual *adj* : usual
usuario, -ria *n* : user
usura *nf* : usury — **usurero, -ra** *n* : usurer
usurpar *vt* : usurp
utensilio *nm* : utensil, tool
útero *nm* : uterus, womb
utilizar {21} *vt* : use, utilize — **útil** *adj* : useful — **útiles** *nmpl* : implements, tools — **utilidad** *nf* : utility, usefulness — **utilitario, -ria** *adj* : utilitarian — **utilización** *nf, pl* **-ciones** : utilization, use
uva *nf* : grape

V

v *nf* : v, 23d letter of the Spanish alphabet
va → **ir**
vaca *nf* : cow
vacaciones *nfpl* **1** : vacation **2 estar de** ~ : be on vacation **3 irse de** ~ : go on vacation
vacante *adj* : vacant — **~** *nf* : vacancy
vaciar {85} *vt* **1** : empty (out) **2** AHUECAR : hollow out **3** : cast, mold (a statue, etc.)

vacilar *vi* **1** : hesitate, waver **2** : flicker (of light) **3** TAMBALEARSE : be unsteady, wobble **4** *fam* : joke, fool around — **vacilación** *nf, pl* **-ciones** : hesitation — **vacilante** *adj* **1** : hesitant **2** OSCILANTE : unsteady
vacío, -cía *adj* : empty — **vacío** *nm* **1** : void **2** : vacuum (in physics) **3** HUECO : space, gap
vacuna *nf* : vaccine — **vacunación** *nf,*

pl **-ciones** : vaccination — **vacunar** *vt* : vaccinate

vacuno, -na *adj* : bovine

vadear *vt* : ford — **vado** *nm* : ford

vagabundear *vi* : wander — **vagabundo, -da** *adj* **1** : vagrant **2** : stray (of a dog, etc.) — ~ *n* : hobo, bum — **vagancia** *nf* **1** : vagrancy **2** PEREZA : laziness, idleness — **vagar** {52} *vi* : roam, wander

vagina *nf* : vagina

vago, -ga *adj* **1** : vague **2** PEREZOSO : lazy, idle — ~ *n* : idler, loafer

vagón *nm*, *pl* **-gones** : car (of a train)

vahído *nm* : dizzy spell

vaho *nm* **1** : breath **2** VAPOR : vapor, steam

vaina *nf* **1** : sheath, scabbard **2** : pod (in botany) **3** *Lat fam* : bother, pain

vainilla *nf* : vanilla

vaivén *nm*, *pl* **-venes 1** : swinging, swaying **2** : coming and going (of people, etc.) **3 vaivenes** *nmpl* : ups and downs

vajilla *nf* : dishes *pl*

vale *nm* **1** : voucher **2** PAGARÉ : IOU — **valedero, -ra** *adj* : valid

valentía *nf* : courage, bravery

valer {84} *vt* **1** : be worth **2** COSTAR : cost **3** GANAR : gain, earn **4** EQUIVALER A : be equal to — *vi* **1** : have value, cost **2** SER VÁLIDO : be valid, count **3** SERVIR : be of use **4 hacerse** ~ : assert oneself **5 más vale** : it's better — **valerse** *vr* **1** ~ **de** : take advantage of **2** ~ **solo** *or* ~ **por sí mismo** : look after oneself

valeroso, -sa *adj* : courageous

valga, etc. → **valer**

valía *nf* : worth

validar *vt* : validate — **validez** *nf* : validity — **válido, -da** *adj* : valid

valiente *adj* **1** : brave **2** (*used ironically*) : fine, great

valija *nf* : case, valise

valioso, -sa *adj* : valuable

valla *nf* **1** : fence **2** : hurdle (in sports) — **vallar** *vt* : put a fence around

valle *nm* : valley

valor *nm* **1** : value, worth **2** VALENTÍA : courage, valor **3 objetos de** ~ : valuables **4 sin** ~ : worthless **5** ~**es** *nmpl* : values, principles **6** ~**es** *nmpl* : securities, bonds — **valoración** *nf*, *pl* **-ciones** : valuation — **valorar** *vt* : evaluate, assess

vals *nm* : waltz

válvula *nf* : valve

vamos → **ir**

vampiro *nm* : vampire

van → **ir**

vanagloriarse *vr* : boast, brag

vándalo *nm* : vandal — **vandalismo** : vandalism

vanguardia *nf* **1** : vanguard **2** : avant-garde (in art, music, etc.) **3 a la** ~ : at/in the forefront

vanidad *nf* : vanity — **vanidoso, -sa** *adj* : vain, conceited

vano, -na *adj* **1** INÚTIL : vain, useless **2** SUPERFICIAL : empty, hollow **3 en vano** : in vain

vapor *nm* **1** : steam, vapor **2 al** ~ : steamed — **vaporizador** *nm* : vaporizer — **vaporizar** {21} *vt* : vaporize

vaquero, -ra *n* : cowboy *m*, cowgirl *f* — **vaqueros** *nmpl* : jeans

vara *nf* **1** : stick, rod **2** : staff (of office)

varado, -da *adj* : stranded

variar {85} *vt* **1** : vary **2** CAMBIAR : change, alter — *vi* : vary, change — **variable** *adj* & *nf* : variable — **variación** *nf*, *pl* **-ciones** : variation — **variado, -da** *adj* : varied — **variante** *nf* : variant

varicela *nf* : chicken pox

varicoso, -sa *adj* : varicose

variedad *nf* : variety

varilla *nf* : rod, stick

vario, -ria *adj* **1** : varied **2** ~**s** *pl* : several

varita *nf* : wand

variz *nf*, *pl* **-rices** *or* **várices** : varicose vein

varón *nm*, *pl* **-rones 1** : man, male **2** NIÑO : boy — **varonil** *adj* : manly

vas → **ir**

vasco, -ca *adj* : Basque — **vasco** *nm* : Basque (language)

vasija *nf* : container, vessel

vaso *nm* **1** : glass **2** : vessel (in anatomy)

vástago *nm* **1** : offspring, descendent **2** BROTE : shoot **3** VARILLA : rod

vasto, -ta *adj* : vast

vaticinar *vt* : prophesy, predict — **vaticinio** *nm* : prophecy

vatio *nm* : watt

vaya, etc. → **ir**

Vd., Vds. → **usted**

ve, etc. → **ir, ver**

vecinal *adj* : local

vecino, -na *n* **1** : neighbor **2** HABITANTE : resident, inhabitant — ~ *adj* : neighboring — **vecindad** *nf* : neighborhood, vicinity — **vecindario** *nm* **1** : neighborhood **2** VECINOS : community, residents *pl*

vedar *vt* : prohibit — **veda** *nf* **1** : prohibition, ban **2** : closed season (for hunting and fishing) — **vedado** *nm* : preserve (for game, etc.)

vega *nf* : fertile lowland

vegetal *nm* : vegetable, plant — ~ *adj* : vegetable — **vegetación** *nf, pl* **-ciones** : vegetation — **vegetar** *vi* : vegetate — **vegetariano, -na** *adj & n* : vegetarian

vehemente *adj* : vehement

vehículo *nm* : vehicle

veinte *adj & nm* : twenty — **veinteavo, -va** *adj* : twentieth — **veinteavo** *nm* : twentieth — **veintena** *nf* : group of twenty, score

vejar *vt* : mistreat, humiliate — **vejación** *nf, pl* **-ciones** : humiliation

vejez *nf* : old age

vejiga *nf* 1 : bladder 2 AMPOLLA : blister

vela *nf* 1 : candle 2 : sail (of a ship) 3 VIGILIA : vigil 4 **pasar la noche en** ~ : have a sleepless night

velada *nf* : evening (party)

velar *vt* 1 : hold a wake over 2 CUIDAR : watch over 3 : blur (a photograph) 4 OCULTAR : veil, mask — *vi* 1 : stay awake 2 ~ **por** : watch over — **velado, -da** *adj* 1 : veiled, hidden 2 : blurred (of a photograph)

velero *nm* : sailing ship

veleta *nf* : weather vane

vello *nm* 1 : body hair 2 PELUSA : down, fuzz — **vellón** *nm, pl* **-llones** : fleece — **velloso, -sa** *adj* : downy, fluffy — **velludo, -da** *adj* : hairy

velo *nm* : veil

veloz *adj, pl* **-loces** : fast, quick — **velocidad** *nf* 1 : speed, velocity 2 MARCHA : gear (of an automobile) — **velocímetro** *nm* : speedometer

vena *nf* 1 : vein 2 : grain (of wood) 3 DISPOSICIÓN : mood 4 **tener** ~ **de** : have a talent for

venado *nm* 1 : deer 2 : venison (in cooking)

vencer {86} *vt* 1 : beat, defeat 2 SUPERAR : overcome — *vi* 1 : win 2 CADUCAR : expire — **vencerse** *vr* : collapse, give way — **vencedor, -dora** *adj* : winning — ~ *n* : winner — **vencido, -da** *adj* 1 : beaten, defeated 2 CADUCADO : expired 3 : due, payable (in finance) 4 **darse por** ~ : give up — **vencimiento** *nm* 1 : expiration 2 : maturity (of a loan)

venda *nf* : bandage — **vendaje** *nm* : bandage, dressing — **vendar** *vt* 1 : bandage 2 ~ **los ojos** : blindfold

vendaval *nm* : gale

vender *vt* : sell — **venderse** *vr* 1 : be sold 2 **se vende** : for sale — **vendedor, -dora** *n* 1 : seller 2 : salesman *m*, saleswoman *f* (in a store)

vendimia *nf* : grape harvest

vendrá, etc. → **venir**

veneno *nm* 1 : poison 2 : venom (of a snake, etc.) — **venenoso, -sa** *adj* : poisonous

venerar *vt* : venerate, revere — **venerable** *adj* : venerable — **veneración** *nf, pl* **-ciones** : veneration, reverence

venéreo, -rea *adj* : venereal

venezolano, -na *adj* : Venezuelan

venga → **venir**

vengar {52} *vt* : avenge — **vengarse** *vr* : get even, take revenge — **venganza** *nf* : vengeance, revenge — **vengativo, -va** *adj* : vindictive, vengeful

venia *nf* 1 : permission 2 : pardon (in law)

venial *adj* : venial, petty

venir {87} *vi* 1 : come 2 LLEGAR : arrive 3 HALLARSE : be, appear 4 QUEDAR : fit 5 **que viene** : coming, next 6 ~ **a ser** : turn out to be 7 ~ **bien** : be suitable — **venirse** *vr* 1 : come 2 ~ **abajo** : fall apart, collapse — **venida** *nf* 1 : arrival, coming 2 REGRESO : return — **venidero, -ra** *adj* : coming

venta *nf* 1 : sale, selling 2 **en** ~ : for sale

ventaja *nf* : advantage — **ventajoso, -sa** *adj* : advantageous

ventana *nf* 1 : window 2 ~ **de la nariz** : nostril — **ventanilla** *nf* 1 : window (of a vehicle or airplane) 2 : ticket window, box office (of a theater, etc.)

ventilar *vt* : ventilate, air (out) — **ventilación** *nf, pl* **-ciones** : ventilation — **ventilador** *nm* : fan, ventilator

ventisca *nf* : blizzard — **ventisquero** *nm* : snowdrift

ventoso, -sa *adj* : windy — **ventosidad** *nf* : wind, flatulence

ventrílocuo, -cua *n* : ventriloquist

ventura *nf* 1 : fortune, luck 2 SATISFACCIÓN : happiness 3 **a la** ~ : at random — **venturoso, -sa** *adj* : fortunate, happy

ver {88} *vt* 1 : see 2 : watch (television, etc.) — *vi* 1 : see 2 **a** ~ *or* **vamos a** ~ : let's see 3 **no tener nada que** ~ **con** : have nothing to do with 4 **ya veremos** : we'll see — **verse** *vr* 1 : see oneself 2 HALLARSE : find oneself 3 ENCONTRARSE : see each other, meet

vera *nf* 1 : side, edge 2 : bank (of a river)

veracidad *nf* : truthfulness

verano *nm* : summer — **veraneante** *nmf* : summer vacationer — **veranear**

vi : spend the summer — **veraniego, -ga** *adj* : summer

veras *nfpl* **de ~** : really

veraz *adj, pl* **-races** : truthful

verbal *adj* : verbal

verbena *nf* : festival, fair

verbo *nm* : verb — **verboso, -sa** *adj* : verbose

verdad *nf* **1** : truth **2 de ~** : really, truly **3 ¿verdad?** : right?, isn't that so? — **verdaderamente** *adv* : really, truly — **verdadero, -dera** *adj* : true, real

verde *adj* **1** : green **2** : dirty, risqué (of a joke, etc.) — **~** *nm* : green — **verdor** *nm* : greenness

verdugo *nm* **1** : executioner, hangman **2** : cruel person, tyrant

verdura *nf* : vegetable(s), green(s)

vereda *nf* **1** : path, trail **2** *Lat* : sidewalk

veredicto *nm* : verdict

vergüenza *nf* **1** : shame **2** TIMIDEZ : bashfulness, shyness — **vergonzoso, -sa** *adj* **1** : shameful **2** TÍMIDO : bashful, shy

verídico, -ca *adj* : true, truthful

verificar {72} *vt* **1** : verify, confirm **2** EXAMINAR : test, check out — **verificarse** *vr* **1** : take place **2** : come true (of a prophecy, etc.) — **verificación** *nf, pl* **-ciones** : verification

verja *nf* **1** : (iron) gate **2** : rails *pl* (of a fence) **3** ENREJADO : grating, grille

vermut *nm, pl* **-muts** : vermouth

vernáculo, -la *adj* : vernacular

verosímil *adj* **1** : probable, likely **2** CREÍBLE : credible

verraco *nm* : boar

verruga *nf* : wart

versar *vi* **~ sobre** : deal with, be about — **versado, -da** *adj* **~ en** : versed in

versátil *adj* **1** : versatile **2** VOLUBLE : fickle

versión *nf, pl* **-siones 1** : version **2** TRADUCCIÓN : translation

verso *nm* **1** : poem, verse **2** : line (of poetry)

vértebra *nf* : vertebra

verter {56} *vt* **1** : pour (out) **2** DERRAMAR : spill **3** TIRAR : dump — *vi* : flow — **vertedero** *nm* **1** : dump, landfill **2** DESAGÜE : drain, outlet

vertical *adj* & *nf* : vertical

vértice *nm* : vertex, apex

vertiente *nf* : slope

vértigo *nm* : vertigo, dizziness — **vertiginoso, -sa** *adj* : dizzy

vesícula *nf* **1** : blister **2 ~ biliar** : gallbladder

vestíbulo *nm* : vestibule, hall, foyer

vestido *nm* **1** : dress **2** ROPA : clothing, clothes *pl*

vestigio *nm* : vestige, trace

vestir {54} *vt* **1** : dress, clothe **2** LLEVAR : wear — *vi* : dress — **vestirse** *vr* : get dressed — **vestimenta** *nf* : clothing — **vestuario** *nm* **1** : wardrobe, clothes *pl* **2** : dressing room (in a theater), locker room (in sports)

veta *nf* **1** : vein, seam **2** : grain (of wood)

vetar *vt* : veto

veteado, -da *adj* : streaked, veined

veterano, -na *adj* & *n* : veteran

veterinaria *nf* : veterinary medicine — **veterinario, -ria** *adj* : veterinary — **~** *n* : veterinarian

veto *nm* : veto

vetusto, -ta *adj* : ancient

vez *nf, pl* **veces 1** : time **2** TURNO : turn **3 a la ~** : at the same time **4 a veces** : sometimes **5 de una ~** : all at once **6 de una ~ para siempre** : once and for all **7 de ~ en cuando** : from time to time **8 dos veces** : twice **9 en ~ de** : instead of **10 una ~** : once

vía *nf* **1** : way, road, route **2** MEDIO : means **3** : track, line (of a railroad) **4** : (anatomical) tract **5 en ~ de** : in the process of — **~** *prep* : via

viable *adj* : viable, feasible — **viabilidad** *nf* : viability

viaducto *nm* : viaduct

viajar *vi* : travel — **viajante** *nmf* : traveling salesperson — **viaje** *nm* : trip, journey — **viajero, -ra** *adj* : traveling — **~** *n* **1** : traveler **2** PASAJERO : passenger

vial *adj* : road, traffic

víbora *nf* : viper

vibrar *vi* : vibrate — **vibración** *nf, pl* **-ciones** : vibration — **vibrante** *adj* : vibrant

vicario, -ria *n* : vicar

vicepresidente, -ta *n* : vice president

viceversa *adv* : vice versa

vicio *nm* **1** : vice **2** MALA COSTUMBRE : bad habit **3** DEFECTO : defect — **viciado, -da** *adj* **1** : corrupt **2** : stuffy, stale (of air, etc.) — **viciar** *vt* **1** : corrupt **2** ESTROPEAR : spoil, pollute — **vicioso, -sa** *adj* : depraved, corrupt

vicisitud *nf* : vicissitude

víctima *nf* : victim

victoria *nf* : victory — **victorioso, -sa** *adj* : victorious

vid *nf* : vine, grapevine

vida *nf* **1** : life **2** DURACIÓN : lifetime **3 de por ~** : for life **4 estar con ~** : be alive

video or **vídeo** nm 1 : video 2 : VCR, videocassette recorder
vidrio nm : glass — **vidriado** nm : glaze — **vidriar** vt : glaze — **vidriera** nf 1 : stained-glass window 2 : glass door 3 Lat : shopwindow — **vidrioso, -sa** adj 1 : delicate (of a subject, etc.) 2 **ojos vidriosos** : glassy eyes
vieira nf : scallop
viejo, -ja adj : old — ~ n 1 : old man m, old woman f 2 **hacerse** ~ : get old
viene, etc. → venir
viento nm : wind
vientre nm 1 : abdomen, belly 2 MATRIZ : womb 3 INTESTINO : bowels pl
viernes nms & pl 1 : Friday 2 **Viernes Santo** : Good Friday
vietnamita adj & nm : Vietnamese
viga nf : beam, girder
vigencia nf 1 : validity 2 **entrar en** ~ : go into effect — **vigente** adj : valid, in force
vigésimo, -ma adj & n : twentieth
vigía nmf : lookout
vigilar vt 1 : look after, watch over — vi : keep watch — **vigilancia** nf 1 : vigilance 2 **bajo** ~ : under surveillance — **vigilante** adj : vigilant — ~ nmf : watchman, guard — **vigilia** nf 1 : wakefulness 2 : vigil (in religion)
vigor nm 1 : vigor 2 **entrar en** ~ : go into effect — **vigorizante** adj : invigorating — **vigoroso, -sa** adj : vigorous
VIH nm : HIV
vil adj : vile, despicable — **vileza** nf 1 : vileness 2 : despicable act — **vilipendiar** vt : revile
villa nf 1 : town, village 2 : villa (house)
villancico nm : (Christmas) carol
villano, -na n : villain
vilo : en ~ : suspended, in the air
vinagre nm : vinegar — **vinagrera** nf : cruet — **vinagreta** nf : vinaigrette
vincular vt : tie, link — **vínculo** nm : link, tie, bond
vindicar vt 1 : vindicate 2 VENGAR : avenge
vino¹, etc. → venir
vino² nm : wine
viña nf or **viñedo** nm : vineyard
vio, etc. → ver
viola nf : viola
violar vt 1 : violate (a law, etc.) 2 : rape (a person) — **violación** nf, pl **-ciones** 1 : violation, offense 2 : rape (of a person)
violencia nf : violence, force — **violentar** vt 1 : force 2 : break into (a house, etc.) — **violentarse** vr 1 : force one-

self 2 AVERGONZARSE : be embarrassed — **violento, -ta** adj 1 : violent 2 INCÓMODO : awkward, embarrassing
violeta adj & nm : violet (color) — ~ nf : violet (flower)
violín nm, pl **-lines** : violin — **violinista** nmf : violinist — **violoncelista** or **violonchelista** nmf : cellist — **violoncelo** or **violonchelo** nm : cello, violoncello
virar vi : turn, change direction — **viraje** nm 1 : turn, swerve 2 CAMBIO : change
virgen adj & nmf, pl **vírgenes** : virgin — **virginal** adj : virginal — **virginidad** nf : virginity
viril adj : virile — **virilidad** nf : virility
virtual adj : virtual
virtud nf 1 : virtue 2 **en** ~ **de** : by virtue of — **virtuoso, -sa** adj : virtuous — ~ n : virtuoso
viruela nf 1 : smallpox 2 **picado de** ~**s** : pockmarked
virulento, -ta adj : virulent
virus nms & pl : virus
visa nf Lat : visa — **visado** nm Spain : visa
vísceras nfpl : entrails — **visceral** adj : visceral
viscoso, -sa adj : viscous — **viscosidad** nf : viscosity
visera nf : visor
visible adj : visible — **visibilidad** nf : visibility
visión nf, pl **-siones** 1 : eyesight 2 APARICIÓN : vision, illusion 3 **PUNTO DE VISTA** : view, perspective — **visionario, -ria** adj & n : visionary
visitar vt : visit — **visita** nf 1 : visit 2 **tener** ~ : have company — **visitante** adj : visiting — ~ nmf : visitor
vislumbrar vt : make out, discern — **vislumbre** nf 1 : glimpse, sign 2 RESPLANDOR : glimmer, gleam
viso nm 1 : sheen 2 **tener** ~**s de** : seem, show signs of
visón nm, pl **-sones** : mink
víspera nf : eve, day before
vista nf 1 : vision, eyesight 2 MIRADA : look, gaze 3 PANORAMA : view, vista 4 : hearing (in court) 5 **a primera** ~ or **a simple** ~ : at first sight 6 **hacer la** ~ **gorda** : turn a blind eye 7 **perder de** ~ : lose sight of — **vistazo** nm 1 : glance 2 **echar un** ~ : have a look
visto, -ta adj 1 : clear, obvious 2 COMÚN : commonly seen 3 **estar bien** ~ : be approved of 4 **estar mal** ~ : be frowned upon 5 **nunca** ~ : unheard-

of **6 por lo visto** : apparently **7 visto que** : since, given that — **visto** nm ~ **bueno** : approval — ~ pp → **ver**

vistoso, -sa adj : colorful, bright

visual adj : visual — **visualizar** {21} vt : visualize

vital adj : vital — **vitalicio, -cia** adj : life, for life — **vitalidad** nf : vitality

vitamina nf : vitamin

viticultor, -tora n : winegrower — **viticultura** nf : wine growing

vitorear vt : cheer, acclaim

vítreo, -trea adj : glassy

vitrina nf **1** : showcase, display case **2** Lat : shopwindow

vituperar vt : censure — **vituperio** nm : censure

viudo, -da n : widower m, widow f — ~ adj : widowed — **viudez** nf : widowerhood, widowhood

viva nm **dar** ~**s** : cheer

vivacidad nf : vivacity, liveliness

vivamente adv **1** : vividly **2** PROFUNDAMENTE : deeply, acutely

vivaz adj, pl **-vaces 1** : lively, vivacious **2** AGUDO : vivid, sharp

víveres nmpl : provisions, supplies

vivero nm **1** : nursery (for plants) **2** : (fish) hatchery, (oyster) bed

viveza nf **1** : liveliness **2** : vividness (of colors, descriptions, etc.) **3** ASTUCIA : sharpness (of mind) — **vívido, -da** adj : vivid

vividor, -dora n : freeloader

vivienda nf **1** : housing **2** MORADA : dwelling

viviente adj : living

vivificar {72} vt : enliven

vivir {19} vi **1** : live, be alive **2** ~ **de** : live on — vt : experience, live (through) — ~ nm **1** : life, lifestyle **2 de mal** ~ : disreputable — **vivo, -va** adj **1** : alive **2** INTENSO : intense, bright **3** ANIMADO : lively **4** ASTUTO : sharp, quick **5 en vivo** : live

vocablo nm : word — **vocabulario** nm : vocabulary

vocación nf, pl **-ciones** : vocation — **vocacional** adj : vocational

vocal adj : vocal — ~ nmf : member (of a committee, etc.) — ~ nf : vowel — **vocalista** nmf : singer, vocalist

vocear v : shout — **vocerío** nm : shouting

vociferar vi : shout

vodka nmf : vodka

volar {19} vi **1** : fly **2** : blow away (of papers, etc.) **3** fam : disappear **4 irse volando** : rush off — vt : blow up — **volador, -dora** adj : flying — **volandas: en** ~ adv phr : in the air —

volante adj : flying — ~ nm **1** : steering wheel **2** : shuttlecock (in badminton) **3** : flounce (of fabric) **4** Lat : flier, circular

volátil adj : volatile

volcán nm, pl **-canes** : volcano — **volcánico, -ca** adj : volcanic

volcar {82} vt **1** : upset, knock over **2** VACIAR : empty out — vi : overturn — **volcarse** vr **1** : overturn, tip over **2** ~ **en** : throw oneself into

voleibol nm : volleyball

voltaje nm : voltage

voltear vt : turn over, turn upside down — **voltearse** vr Lat : turn (around) — **voltereta** nf : somersault

voltio nm : volt

voluble adj : fickle

volumen nm, pl **-lúmenes** : volume — **voluminoso, -sa** adj : voluminous

voluntad nf **1** : will **2** DESEO : wish **3** INTENCIÓN : intention **4 a** ~ : at will **5 buena** ~ : goodwill **6 mala** ~ : ill will **7 fuerza de** ~ : willpower — **voluntario, -ria** adj : voluntary — ~ n : volunteer — **voluntarioso, -sa** adj **1** : willing **2** TERCO : stubborn, willful

voluptuoso, -sa adj : voluptuous

volver {89} vi **1** : return, come or go back **2** ~ **a** : return to, do again **3** ~ **en sí** : come to — vt **1** : turn, turn over, turn inside out **2** CONVERTIR EN : turn (into) **3** ~ **loco** : drive crazy — **volverse** vr **1** : turn (around) **2** HACERSE : become

vomitar vi : vomit — vt **1** : vomit **2** : spew (out) — **vómito** nm **1** : (action of) vomiting **2** : vomit

voraz adj, pl **-races** : voracious

vos pron Lat : you

vosotros, -tras pron Spain : you, yourselves

votar vi : vote — vt : vote for — **votación** nf, pl **-ciones** : vote, voting — **votante** nmf : voter — **voto** nm **1** : vote **2** : vow (in religion)

voy → **ir**

voz nf, pl **voces 1** : voice **2** GRITO : shout, yell **3** VOCABLO : word, term **4** RUMOR : rumor **5 dar voces** : shout **6 en** ~ **alta** : loudly **7 en** ~ **baja** : softly

vuelco nm : upset, overturning

vuelo nm **1** : flight **2** : (action of) flying **3** : flare (of clothing) **4 al** ~ : on the wing

vuelta nf **1** : turn **2** REVOLUCIÓN : circle, revolution **3** CURVA : bend, curve **4** REGRESO : return **5** : round, lap (in sports)

6 PASEO : walk, drive, ride **7** REVÉS : back, other side **8** *Spain* : change **9** **dar ~s** : spin **10 estar de ~** : be back — **vuelto** *nm Lat* : change
vuestro, -tra *adj Spain* : your, of yours — **~** *pron Spain* (*with definite article*) : yours

vulgar *adj* **1** : vulgar **2** CORRIENTE : common — **vulgaridad** *nf* **1** : vulgarity **2** BANALIDAD : banality — **vulgo** *nm* **el ~** : the masses, common people
vulnerable *adj* : vulnerable — **vulnerabilidad** *nf* : vulnerability

WXYZ

w *nf* : w, 24th letter of the Spanish alphabet
wáter *nm Spain* : toilet
whisky *nm, pl* **-skys** *or* **-skies** : whiskey
x *nf* : x, 25th letter of the Spanish alphabet
xenofobia *nf* : xenophobia
xilófono *nm* : xylophone
y¹ *nf* : y, 26th letter of the Spanish alphabet
y² *conj* : and
ya *adv* **1** : already **2** AHORA : (right) now **3** MÁS TARDE : later, soon **4 ~ no** : no longer **5 ~ que** : now that, since, inasmuch as
yacer {90} *vi* : lie (on or in the ground) — **yacimiento** *nm* : bed, deposit
yanqui *adj & nmf* : Yankee
yate *nm* : yacht
yegua *nf* : mare
yelmo *nm* : helmet
yema *nf* **1** : bud, shoot **2** : yolk (of an egg) **3** *or* **~ del dedo** : fingertip
yerba *nf* **1** *or* **~ mate** : maté **2** → **hierba**
yermo, -ma *adj* : barren, deserted — **yermo** *nm* : wasteland
yerno *nm* : son-in-law
yerro *nm* : blunder, mistake
yerto, -ta *adj* : stiff
yesca *nf* : tinder
yeso *nm* **1** : gypsum **2** : plaster (for art, construction)
yo *pron* **1** (*subject*) : I **2** (*object*) : me **3 soy ~** : it is I, it's me — **~** *nm* : ego, self
yodo *nm* : iodine
yoga *nm* : yoga
yogurt *or* **yogur** *nm* : yogurt
yuca *nf* : yucca
yugo *nm* : yoke (of oxen)
yugoslavo, -va *adj* : Yugoslavian
yugular *adj* : jugular
yunque *nm* : anvil
yunta *nf* : yoke

yuxtaponer {60} *vt* : juxtapose — **yuxtaposición** *nf, pl* **-ciones** : juxtaposition
z *nf* : z, 27th letter of the Spanish alphabet
zacate *nm Lat* : grass
zafar *vt Lat* : loosen, untie — **zafarse** *vr* **1** : come undone **2** : get free of (an obligation, etc.)
zafio, -fia *adj* : coarse
zafiro *nm* : sapphire
zaga *nf* **a la ~** *or* **en ~** : behind, in the rear
zaguán *nm, pl* **-guanes** : (entrance) hall
zaherir {76} *vt* : hurt (s.o.'s feelings)
zaino, -na *adj* : chestnut (color)
zalamería *nf* : flattery — **zalamero, -ra** *adj* : flattering — **~** *n* : flatterer
zambullirse {38} *vr* : dive, plunge — **zambullida** *nf* : dive, plunge
zanahoria *nf* : carrot
zancada *nf* : stride, step — **zancadilla** *nf* **1** : trip, stumble **2 hacer una ~ a algn** : trip s.o. up
zancos *nmpl* : stilts
zancudo *nm Lat* : mosquito
zángano, -na *n fam* : lazy person, slacker — **zángano** *nm* : drone (bee)
zanja *nf* : ditch, trench — **zanjar** *vt* : settle, resolve
zapallo *nm Lat* : pumpkin — **zapallito** *nm Lat* : zucchini
zapapico *nm* : pickax
zapato *nm* : shoe — **zapatería** *nf* : shoe store — **zapatero, -ra** *n* : shoemaker, cobbler — **zapatilla** *nf* **1** : slipper **2** : sneaker (for sports, etc.)
zar *nm* : czar
zarandear *vt* **1** : sift **2** SACUDIR : shake
zarcillo *nm* : earring
zarpa *nf* : paw
zarpar *vi* : set sail, raise anchor
zarza *nf* : bramble — **zarzamora** *nf* : blackberry
zigzag *nm, pl* **-zags** *or* **-zagues** : zigzag — **zigzaguear** *vi* : zigzag

zinc *nm* : zinc
zíper *nm Lat* : zipper
zircón *nm, pl* **-cones** : zircon
zócalo *nm* **1** : base (of a column, etc.) **2** : baseboard (of a wall) **3** *Lat* : main square, plaza
zodíaco *nm* : zodiac
zona *nf* : zone, area
zoo *nm* : zoo — **zoología** *nf* : zoology — **zoológico, -ca** *adj* : zoological — **zoológico** *nm* : zoo — **zoólogo, -ga** *n* : zoologist
zopilote *nm Lat* : buzzard
zoquete *nmf fam* : oaf, blockhead

zorrillo *nm Lat* : skunk
zorro, -rra *n* : fox, vixen *f* — ~ *adj* : foxy, sly
zozobra *nf* : anxiety, worry — **zozobrar** *vi* : capsize
zueco *nm* : clog (shoe)
zumbar *vi* : buzz — *vt fam* : hit, beat — **zumbido** *nm* : buzzing
zumo *nf* : juice
zurcir {83} *vt* : darn, mend
zurdo, -da *adj* : left-handed — ~ *n* : left-handed person — **zurda** *nf* : left hand
zutano, -na → **fulano**

English-Spanish
Dictionary

A

a¹ ['eɪ] *n, pl* **a's** *or* **as** ['eɪz] : a *f*, primera letra del alfabeto inglés

a² [ə, 'eɪ] *art* (**an** [ən, 'æn] *before vowel or silent h*) **1** : un *m*, una *f* **2** PER : por, a la, al

aback [ə'bæk] *adv* **be taken ~** : quedarse desconcertado

abacus ['æbəkəs] *n, pl* **abaci** ['æbə,saɪ, -kiː] *or* **abacuses** : ábaco *m*

abandon [ə'bændən] *vt* **1** DESERT : abandonar **2** GIVE UP : renunciar a — **~** *n* : desenfreno *m* — **abandonment** [ə'bændənmənt] *n* : abandono *m*

abashed [ə'bæʃt] *adj* : avergonzado

abate [ə'beɪt] *vi* **abated; abating** : amainar, disminuir

abattoir ['æbə,twɑr] *n* : matadero *m*

abbey ['æbi] *n, pl* **-beys** : abadía *f* — **abbot** ['æbət] *n* : abad *m*

abbreviate [ə'briːvi,eɪt] *vt* **-ated; -ating** : abreviar — **abbreviation** [ə,briːvi'eɪʃən] *n* : abreviatura *f*, abreviación *f*

abdicate ['æbdɪ,keɪt] *v* **-cated; -cating** : abdicar — **abdication** [,æbdɪ'keɪæn] *n* : abdicación *f*

abdomen ['æbdəmən, æb'doːmən] *n* : abdomen *m*, vientre *m* — **abdominal** [æb'dɑmənəl] *adj* : abdominal

abduct [æb'dʌkt] *vt* : secuestrar — **abduction** [æb'dʌkʃən] *n* : secuestro *m*

aberration [,æbə'reɪʃən] *n* : aberración *f*

abet [ə'bet] *vt* **abetted; abetting** *or* **aid and ~** : ser cómplice de

abeyance [ə'beɪənts] *n* : desuso *m*

abhor [əb'hɔr, æb-] *vt* **-horred; -horring** : aborrecer

abide [ə'baɪd] *v* **abode** [ə'boːd] *or* **abided; abiding** *vt* : soportar, tolerar — *vi* **1** DWELL : morar **2 ~ by** : atenerse a

ability [ə'bɪləti] *n, pl* **-ties 1** CAPABILITY : aptitud *f*, capacidad *f* **2** SKILL : habilidad *f*

abject ['æb,dʒekt, æb-] *adj* : miserable, desdichado

ablaze [ə'bleɪz] *adj* : en llamas

able ['eɪbəl] *adj* **abler; ablest 1** CAPABLE : capaz, hábil **2** COMPETENT : competente

abnormal [æb'nɔrməl] *adj* : anormal — **abnormality** [,æbnər'mæləti, -nɔr-] *n, pl* **-ties** : anormalidad *f*

aboard [ə'bord] *adv* : a bordo — **~** *prep* : a bordo de

abode *n* : morada *f*, domicilio *m*

abolish [ə'bɑlɪʃ] *vt* : abolir, suprimir — **abolition** [,æbə'lɪʃən] *n* : abolición *f*

abominable [ə'bɑmənəbəl] *adj* : abominable, aborrecible — **abomination** [ə,bɑmə'neɪʃən] *n* : abominación *f*

aborigine [,æbə'rɪdʒəni] *n* : aborigen *mf*

abort [ə'bɔrt] *vt* : abortar — **abortion** [ə'bɔrʃən] *n* : aborto *m* — **abortive** [ə'bɔrtɪv] *adj* UNSUCCESSFUL : malogrado

abound [ə'baund] *vi* **~ in** : abundar en

about [ə'baut] *adv* **1** APPROXIMATELY : aproximadamente, más o menos **2** AROUND : alrededor **3 be ~ to** : estar a punto de **4 be up and ~** : estar levantado — **~** *prep* **1** AROUND : alrededor de **2** CONCERNING : acerca de, sobre

above [ə'bʌv] *adv* : arriba — **~** *prep* **1** : encima de **2 ~ all** : sobre todo — **aboveboard** [ə'bʌv'bord] *adj* : honrado

abrasive [ə'breɪsɪv] *adj* **1** : abrasivo **2** BRUSQUE : brusco, mordaz

abreast [ə'brest] *adv* **1** : al lado **2 keep ~ of** : mantenerse al corriente de

abridge [ə'brɪdʒ] *vt* **abridged; abridging** : abreviar

abroad [ə'brɔd] *adv* **1** : en el extranjero **2** WIDELY : por todas partes **3 go ~** : ir al extranjero

abrupt [ə'brʌpt] *adj* **1** SUDDEN : repentino **2** BRUSQUE : brusco

abscess ['æb,ses] *n* : absceso *m*

absence ['æbsənts] *n* **1** : ausencia *f* **2** LACK : falta *f*, carencia *f* — **absent** ['æbsənt] *adj* : ausente — **absentee** [,æbsən'tiː] *n* : ausente *mf* — **absentminded** [,æbsənt'maɪndəd] *adj* : distraído, despistado

absolute ['æbsə,luːt, ,æbsə'luːt] *adj* : absoluto — **absolutely** [,æbsə'luːtli] *adv* : absolutamente

absolve [əb'zɑlv, æb-, -'sɑlv] *vt* **-solved; -solving** : absolver

absorb [əb'zɔrb, æb-, -'sɔrb] *vt* : absorber — **absorbent** [əb'zɔrbənt, æb-, -'sɔr-] *adj* : absorbente — **absorption** [əb'zɔrpʃən, æb-, -'sɔrp-] *n* : absorción *f*

abstain [əb'steɪn, æb-] *vi* **~ from** : abstenerse de — **abstinence** ['æbstənənts] *n* : abstinencia *f*

abstract ['æb,strækt, ,æb-] *adj* : abstracto — **~** *vt* : extraer — **~** ['æb,strækt] *n* : resumen *m* — **abstraction** [æb-'stræk∫ən] *n* : abstracción *f*

absurd [əb'sord, -'zərd] *adj* : absurdo — **absurdity** [əb'sərdəṭi, -'zərdəṭi] *n, pl* **-ties** : absurdo *m*

abundant [ə'bʌndənt] *adj* : abundante — **abundance** [ə'bʌndənts] *n* : abundancia *f*

abuse [ə'bju:z] *vt* **abused; abusing 1** MISUSE : abusar de **2** MISTREAT : maltratar **3** REVILE : insultar — **~** [ə'bju:s] *n* **1** : abuso *m* **2** INSULTS : insultos *mpl* — **abusive** [ə'bju:sɪv] *adj* : injurioso

abut [ə'bʌt] *vi* **abutted; abutting ~ on** : colindar con

abyss [ə'bɪs, 'æbɪs] *n* : abismo *m* — **abysmal** [ə'bɪzməl] *adj* : atroz, pésimo

academy [ə'kædəmi] *n, pl* **-mies** : academia *f* — **academic** [,ækə'dɛmɪk] *adj* **1** : académico **2** THEORETICAL : teórico

accelerate [ɪk'sɛlə,reɪt, æk-] *v* **-ated; -ating** : acelerar — **acceleration** [ɪk-,sɛlə'reɪ∫ən, æk-] *n* : aceleración *f*

accent ['æk,sɛnt, æk'sɛnt] *vt* : acentuar — **~** ['æk,sɛnt, sənt] *n* : acento *m* — **accentuate** [ɪk'sɛntʃu,eɪt, æk-] *vt* **-ated; -ating** : acentuar, subrayar

accept [ɪk'sɛpt, æk-] *vt* : aceptar — **acceptable** [ɪk'sɛptəbəl, æk-] *adj* : aceptable — **acceptance** [ɪk'sɛptənts, æk-] *n* **1** : aceptación *f* **2** APPROVAL : aprobación *f*

access ['æk,sɛs] *n* : acceso *m* — **accessible** [ɪk'sɛsəbəl, æk-] *adj* : accesible, asequible

accessory *n, pl* **-ries 1** : accesorio *m* **2** ACCOMPLICE : cómplice *mf*

accident ['æksədənt] *n* **1** MISHAP : accidente *m* **2** CHANCE : casualidad *f* — **accidental** [,æksə'dɛntəl] *adj* : accidental — **accidentally** [,æksə'dɛntəli, -'dɛntli] *adv* **1** BY CHANCE : por casualidad **2** UNINTENTIONALLY : sin querer

acclaim [ə'kleɪm] *vt* : aclamar — **~** *n* : aclamación *f*

acclimatize [ə'klaɪmə,taɪz] *vt* **-tized; -tizing** : aclimatar

accommodate [ə'kɑmə,deɪt] *vt* **-dated; -dating 1** ADAPT : acomodar, adaptar **2** SATISFY : complacer, satisfacer **3** HOLD : tener cabida para — **accomodation** [ə,kɑmə'deɪ∫ən] *n* **1** : adaptación *f* **2 ~s** *npl* LODGING : alojamiento *m*

accompany [ə'kʌmpəni, -kəm-] *vt* **-nied; -nying** : acompañar

accomplice [ə'kɑmpləs, -'kʌm-] *n* : cómplice *mf*

accomplish [ə'kɑmplɪ∫, -'kʌm-] *vt* : re-

alizar, llevar a cabo — **accomplishment** [ə'kɑmplɪ∫mənt, -kʌm-] *n* **1** COMPLETION : realización *f* **2** ACHIEVEMENT : logro *m*, éxito *m*

accord *n* **1** AGREEMENT : acuerdo *m* **2 of one's own ~** : voluntariamente — **accordance** [ə'kɔrdənts] *n* **in ~ with** : conforme a, de acuerdo con — **accordingly** [ə'kɔrdɪŋli] *adv* : en consecuencia — **according to** [ə'kɔrdɪŋ] *prep* : según

accordion [ə'kɔrdiən] *n* : acordeón *m*

accost [ə'kɔst] *vt* : abordar

account [ə'kaʊnt] *n* **1** : cuenta *f* **2** REPORT : relato *m*, informe *m* **3** WORTH : importancia *f* **4 on ~ of** : a causa de, debido a **5 on no ~** : de ninguna manera — **~ vi for** : dar cuenta de, explicar — **accountable** [ə'kaʊntəbəl] *adj* : responsable — **accountant** [ə'kaʊntənt] *n* : contador *m*, -dora *f Lat*; contable *mf Spain* — **accounting** [ə'kaʊntɪŋ] *n* : contabilidad *f*

accrue [ə'kru:] *vi* **-crued; -cruing** : acumularse

accumulate [ə'kju:mjə,leɪt] *v* **-lated; -lating** *vt* : acumular — *vi* : acumularse — **accumulation** [ə,kju:mjə-'leɪ∫ən] *n* : acumulación *f*

accurate ['ækjərət] *adj* : exacto, preciso — **accuracy** ['ækjərəsi] *n* : exactitud *f*, precisión *f*

accuse [ə'kju:z] *vt* **-cused; -cusing** : acusar — **accusation** [,ækjə'zeɪ∫ən] *n* : acusación *f*

accustomed [ə'kʌstəmd] *adj* **1** : acostumbrado **2 become ~ to** : acostumbrarse a

ace ['eɪs] *n* : as *m*

ache ['eɪk] *vi* **ached; aching** : doler — **~** *n* : dolor *m*

achieve [ə'tʃi:v] *vt* **achieved; achieving** : lograr, realizar — **achievement** [ə'tʃi:vmənt] *n* : logro *m*, éxito *m*

acid ['æsəd] *adj* : ácido — **~** *n* : ácido *m*

acknowledge [ɪk'nɑlɪdʒ, æk-] *vt* **-edged; -edging 1** ADMIT : admitir **2** RECOGNIZE : reconocer **3 ~ receipt** : acusar recibo de — **acknowledgment** [ɪk'nɑlɪdʒmənt, æk-] *n* **1** : reconocimiento *m* **2** THANKS : agradecimiento *m* **3 ~ of receipt** : acuse *m* de recibo

acne ['ækni] *n* : acné *m*

acorn ['eɪ,kɔrn, -kərn] *n* : bellota *f*

acoustic [ə'ku:stɪk] *or* **acoustical** [-stɪkəl] *adj* : acústico — **acoustics** [ə'ku:stɪks] *ns & pl* : acústica *f*

acquaint [ə'kweɪnt] *vt* **1 ~ s.o. with**

: poner a algn al corriente de **2 be ~ed with** : conocer a (una persona), saber (un hecho) — **acquaintance** [ə'kweɪntənts] *n* **1** : conocimiento *m* **2** : conocido *m*, -da *f* (persona)

acquire [ə'kwaɪr] *vt* **-quired; -quiring** : adquirir — **acquisition** [ˌækwə'zɪʃən] *n* : adquisición *f*

acquit [ə'kwɪt] *vt* **-quitted; -quitting** : absolver

acre ['eɪkər] *n* : acre *m* — **acreage** ['eɪkərɪdʒ] *n* : superficie *f* en acres

acrid ['ækrəd] *adj* : acre

acrobat ['ækrəˌbæt] *n* : acróbata *mf* — **acrobatic** [ˌækrə'bætɪk] *adj* : acrobático

acronym ['ækrəˌnɪm] *n* : siglas *fpl*

across [ə'krɔs] *adv* **1** : de un lado a otro **2** CROSSWISE : a través **3 go ~** : atravesar — **~** *prep* **1** : a través de **2 ~ the street** : al otro lado de la calle

acrylic [ə'krɪlɪk] *n* : acrílico *m*

act ['ækt] *vi* **1** : actuar **2** PRETEND : fingir **3** FUNCTION : funcionar **4 ~ as** : servir de — *vt* : interpretar (un papel) — **~** *n* **1** ACTION : acto *m*, acción *f* **2** DECREE : ley *f* **3** : acto *m* (en una obra de teatro), número *m* (en un espectáculo) — **acting** *adj* : interino

action ['ækʃən] *n* **1** : acción *f* **2** LAWSUIT : demanda *f* **3 take ~** : tomar medidas

activate ['æktəˌveɪt] *vt* **-vated; -vating** : activar

active ['æktɪv] *adj* **1** : activo **2** LIVELY : enérgico **3 ~ volcano** : volcán *m* en actividad — **activity** [æk'tɪvəti] *n, pl* **-ties** : actividad *f*

actor ['æktər] *n* : actor *m* — **actress** ['æktrəs] *n* : actriz *f*

actual ['æktʃuəl] *adj* : real, verdadero — **actually** ['æktʃuəli, -æəli] *adv* : realmente, en realidad

acupuncture ['ækjuˌpʌŋktʃər] *n* : acupuntura *f*

acute [ə'kjuːt] *adj* **acuter; acutest** **1** : agudo **2** PERCEPTIVE : perspicaz

ad ['æd] → **advertisement**

adamant ['ædəmənt, -ˌmænt] *adj* : inflexible

adapt [ə'dæpt] *vt* : adaptar — *vi* : adaptarse — **adaptable** [ə'dæptəbəl] *adj* : adaptable — **adaptation** [ˌæˌdæp'teɪʃən, -dəp-] *n* : adaptación *f* — **adapter** [ə'dæptər] *n* : adaptador *m*

add ['æd] *vt* **1** : añadir **2** *or* **~ up** : sumar — *vi* : sumar

addict ['ædɪkt] *n* **1** : adicto *m*, -ta *f* **2** *or* **drug ~** : drogadicto *m*, -ta *f*; toxicómano *m*, -na *f* — **addiction** [ə'dɪkʃən] *n* : dependencia *f*

addition [ə'dɪʃən] *n* **1** : suma *f* (en matemáticas) **2** ADDING : adición *f* **3 in ~** : además — **additional** [ə'dɪʃənəl] *adj* : adicional — **additive** ['ædəˌtɪv] *adj* : aditivo *m*

address [ə'dres] *vt* **1** : dirigirse a (una persona) **2** : ponerle la dirección a (una carta) **3** : tratar (un asunto) — **~** [ə'dres, 'æ͵dres] *n* **1** : dirección *f*, domicilio *m* **2** SPEECH : discurso *m*

adept [ə'dept] *adj* : experto, hábil

adequate ['ædɪkwət] *adj* : adecuado, suficiente

adhere [æd'hɪr, əd-] *vi* **-hered; -hering** **1** STICK : adherirse **2 ~ to** : observar — **adherence** [æd'hɪrənts, əd-] *n* **1** : adhesión *f* **2** : observancia *f* (de una ley, etc.) — **adhesive** [æd'hiːsɪv, əd-, -zɪv] *adj* : adhesivo — **~** *n* : adhesivo *m*

adjacent [ə'dʒeɪsənt] *adj* : adyacente, contiguo

adjective ['ædʒɪktɪv] *n* : adjetivo *m*

adjoining [ə'dʒɔɪnɪŋ] *adj* : contiguo, vecino

adjourn [ə'dʒərn] *vt* : aplazar, suspender — *vi* : suspenderse

adjust [ə'dʒʌst] *vt* : ajustar, arreglar — *vi* : adaptarse — **adjustable** [ə'dʒʌstəbəl] *adj* : ajustable — **adjustment** [ə'dʒʌstmənt] *n* : ajuste *m* (a una máquina, etc.), adaptación *f* (de una persona)

ad–lib ['æd'lɪb] *v* **-libbed; -libbing** : improvisar

administer [æd'mɪnəstər, əd-] *vt* : administrar — **administration** [æd͵mɪnə'streɪʃən, əd-] *n* : administración *f* — **administrative** [æd'mɪnəˌstreɪtɪv, əd-] *adj* : administrativo — **administrator** [æd'mɪnəˌstreɪt̬ər, əd-] *n* : administrador *m*, -dora *f*

admirable ['ædmərəbəl] *adj* : admirable

admiral ['ædmərəl] *n* : almirante *m*

admire [æd'maɪr] *vt* **-mired; -miring** : admirar — **admiration** [ˌædmə'reɪʃən] *n* : admiración *f* — **admirer** [æd'maɪrər] *n* : admirador *m*, -dora *f*

admit [æd'mɪt, əd-] *vt* **-mitted; -mitting** **1** : admitir, dejar entrar **2** ACKNOWLEDGE : reconocer — **admission** [æd'mɪʃən] *n* **1** ADMITTANCE : entrada *f*, admisión *f* **2** ACKNOWLEDGMENT : reconocimiento *m* — **admittance** [æd'mɪtənts, əd-] *n* : admisión *f*, entrada *f*

admonish [æd'mɑnɪʃ, əd-] *vt* : amonestar, reprender

ado [ə'duː] *n* **1** : alboroto *m*, bulla *f* **2 without further ~** : sin más (preámbulos)

adolescent [ˌædəlˈɛsənt] n : adolescente mf — **adolescence** [ˌædəlˈɛsənts] n : adolescencia f

adopt [əˈdɑpt] vt : adoptar — **adoption** [əˈdɑpʃən] n : adopción f

adore [əˈdor] vt **adored; adoring 1** : adorar **2** LIKE, LOVE : encantarle (algo a uno) — **adorable** [əˈdorəbəl] adj : adorable — **adoration** [ˌædəˈreɪæən] n : adoración f

adorn [əˈdorn] vt : adornar — **adornment** [əˈdornmənt] n : adorno m

adrift [əˈdrɪft] adj & adv : a la deriva

adroit [əˈdrɔɪt] adj : diestro, hábil

adult [əˈdʌlt, ˌæˌdʌlt] adj : adulto — ~ n : adulto m, -ta f

adultery [əˈdʌltəri] n, pl **-teries** : adulterio m

advance [ædˈvænts, əd-] v **-vanced; -vancing** vt : adelantar — vi : avanzar, adelantarse — ~ n **1** : avance m **2** PROGRESS : adelanto m **3 in** ~ : por adelantado — **advancement** [ædˈvæntsmənt, əd-] n : adelanto m, progreso m

advantage [ədˈvæntɪdʒ, æd-] n **1** : ventaja f **2 take** ~ **of** : aprovecharse de — **advantageous** [ˌædˌvænˈteɪdʒəs, -vən-] adj : ventajoso

advent [ˈædˌvɛnt] n **1** ARRIVAL : llegada f **2 Advent** : Adviento m

adventure [ædˈvɛntʃər, əd-] n : aventura f — **adventurous** [ædˈvɛntʃərəs, əd-] adj **1** : intrépido **2** RISKY : arriesgado

adverb [ˈædˌvərb] n : adverbio m

adversary [ˈædvərˌseri] n, pl **-saries** : adversario m, -ria f

adverse [ædˈvərs, ˈæd-] adj : adverso, desfavorable — **adversity** [ædˈvərsəti, əd-] n, pl **-ties** : adversidad f

advertise [ˈædvərˌtaɪz] v **-tised; -tising** vt : anunciar — vi : hacer publicidad — **advertisement** [ˈædvərˌtaɪzmənt] n : anuncio m — **advertiser** [ˈædvərˌtaɪzər] n : anunciante mf — **advertising** [ˈædvərˌtaɪzɪŋ] n : publicidad f

advice [ædˈvaɪs] n : consejo m

advise [ædˈvaɪz, əd-] vt **-vised; -vising 1** COUNSEL : aconsejar, asesorar **2** RECOMMEND : recomendar **3** INFORM : informar — **advisable** [ædˈvaɪzəbəl, əd-] adj : aconsejable — **adviser** [ædˈvaɪzər, əd-] n : consejero m, -ra f; asesor m, -sora f — **advisory** [ædˈvaɪzəri, əd-] adj : consultivo

advocate [ˈædvəˌkeɪt] vt **-cated; -cating** : recomendar — ~ [ˈædvəkət] n : defensor m, -sora f

aerial [ˈæriəl] adj : aéreo — ~ n : antena f

aerobics [ˌærˈoːbɪks] ns & pl : aeróbic m

aerodynamic [ˌæroːdaɪˈnæmɪk] adj : aerodinámico

aerosol [ˈærəˌsɔl] n : aerosol m

aesthetic [ɛsˈθɛtɪk] adj : estético

afar [əˈfɑr] adv : lejos

affable [ˈæfəbəl] adj : afable

affair [əˈfær] n **1** : asunto m, cuestión f **2** or **love** ~ : amorío m, aventura f

affect [əˈfɛkt, æ-] vt **1** : afectar **2** FEIGN : fingir — **affection** [əˈfɛkʃən] n : afecto m, cariño m — **affectionate** [əˈfɛkʃənət] adj : afectuoso, cariñoso

affinity [əˈfɪnəti] n, pl **-ties** : afinidad f

affirm [əˈfərm] vt : afirmar — **affirmative** [əˈfərmətɪv] adj : afirmativo

affix [əˈfɪks] vt : fijar, pegar

afflict [əˈflɪkt] vt : afligir — **affliction** [əˈflɪkʃən] n : aflicción f

affluent [ˈæˌfluːənt; æˈfluː-, ə-] adj : próspero, adinerado

afford [əˈford] vt **1** : tener los recursos para, permitirse (el lujo de) **2** PROVIDE : brindar

affront [əˈfrʌnt] n : afrenta f

afloat [əˈfloːt] adv & adj : a flote

afoot [əˈfʊt] adj : en marcha

afraid [əˈfreɪd] adj **1 be** ~ : tener miedo **2 I'm** ~ **not** : me temo que no

African [ˈæfrɪkən] adj : africano

after [ˈæftər] adv **1** AFTERWARD : después **2** BEHIND : detrás, atrás — ~ conj : después de (que) — ~ prep **1** : después de **2** ~ **all** : después de todo **3 it's ten** ~ **five** : son las cinco y diez

aftereffect [ˈæftərəˌfɛkt] n : efecto m secundario

aftermath [ˈæftərˌmæθ] n : consecuencias fpl

afternoon [ˌæftərˈnuːn] n : tarde f

afterward [ˈæftərwərd] or **afterwards** [-wərdz] adv : después, más tarde

again [əˈgɛn, -ˈgɪn] adv **1** : otra vez, de nuevo **2** ~ **and** ~ : una y otra vez **3 then** ~ : por otra parte

against [əˈgɛnst, -ˈgɪnst] prep : contra, en contra de

age [ˈeɪdʒ] n **1** : edad f **2** ERA : era f, época f **3 be of** ~ : ser mayor de edad **4 for** ~**s** : hace siglos **5 old** ~ : vejez f — ~ vi **aging; aging** : envejecer — **aged** adj **1** [ˈeɪdʒd, ˈeɪdʒd] OLD : anciano, viejo **2** [ˈeɪdʒd] **children** ~ **10 to 17** : niños de 10 a 17 años

agency [ˈeɪdʒəntsi] n, pl **-cies** : agencia f

agenda [əˈdʒɛndə] n : orden m del día

agent [ˈeɪdʒənt] n : agente mf, representante mf

aggravate [ˈægrəˌveɪt] vt **-vated; -vating**

1 WORSEN : agravar, empeorar **2** ANNOY : irritar

aggregate ['ægrɪgət] *adj* : total, global — **~** *n* : total *m*

aggression [ə'grɛʃən] *n* : agresión *f* — **aggressive** [ə'grɛsɪv] *adj* : agresivo — **aggressor** [ə'grɛsər] *n* : agresor *m*, -sora *f*

aghast [ə'gæst] *adj* : horrorizado

agile ['ædʒəl] *adj* : ágil — **agility** [ə'dʒɪləti] *n, pl* **-ties** : agilidad *f*

agitate ['ædʒə,teɪt] *v* **-tated; -tating** *vt* **1** SHAKE : agitar **2** TROUBLE : inquietar — **agitation** [,ædʒə'teɪʃən] *n* : agitación *f*, inquietud *f*

agnostic [æg'nɑstɪk] *n* : agnóstico *m*, -ca *f*

ago [ə'goː] *adv* **1** : hace **2** long **~** : hace mucho tiempo

agony ['ægəni] *n, pl* **-nies 1** PAIN : dolor *m* **2** ANGUISH : angustia *f* — **agonize** ['ægə,naɪz] *vi* **-nized; -nizing** : atormentarse — **agonizing** ['ægə,naɪzɪŋ] *adj* : angustioso

agree [ə'griː] *v* **agreed; agreeing** *vt* **1** : acordar **2 ~ that** : estar de acuerdo de que — *vi* **1** : estar de acuerdo **2** CORRESPOND : concordar **3 ~ to** : acceder a **4 this climate ~s with me** : este clima me sienta bien — **agreeable** [ə'griːəbəl] *adj* **1** PLEASING : agradable **2** WILLING : dispuesto — **agreement** [ə'griːmənt] *n* : acuerdo *m*

agriculture ['ægrɪ,kʌltʃər] *n* : agricultura *f* — **agricultural** [,ægrɪ'kʌltʃərəl] *adj* : agrícola

aground [ə'graʊnd] *adv* run **~** : encallar

ahead [ə'hɛd] *adv* **1** IN FRONT : delante, adelante **2** BEFOREHAND : por adelantado **3** LEADING : a la delantera **4 get ~** : adelantar — **ahead of** *prep* **1** : delante de, antes de **2 get ~ of** : adelantarse a

aid ['eɪd] *vt* : ayudar — **~** *n* : ayuda *f*, asistencia *f*

AIDS ['eɪdz] *n* : SIDA *m*, sida *m*

ail ['eɪl] *vi* : estar enfermo — **ailment** ['eɪlmənt] *n* : enfermedad *f*

aim ['eɪm] *vt* : apuntar (un arma), dirigir (una observación) — *vi* **1** : apuntar **2** ASPIRE : aspirar — **~** *n* **1** : puntería *f* **2** GOAL : propósito *m*, objetivo *m* — **aimless** ['eɪmləs] *adj* : sin objetivo

air ['ær] *vt* or **~ out** : airear **2** EXPRESS : expresar **3** BROADCAST : emitir — **~** *n* **1** : aire *m* **2 be on the ~** : estar en el aire — **air–conditioning** [,ærkən'dɪʃənɪŋ] *n* : aire *m* acondicionado — **air conditioned** ['ærkən,dɪʃənd] *n*

: climatizado — **aircraft** ['ær,kræft] *ns & pl* **1** : avión *m*, aeronave *f* **2 ~ carrier** : portaaviones *m* — **air force** : fuerza *f* aérea — **airline** ['ær,laɪn] *n* : aerolínea *f*, línea *f* aérea — **airliner** ['ær,laɪnər] *n* : avión *m* de pasajeros — **airmail** *n* : correo *m* aéreo — **airplane** ['ær,pleɪn] *n* : avión *m* — **airport** ['ær,pɔrt] *n* : aeropuerto *m* — **airstrip** ['ær,strɪp] *n* : pista *f* de aterrizaje — **airtight** ['ær,taɪt] *adj* : hermético — **airy** ['æri] *adj* **airier** [-iər]; **-est** : aireado, bien ventilado

aisle ['aɪl] *n* **1** : pasillo *m* **2** : nave *f* lateral (de una iglesia)

ajar [ə'dʒɑr] *adj* : entreabierto

akin [ə'kɪn] *adj* **~ to** : semejante a

alarm [ə'lɑrm] *n* **1** : alarma *f* **2** ANXIETY : inquietud *f* — *vt* : alarmar, asustar — **alarm clock** *n* : despertador *m*

alas [ə'læs] *interj* : ¡ay!

album ['ælbəm] *n* : álbum *m*

alcohol ['ælkə,hɔl] *n* : alcohol *m* — **alcoholic** [,ælkə'hɔlɪk] *adj* : alcohólico — **~** *n* : alcohólico *m*, -ca *f* — **alcoholism** ['ælkəhə,lɪzəm] *n* : alcoholismo *m*

alcove ['æl,koːv] *n* : nicho *m*, hueco *m*

ale ['eɪl] *n* : cerveza *f*

alert [ə'lərt] *adj* **1** WATCHFUL : alerta, atento **2** LIVELY : vivo — **~** *n* : alerta *f* — *vt* : alertar, poner sobre aviso

alfalfa [æl'fælfə] *n* : alfalfa *f*

alga ['ælgə] *n, pl* **-gae** ['æl,dʒiː] : alga *f*

algebra ['ældʒəbrə] *n* : álgebra *f*

alias ['eɪliəs] *adv* : alias — **~** *n* : alias *m*

alibi ['ælə,baɪ] *n* : coartada *f*

alien ['eɪliən] *adj* : extranjero — **~** *n* **1** FOREIGNER : extranjero *m*, -ra *f* **2** EXTRATERRESTRIAL : extraterrestre *mf*

alienate ['eɪliə,neɪt] *vt* **-ated; -ating** : enajenar — **alienation** [,eɪliə'neɪæən] *n* : enajenación *f*

alight [ə'laɪt] *vi* **1** LAND : posarse **2 ~ from** : apearse de

align [ə'laɪn] *vt* : alinear — **alignment** [ə'laɪnmənt] *n* : alineación *f*

alike [ə'laɪk] *adv* : igual, del mismo modo — **~** *adj* : parecido

alimony ['ælə,moʊni] *n, pl* **-nies** : pensión *f* alimenticia

alive [ə'laɪv] *adj* **1** LIVING : vivo, viviente **2** ANIMATED : animado, activo

all ['ɔl] *adv* **1** COMPLETELY : todo, completamente **2 ~ the better** : tanto mejor **3 ~ the more** : aún más, todavía más — **~** *adj* : todo — **~** *pron* **1** : todo, -da **2 ~ in ~** : en general **3 not at ~** : de ninguna manera —

all—around [ˌɔlə'raʊnd] *adj* VERSATILE : completo
allay [ə'leɪ] *vt* 1 ALLEVIATE : aliviar 2 CALM : aquietar
allege [ə'ledʒ] *vt* **-leged; -leging** : alegar — **allegation** [ˌælɪ'geɪʃən] *n* : alegato *m*, acusación *f* — **alleged** [ə'ledʒd, ə'ledʒəd] *adj* : presunto — **allegedly** [ə'ledʒədli] *adv* : supuestamente
allegiance [ə'liːdʒənts] *n* : lealtad *f*
allegory ['æləˌgori] *n, pl* **-ries** : alegoría *f* — **allegorical** [ˌælə'gorɪkəl] *adj* : alegórico
allergy ['ælərdʒi] *n, pl* **-gies** : alergia *f* — **allergic** [ə'lərdʒɪk] *adj* : alérgico
alleviate [ə'liːviˌeɪt] *vt* **-ated; -ating** : aliviar
alley ['æli] *n, pl* **-leys** : callejón *m*
alliance [ə'laɪənts] *n* : alianza *f*
alligator ['æləˌgeɪtər] *n* : caimán *m*
allocate ['æləˌkeɪt] *vt* **-cated; -cating** : asignar — **allocation** [ˌælə'keɪʃən] *n* : asignación *f*, reparto *m*
allot [ə'lɑt] *vt* **-lotted; -lotting** : asignar — **allotment** [ə'lɑtmənt] *n* : reparto *m*, asignación *f*
allow [ə'laʊ] *vt* 1 PERMIT : permitir 2 GRANT : dar, conceder 3 ADMIT : admitir 4 CONCEDE : reconocer — *vi* ~ **for** : tener en cuenta — **allowance** [ə'laʊənts] *n* 1 : pensión *f*, subsidio *m* 2 **make ~s for** : tener en cuenta, disculpar
alloy ['ælˌɔɪ, ə'lɔɪ] *n* : aleación *f*
all right *adv* 1 YES : sí, de acuerdo 2 WELL : bien 3 DEFINITELY : bien, sin duda — ~ *adj* : bien, bueno
allude [ə'luːd] *vi* **-luded; -luding** : aludir
allure [ə'lʊr] *vt* **-lured; -luring** : atraer — **alluring** [ə'lʊrɪŋ] *adj* : atrayente, seductor
allusion [ə'luːʒən] *n* : alusión *f*
ally [ə'laɪ, 'æˌlaɪ] *vi* **-lied; -lying** ~ **oneself with** : aliarse con — ~ ['æˌlaɪ, ə'laɪ] *n* : aliado *m*, -da *f*
almanac ['ɔlməˌnæk, 'æl-] *n* : almanaque *m*
almighty [ɔl'maɪti] *adj* : omnipotente, todopoderoso
almond ['ɑmənd, 'ɑl-, 'æ-, 'æl-] *n* : almendra *f*
almost ['ɔlˌmoːst, ɔl'moːst] *adv* : casi
alms ['ɑmz, 'ɑlmz, 'ælmz] *ns & pl* : limosna *f*
alone [ə'loːn] *adv* : sólo, solamente, únicamente — ~ *adj* : solo
along [ə'lɔŋ] *adv* 1 FORWARD : adelante 2 ~ **with** : con, junto con 3 **all** ~ : desde el principio — ~ *prep* : por, a lo largo de — **alongside** [ə,lɔŋ'saɪd]

adv : al costado — ~ *or* ~ **of** *prep* : al lado de
aloof [ə'luːf] *adj* : distante, reservado
aloud [ə'laʊd] *adv* : en voz alta
alphabet ['ælfəˌbɛt] *n* : alfabeto *m* — **alphabetical** [ˌælfə'bɛtɪkəl] *or* **alphabetic** [-'bɛtɪk] *adj* : alfabético
already [ɔl'rɛdi] *adv* : ya
also ['ɔlˌsoː] *adv* : también, además
altar ['ɔltər] *n* : altar *m*
alter ['ɔltər] *vt* : alterar, modificar — **alteration** [ˌɔltə'reɪʃən] *n* : alteración *f*, modificación *f*
alternate ['ɔltərnət] *adj* : alterno — ~ ['ɔltərˌneɪt] *v* **-nated; -nating** : alternar — **alternating current** ~ : corriente *f* alterna — **alternative** [ɔl'tərnətɪv] *adj* : alternativo — ~ *n* : alternativa *f*
although [ɔl'ðoː] *conj* : aunque
altitude ['æltəˌtuːd, -ˌtjuːd] *n* : altitud *f*
altogether [ˌɔltə'gɛðər] *adv* 1 COMPLETELY : completamente, del todo 2 ON THE WHOLE : en suma, en general
aluminum [ə'luːmənəm] *n* : aluminio *m*
always ['ɔlˌwɪz, -ˌweɪz] *adv* 1 : siempre 2 FOREVER : para siempre
am → **be**
amass [ə'mæs] *vt* : amasar, acumular
amateur ['æmətʃər, -tər, -ˌtʊr, -ˌtjʊr] *adj* : amateur — ~ *n* : amateur *mf*; aficionado *m*, -da *f*
amaze [ə'meɪz] *vt* **amazed; amazing** : asombrar — **amazement** [ə'meɪzmənt] *n* : asombro *m* — **amazing** [ə'meɪzɪŋ] *adj* : asombroso
ambassador [æm'bæsədər] *n* : embajador *m*, -dora *f*
amber ['æmbər] *n* : ámbar *m*
ambiguous [æm'bɪgjʊəs] *adj* : ambiguo — **ambiguity** [ˌæmbə'gjuːəţi] *n, pl* **-ties** : ambigüedad *f*
ambition [æm'bɪʃən] *n* : ambición *f* — **ambitious** [æm'bɪʃəs] *adj* : ambicioso
ambivalence [æm'bɪvələnts] *n* : ambivalencia *f* — **ambivalent** [æm'bɪvələnt] *adj* : ambivalente
amble ['æmbəl] *vi or* ~ **along** : andar sin prisa
ambulance ['æmbjələnts] *n* : ambulancia *f*
ambush ['æmˌbʊʃ] *vt* : emboscar — ~ *n* : emboscada *f*
amen ['eɪ'mɛn, 'ɑ-] *interj* : amén
amenable [ə'miːnəbəl, -'mɛ-] *adj* ~ **to** : receptivo a
amend [ə'mɛnd] *vt* : enmendar — **amendment** [ə'mɛndmənt] *n* : enmienda *f* — **amends** [ə'mɛndz] *ns & pl* **make ~ for** : reparar

amenities [ə'mɛnəţiz, -miː-] *npl* : servicios *mpl*, comodidades *fpl*
American [ə'mɛrɪkən] *adj* : americano
amethyst ['æməθəst] *n* : amatista *f*
amiable ['eɪmiːəbəl] *adj* : amable, agradable
amicable ['æmɪkəbəl] *adj* : amigable, amistoso
amid [ə'mɪd] *or* **amidst** [ə'mɪdst] *prep* : en medio de, entre
amiss [ə'mɪs] *adv* 1 : mal 2 **take sth** ~ : tomar algo a mal — ~ *adj* 1 WRONG : malo 2 **something is** ~ : algo anda mal
ammonia [ə'moɪnjə] *n* : amoníaco *m*
ammunition [æmjə'nɪʃən] *n* : municiones *fpl*
amnesia [æm'niːʒə] *n* : amnesia *f*
amnesty ['æmnəsti] *n, pl* **-ties** : amnistía *f*
among [ə'mʌŋ] *prep* : entre
amorous ['æmərəs] *adj* : amoroso
amount [ə'maʊnt] *vi* 1 ~ **to** : equivaler a 2 ~ **to** TOTAL : sumar, ascender a — ~ *n* : cantidad *f*
amphibian [æm'fɪbiən] *n* : anfibio *m* — **amphibious** [æm'fɪbiəs] *adj* : anfibio
amphitheater ['æmfə'θiːəţər] *n* : anfiteatro *m*
ample ['æmpəl] *adj* **-pler; -plest** 1 SPACIOUS : amplio, extenso 2 ABUNDANT : abundante
amplify ['æmpləfaɪ] *vt* **-fied; -fying** : amplificar — **amplifier** ['æmpləfaɪər] *n* : amplificador *m*
amputate ['æmpjəteɪt] *vt* **-tated; -tating** : amputar — **amputation** [æmpjə'teɪʃən] *n* : amputación *f*
amuse [ə'mjuːz] *vt* **amused; amusing** 1 : hacer reír, divertir 2 ENTERTAIN : entretener — **amusement** [ə'mjuːzmənt] *n* : diversión *f* — **amusing** *adj* : divertido
an → **a²**
analogy [ə'nælədʒi] *n, pl* **-gies** : analogía *f* — **analogous** [ə'næləgəs] *adj* : análogo
analysis [ə'næləsəs] *n, pl* **-yses** [-siːz] : análisis *m* — **analytic** [ænə'lɪţɪk] *or* **analytical** [-ţɪkəl] *adj* : analítico — **analyze** ['ænəlaɪz] *vt* **-lyzed; -lyzing** : analizar
anarchy ['ænərki, -nɑr-] *n* : anarquía *f*
anatomy [ə'næţəmi] *n, pl* **-mies** : anatomía *f* — **anatomic** [ænə'tɑmɪk] *or* **anatomical** [-mɪkəl] *adj* : anatómico
ancestor ['æn,sɛstər] *n* : antepasado *m*, -da *f* — **ancestral** [æn'sɛstrəl] *adj* : ancestral — **ancestry** ['æn,sɛstri] *n* 1 DE-

SCENT : linaje *m*, abolengo *m* 2 ANCESTORS : antepasados *mpl*, -das *fpl*
anchor ['æŋkər] *n* 1 : ancla *f* 2 : presentador *m*, -dora *f* (en televisión) — ~ *vt* 1 : anclar 2 FASTEN : sujetar — *vi* : anclar
anchovy ['æn,tʃoːvi, æn'tʃoː-] *n, pl* **-vies** *or* **-vy** : anchoa *f*
ancient ['eɪntʃənt] *adj* : antiguo, viejo
and ['ænd] *conj* 1 : y (*e* before words beginning with *i-* or *hi-*) 2 **come** ~ **see** : ven a ver 3 **more** ~ **more** : cada vez más 4 **try** ~ **finish it soon** : trata de terminarlo pronto
anecdote ['ænɪk,doːt] *n* : anécdota *f*
anemia [ə'niːmiə] *n* : anemia *f* — **anemic** [ə'niːmɪk] *adj* : anémico
anesthesia [ænəs'θiːʒə] *n* : anestesia *f* — **anesthetic** [ænəs'θɛţɪk] *adj* : anestésico — ~ *n* : anestésico *m*
anew [ə'nuː, -'njuː] *adv* : de nuevo, nuevamente
angel ['eɪndʒəl] *n* : ángel *m* — **angelic** [æn'dʒɛlɪk] *or* **angelical** [-lɪkəl] *adj* : angélico
anger ['æŋgər] *vt* : enojar, enfadar — ~ *n* : ira *f*, enojo *m*, enfado *m*
angle *n* 1 : ángulo *m* 2 POINT OF VIEW : perspectiva *f*, punto *m* de vista — **angler** ['æŋglər] *n* : pescador *m*, -dora *f*
Anglo–Saxon [æŋglo'sæksən] *adj* : anglosajón
angry ['æŋgri] *adj* **-grier; -est** : enojado, enfadado
anguish ['æŋgwɪʃ] *n* : angustia *f*
angular ['æŋgjələr] *adj* 1 : angular 2 ~ **features** : rasgos *mpl* angulosos
animal ['ænəməl] *n* : animal *m*
animate ['ænəmət] *adj* : animado — ['ænə,meɪt] *vt* **-mated; -mating** : animar — **animated** *adj* 1 : animado 2 ~ **cartoon** : dibujos *mpl* animados — **animation** [ænə'meɪʃən] *n* : animación *f*
animosity [ænə'mɑsəţi] *n, pl* **-ties** : animosidad *f*
anise ['ænəs] *n* : anís *m*
ankle ['æŋkəl] *n* : tobillo *m*
annals ['ænəlz] *npl* : anales *mpl*
annex [ə'nɛks, 'æ,nɛks] *vt* : anexar — ~ ['æ,nɛks, -nɪks] *n* : anexo *m*
annihilate [ə'naɪə,leɪt] *vt* **-lated; -lating** : aniquilar — **annihilation** [ə,naɪə'leɪʃən] *n* : aniquilación *f*
anniversary [ænə'vərsəri] *n, pl* **-ries** : aniversario *m*
annotate ['ænəteɪt] *vt* **-tated; -tating** : anotar — **annotation** [ænə'teɪʃən] *n* : anotación *f*
announce [ə'naʊns] *vt* **-nounced;**

-nouncing : anunciar — **announcement** [ə'naʊntsmənt] n : anuncio m — **announcer** [ə'naʊntsər] n : locutor m, -tora f

annoy [ə'nɔɪ] vt : fastidiar, molestar — **annoyance** [ə'nɔɪənts] n : fastidio m, molestia f — **annoying** [ə'nɔɪɪŋ] adj : molesto, fastidioso

annual ['ænjʊəl] adj : anual — ~ n : anuario m

annuity [ə'nuːəti] n, pl -ties : anualidad f

annul [ə'nʌl] vt annulled; annulling : anular — **annulment** [ə'nʌlmənt] n : anulación f

anoint [ə'nɔɪnt] vt : ungir

anomaly [ə'nɑməli] n, pl -lies : anomalía f

anonymous [ə'nɑnəməs] adj : anónimo — **anonymity** [ænə'nɪməti] n : anonimato m

another [ə'nʌðər] adj 1 : otro 2 in ~ minute : en un minuto más — ~ pron : otro, otra

answer ['æntsər] n 1 REPLY : respuesta f, contestación f 2 SOLUTION : solución f — ~ vt 1 : contestar a, responder a 2 ~ the door : abrir la puerta — vi : contestar, responder

ant ['ænt] n : hormiga f

antagonize [æn'tægə,naɪz] vt -nized; -nizing : provocar la enemistad de — **antagonism** [æn'tægə,nɪzəm] n : antagonismo m

antarctic [ænt'ɑrktɪk, -'ɑrtˌɪk] adj : antártico

antelope ['æntəl,oːp] n, pl -lope or -lopes : antílope m

antenna [æn'tenə] n, pl -nae [-,niː, -,naɪ] or -nas : antena f

anthem ['ænθəm] n : himno m

anthology [æn'θɑlədʒi] n, pl -gies : antología f

anthropology [ænθrə'pɑlədʒi] n : antropología f

antibiotic [æntibaɪ'ɑtɪk, æntaɪ-, -bi-] adj : antibiótico — ~ n : antibiótico m

antibody ['ænti,bɑdi] n, pl -bodies : anticuerpo m

anticipate [æn'tɪsə,peɪt] vt -pated; -pating 1 FORESEE : anticipar, prever 2 EXPECT : esperar — **anticipation** [æn,tɪsə'peɪʃən] n : anticipación f, expectación f

antics ['æntɪks] npl : payasadas fpl

antidote ['ænti,doːt] n : antídoto m

antifreeze ['ænti,friːz] n : anticongelante m

antipathy [æn'tɪpəθi] n, pl -thies : antipatía f

antiquated ['æntə,kweɪtəd] adj : anticuado

antique [æn'tiːk] adj : antiguo — ~ n : antigüedad f — **antiquity** [æn'tɪkwə-ti] n, pl -ties : antigüedad f

anti-Semitic [æntisə'mɪtɪk, æntaɪ-] adj : antisemita

antiseptic [æntə'septɪk] adj : antiséptico — ~ n : antiséptico m

antisocial [ænti'soːʃəl, æntaɪ-] adj 1 : antisocial 2 UNSOCIABLE : poco sociable

antithesis [æn'tɪθəsɪs] n, pl -eses [-,siːz] : antítesis f

antlers ['æntlərz] npl : cornamenta f

antonym ['æntə,nɪm] n : antónimo m

anus ['eɪnəs] n : ano m

anvil ['ænvəl, -vɪl] n : yunque m

anxiety [æŋk'zaɪəti] n, pl -eties 1 APPREHENSION : inquietud f, ansiedad f 2 EAGERNESS : anhelo m — **anxious** ['æŋkʃəs] adj 1 WORRIED : inquieto, preocupado 2 EAGER : ansioso — **anxiously** ['æŋkʃəsli] adv : con ansiedad

any ['eni] adv 1 SOMEWHAT : algo, un poco 2 it's not ~ good : no sirve para nada 3 we can't wait ~ longer : no podemos esperar más — ~ adj 1 : alguno 2 (in negative constructions) : ningún 3 WHATEVER : cualquier 4 in ~ case : en todo caso — ~ pron 1 : alguno, -na 2 : ninguno, -na 3 do you want ~ more rice? : ¿quieres más arroz?

anybody ['eni,bʌdi, -,bə-] → anyone

anyhow ['eni,haʊ] adv 1 : de todas formas 2 HAPHAZARDLY : de cualquier modo

anymore [,eni'mor] adv not ~ : ya no

anyone ['eni,wʌn] pron 1 SOMEONE : alguien 2 WHOEVER : quienquiera 3 I don't see ~ : no veo a nadie

anyplace ['eni,pleɪs] → anywhere

anything ['eni,θɪŋ] pron 1 SOMETHING : algo, alguna cosa 2 (in negative constructions) : nada 3 WHATEVER : cualquier cosa, lo que sea

anytime ['eni,taɪm] adv : en cualquier momento

anyway ['eni,weɪ] → anyhow

anywhere ['eni,hwer] adv 1 : en cualquier parte, dondequiera 2 (used in questions) : en algún sitio 3 I can't find it ~ : no lo encuentro por ninguna parte

apart [ə'pɑrt] adv 1 : aparte 2 ~ from : excepto, aparte de 3 fall ~ : deshacerse, hacerse pedazos 4 live ~ : vivir separados 5 take ~ : desmontar, desmantelar

apartment [ə'pɑrtmənt] *n* : apartamento *m*

apathy ['æpəθi] *n* : apatía *f* — **apathetic** [æp'θɛtɪk] *adj* : apático, indiferente

ape *n* : simio *m*

aperture ['æpərtʃər, -,tʃur] *n* : abertura *f*

apex ['eɪˌpɛks] *n, pl* **apexes** *or* **apices** ['eɪpə,siz, 'æ-] : ápice *m*, cumbre *f*

apiece [ə'piːs] *adv* : cada uno

aplomb [ə'plɑm, -'plʌm] *n* : aplomo *m*

apology [ə'pɑlədʒi] *n, pl* **-gies** : disculpa *f* — **apologetic** [ə,pɑlə'dʒɛtɪk] *adj* : lleno de disculpas — **apologize** [ə'pɑlədʒaɪz] *vi* **-gized; -gizing** : disculparse, pedir perdón

apostle [ə'pɑsəl] *n* : apóstol *m*

apostrophe [ə'pɑstrə,fi:] *n* : apóstrofo *m*

appall [ə'pɔl] *vt* : horrorizar — **appalling** [ə'pɔlɪŋ] *adj* : horroroso

apparatus [,æpə'ræ,təs, -reɪ-] *n, pl* **-tuses** *or* **-tus** : aparato *m*

apparel [ə'pærəl] *n* : ropa *f*

apparent [ə'pærənt] *adj* **1** OBVIOUS : claro, evidente **2** SEEMING : aparente — **apparently** [ə'pærəntli] *adv* : al parecer, por lo visto

apparition [,æpə'rɪʃən] *n* : aparición *f*

appeal [ə'piːl] *vi* **1** ~ **for** : solicitar **2** ~ **to** : apelar a (la bondad de algn, etc.) **3** ~ **to** ATTRACT : atraer a — ~ *n* **1** : apelación *f* (en derecho) **2** REQUEST : llamamiento *m* **3** ATTRACTION : atractivo *m* — **appealing** [ə'piːlɪŋ] *adj* : atractivo

appear [ə'pɪr] *vi* **1** : aparecer **2** : comparecer (ante un tribunal), actuar (en el teatro) **3** SEEM : parecer — **appearance** [ə'pɪrənts] *n* **1** : aparición *f* **2** LOOK : apariencia *f*, aspecto *m*

appease [ə'piːz] *vt* **-peased; -peasing** : apaciguar, aplacar

appendix [ə'pɛndɪks] *n, pl* **-dixes** *or* **-dices** [-də,siz] : apéndice *m* — **appendicitis** [ə,pɛndə'saɪtəs] *n* : apendicitis *f*

appetite ['æpə,taɪt] *n* : apetito *m* — **appetizer** ['æpə,taɪzər] *n* : aperitivo *m* — **appetizing** ['æpə,taɪzɪŋ] *adj* : apetitoso

applaud [ə'plɔd] *v* : aplaudir — **applause** [ə'plɔz] *n* : aplauso *m*

apple ['æpəl] *n* : manzana *f*

appliance [ə'plaɪənts] *n* : aparato *m*

apply [ə'plaɪ] *v* **-plied; -plying** *vt* **1** : aplicar **2** ~ **oneself** : aplicarse — *vi* **1** : aplicarse **2** ~ **for** : solicitar, pedir — **applicable** ['æplɪkəbəl, ə'plɪkə-] *adj* : aplicable — **applicant** ['æplɪkənt] *n* : solicitante *mf*; candidato *m*, -ta *f* — **application** [,æplə'keɪʃən] *n* **1** : apli-

cación *f* **2** : solicitud *f* (para un empleo, etc.)

appoint [ə'pɔɪnt] *vt* **1** NAME : nombrar **2** FIX, SET : fijar, señalar — **appointment** [ə'pɔɪntmənt] *n* **1** APPOINTING : nombramiento *m* **2** ENGAGEMENT : cita *f*

apportion [ə'pɔrʃən] *vt* : distribuir, repartir

appraise [ə'preɪz] *vt* **-praised; -praising** : evaluar, valorar — **appraisal** [ə'preɪzəl] *n* : evaluación *f*

appreciate [ə'pri:ʃi,eɪt, -'prɪ-] *v* **-ated; -ating** *vt* **1** VALUE : apreciar **2** UNDERSTAND : darse cuenta de **3 I** ~ **your help** : te agradezco tu ayuda — *vi* : aumentar en valor — **appreciation** [ə,pri:ʃi'eɪʃən, -,prɪ-] *n* **1** GRATITUDE : agradecimiento *m* **2** VALUING : apreciación *f*, valoración *f* — **appreciative** [ə'pri:ʃətɪv, -,prɪ-; ə'pri:ʃi,eɪ-] *adj* **1** : apreciativo **2** GRATEFUL : agradecido

apprehend [,æprɪ'hɛnd] *vt* **1** ARREST : aprehender, detener **2** DREAD : temer **3** COMPREHEND : comprender — **apprehension** [,æprɪ'hɛntʃən] *n* **1** ARREST : detención *f*, aprehensión *f* **2** ANXIETY : aprensión *f*, temor *m* — **apprehensive** [,æprɪ'hɛntsɪv] *adj* : aprensivo, inquieto

apprentice [ə'prɛntɪs] *n* : aprendiz *m*, -diza *f*

approach [ə'proːtʃ] *vt* **1** NEAR : acercarse a **2** : dirigirse a (algn), abordar (un problema, etc.) — *vi* : acercarse — ~ *n* **1** NEARING : acercamiento *m* **2** POSITION : enfoque *m* **3** ACCESS : acceso *m* — **approachable** [ə'proːtʃəbəl] *adj* : accesible, asequible

appropriate [ə'proːpri,eɪt] *vt* **-ated; -ating** : apropiarse de — ~ [ə'proːpri-ət] *adj* : apropiado

approve [ə'pruːv] *vt* **-proved; -proving** : aprobar — **approval** [ə'pruːvəl] *n* : aprobación *f*

approximate [ə'prɑksəmət] *adj* : aproximado — ~ [ə'prɑksə,meɪt] *vt* **-mated; -mating** : aproximarse a — **approximately** [ə'prɑksəmətli] *adv* : aproximadamente

apricot ['æprə,kɑt, 'eɪ-] *n* : albaricoque *m*, chabacano *m* Lat

April ['eɪprəl] *n* : abril *m*

apron ['eɪprən] *n* : delantal *m*

apropos [,æprə'poː, 'æprə,poː] *adv* : a propósito

apt [æpt] *adj* **1** FITTING : apto, apropiado **2** LIABLE : propenso — **aptitude** ['æptə,tuːd, -,tjuːd] *n* : aptitud *f*

aquarium [ə'kwæriəm] n, pl **-iums** or **-ia** [-iə] : acuario m

aquatic [ə'kwɑt̬ɪk, -'kwæ-] adj : acuático

aqueduct ['ækwə,dʌkt] n : acueducto m

Arab ['ærəb] adj — **Arabic** ['ærəbɪk] adj : árabe — ~ n : árabe m (idioma)

arbitrary ['ɑrbə,treri] adj : arbitrario

arbitrate ['ɑrbə,treɪt] v **-trated; -trating** : arbitrar — **arbitration** [,ɑrbə'treɪʃən] n : arbitraje m

arc ['ɑrk] n : arco m

arcade [ɑr'keɪd] n 1 : arcada f 2 **shopping ~** : galería f comercial

arch ['ɑrtʃ] n : arco m — ~ vt : arquear — vi : arquearse

archaeology or **archeology** [,ɑrki-'ɑlədʒi] n : arqueología f — **archaeological** [,ɑrkiə'lɑdʒɪkəl] adj : arqueológico — **archaeologist** [,ɑrki'ɑlə-dʒɪst] n : arqueólogo m, -ga f

archaic [ɑr'keɪɪk] adj : arcaico

archbishop [ɑrtʃ'bɪʃəp] n : arzobispo m

archery ['ɑrtʃəri] n : tiro m al arco

archipelago [,ɑrkə'pelə,goː, ,ɑrtʃə-] n, pl **-goes** or **-gos** [-goːz] : archipiélago m

architecture ['ɑrkə,tektʃər] n : arquitectura f — **architect** ['ɑrkə,tekt] n : arquitecto m, -ta f — **architectural** [,ɑrkə-'tektʃərəl] adj : arquitectónico

archives ['ɑr,kaɪvz] npl : archivo m

archway ['ɑrtʃ,weɪ] n : arco m (de entrada)

arctic ['ɑrktɪk, 'ɑrt̬-] adj : ártico

ardent ['ɑrdənt] adj : ardiente, fervoroso — **ardor** ['ɑrdər] n : ardor m, fervor m

arduous ['ɑrdʒuəs] adj : arduo

are → be

area ['æriə] n 1 REGION : área f, zona f 2 FIELD : campo m 3 ~ **code** : código m de la zona Lat, prefijo m Spain

arena [ə'riːnə] n : arena f, ruedo m

aren't ['ɑrnt, 'ɑrənt] (contraction of **are not**) → **be**

Argentine ['ɑrdʒən,taɪn, -,tiːn] or **Argentinean** or **Argentinian** [,ɑrdʒən'tɪniən] adj : argentino

argue ['ɑr,gjuː] v **-gued; -guing** vi 1 QUARREL : discutir 2 ~ **against** : argumentar contra — vt : argumentar, sostener — **argument** ['ɑrgjəmənt] n 1 QUARREL : disputa f, discusión f 2 REASONING : argumentos mpl

arid ['ærəd] adj : árido — **aridity** [ə'rɪdə-t̬i, æ-] n : aridez f

arise [ə'raɪz] vi **arose** [ə'roːz]; **arisen** [ə'rɪzən]; **arising** 1 : levantarse 2 ~ **from** : surgir de

aristocracy [,ærə'stɑkrəsi] n, pl **-cies** : aristocracia f — **aristocrat** [ə'rɪstə-,kræt] n : aristócrata mf — **aristocratic** [ə,rɪstə'kræt̬ɪk] adj : aristocrático

arithmetic [ə'rɪθmət̬ɪk] n : aritmética f

ark ['ɑrk] n : arca f

arm ['ɑrm] n 1 : brazo m 2 WEAPON : arma f — ~ vt : armar — **armament** ['ɑrməmənt] n : armamento m — **armchair** ['ɑrm,tʃer] n : sillón m — **armed** ['ɑrmd] adj 1 ~ **forces** : fuerzas fpl armadas 2 ~ **robbery** : robo m a mano armada

armistice ['ɑrməstɪs] n : armisticio m

armor or Brit **armour** ['ɑrmər] n : armadura f — **armored** or Brit **armoured** ['ɑrmərd] adj : blindado, acorazado — **armory** or Brit **armoury** ['ɑrmri, 'ɑrməri] : arsenal m

armpit ['ɑrm,pɪt] n : axila f, sobaco m

army ['ɑrmi] n, pl **-mies** : ejército m

aroma [ə'roːmə] n : aroma m — **aromatic** [,ærə'mæt̬ɪk] adj : aromático

around [ə'raʊnd] adv 1 : de circunferencia 2 NEARBY : por ahí 3 APPROXIMATELY : más o menos, aproximadamente 4 **all** ~ : por todos lados, todo alrededor 5 **turn** ~ : voltearse — ~ prep 1 SURROUNDING : alrededor de 2 THROUGHOUT : por 3 NEAR : cerca de 4 ~ **the corner** : a la vuelta de la esquina

arouse [ə'raʊz] vt **aroused; arousing** 1 AWAKE : despertar 2 EXCITE : excitar

arrange [ə'reɪndʒ] vt **-ranged; -ranging** : arreglar, poner en orden — **arrangement** [ə'reɪndʒmənt] n 1 ORDER : arreglo m 2 ~**s** npl : preparativos mpl

array [ə'reɪ] n : selección f, surtido m

arrears [ə'rɪrz] npl 1 : atrasos mpl 2 **be in** ~ : estar atrasado en pagos

arrest [ə'rest] vt : detener — ~ n 1 : arresto m, detención f 2 **under** ~ : detenido

arrive [ə'raɪv] vi **-rived; -riving** : llegar — **arrival** [ə'raɪvəl] n : llegada f

arrogance ['ærəgənts] n : arrogancia f — **arrogant** ['ærəgənt] adj : arrogante

arrow ['æroː] n : flecha f

arsenal ['ɑrsənəl] n : arsenal m

arsenic ['ɑrsənɪk] n : arsénico m

arson ['ɑrsən] n : incendio m premeditado

art ['ɑrt] n 1 : arte m 2 ~**s** npl : letras fpl (en educación) 3 **fine** ~**s** : bellas artes fpl

artefact Brit → **artifact**

artery ['ɑrt̬əri] n, pl **-teries** : arteria f

artful ['ɑrtfəl] adj : astuto, taimado

arthritis [ɑr'θraɪt̬əs] n, pl **-tides** [ɑr'θrɪt̬ə-,diːz] : artritis f — **arthritic** [ɑr'θrɪt̬ɪk] adj : artrítico

artichoke ['ɑrtə,tʃo:k] *n* : alcachofa *f*

article ['ɑrtɪkəl] *n* : artículo *m*

articulate [ɑr'tɪkjə,leɪt] *vt* **-lated; -lating** : articular — ~ [ɑr'tɪkjələt] *adj* **be ~** : expresarse bien

artifact *or Brit* **artefact** ['ɑrtə,fækt] *n* : artefacto *m*

artificial [,ɑrtə'fɪʃəl] *adj* : artificial

artillery [ɑr'tɪləri] *n, pl* **-leries** : artillería *f*

artisan ['ɑrtə,zən, -sən] *n* : artesano *m*, -na *f*

artist ['ɑrtɪst] *n* : artista *mf* — **artistic** [ɑr'tɪstɪk] *adj* : artístico

as ['æz] *adv* **1** : tan, tanto **2 ~ much** : tanto como **3 ~ tall ~** : tan alto como **4 ~ well** : también — ~ *conj* **1** WHILE : mientras **2** (*referring to manner*) : como **3** SINCE : ya que **THOUGH** : por más que — ~ *prep* **1** : de **2** LIKE : como — ~ *pron* : que

asbestos [æz'bestəs, æs-] *n* : asbesto *m*, amianto *m*

ascend [ə'send] *vi* : ascender, subir — *vt* : subir (a) — **ascent** [ə'sent] *n* : ascensión *f*, subida *f*

ascertain [,æsər'teɪn] *vt* : averiguar, determinar

ascribe [ə'skraɪb] *vt* **-cribed; -cribing** : atribuir

as for *prep* : en cuanto a

ash¹ ['æʃ] *n* : ceniza *f*

ash² *n* : fresno *m* (árbol)

ashamed [ə'ʃeɪmd] *adj* : avergonzado, apenado *Lat*

ashore [ə'ʃor] *adv* **1** : en tierra **2 go ~** : desembarcar

ashtray ['æʃ,treɪ] *n* : cenicero *m*

Asian ['eɪʒən, -ʃən] *adj* : asiático

aside [ə'saɪd] *adv* **1** : a un lado **2** APART : aparte **3 set ~** : guardar — **aside from** *prep* **1** BESIDES : además de **2** EXCEPT : aparte de, menos

as if *conj* : como si

ask ['æsk] *vt* **1** : preguntar **2** REQUEST : pedir **3** INVITE : invitar — *vi* : preguntar

askance [ə'skænts] *adv* **look ~** : mirar de soslayo

askew [ə'skju:] *adj* : torcido, ladeado

asleep [ə'sli:p] *adj* **1** : dormido **2 fall ~** : dormirse, quedarse dormido

as of *prep* : desde, a partir de

asparagus [ə'spærəgəs] *n* : espárrago *m*

aspect ['æ,spekt] *n* : aspecto *m*

asphalt ['æs,fɔlt] *n* : asfalto *m*

asphyxiate [æ'sfɪksi,eɪt] *v* **-ated; -ating** *vt* : asfixiar — **asphyxiation** [æ,sfɪksi-'eɪʃən] *n* : asfixia *f*

aspire [ə'spaɪr] *vi* **-pired; -piring** : aspirar — **aspiration** [,æspə'reɪʃən] *n* : aspiración *f*

aspirin ['æsprən, 'æspə-] *n, pl* **aspirin** *or* **aspirins** : aspirina *f*

ass ['æs] *n* **1** : asno *m* **2** IDIOT : imbécil *mf*, idiota *mf*

assail [ə'seɪl] *vt* : atacar, asaltar — **assailant** [ə'seɪlənt] *n* : asaltante *mf*, atacante *mf*

assassin [ə'sæsən] *n* : asesino *m*, -na *f* — **assassinate** [ə'sæsə,neɪt] *vt* **-nated; -nating** : asesinar — **assassination** [ə,sæsən'eɪʃən] *n* : asesinato *m*

assault [ə'sɔlt] *n* **1** : ataque *m*, asalto *m* **2** : agresión *f* (contra algn) — ~ *vt* : atacar, asaltar

assemble [ə'sembəl] *v* **-bled; -bling** *vt* **1** GATHER : reunir, juntar **2** CONSTRUCT : montar — *vi* : reunirse — **assembly** [ə'sembli] *n, pl* **-blies 1** MEETING : reunión *f*, asamblea *f* **2** CONSTRUCTING : montaje *m*

assent [ə'sent] *vi* : asentir, consentir — ~ *n* : asentimiento *m*

assert [ə'sərt] *vt* **1** : afirmar **2 ~ oneself** : hacerse valer — **assertion** [ə'sərʃən] *n* : afirmación *f* — **assertive** [ə'sərtɪv] *adj* : firme, enérgico

assess [ə'ses] *vt* : evaluar, valorar — **assessment** [ə'sesmənt] *n* : evaluación *f*, valoración *f*

asset ['æ,set] *n* **1** : ventaja *f*, recurso *m* **2 ~s** *npl* : bienes *mpl*, activo *m*

assiduous [ə'sɪdʒuəs] *adj* : asiduo

assign [ə'saɪn] *vt* **1** APPOINT : designar, nombrar **2** ALLOT : asignar — **assignment** [ə'saɪnmənt] *n* **1** TASK : misión *f* **2** HOMEWORK : tarea *f* **3** ASSIGNING : asignación *f*

assimilate [ə'sɪmə,leɪt] *vt* **-lated; -lating** : asimilar

assist [ə'sɪst] *vt* : ayudar — **assistance** [ə'sɪstənts] *n* : ayuda *f* — **assistant** [ə'sɪstənt] *n* : ayudante *mf*

associate [ə'so:ʃi,eɪt, -si-] *v* **-ated; -ating** *vt* : asociar — *vi* : asociarse — ~ [ə'so:ʃiət, -siət] *n* : asociado *m*, -da *f*; socio *m*, -cia *f* — **association** [ə,so:ʃi-'eɪʃən, -si-] *n* : asociación *f*

as soon as *conj* : tan pronto como

assorted [ə'sɔrtəd] *adj* : surtido — **assortment** [ə'sɔrtmənt] *n* : surtido *m*, variedad *f*

assume [ə'su:m] *vt* **-sumed; -suming 1** SUPPOSE : suponer **2** UNDERTAKE : asumir **3** TAKE ON : adquirir, tomar — **assumption** [ə'sʌmpʃən] *n* : suposición *f*

assure [ə'ʃur] *vt* **-sured; -suring** : asegurar — **assurance** [ə'ʃurənts] *n* **1**

CERTAINTY : certeza *f*, garantía *f* 2 CON-
FIDENCE : confianza *f*, seguridad *f* (de
sí mismo)
asterisk ['æstə,rɪsk] *n* : asterisco *m*
asthma ['æzmə] *n* : asma *m*
as though → **as if**
as to *prep* : sobre, acerca de
astonish [ə'stɑnɪʃ] *vt* : asombrar — **astonishing** [ə'stɑnɪʃɪŋ] *adj* : asombroso
— **astonishment** [ə'stɑnɪʃmənt] *n*
: asombro *m*
astound [ə'staʊnd] *vt* : asombrar, pasmar — **astounding** [ə'staʊndɪŋ] *adj*
: asombroso, pasmoso
astray [ə'streɪ] *adv* **1 go** ~ : extraviarse
2 lead ~ : llevar por mal camino
astrology [ə'strɑlədʒi] *n* : astrología *f*
astronaut ['æstrə,nɔt] *n* : astronauta *mf*
astronomy [ə'strɑnəmi] *n, pl* **-mies**
: astronomía *f* — **astronomer** [ə-
'strɑnəmər] *n* : astrónomo *m*, -ma *f* —
astronomical [,æstrə'nɑmɪkəl] *adj* : astronómico
astute [ə'stuːt, -'stjuːt] *adj* : astuto, sagaz
— **astuteness** [ə'stuːtnəs, -'stjuːt-] *n*
: astucia *f*
as well as *conj* : tanto como — ~ *prep*
: además de, aparte de
asylum [ə'saɪləm] *n* **1** : asilo *m* **2 insane**
~ : manicomio *m*
at ['æt] *prep* **1** : a **2** ~ **home** : en casa **3**
~ **night** : en la noche, por la noche **4**
~ **two o'clock** : a las dos **5 be angry**
~ : estar enojado con **6 laugh** ~
: reírse de — **at all** *adv* **not** ~ : en absoluto, nada
ate → **eat**
atheist ['eɪθiːɪst] *n* : ateo *m*, atea *f* —
atheism ['eɪθiˌɪzəm] *n* : ateísmo *m*
athlete ['æθˌliːt] *n* : atleta *mf* — **athletic**
[æθ'letɪk] *adj* : atlético — **athletics**
[æθ'letɪks] *ns & pl* : atletismo *m*
atlas ['ætləs] *n* : atlas *m*
atmosphere ['ætməˌsfɪr] *n* **1** : atmósfera
f **2** AMBIENCE : ambiente *m* — **atmospheric** [,ætmə'sfɪrɪk, -'sfer-] *adj* : atmosférico
atom ['ætəm] *n* : átomo *m* — **atomic** [ə-
'tɑmɪk] *adj* : atómico
atomizer ['ætəˌmaɪzər] *n* : atomizador *m*
atone [ə'toːn] *vt* **atoned; atoning** ~ **for**
: expiar
atrocity [ə'trɑsəti] *n, pl* **-ties** : atrocidad
f — **atrocious** [ə'troːʃəs] *adj* : atroz
atrophy ['ætrəfi] *vi* **-phied; -phying**
: atrofiarse
attach [ə'tætʃ] *vt* **1** : sujetar, atar **2** : adjuntar (un documento, etc.) **3** ~ **importance to** : atribuir importancia a **4
become** ~**ed to s.o.** : encariñarse

con algn — **attachment** [ə'tætʃmənt] *n*
1 ACCESSORY : accesorio *m* **2** FOND-
NESS : cariño *m*
attack [ə'tæk] *v* : atacar — ~ *n* : ataque
m — **attacker** [ə'tækər] *n* : agresor *m*,
-sora *f*
attain [ə'teɪn] *vt* : lograr, alcanzar — **attainment** [ə'teɪnmənt] *n* : logro *m*
attempt [ə'tempt] *vt* : intentar — ~ *n*
: intento *m*
attend [ə'tend] *vt* : asistir a — *vi* **1** : asistir **2** ~ **to** : ocuparse de — **attendance** [ə'tendənts] *n* **1** : asistencia *f* **2**
TURNOUT : concurrencia *f* — **atten-
dant** *n* : encargado *m*, -da *f*; asistente
mf
attention [ə'tentʃən] *n* **1** : atención *f* **2**
pay ~ : prestar atención, hacer caso
— **attentive** [ə'tentɪv] *adj* : atento
attest [ə'test] *vt* : atestiguar
attic ['ætɪk] *n* : desván *m*
attire [ə'taɪr] *n* : atavío *m*
attitude ['æʈəˌtuːd, -ˌtjuːd] *n* **1** : actitud *f* **2**
POSTURE : postura *f*
attorney [ə'tərni] *n, pl* **-neys** : abogado
m, -da *f*
attract [ə'trækt] *vt* : atraer — **attraction**
[ə'trækʃən] *n* **1** : atracción *f* **2** APPEAL
: atractivo *m* — **attractive** [ə'træktɪv]
adj : atractivo, atrayente
attribute ['ætrəˌbjuːt] *n* : atributo *m* — ~
[ə'trɪˌbjuːt] *vt* **-tributed; -tributing**
: atribuir, imputar
auburn ['ɔbərn] *adj* : castaño rojizo
auction ['ɔkʃən] *n* : subasta *f* — ~ *vt or*
~ **off** : subastar
audacious [ɔ'deɪʃəs] *adj* : audaz — **audacity** [ɔ'dæsəti] *n, pl* **-ties** : audacia *f*,
atrevimiento *m*
audible ['ɔdəbəl] *adj* : audible
audience ['ɔdiənts] *n* **1** INTERVIEW : audiencia *f* **2** PUBLIC : público *m*
audiovisual [,ɔdio'vɪʒuəl] *adj* : audiovisual
audition [ɔ'dɪʃən] *n* : audición *f*
auditor ['ɔdətər] *n* **1** : auditor *m*, -tora *f*
(de finanzas) **2** STUDENT : oyente *mf*
auditorium [,ɔdə'toriəm] *n, pl* **-riums** *or*
-ria [-riə] : auditorio *m*
augment [ɔg'ment] *vt* : aumentar
augur ['ɔgər] *vi* ~ **well** : ser de buen
agüero
August ['ɔgəst] *n* : agosto *m*
aunt ['ænt, 'ɑnt] *n* : tía *f*
aura ['ɔrə] *n* : aura *f*
auspices ['ɔspəsəz, -ˌsiːz] *npl* : auspicios
mpl
auspicious [ɔ'spɪʃəs] *adj* : propicio,
prometedor

austere [ɔ'stɪr] *adj* : austero — **austerity** [ɔ'sterəti] *n, pl* **-ties** : austeridad *f*
Australian [ɔ'streɪljən] *adj* : australiano
authentic [ə'θentɪk, ɔ-] *adj* : auténtico
author ['ɔθər] *n* : autor *m*, -tora *f*
authority [ə'θɔrəti, ɔ-] *n, pl* **-ties** : autoridad *f* — **authoritarian** [ə,θɔrə'teriən, ə-] *adj* : autoritario — **authoritative** [ə'θɔrə,teɪtɪv, ɔ-] *adj* **1** RELIABLE : autorizado **2** DICTATORIAL : autoritario — **authorization** [,ɔθərə'zeɪʃən] *n* : autorización *f* — **authorize** ['ɔθə,raɪz] *vt* **-rized; -rizing** : autorizar
autobiography [,ɔtobaɪ'agrəfi] *n, pl* **-phies** : autobiografía *f* — **autobiographical** [,ɔtobaɪə'græfɪkəl] *adj* : autobiográfico
autograph ['ɔtə,græf] *n* : autógrafo *m* — ~ *vt* : autografiar
automatic [,ɔtə'mætɪk] *adj* : automático — **automate** ['ɔtə,meɪt] *vt* **-mated; -mating** : automatizar — **automation** [,ɔtə'meɪʃən] *n* : automatización *f*
automobile [,ɔtəmo'biːl, -'moːbiːl] *n* : automóvil *m*
autonomy [ɔ'tɑnəmi] *n, pl* **-mies** : autonomía *f* — **autonomous** [ɔ'tɑnəməs] *adj* : autónomo
autopsy ['ɔ,tɑpsi, -təp-] *n, pl* **-sies** : autopsia *f*
autumn ['ɔtəm] *n* : otoño *m*
auxiliary [ɔg'zɪljəri, -'zɪləri] *adj* : auxiliar — ~ *n, pl* **-ries** : auxiliar *mf*
avail [ə'veɪl] *vt* ~ **oneself of** : aprovecharse de — ~ *n* **to no** ~ : en vano — **available** [ə'veɪləbəl] *adj* : disponible — **availability** [ə,veɪlə'bɪləti] *n, pl* **-ties** : disponibilidad *f*
avalanche ['ævə,læntʃ] *n* : avalancha *f*
avarice ['ævərəs] *n* : avaricia *f*
avenge [ə'vendʒ] *vt* **avenged; avenging** : vengar
avenue ['ævə,nuː, -,njuː] *n* **1** : avenida *f* **2** MEANS : vía *f*
average ['ævrɪdʒ, 'ævə-] *n* : promedio *m* — ~ *adj* **1** MEAN : medio **2** ORDINARY : regular, ordinario — ~ *vt* **-aged; -aging 1** : hacer un promedio de **2** *or* ~ **out** : calcular el promedio de
averse [ə'vərs] *adj* **be** ~ **to** : sentir

aversión por — **aversion** [ə'vərʒən] *n* : aversión *f*
avert [ə'vərt] *vt* **1** AVOID : evitar, prevenir **2** ~ **one's eyes** : apartar los ojos
aviation [,eɪvi'eɪʃən] *n* : aviación *f* — **aviator** ['eɪvi,eɪtər] *n* : aviador *m*, -dora *f*
avid ['ævɪd] *adj* : ávido — **avidly** *adv* : con avidez
avocado [,ævə'kado, ,ɑvə-] *n, pl* **-dos** : aguacate *m*
avoid [ə'vɔɪd] *vt* : evitar — **avoidable** [ə'vɔɪdəbəl] *adj* : evitable
await [ə'weɪt] *vt* : esperar
awake [ə'weɪk] *v* **awoke** [ə'woːk]; **awoken** [ə'woːkən] *or* **awaked; awaking** : despertar — ~ *adj* : despierto — **awaken** [ə'weɪkən] *v* → **awake**
award [ə'wɔrd] *vt* **1** : otorgar, conceder (un premio, etc.) **2** : adjudicar (daños y perjuicios) — ~ *n* **1** PRIZE : premio *m* **2** : adjudicación *f*
aware [ə'wær] *adj* **be** ~ **of** : estar consciente de — **awareness** [ə'wærnəs] *n* : conciencia *f*
away [ə'weɪ] *adv* **1** (*referring to distance*) : de aquí, de distancia **2 far** ~ : lejos **3 give** ~ : regalar **4 go** ~ : irse **5 right** ~ : en seguida **6 take** ~ : quitar — ~ *adj* **1** ABSENT : ausente **2** ~ **game** : partido *m* fuera de casa
awe [ɔ] *n* : temor *m* reverencial — **awesome** ['ɔsəm] *adj* : imponente, formidable
awful ['ɔfəl] *adj* **1** : terrible, espantoso **2 an** ~ **lot** : muchísimo — **awfully** ['ɔfəli] *adv* : terriblemente
awhile [ə'hwaɪl] *adv* : un rato
awkward ['ɔkwərd] *adj* **1** CLUMSY : torpe **2** EMBARRASSING : embarazoso, delicado **3** DIFFICULT : difícil — **awkwardly** *adv* **1** : con dificultad **2** CLUMSILY : de manera torpe
awning ['ɔnɪŋ] *n* : toldo *m*
awry [ə'raɪ] *adj* **1** ASKEW : torcido **2 go** ~ : salir mal
ax *or* **axe** ['æks] *n* : hacha *f*
axiom ['æksiəm] *n* : axioma *m*
axis ['æksɪs] *n, pl* **axes** [-,siːz] : eje *m*
axle ['æksəl] *n* : eje *m*

B

b ['bi:] *n*, *pl* **b's** *or* **bs** ['bi:z] : b, segunda letra del alfabeto inglés

babble ['bæbəl] *vi* **-bled; -bling 1** : balbucear **2** MURMUR : murmurar — **~** *n* : balbuceo *m* (de bebé), murmullo *m* (de voces, de un arroyo)

baboon [bæ'bu:n] *n* : babuino *m*

baby ['beɪbi] *n*, *pl* **-bies** : bebé *m*; niño *m*, -ña *f* — **baby** *vt* **-bied; -bying** : mimar, consentir — **babyish** ['beɪbiʃ] *adj* : infantil — **baby-sit** ['beɪbi-ˌsɪt] *vi* **-sat** [-ˌsæt]; **-sitting** : cuidar a los niños

bachelor ['bætʃələr] *n* **1** : soltero *m* **2** GRADUATE : licenciado *m*, -da *f*

back ['bæk] *n* **1** : espalda *f* **2** REVERSE : reverso *m*, dorso *m*, revés *m* **3** REAR : fondo *m*, parte *f* trasera **4** : defensa *mf* (en deportes) — **~** *adv* **1** : atrás **2** be **~** : estar de vuelta **3** go **~** : volver **4** two years **~** : hace dos años — **~** *adj* **1** REAR : de atrás, trasero **2** OVERDUE : atrasado — **~** *vt* **1** SUPPORT : apoyar **2** *or* **~ up** : darle marcha atrás a (un vehículo) — *vi* **1 ~ down** : volverse atrás **2 ~ up** : retroceder — **backache** ['bæk,eɪk] *n* : dolor *m* de espalda — **backbone** ['bæk,boːn] *n* : columna *f* vertebral — **backfire** ['bæk,faɪr] *vi* **-fired; -firing** : petardear — **background** ['bæk-ˌgraʊnd] *n* **1** : fondo *m* (de un cuadro, etc.), antecedentes *mpl* (de una situación) **2** EXPERIENCE : formación *f* — **backhand** ['bæk,hænd] *adv* : de revés, con el revés — **backhanded** ['bæk,hændəd] *adj* : indirecto — **backing** ['bækɪŋ] *n* : apoyo *m*, respaldo *m* — **backlash** ['bæk,læʃ] *n* : reacción *f* violenta — **backlog** ['bæk,lɔg] *n* : atrasos *mpl* — **backpack** ['bæk,pæk] *n* : mochila *f* — **backstage** [ˌbæk'steɪdʒ, 'bæk-] *adv & adj* : entre bastidores — **backtrack** ['bæk,træk] *vi* : dar marcha atrás — **backup** ['bæk,ʌp] *n* **1** SUPPORT : respaldo *m*, apoyo *m* **2** : copia *f* de seguridad (para computadoras) — **backward** ['bækwərd] *or* **backwards** [-wərdz] *adv* **1** : hacia atrás **2** do it **~** : hacerlo al revés **3** fall **~** : caer de espaldas **4** bend over **~**s : hacer todo lo posible — **backward** *adj* **1** : hacia atrás **2** RETARDED : retrasado

3 SHY : tímido **4** UNDERDEVELOPED : atrasado

bacon ['beɪkən] *n* : tocino *m*, tocineta *f Lat*, bacon *m Spain*

bacteria [bæk'tɪriə] : bacterias *fpl*

bad ['bæd] *adj* **worse** ['wərs]; **worst** ['wərst] **1** : malo **2** ROTTEN : podrido **3** SEVERE : grave **4** from **~** to **worse** : de mal en peor **5** too **~**! : ¡qué lástima! — **~** *adv* → **badly**

badge ['bædʒ] *n* : insignia *f*, chapa *f*

badger ['bædʒər] *n* : tejón *m* — **~** *vt* : acosar

badly ['bædli] *adv* **1** : mal **2** SEVERELY : gravemente **3** want **~** : desear mucho

baffle ['bæfəl] *vi* **-fled; -fling** : desconcertar

bag ['bæg] *n* **1** : bolsa *f*, saco *m* **2** HANDBAG : bolso *m*, cartera *f Lat* **3** SUITCASE : maleta *f* — **~** *vt* **bagged; bagging** : ensacar, poner en una bolsa

baggage ['bægɪdʒ] *n* : equipaje *m*

baggy ['bægi] *adj* **-gier; -est** : holgado

bail ['beɪl] *n* : fianza *f* — **~** *vt* **1** : achicar (agua de un bote) **2** *or* **~ out** RELEASE : poner en libertad bajo fianza **3 ~ out** EXTRICATE : sacar de apuros

bailiff ['beɪləf] *n* : alguacil *mf*

bait ['beɪt] *vt* **1** : cebar **2** HARASS : acosar — **~** *n* : cebo *m*, carnada *f*

bake ['beɪk] *v* **baked; baking** *vt* : cocer al horno — *vi* : cocerse (al horno) — **baker** ['beɪkər] *n* : panadero *m*, -ra *f* — **bakery** ['beɪkəri] *n*, *pl* **-ries** : panadería *f*

balance ['bælənts] *n* **1** SCALES : balanza *f* **2** COUNTERBALANCE : contrapeso *m* **3** EQUILIBRIUM : equilibrio *m* **4** REMAINDER : resto *m* **5** *or* **bank ~** : saldo *m* — **~** *v* **-anced; -ancing** *vt* **1** : hacer el balance de (una cuenta) **2** EQUALIZE : equilibrar **3** WEIGH : sopesar — *vi* **1** : sostenerse en equilibro **2** : cuadrar (dícese de una cuenta)

balcony ['bælkəni] *n*, *pl* **-nies 1** : balcón *m* **2** : galería *f* (de un teatro)

bald ['bɔld] *adj* **1** : calvo **2** WORN : pelado **3** the **~** truth : la pura verdad

bale *n* : bala *f*, fardo *m*

baleful ['beɪlfəl] *adj* : siniestro

balk ['bɔk] *vi* **~ at** : resistirse a

ball ['bɔl] n 1 : pelota f, bola f, balón m 2 DANCE : baile m 3 ~ of string : ovillo m de cuerda

ballad ['bæləd] n : balada f

ballast n : lastre m

ball bearing n : cojinete m de bola

ballerina [bælə'rinə] n : bailarina f

ballet [bæˈleɪ, ˈbæˌleɪ] n : ballet m

ballistic [bəˈlɪstɪk] adj : balístico

balloon n : globo m

ballot n 1 : papeleta f (de voto) 2 VOTING : votación f

ballpoint pen [ˈbɔlˌpɔɪnt] n : bolígrafo m

ballroom [ˈbɔlˌruːm, -ˌrʊm] n : sala f de baile

balm ['bɑm, 'bɑlm] n : bálsamo m — **balmy** ['bɑmi, 'bɑl-] adj **balmier; -est** : templado, agradable

baloney [bəˈloːni] n NONSENSE : tonterías fpl

bamboo [bæmˈbuː] n : bambú m

bamboozle [bæmˈbuːzəl] vt **-zled; -zling** : engañar, embaucar

ban ['bæn] vt **banned; banning** : prohibir — ~ n : prohibición f

banal [bəˈnɑl, bəˈnæl, ˈbeɪnəl] adj : banal

banana [bəˈnænə] n : plátano m, banana f Lat, banano m Lat

band ['bænd] n 1 STRIP : banda f 2 GROUP : banda f, grupo m, conjunto m — vi ~ **together** : unirse, juntarse

bandage ['bændɪdʒ] n : vendaje m, venda f — ~ vt **-daged; -daging** : vendar

bandit ['bændət] n : bandido m, -da f

bandy ['bændi] vt **-died; -dying** ~ **about** : circular, repetir

bang ['bæŋ] vt STRIKE : golpear 2 SLAM : cerrar de un golpe — vi 1 SLAM : cerrarse de un golpe 2 ~ **on** : golpear — ~ n 1 BLOW : golpe m 2 NOISE : estrépito m 3 SLAM : portazo m

bangle ['bæŋgəl] n : brazalete m, pulsera f

bangs ['bæŋz] npl : flequillo m

banish ['bænɪʃ] vt : desterrar

banister ['bænəstər] n : pasamanos m, barandal m

bank ['bæŋk] n 1 : banco m 2 : orilla f, ribera f (de un río) 3 EMBANKMENT : terraplén m — ~ vt : depositar — vi 1 : ladearse (dícese de un avión) 2 : tener una cuenta (en un banco) 3 ~ **on** : contar con — **banker** ['bæŋkər] n : banquero m, -ra f — **banking** ['bæŋkɪŋ] n : banca f

bankrupt ['bæŋˌkrʌpt] adj : en bancarrota, en quiebra — **bankruptcy** ['bæŋˌkrʌptsi] n, pl **-cies** : quiebra f, bancarrota f

banner ['bænər] n : bandera f, pancarta f

banquet ['bæŋkwət] n : banquete m

banter ['bæntər] n : bromas fpl — ~ vi : hacer bromas

baptize [bæpˈtaɪz, ˈbæpˌtaɪz] vt **-tized; -tizing** : bautizar — **baptism** ['bæpˌtɪzəm] n : bautismo m

bar ['bɑr] n 1 : barra f 2 BARRIER : barrera f, obstáculo m 3 COUNTER : mostrador m, barra f 4 TAVERN : bar m 5 **behind ~s** : entre rejas 6 ~ **of soap** : pastilla f de jabón — ~ vt **barred; barring** 1 OBSTRUCT : obstruir, bloquear 2 EXCLUDE : excluir 3 PROHIBIT : prohibir — ~ prep 1 : excepto 2 ~ **none** : sin excepción

barbarian [bɑrˈbæriən] n : bárbaro m, -ra f

barbecue ['bɑrbɪˌkjuː] vt **-cued; -cuing** : asar a la parrilla — ~ n : barbacoa f

barbed wire ['bɑrbdˌwaɪr] n : alambre m de púas

barber ['bɑrbər] n : barbero m, -ra f

bare ['bær] adj 1 : desnudo 2 EMPTY : vacío 3 MINIMUM : mero, esencial — **barefaced** ['bærˌfeɪst] adj : descarado — **barefoot** ['bærˌfʊt] or **barefooted** [-ˌfʊtəd] adv & adj : descalzo — **barely** ['bærli] adv : apenas, por poco

bargain ['bɑrgən] n 1 AGREEMENT : acuerdo m 2 BUY : ganga f — ~ vi 1 : regatear, negociar 2 ~ **for** : contar con

barge ['bɑrdʒ] n : barcaza f — ~ vi **barged; barging** ~ **in** : entrometerse, interrumpir

baritone ['bærəˌtoːn] n : barítono m

bark[1] ['bɑrk] vi : ladrar — ~ n : ladrido m (de un perro)

bark[2] n : corteza f (de un árbol)

barley ['bɑrli] n : cebada f

barn ['bɑrn] n : granero m — **barnyard** ['bɑrnˌjɑrd] n : corral m

barometer [bəˈrɑmətər] n : barómetro m

baron ['bærən] n : barón m — **baroness** ['bærənɪs, -nəs, -ˌnɛs] n : baronesa f

barracks ['bærəks] ns & pl : cuartel m

barrage [bəˈrɑʒ, -ˈrɑdʒ] n 1 : descarga f (de artillería) 2 : aluvión m (de preguntas, etc.)

barrel ['bærəl] n 1 : barril m, tonel m 2 : cañón m (de un arma de fuego)

barren ['bærən] adj : estéril

barricade ['bærəˌkeɪd, ˌbærə'-] vt **-caded; -cading** : cerrar con barricadas — ~ n : barricada f

barrier ['bæriər] n : barrera f

barring ['bɑrɪŋ] prep : salvo

barrio ['bɑrio, 'bær-] n : barrio m

bartender ['bɑr,tendər] *n* : camarero *m*, -ra *f*

barter ['bɑrtər] *vt* : cambiar, trocar — ~ *n* : trueque *m*

base ['beɪs] *n, pl* **bases** : base *f* — ~ *vt* **based; basing** : basar, fundamentar — ~ *adj* **baser; basest** : vil

baseball ['beɪs,bɔl] *n* : beisbol *m*, béisbol *m*

basement ['beɪsmənt] *n* : sótano *m*

bash ['bæʃ] *vt* : golpear violentamente — ~ *n* **1** BLOW : golpe *m* **2** PARTY : fiesta *f*

bashful ['bæʃfəl] *adj* : tímido, vergonzoso

basic ['beɪsɪk] *adj* : básico, fundamental — **basically** ['beɪsɪkli] *adv* : fundamentalmente

basil ['beɪzəl, 'bæzəl] *n* : albahaca *f*

basin ['beɪsən] *n* **1** WASHBOWL : palangana *f*, lavabo *m* **2** : cuenca *f* (de un río)

basis ['beɪsəs] *n, pl* **bases** [-,siːz] : base *f*

bask ['bæsk] *vi* ~ **in the sun** : tostarse al sol

basket ['bæskət] *n* : cesta *f*, cesto *m* — **basketball** ['bæskət,bɔl] *n* : baloncesto *m*, basquetbol *m Lat*

bass¹ ['bæs] *n, pl* **bass** *or* **basses** : róbalo *m* (pesca)

bass² ['beɪs] *n* : bajo *m* (tono, voz, instrumento)

bassoon [bə'suːn, bæ-] *n* : fagot *m*

bastard ['bæstərd] *n* : bastardo *m*, -da *f*

baste ['beɪst] *vt* **basted; basting 1** STITCH : hilvanar **2** : bañar (carne)

bat¹ ['bæt] *n* : murciélago *m* (animal)

bat² *n* : bate *m* — ~ *vt* **batted; batting** : batear

batch ['bætʃ] *n* : hornada *f* (de pasteles, etc.), lote *m* (de mercancías), montón *m* (de trabajo), grupo *m* (de personas)

bath ['bæθ, 'bɑθ] *n, pl* **baths** ['bæðz, 'bæθs, 'bɑðz, 'bɑθs] **1** : baño *m* **2** BATHROOM : baño *m*, cuarto *m* de baño **3 take a** ~ : bañarse — **bathe** ['beɪð] *v* **bathed; bathing** *vt* : bañar, lavar — *vi* : bañarse — **bathrobe** ['bæθ,roːb] *n* : bata *f* (de baño) — **bathroom** ['bæθ,ruːm, -,rʊm] *n* : baño *m*, cuarto *m* de baño — **bathtub** ['bæθ,tʌb] *n* : bañera *f*, tina *f* (de baño)

baton [bə'tɑn] *n* : batuta *f*

battalion [bə'tæljən] *n* : batallón *m*

batter ['bætər] *vt* **1** BEAT : golpear **2** MISTREAT : maltratar — ~ *n* **1** : masa *f* para rebozar **2** HITTER : bateador *m*, -dora *f*

battery ['bætəri] *n, pl* **-teries** : batería *f*, pila *f* (de electricidad)

battle ['bætəl] *n* **1** : batalla *f* **2** STRUGGLE : lucha *f* — ~ *vi* **-tled; -tling** : luchar — **battlefield** ['bætəl,fiːld] *n* : campo *m* de batalla — **battleship** ['bætəl,ʃɪp] *n* : acorazado *m*

bawl ['bɔl] *vi* : llorar a gritos

bay¹ ['beɪ] *n* INLET : bahía *f*

bay² *n or* ~ **leaf** : laurel *m*

bay³ *vi* : aullar — ~ *n* : aullido *m*

bayonet [,beɪə'nɛt, 'beɪə,nɛt] *n* : bayoneta *f*

bay window *n* : ventana *f* en saliente

bazaar [bə'zɑr] *n* **1** : bazar *m* **2** SALE : venta *f* benéfica

be ['biː] *v* **was** ['wəz, 'wɑz], **were** ['wər]; **been** ['bɪn]; **being; am** ['æm], **is** ['ɪz], **are** ['ɑr] *vi* **1** : ser **2** (*expressing location*) : estar **3** (*expressing existence*) : ser, existir **4** (*expressing a state of being*) : estar, tener — *v impers* **1** (*indicating time*) : ser **2** (*indicating a condition*) : hacer, estar — *v aux* **1** (*expressing occurrence*) : ser **2** (*expressing possibility*) : poderse **3** (*expressing obligation*) : deber **4** (*expressing progression*) : estar

beach ['biːtʃ] *n* : playa *f*

beacon ['biːkən] *n* : faro *m*

bead ['biːd] *n* **1** : cuenta *f* **2** DROP : gota *f* **3** ~**s** *npl* NECKLACE : collar *m*

beak ['biːk] *n* : pico *m*

beam ['biːm] *n* **1** : viga *f* (de madera, etc.) **2** RAY : rayo *m* — ~ *vi* SHINE : brillar — *vt* BROADCAST : transmitir, emitir

bean ['biːn] *n* **1** : habichuela *f*, frijol *m* **2** **coffee** ~ : grano *m* **3 string** ~ : judía *f*

bear¹ ['bær] *n, pl* **bears** *or* **bear** : oso *m*, osa *f*

bear² *v* **bore** ['bor]; **borne** ['bɔrn]; **bearing** *vt* **1** CARRY : portar **2** ENDURE : soportar — *vi* ~ **right/left** : doble a la derecha/a la izquierda — **bearable** ['bærəbəl] *adj* : soportable

beard ['bɪrd] *n* : barba *f*

bearer ['bærər] *n* : portador *m*, -dora *f*

bearing ['bærɪŋ] *n* **1** MANNER : comportamiento *m* **2** SIGNIFICANCE : relación *f*, importancia *f* **3 get one's** ~**s** : orientarse

beast ['biːst] *n* : bestia *f*

beat ['biːt] *v* **beat; beaten** ['biːtən] *or* **beat; beating** *vt* **1** HIT : golpear **2** : batir (huevos, etc.) **3** DEFEAT : derrotar — *vi* : latir (dícese del corazón) — ~ *n* **1** : golpe *m* **2** : latido *m* (del corazón) **3** RHYTHM : ritmo *m*, tiempo *m* — **beating** ['biːtɪŋ] *n* **1** : paliza *f* **2** DEFEAT : derrota *f*

beauty ['bjuːţi] *n, pl* **-ties** : belleza *f* —
beautiful ['bjuːţɪfəl] *adj* : hermoso,
lindo — **beautifully** ['bjuːţɪfəli] *adv*
WONDERFULLY : maravillosamente —
beautify ['bjuːţɪˌfaɪ] *vt* **-fied; -fying**
: embellecer
beaver ['biːvər] *n* : castor *m*
because [brˈkʌz, -ˈkɔz] *conj* : porque —
because of *prep* : por, a causa de, debido a
beckon ['bɛkən] *vt* : llamar, hacer señas
a — *vi* : hacer una seña
become [brˈkʌm] *v* **-came** [-ˈkeɪm];
-come; -coming *vi* : hacerse, ponerse
— *vt* SUIT : favorecer — **becoming**
[brˈkʌmɪŋ] *adj* 1 SUITABLE : apropiado 2
FLATTERING : favorecedor
bed ['bɛd] *n* 1 : cama *f* 2 : cauce *m* (de
un río), fondo *m* (del mar) 3 : macizo
m (de flores) 4 **go to** ~ : irse a
la cama — **bedclothes** ['bɛdˌkloːz,
-ˌkloːðz] *npl* : ropa *f* de cama
bedlam ['bɛdləm] *n* : confusión *f*, caos
m
bedraggled [brˈdrægəld] *adj* : desaliñado, sucio
bedridden ['bɛdˌrɪdən] *adj* : postrado en
cama
bedroom ['bɛdˌruːm, -ˌrʊm] *n* : dormitorio *m*, recámara *f Lat*
bedspread ['bɛdˌsprɛd] *n* : colcha *f*
bedtime ['bɛdˌtaɪm] *n* : hora *f* de acostarse
bee ['biː] *n* : abeja *f*
beech ['biːtʃ] *n, pl* **beeches** *or* **beech**
: haya *f*
beef ['biːf] *n* : carne *f* de vaca, carne *f* de
res *Lat* — **beefsteak** ['biːfˌsteɪk] *n*
: bistec *m*
beehive ['biːhaɪv] *n* : colmena *f*
beeline ['biːˌlaɪn] *n* **make a** ~ **for** : irse
derecho a
beep ['biːp] *n* : pitido *m* — ~ *v* : pitar
beer ['bɪr] *n* : cerveza *f*
beet ['biːt] *n* : remolacha *f*
beetle ['biːţəl] *n* : escarabajo *m*
before [brˈfor] *adv* 1 : antes 2 **the**
month ~ : el mes anterior — ~ *prep*
1 (*in space*) : delante de, ante 2 (*in
time*) : antes de — ~ *conj* : antes de
que — **beforehand** [brˈforˌhænd] *adv*
: antes
befriend [brˈfrɛnd] *vt* : hacerse amigo de
beg ['bɛg] *v* **begged; begging** *vt* 1
: pedir, mendigar 2 ENTREAT : suplicar
— *vi* : mendigar, pedir limosna —
beggar ['bɛgər] *n* : mendigo *m*, -ga *f*
begin [brˈgɪn] *v* **-gan** [-ˈgæn]; **-gun**
[-ˈgʌn]; **-ginning** : empezar, comenzar
— **beginner** [brˈgɪnər] *n* : principiante

mf — **beginning** [brˈgɪnɪŋ] *n* : principio *m*, comienzo *m*
begrudge [brˈgrʌdʒ] *vt* **-grudged;**
-grudging 1 : dar de mala gana 2
ENVY : envidiar
behalf [brˈhæf, -ˈhaf] *n* **on** ~ **of** : de
parte de, en nombre de
behave [brˈheɪv] *vi* **-haved; -having**
: comportarse, portarse — **behavior**
[brˈheɪvjər] *n* : comportamiento *m*,
conducta *f*
behind [brˈhaɪnd] *adv* 1 : detrás 2 **fall** ~
: atrasarse — ~ *prep* 1 : atrás de, detrás de 2 **be** ~ **schedule** : ir retrasado 3 **her friends are** ~ **her** : tiene el
apoyo de sus amigos
behold [brˈhoːld] *vt* **-held; -holding**
: contemplar
beige ['beɪʒ] *adj & nm* : beige
being ['biːɪŋ] *n* 1 : ser *m* 2 **come into** ~
: nacer
belated [brˈleɪţəd] *adj* : tardío
belch ['bɛltʃ] *vi* : eructar — ~ *n* : eructo *m*
Belgian ['bɛldʒən] *adj* : belga
belie [brˈlaɪ] *vt* **-lied; -lying** : contradecir, desmentir
belief [bəˈlif] *n* 1 TRUST : confianza *f* 2
CONVICTION : creencia *f*, convicción *f* 3
FAITH : fe *f* — **believable** [bəˈliːvəbəl]
adj : creíble — **believe** [bəˈliːv] *v*
-lieved; -lieving : creer — **believer**
[bəˈliːvər] *n* : creyente *mf*
belittle [brˈlɪţəl] *vt* **-littled; -littling**
: menospreciar
Belizean [bəˈliːziən] *adj* : beliceño *m*,
-ña *f*
bell ['bɛl] *n* 1 : campana *f* 2 : timbre *m*
(de teléfono, de la puerta, etc.)
belligerent [bəˈlɪdʒərənt] *adj* : beligerante
bellow ['bɛˌloː] *vi* : bramar, mugir — *vt*
or ~ **out** : gritar
bellows ['bɛˌloːz] *ns & pl* : fuelle *m*
belly ['bɛli] *n, pl* **-lies** : vientre *m*
belong [brˈlɔŋ] *vi* 1 ~ **to** : pertenecer a,
ser propiedad de 2 ~ **to** : ser miembro de (un club, etc.) 3 **where does it**
~ : ¿dónde va? — **belongings** [br-
ˈlɔŋɪŋz] *npl* : pertenencias *fpl*, efectos
mpl personales
beloved [brˈlʌvəd, -ˈlʌvd] *adj* : querido,
amado — ~ *n* : querido *m*, -da *f*
below [brˈloː] *adv* : abajo — ~ *prep* 1
: abajo de, debajo de 2 ~ **average**
: por debajo del promedio 3 ~ **zero**
: bajo cero
belt ['bɛlt] *n* 1 : cinturón *m* 2 BAND,
STRAP : cinta *f*, correa *f* 3 AREA : frente

m, zona *f* — *vt* **1** : ceñir con un cinturón **2** THRASH : darle una paliza a

bench ['bentʃ] *n* **1** : banco *m* **2** WORKBENCH : mesa *f* de trabajo **3** COURT : tribunal *m*

bend ['bend] *v* **bent** ['bent]; **bending** *vt* : doblar, torcer — *vi* **1** : torcerse **2** ~ **over** : inclinarse — ~ *n* : curva *f*, ángulo *m*

beneath [bɪ'niːθ] *adv* : abajo, debajo — ~ *prep* : bajo, debajo de

benediction [ˌbenə'dɪkʃən] *n* : bendición *f*

benefactor ['benəˌfæktər] *n* : benefactor *m*, -tora *f*

benefit ['benəfɪt] *n* **1** ADVANTAGE : ventaja *f*, provecho *m* **2** AID : asistencia *f*, beneficio *m* — ~ *vt* : beneficiar — *vi* : beneficiarse — **beneficial** [ˌbenə-'fɪʃəl] *adj* : beneficioso — **beneficiary** [ˌbenə'fɪʃiˌeri, -'fɪʃəri] *n*, *pl* -ries : beneficiario *m*, -ria *f*

benevolent [bə'nevələnt] *adj* : benévolo

benign [bɪ'naɪn] *adj* **1** KIND : benévolo, amable **2** : benigno (en medicina)

bent ['bent] *adj* **1** : encorvado **2** be ~ **on** : estar empeñado en — ~ *n* : aptitud *f*, inclinación *f*

bequeath [bɪ'kwiːθ, -'kwiːð] *vt* : legar — **bequest** [bɪ'kwest] *n* : legado *m*

berate [bɪ'reɪt] *vt* -**rated**; -**rating** : reprender, regañar

bereaved [bɪ'riːvd] *adj* : desconsolado, a luto

beret [bə'reɪ] *n* : boina *f*

berry ['beri] *n*, *pl* -ries : baya *f*

berserk [bər'sərk, -'zərk] *adj* **1** : enloquecido **2** go ~ : volverse loco

berth ['bərθ] *n* **1** MOORING : atracadero *m* **2** BUNK : litera *f*

beseech [bɪ'siːtʃ] *vt* -**sought** [-'sɔt] *or* -**seeched**; -**seeching** : suplicar, implorar

beset [bɪ'set] *vt* -**set**; -**setting 1** HARASS : acosar **2** SURROUND : rodear

beside [bɪ'saɪd] *prep* **1** : al lado de, junto a **2** be ~ **oneself** : estar fuera de sí — **besides** [bɪ'saɪdz] *adv* : además — ~ *prep* **1** : además de **2** EXCEPT : excepto

besiege [bɪ'siːdʒ] *vt* -**sieged**; -**sieging** : asediar

best ['best] *adj* (*superlative of* **good**) : mejor — ~ *adv* (*superlative of* **well**) : mejor — ~ *n* **1** at ~ : a lo más **2** do one's ~ : hacer todo lo posible **3** the ~ : lo mejor — **best man** *n* : padrino *m* (de boda)

bestow [bɪ'stoː] *vt* : otorgar, conceder

bet ['bet] *n* : apuesta *f* — ~ *v* **bet**; **betting** *vt* : apostar — *vi* ~ **on sth** : apostarle a algo

betray [bɪ'treɪ] *vt* : traicionar — **betrayal** [bɪ'treɪəl] *n* : traición *f*

better ['betər] *adj* (*comparative of* **good**) **1** : mejor **2** get ~ : mejorar — ~ *adv* (*comparative of* **well**) **1** : mejor **2** all the ~ : tanto mejor — ~ *n* **1** the ~ : el mejor, la mejor **2** get the ~ **of** : vencer a — ~ *vt* **1** IMPROVE : mejorar **2** SURPASS : superar

between [bɪ'twiːn] *prep* : entre — ~ *adv* *or* **in** ~ : en medio

beverage ['bevrɪdʒ, 'bevə-] *n* : bebida *f*

beware [bɪ'wær] *vi* ~ **of** : tener cuidado con

bewilder [bɪ'wɪldər] *vt* : desconcertar — **bewilderment** [bɪ'wɪldərmənt] *n* : desconcierto *m*

bewitch [bɪ'wɪtʃ] *vt* : hechizar, encantar

beyond [bɪ'jɑnd] *adv* : más allá, más lejos (en el espacio), más adelante (en el tiempo) — ~ *prep* : más allá de

bias ['baɪəs] *n* **1** PREJUDICE : prejuicio *m* **2** TENDENCY : inclinación *f*, tendencia *f* — **biased** ['baɪəst] *adj* : parcial

bib ['bɪb] *n* : babero *m* (para niños)

Bible ['baɪbəl] *n* : Biblia *f* — **biblical** ['bɪblɪkəl] *adj* : bíblico

bibliography [ˌbɪbli'ɑgrəfi] *n*, *pl* -**phies** : bibliografía *f*

bicarbonate of soda [ˌbaɪˈkɑrbənət, ˌneɪt] *n* : bicarbonato *m* de soda

biceps ['baɪˌseps] *ns & pl* : bíceps *m*

bicker ['bɪkər] *vi* : reñir

bicycle ['baɪsɪkəl, -sɪ-] *n* : bicicleta *f* — ~ *vi* -**cled**; -**cling** : ir en bicicleta

bid ['bɪd] *vt* **bade** ['bæd, 'beɪd] *or* **bid**; **bidden** ['bɪdən] *or* **bid**; **bidding 1** OFFER : ofrecer **2** ~ **farewell** : decir adios — ~ *n* **1** OFFER : oferta *f* **2** ATTEMPT : intento *m*, tentativa *f*

bide ['baɪd] *vt* **bode** ['boːd] *or* **bided**; **bided**; **biding** ~ **one's time** : esperar el momento oportuno

bifocals ['baɪˌfoːkəlz] *npl* : anteojos *mpl* bifocales

big ['bɪg] *adj* **bigger**; **biggest** : grande

bigamy ['bɪgəmi] *n* : bigamia *f*

bigot ['bɪgət] *n* : intolerante *mf* — **bigotry** ['bɪgətri] *n*, *pl* -**tries** : intolerancia *f*, fanatismo *m*

bike ['baɪk] *n* **1** BICYCLE : bici *f fam* **2** MOTORCYCLE : moto *f*

bikini [bə'kiːni] *n* : bikini *m*

bile ['baɪl] *n* : bilis *f*

bilingual [baɪ'lɪŋgwəl] *adj* : bilingüe

bill ['bɪl] *n* **1** BEAK : pico *m* **2** INVOICE : cuenta *f*, factura *f* **3** BANKNOTE : billete *m* **4** LAW : proyecto *m* de ley, ley *f*

— ~ *vt* : pasarle la cuenta a — **bill-board** ['bɪl,bord] *n* : cartelera *f* — **bill-fold** ['bɪl,fold] *n* : billetera *f*, cartera *f*
billiards ['bɪljərdz] *n* : billar *m*
billion ['bɪljən] *n, pl* **billions** *or* **billion** : mil millones *mpl*
billow ['bɪlo] *vi* : ondular, hincharse
billy goat ['bɪlɪgot] *n* : macho *m* cabrío
bin ['bɪn] *n* : cubo *m*, cajón *m*
binary ['baɪnəri, -neri] *adj* : binario *m*
bind ['baɪnd] *vt* **bound** ['baʊnd]; **bind-ing 1** TIE : atar **2** OBLIGATE : obligar **3** UNITE : unir **4** BANDAGE : vendar **5** : encuadernar (un libro) — **binder** ['baɪndər] *n* FOLDER : carpeta *f* — **bind-ing** ['baɪndɪŋ] *n* : encuadernación *f* (de libros)
binge ['bɪndʒ] *n* : juerga *f fam*
bingo ['bɪŋgo] *n, pl* **-gos** : bingo *m*
binoculars [bə'nakjələrz, baɪ-] *npl* : binoculares *mpl*, gemelos *mpl*
biochemistry [,baɪo'kemɪstri] *n* : bioquímica *f*
biography [baɪ'agrəfi, bi:-] *n, pl* **-phies** : biografía *f* — **biographer** [baɪ'agrəfər] *n* : biógrafo *m*, -fa *f* — **bio-graphical** [baɪə'græfɪkəl] *adj* : biográfico
biology [baɪ'alədʒi] *n* : biología *f* — **bio-logical** [-dʒɪkəl] *adj* : biológico — **biologist** [baɪ'alədʒɪst] *n* : biólogo *m*, -ga
birch ['bərtʃ] *n* : abedul *m*
bird ['bərd] *n* : pájaro *m* (pequeño), ave *f* (grande)
birth ['bərθ] *n* **1** : nacimiento *m*, parto *m* **2 give ~ to** : dar a luz a — **birthday** ['bərθ,deɪ] *n* : cumpleaños *m* — **birth-mark** ['bərθ,mɑrk] *n* : mancha *f* de nacimiento — **birthplace** ['bərθ,pleɪs] *n* : lugar *m* de nacimiento — **birthrate** ['bərθ,reɪt] *n* : índice *m* de natalidad
biscuit ['bɪskət] *n* : bizcocho *m*
bisect ['baɪ,sekt, ,baɪ-] *vt* : bisecar
bisexual [,baɪ'sekʃəwəl, -sekʃəl] *adj* : bisexual
bishop ['bɪʃəp] *n* : obispo *m*
bison ['baɪzən, -sən] *ns & pl* : bisonte *m*
bit[1] ['bɪt] *n* : bocado *m* (de una brida)
bit[2] **1** : trozo *m*, pedazo *m* **2** : bit *m* (de información) **3 a ~** : un poco
bitch ['bɪtʃ] *n* : perra *f* — ~ *vi* COMPLAIN : quejarse, reclamar
bite ['baɪt] *v* **bit** ['bɪt]; **bitten** ['bɪtən]; **bit-ing** *vt* **1** : morder **2** STING : picar — *vi* : morder — ~ *n* **1** : picadura *f* (de un insecto), mordedura *f* (de un animal) **2** SNACK : bocado *m* — **biting** *adj* **1** PEN-ETRATING : cortante, penetrante **2** CAUSTIC : mordaz

bitter ['bɪtər] *adj* **1** : amargo **2 it's ~ cold** : hace un frío glacial **3 to the ~ end** : hasta el final — **bitterness** ['bɪtərnəs] *n* : amargura *f*
bizarre [bə'zar] *adj* : extraño
black ['blæk] *adj* : negro — ~ *n* **1** : negro *m* (color) **2** : negro *m*, -gra *f* (persona) — **black-and-blue** [,blækən'blu:] *adj* : amoratado — **black-berry** ['blæk,beri] *n, pl* **-ries** : mora *f* — **blackbird** ['blæk,bərd] *n* : mirlo *m* — **blackboard** ['blæk,bord] *n* : pizarra *f*, pizarrón *m Lat* — **blacken** ['blækən] *vt* : ennegrecer — **blackmail** ['blæk,meɪl] *n* : chantaje *m* — ~ *vt* : chantajear — **black market** *n* : mercado *m* negro — **blackout** ['blæk,aʊt] *n* **1** : apagón *m* (de poder eléctrico) **2** FAINT : desmayo *m* — **blacksmith** ['blæk,smɪθ] *n* : herrero *m* — **blacktop** ['blæk,tap] *n* : asfalto *m*
bladder ['blædər] *n* : vejiga *f*
blade ['bleɪd] *n* **1** : hoja *f* (de un cuchillo), cuchilla *f* (de un patín) **2** : pala *f* (de un remo, una hélice, etc.) **3 ~ of grass** : brizna *f* (de hierba)
blame ['bleɪm] *vt* **blamed**; **blaming** : culpar, echar la culpa a — ~ *n* : culpa *f* — **blameless** ['bleɪmləs] *adj* : inocente
bland ['blænd] *adj* : soso, insulso
blank ['blæŋk] *adj* **1** : en blanco (dícese de un papel), liso (dícese de una pared) **2** EMPTY : vacío — ~ *n* : espacio *m* en blanco
blanket ['blæŋkət] *n* **1** : manta *f*, cobija *f Lat* **2 ~ of snow** : manto *m* de nieve — ~ *vt* : cubrir
blare ['blær] *vi* **blared**; **blaring** : resonar
blasphemy ['blæsfəmi] *n, pl* **-mies** : blasfemia *f*
blast ['blæst] *n* **1** GUST : ráfaga *f* **2** EX-PLOSION : explosión *f* **3** : toque *m* (de trompeta, etc.) — ~ *vt* BLOW UP : volar — **blast-off** ['blæst,ɔf] *n* : despegue *m*
blatant ['bleɪtənt] *adj* : descarado
blaze ['bleɪz] *n* **1** FIRE : fuego *m* **2** BRIGHTNESS : resplandor *m*, brillantez *f* **3 ~ of anger** : arranque *m* de cólera — ~ *v* **blazed**; **blazing** *vi* : arder, brillar — *vt* **~ a trail** : abrir un camino
blazer ['bleɪzər] *n* : chaqueta *f* deportiva
bleach ['bli:tʃ] *vt* : blanquear, decolorar — ~ *n* : lejía *f*, blanqueador *m Lat*
bleachers ['bli:tʃərz] *ns & pl* : gradas *fpl*
bleak ['bli:k] *adj* **1** DESOLATE : desolado **2** GLOOMY : triste, sombrío
bleary-eyed ['blɪri,aɪd] *adj* : con los ojos nublados
bleat ['bli:t] *vi* : balar — ~ *n* : balido *m*

bleed ['bliːd] v **bled** ['blɛd]; **bleeding** : sangrar

blemish ['blɛmɪʃ] vt : manchar, marcar — ~ n : mancha f, marca f

blend ['blɛnd] vt : mezclar, combinar — ~ n : mezcla f, combinación f — **blender** ['blɛndər] n : licuadora f

bless ['blɛs] vt **blessed** ['blɛst]; **blessing** : bendecir — **blessed** ['blɛsəd] or **blest** ['blɛst] adj : bendito — **blessing** ['blɛsɪŋ] n : bendición f

blew → **blow**

blind ['blaɪnd] adj : ciego — ~ vt 1 : cegar, dejar ciego 2 DAZZLE : deslumbrar — ~ n 1 : persiana f (para una ventana) 2 **the** ~ : los ciegos — **blindfold** ['blaɪnd,foːld] vt : vendar los ojos — ~ n : venda f (para los ojos) — **blindly** ['blaɪndli] adv : ciegamente — **blindness** ['blaɪndnəs] n : ceguera f

blink ['blɪŋk] vi 1 : parpadear 2 FLICKER : brillar intermitentemente — ~ n : parpadeo m — **blinker** ['blɪŋkər] n : intermitente m, direccional f Lat

bliss ['blɪs] n : dicha f, felicidad f (absoluta) — **blissful** ['blɪsfəl] adj : feliz

blister ['blɪstər] n : ampolla f — ~ vi : ampollarse

blitz ['blɪts] n : bombardeo m aéreo

blizzard ['blɪzərd] n : ventisca f (de nieve)

bloated ['bloːtəd] adj : hinchado

blob ['blab] n 1 DROP : gota f 2 SPOT : mancha f

block ['blak] n 1 : bloque m 2 OBSTRUCTION : obstrucción f 3 : manzana f, cuadra f Lat (de edificios) 4 or **building** ~ : cubo m de construcción — ~ vt : obstruir, bloquear — **blockade** [bla'keɪd] n : bloqueo m — **blockage** ['blakɪdʒ] n : obstrucción f

blond or **blonde** ['bland] adj : rubio — ~ n : rubio m, -bia f

blood ['blʌd] n : sangre f — **bloodhound** ['blʌd,haʊnd] n : sabueso m — **blood pressure** n : tensión f (arterial) — **bloodshed** ['blʌd,ʃɛd] n : derramamiento m de sangre — **bloodshot** ['blʌd,ʃat] adj : inyectado de sangre — **bloodstained** ['blʌd,steɪnd] adj : manchado de sangre — **bloodstream** ['blʌd,striːm] n : sangre f, torrente m sanguíneo — **bloody** ['blʌdi] adj **bloodier; -est** : ensangrentado, sangriento

bloom ['bluːm] n 1 : flor f 2 **in full** ~ : en plena floración — ~ vi : florecer

blossom ['blasəm] n : flor f — ~ vi : florecer

blot ['blat] n 1 : borrón m (de tinta, etc.)

2 BLEMISH : mancha f — ~ vt **blotted; blotting** 1 : emborronar 2 DRY : secar

blotch ['blatʃ] n : mancha f, borrón m — **blotchy** ['blatʃi] adj **blotchier; -est** : lleno de manchas

blouse ['blaus, 'blauz] n : blusa f

blow ['bloː] v **blew** ['bluː]; **blown** ['bloːn]; **blowing** vi 1 : soplar 2 SOUND : sonar 3 or ~ **out** : fundirse (dícese de un fusible eléctrico), reventarse (dícese de una llanta) — vt 1 : soplar 2 SOUND : tocar, sonar 3 BUNGLE : echar a perder — ~ n : golpe m — **blowout** ['bloː,aut] n : reventón m — **blow up** vi : estallar, hacer explosión — vt 1 EXPLODE : volar 2 INFLATE : inflar

blubber ['blʌbər] n : esperma f de ballena

bludgeon ['blʌdʒən] vt : aporrear

blue ['bluː] adj **bluer; bluest** 1 : azul 2 MELANCHOLY : triste — ~ n : azul m — **blueberry** ['bluː,bɛri] n, pl **-ries** : arándano m — **bluebird** ['bluː,bərd] n : azulejo m — **blue cheese** n : queso m azul — **blueprint** ['bluː,prɪnt] n PLAN : proyecto m — **blues** ['bluːz] npl 1 SADNESS : tristeza f 2 : blues m (en música)

bluff ['blʌf] vi : hacer un farol — ~ n : farol m

blunder ['blʌndər] vi : meter la pata fam — ~ n : metedura f de pata fam

blunt ['blʌnt] adj 1 DULL : desafilado 2 DIRECT : directo, franco

blur ['blər] n : imagen f borrosa — ~ vt **blurred; blurring** : hacer borroso

blurb ['blərb] n : nota f publicitaria

blurt ['blərt] vt or ~ **out** : espetar

blush ['blʌʃ] n : rubor m — ~ vi : ruborizarse

blustery ['blʌstəri] adj : borrascoso, tempestuoso

boar ['bor] n : cerdo m macho

board ['bord] n 1 PLANK : tabla f, tablón m 2 COMMITTEE : junta f, consejo m 3 : tablero m (de juegos) 4 **room and** ~ : comida y alojamiento — ~ vt 1 : subir a bordo de (una nave, un avión, etc.), subir a (un tren) 2 LODGE : hospedar 3 ~ **up** : cerrar con tablas — **boarder** ['bordər] n : huésped mf

boast ['boːst] n : jactancia f — ~ vi : alardear, jactarse — **boastful** ['boːstfəl] adj : jactancioso

boat ['boːt] n : barco m (grande), barca f (pequeña)

bob ['bab] vi **bobbed; bobbing** or ~ **up and down** : subir y bajar

bobbin ['babən] n : bobina f, carrete m

bobby pin ['babi,pɪn] n : horquilla f

body ['bɑdi] *n, pl* **bodies** 1 : cuerpo *m* 2 CORPSE : cadáver *m* 3 : carrocería (de un automóvil, etc.) 4 COLLECTION : conjunto *m* 5 ~ **of water** : masa *f* de agua — **bodily** *adj* : corporal — **bodyguard** ['bɑdiˌgɑrd] *n* : guardaespaldas *mf*

bog ['bɑg, 'bɔg] *n* : ciénaga *f* — ~ *vt* **bogged; bogging** *or* ~ **down** : empantanarse

bogus ['boːgəs] *adj* : falso

boil ['bɔɪl] *v* : hervir — **boiler** ['bɔɪlər] *n* : caldera *f*

bold ['boːld] *adj* 1 DARING : audaz 2 IMPUDENT : descarado — **boldness** ['boːldnəs] *n* : audacia *f*

Bolivian [bə'lɪviən] *adj* : boliviano *m*, -na *f*

bologna [bə'loːni] *n* : salchicha *f* ahumada

bolster ['boːlstər] *vt* **-stered; -stering** *or* ~ **up** : reforzar

bolt ['boːlt] *n* 1 LOCK : cerrojo *m* 2 SCREW : tornillo *m* 3 ~ **of lightning** : relámpago *m*, rayo *m* — ~ *vt* 1 FASTEN : atornillar 2 LOCK : echar el cerrojo a — *vi* FLEE : salir corriendo

bomb ['bɑm] *n* : bomba *f* — ~ *vt* : bombardear — **bombard** [bɑm'bɑrd, bəm-] *vt* : bombardear — **bombardment** [bɑm'bɑrdmənt] *n* : bombardeo *m* — **bomber** ['bɑmər] *n* : bombardero *m*

bond ['bɑnd] *n* 1 TIE : vínculo *m*, lazo *m* 2 SURETY : fianza *f* 3 : bono *m* (en finanzas) — ~ *vi* STICK : adherirse

bondage ['bɑndɪdʒ] *n* : esclavitud *f*

bone ['boːn] *n* : hueso *m* — ~ *vt* **boned; boning** : deshuesar

bonfire ['bɑnfaɪr] *n* : hoguera *f*

bonus ['boːnəs] *n* 1 PAY : prima *f* 2 BENEFIT : beneficio *m* adicional

bony ['boːni] *adj* **bonier; -est** 1 : huesudo 2 : lleno de espinas (dícese de pescados)

boo ['buː] *n, pl* **boos** : abucheo *m* — ~ *vt* : abuchear

book ['bʊk] *n* 1 : libro *m* 2 NOTEBOOK : libreta *f*, cuaderno *m* — ~ *vt* : reservar — **bookcase** ['bʊkˌkeɪs] *n* : estantería *f* — **bookkeeping** ['bʊkˌkiːpɪŋ] *n* : teneduría *f* de libros, contabilidad *f* — **booklet** ['bʊklət] *n* : folleto *m* — **bookmark** ['bʊkˌmɑrk] *n* : marcador *m* de libros — **bookseller** ['bʊkˌsɛlər] *n* : librero *m*, -ra *f* — **bookshelf** ['bʊkˌʃɛlf] *n, pl* **-shelves** : estante *m* — **bookstore** ['bʊkˌstɔr] *n* : librería *f*

boom ['buːm] *vi* 1 : tronar, resonar 2 PROSPER : estar en auge, prosperar — ~ *n* 1 : bramido *m*, estruendo *m* 2 : auge *m* (económico)

boon ['buːn] *n* : ayuda *f*, beneficio *m*

boost ['buːst] *vt* 1 LIFT : levantar 2 INCREASE : aumentar — ~ *n* 1 INCREASE : aumento *m* 2 ENCOURAGEMENT : estímulo *m*

boot ['buːt] *n* : bota *f*, botín *m* — ~ *vt* 1 : dar una patada a 2 *or* ~ **up** : cargar (un ordenador)

booth ['buːθ] *n, pl* **booths** ['buːðz, 'buːθs] : cabina *f* (de teléfono, de votar), caseta *f* (de información)

booty ['buːti] *n, pl* **-ties** : botín *m*

booze ['buːz] *n* : trago *m*, bebida *f* (alcohólica)

border ['bɔrdər] *n* 1 EDGE : borde *m*, orilla *f* 2 TRIM : ribete *m* 3 FRONTIER : frontera *f*

bore[1] ['bɔr] *vt* **bored; boring** DRILL : taladrar

bore[2] *vt* TIRE : aburrir — ~ *n* : pesado *m*, -da *fam f* (persona), lata *f fam* (cosa, situación) — **boredom** ['bɔrdəm] *n* : aburrimiento *m* — **boring** ['bɔrɪŋ] *adj* : aburrido, pesado

born ['bɔrn] *adj* 1 : nacido 2 **be** ~ : nacer

borough ['bəroː] *n* : distrito *m* municipal

borrow ['bɑroː] *vt* : pedir prestado, tomar prestado

Bosnian ['bɑzniən, 'bɔz-] *adj* : bosnio *m*, -nia *f*

bosom ['bʊzəm, 'buː-] *n* BREAST : pecho *m*, seno *m* — ~ *adj* ~ **friend** : amigo *m* íntimo

boss ['bɔs] *n* : jefe *m*, -fa *f*; patrón *m*, -trona *f* — ~ *vt* SUPERVISE : dirigir — **bossy** ['bɔsi] *adj* **bossier; -est** : autoritario

botany ['bɑtəni] *n* : botánica *f* — **botanical** [bə'tænɪkəl] *adj* : botánico

botch ['bɑtʃ] *vt* : hacer una chapuza de, estropear

both ['boːθ] *adj* : ambos, los dos, las dos — ~ *pron* : ambos *m*, -bas *f*; los dos, las dos

bother ['bɑðər] *vt* 1 TROUBLE : preocupar 2 PESTER : molestar, fastidiar — *vi* ~ **to** : molestarse en — ~ *n* : molestia *f*

bottle ['bɑtəl] *n* 1 : botella *f*, frasco *m* 2 *or* **baby** ~ : biberón *m* — ~ *vt* **bottled; bottling** : embotellar — **bottleneck** ['bɑtəlˌnɛk] *n* : embotellamiento *m*

bottom ['bɑtəm] *n* 1 : fondo *m* (de una caja, del mar, etc.), pie *m* (de una escalera, una montaña, etc.), final *m* (de una lista) 2 BUTTOCKS : nalgas *fpl*, trasero *m* — ~ *adj* : más bajo, inferi-

or, de abajo — **bottomless** ['baṭəmləs]
adj : sin fondo

bough ['bau] *n* : rama *f*

bought → **buy**

bouillon ['buːjɑn; 'buljɑn, -jən] *n* : caldo *m*

boulder ['boːldər] *n* : canto *m* rodado

boulevard ['buləˌvɑrd, 'buː-] *n* : bulevar *m*

bounce ['baunts] *v* **bounced; bouncing** *vt* : hacer rebotar — *vi* : rebotar — ~ *n* : rebote *m*

bound¹ ['baund] *adj* **be** ~ **for** : ir rumbo a

bound² *adj* **1** OBLIGED : obligado **2** DETERMINED : decidido **3 be** ~ **to** : tener que

bound³ *n* **out of** ~**s** : (en) zona prohibida — **boundary** ['baundri, -dəri] *n, pl* **-aries** : límite *m* — **boundless** ['baundləs] *adj* : sin límites

bouquet [boːˈkei, buː-] *n* : ramo *m*

bourgeois ['burˌʒwɑ, burˈʒwɑ] *adj* : burgués

bout ['baut] *n* **1** : combate *m* (en deportes) **2** : ataque *m* (de una enfermedad) **3** : período *m* (de actividad)

bow¹ ['bau] *vi* : inclinarse — *vt* ~ **one's head** : inclinar la cabeza — ['bau] *n* : reverencia *f*, inclinación *f*

bow² ['boː] *n* **1** : arco *m* **2 tie a** ~ : hacer un lazo

bow³ ['bau] *n* : proa *f* (de un barco)

bowels ['bauəlz] *npl* **1** : intestinos *mpl* **2** DEPTHS : entrañas *fpl*

bowl¹ ['boːl] *n* : tazón *m*, cuenco *m*

bowl² *vi* : jugar a los bolos — **bowling** ['boːlɪŋ] *n* : bolos *mpl*

box¹ ['bɑks] *vi* FIGHT : boxear — **boxer** ['bɑksər] *n* : boxeador *m*, -dora *f* — **boxing** ['bɑksɪŋ] *n* : boxeo *m*

box² *n* **1** : caja *f*, cajón *m* **2** : palco *m* (en el teatro) — *vt* : empaquetar — **box office** *n* : taquilla *f*, boletería *f Lat*

boy ['bɔi] *n* : niño *m*, chico *m*

boycott ['bɔiˌkɑt] *vt* : boicotear — ~ *n* : boicot *m*

boyfriend ['bɔiˌfrɛnd] *n* : novio *m*

bra ['brɑ] → **brassiere**

brace ['breis] *n* **1** SUPPORT : abrazadera *f* **2** ~**s** *npl* : aparatos *mpl* (para dientes) — ~ *vi* ~ **oneself for** : prepararse para

bracelet ['breisˌlət] *n* : brazalete *m*

bracket ['brækət] *n* **1** SUPPORT : soporte *m* **2** : corchete *m* (marca de puntuación) **3** CATEGORY : categoría *f* — ~ *vt* **1** : poner entre corchetes **2** CATEGORIZE : catalogar

brag ['bræg] *vi* **bragged; bragging** : jactarse

braid ['breid] *vt* : trenzar — ~ *n* : trenza *f*

braille ['breil] *n* : braille *m*

brain ['brein] *n* **1** : cerebro *m* **2** ~**s** *npl* : inteligencia *f* — **brainstorm** ['breinˌstɔrm] *n* : idea *f* genial — **brainwash** ['breinˌwɑʃ, -ˌwɔʃ] *vt* : lavar el cerebro — **brainy** ['breini] *adj* **brainier; -est** : inteligente, listo

brake ['breik] *n* : freno *m* — ~ *v* **braked; braking** : frenar

bramble ['bræmbəl] *n* : zarza *f*

bran ['bræn] *n* : salvado *m*

branch ['bræntʃ] *n* **1** : rama *f* (de una planta) **2** DIVISION : ramal *m* (de un camino, etc.), sucursal *f* (de una empresa), agencia *f* (del gobierno) — *vi or* ~ **off** : ramificarse, bifurcarse

brand ['brænd] *n* **1** : marca *f* (de ganado) **2** *or* ~ **name** : marca *f* de fábrica — ~ *vt* **1** : marcar (ganado) **2** LABEL : tachar, tildar

brandish ['brændɪʃ] *vt* : blandir

brand-new ['brændˈnuː, -ˈnjuː] *adj* : flamante

brandy ['brændi] *n, pl* **-dies** : brandy *m*, coñac *m*

brass ['bræs] *n* **1** : latón *m* **2** : metales *mpl* (de una orquesta)

brassiere [brəˈzir, brɑ-] *n* : sostén *m*, brasier *m Lat*

brat ['bræt] *n* : mocoso *m*, -sa *f fam*

bravado [brəˈvɑdoː] *n, pl* **-does** *or* **-dos** : bravuconadas *fpl*

brave ['breiv] *adj* **braver; bravest** : valiente, valeroso — ~ *vt* **braved; braving** : afrontar, hacer frente a — ~ *n* : guerrero *m* indio — **bravery** ['breivəri] *n* : valor *m*, valentía *f*

brawl ['brɔl] *n* : pelea *f*, reyerta *f*

brawny ['brɔni] *n* : músculos *mpl* — **brawny** ['brɔni] *adj* **brawnier; -est** : musculoso

bray ['brei] *vi* : rebuznar

brazen ['breizən] *adj* : descarado

Brazilian [brəˈziljən] *adj* : brasileño *m*, -ña *f*

breach ['briːtʃ] *n* **1** VIOLATION : infracción *f*, violación *f* **2** GAP : brecha *f*

bread ['brɛd] *n* **1** : pan *m* **2** ~ **crumbs** : migajas *fpl*

breadth ['brɛtθ] *n* : anchura *f*

break ['breik] *v* **broke** ['broːk]; **broken** ['broːkən]; **breaking** *vt* **1** : romper, quebrar **2** VIOLATE : infringir, violar **3** INTERRUPT : interrumpir **4** SURPASS : batir (un récord, etc.) **5** ~ **a habit** : quitarse una costumbre **6** ~ **the news** : dar la noticia — *vi* **1** : romperse, quebrarse **2** ~ **away** : escapar 3 ~ **down** : estropearse (dícese de una máquina), fallar (dícese de un sistema, etc.) 4 ~ **into** : entrar en 5 ~ **off** : interrumpirse 6 ~ **out of** : escaparse de 7 ~ **up** SEPARATE : separarse — ~ n 1 : ruptura f, fractura f 2 GAP : interrupción f, claro m (entre las nubes) 3 **lucky** ~ : golpe m de suerte 4 **take a** ~ : tomar(se) un descanso — **breakable** ['breɪkəbəl] adj : quebradizo, frágil — **breakdown** ['breɪk-,daun] n 1 : avería f (de máquinas), interrupción f (de comunicaciones), fracaso m (de negociaciones) 2 or **nervous** ~ : crisis f nerviosa

breakfast ['brekfəst] n : desayuno m

breast ['brest] n 1 : seno m (de una mujer) 2 CHEST : pecho m — **breast–feed** ['brest,fiːd] vt **-fed** [-,fed]; **-feeding** : amamantar

breath ['breθ] n : aliento m, respiración f — **breathe** ['briːð] v **breathed**; **breathing** : respirar — **breathless** ['breθləs] adj : sin aliento, jadeante — **breathtaking** ['breθ,teɪkɪŋ] adj : impresionante

breed ['briːd] v **bred** ['bred]; **breeding** vt 1 : criar (animales) 2 ENGENDER : engendrar, producir — vi : reproducirse — ~ n 1 : raza f 2 CLASS : clase f, tipo m

breeze ['briːz] n : brisa f — **breezy** ['briːzi] adj **breezier; -est** 1 WINDY : ventoso 2 NONCHALANT : despreocupado

brevity ['brevəti] n, pl **-ties** : brevedad f

brew ['bruː] vt : hacer (cerveza, etc.), preparar (té) — vi 1 : fabricar cerveza 2 : amenazar (dícese de una tormenta) — **brewery** ['bruːəri, 'bruri] n, pl **-eries** : cervecería f

bribe ['braɪb] n : soborno m — ~ vt **bribed; bribing** : sobornar — **bribery** ['braɪbəri] n, pl **-eries** : soborno m

brick ['brɪk] n : ladrillo m — **bricklayer** ['brɪk,leɪər] n : albañil mf

bride ['braɪd] n : novia f — **bridal** ['braɪdəl] adj : nupcial, de novia — **bridegroom** ['braɪd,gruːm] n : novio m — **bridesmaid** ['braɪdz,meɪd] n : dama f de honor

bridge ['brɪdʒ] n 1 : puente m 2 : caballete m (de la nariz) 3 : bridge m (juego de naipes) — ~ vt **bridged; bridging** 1 : tender un puente sobre 2 ~ **the gap** : salvar las diferencias

bridle ['braɪdəl] n : brida f — ~ vt **-dled; -dling** : embridar

brief ['briːf] adj : breve — ~ n 1 : resumen m, sumario m 2 ~**s** npl UN-

DERPANTS : calzoncillos mpl — ~ vt : dar órdenes a, instruir — **briefcase** ['briːf,keɪs] n : portafolio m, maletín m — **briefly** ['briːfli] adv : brevemente

bright ['braɪt] adj 1 : brillante, claro 2 CHEERFUL : alegre, animado 3 INTELLIGENT : listo, inteligente — **brighten** ['braɪtən] vi 1 : hacerse más brillante 2 or ~ **up** : animarse, alegrarse — vt 1 ILLUMINATE : iluminar 2 ENLIVEN : alegrar, animar

brilliant ['brɪljənt] adj : brillante — **brilliance** ['brɪljənts] n 1 BRIGHTNESS : resplandor m, brillantez f 2 INTELLIGENCE : inteligencia f

brim ['brɪm] n 1 : borde m (de una taza, etc.) 2 : ala f (de un sombrero) — ~ vi **brimmed; brimming** or ~ **over** : desbordarse, rebosar

brine ['braɪn] n : salmuera f

bring ['brɪŋ] vt **brought** ['brɔt]; **bringing** 1 : traer 2 ~ **about** : ocasionar 3 ~ **around** PERSUADE : convencer 4 ~ **back** : devolver 5 ~ **down** : derribar 6 ~ **on** CAUSE : provocar 7 ~ **out** : sacar 8 ~ **to an end** : terminar (con) 9 ~ **up** REAR : criar 10 ~ **up** MENTION : sacar

brink ['brɪŋk] n : borde m

brisk ['brɪsk] adj 1 FAST : rápido 2 LIVELY : enérgico

bristle ['brɪsəl] n : cerda f (de un animal), pelo m (de una planta) — ~ vi **-tled; -tling** : erizarse

British ['brɪtɪʃ] adj : británico

brittle ['brɪtəl] adj **-tler; -tlest** : frágil, quebradizo

broach ['broːtʃ] vt : abordar

broad ['brɔd] adj 1 WIDE : ancho 2 GENERAL : general 3 **in** ~ **daylight** : en pleno día

broadcast ['brɔd,kæst] vt **-cast; -casting** : emitir — ~ n : emisión f

broaden ['brɔdən] vt : ampliar, ensanchar — vi : ensancharse — **broadly** ['brɔdli] adv : en general — **broad-minded** ['brɔd'maɪndəd] adj : de miras amplias, tolerante

broccoli ['brɑkəli] n : brócoli m, brécol m

brochure ['broʊʃʊr] n : folleto m

broil ['brɔɪl] vt : asar a la parrilla

broke ['broʊk] → **break** — ~ adj : pelado fam — **broken** ['broʊkən] adj : roto, quebrado — **brokenhearted** [,broʊkən'hɑrtəd] adj : desconsolado, con el corazón destrozado

broker ['broʊkər] n : corredor m, -dora f

bronchitis [brɑn'kaɪtəs, brɑŋ-] n : bronquitis f

bronze ['brɑnz] n : bronce m
brooch ['broːtʃ, 'bruːtʃ] n : broche m
brood ['bruːd] n : nidada f (de pájaros), camada f (de mamíferos) — vi 1 INCUBATE : empollar 2 ~ about : dar vueltas a, pensar demasiado en
brook ['bruk] n : arroyo m
broom ['bruːm, 'brum] n : escoba f — **broomstick** ['bruːm,stɪk, 'brum-] n : palo m de escoba
broth ['brɔθ] n, pl **broths** ['brɔθs, 'brɔðz] : caldo m
brothel ['brɑθəl, 'brɔ-] n : burdel m
brother ['brʌðər] n : hermano m — **brotherhood** ['brʌðər,hʊd] n : fraternidad f — **brother–in–law** ['brʌðərɪn,lɔ] n, pl **brothers–in–law** : cuñado m — **brotherly** ['brʌðərli] adj : fraternal
brought → **bring**
brow ['brau] n 1 EYEBROW : ceja f 2 FOREHEAD : frente f 3 : cima f (de una colina)
brown ['braun] adj : marrón, castaño (dícese del pelo), moreno (dícese de la piel) — ~ n : marrón m — ~ vt : dorar (en cocinar)
browse ['brauz] vi **browsed; browsing** : mirar, echar un vistazo
bruise ['bruːz] vt **bruised; bruising 1** : contusionar, magullar (a una persona) 2 : machucar (frutas) — ~ n : cardenal m, magulladura f
brunch ['brʌntʃ] n : brunch m
brunet or **brunette** [bruː'net] adj : moreno — ~ n : moreno m, -na f
brunt ['brʌnt] n **bear the ~ of** : aguantar el mayor impacto de
brush ['brʌʃ] n 1 : cepillo m, pincel m (de artista), brocha f (de pintor) 2 UNDERBRUSH : maleza f — ~ vt 1 : cepillar 2 GRAZE : rozar 3 ~ aside : rechazar 4 ~ off DISREGARD : hacer caso omiso de — vi ~ up on : repasar — **brush–off** ['brʌʃ,ɔf] n **give the ~ to** : dar calabazas a
brusque ['brʌsk] adj : brusco
brutal ['bruːtəl] adj : brutal — **brutality** [bruː'tæləti] n, pl **-ties** : brutalidad f
brute ['bruːt] adj : bruto — ~ n : bestia f; bruto m, -ta f
bubble ['bʌbəl] n : burbuja f — ~ vi **-bled; -bling** : burbujear
buck ['bʌk] n, pl **buck** or **bucks 1** : animal m macho, ciervo m (macho) 2 DOLLAR : dólar m — ~ vi 1 : corcovear (dícese de un caballo) 2 ~ up : animarse, levantar el ánimo — vt OPPOSE : oponerse a, ir en contra de
bucket ['bʌkət] n : cubo m
buckle ['bʌkəl] n : hebilla f — ~ v **-led;**

-ling vt 1 FASTEN : abrochar 2 BEND : combar, torcer — vi 1 : combarse, torcerse 2 : doblarse (dícese de las rodillas)
bud ['bʌd] n 1 : brote m 2 or **flower ~** : capullo m — ~ vi **budded; budding** : brotar, hacer brotes
Buddhism ['buː,dɪzəm, 'bu-] n : budismo m — **Buddhist** ['buːdɪst, 'bu-] adj : budista — ~ n : budista mf
buddy ['bʌdi] n, pl **-dies** : compañero m, -ra f
budge ['bʌdʒ] vi **budged; budging 1** MOVE : moverse 2 YIELD : ceder
budget ['bʌdʒət] n : presupuesto m — ~ vi : presupuestar — **budgetary** ['bʌdʒə,teri] adj : presupuestario
buff ['bʌf] n 1 : beige m, color m de ante 2 ENTHUSIAST : aficionado m, -da f — ~ adj : beige — ~ vt POLISH : pulir
buffalo ['bʌfə,lo] n, pl **-lo** or **-loes** : búfalo m
buffet [,bʌ'fei, ,buː-] n 1 : bufé m (comida) 2 SIDEBOARD : aparador m
bug ['bʌg] n 1 INSECT : bicho m, insecto m 2 FLAW : defecto m 3 GERM : microbio m 4 MICROPHONE : micrófono m (oculto) — ~ vt **bugged; bugging 1** PESTER : fastidiar, molestar 2 : ocultar micrófonos en (una habitación, etc.)
buggy ['bʌgi] n, pl **-gies 1** CARRIAGE : calesa f 2 or **baby ~** : cochecito m (para niños)
bugle ['bjuːgəl] n : clarín m, corneta f
build ['bɪld] v **built** ['bɪlt]; **building** vt 1 : construir 2 DEVELOP : desarrollar — vi 1 ~ up INTENSIFY : aumentar, intensificar 2 or ~ up ACCUMULATE : acumularse — ~ n PHYSIQUE : físico m, complexión f — **builder** ['bɪldər] n : constructor m, -tora f — **building** ['bɪldɪŋ] n 1 STRUCTURE : edificio m 2 CONSTRUCTION : construcción f — **built–in** ['bɪlt'ɪn] adj : empotrado
bulb ['bʌlb] n 1 : bulbo m (de una planta) 2 LIGHTBULB : bombilla f
bulge ['bʌldʒ] vi **bulged; bulging** : sobresalir — ~ n : bulto m, protuberancia f
bulk ['bʌlk] n 1 VOLUME : volumen m, bulto m 2 **in ~** : en grandes cantidades — **bulky** ['bʌlki] adj **bulkier; -est** : voluminoso
bull ['bul] n 1 : toro m 2 MALE : macho m
bulldog ['bul,dɔg] n : buldog m
bulldozer ['bul,doːzər] n : bulldozer m
bullet ['bulət] n : bala f
bulletin ['bulətən, -lətən] n : boletín m — **bulletin board** n : tablón m de anuncios

bulletproof ['bulət,pruːf] adj : a prueba de balas

bullfight ['bul,faɪt] n : corrida f (de toros) — **bullfighter** ['bul,faɪtər] n : torero m, -ra f; matador m

bullion ['buljən] n : oro m en lingotes, plata f en lingotes

bull's-eye ['bulz,aɪ] n, pl **bull's-eyes** : diana f

bully ['buli] n, pl **-lies** : matón m — ~ vt **-lied; -lying** : intimidar

bum ['bʌm] n : vagabundo m, -da f

bumblebee ['bʌmbəl,biː] n : abejorro m

bump ['bʌmp] n 1 BULGE : bulto m, protuberancia f 2 IMPACT : golpe m 3 JOLT : sacudida f — ~ vt : chocar contra — vi ~ **into** MEET : encontrarse con — **bumper** ['bʌmpər] n : parachoques mpl — ~ adj : extraordinario, récord — **bumpy** ['bʌmpi] adj **bumpler; -est** 1 : desigual, lleno de baches (dícese de un camino) 2 a ~ **flight** : un vuelo agitado

bun ['bʌn] n : bollo m

bunch ['bʌntʃ] n : grupo m (de personas), racimo m (de frutas, etc.), ramo m (de flores), manojo m (de llaves) — ~ vi or ~ **up** : amontarse, agruparse

bundle ['bʌndəl] n 1 : lío m, bulto m, atado m, haz m (de palos) 2 PARCEL : paquete m 3 ~ **of nerves** : manojo m de nervios — ~ vt **-dled; -dling** or ~ **up** : liar, atar

bungalow ['bʌŋgə,loː] n : casa f de un solo piso

bungle ['bʌŋgəl] vt **-gled; -gling** : echar a perder

bunion ['bʌnjən] n : juanete m

bunk ['bʌŋk] n or **bunk bed** : litera f

bunny ['bʌni] n, pl **-nies** : conejo m, -ja f

buoy ['buːi, 'bɔɪ] n : boya f — ~ vt or ~ **up** HEARTEN : animar, levantar el ánimo a — **buoyant** ['bɔɪənt, 'buːjənt] adj 1 : boyante, flotante 2 LIGHTHEARTED : alegre, optimista

burden ['bərdən] n : carga f — ~ vt ~ **s.o. with** : cargar a algn con — **burdensome** ['bərdənsəm] adj : oneroso

bureau ['bjuro] n 1 : cómoda f (mueble) 2 : departamento m (del gobierno) 3 AGENCY : agencia f — **bureaucracy** [bju'rakrəsi] n, pl **-cies** : burocracia f — **bureaucrat** ['bjurə,kræt] n : burócrata mf — **bureaucratic** [,bjurə'krætɪk] adj : burocrático

burglar ['bərglər] n : ladrón m, -drona f — **burglarize** ['bərglə,raɪz] vt **-ized; -izing** : robar — **burglary** ['bərgləri] n, pl **-glaries** : robo m

burgundy ['bərgəndi] n, pl **-dies** : borgoña m, vino m de Borgoña

burial ['beriəl] n : entierro m

burly ['bərli] adj **-lier; -liest** : fornido

burn ['bərn] v **burned** ['bərnd, 'bərnt] or **burnt** ['bərnt]; **burning** vt 1 : quemar 2 or ~ **down** : incendiar 3 or ~ **up** : consumir — vi 1 : arder (dícese de un fuego), quemarse (dícese de la comida, etc.) 2 : estar encendido (dícese de una luz) 3 ~ **out** : apagarse — ~ n : quemadura f — **burner** ['bərnər] n : quemador m

burnish ['bərnɪʃ] vt : pulir

burp ['bərp] vi : eructar — ~ n : eructo m

burro ['bəro, 'bur-] n, pl **-os** : burro m

burrow ['bəro] n : madriguera f — ~ vi 1 : cavar 2 **into** : hurgar en

bursar ['bərsər] n : tesorero m, -ra f

burst ['bərst] v **burst** or **bursted; bursting** vi : reventarse — vt : reventar — ~ n 1 EXPLOSION : estallido m, explosión f 2 OUTBURST : arranque m, arrebato m 3 ~ **of laughter** : carcajada f

bury ['beri] vt **buried; burying** 1 INTER : enterrar 2 HIDE : esconder

bus ['bʌs] n, pl **buses** or **busses** : autobús m, bus m — ~ v **bused** or **bussed** ['bʌst]; **busing** or **bussing** ['bʌsɪŋ] vt : transportar en autobús — vi : viajar en autobús

bush ['buʃ] n SHRUB : arbusto m, mata f

bushel ['buʃəl] n : medida f de áridos igual a 35.24 litros

bushy ['buʃi] adj **bushier; -est** : poblado, espeso

busily ['bɪzəli] adv : afanosamente

business ['bɪznəs, -nəz] n 1 COMMERCE : negocios mpl, comercio m 2 COMPANY : empresa f, negocio m 3 **it's none of your** ~ : no es asunto tuyo — **businessman** ['bɪznəs,mæn, -nəz-] n, pl **-men** [-mən, -,mɛn] : empresario m, hombre m de negocios — **businesswoman** ['bɪznəs,wumən, -nəz-] n, pl **-women** [-,wɪmən] : empresaria f, mujer f de negocios

bust¹ ['bʌst] vt BREAK : romper

bust² n 1 : busto m (en la escultura) 2 BREASTS : pecho m, senos mpl

bustle ['bʌsəl] vi **-tled; -tling** or ~ **about** : ir y venir, ajetrearse — ~ n or **hustle and** ~ : bullicio m, ajetreo m

busy ['bɪzi] adj **busier; -est** 1 : ocupado 2 BUSTLING : concurrido

but ['bʌt] conj 1 : pero 2 **not one** ~ **two** : no uno sino dos — ~ prep : excepto, menos

butcher ['bʊtʃər] n : carnicero m, -ra f — ~ vt **1** : matar **2** BOTCH : hacer una carnicería de

butler ['bʌtlər] n : mayordomo m

butt ['bʌt] vt : embestir (con los cuernos), darle un cabezazo a — vi ~ **in** : interrumpir — ~ n **1** BUTTING : embestida f (de cuernos) **2** TARGET : blanco m **3** : extremo m, culata f (de un rifle), colilla f (de un cigarrillo)

butter ['bʌtər] n : mantequilla f — ~ vt : untar con mantequilla

buttercup ['bʌtər,kʌp] n : ranúnculo m

butterfly ['bʌtər,flaɪ] n, pl **-flies** : mariposa f

buttocks ['bʌtəks, -,tɑks] npl : nalgas fpl

button ['bʌtən] n : botón m — ~ vt : abotonar — vi or ~ **up** : abotonarse — **buttonhole** ['bʌtən,hoɪl] n : ojal m — ~ vt **-holed; -holing** : acorralar

buy ['baɪ] vt **bought** ['bɔt]; **buying** : comprar — ~ n : compra f — **buyer** ['baɪər] n : comprador m, -dora f

buzz ['bʌz] vi : zumbar — ~ n : zumbido m

buzzard ['bʌzərd] n : buitre m

buzzer ['bʌzər] n : timbre m

by ['baɪ] prep **1** NEAR : cerca de **2** VIA : por **3** PAST : por, por delante de **4** DURING : de, durante **5** (in expressions of time) : para **6** (indicating cause or agent) : por, de, a — ~ adv **1** ~ **and** ~ : poco después **2** ~ **and large** : en general **3** go ~ : pasar **4** stop ~ : pasar por casa

bygone ['baɪ,gɔn] adj : pasado — ~ n **let** ~**s be** ~**s** : lo pasado, pasado está

bypass ['baɪ,pæs] n : carretera f de circunvalación — ~ vt : evitar

by-product ['baɪ,prɑdəkt] n : subproducto m

bystander ['baɪ,stændər] n : espectador m, -dora f

byte ['baɪt] n : byte m, octeto m

byword ['baɪ,wərd] n **be a** ~ **for** : estar sinónimo de

C

c ['si:] n, pl **c's** or **cs** : c, tercera letra del alfabeto inglés

cab ['kæb] n **1** : taxi m **2** : cabina f (de un camión, etc.)

cabbage ['kæbɪdʒ] n : col f, repollo m

cabin ['kæbən] n **1** : cabaña f **2** : cabina f (de un avión, etc.), camarote m (de un barco)

cabinet ['kæbnət] n **1** CUPBOARD : armario m **2** : gabinete m (del gobierno) **3** or **medicine** ~ : botiquín m

cable ['keɪbəl] n : cable m — **cable television** n : televisión f por cable

cackle ['kækəl] vi **-led; -ling 1** CLUCK : cacarear **2** LAUGH : reírse a carcajadas

cactus ['kæktəs] n, pl **cacti** [-,taɪ] or **-tuses** : cactus m

cadence ['keɪdənts] n : cadencia f, ritmo m

cadet [kə'dɛt] n : cadete mf

café [kæ'feɪ, kə-] n : café m, cafetería f — **cafeteria** [,kæfə'tɪriə] n : restaurante m autoservicio, cantina f

caffeine ['kæfi:n] n : cafeína f

cage ['keɪdʒ] n : jaula f — ~ vt **caged; caging** : enjaular

cajole [kə'dʒoːl] vt **-joled; -joling** : engatusar

cake ['keɪk] n **1** : pastel m, torta f **2** : pastilla f (de jabón) **3 take the** ~ : ser el colmo — **caked** ['keɪkt] adj ~ **with** : cubierto de

calamity [kə'læməti] n, pl **-ties** : calamidad f

calcium ['kælsiəm] n : calcio m

calculate ['kælkjə,leɪt] v **-lated; -lating** : calcular — **calculating** ['kælkjə,leɪtɪŋ] adj : calculador — **calculation** [,kælkjə'leɪʃən] n : cálculo m — **calculator** ['kælkjə,leɪtər] n : calculadora f

calendar ['kæləndər] n : calendario m

calf¹ ['kæf, 'kɑf], n, pl **calves** ['kævz, 'kɑvz] **1** : becerro m, -rra f; ternero m, -ra f (de vacunos) **2** : cría f (de otros mamíferos)

calf² n, pl **calves** : pantorrilla f (de la pierna)

caliber or **calibre** ['kæləbər] n : calibre m

call ['kɔl] vi **1** : llamar **2** VISIT : pasar, hacer (una) visita **3** ~ **for** : requerir — vt **1** : llamar **2** ~ **off** : cancelar — ~ n **1** : llamada f **2** SHOUT : grito m **3** VISIT : visita f **4** DEMAND : petición f — **calling** ['kɔlɪŋ] n : vocación f

callous ['kæləs] adj : insensible, cruel

calm ['kɑm, 'kɑlm] n : calma f, tranquilidad f — ~ vt : calmar — vi or ~ **down** : calmarse — ~ adj : tranquilo, en calma — **calmly** ['kɑmli, 'kɑlm-] adv : con calma

calorie ['kæləri] *n* : caloría *f*

came → **come**

camel ['kæməl] *n* : camello *m*

camera ['kæmrə, 'kæmərə] *n* : cámara *f*

camouflage ['kæmə,flɑʒ, -,flɑdʒ] *n* : camuflaje *m* — ~ *vt* **-flaged; -flaging** : camuflar

camp ['kæmp] *n* **1** : campamento *m* **2** FACTION : bando *m* — ~ *vi* : acampar, ir de camping

campaign [kæm'peɪn] *n* : campaña *f* — ~ *vi* : hacer (una) campaña

camping ['kæmpɪŋ] *n* : camping *m*

campus ['kæmpəs] *n* : ciudad *f* universitaria

can¹ ['kæn] *v aux, past* **could** ['kʊd]; *present s & pl* **can 1** (*expressing possibility or permission*) : poder **2** (*expressing knowledge or ability*) : saber **3 that cannot be!** : ¡no puede ser!

can² ['kæn] *n* : lata *f* — ~ *vt* **canned; canning** : enlatar

Canadian [kə'neɪdiən] *adj* : canadiense

canal [kə'næl] *n* : canal *m*

canary [kə'neri] *n, pl* **-naries** : canario *m*

cancel ['kæntsəl] *vt* **-celed** *or* **-celled; -celing** *or* **-celling** : cancelar — **cancellation** [,kæntsə'leɪʃən] *n* : cancelación *f*

cancer ['kæntsər] *n* : cáncer *m* — **cancerous** ['kæntsərəs] *adj* : canceroso

candelabra [,kændə'lɑbrə, -'læ-] *n, pl* **-bra** *or* **-bras** : candelabro *m*

candid ['kændɪd] *adj* : franco

candidate ['kændə,deɪt, -dət] *n* : candidato *m*, -ta *f* — **candidacy** ['kændədəsi] *n, pl* **-cies** : candidatura *f*

candle ['kændəl] *n* : vela *f* — **candlestick** ['kændəl,stɪk] *n* : candelero *m*

candor *or Brit* **candour** ['kændər] *n* : franqueza *f*

candy ['kændi] *n, pl* **-dies** : dulce *m*, caramelo *m*

cane ['keɪn] *n* **1** : bastón *m* (para andar), vara *f* (para castigar) **2** REED : caña *f*, mimbre *m* — ~ *vt* **caned; caning 1** : tapizar con mimbre **2** FLOG : azotar

canine ['keɪ,naɪn] *n or* ~ **tooth** : colmillo *m*, diente *m* canino — ~ *adj* : canino

canister ['kænəstər] *n* : lata *f*, bote *m* Spain

cannibal ['kænəbəl] *n* : caníbal *mf*

cannon ['kænən] *n, pl* **-nons** *or* **-non** : cañón *m*

cannot (can not) ['kæn,ɑt, kə'nɑt] → **can¹**

canny ['kæni] *adj* **cannier; -est** : astuto

canoe [kə'nu:] *n* : canoa *f*, piragua *f* — ~ *vt* **-noed; -noeing** : ir en canoa

canon ['kænən] *n* : canon *m* — **canonize** ['kænə,naɪz] *vt* **-ized; -izing** : canonizar

can opener *n* : abrelatas *m*

canopy ['kænəpi] *n, pl* **-pies** : dosel *m*

can't ['kænt, 'kant] (*contraction of* **can not**) → **can¹**

cantaloupe ['kæntəl,o:p] *n* : melón *m*, cantalupo *m*

cantankerous [kæn'tæŋkərəs] *adj* : irritable, irascible

canteen [kæn'ti:n] *n* **1** FLASK : cantimplora *f* **2** CAFETERIA : cantina *f*

canter ['kæntər] *vi* : ir a medio galope — ~ *n* : medio galope *m*

canvas ['kænvəs] *n* **1** : lona *f* (tela) **2** : lienzo *m* (de pintar)

canvass ['kænvəs] *vt* **1** : solicitar votos de, hacer campaña entre **2** POLL : sondear — ~ *n* **1** : solicitación *f* (de votos) **2** POLL : sondeo *m*

canyon ['kænjən] *n* : cañón *m*

cap *n* **1** : gorra *f*, gorro *m* **2** TOP : tapa *f*, tapón *m* (de botellas) **3** LIMIT : tope *m* — ~ ['kæp] *vt* **capped; capping 1** COVER : tapar, cubrir **2** OUTDO : superar

capable ['keɪpəbəl] *adj* : capaz, competente — **capability** [,keɪpə'bɪləti] *n, pl* **-ties** : capacidad *f*

capacity [kə'pæsəti] *n, pl* **-ties 1** : capacidad *f* **2** ROLE : calidad *f*

cape¹ ['keɪp] *n* : cabo *m* (en geografía)

cape² *n* CLOAK : capa *f*

caper¹ ['keɪpər] *n* : alcaparra *f*

caper² *n* PRANK : broma *f*, travesura *f*

capital ['kæpətəl] *adj* **1** : capital **2** : mayúsculo (dícese de las letras) — ~ *n* **1** *or* ~ **city** : capital *f* **2** WEALTH : capital *m* **3** *or* ~ **letter** : mayúscula *f* — **capitalism** ['kæpətəl,ɪzəm] *n* : capitalismo *m* — **capitalist** ['kæpətəl,ɪst] *or* **capitalistic** [,kæpətəl'ɪstɪk] *adj* : capitalista — **capitalize** ['kæpətə,laɪz] *vt* **-ized; -izing 1** FINANCE : capitalizar **2** : escribir con mayúscula — *vi* ~ **on** : sacar partido de

capitol ['kæpətəl] *n* : capitolio *m*

capitulate [kə'pɪtʃə,leɪt] *vi* **-lated; -lating** : capitular

capsize ['kæp,saɪz, kæp'saɪz] *v* **-sized; -sizing** *vt* : hacer volcar — *vi* : zozobrar, volcar(se)

capsule ['kæpsəl, -su:l] *n* : cápsula *f*

captain ['kæptən] *n* : capitán *m*, -tana *f*

caption ['kæpʃən] *n* **1** : leyenda *f* (al pie de una ilustración) **2** SUBTITLE : subtítulo *m*

captivate ['kæptə,veɪt] *vt* **-vated; -vating** : cautivar, encantar

captive ['kæptɪv] *adj* : cautivo — ~ *n*
: cautivo *m*, -va *f* — **captivity** [kæp-
'tɪvəṭi] *n* : cautiverio *m*

capture ['kæpʃər] *n* 1 : captura *f*, apresamiento *m* — ~ *vt* **-tured; -turing** 1
SEIZE : capturar, apresar 2 ~ **one's interest** : captar el interés de uno

car ['kɑr] *n* 1 : automóvil *m*, coche *m*,
carro *m* *Lat* 2 *or* **railroad** ~ : vagón *m*

carafe [kə'ræf, -'rɑf] *n* : garrafa *f*

caramel ['kɑrməl; 'kærəməl, -ˌmel] *n*
: caramelo *m*, azúcar *f* quemada

carat ['kærət] *n* : quilate *m*

caravan ['kærəˌvæn] *n* : caravana *f*

carbohydrate [ˌkɑrbo'haɪˌdreɪt, -drət] *n*
: carbohidrato *m*, hidrato *m* de carbono

carbon ['kɑrbən] *n* : carbono *m* — **carbon copy** *n* : copia *f*, duplicado *m*

carburetor ['kɑrbəˌreɪṭər, -bjə-] *n* : carburador *m*

carcass ['kɑrkəs] *n* : cuerpo *m* (de un
animal muerto)

card ['kɑrd] *n* 1 : tarjeta *f* 2 *or* **playing**
~ : carta *f*, naipe *m* — **cardboard**
['kɑrdˌbord] *n* : cartón *m*

cardiac ['kɑrdiˌæk] *adj* : cardíaco

cardigan ['kɑrdɪgən] *n* : cárdigan *m*

cardinal ['kɑrdənəl] *n* : cardenal *m* — ~
adj : cardinal, fundamental

care ['kær] *n* 1 : cuidado *m* 2 WORRY
: preocupación 3 **take ~ of** : cuidar
(de) — ~ *vi* **cared; caring** 1 : preocuparse, inquietarse 2 ~ **for** TEND
: cuidar (de), atender 3 ~ **for** LIKE
: querer 4 **I don't** ~ : no me importa

career [kə'rɪr] *n* : carrera *f* — ~ *vi* : ir a
toda velocidad

carefree ['kærˌfri:, ˌkær-] *adj* : despreocupado

careful ['kærfəl] *adj* : cuidadoso —
carefully ['kærfəli] *adv* : con cuidado,
cuidadosamente — **careless** ['kærləs]
adj : descuidado — **carelessness**
['kærləsnəs] *n* : descuido *m*

caress [kə'res] *n* : caricia *f* — ~ *vt*
: acariciar

cargo ['kɑrˌgo:] *n*, *pl* **-goes** *or* **-gos**
: cargamento *m*, carga *f*

caricature ['kærɪkəˌtʃʊr] *n* : caricatura *f*
— ~ *vt* **-tured; -turing** : caricaturizar

caring ['kærɪŋ] *adj* : solícito, afectuoso

carnage ['kɑrnɪdʒ] *n* : matanza *f*, carnicería *f*

carnal ['kɑrnəl] *adj* : carnal

carnation [kɑr'neɪʃən] *n* : clavel *m*

carnival ['kɑrnəvəl] *n* : carnaval *m*

carol ['kærəl] *n* : villancico *m*

carp ['kɑrp] *vi* ~ **at** : quejarse de

carpenter ['kɑrpəntər] *n* : carpintero *m*,

-ra *f* — **carpentry** ['kɑrpəntri] *n* : carpintería *f*

carpet ['kɑrpət] *n* : alfombra *f*

carriage ['kærɪdʒ] *n* 1 : transporte *m* (de
mercancías) 2 BEARING : porte *m* 3 *or*
baby ~ : cochecito *m* 4 *or* **horse-
drawn** ~ : carruaje *m*, coche *m*

carrier ['kæriər] *n* 1 : transportista *mf*,
empresa *f* de transportes 2 : portador
m, -dora *f* (de una enfermedad)

carrot ['kærət] *n* : zanahoria *f*

carry ['kæri] *v* **-ried; -rying** *vt* 1 : llevar
2 TRANSPORT : transportar 3 STOCK
: vender 4 ENTAIL : acarrear, implicar 5
~ **oneself** : portarse — *vi* : oírse
(dícese de sonidos) — **carry away** *vt*
get carried away : exaltarse, entusiasmarse — **carry on** *vt* CONDUCT : realizar — *vi* 1 : portarse inapropiada-
mente 2 CONTINUE : seguir, continuar
— **carry out** *vt* 1 PERFORM : llevar a
cabo, realizar 2 FULFILL : cumplir

cart ['kɑrt] *n* : carreta *f*, carro *m* — ~ *vt*
or ~ **around** : acarrear

cartilage ['kɑrṭəlɪdʒ] *n* : cartílago *m*

carton ['kɑrṭən] *n* : caja *f* (de cartón)

cartoon [kɑr'tu:n] *n* 1 : caricatura *f* 2
COMIC STRIP : historieta *f* 3 *or* **animated** ~ : dibujos *mpl* animados

cartridge ['kɑrtrɪdʒ] *n* : cartucho *m*

carve ['kɑrv] *vt* **carved; carving** 1 : tallar, esculpir 2 : trinchar (carne)

case *n* 1 : caso *m* 2 BOX : caja *f* 3 **in any**
~ : en todo caso 4 **in ~ of** : en caso
de 5 **just in** ~ : por si acaso

cash ['kæʃ] *n* : efectivo *m*, dinero *m* en
efectivo — ~ *vt* : convertir en efectivo, cobrar

cashew ['kæˌʃu:, kə'ʃu:] *n* : anacardo *m*

cashier [kæ'ʃɪr] *n* : cajero *m*, -ra *f*

cashmere ['kæʒˌmɪr, 'kæʃ-] *n* : cachemira *f*

cash register *n* : caja *f* registradora

casino [kə'si:ˌno:] *n*, *pl* **-nos** : casino *m*

cask ['kæsk] *n* : barril *m*

casket ['kæskət] *n* : ataúd *m*

casserole ['kæsəˌro:l] *n* 1 *or* ~ **dish**
: cazuela *f* 2 : guiso *m* (comida)

cassette [kə'set, kæ-] *n* : cassette *mf*

cast ['kæst] *vt* **cast; casting** 1 THROW
: arrojar, lanzar 2 : depositar (un voto)
3 : repartir (papeles dramáticos) 4
MOLD : fundir — ~ *n* 1 : elenco *m*,
reparto *m* (de actores) 2 *or* **plaster** ~
: molde *m* de yeso, escayola *f*

castanets [ˌkæstə'nets] *npl* : castañuelas
fpl

castaway ['kæstəˌweɪ] *n* : náufrago *m*,
-ga *f*

cast iron *n* : hierro *m* fundido

castle ['kæsəl] *n* 1 : castillo *m* 2 : torre *f* (en ajedrez)

castrate ['kæs,treɪt] *vt* **-trated; -trating** : castrar

casual ['kæʒuəl] *adj* 1 CHANCE : casual, fortuito 2 INDIFFERENT : despreocupado 3 INFORMAL : informal — **casually** ['kæʒuəli, 'kæʒəli] *adv* 1 : de manera despreocupada 2 INFORMALLY : informalmente

casualty ['kæʒuəlti, 'kæʒəl-] *n, pl* **-ties** 1 : accidente *m* 2 VICTIM : víctima *f*; herido *m*, -da *f* 3 **casualties** *npl* : bajas *fpl* (militares)

cat ['kæt] *n* : gato *m*, -ta *f*

catalog *or* **catalogue** ['kæṭə,lɔg] *n* : catálogo *m* — ~ *vt* **-loged** *or* **-logued; -loging** *or* **-loguing** : catalogar

catapult ['kæṭə,pʌlt, -,pʊlt] *n* : catapulta *f*

cataract ['kæṭə,rækt] *n* : catarata *f*

catastrophe [kə'tæstrə,fiː] *n* : catástrofe *f* — **catastrophic** [,kæṭə'strɑfɪk] *adj* : catastrófico

catch ['kætʃ, 'ketʃ] *v* **caught** ['kɔt]; **catching** *vt* 1 CAPTURE, TRAP : capturar, atrapar 2 SURPRISE : sorprender 3 GRASP : agarrar, captar 4 SNAG : enganchar 5 : tomar (un tren, etc.) 6 ~ **a cold** : resfriarse — *vi* 1 SNAG : engancharse 2 ~ **fire** : prender fuego — **catching** ['kætʃɪŋ, 'ke-] *adj* : contagioso — **catchy** ['kætʃi, 'ke-] *adj* **catchier; -est** : pegadizo, pegajoso *Lat*

category ['kæṭə,gori] *n, pl* **-ries** : categoría *f* — **categorical** [,kæṭə'gɔrɪkəl] *adj* : categórico

cater ['keɪṭər] *vi* 1 : proveer comida 2 ~ **to** : atender a — **caterer** ['keɪṭərər] *n* : proveedor *m*, -dora *f* de comida

caterpillar ['kæṭər,pɪlər] *n* : oruga *f*

catfish ['kæt,fɪʃ] *n* : bagre *m*

cathedral [kə'θiːdrəl] *n* : catedral *f*

catholic ['kæθəlɪk] *adj* 1 : universal 2 **Catholic** : católico — **catholicism** [kə'θɑlə,sɪzəm] *n* : catolicismo *m*

cattle ['kæṭəl] *npl* : ganado *m* (vacuno)

caught → **catch**

cauldron ['kɔldrən] *n* : caldera *f*

cauliflower ['kɑli,flauər, 'kɔ-] *n* : coliflor *f*

cause ['kɔz] *n* 1 : causa *f* 2 REASON : motivo *m* — ~ *vt* **caused; causing** : causar

caustic ['kɔstɪk] *adj* : cáustico

caution ['kɔʃən] *n* 1 WARNING : advertencia *f* 2 CARE : precaución *f*, cautela *f* — ~ *vt* : advertir — **cautious** ['kɔʃəs] *adj* : cauteloso, precavido —

cautiously ['kɔʃəsli] *adv* : con precaución

cavalier [,kævə'lɪr] *adj* : arrogante, desdeñoso

cavalry ['kævəlri] *n, pl* **-ries** : caballería *f*

cave ['keɪv] *n* : cueva *f* — ~ *vi* **caved; caving** *or* ~ **in** : hundirse

cavern ['kævərn] *n* : caverna *f*

cavity ['kævəṭi] *n, pl* **-ties** 1 : cavidad *f* 2 : caries *f* (dental)

cavort [kə'vɔrt] *vi* : brincar

CD [,siː'diː] *n* : CD *m*, disco *m* compacto

cease ['siːs] *v* **ceased; ceasing** *vt* : dejar de — *vi* : cesar — **cease-fire** ['siːs,faɪr] *n* : alto *m* al fuego — **ceaseless** ['siːsləs] *adj* : incesante

cedar ['siːdər] *n* : cedro *m*

ceiling ['siːlɪŋ] *n* : techo *m*

celebrate ['selə,breɪt] *v* **-brated; -brating** *vt* : celebrar — *vi* : divertirse — **celebrated** ['selə,breɪṭəd] *adj* : célebre — **celebration** [,selə'breɪʃən] *n* 1 : celebración *f* 2 FESTIVITY : fiesta *f* — **celebrity** [sə'lebrəṭi] *n, pl* **-ties** : celebridad *f*

celery ['seləri] *n, pl* **-eries** : apio *m*

cell ['sel] *n* 1 : célula *f* 2 : celda *f* (en una cárcel, etc.)

cellar ['selər] *n* 1 BASEMENT : sótano *m* 2 : bodega *f* (de vinos)

cello ['tʃe,loː] *n, pl* **-los** : violoncelo *m*

cellular ['seljələr] *adj* : celular

cement [sɪ'ment] *n* : cemento *m* — ~ *vt* : cementar

cemetery ['semə,teri] *n, pl* **-teries** : cementerio *m*

censor ['sensər] *vt* : censurar — **censorship** ['sensər,ʃɪp] *n* : censura *f* — **censure** ['sentʃər] *n* : censura *f* — ~ *vt* **-sured; -suring** : censurar, criticar

census ['sensəs] *n* : censo *m*

cent ['sent] *n* : centavo *m*

centennial [sen'teniəl] *n* : centenario *m*

center *or Brit* **centre** ['sentər] *n* : centro *m* — ~ *v* **centered** *or Brit* **centred; centering** *or Brit* **centring** *vt* : centrar — *vi* ~ **on** : centrarse en

centigrade ['sentə,greɪd, 'sɑn-] *adj* : centígrado

centimeter ['sentə,miːṭər, 'sɑn-] *n* : centímetro *m*

centipede ['sentə,piːd] *n* : ciempiés *m*

central ['sentrəl] *adj* 1 : central 2 **a** ~ **location** : un lugar céntrico — **centralize** ['sentrə,laɪz] *vt* **-ized; -izing** : centralizar

centre ['sentər] → **center**

century ['sentʃəri] *n, pl* **-ries** : siglo *m*

ceramics [sə'ræmɪks] *npl* : cerámica *f*

cereal ['sɪriəl] *n* : cereal *m*

ceremony ['serə,moːni] *n, pl* **-nies** : ceremonia *f* — **ceremonial** [,serə'moːniəl] *adj* : ceremonial

certain ['sərtən] *adj* **1** : cierto **2 be ~ of** : estar seguro de **3 for ~** : seguro, con toda seguridad **4 make ~ of** : asegurarse de — **certainly** ['sərtənli] *adv* : desde luego, por supuesto — **certainty** ['sərtənti] *n, pl* **-ties** : certeza *f*, seguridad *f*

certify ['sərtə,faɪ] *vt* **-fied; -fying** : certificar — **certificate** [sər'tɪfɪkət] *n* : certificado *m*, partida *f*, acta *f*

chafe ['tʃeɪf] *v* **chafed; chafing** *vi* : rozarse — *vt* : rozar

chain ['tʃeɪn] *n* **1** : cadena *f* **2 ~ of events** : serie *f* de acontecimientos — **~** *vt* : encadenar

chair ['tʃer] *n* **1** : silla *f* **2** : cátedra *f* (en una universidad) — **~** *vt* : presidir — **chairman** ['tʃermən] *n, pl* **-men** [-mən, -,men] : presidente *m* — **chairperson** ['tʃer,pərsən] *n* : presidente *m*, -ta *f*

chalk ['tʃɔk] *n* : tiza *f*, gis *m Lat*

challenge ['tʃælɪndʒ] *vt* **-lenged; -lenging 1** DISPUTE : disputar, poner en duda **2** DARE : desafiar — **~** *n* : reto *m*, desafío *m* — **challenging** ['tʃælɪndʒɪŋ] *adj* : estimulante

chamber ['tʃeɪmbər] *n* : cámara *f* — **chambermaid** ['tʃeɪmbər,meɪd] *n* : camarera *f*

champagne [ʃæm'peɪn] *n* : champaña *m*, champán *m*

champion ['tʃæmpiən] *n* : campeón *m*, -peona *f* — **~** *vt* : defender — **championship** ['tʃæmpiən,ʃɪp] *n* : campeonato *m*

chance ['tʃænts] *n* **1** LUCK : azar *m*, suerte *f* **2** OPPORTUNITY : oportunidad *f* **3** LIKELIHOOD : probabilidad *f* **4 by ~** : por casualidad **5 take a ~** : arriesgarse — **~** *vt* **chanced; chancing** RISK : arriesgar — **~** *adj* : fortuito

chandelier [,ʃændə'lɪr] *n* : araña *f* (de luces)

change ['tʃeɪndʒ] *v* **changed; changing** *vt* **1** : cambiar **2** SWITCH : cambiar de — *vi* **1** : cambiar **2 or ~ clothes** : cambiarse (de ropa) — **~** *n* : cambio *m* — **changeable** ['tʃeɪndʒəbəl] *adj* : cambiable

channel ['tʃænəl] *n* **1** : canal *m* **2** : cauce *m* (de un río) **3** MEANS : vía *f*, medio *m*

chant ['tʃænt] *v* : cantar — **~** *n* : canto *m*

chaos ['keɪ,ɑs] *n* : caos *m* — **chaotic** [keɪ'ɑtɪk] *adj* : caótico

chap¹ ['tʃæp] *vi* **chapped; chapping** : agrietarse

chap² *n* : tipo *m fam*

chapel ['tʃæpəl] *n* : capilla *f*

chaperon *or* **chaperone** ['ʃæpə,roːn] *n* : acompañante *mf*

chaplain ['tʃæplɪn] *n* : capellán *m*

chapter ['tʃæptər] *n* : capítulo *m*

char ['tʃar] *vt* **charred; charring** : carbonizar

character ['kærɪktər] *n* **1** : carácter *m* **2** : personaje *m* (en una novela, etc.) — **characteristic** [,kærɪktə'rɪstɪk] *adj* : característico — **~** *n* : característica *f* — **characterize** ['kærɪktə,raɪz] *vt* **-ized; -izing** : caracterizar

charcoal ['tʃar,koːl] *n* : carbón *m*

charge ['tʃardʒ] *n* **1** : carga *f* (eléctrica) **2** COST : precio *m* **3** BURDEN : carga *f*, peso *m*, **4** ACCUSATION : cargo *m*, acusación *f* **5 in ~ of** : encargado de **6 take ~ of** : hacerse cargo de — **~** *v* **charged; charging** *vt* **1** : cargar **2** ENTRUST : encargar **3** COMMAND : ordenar, mandar **4** ACCUSE : acusar — *vi* **1** : cargar **2 ~ too much** : cobrar demasiado

charisma [kə'rɪzmə] *n* : carisma *m* — **charismatic** [,kærəz'mætɪk] *adj* : carismático

charity ['tʃærəti] *n, pl* **-ties 1** : organización *f* benéfica **2** GOODWILL : caridad *f*

charlatan ['ʃarlətən] *n* : charlatán *m*, -tana *f*

charm ['tʃarm] *n* **1** : encanto *m* **2** SPELL : hechizo *m* — **~** *vt* : encantar, cautivar — **charming** ['tʃarmɪŋ] *adj* : encantador

chart ['tʃart] *n* **1** MAP : carta *f* **2** DIAGRAM : gráfico *m*, tabla *f* — **~** *vt* : trazar un mapa de

charter ['tʃartər] *n* : carta *f* — **~** *vt* : alquilar, fletar

chase ['tʃeɪs] *n* : persecución *f* — **~** *vt* **chased; chasing 1** PURSUE : perseguir **2 or ~ away** : ahuyentar

chasm ['kæzəm] *n* : abismo *m*

chaste ['tʃeɪst] *adj* **chaster; -est** : casto — **chastity** ['tʃæstəti] *n* : castidad *f*

chat ['tʃæt] *vi* **chatted; chatting** : charlar — **~** *n* : charla *f* — **chatter** ['tʃætər] *vi* **1** : parlotear *fam* **2** : castañetear (dícese de los dientes) — **~** *n* : parloteo *m*, cháchara *f* — **chatterbox** ['tʃætər,baks] *n* : parlanchín *m*, -china *f* — **chatty** ['tʃæti] *adj* **chattier; chattiest 1** : parlanchín **2** INFORMAL : familiar

chauffeur ['ʃoːfər, ʃoˈfər] *n* : chofer *mf*

chauvinist ['ʃoːvənɪst] *or* **chauvinistic**

[ˌʃoːvəˈnɪstɪk] *adj* : chauvinista, patriotero

cheap [ˈtʃiːp] *adj* **1** INEXPENSIVE : barato **2** SHODDY : de baja calidad — ~ *adv* : barato — **cheapen** [ˈtʃiːpən] *vt* : rebajar — **cheaply** [ˈtʃiːpli] *adv* : barato, a precio bajo

cheat [ˈtʃiːt] *vt* : defraudar, estafar — *vi* **1** : hacer trampa(s) **2** ~ **on s.o.** : engañar a algn — ~ *or* **cheater** [ˈtʃiːtər] *n* : tramposo *m*, -sa *f*

check [ˈtʃɛk] *n* **1** RESTRAINT : freno *m* **2** INSPECTION : inspección *f*, comprobación *f* **3** DRAFT : cheque *m* **4** BILL : cuenta *f* **5** : jaque *m* (en ajedrez) **6** : tela *f* a cuadros — ~ *vt* **1** RESTRAIN : frenar, contener **2** INSPECT : revisar **3** VERIFY : comprobar **4** : dar jaque (en ajedrez) **5** ~ **in** : enregistrarse (en un hotel) **6** ~ **out** : irse (de un hotel) **7** ~ **out** VERIFY : verificar, comprobar

checkers [ˈtʃɛkərz] *n* : damas *fpl*

checkmate [ˈtʃɛkˌmeɪt] *n* : jaque *m* mate

checkpoint [ˈtʃɛkˌpɔɪnt] *n* : puesto *m* de control

checkup [ˈtʃɛkˌʌp] *n* : chequeo *m*, examen *m* médico

cheek [ˈtʃiːk] *n* : mejilla *f*

cheer [ˈtʃɪr] *n* **1** CHEERFULNESS : alegría *f* **2** APPLAUSE : aclamación *f* **3** ~s! : ¡salud! — ~ *vt* **1** GLADDEN : alegrar **2** APPLAUD, SHOUT : aclamar, aplaudir — **cheerful** [ˈtʃɪrfəl] *adj* : alegre

cheese [ˈtʃiːz] *n* : queso *m*

cheetah [ˈtʃiːtə] *n* : guepardo *m*

chef [ˈʃɛf] *n* : chef *m*

chemical [ˈkɛmɪkəl] *adj* : químico — ~ *n* : sustancia *f* química — **chemist** [ˈkɛmɪst] *n* : químico *m*, -ca *f* — **chemistry** [ˈkɛmɪstri] *n*, *pl* **-tries** : química *f*

cheque [ˈtʃɛk] *Brit* → **check**

cherish [ˈtʃɛrɪʃ] *vt* **1** : querer, apreciar **2** HARBOR : abrigar (un recuerdo, una esperanza, etc.)

cherry [ˈtʃɛri] *n*, *pl* **-ries** : cereza *f*

chess [ˈtʃɛs] *n* : ajedrez *m*

chest [ˈtʃɛst] *n* **1** BOX : cofre *m* **2** : pecho *m* (del cuerpo) **3** *or* ~ **of drawers** : cómoda *f*

chestnut [ˈtʃɛstˌnʌt] *n* : castaña *f*

chew [ˈtʃuː] *vt* : masticar, mascar — **chewing gum** *n* : chicle *m*

chic [ˈʃiːk] *adj* : elegante

chick [ˈtʃɪk] *n* : polluelo *m*, -la *f* — **chicken** [ˈtʃɪkən] *n* : pollo *m* — **chicken pox** *n* : varicela *f*

chicory [ˈtʃɪkəri] *n*, *pl* **-ries** **1** : endivia *f* (para ensaladas) **2** : achicoria *f* (aditivo de café)

chief [ˈtʃiːf] *adj* : principal — ~ *n* : jefe

m, -fa *f* — **chiefly** [ˈtʃiːfli] *adv* : principalmente

child [ˈtʃaɪld] *n*, *pl* **children** [ˈtʃɪldrən] **1** : niño *m*, -ña *f* **2** OFFSPRING : hijo *m*, -ja *f* — **childbirth** [ˈtʃaɪldˌbərθ] *n* : parto *m* — **childhood** [ˈtʃaɪldˌhʊd] *n* : infancia *f*, niñez *f* — **childish** [ˈtʃaɪldɪʃ] *adj* : infantil — **childlike** [ˈtʃaɪldˌlaɪk] *adj* : infantil, inocente — **childproof** [ˈtʃaɪldˌpruːf] *adj* : a prueba de niños

Chilean [ˈtʃɪliən, tʃɪˈleɪən] *adj* : chileno

chili *or* **chile** *or* **chilli** [ˈtʃɪli] *n*, *pl* **chilies** *or* **chiles** *or* **chillies 1** *or* ~ **pepper** : chile *m* **2** : chile *m* con carne

chill [ˈtʃɪl] *n* **1** CHILLINESS : frío *m* **2** catch a ~ : resfriarse **3** there's a ~ in the air : hace fresco — ~ *adj* : frío — ~ *v* : enfriar — **chilly** [ˈtʃɪli] *adj* **chillier; -est** : fresco, frío

chime [ˈtʃaɪm] *vi* **chimed; chiming** : repicar, sonar — ~ *n* : carillón *m*

chimney [ˈtʃɪmni] *n*, *pl* **-neys** : chimenea *f*

chimpanzee [ˌtʃɪmˌpænˈziː, ˌʃɪm-; tʃɪmˈpænzi, ʃɪm-] *n* : chimpancé *m*

chin [ˈtʃɪn] *n* : barbilla *f*

china [ˈtʃaɪnə] *n* : porcelana *f*, loza *f*

Chinese [ˈtʃaɪˌniːz, -ˈniːs] *adj* : chino — ~ *n* : chino *m* (idioma)

chink [ˈtʃɪŋk] *n* : grieta *f*

chip [ˈtʃɪp] *n* **1** : astilla *f* (de madera o vidrio), lasca *f* (de piedra) **2** : ficha *f* (de póker, etc.) **3** NICK : desportilladura *f* **4** *or* **computer** ~ : chip *m* **5** → **potato chips** — ~ *v* **chipped; chipping** *vt* : desportillar — *vi* **1** : desportillarse **2** ~ **in** : contribuir

chipmunk [ˈtʃɪpˌmʌŋk] *n* : ardilla *f* listada

chiropodist [kəˈrɑpədɪst, ʃə-] *n* : podólogo *m*, -ga *f*

chiropractor [ˈkaɪrəˌpræktər] *n* : quiropráctico *m*, -ca *f*

chirp [ˈtʃərp] *vi* : piar, gorjear

chisel [ˈtʃɪzəl] *n* : cincel *m* (para piedras, etc.), formón *m*, escoplo *m* (para madera) — ~ *vt* **-eled** *or* **-elled; -eling** *or* **-elling** : cincelar, tallar

chit [ˈtʃɪt] *n* : nota *f*

chitchat [ˈtʃɪtˌtʃæt] *n* : cháchara *f* *fam*

chivalrous [ˈʃɪvəlrəs] *adj* : caballeroso — **chivalry** [ˈʃɪvəlri] *n*, *pl* **-ries** : caballerosidad *f*

chive [ˈtʃaɪv] *n* : cebollino *m*

chlorine [ˈklɔriːn] *n* : cloro *m*

chock–full [ˈtʃɑkˈfʊl, ˈtʃʌk-] *adj* : repleto, atestado

chocolate [ˈtʃɑkələt, ˈtʃɔk-] *n* : chocolate *m*

choice [ˈtʃɔɪs] *n* **1** : elección *f*, selección

f **2** PREFERENCE : preferencia *f* — ~
adj choicer; -est : selecto
choir ['kwaɪr] *n* : coro *m*
choke ['tʃoːk] *v* choked; choking *vt* **1**
: asfixiar, estrangular **2** BLOCK : atascar — *vi* : asfixiarse, atragantarse (con
comida) — ~ *n* : estárter *m* (de un
motor)
choose ['tʃuːz] *v* chose ['tʃoːz]; chosen
['tʃoːzən]; choosing *vt* **1** SELECT : escoger, elegir **2** DECIDE : decidir — *vi*
: escoger — choosy *or* choosey
['tʃuːzi] *adj* choosier; -est : exigente
chop ['tʃɑp] *vt* chopped; chopping **1**
: cortar, picar (carne, etc.) **2** ~ down
: talar — ~ *n* : chuleta *f* (de cerdo,
etc.) — choppy ['tʃɑpi] *adj* -pier; -est
: picado, agitado
chopsticks ['tʃɑp,stɪks] *npl* : palillos
mpl
chord ['kɔrd] *n* : acorde *m* (en música)
chore ['tʃor] *n* **1** : tarea *f* **2** household
~s : faenas *fpl* domésticas
choreography [,kori'ɑgrəfi] *n, pl* -phies
: coreografía *f*
chortle ['tʃɔrtəl] *vi* -tled; -tling : reírse
(con satisfacción o júbilo)
chorus ['korəs] **1** : coro *m* (grupo de
personas) **2** REFRAIN : estribillo *m*
chose, chosen → choose
christen ['krɪsən] *vt* : bautizar — christening ['krɪsənɪŋ] *n* : bautizo *m*
Christian ['krɪstʃən] *n* : cristiano *m*, -na *f*
— ~ *adj* : cristiano — Christianity
[,krɪstʃi'ænəti, ,krɪs'tʃæ-] *n* : cristianismo *m*
Christmas ['krɪsməs] *n* : Navidad *f*
chrome ['kroːm] *n* : cromo *m*
chronic ['krɑnɪk] *adj* : crónico
chronicle ['krɑnɪkəl] *n* : crónica *f*
chronology [krə'nɑlədʒi] *n, pl* -gies
: cronología *f* — chronological
[,krɑnəl'ɑdʒɪkəl] *adj* : cronológico
chrysanthemum [krɪ'sænθəməm] *n*
: crisantemo *m*
chubby ['tʃʌbi] *adj* -bier; -est : regordete *fam*, rechoncho *fam*
chuck ['tʃʌk] *vt* : tirar, arrojar
chuckle ['tʃʌkəl] *vi* -led; -ling : reírse
(entre dientes) — ~ *n* : risa *f* ahogada
chum ['tʃʌm] *n* : amigo *m*, -ga *f*; compinche *mf fam* — chummy ['tʃʌmi] *adj*
-mier; -est : muy amigable
chunk ['tʃʌnk] *n* : trozo *m*, pedazo *m*
church ['tʃərtʃ] *n* : iglesia *f*
churn ['tʃərn] *n* : mantequera *f* — ~ *vt*
1 : agitar **2** ~ out : producir en
grandes cantidades
chute ['ʃuːt] *n* **1** : vertedor *m* **2** SLIDE : tobogán *m*

cider ['saɪdər] *n* : sidra *f*
cigar [sɪ'gɑr] *n* : puro *m* — cigarette
[,sɪgə'ret, 'sɪgə,ret] *n* : cigarrillo *m*, cigarro *m*
cinch ['sɪntʃ] *n* it's a ~ : es pan comido
cinema ['sɪnəmə] *n* : cine *m*
cinnamon ['sɪnəmən] *n* : canela *f*
cipher ['saɪfər] *n* **1** ZERO : cero *m* **2** CODE
: cifra *f*
circa ['sərkə] *prep* : hacia
circle ['sərkəl] *n* : círculo *m* — ~ *v*
-cled; -cling *vt* **1** : dar vueltas alrededor de **2** : trazar un círculo alrededor
de (un número, etc.) — *vi* : dar vueltas
circuit ['sərkət] *n* : circuito *m* — cir-
cuitous [sər'kjuːətəs] *adj* : tortuoso
circular ['sərkjələr] *adj* : circular — ~ *n*
LEAFLET : circular *f*
circulate ['sərkjə,leɪt] *v* -lated; -lating *vt*
: hacer circular — *vi* : circular — circulation [,sərkjə'leɪʃən] *n* **1** : circulación *f* **2** : tirada *f* (de una publicación)
circumcise ['sərkəm,saɪz] *vt* -cised;
-cising : circuncidar — circumcision
[,sərkəm'sɪʒən, 'sərkəm,-] *n* : circuncisión *f*
circumference [sər'kʌmpfrənts] *n* : circunferencia *f*
circumspect ['sərkəm,spekt] *adj* : circunspecto, prudente
circumstance ['sərkəm,stænts] *n* **1** : circunstancia *f* **2** under no ~s : bajo
ningún concepto
circus ['sərkəs] *n* : circo *m*
cistern ['sɪstərn] *n* : cisterna *f*
cite ['saɪt] *vt* cited; citing : citar — cita-
tion [saɪ'teɪʃən] *n* : citación *f*
citizen ['sɪtəzən] *n* : ciudadano *m*, -na *f*
— citizenship ['sɪtəzən,ʃɪp] *n* : ciudadanía *f*
citrus ['sɪtrəs] *n, pl* -rus *or* -ruses *or* ~
fruit : cítrico *m*
city ['sɪti] *n, pl* cities : ciudad *f*
civic ['sɪvɪk] *adj* : cívico — civics
['sɪvɪks] *ns & pl* : civismo *m*
civil ['sɪvəl] *adj* : civil — civilian [sə-
'vɪljən] *n* : civil *mf* — civility [sə'vɪləti]
n, pl -ties : cortesía *f* — civilization
[,sɪvələ'zeɪʃən] *n* : civilización *f* — civilize ['sɪvə,laɪz] *vt* -lized; -lizing : civilizar
clad ['klæd] *adj* ~ in : vestido de
claim ['kleɪm] *vt* **1** DEMAND : reclamar **2**
MAINTAIN : afirmar, sostener **3** ~ responsibility : atribuirse la responsabilidad — ~ *n* **1** DEMAND : demanda
f, reclamación *f* **2** ASSERTION : afirmación *f*
clam ['klæm] *n* : almeja *f*

clamber ['klæmbər] *vi* : trepar (con torpeza)

clammy ['klæmi] *adj* **-mier; -est** : húmedo y algo frío

clamor ['klæmər] *n* : clamor *m* — ~ *vi* : clamar

clamp ['klæmp] *n* : abrazadera *f* — ~ *vt* : sujetar con abrazaderas — *vi* ~ **down on** : reprimir

clan ['klæn] *n* : clan *m*

clandestine [klæn'dɛstɪn] *adj* : clandestino

clang ['klæŋ] *n* : ruido *m* metálico

clap ['klæp] *v* **clapped; clapping** *vt* **1** : aplaudir **2** ~ **one's hands** : dar palmadas — *vi* : aplaudir — ~ *n* : palmada *f*

clarify ['klærəˌfaɪ] *vt* **-fied; -fying** : aclarar — **clarification** [ˌklærəfə'keɪʃən] *n* : clarificación *f*

clarinet [ˌklærə'nɛt] *n* : clarinete *m*

clarity ['klærəti] *n* : claridad *f*

clash ['klæʃ] *vi* **1** : chocar, enfrentarse **2** CONFLICT : estar en conflicto — ~ *n* **1** CRASH : choque *m* **2** CONFLICT : conflicto *m*

clasp ['klæsp] *n* : broche *m*, cierre *m* — ~ *vt* **1** : abrazar (a una persona), agarrar (una cosa) **2** FASTEN : abrochar

class ['klæs] *n* : clase *f*

classic ['klæsɪk] *or* **classical** ['klæsɪkəl] *adj* : clásico — **classic** *n* : clásico *m*

classify ['klæsəˌfaɪ] *vt* **-fied; -fying** : clasificar — **classification** [ˌklæsəfə'keɪʃən] *n* : clasificación *f* — **classified** ['klæsəˌfaɪd] *adj* RESTRICTED : secreto

classmate ['klæsˌmeɪt] *n* : compañero *m*, -ra *f* de clase

classroom ['klæsˌruːm] *n* : aula *f*, salón *m* de clase

clatter ['klætər] *vi* : hacer ruido — ~ *n* : estrépito *m*

clause ['klɔz] *n* : cláusula *f*

claustrophobia [ˌklɔstrə'foːbiə] *n* : claustrofobia *f*

claw ['klɔ] *n* : garra *f*, uña *f* (de un gato), pinza *f* (de un crustáceo) — ~ *v* : arañar

clay ['kleɪ] *n* : arcilla *f*

clean ['kliːn] *adj* **1** : limpio **2** UNADULTERATED : puro **3** SPOTLESS : impecable — ~ *vt* : limpiar — ~ *adv* : limpio — **cleaner** ['kliːnər] *n* **1** : limpiador *m*, -dora *f* **2** DRY CLEANER : tintorería *f* — **cleanliness** ['klɛnlinəs] *n* : limpieza *f* — **cleanse** ['klɛnz] *vt* **cleansed; cleansing** : limpiar, purificar

clear ['klɪr] *adj* **1** : claro **2** TRANSPARENT : transparente **3** UNOBSTRUCTED : despejado, libre — ~ *vt* **1** : despejar (una superficie), desatascar (un tubo, etc.) **2** EXONERATE : absolver **3** : saltar por encima de (un obstáculo) **4** ~ **the table** : levantar la mesa **5** ~ **up** RESOLVE : aclarar, resolver — *vi* **1** ~ **up** BRIGHTEN : despejarse (dícese del tiempo, etc.) **2** ~ **up** VANISH : desaparecer (dícese de una infección, etc.) — ~ *adv* **1 make oneself** ~ : explicarse **2 stand** ~ ! : ¡aléjate! — **clearance** ['klɪrənts] *n* **1** SPACE : espacio *m* (libre) **2** AUTHORIZATION : autorización *f* **3** ~ **sale** : liquidación *f* — **clearing** ['klɪrɪŋ] *n* : claro *m* — **clearly** ['klɪrli] *adv* **1** DISTINCTLY : claramente **2** OBVIOUSLY : obviamente

cleaver ['kliːvər] *n* : cuchillo *m* de carnicero

clef ['klɛf] *n* : clave *f*

cleft ['klɛft] *n* : hendidura *f*, grieta *f*

clement ['klɛmənt] *adj* : clemente — **clemency** ['klɛməntsi] *n* : clemencia *f*

clench ['klɛntʃ] *vt* : apretar

clergy ['klərdʒi] *n*, *pl* **-gies** : clero *m* — **clergyman** ['klərdʒimən] *n*, *pl* **-men** [-mən, -ˌmɛn] : clérigo *m* — **clerical** ['klɛrɪkəl] *adj* **1** : clerical **2** ~ **work** : trabajo *m* de oficina

clerk ['klərk, *Brit* 'klɑrk] *n* **1** : oficinista *mf*; empleado *m*, -da *f* de oficina **2** SALESPERSON : dependiente *m*, -ta *f*

clever ['klɛvər] *adj* **1** SKILLFUL : ingenioso, hábil **2** SMART : listo, inteligente — **cleverly** ['klɛvərli] *adv* : ingeniosamente — **cleverness** ['klɛvərnəs] *n* **1** SKILL : ingenio *m* **2** INTELLIGENCE : inteligencia *f*

cliché [kli'ʃeɪ] *n* : cliché *m*

click ['klɪk] *vt* : chasquear — *vi* **1** : chasquear **2** GET ALONG : llevarse bien — ~ *n* : chasquido *m*

client ['klaɪənt] *n* : cliente *m*, -ta *f* — **clientele** [ˌklaɪən'tɛl, ˌkliː-] *n* : clientela *f*

cliff ['klɪf] *n* : acantilado *m*

climate ['klaɪmət] *n* : clima *m*

climax ['klaɪˌmæks] *n* : clímax *m*, punto *m* culminante

climb ['klaɪm] *vt* : escalar, subir a, trepar a — *vi* **1** RISE : subir **2** *or* ~ **up** : subirse, treparse — ~ *n* : subida *f*

clinch ['klɪntʃ] *vt* : cerrar (un acuerdo, etc.)

cling ['klɪŋ] *vi* **clung** ['klʌŋ], **clinging** : adherirse, pegarse

clinic ['klɪnɪk] *n* : clínica *f* — **clinical** ['klɪnɪkəl] *adj* : clínico

clink ['klɪŋk] *vi* : tintinear

clip ['klɪp] *vt* **clipped; clipping 1** CUT

: cortar, recortar **2** FASTEN : sujetar (con un clip) — ~ *n* **1** FASTENER : clip *m* **2** at a good ~ : a buen trote **3** → paper clip — **clippers** ['klɪpərz] *npl* **1** : maquinilla *f* para cortar el pelo **2** *or* nail ~ : cortauñas *m*

cloak ['kloːk] *n* : capa *f*

clock ['klɑk] **1** : reloj *m* (de pared) **2** around the ~ : las veinticuatro horas — **clockwise** ['klɑk,waɪz] *adv & adj* : en el sentido de las agujas del reloj — **clockwork** ['klɑk,wərk] *n* **1** : mecanismo *m* de relojería **2** like ~ : con precisión

clog ['klɑg] *n* : zueco *m* — ~ *v* **clogged; clogging** *vt* : atascar, obstruir — *vi or* ~ up : atascarse

cloister ['klɔɪstər] *n* : claustro *m*

close¹ ['kloːz] *v* **closed; closing** *vt* : cerrar — *vi* **1** : cerrarse **2** TERMINATE : terminar **3** ~ in : acercarse — ~ *n* : final *m*

close² ['kloːs] *adj* **closer; closest 1** NEAR : cercano, próximo **2** INTIMATE : íntimo **3** STRICT : estricto **4** STUFFY : sofocante **5** a ~ game : un juego reñido — ~ *adv* : cerca, de cerca — **closely** ['kloːsli] *adv* : cerca, de cerca — **closeness** ['kloːsnəs] *n* **1** NEARNESS : cercanía *f* **2** INTIMACY : intimidad *f*

closet ['klɑzət] *n* : armario *m*, clóset *m Lat*

closure ['kloːʒər] *n* : cierre *m*

clot ['klɑt] *n* : coágulo *m* — ~ *v* **clotted; clotting** *vt* : coagular, cuajar — *vi* : coagularse

cloth ['klɑθ] *n, pl* **cloths** ['klɔðz, 'klɔθs] **1** FABRIC : tela *f* **2** RAG : trapo *m*

clothe ['kloːð] *vt* **clothed** *or* **clad** ['klæd]; **clothing** : vestir — **clothes** ['kloːz, 'kloːðz] *npl* **1** : ropa *f* **2** put on one's ~ : vestirse — **clothespin** ['kloːz,pɪn] *n* : pinza *f* (para la ropa) — **clothing** ['kloːðɪŋ] *n* : ropa *f*

cloud ['klaʊd] *n* : nube *f* — ~ *vt* : nublar — *vi or* ~ over : nublarse — **cloudy** ['klaʊdi] *adj* **cloudier; -est** : nublado

clout ['klaʊt] *n* **1** BLOW : golpe *m*, tortazo *m fam* **2** INFLUENCE : influencia *f*

clove ['kloːv] *n* **1** : clavo *m* **2** : diente *m* (de ajo)

clover ['kloːvər] *n* : trébol *m*

clown ['klaʊn] *n* : payaso *m*, -sa *f* — ~ *or* ~ **around** *vi* : payasear

cloying ['klɔɪɪŋ] *adj* : empalagoso

club ['klʌb] *n* **1** : garrote *m*, porra *f* **2** ASSOCIATION : club *m* **3** ~s *mpl* : tréboles *mpl* (en los naipes) — ~ *vt* **clubbed; clubbing** : aporrear

cluck ['klʌk] *vi* : cloquear

clue ['kluː] *n* **1** : pista *f*, indicio *m* **2** I haven't got a ~ : no tengo la menor idea

clump ['klʌmp] *n* : grupo *m* (de arbustos)

clumsy ['klʌmzi] *adj* **-sier; -est** : torpe — **clumsiness** ['klʌmzinəs] *n* : torpeza *f*

cluster ['klʌstər] *n* : grupo *m*, racimo *m* (de uvas, etc.) — ~ *vi* : agruparse

clutch ['klʌtʃ] *vt* : agarrar, asir — *vi* ~ at : tratar de agarrarse de — ~ *n* : embrague *m*, clutch *m Lat* (de un automóvil)

clutter ['klʌtər] *vt* : llenar desordenadamente — ~ *n* : desorden *m*, revoltijo *m*

coach ['koːtʃ] *n* **1** CARRIAGE : carruaje *m*, carroza *f* **2** : vagón *m* de pasajeros (de un tren) **3** BUS : autobús *m* **4** : pasaje *m* aéreo de segunda clase **5** TRAINER : entrenador *m*, -dora *f* — ~ *vt* : entrenar (un atleta), dar clases particulares a (un alumno)

coagulate [koˈægjəˌleɪt] *v* **-lated; -lating** *vt* : coagular — *vi* : coagularse

coal ['koːl] *n* : carbón *m*

coalition [ˌkoːəˈlɪʃən] *n* : coalición *f*

coarse ['kors] *adj* **coarser; -est 1** : tosco, basto **2** CRUDE, VULGAR : grosero, ordinario — **coarseness** ['korsnəs] *n* : aspereza *f*, tosquedad *f*

coast ['koːst] *n* : costa *f* — ~ *vi* : ir en punto muerto (dícese de un automóvil), deslizarse (dícese de una bicicleta) — **coastal** ['koːstəl] *adj* : costero

coaster ['koːstər] *n* : posavasos *m*

coast guard *n* : guardacostas *mpl*

coastline ['koːst,laɪn] *n* : litoral *m*

coat ['koːt] *n* **1** : abrigo *m* **2** : pelaje *m* (de un animal) **3** : mano *f* (de pintura) — ~ *vt* : cubrir, revestir — **coating** ['koːtɪŋ] *n* : capa *f* — **coat of arms** *n* : escudo *m* de armas

coax ['koːks] *vt* : engatusar

cob ['kɑb] → **corncob**

cobblestone ['kɑbəl,stoːn] *n* : adoquín *m*

cobweb ['kɑb,wɛb] *n* : telaraña *f*

cocaine [koːˈkeɪn, 'koːˌkeɪn] *n* : cocaína *f*

cock ['kɑk] *n* **1** ROOSTER : gallo *m* **2** FAUCET : grifo *m* **3** : martillo *m* (de un arma de fuego) — ~ *vt* **1** : amartillar (un arma de fuego) **2** ~ one's head : ladear la cabeza — **cockeyed** ['kɑk,aɪd] *adj* **1** ASKEW : ladeado **2** ABSURD : absurdo

cockpit ['kɑk,pɪt] *n* : cabina *f*

cockroach ['kɑk,roːtʃ] *n* : cucaracha *f*

cocktail ['kak,teɪl] *n* : coctel *m*, cóctel *m*

cocky ['kaki] *adj* **cockier; -est** : engreído, arrogante

cocoa ['ko:,ko:] *n* **1** : cacao *m* **2** : chocolate *m* (bebida)

coconut ['ko:ko,nʌt] *n* : coco *m*

cocoon [kə'ku:n] *n* : capullo *m*

cod ['kad] *ns* & *pl* : bacalao *m*

coddle ['kadəl] *vt* **-dled; -dling** : mimar

code ['ko:d] *n* : código *m*

coeducational [,ko:,edʒə'keɪʃənəl] *adj* : mixto

coerce [ko'ərs] *vt* **-erced; -ercing** : coaccionar, forzar — **coercion** [ko-'ərʒən, -ʃən] *n* : coacción *f*

coffee ['kɔfi] *n* : café *m* — **coffeepot** ['kɔfi,pat] *n* : cafetera *f*

coffer ['kɔfər] *n* : cofre *m*

coffin ['kɔfən] *n* : ataúd *m*, féretro *m*

cog ['kag] *n* : diente *m* (de una rueda)

cogent ['ko:dʒənt] *adj* : convincente, persuasivo

cognac ['ko:n,jæk] *n* : coñac *m*

cogwheel ['kag,hwi:l] *n* : rueda *f* dentada

coherent [ko'hɪrənt] *adj* : coherente

coil ['kɔɪl] *vt* : enrollar — *vi* : enrollarse — ~ *n* **1** ROLL : rollo *m* **2** : tirabuzón *m* (de pelo), espiral *f* (de humo)

coin ['kɔɪn] *n* : moneda *f* — ~ *vt* : acuñar

coincide [,ko:ɪn'saɪd, 'ko:ɪn,saɪd] *vi* **-cided; -ciding** : coincidir — **coincidence** [ko'ɪnsədənts] *n* : coincidencia *f*, casualidad *f* — **coincidental** [ko-,ɪnsə'dentəl] *adj* : casual, fortuito

coke ['ko:k] *n* : coque *m* (combustible)

colander ['kaləndər, 'kʌ-] *n* : colador *m*

cold ['ko:ld] *adj* **1** : frío **2 be ~** : tener frío **3 it's ~ today** : hace frío hoy — ~ *n* **1** : frío *m* **2** : resfriado *m* (en medicina) **3 catch a ~** : resfriarse

coleslaw ['ko:l,slɔ] *n* : ensalada *f* de col

colic ['kalɪk] *n* : cólico *m*

collaborate [kə'læbə,reɪt] *vi* **-rated; -rating** : colaborar — **collaboration** [kə,læbə'reɪʃən] *n* : colaboración *f* — **collaborator** [kə'læbə,reɪʃər] *n* : colaborador *m*, -dora *f*

collapse [kə'læps] *vi* **-lapsed; -lapsing** **1** : derrumbarse, hundirse **2** : sufrir un colapso (físico o mental) — ~ *n* **1** FALL : derrumbamiento *m* **2** BREAKDOWN : colapso *m* — **collapsible** [kə-'læpsəbəl] *adj* : plegable

collar ['kalər] *n* : cuello *m* (de camisa, etc.), collar *m* (para animales) — **collarbone** ['kalər,bo:n] *n* : clavícula *f*

colleague ['ka,li:g] *n* : colega *mf*

collect [kə'lekt] *vt* **1** GATHER : reunir **2** : coleccionar, juntar (timbres, etc.) **3**

: recaudar (fondos, etc.) — *vi* **1** ACCUMULATE : acumularse, juntarse **2** CONGREGATE : congregarse, reunirse — ~ *adv* **call ~** : llamar a cobro revertido, llamar por cobrar *Lat* — **collection** [kə'lekʃən] *n* **1** : colección *f* **2** : colecta *f* (de contribuciones) — **collective** [kə'lektɪv] *adj* : colectivo — **collector** [kə'lektər] *n* **1** : coleccionista *mf* **2** : cobrador *m*, -dora *f* (de deudas)

college ['kalɪdʒ] *n* **1** : instituto *m* (a nivel universitario) **2** : colegio *m* (electoral, etc.)

collide [kə'laɪd] *vi* **-lided; -liding** : chocar, colisionar — **collision** [kə-'lɪʒən] *n* : choque *m*, colisión *f*

colloquial [kə'lo:kwiəl] *adj* : coloquial, familiar

cologne [kə'lo:n] *n* : colonia *f*

Colombian [kə'lʌmbiən] *adj* : colombiano

colon[1] ['ko:lən] *n*, *pl* **colons** *or* **cola** [-lə] : colon *m* (en anatomía)

colon[2] *n*, *pl* **colons** : dos puntos *mpl* (signo de puntuación)

colonel ['kərnəl] *n* : coronel *m*

colony ['kaləni] *n*, *pl* **-nies** : colonia *f* — **colonial** [kə'lo:niəl] *adj* : colonial — **colonize** ['kalə,naɪz] *vt* **-nized; -nizing** : colonizar

color *or Brit* **colour** ['kʌlər] *n* : color *m* — ~ *vt* : colorear, pintar — *vi* BLUSH : sonrojarse — **color-blind** *or Brit* **colour-blind** ['kʌlər,blaɪnd] *adj* : daltónico — **colored** *or Brit* **coloured** ['kʌlərd] *adj* : de color — **colorful** *or Brit* **colourful** ['kʌlərfəl] *adj* **1** : de vivos colores **2** PICTURESQUE : pintoresco — **colorless** *or Brit* **colourless** ['kʌlərləs] *adj* : incoloro

colossal [kə'lasəl] *adj* : colosal

colt ['ko:lt] *n* : potro *m*

column ['kaləm] *n* : columna *f* — **columnist** ['kaləm,nɪst, -ləmɪst] *n* : columnista *mf*

coma ['ko:mə] *n* : coma *m*

comb ['ko:m] *n* **1** : peine *m* **2** : cresta *f* (de un gallo) — ~ *vt* : peinar

combat ['kam,bæt] *n* : combate *m* — ~ [kəm'bæt, 'kam,bæt] *vt* **-bated** *or* **-batted; -bating** *or* **-batting** : combatir — **combatant** [kəm'bætənt] *n* : combatiente *mf*

combine [kəm'baɪn] *v* **-bined; -bining** *vt* : combinar — *vi* : combinarse — ~ ['kam,baɪn] *n* HARVESTER : cosechadora *f* — **combination** [,kambə'neɪʃən] *n* : combinación *f*

combustion [kəm'bʌstʃən] *n* : combustión *f*

come ['kʌm] *vi* **came** ['keɪm]; **come**; **coming 1** : venir **2** ARRIVE : llegar **3** ~ **about** : suceder **4** ~ **back** : regresar, volver **5** ~ **from** : venir de, provenir de **6** ~ **in** : entrar **7** ~ **out** : salir **8** ~ **to** REVIVE : volver en sí **9** ~ **on!** : ¡ándale! **10** ~ **up** OCCUR : surgir **11 how** ~? : ¿por qué? — **comeback** ['kʌm,bæk] *n* **1** RETURN : retorno *m* **2** RETORT : réplica *f*

comedy ['kɑmədi] *n, pl* **-dies** : comedia *f* — **comedian** [kə'miːdiən] *n* : cómico *m*, -ca *f*

comet ['kɑmət] *n* : cometa *m*

comfort ['kʌmpfərt] *vt* : consolar — ~ *n* **1** : comodidad *f* **2** SOLACE : consuelo *m* — **comfortable** ['kʌmpfərt̬əbəl, 'kʌmpftə-] *adj* : cómodo

comic ['kɑmɪk] *or* **comical** ['kɑmɪkəl] *adj* : cómico — ~ *n* **1** COMEDIAN : cómico *m*, -ca *f* **2** *or* ~ **book** : revista *f* de historietas, cómic *m* — **comic strip** *n* : tira *f* cómica, historieta *f*

coming ['kʌmɪŋ] *adj* : próximo, que viene

comma ['kɑmə] *n* : coma *f*

command [kə'mænd] *vt* **1** ORDER : ordenar, mandar **2** : estar al mando de (un barco, etc.) **3** ~ **respect** : inspirar (el) respeto — *vi* : dar órdenes — ~ *n* **1** ORDER : orden *f* **2** LEADERSHIP : mando *m* **3** MASTERY : maestría *f*, dominio *m* — **commander** [kə'mændər] *n* : comandante *mf* — **commandment** [kə'mændmənt] *n* : mandamiento *m*

commemorate [kə'mɛmə,reɪt] *vt* **-rated**; **-rating** : conmemorar — **commemoration** [kə,mɛmə'reɪʃən] *n* : conmemoración *f*

commence [kə'mɛnts] *v* **-menced**; **-mencing** : comenzar, empezar — **commencement** [kə'mɛntsmənt] *n* **1** BEGINNING : comienzo *m* **2** GRADUATION : ceremonia *f* de graduación

commend [kə'mɛnd] *vt* **1** ENTRUST : encomendar **2** PRAISE : alabar — **commendable** [kə'mɛndəbəl] *adj* : loable

comment ['kɑ,mɛnt] *n* : comentario *m*, observación *f* — ~ *vi* : hacer comentarios — **commentary** ['kɑmən,tɛri] *n, pl* **-taries** : comentario *m* — **commentator** ['kɑmən,teɪt̬ər] *n* : comentarista *mf*

commerce ['kɑmərs] *n* : comercio *m* — **commercial** [kə'mərʃəl] *adj* : comercial — ~ *n* : anuncio *m*, aviso *m Lat* — **commercialize** [kə'mərʃə,laɪz] *vt* **-ized**; **-izing** : comercializar

commiserate [kə'mɪzə,reɪt] *vi* **-ated**; **-ating** : compadecerse

commission [kə'mɪʃən] *n* : comisión *f* — ~ *vt* : encargar (una obra de arte) — **commissioner** [kə'mɪʃənər] *n* : comisario *m*, -ria *f*

commit [kə'mɪt] *vt* **-mitted**; **-mitting 1** ENTRUST : confiar **2** : cometer (un crimen) **3** : internar (a algn en un hospital) **4** ~ **oneself** : comprometerse **5** ~ **to memory** : aprender de memoria — **commitment** [kə'mɪtmənt] *n* : compromiso *m*

committee [kə'mɪt̬i] *n* : comité *m*, comisión *f*

commodity [kə'mɑdət̬i] *n, pl* **-ties** : artículo *m* de comercio, producto *m*

common ['kɑmən] *adj* **1** : común **2** ORDINARY : ordinario, común y corriente — ~ **in** ~ : en común — **commonly** ['kɑmənli] *adv* : comúnmente — **commonplace** ['kɑmən,pleɪs] *adj* : común, banal — **common sense** *n* : sentido *m* común

commotion [kə'moːʃən] *n* : alboroto *m*, jaleo *m*

commune[1] ['kɑ,mjuːn, kə'mjuːn] *n* : comuna *f* — **communal** [kə'mjuːnəl] *adj* : comunal

commune[2] [kə'mjuːn] *vi* **-muned**; **-muning** ~ **with** : comunicarse con

communicate [kə'mjuːnə,keɪt] *v* **-cated**; **-cating** *vt* : comunicar — *vi* : comunicarse — **communicable** [kə'mjuːnɪkəbəl] *adj* : transmisible — **communication** [kə,mjuːnə'keɪʃən] *n* : comunicación *f* — **communicative** [kə'mjuːnɪ,keɪt̬ɪv, -kət̬ɪv] *adj* : comunicativo

communion [kə'mjuːnjən] *n* : comunión *f*

Communism ['kɑmjə,nɪzəm] *n* : comunismo *m* — **Communist** ['kɑmjə,nɪst] *adj* : comunista — ~ *n* : comunista *mf*

community [kə'mjuːnət̬i] *n, pl* **-ties** : comunidad *f*

commute [kə'mjuːt] *v* **-muted**; **-muting** *vt* : conmutar, reducir (una sentencia) — *vi* : viajar de la residencia al trabajo

compact [kəm'pækt, 'kɑm,pækt] *adj* : compacto — ~ ['kɑm,pækt] *n* **1** *or* ~ **car** : auto *m* compacto **2** *or* **powder** ~ : polvera *f* — **compact disc** ['kɑm,pækt'dɪsk] *n* : disco *m* compacto

companion [kəm'pænjən] *n* : compañero *m*, -ra *f* — **companionship** [kəm'pænjən,ʃɪp] *n* : compañerismo *m*

company ['kʌmpəni] *n, pl* **-nies 1** : compañía *f* **2** GUESTS : visita *f*

compare [kəm'pær] *v* **-pared**; **-paring**

vt : comparar — *vi* ~ **with** : poderse comparar con — **comparable** ['kɑmpərəbəl] *adj* : comparable — **comparative** [kəm'pærəṭiv] *adj* : comparativo, relativo — **comparison** [kəm'pærəsən] *n* : comparación *f*

compartment [kəm'pɑrtmənt] *n* : compartimento *m*

compass ['kʌmpəs, 'kɑm-] *n* **1** : compás *m* **2 points of the** ~ : puntos *mpl* cardinales

compassion [kəm'pæʃən] *n* : compasión *f* — **compassionate** [kəm'pæʃənət] *adj* : compasivo

compatible [kəm'pæṭəbəl] *adj* : compatible, afín — **compatibility** [kəm,pæṭə-'bɪləṭi] *n* : compatibilidad *f*

compel [kəm'pɛl] *vt* **-pelled; -pelling** : obligar — **compelling** [kəm'pɛlɪŋ] *adj* : convincente

compensate ['kɑmpən,seɪt] *v* **-sated; -sating** *vi* ~ **for** : compensar — *vt* : indemnizar, compensar — **compensation** [,kɑmpən'seɪʃən] *n* : compensación *f*, indemnización *f*

compete [kəm'piːt] *vi* **-peted; -peting** : competir — **competent** ['kɑmpəṭənt] *adj* : competente — **competition** [,kɑmpə'tɪʃən] *n* **1** : competencia *f* **2** CONTEST : concurso *m* — **competitor** [kəm'pɛṭəṭər] *n* : competidor *m*, -dora *f*

compile [kəm'paɪl] *vt* **-piled; -piling** : compilar, recopilar

complacency [kəm'pleɪsəntsi] *n* : satisfacción *f* consigo mismo — **complacent** [kəm'pleɪsənt] *adj* : satisfecho de sí mismo

complain [kəm'pleɪn] *vi* : quejarse — **complaint** [kəm'pleɪnt] *n* **1** : queja *f* **2** AILMENT : enfermedad *f*

complement ['kɑmpləmənt] *n* : complemento *m* — ~ ['kɑmplə,mɛnt] *vt* : complementar — **complementary** [,kɑmplə'mɛntəri] *adj* : complementario

complete [kəm'pliːt] *adj* **-pleter; -est 1** WHOLE : completo, entero **2** FINISHED : terminado **3** TOTAL : total — ~ *vt* **-pleted; -pleting** : completar — **completion** [kəm'pliːʃən] *n* : conclusión *f*

complex [kɑm'plɛks, kəm-; 'kɑm,plɛks] *adj* : complejo — ~ ['kɑm,plɛks] *n* : complejo *m*

complexion [kəm'plɛkʃən] *n* : cutis *m*, tez *f*

complexity [kəm'plɛksəṭi, kɑm-] *n, pl* **-ties** : complejidad *f*

compliance [kəm'plaɪənts] *n* **1** : acatamiento *m* **2 in** ~ **with** : conforme a — **compliant** [kəm'plaɪənt] *adj* : sumiso

complicate ['kɑmplə,keɪt] *vt* **-cated;** **-cating** : complicar — **complicated** ['kɑmplə,keɪṭəd] *adj* : complicado — **complication** [,kɑmplə'keɪʃən] *n* : complicación *f*

compliment ['kɑmpləmənt] *n* **1** : cumplido *m* **2** ~**s** *npl* : saludos *mpl* — ~ ['kɑmplə,mɛnt] *vt* : felicitar — **complimentary** [,kɑmplə'mɛntəri] *adj* **1** FLATTERING : halagador, halagüeño **2** FREE : de cortesía, gratis

comply [kəm'plaɪ] *vi* **-plied; -plying** ~ **with** : cumplir, obedecer

component [kəm'poːnənt, 'kɑm,poː-] *n* : componente *m*

compose [kəm'poːz] *vt* **-posed;** **-posing 1** : componer **2** ~ **oneself** : serenarse — **composer** [kəm'poːzər] *n* : compositor *m*, -tora *f* — **composition** [,kɑmpə'zɪʃən] *n* **1** : composición *f* **2** ESSAY : ensayo *m* — **composure** [kəm'poːʒər] *n* : calma *f*

compound¹ [kɑm'paʊnd, kəm-; 'kɑm,paʊnd] *vt* **1** COMPOSE : componer **2** : agravar (un problema, etc.) — ~ ['kɑm,paʊnd; kɑm'paʊnd, kəm-] *adj* : compuesto — ~ ['kɑm,paʊnd] *n* : compuesto *m*

compound² ['kɑm,paʊnd] *n* ENCLOSURE : recinto *m*

comprehend [,kɑmprɪ'hɛnd] *vt* : comprender — **comprehension** [,kɑmprɪ-'hɛntʃən] *n* : comprensión *f* — **comprehensive** [,kɑmprɪ'hɛntsɪv] *adj* **1** INCLUSIVE : inclusivo **2** BROAD : amplio

compress [kəm'prɛs] *vt* : comprimir — **compression** [kəm'prɛʃən] *n* : compresión *f*

comprise [kəm'praɪz] *vt* **-prised;** **-prising** : comprender

compromise ['kɑmprə,maɪz] *n* : acuerdo *m*, arreglo *m* — ~ *v* **-mised; -mising** *vi* : llegar a un acuerdo — *vt* : comprometer

compulsion [kəm'pʌlʃən] *n* **1** COERCION : coacción *f* **2** URGE : impulso *m* — **compulsive** [kəm'pʌlsɪv] *adj* : compulsivo — **compulsory** [kəm'pʌlsəri] *adj* : obligatorio

compute [kəm'pjuːt] *vt* **-puted; -puting** : computar — **computer** [kəm'pjuːṭər] *n* : computadora *f*, computador *m*, ordenador *m* *Spain* — **computerize** [kəm'pjuːṭə,raɪz] *vt* **-ized; -izing** : informatizar

comrade ['kɑm,ræd] *n* : camarada *mf*

con [kɑn] *vt* **conned; conning** : estafar — ~ *n* **1** SWINDLE : estafa *f* **2 the pros and** ~**s** : los pros y los contras

concave [kɑn'keɪv, 'kɑn,keɪv] *adj* : cóncavo

conceal [kən'siːl] vt : ocultar

concede [kən'siːd] vt **-ceded; -ceding** : conceder, admitir

conceit [kən'siːt] n : vanidad f — **conceited** [kən'siːtəd] adj : engreído

conceive [kən'siːv] v **-ceived; -ceiving** vt : concebir — vi ~ **of** : concebir — **conceivable** [kən'siːvəbəl] adj : concebible

concentrate ['kɑntsən,treɪt] v **-trated; -trating** vt : concentrar — vi : concentrarse — **concentration** [,kɑntsən'treɪʃən] n : concentración f

concept ['kɑn,sept] n : concepto m — **conception** [kən'sepʃən] n : concepción f

concern [kən'sərn] vt 1 : concernir 2 ~ **oneself about** : preocuparse por — ~ n 1 AFFAIR : asunto m 2 WORRY : preocupación f 3 BUSINESS : negocio m — **concerned** [kən'sərnd] adj 1 ANXIOUS : ansioso 2 **as far as I'm** ~ : en cuanto a mí — **concerning** [kən'sərnɪŋ] prep : con respecto a

concert ['kɑn,sərt] n : concierto m — **concerted** [kən'sərtəd] adj : concertado

concession [kən'seʃən] n : concesión f

concise [kən'saɪs] adj : conciso

conclude [kən'kluːd] v **-cluded; -cluding** : concluir — **conclusion** [kən'kluːʒən] n : conclusión f — **conclusive** [kən'kluːsɪv] adj : concluyente

concoct [kən'kɑkt, kɑn-] vt 1 PREPARE : confeccionar 2 DEVISE : inventarse, tramar — **concoction** [kən'kɑkʃən] n : mezcla f, brebaje m

concourse ['kɑn,kors] n : vestíbulo m, salón m

concrete [kɑn'kriːt, 'kɑn,kriːt] adj : concreto — ~ ['kɑn,kriːt, kɑn'kriːt] n : hormigón m, concreto m Lat

concur [kən'kər] vi **concurred; concurring** AGREE : estar de acuerdo

concussion [kən'kʌʃən] n : conmoción f cerebral

condemn [kən'dem] vt : condenar — **condemnation** [,kɑn,dem'neɪʃən] n : condenación f

condense [kən'dents] v **-densed; -densing** vt : condensar — vi : condensarse — **condensation** [,kɑn,den'seɪʃən, -dən-] n : condensación f

condescending [,kɑndɪ'sendɪŋ] adj : condescendiente

condiment ['kɑndəmənt] n : condimento m

condition [kən'dɪʃən] n 1 : condición f 2 **in good** ~ : en buen estado — **conditional** [kən'dɪʃənəl] adj : condicional

condolences [kən'doːləntsəz] npl : pésame m

condom ['kɑndəm] n : condón m

condominium [,kɑndə'mɪniəm] n, pl **-ums** : condominio m Lat

condone [kən'doːn] vt **-doned; -doning** : aprobar

conducive [kən'duːsɪv, -'djuː-] adj : propicio, favorable

conduct ['kɑn,dʌkt] n : conducta f — ~ [kən'dʌkt] vt 1 DIRECT, GUIDE : conducir, dirigir 2 CARRY OUT : llevar a cabo 3 ~ **oneself** : conducirse, comportarse — **conductor** [kən'dʌktər] n : revisor m, -sora f (en un tren); cobrador m, -dora f (en un autobús); director m, -tora f (de una orquesta)

cone ['koːn] n 1 : cono m 2 or **ice-cream** ~ : cucurucho m, barquillo m Lat

confection [kən'fekʃən] n : dulce m

confederation [kən,fedə'reɪʃən] n : confederación f

confer [kən'fər] v **-ferred; -ferring** vt : conferir, otorgar — vi ~ **with** : consultar — **conference** ['kɑnfrənts, -fərənts] n : conferencia f

confess [kən'fes] vt : confesar — vi 1 : confesarse 2 ~ **to** : confesar, admitir — **confession** [kən'feʃən] n : confesión f

confetti [kən'feti] n : confeti m

confide [kən'faɪd] v **-fided; -fiding** vi : confiar — **confidence** ['kɑnfədənts] n 1 TRUST : confianza f 2 SELF-ASSURANCE : confianza f en sí mismo 3 SECRET : confidencia f — **confident** ['kɑnfədənt] adj 1 SURE : seguro 2 SELF-ASSURED : confiado, seguro de sí mismo — **confidential** [,kɑnfə'dentʃəl] adj : confidencial

confine [kən'faɪn] vt **-fined; -fining** 1 LIMIT : confinar, limitar 2 IMPRISON : encerrar — **confines** ['kɑn,faɪnz] npl : confines mpl

confirm [kən'fərm] vt : confirmar — **confirmation** [,kɑnfər'meɪʃən] n : confirmación f — **confirmed** adj : inveterado

confiscate ['kɑnfə,skeɪt] vt **-cated; -cating** : confiscar

conflict ['kɑn,flɪkt] n : conflicto m — ~ [kən'flɪkt] vi : estar en conflicto, oponerse

conform [kən'form] vi 1 COMPLY : ajustarse 2 ~ **with** : corresponder a — **conformity** [kən'forməti] n, pl **-ties** : conformidad f

confound [kən'faʊnd, kɑn-] vt : confundir, desconcertar

confront [kən'frʌnt] vt : afrontar, encarar — **confrontation** [kɑnfrən'teɪʃən] n : confrontación f

confuse [kən'fjuːz] vt **-fused; -fusing** : confundir — **confusing** [kən'fjuːzɪŋ] adj : confuso, desconcertante — **confusion** [kən'fjuːʒən] n : confusión f, desconcierto m

congeal [kən'dʒiːl] vi : coagularse

congenial [kən'dʒiːniəl] adj : agradable

congested [kən'dʒɛstəd] adj : congestionado — **congestion** [kən'dʒɛstʃən] n : congestión f

congratulate [kən'grædʒə,leɪt, -'grætʃə-] vt **-lated; -lating** : felicitar — **congratulations** [kən,grædʒə'leɪʃən, -grætʃə-] npl : felicitaciones fpl

congregate ['kɑŋgrɪ,geɪt] vi **-gated; -gating** : congregarse — **congregation** [kɑŋgrɪ'geɪʃən] n : feligreses mpl (en religión)

congress ['kɑŋgrəs] n : congreso m — **congressional** [kən'grɛʃənəl, kɑŋ-] adj : del congreso — **congressman** ['kɑŋgrəsmən] n, pl **-men** [-mən, -,mɛn] : congresista mf

conjecture [kən'dʒɛktʃər] n : conjetura f, presunción f — ~ v **-tured; -turing** vt : conjeturar — vi : hacer conjeturas

conjugal ['kɑndʒɪgəl, kən'dʒuː-] adj : conyugal

conjugate ['kɑndʒə,geɪt] vt **-gated; -gating** : conjugar — **conjugation** [kɑndʒə'geɪʃən] n : conjugación f

conjunction [kən'dʒʌŋkʃən] n 1 : conjunción f 2 **in ~ with** : en combinación con

conjure ['kɑndʒər, 'kʌn-] v **-jured; -juring** vi : hacer juegos de manos — ~ vt or **~ up** : evocar

connect [kə'nɛkt] vi : conectarse — vt 1 JOIN : conectar, juntar 2 ASSOCIATE : asociar — **connection** [kə'nɛkʃən] n 1 : conexión f 2 : enlace m (con un tren, etc.) 3 **~s** npl : relaciones fpl (personas)

connoisseur [kɑnə'sər, -'sur] n : conocedor m, -dora f

connote [kə'noːt] vt **-noted; -noting** : connotar, implicar

conquer ['kɑŋkər] vt : conquistar — **conqueror** ['kɑŋkərər] n : conquistador m, -dora f — **conquest** ['kɑn,kwɛst, 'kɑŋ-] n : conquista f

conscience ['kɑntʃəns] n : conciencia f — **conscientious** [kɑntʃi'ɛntʃəs] adj : concienzudo

conscious ['kɑntʃəs] adj 1 AWARE : consciente f 2 INTENTIONAL : intencional — **consciously** adv : deliberadamente

— **consciousness** ['kɑntʃəsnəs] n 1 AWARENESS : conciencia f 2 **lose ~** : perder el conocimiento

consecrate ['kɑntsə,kreɪt] vt **-crated; -crating** : consagrar — **consecration** [kɑntsə'kreɪʃən] n : consagración f

consecutive [kən'sɛkjətɪv] adj : consecutivo, sucesivo

consensus [kən'sɛntsəs] n : consenso m

consent [kən'sɛnt] vi : consentir — ~ n : consentimiento m

consequence ['kɑntsə,kwɛnts, -kwənts] n 1 : consecuencia f 2 **of no ~** : sin importancia — **consequent** ['kɑntsəkwənt, -,kwɛnt] adj : consiguiente — **consequently** ['kɑntsəkwəntli, -,kwɛnt-] adv : por consiguiente

conserve [kən'sərv] vt **-served; -serving** : conservar, preservar — **conservation** [kɑntsər'veɪʃən] n : conservación f — **conservative** [kən'sərvətɪv] adj 1 : conservador 2 CAUTIOUS : moderado, prudente — ~ n : conservador m, -dora f — **conservatory** [kən'sərvə,tori] n, pl **-ries** : conservatorio m

consider [kən'sɪdər] vt 1 : considerar 2 **all things considered** : teniéndolo todo en cuenta — **considerable** [kən'sɪdərəbəl] adj : considerable — **considerate** [kən'sɪdərət] adj : considerado — **consideration** [kən,sɪdə'reɪʃən] n 1 : consideración f 2 **take into ~** : tener en cuenta — **considering** [kən'sɪdərɪŋ] prep : teniendo en cuenta

consign [kən'saɪn] vt 1 : relegar 2 SEND : enviar — **consignment** [kən'saɪnmənt] n : envío m

consist [kən'sɪst] vi 1 **~ in** : consistir en 2 **~ of** : constar de, componerse de — **consistency** [kən'sɪstəntsi] n, pl **-cies** 1 TEXTURE : consistencia f 2 COHERENCE : coherencia f 3 UNIFORMITY : regularidad f — **consistent** [kən'sɪstənt] adj 1 UNCHANGING : constante, regular 2 **~ with** : consecuente con

console [kən'soːl] vt **-soled; -soling** : consolar — **consolation** [kɑntsə'leɪʃən] n 1 : consuelo m 2 **~ prize** : premio m de consolación

consolidate [kən'sɑlə,deɪt] vt **-dated; -dating** : consolidar — **consolidation** [kən,sɑlə'deɪʃən] n : consolidación f

consonant ['kɑntsənənt] n : consonante f

conspicuous [kən'spɪkjuəs] adj 1 OBVIOUS : visible, evidente 2 STRIKING : llamativo — **conspicuously** [kən'spɪkjuəsli] adv : de manera llamativa

conspire [kən'spair] vi **-spired; -spiring** : conspirar — **conspiracy** [kən'spirəsi] n, pl **-cies** : conspiración f

constant ['kɑntstənt] adj : constante — **constantly** ['kɑntstəntli] adv : constantemente

constellation [ˌkɑntstə'leɪʃən] n : constelación f

constipated ['kɑntstə.peɪtəd] adj : estreñido — **constipation** [ˌkɑntstə'peɪʃən] n : estreñimiento m

constituent [kən'stɪtʃuənt] n **1** COMPONENT : componente m **2** VOTER : elector m, -tora f; votante mf

constitute ['kɑntstə.tu:t, -.tju:t] vt **-tuted; -tuting** : constituir — **constitution** [ˌkɑntstə'tu:ʃən, -'tju:-] n : constitución f — **constitutional** [ˌkɑntstə'tu:ʃənəl, -'tju:-] adj : constitucional

constraint [kən'streɪnt] n : restricción f, limitación f

construct [kən'strʌkt] vt : construir — **construction** [kən'strʌkʃən] n : construcción f — **constructive** [kən'strʌktɪv] adj : constructivo

construe [kən'stru:] vt **-strued; -struing** : interpretar

consul ['kɑntsəl] n : cónsul mf — **consulate** ['kɑntsələt] n : consulado m

consult [kən'sʌlt] v : consultar — **consultant** [kən'sʌltənt] n : asesor m, -sora f; consultor m, -tora f — **consultation** [ˌkɑntsəl'teɪʃən] n : consulta f

consume [kən'su:m] vt **-sumed; -suming** : consumir — **consumer** [kən'su:mər] n : consumidor m, -dora f — **consumption** [kən'sʌmpʃən] n : consumo m

contact ['kɑn.tækt] n : contacto m — ['kɑn.tækt, kən'-] vt : ponerse en contacto con — **contact lens** ['kɑn.tækt'lenz] n : lente mf (de contacto)

contagious [kən'teɪdʒəs] adj : contagioso

contain [kən'teɪn] vt **1** : contener **2** ~ **oneself** : contenerse — **container** [kən'teɪnər] n : recipiente m, envase m

contaminate [kən'tæmə.neɪt] vt **-nated; -nating** : contaminar — **contamination** [kən.tæmə'neɪʃən] n : contaminación f

contemplate ['kɑntəm.pleɪt] v **-plated; -plating** vt **1** : contemplar **2** CONSIDER : considerar, pensar en — vi : reflexionar — **contemplation** [ˌkɑntəm'pleɪʃən] n : contemplación f

contemporary [kən'tempə.reri] adj : contemporáneo — ~ n, pl **-raries** : contemporáneo m, -nea f

contempt [kən'tempt] n : desprecio m —

contemptible [kən'temptəbəl] adj : despreciable — **contemptuous** [kən'temptʃuəs] adj : desdeñoso

contend [kən'tend] vi **1** COMPETE : contender, competir **2** ~ **with** : enfrentarse a — vt : sostener, afirmar — **contender** [kən'tendər] n : contendiente mf

content¹ ['kɑn.tent] n **1** : contenido m **2 table of ~s** : índice m de materias

content² [kən'tent] adj : contento — ~ vt ~ **oneself with** : contentarse con — **contented** [kən'tentəd] adj : satisfecho, contento

contention [kən'tentʃən] n **1** DISPUTE : disputa f **2** OPINION : argumento m, opinión f

contentment [kən'tentmənt] n : satisfacción f

contest [kən'test] vt : disputar — ~ ['kɑn.test] n **1** STRUGGLE : contienda f **2** COMPETITION : concurso m, competencia f — **contestant** [kən'testənt] n : concursante mf, contendiente mf

context ['kɑn.tekst] n : contexto m

continent ['kɑntənənt] n : continente m — **continental** [ˌkɑntən'entəl] adj : continental

contingency [kən'tɪndʒəntsi] n, pl **-cies** : contingencia f

continue [kən'tɪnju:] v **-tinued; -tinuing** : continuar — **continual** [kən'tɪnjuəl] adj : continuo, constante — **continuation** [kən.tɪnju'eɪʃən] n : continuación f — **continuity** [ˌkɑntən'u:əti, -'ju:-] n, pl **-ties** : continuidad f — **continuous** [kən'tɪnjuəs] adj : continuo

contort [kən'tort] vt : retorcer — **contortion** [kən'torʃən] n : contorsión f

contour ['kɑn.tur] n **1** : contorno m **2** or ~ **line** : curva f de nivel

contraband ['kɑntrə.bænd] n : contrabando m

contraception [ˌkɑntrə'sepʃən] n : anticoncepción f — **contraceptive** [ˌkɑntrə'septɪv] adj : anticonceptivo — ~ n : anticonceptivo m

contract ['kɑn.trækt] n : contrato m — ~ [kən'trækt] vt : contraer — vi : contraerse — **contraction** [kən'trækʃən] n : contracción f — **contractor** ['kɑn.træktər, kən'træk-] n : contratista mf

contradiction [ˌkɑntrə'dɪkʃən] n : contradicción f — **contradict** [ˌkɑntrə'dɪkt] vt : contradecir — **contradictory** [ˌkɑntrə'dɪktəri] adj : contradictorio

contraption [kən'træpʃən] n : artilugio m, artefacto m

contrary ['kɑn.treri] n, pl **-traries 1** : contrario **2 on the ~** : al contrario

— ~ ['kɑntreri] *adj* 1 : contrario, opuesto 2 ~ **to** : en contra de
contrast [kən'træst] *v* : contrastar — ~ ['kɑn,træst] *n* : contraste *m*
contribute [kən'trɪbjət] *v* -**uted; -uting** : contribuir — **contribution** [,kɑntrə-'bju:ʃən] *n* : contribución *f* — **contributor** [kən'trɪbjətər] *n* 1 : contribuyente *mf* 2 : colaborador *m*, -dora *f* (en periodismo)
contrite ['kɑn,traɪt, kən'traɪt] *adj* : arrepentido
contrive [kən'traɪv] *vt* -**trived; -triving** 1 DEVISE : idear 2 ~ **to do sth** : lograr hacer algo
control [kən'tro:l] *vt* -**trolled; -trolling** : controlar — ~ *n* 1 : control *m* 2 ~**s** *npl* : mandos *mpl*
controversy ['kɑntrə,vərsi] *n, pl* -**sies** : controversia *f* — **controversial** [kɑntrə'vərʃəl, -siəl] *adj* : polémico
convalescence [kɑnvə'lesənts] *n* : convalecencia *f* — **convalescent** [,kɑnvə-'lesənt] *adj* : convaleciente — ~ *n* : convaleciente *mf*
convene [kən'vi:n] *v* -**vened; -vening** *vt* : convocar — *vi* : reunirse
convenience [kən'vi:njənts] *n* : conveniencia *f*, comodidad *f* — **convenient** [kən'vi:njənt] *adj* : conveniente
convent ['kɑn,vɛnt, -vɛnt] *n* : convento *m*
convention [kən'vɛntʃən] *n* : convención *f* — **conventional** [kən'vɛntʃənəl] *adj* : convencional
converge [kən'vərdʒ] *vi* -**verged; -verging** : converger, convergir
converse[1] [kən'vərs] *vi* -**versed; -versing** : conversar — **conversation** [,kɑnvər'seɪʃən] *n* : conversación *f* — **conversational** [,kɑnvər'seɪʃənəl] *adj* : familiar
converse[2] [kən'vərs, 'kɑn,vərs] *adj* : contrario, opuesto — **conversely** [kən-'vərsli, 'kɑn,vərs-] *adv* : a la inversa
conversion [kən'vərʒən] *n* : conversión *f* — **convert** [kən'vərt] *vt* : convertir — *vi* : convertirse — **convertible** [kən-'vərtəbəl] *adj* : convertible — ~ *n* : descapotable *m*, convertible *m Lat*
convex [kɑn'vɛks, 'kɑn-, kən'-] *adj* : convexo
convey [kən'veɪ] *vt* 1 TRANSPORT : llevar, transportar 2 TRANSMIT : comunicar
convict [kən'vɪkt] *vt* : declarar culpable a — ~ ['kɑn,vɪkt] *n* : presidiario *m*, -ria *f* — **conviction** [kən'vɪkʃən] *n* 1 : condena *f* (de un acusado) 2 BELIEF : convicción *f*

convince [kən'vɪnts] *vt* -**vinced; -vincing** : convencer — **convincing** [kən'vɪntsɪŋ] *adj* : convincente
convoke [kən'vo:k] *vt* -**voked; -voking** : convocar
convoluted ['kɑnvə,lu:t̬əd] *adj* : complicado
convulsion [kən'vʌlʃən] *n* : convulsión *f* — **convulsive** [kən'vʌlsɪv] *adj* : convulsivo
cook ['kʊk] *n* : cocinero *m*, -ra *f* — ~ *vi* : cocinar, guisar — *vt* : preparar (comida) — **cookbook** ['kʊk,bʊk] *n* : libro *m* de cocina
cookie *or* **cooky** ['kʊki] *n, pl* -**ies** : galleta *f* (dulce)
cooking *n* : cocina *f*
cool ['ku:l] *adj* 1 : fresco 2 CALM : tranquilo 3 UNFRIENDLY : frío — ~ *vt* : enfriar — *vi* : enfriarse — ~ *n* 1 : fresco *m* 2 COMPOSURE : calma *f* — **cooler** ['ku:lər] *n* : nevera *f* portátil — **coolness** ['ku:lnəs] *n* : frescura *f*
coop ['ku:p, 'kʊp] *n* : gallinero *m* — ~ *vt or* ~ **up** : encerrar
cooperate [ko'ɑpə,reɪt] *vi* -**ated; -ating** : cooperar — **cooperation** [ko,ɑpə-'reɪʃən] *n* : cooperación *f* — **cooperative** [ko'ɑpərət̬ɪv, -'ɑpə,reɪt̬ɪv] *adj* : cooperativo
coordinate [ko'ɔrdən,eɪt] *v* -**nated; -nating** *vt* : coordinar — **coordination** [ko,ɔrdən'eɪʃən] *n* : coordinación *f*
cop ['kɑp] *n* 1 : poli *mf fam* 2 **the** ~**s** : la poli *fam*
cope ['ko:p] *vi* **coped; coping** 1 : arreglárselas 2 ~ **with** : hacer frente a, poder con
copier ['kɑpiər] *n* : fotocopiadora *f*
copious ['ko:piəs] *adj* : copioso
copper ['kɑpər] *n* : cobre *m*
copy ['kɑpi] *n, pl* **copies** 1 : copia *f* 2 : ejemplar *m* (de un libro), número *m* (de una revista) — ~ *vt* **copied; copying** 1 DUPLICATE : hacer una copia de 2 IMITATE : copiar — **copyright** ['kɑpi,raɪt] *n* : derechos *mpl* de autor
coral ['kɔrəl] *n* : coral *m*
cord ['kɔrd] *n* 1 : cuerda *f* 2 *or* **electric** ~ : cable *m* (eléctrico)
cordial ['kɔrdʒəl] *adj* : cordial
corduroy ['kɔrdə,rɔɪ] *n* : pana *f*
core ['kor] *n* 1 : corazón *m* (de una fruta) 2 CENTER : núcleo *m*, centro *m*
cork ['kɔrk] *n* : corcho *m* — **corkscrew** ['kɔrk,skru:] *n* : sacacorchos *m*
corn ['kɔrn] *n* 1 : grano *m* 2 *or* **Indian** ~ : maíz *m* 3 : callo *m* (del pie) — **corncob** ['kɔrn,kɑb] *n* : mazorca *f*

corner ['kɔrnər] n : ángulo m, rincón m (en una habitación), esquina f (de una intersección) — ~ vt **1** TRAP : acorralar **2** MONOPOLIZE : acaparar (un mercado) — **cornerstone** ['kɔrnər,stoʊn] n : piedra f angular

cornmeal ['kɔrn,miːl] n : harina f de maíz — **cornstarch** ['kɔrn,stɑrtʃ] n : maicena f

corny ['kɔrni] adj : cursi, sentimental

coronary ['kɔrə,nɛri] n, pl **-naries** : trombosis f coronaria

coronation [,kɔrə'neɪʃən] n : coronación f

corporal ['kɔrpərəl] n : cabo m

corporation [,kɔrpə'reɪʃən] n : sociedad f anónima, compañía f — **corporate** ['kɔrpərət] adj : corporativo

corps ['kor] n, pl **corps** ['korz] : cuerpo m

corpse ['kɔrps] n : cadáver m

corpulent ['kɔrpjələnt] adj : obeso, gordo

corpuscle ['kɔr,pʌsəl] n : glóbulo m

corral [kə'ræl] n : corral m — ~ vt **-ralled; -ralling** : acorralar

correct [kə'rɛkt] vt : corregir — ~ adj : correcto — **correction** [kə'rɛkʃən] n : corrección f

correlation [,kɔrə'leɪʃən] n : correlación f

correspond [,kɔrə'spɑnd] vi **1** WRITE : corresponderse **2** ~ **to** : corresponder a — **correspondence** [,kɔrə'spɑndənts] n : correspondencia f

corridor ['kɔrədər, -,dɔr] n : pasillo m

corroborate [kə'rɑbə,reɪt] vt **-rated; -rating** : corroborar

corrode [kə'roːd] v **-roded; -roding** vt : corroer — vi : corroerse — **corrosion** [kə'roːʒən] n : corrosión f — **corrosive** [kə'roːsɪv] adj : corrosivo

corrugated ['kɔrə,geɪtəd] adj : ondulado

corrupt [kə'rʌpt] vt : corromper — ~ adj : corrupto, corrompido — **corruption** [kə'rʌpʃən] n : corrupción f

corset ['kɔrsət] n : corsé m

cosmetic [kɑz'mɛtɪk] n : cosmético m — ~ adj : cosmético

cosmic ['kɑzmɪk] adj : cósmico

cosmopolitan [,kɑzmə'pɑlətən] adj : cosmopolita

cosmos ['kɑzməs, -,moːs, -,mɑs] n : cosmos m

cost ['kɔst] n : costo m, coste m — ~ vi **cost; costing 1** : costar **2 how much does it ~?** : ¿cuánto cuesta?, ¿cuánto vale?

Costa Rican [,kɔstə'riːkən] adj : costarricense

costly ['kɔstli] adj : costoso

costume ['kɑs,tuːm, -,tjuːm] n **1** OUTFIT : traje m **2** DISGUISE : disfraz m

cot ['kɑt] n : catre m

cottage ['kɑtɪdʒ] n : casita f (de campo) — **cottage cheese** n : requesón m

cotton ['kɑtən] n : algodón m

couch ['kaʊtʃ] n : sofá m

cough ['kɔf] vi : toser — ~ n : tos f

could ['kʊd] → **can¹**

council ['kaʊntsəl] n **1** : concejo m **2 or city** ~ : ayuntamiento m — **councillor or councilor** ['kaʊntsələr] n : concejal m, -jala f

counsel n **1** ADVICE : consejo m **2** LAWYER : abogado m, -da f — ~ ['kaʊntsəl] vt **-seled or -selled; -seling or -selling** : aconsejar — **counselor or counsellor** ['kaʊntsələr] n : consejero m, -ra f

count¹ ['kaʊnt] vt : contar — vi **1** : contar **2** ~ **on** : contar con **3 that doesn't ~** : eso no vale — ~ n **1** : recuento m **2 keep ~ of** : llevar la cuenta de

count² n : conde m (noble)

counter¹ ['kaʊntər] n **1** : mostrador m (de un negocio) **2** TOKEN : ficha f (de un juego)

counter² vt : oponerse a — vi : contraatacar — ~ adv ~ **to** : contrario a — **counteract** [kaʊntər'ækt] vt : contrarrestar — **counterattack** ['kaʊntərə,tæk] n : contraataque m — **counterbalance** [kaʊntər'bælənts] n : contrapeso m — **counterclockwise** [kaʊntər'klɑk,waɪz] adv & adj : en sentido opuesto a las agujas del reloj — **counterfeit** ['kaʊntər,fɪt] vt : falsificar — ~ adj : falsificado — n : falsificación f — **counterpart** ['kaʊntər,pɑrt] n : homólogo m (de una persona), equivalente m (de una cosa) — **counterproductive** [,kaʊntərprə'dʌktɪv] adj : contraproducente

countess ['kaʊntɪs] n : condesa f

countless ['kaʊntləs] adj : incontable, innumerable

country ['kʌntri] n, pl **-tries 1** NATION : país m **2** COUNTRYSIDE : campo m — ~ adj : campestre, rural — **countryman** ['kʌntrimən] n, pl **-men** [-mən, -,mɛn] or **fellow ~** : compatriota mf — **countryside** ['kʌntri,saɪd] n : campo m, campiña f

county ['kaʊnti] n, pl **-ties** : condado m

coup ['kuː] n, pl **coups** ['kuːz] or ~ **d'etat** : golpe m (de estado)

couple ['kʌpəl] n **1** : pareja f (de per-

sonas) **2 a ～ of** : un par de — *vt*
-pled; -pling : acoplar, unir
coupon ['ku:pɑn, 'kju:-] *n* : cupón *m*
courage ['kəridʒ] *n* : valor *m* — **coura-**
geous [kə'reidʒəs] *adj* : valiente
courier ['kuriər, 'kəriər] *n* : mensajero *m*,
-ra *f*
course ['kors] *n* **1** : curso *m* **2** : plato *m*
(de una cena) **3** *or* **golf ～** : campo *m*
de golf **4 in the ～ of** : en el transcur-
so de **5 of ～** : desde luego, por
supuesto
court ['kort] *n* **1** : corte *f* (de un rey, etc.)
2 : cancha *f*, pista *f* (en deportes) **3** TRI-
BUNAL : corte *f*, tribunal *m* — *vt*
: cortejar
courteous ['kərtiəs] *adj* : cortés —
courtesy ['kərtəsi] *n, pl* **-sies** : cortesía *f*
courthouse ['kort,haus] *n* : palacio *m* de
justicia, juzgado *m* — **courtroom**
['kort,ruːm] *n* : sala *f* (de un tribunal)
courtship ['kort,ʃip] *n* : cortejo *m*, noviazgo *m*
courtyard ['kort,jɑrd] *n* : patio *m*
cousin ['kʌzən] *n* : primo *m*, -ma *f*
cove ['koːv] *n* : ensenada *f*, cala *f*
covenant ['kʌvənənt] *n* : pacto *m*, convenio *m*
cover ['kʌvər] *vt* **1** : cubrir **2** *or* **～ up**
: encubrir, ocultar **3** TREAT : tratar —
～ n **1** : cubierta *f* **2** SHELTER : abrigo
m, refugio *m* **3** LID : tapa *f* **4** : cubierta
f (de un libro), portada *f* (de una revista) **5 ～s** *npl* BEDCLOTHES : mantas
fpl, cobijas *fpl Lat* **6 take ～** : ponerse
a cubierto **7 under ～ of** : al amparo
de — **coverage** ['kʌvəridʒ] *n* : cobertura *f* — **covert** ['koː,vərt, 'kʌvərt] *adj*
: encubierto — **cover-up** ['kʌvər,ʌp] *n*
: encubrimiento *m*
covet ['kʌvət] *vt* : codiciar — **covetous**
['kʌvətəs] *adj* : codicioso
cow ['kau] *n* : vaca *f* — *～ vt* : intimidar,
acobardar
coward ['kauərd] *n* : cobarde *mf* —
cowardice ['kauərdis] *n* : cobardía *f* —
cowardly ['kauərdli] *adj* : cobarde
cowboy ['kau,bɔi] *n* : vaquero *m*
cower ['kauər] *vi* : encogerse (de miedo)
coy ['kɔi] *adj* : tímido y coqueto
coyote [kaɪ'oːti, 'kaɪ,oːt] *n, pl* **coyotes**
or **coyote** : coyote *m*
cozy ['koːzi] *adj* **-zier; -est** : acogedor
crab ['kræb] *n* : cangrejo *m*, jaiba *f Lat*
crack ['kræk] *v* **1** SPLIT : rajar, partir
2 : cascar (nueces, huevos) **3** : chasquear (un látigo, etc.) **4 ～ down on**
: tomar medidas enérgicas contra —
vi **1** SPLIT : rajarse, agrietarse **2**

: chasquear (dícese de un látigo) **3 ～**
up : sufrir una crisis nerviosa — *～ n*
1 CRACKING : chasquido *m*, crujido *m* **2**
CREVICE : raja *f*, grieta *f* **3 have a ～ at**
: intentar
cracker ['krækər] *n* : galleta *f* (de soda,
etc.)
crackle ['krækəl] *vi* **-led; -ling** : crepitar,
chisporrotear — *～ n* : crujido *m*,
chisporroteo *m*
cradle ['kreidəl] *n* : cuna *f* — *～ vt*
-dled; -dling : acunar
craft ['kræft] *n* **1** TRADE : oficio *m* **2** CUN-
NING : astucia *f* **3** → **craftsmanship 4**
pl usually **craft** BOAT : embarcación *f*
— **craftsman** ['kræftsmən] *n, pl* **-men**
[-mən, -men] : artesano *m*, -na *f* —
craftsmanship ['kræftsmən,ʃip] *n*
: artesanía *f*, destreza *f* — **crafty**
['kræfti] *adj* **craftier; -est** : astuto,
taimado
crag ['kræg] *n* : peñasco *m*
cram ['kræm] *v* **crammed; cramming**
vt **1** STUFF : embutir **2 ～ with** : atiborrar de — *vi* : estudiar a última hora
cramp ['kræmp] *n* **1** : calambre *m*, espasmo *m* (de los músculos) **2 ～s** *npl*
: retorcijones *mpl*
cranberry ['kræn,beri] *n, pl* **-berries**
: arándano *m* (rojo y agrio)
crane ['krein] *n* **1** : grulla *f* (ave) **2** : grúa
f (máquina) — *～ vt* **craned; craning**
: estirar (el cuello)
crank ['kræŋk] *n* **1** : manivela *f* **2** ECCEN-
TRIC : excéntrico *m*, -ca *f* — **cranky**
['kræŋki] *adj* **crankier; -est** : malhumorado
crash ['kræʃ] *vi* **1** : caerse con estrépito
2 COLLIDE : estrellarse, chocar — *vt*
: estrellar — *～ n* **1** DIN : estrépito *m* **2**
COLLISION : choque *m*
crass ['kræs] *adj* : burdo, grosero
crate ['kreit] *n* : cajón *m* (de madera)
crater ['kreitər] *n* : cráter *m*
crave ['kreiv] *vt* **craved; craving** : ansiar — **craving** ['kreiviŋ] *n* : ansia *f*
crawl ['krɔl] *vi* : arrastrarse, gatear
(dícese de un bebé) — *～ n* **at a ～** : a
paso lento
crayon ['krei,ɑn, -ən] *n* : lápiz *m* de cera
craze ['kreiz] *n* : moda *f* pasajera, manía
f
crazy ['kreizi] *adj* **-zier; -est 1** : loco **2**
go ～ : volverse loco — **craziness**
['kreizinəs] *n* : locura *f*
creak ['kriːk] *vi* : chirriar, crujir — *～ n*
: chirrido *m*, crujido *m*
cream ['kriːm] *n* : crema *f*, nata *f Spain*
— **cream cheese** *n* : queso *m* crema

— **creamy** ['kriːmi] *adj* **creamier; -est** : cremoso

crease ['kriːs] *n* : pliegue *m*, raya *f* (del pantalón) — ~ *vt* **creased; creasing** : plegar, poner una raya en (el pantalón)

create [kri'eɪt] *vt* **-ated; -ating** : crear — **creation** [kri'eɪʃən] *n* : creación *f* — **creative** [kri'eɪtɪv] *adj* : creativo — **creator** [kri'eɪtər] *n* : creador *m*, -dora *f*

creature ['kriːtʃər] *n* : criatura *f*, animal *m*

credence ['kriːdənts] *n* lend ~ to : dar crédito a

credentials [krɪ'dentʃəlz] *npl* : credenciales *fpl*

credible ['krɛdəbəl] *adj* : creíble — **credibility** [,krɛdə'bɪləti] *n* : credibilidad *f*

credit ['krɛdɪt] *n* **1** : crédito *m* **2** RECOGNITION : reconocimiento *m* **3** be a ~ to : ser el orgullo de — ~ *vt* **1** BELIEVE : creer **2** : abonar (en una cuenta) **3** ~ s.o. with sth : atribuir algo a algn — **credit card** *n* : tarjeta *f* de crédito

credulous ['krɛdʒələs] *adj* : crédulo

creed ['kriːd] *n* : credo *m*

creek ['kriːk, 'krɪk] *n* : arroyo *m*, riachuelo *m*

creep ['kriːp] *vi* **crept** ['krɛpt]; **creeping 1** CRAWL : arrastrarse **2** SLINK : ir a hurtadillas — ~ *n* **1** CRAWL : paso *m* lento **2** the ~s : escalofríos *mpl* — **creeping** *adj* ~ **plant** : planta *f* trepadora

cremate ['kriːmeɪt] *vt* **-mated; -mating** : incinerar

crescent ['krɛsənt] *n* : media luna *f*

cress ['krɛs] *n* : berro *m*

crest ['krɛst] *n* : cresta *f* — **crestfallen** ['krɛst,fɔlən] *adj* : alicaído

crevice ['krɛvɪs] *n* : grieta *f*

crew ['kruː] *n* **1** : tripulación *f* (de una nave) **2** TEAM : equipo *m*

crib ['krɪb] *n* : cuna *f* (de un bebé)

cricket ['krɪkət] *n* **1** : grillo *m* (insecto) **2** : críquet *m* (juego)

crime ['kraɪm] *n* : crimen *m* — **criminal** ['krɪmənəl] *adj* : criminal — ~ *n* : criminal *mf*

crimp ['krɪmp] *vt* : rizar

crimson ['krɪmzən] *n* : carmesí *m*

cringe ['krɪndʒ] *vi* **cringed; cringing** : encogerse

crinkle ['krɪŋkəl] *vt* **-kled; -kling** : arrugar

cripple ['krɪpəl] *vt* **-pled; -pling 1** DISABLE : lisiar, dejar inválido **2** INCAPACITATE : inutilizar, paralizar

crisis ['kraɪsɪs] *n, pl* **crises** [-,siːz] : crisis *f*

crisp ['krɪsp] *adj* **1** CRUNCHY : crujiente **2** : frío y vigorizante (dícese del aire) — **crispy** ['krɪspi] *adj* **crispier; -est** : crujiente

crisscross ['krɪs,krɔs] *vt* : entrecruzar

criterion [kraɪ'tɪriən] *n, pl* **-ria** [-iə] : criterio *m*

critic ['krɪtɪk] *n* : crítico *m*, -ca *f* — **critical** ['krɪtɪkəl] *adj* : crítico — **criticism** ['krɪtə,sɪzəm] *n* : crítica *f* — **criticize** ['krɪtə,saɪz] *vt* **-cized; -cizing** : criticar

croak ['kroːk] *vi* : croar

crock ['krɑk] *n* : vasija *f* de barro — **crockery** ['krɑkəri] *n* : vajilla *f*, loza *f*

crocodile ['krɑkə,daɪl] *n* : cocodrilo *m*

crony ['kroːni] *n, pl* **-nies** : amigote *m fam*

crook ['krʊk] *n* **1** STAFF : cayado *m* **2** THIEF : ratero *m*, -ra *f*; ladrón *m*, -drona *f* **3** BEND : pliegue *m* — **crooked** ['krʊkəd] *adj* **1** BENT : torcido, chueco *Lat* **2** DISHONEST : deshonesto

crop ['krɑp] *n* **1** WHIP : fusta *f* **2** HARVEST : cosecha *f* **3** : cultivo *m* (de maíz, tabaco, etc.) — ~ *v* **cropped; cropping** *vt* TRIM : recortar, cortar — *vi* ~ **up** : surgir

cross ['krɔs] *n* **1** : cruz *f* **2** HYBRID : cruce *m* — ~ *vt* **1** : cruzar, atravesar **2** CROSSBREED : cruzar **3** *or* ~ **out** : tachar — ~ *adj* **1** : que atraviesa **2** ANGRY : enojado — **crossbreed** ['krɔs,briːd] *vt* **-bred** [-bred]; **-breeding** : cruzar — **cross–examine** *vt* : interrogar — **cross–eyed** ['krɔs,aɪd] *adj* : bizco — **cross fire** *n* : fuego *m* cruzado — **crossing** ['krɔsɪŋ] *n* **1** INTERSECTION : cruce *m*, paso *m* **2** VOYAGE : travesía *f* (del mar) — **cross–reference** [,krɔs'rɛfrənts, -'rɛfərənts] *n* : referencia *f* — **crossroads** ['krɔs,roːdz] *n* : cruce *m* — **cross section** *n* **1** : corte *m* transversal **2** SAMPLE : muestra *f* representativa — **crosswalk** ['krɔs,wɔk] *n* : cruce peatonal, paso *m* de peatones — **crossword puzzle** ['krɔs,wərd] *n* : crucigrama *m*

crotch ['krɑtʃ] *n* : entrepierna *f*

crouch ['kraʊtʃ] *vi* : agacharse

crouton ['kruː,tɑn] *n* : crutón *m*

crow ['kroː] *n* : cuervo *m* — ~ *vi* **crowed** *or Brit* **crew; crowing** : cacarear

crowbar ['kroː,bɑr] *n* : palanca *f*

crowd ['kraʊd] *vi* : amontonarse — *vt* : atestar, llenar — ~ *n* : multitud *f*, muchedumbre *f*

crown ['kraʊn] n 1 : corona f 2 : cima f
(de una colina) — ~ vt : coronar
crucial ['kru:ʃəl] adj : crucial
crucify ['kru:sə‚faɪ] vt -fied; -fying : crucificar — **crucifix** ['kru:sə‚fɪks] n : crucifijo m — **crucifixion** [‚kru:sə'fɪkʃən] n
: crucifixión f
crude ['kru:d] adj **cruder; -est 1** RAW
: crudo **2** VULGAR : grosero **3** ROUGH
: tosco, rudo
cruel ['kru:əl] adj **-eler** or **-eller; -elest**
or **-eliest** : cruel — **cruelty** ['kru:əlti]
n, pl **-ties** : crueldad f
cruet ['kru:ɪt] n : vinagrera f
cruise ['kru:z] vi **cruised; cruising 1**
: hacer un crucero **2** : ir a velocidad de
crucero — ~ n : crucero m — **cruis-
er** ['kru:zər] n **1** WARSHIP : crucero m **2**
: patrulla f (de policía)
crumb ['krʌm] n : miga f, migaja f
crumble ['krʌmbəl] v **-bled; -bling** vt
: desmenuzar — vi : desmenuzarse,
desmoronarse
crumple ['krʌmpəl] vt **-pled; -pling** : arrugar
crunch ['krʌntʃ] vt : ronzar (con los dientes), hacer crujir (con los pies, etc.)
— **crunchy** ['krʌntʃi] adj **crunchier;
-est** : crujiente
crusade [kru:'seɪd] n : cruzada f
crush ['krʌʃ] vt : aplastar, apachurrar
Lat — ~ n **have a ~ on** : estar chiflado por
crust ['krʌst] n : corteza f
crutch ['krʌtʃ] n : muleta f
crux ['krʌks, 'krʊks] n : quid m
cry ['kraɪ] vi **cried; crying 1** SHOUT
: gritar **2** WEEP : llorar — ~ n, pl **cries**
: grito m
crypt ['krɪpt] n : cripta f
crystal ['krɪstəl] n : cristal m
cub ['kʌb] n : cachorro m, -rra f
Cuban ['kju:bən] adj : cubano
cube ['kju:b] n : cubo m — **cubic**
['kju:bɪk] adj : cúbico
cubicle ['kju:bɪkəl] n : cubículo m
cuckoo ['ku‚ku:, 'ku-] n : cuco m, cuclil-
lo m
cucumber ['kju:‚kʌmbər] n : pepino m
cuddle ['kʌdəl] v **-dled; -dling** vi : acurrucarse, abrazarse — vt : abrazar
cudgel ['kʌdʒəl] n : porra f — ~ vt
-geled or **-gelled; -geling** or **-gelling**
: aporrear
cue[1] ['kju:] n SIGNAL : señal f
cue[2] n : taco m (de billar)
cuff[1] ['kʌf] **1** : puño m (de una camisa) **2**
~**s** npl — **handcuffs**
cuff[2] vt : bofetear — ~ n SLAP : bofetada f

cuisine [kwɪ'zi:n] n : cocina f
culinary ['kʌlə‚neri, 'kju:lə-] adj : culinario
cull ['kʌl] vt : seleccionar, entresacar
culminate ['kʌlmə‚neɪt] vi **-nated;
-nating** : culminar — **culmination**
[‚kʌlmə'neɪʃən] n : culminación f
culprit ['kʌlprɪt] n : culpable mf
cult ['kʌlt] n : culto m
cultivate ['kʌltə‚veɪt] vt **-vated; -vating**
: cultivar — **cultivation** [‚kʌltə'veɪʃən]
n : cultivo m
culture ['kʌltʃər] n **1** : cultura f **2** : cultivo m (en biología) — **cultural**
['kʌltʃərəl] adj : cultural — **cultured**
['kʌltʃərd] adj : culto
cumbersome ['kʌmbərsəm] adj : torpe
(y pesado), difícil de manejar
cumulative ['kju:mjələ‚tɪv, -‚leɪtɪv] adj
: acumulativo
cunning ['kʌnɪŋ] adj : astuto, taimado
— ~ n : astucia f
cup ['kʌp] n **1** : taza f **2** TROPHY : copa f
cupboard ['kʌbərd] n : alacena f, armario m
curator ['kjʊr‚eɪtər, kjʊ'reɪtər] n : conservador m, -dora f; director m, -tora f
curb ['kərb] n **1** RESTRAINT : freno m **2**
: borde m de la acera — ~ vt : refre-
nar
curdle ['kərdəl] v **-dled; -dling** vi : cuajarse — vt : cuajar
cure ['kjʊr] n : cura f, remedio m — ~
vt **cured; curing** : curar
curfew ['kər‚fju:] n : toque m de queda
curious ['kjʊriəs] adj : curioso — **curio**
['kjʊri‚o:] n, pl **-rios** : curiosidad f —
curiosity [‚kjʊri'asəti] n, pl **-ties** : curiosidad f
curl ['kərl] vt **1** : rizar **2** COIL : enrollar,
enroscar — vi **1** : rizarse **2** ~ **up**
: acurrucarse — ~ n : rizo m —
curler ['kərlər] n : rulo m — **curly**
['kərli] adj **curlier; -est** : rizado
currant ['kərənt] n **1** : grosella f (fruta) **2**
RAISIN : pasa f de Corinto
currency ['kərəntsi] n, pl **-cies 1** MONEY
: moneda f **2** gain ~ : ganar
aceptación
current ['kərənt] adj **1** PRESENT : actual **2**
PREVALENT : corriente — ~ n : corri-
ente f
curriculum [kə'rɪkjələm] n, pl **-la** [-lə]
: plan m de estudios
curry ['kəri] n, pl **-ries** : curry m
curse ['kərs] n : maldición f — ~ v
cursed; cursing : maldecir
cursor ['kərsər] n : cursor m
cursory ['kərsəri] adj : superficial
curt ['kərt] adj : corto, seco

curtail [kər'teɪl] *vt* : acortar
curtain ['kərtən] *n* : cortina *f* (de una ventana), telón *m* (en un teatro)
curtsy ['kərtsi] *vi* **-sied** *or* **-seyed; -sying** *or* **-seying** : hacer una reverencia — ~ *n* : reverencia *f*
curve ['kərv] *v* **curved; curving** *vi* : hacer una curva — *vt* : encorvar — ~ *n* : curva *f*
cushion ['kʊʃən] *n* : cojín *m* — ~ *vt* : amortiguar
custard ['kʌstərd] *n* : natillas *fpl*
custody ['kʌstədi] *n*, *pl* **-dies 1** : custodia *f* **2 be in ~** : estar detenido — **custodian** [kʌ'stoːdiən] *n* : custodio *m*, -dia *f*; guardián, -diana *f*
custom ['kʌstəm] *n* : costumbre *f* — **customary** ['kʌstəˌmeri] *adj* : habitual, acostumbrado — **customer** ['kʌstəmər] *n* : cliente *m*, -ta *f* — **customs** ['kʌstəmz] *npl* : aduana *f*
cut ['kʌt] *v* **cut; cutting** *vt* **1** : cortar **2** REDUCE : reducir, rebajar **3 ~ oneself** : cortarse **4 ~ up** : cortar en pedazos — *vi* **1** : cortar **2 ~ in** : interrumpir —

~ *n* **1** : corte *m* **2** REDUCTION : rebaja *f*, reducción *f*
cute ['kjuːt] *adj* **cuter; -est** : mono *fam*, lindo
cutlery ['kʌtləri] *n* : cubiertos *mpl*
cutlet ['kʌtlət] *n* : chuleta *f*
cutting ['kʌtɪŋ] *adj* : cortante, mordaz
cyanide ['saɪəˌnaɪd, -nɪd] *n* : cianuro *m*
cycle ['saɪkəl] *n* **1** : ciclo *m* **2** BICYCLE : bicicleta *f* — ~ *vi* **-cled; -cling** : ir en bicicleta — **cyclic** ['saɪklɪk, 'sɪ-] *or* **cyclical** [-klɪkəl] *adj* : cíclico — **cyclist** ['saɪklɪst] *n* : ciclista *mf*
cyclone ['saɪkloːn] *n* : ciclón *m*
cylinder ['sɪləndər] *n* : cilindro *m* — **cylindrical** [sə'lɪndrɪkəl] *adj* : cilíndrico
cymbal ['sɪmbəl] *n* : platillo *m*, címbalo *m*
cynic ['sɪnɪk] *n* : cínico *m*, -ca *f* — **cynical** ['sɪnɪkəl] *adj* : cínico — **cynicism** ['sɪnəˌsɪzəm] *n* : cinismo *m*
cypress ['saɪprəs] *n* : ciprés *m*
cyst ['sɪst] *n* : quiste *m*
czar ['zɑr, 'sɑr] *n* : zar *m*
Czech ['tʃɛk] *adj* : checo — ~ *n* : checo *m* (idioma)

D

d ['diː] *n*, *pl* **d's** *or* **ds** ['diːz] : d *f*, cuarta letra del alfabeto inglés
dab ['dæb] *n* : toque *m* — ~ *vt* **dabbed; dabbing** : dar toques ligeros a, aplicar suavemente
dabble ['dæbəl] *vi* **-bled; -bling ~ in** : interesarse superficialmente en — **dabbler** *n* : aficionado *m*, -da *f*
dad ['dæd] *n* : papá *m fam* — **daddy** ['dædi] *n*, *pl* **-dies** : papá *m fam*
daffodil ['dæfəˌdɪl] *n* : narciso *m*
dagger ['dægər] *n* : daga *f*, puñal *m*
daily ['deɪli] *adj* **-lier; -est** : diario — ~ *adv* : diariamente
dainty ['deɪnti] *adj* **-tier; -est** : delicado
dairy ['dæri] *n*, *pl* **-ies 1** : lechería *f* (tienda) **2** *or* **~ farm** : granja *f* lechera
daisy ['deɪzi] *n*, *pl* **-sies** : margarita *f*
dam ['dæm] *n* : presa *f* — ~ *vt* **dammed; damming** : represar
damage ['dæmɪdʒ] *n* **1** : daño *m*, perjuicio *m* **2 ~s** *npl* : daños y perjuicios *mpl* — ~ *vt* **-aged; -aging** : dañar
damn ['dæm] *vt* **1** CONDEMN : condenar **2** CURSE : maldecir — ~ *n* **not give a ~** : no importarse un comino *fam* — ~ *or* **damned** ['dæmd] *adj* : maldito *fam*
damp ['dæmp] *adj* : húmedo — **dampen** ['dæmpən] *vt* **1** MOISTEN : humede-

cer **2** DISCOURAGE : desalentar, desanimar — **dampness** ['dæmpnəs] *n* : humedad *f*
dance ['dænts] *v* **danced; dancing** : bailar — ~ *n* : baile *m* — **dancer** ['dæntsər] *n* : bailarín *m*, -rina *f*
dandelion ['dændəˌlaɪən] *n* : diente *m* de león
dandruff ['dændrəf] *n* : caspa *f*
dandy ['dændi] *adj* **-dier; -est** : de primera, excelente
danger ['deɪndʒər] *n* : peligro *m* — **dangerous** ['deɪndʒərəs] *adj* : peligroso
dangle ['dæŋgəl] *v* **-gled; -gling** *vi* HANG : colgar, pender — *vt* : hacer oscilar
Danish ['deɪnɪʃ] *adj* : danés — ~ *n* : danés *m* (idioma)
dank ['dæŋk] *adj* : frío y húmedo
dare ['dær] *v* **dared; daring** *vt* : desafiar — *vi* : osar — ~ *n* : desafío *m* — **daredevil** ['dærˌdɛvəl] *n* : persona *f* temeraria — **daring** ['dærɪŋ] *adj* : atrevido, audaz — ~ *n* : audacia *f*
dark ['dɑrk] *adj* **1** : oscuro **2** : moreno (dícese del pelo o de la piel) **3** GLOOMY : sombrío **4 get ~** : hacerse de noche — **darken** ['dɑrkən] *vt* : oscurecer — *vi* : oscurecerse — **darkness** ['dɑrknəs] *n* : oscuridad *f*

darling ['dɑrlɪŋ] n BELOVED : querido m, -da f — ~ adj : querido

darn ['dɑrn] vt : zurcir — ~ adj : maldito fam

dart ['dɑrt] n 1 : dardo m 2 ~s npl : juego m de dardos — ~ vi : precipitarse

dash ['dæʃ] vt 1 SMASH : romper 2 HURL : lanzar 3 ~ off : hacer (algo) rápidamente — vi : lanzarse, irse corriendo — ~ n 1 : guión m largo (signo de puntuación) 2 PINCH : poquito m, pizca f 3 RACE : carrera f — **dashboard** ['dæʃ,bord] n : tablero m de instrumentos — **dashing** ['dæʃɪŋ] adj : gallardo, apuesto

data ['deɪt̬ə, 'dæ-, 'dɑ-] ns & pl : datos mpl — **database** ['deɪt̬ə,beɪs, 'dæ-, 'dɑ-] n : base f de datos

date[1] ['deɪt] n : dátil m (fruta)

date[2] ['deɪt] n 1 : fecha f 2 APPOINTMENT : cita f — ~ v dated; dating vt 1 : fechar (una carta, etc.) 2 : salir con (algn) — vi ~ from : datar de — **dated** ['deɪt̬əd] adj : pasado de moda

daub ['dɑb] vt : embadurnar

daughter ['dɑt̬ər] n : hija f — **daughter-in-law** ['dɑt̬ərin,lɔ] n, pl **daughters-in-law** : nuera f

daunt ['dɔnt] vt : intimidar

dawdle ['dɔdəl] vi -dled; -dling : entretenerse, perder tiempo

dawn ['dɔn] vi 1 : amanecer 2 it ~ed on him that : cayó en la cuenta de que — ~ n : amanecer m

day ['deɪ] n 1 : día m 2 or working ~ : jornada f 3 the ~ before : el día anterior 4 the ~ before yesterday : anteayer 5 the ~ after : el día siguiente 6 the ~ after tomorrow : pasada mañana — **daybreak** ['deɪ,breɪk] n : amanecer m — **daydream** ['deɪ,driːm] n : ensueño m — ~ vi : soñar despierto — **daylight** ['deɪ,laɪt] n : luz f del día — **daytime** ['deɪ,taɪm] n : día m

daze ['deɪz] vt dazed; dazing : aturdir — ~ n in a ~ : aturdido

dazzle ['dæzəl] vt -zled; -zling : deslumbrar

dead ['dɛd] adj 1 LIFELESS : muerto 2 NUMB : entumecido — ~ n 1 in the ~ of night : en plena noche 2 the ~ : los muertos — ~ adv ABSOLUTELY : absolutamente — **deaden** ['dɛdən] vt 1 : atenuar (dolores) 2 MUFFLE : amortiguar — **dead end** ['dɛd'ɛnd] n : callejón m sin salida — **deadline** ['dɛd,laɪn] n : fecha f límite — **deadlock** ['dɛd,lɑk] n : punto m muerto — **deadly**

['dɛdli] adj -lier; -est 1 : mortal, letal 2 ACCURATE : certero, preciso

deaf ['dɛf] adj : sordo — **deafen** ['dɛfən] vt : ensordecer — **deafness** ['dɛfnəs] n : sordera f

deal ['diːl] n 1 TRANSACTION : trato m, transacción f 2 : reparto m (de naipes) 3 a good ~ : mucho — ~ v dealt; dealing vt 1 : dar 2 : repartir, dar (naipes) 3 ~ a blow : asestar un golpe — vi 1 : dar, repartir (en juegos de naipes) 2 ~ in : comerciar en 3 ~ with CONCERN : tratar de 4 ~ with s.o. : tratar con algn — **dealer** ['diːlər] n : comerciante mf — **dealings** npl : trato m, relaciones fpl

dean ['diːn] n : decano m, -na f

dear ['dɪr] adj : querido — ~ n : querido m, -da f — **dearly** ['dɪrli] adv 1 : mucho 2 pay ~ : pagar caro

death ['dɛθ] n : muerte f

debar [dɪ'bɑr] vt : excluir

debate [dɪ'beɪt] n : debate m, discusión f — ~ vt -bated; -bating : debatir, discutir

debit ['dɛbɪt] vt : adeudar, cargar — ~ n : débito m, debe m

debris [də'briː, deɪ-; 'deɪ,briː] n, pl -bris [-'briːz, -,briːz] : escombros mpl

debt ['dɛt] n : deuda f — **debtor** ['dɛt̬ər] n : deudor m, -dora f

debunk [dɪ'bʌŋk] vt : desmentir

debut [deɪ'bjuː, 'deɪ,bjuː] n : debut m — ~ vi : debutar

decade ['dɛ,keɪd, dɛ'keɪd] n : década f

decadence ['dɛkədənts] n : decadencia f — **decadent** ['dɛkədənt] adj : decadente

decal ['diː,kæl, dɪ'kæl] n : calcomanía f

decanter [dɪ'kænt̬ər] n : licorera f

decapitate [dɪ'kæpə,teɪt] vt -tated; -tating : decapitar

decay [dɪ'keɪ] vi 1 DECOMPOSE : descomponerse 2 DETERIORATE : deteriorarse 3 : cariarse (dícese de los dientes) — ~ n 1 : descomposición f 2 : deterioro m (de un edificio, etc.) 3 : caries f (de los dientes)

deceased [dɪ'siːst] adj : difunto — ~ n the ~ : el difunto, la difunta

deceive [dɪ'siːv] vt -ceived; -ceiving : engañar — **deceit** [dɪ'siːt] n : engaño m — **deceitful** [dɪ'siːtfəl] adj : engañoso

December [dɪ'sɛmbər] n : diciembre m

decent ['diːsənt] adj 1 : decente 2 KIND : bueno, amable — **decency** ['diːsəntsi] n, pl -cies : decencia f

deception [dɪ'sɛpʃən] n : engaño m — **deceptive** [dɪ'sɛptɪv] adj : engañoso

decide [dɪ'saɪd] v **-cided; -ciding** vt : decidir — vi : decidirse — **decided** [dɪ'saɪdɪd] adj 1 UNQUESTIONABLE : indudable 2 RESOLUTE : decidido — **decidedly** [dɪ'saɪdədli] adv 1 DEFINITELY : decididamente 2 RESOLUTELY : con decisión

decimal ['desəməl] adj : decimal — ~ n : número m decimal — **decimal point** n : coma f decimal

decipher [dɪ'saɪfər] vt : descifrar

decision [dɪ'sɪʒən] n : decisión f — **decisive** [dɪ'saɪsɪv] adj 1 RESOLUTE : decidido 2 CONCLUSIVE : decisivo

deck ['dek] n 1 : cubierta f (de un barco) 2 or ~ **of cards** : baraja f (de naipes) 3 TERRACE : entarimado m

declare [dɪ'klær] vt **-clared; -claring** : declarar — **declaration** [deklə'reɪʃən] n : declaración f

decline [dɪ'klaɪn] v **-clined; -clining** vt REFUSE : declinar, rehusar — vi DECREASE : disminuir — ~ n 1 DETERIORATION : decadencia f, deterioro m 2 DECREASE : disminución f

decode [di:'ko:d] vt **-coded; -coding** : descodificar

decompose [di:kəm'po:z] vt **-posed; -posing** : descomponer — vi : descomponerse

decongestant [di:kən'dʒestənt] n : descongestionante m

decorate ['dekəreɪt] vt **-rated; -rating** : decorar — **decor** or **décor** [deɪ'kɔr, 'deɪkɔr] n : decoración f — **decoration** [dekə'reɪʃən] n : decoración f — **decorator** ['dekəreɪtər] n : decorador m, -dora f

decoy ['di:kɔɪ, dɪ'-] n : señuelo m

decrease [dɪ'kri:s] v **-creased; -creasing** : disminuir — ~ ['di:kri:s] n : disminución f

decree [dɪ'kri:] n : decreto m — ~ vt **-creed; -creeing** : decretar

decrepit [dɪ'krepɪt] adj 1 FEEBLE : decrépito 2 DILAPIDATED : ruinoso

dedicate ['dedɪkeɪt] vt **-cated; -cating** 1 : dedicar 2 ~ **oneself to** : consagrarse a — **dedication** [dedɪ'keɪʃən] n 1 DEVOTION : dedicación f 2 INSCRIPTION : dedicatoria f

deduce [dɪ'du:s, -'dju:s] vt **-duced; -ducing** : deducir — **deduct** [dɪ'dʌkt] vt : deducir — **deduction** [dɪ'dʌkʃən] n : deducción f

deed ['di:d] n : acción f, hecho m

deem ['di:m] vt : considerar, juzgar

deep ['di:p] adj : hondo, profundo — ~ adv 1 DEEPLY : profundamente 2 ~ **down** : en el fondo 3 **dig** ~ : cavar

hondo — **deepen** ['di:pən] vt : ahondar — vi : hacerse más profundo — **deeply** ['di:pli] adv : hondo, profundamente

deer ['dɪr] ns & pl : ciervo m

deface [dɪ'feɪs] vt **-faced; -facing** : desfigurar

default [dɪ'fɔlt, 'di:fɔlt] n **by** ~ : en rebeldía — vi 1 ~ **on** : no pagar (una deuda) 2 : no presentarse (en deportes)

defeat [dɪ'fi:t] vt 1 BEAT : vencer, derrotar 2 FRUSTRATE : frustrar — ~ n : derrota f

defect [di:'fekt, dɪ'fekt] n : defecto m — ~ [dɪ'fekt] vi : desertar — **defective** [dɪ'fektɪv] adj : defectuoso

defend [dɪ'fend] vt : defender — **defendant** [dɪ'fendənt] n : acusado m, -da f — **defense** or Brit **defence** [dɪ'fens, 'di:fens] n : defensa f — **defenseless** or Brit **defenceless** adj : indefenso — **defensive** [dɪ'fensɪv] adj : defensivo — ~ n **on the** ~ : a la defensiva

defer [dɪ'fər] v **-ferred; -ferring** vt : diferir, aplazar — vi ~ **to** : deferir a — **deference** ['defərəns] n : deferencia f — **deferential** [defə'renʃəl] adj : deferente

defiance [dɪ'faɪəns] n 1 : desafío m 2 **in** ~ **of** : a despecho de — **defiant** [dɪ'faɪənt] adj : desafiante

deficiency [dɪ'fɪʃənsi] n, pl **-cies** : deficiencia f — **deficient** [dɪ'fɪʃənt] adj : deficiente

deficit ['defəsɪt] n : déficit m

defile [dɪ'faɪl] vt **-filed; -filing** 1 DIRTY : ensuciar 2 DESECRATE : profanar

define [dɪ'faɪn] vt **-fined; -fining** : definir — **definite** ['defənɪt] adj 1 : definido 2 CERTAIN : seguro, incuestionable — **definition** [defə'nɪʃən] n : definición f — **definitive** [dɪ'fɪnətɪv] adj : definitivo

deflate [dɪ'fleɪt] v **-flated; -flating** vt : desinflar (una llanta, etc.) — vi : desinflarse

deflect [dɪ'flekt] vt : desviar — vi : desviarse

deform [dɪ'fɔrm] vt : deformar — **deformity** [dɪ'fɔrmət̬i] n, pl **-ties** : deformidad f

defraud [dɪ'frɔd] vt : defraudar

defrost [dɪ'frɔst] vt : descongelar — vi : descongelarse

deft ['deft] adj : hábil, diestro

defy [dɪ'faɪ] vt **-fied; -fying** 1 CHALLENGE : desafiar 2 RESIST : resistir

degenerate [dɪ'dʒenəreɪt] vi : degenerar — ~ [dɪ'dʒenərət] adj : degenerado

degrade [di'greid] *vt* **-graded; -grading** : degradar — **degrading** *adj* : degradante

degree [di'griː] *n* **1** : grado *m* **2** *or* academic ~ : título *m*

dehydrate [diː'haɪˌdreɪt] *vt* **-drated; -drating** : deshidratar

deign ['deɪn] *vi* ~ **to** : dignarse (a)

deity ['diːəti, 'deɪ-] *n, pl* **-ties** : deidad *f*

dejected [di'dʒɛktəd] *adj* : abatido — **dejection** [di'dʒɛkʃən] *n* : abatimiento *m*

delay [di'leɪ] *n* : retraso *m* — ~ *vt* **1** POSTPONE : aplazar **2** HOLD UP : retrasar — *vi* : demorar

delectable [di'lɛktəbəl] *adj* : delicioso

delegate ['dɛlɪgət, -ˌgeɪt] *n* : delegado *m*, -da *f* — ['dɛlɪˌgeɪt] *v* **-gated; -gating** : delegar — **delegation** [ˌdɛlɪ'geɪʃən] *n* : delegación *f*

delete [di'liːt] *vt* **-leted; -leting** : borrar

deliberate [di'lɪbəˌreɪt] *v* **-ated; -ating** : deliberar sobre — *vi* : deliberar — ~ [di'lɪbərət] *adj* : deliberado — **deliberately** [di'lɪbərətli] *adv* INTENTIONALLY : a propósito — **deliberation** [diˌlɪbə'reɪʃən] *n* : deliberación *f*

delicacy ['dɛlɪkəsi] *n, pl* **-cies 1** : delicadeza *f* **2** FOOD : manjar *m*, exquisitez *f* — **delicate** ['dɛlɪkət] *adj* : delicado — **delicatessen** [ˌdɛlɪkə'tɛsən] *n* : charcutería *f*

delicious [di'lɪʃəs] *adj* : delicioso

delight [di'laɪt] *n* : placer *m*, deleite *m* — ~ *vt* : deleitar, encantar — *vi* ~ **in** : deleitarse con — **delightful** [di'laɪtfəl] *adj* : delicioso, encantador

delinquent [di'lɪŋkwənt] *adj* : delincuente — ~ *n* : delincuente *mf*

delirious [di'lɪriəs] *adj* : delirante — **delirium** [di'lɪriəm] *n* : delirio *m*

deliver [di'lɪvər] *vt* **1** DISTRIBUTE : entregar, repartir **2** FREE : liberar **3** : asistir en el parto de (un niño) **4** : pronunciar (un discurso, etc.) **5** DEAL : asestar (un golpe, etc.) — **delivery** [di'lɪvəri] *n, pl* **-eries 1** DISTRIBUTION : entrega *f*, reparto *m* **2** LIBERATION : liberación *f* **3** CHILDBIRTH : parto *m*, alumbramiento *m*

delude [di'luːd] *vt* **-luded; -luding 1** : engañar **2** ~ **oneself** : engañarse

deluge ['dɛljuːdʒ, -juʒ] *n* : diluvio *m*

delusion [di'luːʒən] *n* : ilusión *f*

deluxe [di'lʌks, -'luks] *adj* : de lujo

delve ['dɛlv] *vi* **delved; delving 1** : escarbar **2** ~ **into** PROBE : investigar

demand [di'mænd] *n* **1** REQUEST : petición *f* **2** CLAIM : reclamación *f*, exigencia *f* **3** → **supply** — ~ *vt* : exigir — **demanding** *adj* : exigente

demean [di'miːn] *vt* ~ **oneself** : rebajarse

demeanor [di'miːnər] *n* : comportamiento *m*

demented [di'mɛntəd] *adj* : demente, loco

demise [di'maɪz] *n* : fallecimiento *m*

democracy [di'mɑkrəsi] *n, pl* **-cies** : democracia *f* — **democrat** ['dɛməˌkræt] *n* : demócrata *mf* — **democratic** [ˌdɛmə'krætɪk] *adj* : democrático

demolish [di'mɑlɪʃ] *vt* : demoler — **demolition** [ˌdɛmə'lɪʃən, ˌdiː-] *n* : demolición *f*

demon ['diːmən] *n* : demonio *m*

demonstrate ['dɛmənˌstreɪt] *v* **-strated; -strating** *vt* : demostrar — *vi* RALLY : manifestarse — **demonstration** [ˌdɛmən'streɪʃən] *n* **1** : demostración *f* **2** RALLY : manifestación *f*

demoralize [di'mɔrəˌlaɪz] *vt* **-ized; -izing** : desmoralizar

demote [di'moːt] *vt* **-moted; -moting** : bajar de categoría

demure [di'mjʊr] *adj* : recatado

den ['dɛn] *n* LAIR : guarida *f*

denial [di'naɪəl] *n* **1** : negación *f*, rechazo *m* **2** REFUSAL : denegación *f*

denim ['dɛnəm] *n* : tela *f* vaquera, mezclilla *f Lat*

denomination [diˌnɑmə'neɪʃən] *n* **1** : confesión *f* (religiosa) **2** : valor *m* (de una moneda)

denounce [di'naunts] *vt* **-nounced; -nouncing** : denunciar

dense ['dɛnts] *adj* **denser; -est 1** THICK : denso **2** STUPID : estúpido — **density** ['dɛntsəṭi] *n, pl* **-ties** : densidad *f*

dent ['dɛnt] *vt* : abollar — ~ *n* : abolladura *f*

dental ['dɛntəl] *adj* : dental — **dental floss** *n* : hilo *m* dental — **dentist** ['dɛntɪst] *n* : dentista *mf* — **dentures** ['dɛntʃərz] *npl* : dentadura *f* postiza

deny [di'naɪ] *vt* **-nied; -nying 1** : negar **2** REFUSE : denegar

deodorant [diː'oːdərənt] *n* : desodorante *m*

depart [di'pɑrt] *vi* **1** : salir **2** ~ **from** : apartarse de (la verdad, etc.)

department [di'pɑrtmənt] *n* : sección *f* (de una tienda, etc.), departamento *m* (de una empresa, etc.), ministerio *m* (del gobierno) — **department store** *n* : grandes almacenes *mpl*

departure [di'pɑrtʃər] *n* **1** : salida *f* **2** DEVIATION : desviación *f*

depend [di'pɛnd] *vi* **1** ~ **on** : depender

de 2 ∼ **on s.o.** : contar con algn **3 that** ∼**s** : eso depende — **dependable** [dɪ'pendəbəl] *adj* : digno de confianza — **dependence** [dɪ'pendənts] *n* : dependencia *f* — **dependent** [dɪ'pendənt] *adj* : dependiente

depict [dɪ'pɪkt] *vt* **1** PORTRAY : representar **2** DESCRIBE : describir

deplete [dɪ'plit] *vt* **-pleted; -pleting** : agotar, reducir

deplore [dɪ'plor] *vt* **-plored; -ploring** : deplorar, lamentar — **deplorable** [dɪ'plorəbəl] *adj* : lamentable

deploy [dɪ'plɔɪ] *vt* : desplegar

deport [dɪ'port] *vt* : deportar, expulsar (de un país) — **deportation** [diˌpor-'teɪʃən] *n* : deportación *f*

depose [dɪ'poz] *vt* **-posed; -posing** : deponer

deposit [dɪ'pɑzət] *vt* **-ited; -iting** : depositar — ∼ *n* **1** : depósito *m* **2** DOWN PAYMENT : entrega *f* inicial

depot [*in sense 1 usu* 'de,po:, *2 usu* 'di:-] *n* **1** WAREHOUSE : almacén *m*, depósito *m* **2** STATION : terminal *m*

depreciate [dɪ'priːʃieːt] *vt* **-ated; -ating** : depreciarse — **depreciation** [diˌpriːʃi'eɪʃən] *n* : depreciación *f*

depress [dɪ'pres] *vt* **1** PRESS : apretar **2** : deprimir — **depressed** [dɪ'prest] *adj* : abatido, deprimido — **depressing** [dɪ'presɪŋ] *adj* : deprimente — **depression** [dɪ'preʃən] *n* : depresión *f*

deprive [dɪ'praɪv] *vt* **-prived; -priving** : privar

depth [depθ] *n, pl* **depths** ['depθs, 'deps] **1** : profundidad *f* **2 in the** ∼**s of night** : en lo más profundo de la noche

deputy [depjuti] *n, pl* **-ties** : suplente *mf*; sustituto *m*, -ta *f*

derail [dɪ'reɪl] *vt* : hacer descarrilar

deranged [dɪ'reɪndʒd] *adj* : trastornado

derelict ['derəlɪkt] *adj* : abandonado

deride [dɪ'raɪd] *vt* **-rided; -riding** : burlarse de — **derision** [dɪ'rɪʒən] *n* : mofa *f*

derive [dɪ'raɪv] *vi* **-rived; -riving** : derivar — **derivation** [ˌderə'veɪʃən] *n* : derivación *f*

derogatory [dɪ'rɑgəˌtori] *adj* : despectivo

descend [dɪ'send] *v* : descender, bajar — **descendant** [dɪ'sendənt] *n* : descendiente *mf* — **descent** [dɪ'sent] *n* **1** : descenso *m* **2** LINEAGE : descendencia *f*

describe [dɪ'skraɪb] *vt* **-scribed; -scribing** — **description** [dɪ'skrɪpʃən] *n* : descripción *f* — **descriptive** [dɪ'skrɪptɪv] *adj* : descriptivo

desecrate ['desɪˌkreɪt] *vt* **-crated; -crating** : profanar

desert ['dezərt] *n* : desierto *m* — ∼ *adj* ∼ **island** : isla *f* desierta — ∼ [dɪ'zərt] *vt* : abandonar — *vi* : desertar — **deserter** [dɪ'zərtər] *n* : desertor *m*, -tora *f*

deserve [dɪ'zərv] *vt* **-served; -serving** : merecer

design [dɪ'zaɪn] *vt* **1** DEVISE : diseñar **2** PLAN : proyectar — ∼ *n* **1** : diseño *m* **2** PLAN : plan *m*, proyecto *m*

designate ['dezɪgˌneɪt] *vt* **-nated; -nating** : nombrar, designar

designer [dɪ'zaɪnər] *n* : diseñador *m*, -dora *f*

desire [dɪ'zaɪr] *vt* **-sired; -siring** : desear — ∼ *n* : deseo *m* — **desirable** [dɪ'zaɪrəbəl] *adj* : deseable

desk ['desk] *n* : escritorio *m*, pupitre *m* (en la escuela)

desolate ['desələt, -zə-] *adj* : desolado

despair [dɪ'spær] *vi* : desesperar — ∼ *n* : desesperación *f*

desperate ['despərət] *adj* : desesperado — **desperation** [ˌdespə'reɪʃən] *n* : desesperación *f*

despise [dɪ'spaɪz] *vt* **-spised; -spising** : despreciar — **despicable** [dɪ'spɪkəbəl, 'despɪ-] *adj* : despreciable

despite [də'spaɪt] *prep* : a pesar de

despondent [dɪ'spɑndənt] *adj* : desanimado

dessert [dɪ'zərt] *n* : postre *m*

destination [ˌdestə'neɪʃən] *n* : destino *m* — **destined** ['destənd] *adj* **1** : destinado **2** ∼ **for** : con destino a — **destiny** ['destəni] *n, pl* **-nies** : destino *m*

destitute ['destəˌtuːt, -ˌtjuːt] *adj* : indigente

destroy [dɪ'strɔɪ] *vt* : destruir — **destruction** [dɪ'strʌkʃən] *n* : destrucción *f* — **destructive** [dɪ'strʌktɪv] *adj* : destructivo

detach [dɪ'tætʃ] *vt* : separar — **detached** [dɪ'tætʃt] *adj* **1** : separado **2** IMPARTIAL : objetivo

detail [dɪ'teɪl, 'diˌteɪl] *n* **1** : detalle *m* **2 go into** ∼ : entrar en detalles — ∼ *vt* : detallar — **detailed** *adj* : detallado

detain [dɪ'teɪn] *vt* **1** : detener (un prisionero) **2** DELAY : entretener

detect [dɪ'tekt] *vt* : detectar — **detection** [dɪ'tekʃən] *n* : detección *f*, descubrimiento *m* — **detective** [dɪ'tektɪv] *n* : detective *mf*

detention [dɪ'tentʃən] *n* : detención *m*

deter [dɪ'tər] *vt* **-terred; -terring** : disuadir

detergent [dɪ'tərdʒənt] *n* : detergente *m*

deteriorate [dɪ'tɪriəˌreɪt] vi -rated; -rating : deteriorarse — **deterioration** [dɪˌtɪriə'reɪʃən] n : deterioro m

determine [dɪ'tərmən] vt -mined; -mining : determinar — **determined** [dɪ'tərmənd] adj RESOLUTE : decidido — **determination** [dɪˌtərmə'neɪʃən] n : determinación f

deterrent [dɪ'tərənt] n : medida f disuasiva

detest [dɪ'tɛst] vt : detestar — **detestable** [dɪ'tɛstəbəl] adj : odioso

detonate ['dɛtənˌeɪt] v -nated; -nating vt : hacer detonar — vi EXPLODE : detonar, estallar — **detonation** [ˌdɛtə'neɪʃən, ˌdɛtə, -] n : detonación f

detour ['diːˌtʊr, dɪ'tʊr] n 1 : desviación f 2 **make a ~** : dar un rodeo — ~ vi : desviarse

detract [dɪ'trækt] vi **~ from** : aminorar, restar importancia a

detrimental [ˌdɛtrə'mɛntəl] adj : perjudicial

devalue [dɪ'vælˌjuː] vt -ued; -uing : devaluar

devastate ['dɛvəˌsteɪt] vt -tated; -tating : devastar — **devastating** adj : devastador — **devastation** [ˌdɛvə'steɪʃən] n : devastación f

develop [dɪ'vɛləp] vt 1 : desarrollar 2 **~ an illness** : contraer una enfermedad — vi 1 GROW : desarrollarse 2 HAPPEN : aparecer — **development** [dɪ'vɛləpmənt] n : desarrollo m

deviate ['diːviˌeɪt] v -ated; -ating vi : desviarse — **deviation** [ˌdiːvi'eɪʃən] n : desviación f

device [dɪ'vaɪs] n : dispositivo m, mecanismo m

devil ['dɛvəl] n : diablo m, demonio m — **devilish** ['dɛvəlɪʃ] adj : diabólico

devious ['diːviəs] adj 1 CRAFTY : taimado 2 WINDING : tortuoso

devise [dɪ'vaɪz] vt -vised; -vising : idear, concebir

devoid [dɪ'vɔɪd] adj **~ of** : desprovisto de

devote [dɪ'voːt] vt -voted; -voting : consagrar, dedicar — **devoted** [dɪ'voːtəd] adj : leal — **devotee** [ˌdɛvə'tiː, -'teɪ] n : devoto m, -ta f — **devotion** [dɪ'voːʃən] n 1 : devoción f, dedicación f 2 : oración f (en religión)

devour [dɪ'vaʊər] vt : devorar

devout [dɪ'vaʊt] adj : devoto

dew ['duː, 'djuː] n : rocío m

dexterity [dɛk'stɛrəti] n, pl -ties : destreza f

diabetes [ˌdaɪə'biːtiz] n : diabetes f —

diabetic [ˌdaɪə'bɛtɪk] adj : diabético — **~** n : diabético m, -ca f

diabolic [ˌdaɪə'bɑlɪk] or **diabolical** [-lɪkəl] adj : diabólico

diagnosis [ˌdaɪg'noːsɪs] n, pl -noses [-'noːˌsiːz] : diagnóstico m — **diagnose** ['daɪgˌnoːs, ˌdaɪg'noːs] vt -nosed; -nosing : diagnosticar — **diagnostic** [ˌdaɪg'nɑstɪk] adj : diagnóstico

diagonal [daɪ'ægənəl] adj : diagonal, en diagonal — **~** n : diagonal f

diagram ['daɪəˌgræm] n : diagrama m

dial ['daɪl] n : esfera f (de un reloj), dial m (de un radio, etc.) — **~** v **dialed** or **dialled**; **dialing** or **dialling** : marcar

dialect ['daɪəˌlɛkt] n : dialecto m

dialogue ['daɪəˌlɔg] n : diálogo m

diameter [daɪ'æmətər] n : diámetro m

diamond ['daɪmənd, 'daɪə-] n 1 : diamante m 2 : rombo m (forma) 3 or **baseball ~** : cuadro m, diamante m

diaper ['daɪpər, 'daɪə-] n : pañal m

diaphragm ['daɪəˌfræm] n : diafragma m

diarrhea [ˌdaɪə'riːə] n : diarrea f

diary ['daɪəri] n, pl -ries : diario m

dice ['daɪs] ns & pl : dados mpl (juego)

dictate ['dɪkˌteɪt, dɪk'teɪt] v -tated; -tating : dictar — **dictation** [dɪk'teɪʃən] n : dictado m — **dictator** ['dɪkˌteɪtər] n : dictador m, -dora f — **dictatorship** [dɪk'teɪtərˌʃɪp, 'dɪk,-] n : dictadura f

dictionary ['dɪkʃəˌnɛri] n, pl -naries : diccionario m

did → do

die[1] ['daɪ] vi **died** ['daɪd]; **dying** ['daɪɪŋ] 1 : morir 2 **~ down** : amainar, disminuir 3 **~ out** : extinguirse 4 **be dying for** : morirse por

die[2] ['daɪ] n 1 pl **dice** ['daɪs] : dado m (para jugar) 2 pl **dies** ['daɪz] MOLD : molde m

diesel ['diːzəl, -səl] n : diesel m

diet ['daɪət] n 1 FOOD : alimentación f 2 **go on a ~** : ponerse a régimen — **~** vi : estar a régimen

differ ['dɪfər] vi -ferred; -ferring 1 : diferir, ser distinto 2 DISAGREE : no estar de acuerdo — **difference** ['dɪfrənts, 'dɪfərənts] n : diferencia f — **different** ['dɪfrənt, 'dɪfərənt] adj : distinto, diferente — **differentiate** [ˌdɪfə'rɛntʃiˌeɪt] v -ated; -ating vt : diferenciar — vi : distinguir — **differently** ['dɪfrəntli, 'dɪfərənt-] adv : de otra manera

difficult ['dɪfɪˌkʌlt] adj : difícil — **difficulty** ['dɪfɪˌkʌlti] n, pl -ties : dificultad f

diffident ['dɪfədənt] adj : tímido, que falta confianza

dig ['dɪg] v **dug** ['dʌg]; **digging** vt 1 : cavar 2 ~ **up** : desenterrar — vi : cavar — ~ n 1 GIBE : pulla f 2 EXCAVATION : excavación f

digest ['daɪˌdʒest] n : resumen m — ~ [daɪ'dʒest] vt 1 : digerir 2 SUMMARIZE : resumir — **digestible** [daɪ'dʒestəbəl, dɪ-] adj : digerible — **digestion** [daɪ'dʒestʃən, dɪ-] n : digestión f — **digestive** [daɪ'dʒestɪv, dɪ-] adj : digestivo

digit ['dɪdʒət] n 1 NUMERAL : dígito m, número m 2 FINGER, TOE : dedo m — **digital** ['dɪdʒətəl] adj : digital

dignity ['dɪgnəti] n, pl **-ties** : dignidad f — **dignified** ['dɪgnəˌfaɪd] adj : digno, decoroso

digress [daɪ'gres, də-] vi : desviarse del tema, divagar — **digression** [daɪ'greʃən, də-] n : digresión f

dike ['daɪk] n : dique m

dilapidated [də'læpəˌdeɪtəd] adj : ruinoso

dilate [daɪ'leɪt, 'daɪˌleɪt] v **-lated; -lating** vt : dilatar — vi : dilatarse

dilemma [dɪ'lemə] n : dilema m

diligence ['dɪlədʒənts] n : diligencia f — **diligent** ['dɪlədʒənt] adj : diligente

dilute [daɪ'luːt, də-] vt **-luted; -luting** : diluir

dim ['dɪm] v **dimmed; dimming** vt : atenuar — vi : irse atenuando — ~ adj **dimmer; dimmest** 1 DARK : oscuro 2 FAINT : débil, tenue

dime ['daɪm] n : moneda f de diez centavos

dimension [də'mentʃən, daɪ-] n : dimensión f

diminish [də'mɪnɪʃ] v : disminuir

diminutive [də'mɪnjuˌtɪv] adj : diminuto

dimple ['dɪmpəl] n : hoyuelo m

din ['dɪn] n : estrépito m

dine ['daɪn] vi **dined; dining** : cenar — **diner** ['daɪnər] n 1 : comensal mf (persona) 2 : cafetería f (restaurante)

dingy ['dɪndʒi] adj **-gier; -est** : sucio, deslucido

dinner ['dɪnər] n : cena f, comida f

dinosaur ['daɪnəˌsɔr] n : dinosaurio m

dint ['dɪnt] n **by ~ of** : a fuerza de

dip ['dɪp] v **dipped; dipping** vt : mojar — vi : bajar, descender — ~ n 1 DROP : descenso m, caída f 2 SWIM : chapuzón m 3 SAUCE : salsa f

diploma [də'ploːmə] n, pl **-mas** : diploma m

diplomacy [də'ploːməsi] n : diplomacia f — **diplomat** ['dɪpləˌmæt] n : diplomático m, -ca f — **diplomatic** [ˌdɪplə'mæt̬ɪk] adj : diplomático

dire ['daɪr] adj **direr; direst** 1 : grave, terrible 2 EXTREME : extremo

direct [də'rekt, daɪ-] vt 1 : dirigir 2 ORDER : mandar — ~ adj 1 STRAIGHT : directo 2 FRANK : franco — ~ adv : directamente — **direct current** n : corriente f continua — **direction** [də'rekʃən, daɪ-] n 1 : dirección f 2 ask **~s** : pedir indicaciones — **directly** [də'rekt̬li, daɪ-] adv 1 STRAIGHT : directamente 2 IMMEDIATELY : en seguida — **director** [də'rektər, daɪ-] n 1 : director m, -tora f 2 board of **~s** : directorio m — **directory** [də'rektəri, daɪ-] n, pl **-ries** : guía f (telefónica)

dirt ['dərt] n 1 : suciedad f 2 SOIL : tierra f — **dirty** ['dərt̬i] adj **dirtier; -est** 1 : sucio 2 INDECENT : obsceno, cochino fam

disability [ˌdɪsə'bɪlət̬i] n, pl **-ties** : minusvalía f, invalidez f — **disable** [dɪs'eɪbəl] vt **-abled; -abling** : incapacitar — **disabled** [dɪs'eɪbəld] adj : minusválido

disadvantage [ˌdɪsəd'væntɪdʒ] n : desventaja f

disagree [ˌdɪsə'griː] vi 1 : no estar de acuerdo (con algn) 2 CONFLICT : no coincidir — **disagreeable** [ˌdɪsə'griːəbəl] adj : desagradable — **disagreement** [ˌdɪsə'griːmənt] n 1 : desacuerdo m 2 ARGUMENT : discusión f

disappear [ˌdɪsə'pɪr] vi : desaparecer — **disappearance** [ˌdɪsə'pɪrənts] n : desaparición f

disappoint [ˌdɪsə'pɔɪnt] vt : decepcionar, desilusionar — **disappointment** [ˌdɪsə'pɔɪntmənt] n : decepción f, desilusión f

disapprove [ˌdɪsə'pruːv] vi **-proved; -proving ~ of** : desaprobar — **disapproval** [ˌdɪsə'pruːvəl] n : desaprobación f

disarm [dɪs'ɑrm] vt : desarmar — **disarmament** [dɪs'ɑrməmənt] n : desarme m

disarray [ˌdɪsə'reɪ] n : desorden m

disaster [dɪ'zæstər] n : desastre m — **disastrous** [dɪ'zæstrəs] adj : desastroso

disbelief [ˌdɪsbɪ'liːf] n : incredulidad f

disc → **disk**

discard ['dɪsˌkɑrd, 'dɪsˌkɑrd] vt : desechar, deshacerse de

discern [dɪ'sərn, -'zərn] vt : percibir, discernir — **discernible** [dɪ'sərnəbəl, -'zər-] adj : perceptible

discharge [dɪs'tʃɑrdʒ, 'dɪs-] vt **-charged; -charging** 1 UNLOAD : descargar 2 RELEASE : liberar, poner en libertad 3 DISMISS : despedir 4

CARRY OUT : cumplir con (una obligación) — **~** ['dɪstʃərdʒ, dɪs-] n 1 : descarga f (de electricidad), emisión f (de humo, etc.) 2 DISMISSAL : despido m 3 RELEASE : alta f (de un paciente), puesta f en libertad (de un preso) 4 : supuración f (en medicina)

disciple [dɪ'saɪpəl] n : discípulo m, -la f

discipline ['dɪsəplən] n 1 : disciplina f 2 PUNISHMENT : castigo m — **~** vt -plined; -plining 1 CONTROL : disciplinar 2 PUNISH : castigar

disclaim [dɪs'kleɪm] vt : negar

disclose [dɪs'kloːz] vt -closed; -closing : revelar — **disclosure** [dɪs'kloʒər] n : revelación f

discomfort [dɪs'kʌmfərt] n 1 : incomodidad f 2 PAIN : malestar m 3 UNEASINESS : inquietud f

disconcert [ˌdɪskən'sərt] vt : desconcertar

disconnect [ˌdɪskə'nekt] vt : desconectar

disconsolate [dɪs'kɑntsələt] adj : desconsolado

discontented [ˌdɪskən'tentəd] adj : descontento

discontinue [ˌdɪskən'tɪnjuː] vt -ued; -uing : suspender, descontinuar

discount ['dɪsˌkaʊnt, dɪs'-] n : descuento m, rebaja f — **~** vt 1 : descontar (precios) 2 DISREGARD : descartar

discourage [dɪs'kərɪdʒ] vt -aged; -aging : desalentar, desanimar — **discouragement** [dɪs'kərɪdʒmənt] n : desánimo m, desaliento m

discover [dɪs'kʌvər] vt : descubrir — **discovery** [dɪs'kʌvəri] n, pl -ries : descubrimiento m

discredit [dɪs'kredət] vt : desacreditar — **~** n : descrédito m

discreet [dɪs'kriːt] adj : discreto

discrepancy [dɪs'krepəntsi] n, pl -cies : discrepancia f

discretion [dɪs'kreʃən] n : discreción f

discriminate [dɪs'krɪməˌneɪt] vi -nated; -nating 1 **~** against : discriminar 2 **~** between : distinguir entre — **discrimination** [dɪsˌkrɪmə'neɪʃən] n 1 PREJUDICE : discriminación f 2 DISCERNMENT : discernimiento m

discuss [dɪs'kʌs] vt : hablar de, discutir — **discussion** [dɪs'kʌʃən] n : discusión f

disdain [dɪs'deɪn] n : desdén m — **~** vt : desdeñar

disease [dɪ'ziːz] n : enfermedad f — **diseased** [dɪ'ziːzd] adj : enfermo

disembark [ˌdɪsɪm'bɑrk] vi : desembarcar

disengage [ˌdɪsɪn'geɪdʒ] vt -gaged; -gaging 1 RELEASE : soltar 2 **~** the clutch : desembragar

disentangle [ˌdɪsɪn'tæŋgəl] vt -gled; -gling : desenredar

disfavor [dɪs'feɪvər] n : desaprobación f

disfigure [dɪs'fɪgjər] vt -ured; -uring : desfigurar

disgrace [dɪs'kreɪs] vt -graced; -gracing : deshonrar — **~** n 1 DISHONOR : deshonra f 2 SHAME : vergüenza f — **disgraceful** [dɪs'kreɪsfəl] adj : vergonzoso, deshonroso

disgruntled [dɪs'grʌntəld] adj : descontento

disguise [dɪs'kaɪz] vt -guised; -guising : disfrazar — **~** n : disfraz m

disgust [dɪs'kʌst] n : asco m, repugnancia f — **~** vt : asquear — **disgusting** [dɪs'kʌstɪŋ] adj : asqueroso

dish ['dɪʃ] n 1 : plato m 2 or serving **~** : fuente f 3 wash the **~**es : lavar los platos — **~** vt or **~** up : servir — **dishcloth** ['dɪʃˌkloθ] n : paño m de cocina (para secar), trapo m de fregar (para lavar)

dishearten [dɪs'hɑrtən] vt : desanimar

disheveled or **dishevelled** [dɪ'ʃevəld] adj : desaliñado, despeinado (dícese del pelo)

dishonest [dɪs'ɑnəst] adj : deshonesto — **dishonesty** [dɪs'ɑnəsti] n, pl -ties : falta f de honradez

dishonor [dɪs'ɑnər] n : deshonra f — **~** vt : deshonrar — **dishonorable** [dɪs'ɑnərəbəl] adj : deshonroso

dishwasher ['dɪʃˌwɑʃər] n : lavaplatos m, lavavajillas m

disillusion [ˌdɪsə'luːʒən] vt : desilusionar — **disillusionment** [ˌdɪsə'luːʒənmənt] n : desilusión f

disinfect [ˌdɪsɪn'fekt] vt : desinfectar — **disinfectant** [ˌdɪsɪn'fektənt] n : desinfectante m

disintegrate [dɪs'ɪntəˌgreɪt] vi -grated; -grating : desintegrarse

disinterested [dɪs'ɪntərəstəd, -ˌres-] adj : desinteresado

disk or **disc** ['dɪsk] n : disco m

dislike [dɪs'laɪk] n : aversión f, antipatía f — **~** vt -liked; -liking 1 : tener aversión a 2 I **~** dancing : no me gusta bailar

dislocate ['dɪsloˌkeɪt, dɪs'loː-] vt -cated; -cating : dislocar

dislodge [dɪs'lɑdʒ] vt -lodged; -lodging : sacar, desalojar

disloyal [dɪs'lɔɪəl] adj : desleal — **disloyalty** [dɪs'lɔɪəlti] n, pl -ties : deslealtad f

dismal ['dɪzməl] *adj* : sombrío, deprimente

dismantle [dɪs'mæntəl] *vt* **-tled; -tling** : desmontar, desarmar

dismay [dɪs'meɪ] *vt* : consternar — ~ *n* : consternación *f*

dismiss [dɪs'mɪs] *vt* **1** DISCHARGE : despedir, destituir **2** REJECT : descartar, rechazar — **dismissal** [dɪs'mɪsəl] *n* **1** : despido *m* (de un empleado), destitución *f* (de un funcionario) **2** REJECTION : rechazo *m*

dismount [dɪs'maʊnt] *vi* : desmontar

disobey [ˌdɪsə'beɪ] *v* : desobedecer — **disobedience** [ˌdɪsə'biːdiənts] *n* : desobediencia *f* — **disobedient** [-ənt] *adj* : desobediente

disorder [dɪs'ɔrdər] *n* **1** : desorden *m* **2** AILMENT : afección *f*, problema *m* — **disorderly** [dɪs'ɔrdərli] *adj* : desordenado

disorganize [dɪs'ɔrgənaɪz] *vt* **-nized; -nizing** : desorganizar

disown [dɪs'oɪn] *vt* : renegar de

dispassionate [dɪs'pæʃənət] *adj* : desapasionado

dispatch [dɪs'pætʃ] *vt* : despachar, enviar

dispel [dɪs'pel] *vt* **-pelled; -pelling** : disipar

dispensation [ˌdɪspen'seɪʃən] *n* EXEMPTION : exención *m*, dispensa *f*

dispense [dɪs'pents] *v* **-pensed; -pensing** *vt* : repartir, distribuir — *vi* ~ **with** : prescindir de

disperse [dɪs'pərs] *v* **-persed; -persing** *vt* : dispersar — *vi* : dispersarse

displace [dɪs'pleɪs] *vt* **-placed; -placing** **1** : desplazar **2** REPLACE : reemplazar

display [dɪs'pleɪ] *vt* **1** EXHIBIT : exponer, exhibir **2** ~ **anger** : manifestar la ira — ~ *n* : muestra *f*, exposición *f*

displease [dɪs'pliːz] *vt* **-pleased; -pleasing** : desagradar — **displeasure** [dɪs'pleʒər] *n* : desagrado *m*

dispose [dɪs'poɪz] *v* **-posed; -posing** *vt* : disponer — *vi* ~ **of** : deshacerse de — **disposable** [dɪs'poɪzəbəl] *adj* : desechable — **disposal** [dɪs'poɪzəl] *n* **1** REMOVAL : eliminación *f* **2 have at one's ~** : tener a su disposición — **disposition** [ˌdɪspə'zɪʃən] *n* **1** ARRANGEMENT : disposición *f* **2** TEMPERAMENT : temperamento *m*, carácter *m*

disprove [dɪs'pruːv] *vt* **-proved; -proving** : refutar

dispute [dɪs'pjuːt] *v* **-puted; -puting** *vt* QUESTION : cuestionar — *vi* ARGUE : discutir — ~ *n* : disputa *f*, conflicto *m*

disqualification [dɪsˌkwɑləfə'keɪʃən] *n* : descalificación *f* — **disqualify** [dɪs'kwɑləˌfaɪ] *vt* **-fied; -fying** : descalificar

disregard [ˌdɪsrɪ'gɑrd] *vt* : ignorar, hacer caso omiso de — ~ *n* : indiferencia *f*

disrepair [ˌdɪsrɪ'pær] *n* : mal estado *m*

disreputable [dɪs'repjutəbəl] *adj* : de mala fama

disrespect [ˌdɪsrɪ'spekt] *n* : falta *f* de respeto — **disrespectful** [ˌdɪsrɪ'spektfəl] *adj* : irrespetuoso

disrupt [dɪs'rʌpt] *vt* : trastornar, perturbar — **disruption** [dɪs'rʌpʃən] *n* : trastorno *m*

dissatisfaction [dɪsˌsætəs'fækʃən] *n* : descontento *m* — **dissatisfied** [dɪs'sætəsˌfaɪd] *adj* : descontento

dissect [dɪ'sekt] *vt* : disecar

disseminate [dɪ'seməˌneɪt] *vt* **-nated; -nating** : diseminar, difundir

dissent [dɪ'sent] *vi* : disentir — ~ *n* : disentimiento *m*

dissertation [ˌdɪsər'teɪʃən] THESIS : tesis *f*

disservice [dɪs'sərvɪs] *n* **do a ~ to** : no hacer justicia a

dissident ['dɪsədənt] *n* : disidente *mf*

dissimilar [dɪ'sɪmələr] *adj* : distinto

dissipate ['dɪsəˌpeɪt] *vt* **-pated; -pating** **1** DISPEL : disipar **2** SQUANDER : desperdiciar

dissolve [dɪ'zɑlv] *v* **-solved; -solving** *vt* : disolver — *vi* : disolverse

dissuade [dɪ'sweɪd] *vt* **-suaded; -suading** : disuadir

distance ['dɪstənts] *n* **1** : distancia *f* **2 in the ~** : a lo lejos — **distant** ['dɪstənt] *adj* : distante

distaste [dɪs'teɪst] *n* : desagrado *m* — **distasteful** [dɪs'teɪstfəl] *adj* : desagradable

distend [dɪs'tend] *vt* : dilatar — *vi* : dilatarse

distill [dɪs'tɪl] *or Brit* **distil** *vt* **-tilled; -tilling** : destilar

distinct [dɪs'tɪŋkt] *adj* **1** DIFFERENT : distinto **2** CLEAR : claro — **distinction** [dɪs'tɪŋkʃən] *n* : distinción *f* — **distinctive** [dɪs'tɪŋktɪv] *adj* : distintivo

distinguish [dɪs'tɪŋgwɪʃ] *vt* : distinguir — **distinguished** [dɪs'tɪŋgwɪʃt] *adj* : distinguido

distort [dɪs'tɔrt] *vt* : deformar, distorsionar — **distortion** [dɪs'tɔrʃən] *n* : deformación *f*

distract [dɪs'trækt] *vt* : distraer — **distraction** [dɪs'trækʃən] *n* : distracción *f*

distraught [dɪs'trɔt] *adj* : muy afligido

distress [dɪs'tres] *n* **1** : angustia *f*, aflicción *f* **2 in ~** : en peligro — ~ *vt*

: afligir — **distressing** [dɪ'strɛsɪŋ] *adj*
: penoso

distribute [dɪ'strɪbjuːt, -bjut] *vt* **-uted;**
-uting : distribuir, repartir — **distribu-**
tion [ˌdɪstrə'bjuːʃən] *n* : distribución *f* —
distributor [dɪ'strɪbjuːtər] *n* : distribuidor *m*, -dora *f*

district ['dɪstrɪkt] *n* **1** REGION : región *f*,
zona *f*, barrio *m* (de una ciudad) **2**
: distrito *m* (zona política)

distrust [dɪs'trʌst] *n* : desconfianza *f* —
~ *vt* : desconfiar de

disturb [dɪs'tərb] *vt* **1** BOTHER : molestar,
perturbar **2** WORRY : inquietar — **dis-**
turbance [dɪs'tərbəns] *n* **1** COMMOTION
: alboroto *m*, disturbio *m* **2** INTERRUP-
TION : interrupción *f*

disuse [dɪs'juːs] *n* **fall into ~** : caer en
desuso

ditch ['dɪtʃ] *n* : zanja *f*, cuneta *f* — ~ *vt*
DISCARD : desecharse de, botar

ditto ['dɪtoː] *n, pl* **-tos 1** : ídem *m* **2** ~
marks : comillas *fpl*

dive ['daɪv] *vi* **dived** *or* **dove** ['doːv];
dived; diving 1 : zambullirse, tirarse
al agua **2** DESCEND : bajar en picada
(dícese de un avión, etc.) — ~ *n* **1**
: zambullida *f*, clavado *m* *Lat* **2** DE-
SCENT : descenso *m* en picada — **diver**
['daɪvər] *n* : saltador *m*, -dora *f*

diverge [də'vərdʒ, daɪ-] *vi* **-verged;**
-verging : divergir

diverse [daɪ'vərs, də-, 'daɪˌvərs] *adj* : diverso — **diversify** [daɪ'vərsəˌfaɪ, də-] *v*
-fied; -fying *vt* : diversificar — *vi* : di-
versificarse

diversion [daɪ'vərʒən, də-] *n* **1**
: desviación *f* **2** AMUSEMENT : diver-
sión *f*, distracción *f* — **diversity** [daɪ'vərsəˌti, də-] *n, pl* **-ties**
: diversidad *f*

divert [də'vərt, daɪ-] *vt* **1** : desviar **2** DIS-
TRACT : distraer **3** AMUSE : divertir

divide [də'vaɪd] *v* **-vided; -viding** *vt* : dividir — *vi* : dividirse

dividend ['dɪvəˌdɛnd, -dənd] *n* : dividendo *m*

divine [də'vaɪn] *adj* **-viner; -est** : divino
— **divinity** [də'vɪnəˌti] *n, pl* **-ties** : divinidad *f*

division [dɪ'vɪʒən] *n* : división *f*

divorce [də'voːrs] *n* : divorcio *m* — ~ *v*
-vorced; -vorcing *vt* : divorciar — *vi*
: divorciarse — **divorcée** [dɪˌvorˈseɪ,
-'siː; -'vorˌ-] *n* : divorciada *f*

divulge [də'vʌldʒ, daɪ-] *vt* **-vulged;**
-vulging : revelar, divulgar

dizzy ['dɪzi] *adj* **dizzier; -est 1** : mareado **2 a ~ speed** : una velocidad ver-

tiginosa — **dizziness** ['dɪzinəs] *n*
: mareo *m*, vértigo *m*

DNA [ˌdiːˌɛn'eɪ] *n* : ADN *m*

do ['duː] *v* **did** ['dɪd]; **done** ['dʌn]; **doing;**
does ['dʌz] *vt* **1** : hacer **2** PREPARE
: preparar — *vi* **1** BEHAVE : hacer **2**
FARE : estar, ir, andar **3** SUFFICE : ser
suficiente **4 ~ away with** : abolir,
eliminar **5 how are you doing?**
: ¿cómo estás? — *v aux* **1** (*used in in-*
terrogative sentences) **do you know**
her? : ¿la conoces? **2** (*used in nega-*
tive statements) **I don't know** : yo no
sé **3** (*used as a substitute verb to*
avoid repetition) **do you speak Eng-**
lish? yes, I do : ¿habla inglés? sí

dock ['dɑk] *n* : muelle *m* — ~ *vt* : descontar dinero de (un sueldo) — *vi*
ANCHOR : fondear, atracar

doctor ['dɑktər] *n* **1** : doctor *m*, -tora *f*
(en derecho, etc.) **2** PHYSICIAN : médi-
co *m*, -ca; doctor *m*, -tora *f* — ~ *vt*
ALTER : alterar, falsificar

doctrine ['dɑktrɪn] *n* : doctrina *f*

document ['dɑkjumənt] *n* : documento
m — ['dɑkjuˌmɛnt] *vt* : documentar
— **documentary** [ˌdɑkjuˈmɛntəri] *n, pl*
-ries : documental *m*

dodge ['dɑdʒ] *n* : artimaña *f*, truco *m* —
v **dodged; dodging** *vt* : esquivar,
eludir — *vi* : echarse a un lado

doe ['doː] *n, pl* **does** *or* **doe** : gama *f*,
cierva *f*

does → **do**

dog ['dɔg, 'dɑg] *n* : perro *m*, -rra *f* — ~
vt **dogged; dogging** : perseguir —
dogged ['dɔgəd] *adj* : tenaz

dogma ['dɔgmə] *n* : dogma *m* — **dog-**
matic [dɔg'mætɪk] *adj* : dogmático

doily ['dɔɪli] *n, pl* **-lies** : tapete *m*

doings ['duːɪŋz] *npl* : actividades *fpl*

doldrums ['doːldrəmz, 'dɑl-] *npl* **be in**
the ~ : estar abatido

dole ['doːl] *n* : subsidio *m* de desempleo
— ~ *vt* **doled; doling** *or* **~ out**
: repartir

doleful ['doːlfəl] *adj* : triste, lúgubre

doll ['dɑl, 'dɔl] *n* : muñeco *m*, -ca *f*

dollar ['dɑlər] *n* : dólar *m*

dolphin ['dɑlfən, 'dɔl-] *n* : delfín *m*

domain [do'meɪn, də-] *n* **1** TERRITORY
: dominio *m* **2** FIELD : campo *m*, esfera
f

dome ['doːm] *n* : cúpula *f*

domestic [də'mɛstɪk] *adj* **1** : doméstico
2 INTERNAL : nacional — ~ *n* SERVANT
: empleado *m* doméstico, empleada *f*
doméstica — **domesticate** [də'mɛstɪˌkeɪt] *vt* **-cated; -cating** : domesticar

domination [ˌdɑmə'neɪʃən] *n* : dominación *f* — **dominant** ['dɑmənənt] *adj* : dominante — **dominate** ['dɑmə,neɪt] *v* -**nated; -nating** : dominar — **domineer** [,dɑmə'nɪr] *vi* : dominar, tiranizar

dominos ['dɑmə,noːz] *n* : dominó *m* (juego)

donate ['doː,neɪt, doː-'] *vt* -**nated; -nating** : donar, hacer un donativo de — **donation** [doː'neɪʃən] *n* : donativo *m*

done ['dʌn] → **do** — *adj* 1 FINISHED : terminado, hecho 2 COOKED : cocido

donkey ['dɑŋki, 'dʌŋ-] *n*, *pl* -**keys** : burro *m*

donor ['doːnər] *n* : donante *mf*

don't ['doːnt] (*contraction of* **do not**) → **do**

doodle ['duːdəl] *v* -**dled; -dling** : garabatear — *n* : garabato *m*

doom ['duːm] *n* : perdición *f*, fatalidad *f* — *vt* : condenar

door ['dor] *n* 1 : puerta *f* 2 ENTRANCE : entrada *f* — **doorbell** ['dor,bɛl] *n* : timbre *m* — **doorknob** ['dor,nɑb] *n* : pomo *m* — **doorman** ['dormən] *n*, *pl* -**men** [-mən, -,mɛn] : portero *m* — **doormat** ['dor,mæt] *n* : felpudo *m* — **doorstep** ['dor,stɛp] *n* : umbral *m* — **doorway** ['dor,weɪ] *n* : entrada *f*, portal *m*

dope ['doːp] *n* 1 DRUG : droga *f* 2 IDIOT : idiota *mf* — *vt* **doped; doping** : drogar

dormant ['dormənt] *adj* : inactivo, latente

dormitory ['dormə,tori] *n*, *pl* -**ries** : dormitorio *m*

dose ['doːs] *n* : dosis *f* — **dosage** ['doːsɪdʒ] *n* : dosis *f*

dot ['dɑt] *n* 1 : punto *m* 2 **on the** ~ : en punto

dote ['doːt] *vi* **doted; doting** ~ **on** : adorar

double ['dʌbəl] *adj* : doble — *v* -**bled; -bling** *vt* : doblar — *vi* : doblarse — *adv* : (el) doble — ~ *n* : doble *mf* — **double bass** *n* : contrabajo *m* — **double-cross** [,dʌbəl-'kros] *vt* : traicionar — **doubly** ['dʌbli] *adv* : doblemente

doubt ['daut] *vt* 1 : dudar 2 DISTRUST : desconfiar de, dudar de — ~ *n* : duda *f* — **doubtful** ['dautfəl] *adj* : dudoso — **doubtless** ['dautləs] *adv* : sin duda

dough ['doː] *n* : masa *f* — **doughnut** ['doː,nʌt] *n* : rosquilla *f*, dona *f Lat*

douse ['daus, 'dauz] *vt* **doused; dousing** 1 DRENCH : empapar, mojar 2 EXTINGUISH : apagar

dove[1] ['doːv] → **dive**

dove[2] ['dʌv] *n* : paloma *f*

dowdy ['daudi] *adj* **dowdier; -est** : poco elegante

down ['daun] *adv* 1 DOWNWARD : hacia abajo 2 **come/go** ~ : bajar 3 ~ **here** : aquí abajo 4 ~ : caer 5 **lie** ~ : acostarse 6 **sit** ~ : sentarse — ~ *prep* 1 ALONG : a lo largo de 2 THROUGH : a través de 3 ~ **the hill** : cuesta abajo — ~ *adj* 1 DESCENDING : de bajada 2 DOWNCAST : abatido — ~ *n* : plumón *m* — **downcast** ['daun,kæst] *adj* : triste, abatido — **downfall** ['daun,fɔl] *n* : ruina *f* — **downhearted** ['daun,hɑrtəd] *adj* : desanimado — **downhill** ['daun,hɪl] *adv & adj* : cuesta abajo — **down payment** *n* : entrega *f* inicial — **downpour** ['daun,por] *n* : chaparrón *m* — **downright** ['daun,raɪt] *adv* : absolutamente — ~ *adj* : absoluto, categórico — **downstairs** ['daun'stærz] *adv* : abajo — ~ ['daun,stærz] *adj* : de abajo — **downstream** ['daun'striːm] *adv* : río abajo — **down-to-earth** [,dauntu'ərθ] *adj* : realista — **downtown** [,daun'taun, 'daun,taun] *n* : centro *m* (de la ciudad) — ~ [daun'taun] *adv* : al centro, en el centro — ~ *adj* : del centro — **downward** ['daunwərd] *or* **downwards** [-wərdz] *adv & adj* : hacia abajo

dowry ['dauri] *n*, *pl* -**ries** : dote *f*

doze ['doːz] *vi* **dozed; dozing** : dormitar

dozen ['dʌzən] *n*, *pl* **dozens** *or* **dozen** : docena *f*

drab ['dræb] *adj* **drabber; drabbest** : monótono, apagado

draft ['dræft, 'draft] *n* 1 : corriente *f* de aire 2 *or* **rough** ~ : borrador *m* 3 : conscripción *f* (militar) 4 *or* **beer** ~ : cerveza *f* de barril — ~ *vt* 1 SKETCH : hacer el borrador de 2 CONSCRIPT : reclutar — **drafty** ['dræfti] *adj* **draftier; -est** : con corrientes de aire

drag ['dræg] *v* **dragged; dragging** *vt* 1 : arrastrar 2 DREDGE : dragar — *vi* : arrastrar(se) — ~ *n* 1 RESISTANCE : resistencia *f* (aerodinámica) 2 BORE : pesadez *f*, plomo *m fam*

dragon ['drægən] *n* : dragón *m* — **dragonfly** ['drægən,flaɪ] *n*, *pl* -**flies** : libélula *f*

drain ['dreɪn] *vt* 1 EMPTY : vaciar, drenar 2 EXHAUST : agotar — *vi* 1 : escurrir(se) (se dice de los platos) 2 *or* ~ **away** : desaparecer poco a poco — ~ *n* 1 : desagüe *m* 2 SEWER : alcantarilla *f* 3 DEPLETION : agotamiento *m* — **drainage** ['dreɪnɪdʒ] *n* : drenaje *m* — **drainpipe** ['dreɪn,paɪp] *n* : tubo *m* de desagüe

drama ['drɑmə, 'dræ-] *n* : drama *m* —

dramatic [drə'mæṭɪk] *adj* : dramático — **dramatist** ['dræməṭɪst, 'drɑ-] *n* : dramaturgo *m*, -ga *f* — **dramatize** ['dræmə‚taɪz, 'drɑ-] *vt* **-tized; -tizing** : dramatizar

drank → drink

drape ['dreɪp] *vt* **draped; draping** 1 COVER : cubrir (con tela) 2 HANG : drapear — **drapes** *npl* CURTAINS : cortinas *fpl*

drastic ['dræstɪk] *adj* : drástico

draught ['dræft, 'draft] → **draft**

draw ['drɔ] *v* **drew** ['dru:]; **drawn** ['drɔn]; **drawing** *vt* 1 PULL : tirar de 2 ATTRACT : atraer 3 SKETCH : dibujar, trazar 4 : sacar (una espada, etc.) 5 **~ a conclusion** : llegar a una conclusión 6 **~ up** DRAFT : redactar — *vi* 1 SKETCH : dibujar 2 **~ near** : acercarse — **~** *n* 1 DRAWING : sorteo *m* 2 TIE : empate *m* 3 ATTRACTION : atracción *f* — **drawback** ['drɔ‚bæk] *n* : desventaja *f* — **drawer** ['drɔr, 'drɔər] *n* : gaveta *f*, cajón *m* (en un mueble) — **drawing** ['drɔɪŋ] *n* 1 LOTTERY : sorteo *m* 2 SKETCH : dibujo *m*

drawl ['drɔl] *n* : habla *f* lenta y con vocales prolongadas

dread ['drɛd] *vt* : temer — **~** *n* : pavor *m*, temor *m* — **dreadful** ['drɛdfəl] *adj* : espantoso, terrible

dream ['dri:m] *n* : sueño *m* — *v* **dreamed** ['drɛmpt, 'dri:md] *or* **dreamt** ['drɛmpt]; **dreaming** *vi* : soñar — *vt* 1 : soñar 2 **~ up** : idear — **dreamer** ['dri:mər] *n* : soñador *m*, -dora *f* — **dreamy** ['dri:mi] *adj* **dreamier; -est** : soñador

dreary ['drɪri] *adj* **-rier; -est** : sombrío, deprimente

dredge ['drɛdʒ] *vt* **dredged; dredging** : dragar — **~** *n* : draga *f*

dregs ['drɛgz] *npl* : heces *fpl*

drench ['drɛntʃ] *vt* : empapar

dress ['drɛs] *vt* 1 : vestir 2 : preparar (pollo o pescado), aliñar (ensalada) — *vi* 1 : vestirse 2 **~ up** : ponerse elegante — **~** *n* 1 CLOTHING : ropa *f* 2 : vestido *m* (de mujer) — **dresser** ['drɛsər] *n* : cómoda *f* con espejo — **dressing** ['drɛsɪŋ] *n* 1 : aliño *m* (de ensalada), relleno *m* (de pollo) 2 BANDAGE : vendaje *m* — **dressmaker** ['drɛs‚meɪkər] *n* : modista *mf* — **dressy** ['drɛsi] *adj* **dressier; -est** : elegante

drew → draw

dribble ['drɪbəl] *vi* **-bled; -bling** 1 DRIP : gotear 2 DROOL : babear 3 : driblar (en basquetbol) — **~** *n* 1 TRICKLE : goteo *m*, hilo *m* 2 DROOL : baba *f*

drier, driest → dry

drift ['drɪft] *n* 1 MOVEMENT : movimiento *m* 2 HEAP : montón *m* (de arena, etc.), ventisquero *m* (de nieve) 3 MEANING : sentido *m* — **~** *vi* 1 : ir a la deriva 2 ACCUMULATE : amontonarse

drill ['drɪl] *n* 1 : taladro *m* 2 : ejercicio *m* (en educación), simulacro *m* (de incendio, etc.) — **~** *vt* 1 : perforar, taladrar 2 TRAIN : instruir por repetición — *vi* **~ for** : perforar en busca de

drink ['drɪŋk] *v* **drank** ['dræŋk], **drunk** ['drʌŋk] *or* **drank; drinking** : beber — **~** *n* : bebida *f*

drip ['drɪp] *vi* **dripped; dripping** : gotear — **~** *n* 1 DROP : gota *f* 2 DRIPPING : goteo *m*

drive ['draɪv] *v* **drove** ['droːv]; **driven** ['drɪvən]; **driving** *vt* 1 : manejar 2 IMPEL : impulsar 3 **~ crazy** : volver loco a **~ s.o. to (do sth)** : llevar a algn a (hacer algo) — *vi* : manejar, conducir — **~** *n* 1 : paseo *m* (en coche) 2 CAMPAIGN : campaña *f* 3 VIGOR : energía *f* 4 NEED : instinto *m*

drivel ['drɪvəl] *n* : tonterías *fpl*

driver ['draɪvər] *n* : conductor *m*, -tora *f*; chofer *m*

driveway ['draɪv‚weɪ] *n* : camino *m* de entrada

drizzle ['drɪzəl] *n* : llovizna *f* — **~** *vi* **-zled; -zling** : lloviznar

drone ['droːn] *n* 1 BEE : zángano *m* 2 HUM : zumbido *m* — **~** *vi* **droned; droning** 1 BUZZ : zumbar 2 *or* **~ on** : hablar con monotonía

drool ['druːl] *vi* : babear — **~** *n* : baba *f*

droop ['druːp] *vi* : inclinarse (dícese de la cabeza), encorvarse (dícese de los escombros), marchitarse (dícese de las flores)

drop ['drɑp] *n* 1 : gota *f* (de líquido) 2 DECLINE, FALL : caída *f* — **~** *v* **dropped; dropping** *vt* 1 : dejar caer 2 LOWER : bajar 3 ABANDON : abandonar, dejar 4 **~ off** LEAVE : dejar — *vi* 1 FALL : caer(se) 2 DECREASE : bajar, descender 3 **~ by** *or* **~ in** : pasar

drought ['draut] *n* : sequía *f*

drove → drive

droves ['droːvz] *n* **in ~** : en manada

drown ['draun] *vt* : ahogar — *vi* : ahogarse

drowsy ['drauzi] *adj* **drowsier; -est** : somnoliento

drudgery ['drʌdʒəri] *n, pl* **-eries** : trabajo *m* pesado

drug ['drʌg] *n* 1 MEDICATION : medicamento *m* 2 NARCOTIC : droga *f*, estupefaciente *m* — **~** *vt* **drugged; drugging** : drogar — **drugstore** ['drʌg‚stɔr] *n* : farmacia *f*

drum ['drʌm] n 1 : tambor m 2 or oil ~ : bidón m (de petróleo) — ~ v drummed; drumming vi : tocar el tambor — vt : tamborilear con (los dedos, etc.) — **drumstick** ['drʌm,stɪk] n 1 : palillo m (de tambor) 2 : muslo m (de pollo)

drunk ['drʌŋk] → **drink** — ~ adj : borracho — or **drunkard** ['drʌŋkərd] n : borracho m, -cha f — **drunken** ['drʌŋkən] adj : borracho, ebrio

dry ['draɪ] adj **drier; driest** : seco — ~ v **dried; drying** vt : secar — vi : secarse — **dry-clean** ['draɪˌkliːn] vt : limpiar en seco — **dry cleaner** n : tintorería f (servicio) — **dry cleaning** n : limpieza f en seco — **dryer** ['draɪər] n : secadora f — **dryness** ['draɪnəs] n : sequedad f, aridez f

dual ['duːəl, 'djuː-] adj : doble

dub ['dʌb] vt **dubbed; dubbing 1** CALL : apodar **2** : doblar (una película)

dubious ['duːbiəs, 'djuː-] adj **1** UNCERTAIN : dudoso **2** QUESTIONABLE : sospechoso

duchess ['dʌtʃəs] n : duquesa f

duck ['dʌk] n, pl **duck** or **ducks** : pato m, -ta f — ~ vt **1** LOWER : agachar, bajar **2** EVADE : eludir, esquivar — vi : agacharse — **duckling** ['dʌklɪŋ] n : patito m, -ta f

duct ['dʌkt] n : conducto m

due ['duː, 'djuː] adj **1** PAYABLE : pagadero **2** APPROPRIATE : debido, apropiado **3** EXPECTED : esperado **4** ~ **to** : debido a — ~ n **1** give s.o. their ~ : hacer justicia a algn **2** ~s npl : cuota f — ~ adv ~ **east** : justo al este

duel ['duːəl, 'djuː-] n : duelo m

duet ['duːet, dju-] n : dúo m

dug → **dig**

duke ['duːk, 'djuːk] n : duque m

dull ['dʌl] adj **1** STUPID : torpe **2** BLUNT : desafilado **f 2** BORING : aburrido **4** LACKLUSTER : apagado — ~ vt : entorpecer (los sentidos), aliviar (el dolor)

dumb ['dʌm] adj **1** MUTE : mudo **2** STUPID : estúpido

dumbfound or **dumfound** [ˌdʌmˈfaʊnd] vt : dejar sin habla

dummy ['dʌmi] n, pl **-mies 1** SHAM : imitación f **2** MANNEQUIN : maniquí m **3** IDIOT : tonto m, -ta f

dump ['dʌmp] vt : descargar, verter — ~ n **1** : vertedero m, tiradero m **2** down in the ~s : triste, deprimido

dumpling ['dʌmplɪŋ] n : bola f de masa hervida

dumpy ['dʌmpi] adj **dumpier; -est** : regordete

dunce ['dʌnts] n : burro m, -rra f fam

dune ['duːn, 'djuːn] n : duna f

dung ['dʌŋ] n **1** : excrementos mpl **2** MANURE : estiércol m

dungarees [ˌdʌŋgəˈriː] npl JEANS : vaqueros mpl, jeans mpl

dungeon ['dʌndʒən] n : calabozo m

dunk ['dʌŋk] vt : mojar

duo ['duːoː, 'djuː-] n, pl **duos** : dúo m

dupe ['duːp, djuːp] vt **duped; duping** : engañar — ~ n : inocentón m, -tona f

duplex ['duːˌplɛks, 'djuː-] n : casa f de dos viviendas, dúplex m

duplicate ['duːplɪkət, 'djuː-] adj : duplicado — ~ ['duːplɪˌkeɪt, 'djuː-] vt **-cated; -cating** : duplicar, hacer copias de — ~ ['duːplɪkət, 'djuː-] n : duplicado m, copia f

durable ['dʊrəbəl, 'djʊr-] adj : duradero

duration [dʊˈreɪʃən, dju-] n : duración f

duress [dʊˈres, dju-] n : coacción f

during ['dʊrɪŋ, 'djʊr-] prep : durante

dusk ['dʌsk] n : anochecer m, crepúsculo m

dust ['dʌst] n : polvo m — ~ vt **1** : quitar el polvo a **2** SPRINKLE : espolvorear — **dustpan** ['dʌstˌpæn] n : recogedor m — **dusty** ['dʌsti] adj **dustier; -est** : polvoriento

Dutch ['dʌtʃ] adj : holandés — ~ n **1** : holandés m (idioma) **2** the ~ : los holandeses

duty ['duːti, 'djuː-] n, pl **-ties 1** OBLIGATION : deber m **2** TAX : impuesto m **3** on ~ : de servicio — **dutiful** ['duːtɪfəl, 'djuː-] adj : obediente

dwarf ['dwɔrf] n, pl **dwarfs** ['dwɔrfs] or **dwarves** ['dwɔrvz] : enano m, -na f — ~ vt : hacer parecer pequeño

dwell ['dwɛl] vi **dwelled** or **dwelt** ['dwɛlt]; **dwelling 1** RESIDE : morar, vivir **2** ~ **on** : pensar demasiado en — **dweller** ['dwɛlər] n : habitante mf — **dwelling** ['dwɛlɪŋ] n : morada f, vivienda f

dwindle ['dwɪndəl] vi **-dled; -dling** : disminuir

dye ['daɪ] n : tinte m — ~ vt **dyed; dyeing** : teñir

dying → **die**[1]

dynamic [daɪˈnæmɪk] adj : dinámico

dynamite ['daɪnəˌmaɪt] n : dinamita f

dynamo ['daɪnəˌmoː] n, pl **-mos** : dínamo m

dynasty ['daɪnəsti, -ˌnæs-] n, pl **-ties** : dinastía f

dysentery ['dɪsənˌteri] n, pl **-teries** : disentería f

E

e ['iː] *n, pl* **e's** *or* **es** ['iːz] : e *f*, quinta letra del alfabeto inglés

each ['iːtʃ] *adj* : cada — ~ *pron* **1** : cada uno *m*, cada una *f* **2** ~ **other** : el uno al otro **3 they hate** ~ **other** : se odian — ~ *adv* : cada uno, por persona

eager ['iːgər] *adj* **1** ENTHUSIASTIC : entusiasta **2** IMPATIENT : impaciente — **eagerness** ['iːgərnəs] *n* : entusiasmo *m*, impaciencia *f*

eagle ['iːgəl] *n* : águila *f*

ear ['ɪr] *n* **1** : oreja *f* **2** ~ **of corn** : mazorca *f*, choclo *m Lat* — **eardrum** ['ɪr,drʌm] *n* : tímpano *m*

earl ['ərl] *n* : conde *m*

earlobe ['ɪr,loːb] *n* : lóbulo *m* de la oreja

early ['ərli] *adv* **earlier; -est 1** : temprano **2 as** ~ **as possible** : lo más pronto posible **3 ten minutes** ~ : diez minutos de adelanto — ~ *adj* **earlier; -est 1** FIRST : primero **2** ANCIENT : primitivo, antiguo **3 an** ~ **death** : una muerte prematura **4 be** ~ : llegar temprano **5 in the** ~ **spring** : a principios de la primavera

earmark ['ɪr,mɑrk] *vt* : destinar

earn ['ərn] *vt* **1** : ganar **2** DESERVE : merecer

earnest ['ərnəst] *adj* : serio — ~ *n* **in** ~ : en serio

earnings ['ərnɪŋz] *npl* **1** WAGES : ingresos *mpl* **2** PROFITS : ganancias *fpl*

earphone ['ɪr,foːn] *n* : audífono *m*

earring ['ɪr,rɪŋ] *n* : pendiente *m*, arete *m Lat*

earshot ['ɪr,ʃɑt] *n* **within** ~ : al alcance del oído

earth ['ərθ] *n* **1** : tierra *f* — **earthenware** ['ərθən,wær, -ðən-] *n* : loza *f* — **earthly** ['ərθli] *adj* : terrenal — **earthquake** ['ərθ,kweɪk] *n* : terremoto *m* — **earthworm** ['ərθ,wərm] *n* : lombriz *f* (de tierra) — **earthy** ['ərθi] *adj* **earthier; -est 1** : terroso **2** COARSE, CRUDE : grosero

ease ['iːz] *n* **1** FACILITY : facilidad *f* **2** COMFORT : comodidad *f* **3 feel at** ~ : sentir cómodo — ~ *v* **eased; easing** *vt* **1** ALLEVIATE : aliviar, calmar **2** FACILITATE : facilitar — *vi* **1** : calmarse **2** ~ **up** : disminuir

easel ['iːzəl] *n* : caballete *m*

easily ['iːzəli] *adv* **1** : fácilmente, con fa-

cilidad **2** UNQUESTIONABLY : con mucho, de lejos *Lat*

east ['iːst] *adv* : al este — ~ *adj* : este, del este — ~ *n* **1** : este *m* **2 the East** : el Oriente

Easter ['iːstər] *n* : Pascua *f*

easterly ['iːstərli] *adv & adj* : del este

eastern ['iːstərn] *adj* **1** : del este **2 Eastern** : oriental, del este

easy ['iːzi] *adj* **easier; -est 1** : fácil **2** RELAXED : relajado — **easygoing** [,iːzi'goːɪŋ] *adj* : tolerante, relajado

eat ['iːt] *v* **ate** ['eɪt]; **eaten** ['iːtən]; **eating** *vt* : comer — *vi* **1** : comer **2** ~ **into** CORRODE : corroer **3** ~ **into** DEPLETE : comerse — **eatable** ['iːtəbəl] *adj* : comestible

eaves ['iːvz] *npl* : alero *m* — **eavesdrop** ['iːvz,drɑp] *vi* **-dropped; -dropping** : escuchar a escondidas

ebb ['eb] *n* : reflujo *m* — ~ *vi* **1** : bajar (dícese de la marea) **2** DECLINE : decaer

ebony ['ebəni] *n, pl* **-nies** : ébano *m*

eccentric [ɪk'sentrɪk] *adj* : excéntrico — ~ *n* : excéntrico *m*, -ca *f* — **eccentricity** [,eksen'trɪsəti] *n, pl* **-ties** : excentricidad *f*

echo ['e,koː] *n, pl* **echoes** : eco *m* — ~ *v* **echoed; echoing** *vt* : repetir — *vi* : hacer eco, resonar

eclipse [ɪ'klɪps] *n* : eclipse *m* — ~ *vt* **eclipsed; eclipsing** : eclipsar

ecology [ɪ'kɑlədʒi, ɛ-] *n, pl* **-gies** : ecología *f* — **ecological** [,iːkə'lɑdʒɪkəl, ,ekə-] : ecológico

economy [ɪ'kɑnəmi] *n, pl* **-mies** : economía *f* — **economic** [,iːkə'nɑmɪk, ,ekə-] *or* **economical** [,iːkə'nɑmɪkəl, ,ekə-] *adj* : económico — **economics** [,iːkə'nɑmɪks, ,ekə-] *n* : economía *f* — **economist** [ɪ'kɑnəmɪst] *n* : economista *mf* — **economize** [ɪ'kɑnə,maɪz] *v* **-mized; -mizing** : economizar

ecstasy ['ekstəsi] *n, pl* **-sies** : éxtasis *m* — **ecstatic** [ek'stætɪk, ɪk-] *adj* : extático

Ecuadoran [,ekwə'dɔrən] *or* **Ecuadorean** *or* **Ecuadorian** [,ekwə'dɔriən] *adj* : ecuatoriano

edge ['edʒ] *n* **1** BORDER : borde *m* **2** : filo *m* (de un cuchillo) **3** ADVANTAGE : ventaja *f* — ~ *v* **edged; edging** *vt* : bordear, ribetear — *vi* : avanzar poco a poco — **edgewise** ['edʒ,waɪz] *adv* : de lado — **edgy** ['edʒi] *adj* **edgier; -est** : nervioso

edible ['edəbəl] *adj* : comestible

edit ['edɪt] *vt* **1** : editar, redactar, corregir **2** ~ **out** : suprimir, cortar — **edition** [ɪ'dɪʃən] *n* : edición *f* — **editor** ['edɪtər] *n* : director *m*, -tora *f* (de un periódico); redactor *m*, -tora *f* (de un libro) — **editorial** [,edɪ'toriəl] *n* : editorial *m*

educate ['edʒə,keɪt] *vt* **-cated; -cating 1** TEACH : educar, instruir **2** INFORM : informar — **education** [,edʒə'keɪʃən] *n* : educación *f* — **educational** [,edʒə'keɪʃənəl] *adj* **1** : educativo, instructivo **2** TEACHING : docente — **educator** ['edʒə,keɪtər] *n* : educador *m*, -dora *f*

eel ['iːl] *n* : anguila *f*

eerie ['ɪri] *adj* **-rier; -est** : extraño e inquietante, misterioso

effect [ɪ'fekt] *n* **1** : efecto *m* **2 go into** ~ : entrar en vigor — ~ *vt* : efectuar, llevar a cabo — **effective** [ɪ'fektɪv] *adj* **1** : eficaz **2** ACTUAL : efectivo, vigente — **effectiveness** [ɪ'fektɪvnəs] *n* : eficacia *f*

effeminate [ə'femənət] *adj* : afeminado

effervescent [,efər'vesənt] *adj* : efervescente

efficient [ɪ'fɪʃənt] *adj* : eficiente — **efficiency** [ɪ'fɪʃəntsi] *n, pl* **-cies** : eficiencia *f*

effort ['efərt] *n* **1** : esfuerzo *m* **2 it's not worth the** ~ : no vale la pena — **effortless** ['efərtləs] *adj* : fácil, sin esfuerzo

egg ['eg] *n* : huevo *m* — ~ *vt* ~ **on** : incitar — **eggplant** ['eg,plænt] *n* : berenjena *f* — **eggshell** ['eg,ʃel] *n* : cascarón *m*

ego ['iːgoː] *n, pl* **egos 1** SELF : ego *m*, yo *m* **2** SELF-ESTEEM : amor *m* propio — **egotism** ['iːgə,tɪzəm] *n* : egotismo *m* — **egotist** ['iːgə,tɪst] *n* : egotista *mf* — **egotistic** [,iːgə'tɪstɪk] *or* **egotistical** [-'tɪstɪkəl] *adj* : egotista

eiderdown ['aɪdər,daʊn] *n* **1** DOWN : plumón *m* **2** COMFORTER : edredón *m*

eight ['eɪt] *n* : ocho *m* — ~ *adj* : ocho — **eight hundred** *n* : ochocientos *m*

eighteen [eɪt'tiːn] *n* : dieciocho *m* — ~ *adj* : dieciocho — **eighteenth** [eɪt'tiːnθ] *adj* : decimoctavo — ~ *n* **1** : decimoctavo *m*, -va *f* (en una serie) **2** : dieciochoavo *m*, dieciochoava parte *f*

eighth ['eɪtθ] *n* **1** : octavo *m*, -va *f* (en una serie) **2** : octavo *m*, octava parte *f* — ~ *adj* : octavo

eighty ['eɪti] *n, pl* **eighties** : ochenta *m* — ~ *adj* : ochenta

either ['iːðər, 'aɪ-] *adj* **1** : cualquiera (de los dos) **2** (*in negative constructions*) : ninguno (de los dos) **3** EACH : cada — ~ *pron* **1** : cualquiera *mf* (de los dos) **2** (*in negative constructions*) : ninguno *m*, -na *f* (de los dos) **3** *or* ~ **one** : algún *m*, alguna *f* — ~ *conj* **1** : o **2** (*in negative constructions*) : ni

eject [ɪ'dʒekt] *vt* : expulsar, expeler

eke ['iːk] *vt* **eked; eking** *or* ~ **out** : ganar a duras penas

elaborate [ɪ'læbərət] *adj* **1** DETAILED : detallado **2** COMPLEX : complicado — ~ [ɪ'læbə,reɪt] *v* **-rated; -rating** *vt* : elaborar — *vi* : entrar en detalles

elapse [ɪ'læps] *vi* **elapsed; elapsing** : transcurrir

elastic [ɪ'læstɪk] *adj* : elástico — ~ *n* **1** : elástico *m* **2** RUBBER BAND : goma *f* (elástica) — **elasticity** [ɪ,læs'tɪsəti, iː,læs-] *n, pl* **-ties** : elasticidad *f*

elated [ɪ'leɪtəd] *adj* : regocijado

elbow ['el,boː] *n* : codo *m*

elder ['eldər] *adj* : mayor — ~ *n* **1** : mayor *mf* **2** : anciano *m*, -na *f* (de un tribu, etc.) — **elderly** ['eldərli] *adj* : mayor, anciano

elect [ɪ'lekt] *vt* : elegir — ~ *adj* : electo — **election** [ɪ'lekʃən] *n* : elección *f* — **electoral** [ɪ'lektərəl] *adj* : electoral — **electorate** [ɪ'lektərət] *n* : electorado *m*

electricity [ɪ,lek'trɪsəti] *n, pl* **-ties** : electricidad *f* — **electric** [ɪ'lektrɪk] *or* **electrical** [-trɪkəl] *adj* : eléctrico — **electrician** [ɪ,lek'trɪʃən] *n* : electricista *mf* — **electrify** [ɪ'lektrə,faɪ] *vt* **-fied; -fying** : electrificar — **electrocute** [ɪ'lektrə,kjuːt] *vt* **-cuted; -cuting** : electrocutar

electron [ɪ'lek,trɑn] *n* : electrón *m* — **electronic** [ɪ,lek'trɑnɪk] *adj* : electrónico — **electronic mail** *n* : correo *m* electrónico — **electronics** [ɪ,lek'trɑnɪks] *n* : electrónica *f*

elegant ['elɪgənt] *adj* : elegante — **elegance** ['elɪgənts] *n* : elegancia *f*

element ['eləmənt] *n* **1** : elemento *m* **2** ~**s** *npl* BASICS : elementos *mpl*, rudimentos *mpl* — **elementary** [,elə'mentri] *adj* : elemental — **elementary school** *n* : escuela *f* primaria

elephant ['eləfənt] *n* : elefante *m*, -ta *f*

elevate ['elə,veɪt] *vt* **-vated; -vating** : elevar — **elevator** ['elə,veɪtər] *n* : ascensor *m*

eleven [ɪ'levən] *n* : once *m* — ~ *adj* : once — **eleventh** [ɪ'levənθ] *adj* : undécimo — ~ *n* **1** : undécimo *m*, -ma *f* (en una serie) **2** : onceavo *m*, onceava parte *f*

elf ['elf] *n, pl* **elves** ['elvz] : duende *m*

elicit [ɪ'lɪsət] *vt* : provocar

eligible ['eləzəbəl] *adj* : elegible

eliminate [ɪ'lɪmə,neɪt] *vt* **-nated; -nating** : eliminar — **elimination** [ɪ,lɪmə'neɪ-ʃən] *n* : eliminación *f*

elite [er'li:t, i-] *n* : elite *f*

elk ['elk] *n* : alce *m* (de Europa), uapití *m* (de América)

elliptical [ɪ'lɪptɪkəl, ε-] *or* **elliptic** [-tɪk] *adj* : elíptico

elm ['elm] *n* : olmo *m*

elongate [ɪ'lɔ,ŋeɪt] *vt* **-gated; -gating** : alargar

elope [ɪ'lo:p] *vi* **eloped; eloping** : fugarse — **elopement** [ɪ'lo:pmənt] *n* : fuga *f*

eloquence ['ɛləkwənts] *n* : elocuencia *f* — **eloquent** ['ɛləkwənt] *adj* : elocuente

else ['els] *adv* **1 how ~ ?** : ¿de qué otro modo? **2 where ~ ?** : ¿en qué otro sitio? **3 or ~** : si no, de lo contrario — **~** *adj* **1 everyone ~** : todos los demás **2 nobody ~** : ningún otro, nadie más **3 nothing ~** : nada más **4 what ~ ?** : ¿qué más? — **elsewhere** ['els,ʰwer] *adv* : en otra parte

elude [ɪ'lu:d] *vt* **eluded; eluding** : eludir, esquivar — **elusive** [ɪ'lu:sɪv] *adj* : esquivo

elves → elf

emaciated [ɪ'meɪʃi,eɪtəd] *adj* : esquálido, demacrado

E—mail ['i:,meɪl] **→ electronic mail**

emanate ['ɛmə,neɪt] *vi* **-nated; -nating** : emanar

emancipate [i'mæntsə,peɪt] *vt* **-pated; -pating** : emancipar — **emancipation** [i,mæntsə'peɪʃən] *n* : emancipación *f*

embalm [ɪm'bɑm, εm-, -'bɑlm] *vt* : embalsamar

embankment [ɪm'bæŋkmənt, εm-] *n* : terraplén *m*, dique *m* (de un río)

embargo [ɪm'bɑrɡo, εm-] *n, pl* **-goes** : embargo *m*

embark [ɪm'bɑrk, εm-] *vt* : embarcar — *vi* **1** : embarcarse **2 ~ upon** : emprender — **embarkation** [,εm,bɑr-'keɪʃən] *n* : embarque *m*, embarco *m*

embarrass [ɪm'bærəs, εm-] *vt* : avergonzar — **embarrassing** [ɪm'bærəsɪŋ, εm-] *adj* : embarazoso — **embarrassment** [ɪm'bærəsmənt, εm-] *n* : vergüenza *f*

embassy ['embəsi] *n, pl* **-sies** : embajada *f*

embed [ɪm'bed, εm-] *vt* **-bedded; -bedding** : incrustar, enterrar

embellish [ɪm'belɪʃ, εm-] *vt* : adornar, embellecer — **embellishment** [ɪm-'belɪʃmənt, εm-] *n* : adorno *m*

embers ['embəz] *npl* : ascuas *fpl*

embezzle [ɪm'bezəl, εm-] *vt* **-zled; -zling** : desfalcar, malversar — **embezzlement** [ɪm'bezəlmənt, εm-] *n* : desfalco *m*, malversación *f*

emblem ['embləm] *n* : emblema *m*

embody [ɪm'bɑdi, εm-] *vt* **-bodied; -bodying** : encarnar, personificar

emboss [ɪm'bɑs, εm-, -'bɔs] *vt* : repujar, grabar en relieve

embrace [ɪm'breɪs, εm-] *v* **-braced; -bracing** *vt* : abrazar — *vi* : abrazarse — **~** *n* : abrazo *m*

embroider [ɪm'brɔɪdər, εm-] *vt* : bordar — **embroidery** [ɪm'brɔɪdəri, εm-] *n, pl* **-deries** : bordado *m*

embryo ['embri,o:] *n, pl* **embryos** : embrión *m*

emerald ['emrəld, 'emə-] *n* : esmeralda *f*

emerge [i'mərʤ] *vi* **emerged; emerging** : salir, aparecer — **emergence** [i'mərʤənts] *n* : aparición *f*

emergency [i'mərʤəntsi] *n, pl* **-cies 1** : emergencia *f* **2 ~ exit** : salida *f* de emergencia **3 ~ room** : sala *f* de urgencias, sala *f* de guardia

emery ['eməri] *n, pl* **-eries 1** : esmeril *m* **2 ~ board** : lima *f* de uñas

emigrant ['emɪɡrənt] *n* : emigrante *mf* — **emigrate** ['emə,ɡreɪt] *vi* **-grated; -grating** : emigrar — **emigration** [,emə'ɡreɪʃən] *n* : emigración *f*

eminence ['emənənts] *n* : eminencia *f* — **eminent** ['emənənt] *adj* : eminente

emission [i'mɪʃən] *n* : emisión *f* — **emit** [i'mɪt] *vt* **emitted; emitting** : emitir

emotion [i'mo:ʃən] *n* : emoción *f* — **emotional** [i'mo:ʃənəl] *adj* **1** : emocional **2** MOVING : emotivo

emperor ['empərər] *n* : emperador *m*

emphasis ['emfəsɪs] *n, pl* **-phases** [-,si:z] : énfasis *m* — **emphasize** ['emfə,saɪz] *vt* **-sized; -sizing** : subrayar, hacer hincapié en — **emphatic** [ɪm-'fætɪk, εm-] *adj* : enérgico, categórico

empire ['em,paɪr] *n* : imperio *m*

employ [ɪm'plɔɪ, εm-] *vt* : emplear — **employee** [ɪm,plɔɪ'i:, εm-, -'plɔɪ,i:] *n* : empleado *m*, -da *f* — **employer** [ɪm-'plɔɪər, εm-] *n* : patrón *m*, -trona *f*; empleador *m*, -dora *f* — **employment** [ɪm'plɔɪmənt, εm-] *n* : trabajo *m*, empleo *m*

empower [ɪm'paʊər, εm-] *vt* : autorizar

empress ['emprəs] *n* : emperatriz *f*

empty ['empti] *adj* **emptier; -est 1** : vacío **2** MEANINGLESS : vano — **~** *v*

-tied; -tying vt : vaciar — vi : vaciarse — **emptiness** ['emptinǝs] n : vacío m

emulate ['emjǝ,leɪt] vt **-lated; -lating** : emular

enable [ɪ'neɪbǝl, ɛ-] vt **-abled; -abling** : hacer posible, permitir

enact [ɪ'nækt, ɛ-] vt **1** : promulgar (un ley o un decreto) **2** PERFORM : representar

enamel [ɪ'næmǝl] n : esmalte m

encampment [ɪn'kæmpmǝnt, ɛn-] n : campamento m

encase [ɪn'keɪs, ɛn-] vt **-cased; -casing** : encerrar, revestir

enchant [ɪn'tʃænt, ɛn-] vt : encantar — **enchanting** [ɪn'tʃæntɪŋ, ɛn-] adj : encantador — **enchantment** [ɪn'tʃæntmǝnt, ɛn-] n : encanto m

encircle [ɪn'sǝrkǝl, ɛn-] vt **-cled; -cling** : rodear

enclose [ɪn'kloːz, ɛn-] vt **-closed; -closing 1** SURROUND : encerrar, cercar **2** INCLUDE : adjuntar (a una carta) — **enclosure** [ɪn'kloːʒǝr, ɛn-] n **1** AREA : recinto m **2** : anexo m (con una carta)

encompass [ɪn'kʌmpǝs, ɛn-, -kɑm-] vt **1** ENCIRCLE : cercar **2** INCLUDE : abarcar

encore ['ɑn,kor] n : bis m

encounter [ɪn'kauntǝr, ɛn-] vt : encontrar — ~ n : encuentro m

encourage [ɪn'kǝrɪdʒ, ɛn-] vt **-aged; -aging 1** : animar, alentar **2** FOSTER : promover, fomentar — **encouragement** [ɪn'kǝrɪdʒmǝnt, ɛn-] n **1** : aliento m **2** PROMOTION : fomento m

encroach [ɪn'kroːtʃ, ɛn-] vi ~ **on** : invadir, usurpar, quitar (el tiempo)

encyclopedia [ɪn,saɪklǝ'piːdiǝ, ɛn-] n : enciclopedia f

end ['end] n **1** : fin **2** EXTREMITY : extremo m, punta f **3 come to an** ~ : llegar a su fin **4 in the** ~ : por fin — ~ vt : terminar, poner fin a — vi : terminar(se)

endanger [ɪn'deɪndʒǝr, ɛn-] vt : poner en peligro

endearing [ɪn'dɪrɪŋ, ɛn-] adj : simpático

endeavor or Brit **endeavour** [ɪn'devǝr, ɛn-] vt ~ **to** : esforzarse por — ~ n : esfuerzo m

ending ['endɪŋ] n : final m, desenlace m

endive ['en,daɪv, 'ɑn,diːv] n : endibia f, endivia f

endless ['endlǝs] adj **1** INTERMINABLE : interminable **2** INNUMERABLE : innumerable **3** ~ **possibilities** : posibilidades fpl infinitas

endorse [ɪn'dors, ɛn-] vt **-dorsed; -dorsing 1** SIGN : endosar **2** APPROVE

: aprobar — **endorsement** [ɪn'dorsmǝnt, ɛn-] n APPROVAL : aprobación f

endow [ɪn'dau, ɛn-] vt : dotar

endure [ɪn'dur, ɛn-, -'djur] v **-dured; -during** vt : soportar, aguantar — vi LAST : durar — **endurance** [ɪn'durǝnts, ɛn-, -'djur-] n : resistencia f

enemy ['enǝmi] n, pl **-mies** : enemigo m, -ga f

energy ['enǝrdʒi] n, pl **-gies** : energía f — **energetic** [,enǝr'dʒetɪk] adj : enérgico

enforce [ɪn'fors, ɛn-] vt **-forced; -forcing 1** : hacer cumplir (un ley, etc.) **2** IMPOSE : imponer — **enforced** adj : forzoso — **enforcement** [ɪn'forsmǝnt, ɛn-] n : imposición f del cumplimiento

engage [ɪn'geɪdʒ, ɛn-] v **-gaged; -gaging** vt **1** : captar, atraer (la atención, etc.) **2** ~ **the clutch** : embragar — vi ~ **in** : dedicarse a, entrar en — **engagement** [ɪn'geɪdʒmǝnt, ɛn-] n **1** APPOINTMENT : cita f, hora f **2** BETROTHAL : compromiso m — **engaging** [ɪn'geɪdʒɪŋ, ɛn-] adj : atractivo

engine ['endʒǝn] n **1** : motor m **2** LOCOMOTIVE : locomotora f — **engineer** [,endʒǝ'nɪr] n **1** : ingeniero m, -ra f **2** : maquinista mf (de locomotoras) — ~ vt **1** CONSTRUCT : construir **2** CONTRIVE : tramar — **engineering** [,endʒǝ'nɪrɪŋ] n : ingeniería f

English ['ɪŋglɪʃ, 'ɪŋlɪʃ] adj : inglés — ~ n : inglés m (idioma) — **Englishman** ['ɪŋglɪʃmǝn, 'ɪŋlɪʃ-] n : inglés m — **Englishwoman** ['ɪŋglɪʃ,wumǝn, 'ɪŋlɪʃ-] n : inglesa f

engrave [ɪn'greɪv, ɛn-] vt **-graved; -graving** : grabar — **engraving** [ɪn'greɪvɪŋ, ɛn-] n : grabado m

engross [ɪn'groːs, ɛn-] vt : absorber

engulf [ɪn'gʌlf, ɛn-] vt : envolver

enhance [ɪn'hænts, ɛn-] vt **-hanced; -hancing** : aumentar, mejorar

enjoy [ɪn'dʒoɪ, ɛn-] vt **1** : disfrutar, gozar de **2** ~ **oneself** : divertirse — **enjoyable** [ɪn'dʒoɪǝbǝl, ɛn-] adj : agradable — **enjoyment** [ɪn'dʒoɪmǝnt, ɛn-] n : placer m

enlarge [ɪn'lɑrdʒ, ɛn-] v **-larged; -larging** vt : agrandar, ampliar — vi **1** : agrandarse **2** ~ **upon** : extenderse sobre — **enlargement** [ɪn'lɑrdʒmǝnt, ɛn-] n : ampliación f

enlighten [ɪn'laɪtǝn, ɛn-] vt : aclarar, iluminar

enlist [ɪn'lɪst, ɛn-] vt **1** ENROLL : alistar **2** OBTAIN : conseguir — vi : alistarse

enliven [ɪn'laɪvǝn, ɛn-] vt : animar

enmity ['ɛnməti] *n, pl* **-ties** : enemistad *f*

enormous [ɪ'nɔrməs] *adj* : enorme

enough [ɪ'nʌf] *adj* : bastante, suficiente — ~ *adv* : bastante — ~ *pron* **1** : (lo) suficiente, (lo) bastante **2 it's not ~** : no basta **3 I've had ~** ! : ¡estoy harto!

enquire [ɪn'kwaɪr, ɛn-], **enquiry** ['ɪn,kwaɪri, 'ɛn-, -kwəri; ɪn'kwaɪri, ɛn'-] → **inquire, inquiry**

enrage [ɪn'reɪdʒ, ɛn-] *vt* **-raged; -raging** : enfurecer

enrich [ɪn'rɪtʃ, ɛn-] *vt* : enriquecer

enroll *or* **enrol** [ɪn'roːl, ɛn-] *v* **-rolled; -rolling** *vt* : matricular, inscribir — *vi* : matricularse, inscribirse

ensemble [ɑn'sɑmbəl] *n* : conjunto *m*

ensign ['ɛntsən, 'ɛn,saɪn] *n* **1** FLAG : enseña *f* **2** : alférez *mf* (de fragata)

enslave [ɪn'sleɪv, ɛn-] *vt* **-slaved; -slaving** : esclavizar

ensue [ɪn'suː, ɛn-] *vi* **-sued; -suing** : seguir, resultar

ensure [ɪn'ʃʊr, ɛn-] *vt* **-sured; -suring** : asegurar

entail [ɪn'teɪl, ɛn-] *vt* : suponer, conllevar

entangle [ɪn'tæŋɡəl, ɛn-] *vt* **-gled; -gling** : enredar — **entanglement** [ɪn'tæŋɡəlmənt, ɛn-] *n* : enredo *m*

enter ['ɛntər] *vt* **1** : entrar en **2** RECORD : inscribir — *vi* **1** : entrar **2 ~ into** : firmar (un acuerdo), entablar (negociaciones, etc.)

enterprise ['ɛntər,praɪz] *n* **1** : empresa *f* **2** INITIATIVE : iniciativa *f* — **enterprising** ['ɛntər,praɪzɪŋ] *adj* : emprendedor

entertain [,ɛntər'teɪn] *vt* **1** AMUSE : entretener, divertir **2** CONSIDER : considerar **3 ~ guests** : recibir invitados — **entertainment** [,ɛntər'teɪnmənt] *n* : entretenimiento *m*, diversión *f*

enthrall *or* **enthral** [ɪn'θrɔl, ɛn-] *vt* **-thralled; -thralling** : cautivar, embelesar

enthusiasm [ɪn'θuːzi,æzəm, ɛn-, -'θjuː-] *n* : entusiasmo *m* — **enthusiast** [ɪn'θuːzi,æst, ɛn-, -'θjuː-, -əst] *n* : entusiasta *mf* — **enthusiastic** [ɪn,θuːzi'æstɪk, ɛn-, -θjuː-] *adj* : entusiasta

entice [ɪn'taɪs, ɛn-] *vt* **-ticed; -ticing** : atraer, tentar

entire [ɪn'taɪr, ɛn-] *adj* : entero, completo — **entirely** [ɪn'taɪrli, ɛn-] *adv* : completamente — **entirety** [ɪn'taɪrti, ɛn-, -'taɪrti] *n, pl* **-ties** : totalidad *f*

entitle [ɪn'taɪtəl, ɛn-] *vt* **-tled; -tling 1** NAME : titular **2** AUTHORIZE : dar derecho a — **entitlement** [ɪn'taɪtəlmənt, ɛn-] *n* : derecho *m*

entity ['ɛntəti] *n, pl* **-ties** : entidad *f*

entrails ['ɛn,treɪlz, -trəlz] *npl* : entrañas *fpl*, vísceras *fpl*

entrance[1] [ɪn'trænts, ɛn-] *vt* **-tranced; -trancing** : encantar, fascinar

entrance[2] ['ɛntrənts] *n* : entrada *f* — **entrant** ['ɛntrənt] *n* : participante *mf*

entreat [ɪn'triːt, ɛn-] *vt* : suplicar

entrée *or* **entree** ['ɑn,treɪ, 'ɑn'-] *n* : plato *m* principal

entrepreneur [,ɑntrəprə'nər, -'njʊr] *n* : empresario *m*, -ria *f*

entrust [ɪn'trʌst, ɛn-] *vt* : confiar

entry ['ɛntri] *n, pl* **-tries 1** ENTRANCE : entrada *f* **2** NOTATION : entrada *f*, anotación *f*

enumerate [ɪ'nuːmə,reɪt, ɛ-, -'njuː-] *vt* **-ated; -ating** : enumerar

enunciate [ɪ'nʌntsi,eɪt, ɛ-] *vt* **-ated; -ating 1** STATE : enunciar **2** PRONOUNCE : articular

envelop [ɪn'vɛləp, ɛn-] *vt* : envolver — **envelope** ['ɛnvə,loːp, 'ɑn-] *n* : sobre *m*

envious ['ɛnviəs] *adj* : envidioso — **enviously** *adv* : con envidia

environment [ɪn'vaɪrənmənt, ɛn-, -'vaɪərn-] *n* : medio *m* ambiente — **environmental** [ɪn,vaɪrən'mɛntəl, ɛn-, -,vaɪərn-] *adj* : ambiental — **environmentalist** [ɪn,vaɪrən'mɛntəlɪst, ɛn-, -,vaɪərn-] *n* : ecologista *mf*

envision [ɪn'vɪʒən, ɛn-] *vt* : prever, imaginar

envoy ['ɛn,vɔɪ, 'ɑn-] *n* : enviado *m*, -da *f*

envy ['ɛnvi] *n, pl* **envies** : envidia *f* — ~ *vt* **-vied; -vying** : envidiar

enzyme ['ɛn,zaɪm] *n* : enzima *f*

epic ['ɛpɪk] *adj* : épico — ~ *n* : epopeya *f*

epidemic [,ɛpə'dɛmɪk] *n* : epidemia *f* — ~ *adj* : epidémico

epilepsy ['ɛpə,lɛpsi] *n, pl* **-sies** : epilepsia *f* — **epileptic** [,ɛpə'lɛptɪk] *adj* : epiléptico — ~ *n* : epiléptico *m*, -ca *f*

episode ['ɛpə,soːd] *n* : episodio *m*

epitaph ['ɛpə,tæf] *n* : epitafio *m*

epitome [ɪ'pɪtəmi] *n* : personificación *f* — **epitomize** [ɪ'pɪtə,maɪz] *vt* **-mized; -mizing** : ser la personificación de, personificar

epoch ['ɛpək, 'ɛ,pɑk, 'iː,pɑk] *n* : época *f*

equal ['iːkwəl] *adj* **1** SAME : igual **2 be ~ to** : estar a la altura de (una tarea, etc.) — ~ *n* : igual *mf* — ~ *vt* **equaled** *or* **equalled; equaling** *or* **equalling 1** : igualar **2** : ser igual a (en matemáticas) — **equality** [ɪ'kwɑləti] *n, pl* **-ties** : igualdad *f* — **equalize** ['iːkwə,laɪz] *vt* **-ized; -izing** : igualar — **equally** ['iːkwəli] *adv* **1** : igualmente 2 ~ **important** : igual de importante

equate [ɪ'kweɪt] vt **equated; equating** ~ **with** : equiparar con — **equation** [ɪ'kweɪʒən] n : ecuación f

equator [ɪ'kweɪt̬ər] n : ecuador m

equilibrium [,i:kwə'lɪbriəm, ,ɛ-] n, pl **-riums** or **-ria** [-briə] : equilibrio m

equinox ['i:kwə,nɑks, 'ɛ-] n : equinoccio m

equip [ɪ'kwɪp] vt **equipped; equipping** : equipar — **equipment** [ɪ'kwɪpmənt] n : equipo m

equity ['ɛkwəti] n, pl **-ties 1** FAIRNESS : equidad f **2 equities** npl STOCKS : acciones fpl ordinarias

equivalent [ɪ'kwɪvələnt] adj : equivalente — ~ n : equivalente m

era ['ɪrə, 'ɛrə, 'i:rə] n : era f, época f

eradicate [ɪ'rædə,keɪt] vt **-cated; -cating** : erradicar

erase [ɪ'reɪs] vt **erased; erasing** : borrar — **eraser** [ɪ'reɪsər] n : goma f de borrar, borrador m

erect [ɪ'rɛkt] adj : erguido — ~ vt : erigir, levantar — **erection** [ɪ'rɛkʃən] n **1** BUILDING : construcción f **2** : erección f (en fisiología)

erode [ɪ'roːd] vt **eroded; eroding** : erosionar (el suelo), corroer (metales) — **erosion** [ɪ'roːʒən] n : erosión f, corrosión f

erotic [ɪ'rɑt̬ɪk] adj : erótico

err ['ɛr, 'ər] vi : equivocarse, errar

errand ['ɛrənd] n : mandado m, recado m Spain

erratic [ɪ'ræt̬ɪk] adj : errático, irregular

error ['ɛrər] n : error m — **erroneous** [ɪ'roːniəs, ɛ-] adj : erróneo

erupt [ɪ'rʌpt] vi **1** : hacer erupción (dícese de un volcán) **2** : estallar (dícese de la cólera, la violencia, etc.) — **eruption** [ɪ'rʌpʃən] n : erupción f

escalate ['ɛskə,leɪt] vi **-lated; -lating** : intensificarse

escalator ['ɛskə,leɪt̬ər] n : escalera f mecánica

escapade ['ɛskə,peɪd] n : aventura f

escape [ɪ'skeɪp, ɛ-] v **-caped; -caping** vt : escapar a, evitar — vi : escaparse, fugarse — ~ n **1** : fuga f **2** ~ **from reality** : evasión f de la realidad — **escapee** [ɪ,skeɪ'piː, ,ɛ-] n : fugitivo m, -va f

escort ['ɛs,kɔrt] n **1** GUARD : escolta f **2** COMPANION : acompañante mf — ~ [ɪ'skɔrt, ɛ-] vt **1** : escoltar **2** ACCOMPANY : acompañar

Eskimo ['ɛskə,moː] adj : esquimal

especially [ɪ'spɛʃəli] adv : especialmente

espionage ['ɛspiə,nɑʒ, -,nɑdʒ] n : espionaje m

espresso [ɛ'sprɛ,soː] n, pl **-sos** : café m exprés

essay ['ɛ,seɪ] n : ensayo m (literario), composición f (académica)

essence ['ɛsənts] n : esencia f — **essential** [ɪ'sɛntʃəl] adj : esencial — ~ n **1** : elemento m esencial **2 the ~s** : lo indispensable

establish [ɪ'stæblɪʃ, ɛ-] vt : establecer — **establishment** [ɪ'stæblɪʃmənt, ɛ-] n : establecimiento m

estate [ɪ'steɪt, ɛ-] n **1** POSSESSIONS : bienes mpl **2** LAND, PROPERTY : finca f

esteem [ɪ'sti:m, ɛ-] n : estima f — ~ vt : estimar

esthetic [ɛs'θɛt̬ɪk] → **aesthetic**

estimate ['ɛstə,meɪt] vt **-mated; -mating** : calcular, estimar — ~ ['ɛstəmət] n **1** : cálculo m (aproximado) **2** or ~ **of costs** : presupuesto m — **estimation** [,ɛstə'meɪʃən] n **1** JUDGMENT : juicio m **2** ESTEEM : estima f

estuary ['ɛstʃu,weri] n, pl **-aries** : estuario m, ría f

eternal [ɪ'tərnəl, iː-] adj : eterno — **eternity** [ɪ'tərnəti, iː-] n, pl **-ties** : eternidad f

ether ['iːθər] n : éter m

ethical ['ɛθɪkəl] adj : ético — **ethics** ['ɛθɪks] ns & pl : ética f, moralidad f

ethnic ['ɛθnɪk] adj : étnico

etiquette ['ɛt̬ɪkət, -,kɛt] n : etiqueta f

Eucharist ['juːkərɪst] n : Eucaristía f

eulogy ['juːlədʒi] n, pl **-gies** : elogio m, panegírico m

euphemism ['juːfə,mɪzəm] n : eufemismo m

euphoria [ju'foriə] n : euforia f

European [,jurə'piːən, -,piːn] adj : europeo

evacuate [ɪ'vækju,eɪt] vt **-ated; -ating** : evacuar — **evacuation** [ɪ,vækju-'eɪʃən] n : evacuación f

evade [ɪ'veɪd] vt **evaded; evading** : evadir, eludir

evaluate [ɪ'vælju,eɪt] vt **-ated; -ating** : evaluar

evaporate [ɪ'væpə,reɪt] vi **-rated; -rating** : evaporarse

evasion [ɪ'veɪʒən] n : evasión f — **evasive** [ɪ'veɪsɪv] adj : evasivo

eve ['iːv] n : víspera f

even ['iːvən] adj **1** REGULAR, STEADY : regular, constante **2** LEVEL : plano, llano **3** SMOOTH : liso **4** EQUAL : igual **5** ~ **number** : número m par **6 get ~ with** : desquitarse con — ~ adv **1** : hasta, incluso **2** ~ **better** : aún

mejor, todavía mejor **3 ~ if** : aunque
4 ~ so : aun así **— ~** vt : igualar —
vi or **out** : nivelarse

evening ['i:vnɪŋ] n : tarde f, noche f

event [ɪ'vɛnt] n **1** : acontecimiento m,
suceso m **2** : prueba f (en deportes) **3**
in the ~ of : en caso de — **eventful**
[ɪ'vɛntfəl] adj : lleno de incidentes

eventual [ɪ'vɛntʃʊəl] adj : final — **even-**
tuality [ɪ,vɛntʃʊ'æləti] n, pl **-ties**
: eventualidad f — **eventually** [ɪ-
'vɛntʃʊəli] adv : al fin, finalmente

ever ['ɛvər] adv **1** ALWAYS : siempre **2 ~**
since : desde entonces **3 hardly ~**
: casi nunca **4 have you ~** done it?
: ¿lo has hecho alguna vez?

evergreen ['ɛvər,ɡriːn] n : planta f de
hoja perenne

everlasting [,ɛvər'læstɪŋ] adj : eterno

every ['ɛvri] adj **1** EACH : cada **2 ~**
month : todos los meses **3 ~ other**
day : cada dos días — **everybody**
['ɛvri,bʌdi, -,ba-] pron : todos mpl, -das
fpl; todo el mundo — **everyday** [,ɛvri-
'deɪ, 'ɛvri,-] adj : cotidiano, de todos los
días — **everyone** ['ɛvri,wʌn] → **every-**
body — **everything** ['ɛvri θɪŋ] pron
: todo — **everywhere** ['ɛvri ,hwɛr] adv
: en todas partes, por todas partes

evict [ɪ'vɪkt] vt : desahuciar, desalojar —
eviction [ɪ'vɪkʃən] n : desahucio m

evidence ['ɛvədənts] n **1** PROOF : prue-
bas fpl **2** TESTIMONY : testimonio m,
declaración f — **evident** ['ɛvidənt] adj
: evidente — **evidently** ['ɛvidəntli, ,ɛvi-
'dɛntli] adv **1** OBVIOUSLY : obviamente
2 APPARENTLY : evidentemente, al
parecer

evil ['i:vəl, -vɪl] adj **eviler** or **eviller**;
evilest or **evillest** : malvado, malo —
~ n : mal m, maldad f

evoke [ɪ'voːk] vt **evoked; evoking**
: evocar

evolution [,ɛvə'luːʃən, ,iː-] n : evolución
f, desarrollo m — **evolve** [ɪ'vɑlv] vi
evolved; evolving : evolucionar, desarrollarse

exact [ɪɡ'zækt, ɛɡ-] adj : exacto, preciso
— ~ vt : exigir — **exacting** [ɪɡ-
'zæktɪŋ, ɛɡ-] adj : exigente — **exactly**
[ɪɡ'zæktli, ɛɡ-] adv : exactamente

exaggerate [ɪɡ'zædʒə,reɪt, ɛɡ-] v **-ated;**
-ating : exagerar — **exaggeration** [ɪɡ-
,zædʒə'reɪʃən, ɛɡ-] n : exageración f

examine [ɪɡ'zæmən, ɛɡ-] vt **-ined;**
-ining 1 : examinar **2** INSPECT : revisar
3 QUESTION : interrogar — **exam** [ɪɡ-
'zæm, ɛɡ-] n : examen m — **examina-**
tion [ɪɡ,zæmə'neɪʃən, ɛɡ-] n : examen
m

example [ɪɡ'zæmpəl, ɛɡ-] n : ejemplo m

exasperate [ɪɡ'zæspə,reɪt, ɛɡ-] vt **-ated;**
-ating : exasperar — **exasperation**
[ɪɡ,zæspə'reɪʃən, ɛɡ-] n : exasperación f

excavate ['ɛkskə,veɪt] vt **-vated; -vating**
: excavar — **excavation** [,ɛkskə'veɪʃən]
n : excavación f

exceed [ɪk'siːd, ɛk-] vt : exceder, sobrepasar — **exceedingly** [ɪk'siːdɪŋli,
ɛk-] adv : extremadamente

excel [ɪk'sɛl, ɛk-] v **-celled; -celling** vi
: sobresalir — vt SURPASS : superar —
excellence ['ɛksələnts] n : excelencia f
— **excellent** ['ɛksələnt] adj : excelente

except [ɪk'sɛpt] prep or **for** : excepto, menos, salvo — **~** vt : exceptuar
— **exception** [ɪk'sɛpʃən] n : excepción
f — **exceptional** [ɪk'sɛpʃənəl] adj : excepcional

excerpt ['ɛk,sərpt, 'ɛɡ,zərpt] n : extracto
m

excess [ɪk'sɛs, 'ɛk,sɛs] n : exceso m —
~ ['ɛk,sɛs, ɪk'sɛs] adj : excesivo, de
sobra — **excessive** [ɪk'sɛsɪv, ɛk-] adj
: excesivo

exchange [ɪks'tʃeɪndʒ, ɛks-; 'ɛks,tʃeɪndʒ]
n **1** : intercambio m **2** : cambio m (en
finanzas) — **~** vt **-changed; -chang-**
ing : cambiar, intercambiar

excise ['ɛk,saɪz, ɛk-] n **~ tax** : impuesto
m interno, impuesto m sobre el con-
sumo

excite [ɪk'saɪt, ɛk-] vt **-cited; -citing**
: excitar, emocionar — **excited** [ɪk-
'saɪtəd, ɛk-] adj : excitado, entusias-
mado — **excitement** [ɪk'saɪtmənt, ɛk-]
n : entusiasmo m, emoción f

exclaim [ɪks'kleɪm, ɛks-] v : exclamar —
exclamation [,ɛksklə'meɪʃən] n : exclamación f — **exclamation point** n
: signo m de admiración

exclude [ɪks'kluːd, ɛks-] vt **-cluded;**
-cluding : excluir — **excluding** [ɪks-
'kluːdɪŋ, ɛks-] prep : excepto, con excepción de — **exclusion** [ɪks'kluːʒən,
ɛks-] n : exclusión f — **exclusive** [ɪks-
'kluːsɪv, ɛks-] adj : exclusivo

excrement ['ɛkskrəmənt] n : excremento m

excruciating [ɪk'skruːʃi,eɪtɪŋ, ɛk-] adj
: insoportable, atroz

excursion [ɪk'skərʒən, ɛk-] n : excursión f

excuse [ɪk'skjuːz, ɛk-] vt **-cused;**
-cusing 1 : perdonar **2 ~ me**
: perdóne, perdón — **~** [ɪk'skjuːs, ɛk-]
n : excusa f

execute ['ɛksɪ,kjuːt] vt **-cuted; -cuting**
1 : ejecutar — **execution** [,ɛksɪ'kjuːʃən] n
: ejecución f — **executioner** [,ɛksɪ-
'kjuːʃənər] n : verdugo m

executive [ɪgˈzɛkjə̣tɪv, ɛg-] *adj* : ejecutivo — ~ *n* **1** MANAGER : ejecutivo *m*, -va *f* **2** *or* ~ **branch** : poder *m* ejecutivo

exemplify [ɪgˈzɛmpləˌfaɪ, ɛg-] *vt* **-fied; -fying** : ejemplificar — **exemplary** [ɪgˈzɛmpləri, ɛg-] *adj* : ejemplar

exempt [ɪgˈzɛmpt, ɛg-] *adj* : exento — ~ *vt* : dispensar — **exemption** [ɪgˈzɛmpʃən, eg-] *n* : exención *f*

exercise [ˈɛksərˌsaɪz] *n* : ejercicio *m* — ~ *v* **-cised; -cising** *vt* USE : ejercer, hacer uso de — *vi* : hacer ejercicio

exert [ɪgˈzərt, ɛg-] *vt* **1** : ejercer **2** ~ **oneself** : esforzarse — **exertion** [ɪgˈzərʃən, ɛg-] *n* : esfuerzo *m*

exhale [ɛksˈheɪl] *v* **-haled; -haling** : exhalar

exhaust [ɪgˈzɔst, ɛg-] *vt* : agotar — ~ *n* **1** *or* ~ **fumes** : gases *mpl* de escape **2** *or* ~ **pipe** : tubo *m* de escape — **exhaustion** [ɪgˈzɔstʃən, ɛg-] *n* : agotamiento *m* — **exhaustive** [ɪgˈzɔstɪv, ɛg-] *adj* : exhaustivo

exhibit [ɪgˈzɪbət, ɛg-] *vt* **1** DISPLAY : exponer **2** SHOW : mostrar — ~ *n* **1** : objeto *m* expuesto **2** EXHIBITION : exposición *f* — **exhibition** [ˌɛksəˈbɪʃən] *n* : exposición *f*

exhilarate [ɪgˈzɪləˌreɪt, ɛg-] *vt* **-rated; -rating** : alegrar — **exhilaration** [ɪgˌzɪləˈreɪʃən, ɛg-] *n* : regocijo *m*

exile [ˈɛgˌzaɪl, ˈɛksˌaɪl] *n* **1** : exilio *m* **2** OUTCAST : exiliado *m*, -da *f* — ~ *vt* **exiled; exiling** : exiliar

exist [ɪgˈzɪst, ɛg-] *vi* : existir — **existence** [ɪgˈzɪstənts, ɛg-] *n* : existencia *f* — **existing** *adj* : existente

exit [ˈɛgzət, ˈɛksət] *n* : salida *f* — ~ *vi* : salir

exodus [ˈɛksədəs] *n* : éxodo *m*

exonerate [ɪgˈzɑnəˌreɪt, ɛg-] *vt* **-ated; -ating** : exonerar, disculpar

exorbitant [ɪgˈzɔrbətənt, ɛg-] *adj* : exorbitante, excesivo

exotic [ɪgˈzɑtɪk, ɛg-] *adj* : exótico

expand [ɪkˈspænd, ɛk-] *vt* **1** : ampliar, extender **2** : dilatar (metales, etc.) — *vi* **1** : ampliarse, extenderse **2** : dilatarse (dícese de metales, etc.) — **expanse** [ɪkˈspænts, ɛk-] *n* : extensión *f* — **expansion** [ɪkˈspæntʃən, ɛk-] *n* : expansión *f*

expatriate [ɛksˈpeɪtriət, -ˌeɪt] *n* : expatriado *m*, -da *f* — ~ *adj* : expatriado

expect [ɪkˈspɛkt, ɛk-] *vt* **1** : esperar **2** REQUIRE : contar con — *vi* **be expecting** : estar embarazada — **expectancy** [ɪkˈspɛktəntsi, ɛk-] *n, pl* **-cies** : esperanza *f* — **expectant** [ɪkˈspɛktənt, ɛk-] *adj* **1**

: expectante **2** ~ **mother** : futura madre *f* — **expectation** [ˌɛkspɛkˈteɪʃən] *n* : esperanza *f*

expedient [ɪkˈspiːdiənt, ɛk-] *adj* : conveniente — ~ *n* : expediente *m*, recurso *m*

expedition [ˌɛkspəˈdɪʃən] *n* : expedición *f*

expel [ɪkˈspɛl, ɛk-] *vt* **-pelled; -pelling** : expulsar (a una persona), expeler (humo, etc.)

expend [ɪkˈspɛnd, ɛk-] *vt* : gastar — **expendable** [ɪkˈspɛndəbəl, ɛk-] *adj* : prescindible — **expenditure** [ɪkˈspɛndɪtʃər, ɛk-, -ˌtʃʊr] *n* : gasto *m* — **expense** [ɪkˈspɛnts, ɛk-] *n* **1** : gasto *m* **2** ~ **s** *npl* : gastos *mpl*, expensas *fpl* **3** **at the** ~ **of** : a expensas de — **expensive** [ɪkˈspɛntsɪv, ɛk-] *adj* : caro

experience [ɪkˈspɪriənts, ɛk-] *n* : experiencia *f* — ~ *vt* **-enced; -encing** : experimentar — **experienced** [ɪkˈspɪriəntst, ɛk-] *adj* : experimentado — **experiment** [ɪkˈspɛrəmənt, ɛk-, -ˌspɪr-] *n* : experimento *m* — ~ *vi* : experimentar — **experimental** [ɪkˌspɛrəˈmɛntəl, ɛk-, -ˌspɪr-] *adj* : experimental

expert [ˈɛkˌspərt, ɪkˈspərt] *adj* : experto — ~ [ˈɛkˌspərt] *n* : experto *m*, -ta *f* — **expertise** [ˌɛkspərˈtiːz] *n* : pericia *f*, competencia *f*

expire [ɪkˈspaɪr, ɛk-] *vi* **-pired; -piring 1** : caducar, vencer **2** DIE : expirar, morir — **expiration** [ˌɛkspəˈreɪʃən] *n* : vencimiento *m*, caducidad *f*

explain [ɪkˈspleɪn, ɛk-] *vt* : explicar — **explanation** [ˌɛkspləˈneɪʃən] *n* : explicación *f* — **explanatory** [ɪkˈsplænəˌtori, ɛk-] *adj* : explicativo

explicit [ɪkˈsplɪsət, ɛk-] *adj* : explícito

explode [ɪkˈsploːd, ɛk-] *v* **-ploded; -ploding** *vt* : hacer explotar — *vi* : explotar, estallar

exploit [ˈɛkˌsplɔɪt] *n* : hazaña *f*, proeza *f* — ~ [ɪkˈsplɔɪt, ɛk-] *vt* : explotar — **exploitation** [ˌɛksplɔɪˈteɪʃən] *n* : explotación *f*

exploration [ˌɛkspləˈreɪʃən] *n* : exploración *f* — **explore** [ɪkˈsplor, ɛk-] *vt* **-plored; -ploring** : explorar — **explorer** [ɪkˈsplorər, ɛk-] *n* : explorador *m*, -dora *f*

explosion [ɪkˈsploːʒən, ɛk-] *n* : explosión *f* — **explosive** [ɪkˈsploːsɪv, ɛk-] *adj* : explosivo — ~ *n* : explosivo *m*

export [ˈɛkˌsport, ˈɛkˌsport] *vt* : exportar — ~ [ˈɛkˌsport] *n* : exportación *f*

expose [ɪkˈspoːz, ɛk-] *vt* **-posed; -posing 1** : exponer **2** REVEAL : descubrir, revelar — **exposed** [ɪkˈspoːzd, ɛk-] *adj*

express [ɪk'spres, ek-] *adj* **1** SPECIFIC
: expreso, específico **2** FAST : expreso,
rápido — ~ *adv* : por correo urgente
— ~ *n or* ~ **train** : expreso *m* — ~
vt : expresar — **expression** [ɪk-
'spreʃən, ek-] *n* : expresión *f* — **expressive** [ɪk'spresɪv, ek-] *adj* : expresivo — **expressly** [ɪk'spresli, ek-] *adv*
: expresamente — **expressway** [ɪk-
'spres,weɪ, ek-] *n* : autopista *f*
expulsion [ɪk'spʌlʃən, ek-] *n* : expulsión
f
exquisite [ek'skwɪzət, 'ek,skwɪ-] *adj* : exquisito
extend [ɪk'stend, ek-] *vt* **1** STRETCH : extender **2** LENGTHEN : prolongar **3** EN-
LARGE : ampliar **4** ~ **one's hand**
: tender la mano — *vi* : extenderse —
extension [ɪk'stentʃən, ek-] *n* **1** : extensión *f* **2** LENGTHENING : prolongación *f* **3** ANNEX : ampliación *f*, anexo
m **4** ~ **cord** : alargador *m* — **extensive** [ɪk'stentsɪv, ek-] *adj* : extenso —
extent [ɪk'stent, ek-] *n* **1** SIZE : extensión *f* **2** DEGREE : alcance *m*, grado *m* **3**
to a certain ~ : hasta cierto punto
extenuating [ɪk'stenjə,weɪtɪŋ, ek-] *adj*
~ **circumstances** : circunstancias
fpl atenuantes
exterior [ek'stɪriər] *adj* : exterior — ~ *n*
: exterior *m*
exterminate [ɪk'stərmə,neɪt, ek-] *vt*
-nated; -nating : exterminar — **extermination** [ɪk,stərmə'neɪʃən, ek-] *n* : exterminación *f*
external [ɪk'stərnəl, ek-] *adj* : externo —
externally [ɪk'stərnəli, ek-] *adv* : exteriormente
extinct [ɪk'stɪŋkt, ek-] *adj* : extinto —
extinction [ɪk'stɪŋkʃən, ek-] *n* : extinción *f*
extinguish [ɪk'stɪŋgwɪʃ, ek-] *vt* : extinguir, apagar — **extinguisher** [ɪk-
'stɪŋgwɪʃər, ek-] *n* : extintor *m*
extol [ɪk'stoʊl, ek-] *vt* **-tolled; -tolling**
: ensalzar, alabar
extort [ɪk'stort, ek-] *vt* : arrancar (algo a
algn) por la fuerza — **extortion** [ɪk-
'storʃən, ek-] *n* : extorsión *f*
extra ['ekstrə] *adj* : suplementario, de

más — ~ *n* : extra *m* — ~ *adv* **1**
: extra, más **2** ~ **special** : super especial
extract [ɪk'strækt, ek-] *vt* : extraer, sacar
— ~ ['ek,strækt] *n* : extracto *m* — **extraction** [ɪk'strækʃən, ek-] *n* : extracción *f*
extracurricular [,ekstrəkə'rɪkjələr] *adj*
: extracurricular
extradite ['ekstrə,daɪt] *vt* **-dited; -diting**
: extraditar
extraordinary [ɪk'strordən,eri, ,ekstrə-
'ord-] *adj* : extraordinario
extraterrestrial [,ekstrətə'restriəl] *adj*
: extraterrestre — ~ *n* : extraterrestre
mf
extravagant [ɪk'strævɪgənt, ek-] *adj* **1**
WASTEFUL : despilfarrador, derrocha-
dor **2** EXAGGERATED : extravagante,
exagerado — **extravagance** [ɪk-
'strævɪgənts, ek-] *n* **1** WASTEFULNESS
: derroche *m*, despilfarro *m* **2** LUXURY
: lujo *m* **3** EXAGGERATION : extravagancia *f*
extreme [ɪk'strim, ek-] *adj* : extremo —
~ *n* : extremo *m* — **extremely** [ɪk-
'strɪmli, ek-] *adv* : extremadamente —
extremity [ɪk'streməti, ek-] *n, pl* **-ties**
: extremidad *f*
extricate ['ekstrə,keɪt] *vt* **-cated; -cating**
: librar, (lograr) sacar
extrovert ['ekstrə,vərt] *n* : extrovertido
m, -da *f* — **extroverted** ['ekstrə,vərtəd]
adj : extrovertido
exuberant [ɪg'zuːbərənt, eg-] *adj* **1** JOY-
OUS : eufórico **2** LUSH : exuberante —
exuberance [ɪg'zuːbərənts, eg-] *n* **1**
JOYOUSNESS : euforia *f* **2** VIGOR : exuberancia *f*
exult [ɪg'zʌlt, eg-] *vi* : exultar
eye ['aɪ] *n* **1** : ojo *m* **2** VISION : visión *f*,
vista *f* **3** GLANCE : mirada *f* — ~ *vt*
eyed; eyeing *or* **eying** : mirar — **eyeball** ['aɪ,bɔl] *n* : globo *m* ocular — **eyebrow** ['aɪ,braʊ] *n* : ceja *f* — **eyeglasses** ['aɪglæsəz] *npl* : anteojos *mpl*,
lentes *mpl* — **eyelash** ['aɪ,læʃ] *n* : pestaña *f* — **eyelid** ['aɪ,lɪd] *n* : párpado *m*
— **eyesight** ['aɪ,saɪt] *n* : vista *f*, visión *f*
— **eyesore** ['aɪ,sor] *n* : monstruosidad
f — **eyewitness** ['aɪ'wɪtnəs] *n* : testigo
mf ocular

F

f ['ɛf] *n*, *pl* **f's** *or* **fs** ['ɛfs] : f, sexta letra del alfabeto inglés
fable ['feɪbəl] *n* : fábula *f*
fabric ['fæbrɪk] *n* : tela *f*, tejido *m*
fabulous ['fæbjələs] *adj* : fabuloso
facade [fə'sɑd] *n* : fachada *f*
face ['feɪs] *n* **1** : cara *f*, rostro *m* (de una persona) **2** APPEARANCE : fisonomía *f*, aspecto *m* **3** : cara *f* (de una moneda), fachada *f* (de un edificio) **4** ~ **value** : valor *m* nominal **5 in the ~ of** : en medio de, ante **6 lose ~** : desprestigiarse **7 make ~s** : hacer muecas — **~ faced; facing** *vt* **1** : estar frente a **2** CONFRONT : enfrentarse a **3** OVERLOOK : dar a — *vi* **to the north** : mirar hacia el norte — **facedown** ['feɪs,daʊn] *adv* : boca abajo — **faceless** ['feɪsləs] *adj* : anónimo — **face-lift** ['feɪs,lɪft] *n* : estiramiento *m* facial
facet ['fæsət] *n* : faceta *f*
face–to–face *adv & adj* : cara a cara
facial ['feɪʃəl] *adj* : de la cara, facial — ~ *n* : limpieza *f* de cutis
facetious [fə'si:ʃəs] *adj* : gracioso, burlón
facility [fə'sɪləti] *n*, *pl* **-ties 1** EASE : facilidad *f* **2** CENTER : centro *m* **3 facilities** *npl* : comodidades *fpl*, servicios *mpl*
facsimile [fæk'sɪməli] *n* : facsímile *m*, facsímil *m*
fact ['fækt] *n* **1** : hecho *m* **2 in ~** : en realidad, de hecho
faction ['fækʃən] *n* : facción *m*, bando *m*
factor ['fæktər] *n* : factor *m*
factory ['fæktəri] *n*, *pl* **-ries** : fábrica *f*
factual ['fæktʃʊəl] *adj* : basado en hechos
faculty ['fækəlti] *n*, *pl* **-ties** : facultad *f*
fad ['fæd] *n* : moda *f* pasajera, manía *f*
fade ['feɪd] *v* **faded; fading** *vi* **1** WITHER : marchitarse **2** DISCOLOR : desteñirse, decolorarse **3** DIM : apagarse **4** VANISH : desvanecerse — *vt* : desteñir
fail ['feɪl] *vi* **1** : fracasar (dícese de una empresa, un matrimonio, etc.) **2** BREAK DOWN : fallar **3 ~ in** : faltar a, no cumplir con **4** FLUNK : suspender *Spain*, ser reprobado *Lat* **5 ~ to do sth** : no hacer algo — *vt* **1** DISAPPOINT : fallar **2** FLUNK : suspender *Spain*, reprobar *Lat* — **~** *n* **without ~** : sin

falta — **failing** ['feɪlɪŋ] *n* : defecto *m* — **failure** ['feɪljər] *n* **1** : fracaso *m* **2** BREAKDOWN : falla *f*
faint ['feɪnt] *adj* **1** WEAK : débil **2** INDISTINCT : tenue, indistinto **3 feel ~** : estar mareado — **~** *vi* : desmayarse — **~** *n* : desmayo *m* — **fainthearted** ['feɪnt'hɑrtəd] *adj* : cobarde, pusilánime — **faintly** ['feɪntli] *adv* **1** WEAKLY : débilmente **2** SLIGHTLY : ligeramente, levemente
fair[1] ['fær] *n* : feria *f*
fair[2] *adj* **1** BEAUTIFUL : bello, hermoso **2** : bueno (dícese del tiempo) **3** JUST : justo **4** : rubio (dícese del pelo), blanco (dícese de la tez) **5** ADEQUATE : adecuado — **~** *adv* **play** : jugar limpio — **fairly** ['færli] *adv* **1** JUSTLY : justamente **2** QUITE : bastante — **fairness** ['færnəs] *n* : justicia *f*
fairy ['færi] *n*, *pl* **fairies 1** : hada *f* **2 ~ tale** : cuento *m* de hadas
faith ['feɪθ] *n*, *pl* **faiths** ['feɪθs, 'feɪðz] : fe *f* — **faithful** ['feɪθfəl] *adj* : fiel — **faithfully** *adv* : fielmente — **faithfulness** ['feɪθfəlnəs] *n* : fidelidad *f*
fake ['feɪk] *v* **faked; faking** *vt* **1** FALSIFY : falsificar, falsear **2** FEIGN : fingir — *vi* PRETEND : fingir — **~** *adj* : falso — **~** *n* **1** IMITATION : falsificación *f* **2** IMPOSTOR : impostor *m*, -tora *f*
falcon ['fælkən, 'fɒl-] *n* : halcón *m*
fall ['fɒl] *vi* **fell** ['fɛl]; **fallen** ['fɒlən]; **falling 1** : caer, bajar (dícese de los precios), descender (dícese de la temperatura) **2 ~ asleep** : dormirse **3 ~ back** : retirarse **4 ~ back on** : recurrir a **5 ~ down** : caerse **6 ~ in love** : enamorarse **7 ~ out** QUARREL : pelearse **8 ~ through** : fracasar — **~** *n* **1** : caída *f*, bajada *f* (de precios), descenso *m* (de temperatura) **2** AUTUMN : otoño *m* **3 ~s** *npl* WATERFALL : cascada *f*, catarata *f*
fallacy ['fæləsi] *n*, *pl* **-cies** : concepto *m* erróneo
fallible ['fæləbəl] *adj* : falible
fallow ['fælo] *adj* **lie ~** : estar en barbecho
false ['fɒls] *adj* **falser; falsest 1** : falso **2 ~ alarm** : falsa alarma *f* **3 ~ teeth** : dentadura *f* postiza — **falsehood** ['fɒls,hʊd] *n* : mentira — **falseness**

['fɔlsnəs] n : falsedad f — **falsify** ['fɔlsə,faɪ] vt -**fied; -fying** : falsificar, falsear

falter ['fɔltər] vi -**tered; -tering 1** STUMBLE : tambalearse **2** WAVER : vacilar

fame ['feɪm] n : fama f

familiar [fə'mɪljər] adj **1** : familiar **2 be ~ with** : estar familiarizado con — **familiarity** [fə,mɪli'ærəti, -,mɪl'jær-] n, pl -**ties** : familiaridad f — **familiarize** [fə'mɪljə,raɪz] vt -**ized; -izing ~ oneself** : familiarizarse

family ['fæmli, 'fæmə-] n, pl -**lies** : familia f

famine ['fæmən] n : hambre f, hambruna f

famished ['fæmɪʃt] adj : famélico

famous ['feɪməs] adj : famoso

fan ['fæn] n **1** : ventilador m, abanico m **2** : aficionado m, -da f (a un pasatiempo); admirador m, -dora f (de una persona) — ~ vt **fanned; fanning** : abanicar (a una persona), avivar (un fuego)

fanatic [fə'nætɪk] or **fanatical** [-tɪkəl] adj : fanático — ~ n : fanático m, -ca f — **fanaticism** [fə'nætə,sɪzəm] n : fanatismo m

fancy ['fænsi] vt -**cied; -cying 1** IMAGINE : imaginarse **2** DESIRE : apetecerle (algo a uno) — ~ adj -**cier; -est 1** ELABORATE : elaborado **2** LUXURIOUS : lujoso, elegante — ~ n, pl -**cies 1** WHIM : capricho m **2** IMAGINATION : imaginación f **3 take a ~ to** : aficionarse a (una cosa), tomar cariño a (una persona) — **fanciful** ['fænsɪfəl] adj **1** CAPRICIOUS : caprichoso **2** IMAGINATIVE : imaginativo

fanfare ['fæn,fær] n : fanfarria f

fang ['fæŋ] n : colmillo m (de un animal), diente m (de una serpiente)

fantasy ['fæntəsi] n, pl -**sies** : fantasía f — **fantasize** ['fæntə,saɪz] vi -**sized; -sizing** : fantasear — **fantastic** [fæn'tæstɪk] adj : fantástico

far ['fɑr] adv **farther** ['fɑrðər] or **further** ['fər-]; **farthest** or **furthest** [-ðəst] **1** : lejos **2** MUCH : muy, mucho **3 as ~ as** : hasta (un lugar), con respecto a (un tema) **4 by ~** : con mucho **5 ~ and wide** : por todas partes **6 ~ away** : a lo lejos **7 ~ from it!** : ¡todo lo contrario! **8 so ~** : hasta ahora, todavía — ~ adj **farther** or **further; farthest** or **furthest 1** REMOTE : lejano **2** EXTREME : extremo — **faraway** ['fɑrə,weɪ] adj : remoto, lejano

farce ['fɑrs] n : farsa f

fare ['fær] vi **fared; faring** : irle a uno —

~ n **1** : precio m del pasaje **2** FOOD : comida f

farewell [fær'wel] n : despedida f — ~ adj : de despedida

far-fetched ['fɑr'fetʃt] adj : improbable, exagerado

farm ['fɑrm] n : granja f, hacienda f — ~ vt : cultivar (la tierra), criar (animales) — vi : ser agricultor — **farmer** ['fɑrmər] n : agricultor m, -tora f; granjero m, -jera f — **farmhand** ['fɑrm,hænd] n : peón m — **farmhouse** ['fɑrm,haʊs] n : granja f, casa f de hacienda — **farming** ['fɑrmɪŋ] n : agricultura f, cultivo m (de plantas), crianza f (de animales) — **farmyard** ['fɑrm,jɑrd] n : corral m

far-off ['fɑr,ɔf, -'ɔf] adj : lejano

far-reaching ['fɑr'riːtʃɪŋ] adj : de gran alcance

farsighted ['fɑr,saɪtəd] adj **1** : hipermétrope **2** PRUDENT : previsor

farther ['fɑrðər] adv **1** : más lejos **2** MORE : más — adj : más lejano — **farthest** adv **1** : lo más lejos **2** MOST : más — adj : más lejano

fascinate ['fæsən,eɪt] vt -**nated; -nating** : fascinar — **fascination** [,fæsən'eɪʃən] n : fascinación f

fascism ['fæʃ,ɪzəm] n : fascismo m — **fascist** ['fæʃɪst] adj : fascista — ~ n : fascista mf

fashion ['fæʃən] n **1** MANNER : manera f **2** STYLE : moda f **3 out of ~** : pasada de moda — **fashionable** ['fæʃənəbəl] adj : de moda

fast[1] ['fæst] vi : ayunar — ~ n : ayuno m

fast[2] adj **1** SWIFT : rápido **2** SECURE : firme, seguro **3** : adelantado (dícese de un reloj) **4 ~ friends** : amigos mpl leales — ~ adv **1** SECURELY : firmemente **2** SWIFTLY : rápidamente **3 ~ asleep** : profundamente dormido

fasten ['fæsən] vt : sujetar (papeles, etc.), abrochar (una blusa, etc.), cerrar (una maleta, etc.) — vi : abrocharse, cerrar — **fastener** ['fæsənər] n : cierre m

fat ['fæt] adj **fatter; fattest 1** : gordo **2** THICK : grueso — ~ n : grasa f

fatal ['feɪtəl] adj **1** : mortal **2** FATEFUL : fatal, fatídico — **fatality** [feɪt'æləti, fə-] n, pl -**ties** : víctima f mortal

fate ['feɪt] n **1** : destino m **2** LOT : suerte f — **fateful** ['feɪtfəl] adj : fatídico

father ['fɑðər] n : padre m — ~ vt : engendrar — **fatherhood** ['fɑðər,hʊd] n : paternidad f — **father-in-law** ['fɑðərɪn,lɔ] n, pl **fathers-in-law** : suegro *m* — **fatherly** ['fɑðərli] *adj* : paternal

fathom ['fæðəm] *vt* : comprender

fatigue [fə'tiːɡ] *n* : fatiga *f* — ~ *vt* -tigued; -tiguing : fatigar

fatten ['fætən] *vt* : engordar — **fattening** *adj* : que engorda

fatty ['fæti] *adj* fattier; -est : graso

faucet ['fɔsət] *n* : llave *f* Lat, grifo *m* Spain

fault ['fɔlt] *n* 1 FLAW : defecto *m* 2 RESPONSIBILITY : culpa *f* 3 : falla *f* (geológica) — *vt* : encontrar defectos a — **faultless** ['fɔltləs] *adj* : impecable — **faulty** ['fɔlti] *adj* faultier; -est : defectuoso

fauna ['fɔnə] *n* : fauna *f*

favor *or Brit* **favour** ['feɪvər] *n* 1 : favor *m* 2 **in ~ of** : a favor de — ~ *vt* 1 : favorecer 2 SUPPORT : estar a favor de 3 PREFER : preferir — **favorable** *or Brit* **favourable** ['feɪvərəbəl] *adj* : favorable — **favorite** *or Brit* **favourite** ['feɪvərət] *n* : favorito *m*, -ta *f* — ~ *adj* : favorito — **favoritism** *or Brit* **favouritism** ['feɪvərə,tɪzəm] *n* : favoritismo *m*

fawn[1] ['fɔn] *vi* **~ over** : adular

fawn[2] *n* : cervato *m*

fax ['fæks] *n* : fax *m* — ~ *vt* : faxear, enviar por fax

fear ['fɪr] *v* : temer — ~ *n* 1 : miedo *m*, temor *m* 2 **for ~ of** : por temor a — **fearful** ['fɪrfəl] *adj* 1 FRIGHTENING : espantoso 2 AFRAID : temeroso

feasible ['fiːzəbəl] *adj* : viable, factible

feast ['fiːst] *n* 1 BANQUET : banquete *m*, festín *m* 2 FESTIVAL : fiesta *f* — ~ *vi* 1 : banquetear 2 **~ upon** : darse un festín de

feat ['fiːt] *n* : hazaña *f*

feather ['feðər] *n* : pluma *f*

feature ['fiːtʃər] *n* 1 : rasgo *m* (de la cara) 2 CHARACTERISTIC : característica *f* 3 : artículo *m* (en un periódico) 4 **~ film** : largometraje *m* — *v* **-tured; -turing** *vt* 1 PRESENT : presentar 2 EMPHASIZE : destacar — *vi* : figurar

February ['fɛbjuˌɛri, 'fɛbu-, 'fɛbru-] *n* : febrero *m*

feces ['fiːˌsiːz] *npl* : excremento *mpl*

federal ['fɛdrəl, -dərəl] *adj* : federal — **federation** [ˌfɛdə'reɪʃən] *n* : federación *f*

fed up *adj* : harto

fee ['fiː] *n* 1 : honorarios *mpl* 2 **entrance ~** : entrada *f*

feeble ['fiːbəl] *adj* **-bler; -blest** 1 : débil 2 **a ~ excuse** : una pobre excusa

feed ['fiːd] *v* **fed** ['fɛd]; **feeding** *vt* 1 : dar de comer a, alimentar 2 SUPPLY : alimentar — *vi* : comer, alimentarse — ~ *n* : pienso *m*

feel ['fiːl] *v* **felt** ['fɛlt]; **feeling** *vt* 1 : sentir (una sensación, etc.) 2 TOUCH : tocar, palpar 3 BELIEVE : creer — *vi* 1 : sentirse (bien, cansado, etc.) 2 SEEM : parecer 3 **~ hot/thirsty** : tener calor/sed 4 **~ like doing** : tener ganas de hacer — ~ *n* : tacto *m*, sensación *f* — **feeling** ['fiːlɪŋ] *n* 1 SENSATION : sensación *f* 2 EMOTION : sentimiento *m* 3 OPINION : opinión *f* 4 **hurt s.o.'s ~s** : herir los sentimientos de algn

feet → foot

feign ['feɪn] *vt* : fingir

feline ['fiːˌlaɪn] *adj* : felino — ~ *n* : felino *m*, -na *f*

fell[1] **→ fall**

fell[2] ['fɛl] *vt* : talar (un árbol)

fellow ['fɛˌloː] *n* 1 COMPANION : compañero *m*, -ra *f* 2 MEMBER : socio *m*, -cia *f* 3 MAN : tipo *m* — **fellowship** ['fɛloˌʃɪp] *n* 1 : compañerismo *m* 2 ASSOCIATION : fraternidad *f* 3 GRANT : beca *f*

felon ['fɛlən] *n* : criminal *mf* — **felony** ['fɛləni] *n*, *pl* -nies : delito *m* grave

felt[1] **→ feel**

felt[2] ['fɛlt] *n* : fieltro *m*

female ['fiːˌmeɪl] *adj* : femenino — ~ *n* 1 : hembra *f* (animal) 2 WOMAN : mujer *f*

feminine ['fɛmənən] *adj* : femenino — **femininity** [ˌfɛmə'nɪnət̬i] *n* : femineidad *f* — **feminism** ['fɛməˌnɪzəm] *n* : feminismo *m* — **feminist** ['fɛmənɪst] *adj* : feminista — ~ *n* : feminista *mf*

fence ['fɛns] *n* : cerca *f*, valla *f*, cerco *m* Lat — ~ *v* **fenced; fencing** *vi or* **~ in** : vallar, cercar — *vi* : hacer esgrima — **fencing** ['fɛnsɪŋ] *n* : esgrima *m* (deporte)

fend ['fɛnd] *vt* **~ off** : rechazar (un enemigo), eludir (una pregunta) — *vi* **~ for oneself** : valerse por sí mismo

fender ['fɛndər] *n* : guardabarros *mpl*

fennel ['fɛnəl] *n* : hinojo *m*

ferment [fər'mɛnt] *v* : fermentar — **fermentation** [ˌfərmən'teɪʃən, -mɛn-] *n* : fermentación *f*

fern ['fərn] *n* : helecho *m*

ferocious [fə'roːʃəs] *adj* : feroz — **ferocity** [fə'rɑsət̬i] *n* : ferocidad *f*

ferret ['fɛrət] *n* : hurón *m* — ~ *vt* **~ out** : descubrir

Ferris wheel ['fɛrɪs] *n* : noria *f*

ferry ['fɛri] *vt* **-ried; -rying** : transportar — ~ *n*, *pl* **-ries** : ferry *m*

fertile ['fərṭəl] *adj* : fértil — **fertility** [fər'tɪləṭi] *n* : fertilidad *f* — **fertilize** ['fərṭəlˌaɪz] *vt* **-ized; -izing** : fecundar (un huevo), abonar (el suelo) — **fertilizer** ['fərṭəlˌaɪzər] *n* : fertilizante *m*, abono *m*

fervent ['fərvənt] *adj* : ferviente — **fervor** *or Brit* **fervour** ['fərvər] *n* : fervor *m*

fester ['fɛstər] *vi* : enconarse

festival ['fɛstəvəl] *n* **1** : fiesta *f* **2** film ~ : festival *m* de cine — **festive** ['fɛstɪv] *adj* : festivo — **festivity** [fɛs'tɪvəṭi] *n*, *pl* **-ties** : festividad *f*

fetch ['fɛʧ] *vt* **1** : ir a buscar **2** : venderse por (un precio)

fête ['feɪt, 'fɛt] *n* : fiesta *f*

fetid ['fɛṭəd] *adj* : fétido

fetish ['fɛṭɪʃ] *n* : fetiche *m*

fetters ['fɛṭərz] *npl* : grillos *mpl* — **fetter** ['fɛṭər] *vt* : encadenar

fetus ['fiːṭəs] *n* : feto *m*

feud ['fjuːd] *n* : enemistad *f* (entre familiares) — ~ *vi* : pelear

feudal ['fjuːdəl] *adj* : feudal — **feudalism** ['fjuːdəlˌɪzəm] *n* : feudalismo *m*

fever ['fiːvər] *n* : fiebre *f* — **feverish** ['fiːvərɪʃ] *adj* : febril

few ['fjuː] *adj* **1** : pocos **2 a ~ times** : varias veces — ~ *pron* **1** : pocos **2 a ~** : algunos, unos cuantos **3 quite a ~** : muchos — **fewer** ['fjuːər] *adj & pron* : menos

fiancé, fiancée [ˌfiːɑnˈseɪ, ˈfiːɑnˌseɪ] *n* : prometido *m*, -da *f*; novio *m*, -via *f*

fiasco [fiˈæsˌkoː] *n*, *pl* **-coes** : fiasco *m*

fib ['fɪb] *n* : mentirilla *f* — ~ *vi* **fibbed; fibbing** : decir mentirillas

fiber *or* **fibre** ['faɪbər] *n* : fibra *f* — **fiberglass** ['faɪbərˌglæs] *n* : fibra *f* de vidrio — **fibrous** ['faɪbrəs] *adj* : fibroso

fickle ['fɪkəl] *adj* : inconstante

fiction ['fɪkʃən] *n* : ficción *f* — **fictional** ['fɪkʃənəl] *or* **fictitious** [fɪk'tɪʃəs] *adj* : ficticio

fiddle ['fɪdəl] *n* : violín *m* — ~ *vi* **-dled; -dling 1** : tocar el violín **2 ~ with** : juguetear con

fidelity [fəˈdɛləṭi, faɪ-] *n*, *pl* **-ties** : fidelidad *f*

fidget ['fɪʤət] *vi* **1** : estarse inquieto, moverse **2 ~ with** : juguetear con — **fidgety** ['fɪʤəṭi] *adj* : inquieto, nervioso

field ['fiːld] *n* : campo *m* — ~ *vt* : interceptar (una pelota), sortear (una pregunta) — **field glasses** *n* : binoculares *mpl*, gemelos *mpl* — **field trip** *n* : viaje *m* de estudio

fiend ['fiːnd] *n* **1** : demonio *m* **2** FANATIC

: fanático *m*, -ca *f* — **fiendish** ['fiːndɪʃ] *adj* : diabólico

fierce ['fɪrs] *adj* **fiercer; -est 1** : feroz **2** INTENSE : fuerte (dícese del viento), acalorado (dícese de un debate) — **fierceness** ['fɪrsnəs] *n* : ferocidad *f*

fiery ['faɪəri] *adj* **fierier; -est 1** BURNING : llameante **2** SPIRITED : ardiente, fogoso — **fieriness** ['faɪərinəs] *n* : pasión *f*, ardor *m*

fifteen [fɪfˈtiːn] *n* : quince *m* — ~ *adj* : quince — **fifteenth** [fɪfˈtiːnθ] *adj* : decimoquinto — ~ *n* **1** : decimoquinto *m*, -ta *f* (en una serie) **2** : quinceavo *m* (en matemáticas)

fifth ['fɪfθ] *n* **1** : quinto *m*, -ta *f* (en una serie) **2** : quinto *m* (en matemáticas) — ~ *adj* : quinto

fiftieth ['fɪftiːəθ] *adj* : quincuagésimo — ~ *n* **1** : quincuagésimo *m*, -ma *f* (en una serie) **2** : cincuentavo *m* (en matemáticas)

fifty ['fɪfti] *n*, *pl* **-ties** : cincuenta *m* — ~ *adj* : cincuenta — **fifty-fifty** [ˌfɪftiˈfɪfti] *adv* : a medias, mitad y mitad — ~ *adj* **a ~ chance** : un cincuenta por ciento de posibilidades

fig ['fɪg] *n* : higo *m*

fight ['faɪt] *v* **fought** ['fɔt]; **fighting** *vi* **1** BATTLE : luchar **2** QUARREL : pelear **3 ~ back** : defenderse — *vt* : luchar contra — ~ *n* **1** STRUGGLE : lucha *f* **2** QUARREL : pelea *f* — **fighter** ['faɪṭər] *n* **1** : luchador *m*, -dora *f* **2** *or* **~ plane** : avión *m* de caza

figment ['fɪgmənt] *n* **~ of the imagination** : producto *m* de la imaginación

figurative ['fɪgjərəṭɪv, -gə-] *adj* : figurado

figure ['fɪgjər, -gər] *n* **1** NUMBER : número *m*, cifra *f* **2** PERSON, SHAPE : figura *f* **3 ~ of speech** : figura *f* retórica **4 watch one's ~** : cuidar la línea — ~ *v* **-ured; -uring** *vt* : calcular — *vi* **1** : figurar **2 that ~s!** : ¡no me extraña! — **figurehead** ['fɪgjərˌhɛd, -gər] *n* : testaferro *m* — **figure out** *vt* **1** UNDERSTAND : entender **2** RESOLVE : resolver

file[1] ['faɪl] *n* : lima *f* (instrumento) — ~ *vt* **filed; filing** : limar

file[2] *vt* **filed; filing 1** : archivar (documentos) **2 ~ charges** : presentar cargos — ~ *n* : archivo *m*

file[3] *n* LINE : fila *f* — ~ *vi* **in/out** : entrar/salir en fila

fill ['fɪl] *vt* **1** : llenar, rellenar **2** : cumplir con (un requisito) **3** : tapar (un agujero), empastar (un diente) — *vi* **1 ~ in for** : reemplazar **2** *or* **~ up**

: llenarse — **~** *n* **1 eat one's ~**
: comer lo suficiente **2 have one's ~**
of : estar harto de

fillet ['fɪlət, fɪ'leɪ, 'fɪˌleɪ] *n* : filete *m*

filling ['fɪlɪŋ] *n* **1** : relleno *m* **2** : empaste
m (de dientes) **3 ~ station → service
station**

filly ['fɪli] *n*, *pl* **-lies** : potra *f*

film ['fɪlm] *n* **1** : película *f* — **~** *vt* : filmar

filter ['fɪltər] *n* : filtro *m* — **~** *vt* : filtrar

filth ['fɪlθ] *n* : mugre *f* — **filthy** ['fɪlθi] *adj*
filthier; -est 1 : mugriento **2** OBSCENE
: obsceno

fin ['fɪn] *n* : aleta *f*

final ['faɪnəl] *adj* **1** LAST : último **2** DE-
FINITIVE : definitivo **3** ULTIMATE : final
— **~** *n* **1** : final *f* (en deportes) **2 ~s**
npl : exámenes *mpl* finales — **finalist**
['faɪnəlɪst] *n* : finalista *mf* — **finalize**
['faɪnəlˌaɪz] *vt* **-ized; -izing** : finalizar
— **finally** ['faɪnəli] *adv* : finalmente

finance [fə'nænts, 'faɪˌnænts] *n* **1** : finanzas *fpl* **2 ~s** *npl* : recursos *mpl* fi-
nancieros — **~** *vt* **-nanced; -nancing**
: financiar — **financial** [fə'nænt∫əl,
faɪ-] *adj* : financiero — **financially** [fə-
'nænt∫əli, faɪ-] *adv* : económicamente

find ['faɪnd] *vt* **found** ['faʊnd]; **finding 1**
LOCATE : encontrar **2** REALIZE : darse
cuenta de **3 ~ guilty** : declarar culpable **4** *or* **~ out** : descubrir — *vi* **~
out** : enterarse — **~** *n* : hallazgo *m* —
finding ['faɪndɪŋ] *n* **1** FIND : hallazgo *m*
2 ~s *npl* : conclusiones *fpl*

fine¹ ['faɪn] *n* : multa *f* — **~** *vt* **fined;
fining** : multar

fine² *adj* **finer; -est 1** DELICATE : fino **2**
EXCELLENT : excelente **3** SUBTLE : sutil
4 : bueno (dícese del tiempo) **5 ~
print** : letra *f* menuda **6 it's ~ with
me** : me parece bien — **~** *adv* OK
: bien — **fine arts** *npl* : bellas artes *fpl*
— **finely** ['faɪnli] *adv* **1** EXCELLENTLY
: excelentemente **2** PRECISELY : con
precisión **3** MINUTELY : fino, menudo

finger ['fɪŋgər] *n* : dedo *m* — **~** *vt*
: tocar, toquetear — **fingernail** ['fɪŋ-
gərˌneɪl] *n* : uña *f* — **fingerprint** ['fɪŋ-
gərˌprɪnt] *n* : huella *f* digital — **fingertip** ['fɪŋgərˌtɪp] *n* : punta *f* del dedo

finicky ['fɪnɪki] *adj* : maniático, mañoso
Lat

finish ['fɪnɪʃ] *v* : acabar, terminar — **~**
n **1** END : fin *m*, final *m* **2** *or* **~ line**
: meta *f* **3** SURFACE : acabado *m*

finite ['faɪˌnaɪt] *adj* : finito

fir ['fər] *n* : abeto *m*

fire ['faɪr] *n* **1** : fuego *m* **2** CONFLAGRA-
TION : incendio *m* **3 catch ~** : incendiarse (dícese de bosques, etc.), prenderse (dícese de fósforos, etc.) **4 on
~** : en llamas **5 open ~ on** : abrir
fuego sobre — **~** *vt* **fired; firing 1**
DISMISS : despedir **2** SHOOT : disparar
— *vi* : disparar — **fire alarm** *n* : alarma *f* contra incendios — **firearm** ['faɪr-
ˌɑrm] *n* : arma *f* de fuego — **firecracker** ['faɪrˌkrækər] *n* : petardo *m* — **fire
engine** *n* : carro *m* de bomberos *Lat*,
coche *m* de bomberos *Spain* — **fire
escape** *n* : escalera *f* de incendios —
fire extinguisher *n* : extintor *m* (de
incendios) — **firefighter** ['faɪrˌfaɪtər] *n*
: bombero *m*, -ra *f* — **firefly** ['faɪrˌflaɪ]
n, *pl* **-flies** : luciérnaga *f* — **firehouse**
→ **fire station** — **fireman** ['faɪrmən] *n*,
pl **-men** [-mən, -ˌmɛn] → **firefighter** —
fireplace ['faɪrˌpleɪs] *n* : hogar *m*,
chimenea *f* — **fireproof** ['faɪrˌpruːf] *adj*
: ignífugo — **fireside** ['faɪrˌsaɪd] *n*
: hogar *m* — **fire station** *n* : estación *f*
de bomberos *Lat*, parque *m* de
bomberos *Spain* — **firewood** ['faɪr-
ˌwʊd] *n* : leña *f* — **fireworks** ['faɪrˌwərk]
npl : fuegos *mpl* artificiales

firm¹ ['fərm] *n* : empresa *f*

firm² *adj* : firme — **firmly** ['fərmli] *adv*
: firmemente — **firmness** ['fərmnəs] *n*
: firmeza *f*

first ['fərst] *adj* **1** : primero **2 at ~ sight**
: a primera vista **3 for the ~ time**
: por primera vez — **~** *adv* **1**
: primero **2 ~ and foremost** : ante
todo **3 ~ of all** : en primer lugar —
~ *n* **1** : primero *m*, -ra *f* **2 at ~** : al
principio — **first aid** *n* : primeros aux-
ilios *mpl* — **first-class** ['fərst'klæs]
adv : en primera — **~** *adj* : de
primera *f* — **firsthand** ['fərst'hænd] *adv*
: directamente — **~** *adj* : de primera
mano — **firstly** ['fərstli] *adv* : en
primer lugar — **first name** *n* : nombre
m de pila — **first-rate** ['fərst'reɪt] *adj*
→ **first-class**

fiscal ['fɪskəl] *adj* : fiscal

fish ['fɪʃ] *n*, *pl* **fish** *or* **fishes** : pez *m*
(vivo), pescado *m* (para comer) — **~**
vi **1** : pescar **2 ~ for** SEEK : buscar **3
go ~ing** : ir de pesca — **fisherman**
['fɪʃərmən] *n*, *pl* **-men** [-mən, -ˌmɛn]
: pescador *m*, -dora *f* — **fishhook** ['fɪʃ-
ˌhʊk] *n* : anzuelo *m* — **fishing** ['fɪʃɪŋ] *n*
: pesca *f* — **fishing pole** *n* : caña *f* de
pescar — **fish market** *n* : pescadería *f*
— **fishy** ['fɪʃi] *adj* **fishier; -est 1** : a
pescado (dícese de sabores, etc.) **2**
SUSPICIOUS : sospechoso

fist ['fɪst] *n* : puño *m*

fit¹ ['fɪt] *n* **1** : ataque *m* **2 he had a ~**
: le dio un ataque

fit² *adj* **fitter; fittest 1** SUITABLE : apropiado **2** HEALTHY : en forma **3 be ~ for** : ser apto para — *v* **fitted; fitting** *vt* **1** : encajar en (un hueco, etc.) **2** (*relating to clothing*) : quedar bien a **3** SUIT : ser apropiado para **4** MATCH : coincidir con **5** *or* **~ out** : equipar — *vi* **1** : caber (en una caja, etc.), encajar (en un hueco, etc.) **2** *or* **~ in** BELONG : encajar **3 this dress doesn't ~** : este vestido no me queda bien — **~ it's a good fit** : me queda bien — **fitful** ['fɪtfəl] *adj* : irregular — **fitness** ['fɪtnəs] *n* **1** HEALTH : salud *f* **2** SUITABILITY : idoneidad *f* — **fitting** ['fɪtɪŋ] *adj* : apropiado

five ['faɪv] *adj* : cinco — *n* — *adj* : cinco — **five hundred** *n* : quinientos — *~ adj* : quinientos

fix ['fɪks] *vt* **1** ATTACH : fijar, sujetar **2** REPAIR : arreglar **3** PREPARE : preparar — *n* PREDICAMENT : aprieto *m*, apuro *m* — **fixed** ['fɪkst] *adj* : fijo — **fixture** ['fɪkstʃər] *n* : instalación *f*

fizz ['fɪz] *vi* **1** : burbujear — *~ n* : efervescencia *f*

fizzle ['fɪzəl] *vi* **-zled; -zling** *or* **~ out** : quedar en nada

flabbergasted ['flæbər,gæstəd] *adj* : estupefacto, pasmado

flabby ['flæbi] *adj* **-bier; -est** : fofo

flaccid ['flæksəd, 'flæsəd] *adj* : fláccido

flag¹ ['flæg] *vi* WEAKEN : flaquear

flag² *n* : bandera *f* — *vt* **flagged; flagging** *or* **~ down** : hacer señales de parada a — **flagpole** ['flæg,poːl] *n* : asta *f*

flagrant ['fleɪgrənt] *adj* : flagrante

flair ['flær] *n* : don *m*, facilidad *f*

flake ['fleɪk] *n* : copo *m* (de nieve), escama *f* (de pintura, de la piel) — *~ vi* **flaked; flaking** : pelarse

flamboyant [flæm'bɔɪənt] *adj* : extravagante

flame ['fleɪm] *n* **1** : llama *f* **2 burst into ~s** : estallar en llamas **3 go up in ~s** : incendiarse

flamingo [flə'mɪŋgo] *n, pl* **-gos** : flamenco *m*

flammable ['flæməbəl] *adj* : inflamable

flank ['flæŋk] *n* : ijada *m* (de un animal), flanco *m* (militar) — *~ vt* : flanquear

flannel ['flænəl] *n* : franela *f*

flap ['flæp] *n* : solapa *f* (de un sobre, un libro, etc.), tapa *f* (de un recipiente) — *~ v* **flapped; flapping** *vi* : agitarse — *vt* : batir, agitar

flapjack ['flæp,dʒæk] → **pancake**

flare ['flær] *vi* **flared; flaring 1 ~ up** BLAZE : llamear **2 ~ up** EXPLODE,

ERUPT : estallar, explotar — *~ n* **1** BLAZE : llamarada *f* **2** SIGNAL : (luz *f* de) bengala *f*

flash ['flæʃ] *vi* **1** : brillar, destellar **2 ~ past** : pasar como un rayo — *vt* **1** : dirigir (una luz) **2** SHOW : mostrar **3 ~ a smile** : sonreír — *~ n* **1** : destello *m* **2 ~ of lightning** : relámpago *m* **3 in a ~** : de repente — **flashlight** ['flæʃ,laɪt] *n* : linterna *f* — **flashy** ['flæʃi] *adj* **flashier; -est** : ostentoso

flask ['flæsk] *n* : frasco *m*

flat ['flæt] *adj* **flatter; flattest 1** LEVEL : plano, llano **2** DOWNRIGHT : categórico **3** FIXED : fijo **4** MONOTONOUS : monótono **5** : bemol (en la música) **6 ~ tire** : neumático *m* desinflado — *~ n* **1** : bemol *m* (en la música) **2** *Brit* APARTMENT : apartamento *m*, departamento *m* *Lat* **3** PUNCTURE : pinchazo *m* — *~ adv* **1 ~ broke** : pelado **2 in one hour ~** : en una hora justa — **flatly** ['flætli] *adv* : categóricamente — **flat-out** ['flæt,aʊt] *adj* **1** : frenético **2** DOWNRIGHT : categórico — **flatten** ['flætən] *vt* **1** LEVEL : aplanar, allanar **2** KNOCK DOWN : arrasar

flatter ['flætər] *vt* **1** : halagar **2** BECOME : favorecer — **flatterer** ['flætərər] *n* : adulador *m*, -dora *f* — **flattering** ['flætərɪŋ] *adj* **1** : halagador **2** BECOMING : favorecedor — **flattery** ['flætəri] *n, pl* **-ries** : halagos *mpl*

flaunt ['flɔnt] *vt* : hacer alarde de

flavor *or Brit* **flavour** ['fleɪvər] *n* : gusto *m*, sabor *m* — *~ vt* : sazonar — **flavorful** *or Brit* **flavourful** ['fleɪvərfəl] *adj* : sabroso — **flavoring** *or Brit* **flavouring** ['fleɪvərɪŋ] *n* : condimento *m*, sazón *f*

flaw ['flɔ] *n* : defecto *m* — **flawless** ['flɔləs] *adj* : perfecto

flax ['flæks] *n* : lino *m*

flea ['fliː] *n* : pulga *f*

fleck ['flɛk] *n* **1** PARTICLE : mota *f* **2** SPOT : pinta *f*

flee ['fliː] *v* **fled** ['flɛd]; **fleeing** *vi* : huir — *vt* : huir de

fleece ['fliːs] *n* : vellón *m* — *~ vt* **fleeced; fleecing 1** SHEAR : esquilar **2** DEFRAUD : desplumar

fleet ['fliːt] *n* : flota *f*

fleeting ['fliːtɪŋ] *adj* : fugaz

Flemish ['flɛmɪʃ] *adj* : flamenco

flesh ['flɛʃ] *n* **1** : carne *f* **2** PULP : pulpa *f* **3 in the ~** : en persona — **fleshy** ['flɛʃi] *adj* **fleshier; -est 1** : gordo **2** PULPY : carnoso

flew → fly

flex ['flɛks] *vt* : flexionar — **flexibility**

[ˌflɛksəˈbɪləţi] n, pl **-ties** : flexibilidad f — **flexible** [ˈflɛksəbəl] adj : flexible

flick [ˈflɪk] n : golpecito m — ~ vt : dar un golpecito a — vi ~ **through** : hojear

flicker [ˈflɪkər] vi : parpadear — ~ n 1 : parpadeo m 2 a ~ **of hope** : un rayo de esperanza

flier [ˈflaɪər] n 1 AVIATOR : aviador m, -dora f 2 or **flyer** LEAFLET : folleto m, volante m Lat

flight[1] [ˈflaɪt] n 1 : vuelo m 2 TRAJECTORY : trayectoria f 3 ~ **of stairs** : tramo m

flight[2] n ESCAPE : huida f

flimsy [ˈflɪmzi] adj **flimsier; -est 1** LIGHT : ligero 2 SHAKY : poco sólido 3 a ~ **excuse** : una excusa floja

flinch [ˈflɪntʃ] vi ~ **from** : encogerse ante

fling [ˈflɪŋ] vt **flung** [ˈflʌŋ]; **flinging 1** : arrojar 2 ~ **open** : abrir de un golpe — ~ n 1 AFFAIR : aventura f 2 **have a** ~ **at** : intentar

flint [ˈflɪnt] n : pedernal m

flip [ˈflɪp] v **flipped; flipping** vt 1 or ~ **over** : dar la vuelta a 2 ~ **a coin** : echarlo a cara o cruz — vi 1 or ~ **over** : volcarse 2 ~ **through** : hojear — ~ n SOMERSAULT : voltereta f

flippant [ˈflɪpənt] adj : ligero, frívolo

flipper [ˈflɪpər] n : aleta f

flirt [ˈflərt] vi : coquetear — ~ n : coqueto m, -ta f — **flirtatious** [flərˈteɪʃəs] adj : coqueto

flit [ˈflɪt] vi **flitted; flitting** : revolotear

float [ˈfloːt] n 1 : flotador m 2 : carroza f (en un desfile) — ~ vi : flotar — vt : hacer flotar

flock [ˈflɑk] n : rebaño m (de ovejas), bandada f (de pájaros) — ~ vi : congregarse

flog [ˈflɑg] vt **flogged; flogging** : azotar

flood [ˈflʌd] n 1 : inundación f 2 : torrente m (de palabras, de lágrimas, etc.) — ~ vt : inundar — **floodlight** [ˈflʌdˌlaɪt] n : foco m

floor [ˈflor] n 1 : suelo m, piso m Lat 2 STORY : piso m 3 **dance** ~ : pista f de baile 4 **ground** ~ : planta f baja — ~ vt 1 KNOCK DOWN : derribar 2 NONPLUS : desconcertar — **floorboard** [ˈflorˌbord] n : tabla f del suelo

flop [ˈflɑp] vi **flopped; flopping 1** FLAP : agitarse 2 COLLAPSE : dejarse caer 3 FAIL : fracasar — ~ n FAILURE : fracaso m — **floppy** [ˈflɑpi] adj **-pier; -est** : flojo, flexible — **floppy disk** n : diskette m, disquete m

flora [ˈflorə] n : flora f — **floral** [ˈflorəl]

adj : floral — **florid** [ˈflorɪd] adj 1 FLOWERY : florido 2 RUDDY : rojizo — **florist** [ˈflorɪst] n : florista mf

floss [ˈflɔs] n → **dental floss**

flounder[1] [ˈflaʊndər] n, pl **flounder** or **flounders** : platija f

flounder[2] vi 1 or ~ **about** : resbalarse, revolcarse 2 : titubear (en un discurso)

flour [ˈflaʊər] n : harina f

flourish [ˈflərɪʃ] vi : florecer — vt BRANDISH : blandir — ~ n : floritura f — **flourishing** [ˈflərɪʃɪŋ] adj : floreciente

flout [ˈflaʊt] vt : desacatar, burlarse de

flow [ˈfloː] vi : fluir, correr — ~ n 1 : flujo m, circulación f 2 : corriente f (de información, etc.)

flower [ˈflaʊər] n : flor f — ~ vi : florecer — **flowered** [ˈflaʊərd] adj : floreado — **flowerpot** [ˈflaʊərˌpat] n : maceta f — **flowery** [ˈflaʊəri] adj : florido

flown → **fly**

flu [ˈflu:] n : gripe f

fluctuate [ˈflʌktʃuˌeɪt] vi **-ated; -ating** : fluctuar — **fluctuation** [ˌflʌktʃuˈeɪʃən] n : fluctuación f

fluency [ˈflu:ənsi] n : fluidez f — **fluent** [ˈflu:ənt] adj 1 : fluido 2 **be** ~ **in** : hablar con fluidez — **fluently** [ˈflu:əntli] adv : con fluidez

fluff [ˈflʌf] n : pelusa f — **fluffy** [ˈflʌfi] adj **fluffier; -est** : de pelusa, velloso

fluid [ˈflu:ɪd] adj : fluido — ~ n : fluido m

flung → **fling**

flunk [ˈflʌŋk] vt : reprobar Lat, suspender Spain — vi : ser reprobado Lat, suspender Spain

fluorescence [ˌflʊrˈɛsənts, ˌflor-] n : fluorescencia f — **fluorescent** [ˌflʊrˈɛsənt, ˌflor-] adj : fluorescente

flurry [ˈfləri] n, pl **-ries 1** GUST : ráfaga f 2 or **snow** ~ : nevisca f 3 ~ **of questions** : aluvión m de preguntas

flush [ˈflʌʃ] vi BLUSH : ruborizarse, sonrojarse — vt ~ **the toilet** : tirar de la cadena, jalarle a la cadena Lat — ~ n BLUSH : rubor m, sonrojo m — ~ adj ~ **with** : a nivel con, a ras de — ~ adv : al mismo nivel, a ras

fluster [ˈflʌstər] vt : poner nervioso

flute [ˈfluːt] n : flauta f

flutter [ˈflʌtər] vi 1 FLIT : revolotear 2 WAVE : ondear 3 or ~ **about** : ir y venir — ~ n 1 : revoloteo m (de alas) 2 STIR : revuelo m

flux [ˈflʌks] n **be in a state of** ~ : cambiar continuamente

fly[1] [ˈflaɪ] v **flew** [ˈfluː]; **flown** [ˈfloːn]; **flying** vi 1 : volar 2 TRAVEL : ir en avión 3 WAVE : ondear 4 RUSH : correr 5 ~

by : pasar volando — *vt* **1** PILOT : pilotar **2** : hacer volar (una cometa), enarbolar (una bandera) — ~ *n, pl* **flies** : bragueta *f* (de un pantalón)

fly² *n, pl* **flies** : mosca *f* (insecto)

flyer → **flier**

flying saucer *n* : platillo *m* volador *Lat*, platillo *m* volante *Spain*

flyswatter ['flaɪˌswɑtər] *n* : matamoscas *m*

foal ['foːl] *n* : potro *m*, -tra *f*

foam ['foːm] *n* : espuma *f* — ~ *vi* : hacer espuma — **foamy** ['foːmi] *adj* **foamier; -est** : espumoso

focus ['foːkəs] *n, pl* **-ci** ['foːˌsaɪ, -ˌkaɪ] **1** : foco *m* **2 be in ~** : estar enfocado **3 ~ of attention** : centro *m* de atención — ~ *v* **-cused** *or* **-cussed; -cusing** *or* **-cussing** *vt* **1** : enfocar **2** : centrar (la atención, etc.) — *vi* **~ on** : enfocar (con los ojos), concentrarse en (con la mente)

fodder ['fɑdər] *n* : forraje *m*

foe ['foː] *n* : enemigo *m*, -ga *f*

fog ['fɔg, 'fɑg] *n* : niebla *f* — ~ *v* **fogged; fogging** *vt* : empañar — *vi* **~ up** : empañarse — **foggy** ['fɔgi, 'fɑ-] *adj* **foggier; -est** : nebuloso — **foghorn** ['fɔgˌhɔrn, 'fɑg-] *n* : sirena *f* de niebla

foil¹ ['fɔɪl] *vt* : frustrar

foil² *n or* **aluminum ~** : papel *m* de aluminio

fold¹ ['foːld] *n* **1** : redil *m* (para ovejas) **2 return to the ~** : volver al redil

fold² *vt* **1** : doblar, plegar **2 ~ one's arms** : cruzar los brazos — *vi* **1** *or* **~ up** : doblarse, plegarse **2** FAIL : fracasar — ~ *n* : pliegue *m* — **folder** ['foːldər] *n* : carpeta *f*

follage ['foːliːdʒ, -lɪdʒ] *n* : follaje *m*

folk ['foːk] *n, pl* **folk** *or* **folks 1** : gente *f* **2 ~s** *npl* PARENTS : padres *mpl* — ~ *adj* **1** : popular **2 ~ dance** : danza *f* folklórica — **folklore** ['foːkˌlor] *n* : folklore *m*

follow ['fɑlo] *vt* **1** : seguir **2** UNDERSTAND : entender **3 ~ up** : seguir — *vi* **1** : seguir **2** UNDERSTAND : entender **3 ~ up on** : seguir con — **follower** ['fɑloər] *n* : seguidor *m*, -dora *f* — **following** ['fɑloɪŋ] *adj* : siguiente — ~ *n* : seguidores *mpl* — ~ *prep* : después de

folly ['fɑli] *n, pl* **-lies** : locura *f*

fond ['fɑnd] *adj* **1** : cariñoso **2 be ~ of sth** : ser aficionado a algo **3 be ~ of s.o.** : tener cariño a algn

fondle ['fɑndəl] *vt* **-dled; -dling** : acariciar

fondness ['fɑndnəs] *n* **1** LOVE : cariño *m* **2** LIKING : afición *f*

food ['fuːd] *n* **1** : comida *f*, alimento *m* — **foodstuffs** ['fuːdˌstʌfs] *npl* : comestibles *mpl*

fool ['fuːl] *n* **1** : idiota *mf* **2** JESTER : bufón *m*, -fona *f* — ~ *vi* **1** JOKE : bromear **2 ~ around** : perder el tiempo — *vt* TRICK : engañar — **foolhardy** ['fuːlˌhɑrdi] *adj* : temerario — **foolish** ['fuːlɪʃ] *adj* : tonto — **foolishness** ['fuːlɪʃnəs] *n* : tontería *f* — **foolproof** ['fuːlˌpruːf] *adj* : infalible

foot ['fut] *n, pl* **feet** ['fiːt] : pie *m* — **footage** ['fʊtɪdʒ] *n* : secuencias *fpl* (cinemáticas) — **football** ['fʊtˌbɔl] *n* : fútbol *m* americano — **footbridge** ['fʊtˌbrɪdʒ] *n* : pasarela *f*, puente *m* peatonal — **foothills** ['fʊtˌhɪlz] *npl* : estribaciones *fpl* — **foothold** ['fʊtˌhoːld] *n* : punto *m* de apoyo — **footing** ['fʊtɪŋ] *n* **1** BALANCE : equilibrio *m* **2 on equal ~** : en igualdad — **footlights** ['fʊtˌlaɪts] *npl* : candilejas *fpl* — **footnote** ['fʊtˌnoːt] *n* : nota *f* al pie de la página — **footpath** ['fʊtˌpæθ] *n* : sendero *m* — **footprint** ['fʊtˌprɪnt] *n* : huella *f* — **footstep** ['fʊtˌstep] *n* : paso *m* — **footstool** ['fʊtˌstuːl] *n* : escabel *m* — **footwear** ['fʊtˌwær] *n* : calzado *m*

for ['fɔr] *prep* **1** (*indicating purpose, etc.*) : para **2** (*indicating motivation, etc.*) : por **3** (*indicating duration*) : durante **4 we walked ~ 3 miles** : andamos 3 millas **5** AS FOR : con respecto a — ~ *conj* : puesto que, porque

forage ['fɔrɪdʒ] *n* : forraje *m* — ~ *vi* **-aged; -aging 1** : forrajear **2 ~ for** : buscar

foray ['fɔrˌeɪ] *n* : incursión *f*

forbid [fərˈbɪd] *vt* **-bade** [-ˈbæd, -ˈbeɪd] *or* **-bad** [-ˈbæd]; **-bidden** [-ˈbɪdən]; **-bidding** : prohibir — **forbidding** [fərˈbɪdɪŋ] *adj* : intimidante, severo

force ['fɔrs] *n* **1** : fuerza *f* **2 by ~** : por la fuerza **3 in ~** : en vigor, en vigencia **4 armed ~s** : fuerzas *fpl* armadas — ~ *vt* **forced; forcing 1** : forzar **2** OBLIGATE : obligar — **forced** ['fɔrst] *adj* : forzado, forzoso — **forceful** ['fɔrsfəl] *adj* : fuerte, energético

forceps ['fɔrsəps, -ˌseps] *ns & pl* : fórceps *m*

forcibly [-bli] *adv* : por la fuerza

ford ['fɔrd] *n* : vado *m* — ~ *vt* : vadear

fore ['fɔr] *n* **come to the ~** : empezar a destacarse

forearm ['fɔrˌɑrm] *n* : antebrazo *m*

foreboding [fɔrˈboːdɪŋ] *n* : premonición *f*, presentimiento *m*

forecast ['fɔr,kæst] vt **-cast; -casting** : predecir, pronosticar — ~ n : predicción f, pronóstico m

forefathers ['fɔr,fɑðərz] n : antepasados mpl

forefinger ['fɔr,fɪŋgər] n : índice m, dedo m índice

forefront ['fɔr,frʌnt] n **at/in the** ~ : a la vanguardia

forego [for'goː] → **forgo**

foregone [for'gɔn] adj ~ **conclusion** : resultado m inevitable

foreground ['fɔr,graʊnd] n : primer plano m

forehead ['fɔrəd, 'fɔr,hɛd] n : frente f

foreign ['fɔrən] adj **1** : extranjero **2** ~ **trade** : comercio m exterior — **foreigner** ['fɔrənər] n : extranjero m, -ra f

foreman ['fɔrmən] n, pl **-men** [-mən, -,mɛn] : capataz mf

foremost ['fɔr,moːst] adj : principal — ~ adv **first and** ~ : ante todo

forensic [fə'rɛntsɪk] adj : forense

forerunner ['fɔr,rʌnər] n : precursor m, -sora f

foresee [for'siː] vt **-saw; -seen; -seeing** : prever — **foreseeable** [for'siːəbəl] adj : previsible

foreshadow [for'ʃædoː] vt : presagiar

foresight ['fɔr,saɪt] n : previsión f

forest ['fɔrəst] n : bosque m — **forestry** ['fɔrəstri] n : silvicultura f

foretaste ['fɔr,teɪst] n : anticipo m

foretell [for'tɛl] vt **-told; -telling** : predecir

forethought ['fɔr,θɔt] n : reflexión f previa

forever [fər'ɛvər] adv **1** ETERNALLY : para siempre **2** CONTINUALLY : siempre, constantemente

forewarn [for'wɔrn] vt : advertir, prevenir

foreword ['fɔrwərd] n : prólogo m

forfeit ['fɔrfət] n **1** PENALTY : pena f **2** : prenda f (en un juego) — ~ vt : perder

forge ['fɔrdʒ] n : forja f — ~ v **forged; forging** vt **1** : forjar (metal, etc.) **2** COUNTERFEIT : falsificar — vi ~ **ahead** : avanzar, seguir adelante — **forger** ['fɔrdʒər] n : falsificador m, -dora f — **forgery** ['fɔrdʒəri] n, pl **-eries** : falsificación f

forget [fər'gɛt] v **-got** [-'gɑt]; **-gotten** [-'gɑtən] or **-got; -getting** vt : olvidar, olvidarse de — vi **1** : olvidarse **2 I forgot** : se me olvidó — **forgetful** [fər'gɛtfəl] adj : olvidadizo

forgive [fər'gɪv] vt **-gave** [-'geɪv]; **-given** [-'gɪvən]; **-giving** : perdonar — **forgiveness** [fər'gɪvnəs] n : perdón m

forgo or **forego** [for'goː] vt **-went; -gone; -going** : privarse de, renunciar a

fork ['fɔrk] n **1** : tenedor m **2** PITCHFORK : horca f **3** : bifurcación f (de un camino, etc.) — vi : ramificarse, bifurcarse — vt ~ **over** : desembolsar

forlorn [fər'lɔrn] adj : triste

form ['fɔrm] n **1** : forma f **2** DOCUMENT : formulario m **3** KIND : tipo m — ~ vt **1** : formar **2** ~ **a habit** : adquirir un hábito — vi : formarse

formal ['fɔrməl] adj : formal — ~ n **1** BALL : baile m (formal) **2** or ~ **dress** : traje m de etiqueta — **formality** [fɔr'mælə,ti] n, pl **-ties** : formalidad f

format ['fɔr,mæt] n : formato m — ~ vt **-matted; -matting** : formatear

formation [fɔr'meɪʃən] n **1** : formación f **2** SHAPE : forma f

former ['fɔrmər] adj **1** PREVIOUS : antiguo, anterior **2** : primero (de dos) — **formerly** ['fɔrmərli] adv : anteriormente, antes

formidable ['fɔrmədəbəl, fɔr'mɪdə-] adj : formidable

formula ['fɔrmjələ] n, pl **-las** or **-lae** [-,liː, -,laɪ] **1** : fórmula f **2** or **baby** ~ : preparado m para biberón

forsake [fər'seɪk] vt **-sook** [-'sʊk]; **-saken** [-'seɪkən]; **-saking** : abandonar

fort ['fɔrt] n : fuerte m

forth ['fɔrθ] adv **1 and so** ~ : etcétera **2 back and** ~ → **back 3 from this day** ~ : de hoy en adelante — **forthcoming** [forθ'kʌmɪŋ, 'forθ,-] adj **1** COMING : próximo **2** OPEN : comunicativo — **forthright** ['fɔrθ,raɪt] adj : directo, franco

fortieth ['fɔrtiəθ] adj : cuadragésimo — ~ n **1** : cuadragésimo m, -ma f (en una serie) **2** : cuarentavo m, cuarentava parte f

fortify ['fɔrtə,faɪ] vt **-fied; -fying** : fortificar — **fortification** [,fɔrtəfə'keɪʃən] n : fortificación f

fortitude ['fɔrtə,tuːd, -,tjuːd] n : fortaleza f

fortnight ['fɔrt,naɪt] n : quince días mpl, quincena f

fortress ['fɔrtrəs] n : fortaleza f

fortunate ['fɔrtʃənət] adj : afortunado — **fortunately** ['fɔrtʃənətli] adv : afortunadamente — **fortune** ['fɔrtʃən] n : fortuna f — **fortune-teller** ['fɔrtʃən,tɛlər] n : adivino m, -na f

forty ['fɔrti] n, pl **forties** : cuarenta m — ~ adj : cuarenta

forum ['forəm] *n*, *pl* **-rums** : foro *m*

forward ['fɔrwərd] *adj* **1** : hacia adelante (en dirección), delantero (en posición) **2** BRASH : descarado — ~ *adv* **1** : (hacia) adelante **2 from this day** ~ : de aquí en adelante — ~ *vt* : remitir, enviar — ~ *n* : delantero *m*, -ra *f* (en deportes) — **forwards** ['fɔrwərdz] *adv* → **forward**

fossil ['fɑsəl] *n* : fósil *m*

foster ['fɔstər] *adj* : adoptivo — ~ *vt* : promover, fomentar

fought → **fight**

foul ['faʊl] *adj* **1** REPULSIVE : asqueroso **2** ~ **language** : palabrotas *fpl* **3** ~ **play** : actos *mpl* criminales **4** ~ **weather** : mal tiempo *m* — ~ *n* : falta *f* (en deportes) — ~ *vi* : cometer faltas (en deportes) — ~ *vt* : ensuciar

found¹ ['faʊnd] → **find**

found² *vt* : fundar, establecer — **foundation** [faʊn'deɪʃən] *n* **1** : fundación *f* **2** BASIS : fundamento *m* **3** : cimientos *mpl* (de un edificio)

founder¹ ['faʊndər] *n* : fundador *m*, -dora *f*

founder² *vi* SINK : hundirse

fountain ['faʊntən] *n* : fuente *f*

four ['fɔr] *n* : cuatro *m* — ~ *adj* : cuatro — **fourfold** ['fɔr,foːld, -'foːld] *adj* : cuadruple — **four hundred** *adj* : cuatrocientos — ~ *n* : cuatrocientos *m*

fourteen [fɔr'tiːn] *n* : catorce *m* — ~ *adj* : catorce — **fourteenth** [fɔr'tiːnθ] *adj* : decimocuarto — ~ *n* **1** : decimocuarto *m*, -ta *f* (en una serie) **2** : catorceavo *m*, catorceava parte *f*

fourth [fɔrθ] *n* **1** : cuarto *m*, -ta *f* (en una serie) **2** : cuarto *m*, cuarta parte *f* — ~ *adj* : cuarto

fowl ['faʊl] *n*, *pl* **fowl** *or* **fowls** : ave *f*

fox ['fɑks] *n*, *pl* **foxes** : zorro *m*, -rra *f* — ~ *vt* TRICK : engañar — **foxy** ['fɑksi] *adj* **foxier; -est** SHREWD : astuto

foyer ['fɔɪər, 'fɔɪjeɪ] *n* : vestíbulo *m*

fraction ['frækʃən] *n* : fracción *f*

fracture ['fræktʃər] *n* : fractura *f* — ~ *vt* **-tured; -turing** : fracturar

fragile ['frædʒəl, -,dʒaɪl] *adj* : frágil

fragment ['frægmənt] *n* : fragmento *m*

fragrant ['freɪgrənt] *adj* : fragante — **fragrance** ['freɪgrənts] *n* : fragancia *f*, aroma *m*

frail ['freɪl] *adj* : débil, delicado

frame ['freɪm] *n* *vt* **framed; framing 1** ENCLOSE : enmarcar **2** COMPOSE, DRAFT : formular **3** INCRIMINATE : incriminar — ~ *n* **1** : armazón *mf* (de un edificio, etc.) **2** : marco *m* (de un cuadro, una puerta, etc.) **3** *or* ~**s** *npl* : montura *f*

(para anteojos) **4** ~ **of mind** : estado *m* de ánimo — **framework** ['freɪm,wɜrk] *n* : armazón *f*

franc ['fræŋk] *n* : franco *m*

frank ['fræŋk] *adj* : franco — **frankly** *adv* : francamente — **frankness** ['fræŋknəs] *n* : franqueza *f*

frantic ['fræntɪk] *adj* : frenético

fraternal [frə'tərnəl] *adj* : fraterno, fraternal — **fraternity** [frə'tərnəti] *n*, *pl* **-ties** : fraternidad *f* — **fraternize** ['frætər,naɪz] *vi* **-nized; -nizing** : confraternizar

fraud ['frɔd] *n* **1** DECEIT : fraude *m* **2** IMPOSTOR : impostor *m*, -tora *f* — **fraudulent** ['frɔdʒələnt] *adj* : fraudulento

fraught ['frɔt] *adj* ~ **with** : lleno de, cargado de

fray¹ ['freɪ] *n* **1 join the** ~ : salir a la palestra **2 return to the** ~ : volver a la carga

fray² *vt* : crispar (los nervios) — *vi* : deshilacharse

freak ['friːk] *n* **1** ODDITY : fenómeno *m* **2** ENTHUSIAST : entusiasta *mf* — **freakish** ['friːkɪʃ] *adj* : anormal

freckle ['frekəl] *n* : peca *f*

free ['friː] *adj* **freer; freest 1** : libre **2** *or* ~ **of charge** : gratuito, gratis **3** LOOSE : suelto — ~ *vt* **freed; freeing 1** : liberar, poner en libertad **2** RELEASE, UNFASTEN : soltar, desatar — ~ *adv* *or* **for** ~ : gratis — **freedom** ['friːdəm] *n* : libertad *f* — **freelance** ['friː,lænts] *adj* : por cuenta propia — **freely** ['friːli] *adv* **1** : libremente **2** LAVISHLY : con generosidad — **freeway** ['friː,weɪ] *n* : autopista *f* — **free will** *n* **1** : libre albedrío *m* **2 of one's own** ~ : por su propia voluntad

freeze ['friːz] *v* **froze** ['froːz]; **frozen** ['froːzən]; **freezing** *vi* **1** : congelarse, helarse **2** STOP : quedarse inmóvil — *vt* : helar (agua, etc.), congelar (alimentos, precios, etc.) — **freeze-dry** ['friːz,draɪ] *vt* **-dried; -drying** : liofilizar — **freezer** ['friːzər] *n* : congelador *m* — **freezing** ['friːzɪŋ] *adj* **1** CHILLY : helado **2 it's freezing!** : ¡hace un frío espantoso!

freight ['freɪt] *n* **1** SHIPPING : porte *m*, flete *m* *Lat* **2** CARGO : carga *f*

French ['frentʃ] *adj* : francés — ~ *n* **1** : francés *m* (idioma) **2 the** ~ *npl* : los franceses — **Frenchman** ['frentʃmən] *n* : francés *m* — **Frenchwoman** ['frentʃ,wʊmən] *n* : francesa *f* — **french fries** ['frentʃ,fraɪz] *npl* : papas *fpl* fritas

frenetic [frɪ'nɛtɪk] *adj* : frenético

frenzy ['frenzi] *n, pl* **-zies** : frenesí *m* — **frenzied** ['frenzid] *adj* : frenético

frequent [fri'kwent, 'fri:kwənt] *vt* : frecuentar — **~** ['fri:kwənt] *adj* : frecuente — **frequency** ['fri:kwəntsi] *n, pl* **-cies** : frecuencia *f* — **frequently** *adv* : a menudo, frecuentemente

fresco ['fresko:] *n, pl* **-coes** : fresco *m*

fresh ['freʃ] *adj* 1 : fresco 2 IMPUDENT : descarado 3 CLEAN : limpio 4 NEW : nuevo 5 **~ water** : agua *m* dulce — **freshen** ['freʃən] *vt* : refrescar — *vi* **~ up** : arreglarse — **freshly** ['freʃli] *adv* : recién — **freshman** ['freʃmən] *n, pl* **-men** [-mən, -ˌmen] : estudiante *mf* de primer año — **freshness** ['freʃnəs] *n* : frescura *f*

fret ['fret] *vi* **fretted; fretting** : preocuparse — **fretful** ['fretfəl] *adj* : nervioso, irritable

friar ['fraɪər] *n* : fraile *m*

friction ['frɪkʃən] *n* : fricción *f*

Friday ['fraɪˌdeɪ, -di] *n* : viernes *m*

friend ['frend] *n* : amigo *m*, -ga *f* — **friendliness** ['frendlinəs] *n* : simpatía *f* — **friendly** ['frendli] *adj* **-lier; -est** : simpático, amable — **friendship** ['frendʃɪp] *n* : amistad *f*

frigate ['frɪgət] *n* : fragata *f*

fright ['fraɪt] *n* : miedo *m*, susto *m* — **frighten** ['fraɪtən] *vt* : asustar, espantar — **frightened** ['fraɪtənd] *adj* 1 : asustado, temeroso 2 **be ~ of** : tener miedo de — **frightening** ['fraɪtənɪŋ] *adj* : espantoso — **frightful** ['fraɪtfəl] *adj* : espantoso, terrible

frigid ['frɪdʒɪd] *adj* : frío, glacial

frill ['frɪl] *n* 1 RUFFLE : volante *m* 2 LUXURY : lujo *m*

fringe ['frɪndʒ] *n* 1 : fleco *m* 2 EDGE : periferia *f*, margen *m* 3 **~ benefits** : incentivos *mpl*, extras *mpl*

frisk ['frɪsk] *vt* SEARCH : cachear, registrar — **frisky** ['frɪski] *adj* **friskier; -est** : retozón, juguetón

fritter ['frɪtər] *n* : buñuelo *m* — *vt or* **~ away** : malgastar (dinero), desperdiciar (tiempo)

frivolous ['frɪvələs] *adj* : frívolo — **frivolity** [frɪ'vɑləti] *n, pl* **-ties** : frivolidad *f*

frizzy ['frɪzi] *adj* **frizzier; -est** : rizado, crespo

fro ['fro:] *adv* **to and ~** → **to**

frock ['frɑk] *n* : vestido *m*

frog ['frɔg, 'frɑg] *n* 1 : rana *f* 2 **have a ~ in one's throat** : tener carraspera

frolic ['frɑlɪk] *vi* **-icked; -icking** : retozar

from ['frʌm, 'frɑm] *prep* 1 : de 2 (*indicating a starting point*) : desde 3 (*indicating a cause*) : de, por 4 **~ now on** : a partir de ahora

front ['frʌnt] *n* 1 : parte *f* delantera 2 : delantera *f* (de un vestido, etc.), fachada *f* (de un edificio), frente *m* (militar) 3 **cold ~** : frente *m* frío 4 **in ~ of** : delante de, adelante de — *Lat* — *vi or* **~ on** : dar a, estar orientado a — *adj* 1 : delantero, de adelante 2 **the ~ row** : la primera fila

frontier [ˌfrʌn'tɪr] *n* : frontera *f*

frost ['frɔst] *n* 1 : helada *f* 2 : escarcha *f* (en una superficie) — *vt* ICE : bañar (pasteles) — **frostbite** ['frɔstˌbaɪt] *n* : congelación *f* — **frosting** ['frɔstɪŋ] *n* ICING : baño *m* — **frosty** ['frɔsti] *adj* **frostier; -est** 1 : cubierto de escarcha 2 CHILLY : helado, frío

froth ['frɔθ] *n, pl* **froths** ['frɔθs, 'frɔðz] : espuma *f* — **frothy** ['frɔθi] *adj* **frothier; -est** : espumoso

frown ['fraʊn] *vi* 1 : fruncir el ceño, fruncir el entrecejo 2 **~ at** : mirar con ceño 3 **~ upon** : desaprobar — **~** *n* : ceño *m* (fruncido)

froze, frozen → **freeze**

frugal ['fru:gəl] *adj* : frugal

fruit ['fru:t] *n* 1 : fruta *f* 2 PRODUCT, RESULT : fruto *m* — **fruitcake** ['fru:tˌkeɪk] *n* : pastel *m* de frutas — **fruitful** ['fru:tfəl] *adj* : fructífero — **fruition** [fru'ɪʃən] *n* **come to ~** : realizarse — **fruitless** ['fru:tləs] *adj* : infructuoso — **fruity** ['fru:ti] *adj* **fruitier; -est** : (con sabor) a fruta

frustrate ['frʌsˌtreɪt] *vt* **-trated; -trating** : frustrar — **frustrating** ['frʌsˌtreɪtɪŋ] *adj* : frustrante — **frustration** [ˌfrʌs'treɪʃən] *n* : frustración *f*

fry ['fraɪ] *vt* **fried; frying** : freír — **~** *n, pl* **fries** 1 **small ~** : gente *f* de poca monta 2 **fries** *npl* → **french fries** — **frying pan** *n* : sartén *mf*

fudge ['fʌdʒ] *n* : dulce *m* blando de chocolate y leche

fuel ['fju:əl] *n* : combustible *m* — *vt* **-eled** *or* **-elled; -eling** *or* **-elling** 1 : alimentar (un horno), abastecer de combustible (un avión) 2 STIMULATE : estimular

fugitive ['fju:dʒətɪv] *n* : fugitivo *m*, -va *f*

fulfill *or* **fulfil** [fʊl'fɪl] *vt* **-filled; -filling** 1 : cumplir con (una obligación), desarrollar (potencial) 2 FILL, MEET : cumplir — **fulfillment** [fʊl'fɪlmənt] *n* 1 ACCOMPLISHMENT : cumplimiento *m* 2 SATISFACTION : satisfacción *f*

full ['fʊl, 'fɑl] *adj* 1 FILLED : lleno 2 COMPLETE : complete, detallado 3 : redondo (dícese de la cara), amplio (dícese de ropa) **4 at ~ speed** : a toda velocidad **5 in ~ bloom** : en plena flor — **~** adv **1** DIRECTLY : de lleno **2 know ~ well** : saber muy bien — **~** n **1 pay in ~** : pagar en su totalidad **2 to the ~** : al máximo — **full–fledged** ['fʊl'flɛdʒd] adj : hecho y derecho — **fully** ['fʊli] adv **1** COMPLETELY : completamente **2** AT LEAST : al menos, por lo menos

fumble ['fʌmbəl] vi **-bled; -bling 1** RUMMAGE : hurgar **2 ~ with** : manejar con torpeza

fume ['fjuːm] vi **fumed; fuming 1** SMOKE : echar humo, humear **2** RAGE : estar furioso — **fumes** npl : gases mpl

fumigate ['fjuːməˌgeɪt] vt **-gated; -gating** : fumigar

fun ['fʌn] n **1** AMUSEMENT : diversión f **2 have ~** : divertirse **3 make ~ of** : reírse de, burlarse de — **~** adj : divertido

function ['fʌŋkʃən] n **1** : función f **2** GATHERING : recepción f, reunión f social — **~** vi : funcionar — **functional** ['fʌŋkʃənəl] adj : funcional

fund ['fʌnd] n **1** : fondo m **2 ~s** npl RESOURCES : fondos mpl — **~** vt : financiar

fundamental [ˌfʌndəˈmɛntəl] adj : fundamental — **fundamentals** npl : fundamentos mpl

funeral ['fjuːnərəl] adj : funeral, fúnebre — **~** n : funeral m, funerales mpl — **funeral home** or **funeral parlor** n : funeraria f

fungus ['fʌŋgəs] n, pl **fungi** ['fʌndʒaɪ, 'fʌŋgaɪ] : hongo m

funnel ['fʌnəl] n **1** : embudo m **2** SMOKESTACK : chimenea f

funny ['fʌni] adj **funnier; -est 1** : divertido, gracioso **2** STRANGE : extraño, raro — **funnies** ['fʌniz] npl : tiras fpl cómicas

fur ['fər] n **1** : pelaje m, pelo m (de un animal) **2** or **~ coat** : (prenda f de) piel f — **~** adj : de piel

furious ['fjʊriəs] adj : furioso

furnace ['fərnəs] n : horno m

furnish ['fərnɪʃ] vt **1** SUPPLY : proveer **2** : amueblar (una casa, etc.) — **furnishings** ['fərnɪʃɪŋz] npl : muebles mpl, mobiliario m — **furniture** ['fərnɪtʃər] n : muebles mpl, mobiliario m

furrow ['fəroː] n : surco m

furry ['fəri] adj **furrier; -est** : peludo (dícese de un animal), de peluche (dícese de un juguete, etc.)

further ['fərðər] adv **1** FARTHER : más lejos **2** MOREOVER : además **3** MORE : más — **~** vt : promover, fomentar — adj **1** FARTHER : más lejano **2** ADDITIONAL : adicional, más **3 until ~ notice** : hasta nuevo aviso — **furthermore** ['fərðərˌmor] adv : además — **furthest** ['fərðəst] → **farthest**

furtive ['fərtɪv] adj : furtivo

fury ['fjʊri] n, pl **-ries** : furia f

fuse¹ or **fuze** ['fjuːz] n : mecha f (de una bomba, etc.)

fuse² v **fused; fusing** vt **1** MELT : fundir **2** UNITE : fusionar — vi : fundirse, fusionarse — **~** n **1** : fusible m **2 blow a ~** : fundir un fusible — **fusion** ['fjuːʒən] n : fusión f

fuss ['fʌs] n **1** : jaleo m, alboroto m **2 make a ~** : armar un escándalo — **~** vi **1** WORRY : preocuparse **2** COMPLAIN : quejarse — **fussy** ['fʌsi] adj **fussier; -est 1** IRRITABLE : irritable **2** ELABORATE : recargado **3** FINICKY : quisquilloso

futile ['fjuːtəl, 'fjuːˌtaɪl] adj : inútil, vano — **futility** [fjuːˈtɪləti] n, pl **-ties** : inutilidad f

future ['fjuːtʃər] adj : futuro — **~** n : futuro m

fuze → **fuse¹**

fuzz ['fʌz] n : pelusa f — **fuzzy** ['fʌzi] adj **fuzzier; -est 1** FURRY : con pelusa, peludo **2** BLURRY : borroso **3** VAGUE : confuso

G

g ['dʒiː] n, pl **g's** or **gs** ['dʒiːz] : g f, séptima letra del alfabeto inglés

gab ['gæb] vi **gabbed; gabbing** : charlar, cotorrear fam — **~** n CHATTER : charla f

gable ['geɪbəl] n : aguilón m

gadget ['gædʒət] n : artilugio m

gag ['gæg] v **gagged; gagging** vt : amordazar — vi CHOKE : atragantarse — **~** n **1** : mordaza f **2** JOKE : chiste m

gage → **gauge**

gaiety ['geɪəti] n, pl **-eties** : alegría f — **gaily** ['geɪli] adv : alegremente

gain ['geɪn] n **1** PROFIT : ganancia f **2** INCREASE : aumento m — **~** vt **1** OBTAIN : ganar, adquirir **2 ~ weight** : aumentar de peso — *vi* **1** PROFIT : beneficiarse **2** : adelantar(se) (dícese de un reloj) — **gainful** ['geinfəl] *adj* : lucrativo

gait ['geit] *n* : modo *m* de andar

gala ['geilə, 'gæ-, 'ga-] *n* : fiesta *f*

galaxy ['gæləksi] *n*, *pl* **-axies** : galaxia *f*

gale ['geil] *n* **1** : vendaval *f* **2** ~**s of laughter** : carcajadas *fpl*

gall ['gɔl] *n* **have the** ~ **to** : tener el descaro de

gallant ['gælənt] *adj* **1** BRAVE : valiente **2** CHIVALROUS : galante

gallbladder ['gɔl,blædər] *n* : vesícula *f* biliar

gallery ['gæləri] *n*, *pl* **-leries** : galería *f*

gallon ['gælən] *n* : galón *m*

gallop ['gæləp] *vi* : galopar — ~ *n* : galope *m*

gallows ['gæ,lo:z] *n*, *pl* **-lows** *or* **-lowses** [-,lo:zəz] : horca *f*

gallstone ['gɔl,sto:n] *n* : cálculo *m* biliar

galore [gə'lor] *adj* : en abundancia

galoshes [gə'laʃ] *n* : galochas *fpl*, chanclos *mpl*

galvanize ['gælvən,aiz] *vt* **-nized**; **-nizing** : galvanizar

gamble ['gæmbəl] *v* **-bled**; **-bling** *vi* : jugar — *vt* : jugarse — ~ *n* **1** BET : apuesta *f* **2** RISK : riesga *f* — **gambler** ['gæmbələr] *n* : jugador *m*, -dora *f*

game ['geim] *n* **1** : juego *m* **2** MATCH : partido *m* **3** *or* ~ **animals** : caza *f* — ~ *adj* READY : listo, dispuesto

gamut ['gæmət] *n* : gama *f*

gang ['gæŋ] *n* : banda *f*, pandilla *f* — ~ *vi* ~ **up on** : unirse contra

gangplank ['gæŋ,plæŋk] *n* : pasarela *f*

gangrene ['gæŋ,gri:n, 'gæn-; gæŋ'-, gæn'-] *n* : gangrena *f*

gangster ['gæŋstər] *n* : gángster *mf*

gangway ['gæŋ,wei] *n* → **gangplank**

gap ['gæp] *n* **1** OPENING : espacio *m* **2** INTERVAL : intervalo *m* **3** DISPARITY : brecha *f*, distancia *f* **4** DEFICIENCY : laguna *f*

gape ['geip] *vi* **gaped**; **gaping 1** OPEN : estar abierto **2** STARE : mirar boquiabierto

garage [gə'raʒ, -'radʒ] *n* : garaje *m* — ~ *vt* **-raged**; **-raging** : dejar en un garaje

garb ['garb] *n* : vestido *m*

garbage ['garbidʒ] *n* : basura *f* — **garbage can** *n* : cubo *m* de la basura

garble ['garbəl] *vt* **-bled**; **-bling** : tergiversar — **garbled** ['garbəld] *adj* : confuso, incomprensible

garden ['gardən] *n* : jardín *m* — ~ *vi* : trabajar en el jardín — **gardener** ['gardənər] *n* : jardinero *m*, -ra *f* — **gardening** ['gardəniŋ] *n* : jardinería *f*

gargle ['gargəl] *vi* **-gled**; **-gling** : hacer gárgaras

garish ['gæriʃ] *adj* : chillón

garland ['garlənd] *n* : guirnalda *f*

garlic ['garlik] *n* : ajo *m*

garment ['garmənt] *n* : prenda *f*

garnish ['garniʃ] *vt* : guarnecer — ~ *n* : adorno *m*, guarnición *f*

garret ['gærət] *n* : buhardilla *f*

garrison ['gærəsən] *n* : guarnición *f*

garrulous ['gærələs] *adj* : charlatán, parlanchín

garter ['gartər] *n* : liga *f*

gas ['gæs] *n*, *pl* **gases** ['gæsəz] **1** : gas *m* **2** GASOLINE : gasolina *f* — ~ *v* **gassed**; **gassing** *vt* : asfixiar con gas — *vi* ~ **up** : llenar el tanque con gasolina

gash ['gæʃ] *n* : tajo *m* — ~ *vt* : hacer un tajo en, cortar

gasket ['gæskət] *n* : junta *f*

gasoline ['gæsə,li:n, ,gæsə'-] *n* : gasolina *f*

gasp ['gæsp] *vi* **1** : dar un grito ahogado **2** PANT : jadear — ~ *n* : grito *m* ahogado

gas station *n* : gasolinera *f*

gastric ['gæstrik] *adj* : gástrico

gastronomy [gæs'tranəmi] *n* : gastronomía *f*

gate ['geit] *n* **1** DOOR : puerta *f* **2** BARRIER : barrera *f* — **gateway** ['geit,wei] *n* : puerta *f*

gather ['gæðər] *vt* **1** ASSEMBLE : reunir **2** COLLECT : recoger **3** CONCLUDE : deducir **4** : fruncir (una tela) **5** ~ **speed** : acelerar — *vi* : reunirse (dícese de personas), acumularse (dícese de cosas) — **gathering** ['gæðəriŋ] *n* : reunión *f*

gaudy ['gɔdi] *adj* **gaudier**; **-est** : chillón, llamativo

gauge ['geidʒ] *n* **1** INDICATOR : indicador *m* **2** CALIBER : calibre *m* — ~ *vt* **gauged**; **gauging 1** MEASURE : medir **2** ESTIMATE : calcular, evaluar

gaunt ['gɔnt] *adj* : demacrado, descarnado

gauze ['gɔz] *n* : gasa *f*

gave → **give**

gawky ['gɔki] *adj* **gawkier**; **-est** : desgarbado

gay ['gei] *adj* **1** : alegre **2** HOMOSEXUAL : gay, homosexual

gaze ['geiz] *vi* **gazed**; **gazing** : mirar (fijamente) — ~ *n* : mirada *f*

gazelle [gə'zel] *n* : gacela *f*

gazette [gə'zet] *n* : gaceta *f*

gear ['gir] *n* **1** EQUIPMENT : equipo *m* **2** POSSESSIONS : efectos *mpl* personales

3 : marcha f (de un vehículo) 4 or ~ **wheel** : rueda f dentada — ~ vt : orientar, adaptar — vi ~ **up** : prepararse — **gearshift** ['gɪr,ʃɪft] n : palanca f de cambio, palanca f de velocidades Lat

geese → **goose**

gelatin ['dʒɛlətən] n : gelatina f

gem ['dʒem] n : gema f, piedra f preciosa — **gemstone** ['dʒem,stoːn] n : piedra f preciosa

gender ['dʒendər] n 1 SEX : sexo m 2 : género m (en la gramática)

gene ['dʒiːn] n : gen m, gene m

genealogy [,dʒiːni'alədʒi, ,dʒe-, -'æ-] n, pl -**gies** : genealogía f

general ['dʒenrəl, 'dʒenə-] adj : general — ~ n 1 : general mf (militar) 2 **in** ~ : en general, por lo general — **generalize** ['dʒenrə,laɪz, 'dʒenərə-] v -**ized**; -**izing** : generalizar — **generally** ['dʒenrəli, 'dʒenərə-] adv : generalmente, en general — **general practitioner** n : médico m, -ca f de cabecera

generate ['dʒenə,reɪt] vt -**ated**; -**ating** : generar — **generation** [dʒenə'reɪʃən] n : generación f — **generator** ['dʒenə,reɪtər] n : generador m

generous ['dʒenərəs] adj 1 : generoso 2 AMPLE : abundante — **generosity** [,dʒenə'rasəti] n, pl -**ties** : generosidad f

genetic [dʒə'netɪk] adj : genético — **genetics** [dʒə'netɪks] n : genética f

genial ['dʒiːniəl] adj : afable, simpático

genital ['dʒenətəl] adj : genital — **genitals** ['dʒenətəlz] npl : genitales mpl

genius ['dʒiːnjəs] n : genio m

genocide ['dʒenə,saɪd] n : genocidio m

genteel [dʒen'tiːl] adj : refinado

gentle ['dʒentəl] adj -**tler**; -**tlest** 1 MILD : suave, dulce 2 LIGHT : ligero 3 a ~ **hint** : una indirecta discreta — **gentleman** ['dʒentəlmən] n, pl -**men** [-mən, -,men] 1 MAN : caballero m, señor m 2 **a perfect** ~ : un perfecto caballero — **gentleness** ['dʒentəlnəs] n : delicadeza f, ternura f

genuine ['dʒenjuwən] adj 1 AUTHENTIC : verdadero, auténtico 2 SINCERE : sincero

geography [dʒi'agrəfi] n, pl -**phies** : geografía f — **geographic** [,dʒiːə'græfɪk] or **geographical** [-fɪkəl] adj : geográfico

geology [dʒi'alədʒi] n : geología f — **geologic** [,dʒiːə'ladʒɪk] or **geological** [-dʒɪkəl] adj : geológico

geometry [dʒi'amətri] n, pl -**tries** : geometría f — **geometric** [,dʒiːə'metrɪk] or **geometrical** [-trɪkəl] adj : geométrico

geranium [dʒə'reɪniəm] n : geranio m

geriatric [,dʒeri'ætrɪk] adj : geriátrico — **geriatrics** [,dʒeri'ætrɪks] n : geriatría f

germ ['dʒərm] n 1 : germen m 2 MICROBE : microbio m

German ['dʒərmən] adj : alemán — ~ n : alemán m (idioma)

germinate ['dʒərmə,neɪt] v -**nated**; -**nating** vi : germinar — vt : hacer germinar

gestation [dʒe'steɪʃən] n : gestación f

gesture ['dʒestʃər] n : gesto m — ~ vi -**tured**; -**turing** 1 : hacer gestos 2 ~ **to** : hacer señas a

get ['get] v **got** ['gɑt]; **got** or **gotten** ['gɑtən]; **getting** vt 1 OBTAIN : conseguir, obtener 2 RECEIVE : recibir 3 EARN : ganar 4 FETCH : traer 5 CATCH : coger, agarrar Lat 6 UNDERSTAND : entender 7 PREPARE : preparar 8 ~ **one's hair cut** : cortarse el pelo 9 ~ **s.o. to do sth** : lograr que uno haga algo 10 **have got** : tener 11 **have got to** : tener que — vi 1 BECOME : ponerse, hacerse 2 GO, MOVE : ir 3 PROGRESS : avanzar 4 ~ **ahead** : progresar 5 ~ **at** MEAN : querer decir 6 ~ **away** : escaparse 7 ~ **away with** : salir impune de 8 ~ **back at** : desquitarse con 9 ~ **by** : arreglárselas 10 ~ **home** : llegar a casa 11 ~ **out** : salir 12 ~ **over** : reponerse de, consolarse de 13 ~ **together** : reunirse 14 ~ **up** : levantarse — **getaway** ['getə,weɪ] n : fuga f, huida f — **get-together** n : reunión f

geyser ['gaɪzər] n : géiser m

ghastly ['gæstli] adj -**lier**; -**est** : horrible, espantoso

ghetto ['getoː] n, pl -**tos** or -**toes** : gueto m

ghost ['goːst] n : fantasma f, espectro m — **ghostly** ['goːstli] adv : fantasmal

giant ['dʒaɪənt] n : gigante m, -ta f — ~ adj : gigantesco

gibberish ['dʒɪbərɪʃ] n : galimatías m, jerigonza f

gibe ['dʒaɪb] vi **gibed**; **gibing** ~ **at** : mofarse de — ~ n : pulla f, mofa f

giblets ['dʒɪbləts] npl : menudillos mpl

giddy ['gɪdi] adj -**dier**; -**est** : mareado, vertiginoso — **giddiness** ['gɪdinəs] n : vértigo m

gift ['gɪft] n 1 PRESENT : regalo m 2 TALENT : don m — **gifted** ['gɪftəd] adj : talentoso, de talento

gigantic [dʒaɪ'gæntɪk] adj : gigantesco

giggle ['gɪgəl] vi -**gled**; -**gling** : reírse tontamente — ~ n : risa f tonta

gild ['gɪld] vt **gilded** ['gɪldəd] or **gilt** ['gɪlt]; **gilding** : dorar

gill ['gɪl] n : agalla f, branquia f

gilt ['gɪlt] adj : dorado

gimmick ['gɪmɪk] n : truco m, ardid m

gin ['dʒɪn] n : ginebra f

ginger ['dʒɪndʒər] n : jengibre m — **ginger ale** n : refresco m de jengibre — **gingerbread** ['dʒɪndʒər,brɛd] n : pan m de jengibre — **gingerly** ['dʒɪndʒərli] adv : con cuidado, cautelosamente

giraffe [dʒəˈræf] n : jirafa f

girder ['gərdər] n : viga f

girdle ['gərdəl] n CORSET : faja f

girl ['gərl] n 1 : niña f, muchacha f, chica f — **girlfriend** ['gərl,frɛnd] n : novia f, amiga f

girth ['gərθ] n : circunferencia f

gist ['dʒɪst] n **get the ~ of** : comprender lo esencial de

give ['gɪv] v **gave** ['geɪv]; **given** ['gɪvən]; **giving** vt 1 : dar 2 INDICATE : señalar 3 PRESENT : presentar 4 **~ away** : regalar 5 **~ back** : devolver 6 **~ out** : repartir 7 **~ up smoking** : dejar de fumar — vi 1 YIELD : ceder 2 COLLAPSE : romperse 3 **~ out** : agotarse 4 **~ up** : rendirse — **~** n : elasticidad f — **given** ['gɪvən] adj 1 SPECIFIED : determinado 2 INCLINED : dado, inclinado — **given name** n : nombre m de pila

glacier ['gleɪʃər] n : glaciar m

glad ['glæd] adj **gladder; gladdest** 1 : alegre, contento 2 **to be ~** : alegrarse 3 **~ to meet you!** : ¡mucho gusto! — **gladden** ['glædən] vt : alegrar — **gladly** ['glædli] adv : con mucho gusto — **gladness** ['glædnəs] n : alegría f, gozo m

glade ['gleɪd] n : claro m

glamor or **glamour** ['glæmər] n : atractivo m, encanto m — **glamorous** ['glæmərəs] adj : atractivo

glance ['glænts] vi **glanced; glancing** 1 **~ at** : mirar, dar un vistazo a 2 **~ off** : rebotar en — **~** n : mirada f, vistazo m

gland ['glænd] n : glándula f

glare ['glær] vi **glared; glaring** 1 : brillar, relumbrar 2 **~ at** : lanzar una mirada feroz a — **~** n 1 : luz f deslumbrante 2 STARE : mirada f feroz — **glaring** ['glærɪŋ] adj 1 BRIGHT : deslumbrante 2 FLAGRANT : flagrante

glass ['glæs] n 1 : vidrio m, cristal m 2 **a ~ of milk** : un vaso de leche 3 **~es** npl SPECTACLES : anteojos mpl, lentes fpl — **~** adj : de vidrio — **glassware** ['glæs,wær] n : cristalería f — **glassy**

['glæsi] adj **glassier; -est** 1 : vítreo 2 **~ eyes** : ojos mpl vidriosos

glaze ['gleɪz] vt **glazed; glazing** 1 : poner vidrios a (una ventana, etc.) 2 : vidriar (cerámica) 3 ICE : glasear — **~** n 1 : vidriado m, barniz m (de cerámica) 2 ICING : glaseado m

gleam ['gli:m] n 1 : destello m 2 **a ~ of hope** : un rayo de esperanza — **~** vi : destellar, relucir

glee ['gli:] n : alegría f — **gleeful** ['gli:fəl] adj : lleno de alegría

glib ['glɪb] adj **glibber; glibbest** 1 : de mucha labia 2 **a ~ reply** : una respuesta simplista — **glibly** ['glɪbli] adv : con mucha labia

glide ['glaɪd] vi **glided; gliding** : deslizarse (en una superficie), planear (en el aire) — **glider** ['glaɪdər] n : planeador m

glimmer ['glɪmər] vi : brillar con luz trémula — **~** n : luz f trémula, luz f tenue

glimpse ['glɪmps] vt **glimpsed; glimpsing** : vislumbrar — **~** n : vislumbre f

glint ['glɪnt] vi : destellar — **~** n : destello m

glisten ['glɪsən] vi : brillar

glitter ['glɪtər] vi : relucir, brillar

gloat ['gloːt] vi **~ over** : regodearse con

globe ['gloːb] n : globo m — **global** ['gloːbəl] adj : global, mundial

gloom ['glu:m] n 1 DARKNESS : oscuridad f 2 SADNESS : tristeza f — **gloomy** ['glu:mi] adj **gloomier; -est** 1 DARK : sombrío, tenebroso 2 DISMAL : deprimente, lúgubre 3 PESSIMISTIC : pesimista

glory ['glori] n, pl **-ries** : gloria f — **glorify** ['glorəˌfaɪ] vt **-fied; -fying** : glorificar — **glorious** ['gloriəs] adj : glorioso, espléndido

gloss ['glɔs, 'glɑs] n : lustre m, brillo m — **~** vt **~ over** : minimizar (la importancia de algo)

glossary ['glɔsəri, 'glɑ-] n, pl **-ries** : glosario m

glossy ['glɔsi, 'glɑ-] adj **glossier; -est** : lustroso, brillante

glove ['glʌv] n : guante m

glow ['gloː] vi 1 : brillar, resplandecer 2 **~ with health** : rebosar de salud — **~** n : resplandor m, brillo m

glue ['glu:] n : pegamento m, cola f — **~** vt **glued; gluing** or **glueing** : pegar

glum ['glʌm] adj **glummer; glummest** : sombrío, triste

glut ['glʌt] n : superabundancia f, exceso m

glutton ['glʌtən] n : glotón m, -tona f —
gluttonous ['glʌtənəs] adj : glotón —
gluttony ['glʌtəni] n, pl **-tonies** : glotonería f
gnarled ['nɑrld] adj : nudoso
gnash ['næʃ] vt ~ **one's teeth** : hacer
rechinar los dientes
gnat ['næt] n : jején m
gnaw ['nɔ] vt : roer
go ['goː] v **went** ['went]; **gone** ['gɔn,
'gɑn]; **going; goes** ['goːz] vi 1 : ir 2
LEAVE : irse, salir 3 EXTEND : ir, extenderse 4 SELL : venderse 5 FUNCTION
: funcionar, marchar 6 DISAPPEAR : desaparecer 7 ~ **back on one's word**
: faltar a su palabra 8 ~ **crazy** : volverse loco 9 ~ **for** LIKE : gustar 10 ~
off EXPLODE : estallar 11 ~ **with**
MATCH : armonizar con 12 ~ **without**
: pasar sin — v aux **be going to** : ir a
— ~ n, pl **goes have a** ~ **at** : intentar
goad ['goːd] vt : aguijonear (un animal),
incitar (a una persona)
goal ['goːl] n 1 AIM : meta m, objetivo m
2 : gol m (en deportes) — **goalkeeper**
['goːlˌkiːpər] or **goalie** ['goːli] n : portero
m, -ra f; arquero m, -ra f
goat ['goːt] n : cabra f
goatee [goːˈtiː] n : barbita f de chivo
gobble ['gɑbəl] vt **-bled; -bling** or ~
up : engullir
goblet ['gɑblət] n : copa f
goblin ['gɑblən] n : duende m
god ['gɑd, 'gɔd] n 1 : dios m 2 **God**
: Dios m — **goddess** ['gɑdəs, 'gɔ-] n
: diosa f — **godchild** ['gɑd,tʃaɪld, 'gɔd-]
n, pl **-children** : ahijado m, -da f —
godfather ['gɑdˌfɑðər, 'gɔd-] n : padrino m — **godmother** ['gɑd,mʌðər, 'gɔd-]
n : madrina f — **godparents** ['gɑd-
ˌpærənt, 'gɔd-] n : padrinos mpl —
godsend ['gɑd,send, 'gɔd-] n : bendición f (del cielo)
goes → go
goggles ['gɑgəlz] npl : gafas fpl (protec-
toras), anteojos mpl
goings-on [goːɪŋz'ɑn, -'ɔn] npl : sucesos
mpl
got → get
gold ['goːld] n : oro m — **golden**
['goːldən] adj 1 : (hecho) de oro 2 : dorado, de color oro — **goldfish** ['goːld-
ˌfɪʃ] n : pez m de colores — **goldsmith**
['goːld,smɪθ] n : orfebre mf
golf ['gɑlf, 'gɔlf] n : golf m — ~ vi
: jugar (al) golf — **golf ball** n : pelota
f de golf — **golf course** n : campo m
de golf — **golfer** ['gɑlfər, 'gɔl-] n
: golfista mf

gone ['gɔn] adj 1 : ido, pasado 2 DEAD
: muerto 3 LOST : desaparecido
good ['gud] adj **better** ['betər]; **best**
['best] 1 : bueno 2 KIND : amable 3 ~
afternoon (evening) : buenas tardes
be ~ **at** : tener facilidad para 5 **feel**
~ : sentirse bien 6 ~ **for a cold**
: beneficioso para los resfriados 7
have a ~ **time** : divertirse 8 ~
morning : buenos días 9 ~ **night**
: buenas noches — ~ n 1 : bien m 2
GOODNESS : bondad f 3 — **s** npl PROP-
ERTY : bienes mpl 4 **~s** npl WARES
: mercancías fpl, mercaderías fpl 5 **for**
~ : para siempre — ~ adv : bien —
good-bye or **good-by** [gud'baɪ] n
: adiós m — **Good Friday** n : Viernes
m Santo — **good-looking** ['gud'lukɪŋ]
adj : bello, guapo — **goodness**
['gudnəs] n 1 : bondad f 2 **thank** ~ !
: ¡gracias a Dios!, ¡menos mal! —
goodwill [gud'wɪl] n : buena voluntad
f — **goody** ['gudi] n, pl **goodies**
: golosina f
gooey ['guːi] adj **gooier; gooiest** : pegajoso
goof n ['guːf] : pifia f fam — ~ vi 1 or
~ **up** : cometer un error 2 ~ **around**
: hacer tonterías
goose ['guːs] n, pl **geese** ['giːs] : ganso
m, -sa f; oca f — **goose bumps** or
goose pimples npl : carne f de gallina
gopher ['goːfər] n : taltuza f
gore¹ ['gor] n BLOOD : sangre f
gore² vt **gored; goring** : cornear
gorge ['gɔrdʒ] n RAVINE : cañon m — ~
vt **gorged; gorging** ~ **oneself** : hartarse
gorgeous ['gɔrdʒəs] adj : magnífico, espléndido
gorilla [gəˈrɪlə] n : gorila m
gory ['gori] adj **gorier; -est** : sangriento
gospel ['gɑspəl] n 1 : evangelio m 2 **the**
Gospel : el Evangelio
gossip ['gɑsɪp] n 1 : chismoso m, -sa f
(persona) 2 RUMOR : chisme m — ~
vi : chismear, contar chismes — **gossipy** ['gɑsɪpi] adj : chismoso
got → get
Gothic ['gɑθɪk] adj : gótico
gotten → get
gourmet ['gur,meɪ, gur'meɪ] n : gastrónomo m, -ma f
gout ['gaut] n : gota f
govern ['gʌvərn] v : gobernar — **governess** ['gʌvərnəs] n : institutriz f —
government ['gʌvərmənt] n : gobierno
m — **governor** ['gʌvənər, 'gʌvərnər] n
: gobernador m, -dora f

gown ['gaʊn] n 1 : vestido m 2 : toga f (de magistrados, etc.)

grab ['græb] v **grabbed; grabbing** vt : agarrar, arrebatar

grace ['greɪs] n 1 : gracia f 2 say ~ : bendecir la mesa — ~ vt **graced; gracing** 1 HONOR : honrar 2 ADORN : adornar — **graceful** ['greɪsfəl] adj : lleno de gracia, grácil — **gracious** ['greɪʃəs] adj : cortés, gentil

grade ['greɪd] n 1 QUALITY : calidad f 2 RANK : grado m, rango m (militar) 3 YEAR : grado m, año m (a la escuela) 4 MARK : nota f 5 SLOPE : cuesta f — ~ vt **graded; grading** 1 CLASSIFY : clasificar 2 MARK : calificar (exámenes, etc.) — **grade school** → **elementary school**

gradual ['grædʒʊəl] adj : gradual — **gradually** ['grædʒʊəli, 'grædʒəli] adv : gradualmente, poco a poco

graduate ['grædʒʊət] n : licenciado m, -da f (de la universidad), bachiller mf (de la escuela secundaria) — ~ ['grædʒʊˌeɪt] v **-ated; -ating** vi : graduarse, licenciarse — vt CALIBRATE : graduar — **graduation** [ˌgrædʒʊˈeɪʃən] n : graduación f

graffiti [grəˈfiːti, græ-] npl : graffiti mpl

graft ['græft] n : injerto m — ~ vt : injertar

grain ['greɪn] n 1 : grano m 2 CEREALS : cereales mpl 3 : veta f, vena f (de madera)

gram ['græm] n : gramo m

grammar ['græmər] n : gramática f — **grammar school** → **elementary school**

grand ['grænd] adj 1 : magnífico, espléndido 2 FABULOUS, GREAT : fabuloso, estupendo — **grandchild** ['grænd,tʃaɪld] n, pl **-children** : nieto m, -ta f — **granddaughter** ['grænd,dɔtər] n : nieta f — **grandeur** ['grændʒər] n : grandiosidad f — **grandfather** ['grænd,fɑðər] n : abuelo m — **grandiose** ['grændiˌoʊs, ˌgrændi'-] adj : grandioso — **grandmother** ['grænd,mʌðər] n : abuela f — **grandparents** ['grænd,pærənt] npl : abuelos mpl — **grandson** ['grænd,sʌn] n : nieto m — **grandstand** ['grænd,stænd] n : tribuna f

granite ['grænɪt] n : granito m

grant ['grænt] vt 1 : conceder 2 ADMIT : reconocer, admitir 3 take for granted : dar (algo) por sentado — ~ n 1 SUBSIDY : subvención f 2 SCHOLARSHIP : beca f

grape ['greɪp] n : uva f

grapefruit ['greɪp,fruːt] n : toronja f, pomelo m

grapevine ['greɪp,vaɪn] n 1 : vid f, parra f 2 **I heard it through the** ~ : me lo dijo un pajarito fam

graph ['græf] n : gráfica f, gráfico m — **graphic** ['græfɪk] adj : gráfico

grapple ['græpəl] vi **-pled; -pling** ~ **with** : forcejear con (una persona), luchar con (un problema)

grasp ['græsp] vt 1 : agarrar 2 UNDERSTAND : comprender, captar — ~ n 1 : agarre m 2 UNDERSTANDING : comprensión f 3 REACH : alcance m

grass ['græs] n 1 : hierba f (planta) 2 LAWN : césped m, pasto m Lat — **grasshopper** ['græs,hɑpər] n : saltamontes m — **grassy** ['græsi] adj **grassier; -est** : cubierto de hierba

grate[1] ['greɪt] v **grated; -ing** vt 1 : rallar (en cocina) 2 ~ **one's teeth** : hacer rechinar los dientes — vi RASP : chirriar

grate[2] n GRATING : reja f, rejilla f

grateful ['greɪtfəl] adj : agradecido — **gratefully** ['greɪtfəli] adv : con agradecimiento — **gratefulness** ['greɪtfəlnəs] n : gratitud f, agradecimiento m

grater ['greɪtər] n : rallador m

gratify ['grætəˌfaɪ] vt **-fied; -fying** 1 PLEASE : complacer 2 SATISFY : satisfacer

grating ['greɪtɪŋ] n : reja f, rejilla f

gratitude ['grætəˌtuːd, -ˌtjuːd] n : gratitud f

gratuitous [grəˈtuːətəs] adj : gratuito

grave[1] ['greɪv] n : tumba f, sepultura f

grave[2] adj **graver; -est** : grave

gravel ['grævəl] n : grava f, gravilla f

gravestone ['greɪv,stoʊn] n : lápida f — **graveyard** ['greɪv,jɑrd] n : cementerio m

gravity ['grævəti] n, pl **-ties** : gravedad f

gravy ['greɪvi] n, pl **-vies** : salsa f (preparada con jugo de carne)

gray ['greɪ] adj 1 : gris 2 ~ **hair** : pelo m canoso — ~ n : gris m — ~ vi or **turn** ~ : encanecer, ponerse gris

graze[1] ['greɪz] vi **grazed; grazing** : pastar, pacer

graze[2] vt 1 TOUCH : rozar 2 SCRATCH : rasguñar

grease ['griːs] n : grasa f — ~ ['griːs, 'griːz] vt **greased; greasing** : engrasar — **greasy** ['griːsi, -zi] adj **greasier; -est** 1 OILY : grasiento, graso, grasoso

great ['greɪt] adj 1 : grande 2 FANTASTIC : estupendo, fabuloso — **great-grandchild** [greɪt'grænd,tʃaɪld] n, pl

-children [-,t∫ɪldrən] : bisnieto m, -ta f
— **great—grandfather** [,greɪt'grænd-
,fɑðər] n : bisabuelo m — **great—
grandmother** [,greɪt'grænd,mʌðər] n
: bisabuela f — **greatly** ['greɪtli] adv 1
MUCH : mucho 2 VERY : muy — **greatness** ['greɪtnəs] n : grandeza f

greed ['griːd] n 1 : codicia f, avaricia f 2
GLUTTONY : glotonería f — **greedily**
['griːdəli] adv : con avaricia — **greedy**
['griːdi] adj **greedier; -est** 1 : codicioso, avaro 2 GLUTTONOUS : glotón

Greek ['griːk] adj : griego m, -ga f — ~ n
: griego m (idioma)

green ['griːn] adj 1 : verde 2 INEXPERI-
ENCED : novato — ~ n 1 : verde m
(color) 2 ~s npl : verduras fpl —
greenery ['griːnəri] n, pl **-eries** : vegetación f — **greenhouse** ['griːn,haʊs]
n : invernadero m

greet ['griːt] vt 1 : saludar 2 WELCOME
: recibir — **greeting** ['griːtɪŋ] n 1
: saludo m 2 ~s npl REGARDS : saludos mpl, recuerdos mpl

gregarious [grɪ'gæriəs] adj : sociable

grenade [grə'neɪd] n : granada f

grew → grow

grey → gray

greyhound ['greɪ,haʊnd] n : galgo m

grid ['grɪd] n 1 GRATING : rejilla f 2 NET-
WORK : red f 3 : cuadriculado m (de un
mapa)

griddle ['grɪdəl] n : plancha f

grief ['griːf] n : dolor m, pesar m —
grievance ['griːvəns] n : queja f —
grieve ['griːv] v **grieved; grieving** vt
: entristecer — vi ~ **for** : llorar (a),
lamentar — **grievous** ['griːvəs] adj
: grave, doloroso

grill ['grɪl] vt 1 : asar a la parrilla 2 IN-
TERROGATE : interrogar — ~ n 1 : parrilla f (para cocinar) — **grille** or **grill**
['grɪl] GRATING : reja f, rejilla f

grim ['grɪm] adj **grimmer; grimmest** 1
STERN : severo 2 GLOOMY : sombrío

grimace ['grɪməs, grɪ'meɪs] n : mueca f
— ~ vi **-maced; -macing** : hacer
muecas

grime ['graɪm] n : mugre f, suciedad f —
grimy ['graɪmi] adj **grimier; -est** : mugriento, sucio

grin ['grɪn] vi **grinned; grinning** : sonreír (abiertamente) — ~ n : sonrisa f
(abierta)

grind ['graɪnd] v **ground** ['graʊnd];
grinding vt 1 : moler (el café, etc.) 2
SHARPEN : afilar 3 ~ **one's teeth**
: rechinar los dientes — vi ~ : rechinar
— ~ **n the daily** : la rutina diaria
— **grinder** ['graɪndər] n : molinillo m

grip ['grɪp] vt **gripped; gripping** 1
: agarrar, asir 2 INTEREST : captar el interés de — ~ n 1 GRASP : agarre m 2
CONTROL : control m, dominio m 3
HANDLE : empuñadura f 4 **come to
~s with** : llegar a entender de

gripe ['graɪp] vi **griped; griping** : quejarse — ~ n : queja f

grisly ['grɪzli] adj **-lier; -est** : espeluznante, horrible

gristle ['grɪsəl] n : cartílago m

grit ['grɪt] n 1 : arena f, grava f 2 GUTS
: agallas fpl fam 3 ~s npl : sémola f
de maíz — ~ vt **gritted; gritting** ~
one's teeth : acorazarse

groan ['groʊn] vi : gemir — ~ n : gemido m

grocery ['groʊsəri, -fəri] n, pl **-ceries**
or ~ **store** : tienda f de comestibles,
tienda f de abarrotes Lat — **groceries**
npl : comestibles mpl, abarrotes mpl
Lat — **grocer** ['groʊsər] n : tendero m,
-ra f

groggy ['grɑgi] adj **-gier; -est** : atonta-
do, grogui fam

groin ['grɔɪn] n : ingle f

groom ['gruːm, 'grʊm] n BRIDEGROOM
: novio m — ~ vt 1 : almohazar (un
animal) 2 PREPARE : preparar

groove ['gruːv] n : ranura f, surco m

grope ['groʊp] vi **groped; groping** 1
: andar a tientas 2 ~ **for** : buscar a
tientas

gross ['groʊs] adj 1 SERIOUS : grave 2
OBESE : obeso 3 TOTAL : bruto 4 VUL-
GAR : grosero, basto — ~ n 1 or ~
income : ingresos mpl brutos 2 pl ~
: gruesa f (12 docenas) — **grossly**
['groʊsli] adv 1 EXTREMELY : enormemente 2 CRUDELY : groseramente

grotesque [groʊ'tesk] adj : grotesco

grouch ['graʊt∫] n : gruñón m, -ñona f
fam — **grouchy** ['graʊt∫i] adj **grouch-
ier; -est** : gruñón fam

ground¹ ['graʊnd] → grind

ground² n 1 : suelo m, tierra f 2 or ~s
LAND : terreno m 3 ~s REASON : razón
f, motivos mpl 4 ~s DREGS : pozo m
(de café) — ~ vt 1 BASE : fundar,
basar 2 : conectar a tierra (un aparato
eléctrico) 3 : restringir (un avión o un
piloto) a la tierra — **groundhog**
['graʊnd,hɔg] n : marmota f (de América) — **groundless** ['graʊndləs] adj
: infundado — **groundwork** ['graʊnd-
,wɜrk] n : trabajo m preparatorio

group ['gruːp] n : grupo m — ~ vt
: agrupar — vi or ~ **together** : agruparse

grove ['groʊv] n : arboleda f

grovel ['grʌvəl, 'grʌ-] vi **-eled** or **-elled**; **-eling** or **-elling** : arrastrarse, humillarse

grow ['groː] v **grew** ['gruː]; **grown** ['groːn]; **growing** vi 1 : crecer 2 INCREASE : aumentar 3 BECOME : volverse, ponerse 4 ~ **dark** : oscurecerse 5 ~ **up** : hacerse mayor — vt 1 CULTIVATE : cultivar 2 : dejarse crecer (el pelo, etc.) — **grower** ['groːər] n : cultivador m, -dora f

growl ['graul] vi : gruñir — ~ n : gruñido m

grown-up ['groːnˌəp] adj : mayor — ~ n : persona f mayor

growth ['groːθ] n 1 : crecimiento m 2 INCREASE : aumento m 3 DEVELOPMENT : desarrollo m 4 TUMOR : tumor m

grub ['grʌb] n 1 LARVA : larva f 2 FOOD : comida f

grubby ['grʌbi] adj **grubbier; -est** : mugriento, sucio

grudge ['grʌdʒ] vt **grudged; grudging** : dar de mala gana — ~ n **hold a** ~ : guardar rencor

grueling or **gruelling** ['gruːlɪŋ, 'gruːə-] adj : extenuante, agotador

gruesome ['gruːsəm] adj : horripilante

gruff ['grʌf] adj 1 BRUSQUE : brusco 2 HOARSE : bronco

grumble ['grʌmbəl] vi **-bled; -bling** : refunfuñar, rezongar

grumpy ['grʌmpi] adj **grumpier; -est** : malhumorado, gruñón fam

grunt ['grʌnt] vi : gruñir — ~ n : gruñido m

guarantee [ˌgærən'tiː] n : garantía f — ~ vt **-teed; -teeing** : garantizar

guard ['gɑrd] n 1 : guardia f 2 PRECAUTION : protección f — ~ vt : proteger, vigilar — vi ~ **against** : protegerse contra — **guardian** ['gɑrdiən] n 1 : tutor m, -tora f (de niños) 2 PROTECTOR : guardián m, -diana f

guava ['gwɑvə] n : guayaba f

guerrilla or **guerilla** [gə'rɪlə] n 1 : guerrillero m, -ra f 2 ~ **warfare** : guerra f de guerrillas

guess ['gɛs] vt 1 : adivinar 2 SUPPOSE : suponer, creer — vi ~ **at** : adivinar — ~ n : conjetura f, suposición f

guest ['gɛst] n 1 : invitado m, -da f 2 : huésped mf (a un hotel)

guide ['gaɪd] n : guía mf (persona), guía f (libro, etc.) — ~ vt **guided; guiding** : guiar — **guidance** ['gaɪdənts] n : orientación f — **guidebook** ['gaɪdˌbuk] n : guía f — **guideline** ['gaɪdˌlaɪn] n : pauta f, directriz f

guild ['gɪld] n : gremio m

guile ['gaɪl] n : astucia f

guilt ['gɪlt] n : culpa f, culpabilidad f — **guilty** ['gɪlti] adj **guiltier; -est** : culpable

guinea pig ['gɪni-] n : conejillo m de Indias, cobaya f

guise ['gaɪz] n : apariencia f

guitar [gə'tɑr, gɪ-] n : guitarra f

gulf ['gʌlf] n 1 : golfo m 2 ABYSS : abismo m

gull ['gʌl] n : gaviota f

gullet ['gʌlət] n 1 THROAT : garganta f 2 ESOPHAGUS : esófago m

gullible ['gʌlɪbəl] adj : crédulo

gully ['gʌli] n, pl **-lies** : barranco m

gulp ['gʌlp] vt or ~ **down** : tragarse, engullir — vi : tragar saliva — ~ n : trago m

gum¹ ['gʌm] n : encía f (de la boca)

gum² n 1 : resina f (de plantas) 2 CHEWING GUM : goma f de mascar, chicle m

gumption ['gʌmpʃən] n : iniciativa f, agallas fpl fam

gun ['gʌn] n 1 FIREARM : arma f de fuego 2 or **spray** ~ : pistola f 3 → cannon, pistol, revolver, rifle — ~ vt **gunned; gunning** 1 or ~ **down** : matar a tiros, asesinar 2 ~ **the engine** : acelerar (el motor) — **gunboat** ['gʌnˌboːt] n : cañonero m — **gunfire** ['gʌnˌfaɪr] n : disparos mpl — **gunman** ['gʌnmən] n, pl **-men** [-mən, -ˌmɛn] : pistolero m, gatillero m Lat — **gunpowder** ['gʌnˌpaudər] n : pólvora f — **gunshot** ['gʌnˌʃɑt] n : disparo m, tiro m

gurgle ['gərgəl] vi **-gled; -gling** 1 : borbotar, gorgotear 2 : gorjear (dícese de un niño)

gush ['gʌʃ] vi 1 SPOUT : salir a chorros 2 ~ **with praise** : deshacerse en elogios

gust ['gʌst] n : ráfaga f

gusto ['gʌsˌtoː] n, pl **gustoes** : entusiasmo m

gusty ['gʌsti] adj **gustier; -est** : racheado, ventoso

gut ['gʌt] n 1 : intestino m 2 ~s npl INNARDS : tripas fpl 3 ~s npl COURAGE : agallas fpl fam — ~ vt **gutted; gutting** 1 EVISCERATE : destripar (un pollo, etc.), limpiar (un pescado) 2 : destruir el interior de (un edificio)

gutter ['gʌtər] n : canaleta f (de un techo), cuneta f (de una calle)

guy ['gaɪ] n : tipo m fam

guzzle ['gʌzəl] vt **-zled; -zling** : chupar fam, tragar

gym ['dʒɪm] or **gymnasium** [dʒɪm'neɪziəm, -ʒəm] n, pl **-siums** or **-sia** [-ziːə, -ʒə] : gimnasio m — **gymnast**

H

h ['eɪt∫] *n*, *pl* **h's** *or* **hs** ['eɪt∫əz] : h *f*, octava letra del alfabeto inglés
habit ['hæbɪt] *n* **1** CUSTOM : hábito *m*, costumbre *f* **2** : hábito *m* (religioso)
habitat ['hæbɪˌtæt] *n* : hábitat *m*
habitual [hə'bɪt∫ʊəl] *adj* **1** CUSTOMARY : habitual **2** INVETERATE : empedernido
hack¹ ['hæk] *n* **1** : caballo *m* de alquiler **2** *or* ~ **writer** : escritorzuelo *m*, -la *f*
hack² *vt* : cortar — *vi or* ~ **into** : piratear (un sistema informático)
hackneyed ['hæknid] *adj* : manido, trillado
hacksaw ['hækˌsɔ] *n* : sierra *f* para metales
had → **have**
haddock ['hædək] *ns & pl* : eglefino *m*
hadn't ['hædənt] (*contraction of* **had not**) → **have**
hag ['hæg] *n* : bruja *f*
haggard ['hægərd] *adj* : demacrado
haggle ['hægəl] *vi* **-gled; -gling** : regatear
hail¹ ['heɪl] *vt* **1** GREET : saludar **2** : llamar (un taxi)
hail² *n* : granizo *m* (en meteorología) — ~ *vi* : granizar — **hailstone** ['heɪlˌstoʊn] *n* : piedra *f* de granizo
hair ['hær] *n* **1** : pelo *m*, cabello *m* **2** : vello *m* (en las piernas, etc.) — **hairbrush** ['hærˌbrʌ∫] *n* : cepillo *m* (para el pelo) — **haircut** ['hærˌkʌt] *n* **1** : corte *m* de pelo **2 get a** ~ : cortarse el pelo — **hairdo** ['hærˌduː] *n*, *pl* **-dos** : peinado *m* — **hairdresser** ['hærˌdresər] *n* : peluquero *m*, -ra *f* — **hairless** ['hærləs] *adj* : sin pelo, calvo — **hairpin** ['hærˌpɪn] *n* : horquilla *f* — **hair-raising** ['hærˌreɪzɪŋ] *adj* : espeluznante — **hairstyle** ['hærˌstaɪl] — **hairdo** — **hair spray** : laca *f* (para el pelo) — **hairy** ['hæri] *adj* **hairier; -est** : peludo, velludo
hale ['heɪl] *adj* : saludable, robusto
half ['hæf, 'haf] *n*, *pl* **halves** ['hævz, 'havz] **1** : mitad *f* **2** *or* **halftime** : tiempo *m* (en deportes) **3 in** ~ : por la mitad — ~ *adj* **1** : medio **2** ~ **an hour** : una media hora — ~ *adv* : medio — **half brother** *n* : medio hermano *m*, hermanastro *m* — **halfhearted** ['hæf'hɑrtəd] *adj* : sin ánimo, poco entusiasta — **half sister** *n* : media her-

mana *f*, hermanastra *f* — **halfway** ['hæf'weɪ] *adv* : a medio camino — ~ *adj* : medio
halibut ['hælɪbət] *ns & pl* : halibut *m*
hall ['hɔl] *n* **1** HALLWAY : corredor *m*, pasillo *m* **2** AUDITORIUM : sala *f* **3** LOBBY : vestíbulo *m* **4** DORMITORY : residencia *f* universitaria
hallmark ['hɔlˌmɑrk] *n* : sello *m* (distintivo)
Halloween [ˌhælə'wiːn, ˌhɑ-] *n* : víspera *f* de Todos los Santos
hallucination [həˌluːsən'eɪ∫ən] *n* : alucinación *f*
hallway ['hɔlˌweɪ] *n* **1** ENTRANCE : entrada *f* **2** CORRIDOR : corredor *m*, pasillo *m*
halo ['heɪˌloː] *n*, *pl* **-los** *or* **-loes** : aureola *f*, halo *m*
halt ['hɔlt] *n* **1 call a** ~ **to** : poner fin a **2 come to a** ~ : pararse — ~ *vi* : pararse — *vt* : parar
halve ['hæv, 'hav] *vt* **halved; halving 1** DIVIDE : partir por la mitad **2** REDUCE : reducir a la mitad — **halves** → **half**
ham ['hæm] *n* : jamón *m*
hamburger ['hæmˌbərgər] *or* **hamburg** [-ˌbərg] *n* **1** : carne *f* molida **2** *or* ~ **patty** : hamburguesa *f*
hammer ['hæmər] *n* : martillo *m* — ~ *v* : martillar, martillear
hammock ['hæmək] *n* : hamaca *f*
hamper¹ ['hæmpər] *vt* : obstaculizar, dificultar
hamper² *n* : cesto *m*, canasta *f* (para ropa sucia)
hamster ['hæmpstər] *n* : hámster *m*
hand ['hænd] *n* **1** : mano *f* **2** : manecilla *f*, aguja *f* (de un reloj, etc.) **3** HANDWRITING : letra *f*, escritura *f* **4** WORKER : obrero *m*, -ra *f* **5 by** ~ : a mano **6 lend a** ~ : echar una mano **7 on** ~ : a mano, disponible **8 on the other** ~ : por otro lado — ~ *vt* **1** : pasar, dar **2** ~ **out** : distribuir **3** ~ **over** : entregar — **handbag** ['hændˌbæg] *n* : cartera *f Lat*, bolso *m Spain* — **handbook** ['hændˌbʊk] *n* : manual *m* — **handcuffs** ['hændˌkʌfs] *npl* : esposas *fpl* — **handful** ['hændˌfʊl] *n* : puñado *m* — **handgun** ['hændˌgʌn] *n* : pistola *f*, revólver *m*
handicap ['hændiˌkæp] *n* **1** : minusvalía *f*

(física) 2 : hándicap *m* (en deportes) —
~ *vt* -**capped**; -**capping 1** : asignar
un handicap a (en deportes) 2 HAMPER
: obstaculizar — **handicapped**
['hændi,kæpt] *adj* : minusválido

handicrafts ['hændi,kræfts] *npl* : arte-
sanía(s) *f(pl)*

handiwork ['hændi,wərk] *n* : trabajo *m*
(manual)

handkerchief ['hæŋkərtʃəf, -tʃi:f] *n, pl*
-**chiefs** : pañuelo *m*

handle ['hændəl] *n* : asa *f* (de una taza,
etc.), mango *m* (de un utensilio),
pomo *m* (de una puerta), tirador *m* (de
un cajón) — ~ *vt* -**dled**; -**dling 1**
TOUCH : tocar 2 MANAGE : tratar, manejar — **handlebars** ['hændəl,bɑrz] *npl*
: manillar *m*, manubrio *m* Lat

handmade ['hænd,meid] *adj* : hecho a
mano

handout ['hænd,aut] *n* 1 ALMS : dádiva *f*,
limosna *f* 2 LEAFLET : folleto *m*

handrail ['hænd,reil] *n* : pasamanos *m*

handshake ['hænd,ʃeik] *n* : apretón *m*
de manos

handsome ['hæntsəm] *adj* -**somer**; -**est**
1 ATTRACTIVE : apuesto, guapo 2 GEN-
EROUS : generoso 3 SIZABLE : considerable

handwriting ['hænd,raitɪŋ] *n* : letra *f*, escritura *f* — **handwritten** ['hænd,ritən]
adj : escrito a mano

handy ['hændi] *adj* **handier**; -**est 1**
NEARBY : a mano 2 USEFUL : práctico,
útil 3 DEFT : habilidoso — **handyman**
['hændimæn] *n, pl* -**men** [-mən, -,mɛn]
: hombre *m* habilidoso

hang ['hæŋ] *v* **hung** ['hʌŋ]; **hanging** *vt* 1
: colgar 2 (*past tense often* **hanged**)
EXECUTE : ahorcar 3 ~ **one's head**
: bajar la cabeza — *vi* 1 : colgar, pender 2 : caer (dícese de la ropa, etc.) 3
~ **up on s.o.** : colgar a algn — ~ *n*
1 DRAPE : caída *f* 2 **get the** ~ **of**
: agarrar la onda de

hangar ['hæŋər, 'hæŋgər] *n* : hangar *m*

hanger ['hæŋər] *n* : percha *f*, gancho *m*
(para ropa) Lat

hangover ['hæŋ,ovər] *n* : resaca *f*

hanker ['hæŋkər] *vi* ~ **for** : tener ansias
de — **hankering** ['hæŋkərɪŋ] *n* : ansia *f*,
anhelo *m*

haphazard [hæp'hæzərd] *adj* : casual,
fortuito

happen ['hæpən] *vi* 1 : pasar, suceder,
ocurrir 2 ~ **to do sth** : hacer algo por
casualidad 3 **it so happens that...**
: da la casualidad de que... — **hap-
pening** ['hæpənɪŋ] *n* : suceso *m*, acontecimiento *m*

happy ['hæpi] *adj* -**pier**; -**est 1** : feliz 2
be ~ : alegrarse 3 **be** ~ **with** : estar
contento con 4 **be** ~ **to do sth** : hacer
algo con mucho gusto — **happily**
['hæpəli] *adv* : alegremente — **happiness** ['hæpinəs] *n* : felicidad *f* —
happy-go-lucky ['hæpigo'lʌki] *adj*
: despreocupado

harass [hə'ræs, 'hærəs] *vt* : acosar — **harassment** [hə'ræsmənt, 'hærəsmənt] *n*
: acoso *m*

harbor *or Brit* **harbour** ['hɑrbər] *n*
: puerto *m* — ~ *vt* 1 SHELTER : albergar
2 ~ **a grudge against** : guardar rencor a

hard ['hɑrd] *adj* 1 : duro 2 DIFFICULT
: difícil 3 **be a** ~ **worker** : ser muy
trabajador 4 ~ **liquor** : bebidas *fpl*
fuertes 5 ~ **water** : agua *f* dura —
adv 1 FORCEFULLY : fuerte 2 **work** ~
: trabajar duro 3 **take sth** ~ : tomarse
algo muy mal — **harden** ['hɑrdən] *vt*
: endurecer — **hardheaded** [,hɑrd-
'hɛdəd] *adj* : testarudo, terco —
hard-hearted [,hɑrd'hɑrtəd] *adj* : duro
de corazón — **hardly** ['hɑrdli] *adv* 1
: apenas 2 ~ **ever** : casi nunca —
hardness ['hɑrdnəs] *n* 1 : dureza *f* 2
DIFFICULTY : dificultad *f* — **hardship**
['hɑrd,ʃip] *n* : dificultad *f* — **hardware**
['hɑrd,wær] *n* 1 : ferretería *f* 2 : hardware *m* (en informática) — **hardwork-
ing** ['hɑrd'wərkɪŋ] *adj* : trabajador

hardy ['hɑrdi] *adj* -**dier**; -**est** : fuerte (dícese de personas), resistente (dícese
de las plantas)

hare ['hær] *n, pl* **hare** *or* **hares** : liebre *f*

harm ['hɑrm] *n* : daño *m* — ~ *vt* : hacer
daño a (una persona), dañar (una
cosa), perjudicar (la reputación de
algn, etc.) — **harmful** ['hɑrmfəl] *adj*
: perjudicial — **harmless** ['hɑrmləs]
adj : inofensivo

harmonica [hɑr'mɑnikə] *n* : armónica *f*

harmony ['hɑrməni] *n, pl* -**nies** : armonía *f* — **harmonious** [hɑr'moniəs] *adj*
: armonioso — **harmonize** ['hɑrmə-
,naiz] *v* -**nized**; -**nizing** : armonizar

harness ['hɑrnəs] *n* : arnés *m* — ~ *vt* 1
: enjaezar 2 UTILIZE : utilizar

harp ['hɑrp] *n* : arpa *m* — ~ *vi* ~ **on**
: insistir sobre

harpoon [hɑr'pun] *n* : arpón *m*

harpsichord ['hɑrpsi,kord] *n* : clavicémbalo *m*

harsh ['hɑrʃ] *adj* 1 ROUGH : áspero 2 SE-
VERE : duro, severo 3 : fuerte (dícese
de una luz), discordante (dícese de
sonidos) — **harshness** ['hɑrʃnəs] *n*
: severidad *f*

harvest ['hɑrvəst] n : cosecha f — ~ v : cosechar

has → **have**

hash ['hæʃ] vt 1 CHOP : picar 2 ~ **over** DISCUSS : discutir — ~ n : picadillo m (comida)

hasn't ['hæzənt] (contraction of has not) → **has**

hassle ['hæsəl] n : problemas mpl, lío m — ~ vt -**sled; -sling** : fastidiar

haste ['heɪst] n 1 : prisa f, apuro m Lat 2 **make** ~ : darse prisa, apurarse Lat — **hasten** ['heɪsən] vt : acelerar — vi : apresurarse, apurarse Lat — **hasty** ['heɪsti] adj **hastier; -est** : precipitado

hat ['hæt] n : sombrero m

hatch ['hætʃ] n : escotilla f — ~ vt 1 : empollar (huevos) 2 CONCOCT : tramar — vi : salir del cascarón

hatchet ['hætʃət] n : hacha f

hate ['heɪt] n : odio m — ~ vt **hated; hating** : odiar, aborrecer — **hateful** ['heɪtfəl] adj : odioso, aborrecible — **hatred** ['heɪtrəd] n : odio m

haughty ['hɔṭi] adj -**tier; -est** : altanero, altivo

haul ['hɔl] vt : arrastrar, jalar Lat — ~ n 1 CATCH : redada f (de peces) 2 LOOT : botín m 3 **a long** ~ : un trayecto largo

haunch ['hɔntʃ] n : cadera f (de una persona), anca f (de un animal)

haunt ['hɔnt] vt 1 : frecuentar, rondar 2 TROUBLE : inquietar — ~ n : sitio m predilecto — **haunted** ['hɔntəd] adj : embrujado

have ['hæv, in sense 3 as an auxiliary verb usu hæf] v **had** ['hæd]; **having**; **has** ['hæz, in sense 3 as an auxiliary verb usu hæs] vt 1 : tener 2 CONSUME : comer, tomar 3 ALLOW : permitir 4 : dar (una fiesta, etc.), convocar (una reunión) 5 ~ **one's hair cut** : cortarse el pelo 6 ~ **sth done** : mandar hacer algo — v **aux** 1 : haber 2 ~ **just done sth** : acabar de hacer algo 4 **you've finished, haven't you?** : has terminado, ¿no?

haven ['heɪvən] n : refugio m

havoc ['hævək] n : estragos mpl

hawk[1] ['hɔk] n : halcón m

hawk[2] vt : pregonar (mercancías)

hay ['heɪ] n : heno m — **hay fever** n : fiebre f del heno — **haystack** ['heɪ,stæk] n : almiar m — **haywire** ['heɪ,waɪr] adj **go** ~ : estropearse

hazard ['hæzərd] n : peligro m, riesgo m — ~ vt : arriesgar, aventurar — **hazardous** ['hæzərdəs] adj : arriesgado, peligroso

haze ['heɪz] n : bruma f, neblina f

hazel ['heɪzəl] n : color m avellana — **hazelnut** ['heɪzəl,nʌt] n : avellana f

hazy ['heɪzi] adj **hazier; -est** : nebuloso

he ['hi:] pron : él

head ['hɛd] n 1 : cabeza f 2 END, TOP : cabeza f (de un clavo, etc.), cabecera f (de una mesa) 3 LEADER : jefe m, -fa f 4 **be out of one's** ~ : estar loco 5 **come to a** ~ : llegar a un punto crítico 6 ~**s or tails** : cara o cruz 7 **per** ~ : por cabeza — ~ adj MAIN : principal — ~ vt : encabezar — vi : dirigirse — **headache** ['hɛd,eɪk] n : dolor m de cabeza — **headband** ['hɛd,bænd] n : cinta f del pelo — **headdress** ['hɛd,drɛs] n : tocado m — **headfirst** ['hɛd-'fərst] adv : de cabeza — **heading** ['hɛdɪŋ] n : encabezamiento m, título m — **headland** ['hɛdlənd, -,lænd] n : cabo m — **headlight** ['hɛd,laɪt] n : faro m — **headline** ['hɛd,laɪn] n : titular m — **headlong** ['hɛd,lɔŋ] adv HEADFIRST : de cabeza 2 HASTILY : precipitadamente — **headmaster** ['hɛd,mæstər] n : director m — **headmistress** ['hɛd-,mɪstrəs, -,mɪs-] n : directora f — **head-on** ['hɛd'ɔn, -'ɔn] adv & adj : de frente — **headphones** ['hɛd,fonz] npl : auriculares mpl, audífonos mpl Lat — **headquarters** ['hɛd,kwɔrtərz] ns & pl : oficina f central (de una compañía), cuartel m general (de los militares) — **head start** n : ventaja f — **headstrong** ['hɛd'strɔŋ] adj : testarudo, obstinado — **headwaiter** ['hɛd-'weɪtər] n : jefe m, -fa f de comedor — **headway** ['hɛd,weɪ] n 1 : progreso m 2 **make** ~ : avanzar — **heady** ['hɛdi] adj **headier; -est** : embriagador

heal ['hi:l] vt : curar — vi : cicatrizar

health ['hɛlθ] n : salud f — **healthy** ['hɛlθi] adj **healthier; -est** : sano, saludable

heap ['hi:p] n : montón m — ~ vt : amontonar

hear ['hɪr] v **heard** ['hərd]; **hearing** vt : oír — vi 1 : oír 2 ~ **about** : enterarse de 3 ~ **from** : tener noticias de — **hearing** ['hɪrɪŋ] n 1 : oído m 2 : vista f (en un tribunal) — **hearing aid** n : audífono m — **hearsay** ['hɪr,seɪ] n : rumores mpl

hearse ['hərs] n : coche m fúnebre

heart ['hɑrt] n 1 : corazón m 2 **at** ~ : en el fondo 3 **by** ~ : de memoria 4 **lose** ~ : descorazonarse 5 **take** ~ : animarse — **heartache** ['hɑrt,eɪk] n : pena f, dolor m — **heart attack** n : infarto m, ataque m al corazón — **heartbeat**

['hɑrt,biːt] *n* : latido *m* (del corazón) — **heartbreak** ['hɑrt,breɪk] *n* : congoja *f*, angustia *f* — **heartbroken** ['hɑrt,broːkən] *adj* : desconsolado — **heartburn** ['hɑrt,bərn] *n* : acidez *f* estomacal

hearth ['hɑrθ] *n* : hogar *m*

heartily ['hɑrṭəli] *adv* : de buena gana

heartless ['hɑrtləs] *adj* : de mal corazón, cruel

hearty ['hɑrṭi] *adj* **heartier; -est 1** : cordial, caluroso **2** : abundante (dícese de una comida)

heat ['hiːt] *vt* : calentar — *vi or* ~ **up** : calentarse — ~ *n* **1** : calor *m* **2** HEATING : calefacción *f* — **heated** ['hiːṭəd] *adj* : acalorado — **heater** ['hiːṭər] *n* : calentador *m*

heath ['hiːθ] *n* : brezal *m*

heathen ['hiːðən] *adj* : pagano — ~ *n*, *pl* **-thens** *or* **-then** : pagano *m*, -na *f*

heather ['hɛðər] *n* : brezo *m*

heave ['hiːv] *v* **heaved** *or* **hove** ['hoːv]; **heaving** *vt* **1** LIFT : levantar (con esfuerzo) **2** HURL : lanzar, tirar **3** ~ **a sigh** : suspirar — ~ *vi or* ~ **up** : levantarse

heaven ['hɛvən] *n* : cielo *m* — **heavenly** ['hɛvənli] *adj* **1** : celestial **2** ~ **body** : cuerpo *m* celeste

heavy ['hɛvi] *adj* **heavier; -est 1** : pesado **2** INTENSE : fuerte **3** ~ **sigh** : suspiro *m* profundo **4** ~ **traffic** : tráfico *m* denso — **heavily** ['hɛvəli] *adv* **1** : pesadamente **2** EXCESSIVELY : mucho — **heaviness** ['hɛvinəs] *n* : peso *m*, pesadez *f* — **heavyweight** ['hɛvi,weɪt] *n* : peso *m* pesado

Hebrew ['hiː,bruː] *adj* : hebreo — ~ *n* : hebreo *m* (idioma)

heckle ['hɛkəl] *vt* **-led; -ling** : interrumpir (a un orador) con preguntas molestas

hectic ['hɛktɪk] *adj* : agitado, ajetreado

he'd ['hiːd] (*contraction of* **he had** *or* **he would**) → **have, would**

hedge ['hɛdʒ] *n* : seto *m* vivo — ~ *v* **hedged; hedging** *vt* ~ **one's bets** : cubrirse — *vi* : contestar con evasivas — **hedgehog** ['hɛdʒ,hɔg, -hɑg] *n* : erizo *m*

heed ['hiːd] *vt* : prestar atención a, hacer caso de — ~ *n* **take** ~ : tener cuidado — **heedless** ['hiːdləs] *adj* **be** ~ **of** : hacer caso omiso de

heel ['hiːl] *n* : talón *m* (del pie), tacón *m* (de un zapato)

hefty ['hɛfti] *adj* **heftier; -est** : robusto y pesado

heifer ['hɛfər] *n* : novilla *f*

height ['haɪt] *n* **1** : estatura *f* (de una persona), altura *f* (de un objeto) **2** PEAK : cumbre *f* **3 the** ~ **of folly** : el colmo de la locura **4 what is your** ~ **?** : ¿cuánto mides? — **heighten** ['haɪtən] *vt* : aumentar, intensificar

heir ['ær] *n* : heredero *m*, -ra *f* — **heiress** ['ærəs] *n* : heredera *f* — **heirloom** ['ær,luːm] *n* : reliquia *f* de familia

held → **hold**

helicopter ['hɛlə,kɑptər] *n* : helicóptero *m*

hell ['hɛl] *n* : infierno *m* — **hellish** ['hɛlɪʃ] *adj* : infernal

he'll ['hiːl, 'hɪl] (*contraction of* **he shall** *or* **he will**) → **shall, will**

hello [hə'loː, hɛ-] *interj* : ¡hola!

helm ['hɛlm] *n* : timón *m*

helmet ['hɛlmət] *n* : casco *m*

help ['hɛlp] *vt* **1** : ayudar **2** ~ **oneself** : servirse **3 I can't** ~ **it** : no lo puedo remediar — ~ *n* **1** : ayuda *f* **2** STAFF : personal *m* **3 help!** : ¡socorro!, ¡auxilio! — **helper** ['hɛlpər] *n* : ayudante *mf* — **helpful** ['hɛlpfəl] *adj* **1** OBLIGING : servicial, amable **2** USEFUL : útil — **helping** ['hɛlpɪŋ] *n* : porción *f* — **helpless** ['hɛlpləs] *adj* **1** POWERLESS : incapaz **2** DEFENSELESS : indefenso

hem ['hɛm] *n* : dobladillo *m* — ~ *vt* **hemmed; hemming** ~ **in** : encerrar

hemisphere ['hɛmə,sfɪr] *n* : hemisferio *m*

hemorrhage ['hɛmərɪdʒ] *n* : hemorragia *f*

hemorrhoids ['hɛmə,rɔɪdz, 'hɛm,rɔɪdz] *npl* : hemorroides *fpl*, almorranas *fpl*

hemp ['hɛmp] *n* : cáñamo *m*

hen ['hɛn] *n* : gallina *f*

hence ['hɛnts] *adv* **1** : de aquí, de ahí **2** THEREFORE : por lo tanto **3 ten years** ~ : de aquí a 10 años — **henceforth** ['hɛnts,forθ, ,hɛnts'-] *adv* : de ahora en adelante

henpeck ['hɛn,pɛk] *vt* : dominar (al marido)

hepatitis [,hɛpə'taɪṭəs] *n*, *pl* **-titides** [-'tɪṭə,diːz] : hepatitis *f*

her ['hər] *adj* : su, sus — ~ ['hər, ər] *pron* **1** (*used as direct object*) : la **2** (*used as indirect object*) : le, se **3** (*used as object of a preposition*) : ella

herald ['hɛrəld] *vt* : anunciar

herb ['ərb, 'hərb] *n* : hierba *f*

herd ['hərd] *n* : manada *f* — ~ *vt* : conducir (en manada) — *vi or* ~ **together** : reunir

here ['hɪr] *adv* **1** : aquí, acá **2** ~ **you are!** : ¡toma! — **hereabouts** ['hɪrə,baʊts] *or* **hereabout** [-,baʊt] *adv* : por aquí (cerca) — **hereafter** [hɪr'æftər]

adv : en el futuro — **hereby** ['hɪr'baɪ]
adv : por este medio

hereditary [həˈrɛdəˌtɛri] *adj* : hereditario
— **heredity** [həˈrɛdəti] *n* : herencia *f*

heresy ['hɛrəsi] *n, pl* -**sies** : herejía *f*

herewith [hɪrˈwɪθ] *adv* : adjunto

heritage ['hɛrətɪdʒ] *n* 1 : herencia *f* 2
: patrimonio *m* (nacional)

hermit ['hərmət] *n* : ermitaño *m*, -ña *f*

hernia ['hərniə] *n, pl* -**nias** *or* -**niae**
[-niˌiː, -niˌaɪ] : hernia *f*

hero ['hiːroʊ, 'hɪrˌoɪ] *n, pl* -**roes** : héroe *m*
— **heroic** [hɪˈroʊɪk] *adj* : heroico —
heroine ['hɛroən] *n* : heroína *f* —
heroism ['hɛroˌɪzəm] *n* : heroísmo *m*

heron ['hɛrən] *n* : garza *f*

herring ['hɛrɪŋ] *n, pl* -**ring** *or* -**rings**
: arenque *m*

hers ['hərz] *pron* 1 : (el) suyo, (la) suya,
(los) suyos, (las) suyas 2 **some
friends of ~** : unos amigos suyos,
unos amigos de ella — **herself** [hər-
'sɛlf] *pron* 1 (*used reflexively*) : se 2
(*used emphatically*) : ella misma

he's ['hiːz] (*contraction of* **he is** *or* **he
has**) → **be, have**

hesitant ['hɛzətənt] *adj* : titubeante,
vacilante — **hesitate** ['hɛzəˌteɪt] *vi*
-**tated; -tating** : vacilar, titubear —
hesitation [ˌhɛzəˈteɪʃən] *n* : vacilación
f, titubeo *m*

heterosexual [ˌhɛtəroʊˈsɛkʃʊəl] *adj* : heterosexual — **~** *n* : heterosexual *mf*

hexagon ['hɛksəˌgɑn] *n* : hexágono *m*

hey ['heɪ] *interj* : ¡eh!, ¡oye!

heyday ['heɪˌdeɪ] *n* : auge *m*, apogeo *m*

hi ['haɪ] *interj* : ¡hola!

hibernate ['haɪbərˌneɪt] *vi* -**nated; -nat-
ing** : hibernar

hiccup ['hɪkəp] *n* **have the ~s** : tener
hipo — **~** *vi* -**cuped; -cuping** : tener
hipo

hide[1] ['haɪd] *n* : piel *f*, cuero *m*

hide[2] *v* **hid** ['hɪd]; **hidden** ['hɪdən] *or*
hid; hiding *vt* 1 : esconder 2 : ocultar
(motivos, etc.) — *vi* : esconderse —
hide-and-seek ['haɪdəndˌsiːk] *n* : escondite *m*, escondidas *fpl Lat*

hideous ['hɪdiəs] *adj* : horrible, espantoso

hideout ['haɪdˌaʊt] *n* : escondite *m*, guarida *f*

hierarchy ['haɪəˌrɑrki] *n, pl* -**chies** : jerarquía *f* — **hierarchical** [ˌhaɪəˈrɑrkɪkəl]
adj : jerárquico

high ['haɪ] *adj* 1 : alto 2 INTOXICATED
: borracho, drogado 3 **a ~ voice** : una
voz aguda 4 **it's two feet ~** : tiene
dos pies de alto 5 **~ winds** : fuertes
vientos *mpl* — **~** *adv* : alto — **~** *n*

: récord *m*, máximo *m* — **higher**
['haɪər] *adj* 1 : superior 2 **~ education** : enseñanza *f* superior — **highlight** ['haɪˌlaɪt] *n* : punto *m* culminante
— **highly** ['haɪli] *adv* 1 VERY : muy,
sumamente 2 **think ~ of** : tener en
mucho a — **Highness** ['haɪnəs] *n*
His/Her ~ : Su Alteza *f* — **high
school** *n* : escuela *f* superior, escuela *f*
secundaria — **high-strung** ['haɪˈstrʌŋ]
adj : nervioso, excitable — **highway**
['haɪˌweɪ] *n* : carretera *f*

hijack ['haɪˌdʒæk] *vt* : secuestrar — **hijacker** ['haɪˌdʒækər] *n* : secuestrador
m, -dora *f* — **hijacking** *n* : secuestro
m

hike ['haɪk] *v* **hiked; hiking** *vi* : ir de
caminata — *vt or* **~ up** RAISE : subir
— **~** *n* : caminata *f*, excursión *f* —
hiker ['haɪkər] *n* : excursionista *mf*

hilarious [hɪˈlæriəs, haɪ-] *adj* : muy divertido — **hilarity** [hɪˈlærəti, haɪ-] *n*
: hilaridad *f*

hill ['hɪl] *n* 1 : colina *f*, cerro *m* 2 SLOPE
: cuesta *f* — **hillside** ['hɪlˌsaɪd] *n*
: ladera *f*, cuesta *f* — **hilly** ['hɪli] *adj*
hillier; -est : accidentado

hilt ['hɪlt] *n* : puño *m*

him ['hɪm, əm] *pron* 1 (*used as direct object*) : lo 2 (*used as indirect object*)
: le, se 3 (*used as object of a preposition*) : él — **himself** ['hɪmˈsɛlf] *pron* 1
(*used reflexively*) : se 2 (*used emphatically*) : él mismo

hind ['haɪnd] *adj* : trasero, posterior

hinder ['hɪndər] *vt* : dificultar, estorbar
— **hindrance** ['hɪndrənts] *n* : obstáculo
m

hindsight ['haɪndˌsaɪt] *n* **in ~** : en retrospectiva

Hindu ['hɪnˌduː] *adj* : hindú

hinge ['hɪndʒ] *n* : bisagra *f*, gozne *m* —
~ *vi* **hinged; hinging ~ on** : depender de

hint ['hɪnt] *n* 1 : indirecta *f* 2 TIP : consejo *m* 3 TRACE : asomo *m*, toque *m* —
~ *vt* : dar a entender — *vi* **~ at** : insinuar

hip ['hɪp] *n* : cadera *f*

hippopotamus [ˌhɪpəˈpɑtəməs] *n, pl*
-**muses** *or* -**mi** [-ˌmaɪ] : hipopótamo *m*

hire ['haɪr] *n* 1 : alquiler *m* 2 **for ~** : se
alquila — **~** *vt* **hired; hiring** 1 EM-
PLOY : contratar, emplear 2 RENT
: alquilar

his ['hɪz, ɪz] *adj* : su, sus, de él — **~**
pron 1 : (el) suyo, (la) suya, (los)
suyos, (las) suyas 2 **some friends of
~** : unos amigos suyos, unos amigos
de él

Hispanic ['hr'spænɪk] *adj* : hispano, hispánico

hiss ['hɪs] *vi* : silbar — *n* : silbido *m*

history ['hɪstəri] *n, pl* **-ries 1** : historia *f* **2** BACKGROUND : historial *m* — **historian** [hr'storiən] *n* : historiador *m*, -dora *f* — **historic** [hr'storɪk] *or* **historical** [-ɪkəl] *adj* : histórico

hit ['hɪt] *v* **hit; hitting** *vt* **1** : golpear, pegar **2** : dar (con un proyectil) **3** AFFECT : afectar **4** REACH : alcanzar **5 the car ~ a tree** : el coche chocó contra un árbol — *vi* : pegar — *~ n* **1** : golpe *m* **2** SUCCESS : éxito *m*

hitch ['hɪtʃ] *vt* **1** ATTACH : enganchar **2** *or* **~ up** RAISE : subirse **3 ~ a ride** : hacer autostop — *~ n* PROBLEM : problema *m* — **hitchhike** ['hɪtʃ,haɪk] *vi* **-hiked; -hiking** : hacer autostop — **hitchhiker** ['hɪtʃ,haɪkər] *n* : autostopista *mf*

hitherto ['hɪðər,tu:, ,hɪðər'-] *adv* : hasta ahora

HIV [,eɪtʃ,aɪ'vi:] *n* : VIH *m*, virus del sida

hive ['haɪv] *n* : colmena *f*

hives ['haɪvz] *ns & pl* : urticaria *f*

hoard ['hord] *n* : tesoro *m* (de dinero), reserva *f* (de provisiones) — *~ vt* : acumular

hoarse ['hors] *adj* **hoarser; -est** : ronco

hoax ['hoːks] *n* : engaño *m*

hobble ['habəl] *vi* **-bled; -bling** : cojear

hobby ['habi] *n, pl* **-bies** : pasatiempo *m*

hobo ['hoːboː] *n, pl* **-boes** : vagabundo *m*, -da *f*

hockey ['haki] *n* : hockey *m*

hoe ['hoː] *n* : azada *f* — *~ vt* **hoed; hoeing** : azadonar

hog ['hɔg, 'hag] *n* : cerdo *m* — *~ vt* **hogged; hogging** MONOPOLIZE : acaparar

hoist ['hɔɪst] *vt* **1** : izar (una vela, etc.) **2** LIFT : levantar — *~ n* : grúa *f*

hold¹ ['hoːld] *n* : bodega *f* (en un barco o un avión)

hold² *v* **held** ['held]; **holding** *vt* **1** GRIP : agarrar **2** POSSESS : tener **3** SUPPORT : sostener **4** : celebrar (una reunión, etc.), mantener (una conversación) **5** CONTAIN : contener **6** CONSIDER : considerar **7** *or* **~ back** : detener **8 ~ hands** : agarrarse de la mano **9 ~ up** ROB : atracar **10 ~ up** DELAY : retrasar — *vi* **1** LAST : durar, continuar **2** APPLY : ser válido — *~ n* **1** GRIP : agarre *m* **2 get ~ of** : conseguir **3 get ~ of oneself** : controlarse — **holder** ['hoːldər] *n* : tenedor *m*, -dora *f* — **holdup** ['hoːld-

ʌp] *n* **1** ROBBERY : atraco *m* **2** DELAY : retraso *m*, demora *f*

hole ['hoːl] *n* : agujero *m*, hoyo *m*

holiday ['halə,deɪ] *n* **1** : día *m* feriado, fiesta *f* **2** *Brit* VACATION : vacaciones *fpl*

holiness ['hoːlinəs] *n* : santidad *f*

holler ['halər] *vi* : gritar — *~ n* : grito *m*

hollow ['haloː] *n* **1** : hueco *m* **2** VALLEY : hondonada *f* — *~ adj* **-lower; -est 1** : hueco **2** FALSE : vacío, falso — *~ vt or ~ out* : ahuecar

holly ['hali] *n, pl* **-lies** : acebo *m*

holocaust ['halə,kɔst, 'hoː-, 'hɔ-] *n* : holocausto *m*

holster ['hoːlstər] *n* : pistolera *f*

holy ['hoːli] *adj* **-lier; -est** : santo, sagrado

homage ['amɪdʒ, 'ha-] *n* : homenaje *m*

home ['hoːm] *n* **1** : casa *f* **2** FAMILY : hogar *m* **3** INSTITUTION : residencia *f*, asilo *m* **4 at ~ and abroad** : dentro y fuera del país — *~ adv* **go ~** : ir a casa — **homeland** ['hoːm,lænd] *n* : patria *f* — **homeless** ['hoːmləs] *adj* : sin hogar — **homely** ['hoːmli] *adj* **-lier; -est 1** DOMESTIC : casero **2** UGLY : feo — **homemade** ['hoːm'meɪd] *adj* : casero, hecho en casa — **homemaker** ['hoːm,meɪkər] *n* : ama *f* de casa — **home run** *n* : jonrón *m* — **homesick** ['hoːm,sɪk] *adj* **be ~** : echar de menos a la familia — **homeward** ['hoːmwərd] *adj* : de vuelta, de regreso — **homework** ['hoːm,wərk] *n* : tarea *f*, deberes *mpl* — **homey** ['hoːmi] *adj* **homier; -est** : hogareño, acogedor

homicide ['hamə,saɪd, 'hoː-] *n* : homicidio *m*

homogeneous [,hoːmə'dʒiːniːəs, -njəs] *adj* : homogéneo

homosexual [,hoːmə'sekʃəl] *adj* : homosexual — *~ n* : homosexual *mf* — **homosexuality** [,hoːmə,sekʃu'æləţi] *n* : homosexualidad *f*

honest ['anəst] *adj* **1** : honrado **2** FRANK : sincero — **honestly** *adv* : sinceramente — **honesty** ['anəsti] *n, pl* **-ties** : honradez *f*

honey ['hʌni] *n, pl* **-eys** : miel *f* — **honeycomb** ['hʌni,koːm] *n* : panal *m* — **honeymoon** ['hʌni,mu:n] *n* : luna *f* de miel

honk ['haŋk, 'hɔŋk] *vi* : tocar la bocina — *~ n* : bocinazo *m*

honor *or Brit* **honour** ['anər] *n* : honor *m* — *~ vt* **1** : honrar **2** : aceptar (un cheque, etc.), cumplir con (una promesa) — **honorable** *or Brit* **honourable** ['anərəbəl] *adj* : honorable, honroso — **honorary** ['anə,reri] *adj* : honorario

hood ['hʊd] *n* 1 : capucha *f* (de un abrigo, etc.) 2 : capó *m* (de un automóvil)

hoodlum ['hʊdləm, 'huːd-] *n* : matón *m*

hoodwink ['hʊd,wɪŋk] *vt* : engañar

hoof ['hʊf, 'huːf] *n, pl* **hooves** ['hʊvz, 'huːvz] *or* **hoofs** : pezuña *f* (de una vaca, etc.), casco *m* (de un caballo)

hook ['hʊk] *n* 1 : gancho *m* 2 *or* ~ **and eye** : corchete *m* 3 → **fishhook** 4 **off the** ~ : descolgado — ~ *vt* : enganchar — *vi* : engancharse

hoop ['huːp] *n* : aro *m*

hooray [hʊ'reɪ] → **hurrah**

hoot ['huːt] *vi* 1 : ulular (dícese de un búho) 2 ~ **with laughter** : reírse a carcajadas — ~ *n* 1 : ululato *m* (de un búho) 2 **I don't give a** ~ : me importa un comino

hop¹ ['hɑp] *vi* **hopped; hopping** : saltar a la pata coja — ~ *n* : salto *m* a la pata coja

hop² *n* — **s** : lúpulo *m* (planta)

hope ['hoːp] *v* **hoped; hoping** *vi* : esperar — *vt* : esperar que — ~ *n* : esperanza *f* — **hopeful** ['hoːpfəl] *adj* : esperanzado — **hopefully** *adv* 1 : con esperanza 2 ~ **it will help** : se espera que ayude — **hopeless** ['hoːpləs] *adj* : desesperado — **hopelessly** ['hoːpləsli] *adv* : desesperadamente

horde ['hord] *n* : horda *f*

horizon [hə'raɪzən] *n* : horizonte *m* — **horizontal** [horə'zɑntəl] *adj* : horizontal

hormone ['hor,moːn] *n* : hormona *f*

horn ['horn] *n* 1 : cuerno *m* (de un animal) 2 : trompa *f* (instrumento musical) 3 : bocina *f*, claxon *m* (de un vehículo)

hornet ['hornət] *n* : avispón *m*

horoscope ['horə,skoːp] *n* : horóscopo *m*

horror ['horər] *n* : horror *m* — **horrendous** [hə'rendəs] *adj* : horrendo — **horrible** ['horəbəl] *adj* : horrible — **horrid** ['horɪd] *adj* : horroroso, horrible — **horrify** ['horə,faɪ] *vt* **-fied; -fying** : horrorizar

hors d'oeuvre [or'dərv] *n, pl* **hors d'oeuvres** [-'dərvz] : entremés *m*

horse ['hors] *n* : caballo *m* — **horseback** ['hors,bæk] *n* **on** ~ : a caballo — **horsefly** ['hors,flaɪ] *n, pl* **-flies** : tábano *m* — **horseman** ['horsmən] *n, pl* **-men** [-mən, -,men] : jinete *m* — **horseplay** ['hors,pleɪ] *n* : payasadas *fpl* — **horsepower** ['hors,paʊər] *n* : caballo *m* de fuerza — **horseradish** ['hors,rædɪʃ] *n* : rábano *m* picante — **horseshoe** ['hors,ʃuː] *n* : herradura *f* — **horse-**

woman ['hors,wʊmən] *n, pl* **-women** [-,wɪmən] : jinete *f*

horticulture ['hortə,kʌltʃər] *n* : horticultura *f*

hose ['hoːz] *n* 1 *pl* **hoses** : manguera *f*, manga *f* 2 **hose** *pl* STOCKINGS : medias *fpl* — ~ *vt* **hosed; hosing** : regar (con manguera) — **hosiery** ['hoːʒəri, 'hoːʒə-] *n* : calcetería *f*

hospice ['hɑspəs] *n* : hospicio *m*

hospital ['hɑs,pɪtəl] *n* : hospital *m* — **hospitable** [hɑ'spɪtəbəl, 'hɑs,pɪ-] *adj* : hospitalario — **hospitality** [hɑspə'tæləti] *n, pl* **-ties** : hospitalidad *f* — **hospitalize** ['hɑs,pɪtəl,aɪz] *vt* **-ized; -izing** : hospitalizar

host¹ ['hoːst] *n* **a** ~ **of** : toda una serie de

host² *n* 1 : anfitrión *m*, -triona *f* 2 : presentador *m*, -dora *f* (de televisión, etc.) — ~ *vt* : presentar (un programa de televisión, etc.)

host³ *n* EUCHARIST : hostia *f*, Eucaristía *f*

hostage ['hɑstɪdʒ] *n* : rehén *m*

hostel ['hɑstəl] *n or* **youth** ~ : albergue *m* juvenil

hostess ['hoːstɪs] *n* : anfitriona *f*

hostile ['hɑstəl, -,taɪl] *adj* : hostil — **hostility** [hɑs'tɪləti] *n, pl* **-ties** : hostilidad *f*

hot ['hɑt] *adj* **hotter; hottest** 1 : caliente, caluroso (dícese del tiempo), cálido (dícese del clima) 2 SPICY : picante 3 **feel** ~ : tener calor 4 **have a** ~ **temper** : tener mal genio 5 ~ **news** : noticias *fpl* de última hora 6 **it's** ~ **today** : hace calor

hot dog *n* : perro *m* caliente

hotel [hoː'tel] *n* : hotel *m*

hotheaded ['hɑt,hedəd] *adj* : exaltado

hound ['haʊnd] *n* : perro *m* (de caza) — ~ *vt* : acosar, perseguir

hour ['aʊər] *n* : hora *f* — **hourglass** ['aʊər,glæs] *n* : reloj *m* de arena — **hourly** ['aʊərli] *adv & adj* : cada hora, por hora

house ['haʊs] *n, pl* **houses** ['haʊzəz, -səz] 1 : casa *f* 2 : cámara *f* (del gobierno) 3 **publishing** ~ : editorial *f* — ~ ['haʊz] *vt* **housed; housing** : albergar — **houseboat** ['haʊs,boːt] *n* : casa *f* flotante — **housefly** ['haʊs,flaɪ] *n, pl* **-flies** : mosca *f* común — **household** ['haʊs,hoːld] *adj* 1 : doméstico 2 ~ **name** : nombre *m* muy conocido — ~ *n* : casa *f* — **housekeeper** ['haʊs,kiːpər] *n* : ama *f* de llaves — **housekeeping** ['haʊs,kiːpɪŋ] *n* : gobierno *m* de la casa — **housewarming** ['haʊs,wormɪŋ] *n* : fiesta *f* de estreno de

una casa — **housewife** ['haʊs,waɪf] n,
pl **-wives** : ama f de casa — **housework** ['haʊs,wərk] n : faenas fpl domésticas — **housing** ['haʊzɪŋ] n 1 : viviendas fpl 2 CASE : caja f protectora

hove → **heave**

hovel ['hʌvəl, 'hɑ-] n : casucha f, tugurio
m

hover ['hʌvər, 'hɑ-] vi 1 : cernerse 2 ~
about : rondar

how ['haʊ] adv 1 : cómo 2 (used in exclamations) : qué 3 ~ **are you?**
: ¿cómo está Ud.? 4 ~ **come** : por
qué 5 ~ **much** : cuánto 6 ~ **do you
do?** : mucho gusto 7 ~ **old are you?**
: ¿cuántos años tienes? — ~ conj
: como

however [haʊ'ɛvər] conj 1 : de cualquier
manera que 2 ~ **you like** : como
quieras — ~ adv 1 NEVERTHELESS
: sin embargo, no obstante 2 ~ **difficult it is** : por difícil que sea 3 ~
hard I try : por más que me esfuerce

howl ['haʊl] vi : aullar — ~ n : aullido
m

hub ['hʌb] n 1 CENTER : centro m 2
: cubo m (de una rueda)

hubbub ['hʌ,bʌb] n : alboroto m, jaleo m

hubcap ['hʌb,kæp] n : tapacubos m

huddle ['hʌdəl] vi **-dled; -dling** or ~
together : apiñarse

hue ['hjuː] n : color m, tono m

huff ['hʌf] n **be in a** ~ : estar enojado

hug ['hʌg] vt **hugged; hugging** : abrazar — ~ n : abrazo m

huge ['hjuːdʒ] adj **huger; hugest** : inmenso, enorme

hull ['hʌl] n : casco m (de un barco, etc.)

hum ['hʌm] v **hummed; humming** vi 1
: tararear 2 BUZZ : zumbar — vt
: tararear (una melodía) — ~ n
: zumbido m

human ['hjuːmən, 'juː-] adj : humano —
~ n : (ser m) humano m — **humane**
[hjuː'meɪn, juː-] adj : humano, humanitario — **humanitarian** [hjuːˌmænə-
'teriən, juː-] adj : humanitario — **humanity** [hjuː'mænət̬i, juː-] n, pl **-ties**
: humanidad f

humble ['hʌmbəl] vt **-bled; -bling** 1
: humillar 2 ~ **oneself** : humillarse
— ~ adj **-bler; -blest** : humilde

humdrum ['hʌm,drʌm] adj : monótono,
rutinario

humid ['hjuːməd, 'juː-] adj : húmedo —
humidity [hjuː'mɪdət̬i, juː-] n, pl **-ties**
: humedad f

humiliate [hjuː'mɪliˌeɪt, juː-] vt **-ated;
-ating** : humillar — **humiliating** [hjuː-
'mɪliˌeɪt̬ɪŋ, juː-] adj : humillante — **hu-**

miliation [hjuːˌmɪli'eɪʃən, juː-] n : humillación f — **humility** [hjuː'mɪlət̬i,
juː-] n : humildad f

humor or Brit **humour** ['hjuːmər, 'juː-] n
: humor m — ~ vt : seguir la corriente
a, complacer — **humorous** ['hjuːmərəs,
'juː-] adj : humorístico, cómico

hump ['hʌmp] n : joroba f

hunch ['hʌntʃ] vi or ~ **over** : encorvarse — ~ n : presentimiento m

hundred ['hʌndrəd] adj : cien, ciento —
~ n, pl **-dreds** or **-dred** : ciento m —
hundredth ['hʌndrədθ] adj : centésimo
— ~ n 1 : centésimo m, -ma f (en una
serie) 2 : centésimo m (en matemáticas)

hung → **hang**

Hungarian [hʌŋ'gæriən] adj : húngaro
— ~ n : húngaro m (idioma)

hunger ['hʌŋgər] n : hambre m — ~ vi
1 : tener hambre 2 ~ **for** : ansiar, anhelar — **hungry** ['hʌŋgri] adj **-grier;
-est** 1 : hambriento 2 **be** ~ : tener
hambre

hunk ['hʌŋk] n : pedazo m (grande)

hunt ['hʌnt] vt 1 : cazar 2 ~ **for** : buscar
— ~ n 1 : caza f, cacería f 2 SEARCH
: búsqueda f, busca f — **hunter**
['hʌntər] n : cazador m, -dora f — **hunting** ['hʌntɪŋ] n : caza f 2 **go** ~ : ir de
caza

hurdle ['hərdəl] n 1 : valla f (en deportes) 2 OBSTACLE : obstáculo m

hurl ['hərl] vt : lanzar, arrojar

hurrah [hʊ'rɑ, -'rɔ] interj : ¡hurra!

hurricane ['hərəˌkeɪn] n : huracán m

hurry ['həri] n : prisa f, apuro f Lat — v
-ried; -rying vi : darse prisa, apurarse
Lat — vt : apurar, dar prisa a — **hur-
ried** ['hərid] adj : apresurado — **hurriedly** ['həridli] adv : apresuradamente, de prisa

hurt ['hərt] v **hurt; hurting** vt 1 INJURE
: hacer daño a, lastimar 2 OFFEND
: ofender, herir — vi 1 : doler 2 **my
foot** ~**s** : me duele el pie — ~ n 1
INJURY : herida f 2 DISTRESS : dolor m,
pena f — **hurtful** ['hərtfəl] adj : hiriente, doloroso

hurtle ['hərt̬əl] vi **-tled; -tling** : lanzarse,
precipitarse

husband ['hʌzbənd] n : esposo m, marido m

hush ['hʌʃ] vt : hacer callar, acallar —
~ n : silencio m

husk ['hʌsk] n : cáscara f

husky[1] ['hʌski] adj **-kier; -est** HOARSE
: ronco

husky[2] n, pl **-kies** : perro m, -rra f esquimal

husky³ *adj* BURLY : fornido

hustle ['həsəl] *v* **-tled; -tling** *vt* : dar prisa a, apurar *Lat* — *vi* : darse prisa, apurarse *Lat* — ~ *n* ~ **and bustle** : ajetreo *m*, bullicio *m*

hut ['hʌt] *n* : cabaña *f*

hutch ['hʌtʃ] *n or* **rabbit** ~ : conejera *f*

hyacinth ['haɪəsɪnθ] *n* : jacinto *m*

hybrid ['haɪbrɪd] *n* : híbrido *m* — ~ *adj* : híbrido

hydrant ['haɪdrənt] *n or* **fire** ~ : boca *f* de incendios

hydraulic [haɪˈdrɑːlɪk] *adj* : hidráulico

hydroelectric [ˌhaɪdroʊˈlektrɪk] *adj* : hidroeléctrico

hydrogen ['haɪdrədʒən] *n* : hidrógeno *m*

hyena [haɪˈiːnə] *n* : hiena *f*

hygiene ['haɪdʒiːn] *n* : higiene *f* — **hygienic** [haɪˈdʒenɪk, -'dʒiː-; ˌhaɪdʒiˈenɪk] *adj* : higiénico

hymn ['hɪm] *n* : himno *m*

hyperactive [ˌhaɪpərˈæktɪv] *adj* : hiperactivo

hyphen ['haɪfən] *n* : guión *m*

hypnosis [hɪpˈnoːsɪs] *n, pl* **-noses** [-ˌsiːz] : hipnosis *f* — **hypnotic** [hɪpˈnɑtɪk] *adj* : hipnótico — **hypnotism** ['hɪpnəˌtɪzəm] *n* : hipnotismo *m* — **hypnotize** ['hɪpnəˌtaɪz] *vt* **-tized; -tizing** : hipnotizar

hypochondriac [ˌhaɪpəˈkɑndriˌæk] *n* : hipocondríaco *m*, -ca *f*

hypocrisy [hɪpˈɑkrəsi] *n, pl* **-sies** : hipocresía *f* — **hypocrite** ['hɪpəˌkrɪt] *n* : hipócrita *mf* — **hypocritical** [ˌhɪpəˈkrɪtɪkəl] *adj* : hipócrita

hypothesis [haɪˈpɑθəsɪs] *n, pl* **-eses** [-ˌsiːz] : hipótesis *f* — **hypothetical** [ˌhaɪpəˈθetɪkəl] *adj* : hipotético

hysteria [hɪsˈteriə, -tɪr-] *n* : histeria *f*, histerismo *m* — **hysterical** [hɪsˈterɪkəl] *adj* : histérico

I

i ['aɪ] *n, pl* **i's** *or* **is** ['aɪz] : i *f*, novena letra del alfabeto inglés

I ['aɪ] *pron* : yo

ice ['aɪs] *n* : hielo *m* — ~ *v* **iced; icing** *vt* **1** FREEZE : congelar **2** CHILL : enfriar **3** : bañar (pasteles, etc.) — ~ *vi or* ~ **up** : helarse, congelarse — **iceberg** ['aɪsˌbərg] *n* : iceberg *m* — **icebox** ['aɪsˌbɑks] → **refrigerator** — **ice-cold** ['aɪsˈkoːld] *adj* : helado — **ice cream** *n* : helado *m* — **ice cube** *n* : cubito *m* de hielo — **ice-skate** ['aɪsˌskeɪt] *vi* **-skated; -skating** : patinar — **ice skate** *n* : patín *m* de cuchilla — **icicle** ['aɪsɪkəl] *n* : carámbano *m* — **icing** ['aɪsɪŋ] *n* : baño *m*

icon ['aɪˌkɑn, -kən] *n* : icono *m*

icy ['aɪsi] *adj* **icier; -est 1** : cubierto de hielo (dícese de pavimento, etc.) **2** FREEZING : helado

I'd ['aɪd] (*contraction of* **I should** *or* **I would**) → **should, would**

idea [aɪˈdiːə] *n* : idea *f*

ideal [aɪˈdiːəl] *adj* : ideal — ~ *n* : ideal *m* — **idealist** [aɪˈdiːəlɪst] *n* : idealista *mf* — **idealistic** [aɪˌdiːəˈlɪstɪk] *adj* : idealista — **idealize** [aɪˈdiːəˌlaɪz] *vt* **-ized; -izing** : idealizar

identity [aɪˈdentəti] *n, pl* **-ties** : identidad *f* — **identical** [aɪˈdentɪkəl] *adj* : idéntico — **identify** [aɪˈdentəˌfaɪ] *v* **-fied; -fying** *vt* : identificar — *vi* ~ **with** : identificarse con — **identifica-** **tion** [aɪˌdentəfəˈkeɪʃən] *n* **1** : identificación *f* **2** ~ **card** : carnet *m*, carné *m*

ideology [ˌaɪdiˈɑlədʒi, ˌɪ-] *n, pl* **-gies** : ideología *f* — **ideological** [ˌaɪdiəˈlɑdʒɪkəl, ˌɪ-] *adj* : ideológico

idiocy ['ɪdiəsi] *n, pl* **-cies** : idiotez *f*

idiom ['ɪdiəm] *n* EXPRESSION : modismo *m* — **idiomatic** [ˌɪdiəˈmætɪk] *adj* : idiomático

idiosyncrasy [ˌɪdioʊˈsɪŋkrəsi] *n, pl* **-sies** : idiosincrasia *f*

idiot ['ɪdiət] *n* : idiota *mf* — **idiotic** [ˌɪdiˈɑtɪk] *adj* : idiota

idle ['aɪdəl] *adj* **idler; idlest 1** LAZY : haragán, holgazán **2** INACTIVE : parado (dícese de una máquina) **3** UNEMPLOYED : desocupado **4** VAIN : frívolo, vano **5 out of** ~ **curiosity** : por pura curiosidad — ~ *v* **idled; idling** *vi* : andar al ralentí (dícese de un motor) — *vt* ~ **away the hours** : pasar el rato — **idleness** ['aɪdəlnəs] *n* : ociosidad *f*

idol ['aɪdəl] *n* : ídolo *m* — **idolize** ['aɪdəˌlaɪz] *vt* **-ized; -izing** : idolatrar

idyllic [aɪˈdɪlɪk] *adj* : idílico

if ['ɪf] *conj* **1** : si **2** THOUGH : aunque, si bien **3** ~ **so** : si es así

igloo ['ɪgluː] *n, pl* **-loos** : iglú *m*

ignite [ɪgˈnaɪt] *v* **-nited; -niting** *vt* : encender — *vi* : encenderse — **ignition** [ɪgˈnɪʃən] *n* **1** : ignición *f* **2** *or* ~ **switch** : encendido *m*

ignore [ɪg'nor] vt **-nored; -noring** : ignorar, no hacer caso de — **ignorance** [ˈɪgnərənts] n : ignorancia f — **ignorant** [ˈɪgnərənt] adj **1** : ignorante **2 be ~ of** : desconocer, ignorar

ilk [ˈɪlk] n : tipo m, clase f

ill [ˈɪl] adj **worse** [ˈwərs]; **worst** [ˈwərst] **1** SICK : enfermo **2** BAD : malo — adv **worse; worst** : mal — **ill-advised** [ˌɪlædˈvaɪzd, -əd-] adj : imprudente — **ill at ease** adj : incómodo

I'll [ˈaɪl] (contraction of **I shall** or **I will**) → **shall, will**

illegal [ɪlˈliːgəl] adj : ilegal

illegible [ɪlˈlɛdʒəbəl] adj : ilegible

illegitimate [ˌɪlɪˈdʒɪtəmət] adj : ilegítimo — **illegitimacy** [ˌɪlɪˈdʒɪtəməsi] n : ilegitimidad f

illicit [ɪlˈlɪsət] adj : ilícito

illiterate [ɪlˈlɪtərət] adj : analfabeto — **illiteracy** [ɪlˈlɪtərəsi] n, pl **-cies** : analfabetismo m

ill-mannered [ˌɪlˈmænərd] adj : descortés, maleducado

ill-natured [ˌɪlˈneɪtʃərd] adj : de mal genio

illness [ˈɪlnəs] n : enfermedad f

illogical [ɪlˈlɑdʒɪkəl] adj : ilógico

ill-treat [ˌɪlˈtriːt] vt : maltratar

illuminate [ɪlˈuːməˌneɪt] vt **-nated; -nating** : iluminar — **illumination** [ɪˌluːməˈneɪʃən] n : iluminación f

illusion [ɪlˈuːʒən] n : ilusión f — **illusory** [ɪlˈuːsəri, -zəri] adj : ilusorio

illustrate [ˈɪləsˌtreɪt] v **-trated; -trating** : ilustrar — **illustration** [ˌɪləˈstreɪʃən] n **1** : ilustración f **2** EXAMPLE : ejemplo m — **illustrative** [ɪˈlʌstrətɪv, ˈɪləˌstreɪtɪv] adj : ilustrativo

illustrious [ɪˈlʌstriəs] adj : ilustre, glorioso

ill will n : animadversión f, mala voluntad f

I'm [ˈaɪm] (contraction of **I am**) → **be**

image [ˈɪmɪdʒ] n : imagen f — **imaginary** [ˈɪmædʒəˌneri] adj : imaginario — **imagination** [ɪˌmædʒəˈneɪʃən] n : imaginación f — **imaginative** [ɪˈmædʒənətɪv, -əˌneɪtɪv] adj : imaginativo — **imagine** [ɪˈmædʒən] vt **-ined; -ining** : imaginar(se)

imbalance [ɪmˈbælənts] n : desequilibrio m

imbecile [ˈɪmbəsəl, -ˌsɪl] n : imbécil mf

imbue [ɪmˈbjuː] vt **-bued; -buing** : imbuir

imitation [ˌɪməˈteɪʃən] n : imitación f — ~ adj : de imitación, artificial — **imitate** [ˈɪməˌteɪt] vt **-tated; -tating** : imitar, remedar — **imitator** [ˈɪməˌteɪtər] n : imitador m, -dora f

immaculate [ɪˈmækjələt] adj : inmaculado

immaterial [ˌɪməˈtɪriəl] adj : irrelevante, sin importancia

immature [ˌɪməˈtʃur, -ˈtjur, -ˈtur] adj : inmaduro — **immaturity** [ˌɪməˈtʃurəti, -ˈtjur-, -ˈtur-] n, pl **-ties** : inmadurez f

immediate [ɪˈmiːdiət] adj : inmediato — **immediately** [ɪˈmiːdiətli] adv : inmediatamente

immense [ɪˈmɛnts] adj : inmenso — **immensity** [ɪˈmɛntsəti] n, pl **-ties** : inmensidad f

immerse [ɪˈmərs] vt **-mersed; -mersing** : sumergir — **immersion** [ɪˈmərʒən] n : inmersión f

immigrate [ˈɪməˌgreɪt] vi **-grated; -grating** : inmigrar — **immigrant** [ˈɪmɪgrənt] n : inmigrante mf — **immigration** [ˌɪməˈgreɪʃən] n : inmigración f

imminent [ˈɪmənənt] adj : inminente — **imminence** [ˈɪmənənts] n : inminencia f

immobile [ɪmˈoːbəl] adj : inmóvil — **immobilize** [ɪˈmoːbəˌlaɪz] vt **-lized; -lizing** : inmovilizar

immoral [ɪˈmɔrəl] adj : inmoral — **immorality** [ˌɪmɔˈrælət̬i, ˌɪmə-] n, pl **-ties** : inmoralidad f

immortal [ɪˈmɔrtəl] adj : inmortal — ~ n : inmortal mf — **immortality** [ˌɪmɔrˈtælət̬i] n : inmortalidad f

immune [ɪˈmjuːn] adj : inmune — **immunity** [ɪˈmjuːnət̬i] n, pl **-ties** : inmunidad f — **immunization** [ˌɪmjunəˈzeɪʃən] n : inmunización f — **immunize** [ˈɪmjuˌnaɪz] vt **-nized; -nizing** : inmunizar

imp [ˈɪmp] n RASCAL : diablillo m

impact [ˈɪmˌpækt] n : impacto m

impair [ɪmˈpær] vt : dañar, perjudicar

impart [ɪmˈpɑrt] vt : impartir (información), conferir (una calidad, etc.)

impartial [ɪmˈpɑrʃəl] adj : imparcial — **impartiality** [ɪmˌpɑrʃiˈælət̬i] n, pl **-ties** : imparcialidad f

impassable [ɪmˈpæsəbəl] adj : intransitable

impasse [ˈɪmˌpæs] n : impasse m

impassioned [ɪmˈpæʃənd] adj : apasionado

impassive [ɪmˈpæsɪv] adj : impasible

impatience [ɪmˈpeɪʃənts] n : impaciencia f — **impatient** [ɪmˈpeɪʃənt] adj : impaciente — **impatiently** [ɪmˈpeɪʃəntli] adv : con impaciencia

impeccable [ɪmˈpekəbəl] adj : impecable

impede [ɪm'piːd] *vt* **-peded; -peding** : dificultar — **impediment** [ɪm'pedəmənt] *n* : impedimento *m*, obstáculo *m*

impel [ɪm'pel] *vt* **-pelled; -pelling** : impeler

impending [ɪm'pendɪŋ] *adj* : inminente

impenetrable [ɪm'penətrəbəl] *adj* : impenetrable

imperative [ɪm'perətɪv] *adj* **1** COMMANDING : imperativo **2** NECESSARY : imprescindible — **~** *n* : imperativo *m*

imperceptible [ˌɪmpər'septəbəl] *adj* : imperceptible

imperfection [ˌɪmpər'fekʃən] *n* : imperfección *f* — **imperfect** [ɪm'pərfɪkt] *adj* : imperfecto — **~** *n or* **~ tense** : imperfecto *m*

imperial [ɪm'pɪriəl] *adj* : imperial — **imperialism** [ɪm'pɪriəˌlɪzəm] *n* : imperialismo *m* — **imperious** [ɪm'pɪriəs] *adj* : imperioso

impersonal [ɪm'pərsənəl] *adj* : impersonal

impersonate [ɪm'pərsənˌeɪt] *vt* **-ated; -ating** : hacerse pasar por, imitar — **impersonation** [ɪmˌpərsən'eɪʃən] *n* : imitación *f* — **impersonator** [ɪm'pərsənˌeɪtər] *n* : imitador *m*, -dora *f*

impertinent [ɪm'pərtənənt] *adj* : impertinente — **impertinence** [ɪm'pərtənənts] *n* : impertinencia *f*

impervious [ɪm'pərviəs] *adj* **~ to** : impermeable a

impetuous [ɪm'petʃʊəs] *adj* : impetuoso, impulsivo

impetus ['ɪmpətəs] *n* : ímpetu *m*, impulso *m*

impinge [ɪm'pɪndʒ] *vi* **-pinged; -pinging ~ on** : afectara, incidir en

impish ['ɪmpɪʃ] *adj* : pícaro, travieso

implant [ɪm'plænt] *vt* : implantar

implausible [ɪm'plɔzəbəl] *adj* : inverosímil

implement ['ɪmpləmənt] *n* : instrumento *m*, implemento *m* Lat — **~** ['ɪmpləˌment] *vt* : poner en práctica

implicate ['ɪmpləˌkeɪt] *vt* **-cated; -cating** : implicar — **implication** [ˌɪmpləˈkeɪʃən] *n* **1** INVOLVEMENT : implicación *f* **2** CONSEQUENCE : consecuencia *f* **3** by **~** : de forma indirecta

implicit [ɪm'plɪsət] *adj* **1** : implícito **2** UNQUESTIONING : absoluto, incondicional

implore [ɪm'plor] *vt* **-plored; -ploring** : implorar, suplicar

imply [ɪm'plaɪ] *vt* **-plied; -plying 1** HINT : insinuar **2** ENTAIL : implicar

impolite [ˌɪmpə'laɪt] *adj* : descortés, maleducado

import [ɪm'port] *vt* : importar (mercancías) — **important** [ɪm'portənt] *adj* : importante — **importance** [ɪm'portənts] *n* : importancia *f* — **importation** [ˌɪmpor'teɪʃən] *n* : importación *f* — **importer** [ɪm'portər] *n* : importador *m*, -dora *f*

impose [ɪm'poz] *v* **-posed; -posing** *vt* : imponer — *vi* **~ on** : importunar, molestar — **imposing** [ɪm'pozɪŋ] *adj* : imponente — **imposition** [ˌɪmpə'zɪʃən] *n* **1** ENFORCEMENT : imposición *f* **2 be an ~ on** : molestar

impossible [ɪm'pasəbəl] *adj* : imposible — **impossibility** [ɪmˌpasə'bɪləti] *n, pl* **-ties** : imposibilidad *f*

impostor *or* **imposter** [ɪm'pastər] *n* : impostor *m*, -tora *f*

impotent ['ɪmpətənt] *adj* : impotente — **impotence** ['ɪmpətənts] *n* : impotencia *f*

impound [ɪm'paʊnd] *vt* : incautar, embargar

impoverished [ɪm'pavərɪʃt] *adj* : empobrecido

impracticable [ɪm'præktɪkəbəl] *adj* : impracticable

impractical [ɪm'præktɪkəl] *adj* : poco práctico

imprecise [ˌɪmprɪ'saɪs] *adj* : impreciso — **imprecision** [ˌɪmprɪ'sɪʒən] *n* : imprecisión *f*

impregnable [ɪm'pregnəbəl] *adj* : impenetrable

impregnate [ɪm'pregˌneɪt] *vt* **-nated; -nating 1** : impregnar **2** FERTILIZE : fecundar

impress [ɪm'pres] *vt* **1** : causar una buena impresión a **2** AFFECT : impresionar **3 ~ sth on s.o.** : recalcar algo a algn — *vi* : impresionar — **impression** [ɪm'preʃən] *n* : impresión *f* — **impressionable** [ɪm'preʃənəbəl] *adj* : impresionable — **impressive** [ɪm'presɪv] *adj* : impresionante

imprint [ɪm'prɪnt, 'ɪm-] *vt* : imprimir — **~** ['ɪmprɪnt] *n* MARK : impresión *f*, huella *f*

imprison [ɪm'prɪzən] *vt* : encarcelar — **imprisonment** [ɪm'prɪzənmənt] *n* : encarcelamiento *m*

improbable [ɪm'prabəbəl] *adj* : improbable — **improbability** [ɪmˌprabə'bɪləti] *n, pl* **-ties** : improbabilidad *f*

impromptu [ɪm'pramp.tuː, -'tjuː] *adj* : improvisado

improper [ɪm'prapər] *adj* **1** UNSEEMLY : indecoroso **2** INCORRECT : impropio

— **impropriety** [ˌɪmprə'praɪəti] n, pl -eties : inconveniencia f

improve [ɪm'pruːv] v -proved; -proving : mejorar — **improvement** [ɪm'pruːvmənt] n : mejora f

improvise ['ɪmprə,vaɪz] v -vised; -vising : improvisar — **improvisation** [ˌɪmprəvə'zeɪʃən, ˌɪmprəvə-] n : improvisación f

impudent ['ɪmpjədənt] adj : insolente — **impudence** ['ɪmpjədənts] n : insolencia f

impulse ['ɪmpʌls] n 1 : impulso m 2 on ~ : sin reflexionar — **impulsive** [ɪm'pʌlsɪv] adj : impulsivo — **impulsiveness** [ɪm'pʌlsɪvnəs] n : impulsividad f

impunity [ɪm'pjuːnəti] n 1 : impunidad f 2 with ~ : impunemente

impure [ɪm'pjʊr] adj : impuro — **impurity** [ɪm'pjʊrəti] n, pl -ties : impureza f

in ['ɪn] prep 1 : en 2 DURING : por, en Lat 3 WITHIN : dentro de 4 dressed ~ red : vestido de rojo 5 ~ the rain : bajo la lluvia 6 ~ the sun : al sol 7 ~ this way : de esta manera 8 the best ~ the world : el mejor del mundo 9 written ~ ink/French : escrito con tinta/en francés — adv 1 INSIDE : dentro, adentro 2 be ~ : estar (en casa) 3 be ~ on : participar en 4 come in! : ¡entre!, ¡pase! 5 he's ~ for a shock : se va a llevar un shock — ~ adj : de moda

inability [ˌɪnə'bɪləti] n, pl -ties : incapacidad f

inaccessible [ˌɪnɪk'sesəbəl] adj : inaccesible

inaccurate [ɪn'ækjərət] n : inexacto

inactive [ɪn'æktɪv] n : inactivo — **inactivity** [ˌɪnæk'tɪvəti] n, pl -ties : inactividad f

inadequate [ɪn'ædɪkwət] adj : insuficiente

inadvertently [ˌɪnəd'vərtəntli] adv : sin querer

inadvisable [ˌɪnæd'vaɪzəbəl] adj : desaconsejable

inane ['ɪnem] adj **inaner; -est** : estúpido, tonto

inanimate [ɪn'ænəmət] adj : inanimado

inapplicable [ɪn'æplɪkəbəl, ˌɪnə'plɪkəbəl] adj : inaplicable

inappropriate [ˌɪnə'proːpriət] adj : impropio, inoportuno

inarticulate [ˌɪnɑr'tɪkjələt] adj : incapaz de expresarse

inasmuch as [ˌɪnæz'mʌtʃæz] conj : ya que, puesto que

inattentive [ˌɪnə'tentɪv] adj : poco atento

inaudible [ɪn'odəbəl] adj : inaudible

inaugural [ɪ'nɔgjərəl, -gərəl] adj 1 : inaugural 2 ~ address : discurso m de investidura — **inaugurate** [ɪ'nɔgjə,reɪt, -gə-] vt -rated; -rating : investir (a un presidente, etc.) 2 BEGIN : inaugurar — **inauguration** [ɪ,nɔgjə'reɪʃən, -gə-] n : investidura f (de una persona), inauguración f (de un edificio, etc.)

inborn ['ɪn,bɔrn] adj : innato

inbred ['ɪn,bred] adj INNATE : innato

incalculable [ɪn'kælkjələbəl] adj : incalculable

incapable [ɪn'keɪpəbəl] adj : incapaz — **incapacitate** [ˌɪnkə'pæsə,teɪt] vt -tated; -tating : incapacitar — **incapacity** [ˌɪnkə'pæsəti] n, pl -ties : incapacidad f

incarcerate [ɪn'kɑrsə,reɪt] vt -ated; -ating : encarcelar

incarnate [ɪn'kɑrnət, -,neɪt] adj : encarnado — **incarnation** [ˌɪn,kɑr'neɪʃən] n : encarnación f

incendiary [ɪn'sendi,eri] adj : incendiario

incense¹ [ˌɪn,sents] n : incienso m

incense² [ɪn'sents] vt -censed; -censing : indignar, enfurecer

incentive [ɪn'sentɪv] n : incentivo m

inception [ɪn'sepʃən] n : comienzo m, principio m

incessant [ɪn'sesənt] adj : incesante

incest ['ɪn,sest] n : incesto m — **incestuous** [ɪn'sestʃuəs] adj : incestuoso

inch ['ɪntʃ] n : pulgada f — ~ v : avanzar poco a poco

incident ['ɪnsədənt] n : incidente m — **incidence** ['ɪnsədənts] n : índice m (de crímenes, etc.) — **incidental** [ˌɪnsə'dentəl] adj 1 MINOR : incidental 2 CHANCE : casual — **incidentally** [ˌɪnsə'dentəli, -'dentli] adv : a propósito

incinerate [ɪn'sɪnə,reɪt] vt -ated; -ating : incinerar — **incinerator** [ɪn'sɪnə,reɪtər] n : incinerador m

incision [ɪn'sɪʒən] n : incisión f

incite [ɪn'saɪt] vt -cited; -citing : incitar, instigar

incline [ɪn'klaɪn] v -clined; -clining vt 1 BEND : inclinar 2 be ~ed to : inclinarse a, tender a — ~ vi : inclinarse — ~ ['ɪn,klaɪn] n : pendiente f — **inclination** [ˌɪnklə'neɪʃən] n 1 : inclinación f 2 DESIRE : deseo m, ganas fpl

include [ɪn'kluːd] vt -cluded; -cluding : incluir — **inclusion** [ɪn'kluːʒən] n : inclusión f — **inclusive** [ɪn'kluːsɪv] adj : inclusivo

incognito [ˌɪn,kag'niːto, ɪn'kagnə,to] adv & adj : de incógnito

incoherent [ˌɪnko'hɪrənt, -'her-] adj : incoherente — **Incoherence** [,ınko-'hırənts, -'her-] n : incoherencia f

income ['ın,kʌm] n : ingresos mpl — **income tax** n : impuesto m sobre la renta

incomparable [ın'kɑmpərəbəl] adj : incomparable

incompatible [,ınkəm'pætəbəl] adj : incompatible

incompetent [ın'kɑmpətənt] adj : incompetente — **incompetence** [ın-'kɑmpətənts] n : incompetencia f

incomplete [,ınkəm'pliːt] adj : incompleto

incomprehensible [,ınkɑmprı'hentsə-bəl] adj : incomprensible

inconceivable [,ınkən'siːvəbəl] adj : inconcebible

inconclusive [,ınkən'kluːsıv] adj : no concluyente

incongruous [ın'kɑngruəs] adj : incongruente

inconsiderate [,ınkən'sıdərət] adj : desconsiderado

inconsistent [,ınkən'sıstənt] adj 1 : inconsecuente 2 be ~ with : no concordar con — **Inconsistency** [,ınkən-'sıstəntsi] n, pl -cles : inconsecuencia f

inconspicuous [,ınkən'spıkjuəs] adj : que no llama la atención

inconvenient [,ınkən'viːnjənt] adj : incómodo, inconveniente — **inconvenience** [,ınkən'viːnjənts] n 1 BOTHER : incomodidad f, molestia f 2 DRAWBACK : inconveniente m — ~ vt -nienced; -niencing vt : importunar, molestar

incorporate [ın'kɔrpə,reıt] vt -rated; -rating : incorporar

incorrect [,ınkə'rekt] adj : incorrecto

increase ['ın,kriːs, ın'kriːs] n : aumento m — ~ [ın'kriːs, 'ın,kriːs] v -creased; -creasing : aumentar — **Increasingly** [ın'kriːsınli] adv : cada vez más

incredible [ın'kredəbəl] adj : increíble

incredulous [ın'kredʒələs] adj : incrédulo

incriminate [ın'krımə,neıt] vt -nated; -nating : incriminar

incubator ['ınkjʊ,beıtər, 'ın-] n : incubadora f

incumbent [ın'kʌmbənt] n : titular mf

incur [ın'kər] vt **incurred; incurring** : provocar (al enojo, etc.), incurrir en (gastos)

incurable [ın'kjʊrəbəl] adj : incurable

indebted [ın'dɛţəd] adj 1 : endeudado 2 be ~ to s.o. : estar en deuda con algn

indecent [ın'diːsənt] adj : indecente — **Indecency** [ın'diːsəntsi] n, pl -cles : indecencia f

indecisive [,ındı'saısıv] adj : indeciso

indeed [ın'diːd] adv 1 TRULY : verdaderamente, sin duda 2 IN FACT : en efecto 3 ~? : ¿de veras?

indefinite [ın'defənət] adj 1 : indefinido 2 VAGUE : impreciso — **indefinitely** [ın'defənətli] adv : indefinidamente

indelible [ın'deləbəl] adj : indeleble

indent [ın'dent] vt : sangrar (un párrafo) — **indentation** [,ınden'teıʃən] n DENT, NOTCH : mella f

independent [,ındə'pendənt] adj : independiente — **Independence** [,ındə-'pendənts] n : independencia f

indescribable [,ındı'skraıbəbəl] adj : indescriptible

indestructible [,ındı'strʌktəbəl] adj : indestructible

index ['ın,dɛks] n, pl -dexes or -dices ['ındə,siːz] : índice m — ~ vt : incluir en un índice — **index finger** n : dedo m índice

Indian ['ındiən] adj : indio m, -dia f

indication [,ındə'keıʃən] n : indicio m, señal f — **indicate** ['ındə,keıt] vt -cated; -cating : indicar — **indicative** [ın'dıkətıv] adj : indicativo — **indicator** ['ındə,keıtər] n : indicador m

indict [ın'daıt] vt : acusar (de un crimen) — **indictment** [ın'daıtmənt] n : acusación f

indifferent [ın'dıfrənt, -'dıfə-] adj 1 : indiferente 2 MEDIOCRE : mediocre — **indifference** [ın'dıfrənts, -'dıfə-] n : indiferencia f

indigenous [ın'dıdʒənəs] adj : indígena

indigestion [,ındar'dʒestʃən, -dı-] n : indigestión f — **indigestible** [,ındar'dʒestəbəl, -dı-] adj : indigesto

indignation [,ındıg'neıʃən] n : indignación f — **indignant** [ın'dıgnənt] adj : indignado — **indignity** [ın'dıgnəţi] n, pl -ties : indignidad f

indigo ['ındı,goː] n, pl -gos or -goes : añil m

indirect [,ındə'rekt, -daı-] adj : indirecto

indiscreet [,ındı'skriːt] adj : indiscreto — **indiscretion** [,ındı'skreʃən] n : indiscreción f

indiscriminate [,ındı'skrımənət] adj : indiscriminado

indispensable [,ındı'spentsəbəl] adj : indispensable, imprescindible

indisputable [,ındı'spjuːţəbəl, ın'dıspjuː-ţə-] adj : indiscutible

indistinct [,ındı'stınkt] adj : indistinto

individual [,ındə'vıdʒuəl] adj 1 : individual 2 PARTICULAR : particular — ~ n : individuo m — **individuality** [,ındə-,vıdʒu'æləţi] n, pl -ties : individualidad *f* — **individually** [ˌɪndə'vɪdʒuəli, -dʒəli] *adv* : individualmente

indoctrinate [ɪn'dɑktrəˌneɪt] *vt* **-nated;** **-nating** : adoctrinar — **indoctrination** [ɪnˌdɑktrə'neɪʃən] *n* : adoctrinamiento *m*

indoor [ɪn'dor] *adj* 1 : (de) interior 2 ~ **plant** : planta *f* de interior 3 ~ **pool** : piscina *f* cubierta 4 ~ **sports** : deportes *mpl* bajo techo — **indoors** ['ɪn'dorz] *adv* : adentro, dentro

induce [ɪn'du:s, -'dju:s] *vt* **-duced;** **-ducing** 1 : inducir 2 CAUSE : provocar — **inducement** [ɪn'du:smənt, -'dju:s-] *n* : incentivo *m*

indulge [ɪn'dʌldʒ] *v* **-dulged; -dulging** *vt* 1 GRATIFY : satisfacer 2 PAMPER : consentir — *vi* ~ **in** : permitirse — **indulgence** [ɪn'dʌldʒənts] *n* 1 : indulgencia *f* 2 SATISFYING : satisfacción *f* — **indulgent** [ɪn'dʌldʒənt] *adj* : indulgente

industry ['ɪndəstri] *n, pl* **-tries** 1 : industria *f* 2 DILIGENCE : diligencia *f* — **industrial** [ɪn'dʌstriəl] *adj* : industrial — **industrialize** [ɪn'dʌstriəˌlaɪz] *vt* **-ized;** **-izing** : industrializar — **industrious** [ɪn'dʌstriəs] *adj* : diligente, trabajador

inebriated [ɪ'ni:briˌeɪtəd] *adj* : ebrio, embriagado

inedible [ɪn'edəbəl] *adj* : no comestible

ineffective [ˌɪnɪ'fektɪv] *adj* 1 : ineficaz 2 INCOMPETENT : incompetente — **ineffectual** [ˌɪnɪ'fektʃuəl] *adj* : inútil, ineficaz

inefficient [ˌɪnɪ'fɪʃənt] *adj* 1 : ineficiente 2 INCOMPETENT : incompetente — **inefficiency** [ˌɪnɪ'fɪʃəntsi] *n, pl* **-cies** : ineficiencia *f*

ineligible [ɪ'nelədʒəbəl] *adj* : ineligible

inept [ɪ'nept] *adj* 1 : inepto 2 ~ **at** : incapaz para

inequality [ˌɪnɪ'kwɑləti] *n, pl* **-ties** : desigualdad *f*

inert [ɪ'nərt] *adj* : inerte — **inertia** [ɪ'nər-ʃə] *n* : inercia *f*

inescapable [ˌɪnɪ'skeɪpəbəl] *adj* : ineludible

inevitable [ɪ'nevətəbəl] *adj* : inevitable — **inevitably** [-bli] *adv* : inevitablemente

inexcusable [ˌɪnɪk'skju:zəbəl] *adj* : inexcusable

inexpensive [ˌɪnɪk'spentsɪv] *adj* : barato, económico

inexperienced [ˌɪnɪk'spɪriəntst] *adj* : inexperto

inexplicable [ˌɪnɪk'splɪkəbəl] *adj* : inexplicable

infallible [ɪn'fæləbəl] *adj* : infalible

infamous ['ɪnfəməs] *adj* : infame

infancy ['ɪnfəntsi] *n, pl* **-cies** : infancia *f* — **infant** ['ɪnfənt] *n* : bebé *m*; niño *m*, -ña *f* — **infantile** ['ɪnfənˌtaɪl, -təl, -ˌti:l] *adj* : infantil

infantry ['ɪnfəntri] *n, pl* **-tries** : infantería *f*

infatuated [ɪn'fætʃuˌeɪtəd] *adj* be ~ **with** : estar encaprichado con — **infatuation** [ɪnˌfætʃu'eɪʃən] *n* : encaprichamiento *m*

infect [ɪn'fekt] *vt* : infectar — **infection** [ɪn'fekʃən] *n* : infección *f* — **infectious** [ɪn'fekʃəs] *adj* : contagioso

infer [ɪn'fər] *vt* **inferred; inferring** : deducir, inferir — **inference** ['ɪnfərənts] *n* : deducción *f*

inferior [ɪn'fɪriər] *adj* : inferior — ~ *n* : inferior *mf* — **inferiority** [ɪnˌfɪri'ɔrəti] *n, pl* **-ties** : inferioridad *f*

infernal [ɪn'fərnəl] *adj* : infernal — **inferno** [ɪn'fərˌno:] *n, pl* **-nos** : infierno *m*

infertile [ɪn'fərtəl, -ˌtaɪl] *adj* : estéril — **infertility** [ˌɪnfər'tɪləti] *n* : esterilidad *f*

infest [ɪn'fest] *vt* : infestar

infidelity [ˌɪnfə'deləti, -faɪ-] *n, pl* **-ties** : infidelidad *f*

infiltrate [ɪn'fɪlˌtreɪt, 'ɪnˌfɪl-] *v* **-trated; -trating** *vt* : infiltrar — *vi* : infiltrarse

infinite ['ɪnfənət] *adj* : infinito

infinitive [ɪn'fɪnətɪv] *n* : infinitivo *m*

infinity [ɪn'fɪnəti] *n, pl* **-ties** 1 : infinito *m* 2 **an ~ of** : una infinidad de

infirm [ɪn'fərm] *adj* : enfermizo, endeble — **infirmary** [ɪn'fərməri] *n, pl* **-ries** : enfermería *f* — **infirmity** [ɪn'fərməti] *n, pl* **-ties** 1 FRAILTY : endeblez *f* 2 AILMENT : enfermedad *f*

inflame [ɪn'fleɪm] *vt* **-flamed; -flaming** : inflamar — **inflammable** [ɪn'flæməbəl] *adj* : inflamable — **inflammation** [ˌɪnflə'meɪʃən] *n* : inflamación *f* — **inflammatory** [ɪn'flæməˌtori] *adj* : inflamatorio

inflate [ɪn'fleɪt] *vt* **-flated; -flating** : inflar — **inflation** [ɪn'fleɪʃən] *n* : inflación *f* — **inflationary** [ɪn'fleɪʃəˌneri] *adj* : inflacionario, inflacionista

inflexible [ɪn'fleksɪbəl] *adj* : inflexible

inflict [ɪn'flɪkt] *vt* : infligir

influence ['ɪnˌfluənts, ɪn'fluənts] *n* 1 : influencia *f* 2 **under the ~** : embriagado — ~ *vt* **-enced; -encing** : influir en, influenciar — **influential** [ˌɪnflu-'entʃəl] *adj* : influyente

influenza [ˌɪnflu'enzə] *n* : gripe *f*, influenza *f*

influx ['ɪnˌflʌks] *n* : afluencia *f*

inform [ɪn'form] *vt* 1 : informar 2 **keep me ~ed** : manténme al corriente — *vi* ~ **on** : delatar, denunciar

informal [ɪnˈfɔrməl] *adj* **1** : informal **2** : familiar (dícese del lenguaje) — **informality** [ˌɪnfɔrˈmæləṭi, -fər-] *n, pl* **-ties** : falta *f* de ceremonia — **informally** [ɪnˈfɔrməli] *adv* : de manera informal

information [ˌɪnfərˈmeɪʃən] *n* : información *f* — **informative** [ɪnˈfɔrməṭɪv] *adj* : informativo — **informer** [ɪnˈfɔrmər] *n* : informante *mf*

infrared [ˌɪnfrəˈred] *adj* : infrarrojo

infrastructure [ˈɪnfrəˌstrʌktʃər] *n* : infraestructura *f*

infrequent [ɪnˈfriːkwənt] *adj* : infrecuente — **infrequently** [ɪnˈfriːkwəntli] *adv* : raramente

infringe [ɪnˈfrɪndʒ] *v* **-fringed; -fringing** *vt* : infringir — *vi* ~ **on** : violar — **infringement** [ɪnˈfrɪndʒmənt] *n* : violación *f*

infuriate [ɪnˈfjʊriˌeɪt] *vt* **-ated; -ating** : enfurecer, poner furioso — **infuriating** [ɪnˈfjʊriˌeɪtɪŋ] *adj* : exasperante

infuse [ɪnˈfjuːz] *vt* **-fused; -fusing** : infundir — **infusion** [ɪnˈfjuːʒən] *n* : infusión *f*

ingenious [ɪnˈdʒiːnjəs] *adj* : ingenioso — **ingenuity** [ˌɪndʒəˈnuːəṭi, -njuː-] *n, pl* **-ities** : ingenio

ingenuous [ɪnˈdʒɛnjuəs] *adj* : ingenuo

ingest [ɪnˈdʒɛst] *vt* : ingerir

ingot [ˈɪŋgət] *n* : lingote *m*

ingrained [ɪnˈgreɪnd] *adj* : arraigado

ingratiate [ɪnˈgreɪʃiˌeɪt] *vt* **-ated; -ating** ~ **oneself with** : congraciarse con — **ingratitude** [ɪnˈgræṭəˌtuːd, -ˌtjuːd] *n* : ingratitud *f*

ingredient [ɪnˈgriːdiənt] *n* : ingrediente *m*

ingrown [ˈɪnˌgroːn] *adj* ~ **nail** : uña *f* encarnada

inhabit [ɪnˈhæbət] *vt* : habitar — **inhabitant** [ɪnˈhæbəṭənt] *n* : habitante *mf*

inhale [ɪnˈheɪl] *v* **-haled; -haling** *vt* : inhalar, aspirar — *vi* : inspirar

inherent [ɪnˈhɪrənt, -ˈher-] *adj* : inherente — **inherently** [ɪnˈhɪrəntli, -ˈher-] *adv* : intrínsecamente

inherit [ɪnˈherət] *vt* : heredar — **inheritance** [ɪnˈherəṭənts] *n* : herencia *f*

inhibit [ɪnˈhɪbət] *vt* IMPEDE : inhibir — **inhibition** [ˌɪnhəˈbɪʃən, ˌɪnə-] *n* : inhibición *f*

inhuman [ɪnˈhjuːmən, -ˈjuː-] *adj* : inhumano — **inhumane** [ˌɪnhjuˈmeɪn, -ˈjuː-] *adj* : inhumano — **inhumanity** [ˌɪnhjuˈmænəṭi, -ˈjuː-] *n, pl* **-ties** : inhumanidad *f*

initial [ɪˈnɪʃəl] *adj* : inicial — *n* : inicial *f* — *vt* **-tialed** *or* **-tialled; -tialing** *or* **-tialling** : poner las iniciales a

initiate [ɪˈnɪʃiˌeɪt] *vt* **-ated; -ating** **1** BEGIN : iniciar **2** ~ **s.o. into sth** : iniciar a algn en algo — **initiation** [ɪˌnɪʃiˈeɪʃən] *n* : iniciación *f* — **initiative** [ɪˈnɪʃəṭɪv] *n* : iniciativa *f*

inject [ɪnˈdʒɛkt] *vt* : inyectar — **injection** [ɪnˈdʒɛkʃən] *n* : inyección *f*

injure [ˈɪndʒər] *vt* **-jured; -juring** **1** : herir **2** ~ **oneself** : hacerse daño — **injurious** [ɪnˈdʒʊriəs] *adj* : perjudicial — **injury** [ˈɪndʒəri] *n, pl* **-ries 1** : herida *f* **2** HARM : perjuicio *m*

injustice [ɪnˈdʒʌstəs] *n* : injusticia *f*

ink [ˈɪŋk] *n* : tinta *f* — **inkwell** [ˈɪŋkˌwel] *n* : tintero *m*

inland [ˈɪnˌlænd, -lənd] *adj* : interior — ~ *adv* : hacia el interior, tierra adentro

in–laws [ˈɪnˌlɔz] *npl* : suegros *mpl*

inlet [ˈɪnˌlet, -lət] *n* : ensenada *f*, cala *f*

inmate [ˈɪnˌmeɪt] *n* **1** PATIENT : paciente *mf* **2** PRISONER : preso *m*, -sa *f*

inn [ˈɪn] *n* : posada *f*, hostería *f*

innards [ˈɪnərdz] *npl* : entrañas *fpl*, tripas *fpl fam*

innate [ɪˈneɪt] *adj* : innato

inner [ˈɪnər] *adj* : interior, interno — **innermost** [ˈɪnərˌmoːst] *adj* : más íntimo, más profundo

inning [ˈɪnɪŋ] *n* : entrada *f*

innocent [ˈɪnəsənt] *adj* : inocente — ~ *n* : inocente *mf* — **innocence** [ˈɪnəsənts] *n* : inocencia *f*

innocuous [ɪˈnɑkjəwəs] *adj* : inocuo

innovate [ˈɪnəˌveɪt] *vi* **-vated; -vating** : innovar — **innovation** [ˌɪnəˈveɪʃən] *n* : innovación *f* — **innovative** [ˈɪnəˌveɪṭɪv] *adj* : innovador — **innovator** [ˈɪnəˌveɪṭər] *n* : innovador *m*, -dora *f*

innuendo [ˌɪnjuˈendo] *n, pl* **-dos** *or* **-does** : insinuación *f*, indirecta *f*

innumerable [ɪˈnuːmərəbəl, -ˈnjuː-] *adj* : innumerable

inoculate [ɪˈnɑkjəˌleɪt] *vt* **-lated; -lating** : inocular — **inoculation** [ɪˌnɑkjəˈleɪʃən] *n* : inoculación *f*

inoffensive [ˌɪnəˈfentsɪv] *adj* : inofensivo

inpatient [ˈɪnˌpeɪʃənt] *n* : paciente *mf* hospitalizado

input [ˈɪnˌpʊt] *n* **1** : contribución *f* **2** : entrada *f* (de datos) — ~ *vt* **-putted** *or* **-put; -putting** : entrar (datos, etc.)

inquire [ɪnˈkwaɪr] *v* **-quired; -quiring** *vt* : preguntar — *vi* **1** ~ **about** : informarse sobre **2** ~ **into** : investigar — **inquiry** [ˈɪnˌkwaɪri, ɪnˈkwaɪri; ˈɪnkwəri, -ˌri-] *n, pl* **-ries 1** QUESTION : pregunta *f* **2** INVESTIGATION : investigación *f*

Inquisition [ˌɪnkwəˈzɪʃən, ˌɪŋ-] *n* : inquisición f — **inquisitive** [ɪn'kwɪzət̮ɪv] adj : curioso

insane [ɪn'seɪn] adj : loco — **insanity** [ɪn'sænət̮i] n, pl -**ties** : locura f

insatiable [ɪn'seɪʃəbəl] adj : insaciable

inscribe [ɪn'skraɪb] vt -**scribed**; -**scribing** : inscribir — **inscription** [ɪn'skrɪpʃən] n : inscripción f

inscrutable [ɪn'skruːt̮əbəl] adj : inescrutable

insect ['ɪn.sekt] n : insecto m — **insecticide** [ɪn'sektə.saɪd] n : insecticida m

insecure [ˌɪnsɪ'kjʊr] adj : inseguro, poco seguro — **insecurity** [ˌɪnsɪ'kjʊrət̮i] n, pl -**ties** : inseguridad f

insensitive [ɪn'sensət̮ɪv] adj : insensible — **insensitivity** [ɪn.sensə'tɪvət̮i] n, pl -**ties** : insensibilidad f

inseparable [ɪn'sepərəbəl] adj : inseparable

insert [ɪn'sərt] vt : insertar (texto), introducir (una moneda, etc.)

inside [ɪn'saɪd, 'ɪn.saɪd] n 1 : interior m 2 ~ **out** : al revés — ~ adv : dentro, adentro — ~ adj : interior — ~ prep 1 or ~ **of** : dentro de 2 ~ **an hour** : en menos de una hora

insidious [ɪn'sɪdiəs] adj : insidioso

insight ['ɪn.saɪt] n : perspicacia f

insignia [ɪn'sɪgniə] or **insigne** [-.ni] n, pl -**nia** or -**nias** : insignia f, enseña f

insignificant [ˌɪnsɪg'nɪfɪkənt] adj : insignificante

insincere [ˌɪnsɪn'sɪr] adj : insincero

insinuate [ɪn'sɪnjuˌeɪt] vt -**ated**; -**ating** : insinuar — **insinuation** [ɪn.sɪnju'eɪʃən] n : insinuación f

insipid [ɪn'sɪpəd] adj : insípido

insist [ɪn'sɪst] v : insistir — **insistent** [ɪn'sɪstənt] adj : insistente

insofar as [ˌɪnsə'fɑːræz] conj : en la medida en que

insole ['ɪn.soʊl] n : plantilla f

insolent ['ɪnsələnt] adj : insolente — **insolence** ['ɪnsələns] n : insolencia f

insolvent [ɪn'sɑlvənt] adj : insolvente

insomnia [ɪn'sɑmniə] n : insomnio m

inspect [ɪn'spekt] vt : inspeccionar, revisar — **inspection** [ɪn'spekʃən] n : inspección f — **inspector** [ɪn'spektər] n : inspector m, -tora f

inspire [ɪn'spaɪr] vt -**spired**; -**spiring** : inspirar — **inspiration** [ˌɪnspə'reɪʃən] n : inspiración f — **inspirational** [ˌɪnspə'reɪʃənəl] adj : inspirador

instability [ˌɪnstə'bɪlət̮i] n, pl -**ties** : inestabilidad f

install [ɪn'stɔl] vt -**stalled**; -**stalling** : instalar — **installation** [ˌɪnstə'leɪʃən] n : instalación f — **installment** [ɪn-

'stɔlmənt] n 1 PAYMENT : plazo m, cuota f 2 : entrega f (de una publicación o telenovela)

instance ['ɪnstənts] n 1 : ejemplo m 2 **for** ~ : por ejemplo 3 **in this** ~ : en este caso

instant ['ɪnstənt] n : instante m — ~ adj 1 IMMEDIATE : inmediato 2 ~ **coffee** : café m instantáneo — **instantaneous** [ˌɪnstən'teɪniəs] adj : instantáneo — **instantly** ['ɪnstəntli] adv : al instante, instantáneamente

instead [ɪn'sted] adv 1 : en cambio 2 **I went** ~ : fui en su lugar — **instead of** prep : en vez de, en lugar de

instep ['ɪn.step] n : empeine m

instigate ['ɪnstəˌgeɪt] vt -**gated**; -**gating** : instigar a — **instigation** [ˌɪnstə'geɪʃən] n : instigación f — **instigator** ['ɪnstəˌgeɪt̮ər] n : instigador m, -dora f

instill [ɪn'stɪl] or Brit **instil** vt -**stilled**; -**stilling** : inculcar, infundir

instinct ['ɪnstɪŋkt] n : instinto m — **instinctive** [ɪn'stɪŋktɪv] or **instinctual** [ɪn'stɪŋktʃuəl] adj : instintivo

institute ['ɪnstəˌtuːt, -ˌtjuːt] vt -**tuted**; -**tuting** 1 : instituir 2 INITIATE : iniciar — ~ n : instituto m — **institution** [ˌɪnstə'tuːʃən, -'tjuː-] n : institución f

instruct [ɪn'strʌkt] vt 1 : instruir 2 COMMAND : mandar — **instruction** [ɪn'strʌkʃən] n : instrucción f — **instructor** [ɪn'strʌktər] n : instructor m, -tora f

instrument ['ɪnstrəmənt] n : instrumento m — **instrumental** [ˌɪnstrə'mentəl] adj 1 : instrumental 2 **be** ~ **in** : jugar un papel fundamental en

insubordinate [ˌɪnsə'bɔrdənət] adj : insubordinado — **insubordination** [ˌɪnsəˌbɔrdən'eɪʃən] n : insubordinación f

insufferable [ɪn'sʌfərəbəl] adj : insoportable

insufficient [ˌɪnsə'fɪʃənt] adj : insuficiente

insular ['ɪntsʊlər, -sjʊ-] adj 1 : insular 2 NARROW-MINDED : estrecho de miras

insulate ['ɪntsəˌleɪt] vt -**lated**; -**lating** : aislar — **insulation** [ˌɪntsə'leɪʃən] n : aislamiento m

insulin ['ɪntsələn] n : insulina f

insult [ɪn'sʌlt] vt : insultar — ~ ['ɪn.sʌlt] n : insulto m — **insulting** [ɪn'sʌltɪŋ] : insultante, ofensivo

insure [ɪn'ʃʊr] vt -**sured**; -**suring** : asegurar — **insurance** [ɪn'ʃʊrənts, 'ɪn.ʃʊr-] n : seguro m

insurmountable [ˌɪnsər'maʊntəbəl] adj : insuperable

intact [ɪn'tækt] adj : intacto

intake ['ɪn,teɪk] *n* : consumo *m* (de alimentos), entrada *f* (de aire, etc.)

intangible [ɪn'tændʒəbəl] *adj* : intangible

integral ['ɪntɪgrəl] *adj* : integral

integrate ['ɪntəgreɪt] *v* **-grated; -grating** *vt* : integrar — *vi* : integrarse

integrity [ɪn'tegrəti] *n* : integridad *f*

intellect ['ɪntəˌlekt] *n* : intelecto *m* — **intellectual** [ˌɪntə'lektʃuəl] *adj* : intelectual — **~** *n* : intelectual *mf* — **intelligence** [ɪn'telədʒənts] *n* : inteligencia *f* — **intelligent** [ɪn'telədʒənt] *adj* : inteligente — **intelligible** [ɪn'telədʒəbəl] *adj* : inteligible

intend [ɪn'tend] *vt* **1** be **~ed for** : ser para **2 ~ to do** : pensar hacer, tener la intención de hacer — **intended** [ɪn'tendəd] *adj* : intencionado, deliberado

intense [ɪn'tents] *adj* : intenso — **intensely** [ɪn'tentsli] *adv* : sumamente, profundamente — **intensify** [ɪn'tentsəˌfaɪ] *v* **-fied; -fying** *vt* : intensificar — *vi* : intensificarse — **intensity** [ɪn'tentsəti] *n*, *pl* **-ties** : intensidad *f* — **intensive** [ɪn'tentsɪv] *adj* : intensivo

intent [ɪn'tent] *n* : intención *f* — **~** *adj* **1** : atento, concentrado **2 ~ on doing** : resuelto a hacer — **intention** [ɪn'tentʃən] *n* : intención *f* — **intentional** [ɪn'tentʃənəl] *adj* : intencional, deliberado — **intently** [ɪn'tentli] *adv* : atentamente, fijamente

interact [ˌɪntər'ækt] *vi* **1** : interactuar **2 ~ with** : relacionarse con — **interaction** [ˌɪntər'ækʃən] *n* : interacción *f* — **interactive** [ˌɪntər'æktɪv] *adj* : interactivo

intercede [ˌɪntər'siːd] *vi* **-ceded; -ceding** : interceder

intercept [ˌɪntər'sept] *vt* : interceptar

interchange [ˌɪntər'tʃeɪndʒ] *vt* **-changed; -changing** : intercambiar — **~** ['ɪntərˌtʃeɪndʒ] *n* **1** : intercambio *m* **2** JUNCTION : enlace *m* — **interchangeable** [ˌɪntər'tʃeɪndʒəbəl] *adj* : intercambiable

intercourse ['ɪntərˌkors] *n* : relaciones *fpl* (sexuales)

interest ['ɪntrəst, -tərest] *n* : interés *m* — **~** *vt* : interesar — **interested** [-əd] *adj* : interesado — **interesting** ['ɪntrəstɪŋ, -tərestɪŋ] *adj* : interesante

interface ['ɪntərˌfeɪs] *n* : interfaz *mf* (de una computadora)

interfere [ˌɪntər'fɪr] *vi* **-fered; -fering 1 ~ in** : entrometerse en, interferir en **2 ~ with** DISRUPT : afectar (una actividad, etc.) — **interference** [ˌɪntər'fɪrənts] *n* **1** : interferencia *f* **2** : intromisión *f* (en el radio, etc.)

interim ['ɪntərəm] *n* **1** : interín *m* **2 in the ~** : mientras tanto — **~** *adj* : interino, provisional

interior [ɪn'tɪriər] *adj* : interior — **~** *n* : interior *m*

interjection [ˌɪntər'dʒekʃən] *n* : interjección *f*

interlock [ˌɪntər'lɑk] *vt* : engranar

interloper [ˌɪntər'loːpər] *n* : intruso *m*, -sa *f*

interlude ['ɪntərˌluːd] *n* **1** : intervalo *m* **2** : interludio *m* (en música, etc.)

intermediate [ˌɪntər'miːdiət] *adj* : intermedio — **intermediary** [ˌɪntər'miːdiˌeri] *n*, *pl* **-aries** : intermediario *m*, -ria *f*

interminable [ɪn'tərmənəbəl] *adj* : interminable

intermission [ˌɪntər'mɪʃən] *n* : intervalo *m*, intermedio *m*

intermittent [ˌɪntər'mɪtənt] *adj* : intermitente

intern[1] ['ɪn,tərn, ɪn'tərn] *vt* : confinar

intern[2] ['ɪn,tərn] *vi* : hacer las prácticas — **~** *n* : interno *m*, -na *f*

internal [ɪn'tərnəl] *adj* : interno

international [ˌɪntər'næʃənəl] *adj* : internacional

interpret [ɪn'tərprət] *vt* : interpretar — **interpretation** [ɪnˌtərprə'teɪʃən] *n* : interpretación *f* — **interpreter** [ɪn'tərprətər] *n* : intérprete *mf*

interrogate [ɪn'terəˌgeɪt] *vt* **-gated; -gating** : interrogar — **interrogation** [ɪnˌterə'geɪʃən] *n* QUESTIONING : interrogatorio *m* — **interrogative** [ˌɪntə'rɑgətɪv] *adj* : interrogativo

interrupt [ˌɪntə'rʌpt] *v* : interrumpir — **interruption** [ˌɪntə'rʌpʃən] *n* : interrupción *f*

intersect [ˌɪntər'sekt] *vt* : cruzar (dícese de calles), cortar (dícese de líneas) — *vi* : cruzarse, cortarse — **intersection** [ˌɪntər'sekʃən] *n* : cruce *m*, intersección *f*

intersperse [ˌɪntər'spərs] *vt* **-spersed; -spersing** : intercalar

interstate [ˌɪntər'steɪt] *n or* **~ highway** : carretera *f* interestatal

intertwine [ˌɪntər'twaɪn] *vi* **-twined; -twining** : entrelazarse

interval ['ɪntərvəl] *n* : intervalo *m*

intervene [ˌɪntər'viːn] *vi* **-vened; -vening 1** : intervenir **2** ELAPSE : transcurrir, pasar — **intervention** [ˌɪntər'ventʃən] *n* : intervención *f*

interview ['ɪntərˌvjuː] *n* : entrevista *f* — **~** *vt* : entrevistar — **interviewer** ['ɪntərˌvjuːər] *n* : entrevistador *m*, -dora *f*

intestine [ɪn'tɛstən] n : intestino m — **intestinal** [ɪn'tɛstənəl] adj : intestinal

intimate[1] ['ɪntə,meɪt] vt **-mated; -mating** : insinuar, dar a entender

intimate[2] ['ɪntəmət] adj : íntimo — **intimacy** ['ɪntəməsi] n, pl **-cies** : intimidad f

intimidate [ɪn'tɪmə,deɪt] vt **-dated; -dating** : intimidar — **intimidation** [ɪn,tɪmə'deɪʃən] n : intimidación f

into ['ɪn,tuː] prep 1 : en, a 2 bump ∼ : darse contra 3 (used in mathematics) 3 ∼ 12 : 12 dividido por 3

intolerable [ɪn'tɑlərəbəl] adj : intolerable — **intolerance** [ɪn'tɑlərənts] n : intolerancia f — **intolerant** [ɪn'tɑlərənt] adj : intolerante

intoxicate [ɪn'tɑksə,keɪt] vt **-cated; -cating** : embriagar — **intoxicated** [ɪn'tɑksə,keɪtəd] adj 1 : embriagado 2 ∼ **with** : ebrio de

intransitive [ɪn'træntsətɪv, -'trænzə-] adj : intransitivo

intravenous [,ɪntrə'viːnəs] adj : intravenoso

intrepid [ɪn'trɛpəd] adj : intrépido

intricate ['ɪntrɪkət] adj : complicado, intrincado — **intricacy** ['ɪntrɪkəsi] n, pl **-cies** : complejidad f

intrigue ['ɪn,triːg, ɪn'triːg] n : intriga f — ∼ [ɪn'triːg] v **-trigued; -triguing** : intrigar — **intriguing** [ɪn'triːgɪŋli] adj : intrigante

intrinsic [ɪn'trɪnzɪk, -'trɪntsɪk] adj : intrínseco

introduce [,ɪntrə'duːs, -'djuːs] vt **-duced; -ducing** 1 : introducir 2 : presentar (a una persona) — **introduction** [,ɪntrə'dʌkʃən] n 1 : introducción f 2 : presentación f (de una persona) — **introductory** [,ɪntrə'dʌktəri] adj : introductorio

introvert ['ɪntrə,vərt] n : introvertido m, -da f — **introverted** ['ɪntrə,vərtəd] adj : introvertido

intrude [ɪn'truːd] vi **-truded; -truding** 1 : entrometerse 2 ∼ **on s.o.** : molestar a algn — **intruder** [ɪn'truːdər] n : intruso m, -sa f — **intrusion** [ɪn'truːʒən] n : intrusión f — **intrusive** [ɪn'truːsɪv] adj : intruso

intuition [,ɪntu'ɪʃən, -tju-] n : intuición f — **intuitive** [ɪn'tuːətɪv, -'tjuː-] adj : intuitivo

inundate ['ɪnən,deɪt] vt **-dated; -dating** : inundar

invade [ɪn'veɪd] vt **-vaded; -vading** : invadir

invalid[1] [ɪn'væləd] adj : inválido

invalid[2] ['ɪnvələd] n : inválido m, -da f

invaluable [ɪn'væljəbəl, -'væljuə-] adj : inestimable, invalorable Lat

invariable [ɪn'væriəbəl] adj : invariable

invasion [ɪn'veɪʒən] n : invasión f

invent [ɪn'vɛnt] vt : inventar — **invention** [ɪn'vɛntʃən] n : invención f — **inventive** [ɪn'vɛntɪv] adj : inventivo — **inventor** [ɪn'vɛntər] n : inventor m, -tora f

inventory ['ɪnvən,tɔri] n, pl **-ries** : inventario m

invert [ɪn'vərt] vt : invertir

invertebrate [ɪn'vərtəbrət, -,breɪt] adj : invertebrado — ∼ n : invertebrado m

invest [ɪn'vɛst] vt : invertir

investigate [ɪn'vɛstə,geɪt] v **-gated; -gating** : investigar — **investigation** [ɪn,vɛstə'geɪʃən] n : investigación f — **investigator** [ɪn'vɛstə,geɪtər] n : investigador m, -dora f

investment [ɪn'vɛstmənt] n : inversión f — **investor** [ɪn'vɛstər] n : inversor m, -sora f

inveterate [ɪn'vɛtərət] adj : inveterado

invigorating [ɪn'vɪgə,reɪtɪŋ] adj : vigorizante

invincible [ɪn'vɪntsəbəl] adj : invencible

invisible [ɪn'vɪzəbəl] adj : invisible

invitation [,ɪnvə'teɪʃən] n : invitación f — **invite** [ɪn'vaɪt] vt **-vited; -viting** 1 : invitar 2 SEEK : buscar (problemas, etc.) — **inviting** [ɪn'vaɪtɪŋ] adj : atrayente

invoice ['ɪn,vɔɪs] n : factura f

invoke [ɪn'voːk] vt **-voked; -voking** : invocar

involuntary [ɪn'vɑlən,tɛri] adj : involuntario

involve [ɪn'vɑlv] vt **-volved; -volving** 1 CONCERN : concernir, afectar 2 ENTAIL : suponer — **involved** [ɪn'vɑlvd] adj 1 COMPLEX : complicado 2 CONCERNED : afectado — **involvement** [ɪn'vɑlvmənt] n : participación f

invulnerable [ɪn'vʌlnərəbəl] adj : invulnerable

inward ['ɪnwərd] adj INNER : interior, interno — ∼ or **inwards** [-wərdz] adv : hacia adentro, hacia el interior

iodine ['aɪə,daɪn, -dən] n : yodo m, tintura f de yodo

ion ['aɪən, 'aɪ,ɑn] n : ion m

iota [aɪ'oːtə] n : pizca f, ápice m

IOU [,aɪ,o'juː] n : pagaré m, vale m

Iranian ['reɪniən, -'ræ-, -'rɑ-; aɪ'-] adj : iraní

Iraqi ['rɑki, -'ræk-] adj : iraquí

ire ['aɪr] n : ira f — **irate** [aɪ'reɪt] adj : furioso

iris ['aɪrəs] n, pl **irises** or **irides** ['aɪrə-

,diːz, 'ir-] **1 :** iris *m* (del ojo) **2 :** lirio *m* (planta)

Irish ['aɪrɪʃ] *adj* : irlandés

irksome ['ərksəm] *adj* : irritante, fastidioso

iron ['aɪərn] *n* **1 :** hierro *m*, fierro *m Lat* (metal) **2 :** plancha *f* (para la ropa) — ~ *v* : planchar

ironic [aɪ'rɑnɪk] *or* **ironical** [-nɪkəl] *adj* : irónico

ironing board *n* : tabla *f* (de planchar)

irony ['aɪrəni] *n, pl* -nies : ironía *f*

irrational [ɪ'ræʃənəl] *adj* : irracional

irreconcilable [ɪ,rekən'saɪləbəl] *adj* : irreconciliable

irrefutable [,ɪrɪ'fjuːtəbəl, ɪ'refjə-] *adj* : irrefutable

irregular [ɪ'regjələr] *adj* : irregular — **irregularity** [ɪ,regjə'lærəti] *n, pl* -ties : irregularidad *f*

irrelevant [ɪ'reləvənt] *adj* : irrelevante

irreparable [ɪ'repərəbəl] *adj* : irreparable

irreplaceable [,ɪrɪ'pleɪsəbəl] *adj* : irreemplazable

irresistible [,ɪrɪ'zɪstəbəl] *adj* : irresistible

irresolute [ɪ'rezə,luːt] *adj* : irresoluto

irrespective of [,ɪrɪ'spektɪvəv] *prep* : sin tener en cuenta

irresponsible [,ɪrɪ'spɑntsəbəl] *adj* : irresponsable — **irresponsibility** [,ɪrɪ,spɑntsə'bɪləţi] *n, pl* -ties : irresponsabilidad *f*

irreverent [ɪ'revərənt] *adj* : irreverente

irreversible [,ɪrɪ'vərsəbəl] *adj* : irreversible, irrevocable

irrigate ['ɪrə,geɪt] *vt* -gated; -gating : irrigar, regar — **irrigation** [,ɪrə'geɪʃən] *n* : irrigación *f*, riego *m*

irritate ['ɪrə,teɪt] *vt* -tated; -tating : irritar — **irritable** ['ɪrəţəbəl] *adj* : irritable — **irritably** ['ɪrəţəbli] *adv* : con irritación — **irritating** ['ɪrə,teɪţɪŋ] *adj* : irritante — **irritation** [,ɪrə'teɪʃən] *n* : irritación *f*

is → **be**

Islam [ɪs'lɑm, ɪz-, -'læm; 'ɪs,lɑm, 'ɪz-, -,læm] *n* : el Islam — **Islamic** [ɪs'lɑmɪk, ɪz-, -'læ-] *adj* : islámico

island ['aɪlənd] *n* : isla *f* — **isle** ['aɪl] *n* : isla *f*

isolate ['aɪsə,leɪt] *vt* -lated; -lating : aislar — **isolation** [,aɪsə'leɪʃən] *n* : aislamiento *m*

Israeli [ɪz'reɪli] *adj* : israelí

issue ['ɪ,ʃuː] *n* **1** MATTER : asunto *m*, cuestión *f* **2 :** número *m* (de una revista, etc.) **3 make an** ~ **of :** insistir demasiado sobre **4 take** ~ **with :** disentir de — ~ *v* **-sued; -suing** *vi* **from :** surgir de — *vt* **1 :** emitir (sellos, etc.), distribuir (provisiones, etc.) **2** PUBLISH : publicar

isthmus ['ɪsməs] *n* : istmo *m*

it ['ɪt] *pron* **1** (*as subject*) : él, ella **2** (*as indirect object*) : le, se **3** (*as direct object*) : lo, la **4** (*as object of a preposition*) : él, ella **5 it's raining :** está lloviendo **6 it's 8 o'clock :** son las ocho **7 it's hot out :** hace calor **8** ~ **is necessary :** es necesario **9 who is** ~**? :** ¿quién es? **10 it's me :** soy yo

Italian [ɪ'tæliən, aɪ-] *adj* : italiano — ~ *n* : italiano *m* (idioma)

italics ['ɪtælɪks, aɪ-] *n* : cursiva *f*

itch ['ɪtʃ] *vi* **1 :** picar **2 be** ~**ing to :** morirse por — ~ *n* : picazón *f* — **itchy** ['ɪtʃi] *adj* **itchier; -est :** que pica

it'd ['ɪţəd] (*contraction of* it had *or* it would*) → have, would

item ['aɪţəm] *n* **1 :** artículo *m* **2 :** punto *m* (en una agenda) **3** ~ **of clothing :** prenda *f* de vestir **4 news** ~ : noticia *f* — **itemize** ['aɪţə,maɪz] *vt* -ized; -izing : detallar, enumerar

itinerant [aɪ'tɪnərənt] *adj* : ambulante

itinerary [aɪ'tɪnə,reri] *n, pl* -aries : itinerario *m*

it'll ['ɪţəl] (*contraction of* it shall *or* it will) → **shall, will**

its ['ɪts] *adj* : su, sus

it's ['ɪts] (*contraction of* it is *or* it has) → **be, have**

itself [ɪt'self] *pron* **1** (*used reflexively*) : se **2** (*used for emphasis*) : (él) mismo, (ella) misma, sí (mismo) **3 by** ~ : solo

I've ['aɪv] (*contraction of* I have) → **have**

ivory ['aɪvəri] *n, pl* -ries : marfil *m*

ivy ['aɪvi] *n, pl* **ivies :** hiedra *f*

perforate ['pərfə,reɪt] *vt* -**rated; -rating** : perforar

perform [pər'fɔrm] *vt* **1** CARRY OUT : realizar, hacer **2** : representar (una obra teatral), interpretar (una obra musical) — *vi* **1** FUNCTION : funcionar **2** ACT : actuar — **performance** [pər'fɔrmənts] *n* **1** : realización *f* **2** INTERPRETATION : interpretación *f* **3** PRESENTATION : representación *f* — **performer** [pər'fɔrmər] *n* : actor *m*, -triz *f*; intérprete *mf* (de música)

perfume ['pər,fjuːm, pər'-] *n* : perfume *m*

perhaps [pər'hæps] *adv* : tal vez, quizá, quizás

peril ['perəl] *n* : peligro *m* — **perilous** ['perələs] *adj* : peligroso

perimeter [pə'rɪmətər] *n* : perímetro *m*

period ['pɪriəd] *n* **1** : período *m* (de tiempo) **2** : punto *m* (en puntuación) **3** ERA : época *f* — **periodic** [,pɪri'ɑdɪk] *adj* : periódico — **periodical** [,pɪri'ɑdɪkəl] *n* : revista *f*

peripheral [pə'rɪfərəl] *adj* : periférico

perish ['perɪʃ] *vi* : perecer — **perishable** ['perɪʃəbəl] *adj* : perecedero — **perishables** ['perɪʃəbəlz] *npl* : productos *mpl* perecederos

perjury ['pərdʒəri] *n* : perjurio *m*

perk ['pərk] *vi* ~ **up** : animarse, reanimarse — ~ *n* : extra *m* — **perky** ['pərki] *adj* **perkier; -est** : alegre

permanence ['pərmənənts] *n* : permanencia *f* — **permanent** ['pərmənənt] *adj* : permanente — ~ *n* : permanente *f*

permeate ['pərmi,eɪt] *v* -**ated; -ating** : penetrar

permission [pər'mɪʃən] *n* : permiso *m* — **permissible** [pər'mɪsəbəl] *adj* : permisible — **permissive** [pər'mɪsɪv] *adj* : permisivo — **permit** [pər'mɪt] *vt* -**mitted; -mitting** : permitir — ~ ['pər,mɪt, pər'-] *n* : permiso *m*

peroxide [pə'rɑk,saɪd] *n* : peróxido *m*

perpendicular [,pərpən'dɪkjələr] *adj* : perpendicular

perpetrate ['pərpə,treɪt] *vt* -**trated; -trating** : cometer — **perpetrator** ['pərpə,treɪtər] *n* : autor *m*, -tora *f* (de un delito)

perpetual [pər'petʃuəl] *adj* : perpetuo

perplex [pər'pleks] *vt* : dejar perplejo — **perplexing** [pər'pleksɪŋ] *adj* : desconcertante — **perplexity** [pər'pleksəti] *n*, *pl* -**ties** : perplejidad *f*

persecute ['pərsɪ,kjuːt] *vt* -**cuted; -cuting** : perseguir — **persecution** [,pərsɪ'kjuːʃən] *n* : persecución *f*

persevere [,pərsə'vɪr] *vi* -**vered; -vering** : perseverar — **perseverance** [,pərsə'vɪrənts] *n* : perseverancia *f*

persist [pər'sɪst] *vi* : persistir — **persistence** [pər'sɪstənts] *n* : persistencia *f* — **persistent** [pər'sɪstənt] *adj* : persistente

person ['pərsən] *n* : persona *f* — **personal** ['pərsənəl] *adj* : personal — **personality** [,pərsən'æləti] *n*, *pl* -**ties** : personalidad *f* — **personally** ['pərsənəli] *adv* : personalmente, en persona — **personnel** [,pərsən'el] *n* : personal *m*

perspective [pər'spektɪv] *n* : perspectiva *f*

perspiration [,pərspə'reɪʃən] *n* : transpiración *f* — **perspire** [pər'spaɪr] *vi* -**spired; -spiring** : transpirar

persuade [pər'sweɪd] *vt* -**suaded; -suading** : persuadir — **persuasion** [pər'sweɪʒən] *n* : persuasión *f*

pertain [pər'teɪn] *vi* ~ **to** : estar relacionado con — **pertinent** ['pərtənənt] *adj* : pertinente

perturb [pər'tərb] *vt* : perturbar

Peruvian [pə'ruːviən] *adj* : peruano

pervade [pər'veɪd] *vt* -**vaded; -vading** : penetrar — **pervasive** [pər'veɪsɪv, -zɪv] *adj* : penetrante

perverse [pər'vərs] *adj* **1** CORRUPT : perverso **2** STUBBORN : obstinado — **pervert** ['pər,vərt] *n* : pervertido *m*, -da *f*

peso ['peɪ,soː] *n*, *pl* -**sos** : peso *m*

pessimism ['pesə,mɪzəm] *n* : pesimismo *m* — **pessimist** ['pesəmɪst] *n* : pesimista *mf* — **pessimistic** [,pesə'mɪstɪk] *adj* : pesimista

pest ['pest] *n* **1** : insecto *m* nocivo, animal *m* nocivo **2** : peste *f fam* (persona) — **pester** ['pestər] *vt* -**tered; -tering** : molestar

pesticide ['pestə,saɪd] *n* : pesticida *m*

pet ['pet] *n* **1** : animal *m* doméstico **2** FAVORITE : favorito *m*, -ta *f* — ~ *vt* **petted; petting** : acariciar

petal ['petəl] *n* : pétalo *m*

petite [pə'tiːt] *adj* : chiquita

petition [pə'tɪʃən] *n* : petición *f* — ~ *vt* : dirigir una petición a

petrify ['petrə,faɪ] *vt* -**fied; -fying** : petrificar

petroleum [pə'troːliəm] *n* : petróleo *m*

petticoat ['peti,koːt] *n* : enagua *f*, fondo *m Lat*

petty ['peti] *adj* -**tier; -est** **1** UNIMPORTANT : insignificante, nimio **2** MEAN : mezquino — **pettiness** ['petinəs] *n* : mezquindad *f*

petulant ['petʃələnt] *adj* : irritable, de mal genio

pew ['pjuː] *n* : banco *m* (de iglesia)

pewter ['pjuːt̬ər] n : peltre m
phallic ['fælɪk] adj : fálico
phantom ['fæntəm] n : fantasma m
pharmacy ['fɑrməsi] n, pl **-cies** : farmacia f — **pharmacist** ['fɑrməsɪst] n : farmacéutico m, -ca f
phase ['feɪz] n : fase f — ~ vt **phased; phasing 1 ~ in** : introducir progresivamente **2 ~ out** : retirar progresivamente
phenomenon [fɪ'nɑmənɑn, -nən] n, pl **-na** [-nə] or **-nons** : fenómeno m — **phenomenal** [fɪ'nɑmənəl] adj : fenomenal
philanthropy [fə'lænθrəpi] n, pl **-pies** : filantropía f — **philanthropist** [fə'lænθrəpɪst] n : filántropo m, -pa f
philosophy [fə'lɑsəfi] n, pl **-phies** : filosofía f — **philosopher** [fə'lɑsəfər] n : filósofo m, -fa f
phlegm ['flɛm] n : flema f
phobia ['foːbiə] n : fobia f
phone ['foːn] → **telephone**
phonetic [fə'nɛt̬ɪk] adj : fonético
phony or **phoney** ['foːni] adj **-nier; -est** : falso — ~ n, pl **-nies** : farsante mf
phosphorus ['fɑsfərəs] n : fósforo m
photo ['foːt̬oː] n, pl **-tos** : foto f — **photocopier** ['foːt̬oːkɑpiər] n : fotocopiadora f — **photocopy** ['foːt̬oːkɑpi] n, pl **-copies** : fotocopia f — ~ vt **-copied; -copying** : fotocopiar — **photograph** ['foːt̬əgræf] n : fotografía f, foto f — ~ vt : fotografiar — **photographer** [fə'tɑgrəfər] n : fotógrafo m, -fa f — **photographic** [ˌfoːt̬ə'græfɪk] adj : fotográfico — **photography** [fə'tɑgrəfi] n : fotografía f
phrase ['freɪz] n : frase f — ~ vt **phrased; phrasing** : expresar
physical ['fɪzɪkəl] adj : físico — ~ n : reconocimiento m médico
physician [fə'zɪʃən] n : médico m, -ca f
physics ['fɪzɪks] ns & pl : física f — **physicist** ['fɪzəsɪst] n : físico m, -ca f
physiology [ˌfɪzi'ɑlədʒi] n : fisiología f
physique [fə'ziːk] n : físico m
piano [pi'ænoː] n, pl **-anos** : piano m — **pianist** [pi'ænɪst, 'piːənɪst] n : pianista mf
pick ['pɪk] vt **1** CHOOSE : escoger **2** GATHER : recoger **3** REMOVE : quitar (poco a poco) **4 ~ a fight** : buscar camorra — vi **1 ~ and choose** : ser exigente **2 ~ on** : meterse con — ~ n **1** CHOICE : selección f **2** or **pickax** ['pɪkˌæks] : pico m **3 the ~ of** : lo mejor de
picket ['pɪkət] n **1** STAKE : estaca f **2** or **~ line** : piquete m — ~ v : piquetear
pickle ['pɪkəl] n **1** : pepinillo m (encurtido) **2** JAM : lío m fam, apuro m — ~ vt **-led; -ling** : encurtir
pickpocket ['pɪkˌpɑkət] n : carterista mf
pickup ['pɪkˌəp] n **1** IMPROVEMENT : mejora f **2** or **~ truck** : camioneta f — **pick up** vt **1** LIFT : levantar **2** TIDY : arreglar, ordenar — vi IMPROVE : mejorar
picnic ['pɪkˌnɪk] n : picnic m — ~ vi **-nicked; -nicking** : ir de picnic
picture ['pɪktʃər] n **1** PAINTING : cuadro m **2** DRAWING : dibujo m **3 a ~** PHOTO : fotografía f **4** IMAGE : imagen f **5** MOVIE : película f — ~ vt **-tured; -turing 1** DEPICT : representar **2** IMAGINE : imaginarse — **picturesque** [ˌpɪktʃə'resk] adj : pintoresco
pie ['paɪ] n : pastel m (con fruta o carne), empanada f (con carne)
piece ['piːs] n **1** : pieza f **2** FRAGMENT : trozo m, pedazo m **3 a ~ of advice** : un consejo — ~ vt **pieced; piecing** or **~ together** : juntar, componer — **piecemeal** ['piːsˌmiːl] adv : poco a poco — ~ adj : poco sistemático
pier ['pɪr] n : muelle m
pierce ['pɪrs] vt **pierced; piercing** : perforar — **piercing** adj : penetrante
piety ['paɪət̬i] n, pl **-eties** : piedad f
pig ['pɪg] n : cerdo m, -da f; puerco m, -ca f
pigeon ['pɪdʒən] n : paloma f — **pigeonhole** ['pɪdʒənˌhoːl] n : casilla f
piggyback ['pɪgiˌbæk] adv & adj : a cuestas
pigment ['pɪgmənt] n : pigmento m
pigpen ['pɪgˌpɛn] n : pocilga f
pigtail ['pɪgˌteɪl] n : coleta f, trenza f
pile¹ ['paɪl] n HEAP : montón m, pila f — ~ v **piled; piling** vt : amontonar, apilar — vi **~ up** : amontonarse, acumularse
pile² n NAP : pelo m (de telas)
pilfer ['pɪlfər] v : robar, hurtar
pilgrim ['pɪlgrəm] n : peregrino m, -na f — **pilgrimage** ['pɪlgrəmɪdʒ] n : peregrinación f
pill ['pɪl] n : pastilla f, píldora f
pillage ['pɪlɪdʒ] n : saqueo m — ~ vt **-laged; -laging** : saquear
pillar ['pɪlər] n : pilar m, columna f
pillow ['pɪloː] n : almohada f — **pillowcase** ['pɪloːˌkeɪs] n : funda f (de almohada)
pilot ['paɪlət] n : piloto mf — ~ vt : pilotar, pilotear — **pilot light** n : piloto m
pimp ['pɪmp] n : proxeneta m
pimple ['pɪmpəl] n : grano m
pin ['pɪn] n **1** : alfiler m **2** BROOCH

: broche *m* **3** *or* **bowling ~** : bolo *m*
— **~** *vt* **pinned; pinning 1** FASTEN
: prender, sujetar (con alfileres) **2** *or*
~ down : inmovilizar
pincers ['pɪntsərz] *npl* : tenazas *fpl*
pinch ['pɪntʃ] *vt* **1** : pellizcar **2** STEAL
: robar — *vi* : apretar — **~** *n* **1** : pellizco *m* **2** BIT : pizca *f* **3 in a ~** : en
caso necesario
pine¹ ['paɪn] *n* : pino *m* (árbol)
pine² *vi* **pined; pining 1** LANGUISH
: languidecer **2 ~ for** : suspirar por
pineapple ['paɪnˌæpəl] *n* : piña *f*, ananás
m
pink ['pɪŋk] *n* : rosa *m*, rosado *m* — **~**
adj : rosa, rosado
pinnacle ['pɪnɪkəl] *n* : pináculo *m*
pinpoint ['pɪnˌpɔɪnt] *vt* : localizar, precisar
pint ['paɪnt] *n* : pinta *f*
pioneer [ˌpaɪə'nɪr] *n* : pionero *m*, -ra *f*
pious ['paɪəs] *adj* : piadoso
pipe ['paɪp] *n* **1** : tubo *m*, caño *m* **2** : pipa
f (para fumar) — **pipeline** ['paɪpˌlaɪn] *n*
1 : conducto *m*, oleoducto *m* (para
petróleo)
piquant ['piːkənt, 'pɪkwənt] *adj* : picante
pique ['piːk] *n* : resentimiento *m*
pirate ['paɪrət] *n* : pirata *mf*
pistachio [pə'stæʃiˌoː, -'sta-] *n*, *pl* **-chios**
: pistacho *m*
pistol ['pɪstəl] *n* : pistola *f*
piston ['pɪstən] *n* : pistón *m*
pit ['pɪt] *n* **1** HOLE : hoyo *m*, fosa *f* **2** MINE
: mina *f* **3** : hueso *m* (de una fruta) **4 ~
of the stomach** : boca *f* del estómago
— **~** *vt* **pitted; pitting 1** : marcar de
hoyos **2** : deshuesar (una fruta) **3 ~
against** : enfrentar a
pitch ['pɪtʃ] *vt* **1** : armar (una tienda) **2**
THROW : lanzar — *vi* **1** *or* **~ forward**
: caerse **2** LURCH : cabecear (dícese de
un barco o un avión) — **~** *n* **1** DEGREE, LEVEL : grado *m*, punto *m* **2**
TONE : tono *m* **3** THROW : lanzamiento
m **4** *or* **sales ~** : presentación *f* (de
un vendedor)
pitcher ['pɪtʃər] *n* **1** JUG : jarro *m* **2** : lanzador *m*, -dora *f* (en béisbol, etc.)
pitchfork ['pɪtʃˌfɔrk] *n* : horquilla *f*,
horca *f*
pitfall ['pɪtˌfɔl] *n* : riesgo *m*, dificultad *f*
pith ['pɪθ] *n* **1** : médula *f* (de un hueso,
etc.) **2** CORE : meollo *m* — **pithy** ['pɪθi]
adj **pithier; -est** : conciso y sustancioso
pity ['pɪti] *n*, *pl* **pities 1** COMPASSION
: compasión *f* **2 what a ~!** : ¡qué lástima! — **~** *vt* **pitied; pitying** : compadecerse de — **pitiful** ['pɪtɪfəl] *adj*

: lastimoso — **pitiless** ['pɪtɪləs] *adj*
: despiadado
pivot ['pɪvət] *n* : pivote *m* — **~** *vi* **1**
: girar sobre un eje **2 ~ on** : depender
de
pizza ['piːtsə] *n* : pizza *f*
placard ['plækərd, -ˌkɑrd] *n* POSTER : cartel *m*, póster *m*
placate ['pleɪkeɪt, 'plæ-] *vt* **-cated;
-cating** : apaciguar
place ['pleɪs] *n* **1** : sitio *m*, lugar *m* **2**
SEAT : asiento *m* **3** POSITION : puesto *m*
4 ROLE : papel *m* **5 take ~** : tener
lugar **6 take the ~ of** : sustituir a —
~ *vt* **placed; placing 1** PUT, SET
: poner, colocar **2** IDENTIFY : identificar, recordar **3 ~ an order** : hacer
un pedido — **placement** ['pleɪsmənt] *n*
: colocación *f*
placid ['plæsəd] *adj* : plácido, tranquilo
plagiarism ['pleɪdʒəˌrɪzəm] *n* : plagio *m*
— **plagiarize** ['pleɪdʒəˌraɪz] *vt* **-rized;
-rizing** : plagiar
plague ['pleɪg] *n* **1** : plaga *f* (de insectos,
etc.) **2** : peste *f* (en medicina)
plaid ['plæd] *n* : tela *f* escocesa — **~** *adj*
: escocés
plain ['pleɪn] *adj* **1** SIMPLE : sencillo **2**
CLEAR : claro, evidente **3** CANDID
: franco **4** HOMELY : poco atractivo **5 in
~ sight** : a la vista (de todos) — **~** *n*
: llanura *f*, planicie *f* — **plainly** ['pleɪnli] *adv* **1** CLEARLY : claramente **2**
FRANKLY : francamente **3** SIMPLY : sencillamente
plaintiff ['pleɪntɪf] *n* : demandante *mf*
plan ['plæn] *n* **1** : plan *m*, proyecto *m* **2**
DIAGRAM : plano *m* — *v* **planned;
planning** *vt* **1** : planear, proyectar **2**
INTEND : tener planeado — *vi* : hacer
planes
plane¹ ['pleɪn] *n* **1** LEVEL : plano *m*,
nivel *m* **2** AIRPLANE : avión *m*
plane² *n* *or* **carpenter's ~** : cepillo *m*
planet ['plænət] *n* : planeta *m*
plank ['plæŋk] *n* : tabla *f*
planning ['plænɪŋ] *n* : planificación *f*
plant ['plænt] *vt* : plantar (flores, árboles), sembrar (semillas) — **~** *n* **1**
: planta *f* **2** FACTORY : fábrica *f*
plantain ['plæntən] *n* : plátano *m* (grande)
plantation [plæn'teɪʃən] *n* : plantación *f*
plaque ['plæk] *n* : placa *f*
plaster ['plæstər] *n* : yeso *m* — **~** *vt* **1**
: enyesar **2** COVER : cubrir — **plaster
cast** *n* : escayola *f*
plastic ['plæstɪk] *adj* **1** : de plástico **2**
FLEXIBLE : plástico, flexible **3 ~ surgery** : cirugía *f* plástica — **~** *n* : plástico *m*

plate 334 pneumatic

plate ['pleɪt] *n* **1** SHEET : placa *f* **2** DISH : plato *m* **3** ILLUSTRATION : lámina *f* — ~ *vt* **plated; plating** : chapar (en metal)

plateau [plæ'toː] *n*, *pl* **-teaus** *or* **-teaux** ['-toːz] : meseta *f*

platform ['plætˌfɔrm] *n* **1** : plataforma *f* **2** : andén *m* (de una estación de ferrocarril) **3** *or* **political** ~ : programa *m* electoral

platinum ['plætənəm] *n* : platino *m*

platitude ['plætəˌtuːd, -ˌtjuːd] *n* : lugar *m* común

platoon [plə'tuːn] *n* : sección *f* (en el ejército)

platter ['plæt̬ər] *n* : fuente *f*

plausible ['plɔːzəbəl] *adj* : creíble, verosímil

play ['pleɪ] *n* **1** : juego *m* **2** DRAMA : obra *f* de teatro — ~ *vi* **1** : jugar **2** ~ **in a band** : tocar en un grupo — *vt* **1** : jugar (deportes, etc.), jugar a (juegos) **2** : tocar (música o un instrumento) **3** ~ **the role of** : representar el papel de — **player** ['pleɪər] *n* **1** : jugador *m*, -dora *f* **2** ACTOR : actor *m*, actriz *f* **3** MUSICIAN : músico *m*, -ca *f* — **playful** ['pleɪfəl] *adj* : juguetón — **playground** ['pleɪˌɡraʊnd] *n* : patio *m* de recreo — **playing card** *n* : naipe *m*, carta *f* — **playmate** ['pleɪˌmeɪt] *n* : compañero *m*, -ra *f* de juego — **play-off** ['pleɪˌɔf] *n* : desempate *m* — **playpen** ['pleɪˌpɛn] *n* : corral *m* (para niños) — **plaything** ['pleɪˌθɪŋ] *n* : juguete *m* — **playwright** ['pleɪˌraɪt] *n* : dramaturgo *m*, -ga *f*

plea ['pliː] *n* **1** : acto *m* de declararse (en derecho) **2** APPEAL : ruego *m*, súplica *f* — **plead** ['pliːd] *v* **pleaded** *or* **pled** ['plɛd]; **pleading** *vi* **1** ~ **for** : suplicar **2** ~ **guilty** : declararse culpable **3** ~ **not guilty** : negar la acusación — *vt* **1** : alegar, pretextar **2** ~ **a case** : defender un caso

pleasant ['plɛzənt] *adj* : agradable, grato — **please** ['pliːz] *v* **pleased; pleasing** *vt* GRATIFY : complacer **2** SATISFY : satisfacer — *vi* **1** : agradar **2** **do as you** ~ : haz lo que quieras — ~ *adv* : por favor — **pleased** ['pliːzd] *adj* : contento — **pleasing** ['pliːzɪŋ] *adj* : agradable — **pleasure** ['plɛʒər] *n* : placer *m*, gusto *m*

pleat ['pliːt] *vt* : plisar — ~ *n* : pliegue *m*

pledge ['plɛdʒ] *n* **1** SECURITY : prenda *f* **2** PROMISE : promesa *f* — ~ *vt* **pledged; pledging** **1** PAWN : empeñar **2** PROMISE : prometer

plenty ['plɛnti] *n* **1** : abundancia *f* **2** ~ **of time** : tiempo *m* de sobra — **plentiful** ['plɛntɪfəl] *adj* : abundante

pliable ['plaɪəbəl] *adj* : flexible

pliers ['plaɪərz] *npl* : alicates *mpl*

plight ['plaɪt] *n* : situación *f* difícil

plod ['plɑd] *vi* **plodded; plodding** **1** : caminar con paso pesado **2** DRUDGE : trabajar laboriosamente

plot ['plɑt] *n* **1** LOT : parcela *f* **2** : argumento *m* (de una novela, etc.) **3** CONSPIRACY : complot *m*, intriga *f* — ~ *v* **plotted; plotting** *vt* : tramar (un plan), trazar (una gráfica, etc.) — *vi* CONSPIRE : conspirar

plow *or* **plough** ['plaʊ] *n* **1** : arado *m* **2** → **snowplow** — ~ *v* : arar

ploy ['plɔɪ] *n* : estratagema *f*

pluck ['plʌk] *vt* **1** : arrancar **2** : desplumar (un pollo, etc.) **3** : recoger (flores) **4** ~ **one's eyebrows** : depilarse las cejas

plug ['plʌɡ] *n* **1** STOPPER : tapón *m* **2** : enchufe *m* (eléctrico) — ~ *vt* **plugged; plugging 1** BLOCK : tapar **2** ADVERTISE : dar publicidad a **3** ~ **in** : enchufar

plum ['plʌm] *n* : ciruela *f*

plumb ['plʌm] *adj* : a plomo, vertical — **plumber** ['plʌmər] *n* : fontanero *m*, -ra *f*; plomero *m*, -ra *f Lat* — **plumbing** ['plʌmɪŋ] *n* **1** : fontanería *f*, plomería *f Lat* **2** PIPES : cañerías *fpl*

plume ['pluːm] *n* : pluma *f*

plummet ['plʌmət] *vi* : caer en picado

plump ['plʌmp] *adj* : rechoncho *fam*

plunder ['plʌndər] *vi* : saquear, robar — ~ *n* : botín *m*

plunge ['plʌndʒ] *v* **plunged; plunging** *vt* **1** IMMERSE : sumergir **2** THRUST : hundir — *vi* **1** : zambullirse (en el agua) **2** DESCEND : descender en picada — ~ *n* **1** DIVE : zambullida *f* **2** DROP : descenso *m* abrupto

plural ['plʊrəl] *adj* : plural — ~ *n* : plural *m*

plus ['plʌs] *adj* : positivo — ~ *n* **1** *or* ~ **sign** : signo *m* (de) más **2** ADVANTAGE : ventaja *f* — ~ *prep* : más — ~ *conj* : y, además

plush ['plʌʃ] *n* : felpa *f* — ~ *adj* **1** : de felpa **2** LUXURIOUS : lujoso

plutonium [pluː'toːniəm] *n* : plutonio *m*

ply ['plaɪ] *vt* **plied; plying 1** : ejercer (un oficio) **2** ~ **with questions** : acosar con preguntas

plywood ['plaɪˌwʊd] *n* : contrachapado *m*

pneumatic [nʊ'mætɪk, njʊ-] *adj* : neumático

pneumonia [nʊ'moːnjə, njʊ-] n : pulmonía f

poach¹ ['poːtʃ] vt : cocer a fuego lento

poach² vt or ~ **game** : cazar ilegalmente — **poacher** ['poːtʃər] n : cazador m furtivo, cazadora f furtiva

pocket ['pakət] n : bolsillo m — ~ vt : meterse en el bolsillo — **pocketbook** ['pakət,bʊk] n : cartera f, bolsa f Lat — **pocketknife** ['pakət,naɪf] n, pl -**knives** : navaja f

pod ['pad] n : vaina f

poem ['poːəm] n : poema m — **poet** ['poːət] n : poeta m — **poetic** [po'ɛtɪk] or **poetical** [-tɪkəl] adj : poético — **poetry** ['poːətri] n : poesía f

poignant ['pɔɪnjənt] adj : conmovedor

point ['pɔɪnt] n 1 : punto m 2 PURPOSE : sentido m 3 TIP : punta f 4 FEATURE : cualidad f 5 **be beside the** ~ : no venir al caso 6 **there's no** ~ ... : no sirve de nada — ~ vt 1 AIM : apuntar 2 or ~ **out** : señalar, indicar — vi ~ **at** : señalar (con el dedo) — **point-blank** ['pɔɪnt'blæŋk] adv : a quemarropa — **pointer** ['pɔɪntər] n 1 NEEDLE : aguja f 2 : perro m de muestra 3 TIP : consejo m — **pointless** ['pɔɪntləs] adj : inútil — **point of view** n : perspectiva f, punto m de vista

poise ['pɔɪz] n 1 : elegancia f 2 COMPOSURE : aplomo m

poison ['pɔɪzən] n : veneno m — ~ vt : envenenar — **poisonous** ['pɔɪzənəs] adj : venenoso (dícese de una culebra, etc.), tóxico (dícese de una sustancia)

poke ['poːk] vt **poked**; **poking** 1 JAB : golpear (con la punta de algo), dar 2 THRUST : introducir, asomar — ~ n : golpe m abrupto (con la punta de algo)

poker¹ ['poːkər] n : atizador m (para el fuego)

poker² n : póquer m (juego de naipes)

polar ['poːlər] adj : polar — **polar bear** n : oso m blanco — **polarize** ['poːlə,raɪz] vt -**ized**; -**izing** : polarizar

pole¹ ['poːl] n : palo m, poste m

pole² n : polo m (en geografía)

police [pə'liːs] vt -**liced**; -**licing** : mantener el orden en — ~ ns & pl the ~ : la policía — **policeman** [pə'liːsmən] n, pl -**men** [-mən, -,mɛn] : policía m — **police officer** n : policía mf, agente mf de policía — **policewoman** [pə'liːs,wʊmən] n, pl -**women** [-,wɪmən] : (mujer f) policía f

policy ['paləsi] n, pl -**cies** 1 : política f 2 or **insurance** ~ : póliza f de seguros

polio ['poːliˌoː] or **poliomyelitis** [,poːliˌoː,maɪə'laɪtəs] n : polio f, poliomielitis f

polish ['palɪʃ] vt 1 : limpiar (zapatos), encerar (un suelo) — ~ n 1 LUSTER : brillo m, lustre m 2 : betún m (para zapatos), cera f (para suelos y muebles), esmalte m (para las uñas)

Polish ['poːlɪʃ] adj : polaco — ~ n : polaco m (idioma)

polite [pə'laɪt] adj -**liter**; -**est** : cortés — **politeness** [pə'laɪtnəs] n : cortesía f

political [pə'lɪtɪkəl] adj : político — **politician** [,palə'tɪʃən] n : político m, -ca f — **politics** ['palətɪks] ns & pl : política f

polka ['poːlkə, 'poːkə] n : polka f — **polka dot** ['poːkə] n : lunar m

poll ['poːl] n 1 : encuesta f, sondeo m 2 **the** ~**s** : las urnas — ~ vt 1 : obtener (votos) 2 CANVASS : encuestar, sondear

pollen ['palən] n : polen m

pollute [pə'luːt] vt -**luted**; -**luting** : contaminar — **pollution** [pə'luːʃən] n : contaminación f

polyester ['pali,ɛstər, ,pali'-] n : poliéster m

polygon ['pali,gan] n : polígono m

pomegranate ['pamə,grænət, 'pam,grænət] n : granada f

pomp ['pamp] n : pompa f — **pompous** ['pampəs] adj : pomposo

pond ['pand] n : charca f (natural), estanque m (artificial)

ponder ['pandər] vt : considerar — vi ~ **over** : reflexionar sobre

pony ['poːni] n, pl -**nies** : poni m — **ponytail** ['poːni,teɪl] n : cola f de caballo

poodle ['puːdəl] n : caniche m

pool ['puːl] n 1 PUDDLE : charco m 2 : fondo m común (de recursos) 3 BILLIARDS : billar m 4 or **swimming** ~ : piscina f — ~ vt : hacer un fondo común de

poor ['pʊr, 'por] adj 1 : pobre 2 INFERIOR : malo 3 **the** ~ : los pobres — **poorly** ['pʊrli, 'por-] adv : mal

pop¹ ['pap] v **popped**; **popping** vt 1 : hacer reventar 2 ~ **sth into** : meter algo en — vi 1 BURST : reventarse, estallar 2 ~ **in** : entrar (un momento) 3 ~ **out** APPEAR : aparecer — ~ n 1 : ruido m seco 2 → **soda pop**

pop² or ~ **music** : música f popular

popcorn ['pap,korn] n : palomitas fpl

pope ['poːp] n : papa m

poplar ['paplər] n : álamo m

poppy ['papi] n, pl -**pies** : amapola f

popular ['papjələr] adj : popular — **pop-**

ularity [,papjə'lærəti] n : popularidad f — **popularize** ['papjələ,raiz] vt **-ized;** **-izing** : popularizar

populate ['papjə,leit] vt **-lated; -lating** : poblar — **population** [,papjə'leiʃən] n : población f

porcelain ['porsələn] n : porcelana f

porch ['portʃ] n : porche m

porcupine ['pɔrkjə,pain] n : puerco m espín

pore[1] ['por] vi **pored; poring** ~ **over** : estudiar esmeradamente

pore[2] n : poro m

pork ['pork] n : carne f de cerdo

pornography [por'nagrəfi] n : pornografía f — **pornographic** [,pɔrnə-'græfik] adj : pornográfico

porous ['porəs] adj : poroso

porpoise ['pɔrpəs] n : marsopa f

porridge ['pɔridʒ] n : avena f (cocida), gachas fpl (de avena)

port[1] ['port] n HARBOR : puerto m

port[2] n or ~ **side** : babor m

port[3] n : oporto m (vino)

portable ['pɔrtəbəl] adj : portátil

portent ['pɔr,tent] n : presagio m

porter ['pɔrtər] n : maletero m, mozo m (de estación)

portfolio [port'fo:li,o] n, pl **-lios** : cartera f

porthole ['port,ho:l] n : portilla f

portion ['pɔrʃən] n : porción f

portrait ['pɔrtrət, -,treit] n : retrato m

portray [por'trei] vt **1** : representar, retratar **2** : interpretar (un personaje)

Portuguese [,pɔrtʃə'gi:z, -'gi:s] adj : portugués — ~ n : portugués m (idioma)

pose ['po:z] v **posed; posing** vt : plantear (una pregunta, etc.), representar (una amenaza) — vi **1** : posar **2** ~ **as** : hacerse pasar por — ~ n : pose f

posh ['paʃ] adj : elegante, de lujo

position [pə'ziʃən] n **1** : posición f **2** JOB : puesto m — ~ vt : colocar, situar

positive ['pazətiv] adj **1** : positivo **2** CERTAIN : seguro

possess [pə'zes] vt : poseer — **possession** [pə'zeʃən] n **1** : posesión f **2** ~**s** npl BELONGINGS : bienes mpl — **possessive** [pə'zesiv] adj : posesivo

possible ['pasəbəl] adj : posible — **possibility** [,pasə'biləti] n, pl **-ties** : posibilidad f — **possibly** ['pasəbli] adv : posiblemente

post[1] ['po:st] n POLE : poste m, palo m

post[2] n POSITION : puesto m

post[3] vt **1** MAIL : echar al correo **2 keep** ~**ed** : tener al corriente — **postage** ['po:stidʒ] n

: franqueo m — **postal** ['po:stəl] adj : postal — **postcard** ['po:st,kard] n : tarjeta f postal

poster ['po:stər] n : cartel m

posterity [pa'sterəti] n : posteridad f

posthumous ['pastʃəməs] adj : póstumo

postman ['po:stmən, -,mæn] → **mailman**

— post office n : oficina f de correos

postpone [,po:st'po:n] vt **-poned;** **-poning** : aplazar — **postponement** [,po:st'po:nmənt] n : aplazamiento m

postscript ['po:st,skript] n : posdata f

posture ['pastʃər] n : postura f

postwar [,po:st'wɔr] adj : de (la) posguerra

pot ['pat] n **1** : olla f (de cocina) **2** FLOWERPOT : maceta f **3** ~**s and pans** : cacharros mpl

potassium [pə'tæsiəm] n : potasio m

potato [pə'teito] n, pl **-toes** : patata f, papa f Lat

potent ['po:tənt] adj **1** POWERFUL : poderoso **2** EFFECTIVE : eficaz

potential [pə'tentʃəl] adj : potencial — ~ n : potencial m

pothole ['pat,ho:l] n : bache m

potion ['po:ʃən] n : poción f

pottery ['patəri] n, pl **-teries** : cerámica f

pouch ['pautʃ] n **1** BAG : bolsa f pequeña **2** : bolsa f (de un animal)

poultry ['po:ltri] n : aves fpl de corral

pounce ['paunts] vi **pounced; pouncing** : abalanzarse

pound[1] ['paund] n : libra f (unidad de dinero o de peso)

pound[2] n or dog ~ : perrera f

pound[3] vt **1** CRUSH : machacar **2** HIT : golpear — vi : palpitar (dícese del corazón)

pour ['por] vt : verter — vi **1** FLOW : fluir, salir **2 it's** ~**ing** : está lloviendo a cántaros

pout ['paut] vi : hacer pucheros — ~ n : puchero m

poverty ['pavərti] n : pobreza f

powder ['paudər] vt **1** : empolvar **2** CRUSH : pulverizar — ~ n **1** : polvo m **2** or **face** ~ : polvos mpl — **powdery** ['paudəri] adj : polvoriento

power ['pauər] n **1** CONTROL : poder m **2** ABILITY : capacidad f **3** STRENGTH : fuerza f **4** : potencia f (política) **5** ENERGY : energía f **6** ELECTRICITY : electricidad f — ~ vt : impulsar — **powerful** ['pauərfəl] adj : poderoso — **powerless** ['pauərləs] adj : impotente

practical ['præktikəl] adj : práctico — **practically** ['præktikli] adv : casi, prácticamente

practice or **practise** ['præktəs] v **-ticed**

or -**tised**; -**ticing** *or* -**tising** *vt* **1** : practicar **2** : ejercer (una profesión) — *vi* : practicar — **practice** *n* **1** : práctica *f* **2** CUSTOM : costumbre *f* **3** : ejercicio *m* (de una profesión) **4 be out of ~** : no estar en forma — **practitioner** [præk-'tɪʃənər] *n* **1** : profesional *mf* **2 general ~** : médico *m*, -ca *f* de medicina general

pragmatic [præg'mætɪk] *adj* : pragmático

prairie ['preri] *n* : pradera *f*

praise ['preɪz] *vt* **praised**; **praising** : elogiar, alabar — **~** *n* : elogio *m*, alabanza *f* — **praiseworthy** ['preɪz,wərði] *adj* : loable

prance ['prænts] *vi* **pranced**; **prancing** : hacer cabriolas

prank ['præŋk] *n* : travesura *f*

prawn ['prɔn] *n* : gamba *f*

pray ['preɪ] *vi* **1** : rezar **2 ~ for** : rogar — **prayer** ['prer] *n* : oración *f*

preach ['priːtʃ] *v* : predicar — **preacher** ['priːtʃər] *n* MINISTER : pastor *m*, -tora *f*

precarious [prɪ'kæriəs] *adj* : precario

precaution [prɪ'kɔʃən] *n* : precaución *f*

precede [prɪ'siːd] *vt* -**ceded**; -**ceding** : preceder a — **precedence** ['presə-dənts, prɪ'siːdənts] *n* : precedencia *f* — **precedent** ['presədənt] *n* : precedente *m*

precinct ['priː,sɪŋkt] *n* **1** DISTRICT : distrito *m* **2 ~s** *npl* : recinto *m*

precious ['preʃəs] *adj* : precioso

precipice ['presəpəs] *n* : precipicio *m*

precipitate [prɪ'sɪpə,teɪt] *vt* -**tated**; -**tating** : precipitar — **precipitation** [prɪ,sɪpə'teɪʃən] *n* **1** HASTE : precipitación *f* **2** : precipitaciones *fpl* (en meteorología)

precise [prɪ'saɪs] *adj* : preciso — **precisely** *adv* : precisamente — **precision** [prɪ'sɪʒən] *n* : precisión *f*

preclude [prɪ'kluːd] *vt* -**cluded**; -**cluding** **1** PREVENT : impedir **2** EXCLUDE : excluir

precocious [prɪ'koːʃəs] *adj* : precoz

preconceived [,priːkən'siːv] *adj* : preconcebido

predator ['predətər] *n* : depredador *m*

predecessor ['predə,sesər, 'priː-] *n* : antecesor *m*, -sora *f*; predecesor *m*, -sora *f*

predicament [prɪ'dɪkəmənt] *n* : apuro *m*

predict [prɪ'dɪkt] *vt* : pronosticar, predecir — **predictable** [prɪ'dɪktəbəl] *adj* : previsible — **prediction** [prɪ'dɪkʃən] *n* : pronóstico *m*, predicción *f*

predispose [,priːdɪ'spoːz] *vt* -**posed**; -**posing** : predisponer

predominant [prɪ'dɑmənənt] *adj* : predominante

preeminent [pri'emənənt] *adj* : preeminente

preempt [pri'empt] *vt* : adelantarse a (un ataque, etc.)

preen ['priːn] *vt* **1** : arreglarse (las plumas) **2 ~ oneself** : acicalarse

prefabricated [,priː'fæbrə,keɪtəd] *adj* : prefabricado

preface ['prefəs] *n* : prefacio *m*, prólogo *m*

prefer [prɪ'fər] *vt* -**ferred**; -**ferring** : preferir — **preferable** ['prefərəbəl] *adj* : preferible — **preference** ['prefrənts, 'prefər-] *n* : preferencia *f* — **preferential** [,prefə'rentʃəl] *adj* : preferente

prefix ['priː,fɪks] *n* : prefijo *m*

pregnancy ['pregnəntsi] *n*, *pl* -**cies** : embarazo *m* — **pregnant** ['pregnənt] *adj* : embarazada

prehistoric [,priːhɪs'tɔrɪk] *or* **prehistorical** [-ɪkəl] *adj* : prehistórico

prejudice ['predʒədəs] *n* **1** BIAS : prejuicio *m* **2** HARM : perjuicio *m* — **~** *vt* -**diced**; -**dicing** **1** BIAS : predisponer **2** HARM : perjudicar — **prejudiced** ['predʒədəst] *adj* : parcial

preliminary [prɪ'lɪmə,neri] *adj* : preliminar

prelude ['pre,luːd, 'prel,juːd, 'preɪ,luːd, 'priː-] *n* : preludio *m*

premarital [,priː'mærətəl] *adj* : prematrimonial

premature [,priːmə'tur, -'tjur, -'tʃur] *adj* : prematuro

premeditated [prɪ'medə,teɪtəd] *adj* : premeditado

premier [prɪ'mɪr, -'mjɪr; 'priːmiər] *adj* : principal — **~** *n* PRIME MINISTER : primer ministro *m*, primera ministra *f*

premiere [prɪ'mjer, -'mɪr] *n* : estreno *m*

premise ['premɪs] *n* **1** : premisa *f* (de un argumento) **2 ~s** *npl* : recinto *m*, local *m*

premium ['priːmiəm] *n* **1** : premio *m* **2** *or* **insurance ~** : prima *f* (de seguro)

preoccupied [pri'ɑkjə,paɪd] *adj* : preocupado

prepare [prɪ'pær] *v* -**pared**; -**paring** *vt* : preparar — *vi* : prepararse — **preparation** [,prepə'reɪʃən] *n* **1** : preparación *f* **2 ~s** *npl* ARRANGEMENTS : preparativos *mpl* — **preparatory** [prɪ'pærə,tori] *adj* : preparatorio

prepay [,priː'peɪ] *vt* -**paid**; -**paying** : pagar por adelantado

preposition [,prepə'zɪʃən] *n* : preposición *f*

preposterous [pri'pɑstərəs] *adj* : absurdo, ridículo

prerequisite [pri'rɛkwəzət] *n* : requisito *m* previo

prerogative [pri'rɑgət̬ɪv] *n* : prerrogativa *f*

prescribe [pri'skraɪb] *vt* **-scribed; -scribing** 1 : prescribir 2 : recetar (en medicina) — **prescription** [pri-'skrɪpʃən] *n* : receta *f*

presence ['prɛzənts] *n* : presencia *f*

present[1] ['prɛzənt] *adj* 1 CURRENT : actual 2 be ∼ at : estar presente en — ∼ *n* 1 : presente *m* 2 at ∼ : actualmente

present[2] ['prɛzənt] *n* GIFT : regalo *m* — [prɪ'zɛnt] *vt* 1 INTRODUCE : presentar 2 GIVE : entregar — **presentation** [ˌpriːzɛn'teɪʃən, ˌprɛzən-] *n* 1 : presentación *f* 2 or ∼ **ceremony** : ceremonia *f* de entrega

presently ['prɛzəntli] *adv* 1 SOON : dentro de poco 2 NOW : actualmente

preserve [pri'zərv] *vt* **-served; -serving** 1 : conservar 2 MAINTAIN : mantener — ∼ *n* 1 JAM : confitura *f* 2 or **game** ∼ : coto *m* de caza — **preservation** [ˌprɛzər'veɪʃən] *n* : preservación *f*, conservación *f* — **preservative** [prɪ'zərvə-t̬ɪv] *n* : conservante *m*

president ['prɛzədənt] *n* : presidente *m*, -ta *f* — **presidency** ['prɛzədəntsi] *n, pl* **-cies** : presidencia *f* — **presidential** [ˌprɛzə'dɛntʃəl] *adj* : presidencial

press ['prɛs] *n* : prensa *f* — ∼ *vt* 1 : apretar 2 IRON : planchar — *vi* 1 : apretar 2 URGE : presionar — **pressing** ['prɛsɪŋ] *adj* : urgente — **pressure** ['prɛʃər] *n* : presión *f* — ∼ *vt* **-sured; -suring** : presionar, apremiar

prestige [prɛ'stiːʒ, -'stiːdʒ] *n* : prestigio *m* — **prestigious** [prɛ'stɪdʒəs] *adj* : prestigioso

presume [prɪ'zuːm] *vt* **-sumed; -suming** : presumir — **presumably** [prɪ'zuːməbli] *adv* : es de suponer, supuestamente — **presumption** [prɪ-'zʌmpʃən] *n* : presunción *f* — **presumptuous** [prɪ'zʌmptʃuəs] *adj* : presuntuoso

pretend [prɪ'tɛnd] *vt* 1 CLAIM : pretender 2 FEIGN : fingir — *vi* : fingir — **pretense** *or* **pretence** ['priː.tɛnts, prɪ'tɛnts] *n* 1 CLAIM : pretensión *f* 2 **under false** ∼**s** : con pretextos falsos — **pretentious** [prɪ'tɛntʃəs] *adj* : pretencioso

pretext ['priː.tɛkst] *n* : pretexto *m*

pretty ['prɪt̬i] *adj* **-tier; -est** : lindo, bonito — ∼ *adv* FAIRLY : bastante

pretzel ['prɛtsəl] *n* : galleta *f* salada

prevail [prɪ'veɪl] *vi* 1 TRIUMPH : prevalecer 2 PREDOMINATE : predominar 3 ∼ **upon** : persuadir — **prevalent** ['prɛvələnt] *adj* : extendido

prevent [prɪ'vɛnt] *vt* : impedir — **prevention** [prɪ'vɛntʃən] *n* : prevención *f* — **preventive** [prɪ'vɛntɪv] *adj* : preventivo

preview ['priː.vjuː] *n* : preestreno *m*

previous ['priːviəs] *adj* : previo, anterior — **previously** ['priːviəsli] *adv* : anteriormente

prey ['preɪ] *n, pl* **preys** : presa *f* — **prey on** *vt* 1 : alimentarse de 2 ∼ **on one's mind** : atormentar a algn

price ['praɪs] *n* : precio *m* — ∼ *vt* **priced; pricing** : poner un precio a — **priceless** ['praɪsləs] *adj* : inestimable

prick ['prɪk] *n* : pinchazo *m* — ∼ *vt* 1 : pinchar 2 ∼ **up one's ears** : levantar las orejas — **prickly** ['prɪkəli] *adj* : espinoso

pride ['praɪd] *n* : orgullo *m* — ∼ *vt* **prided; priding** ∼ **oneself on** : enorgullecerse de

priest ['priːst] *n* : sacerdote *m* — **priesthood** ['priːst.hʊd] *n* : sacerdocio *m*

prim ['prɪm] *adj* **primmer; primmest** : remilgado

primary ['praɪ.mɛri, 'praɪməri] *adj* 1 FIRST : primario 2 PRINCIPAL : principal — **primarily** [praɪ'mɛrəli] *adv* : principalmente

prime[1] ['praɪm] *vt* **primed; priming** 1 : cebar (un arma de fuego, etc.) 2 PREPARE : preparar

prime[2] *n* **the** ∼ **of one's life** : la flor de la vida — ∼ *adj* 1 MAIN : principal, primero 2 EXCELLENT : excelente — **prime minister** *n* : primero ministro *m*, primera ministra *f*

primer[1] ['praɪmər] *n* : base *f* (de pintura)

primer[2] ['prɪmər] *n* READER : cartilla *f*

primitive ['prɪmət̬ɪv] *adj* : primitivo

primrose ['prɪm.roːz] *n* : primavera *f*

prince ['prɪnts] *n* : príncipe *m* — **princess** ['prɪntsəs, 'prɪn.sɛs] *n* : princesa *f*

principal ['prɪntsəpəl] *adj* : principal — ∼ *n* : director *m*, -tora *f* (de un colegio)

principle ['prɪntsəpəl] *n* : principio *m*

print ['prɪnt] *n* 1 MARK : huella *f* 2 LETTERING : letra *f* 3 ENGRAVING : grabado *m* 4 : estampado *m* (de tela) 5 : copia *f* (en fotografía) 6 **out of** ∼ : agotado — ∼ *vt* : imprimir (libros, etc.) — *vi* : escribir con letra de molde — **printer** ['prɪntər] *n* 1 : impresor *m*, -sora *f* (persona) 2 : impresora *f* (máquina) — **printing** ['prɪntɪŋ] *n* 1 : impresión *f* 2

: imprenta *f* (profesión) **3** LETTERING
: letras *fpl* de molde

prior ['praɪər] *adj* **1** : previo **2** ~ **to**
: antes de — **priority** [praɪ'ɔrəʈi] *n, pl*
-ties : prioridad *f*

prison ['prɪzən] *n* : prisión *f*, cárcel *f* —
prisoner ['prɪzənər] *n* **1** : preso *m*, -sa *f*
2 ~ **of war** : prisionero *m*, -ra *f* de
guerra

privacy ['praɪvəsi] *n, pl* **-cies** : intimidad
f — **private** ['praɪvət] *adj* **1** : privado **2**
SECRET : secreto — ~ *n* : soldado *m*
raso — **privately** ['praɪvətli] *adv* : en
privado

privilege ['prɪvlɪdʒ, 'prɪvə-] *n* : privilegio
m — **privileged** ['prɪvlɪdʒd, 'prɪvə-] *adj*
: privilegiado

prize ['praɪz] *n* : premio *m* — ~ *adj*
: premiado — ~ *vt* **prized**; **prizing**
: valorar, apreciar — **prizefighter**
['praɪz,faɪtər] *n* : boxeador *m*, -dora *f*
profesional — **prizewinning** ['praɪz-
,wɪnɪŋ] *adj* : premiado

pro ['pro:] *n* **1** ~ **professional 2 the** ~**s**
and cons : los pros y los contras

probability [,prɑbə'bɪləʈi] *n, pl* **-ties**
: probabilidad *f* — **probable** ['prɑbə-
bəl] *adj* : probable — **probably** [-bli]
adv : probablemente

probation [pro'beɪʃən] *n* **1** : período *m*
de prueba (de un empleado, etc.) **2**
: libertad *f* condicional (de un preso)

probe ['pro:b] *n* **1** : sonda *f* (en medicina, etc.) **2** INVESTIGATION : investigación *f* — ~ *vt* **probed**; **probing** **1**
: sondar **2** INVESTIGATE : investigar

problem ['prɑbləm] *n* : problema *m*

procedure [prə'si:dʒər] *n* : procedimiento *m*

proceed [pro'si:d] *vi* **1** ACT : proceder **2**
CONTINUE : continuar **3** ADVANCE
: avanzar — **proceedings** [pro'si:dɪŋz]
npl **1** EVENTS : actos *mpl* **2** : proceso *m*
(en derecho) — **proceeds** ['pro:,si:dz]
npl : ganancias *fpl*

process ['prɑ,ses, 'pro:-] *n, pl* **-cesses**
['prɑ,sesəz, 'pro:-, -,sɔsəz, -sə,si:z] **1** : proceso *m* **2 in the** ~ **of** : en vías de —
~ *vt* : procesar — **procession** [prə-
'seʃən] *n* : desfile *m*

proclaim [pro'kleɪm] *vt* : proclamar —
proclamation [,prɑklə'meɪʃən] *n* : proclamación *f*

procrastinate [prə'kræstə,neɪt] *vi* **-nated**;
-nating : demorar, aplazar

procure [prə'kjʊr] *vt* **-cured**; **-curing**
: obtener

prod ['prɑd] *vt* **prodded**; **prodding**
: pinchar, aguijonear

prodigal ['prɑdɪgəl] *adj* : pródigo

prodigy ['prɑdədʒi] *n, pl* **-gies** : prodigio
m

produce [prə'du:s, -'dju:s] *vt* **-duced**;
-ducing **1** : producir **2** CAUSE : causar
3 SHOW : presentar, mostrar **4** : poner
en escena (una obra de teatro) — ~
['prɑ,du:s, 'pro:-, -,dju:s] *n* : productos
mpl agrícolas — **producer** [prə'du:sər,
-'dju:-] *n* : productor *m*, -tora *f* — **product** ['prɑdʌkt] *n* : producto *m* — **productive** [prə'dʌktɪv] *adj* : productivo

profane [pro'feɪn] *adj* **1** : profano **2** IR-
REVERENT : blasfemo — **profanity**
[pro'fænəʈi] *n, pl* **-ties** : blasfemia *f*

profess [prə'fes] *vt* : profesar — **profession** [prə'feʃən] *n* : profesión *f* —
professional [prə'feʃənəl] *adj* : profesional — ~ *n* : profesional *mf* —
professor [prə'fesər] *n* : profesor *m*,
-sora *f*

proficiency [prə'fɪʃəntsi] *n* : competencia *f* — **proficient** [prə'fɪʃənt] *adj*
: competente

profile ['pro:,faɪl] *n* **1** : perfil *m* **2 keep a**
low ~ : no llamar la atención

profit ['prɑfət] *n* : beneficio *m*, ganancia
f — ~ *vi* : sacar provecho (de), beneficiarse (de) — **profitable** ['prɑfəʈəbəl]
adj : provechoso

profound [prə'faʊnd] *adj* : profundo

profuse [prə'fju:s] *adj* : profuso — **profusion** [prə'fju:ʒən] *n* : profusión *f*

prognosis [prɑg'no:sɪs] *n, pl* **-noses**
[-,si:z] : pronóstico *m*

program ['pro:,græm, -grəm] *n* : programa *m* — ~ *vt* **-grammed** *or*
-gramed; **-gramming** *or* **-graming**
: programar

progress ['prɑgrəs, -,gres] *n* **1** : progreso
m **2** ADVANCE : avance *m* — ~ [prə-
'gres] *vi* : progresar, avanzar — **progressive** [prə'gresɪv] *adj* **1** : progresista (dícese de la política, etc.) **2**
INCREASING : progresiva

prohibit [pro'hɪbət] *vt* : prohibir — **prohibition** [,pro:ə'bɪʃən, ,pro:hə-] *n* : prohibición *f*

project ['prɑdʒɛkt, -dʒɪkt] *n* : proyecto *m*
— ~ [prə'dʒɛkt] *vt* : proyectar — *vi*
PROTRUDE : sobresalir — **projectile**
[prə'dʒɛktəl, -,taɪl] *n* : proyectil *m* —
projection [prə'dʒɛkʃən] *n* **1** : proyección *f* **2** PROTRUSION : saliente *m* —
projector [prə'dʒɛktər] *n* : proyector *m*

proliferate [prə'lɪfə,reɪt] *vi* **-ated**; **-ating**
: proliferar — **proliferation** [prə,lɪfə-
'reɪʃən] *n* : proliferación *f* — **prolific**
[prə'lɪfɪk] *adj* : prolífico

prologue ['pro:,lɔg] *n* : prólogo *m*

prolong [pro'lɔŋ] *vt* : prolongar

prom ['prɑm] *n* : baile *m* formal (en un colegio)

prominent ['prɑmənənt] *adj* : prominente — **prominence** ['prɑmənənts] *n* **1** : prominencia *f* **2** IMPORTANCE : eminencia *f*

promiscuous [prə'mɪskjʊəs] *adj* : promiscuo

promise ['prɑməs] *n* : promesa *f* — ~ *v* **-ised; -ising** : prometer — **promising** ['prɑməsɪŋ] *adj* : prometedor

promote [prə'moːt] *vt* **-moted; -moting** **1** : ascender (a un alumno o un empleado) **2** FURTHER : promover, fomentar **3** ADVERTISE : promocionar — **promoter** [prə'moːtər] *n* : promotor *m*, -tora *f*; empresario *m*, -ria *f* (en deportes) — **promotion** [prə'moːʃən] *n* **1** : ascenso *m* (de un alumno o un empleado) **2** ADVERTISING : publicidad *f*, propaganda *f*

prompt ['prɑmpt] *vt* **1** INCITE : provocar (una cosa), inducir (a una persona) **2** : apuntar (a un actor, etc.) — ~ *adj* **1** : rápido **2** PUNCTUAL : puntual

prone ['proːn] *adj* **1** : boca abajo, decúbito prono **2** be ~ to : ser propenso a

prong ['prɔŋ] *n* : punta *f*, diente *m*

pronoun ['proːnaʊn] *n* : pronombre *m*

pronounce [prə'naʊnts] *vt* **-nounced; -nouncing** : pronunciar — **pronouncement** [prə'naʊntsmənt] *n* : declaración *f* — **pronunciation** [prə-ˌnʌntsi'eɪʃən] *n* : pronunciación *f*

proof ['pruːf] *n* : prueba *f* — ~ *adj* — **against** : a prueba de — **proofread** ['pruːfˌriːd] *vt* **-read; -reading** : corregir

prop ['prɑp] *n* **1** SUPPORT : puntal *m*, apoyo *m* **2** : accesorio *m* (en teatro) — ~ *vt* **propped; propping 1** ~ **against** : apoyar contra **2** ~ **up** SUPPORT : apoyar

propaganda [ˌprɑpə'gændə, ˌproː-] *n* : propaganda *f*

propagate ['prɑpəˌgeɪt] *v* **-gated; -gating** *vt* : propagar — *vi* : propagarse

propel [prə'pɛl] *vt* **-pelled; -pelling** : propulsar — **propeller** [prə'pɛlər] *n* : hélice *f*

propensity [prə'pɛntsəti] *n, pl* **-ties** : propensión *f*

proper ['prɑpər] *adj* **1** SUITABLE : apropiado **2** REAL : verdadero **3** CORRECT : correcto **4** GENTEEL : cortés **5** ~ **name** : nombre *m* propio — **properly** ['prɑpərli] *adv* : correctamente

property ['prɑpərti] *n, pl* **-ties 1** : propiedad *f* **2** BUILDING : inmueble *m* **3** LAND, LOT : parcela *f*

prophet ['prɑfət] *n* : profeta *m*, profetisa *f* — **prophecy** ['prɑfəsi] *n, pl* **-cies** : profecía *f* — **prophesy** ['prɑfəˌsaɪ] *v* **-sied; -sying** *vt* : profetizar — *vi* : hacer profecías — **prophetic** [prə'fɛtɪk] *adj* : profético

proportion [prə'porʃən] *n* **1** : proporción *f* **2** SHARE : parte *f* — **proportional** [prə'porʃənəl] *adj* : proporcional — **proportionate** [prə'porʃənət] *adj* : proporcional

proposal [prə'poːzəl] *n* : propuesta *f*

propose [prə'poːz] *v* **-posed; -posing** *vt* **1** SUGGEST : proponer **2** ~ **to do sth** : pensar hacer algo — *vi* : proponer matrimonio — **proposition** [ˌprɑpə-'zɪʃən] *n* : proposición *f*

proprietor [prə'praɪətər] *n* : propietario *m*, -ria *f*

propriety [prə'praɪəti] *n, pl* **-eties** : decencia *f*, decoro *m*

propulsion [prə'pʌlʃən] *n* : propulsión *f*

prose ['proːz] *n* : prosa *f*

prosecute ['prɑsɪˌkjuːt] *vt* **-cuted; -cuting** : procesar — **prosecution** [ˌprɑsɪ'kjuːʃən] *n* **1** : procesamiento *m* **2** **the ~** : la acusación *f* — **prosecutor** ['prɑsɪˌkjuːtər] *n* : acusador *m*, -dora *f*

prospect ['prɑspɛkt] *n* **1** : perspectiva *f* **2** POSSIBILITY : posibilidad *f* — **prospective** [prə'spɛktɪv, 'prɑˌspɛk-] *adj* : futuro, posible

prosper ['prɑspər] *vi* : prosperar — **prosperity** [prɑ'spɛrəti] *n* : prosperidad *f* — **prosperous** ['prɑspərəs] *adj* : próspero

prostitute ['prɑstəˌtuːt, -ˌtjuːt] *n* : prostituta *f* — **prostitution** [ˌprɑstə'tuːʃən, -ˌtjuː-] *n* : prostitución *f*

prostrate ['prɑˌstreɪt] *adj* : postrado

protagonist [proː'tægənɪst] *n* : protagonista *mf*

protect [prə'tɛkt] *vt* : proteger — **protection** [prə'tɛkʃən] *n* : protección *f* — **protective** [prə'tɛktɪv] *adj* : protector — **protector** [prə'tɛktər] *n* : protector *m*, -tora *f*

protégé ['proːtəˌʒeɪ] *n* : protegido *m*, -da *f*

protein ['proːˌtiːn] *n* : proteína *f*

protest ['proːˌtɛst] *n* : protesta *f* — ~ [proː'tɛst] *vt* : protestar — *vi* ~ **against** : protestar contra — **Protestant** ['prɑtəstənt] *n* : protestante *mf* — **protester** *or* **protestor** ['proːˌtɛstər, proː'-] *n* : manifestante *mf*

protocol ['proːtəˌkɔl] *n* : protocolo *m*

prototype ['proːtəˌtaɪp] *n* : prototipo *m*

protract [proː'trækt] *vt* : prolongar

protrude [proː'truːd] *vi* **-truded; -truding** : sobresalir

proud ['praud] *adj* : orgulloso
prove ['pruːv] *v* **proved; proved** *or* **proven** ['pruːvən]; **proving** *vt* : probar — *vi* : resultar
proverb ['prɑˌvərb] *n* : proverbio *m*, refrán *m* — **proverbial** [prə'vərbiəl] *adj* : proverbial
provide [prə'vaid] *v* **-vided; -viding** *vt* : proveer — *vi* ~ **for** SUPPORT : mantener — **provided** [prə'vaidəd] *or* **that** *conj* : con tal (de) que, siempre que — **providence** ['prɑvədənts] *n* : providencia *f*
province ['prɑvɪnts] *n* **1** : provincia *f* **2** SPHERE : campo *m*, competencia *f* — **provincial** [prə'vɪntʃəl] *adj* : provinciano
provision [prə'vɪʒən] *n* **1** : provisión *f*, suministro *m* **2** STIPULATION : condición *f* **3** ~**s** *npl* : víveres *mpl* — **provisional** [prə'vɪʒənəl] *adj* : provisional — **proviso** [prə'vaizoː] *n*, *pl* **-sos** *or* **-soes** : condición *f*
provoke [prə'voːk] *vt* **-voked; -voking** : provocar — **provocation** [prɑvə'keiʃən] *n* : provocación *f* — **provocative** [prə'vɑkətɪv] *adj* : provocador, provocativo
prow ['prau] *n* : proa *f*
prowess ['prauəs] *n* **1** BRAVERY : valor *m* **2** SKILL : habilidad *f*
prowl ['praul] *vi* : merodear, rondar — *vt* : merodear por — **prowler** ['praulər] *n* : merodeador *m*, -dora *f*
proximity [prɑk'sɪməti] *n* : proximidad *f* — **proxy** ['prɑksi] *n*, *pl* **proxies** by ~ : por poder
prude ['pruːd] *n* : mojigato *m*, -ta *f*
prudence ['pruːdənts] *n* : prudencia *f* — **prudent** ['pruːdənt] *adj* : prudente
prune¹ ['pruːn] *n* : ciruela *f* pasa
prune² *vt* **pruned; pruning** : podar (arbustos, etc.)
pry ['prai] *v* **pried; prying** *vi* ~ **into** : entrometerse en — *vt* *or* ~ **open** : abrir (a la fuerza)
psalm ['sɑm, 'sɑlm] *n* : salmo *m*
pseudonym ['suːdəˌnɪm] *n* : seudónimo *m*
psychiatry [sə'kaiətri, sai-] *n* : psiquiatría *f* — **psychiatric** [ˌsaiki'ætrɪk] *adj* : psiquiátrico — **psychiatrist** [sə'kaiətrɪst, sai-] *n* : psiquiatra *mf*
psychic ['saikɪk] *adj* : psíquico
psychoanalysis [ˌsaikoə'næləsɪs] *n*, *pl* **-yses** : psicoanálisis *m* — **psychoanalyst** [ˌsaiko'ænəlɪst] *n* : psicoanalista *mf* — **psychoanalyze** [ˌsaiko'ænəlˌaiz] *vt* **-lyzed; -lyzing** : psicoanalizar
psychology [sai'kɑlədʒi] *n*, *pl* **-gies**

: psicología *f* — **psychological** [ˌsaikə'lɑdʒɪkəl] *adj* : psicológico — **psychologist** [sai'kɑlədʒɪst] *n* : psicólogo *m*, -ga *f*
psychopath ['saikəˌpæθ] *n* : psicópata *mf*
psychotherapy [ˌsaiko'θerəpi] *n*, *pl* **-pies** : psicoterapia *f*
psychotic [sai'kɑtɪk] *adj* : psicótico
puberty ['pjuːbərti] *n* : pubertad *f*
pubic ['pjuːbɪk] *adj* : púbico
public ['pʌblɪk] *adj* : público — ~ *n* : público *m* — **publication** [ˌpʌblə'keiʃən] *n* : publicación *f* — **publicity** [pə'blisəti] *n* : publicidad *f* — **publicize** ['pʌbləˌsaiz] *vt* **-cized; -cizing** : publicitar, divulgar
publish ['pʌblɪʃ] *vt* : publicar — **publisher** ['pʌblɪʃər] *n* **1** : editor *m*, -tora *f* (persona) **2** : casa *f* editorial (negocio)
pucker ['pʌkər] *vt* : fruncir, arrugar — *vi* : arrugarse
pudding ['pudɪŋ] *n* : budín *m*, pudín *m*
puddle ['pʌdəl] *n* : charco *m*
pudgy ['pʌdʒi] *adj* **pudgier; -est** : rechoncho *fam*
Puerto Rican [ˌpwertə'riːkən, ˌportə-] *adj* : puertorriqueño
puff ['pʌf] *vi* **1** BLOW : soplar **2** PANT : resoplar **3** ~ **up** SWELL : hincharse — *vt* ~ **out** : hinchar — ~ *n* **1** : bocanada *f* (de humo) **2** : chupada *f* (a un cigarrillo) **3** *or* **cream** ~ : pastelito *m* de crema **4** *or* **powder** ~ : borla *f* — **puffy** ['pʌfi] *adj* **puffier; -est** : hinchado
pull ['pul, 'pʌl] *vt* **1** : tirar de **2** EXTRACT : sacar **3** TEAR : desgarrarse (un músculo, etc.) **4** ~ **off** REMOVE : quitar **5** ~ **oneself together** : calmarse **6** ~ **up** : levantar, subir — *vi* **1** : tirar **2** ~ **through** RECOVER : reponerse **3** ~ **together** COOPERATE : reunir **4** ~ **up** STOP : parar — ~ *n* **1** : tirón *m* **2** INFLUENCE : influencia *f* — **pulley** ['puli] *n*, *pl* **-leys** : polea *f* — **pullover** ['pulˌoːvər] *n* : suéter *m*
pulp ['pʌlp] *n* **1** : pulpa *f* (de frutas, etc.) **2** *or* **wood** ~ : pasta *f* de papel
pulpit ['pulpɪt] *n* : púlpito *m*
pulsate ['pʌlseit] *vi* **-sated; -sating** : palpitar — **pulse** ['pʌls] *n* : pulso *m*
pulverize ['pʌlvəˌraiz] *vt* **-ized; -izing** : pulverizar
pummel ['pʌməl] *vt* **-meled; -meling** : aporrear
pump¹ ['pʌmp] *n* : bomba *f* — ~ *vt* **1** : bombear **2** ~ **up** : inflar
pump² *n* SHOE : zapato *m* de tacón
pumpernickel ['pʌmpərˌnɪkəl] *n* : pan *m* negro de centeno

pumpkin ['pʌmpkɪn, 'pʌŋkən] *n* : calabaza *f*, zapallo *m Lat*

pun ['pʌn] *n* : juego *m* de palabras — ~ *vi* **punned; punning** : hacer juegos de palabras

punch[1] ['pʌntʃ] *vt* **1** : dar un puñetazo a **2** PERFORATE : perforar (papeles, etc.), picar (un boleto) — ~ *n* **1** : golpe *m*, puñetazo *m* **2** *or* **paper** ~ : perforadora *f*

punch[2] *n* : ponche *m* (bebida)

punctual ['pʌŋktʃʊəl] *adj* : puntual — **punctuality** [,pʌŋktʃʊˈæləti] *n* : puntualidad *f*

punctuate ['pʌŋktʃʊ,eɪt] *vt* **-ated; -ating** : puntuar — **punctuation** [,pʌŋktʃʊˈeɪʃən] *n* : puntuación *f*

puncture ['pʌŋktʃər] *n* : pinchazo *m*, ponchadura *f Lat* — ~ *vt* **-tured; -turing** : pinchar, ponchar *Lat*

pungent ['pʌndʒənt] *adj* : acre

punish ['pʌnɪʃ] *vt* : castigar — **punishment** ['pʌnɪʃmənt] *n* : castigo *m* — **punitive** ['pjuːnətɪv] *adj* : punitivo

puny ['pjuːni] *adj* **-nier; -est** : enclenque

pup ['pʌp] *n* : cachorro *m*, -rra *f* (de un perro); cría *f* (de otros animales)

pupil[1] ['pjuːpəl] *n* : alumno *m*, -na *f* (de colegio)

pupil[2] *n* : pupila *f* (del ojo)

puppet ['pʌpət] *n* : títere *m*

puppy ['pʌpi] *n, pl* **-pies** : cachorro *m*, -rra *f*

purchase ['pərtʃəs] *vt* **-chased; -chasing** : comprar — ~ *n* : compra *f*

pure ['pjʊr] *adj* **purer; purest** : puro

puree [pjʊˈreɪ, -riː] *n* : puré *m*

purely ['pjʊrli] *adv* : puramente

purgatory ['pərgə,tori] *n, pl* **-ries** : purgatorio *m* — **purge** ['pərdʒ] *vt* **purged; purging** : purgar — ~ *n* : purga *f*

purify ['pjʊrə,faɪ] *vt* **-fied; -fying** : purificar — **purification** [,pjʊrəfəˈkeɪʃən] *n* : purificación *f*

puritanical [,pjʊrəˈtænɪkəl] *adj* : puritano

purity ['pjʊrəti] *n* : pureza *f*

purple ['pərpəl] *n* : morado *m*

purport [pərˈport] *vt* ~ **to be** : pretender ser

purpose ['pərpəs] *n* **1** : propósito *m* **2** RESOLUTION : determinación *f* **3 on** ~ : a propósito — **purposeful** ['pərpəsfəl] *adj* : resuelto — **purposely** ['pərpəsli] *adv* : a propósito

purr ['pər] *n* : ronroneo *m* — ~ *vi* : ronronear

purse ['pərs] *n* **1** *or* **change** ~ : monedero *m* **2** HANDBAG : cartera *f*, bolso *m Spain*, bolsa *f Lat* — ~ *vt* **pursed; pursing** : fruncir

pursue [pərˈsuː] *vt* **-sued; -suing 1** CHASE : perseguir **2** SEEK : buscar — **pursuer** [pərˈsuːər] *n* : perseguidor *m*, -dora *f* — **pursuit** [pərˈsuːt] *n* **1** CHASE : persecución *f* **2** SEARCH : búsqueda *f* **3** OCCUPATION : actividad *f*

pus ['pʌs] *n* : pus *m*

push ['pʊʃ] *vt* **1** SHOVE : empujar **2** PRESS : apretar **3** URGE : presionar **4** ~ **around** BULLY : mangonear — *vi* **1** : empujar **2** ~ **for** : presionar para — ~ *n* **1** SHOVE : empujón *m* **2** DRIVE : dinamismo *m* **3** EFFORT : esfuerzo *m* — **pushy** ['pʊʃi] *adj* **pushier; -est** : mandón, prepotente

pussy ['pʊsi] *n, pl* **pussies** : gatito *m*, -ta *f*; minino *m*, -na *f*

put ['pʊt] *v* **put; putting** *vt* **1** : poner **2** INSERT : meter **3** EXPRESS : decir **4** ~ **one's mind to sth** : proponerse hacer algo — *vi* ~ **up with** : aguantar — **put away** *vt* **1** STORE : guardar **2** *or* ~ **aside** : dejar a un lado — **put down** *vt* **1** SUPPRESS : aplastar, sofocar **2** ATTRIBUTE : atribuir — **put off** *vt* DEFER : aplazar, posponer — **put on** *vt* **1** ASSUME : adoptar **2** PRESENT : presentar (una obra de teatro, etc.) **3** WEAR : ponerse — **put out** *vt* INCONVENIENCE : incomodar — **put up** *vt* **1** BUILD : construir **2** LODGE : alojar **3** PROVIDE : poner (dinero)

putrefy ['pjuːtrə,faɪ] *vi* **-fied; -fying** : pudrirse

putty ['pʌti] *n, pl* **-ties** : masilla *f*

puzzle ['pʌzəl] *v* **-zled; -zling** *vt* : confundir, dejar perplejo — *vi* ~ **over** : tratar de descifrar — ~ *n* **1** : rompecabezas *m* **2** MYSTERY : enigma *m*

pylon ['paɪlɑn, -lən] *n* : pilón *m*

pyramid ['pɪrə,mɪd] *n* : pirámide *f*

python ['paɪ,θɑn, -θən] *n* : pitón *f*

Q

q ['kjuː] *n, pl* **q's** *or* **qs** ['kjuːz] : q *f*, decimoséptima letra del alfabeto inglés

quack¹ ['kwæk] *vi* : graznar (dícese del pato) — **~** *n* : graznido *m*

quack² *n* CHARLATAN : charlatán *m*, -tana *f*

quadruple [kwɑ'druːpəl, -'drʌ-; 'kwɑdrə-] *v* **-pled; -pling** *vt* : cuadruplicar — *vi* : cuadruplicarse

quagmire ['kwæg,maɪr, 'kwɑg-] *n* : atolladero *m*

quail ['kweɪl] *n, pl* **quail** *or* **quails** : codorniz *f*

quaint ['kweɪnt] *adj* **1** ODD : curioso 2 PICTURESQUE : pintoresco

quake ['kweɪk] *vi* **quaked; quaking** : temblar — **~** *n* → **earthquake**

qualify ['kwɑlə,faɪ] *v* **-fied; -fying** *vt* **1** LIMIT : matizar 2 : calificar (en gramática) 3 EQUIP : habilitar — *vi* **1** : titularse (de abogado, etc.) 2 : clasificarse (en deportes) — **qualification** [,kwɑləfə'keɪʃən] *n* **1** REQUIREMENT : requisito *m* **2** **~s** *npl* ABILITY : capacidad *f* **3 without ~** : sin reservas — **qualified** ['kwɑlə,faɪd] *adj* : capacitado

quality ['kwɑləti] *n, pl* **-ties 1** : calidad *f* **2** PROPERTY : cualidad *f*

qualm ['kwɑm, 'kwɑlm, 'kwɔm] *n* **1** DOUBT : duda *f* **2 have no ~s about** : no tener ningún escrúpulo en

quandary ['kwɑndri] *n, pl* **-ries** : dilema *m*

quantity ['kwɑntəti] *n, pl* **-ties** : cantidad *f*

quarantine ['kwɔrən,tiːn] *n* : cuarentena *f* — **~** *vt* **-tined; -tining** : poner en cuarentena

quarrel ['kwɔrəl] *n* : pelea *f*, riña *f* — *vi* **-reled** *or* **-relled; -reling** *or* **-relling** : pelearse, reñir — **quarrelsome** ['kwɔrəlsəm] *adj* : pendenciero

quarry¹ ['kwɔri] *n, pl* **quarries** PREY : presa *f*

quarry² *n, pl* **quarries** EXCAVATION : cantera *f*

quart ['kwɔrt] *n* : cuarto *m* de galón

quarter ['kwɔrtər] *n* **1** : cuarto *m* (en matemáticas) 2 : moneda *f* de 25 centavos 3 DISTRICT : barrio *m* **4 ~ after three** : las tres y cuarto **5 ~s** *npl* LODGING : alojamiento *m* — *vt* **1**

: dividir en cuatro partes 2 : acuartelar (tropas) — **quarterly** ['kwɔrtərli] *adv* : cada tres meses — **~** *adj* : trimestral — **~** *n, pl* **-lies** : publicación *f* trimestral

quartet [kwɔr'tɛt] *n* : cuarteto *m*

quartz ['kwɔrts] *n* : cuarzo *m*

quash ['kwɑʃ, 'kwɔʃ] *vt* **1** ANNUL : anular 2 SUPPRESS : aplastar, sofocar

quaver ['kweɪvər] *vi* : temblar

quay ['kiː, 'keɪ, 'kweɪ] *n* : muelle *m*

queasy ['kwiːzi] *adj* **-sier; -est** : mareado

queen ['kwiːn] *n* : reina *f*

queer ['kwɪr] *adj* ODD : extraño

quell ['kwɛl] *vt* SUPPRESS : sofocar, aplastar

quench ['kwɛntʃ] *vt* **1** EXTINGUISH : apagar 2 **~ one's thirst** : quitar la sed

query ['kwɪri, 'kwɛr-] *n, pl* **-ries** : pregunta *f* — **~** *vt* **-ried; -rying 1** ASK : preguntar 2 QUESTION : cuestionar

quest ['kwɛst] *n* : búsqueda *f*

question ['kwɛstʃən] *n* **1** QUERY : pregunta *f* **2** ISSUE : cuestión *f* **3 be out of the ~** : ser indiscutible **4 call into ~** : poner en duda **5 without ~** : sin duda — **~** *vt* **1** ASK : preguntar 2 DOUBT : cuestionar 3 INTERROGATE : interrogar — *vi* : preguntar — **questionable** ['kwɛstʃənəbəl] *adj* : discutible — **question mark** *n* : signo *m* de interrogación — **questionnaire** [,kwɛstʃə'nær] *n* : cuestionario *m*

queue ['kjuː] *n* : cola *f* — **~** *vi* **queued; queuing** *or* **queueing** : hacer cola

quibble ['kwɪbəl] *vi* **-bled; -bling** : discutir, quejarse por nimiedades

quick ['kwɪk] *adj* **1** : rápido 2 CLEVER : agudo — **~** *n* **to the ~** : en lo vivo — **~** *adv* : rápidamente — **quicken** ['kwɪkən] *vt* : acelerar — **quickly** ['kwɪkli] *adv* : rápidamente — **quicksand** ['kwɪk,sænd] *n* : arena *f* movediza — **quick-tempered** ['kwɪk'tɛmpərd] *adj* : irascible — **quick-witted** ['kwɪk-'wɪtəd] *adj* : agudo

quiet ['kwaɪət] *n* **1** : silencio *m* **2** CALM : tranquilidad *f* — **~** *adj* **1** : silencioso 2 CALM : tranquilo 3 RESERVED : callado 4 : discreto (dícese de colores, etc.) — **~** *vt* **1** SILENCE : hacer callar 2 CALM : calmar — *vi* *or* **~ down** : cal-

marse — **quietly** *adv* **1** : silenciosamente **2** CALMLY : tranquilamente
quilt ['kwɪlt] *n* : edredón *m*
quintet [kwɪn'tet] *n* : quinteto *m*
quip ['kwɪp] *n* : ocurrencia *f*, salida *f* — ~ *vi* **quipped; quipping** : decir bromeando
quirk ['kwərk] *n* : peculiaridad *f*
quit ['kwɪt] *v* **quit; quitting** *vt* **1** LEAVE : dejar, abandonar **2** ~ **doing** : dejar de hacer — *vi* **1** STOP : parar **2** RESIGN : dimitir, renunciar
quite ['kwaɪt] *adv* **1** COMPLETELY : completamente **2** RATHER : bastante

quits ['kwɪts] *adj* **call it** ~ : quedar en paz
quiver ['kwɪvər] *vi* : temblar
quiz ['kwɪz] *n, pl* **quizzes** TEST : prueba *f* — ~ *vt* **quizzed; quizzing** : interrogar
quota ['kwoʊtə] *n* : cuota *f*, cupo *m*
quotation [kwo'teɪʃən] *n* **1** : cita *f* **2** ESTIMATE : presupuesto *m* — **quotation marks** *npl* : comillas *fpl* — **quote** ['kwoːt] *vt* **quoted; quoting 1** CITE : citar **2** : cotizar (en finanzas) — ~ *n* **1** → quotation **2** ~s *npl* → quotation marks
quotient ['kwoːʃənt] *n* : cociente *m*

R

r ['ɑr] *n, pl* **r's** *or* **rs** ['ɑrz] : r *f*, decimoctava letra del alfabeto inglés
rabbi ['ræbaɪ] *n* : rabino *m*, -na *f*
rabbit ['ræbət] *n, pl* **-bit** *or* **-bits** : conejo *m*, -ja *f*
rabble ['ræbəl] *n* : chusma *f*, populacho *m*
rabies ['reɪbiːz] *ns & pl* : rabia *f* — **rabid** ['ræbɪd] *adj* **1** : rabioso **2** FANATIC : fanático
raccoon [ræ'kuːn] *n, pl* **-coon** *or* **-coons** : mapache *m*
race¹ ['reɪs] *n* **1** : raza *f* **2 human** ~ : género *m* humano
race² *n* : carrera *f* (competitiva) — ~ *vi* **raced; racing 1** : correr (en una carrera) **2** RUSH : ir corriendo — **racehorse** ['reɪs,hɔrs] *n* : caballo *m* de carreras — **racetrack** ['reɪs,træk] *n* : pista *f* (de carreras)
racial ['reɪʃəl] *adj* : racial — **racism** ['reɪ,sɪzəm] *n* : racismo *m* — **racist** ['reɪsɪst] *n* : racista *mf*
rack ['ræk] *n* **1** SHELF : estante *m* **2** luggage ~ : portaequipajes *m* — ~ *vt* **1** ~ed with : atormentado por **2** ~ one's brains : devanarse los sesos
racket¹ ['rækət] *n* : raqueta *f* (en deportes)
racket² *n* **1** DIN : alboroto *m*, bulla *f* **2** SWINDLE : estafa *f*
racy ['reɪsi] *adj* **racier; -est** : subido de tono, picante
radar ['reɪ,dɑr] *n* : radar *m*
radiant ['reɪdiənt] *adj* : radiante — **radiance** ['reɪdiənts] *n* : resplandor *m* — **radiate** ['reɪdi,eɪt] *v* **-ated; -ating** *vt* : irradiar — *vi* **1** : irradiar **2** *or* ~ out : extenderse (desde un centro) — **radi-**

-ation [reɪdi'eɪʃən] *n* : radiación *f* — **radiator** ['reɪdi,eɪtər] *n* : radiador *m*
radical ['rædɪkəl] *adj* : radical — ~ *n* : radical *mf*
radii → radius
radio ['reɪdi,oː] *n, pl* **-dios** : radio *mf* (aparato), radio *f* (medio) — ~ *vt* : transmitir por radio — **radioactive** ['reɪdio'æktɪv] *adj* : radioactivo, radiactivo
radish ['rædɪʃ] *n* : rábano *m*
radius ['reɪdiəs] *n, pl* **radii** [-di,aɪ] : radio *m*
raffle ['ræfəl] *vt* **-fled; -fling** : rifar — ~ *n* : rifa *f*
raft ['ræft] *n* : balsa *f*
rafter ['ræftər] *n* : cabrio *m*
rag ['ræg] *n* **1** : trapo *m* **2** ~s *npl* TATTERS : harapos *mpl*, andrajos *mpl*
rage ['reɪdʒ] *n* **1** : cólera *f*, rabia *f* **2 be all the** ~ : hacer furor — ~ *vi* **raged; raging 1** : estar furioso **2** : bramar (dícese del viento, etc.)
ragged ['rægəd] *adj* **1** UNEVEN : irregular **2** TATTERED : andrajoso, harapiento
raid ['reɪd] *n* **1** : invasión *f* (militar) **2** : asalto *m* (por delincuentes), redada *f* (por la policía) — ~ *vt* **1** INVADE : invadir **2** ROB : asaltar **3** : asaltar, hacer una redada en (dícese de la policía) — **raider** ['reɪdər] *n* ATTACKER : asaltante *mf*
rail¹ ['reɪl] *vi* ~ **at s.o.** : recriminar a algn
rail² *n* **1** BAR : barra *f* **2** HANDRAIL : pasamanos *m* **3** TRACK : riel *m* **4 by** ~ : por ferrocarril — **railing** ['reɪlɪŋ] *n* **1** : baranda *f* (de un balcón), pasamanos *m* (de una escalera) **2**

RAILS : reja f — **railroad** ['reɪlˌroːd] n : ferrocarril m — **railway** ['reɪlˌweɪ] → **railroad**

rain ['reɪn] n : lluvia f — ~ vi : llover — **rainbow** ['reɪnˌboː] n : arco m iris — **raincoat** ['reɪnˌkoːt] n : impermeable m — **rainfall** ['reɪnˌfɔl] n : precipitación f — **rainy** ['reɪni] adj **rainier; -est** : lluvioso

raise ['reɪz] vt **raised; raising 1** : levantar **2** COLLECT : recaudar **3** REAR : criar **4** GROW : cultivar **5** INCREASE : aumentar **6** : sacar (objeciones, etc.) — ~ n : aumento m

raisin ['reɪzən] n : pasa f

rake ['reɪk] n : rastrillo m — ~ vt **raked; raking** : rastrillar

rally ['ræli] v **-lied; -lying** vi **1** : unirse, reunirse **2** RECOVER : recuperarse — vt : conseguir (apoyo), unir a (la gente) — ~ n, pl **-lies** : reunión f, mitin m

ram n ['ræm] : carnero m (animal) — ~ vt **rammed; ramming 1** CRAM : meter con fuerza **2** or ~ **into** : chocar contra

RAM ['ræm] n : RAM f

ramble ['ræmbəl] vi **-bled; -bling 1** WANDER : pasear **2** or ~ **on** : divagar — ~ n : paseo m, excursión f

ramp ['ræmp] n : rampa f

rampage ['ræmˌpeɪdʒ, ˌræmˈpeɪdʒ] vi **-paged; -paging** : andar arrasando todo — ~ ['ræmˌpeɪdʒ] n : frenesí m (de violencia)

rampant ['ræmpənt] adj : desenfrenado

rampart ['ræmˌpɑrt] n : muralla f

ramshackle ['ræmˌʃækəl] adj : destartalado

ran → **run**

ranch ['ræntʃ] n : hacienda f — **rancher** ['ræntʃər] n : hacendado m, -da f

rancid ['ræntsɪd] adj : rancio

rancor ['ræŋkər] n : rencor m

random ['rændəm] adj **1** : aleatorio **2 at** ~ : al azar

rang → **ring**

range ['reɪndʒ] n **1** GRASSLAND : pradera f **2** STOVE : cocina f **3** VARIETY : gama f **4** SCOPE : amplitud f **5** or **mountain** ~ : cordillera f — ~ vi **ranged; ranging 1** EXTEND : extenderse **2** ~ **from...to...** : variar entre...y... — **ranger** ['reɪndʒər] n or **forest** ~ : guardabosque mf

rank¹ ['ræŋk] adj **1** SMELLY : fétido **2** OUTRIGHT : completo

rank² n **1** ROW : fila f **2** : rango m (militar) **3** ~**s** npl : soldados mpl rasos **4 the** ~ **and file** : las bases — ~ vt RATE : clasificar — vi : clasificarse

rankle ['ræŋkəl] vi **-kled; -kling** : causar rencor, doler

ransack ['rænˌsæk] vt **1** SEARCH : registrar **2** LOOT : saquear

ransom ['ræntsəm] n : rescate m — ~ vt : rescatar

rant ['rænt] vi or ~ **and rave** : despotricar

rap¹ ['ræp] n KNOCK : golpecito m — ~ v **rapped; rapping** : golpear

rap² n or ~ **music** : rap m

rapacious [rəˈpeɪʃəs] adj : rapaz

rape ['reɪp] vt **raped; raping** : violar — ~ n : violación f

rapid ['ræpɪd] adj : rápido — **rapids** ['ræpɪdz] npl : rápidos mpl

rapist ['reɪpɪst] n : violador m, -dora f

rapport [ræˈpor] n **have a good** ~ : entenderse bien

rapt ['ræpt] adj : absorto, embelesado — **rapture** ['ræptʃər] n : éxtasis m

rare ['rær] adj **rarer; rarest 1** FINE : excepcional **2** UNCOMMON : raro **3** : poco cocido (dícese de la carne) — **rarely** ['rærli] adv : raramente — **rarity** ['ræro-ți] n, pl **-ties** : rareza f

rascal ['ræskəl] n : pillo m, -lla f; pícaro m, -ra f

rash¹ ['ræʃ] adj : imprudente, precipitado

rash² n : sarpullido m, erupción f

rasp ['ræsp] vt SCRAPE : raspar — ~ n : escofina f

raspberry ['ræzˌbɛri] n, pl **-ries** : frambuesa f

rat ['ræt] n : rata f

rate ['reɪt] n **1** PACE : velocidad f, ritmo m **2** : tipo m, tasa m (de interés, etc.) **3** PRICE : tarifa f **4 at any** ~ : de todos modos **5 birth** ~ : índice m de natalidad — ~ vt **rated; rating 1** REGARD : considerar **2** DESERVE : merecer

rather ['ræðər, 'rʌ-, 'rɑ-] adv **1** FAIRLY : bastante **2 I'd** ~... : prefiero... **3** or ~ : o mejor dicho

ratify ['ræțəˌfaɪ] vt **-fied; -fying** : ratificar — **ratification** [ˌræțəfəˈkeɪʃən] n : ratificación f

rating ['reɪțɪŋ] n **1** : clasificación f **2** ~**s** npl : índice m de audiencia

ratio ['reɪʃio] n, pl **-tios** : proporción f

ration ['ræʃən, 'reɪʃən] n **1** : ración f **2** ~**s** npl PROVISIONS : víveres mpl — ~ vt **rationed; rationing** : racionar

rational ['ræʃənəl] adj : racional — **rationale** [ˌræʃəˈnæl] n : lógica f, razones fpl — **rationalize** ['ræʃənəˌlaɪz] vt **-ized; -izing** : racionalizar

rattle ['ræțəl] v **-tled; -tling** vi : traquetear — vt **1** SHAKE : agitar **2** UPSET : de-

sconcertar 3 ~ **off** : decir de corrido
— ~ n 1 : traqueteo m 2 or baby's ~
: sonajero m — **rattlesnake** ['ræt̬əl-
ˌsneɪk] n : serpiente f de cascabel

raucous ['rɔkəs] adj 1 HOARSE : ronco 2
BOISTEROUS : bullicioso

ravage ['rævɪdʒ] vt **-aged; -aging** : estragar, asolar — **ravages** ['rævɪdʒəz]
npl : estragos mpl

rave ['reɪv] vi **raved; raving** 1 : delirar 2
~ **about** : hablar con entusiasmo
sobre

raven ['reɪvən] n : cuervo m

ravenous ['rævənəs] adj 1 HUNGRY
: hambriento 2 VORACIOUS : voraz

ravine [rə'vin] n : barranco m

ravishing ['rævɪʃɪŋ] adj : encantador

raw ['rɔ] adj **rawer; rawest** 1 UNCOOKED
: crudo 2 INEXPERIENCED : inexperto 3
CHAFED : en carne viva 4 : frío y
húmedo (dícese del tiempo) 5 ~ **deal**
: trato m injusto 6 ~ **materials** : materias fpl primas

ray ['reɪ] n : rayo m

rayon ['reɪˌɑn] n : rayón m

raze ['reɪz] vt **razed; razing** : arrasar

razor ['reɪzər] n : maquinilla f de afeitar
— **razor blade** n : hoja f de afeitar

reach ['ritʃ] vt 1 : alcanzar 2 or ~ **out**
: extender 3 : llegar a (un acuerdo, un
límite, etc.) 4 CONTACT : contactar —
vi 1 : extenderse 2 ~ **for** : tratar de
agarrar — ~ n 1 : alcance m 2 **within**
~ : al alcance

react [ri'ækt] vi : reaccionar — **reaction**
[ri'ækʃən] n : reacción f — **reactionary**
[ri'ækʃəˌneri] adj : reaccionario — ~
n, pl **-ries** : reaccionario m, -ria f — **reactor** [ri'æktər] n : reactor m

read ['rid] v **read** ['rɛd]; **reading** vt 1
: leer 2 INTERPRET : interpretar 3 SAY
: decir 4 INDICATE : marcar — vi 1
: leer 2 **it** ~s **as follows** : dice lo
siguiente — **readable** ['ridəbəl] adj
: legible — **reader** ['ridər] n : lector m,
-tora f

readily ['rɛdəli] adv 1 WILLINGLY : de
buena gana 2 EASILY : fácilmente

reading ['ridɪŋ] n : lectura f

readjust [ˌriə'dʒʌst] vt : reajustar — vi
: volverse a adaptar

ready ['rɛdi] adj **readier; -est** 1 : listo,
preparado 2 WILLING : dispuesto 3
AVAILABLE : disponible 4 **get** ~
: prepararse — ~ vt **readied; ready-
ing** : preparar

real ['ril] adj 1 : verdadero, real 2 GEN-
UINE : auténtico — ~ adv VERY : muy
— **real estate** n : propiedad f inmobi-
liaria, bienes mpl raíces — **realism**
['riəˌlɪzəm] n : realismo m — **realist**
['riəlɪst] n : realista mf — **realistic**
[ˌriə'lɪstɪk] adj : realista — **reality** [ri-
'æləti] n, pl **-ties** : realidad f

realize ['riəˌlaɪz] vt **-ized; -izing** 1
: darse cuenta de 2 ACHIEVE : realizar
— **realization** [ˌriələ'zeɪʃən] n 1 : comprensión f 2 FULFILLMENT : realización
f

really ['rɪli, 'ri-] adv : verdaderamente

realm ['rɛlm] n 1 KINGDOM : reino m 2
SPHERE : esfera f

ream ['rim] n : resma f (de papel)

reap ['rip] v : cosechar

reappear [ˌriə'pɪr] vi : reaparecer

rear¹ ['rɪr] vt 1 RAISE : levantar 2 : criar
(niños, etc.) — vi or ~ **up** : encabritarse

rear² n 1 BACK : parte f de atrás 2 BUT-
TOCKS : trasero m fam — ~ adj
: trasero, posterior

rearrange [ˌriə'reɪndʒ] vt **-ranged;
-ranging** : reorganizar, cambiar

reason ['rizən] n : razón f — ~ vt
THINK : pensar — vi : razonar — **reasonable** ['rizənəbəl] adj : razonable —
reasoning ['rizənɪŋ] n : razonamiento
m

reassure [ˌriə'ʃur] vt **-sured; -suring**
: tranquilizar — **reassurance** [ˌriə-
'ʃurənts] n : (palabras fpl de) consuelo
m

rebate ['riˌbeɪt] n : reembolso m

rebel ['rɛbəl] n : rebelde mf — ~ [rɪ'bɛl]
vi **-belled; -belling** : rebelarse — **rebellion** [rɪ'bɛljən] n : rebelión f — **rebellious** [rɪ'bɛljəs] adj : rebelde

rebirth [ˌriˈbərθ] n : renacimiento m

rebound ['riˌbaʊnd, ˌriˈbaʊnd] vi : rebotar — ~ ['riˌbaʊnd] n : rebote m

rebuff [rɪ'bʌf] vt : rechazar — ~ n : desaire m

rebuild [ˌriˈbɪld] vt **-built; -building** : reconstruir

rebuke [rɪ'bjuk] vt **-buked; -buking**
: reprender — ~ n : reprimenda f

rebut [rɪ'bʌt] vt **-butted; -butting** : rebatir — **rebuttal** [rɪ'bʌt̬əl] n : refuta-
ción f

recall [rɪ'kɔl] vt 1 : llamar (al servicio,
etc.) 2 REMEMBER : recordar 3 REVOKE
: revocar — ~ [rɪ'kɔl, 'riˌkɔl] n 1 : retirada f 2 MEMORY : memoria f

recant [rɪ'kænt] vi : retractarse

recapitulate [ˌrikə'pɪtʃəˌleɪt] v **-lated;
-lating** : recapitular

recapture [ˌriˈkæptʃər] vt **-tured; -tur-
ing** 1 : recobrar 2 RELIVE : revivir

recede [ri'sid] vi **-ceded; -ceding** : retirarse

receipt [ri'si:t] n 1 : recibo m 2 ~s npl : ingresos mpl

receive [ri'si:v] vt -ceived; -ceiving : recibir — receiver [ri'si:vər] n 1 : receptor m (de radio, etc.) 2 or telephone ~ : auricular m

recent ['ri:sənt] adj : reciente — recently [-li] adv : recientemente

receptacle [ri'septikəl] n : receptáculo m, recipiente m

reception [ri'sepʃən] n : recepción f — receptionist [ri'sepʃənɪst] n : recepcionista mf — receptive [ri'septɪv] adj : receptivo

recess ['ri:ses, rɪ'ses] n 1 ALCOVE : hueco m 2 : recreo m (escolar) 3 ADJOURNMENT : suspensión f de actividades Spain, receso m Lat — recession [ri'seʃən] n : recesión f

recharge [ˌri:'tʃɑrdʒ] vt -charged; -charging : recargar — rechargeable [ˌri:'tʃɑrdʒəbəl] adj : recargable

recipe ['resəpi:] n : receta f

recipient [ri'sɪpiənt] n : recipiente mf

reciprocal [ri'sɪprəkəl] adj : recíproco

recite [ri'saɪt] vt -cited; -citing 1 : recitar (un poema, etc.) 2 LIST : enumerar — recital [ri'saɪtəl] n : recital m

reckless ['rekləs] adj : imprudente — recklessness ['rekləsnəs] n : imprudencia f

reckon ['rekən] vt 1 COMPUTE : calcular 2 CONSIDER : considerar — reckoning ['rekənɪŋ] n : cálculos mpl

reclaim [ri'kleɪm] vt 1 : reclamar 2 RECOVER : recuperar

recline [ri'klaɪn] vi -clined; -clining : reclinarse — reclining adj : reclinable (dícese de un asiento, etc.)

recluse ['re.klu:s, ri'klu:s] n : solitario m, -ria f

recognition [ˌrekɪg'nɪʃən] n : reconocimiento m — recognizable ['rekɪgˌnaɪzəbəl] adj : reconocible — recognize ['rekɪgˌnaɪz] vt -nized; -nizing : reconocer

recoil [ri'kɔɪl] vi : retroceder — ~ ['ri:ˌkɔɪl, ri'-] n : culatazo m (de un arma de fuego)

recollect [ˌrekə'lekt] v : recordar — recollection [ˌrekə'lekʃən] n : recuerdo m

recommend [ˌrekə'mend] vt : recomendar — recommendation [ˌrekəmən'deɪʃən] n : recomendación f

reconcile ['rekən.saɪl] v -ciled; -ciling 1 : reconciliar (personas), conciliar (datos, etc.) 2 ~ oneself to : resignarse a — vi MAKE UP : reconciliarse — reconciliation [ˌrekənˌsɪli'eɪʃən] n : reconciliación f

reconnaissance [ri'kɑnəzənɪs, -sənɪs] n : reconocimiento m (militar)

reconsider [ˌri:kən'sɪdər] vt : reconsiderar

reconstruct [ˌri:kən'strʌkt] vt : reconstruir

record [ri'kɔrd] vt 1 WRITE DOWN : anotar, apuntar 2 REGISTER : registrar 3 : grabar (música, etc.) — ~ ['rekərd] n 1 DOCUMENT : documento m 2 REGISTER : registro m 3 HISTORY : historial m 4 : disco m (de música, etc.) 5 criminal ~ : antecedentes mpl penales 6 world ~ : récord m mundial — recorder [ri'kɔrdər] n 1 : flauta f dulce 2 or tape ~ : grabadora f — recording [-ɪŋ] n : disco m — record player n : tocadiscos m

recount¹ [ri'kaʊnt] vt NARRATE : narrar, relatar

recount² ['ri:ˌkaʊnt, ˌri'-] vt : volver a contar (votos, etc.) — ~ n : recuento m

recourse ['ri:ˌkors, ri'-] n 1 : recurso m 2 have ~ to : recurrir a

recover [ri'kʌvər] vt : recobrar — vi RECUPERATE : recuperarse — recovery [ri'kʌvəri] n, pl -eries : recuperación f

recreation [ˌrekri'eɪʃən] n : recreo m — recreational [ˌrekri'eɪʃənəl] adj : de recreo

recruit [ri'kru:t] vt : reclutar — ~ n : recluta mf — recruitment [ri'kru:tmənt] n : reclutamiento m

rectangle ['rek.tæŋgəl] n : rectángulo m — rectangular [rek'tæŋgjələr] adj : rectangular

rectify ['rektə.faɪ] vt -fied; -fying : rectificar

rector ['rektər] n 1 : párroco m (clérigo) 2 : rector m, -tora f (de una universidad) — rectory ['rektəri] n, pl -ries : rectoría f

rectum ['rektəm] n, pl -tums or -ta [-tə] : recto m

recuperate [ri'ku:pə.reɪt, -'kju:-] v -ated; -ating vt : recuperar — vi : recuperarse — recuperation [ri.ku:pə'reɪʃən, -.kju:-] n : recuperación f

recur [ri'kər] vi -curred; -curring : repetirse — recurrence [ri'kərənɪs] n : repetición f — recurrent [ri'kərənt] adj : que se repite

recycle [ri'saɪkəl] vt -cled; -cling : reciclar

red ['red] adj : rojo — ~ n : rojo m — redden ['redən] vt : enrojecer — vi : enrojecerse — reddish ['redɪʃ] adj : rojizo

redecorate [ˌri:'dekə.reɪt] vt -rated; -rating : pintar de nuevo

redeem [ri'di:m] vt 1 SAVE : salvar,

rescatar **2** : desempeñar (de un monte de piedad) **3** : canjear (cupones, etc.) **— redemption** [ri'dempʃən] *n* : redención *f*

red–handed ['red'hændəd] *adv or adj* : con las manos en la masa

redhead ['red,hed] *n* : pelirrojo *m*, -ja *f*

red–hot ['red'hɑt] *adj* : al rojo vivo

redness ['rednəs] *n* : rojez *f*

redo [ri:'du:] *vt* **-did** [-'dɪd]; **-done** [-'dʌn]; **-doing** : hacer de nuevo

redouble [ri'dʌbəl] *vt* **-bled**; **-bling** : redoblar

red tape *n* : papeleo *m*

reduce [ri'du:s, -'dju:s] *v* **-duced**; **-ducing** *vt* : reducir — *vi* SLIM : adelgazar — **reduction** [ri'dʌkʃən] *n* : reducción *f*

redundant [ri'dʌndənt] *adj* : redundante

reed ['ri:d] *n* **1** : caña *f* **2** : lengüeta *f* (de un instrumento)

reef ['ri:f] *n* : arrecife *m*

reek ['ri:k] *vi* : apestar

reel ['ri:l] *n* : carrete *m* (de hilo, etc.) — ~ *vt* **1** ~ **in** : enrollar (un sedal), sacar (un pez) del agua **2** ~ **off** : enumerar — *vi* **1** SPIN : dar vueltas STAGGER : tambalearse

reestablish [,ri:ə'stæblɪʃ] *vt* : restablecer

refer [ri'fər] *v* **-ferred**; **-ferring** *vt* **1** DIRECT : enviar, mandar **2** SUBMIT : remitir — *vi* **to 1** MENTION : referirse a **2** CONSULT : consultar

referee [,refə'ri:] *n* : árbitro *m*, -tra *f* — ~ *v* **-eed**; **-eeing** : arbitrar

reference ['refrənts, 'refə-] *n* **1** : referencia *f* **2** CONSULTATION : consulta *f* **3** *or* ~ **book** : libro *m* de consulta **4 in** ~ **to** : con referencia a

refill [ri:'fɪl] *vt* : rellenar — ~ ['ri:,fɪl] *n* : recambio *m*

refine [ri'faɪn] *vt* **-fined**; **-fining** : refinar — **refined** [ri'faɪnd] *adj* : refinado — **refinement** [ri'faɪnmənt] *n* : refinamiento *m* — **refinery** [ri'faɪnəri] *n*, *pl* **-eries** : refinería *f*

reflect [ri'flekt] *vt* : reflejar — *vi* **1** : reflejarse **2** ~ **badly on** : desacreditar **3** ~ **upon** : reflexionar sobre — **reflection** [ri'flekʃən] *n* **1** : reflexión *f* **2** IMAGE : reflejo *m* — **reflector** [ri'flektər] *n* : reflector *m*

reflex ['ri:,fleks] *n* : reflejo *m*

reflexive [ri'fleksɪv] *adj* : reflexivo

reform [ri'fɔrm] *vt* : reformar — *vi* : reformarse — ~ *n* : reforma *f* — **reformer** [ri'fɔrmər] *n* : reformador *m*, -dora *f*

refrain¹ [ri'freɪn] *vi* ~ **from** : abstenerse de

refrain² *n* : estribillo *m* (en música)

refresh [ri'frɛʃ] *vt* : refrescar — **refreshments** [ri'frɛʃmənts] *npl* : refrigerio *m*

refrigerate [ri'frɪdʒə,reɪt] *vt* **-ated**; **-ating** : refrigerar — **refrigeration** [ri,frɪdʒə'reɪʃən] *n* : refrigeración *f* — **refrigerator** [ri'frɪdʒə,reɪtər] *n* : nevera *f*, refrigerador *m* *Lat*, frigorífico *m* *Spain*

refuel [ri:'fju:əl] *v* **-eled** *or* **-elled**; **-eling** *or* **-elling** *vt* : llenar de carburante — *vi* : repostar

refuge ['re,fju:dʒ] *n* : refugio *m* — **refugee** [,refju'dʒi:] *n* : refugiado *m*, -da *f*

refund [ri'fʌnd, 'ri,fʌnd] *vt* : reembolsar — ~ ['ri:,fʌnd] *n* : reembolso *m*

refurbish [ri'fərbɪʃ] *vt* : renovar, restaurar

refuse¹ [ri'fju:z] *v* **-fused**; **-fusing** *vt* **1** : rehusar, rechazar **2** ~ **to do sth** : negarse a hacer algo — *vi* : negarse — **refusal** [ri'fju:zəl] *n* : negativa *f*

refuse² ['re,fju:s, -,fju:z] *n* : residuos *mpl*, desperdicios *mpl*

refute [ri'fju:t] *vt* **-futed**; **-futing** : refutar

regain [ri:'geɪn] *vt* : recuperar, recobrar

regal ['ri:gəl] *adj* : regio, majestuoso — **regalia** [ri'geɪljə] *n* : ropaje *m*, insignias *fpl*

regard [ri'gɑrd] *n* **1** : consideración *f* **2** ESTEEM : estima *f* **3 in this** ~ : en este sentido **4** ~s *npl* : saludos *mpl* **5 with** ~ **to** : respecto a — ~ *vt* **1** : mirar (con recelo, etc.) **2** HEED : tener en cuenta **3** ESTEEM : estimar **4 as** ~s : en lo que se refiere a **5** ~ **as** : considerar — **regarding** [ri'gɑrdɪŋ] *prep* : respecto a — **regardless** [ri'gɑrdləs] *adv* : a pesar de todo — **regardless of** *prep* **1** : sin tener en cuenta **2** IN SPITE OF : a pesar de

regent ['ri:dʒənt] *n* : regente *mf*

regime [reɪ'ʒi:m, rɪ-] *n* : régimen *m* — **regimen** ['redʒəmən] *n* : régimen *m*

regiment ['redʒəmənt] *n* : regimiento *m*

region ['ri:dʒən] *n* : región *f* — **regional** ['ri:dʒənəl] *adj* : regional

register ['redʒəstər] *n* : registro *m* — ~ *vt* **1** : registrar (a personas), matricular (vehículos) **2** SHOW : marcar, manifestar **3** : certificar (correo) — *vi* ENROLL : inscribirse, matricularse — **registrar** ['redʒə,strɑr] *n* : registrador *m*, -dora *f* oficial — **registration** [,redʒə'streɪʃən] *n* **1** : inscripción *f*, matriculación *f* **2** *or* ~ **number** : número *m* de matrícula — **registry** ['redʒəstri] *n*, *pl* **-tries** : registro *m*

regret [ri'gret] *vt* **-gretted**; **-gretting** : lamentar — ~ *n* **1** REMORSE : arrepentimiento *m* **2** SORROW : pesar *m*

— **regrettable** [ri'grɛtəbəl] *adj* : lamentable

regular ['rɛgjələr] *adj* **1** : regular **2** CUSTOMARY : habitual — ~ *n* : cliente *mf* habitual — **regularity** [‚rɛgjə'lærəti] *n*, *pl* **-ties** : regularidad *f* — **regularly** ['rɛgjələrli] *adv* : regularmente — **regulate** ['rɛgjə‚leɪt] *vt* **-lated; -lating** : regular — **regulation** [‚rɛgjə'leɪʃən] *n* **1** CONTROL : regulación *f* **2** RULE : regla *f*

rehabilitate [‚ri:hə'bilə‚teɪt, ‚ri:ə-] *vt* **-tated; -tating** : rehabilitar — **rehabilitation** [‚ri:hə‚bilə'teɪʃən, ‚ri:ə-] *n* : rehabilitación *f*

rehearse [ri'hərs] *v* **-hearsed; -hearsing** : ensayar — **rehearsal** [ri'hərsəl] *n* : ensayo *m*

reign ['reɪn] *n* : reinado *m* — ~ *vi* : reinar

reimburse [‚ri:əm'bərs] *vt* **-bursed; -bursing** : reembolsar — **reimbursement** [‚ri:əm'bərsmənt] *n* : reembolso *m*

rein ['reɪn] *n* : rienda *f*

reincarnation [‚ri:ɪn‚kɑr'neɪʃən] *n* : reencarnación *f*

reindeer ['reɪn‚dɪr] *n* : reno *m*

reinforce [‚ri:ən'fors] *vt* **-forced; -forcing** : reforzar — **reinforcement** [‚ri:ən'forsmənt] *n* : refuerzo *m*

reinstate [‚ri:ən'steɪt] *vt* **-stated; -stating 1** : restablecer **2** : restituir (a algn en su cargo)

reiterate [ri'ɪtə‚reɪt] *vt* **-ated; -ating** : reiterar

reject [ri'dʒɛkt] *vt* : rechazar — **rejection** [ri'dʒɛkʃən] *n* : rechazo *m*

rejoice [ri'dʒɔɪs] *vi* **-joiced; -joicing** : regocijarse

rejuvenate [ri'dʒu:və‚neɪt] *vt* **-nated; -nating** : rejuvenecer

rekindle [‚ri:'kɪndəl] *vt* **-dled; -dling** : reavivar

relapse ['ri:‚læps, ri'læps] *n* : recaída *f* — ~ [ri'læps] *vi* **-lapsed; -lapsing** : recaer

relate [ri'leɪt] *v* **-lated; -lating** *vt* **1** TELL : relatar **2** ASSOCIATE : relacionar — *vi* ~ **to 1** CONCERN : estar relacionado con **2** UNDERSTAND : identificarse con **3** : relacionarse con (socialmente) — **related** [ri'leɪtəd] *adj* ~ **to** : emparentado con — **relation** [ri'leɪʃən] *n* **1** CONNECTION : relación *f* **2** RELATIVE : pariente *mf* **3 in** ~ **to** : en relación con **4** ~**s** *npl* : relaciones *fpl* — **relationship** [ri'leɪʃən‚ɪp] *n* **1** : relación *f* **2** KINSHIP : parentesco *m* — **relative** ['rɛlətɪv] *n* : pariente *mf* — ~ *adj* : relativo — **relatively** *adv* : relativamente

relax [ri'læks] *vt* : relajar — *vi* : relajarse — **relaxation** [‚ri:‚læk'seɪʃən] *n* **1** : relajación *f* **2** RECREATION : esparcimiento *m*

relay ['ri:‚leɪ] *n* **1** : relevo *m* **2** *or* ~ **race** : carrera *f* de relevos — ~ ['ri:‚leɪ, ri'leɪ] *vt* **-layed; -laying** : transmitir

release [ri'li:s] *vt* **-leased; -leasing 1** FREE : liberar, poner en libertad **2** : soltar (un freno, etc.) **3** EMIT : despedir **4** : sacar (un libro, etc.), estrenar (una película) — ~ *n* **1** : liberación *f* **2** : estreno *m* (de una película), publicación *f* (de un libro) **3** : fuga *f* (de gases)

relegate ['rɛlə‚geɪt] *vt* **-gated; -gating** : relegar

relent [ri'lɛnt] *vi* : ceder — **relentless** [ri'lɛntləs] *adj* : implacable

relevant ['rɛləvənt] *adj* : pertinente — **relevance** ['rɛləvənts] *n* : pertinencia *f*

reliable [ri'laɪəbəl] *adj* : fiable (dícese de personas), fidedigno (dícese de información, etc.) — **reliability** [ri‚laɪə'bilə‚ti] *n*, *pl* **-ties** : fiabilidad *f* (de una cosa), responsabilidad *f* (de una persona) — **reliance** [ri'laɪənts] *n* **1** : dependencia *f* **2** TRUST : confianza *f* — **reliant** [ri'laɪənt] *adj* : dependiente

relic ['rɛlɪk] *n* : reliquia *f*

relief [ri'li:f] *n* **1** : alivio *m* **2** AID : ayuda *f* **3** : relieve *m* (en la escultura) **4** REPLACEMENT : relevo *m* — **relieve** [ri'li:v] *vt* **-lieved; -lieving 1** : aliviar **2** REPLACE : relevar (a algn) **3** ~ **s.o. of** : liberar a algn de

religion [ri'lɪdʒən] *n* : religión *f* — **religious** [ri'lɪdʒəs] *adj* : religioso

relinquish [ri'lɪŋkwɪʃ, -'lɪn-] *vt* : renunciar a, abandonar

relish ['rɛlɪʃ] *n* **1** : salsa *f* (condimento) **2 with** ~ : con gusto — ~ *vt* : saborear

relocate [‚ri:'lo‚keɪt, ‚ri:lo'keɪt] *vt* **-cated; -cating** : trasladar — *vi* : trasladarse — **relocation** [‚ri:lo'keɪʃən] *n* : traslado *m*

reluctance [ri'lʌktənts] *n* : reticencia *f*, desgana *f* — **reluctant** [ri'lʌktənt] *adj* : reacio, reticente — **reluctantly** [ri'lʌktəntli] *adv* : a regañadientes

rely [ri'laɪ] *vi* **-lied; -lying** ~ **on 1** DEPEND ON : depender de **2** TRUST : confiar (en)

remain [ri'meɪn] *vi* **1** : quedar **2** STAY : quedarse **3** CONTINUE : seguir, continuar — **remainder** [ri'meɪndər] *n* : resto *m* — **remains** [ri'meɪnz] *npl* : restos *mpl*

remark [ri'mɑrk] *n* : comentario *m*, observación *f* — ~ *vt* : observar — *vi* ~

on : observar — **remarkable** [ri-'markəbəl] *adj* : extraordinario, notable

remedy ['remədi] *n, pl* **-dies** : remedio *m* — ~ *vt* **-died; -dying** : remediar — **remedial** [ri'mi:diəl] *adj* : correctivo

remember [ri'membər] *vt* 1 : acordarse de, recordar 2 ~ **to** : acordarse de — *vi* : acordarse, recordar — **remembrance** [ri'membrənts] *n* : recuerdo *m*

remind [ri'maind] *vt* : recordar — **reminder** [ri'maindər] *n* : recordatorio *m*

reminiscence [remə'nisənts] *n* : recuerdo *m*, reminiscencia *f* — **reminisce** [remə'nis] *vi* **-nisced; -niscing** : rememorar los viejos tiempos — **reminiscent** [remə'nisənt] *adj* **be ~ of** : recordar

remiss [ri'mis] *adj* : negligente, remiso

remit [ri'mit] *vt* **-mitted; -mitting** 1 PARDON : perdonar 2 : enviar (dinero) — **remission** [ri'miʃən] *n* : remisión *f*

remnant ['remnənt] *n* 1 : resto *m* 2 TRACE : vestigio *m*

remorse [ri'mors] *n* : remordimiento *m* — **remorseful** [ri'morsfəl] *adj* : arrepentido

remote [ri'mo:t] *adj* **-moter; -est** 1 : remoto 2 ALOOF : distante 3 ~ **from** : apartado de, alejado de — **remote control** *n* : control *m* remoto — **remotely** [ri'mo:tli] *adv* SLIGHTLY : remotamente

remove [ri'mu:v] *vt* **-moved; -moving** 1 : quitar (una tapa, etc.), quitarse (ropa) 2 EXTRACT : sacar 3 DISMISS : destituir 4 ELIMINATE : eliminar — **removable** [ri'mu:vəbəl] *adj* : separable, de quita y pon — **removal** [ri'mu:vəl] *n* 1 : eliminación *f* 2 EXTRACTION : extracción *f*

remunerate [ri'mju:nə,reit] *vt* **-ated; -ating** : remunerar

render ['rendər] *vt* 1 : rendir (homenaje), prestar (ayuda) 2 MAKE : hacer 3 TRANSLATE : traducir

rendezvous ['randi,vu:, -dei-] *ns & pl* : cita *f*

rendition [ren'dıʃən] *n* : interpretación *f*

renegade ['reni,geid] *n* : renegado *m*, -da *f*

renew [ri'nu:, -'nju:] *vt* 1 : renovar 2 RESUME : reanudar — **renewal** [ri'nu:əl, -'nju:-] *n* : renovación *f*

renounce [ri'naunts] *vt* **-nounced; -nouncing** : renunciar a

renovate ['renə,veit] *vt* **-vated; -vating** : renovar — **renovation** [renə'veiʃən] *n* : renovación *f*

renown [ri'naun] *n* : renombre *m* — **renowned** [ri'naund] *adj* : célebre, renombrado

rent ['rent] *n* 1 : alquiler *m*, arrendamiento *m*, renta *f* 2 **for ~** : se alquila — ~ *vt* : alquilar — **rental** ['rentəl] *n* : alquiler *m* — ~ *adj* : de alquiler — **renter** ['rentər] *n* : arrendatario *m*, -ria *f*

renunciation [ri,nʌntsi'eiʃən] *n* : renuncia *f*

reopen [ri'o:pən] *vt* : volver a abrir

reorganize [ri'orgən,aiz] *vt* **-nized; -nizing** : reorganizar — **reorganization** [ri,orgənə'zeiʃən] *n* : reorganización *f*

repair [ri'pær] *vt* : reparar, arreglar — ~ *n* 1 : reparación *f*, arreglo *m* 2 **in bad ~** : en mal estado

repay [ri'pei] *vt* **-paid; -paying** 1 : devolver (dinero), pagar (una deuda) 2 : corresponder a (un favor, etc.)

repeal [ri'pi:l] *vt* : abrogar, revocar — ~ *n* : abrogación *f*, revocación *f*

repeat [ri'pi:t] *vt* : repetir — ~ *n* : repetición *f* — **repeatedly** [ri'pi:tədli] *adv* : repetidas veces

repel [ri'pel] *vt* **-pelled; -pelling** : repeler — **repellent** [ri'pelənt] *n* : repelente *m*

repent [ri'pent] *vi* : arrepentirse — **repentance** [ri'pentənts] *n* : arrepentimiento *m*

repercussion [ri:pər'kʌʃən, repər-] *n* : repercusión *f*

repertoire ['repər,twar] *n* : repertorio *m*

repetition [repə'tiʃən] *n* : repetición *f* — **repetitious** [repə'tiʃəs] *adj* : repetitivo — **repetitive** [ri'petətiv] *adj* : repetitivo

replace [ri'pleis] *vt* **-placed; -placing** 1 : reponer 2 SUBSTITUTE : reemplazar, sustituir 3 EXCHANGE : cambiar — **replacement** [ri'pleismənt] *n* 1 : sustitución *f* 2 : sustituto *m*, -ta *f* (persona) 3 **or ~ part** : repuesto *m*

replenish [ri'pleniʃ] *vt* 1 : reponer 2 REFILL : rellenar

replete [ri'pli:t] *adj* ~ **with** : repleto de

replica ['replikə] *n* : réplica *f*

reply [ri'plai] *vi* **-plied; -plying** : contestar, responder — ~ *n, pl* **-plies** : respuesta *f*

report [ri'port] *n* 1 : informe *m* 2 RUMOR : rumor *m* 3 **or news** ~ : reportaje *m* 4 **weather ~** : boletín *m* meteorológico — ~ *vt* 1 RELATE : anunciar 2 ~ **a crime** : denunciar un delito 3 *or* ~ **on** : informar sobre — *vi* 1 : informar 2 ~ **for duty** : presentarse — **report card** *n* : boletín *m* de calificaciones — **reportedly** [ri'portədli] *adv*

: según se dice — **reporter** [rɪ'portər] *n* : periodista *mf*; reportero *m*, -ra *f*

repose [rɪ'poːz] *vi* **-posed; -posing** : reposar — **~** *n* : reposo *m*

reprehensible [ˌreprɪ'hentsəbəl] *adj* : reprensible

represent [ˌreprɪ'zent] *vt* **1** : representar **2** PORTRAY : presentar — **representation** [ˌreprɪzen'teɪʃən, -zən-] *n* : representación *f* — **representative** [ˌreprɪ'zentətɪv] *adj* : representativo — **~** *n* : representante *mf*

repress [rɪ'pres] *vt* : reprimir — **repression** [rɪ'preʃən] *n* : represión *f*

reprieve [rɪ'priːv] *n* : indulto *m*

reprimand ['reprəˌmænd] *n* : reprimenda *f* — **~** *vt* : reprender

reprint [rɪ'prɪnt] *vt* : reimprimir — **~** ['riːˌprɪnt, rɪ'prɪnt] *n* : reedición *f*

reprisal [rɪ'praɪzəl] *n* : represalia *f*

reproach [rɪ'proːtʃ] *n* : reproche *m* **beyond ~** : irreprochable — **~** *vt* : reprochar — **reproachful** [rɪ'proːtʃfəl] *adj* : de reproche

reproduce [ˌriːprə'duːs, -'djuːs] *v* **-duced; -ducing** *vt* : reproducir — *vi* : reproducirse — **reproduction** [ˌriːprə'dʌkʃən] *n* : reproducción *f* — **reproductive** [ˌriːprə'dʌktɪv] *adj* : reproductor

reproof [rɪ'pruːf] *n* : reprobación *f*

reptile ['reptaɪl] *n* : reptil *m*

republic [rɪ'pʌblɪk] *n* : república *f* — **republican** [rɪ'pʌblɪkən] *n* : republicano *m*, -na *f* — **~** *adj* : republicano

repudiate [rɪ'pjuːdiˌeɪt] *vt* **-ated; -ating** : repudiar

repugnant [rɪ'pʌgnənt] *adj* : repugnante, asqueroso — **repugnance** [rɪ'pʌgnənts] *n* : repugnancia *f*

repulse [rɪ'pʌls] *vt* **-pulsed; -pulsing** : repeler, rechazar — **repulsive** [rɪ'pʌlsɪv] *adj* : repulsivo

reputation [ˌrepjə'teɪʃən] *n* : reputación *f* — **reputable** ['repjətəbəl] *adj* : de confianza, acreditado — **reputed** [rɪ'pjuːtəd] *adj* : supuesto

request [rɪ'kwest] *n* : petición *f* — **~** *vt* : pedir

requiem ['rekwiəm, 'reɪ-] *n* : réquiem *m*

require [rɪ'kwaɪr] *vt* **-quired; -quiring 1** CALL FOR : requerir **2** NEED : necesitar — **requirement** [rɪ'kwaɪrmənt] *n* **1** NEED : necesidad *f* **2** DEMAND : requisito *m* — **requisite** ['rekwəzɪt] *adj* : necesario

resale ['riːˌseɪl, ˌriː'seɪl] *n* : reventa *f*

rescind [rɪ'sɪnd] *vt* : rescindir (un contrato), revocar (una ley, etc.)

rescue ['reskjuː] *vt* **-cued; -cuing** : rescatar, salvar — **~** *n* : rescate *m* —

rescuer ['reskjuər] *n* : salvador *m*, -dora *f*

research [rɪ'sərtʃ, 'riːˌsərtʃ] *n* : investigación *f* — **~** *vt* : investigar — **researcher** [rɪ'sərtʃər, 'riː-] *n* : investigador *m*, -dora *f*

resemble [rɪ'zembəl] *vt* **-sembled; -sembling** : parecerse a — **resemblance** [rɪ'zembləns] *n* : parecido *m*

resent [rɪ'zent] *vt* : resentirse de, ofenderse por — **resentful** [rɪ'zentfəl] *adj* : resentido — **resentment** [rɪ'zentmənt] *n* : resentimiento *m*

reserve [rɪ'zərv] *vt* **-served; -serving** : reservar — **~** *n* **1** : reserva *f* **2 ~s** *npl* : reservas *fpl* (militares) — **reservation** [ˌrezər'veɪʃən] *n* : reserva *f* — **reserved** [rɪ'zərvd] *adj* : reservado — **reservoir** ['rezərˌvwɑr, -ˌvwɔr, -ˌvɔr] *n* : embalse *m*

reset [ˌriː'set] *vt* **-set; -setting** : volver a poner (un reloj, etc.)

residence ['rezədənts] *n* : residencia *f* — **reside** [rɪ'zaɪd] *vi* **-sided; -siding** : residir — **resident** ['rezədənt] *adj* : residente — **~** *n* : residente *mf* — **residential** [ˌrezə'dentʃəl] *adj* : residencial

residue ['rezəˌduː, -ˌdjuː] *n* : residuo *m*

resign [rɪ'zaɪn] *vt* **1** QUIT : dimitir **2 ~ oneself to** : resignarse a — **resignation** [ˌrezɪg'neɪʃən] *n* **1** : dimisión *f* **2** ACCEPTANCE : resignación *f*

resilient [rɪ'zɪljənt] *adj* **1** : resistente (dícese de personas) **2** ELASTIC : elástico — **resilience** [rɪ'zɪljənts] *n* **1** : resistencia *f* **2** ELASTICITY : elasticidad *f*

resin ['rezən] *n* : resina *f*

resist [rɪ'zɪst] *vt* : resistir — *vi* : resistirse — **resistance** [rɪ'zɪstənts] *n* : resistencia *f* — **resistant** [rɪ'zɪstənt] *adj* : resistente

resolve [rɪ'zɑlv] *vt* **-solved; -solving** : resolver — **~** *n* : resolución *f* — **resolution** [ˌrezə'luːʃən] *n* **1** : resolución *f* **2** DECISION, INTENTION : propósito *m* — **resolute** ['rezəˌluːt] *adj* : resuelto

resonance ['rezənənts] *n* : resonancia *f* — **resonant** ['rezənənt] *adj* : resonante

resort [rɪ'zɔrt] *n* **1** RECOURSE : recurso *m* **2** *or* **tourist ~** : centro *m* turístico — **~** *vi* **~ to** : recurrir a

resounding [rɪ'zaʊndɪŋ] *adj* **1** RESONANT : resonante **2** ABSOLUTE : rotundo

resource ['riːˌsɔrs, rɪ'sɔrs] *n* : recurso *m* — **resourceful** [rɪ'sɔrsfəl, -'zɔrs-] *adj* : ingenioso

respect [rɪ'spekt] *n* **1** ESTEEM : respeto *m* **2 in some ~s** : en algún sentido **3 pay one's ~s** : presentar uno sus respetos **4 with ~ to** : (con) respecto a — **~** vt : respetar — **respectable** [ri'spektəbəl] adj : respetable — **respectful** [ri'spektfəl] adj : respetuoso — **respective** [ri'spektiv] adj : respectivo — **respectively** adv : respectivamente

respiration [,respə'reiʃən] n : respiración f — **respiratory** ['respərə,tori, ri-'spai:rə-] adj : respiratorio

respite ['respit, ri'spait] n : respiro m

response [ri'spanʦ] n : respuesta f — **respond** [ri'spand] vi : responder — **responsibility** [ri,spanʦə'biləʈi] n, **-ties** : responsabilidad f — **responsible** [ri'spanʦəbəl] adj : responsable — **responsive** [ri'spanʦiv] adj : sensible, receptivo

rest¹ ['rest] n **1** : descanso m **2** SUPPORT : apoyo m **3** : silencio m (en música) — **~** vi **1** : descansar **2** LEAN : apoyarse **3 ~ on** DEPEND ON : depender de — vt **1** RELAX : descansar **2** LEAN : apoyar

rest² n REMAINDER : resto m

restaurant ['restə,rant, -rənt] n : restaurante m

restful ['restfəl] adj : tranquilo, apacible

restitution [,restə'tu:ʃən, -'tju:-] n : restitución f

restless ['restləs] adj : inquieto, agitado

restore [ri'stor] vt **-stored; -storing 1** RETURN : devolver **2** REESTABLISH : restablecer **3** REPAIR : restaurar — **restoration** [,restə'reiʃən] n **1** : restablecimiento m **2** REPAIR : restauración f

restrain [ri'strein] vt **1** : contener **2 ~ oneself** : contenerse — **restrained** [ri'streind] adj : comedido, moderado — **restraint** [ri'streint] n **1** : restricción f **2** SELF-CONTROL : moderación f, control m de sí mismo

restriction [ri'strikʃən] n : restricción f — **restrict** [ri'strikt] vt : restringir — **restricted** [ri'striktəd] adj : restringido — **restrictive** [ri'striktiv] adj : restrictivo

result [ri'zʌlt] vi : resultar — **~** n **1** : resultado m **2 as a ~ of** : como consecuencia de

resume [ri'zu:m] v **-sumed; -suming** vt : reanudar — vi : reanudarse

résumé or **resume** or **resumé** ['rezə,mei, ,rezə'-] n : currículum m (vitae)

resumption [ri'zʌmpʃən] n : reanudación f

resurgence [ri'sərdʒənʦ] n : resurgimiento m

resurrection [,rezə'rekʃən] n : resurrección f — **resurrect** [,rezə'rekt] vt : resucitar

resuscitate [ri'sʌsə,teit] vt **-tated; -tating** : resucitar

retail ['ri:,teil] vt : vender al por menor — **~** n : venta f al por menor — **~** adj : detallista, minorista — **~** adv : al detalle, al por menor — **retailer** ['ri:,teilər] n : detallista mf, minorista mf

retain [ri'tein] vt : retener

retaliate [ri'tæli,eit] vi **-ated; -ating** : tomar represalias — **retaliation** [ri,tæli'eiʃən] n : represalias fpl

retard [ri'tard] vt : retardar, retrasar — **retarded** [ri'tardəd] adj : retrasado

retention [ri'tenʃən] n : retención f

reticence ['retəsənʦ] n : reticencia f — **reticent** ['retəsənt] adj : reticente

retina ['retənə] n, pl **-nas** or **-nae** [-əni, -ə,nai] : retina f

retinue ['retən,u:, -,ju:] n : séquito m

retire [ri'tair] vi **-tired; -tiring 1** WITHDRAW : retirarse **2** : jubilarse, retirarse (de un trabajo) **3** : acostarse (en la cama) — **retirement** [ri'tairmənt] n : jubilación f — **retiring** [ri'tairiŋ] adj SHY : retraído

retort [ri'tort] vt : replicar — **~** n : réplica f

retrace [ri,treis] vt **-traced; -tracing ~ one's steps** : volver sobre sus pasos

retract [ri'trækt] vt **1** WITHDRAW : retirar **2** : retraer (garras, etc.) — vi : retractarse

retrain [ri,trein] vt : reciclar

retreat [ri'tri:t] n **1** : retirada f **2** REFUGE : refugio m — **~** vi : retirarse

retribution [,retrə'bju:ʃən] n : castigo m

retrieve [ri'tri:v] vt **-trieved; -trieving 1** : cobrar, recuperar **2** RESCUE : salvar — **retrieval** [ri'tri:vəl] n : recuperación f — **retriever** [ri'tri:vər] n : perro m cobrador

retroactive [,retro'æktiv] adj : retroactivo

retrospect ['retrə,spekt] n **in ~** : mirando hacia atrás — **retrospective** [,retrə-'spektiv] adj : retrospectivo

return [ri'tərn] vi **1** : volver, regresar **2** REAPPEAR : reaparecer — vt **1** : devolver **2** YIELD : producir — **~** n **1** : regreso m, vuelta f **2** : devolución f (de algo prestado) **3** YIELD : rendimiento m **4 in ~ for** : a cambio de **5** or **tax ~** : declaración f de impuestos — **~** adj : de vuelta

reunite [,ri:ju'nait] vt **-nited; -niting** : reunir — **reunion** [ri'ju:njən] n : reunión f

revamp [,ri'væmp] vt : renovar

reveal [ri'vi:l] vt **1** : revelar **2** SHOW : dejar ver

revel ['rɛvəl] *vi* -eled *or* -elled; -eling *or* -elling ~ **in** : deleitarse en

revelation [ˌrɛvəˈleɪʃən] *n* : revelación *f*

revelry ['rɛvəlri] *n, pl* -ries : jolgorio *m*, regocijos *mpl*

revenge [rɪˈvɛndʒ] *vt* -venged; -venging — ~ *n* 1 : venganza *f* 2 take ~ on : vengarse de

revenue ['rɛvəˌnuː, -ˌnjuː] *n* : ingresos *mpl*

reverberate [rɪˈvɜrbəˌreɪt] *vi* -ated; -ating : retumbar, resonar

reverence ['rɛvərənts] *n* : reverencia *f*, veneración *f* — **revere** [rɪˈvɪr] *vt* -vered; -vering : venerar — **reverend** ['rɛvərənd] *adj* : reverendo — **reverent** ['rɛvərənt] *adj* : reverente

reverie ['rɛvəri] *n, pl* -eries : ensueño *m*

reverse [rɪˈvɜrs] *adj* : inverso, contrario — ~ *v* -versed; -versing *vt* 1 : invertir 2 : cambiar (una política), revocar (una decisión) 3 : dar marcha atrás a (un automóvil) — *vi* : invertirse — ~ *n* 1 BACK : dorso *m*, revés *m* 2 *or* ~ **gear** : marcha *f* atrás 3 **the** ~ : lo contrario — **reversible** [rɪˈvɜrsəbəl] *adj* : reversible — **reversal** ['rɛvərsəl] *n* 1 : inversión *f* 2 CHANGE : cambio *m* total 3 SETBACK : revés *m* — **revert** [rɪˈvɜrt] *vi* : revertir

review [rɪˈvjuː] *n* 1 : revisión *f* 2 OVERVIEW : resumen *m* 3 CRITIQUE : reseña *f*, crítica *f* 4 : repaso *m* (para un examen) — ~ *vt* 1 EXAMINE : examinar 2 : repasar (una lección) 3 CRITIQUE : reseñar — **reviewer** [rɪˈvjuːər] *n* : crítico *m*, -ca *f*

revile [rɪˈvaɪl] *vt* -viled; -viling : injuriar

revise [rɪˈvaɪz] *vt* -vised; -vising 1 : modificar (una política, etc.) 2 : revisar, corregir (una publicación) — **revision** [rɪˈvɪʒən] *n* : corrección *f*, modificación *f*

revive [rɪˈvaɪv] *v* -vived; -viving *vt* 1 : reanimar, reactivar 2 : resucitar (a una persona) 3 RESTORE : restablecer — *vi* 1 : reanimarse, reactivarse 2 COME TO : volver en sí — **revival** [rɪˈvaɪvəl] *n* : reanimación *f*, reactivación *f*

revoke [rɪˈvoːk] *vt* -voked; -voking : revocar

revolt [rɪˈvoːlt] *vi* : rebelarse, sublevarse — *vt* : dar asco a — ~ *n* : revuelta *f*, sublevación *f* — **revolting** [rɪˈvoːltɪŋ] *adj* : asqueroso

revolution [ˌrɛvəˈluːʃən] *n* : revolución *f* — **revolutionary** [ˌrɛvəˈluːʃənˌɛri] *adj* : revolucionario — ~ *n, pl* -aries : revolucionario *m*, -ria *f* — **revolutionize** [ˌrɛvəˈluːʃənˌaɪz] *vt* -ized; -izing : revolucionar

revolve [rɪˈvalv] *v* -volved; -volving *vt* : hacer girar — *vi* : girar

revolver [rɪˈvalvər] *n* : revólver *m*

revue [rɪˈvjuː] *n* : revista *f* (teatral)

revulsion [rɪˈvʌlʃən] *n* : repugnancia *f*

reward [rɪˈword] *vt* : recompensar — ~ *n* : recompensa *f*

rewrite [ˌriːˈraɪt] *vt* -wrote; -written; -writing : volver a escribir

rhetoric ['rɛtərɪk] *n* : retórica *f* — **rhetorical** [rɪˈtorɪkəl] *adj* : retórico

rheumatism ['ruːməˌtɪzəm, 'ruː-] *n* : reumatismo *m* — **rheumatic** [ruˈmætɪk] *adj* : reumático

rhino ['raɪˌnoː] *n, pl* -no *or* -nos → **rhinoceros** — **rhinoceros** [raɪˈnɑsərəs] *n, pl* -noceroses *or* -noceros *or* -noceri [-ˌraɪ] : rinoceronte *m*

rhubarb ['ruːˌbɑrb] *n* : ruibarbo *m*

rhyme ['raɪm] *n* 1 : rima *f* 2 VERSE : verso *m* (en rima) — ~ *vi* **rhymed; rhyming** : rimar

rhythm ['rɪðəm] *n* : ritmo *m* — **rhythmic** ['rɪðmɪk] *or* **rhythmical** [-mɪkəl] *adj* : rítmico

rib ['rɪb] *n* : costilla *f* — ~ *vt* TEASE : tomar el pelo a

ribbon ['rɪbən] *n* : cinta *f*

rice ['raɪs] *n* : arroz *m*

rich ['rɪtʃ] *adj* 1 : rico 2 ~ **foods** : comidas *fpl* pesadas — **riches** ['rɪtʃəz] *npl* : riquezas *fpl* — **richness** ['rɪtʃnəs] *n* : riqueza *f*

rickety ['rɪkəti] *adj* : desvencijado, destartalado

ricochet ['rɪkəˌʃeɪ, -ˌʃɛt] *n* : rebote *m* — ~ *vi* -cheted [-ˌʃeɪd] *or* -chetted [-ˌʃɛtəd]; -cheting [-ˌʃeɪŋ] *or* -chetting [-ˌʃɛtɪŋ] : rebotar

rid ['rɪd] *vt* **rid; ridding** 1 : librar 2 get ~ **of** : deshacerse de — **riddance** ['rɪdənts] *n* good ~! : ¡adiós y buen viaje!

riddle¹ ['rɪdəl] *n* : acertijo *m*, adivinanza *f*

riddle² *vt* -dled; -dling 1 : acribillar 2 **riddled with** : lleno de

ride ['raɪd] *v* **rode** ['roːd]; **ridden** ['rɪdən]; **riding** *vt* 1 : montar (a caballo, en bicicleta), ir (en autobús, etc.) 2 TRAVERSE : recorrer — *vi* 1 *or* ~ **horseback** : montar a caballo 2 : ir (en auto, etc.) — ~ *n* 1 : paseo *m*, vuelta *f* 2 : aparato *m* (en un parque de diversiones) — **rider** ['raɪdər] *n* 1 : jinete *mf* (a caballo) 2 CYCLIST : ciclista *mf*, motociclista *mf*

ridge ['rɪdʒ] *n* : cadena *f* (de montañas)

ridiculous [rəˈdɪkjələs] *adj* : ridículo — **ridicule** ['rɪdəˌkjuːl] *n* : burlas *fpl* — ~ *vt* -culed; -culing : ridiculizar

rife ['raɪf] *adj* **1** : extendido **2 be ~ with** : estar plagado de

rifle¹ ['raɪfəl] *vi* **-fled; -fling ~ through** : revolver

rifle² *n* : rifle *m*, fusil *m*

rift ['rɪft] *n* **1** : grieta *f* **2** : ruptura *f* (entre personas)

rig¹ ['rɪg] *vt* : amañar (una elección)

rig² *vt* **rigged; rigging 1** : aparejar (un barco) **2** EQUIP : equipar **3** *or* **~ out** DRESS : vestir **4** *or* **~ up** CONSTRUCT : construir — **~** *n* **1** : aparejo *m* (de un barco) **2** *or* **oil ~** : plataforma *f* petrolífera — **rigging** ['rɪgɪŋ, -gən] *n* : aparejo *m*

right ['raɪt] *adj* JUST : bueno, justo **2** CORRECT : correcto **3** APPROPRIATE : apropiado, adecuado **4** STRAIGHT : recto **5 be ~** : tener razón **6 — right–hand — ~** *n* **1** GOOD : bien *m* **2** ENTITLEMENT : derecho *m* **3 on the ~** : a la derecha **4** *or* **~ side** : derecha *f* — **~** *adv* **1** WELL : bien **2** PRECISELY : justo **3** DIRECTLY : derecho **4** IMMEDIATELY : inmediatamente **5** COMPLETELY : completamente **6** *or* **to the ~** : a la derecha — **~** *vt* **1** STRAIGHTEN : enderezar **2 ~ a wrong** : reparar un daño — **right angle** *n* : ángulo *m* recto — **righteous** ['raɪtʃəs] *adj* : recto, honrado — **rightful** ['raɪtfəl] *adj* : legítimo — **right–hand** ['raɪt'hænd] *adj* : derecho — **right–handed** ['raɪt'hændəd] *adj* : diestro — **rightly** ['raɪtli] *adv* **1** : justamente **2** CORRECTLY : correctamente — **right–wing** ['raɪt'wɪŋ] *adj* : derechista

rigid ['rɪdʒəd] *adj* : rígido

rigor *or Brit* **rigour** ['rɪgər] *n* : rigor *m* — **rigorous** ['rɪgərəs] *adj* : riguroso

rim ['rɪm] *n* **1** EDGE : borde *m* **2** : llanta *f* (de una rueda) **3** : montura *f* (de anteojos)

rind ['raɪnd] *n* : corteza *f*

ring¹ ['rɪŋ] *v* **rang** ['ræŋ]; **rung** ['rʌŋ]; **ringing** *vi* **1** : sonar (dícese de un timbre, etc.) **2** RESOUND : resonar — *vt* : tocar (un timbre, etc.) — **~** *n* **1** : toque *m* (de un timbre, etc.) **2** CALL : llamada *f* (por teléfono)

ring² *n* **1** : anillo *m*, sortija *f* **2** BAND, HOOP : aro *m* **3** CIRCLE : círculo *m* **4** *or* **boxing ~** : cuadrilátero *m* **5** NETWORK : red *f* — **~** *vt* : cercar, rodear — **ringleader** ['rɪŋˌliːdər] *n* : cabecilla *mf*

ringlet ['rɪŋlət] *n* : rizo *m*, bucle *m*

rink ['rɪŋk] *n* : pista *f* (de patinaje)

rinse ['rɪnts] *vt* **rinsed; rinsing** : enjuagar — **~** *n* : enjuague *m*

riot ['raɪət] *n* : disturbio *m* — **~** *vi* : causar disturbios — **rioter** ['raɪətər] *n* : alborotador *m*, -dora *f*

rip ['rɪp] *v* **ripped; ripping** *vt* **1** : rasgar, desgarrar **2 ~ off** : arrancar — *vi* : rasgarse — **~** *n* : rasgón *m*, desgarrón *m*

ripe ['raɪp] *adj* **riper; ripest 1** : maduro **2 ~ for** : listo para — **ripen** ['raɪpən] *v* : madurar — **ripeness** ['raɪpnəs] *n* : madurez *f*

rip-off ['rɪpˌɔf] *n* : timo *m fam*

ripple ['rɪpəl] *v* **-pled; -pling** *vi* : rizarse (dícese de agua) — *vt* : rizar — **~** *n* : onda *f*, rizo *m*

rise ['raɪz] *vi* **rose** ['roːz]; **risen** ['rɪzən]; **rising 1** GET UP : levantarse **2** : salir (dícese del sol, etc.) **3** ASCEND : subir **4** INCREASE : aumentar **5 ~ up** REBEL : sublevarse — **~** *n* **1** ASCENT : subida *f* **2** INCREASE : aumento *m* **3** SLOPE : cuesta *f* — **riser** ['raɪzər] *n* **1 early ~** : madrugador *m*, -dora *f* **2 late ~** : dormilón *m*, -lona *f*

risk ['rɪsk] *n* : riesgo *m* — *vt* : arriesgar — **risky** ['rɪski] *adj* **riskier; -est** : arriesgado, riesgoso *Lat*

rite ['raɪt] *n* : rito *m* — **ritual** ['rɪtʃuəl] *adj* : ritual — **~** *n* : ritual *m*

rival ['raɪvəl] *n* : rival *mf* — **~** *adj* : rival — **~** *vt* **-valed** *or* **-valled; -valing** *or* **-valling** : rivalizar con — **rivalry** ['raɪvəlri] *n, pl* **-ries** : rivalidad *f*

river ['rɪvər] *n* : río *m*

rivet ['rɪvət] *n* : remache *m* — **~** *vt* **1** : remachar **2** FIX : fijar (los ojos, etc.) **3 be ~ed by** : estar fascinado con

roach ['roːtʃ] → **cockroach**

road ['roːd] *n* **1** : carretera *f* **2** STREET : calle *f* **3** PATH : camino *m* — **roadblock** ['roːdˌblɑk] *n* : control *m* — **roadside** ['roːdˌsaɪd] *n* : borde *m* de la carretera — **roadway** ['roːdˌweɪ] *n* : carretera *f*

roam ['roːm] *vi* : vagar — *vt* : vagar por

roar ['ror] *vi* **1** : rugir **2 ~ with laughter** : reírse a carcajadas — *vt* : decir a gritos — **~** *n* : rugido *m* (de un animal), estruendo *m* (de un avión, etc.)

roast ['roːst] *vt* : asar (carne, etc.), tostar (café, etc.) — *vi* : asarse — **~** *n* : asado *m* — **~** *adj* : asado — **roast beef** *n* : rosbif *m*

rob ['rɑb] *v* **robbed; robbing** *vt* **1** : robar **2 ~ of** : privar de — *vi* : robar — **robber** ['rɑbər] *n* : ladrón *m*, -drona *f* — **robbery** ['rɑbəri] *n, pl* **-beries** : robo *m*

robe ['roːb] *n* **1** : toga *f* (de un magistrado, etc.) **2** → **bathrobe**

robin ['rɑbən] *n* : petirrojo *m*

robot ['ro:bɑt, -bət] n : robot m

robust [ro'bʌst, 'ro:bʌst] adj : robusto

rock¹ ['rɑk] vt 1 : acunar (a un niño), mecer (una cuna) 2 SHAKE : sacudir — vi : mecerse — ~ n or ~ **music** : música f rock

rock² n 1 : roca f (sustancia) 2 BOULDER : peña f, peñasco m 3 STONE : piedra f

rocket ['rɑkət] n : cohete m

rocking chair n : mecedora f

rocky ['rɑki] adj **rockier; -est** 1 : rocoso 2 SHAKY : tambaleante

rod ['rɑd] n 1 : varilla f 2 or **fishing** ~ : caña f de pescar

rode → **ride**

rodent ['ro:dənt] n : roedor m

rodeo ['ro:di,o:, ro'dei,o:] n, pl **-deos** : rodeo m

roe ['ro:] n : hueva f

rogue ['ro:g] n : pícaro m, -ra f

role ['ro:l] n : papel m

roll ['ro:l] n 1 : rollo m (de película, etc.) 2 LIST : lista f 3 : redoble m (de un tambor) 4 SWAYING : balanceo m 5 BUN : pancito m Lat, panecillo m Spain — ~ vt 1 : hacer rodar 2 or ~ **out** : estirar (masa) 3 ~ **up** : enrollar (papel, etc.), arremangar (una manga) — vi 1 : rodar 2 SWAY : balancearse 3 ~ **around** : revolcarse 4 ~ **over** : darse la vuelta — **roller** ['ro:lər] n 1 : rodillo m 2 CURLER : rulo m — **roller coaster** ['ro:lər,ko:stər] n : montaña f rusa — **roller–skate** ['ro:lər,skeit] vi **-skated; -skating** : patinar (sobre ruedas) — **roller skate** n : patín m (de ruedas)

Roman ['ro:mən] adj : romano — **Roman Catholic** adj : católico

romance [ro'mæns, 'ro:,mæns] n 1 : novela f romántica 2 AFFAIR : romance m

Romanian [ru'meiniən, ro-] adj : rumano — ~ n : rumano m (idioma)

romantic [ro'mæntik] adj : romántico

romp ['rɑmp] n : retozo m — vi : retozar

roof ['ru:f, 'rʊf] n, pl **roofs** ['ru:fs, 'rʊfs; 'ru:vz, 'rʊvz] 1 : tejado m, techo m 2 ~ **of the mouth** : paladar m — **roofing** ['ru:fiŋ, 'rʊfiŋ] n : techumbre f — **rooftop** ['ru:f,tɑp, 'rʊf-] n : tejado m, techo m

rook¹ ['rʊk] n : grajo m (ave)

rook² n : torre f (en ajedrez)

rookie ['rʊki] n : novato m, -ta f

room ['ru:m, 'rʊm] n 1 : cuarto m, habitación f 2 BEDROOM : dormitorio m 3 SPACE : espacio m 4 OPPORTUNITY : posibilidad f — **roommate** ['ru:m-, meit, 'rʊm-] n : compañero m, -ra f de

cuarto — **roomy** ['ru:mi, 'rʊmi] adj **roomier; -est** : espacioso

roost ['ru:st] n : percha f — ~ vi : posarse — **rooster** ['ru:stər, 'rʊs-] n : gallo m

root¹ ['ru:t, 'rʊt] n : raíz f — ~ vt ~ **out** : extirpar

root² vi ~ **around in** : hurgar en

root³ vi ~ **for** SUPPORT : alentar

rope ['ro:p] n : cuerda f — ~ vt **roped; roping** 1 : atar (con cuerda) 2 ~ **off** : acordonar

rosary ['ro:zəri] n, pl **-ries** : rosario m

rose¹ → **rise**

rose² ['ro:z] n : rosa f (flor), rosa m (color) — ~ adj : rosa — **rosebush** ['ro:z,bʊʃ] n : rosal m

rosemary ['ro:z,meri] n, pl **-maries** : romero m

Rosh Hashanah [rɑʃhɑ'ʃɑnə, ,ro:ʃ-] n : el Año Nuevo judío

roster ['rɑstər] n : lista f

rostrum ['rɑstrəm] n, pl **-tra** or **-trums** [-trə] : tribuna f

rosy ['ro:zi] adj **rosier; -est** 1 : sonrosado 2 PROMISING : halagüeno

rot ['rɑt] v **rotted; rotting** vi : pudrirse — vt : pudrir — ~ n : putrefacción f

rotary ['ro:təri] adj : rotativo — ~ n : rotonda f, glorieta f Spain

rotate ['ro:teit] v **-tated; -tating** vi : girar — vt 1 : girar 2 ALTERNATE : alternar — **rotation** [ro'teiʃən] n : rotación f

rote ['ro:t] n **by** ~ : de memoria

rotor ['ro:tər] n : rotor m

rotten ['rɑtən] adj 1 : podrido 2 BAD : malo

rouge ['ru:ʒ, 'ru:dʒ] n : colorete m

rough ['rʌf] adj 1 COARSE : áspero 2 RUGGED : accidentado 3 CHOPPY : agitado 4 DIFFICULT : duro 5 FORCEFUL : brusco 6 APPROXIMATE : aproximado 7 UNREFINED : tosco 8 ~ **draft** : borrador m — ~ vt 1 ~ **roughen** 2 ~ **up** BEAT : dar una paliza a — **roughage** ['rʌfidʒ] n : fibra f — **roughen** ['rʌfən] vt : poner áspero — vi : ponerse áspero — **roughly** ['rʌfli] adv 1 : bruscamente 2 ABOUT : aproximadamente — **roughness** ['rʌfnəs] n COARSENESS : aspereza f

roulette [ru:'let] n : ruleta f

round ['raʊnd] adj : redondo — ~ adv → **around** — ~ n 1 : círculo m 2 : ronda f (de bebidas, negociaciones, etc.) 3 : asalto m (en boxeo), vuelta f (en juegos) 4 ~ **of applause** : aplauso m 5 ~**s** npl : visitas fpl (de un médico), rondas fpl (de un policía, etc.) — ~ vt 1 TURN : doblar 2 ~ **off**

: redondear 3 ~ off *or* ~ out COM-
PLETE : rematar 4 ~ up GATHER : reunir (personas), rodear (ganado) — ~
prep → **around** — **roundabout**
['raʊndə,baʊt] *adj* : indirecto —
round–trip ['raʊnd,trɪp] *n* : viaje *m* de
ida y vuelta — **roundup** ['raʊnd,ʌp] *n*
: rodeo *m* (de animales), redada *f* (de
delincuentes, etc.)
rouse ['raʊz] *vt* **roused; rousing 1**
AWAKEN : despertar **2** EXCITE : excitar
rout ['raʊt] *n* : derrota *f* aplastante — ~
vt : derrotar
route ['ru:t, 'raʊt] *n* **1** : ruta *f* **2** *or* **delivery ~** : recorrido *m*
routine [ru:'ti:n] *n* : rutina *f* — ~ *adj*
: rutinario
rove ['ro:v] *v* **roved; roving** *vi* : errar,
vagar — *vt* : errar por
row¹ ['ro:] *vt* **1** : llevar a remo **2 ~ a
boat** : remar — *vi* : remar
row² *n* **1** : fila *f* (de gente o asientos),
hilera *f* (de casas, etc.) **2 in a ~**
SUCCESSIVELY : seguido
row³ ['raʊ] *n* **1** RACKET : bulla *f* **2** QUAR-
REL : pelea *f*
rowboat ['ro:,bo:t] *n* : bote *m* de remos
rowdy ['raʊdi] *adj* **-dier; -est** : escandaloso, alborotador — ~ *n, pl* **-dies**
: alborotador *m*, -dora *f*
royal ['rɔɪəl] *adj* : real — **royalty** ['rɔɪəlti]
n, pl **-ties 1** : realeza *f* **2 royalties** *npl*
: derechos *mpl* de autor
rub ['rʌb] *v* **rubbed; rubbing** *vt* **1** : frotar **2** CHAFE : rozar **3 ~ in** : aplicar
frotando — *vi* **1 ~ against** : rozar **2
~ off** : salir (al frotar) — ~ *n* : fro-
tamiento *m*
rubber ['rʌbər] *n* **1** : goma *f*, caucho *m* **2
~s** *npl* : chanclos *mpl* — **rubber
band** *n* : goma *f* (elástica) — **rubber
stamp** : sello *m* (de goma) — **rub-
bery** ['rʌbəri] *adj* : gomoso
rubbish ['rʌbɪʃ] *n* **1** : basura *f* **2** NON-
SENSE : tonterías *fpl*
rubble ['rʌbəl] *n* : escombros *mpl*
ruby ['ru:bi] *n, pl* **-bies** : rubí *m*
rudder ['rʌdər] *n* : timón *m*
ruddy ['rʌdi] *adj* **-dier; -est** : rubicundo
rude ['ru:d] *adj* **ruder; rudest 1** IMPO-
LITE : grosero, mal educado **2** ABRUPT
: brusco — **rudely** ['ru:dli] *adv*
: groseramente — **rudeness** ['ru:dnəs]
n : mala educación *f*
rudiment ['ru:dəmənt] *n* : rudimento *m*
— **rudimentary** [,ru:də'mentəri] *adj*
: rudimentario
rue ['ru:] *vt* **rued; ruing** : lamentar —
rueful ['ru:fəl] *adj* : triste, arrepentido
ruffle ['rʌfəl] *vt* **-fled; -fling 1** : des-

peinar (pelo), erizar (plumas) **2** VEX
: alterar, contrariar — ~ *n* : volante *m*
(de un vestido, etc.)
rug ['rʌg] *n* : alfombra *f*, tapete *m*
rugged ['rʌgəd] *adj* **1** : escabroso (dícese del terreno), escarpado (dícese de
montañas) **2** HARSH : duro **3** STURDY
: fuerte
ruin ['ru:ən] *n* : ruina *f* — ~ *vt* : arruinar
rule ['ru:l] *n* **1** : regla *f* **2** CONTROL : dominio *m* **3 as a ~** : por lo general —
~ *v* **ruled; ruling** *vt* **1** GOVERN : gobernar **2** : fallar (dícese de un juez) **3 ~
out** : descartar — *vi* : gobernar, reinar
— **ruler** ['ru:lər] *n* **1** : gobernante *mf*;
soberano *m*, -na *f* **2** : regla *f* (para
medir) — **ruling** ['ru:lɪŋ] *n* VERDICT
: fallo *m*
rum ['rʌm] *n* : ron *m*
Rumanian [rʊ'meɪniən] → **Romanian**
rumble ['rʌmbəl] *vi* **-bled; -bling 1** : retumbar **2** : hacer ruidos (dícese del estómago) — ~ *n* : retumbo *m*, estruendo *m*
rummage ['rʌmɪdʒ] *vi* **-maged; -maging**
: hurgar
rumor ['ru:mər] *n* : rumor *m* — ~ *vt* **be
~ed** : rumorearse
rump ['rʌmp] *n* **1** : grupa *f* (de un animal) **2 ~ steak** : filete *m* de cadera
rumpus ['rʌmpəs] *n* : lío *m*, jaleo *m* fam
run ['rʌn] *v* **ran** ['ræn]; **run; running** *vi* **1**
: correr **2** FUNCTION : funcionar **3** LAST
: durar **4** : desteñir (dícese de colores)
5 EXTEND : correr, extenderse **6** : presentarse (como candidato) **7 ~ away**
: huir **8 ~ into** ENCOUNTER : tropezar
con **9 ~ into** HIT : chocar contra **10
~ late** : ir retrasado **11 ~ out of**
: quedarse sin **12 ~ over** : atropellar
— *vt* **1** : correr **2** OPERATE : hacer funcionar **3** : hacer correr (agua) **4** MAN-
AGE : dirigir **5 ~ a fever** : tener fiebre
— ~ *n* **1** : carrera *f* **2** TRIP : viaje *m*,
paseo *m* (en coche) **3** SERIES : serie *f* **4
in the long ~** : a la larga **5 in the
short ~** : a corto plazo — **runaway**
['rʌnə,weɪ] *n* : fugitivo *m*, -va *f* — ~
adj : fugitivo — **rundown** ['rʌn,daʊn]
: resumen *m* — **run–down** ['rʌn'daʊn]
adj **1** : destartalado **2** EXHAUSTED
: agotado
rung¹ → **ring¹**
rung² ['rʌŋ] *n* : peldaño *m* (de una escalera, etc.)
runner ['rʌnər] *n* **1** : corredor *m*, -dora *f*
2 : patín *m* (de un trineo), riel *m* (de un
cajón, etc.) — **runner–up** [,rʌnər'ʌp] *n,
pl* **runners–up** : subcampeón *m*,
-peona *f* — **running** ['rʌnɪŋ] *adj* **1**

FLOWING : corriente **2** CONTINUOUS : continuo **3** CONSECUTIVE : seguido

runt ['rʌnt] *n* : animal *m* más pequeño (de una camada)

runway ['rʌn,weɪ] *n* : pista *f* de aterrizaje

rupture ['rʌptʃər] *n* : ruptura *f* — ~ *v* **-tured; -turing** *vt* : romper — *vi* : reventar

rural ['rʊrəl] *adj* : rural

ruse ['ruːs, 'ruːz] *n* : ardid *m*

rush[1] ['rʌʃ] *n* : junco *m* (planta)

rush[2] *vi* : ir de prisa — *vt* **1** : apresurar, apurar **2** ATTACK : asaltar **3** : llevar rápidamente (al hospital, etc.) — ~ *n* **1** : prisa *f*, apuro *m* **2** : ráfaga *f* (de aire), torrente *m* (de agua) — ~ *adj* : urgente — **rush hour** *n* : hora *f* punta

russet ['rʌsət] *n* : color *m* rojizo

Russian ['rʌʃən] *adj* : ruso — ~ *n* : ruso *m* (idioma)

rust ['rʌst] *n* : herrumbre *f*, óxido *m* — ~ *vi* : oxidarse — *vt* : oxidar

rustic ['rʌstɪk] *adj* : rústico

rustle ['rʌsəl] *v* **-tled; -tling** *vt* **1** : hacer susurrar **2** : robar (ganado) — *vi* : susurrar — ~ *n* : susurro *m*

rusty ['rʌsti] *adj* **rustier; -est** : oxidado

rut ['rʌt] *n* **1** : surco *m* **2 be in a ~** : ser esclavo de la rutina

ruthless ['ruːθləs] *adj* : despiadado, cruel

rye ['raɪ] *n* : centeno *m*

S

s ['es] *n, pl* **s's** *or* **ss** ['esəz] : s *f*, decimonovena letra del alfabeto inglés

Sabbath ['sæbəθ] *n* **1** : sábado *m* (día santo judío) **2** : domingo *m* (día santo cristiano)

sabotage ['sæbə,taʒ] *n* : sabotaje *m* — ~ *vt* **-taged; -taging** : sabotear

saccharin ['sækərən] *n* : sacarina *f*

sack ['sæk] *n* : saco *m* — ~ *vt* **1** FIRE : despedir **2** PLUNDER : saquear

sacrament ['sækrəmənt] *n* : sacramento *m*

sacred ['seɪkrəd] *adj* : sagrado

sacrifice ['sækrə,faɪs] *n* : sacrificio *m* — ~ *vt* **-ficed; -ficing** : sacrificar

sacrilege ['sækrəlɪdʒ] *n* : sacrilegio *m* — **sacrilegious** [,sækrə'lɪdʒəs, -'liː-] *adj* : sacrílego

sad ['sæd] *adj* **sadder; saddest** : triste — **sadden** ['sædən] *vt* : entristecer

saddle ['sædəl] *n* : silla *f* (de montar) — ~ *vt* **-dled; -dling 1** : ensillar (un caballo, etc.) **2 ~ s.o. with sth** : cargar a algn con algo

sadistic [sə'dɪstɪk] *adj* : sádico

sadness ['sædnəs] *n* : tristeza *f*

safari [sə'fɑri, -'fær-] *n* : safari *m*

safe ['seɪf] *adj* **safer; safest 1** : seguro **2** UNHARMED : ileso **3** CAREFUL : prudente **4 ~ and sound** : sano y salvo — ~ *n* : caja *f* fuerte — **safeguard** ['seɪf,gɑrd] *n* : salvaguarda *f* — ~ *vt* : salvaguardar — **safely** ['seɪfli] *adv* **1** : sin peligro **2** : llegar sin novedad — **safety** ['seɪfti] *n, pl* **-ties** : seguridad *f* — **safety belt** *n* : cinturón *m* de seguridad — **safety pin** *n* : imperdible *m*

saffron ['sæfrən] *n* : azafrán *m*

sag ['sæg] *vi* **sagged; sagging 1** : combarse **2** GIVE : aflojarse **3** FLAG : flaquear

saga ['sɑgə, 'sæ-] *n* : saga *f*

sage[1] ['seɪdʒ] *n* : salvia *f* (planta)

sage[2] *adj* **sager; -est** : sabio — ~ *n* : sabio *m*, -bia *f*

said → **say**

sail ['seɪl] *n* **1** : vela *f* (de un barco) **2 go for a ~** : salir a navegar **3 set ~** : zarpar — ~ *vi* : navegar — *vt* : gobernar (un barco), navegar (el mar) — **sailboat** ['seɪl,boːt] *n* : velero *m* — **sailor** ['seɪlər] *n* : marinero *m*

saint ['seɪnt, *before a name* ,seɪnt *or* sənt] *n* : santo *m*, -ta *f* — **saintly** ['seɪntli] *adj* **saintlier; -est** : santo

sake ['seɪk] *n* **1 for goodness' ~!** : ¡por Dios! **2 for the ~ of** : por (el bien de)

salad ['sæləd] *n* : ensalada *f*

salamander ['sælə,mændər] *n* : salamandra *f*

salami [sə'lɑmi] *n* : salami *m*

salary ['sæləri] *n, pl* **-ries** : sueldo *m*

sale ['seɪl] *n* **1** : venta *f* **2 for ~** : se vende **3 on ~** : de rebaja — **salesman** ['seɪlzmən] *n, pl* **-men** [-mən, -,men] : vendedor *m*, dependiente *m* — **saleswoman** ['seɪlz,wʊmən] *n, pl* **-women** [-,wɪmən] : vendedora *f*, dependienta *f*

salient ['seɪljənt] *adj* : saliente

saliva [sə'laɪvə] *n* : saliva *f*

sallow ['sæloː] *adj* : amarillento, cetrino

salmon ['sæmən] *ns & pl* : salmón *m*

salon [sə'lɑn, 'sæ,lɑn] *n* → **beauty salon**

saloon [sə'luːn] n : bar m

salsa ['sɔlsə, 'sɑl-] n : salsa f mexicana, salsa f picante

salt ['sɔlt] n : sal f — ~ vt : salar — saltwater ['sɔlt,wɔtər, -wɑ-] adj : de agua salada — salty ['sɔlti] adj saltier; -est : salado

salute [sə'luːt] v -luted; -luting vt : saludar — vi : hacer un saludo — ~ n : saludo m

salvage ['sælvɪdʒ] n : salvamento m — ~ vt -vaged; -vaging : salvar

salvation [sæl'veɪʃən] n : salvación f

salve ['sæv, 'sav] n : ungüento m

same ['seɪm] adj 1 : mismo 2 be the ~ (as) : ser igual (que) 3 the ~ thing (as) : la misma cosa (que) — ~ pron 1 all the ~ : igual 2 the ~ : lo mismo — ~ adv the ~ : igual

sample ['sæmpəl] n : muestra f — ~ vt -pled; -pling : probar

sanatorium [,sænə'tɔriəm] n, pl -riums or -ria [-iə] : sanatorio m

sanctify ['sæŋktə,faɪ] vt -fied; -fying : santificar

sanction ['sæŋkʃən] n : sanción f — ~ vt : sancionar

sanctity ['sæŋktəti] n, pl -ties : santidad f

sanctuary ['sæŋktʃʊˌɛri] n, pl -aries : santuario m

sand ['sænd] n : arena f — ~ vt : lijar (madera)

sandal ['sændəl] n : sandalia f

sandpaper ['sænd,peɪpər] n : papel m de lija — ~ vt : lijar

sandwich ['sænd,wɪtʃ] n : sandwich m, bocadillo m Spain — ~ vt ~ between : meter entre

sandy ['sændi] adj sandier; -est : arenoso

sane ['seɪn] adj saner; sanest 1 : cuerdo 2 SENSIBLE : sensato

sang → sing

sanitarium [,sænə'tɛriəm] n, pl -iums or -ia [-iə] → sanatorium

sanitary ['sænəteri] adj 1 : sanitario 2 HYGIENIC : higiénico — sanitary napkin n : compresa f (higiénica) — sanitation [,sænə'teɪʃən] n : sanidad f

sanity ['sænəti] n : cordura f

sank → sink

Santa Claus ['sæntə,klɔz] n : Papá m Noel

sap¹ ['sæp] n 1 : savia f (de una planta) 2 SUCKER : inocentón m, -tona f

sap² vt sapped; sapping : minar (la fuerza, etc.)

sapphire ['sæˌfaɪr] n : zafiro m

sarcasm ['sɑrˌkæzəm] n : sarcasmo m — sarcastic [sɑr'kæstɪk] adj : sarcástico

sardine [sɑr'diːn] n : sardina f

sash ['sæʃ] n : faja f (de un vestido), fajín m (de un uniforme)

sat → sit

satanic [sə'tænɪk, seɪ-] adj : satánico

satchel ['sætʃəl] n : cartera f

satellite ['sætə,laɪt] n : satélite m

satin ['sætən] n : raso m

satire ['sæˌtaɪr] n : sátira f — satiric [sə-'tɪrɪk] or satirical [-ɪkəl] adj : satírico

satisfaction [,sætəs'fækʃən] n : satisfacción f — satisfactory [,sætəs'fæktəri] adj : satisfactorio — satisfy ['sætəs-ˌfaɪ] v -fied; -fying vt 1 : satisfacer 2 CONVINCE : convencer — satisfying adj : satisfactorio

saturate ['sætʃəˌreɪt] vt -rated; -rating 1 : saturar 2 DRENCH : empapar — saturation [,sætʃə'reɪʃən] n : saturación f

Saturday ['sætərˌdeɪ, -di] n : sábado m

Saturn ['sætərn] n : Saturno m

sauce ['sɔs] n : salsa f — saucepan ['sɔsˌpæn] n : cacerola f — saucer ['sɔsər] n : platillo m — saucy ['sɔsi] adj saucier; -est IMPUDENT : descarado

sauna ['sɔnə, 'saʊnə] n : sauna mf

saunter ['sɔntər, 'san-] vi : pasear

sausage ['sɔsɪdʒ] n : salchicha f

sauté [sɔ'teɪ, soʊ-] vt -téed or -téd; -téing : saltear, sofreír

savage ['sævɪdʒ] adj : salvaje, feroz — ~ n : salvaje mf — savagery ['sævɪdʒri, -dʒəri] n, pl -ries : ferocidad f

save ['seɪv] vt saved; saving 1 RESCUE : salvar 2 RESERVE : guardar 3 : ahorrar (dinero, tiempo, etc.) — ~ prep EXCEPT : salvo

savior ['seɪvjər] n : salvador m, -dora f

savor ['seɪvər] vt : saborear — savory ['seɪvəri] adj : sabroso

saw¹ → see

saw² ['sɔ] n : sierra f — ~ vt sawed; sawed or sawn; sawing : serrar — sawdust ['sɔˌdʌst] n : serrín m, aserrín m

saxophone ['sæksəˌfoːn] n : saxofón m

say ['seɪ] v said ['sɛd]; saying; says ['sɛz] vt 1 : decir 2 INDICATE : marcar (dícese de relojes, etc.) — vi 1 : decir 2 that is to ~ : es decir — ~ n, pl says ['seɪz] 1 have no ~ : no tener ni voz ni voto 2 have one's ~ : dar su opinión — saying ['seɪɪŋ] n : refrán m

scab ['skæb] n 1 : costra f (de una herida) 2 STRIKEBREAKER : esquirol mf

scaffold ['skæfəld, -ˌfoːld] n : andamio m (en construcción)

scald ['skɔld] vt : escaldar

scale¹ ['skeɪl] *n* : balanza *f* (para pesar)
scale² *n* : escama *f* (de un pez, etc.) — **~** *vt* scaled; scaling : escamar
scale³ *vt* scaled; scaling 1 CLIMB : escalar 2 — **down** : reducir — *n* : escala *f* (musical, salarial, etc.)
scallion ['skæljən] *n* : cebolleta *f*
scallop ['skɑləp, 'skæ-] *n* : vieira *f*
scalp ['skælp] *n* : cuero *m* cabelludo
scam ['skæm] *n* 1 : estafa *f*, timo *m fam*
scamper ['skæmpər] *vi* **~ away** : irse corriendo
scan ['skæn] *vt* scanned; scanning 1 : escandir (versos) 2 EXAMINE : escudriñar 3 SKIM : echar un vistazo a 4 : escanear (en informática)
scandal ['skændəl] *n* 1 : escándalo *m* 2 GOSSIP : habladurías *fpl* — **scandalous** ['skændələs] *adj* : escandaloso
Scandinavian [,skændə'neɪviən] *adj* : escandinavo
scant ['skænt] *adj* : escaso
scapegoat ['skeɪp,goːt] *n* : chivo *m* expiatorio
scar ['skɑr] *n* : cicatriz *f* — **~** *v* scarred; scarring *vt* : dejar una cicatriz en — *vi* : cicatrizar
scarce ['skers] *adj* scarcer; -est : escaso — **scarcely** ['skersli] *adv* : apenas — **scarcity** ['skersəṭi] *n, pl* -ties : escasez *f*
scare ['sker] *vt* scared; scaring 1 : asustar 2 be **~d of** : tener miedo a — **~** *n* 1 FRIGHT : susto *m* 2 ALARM : pánico *m* — **scarecrow** ['sker,kroː] *n* : espantapájaros *m*, espantajo *m*
scarf ['skɑrf] *n, pl* scarves ['skɑrvz] *or* scarfs 1 : bufanda *f* 2 KERCHIEF : pañuelo *m*
scarlet ['skɑrlət] *adj* : escarlata — **scarlet fever** *n* : escarlatina *f*
scary ['skeri] *adj* scarier; -est : que da miedo
scathing ['skeɪðɪŋ] *adj* : mordaz
scatter ['skæṭər] *vt* 1 STREW : esparcir 2 DISPERSE : dispersar — *vi* : dispersarse
scavenger ['skævəndʒər] *n* : carroñero *m*, -ra *f* (animal)
scenario [sə'næri,oː, -'nɑr-] *n, pl* -ios 1 : guión *m* (cinemático) 2 the **worst-case ~** : el peor de los casos
scene ['siːn] *n* 1 : escena *f* 2 behind the **~s** : entre bastidores 3 make a **~** : armar un escándalo — **scenery** ['siːnəri] *n, pl* -eries 1 : decorado *m* 2 LANDSCAPE : paisaje *m* — **scenic** ['siːnɪk] *adj* : pintoresco
scent ['sent] *n* 1 : aroma *m* 2 PERFUME : perfume *m* 3 TRAIL : rastro *m* — **scented** ['sentəd] *adj* : perfumado

sceptic ['skeptɪk] → **skeptic**
schedule ['ske,dʒuːl, -dʒəl, *esp Brit* 'ʃed-juːl] *n* 1 : programa *m* 2 TIMETABLE : horario *m* 3 behind **~** : atrasado, con retraso 4 on **~** : según lo previsto — **~** *vt* -uled; -uling : planear, programar
scheme ['skiːm] *n* 1 PLAN : plan *m* 2 PLOT : intriga *f* 3 DESIGN : esquema *f* — **~** *vi* schemed; scheming : intrigar
schism ['sɪzəm, 'skɪ-] *n* : cisma *m*
schizophrenia [,skɪtsə'friːniə, ,skɪzə-, -'frɛ-] *n* : esquizofrenia *f* — **schizophrenic** [,skɪtsə'frɛnɪk, ,skɪzə-] *adj* : esquizofrénico
scholar ['skɑlər] *n* : erudito *m*, -ta *f* — **scholarly** ['skɑlərli] *adj* : erudito — **scholarship** ['skɑlər,ʃɪp] *n* 1 : erudición *f* 2 GRANT : beca *f*
school¹ ['skuːl] *n* : banco *m* (de peces)
school² *n* 1 : escuela *f* 2 COLLEGE : universidad *f* 3 DEPARTMENT : facultad *f* — **~** *vt* : instruir — **schoolboy** ['skuːl,bɔɪ] *n* : colegial *m* — **schoolgirl** ['skuːl,gərl] *n* : colegiala *f* — **schoolteacher** ['skuːl,tiːtʃər] *n* → **teacher**
science ['saɪənts] *n* : ciencia *f* — **scientific** [,saɪən'tɪfɪk] *adj* : científico — **scientist** ['saɪəntɪst] *n* : científico *m*, -ca *f*
scissors ['sɪzərz] *npl* : tijeras *fpl*
scoff ['skɑf] *vi* **~ at** : burlarse de, mofarse de
scold ['skoːld] *vt* : regañar
scoop ['skuːp] *n* 1 : pala *f* 2 : noticia *f* exclusiva (en periodismo) — **~** *vt* 1 : sacar (con pala) 2 — **out** : ahuecar 3 — **up** : recoger
scoot ['skuːt] *vi* : ir rápidamente — **scooter** ['skuːṭər] *n* 1 : patinete *m* 2 *or* motor **~** : escúter *m*
scope ['skoːp] *n* 1 RANGE : alcance *m* 2 OPPORTUNITY : posibilidades *fpl*
scorch ['skɔrtʃ] *vt* : chamuscar
score ['skor] *n, pl* scores 1 : tanteo *m* (en deportes) 2 RATING : puntuación *f* 3 : partitura *f* (musical) 4 *or pl* score TWENTY : veintena *f* 5 keep **~** : llevar la cuenta 6 on that **~** : en ese sentido — **~** *v* scored; scoring *vt* 1 : marcar, anotarse *Lat* (un tanto) 2 : sacar (una nota) — *vi* : marcar (en deportes)
scorn ['skɔrn] *n* : desdén *m* — **~** *vt* : desdeñar — **scornful** ['skɔrnfəl] *adj* : desdeñoso
scorpion ['skɔrpiən] *n* : alacrán *m*, escorpión *m*
Scot ['skɑt] *n* : escocés *m*, -cesa *f* — **Scotch** ['skɑtʃ] *adj* → **Scottish** — **~** *n or* **~ whiskey** : whisky *m* escocés — **Scottish** ['skɑtɪʃ] *adj* : escocés

scoundrel ['skaʊndrəl] *n* : sinvergüenza *mf*

scour ['skaʊər] *vt* **1** SCRUB : fregar **2** SEARCH : registrar

scourge ['skərdʒ] *n* : azote *m*

scout ['skaʊt] *n* : explorador *m*, -dora *f*

scowl ['skaʊl] *vi* : fruncir el ceño — ~ *n* : ceño *m* fruncido

scram ['skræm] *vi* **scrammed; scramming** : largarse

scramble ['skræmbəl] *v* -**bled; -bling** *vi* **1** CLAMBER : trepar **2** ~ **for** : pelearse por — *vt* : mezclar — ~ *n* : rebatiña *f*, pelea *f* — **scrambled eggs** *npl* : huevos *mpl* revueltos

scrap¹ ['skræp] *n* **1** PIECE : pedazo *m* **2** *or* ~ **metal** : chatarra *f* **3** ~**s** *npl* : sobras — ~ *vt* **scrapped; scrapping** : desechar

scrap² *n* FIGHT : pelea *f*

scrapbook ['skræp,bʊk] *n* : álbum *m* de recortes

scrape ['skreɪp] *v* **scraped; scraping** *vt* **1** : raspar **2** : rasparse (la rodilla, etc.) **3** *or* ~ **off** : raspar **4** ~ **together** : reunir — *vi* **1** RUB : rozar **2** ~ **by** : arreglárselas — ~ *n* **1** : rasguño *m* **2** PREDICAMENT : apuro *m*

scratch ['skrætʃ] *vt* **1** CLAW : arañar **2** MARK : rayar **3** : rascarse (la cabeza, etc.) **4** ~ **out** : tachar — ~ *n* **1** : arañazo *m* **2** MARK : rayón *m* **3** **start from** ~ : empezar desde cero

scrawl ['skrɔl] *v* : garabatear — ~ *n* : garabato *m*

scrawny ['skrɔni] *adj* **scrawnier; -est** : escuálido

scream ['skriːm] *vi* : gritar, chillar — ~ *n* : grito *m*, chillido *m*

screech ['skriːtʃ] *n* **1** : chillido *m* (de personas) **2** : chirrido *m* (de frenos, etc.) — ~ *vi* **1** : chillar **2** : chirriar (dícese de los frenos, etc.)

screen ['skriːn] *n* **1** : pantalla *f* **2** PARTITION : mampara *f* **3** *or* **window** ~ : mosquitero *m* — ~ *vt* **1** SHIELD : proteger **2** HIDE : ocultar **3** : seleccionar (candidatos, etc.)

screw ['skruː] *n* : tornillo *m* — ~ *vt* **1** : atornillar **2** ~ **up** RUIN : fastidiar — **screwdriver** ['skruː,draɪvər] *n* : destornillador *m*

scribble ['skrɪbəl] *v* -**bled; -bling** : garabatear — ~ *n* : garabato *m*

script ['skrɪpt] *n* **1** HANDWRITING : escritura *f* **2** : guión *m* (de cine, etc.) — **scripture** ['skrɪptʃər] *n* **1** : escritos *mpl* sagrados **2 the Scriptures** *npl* : las Escrituras *fpl*

scroll ['skroːl] *n* : rollo *m* (de pergamino, etc.)

scrounge ['skraʊndʒ] *v* **scrounged; scrounging** *vt* : gorrear *fam* — *vi* ~ **around for sth** : andar buscando algo

scrub¹ ['skrʌb] *n* UNDERBRUSH : maleza *f*

scrub² *vt* **scrubbed; scrubbing** SCOUR : fregar — ~ *n* : fregado *m*

scruff ['skrʌf] *n* **by the** ~ **of the neck** : por el pescuezo

scruple ['skruːpəl] *n* : escrúpulo *m* — **scrupulous** ['skruːpjələs] *adj* : escrupuloso

scrutiny ['skruːtəni] *n, pl* -**nies** : análisis *m* cuidadoso — **scrutinize** ['skruːtən,aɪz] *vt* -**nized; -nizing** : escudriñar

scuff ['skʌf] *vt* : raspar, rayar

scuffle ['skʌfəl] *n* : refriega *f*

sculpture ['skʌlptʃər] *n* : escultura *f* — **sculpt** ['skʌlpt] *v* : esculpir — **sculptor** ['skʌlptər] *n* : escultor *m*, -tora *f*

scum ['skʌm] *n* **1** FROTH : espuma *f* **2** : escoria *f* (dícese de personas)

scurry ['skəri] *vi* -**ried; -rying** : corretear

scuttle¹ ['skʌtəl] *n* : cubo *m* (para carbón)

scuttle² *vt* -**tled; -tling** : hundir (un barco)

scuttle³ *vi* SCAMPER : corretear

sea ['siː] *n* **1** : mar *mf* **2 at** ~ : en el mar — ~ *adj* : del mar — **seafarer** ['siː,færər] *n* : marinero *m* — **seafood** ['siː,fuːd] *n* : mariscos *mpl* — **seagull** ['siː,gʌl] *n* : gaviota *f*

seal¹ ['siːl] *n* : foca *f* (animal)

seal² *n* **1** STAMP : sello *m* **2** CLOSURE : cierre *m* (hermético) — ~ *vt* : sellar

seam ['siːm] *n* **1** : costura *f* **2** VEIN : veta *f*

seaman ['siːmən] *n, pl* -**men** [-mən, -ˌmɛn] : marinero *m*

seamy ['siːmi] *adj* **seamier; -est** : sórdido

seaplane ['siː,pleɪn] *n* : hidroavión *m*

seaport ['siː,port] *n* : puerto *m* marítimo

search ['sərtʃ] *vt* : registrar — *vi* ~ **for** : buscar — ~ *n* **1** : registro *m* **2** HUNT : búsqueda *f* — **searchlight** ['sərtʃ,laɪt] *n* : reflector *m*

seashell ['siːˌʃɛl] *n* : concha *f* (marina) — **seashore** ['siːˌʃor] *n* : orilla *f* del mar — **seasick** ['siːˌsɪk] *adj* **1** : mareado **2 be** ~ : marearse — **seasickness** ['siːˌsɪknəs] *n* : mareo *m*

season ['siːzən] *n* **1** : estación *f* (del año) **2** : temporada *f* (en deportes, etc.) — ~ *vt* **1** FLAVOR : sazonar **2** : secar (madera) — **seasonal** ['siːzənəl] *adj*

: estacional — **seasoned** adj EXPERIENCED : veterano — **seasoning** ['si:zənɪŋ] n : condimento m

seat ['si:t] n 1 : asiento m 2 : fondillos mpl (de un pantalón) 3 BUTTOCKS : trasero m 4 CENTER : sede f — ~ vt 1 be ~ed : sentarse 2 **the bus** ~**s** 30 : el autobús tiene cabida para 30 — **seat belt** n : cinturón m de seguridad

seaweed ['si:wi:d] n : alga f marina

secede [sɪ'si:d] vi -**ceded**; -**ceding** : separarse (de una nación, etc.)

secluded [sɪ'klu:dəd] adj : aislado — **seclusion** [sɪ'klu:ʒən] n : aislamiento m

second ['sekənd] adj : segundo — ~ or **secondly** ['sekəndli] adv : en segundo lugar — ~ n 1 : segundo m, -da f 2 MOMENT : segundo m 3 **have** ~**s** : repetir (en una comida) — ~ vt : secundar — **secondary** ['sekən,deri] adj : secundario — **secondhand** ['sekənd'hænd] adj : de segunda mano — **second-rate** ['sekənd'reɪt] adj : mediocre

secret ['si:krət] adj : secreto — ~ n : secreto m — **secrecy** ['si:krəsi] n, pl -**cies** : secreto m

secretary ['sekrə,teri] n, pl -**taries** 1 : secretario m, -ria f 2 : ministro m, -tra f (del gobierno)

secretion [sɪ'kri:ʃən] n : secreción f — **secrete** [sɪ'kri:t] vt -**creted**; -**creting** : secretar

secretive ['si:krətɪv, sɪ'kri:tɪv] adj : reservado — **secretly** ['si:krətli] adv : en secreto

sect ['sekt] n : secta f

section ['sekʃən] n : sección f, parte f

sector ['sektər] n : sector m

secular ['sekjələr] adj : secular

security [sɪ'kjurət̬i] n, pl -**ties** 1 : seguridad f 2 GUARANTEE : garantía f 3 **securities** npl : valores mpl — **secure** [sɪ'kjur] adj -**curer**; -**est** : seguro — ~ vt -**cured**; -**curing** 1 FASTEN : asegurar 2 GET : conseguir

sedan [sɪ'dæn] n : sedán m

sedate [sɪ'deɪt] adj : sosegado

sedative ['sedət̬ɪv] adj : sedante — ~ n : sedante m

sedentary ['sedən,teri] adj : sedentario

sediment ['sedəmənt] n : sedimento m

seduce [sɪ'du:s, -'dju:s] vt -**duced**; -**ducing** : seducir — **seduction** [sɪ'dʌkʃən] n : seducción f — **seductive** [sɪ'dʌktɪv] adj : seductor

see ['si:] v **saw** ['sɔ]; **seen** ['si:n]; **seeing** vt 1 : ver 2 UNDERSTAND : entender 3 ESCORT : acompañar 4 ~ **s.o. off** : despedirse de algn 5 ~ **sth through** : ll

evar algo a cabo 6 ~ **you later!** : ¡hasta luego! — vi 1 : ver 2 UNDERSTAND : entender 3 **let's** ~ : vamos a ver 4 ~ **to** : ocuparse de

seed ['si:d] n, pl **seed** or **seeds** 1 : semilla f 2 SOURCE : germen m — **est** SQUALID : sórdido

seedy ['si:di] adj **seedier**; -**est** SQUALID : sórdido

seek ['si:k] v **sought** ['sɔt]; **seeking** vt 1 or ~ **out** : buscar 2 REQUEST : pedir 3 ~ **to** : tratar de — vi SEARCH : buscar

seem ['si:m] vi : parecer

seep ['si:p] vi : filtrarse

seesaw ['si:,sɔ] n : balancín m

seethe ['si:ð] vi **seethed**; **seething** : rabiar, estar furioso

segment ['segmənt] n : segmento m

segregate ['segri,geɪt] vt -**gated**; -**gating** : segregar — **segregation** [,segri'geɪʃən] n : segregación f

seize ['si:z] v **seized**; **seizing** vt 1 GRASP : agarrar 2 CAPTURE : tomar 3 : aprovechar (una oportunidad) — vi or ~ **up** : agarrotarse — **seizure** ['si:ʒər] n 1 CAPTURE : toma f 2 : ataque m (en medicina)

seldom ['seldəm] adv : pocas veces, raramente

select [sə'lekt] adj : selecto — ~ vt : seleccionar — **selection** [sə'lekʃən] n : selección f — **selective** [sə'lektɪv] adj : selectivo

self ['self] n, pl **selves** ['selvz] 1 : ser m 2 **her better** ~ : su lado bueno — **self-addressed** [,self'drest] adj : con la dirección del remitente — **self-assured** [,selfə'ʃurd] adj : seguro de sí mismo — **self-centered** [,self'sentərd] adj : egocéntrico — **self-confidence** [,self'kanfədənts] n : confianza f en sí mismo — **self-confident** [,self'kanfədənt] adj : seguro de sí mismo — **self-conscious** [,self'kantʃəs] adj : cohibido — **self-control** [,selfkən'troːl] n : dominio m de sí mismo — **self-defense** [,selfdɪ'fents] n : defensa f propia — **self-employed** [,selfim'plɔid] adj : que trabaja por cuenta propia — **self-esteem** [,selfɪ'sti:m] n : amor m propio — **self-evident** [,self'evədənt] adj : evidente — **self-help** [,self'help] n : autoayuda f — **self-important** [,selfim'pɔrtənt] adj : presumido — **self-interest** [,self'intrəst, -tə,rest] n : interés m personal — **selfish** ['selfɪʃ] adj : egoísta — **selfishness** ['selfɪʃnəs] n : egoísmo m — **selfless** ['selfləs] adj : desinteresado — **self-pity** [,self'pit̬i] n, pl -**ties** : autocompasión f — **self-portrait** [,self 'portrat] n : autorretrato m — **self-respect** [ˌselfrɪ'spekt] n : amor m propio — **self-righteous** [ˌselfraɪtʃəs] adj : santurrón — **self-service** [ˌself-'sɜrvɪs] adj : de autoservicio — **self-sufficient** [ˌselfsə'fɪʃənt] adj : autosuficiente — **self-taught** [ˌselftɔt] adj : autodidacta

sell ['sel] v **sold** ['soːld]; **selling** vt : vender — vi : venderse — **seller** ['selər] n : vendedor m, -dora f

selves → self

semantics [sɪ'mæntɪks] ns & pl : semántica f

semblance ['sembləns] n : apariencia f

semester [sə'mestər] n : semestre m

semicolon ['semɪˌkoːlən, ˌse.maɪ-] n : punto y coma m

semifinal ['semɪfaɪnəl, 'se.maɪ-] n : semifinal f

seminary ['semərneri] n, pl **-naries** : seminario m — **seminar** ['seməˌnɑr] n : seminario m

senate ['senət] n : senado m — **senator** ['senətər] n : senador m, -dora f

send ['send] vt **sent** ['sent]; **sending** 1 : mandar, enviar 2 ~ **away for** : pedir 3 ~ **back** : devolver (mercancías, etc.) 4 ~ **for** : mandar a buscar — **sender** ['sendər] n : remitente mf

senile ['siːnaɪl] adj : senil — **senility** [sɪ'nɪləti] n : senilidad f

senior ['siːnjər] n 1 SUPERIOR : superior m 2 : estudiante mf de último año (en educación) 3 or ~ **citizen** : persona f mayor 4 **be s.o.'s** ~ : ser mayor que algn — ~ adj 1 : superior (en rango) 2 ELDER : mayor — **seniority** [ˌsiː-'njɔrəti] n : antigüedad f

sensation [sen'seɪʃən] n : sensación f — **sensational** [sen'seɪʃənəl] adj : sensacional

sense ['sents] n 1 : sentido m 2 FEELING : sensación f 3 COMMON SENSE : sentido m común 4 **make** ~ : tener sentido — ~ vt **sensed**; **sensing** : sentir — **senseless** ['sentsləs] adj 1 : sin sentido 2 UNCONSCIOUS : inconsciente — **sensible** ['sentsəbəl] adj : sensato, práctico — **sensibility** [ˌsentsə'bɪləti] n, pl **-ties** : sensibilidad f — **sensitive** ['sentsətɪv] adj 1 : sensible 2 TOUCHY : susceptible — **sensitivity** [ˌsentsə-'tɪvəti] n, pl **-ties** : sensibilidad f — **sensual** ['sentʃuəl] adj : sensual — **sensuous** ['sentʃuəs] adj : sensual

sent → send

sentence ['sentənts, -ənz] n 1 : frase f 2 JUDGMENT : sentencia f — ~ vt **-tenced**; **-tencing** : sentenciar

sentiment ['sentəmənt] n 1 : sentimiento m 2 BELIEF : opinión f — **sentimental** [ˌsentə'mentəl] adj : sentimental — **sentimentality** [ˌsentəmen'tæləti] n, pl **-ties** : sentimentalismo m

sentry ['sentri] n, pl **-tries** : centinela m

separation [ˌsepə'reɪʃən] n : separación f — **separate** ['sepəˌreɪt] v **-rated**; **-rating** vt 1 : separar 2 DISTINGUISH : distinguir — vi : separarse — ~ ['seprət, 'sepə-] adj 1 : separado 2 DETACHED : aparte 3 DISTINCT : distinto — **separately** ['seprətli, 'sepə-] adv : por separado

September [sep'tembər] n : septiembre m, setiembre m

sequel ['siːkwəl] n 1 : continuación f 2 CONSEQUENCE : secuela f

sequence ['siːkwənts] n 1 ORDER : orden m 2 : secuencia f (de números o escenas)

Serb ['sɜrb] or **Serbian** ['sɜrbiən] adj : serbio

serene [sə'rim] adj : sereno — **serenity** [sə'renəti] n : serenidad f

sergeant ['sɑrdʒənt] n : sargento mf

serial ['sɪriəl] adj : seriado — ~ n : serial m — **series** ['sɪrˌiz] n, pl **series** : serie f

serious ['sɪriəs] adj : serio — **seriously** ['sɪriəsli] adv 1 : seriamente 2 GRAVELY : gravemente 3 **take** ~ : tomar en serio

sermon ['sɜrmən] n : sermón m

serpent ['sɜrpənt] n : serpiente f

servant ['sɜrvənt] n : criado m, -da f

serve ['sɜrv] v **served**; **serving** vi 1 : servir 2 : sacar (en deportes) 3 ~ **as** : servir de — vt 1 : servir 2 ~ **time** : cumplir una condena — **server** ['sɜrvər] n 1 WAITER : camarero m, -ra f 2 : servidor m (en informática)

service ['sɜrvəs] n 1 : servicio m 2 CEREMONY : oficio m 3 MAINTENANCE : revisión f 4 **armed** ~**s** : fuerzas fpl armadas — ~ vt **-viced**; **-vicing** : revisar (un vehículo, etc.) — **serviceman** ['sɜrvəsˌmæn, -mən] n, pl **-men** [-mən, -ˌmen] : militar m — **service station** n : estación f de servicio — **serving** ['sɜrvɪŋ] n : porción f, ración f

session ['seʃən] n : sesión f

set ['set] n 1 : juego m (de platos, etc.) 2 : set m (en tenis, etc.) 3 or **stage** ~ : decorado m 4 **television** ~ : aparato m de televisión — ~ v **set**; **setting** vt 1 or ~ **down** : poner 2 : poner en hora (un reloj) 3 FIX : fijar (una fecha, etc.) 4 ~ **fire to** : prender fuego a 5 ~ **free** : poner en libertad 6 ~ **off**

: hacer sonar (una alarma), hacer estallar (una bomba) **7** ~ **out to (do sth)** : proponerse (hacer algo) **8** ~ **up** ASSEMBLE : montar, armar **9** ~ **up** ESTABLISH : establecer — vi **1** : cuajarse (dícese de la gelatina, etc.), fraguar (dícese del cemento) **2** : ponerse (dícese del sol, etc.) **3** ~ **in** BEGIN : empezar **4** ~ **off** or ~ **out** : salir (de viaje) — ~ adj **1** FIXED : fijo **2** READY : listo, preparado — **setback** ['set,bæk] n : revés m — **setting** ['setɪŋ] n **1** : posición f (de un control) **2** MOUNTING : engaste m (de joyas) **3** SCENE : escenario m

settle ['setəl] v **settled; settling** vi **1** : asentarse (dícese de polvo, colonos, etc.) **2** ~ **down** RELAX : calmarse **3** ~ **for** : conformarse con **4** ~ **in** : instalarse — vt **1** DECIDE : fijar, decidir **2** RESOLVE : resolver **3** PAY : pagar **4** CALM : calmar **5** COLONIZE : colonizar — **settlement** ['setəlmənt] n **1** PAYMENT : pago m **2** COLONY : colonia f, poblado m **3** AGREEMENT : acuerdo m — **settler** ['setələr] n : colono m, -na f

seven ['sevən] adj : siete — ~ n : siete m — **seven hundred** adj : setecientos — ~ n : setecientos m — **seventeen** [,sevən'tiːn] adj : diecisiete — ~ n : diecisiete m — **seventeenth** [,sevən-'tiːnθ] adj : decimoséptimo — ~ n **1** : decimoséptimo m, -ma f (en una serie) **2** : diecisieteavo m (en matemáticas) — **seventh** ['sevənθ] adj : séptimo — ~ n **1** : séptimo m, -ma f (en una serie) **2** : séptimo m (en matemáticas) — **seventieth** ['sevəntiəθ] adj : septuagésimo — ~ n **1** : septuagésimo m, -ma f (en una serie) **2** : setentavo m (en matemáticas) — **seventy** ['sevənti] adj : setenta — ~ n, pl **-ties** : setenta m

sever ['sevər] vt **-ered; -ering** : cortar, romper

several ['sevrəl, 'sevə-] adj : varios — ~ pron : varios, varias

severance ['sevrənts, sevə-] n : ruptura f

severe [sə'vir] adj **severer; -est 1** : severo **2** SERIOUS : grave — **severely** adv **1** : severamente **2** SERIOUSLY : gravemente — **severity** [sə'verəti] n **1** : severidad f **2** SERIOUSNESS : gravedad f

sew ['soː] v **sewed; sewn** ['soːn] or **sewed; sewing** : coser

sewer ['suːər] n : cloaca f — **sewage** ['suːɪdʒ] n : aguas fpl negras

sewing ['soːɪŋ] n : costura f

sex ['seks] n **1** : sexo m **2** INTERCOURSE

: relaciones fpl sexuales — **sexism** ['sek,sɪzəm] n : sexismo m — **sexist** ['seksɪst] adj : sexista — **sexual** ['sekʃuəl] adj : sexual — **sexuality** [,sekʃu'æləti] n : sexualidad f — **sexy** ['seksi] adj **sexier; -est** : sexy

shabby ['ʃæbi] adj **shabbier; -est 1** WORN : gastado **2** UNFAIR : malo, injusto

shack ['ʃæk] n : choza f

shackle ['ʃækəl] n : grillete m

shade ['ʃeɪd] n **1** : sombra f **2** : tono m (de un color) **3** NUANCE : matiz m **4** or **lampshade** : pantalla f **5** or **window** ~ : persiana f — ~ vt **shaded; shading** : proteger de la luz — **shadow** ['ʃædoː] n : sombra f — **shadowy** ['ʃædowi] adj INDISTINCT : vago — **shady** ['ʃeɪdi] adj **shadier; -est 1** : sombreado **2** DISREPUTABLE : sospechoso

shaft ['ʃæft] n **1** : asta f (de una flecha, etc.) **2** HANDLE : mango m **3** AXLE : eje m **4** : rayo m (de luz) **5** or **mine** ~ : pozo m

shaggy ['ʃægi] adj **shaggier; -est** : peludo

shake ['ʃeɪk] v **shook** ['ʃuk]; **shaken** ['ʃeɪkən]; **shaking** vt **1** : sacudir **2** MIX : agitar **3** ~ **hands with s.o.** : dar la mano a algn **4** ~ **one's head** : negar con la cabeza **5** ~ **up** UPSET : afectar — vi : temblar — ~ n **1** : sacudida f **2** → **handshake** — **shaker** ['ʃeɪkər] n **1 salt** ~ : salero m **2 pepper** ~ : pimentero m — **shaky** ['ʃeɪki] adj **shakier; -est 1** : tembloroso **2** UNSTABLE : poco firme

shall ['ʃæl] v aux, past **should** ['ʃud]; pres sing & pl **shall 1** (expressing volition or futurity) → **will 2** (expressing possibility or obligation) → **should 3** ~ **we go?** : ¿nos vamos?

shallow ['ʃæloː] adj **1** : poco profundo **2** SUPERFICIAL : superficial

sham ['ʃæm] n : farsa f — ~ v **shammed; shamming** : fingir

shambles ['ʃæmbəlz] ns & pl : caos m, desorden m

shame ['ʃeɪm] n **1** : vergüenza f **2 what a** ~! : ¡qué lástima! — ~ vt **shamed; shaming** : avergonzar — **shameful** ['ʃeɪmfəl] adj : vergonzoso — **shameless** ['ʃeɪmləs] adj : desvergonzado

shampoo [ʃæm'puː] vt : lavar (el pelo) — ~ n, pl **-poos** : champú m

shamrock ['ʃæm,rɑk] n : trébol m

shan't ['ʃænt] (contraction of **shall not**) → **shall**

shape ['ʃeɪp] v **shaped; shaping** vt 1 : formar 2 DETERMINE : determinar 3 **be ~d like** : tener forma de — vi or **~ up** : tomar forma — ~ n 1 : forma f 2 **get in** : ponerse en forma — **shapeless** ['ʃeɪpləs] adj : informe

share ['ʃer] n 1 : porción f 2 : acción f (en una compañía) — ~ v **shared; sharing** vt 1 : compartir 2 DIVIDE : dividir — vi : compartir — **shareholder** ['ʃer,hoʊldər] n : accionista mf

shark ['ʃɑrk] n : tiburón m

sharp ['ʃɑrp] adj 1 : afilado 2 POINTY : puntiagudo 3 ACUTE : agudo 4 HARSH : duro, severo 5 CLEAR : nítido 6 : sostenido (en música) 7 **a ~ curve** : una curva cerrada — ~ adv **at two o'clock ~** : a las dos en punto — ~ n : sostenido (en música) — **sharpen** ['ʃɑrpən] vt : afilar (un cuchillo, etc.), sacar punta a (un lápiz) — **sharpener** ['ʃɑrpənər] n 1 or **knife ~** : afilador m 2 or **pencil ~** : sacapuntas m — **sharply** ['ʃɑrpli] adv : bruscamente

shatter ['ʃætər] vt 1 : hacer añicos 2 DEVASTATE : destrozar — vi : hacerse añicos

shave ['ʃeɪv] v **shaved; shaved** or **shaven** ['ʃeɪvən]; **shaving** vt 1 : afeitar 2 SLICE : cortar — vi : afeitarse — ~ n : afeitada f — **shaver** ['ʃeɪvər] n : máquina f de afeitar

shawl ['ʃɔl] n : chal m

she ['ʃi] pron : ella

sheaf ['ʃif] n, pl **sheaves** ['ʃivz] 1 : gavilla f 2 : fajo m (de papeles)

shear ['ʃɪr] vt **sheared; sheared** or **shorn** ['ʃɔrn]; **shearing** : esquilar — **shears** ['ʃɪrz] npl : tijeras fpl (grandes)

sheath ['ʃiθ] n, pl **sheaths** ['ʃiðz, 'ʃiθs] : funda f, vaina f

shed[1] ['ʃed] v **shed; shedding** vt 1 : derramar (lágrimas, etc.) 2 : mudar (de piel, etc.), quitarse (ropa) 3 **~ light on** : aclarar

shed[2] n : cobertizo m

she'd ['ʃid] (contraction of **she had** or **she would**) → **have, would**

sheen ['ʃin] n : brillo m, lustre m

sheep ['ʃip] n, pl **sheep** : oveja f — **sheepish** ['ʃipɪʃ] adj : avergonzado

sheer ['ʃɪr] adj 1 THIN : transparente 2 PURE : puro 3 STEEP : escarpado

sheet ['ʃit] n 1 : sábana f (de la cama) 2 : hoja f (de papel) 3 : capa f (de hielo, etc.) 4 PLATE : placa f, lámina f

shelf ['ʃelf] n, pl **shelves** ['ʃelvz] : estante m

shell ['ʃel] n 1 : concha f 2 : caparazón m (de un crustáceo, etc.) 3 : cáscara f (de un huevo, etc.) 4 : armazón mf (de un edificio, etc.) 5 POD : vaína f 6 MISSILE : proyectil m — ~ vt 1 : pelar (nueces, etc.) 2 BOMBARD : bombardear

she'll ['ʃil, 'ʃɪl] (contraction of **she shall** or **she will**) → **shall, will**

shellfish ['ʃel,fɪʃ] n : marisco m

shelter ['ʃeltər] n 1 : refugio m 2 **take ~** : refugiarse — ~ vt 1 PROTECT : proteger 2 HARBOR : albergar

shelve ['ʃelv] vt **shelved; shelving** DEFER : dar carpetazo a

shepherd ['ʃepərd] n : pastor m — ~ vt GUIDE : conducir, guiar

sherbet ['ʃərbət] n : sorbete m

sheriff ['ʃerɪf] n : sheriff mf

sherry ['ʃeri] n, pl **-ries** : jerez m

she's ['ʃiz] (contraction of **she is** or **she has**) → **be, have**

shield ['ʃild] n : escudo m — ~ vt : proteger

shier, shiest → **shy**

shift ['ʃɪft] vt 1 MOVE : mover 2 SWITCH : transferir — vi 1 CHANGE : cambiar 2 MOVE : moverse 3 or **~ gears** : cambiar de velocidad — ~ n 1 CHANGE : cambio m 2 : turno m (de trabajo) — **shiftless** ['ʃɪftləs] adj : holgazán — **shifty** ['ʃɪfti] adj **shiftier; -est** : sospechoso

shimmer ['ʃɪmər] vi : brillar, relucir

shin ['ʃɪn] n : espinilla f

shine ['ʃaɪn] v **shone** ['ʃoʊn] or **shined**; **shining** vi : brillar — vt 1 : alumbrar (una luz) 2 POLISH : sacar brillo a — ~ n : brillo m

shingle ['ʃɪŋgəl] n : teja f plana y delgada (en construcción) — ~ vt **-gled; -gling** : techar — **shingles** ['ʃɪŋgəlz] npl : herpes m

shiny ['ʃaɪni] adj **shinier; -est** : brillante

ship ['ʃɪp] n 1 : barco m, buque m 2 → **spaceship** — ~ vt **shipped; shipping** : transportar, enviar (por barco) — **shipbuilding** ['ʃɪp,bɪldɪŋ] n : construcción f naval — **shipment** ['ʃɪpmənt] n : envío m — **shipping** ['ʃɪpɪŋ] n 1 : transporte m 2 SHIPS : barcos mpl — **shipshape** ['ʃɪp,ʃeɪp] adj : ordenado — **shipwreck** ['ʃɪp,rek] n : naufragio m — ~ vt **be ~ed** : naufragar — **shipyard** ['ʃɪp,jɑrd] n : astillero m

shirk ['ʃərk] vt : esquivar

shirt ['ʃərt] n : camisa f

shiver ['ʃɪvər] vi : temblar (del frío, etc.) — ~ n : escalofrío m

shoal ['ʃoʊl] n : banco m

shock ['ʃak] n 1 IMPACT : choque m 2
SURPRISE, UPSET : golpe m emocional 3
: shock m (en medicina) 4 or electric
~ : descarga f (eléctrica) — vt
: escandalizar — **shock absorber** n
: amortiguador m — **shocking** ['ʃakɪŋ]
adj : escandaloso

shoddy ['ʃadi] adj **shoddier; -est** : de
mala calidad

shoe ['ʃuː] n : zapato m — ~ vt **shod**
['ʃad]; **shoeing** : herrar (un caballo)
— **shoelace** ['ʃuːleɪs] n : cordón m (de
zapato) — **shoemaker** ['ʃuːmeɪkər] n
: zapatero m, -ra f

shone → **shine**

shook → **shake**

shoot ['ʃuːt] v **shot** ['ʃat]; **shooting** vt
: disparar 2 : echar (una mirada) 3
PHOTOGRAPH : fotografiar 4 FILM
: rodar — vi 1 : disparar 2 ~ **by**
: pasar como una bala — ~ n : brote
m, retoño m (de una planta) — **shooting star** n : estrella f fugaz

shop ['ʃap] n 1 : tienda f 2 WORKSHOP
: taller m — ~ vi **shopped; shopping 1** : hacer compras **2 go shopping** : ir de compras — **shopkeeper**
['ʃapˌkiːpər] n : tendero m, -ra f —
shoplift ['ʃapˌlɪft] vi : hurtar mercancía
(en tiendas) — **shoplifter** ['ʃapˌlɪftər] n
: ladrón m, -drona f (que roba en tiendas) — **shopper** ['ʃapər] n : comprador m, -dora f

shore ['ʃor] n : orilla f

shorn → **shear**

short ['ʃort] adj 1 : corto 2 : bajo (de estatura) 3 CURT : brusco 4 **a ~ time
ago** : hace poco 5 **be ~ of** : estar
corto de — ~ adv 1 **stop ~** : parar
en seco 2 **fall ~** : quedarse corto —
shortage ['ʃortɪdʒ] n : escasez f, carencia f — **shortcake** ['ʃortˌkeɪk] n : tarta f
de fruta — **shortcoming** ['ʃortˌkʌmɪŋ]
n : defecto m — **shortcut** ['ʃortˌkʌt] n
: atajo m — **shorten** ['ʃortən] vt : acortar — **shorthand** ['ʃortˌhænd] n
: taquigrafía f — **short-lived** ['ʃort-
'lɪvd, -'laɪvd] adj : efímero — **shortly**
['ʃortli] adv : dentro de poco — **shortness** ['ʃortnəs] n 1 : lo corto (de una
cosa), baja estatura f (de una persona)
2 **~ of breath** : falta f de aliento —
shorts npl : shorts mpl, pantalones
mpl cortos — **shortsighted** ['ʃort,saɪ-
təd] → **nearsighted**

shot ['ʃat] n 1 : disparo m, tiro m 2 : tiro
m (en deportes) 3 ATTEMPT : intento m
4 PHOTOGRAPH : foto f 5 INJECTION : inyección f 6 : trago m (de licor) —
shotgun ['ʃatˌgʌn] n : escopeta f

should ['ʃʊd] past of **shall 1 if she ~
call** : si llama 2 **I ~ have gone** : de-
bería haber ido 3 **they ~ arrive soon**
: deben llegar pronto 4 **what ~ we
do?** : ¿qué hacemos?

shoulder ['ʃoːldər] n 1 : hombro m 2
: arcén m (de una carretera) — ~ vt
: cargar con (la responsabilidad, etc.)
— **shoulder blade** n : omóplato m

shouldn't ['ʃʊdənt] (contraction of
should not) → **should**

shout ['ʃaʊt] v : gritar — ~ n : grito m

shove ['ʃʌv] v **shoved; shoving** : empujar — ~ n : empujón m

shovel ['ʃʌvəl] n : pala f — ~ vt -**veled**
or -**velled; -veling** or -**velling 1**
: mover (tierra, etc.) con una pala 2
DIG : cavar (con una pala)

show ['ʃoː] v **showed; shown** ['ʃoːn] or
showed; showing vt 1 : mostrar 2
TEACH : enseñar 3 PROVE : demostrar 4
ESCORT : acompañar 5 : proyectar (una
película), dar (un programa de televisión) 6 ~ **off** : hacer alarde de — vi
1 : notarse, verse 2 ~ **off** : lucirse 3
~ **up** ARRIVE : aparecer — ~ n 1
: demostración f 2 EXHIBITION : exposición f 3 : espectáculo m (teatral),
programa m (de televisión, etc.) —
showdown ['ʃoːˌdaʊn] n : confrontación f

shower ['ʃaʊər] n 1 : ducha f 2 : chaparrón m (en meteorología) 3 PARTY : fiesta f — ~ vt 1 SPRAY : regar 2 ~ **s.o.
with** : colmar a algn de — vi 1 : ducharse 2 RAIN : llover

showy ['ʃoːi] adj **showier; -est** : llamativo, ostentoso

shrank → **shrink**

shrapnel ['ʃræpnəl] ns & pl : metralla f

shred ['ʃred] n 1 : tira f (de tela, etc.) 2
IOTA : pizca f — ~ vt **shredded;
shredding 1** : hacer tiras 2 GRATE
: rallar

shrewd ['ʃruːd] adj : astuto

shriek ['ʃriːk] vi : chillar — ~ n : chillido m, alarido m

shrill ['ʃrɪl] adj : agudo, estridente

shrimp ['ʃrɪmp] n : camarón m

shrine ['ʃraɪn] n 1 TOMB : sepulcro m 2
SANCTUARY : santuario m

shrink ['ʃrɪŋk] v **shrank** ['ʃræŋk];
shrunk ['ʃrʌŋk] or **shrunken**
['ʃrʌŋkən]; **shrinking** vt : encoger — vi
1 : encogerse (dícese de ropa), reducirse (dícese de números, etc.) 2 ~
back : retroceder

shrivel ['ʃrɪvəl] vi -**veled** or -**velled**;
-**veling** or -**velling** or ~ **up** : arrugarse, marchitarse

shroud ['ʃraʊd] n 1 : sudario m, mortaja f 2 VEIL : velo m — ~ vt : envolver
shrub ['ʃrʌb] n : arbusto m, mata f
shrug ['ʃrʌg] vi **shrugged; shrugging** : encogerse de hombros
shrunk → **shrink**
shudder ['ʃʌdər] vi : estremecerse — ~ n : estremecimiento m
shuffle ['ʃʌfəl] v **-fled; -fling** vt : barajar (naipes), revolver (papeles, etc.) — vi : caminar arrastrando los pies
shun ['ʃʌn] vi **shunned; shunning** : evitar, esquivar
shut ['ʃʌt] v **shut; shutting** vt 1 CLOSE : cerrar 2 ~ **off** → **turn off** 3 ~ **up** CONFINE : encerrar — vi 1 or ~ **down** : cerrarse 2 ~ **up!** : ¡cállate! — **shutter** ['ʃʌtər] n 1 or **window** ~ : contraventana f 2 : obturador m (de una cámara)
shuttle ['ʃʌtəl] n 1 : lanzadera f (para tejer) 2 or ~ **bus** : autobús m (de corto recorrido) 3 → **space shuttle** — ~ v **-tled; -tling** vt : transportar — vi : ir y venir
shy ['ʃaɪ] adj **shier** or **shyer** ['ʃaɪər]; **shiest** or **shyest** ['ʃaɪəst] : tímido — ~ vi **shied; shying** or ~ **away** : retroceder — **shyness** ['ʃaɪnəs] n : timidez f
sibling ['sɪblɪŋ] n : hermano m, hermana f
sick ['sɪk] adj 1 : enfermo 2 be ~ VOMIT : vomitar 3 be ~ **of** : estar harto de 4 **feel** ~ : tener náuseas — **sicken** ['sɪkən] vt DISGUST : dar asco a — **sickening** ['sɪkənɪŋ] adj : nauseabundo
sickle ['sɪkəl] n : hoz f
sickly ['sɪkli] adj **sicklier; -est** 1 UNHEALTHY : enfermizo 2 → **sickening** — **sickness** ['sɪknəs] n : enfermedad f
side ['saɪd] n 1 : lado m 2 : costado m (de una persona), ijada f (de un animal) 3 : parte f (en una disputa, etc.) 4 ~ **by** ~ : uno al lado de otro 5 **take** ~**s** : tomar partido — vi ~ **with** : ponerse de parte de — **sideboard** ['saɪd,bord] n : aparador m — **sideburns** ['saɪd,bərnz] npl : patillas fpl — **side effect** n : efecto m secundario — **sideline** ['saɪd,laɪn] n : línea f de banda (en deportes) — **sidestep** ['saɪd,stɛp] vt **-stepped; -stepping** : eludir, esquivar — **sidetrack** ['saɪd,træk] vt **get ~ed** : distraerse — **sidewalk** ['saɪd,wɔk] n : acera f — **sideways** ['saɪd,weɪz] adj & adv : de lado — **siding** ['saɪdɪŋ] n : revestimiento m exterior
siege ['siːdʒ, 'siːʒ] n : sitio m

sieve ['sɪv] n : tamiz m, cedazo m
sift ['sɪft] vt 1 : cerner, tamizar 2 or ~ **through** : pasar por el tamiz
sigh ['saɪ] vi : suspirar — ~ n : suspiro m
sight ['saɪt] n 1 : vista f 2 SPECTACLE : espectáculo m 3 : lugar m de interés (turístico) 4 **catch** ~ **of** : avistar — ~ vt : avistar — **sightseer** ['saɪt,siːər] n : turista mf
sign ['saɪn] n 1 : signo m 2 NOTICE : letrero m 3 GESTURE : seña f, señal f — ~ vt : firmar (un cheque, etc.) — vi 1 : firmar 2 ~ **up** ENROLL : inscribirse
signal ['sɪgnəl] n : señal f — ~ v **-naled** or **-nalled; -naling** or **-nalling** vt 1 : hacer señas a 2 INDICATE : señalar — vi 1 : hacer señas 2 : señalizar (en un vehículo)
signature ['sɪgnətʃʊr] n : firma f
significance [sɪg'nɪfɪkənts] n 1 : significado m 2 IMPORTANCE : importancia f — **significant** [sɪg'nɪfɪkənt] adj : importante — **signify** ['sɪgnə,faɪ] vt **-fied; -fying** : significar
sign language n : lenguaje m gestual — **signpost** ['saɪn,poːst] n : poste m indicador
silence ['saɪlənts] n : silencio m — ~ vt **-lenced; -lencing** : silenciar — **silent** ['saɪlənt] adj 1 : silencioso 2 MUM : callado 3 : mudo (dícese de películas y letras)
silhouette [,sɪlə'wɛt] n : silueta f — ~ vt **-etted; -etting** be ~**d against** : perfilarse contra
silicon ['sɪlɪkən, -,kɑn] n : silicio m
silk ['sɪlk] n : seda f — **silky** ['sɪlki] adj **silkier; -est** : sedoso
sill ['sɪl] n : alféizar m (de una ventana), umbral m (de una puerta)
silly ['sɪli] adj **sillier; -est** : tonto, estúpido
silt ['sɪlt] n : cieno m
silver ['sɪlvər] n 1 : plata f 2 → **silverware** — ~ adj : de plata — **silverware** ['sɪlvər,wær] n : plata f — **silvery** ['sɪlvəri] adj : plateado
similar ['sɪmələr] adj : similar, parecido — **similarity** [,sɪmə'lærəti] n, pl **-ties** : semejanza f, parecido m
simmer ['sɪmər] v : hervir a fuego lento
simple ['sɪmpəl] adj **simpler; -plest** 1 : simple 2 EASY : sencillo — **simplicity** [sɪm'plɪsəti] n : simplicidad f, sencillez f — **simplify** ['sɪmplə,faɪ] vt **-fied; -fying** : simplificar — **simply** ['sɪmpli] adv 1 : sencillamente 2 ABSOLUTELY : realmente

simulate ['sɪmjəˌleɪt] *vt* **-lated; -lating** : simular

simultaneous [ˌsaɪməl'teɪniəs] *adj* : simultáneo

sin ['sɪn] *n* : pecado *m* — ~ *vi* **sinned; sinning** : pecar

since ['sɪns] *adv* **1** *or* ~ **then** : desde entonces **2 long** ~ : hace mucho — ~ *conj* **1** : desde que **2** BECAUSE : ya que, como **3 it's been years** ~... : hace años que... — ~ *prep* : desde

sincere [sɪn'sɪr] *adj* **-cerer; -est** : sincero — **sincerely** *adv* : sinceramente — **sincerity** [sɪn'serəţi] *n* : sinceridad *f*

sinful ['sɪnfəl] *adj* : pecador (dícese de las personas), pecaminoso (dícese de las acciones)

sing ['sɪŋ] *v* **sang** ['sæŋ] *or* **sung** ['sʌŋ]; **sung; singing** : cantar

singe ['sɪndʒ] *vt* **singed; singeing** : chamuscar

singer ['sɪŋər] *n* : cantante *mf*

single ['sɪŋgəl] *adj* **1** : solo, único **2** UNMARRIED : soltero **3 every** ~ **day** : cada día, todos los días — ~ *n* **1** : soltero *m*, -ra *f* **2** *or* ~ **room** : habitación *f* individual — ~ *vt* **-gled; -gling** *or* ~ **out** SELECT : escoger **2** DISTINGUISH : señalar — **single-handed** ['sɪŋgəl'hændəd] *adj* : sin ayuda, solo

singular ['sɪŋgjələr] *adj* : singular — ~ *n* : singular *m*

sinister ['sɪnəstər] *adj* : siniestro

sink ['sɪŋk] *v* **sank** ['sæŋk] *or* **sunk** ['sʌŋk]; **sunk; sinking** *vi* **1** : hundirse (en un líquido) **2** DROP : bajar, caer — *vt* **1** : hundir **2** ~ **sth into** : clavar algo en — ~ *n* **1** *or* **kitchen** ~ : fregadero *m* **2** *or* **bathroom** ~ : lavabo *m*, lavamanos *m*

sinner ['sɪnər] *n* : pecador *m*, -dora *f*

sip ['sɪp] *v* **sipped; sipping** *vt* : sorber — *vi* : beber a sorbos — ~ *n* : sorbo *m*

siphon ['saɪfən] *n* : sifón *m* — ~ *vt* : sacar con sifón

sir ['sər] *n* **1** (*in titles*) : sir *m* **2** (*as a form of address*) : señor *m* **3 Dear Sir** : Estimado señor

siren ['saɪrən] *n* : sirena *f*

sirloin ['sərˌlɔɪn] *n* : solomillo *m*

sissy ['sɪsi] *n, pl* **-sies** : mariquita *mf fam*

sister ['sɪstər] *n* : hermana *f* — **sister-in-law** ['sɪstərɪnˌlɔ] *n, pl* **sisters-in-law** : cuñada *f*

sit ['sɪt] *v* **sat** ['sæt]; **sitting** *vi* **1** *or* ~ **down** : sentarse **2** LIE : estar (ubicado) **3** MEET : estar en sesión **4** *or* ~ **up** : incorporarse — *vt* : sentar

site ['saɪt] *n* **1** : sitio *m*, lugar *m* **2** LOT : solar *m*

sitting room → **living room**

sitter ['sɪţər] → **baby-sitter**

situated ['sɪtʃuˌeɪţəd] *adj* : ubicado, situado — **situation** [ˌsɪtʃu'eɪʃən] *n* : situación *f*

six ['sɪks] *adj* : seis — ~ *n* : seis *m* — **six hundred** *adj* : seiscientos — ~ *n* : seiscientos — **sixteen** [sɪks'tiːn] *adj* : dieciséis — ~ *n* : dieciséis *m* — **sixteenth** [sɪks'tiːnθ] *adj* : decimosexto — ~ *n* **1** : decimosexto *m*, -ta *f* (en una serie) **2** : dieciseisavo *m*, dieciseisava parte *f* — **sixth** ['sɪksθ, 'sɪkst] *adj* : sexto — ~ *n* **1** : sexto *m*, -ta *f* (en una serie) **2** : sexto *m* (en matemáticas) — **sixtieth** ['sɪkstiˌəθ] *adj* : sexagésimo — ~ *n* **1** : sexagésimo *m*, -ma *f* (en una serie) **2** : sesentavo *m* (en matemáticas) — **sixty** ['sɪksti] *adj* : sesenta — ~ *n, pl* **-ties** : sesenta *m*

size ['saɪz] *n* **1** : tamaño *m*, talla *f* (de ropa), número *m* (de zapatos) **2** EXTENT : magnitud *f* — ~ *vt* **sized; sizing** ~ **up** : evaluar — **sizable** *or* **sizeable** ['saɪzəbəl] *adj* : considerable

sizzle ['sɪzəl] *vi* **-zled; -zling** : chisporrotear

skate¹ ['skeɪt] *n* : raya *f* (pez)

skate² *n* : patín *m* — ~ *vi* **skated; skating** : patinar — **skateboard** ['skeɪtˌbord] *n* : monopatín *m* — **skater** ['skeɪtər] *n* : patinador *m*, -dora *f*

skeleton ['skelətən] *n* : esqueleto *m*

skeptic ['skeptɪk] *n* : escéptico *m*, -ca *f* — **skeptical** ['skeptɪkəl] *adj* : escéptico — **skepticism** ['skeptəˌsɪzəm] *n* : escepticismo *m*

sketch ['sketʃ] *n* **1** : esbozo *m*, bosquejo *m* **2** SKIT : sketch — ~ *vt* : bosquejar — *vi* : hacer bosquejos — **sketchy** ['sketʃi] *adj* **sketchier; -est** : incompleto

skewer ['skjuːər] *n* : brocheta *f*, broqueta *f*

ski ['skiː] *n, pl* **skis** : esquí *m* — ~ *vi* **skied; skiing** : esquiar

skid ['skɪd] *n* : derrape *m*, patinazo *m* — ~ *vi* **skidded; skidding** : derrapar, patinar

skier ['skiːər] *n* : esquiador *m*, -dora *f*

skill ['skɪl] *n* **1** : habilidad *f*, destreza *f* **2** TECHNIQUE : técnica *f* — **skilled** ['skɪld] *adj* : hábil

skillet ['skɪlət] *n* : sartén *mf*

skillful ['skɪlfəl] *adj* : hábil, diestro

skim ['skɪm] *vt* **skimmed; skimming 1** : espumar (sopa, etc.), descremar (leche) **2** : pasar rozando (una superficie) **3** *or* **~ through** : echar un vistazo a — **~** *adj* : descremado

skimp ['skɪmp] *vi* **~ on** : escatimar — **skimpy** ['skɪmpi] *adj* **skimpier; -est** **1** : exiguo, escaso **2** : brevísimo (dícese de ropa)

skin ['skɪn] *n* : piel *f* — **~** *vt* **skinned; skinning** : despellejar — **skin diving** *n* : buceo *m*, submarinismo *m* — **skinny** ['skɪni] *adj* **skinnier; -est** : flaco

skip ['skɪp] *v* **skipped; skipping** *vi* : ir brincando — *vt* OMIT : saltarse — **~** *n* : brinco *m*, salto *m*

skipper ['skɪpər] *n* : capitán *m*, -tana *f*

skirmish ['skərmɪʃ] *n* : escaramuza *f*

skirt ['skərt] *n* : falda *f* — **~** *vt* **1** BORDER : bordear **2** EVADE : eludir

skull ['skʌl] *n* : cráneo *m* (de una persona viva), calavera *f* (de un esqueleto)

skunk ['skʌŋk] *n* : mofeta *f*, zorrillo *m* *Lat*

sky ['skaɪ] *n*, *pl* **skies** : cielo *m* — **skylight** ['skaɪ.laɪt] *n* : claraboya *f*, tragaluz *m* — **skyline** ['skaɪ.laɪn] *n* : horizonte *m* — **skyscraper** ['skaɪ.skreɪpər] *n* : rascacielos *m*

slab ['slæb] *n* : bloque *m* (de piedra, etc.)

slack ['slæk] *adj* **1** LOOSE : flojo **2** CARELESS : descuidado — **~** *n* **1 take up the ~** : tensar (una cuerda, etc.) **2 ~s** *npl* : pantalones *mpl* — **slacken** ['slækən] *vt* : aflojar — *vi* : aflojarse

slain → slay

slam ['slæm] *n* : golpe *m*, portazo *m* (de una puerta) — **~** *v* **slammed; slamming** *vt* **1** *or* **~ down** : tirar, plantar **2** *or* **~ shut** : cerrar de golpe **3 ~ the door** : dar un portazo — *vi* **1** : cerrarse de golpe **2 ~ into** : chocar contra

slander ['slændər] *vt* : calumniar, difamar — **~** *n* : calumnia *f*, difamación *f*

slang ['slæŋ] *n* : argot *m*

slant ['slænt] *n* : inclinación *f* — **~** *vi* : inclinarse

slap ['slæp] *vt* **slapped; slapping 1** : dar una bofetada a **2 ~ s.o. on the back** : dar una palmada en la espalda a algn — **~** *n* : bofetada *f*, cachetada *f* *Lat*

slash ['slæʃ] *vt* **1** : hacer un tajo en **2** : rebajar (precios) drásticamente — **~** *n* : tajo *m*

slat ['slæt] *n* : tablilla *f*

slate ['sleɪt] *n* : pizarra *f*

slaughter ['slɔtər] *n* : matanza *f* — **~** *vt* **1** : matar (animales) **2** MASSACRE : masacrar — **slaughterhouse** ['slɔtər.haʊs] *n* : matadero *m*

slave ['sleɪv] *n* : esclavo *m*, -va *f* — **~** *vi*

slaved; slaving : trabajar como un burro — **slavery** ['sleɪvəri] *n* : esclavitud *f*

Slavic ['slɑvɪk, 'slæ-] *adj* : eslavo

slay ['sleɪ] *vt* **slew** ['slu:]; **slain** ['sleɪn]; **slaying** : asesinar

sleazy ['slizi] *adj* **sleazier; -est** : sórdido

sled ['sled] *n* : trineo *m*

sledgehammer ['sledʒ.hæmər] *n* : almádena *f*

sleek ['slik] *adj* : liso y brillante

sleep ['slip] *n* **1** : sueño *m* **2 go to ~** : dormirse — **~** *vi* **slept** ['slept]; **sleeping** : dormir — **sleeper** ['slipər] *n* **be a light ~** : tener el sueño ligero — **sleepless** ['sliplas] *adj* **have a ~ night** : pasar la noche en blanco — **sleepwalker** ['slip.wɔkər] *n* : sonámbulo *m*, -la *f* — **sleepy** ['slipi] *adj* **sleepier; -est 1** : somnoliento, soñoliento **2 be ~** : tener sueño

sleet ['slit] *n* : aguanieve *f* — **~** *vi* : caer aguanieve

sleeve ['sliv] *n* : manga *f* — **sleeveless** ['slivlas] *adj* : sin mangas

sleigh ['sleɪ] *n* : trineo *m*

slender ['slendər] *adj* : delgado

slew ['slu:] → **slay**

slice ['slaɪs] *vt* **sliced; slicing** : cortar — **~** *n* : trozo *m*, rebanada *f* (de pan, etc.), tajada *f* (de carne)

slick ['slɪk] *adj* SLIPPERY : resbaladizo, resbaloso *Lat*

slide ['slaɪd] *v* **slid** ['slɪd]; **sliding** ['slaɪdɪŋ] *vi* : deslizarse — *vt* : deslizar — **~** *n* **1** : deslizamiento *m* **2** : tobogán *m* (para niños) **3** : diapositiva *f* (fotográfica) **4** DECLINE : descenso *m*

slier, sliest → sly

slight ['slaɪt] *adj* **1** : ligero, leve **2** SLENDER : delgado — **~** *vt* : desairar — **slightly** ['slaɪtli] *adv* : ligeramente, un poco

slim ['slɪm] *adj* **slimmer; slimmest 1** : delgado **2 a ~ chance** : escasas posibilidades *fpl* — **~** *v* **slimmed; slimming** : adelgazar

slime ['slaɪm] *n* **1** : baba *f* (de un caracol, etc.) **2** MUD : limo *m* — **slimy** ['slaɪmi] *adj* **slimier; -est** : viscoso

sling ['slɪŋ] *vt* **slung** ['slʌŋ]; **slinging 1** THROW : lanzar **2** HANG : colgar — **~** *n* **1** : honda *f* **2** : cabestrillo *m* (en medicina) — **slingshot** ['slɪŋ.ʃɑt] *n* : tirachinas *m*

slink ['slɪŋk] *vi* **slunk** ['slʌŋk]; **slinking** : andar furtivamente

slip¹ ['slɪp] *v* **slipped; slipping** *vi* **1** SLIDE : resbalarse **2 let sth ~** : dejar escapar algo **3 ~ away** : escabullirse **4 ~ up** : equivocarse — *vt* **1** : deslizar **2 ~ into** : ponerse (una prenda) **3** it slipped my mind : se me olvidó — ~ *n* **1** MISTAKE : error *m*, desliz *m* **2 ~ of the tongue** : lapsus *m* **3** PETTICOAT : enagua *f*

slip² *n* ~ **of paper** : papelito *m*

slipper ['slɪpər] *n* : zapatilla *f*, pantufla *f*

slippery ['slɪpəri] *adj* **slipperier; -est** : resbaladizo, resbaloso *Lat*

slit ['slɪt] *n* **1** OPENING : rendija *f* **2** CUT : corte *m*, raja *f* — ~ *vt* **slit; slitting** : cortar

slither ['slɪðər] *vi* : deslizarse

sliver ['slɪvər] *n* : astilla *f*

slogan ['sloːgən] *n* : eslogan *m*

slop ['slap] *v* **slopped; slopping** *vt* : derramar — *vi* : derramarse

slope ['sloːp] *vi* **sloped; sloping** : inclinarse — ~ *n* : pendiente *f*, declive *m*

sloppy ['slapi] *adj* **sloppier; -est 1** CARELESS : descuidado **2** UNKEMPT : desaliñado

slot ['slat] *n* : ranura *f*

sloth ['slɔθ, 'sloθ] *n* : pereza *f*

slouch ['slautʃ] *vi* : andar con los hombros caídos (en una silla)

slovenly ['slʌvənli, 'slʌv-] *adj* : desaliñado

slow ['sloː] *adj* **1** : lento **2** be ~ : estar atrasado (dícese de un reloj) — ~ → **slowly** — ~ *vt* : retrasar, retardar — *vi or* ~ **down** : ir más despacio — **slowly** ['sloːli] *adv* : lentamente, despacio — **slowness** ['sloːnəs] *n* : lentitud *f*

sludge ['slʌdʒ] *n* SEWAGE : aguas *fpl* negras

slug¹ ['slʌg] *n* **1** : babosa *f* (molusco) **2** BULLET : bala *f* **3** TOKEN : ficha *f*

slug² *vt* **slugged; slugging** : pegar un porrazo a

sluggish ['slʌgɪʃ] *adj* : lento

slum ['slʌm] *n* : barrio *m* bajo

slumber ['slʌmbər] *vi* : dormir — ~ *n* : sueño *m*

slump ['slʌmp] *vi* **1** DROP : bajar **2** COLLAPSE : dejarse caer **3** → **slouch** — ~ *n* : bajón *m*

slung → **sling**

slunk → **slink**

slur¹ ['slər] *n* ASPERSION : calumnia *f*, difamación *f*

slur² *vt* **slurred; slurring** : arrastrar (las palabras)

slurp ['slərp] *v* : beber haciendo ruido — ~ *n* : sorbo *m* (ruidoso)

slush ['slʌʃ] *n* : nieve *f* medio derretida

sly ['slaɪ] *adj* **slier** ['slaɪər]; **sliest** ['slaɪəst] **1** : astuto, taimado **2 on the ~** : a escondidas

smack¹ ['smæk] *vi* ~ **of** : oler a

smack² *vt* **1** : pegar una bofetada a **2** KISS : besar **3 ~ one's lips** : relamerse — ~ *n* : **1** SLAP : bofetada *f* **2** KISS : beso *m* — ~ *adv* : justo, exactamente

small ['smɔl] *adj* : pequeño, chico — **smallpox** ['smɔl,paks] *n* : viruela *f*

smart ['smart] *adj* **1** : listo, inteligente **2** STYLISH : elegante — *vi* STING : escocer — **smartly** ['smartli] *adv* : elegantemente

smash ['smæʃ] *n* **1** BLOW : golpe *m* **2** COLLISION : choque *m* **3** BANG, CRASH : estrépito *m* — ~ *vt* **1** BREAK : romper **2** DESTROY : aplastar — *vi* **1** SHATTER : hacerse pedazos **2 ~ into** : estrellarse contra

smattering ['smætərɪŋ] *n* : nociones *fpl*

smear ['smɪr] *n* : mancha *f* — ~ *vt* **1** : embadurnar (de pinta, etc.), untar (de aceite, etc.) **2** SMUDGE : manchar

smell ['smɛl] *v* **smelled** *or* **smelt** ['smɛlt]; **smelling** : oler — ~ *n* **1** : (sentido *m* del) olfato *m* **2** ODOR : olor *m* — **smelly** ['smɛli] *adj* **smellier; -est** : maloliente

smelt ['smɛlt] *vt* : fundir

smile ['smaɪl] *vi* **smiled; smiling** : sonreír — ~ *n* : sonrisa *f*

smirk ['smərk] *vi* : sonreír con suficiencia — ~ *n* : sonrisa *f* satisfecha

smitten ['smɪtən] *adj* **be ~ with** : estar enamorado de

smith ['smɪθ] → **blacksmith**

smock ['smak] *n* : blusón *m*, bata *f*

smog ['smag, 'smɔg] *n* : smog *m*

smoke ['smoːk] *n* : humo *m* — ~ *v* **smoked; smoking** *vi* **1** : humear (dícese de fuegos, etc.) **2** : fumar (dícese de personas) — *vt* **1** : ahumar (carne, etc.) **2** : fumar (cigarrillos) — **smoker** ['smoːkər] *n* : fumador *m*, -dora *f* — **smokestack** ['smoːk,stæk] *n* : chimenea *f* — **smoky** ['smoːki] *adj* **smokier; -est 1** : lleno de humo **2** : a humo (dícese de sabores, etc.)

smolder ['smoːldər] *vi* : arder (sin llama)

smooth ['smuːð] *adj* **1** : liso (dícese de superficies), suave (dícese de movimientos), tranquilo (dícese del mar) **2** : sin grumos (dícese de salsas, etc.) — ~ *vt* : alisar — **smoothly** ['smuːðli] *adv* : suavemente — **smoothness** ['smuːðnəs] *n* : suavidad *f*

smother ['smʌðər] *vt* : asfixiar (a algn), sofocar (llamas, etc.)

smudge ['smʌdʒ] *v* **smudged; smudg-**

ing vt : emborronar — vi : correrse —
~ n : mancha f, borrón m
smug ['smʌg] adj **smugger; smuggest**
: suficiente
smuggle ['smʌgəl] vt **-gled; -gling**
: pasar de contrabando — **smuggler**
['smʌglər] n : contrabandista mf
snack ['snæk] n : refrigerio m, tentempié m fam
snag ['snæg] n : problema m — ~ v
snagged; snagging vt : enganchar —
vi : engancharse
snail ['sneɪl] n : caracol m
snake ['sneɪk] n : culebra f, serpiente f
snap ['snæp] v **snapped; snapping** vi 1
BREAK : romperse 2 : intentar morder
(dícese de un perro, etc.) 3 ~ at : contestar bruscamente a — vt 1 BREAK
: romper 2 ~ one's fingers
: chasquear los dedos 3 ~ open/shut
: abrir/cerrar de golpe — ~ n 1
: chasquido m 2 FASTENER : broche m
(de presión) 3 be a ~ : ser facilísimo
— **snappy** ['snæpi] adj **snappier; -est**
1 FAST : rápido 2 STYLISH : elegante —
snapshot ['snæp,ʃɑt] n : instantánea f
snare ['snær] n : trampa f — ~ vt
snared; snaring : atrapar
snarl[1] ['snɑrl] vi TANGLE : enmarañar,
enredar — ~ n : enredo m, maraña f
snarl[2] vi GROWL : gruñir — n : gruñido m
snatch ['snætʃ] vt : arrebatar
sneak ['snik] vi : ir a hurtadillas — vt
: hacer furtivamente — ~ n : soplón
m, -plona f fam — **sneakers** ['sni:kərz]
npl : tenis mpl, zapatillas fpl —
sneaky ['sni:ki] adj **sneakier; -est**
: solapada
sneer ['snɪr] vi : sonreír con desprecio
— ~ n : sonrisa f de desprecio
sneeze ['sni:z] vi **sneezed; sneezing**
: estornudar — ~ n : estornudo m
snide ['snaɪd] adj : sarcástico
sniff ['snɪf] vi : oler — vt 1 : oler 2
→ **sniffle** — ~ n : aspiración f por la
nariz — **sniffle** ['snɪfəl] vi **-fled; -fling**
: sorberse la nariz — **sniffles** ['snɪfəlz]
npl have the ~ : estar resfriado
snip ['snɪp] n : tijeretada f — ~ vt
snipped; snipping : cortar (con tijeras)
snivel ['snɪvəl] vi **-veled** or **-velled;
-veling** or **-velling** : lloriquear
snob ['snɑb] n : esnob mf — **snobbish**
['snɑbɪʃ] adj : esnob
snoop ['snu:p] vi : husmear — ~ n : fisgón m, -gona f
snooze ['snu:z] vi **snoozed; snoozing**
: dormitar — ~ n : siestecita f, siesti-
ta f

snore ['snor] vi **snored; snoring** : roncar — ~ n : ronquido m
snort ['snɔrt] vi : bufar — ~ n : bufido
m
snout ['snaʊt] n : hocico m, morro m
snow ['sno:] n : nieve f — vi : nevar
— **snowfall** ['sno:,fɔl] n — **snowflake** ['sno:,fleɪk] n : copo m de
nieve — **snowman** ['sno:,mæn] n
: muñeco m de nieve — **snowplow**
['sno:,plaʊ] n : quitanieves m — **snow-
shoe** ['sno:,ʃu:] n : raqueta f (para
nieve) — **snowstorm** ['sno:,stɔrm] n
: tormenta f de nieve — **snowy** ['sno:i]
adj **snowier; -est** 1 a ~ **day** : un día
nevoso 2 ~ **mountains** : montañas
fpl nevadas
snub ['snʌb] vt **snubbed; snubbing**
: desairar — ~ n : desaire m
snuff ['snʌf] vt or ~ **out** : apagar
snug ['snʌg] adj **snugger; snuggest** 1
: cómodo 2 TIGHT : ajustado — **snug-
gle** ['snʌgəl] vi **-gled; -gling** : acurrucarse
so ['so:] adv 1 LIKEWISE : también 2
THUS : así 3 THEREFORE : por lo tanto 4
or ~ **much** : tanto 5 or ~ **very** : tan
6 **and** ~ **on** : etcétera 7 **I think** ~
: creo que sí 8 **I told you** ~ : te lo dije
— ~ conj 1 THEREFORE : así que 2 or
~ **that** : para que 3 ~ **what?** : ¿y
qué? — ~ adj TRUE : cierto — ~
pron or ~ : más o menos
soak ['so:k] vi : estar en remojo — vt 1
: poner en remojo 2 ~ **up** : absorber
— ~ n : remojo m
soap ['so:p] n : jabón m — ~ vt or ~
up : enjabonar — **soapy** ['so:pi]
soapier; -est adj : jabonoso
soar ['sor] vi 1 : planear 2 SKYROCKET
: dispararse
sob ['sɑb] vi **sobbed; sobbing** : sollozar — ~ n : sollozo m
sober ['so:bər] adj 1 : sobrio 2 SERIOUS
: serio — **sobriety** [sə'braɪəti, so-] n 1
: sobriedad f 2 SERIOUSNESS : seriedad
f
so-called ['so:,kɔld] adj : supuesto, presunto
soccer ['sɑkər] n : futbol m, fútbol m
social ['so:ʃəl] adj : social — ~ n : reunión f social — **sociable** ['so:ʃəbəl]
adj : sociable — **socialism** ['so:ʃə-
,lɪzəm] n : socialismo m — **socialist**
['so:ʃəlɪst] n : socialista mf — ~ adj
: socialista — **socialize** ['so:ʃə,laɪz] v
-ized; -izing vt : socializar — vi
with : alternar con — **society** [sə-
'saɪəti] n, pl **-eties** : sociedad f — **sociology** [,so:si'ɑlədʒi] n : sociología f

sock¹ ['sɑk] *n*, *pl* **socks** *or* **sox** ['sɑks] : calcetín *m*

sock² *vt* : pegar, golpear — **~** *n* PUNCH : puñetazo *m*

socket ['sɑkət] *n* **1** *or* **electric ~** : enchufe *m*, toma *f* de corriente **2** *or* **eye ~** : órbita *f*, cuenca *f* **3** : glena *f* (de una articulación)

soda ['soːdə] *n* **1** *or* **~ pop** : refresco *m*, gaseosa *f* **2** *or* **~ water** : soda *f*

sodium ['soːdiəm] *n* : sodio *m*

sofa ['soːfə] *n* : sofá *m*

soft ['sɔft] *adj* **1** : blando **2** SMOOTH : suave — **softball** ['sɔft,bɔl] *n* : softbol *m* — **soft drink** *n* : refresco *m* — **soften** ['sɔfən] *vt* **1** : ablandar **2** EASE, SMOOTH : suavizar — *vi* **1** : ablandarse **2** EASE : suavizarse — **softly** ['sɔftli] *adv* : suavemente — **software** ['sɔft,wær] *n* : software *m*

soggy ['sɑgi] *adj* **soggier; -est** : empapado

soil ['sɔil] *vt* : ensuciar — **~** *n* DIRT : tierra *f*

solace ['sɑləs] *n* : consuelo *m*

solar ['soːlər] *adj* : solar

sold → **sell**

solder ['sɑdər, 'soː-] *n* : soldadura *f* — **~** *vt* : soldar

soldier ['soːldʒər] *n* : soldado *mf*

sole¹ ['soːl] *n* : lenguado *m* (pez)

sole² *n* : planta *f* (del pie), suela *f* (de un zapato)

sole³ *adj* : único — **solely** ['soːli] *adv* : únicamente, sólo

solemn ['sɑləm] *adj* : solemne — **solemnity** [sə'lɛmnəti] *n*, *pl* **-ties** : solemnidad *f*

solicit [sə'lɪsət] *vt* : solicitar

solid ['sɑləd] *adj* **1** : sólido **2** UNBROKEN : continuo **3** ~ **gold** : oro *m* macizo **4** **two ~ hours** : dos horas seguidas — **~** *n* : sólido *m* — **solidarity** [sɑlə'dærəti] *n* : solidaridad *f* — **solidify** [sə'lɪdə,faɪ] *v* **-fied; -fying** *vt* : solidificar — *vi* : solidificarse — **solidity** [sə'lɪdəti] *n*, *pl* **-ties** : solidez *f*

solitary ['sɑlə,tɛri] *adj* : solitario — **solitude** ['sɑlə,tuːd, -,tjuːd] *n* : soledad *f*

solo ['soːloː] *n*, *pl* **solos** : solo *m* — **soloist** ['soːloɪst] *n* : solista *mf*

solution [sə'luːʃən] *n* : solución *f* — **soluble** ['sɑljəbəl] *adj* : soluble — **solve** ['sɑlv] *vt* **solved; solving** : resolver — **solvent** ['sɑlvənt] *n* : solvente *m*

somber ['sɑmbər] *adj* : sombrío

some ['sʌm] *adj* **1** (*of unspecified identity*) : un **2** (*of an unspecified amount*) : algo de, un poco de **3** (*of an unspecified number*) : unos **4** CERTAIN : al-

gunos **5 that was ~ game!** : ¡fue un partidazo! — **~** *pron* **1** SEVERAL : algunos, unos **2** PART : un poco, algo — **~** *adv* **twenty people** : unas veinte personas — **somebody** ['sʌm,bɑdi, -,bɑdi] *pron* : alguien — **someday** ['sʌm,deɪ] *adv* : algún día — **somehow** ['sʌm,haʊ] *adv* **1** : de algún modo **2 ~ or other** : de alguna manera u otra — **someone** ['sʌm,wʌn] *pron* : alguien

somersault ['sʌmər,sɔlt] *n* : voltereta *f*, salto *m* mortal

something ['sʌmθɪŋ] *pron* **1** : algo **2 ~ else** : otra cosa — **sometime** ['sʌm,taɪm] *adv* **1** : algún día, en algún momento **2 ~ next month** : (durante) el mes que viene — **sometimes** ['sʌm,taɪmz] *adv* : a veces — **somewhat** ['sʌm,hwʌt, -,hwɑt] *adv* : algo — **somewhere** ['sʌm,hwɛr] *adv* **1** : en alguna parte, en algún lado **2 ~ around** : alrededor de **3 ~ else** → **elsewhere**

son ['sʌn] *n* : hijo *m*

song ['sɔŋ] *n* : canción *f*

son–in–law ['sʌnɪn,lɔ] *n*, *pl* **sons–in–law** : yerno *m*

sonnet ['sɑnət] *n* : soneto *m*

soon ['suːn] *adv* **1** : pronto **2** SHORTLY : dentro de poco **3 as ~ as** : en cuanto **4 as ~ as possible** : lo más pronto posible **5 ~ after** : poco después **6 ~er or later** : tarde o temprano **7 the ~er the better** : cuanto antes mejor

soot ['sʊt, 'suːt, 'sʌt] *n* : hollín *m*

soothe ['suːð] *vt* **soothed; soothing 1** CALM : calmar **2** RELIEVE : aliviar

sop ['sɑp] *vt* **sopped; sopping ~ up** : absorber

sophistication [sə,fɪstə'keɪʃən] *n* : sofisticación *f* — **sophisticated** [sə'fɪstə,keɪtəd] *adj* : sofisticado

sophomore ['sɑf,mor, 'sɑfə,mor] *n* : estudiante *mf* de segundo año

soprano [sə'prænoː] *n*, *pl* **-nos** : soprano *mf*

sorcerer ['sɔrsərər] *n* : hechicero *m*, brujo *m* — **sorcery** ['sɔrsəri] *n* : hechicería *f*, brujería *f*

sordid ['sɔrdəd] *adj* : sórdido

sore ['sor] *adj* **sorer; sorest 1** : dolorido **2** ANGRY : enfadado **3 ~ throat** : dolor *m* de garganta **4 I have a ~ throat** : me duele la garganta — **~** *n* : llaga *f* — **sorely** ['sorli] *adv* : muchísimo — **soreness** ['sornəs] *n* : dolor *m*

sorrow ['sɑr,oː] *n* : pesar *m*, pena *f* — **sorry** ['sɑri] *adj* **sorrier; -est 1** PITIFUL : lamentable **2 feel ~ for** : compadecer **3 I'm ~** : lo siento

sort ['sɔrt] n 1 : tipo m, clase f 2 **a ~ of** : una especie de — ~ vt : clasificar —
sort of adv 1 SOMEWHAT : algo 2 MORE OR LESS : más o menos
SOS [ˌɛsˌoːˈɛs] n : SOS m
so-so ['soːˌsoː] adj & adv : así así fam
soufflé [suːˈfleɪ] n : suflé m
sought → **seek**
soul ['soːl] n : alma f
sound[1] ['saʊnd] adj 1 HEALTHY : sano 2 FIRM : sólido 3 SENSIBLE : lógico 4 **a ~ sleep** : un sueño profundo 5 **safe and ~** : sano y salvo
sound[2] n : sonido m — vt : hacer sonar, tocar (una trompeta, etc.) — vi 1 : sonar 2 SEEM : parecer
sound[3] n CHANNEL : brazo m de mar — ~ vt 1 : sondar (en navegación) 2 or **~ out** : sondear
soundly ['saʊndli] adv 1 SOLIDLY : sólidamente 2 DEEPLY : profundamente
soundproof ['saʊndˌpruːf] adj : insonorizado
soup ['suːp] n : sopa f
sour ['saʊər] adj 1 : agrio 2 **~ milk** : leche f cortada — ~ vt : agriar
source ['sɔrs] n : fuente f, origen m
south ['saʊθ] adv : al sur — ~ adj : (del) sur — ~ n : sur m — **South African** adj : sudafricano — **South American** adj : sudamericano — **southeast** [saʊθˈiːst] adv : hacia el sureste — ~ adj : (del) sureste — ~ n : sureste m, sudeste m — **southeastern** [saʊθˈiːstərn] adj → **southeast** — **southerly** ['sʌðərli] adv & adj : del sur — **southern** ['sʌðərn] adj : del sur, meridional — **southwest** [saʊθˈwest] adv : hacia el suroeste — ~ adj : (del) suroeste — ~ n : suroeste m, sudoeste m — **southwestern** [saʊθˈwestərn] adj → **southwest**
souvenir [ˌsuːvəˈnɪr, 'suːvəˌ-] n : recuerdo m
sovereign ['sɑvərən] n : soberano m, -na f — ~ adj : soberano — **sovereignty** ['sɑvərənti] n, pl **-ties** : soberanía f
Soviet ['soːviˌɛt, 'sɑ-, -viət] adj : soviético
sow[1] ['saʊ] n : cerda f
sow[2] ['soː] vt **sowed; sown** ['soːn] or **sowed; sowing** : sembrar
sox → **sock**
soybean ['sɔɪˌbiːn] n : soya f, soja f
spa ['spɑ] n : balneario m
space ['speɪs] n 1 : espacio m 2 ROOM, SPOT : sitio m, lugar m — ~ vt **spaced; spacing** : espaciar — **spaceship** ['speɪsˌʃɪp] n : nave f espacial — **space shuttle** n : transbor-

dador m espacial — **spacious** ['speɪʃəs] adj : espacioso, amplio
spade[1] ['speɪd] n SHOVEL : pala f
spade[2] n : pica f (naipe)
spaghetti [spəˈɡɛti] n : espaguetis mpl
span ['spæn] n 1 PERIOD : espacio m 2 : luz f (entre dos soportes) — ~ vt **spanned; spanning** 1 : abarcar (un período) 2 CROSS : extenderse sobre
Spaniard ['spænjərd] n : español m, -ñola f
spaniel ['spænjəl] n : spaniel m
Spanish ['spænɪʃ] adj : español — ~ n : español m (idioma)
spank ['spæŋk] vt : dar palmadas a (en las nalgas)
spar ['spɑr] vi **sparred; sparring** : entrenarse (en boxeo)
spare ['spær] vt **spared; sparing** 1 PARDON : perdonar 2 SAVE : ahorrar 3 **can you ~ a dollar?** : ¿me das un dólar? 4 **I can't ~ the time** : no tengo tiempo 5 **~ no expense** : no reparar en gastos 6 **to ~** : de sobra — ~ adj 1 : de repuesto 2 EXCESS : de más 3 LEAN : delgado — ~ n or **~ part** : repuesto m — **spare time** n : tiempo m libre — **sparing** ['spærɪŋ] adj : parco, económico
spark ['spɑrk] n : chispa f — ~ vi : chispear, echar chispas — vt : despertar (interés), provocar (crítica) — **sparkle** ['spɑrkəl] vi **-kled; -kling** : destellar, centellear — ~ n : destello m, centelleo m — **spark plug** n : bujía f
sparrow ['spæroː] n : gorrión m
sparse ['spɑrs] adj **sparser; -est** : escaso
spasm ['spæzəm] n : espasmo m
spat[1] → **spit**
spat[2] n QUARREL : disputa f, pelea f
spatter ['spætər] vt : salpicar
spawn ['spɔn] vi : desovar — vt : engendrar, producir — ~ n : hueva f
speak ['spiːk] v **spoke** ['spoːk]; **spoken** ['spoːkən]; **speaking** vi 1 : hablar 2 **~ out against** : denunciar 3 **~ up** : hablar más alto 4 **~ up for** : defender — vt 1 : decir 2 : hablar (un idioma) — **speaker** ['spiːkər] n 1 ORATOR : orador m, -dora f 2 : hablante mf (de un idioma) 3 LOUDSPEAKER : altavoz m
spear ['spɪr] n : lanza f — **spearhead** ['spɪrˌhed] n : punta f de lanza — ~ vt : encabezar — **spearmint** ['spɪrˌmɪnt] n : menta f verde
special ['speʃəl] adj : especial — **specialist** ['speʃəlɪst] n : especialista mf — **specialization** [ˌspeʃələˈzeɪʃən] n : especialización f — **specialize** ['speʃə-

,laɪz] *vi* **-ized; -izing** : especializarse — **specially** *adv* : especialmente — **specialty** ['speʃəlʈi] *n, pl* **-ties** : especialidad *f*

species ['spiːʃiːz, -siːz] *ns & pl* : especie *f*

specify ['spesəfaɪ] *vt* **-fied; -fying** : especificar — **specific** [sprˈsɪfɪk] *adj* : específico — **specifically** [sprˈsɪfɪkli] *adv* 1 : específicamente 2 EXPLICITLY : expresamente — **specification** [spesəfəˈkeɪʃən] *n* : especificación *f*

specimen ['spesəmən] *n* : espécimen *m*

speck ['spek] *n* 1 SPOT : mancha *f* 2 BIT : mota *f* — **speckled** ['spekəld] *adj* : moteado

spectacle ['spektɪkəl] *n* 1 : espectáculo *m* 2 **~s** *npl* GLASSES : gafas *fpl*, lentes *fpl*, anteojos *mpl* — **spectacular** [spekˈtækjələr] *adj* : espectacular — **spectator** ['spekˌteɪtər] *n* : espectador *m*, -dora *f*

specter *or* **spectre** ['spektər] *n* : espectro *m*

spectrum ['spektrəm] *n, pl* **-tra** [-trə] *or* **-trums** 1 : espectro *m* 2 RANGE : gama *f*

speculation [spekjəˈleɪʃən] *n* : especulación *f*

speech ['spiːtʃ] *n* 1 : habla *f* 2 ADDRESS : discurso *m* — **speechless** ['spiːtʃləs] *adj* : mudo

speed ['spiːd] *n* 1 : rapidez *f* 2 VELOCITY : velocidad *f* — **~** *v* **sped** ['sped] *or* **speeded; speeding** *vi* 1 : conducir a exceso de velocidad 2 **~ off** : irse a toda velocidad 3 **~ up** : acelerarse — *vt or* **~ up** : acelerar — **speed limit** *n* : velocidad *f* máxima — **speedometer** [sprˈdɑmətər] *n* : velocímetro *m* — **speedy** ['spiːdi] *adj* **speedier, -est** : rápido

spell[1] ['spel] *vt* 1 : escribir (las letras de) 2 *or* **~ out** : deletrear 3 MEAN : significar

spell[2] *n* ENCHANTMENT : hechizo *m*

spell[3] *n* : período *m* (de tiempo)

spellbound ['spel,baʊnd] *adj* : embelesado

spelling ['spelɪŋ] *n* : ortografía *f*

spend ['spend] *vt* **spent** ['spent]; **spending** 1 : gastar (dinero) 2 : pasar (las vacaciones, etc.) 3 **~ time on** : dedicar tiempo a

sperm ['spərm] *n, pl* **sperm** *or* **sperms** : esperma *mf*

spew ['spjuː] *vt* : vomitar, arrojar (lava, etc.)

sphere ['sfɪr] *n* : esfera *f* — **spherical** ['sfɪrɪkəl, 'sfer-] *adj* : esférico

spice ['spaɪs] *n* : especia *f* — **~** *vt* **spiced; spicing** : condimentar, sazonar — **spicy** ['spaɪsi] *adj* **spicier; -est** : picante

spider ['spaɪdər] *n* : araña *f*

spigot ['spɪgət, -kət] *n* : grifo *m* *Spain*, llave *f* *Lat*

spike ['spaɪk] *n* 1 : clavo *m* (grande) 2 POINT : punta *f* — **spiky** ['spaɪki] *adj* : puntiagudo

spill ['spɪl] *vt* : derramar — *vi* : derramarse

spin ['spɪn] *v* **spun** ['spʌn]; **spinning** *vi* : girar — *vt* 1 : hilar (lana, etc.) 2 TWIRL : hacer girar — **~** *n* 1 : vuelta *f*, giro *m* 2 **go for a ~** : dar una vuelta (en auto)

spinach ['spɪnɪtʃ] *n* : espinacas *fpl*

spinal cord ['spaɪnəl] *n* : médula *f* espinal

spindle ['spɪndəl] *n* : huso *m* (para hilar) — **spindly** ['spɪndli] *adj* : larguirucho *fam*

spine ['spaɪn] *n* 1 : columna *f* vertebral 2 QUILL : púa *f* 3 THORN : espina *f* 4 : lomo *m* (de un libro)

spinster ['spɪnstər] *n* : soltera *f*

spiral ['spaɪrəl] *adj* : de espiral, en espiral — **~** *n* : espiral *f* — *vi* **-raled** *or* **-ralled; -raling** *or* **-ralling** : ir en espiral

spire ['spaɪr] *n* : aguja *f*

spirit ['spɪrət] *n* 1 : espíritu *m* 2 **in good ~s** : animado 3 **~s** *npl* : licores *mpl* — **spirited** ['spɪrətəd] *adj* : animado — **spiritual** ['spɪrɪtʃuəl, -tʃəl] *adj* : espiritual — **spirituality** [spɪrɪtʃuˈæləʈi] *n, pl* **-ties** : espiritualidad *f*

spit[1] ['spɪt] *n* ROTISSERIE : asador *m*

spit[2] *v* **spit** *or* **spat** ['spæt]; **spitting** : escupir — *n* SALIVA : saliva *f*

spite ['spaɪt] *n* 1 : rencor *m* 2 **in ~ of** : a pesar de — **~** *vt* **spited; spiting** : fastidiar — **spiteful** ['spaɪtfəl] *adj* : rencoroso

spittle ['spɪtəl] *n* : saliva *f*

splash ['splæʃ] *vt* : salpicar — *vi* 1 : salpicar 2 *or* **~ about** : chapotear — **~** *n* 1 : salpicadura *f* 2 : mancha *f* (de color, etc.)

splatter ['splætər] → **spatter**

spleen ['spliːn] *n* : bazo *m* (órgano)

splendor ['splendər] *n* : esplendor *m* — **splendid** ['splendəd] *adj* : espléndido

splint ['splɪnt] *n* : tablilla *f*

splinter ['splɪntər] *n* : astilla *f* — *vi* : astillarse

split ['splɪt] *v* **split; splitting** *vt* 1 : partir 2 BURST : reventar 3 *or* **~ up** : dividir — *vi* 1 : partirse, rajarse 2 *or* **~ up**

: dividirse — ~ *n* 1 CRACK : rajadura *f* 2 *or* ~ **seam** : descosido *m* 3 DIVISION : división *f*

splurge ['splərdʒ] *vi* **splurged; splurging** : derrochar dinero

spoil ['spɔɪl] *vt* **spoiled** *or* **spoilt** ['spɔɪlt]; **spoiling** 1 RUIN : estropear 2 PAMPER : consentir, mimar — **spoils** *npl* : botín *m*

spoke[1] ['spoːk] → **speak**

spoke[2] *n* : rayo *m* (de una rueda)

spoken → **speak**

spokesman ['spoːksmən] *n*, *pl* **-men** [-mən, -men] : portavoz *mf* — **spokeswoman** ['spoːks,wumən] *n*, *pl* **-women** [-,wimən] : portavoz *f*

sponge ['spʌndʒ] *n* : esponja *f* — ~ *vt* **sponged; sponging** : limpiar con una esponja — **spongy** ['spʌndʒi] *adj* **spongier; -est** : esponjoso

sponsor ['spɑntsər] *n* : patrocinador *m*, -dora *f* — ~ *vt* : patrocinar — **sponsorship** ['spɑntsər,ʃɪp] *n* : patrocinio *m*

spontaneity [,spɑntə'niːəti, -'neɪ-] *n* : espontaneidad *f* — **spontaneous** [spɑn'teɪniəs] *adj* : espontáneo

spooky ['spuːki] *adj* **spookier; -est** : espeluzante

spool ['spuːl] *n* : carrete *m*

spoon ['spuːn] *n* : cuchara *f* — **spoonful** ['spuːn,fʊl] *n* : cucharada *f*

sporadic [spə'rædɪk] *adj* : esporádico

spore ['spɔr] *n* : espora *f*

sport ['spɔrt] *n* 1 : deporte *m* 2 **be a good** ~ : tener espíritu deportivo — **sportsman** ['spɔrtsmən] *n*, *pl* **-men** [-mən, -men] : deportista *m* — **sportswoman** ['spɔrts,wumən] *n*, *pl* **-women** [-,wimən] : deportista *f* — **sporty** ['spɔrti] *adj* **sportier; -est** : deportivo

spot ['spɑt] *n* 1 : mancha *f* 2 DOT : punto *m* 3 PLACE : lugar *m*, sitio *m* 4 **in a tight** ~ : en apuros 5 **on the** ~ INSTANTLY : en ese mismo momento — ~ *vt* **spotted; spotting** 1 STAIN : manchar 2 DETECT, NOTICE : ver, descubrir — **spotless** ['spɑtləs] *adj* : impecable — **spotlight** ['spɑt,laɪt] *n* 1 : foco *m*, reflector *m* 2 **be in the** ~ : ser el centro de atención — **spotty** ['spɑti] *adj* **spottier; -est** : irregular

spouse ['spaʊs] *n* : cónyuge *mf*

spout ['spaʊt] *vi* : salir a chorros — ~ *n* 1 : pico *m* (de una jarra, etc.) 2 STREAM : chorro *m*

spray[1] ['spreɪ] *n* BOUQUET : ramillete *m*

spray[2] *n* 1 MIST : rocío *m* 2 *or* **aerosol** ~ : spray *m* 3 *or* ~ **bottle** : atomizador *m* — ~ *vt* : rociar (una superficie), pulverizar (un líquido)

spread ['spred] *v* **spread; spreading** *vt* 1 : propagar (enfermedades), difundir (noticias, etc.) 2 *or* ~ **out** : extender 3 : untar (con mantequilla, etc.) — *vi* 1 : propagarse, difundirse 2 *or* ~ **out** : extenderse — ~ *n* 1 : propagación *f*, difusión *f* 2 PASTE : pasta *f* (para untar) — **spreadsheet** ['spred,ʃiːt] *n* : hoja *f* de cálculo

spree ['spriː] *n* **go on a** ~ : ir de juerga *fam*

sprig ['sprɪg] *n* : ramito *m*

sprightly ['spraɪtli] *adj* **sprightlier; -est** : vivo

spring ['sprɪŋ] *v* **sprang** ['spræŋ] *or* **sprung** ['sprʌŋ]; **sprung; springing** *vi* 1 : saltar 2 ~ **from** : surgir de 3 ~ **up** : surgir — *vt* 1 ACTIVATE : accionar 2 ~ **a leak** : hacer agua 3 ~ **sth on s.o.** : sorprender a algn con algo — ~ *n* 1 : manantial *m* (de aguas) 2 : primavera *f* (estación) 3 LEAP : salto *m* 4 RESILIENCE : elasticidad *f* 5 : resorte *m* (mecanismo) 6 *or* **bedspring** : muelle *m* — **springboard** ['sprɪŋ,bɔrd] *n* : trampolín *m* — **springtime** ['sprɪŋ,taɪm] *n* : primavera *f* — **springy** ['sprɪŋi] *adj* **springier; -est** : mullido

sprinkle ['sprɪŋkəl] *vt* **-kled; -kling** 1 : salpicar, rociar 2 DUST : espolvorear — ~ *vi* : lloviznar *f* — **sprinkler** ['sprɪŋkələr] *n* : aspersor *m*

sprint ['sprɪnt] *vi* 1 : correr 2 : esprintar (en deportes) — ~ *n* : esprint *m* (en deportes)

sprout ['spraʊt] *vi* : brotar — ~ *n* : brote *m*

spruce[1] ['spruːs] *vt* **spruced; sprucing** ~ **up** : arreglar

spruce[2] *n* : picea *f* (árbol)

spry ['spraɪ] *adj* **sprier** *or* **spryer** ['spraɪər]; **spriest** *or* **spryest** ['spraɪəst] : ágil, activo

spun → **spin**

spur ['spər] *n* 1 : espuela *f* 2 STIMULUS : acicate *m* 3 **on the** ~ **of the moment** : sin pensarlo — ~ *vt* **spurred; spurring** *or* ~ **on** 1 : espolear (un caballo) 2 MOTIVATE : motivar

spurn ['spərn] *vt* : desdeñar, rechazar

spurt[1] ['spərt] *vi* : salir a chorros — ~ *n* : chorro *m*

spurt[2] *n* 1 : arranque *m* (de energía, etc.) 2 **work in** ~**s** : trabajar por rachas

spy ['spaɪ] v **spied; spying** vt : ver, divisar — vi ~ **on s.o.** : espiar a algn — ~ n : espía mf

squabble ['skwɑbəl] n : riña f, pelea f — ~ vi **-bled; -bling** : reñir, pelearse

squad ['skwɑd] n : pelotón m (militar), brigada f (de policías)

squadron ['skwɑdrən] n : escuadrón m (de soldados), escuadra f (de aviones o naves)

squalid ['skwɑlɪd] adj : miserable

squall ['skwɔl] n : turbión m

squalor ['skwɑlər] n : miseria f

squander ['skwɑndər] vt : derrochar (dinero, etc.), desperdiciar (oportunidades, etc.)

square ['skwær] n 1 : cuadrado m 2 : plaza f (de una ciudad) — ~ adj **squarer; -est** 1 : cuadrado 2 HONEST : justo 3 EVEN : en paz 4 a ~ **meal** : una comida decente — ~ vt **squared; squaring** 1 : elevar al cuadrado (un número) 2 : saldar (una cuenta) — **square root** n : raíz f cuadrada

squash¹ ['skwɑʃ, 'skwɔʃ] vt 1 : aplastar 2 : acallar (protestas, etc.) — ~ n : squash m (deporte)

squash² n, pl **squashes** or **squash** : calabaza f (vegetal)

squat ['skwɑt] vi **squatted; squatting** 1 or ~ **down** : ponerse en cuclillas 2 : ocupar un lugar sin derecho — ~ adj **squatter; squattest** : achaparrado

squawk ['skwɔk] n : graznido m — ~ vi : graznar

squeak ['skwik] vi : chillar 2 CREAK : chirriar — ~ n 1 : chillido m 2 CREAK : chirrido m — **squeaky** ['skwiki] adj **squeakier; -est** : chirriante

squeal ['skwil] vi 1 : chillar (dícese de personas, etc.), chirriar (dícese de frenos, etc.) 2 PROTEST : quejarse — ~ n : chillido m (de una persona), chirrido m (de frenos, etc.)

squeamish ['skwimɪʃ] adj : impresionable, delicado

squeeze ['skwiz] vt **squeezed; squeezing** 1 : apretar 2 : exprimir (frutas, etc.) 3 : extraer (jugo, etc.) — ~ n : apretón m

squid ['skwɪd] n, pl **squid** or **squids** : calamar m

squint ['skwɪnt] vi : entrecerrar los ojos — ~ n : estrabismo m

squirm ['skwərm] vi : retorcerse

squirrel ['skwərəl] n : ardilla f

squirt ['skwərt] vt : lanzar un chorro de — vi : salir a chorros — ~ n : chorrito m

stab ['stæb] n 1 : puñalada f 2 ~ **of pain** : pinchazo m 3 **take a** ~ **at** : intentar — ~ vt **stabbed; stabbing** 1 KNIFE : apuñalar 2 STICK : clavar

stable ['steɪbəl] n 1 : establo m (para ganado) 2 or **horse** ~ : caballeriza f — ~ adj **-bler; -blest** : estable — **stability** [stə'bɪləti] n, pl **-ties** : estabilidad f — **stabilize** ['steɪbə,laɪz] vt **-lized; -lizing** : estabilizar

stack ['stæk] n : montón m, pila f — ~ vt : amontonar, apilar

stadium ['steɪdiəm] n, pl **-dia** or **-diums** : estadio m

staff ['stæfs, stævz] n, pl **staffs** or **staves** ['stævz, 'steɪvz] 1 : bastón m 2 pl **staffs** PERSONNEL : personal m 3 pl **staffs** : pentagrama m (en música) — ~ vt ['stæf] vt : proveer de personal

stag ['stæg] n, pl **stags** or **stag** : ciervo m, venado m — ~ adj : sólo para hombres — ~ adv **go** ~ : ir solo

stage ['steɪdʒ] n 1 : escenario m (de un teatro) 2 PHASE : etapa f 3 **the** ~ : el teatro — ~ vt **staged; staging** 1 : poner en escena 2 ARRANGE : montar — **stagecoach** ['steɪdʒ,koʊtʃ] n : diligencia f

stagger ['stægər] vi : tambalearse — vt 1 : escalonar (turnos, etc.) 2 **be** ~ **ed by** : quedarse estupefacto por — ~ n : tambaleo m — **staggering** ['stægərɪŋ] adj : asombroso

stagnant ['stægnənt] adj : estancado — **stagnate** ['stæg,neɪt] vi **-nated; -nating** : estancarse

stain ['steɪn] vt 1 : manchar 2 : teñir (madera) — ~ n 1 : mancha f 2 DYE : tinte m, tintura f — **stainless steel** ['steɪnləs-] n : acero m inoxidable

stair ['stær] n 1 STEP : escalón m, peldaño m 2 ~ **s** npl : escalera(s) f(pl) — **staircase** ['stær,keɪs] n : escalera(s) f(pl) — **stairway** ['stær,weɪ] n : escalera(s) f(pl)

stake ['steɪk] n 1 POST : estaca f 2 BET : apuesta f 3 INTEREST : intereses mpl 4 **be at** ~ : estar en juego — ~ vt **staked; staking** 1 : estacar 2 BET : jugarse 3 ~ **a claim to** : reclamar

stale ['steɪl] adj **staler; stalest** 1 : duro (dícese del pan) 2 OLD : viejo 3 STUFFY : viciado

stalk¹ ['stɔk] n : tallo m (de una planta)

stalk² vt : acechar — vi or ~ **off** : irse con altivez

stall¹ ['stɔl] n 1 : compartimiento m (de un establo) 2 STAND : puesto m — ~ vt : parar (un motor) — vi : pararse

stall² vt DELAY : entretener — vi : andar con rodeos

stallion ['stæljən] n : caballo m semental

stalwart ['stɔlwərt] adj 1 STRONG : fornido 2 ~ **supporter** : partidario m leal

stamina ['stæmənə] n : resistencia f

stammer ['stæmər] vi : tartamudear — ~ n : tartamudeo m

stamp ['stæmp] n 1 SEAL : sello m 2 DIE : cuño m 3 or **postage** ~ : sello m, estampilla f Lat, timbre m Lat — ~ vt 1 : franquear (una carta) 2 IMPRINT : sellar 3 MINT : acuñar 4 ~ **one's foot** : dar una patada (en el suelo)

stampede [stæm'piːd] n : estampida f — ~ vi **-peded; -peding** : salir en estampida

stance ['stæns] n : postura f

stand ['stænd] v **stood** ['stʊd]; **standing** vi 1 : estar de pie, estar parado Lat 2 BE : estar 3 CONTINUE : seguir vigente 4 LIE, REST : reposar 5 ~ **aside** or ~ **back** : apartarse 6 ~ **out** : sobresalir 7 or ~ **up** : ponerse de pie, pararse Lat — vt 1 PLACE : poner, colocar 2 ENDURE : soportar 3 ~ **a chance** : tener una posibilidad — **stand by** vt 1 : mantener (una promesa, etc.) 2 SUPPORT : apoyar — **stand for** vt 1 MEAN : significar 2 PERMIT : permitir — **stand up** vi 1 ~ **for** : defender 2 ~ **up to** : resistir a — ~ n 1 RESISTANCE : resistencia f 2 STALL : puesto m 3 BASE : base f 4 POSITION : posición f 5 ~ s npl : tribuna f

standard ['stændərd] n 1 : norma f 2 BANNER : estandarte m 3 CRITERION : criterio m 4 ~ **of living** : nivel m de vida — ~ adj : estándar — **standardize** ['stændər,daɪz] vt **-ized; -izing** : estandarizar

standing ['stændɪŋ] n 1 RANK : posición f 2 DURATION : duración f

standpoint ['stænd,pɔɪnt] n : punto m de vista

standstill ['stænd,stɪl] n 1 **be at a** ~ : estar paralizado 2 **come to a** ~ : pararse

stank → **stink**

stanza ['stænzə] n : estrofa f

staple¹ ['steɪpəl] n : producto m principal — ~ adj : principal, básico

staple² ['steɪpəl] n : grapa f (para papeles) — ~ vt **-pled; -pling** : grapar, engrapar Lat — **stapler** ['steɪplər] n : grapadora f, engrapadora f Lat

star ['stɑr] n : estrella f — ~ v **starred**; **starring** vt FEATURE : estar protagonizado por — vi **in** : protagonizar

starboard ['stɑrbərd] n : estribor m

starch ['stɑrtʃ] vt : almidonar — ~ n 1 : almidón m 2 : fécula f (comida)

stardom ['stɑrdəm] n : estrellato m

stare ['stær] vi **stared**; **staring** : mirar fijamente — ~ n : mirada f fija

starfish ['stɑr,fɪʃ] n : estrella f de mar

stark ['stɑrk] adj 1 PLAIN : austero 2 HARSH : severo, duro 3 SHARP : marcado — ~ adv 1 : completamente 2 ~ **naked** : en cueros (vivos)

starlight ['stɑr,laɪt] n : luz f de las estrellas

starling ['stɑrlɪŋ] n : estornino m

starry ['stɑri] adj **starrier; -est** : estrellado

start ['stɑrt] vi 1 : empezar, comenzar 2 SET OUT : salir 3 JUMP : sobresaltarse 4 or ~ **up** : arrancar — vt 1 : empezar, comenzar 2 CAUSE : provocar 3 or ~ **up** ESTABLISH : montar 4 or ~ **up** : arrancar (un motor, etc.) — ~ n 1 : principio m 2 **get an early** ~ : salir temprano 3 **give s.o. a** ~ : asustar a algn — **starter** ['stɑrtər] n : motor m de arranque (de un vehículo)

startle ['stɑrtəl] vt **-tled; -tling** : asustar

starve ['stɑrv] v **starved; starving** vi : morirse de hambre — vt : privar de comida — **starvation** [stɑr'veɪʃən] n : inanición f, hambre f

stash ['stæʃ] vt : esconder

state ['steɪt] n 1 : estado m 2 **the States** : los Estados Unidos — ~ vt **stated; stating** 1 SAY : decir 2 REPORT : exponer — **stately** ['steɪtli] adj **statelier; -est** : majestuoso — **statement** ['steɪtmənt] n 1 : declaración f 2 or **bank** ~ : estado m de cuenta — **statesman** ['steɪtsmən] n, pl **-men** [-mən, -mɛn] : estadista mf

static ['stætɪk] adj : estático — ~ n : estática f

station ['steɪʃən] n 1 : estación f (de trenes, etc.) 2 RANK : condición f (social) 3 : canal m (de televisión), emisora f (de radio) 4 → **fire station**, **police station** — ~ vt : apostar, estacionar — **stationary** ['steɪʃə,nɛri] adj : estacionario

stationery ['steɪʃə,nɛri] n : papel m y sobres mpl (para cartas)

station wagon n : camioneta f (familiar)

statistic [stə'tɪstɪk] n : estadística f — **statistical** [stə'tɪstɪkəl] adj : estadístico

statue ['stætʃu] n : estatua f

stature ['stætʃər] n : estatura f, talla f

status ['steɪtəs, 'stæ-] n 1 : situación f 2 or **social** ~ : estatus m 3 **marital** ~ : estado m civil

statute ['stæ,tʃuːt] n : estatuto m

staunch ['stɔntʃ] adj : leal

stave ['steɪv] vt **staved** or **stove** ['stoːv]; **staving 1 ~ in** : romper **2 ~ off** : evitar

staves → **staff**

stay[1] ['steɪ] vi **1** REMAIN : quedarse, permanecer **2** LODGE : alojarse **3 ~ awake** : mantenerse despierto **4 ~ in** : quedarse en casa — vt : suspender (una ejecución, etc.) — ~ n **1** : estancia f, estadía f Lat **2** SUSPENSION : suspensión f

stay[2] n SUPPORT : soporte m

stead ['sted] n **1 in s.o.'s ~** : en lugar de algn **2 stand s.o. in good ~** : ser muy útil a algn — **steadfast** ['sted,fæst] adj **1** FIXEDLY : firme **2** LOYAL : leal, fiel — **steadily** ['stedəli] adv **1** : progresivamente **2** INCESSANTLY : sin parar **3** FIXEDLY : fijamente — **steady** ['stedi] adj **steadier; -est 1** FIRM, SURE : firme, seguro **2** FIXED : fijo **3** DEPENDABLE : responsable **4** CONSTANT : constante — ~ vt **steadied; steadying 1** : mantener firme **2** : calmar (los nervios)

steak ['steɪk] n : bistec m, filete m

steal ['stiːl] v **stole** ['stoːl]; **stolen** ['stoːlən]; **stealing** vt : robar — vi **1** : robar **2 ~ away** : escabullirse

stealth ['stelθ] n : sigilo m — **stealthy** ['stelθi] adj **stealthier; -est** : furtivo, sigiloso

steam ['stiːm] n **1** : vapor m **2 let off ~** : desahogarse — vi : echar vapor — vt **1** : cocer al vapor **2 ~ up** : empañar — **steam engine** n : motor m de vapor — **steamship** ['stiːm,ʃɪp] n : (barco m de) vapor m — **steamy** ['stiːmi] adj **steamier; -est 1** : lleno de vapor **2** PASSIONATE : tórrido

steel ['stiːl] n : acero m — vt **~ oneself** : armarse de valor — ~ adj : de acero

steep[1] ['stiːp] adj **1** : empinado **2** CONSIDERABLE : considerable **3** : muy alto (dícese de precios)

steep[2] vt : dejar (té, etc.) en infusión

steeple ['stiːpəl] n : aguja f, campanario m

steer[1] ['stɪr] n : buey m

steer[2] vt : dirigir (un auto, etc.), pilotear (un barco) — **steering wheel** n : volante m

stem[1] ['stem] n : tallo m (de una planta), pie m (de una copa) — vi **~ from** : provenir de

stem[2] vt **stemmed; stemming** : contener, detener

stench ['stentʃ] n : hedor m, mal olor m

stencil ['stensəl] n : plantilla f (para marcar)

step ['step] n **1** : paso m **2** RUNG, STAIR : escalón m **3 ~ by ~** : paso por paso **4 take ~s** : tomar medidas **5 watch your ~** : mira por dónde caminas — ~ vi **stepped; stepping 1** : dar un paso **2 ~ back** : retroceder **3 ~ down** RESIGN : retirarse **4 ~ in** : intervenir **5 ~ out** : salir (por un momento) **6 ~ this way** : pase por aquí — **step up** vt INCREASE : aumentar

stepbrother ['step,brʌðər] n : hermanastro m — **stepdaughter** ['step,dɔtər] n : hijastra f — **stepfather** ['step,fɑðər, -fa-] n : padrastro m

stepladder ['step,lædər] n : escalera f de tijera

stepmother ['step,mʌðər] n : madrastra f — **stepsister** ['step,sɪstər] n : hermanastra f — **stepson** ['step,sʌn] n : hijastro m

stereo ['steri,oː, 'stɪr-] n, pl **stereos** : estéreo m — ~ adj : estéreo

stereotype ['steriə,taɪp, 'stɪr-] vt **-typed; -typing** : estereotipar — ~ n : estereotipo m

sterile ['sterəl] adj : estéril — **sterility** [stə'rɪləti] n : esterilidad f — **sterilization** [,sterələ'zeɪʃən] n : esterilización f — **sterilize** ['sterə,laɪz] vt **-ized; -izing** : esterilizar

sterling ['stərlɪŋ] adj : excelente — **sterling silver** n : plata f de ley

stern[1] ['stərn] adj : severo, adusto

stern[2] n : popa f

stethoscope ['steθə,skoːp] n : estetoscopio m

stew ['stuː, 'stjuː] n : estofado m, guiso m — ~ vt : estofar, guisar — vi **1** : cocer **2** FRET : preocuparse

steward ['stuːərd, 'stjuː-] n **1** : administrador m, -dora f **2** : auxiliar m de vuelo (en un avión) **3** : camarero m (en un barco) — **stewardess** ['stuːərdəs, 'stjuː-] n **1** : auxiliar f de vuelo, azafata f (en un avión) **2** : camarera f (en un barco)

stick[1] ['stɪk] n **1** : palo m **2** TWIG : ramita f (suelta) **3** WALKING STICK : bastón m

stick[2] v **stuck** ['stʌk]; **sticking** vt **1** : pegar **2** STAB : clavar **3** PUT : poner **4 ~ out** : sacar (la lengua, etc.) — vi **1** : pegarse **2** JAM : atascarse **3 ~ around** : quedarse **4 ~ out** PROTRUDE : sobresalir **5 ~ out** SHOW : asomar **6 ~ up** : sobresalir **7 ~ up for** : defender — **sticker** ['stɪkər] n : etiqueta f adhesiva — **stickler** ['stɪklər] *n* **be a ~ for** : insistir mucho en — **sticky** ['stɪki] *adj* **stickier; -est** : pegajoso

stiff ['stɪf] *adj* **1** RIGID : rígido, tieso **2** STILTED : forzado **3** STRONG : fuerte **4** DIFFICULT : difícil **5** : entumecido (dícese de músculos) — **stiffen** ['stɪfən] *vt* : fortalecer, hacer más duro — *vi* **1** HARDEN : endurecerse **2** : entumecerse (dícese de músculos) — **stiffness** ['stɪfnəs] *n* : rigidez *f*

stifle ['staɪfəl] *vt* **-fled; -fling** : sofocar

stigmatize ['stɪgmətaɪz] *vt* **-tized; -tizing** : estigmatizar

still ['stɪl] *adj* **1** : inmóvil **2** SILENT : callado — *adv* **1** : todavía, aún **2** NEVERTHELESS : de todos modos, aún así **3 sit ~!** : ¡quédate quieto! — *vt* : quietud *f*, calma *f* — **stillborn** ['stɪl-bɔrn] *adj* : nacido muerto — **stillness** ['stɪlnəs] *n* : calma *f*, silencio *m*

stilt ['stɪlt] *n* : zanco *m* — **stilted** ['stɪltəd] *adj* : forzado

stimulate ['stɪmjəleɪt] *vt* **-lated; -lating** : estimular — **stimulant** ['stɪmjələnt] *n* : estimulante *m* — **stimulation** [ˌstɪmjəˈleɪʃən] *n* : estimulación *f* — **stimulus** ['stɪmjələs] *n, pl* **-li** [-ˌlaɪ] : estímulo *m*

sting ['stɪŋ] *v* **stung** ['stʌŋ], **stinging** : picar — *~ n* : picadura *f* — **stinger** ['stɪŋər] *n* : aguijón *m*

stingy ['stɪndʒi] *adj* **stingier; -est** : tacaño — **stinginess** ['stɪndʒinəs] *n* : tacañería *f*

stink ['stɪŋk] *vi* **stank** ['stæŋk] *or* **stunk** ['stʌŋk]; **stunk; stinking** : apestar, oler mal — *~ n* : hedor *m*, peste *f fam*

stint ['stɪnt] *vi* **~ on** : escatimar — *~ n* : período *m*

stipulate ['stɪpjəleɪt] *vt* **-lated; -lating** : estipular

stir ['stər] *v* **stirred; stirring** *vt* **1** : remover, revolver **2** MOVE : mover **3** INCITE : incitar **4** *or* **~ up** : despertar (memorias, etc.), provocar (ira, etc.) — *vi* : moverse, agitarse — *~ n* COMMOTION : revuelo *m*

stirrup ['stərəp, 'stɪr-] *n* : estribo *m*

stitch ['stɪtʃ] *n* **1** : puntada *f* **2** PAIN : punzada *f* (en el costado) — *~ v* : coser

stock ['stak] *n* **1** INVENTORY : existencias *fpl* **2** SECURITIES : acciones *fpl* **3** ANCESTRY : linaje *m*, estirpe *f* **4** BROTH : caldo *m* **5 out of ~** : agotado **6 take ~ of** : evaluar — *vi* **~ up on** : abastecerse de — **stockbroker** ['stak,broːkər] *n* : corredor *m*, -dora *f* de bolsa

stocking ['stakɪŋ] *n* : media *f*

stock market *n* : bolsa *f* — **stockpile** ['stak,paɪl] *n* : reservas *fpl* — *~ vt* **-piled; -piling** : almacenar — **stocky** ['staki] *adj* **stockier; -est** : robusto, fornido

stodgy ['stadʒi] *adj* **stodgier; -est 1** DULL : pesado **2** OLD-FASHIONED : anticuado

stoic ['stoɪk] *n* : estoico *m*, -ca *f* — *~ or* **stoical** [-ɪkəl] *adj* : estoico — **stoicism** ['stoɪəˌsɪzəm] *n* : estoicismo *m*

stoke ['stoːk] *vt* **stoked; stoking** : echar carbón o leña a

stole[1] ['stoːl] → **steal**

stole[2] *n* : estola *f*

stolen → **steal**

stomach ['stʌmɪk] *n* : estómago *m* — *~ vt* : aguantar, soportar — **stomachache** ['stʌmɪkˌeɪk] *n* : dolor *m* de estómago

stone ['stoːn] *n* **1** : piedra *f* **2** : hueso *m* (de una fruta) — *~ vt* **stoned; stoning** : apedrear — **stony** ['stoːni] *adj* **stonier; -est 1** : pedregoso **2 a ~ silence** : un silencio sepulcral

stood → **stand**

stool ['stuːl] *n* : taburete *m*

stoop ['stuːp] *vi* **1** : agacharse **2 ~ to** : rebajarse a — *~ n* **have a ~** : ser encorvado

stop ['stap] *v* **stopped; stopping** *vt* **1** PLUG : tapar **2** PREVENT : impedir **3** HALT : parar, detener **4** CEASE : dejar de — *vi* **1** : detenerse, parar **2** CEASE : cesar, dejar **3 ~ by** : visitar — *~ n* **1** : parada *f*, alto *m* **2 come to a ~** : pararse, detenerse **3 put a ~ to** : poner fin a — **stopgap** ['stap,gæp] *n* : arreglo *m* provisorio — **stoplight** ['stap,laɪt] *n* : semáforo *m* — **stoppage** ['stapɪdʒ] *n or* **work ~** : paro *m* — **stopper** ['stapər] *n* : tapón *m*

store ['stor] *vt* **stored; storing** : guardar (comida, etc.), almacenar (datos, mercancías, etc.) — *~ n* **1** SUPPLY : reserva *f* **2** SHOP : tienda *f* — **storage** ['storɪdʒ] *n* : almacenamiento *m* — **storehouse** ['stor,haʊs] *n* : almacén *m* — **storekeeper** ['stor,kiːpər] *n* : tendero *m*, -ra *f* — **storeroom** ['stor,ruːm, -ˌrʊm] *n* : almacén *m*

stork ['stork] *n* : cigüeña *f*

storm ['storm] *n* : tormenta *f*, tempestad *f* — *~ vi* **1** RAGE : ponerse furioso **2 ~ in/out** : entrar/salir furioso — *vt* ATTACK : asaltar — **stormy** ['stormi] *adj* **stormier; -est** : tormentoso

story[1] ['stori] *n, pl* **stories 1** TALE : cuento *m* **2** ACCOUNT : historia *f* **3** RUMOR : rumor *m*

story² *n* FLOOR : piso *m*, planta *f*

stout ['staut] *adj* **1** BRAVE : valiente **2** RESOLUTE : tenaz **3** STURDY : fuerte **4** FAT : corpulento

stove¹ ['sto:v] *n* **1** : estufa *f* (para calentar) **2** RANGE : cocina *f*

stove² → **stave**

stow ['sto:] *vt* **1** : guardar **2** LOAD : cargar — *vi* **away** : viajar de polizón —

stowaway ['sto:ə,weɪ] *n* : polizón *m*

straddle ['strædəl] *vt* -**dled; -dling** : sentarse a horcajadas sobre

straggle ['strægəl] *vi* -**gled; -gling** : rezagarse, quedarse atrás — **straggler** ['strægələr] *n* : rezagado *m*, -da *f*

straight ['streɪt] *adj* **1** : recto, derecho **2** : lacio (dícese del pelo) **3** HONEST : franco **4** TIDY : arreglado — *adv* **1** DIRECTLY : derecho **2** EXACTLY : justo **3** CLEARLY : con claridad **4** FRANKLY : con franqueza — **straightaway** ['streɪt,weɪ, -,weɪ] *adv* : inmediatamente — **straighten** ['streɪtən] *vt* **1** : enderezar **2** ~ **up** : arreglar — **straightforward** [streɪt'fɔrwərd] *adj* **1** FRANK : franco **2** CLEAR : claro, sencillo

strain¹ ['streɪn] *n* **1** LINEAGE : linaje *m* **2** STREAK : veta *f* **3** VARIETY : variedad *f* **4** ~**s** *npl* : acordes *mpl* (de música)

strain² *vt* **1** : forzar (la vista o la voz) **2** FILTER : colar **3** : tensar (relaciones, etc.) **4** ~ **a muscle** : sufrir un esguince **5** ~ **oneself** : hacerse daño — *vi* : esforzarse (por) — ~ *n* **1** STRESS : tensión *f* **2** SPRAIN : esguince *m* — **strainer** ['streɪnər] *n* : colador *m*

strait ['streɪt] *n* **1** : estrecho *m* **2** **in dire** ~**s** : en grandes apuros

strand¹ ['strænd] *vt* **be** ~**ed** : quedar(se) varado

strand² *n* **1** : hebra *f* **2** **a** ~ **of hair** : un pelo

strange ['streɪndʒ] *adj* **stranger; -est** **1** : extraño, raro **2** UNFAMILIAR : desconocido — **strangely** ['streɪndʒli] *adv* : de manera extraña — **strangeness** ['streɪndʒnəs] *n* **1** : rareza *f* **2** UNFAMILIARITY : lo desconocido — **stranger** ['streɪndʒər] *n* : desconocido *m*, -da *f*

strangle ['stræŋgəl] *vt* -**gled; -gling** : estrangular

strap ['stræp] *n* **1** : correa *f* **2** *or* **shoulder** ~ : tirante *m* — ~ *vt* **strapped; strapping** : sujetar con una correa — **strapless** ['stræpləs] *adj* : sin tirantes — **strapping** ['stræpɪŋ] *adj* : robusto, fornido

strategy ['stræṭədʒi] *n*, *pl* -**gies** : estrategia *f* — **strategic** [strə'ti:dʒɪk] *adj* : estratégico

straw ['strɔ] *n* **1** : paja *f* **2** *or* **drinking** ~ : pajita *f* **3** **the last** ~ : el colmo

strawberry ['strɔ,beri] *n*, *pl* -**ries** : fresa *f*

stray ['streɪ] *n* : animal *m* perdido — ~ *vi* **1** : perderse, extraviarse **2** : apartarse (de un grupo, etc.) **3** DEVIATE : desviarse — ~ *adj* : perdido

streak ['stri:k] *n* **1** : raya *f* **2** VEIN : veta *f* **3** ~ **of luck** : racha *f* de suerte — *vi* ~ **by** : pasar como una flecha

stream ['stri:m] *n* **1** : arroyo *m*, riachuelo *m* **2** FLOW : chorro *m*, corriente *f* — *vi* ~ : correr — **streamer** ['stri:mər] *n* **1** PENNANT : banderín *m* **2** : serpentina *f* (de papel) — **streamlined** ['stri:m,laɪnd] *adj* **1** : aerodinámico **2** EFFICIENT : eficiente

street ['stri:t] *n* : calle *f* — **streetcar** ['stri:t,kar] *n* : tranvía *m* — **streetlight** ['stri:t,laɪt] *n* : farol *m*

strength ['streŋkθ] *n* **1** : fuerza *f* **2** FORTITUDE : fortaleza *f* **3** TOUGHNESS : resistencia *f*, solidez *f* **4** INTENSITY : intensidad *f* **5** ~**s and weaknesses** : virtudes y defectos — **strengthen** ['streŋkθən] *vt* **1** : fortalecer **2** REINFORCE : reforzar **3** INTENSIFY : intensificar

strenuous ['strenjuəs] *adj* **1** : enérgico **2** ARDUOUS : duro, riguroso

stress ['stres] *n* **1** : tensión *f* **2** EMPHASIS : énfasis *m* **3** : acento *m* (en lingüística) — *vt* **1** EMPHASIZE : enfatizar **2** *or* ~ **out** : estresar — **stressful** ['stresfəl] *adj* : estresante

stretch ['stretʃ] *vt* **1** : estirar (músculos, elástico, etc.) **2** EXTEND : extender **3** ~ **the truth** : forzar la verdad — *vi* **1** : estirarse **2** EXTEND : extenderse — ~ *n* **1** : extensión *f* **2** ELASTICITY : elasticidad *f* **3** EXPANSE : tramo *m* **4** : período *m* (de tiempo) — **stretcher** ['stretʃər] *n* : camilla *f*

strew ['stru:] *vt* **strewed; strewed** *or* **strewn** ['stru:n] : esparcir (semillas, etc.), desparramar (papeles, etc.)

stricken ['strɪkən] *adj* ~ **with** : aquejado de (una enfermedad), afligido por (tristeza, etc.)

strict ['strɪkt] *adj* : estricto — **strictly** *adv* ~ **speaking** : en rigor

stride ['straɪd] *vi* **strode** ['stro:d]; **stridden** ['strɪdən]; **striding** : ir dando zancadas — ~ *n* **1** : zancada *f* **2** **make great** ~**s** : hacer grandes progresos

strident ['straɪdənt] *adj* : estridente

strife ['straɪf] *n* : conflictos *mpl*

strike ['straɪk] v **struck** ['strʌk]; **struck**, **striking** vt **1** HIT : golpear **2** or ~ **against** : chocar contra **3** or ~ **out** DELETE : tachar **4** : dar (la hora) **5** IMPRESS : impresionar **6** : descubrir (oro o petróleo) **7** it ~s me as... : me parece... **8** ~ **up** START : entablar — vi **1** : golpear **2** ATTACK : atacar **3** : declararse en huelga **4** : sobrevenir (dícese de una enfermedad, etc.) — ~ n **1** BLOW : golpe m **2** : huelga f, paro m Lat (de trabajadores) **3** ATTACK : ataque m — **strikebreaker** ['straɪk‚breɪkər] n : esquirol mf — **striker** ['straɪkər] n : huelguista mf — **striking** ['straɪkɪŋ] adj : notable, llamativo

string ['strɪŋ] n **1** : cordel m **2** : sarta f (de perlas, insultos, etc.), serie f (de eventos, etc.) **3** ~s npl : cuerdas fpl (en música) — ~ vt **strung** ['strʌŋ]; **stringing 1** : ensartar **2** or ~ **up** : colgar — **string bean** n : habichuela f verde

stringent ['strɪndʒənt] adj : estricto, severo

strip¹ ['strɪp] v **stripped**; **stripping** vt **1** REMOVE : quitar **2** UNDRESS : desnudar **3** ~ **s.o. of sth** : despojar a algn de algo — vi UNDRESS : desnudarse

strip² n : tira f

stripe ['straɪp] n : raya f, lista f — **striped** ['straɪpt, 'straɪpəd] adj : a rayas, rayado

strive ['straɪv] vi **strove** ['stroːv]; **striven** ['strɪvən] or **strived**; **striving 1** ~ **for** : luchar por **2** ~ **to** : esforzarse por

strode → **stride**

stroke ['stroːk] vt **stroked**; **stroking** : acariciar — ~ n **1** : golpe m **2** : derrame m cerebral (en medicina)

stroll ['stroːl] vi : pasearse — ~ n : paseo m — **stroller** ['stroːlər] n : cochecito m (para niños)

strong ['strɔŋ] adj : fuerte — **stronghold** ['strɔŋ‚hoːld] n : bastión m — **strongly** ['strɔŋli] adv **1** DEEPLY : profundamente **2** WHOLEHEARTEDLY : totalmente **3** VIGOROUSLY : enérgicamente

strove → **strive**

struck → **strike**

structure ['strʌktʃər] n : estructura f — **structural** ['strʌktʃərəl] adj : estructural

struggle ['strʌgəl] vi **-gled**; **-gling 1** : forcejear **2** STRIVE : luchar — ~ n : lucha f

strum ['strʌm] vt **strummed**; **strumming** : rasguear

strung → **string**

strut ['strʌt] vi **strutted**; **strutting** : pavonearse — ~ n : puntal m (en construcción)

stub ['stʌb] n : colilla f (de un cigarrillo), cabo m (de un lápiz, etc.), talón m (de un cheque) — ~ vt **stubbed**; **stubbing** ~ **one's toe** : darse en el dedo

stubble ['stʌbəl] n : barba f de varios días

stubborn ['stʌbərn] adj **1** : terco, obstinado **2** PERSISTENT : tenaz

stucco ['stʌkoː] n, pl **stuccos** or **stuccoes** : estuco m

stuck → **stick** — **stuck-up** ['stʌk‚ʌp] adj : engreído, creído fam

stud¹ ['stʌd] n : semental m (animal)

stud² n **1** NAIL, TACK : tachuela f, tachón m **2** or ~ **earring** : arete m Lat, pendiente m Spain **3** : montante m (en construcción)

student ['stuːdənt, 'stjuː-] n : estudiante mf; alumno m, -na f (de un colegio) — **studio** ['stuːdi‚oː, 'stjuː-] n, pl **studios** : estudio m — **study** ['stʌdi] n, pl **studies** : estudio m — ~ v **studied**; **studying** : estudiar — **studious** ['stuːdiəs, 'stjuː-] adj : estudioso

stuff ['stʌf] n **1** : cosas fpl **2** MATTER, SUBSTANCE : cosa f **3 know one's** ~ : ser experto — ~ vt **1** FILL : rellenar **2** CRAM : meter — **stuffing** ['stʌfɪŋ] n : relleno m — **stuffy** ['stʌfi] adj **stuffier**, **-est 1** STODGY : pesado, aburrido **2** : tapado (dícese de la nariz) **3** ~ **rooms** : salas fpl mal ventiladas

stumble ['stʌmbəl] vi **-bled**; **-bling 1** : tropezar **2** ~ **across** or **upon** : tropezar con

stump ['stʌmp] n **1** : muñón m (de una pierna, etc.) **2** or **tree** ~ : tocón m — ~ vt : dejar perplejo

stun ['stʌn] vt **stunned**; **stunning 1** : aturdir (con un golpe) **2** ASTONISH : dejar atónito

stung → **sting**

stunk → **stink**

stunning ['stʌnɪŋ] adj **1** : increíble, sensacional **2** STRIKING : imponente

stunt¹ ['stʌnt] vt : atrofiar

stunt² n : proeza f (acrobática)

stupendous [stu'pendəs, stju-] adj : estupendo

stupid ['stuːpəd, 'stjuː-] adj **1** : estúpido **2** SILLY : tonto, bobo — **stupidity** [stu'pɪdəti, stju-] n : tontería f, estupidez f

sturdy ['stərdi] adj **sturdier**, **-est 1** : fuerte, resistente **2** ROBUST : robusto

stutter ['stʌtər] vi : tartamudear — ~ n : tartamudeo m

sty ['staɪ] n **1** pl **sties** PIGPEN : pocilga f

2 *pl* **sties** *or* **styes** : orzuelo *m* (en el ojo)

style ['staɪl] *n* 1 : estilo *m* 2 FASHION : moda *f* 3 **be in —** : estar de moda — **~** *vt* **styled; styling** : peinar (pelo), diseñar (vestidos, etc.) — **stylish** ['staɪlɪʃ] *adj* : elegante, chic — **stylist** ['staɪlɪst] *n* : estilista *mf*

suave ['swɑv] *adj* : refinado y afable

sub¹ ['sʌb] *vi* **subbed; subbing →** **substitute — ~** *n* → **substitute**

sub² *n* → **submarine**

subconscious [.sʌb'kɑntʃəs] *adj* : subconsciente — **~** *n* : subconsciente *m*

subdivide [.sʌbdə'vaɪd, 'sʌbdə,vaɪd] *vt* **-vided; -viding** : subdividir — **subdivision** ['sʌbdə,vɪʒən] *n* : subdivisión *f*

subdue [səb'duː, -'djuː] *vt* **-dued; -duing** 1 CONQUER : sojuzgar 2 CONTROL : dominar 3 SOFTEN : atenuar — **subdued** *adj* : apagado

subject ['sʌbdʒɪkt] *n* 1 : sujeto *m* 2 : súbdito *m*, -ta *f* (de un gobierno) 3 TOPIC : tema *m* — **~** *adj* 1 : sometido 2 **~** **to** : sujeto a — **~** [səb'dʒɛkt] *vt* **~ to** : someter a — **subjective** [səb'dʒɛktɪv] *adj* : subjetivo

subjunctive [səb'dʒʌŋktɪv] *n* : subjuntivo *m* — **subjunctive** *adj* : subjuntivo

sublime [sə'blaɪm] *adj* : sublime

submarine ['sʌbmə,riːn, ,sʌbmə'-] : submarino — **~** *n* : submarino *m*

submerge [səb'mərdʒ] *v* **-merged; -merging** *vt* : sumergir — *vi* : sumergirse

submit [səb'mɪt] *v* **-mitted; -mitting** *vi* 1 YIELD : rendirse 2 **~ to** : someterse a — *vt* : presentar — **submission** [səb'mɪʃən] *n* 1 : sumisión *f* 2 PRESENTATION : presentación *f* — **submissive** [səb'mɪsɪv] *adj* : sumiso

subordinate [sə'bordənət] *adj* : subordinado — **~** *n* : subordinado *m*, -da *f* — **~** [sə'bordən,eɪt] *vt* **-nated; -nating** : subordinar

subpoena [sə'piːnə] *n* : citación *f*

subscribe [səb'skraɪb] *vi* **-scribed; -scribing ~ to** : suscribirse a (una revista, etc.), suscribir (una opinión, etc.) — **subscriber** [səb'skraɪbər] *n* : suscriptor *m*, -tora *f* (de una revista, etc.); abonado *m*, -da *f* (de un servicio) — **subscription** [səb'skrɪpʃən] *n* : suscripción *f*

subsequent ['sʌbsɪkwənt, -sə,kwent] *adj* 1 : subsiguiente 2 **~ to** : posterior a — **subsequently** ['sʌb,kwentli, -kwənt-] *adv* : posteriormente

subservient [səb'sərviənt] *adj* : servil

subside [səb'saɪd] *vi* **-sided; -siding** 1

SINK : hundirse 2 : amainar (dícese de tormentas, pasiones, etc.), remitir (dícese de fiebres, etc.)

subsidiary [səb'sɪdi,eri] *adj* : secundario — **~** *n*, *pl* **-ries** : filial *f*

subsidy ['sʌbsədi] *n*, *pl* **-dies** : subvención *f* — **subsidize** ['sʌbsə,daɪz] *vt* **-dized; -dizing** : subvencionar

subsistence [səb'sɪstənts] *n* : subsistencia *f* — **subsist** [səb'sɪst] *vi* : subsistir

substance ['sʌbstənts] *n* : sustancia *f*

substandard [,sʌb'stændərd] *adj* : inferior

substantial [səb'stæntʃəl] *adj* 1 CONSIDERABLE : considerable 2 STURDY : sólido 3 : sustancioso (dícese de una comida, etc.) — **substantially** [səb'stæntʃəli] *adv* : considerablemente

substitute ['sʌbstə,tuːt, -,tjuːt] *n* : sustituto *m*, -ta *f* (de una persona); sucedáneo *m* (de una cosa) — **~** *vt* **-tuted; -tuting** : sustituir — **substitution** [,sʌbstə'tuːʃən, -'tjuː-] *n* : sustitución *f*

subterranean [,sʌbtə'reɪniən] *adj* : subterráneo

subtitle ['sʌb,taɪtəl] *n* : subtítulo *m*

subtle ['sʌtəl] *adj* **-tler; -tlest** : sutil — **subtlety** ['sʌtəlti] *n*, *pl* **-ties** : sutileza *f*

subtraction [səb'trækʃən] *n* : resta *f* — **subtract** [səb'trækt] *vt* : restar

suburb ['sʌ,bərb] *n* 1 : barrio *m* residencial, suburbio *m* 2 **the ~s** : las afueras — **suburban** [sə'bərbən] *adj* : de las afueras (de una ciudad)

subversion [səb'vərʒən] *n* : subversión *f* — **subversive** [səb'vərsɪv] *adj* : subversivo

subway ['sʌb,weɪ] *n* : metro *m*

succeed [sək'siːd] *vt* : suceder a — *vi* : tener éxito (dícese de personas), dar resultado (dícese de planes, etc.) — **success** [sək'sɛs] *n* : éxito *m* — **successful** [sək'sɛsfəl] *adj* : de éxito, exitoso *Lat* — **successfully** *adv* : con éxito

succession [sək'sɛʃən] *n* 1 : sucesión *f* 2 **in ~** : sucesivamente, seguidos — **successive** [sək'sɛsɪv] *adj* : sucesivo — **successor** [sək'sɛsər] *n* : sucesor *m*, -sora *f*

succinct [sək'sɪŋkt, sə'sɪŋkt] *adj* : sucinto

succulent ['sʌkjələnt] *adj* : suculento

succumb [sə'kʌm] *vi* : sucumbir

such ['sʌtʃ] *adj* 1 : tal 2 **~ as** : como 3 **~ a pity!** : ¡qué lástima! — **~** *pron* 1 : tal 2 **and ~** : y cosas por el estilo 3 **as ~** : como tal — **~** *adv* 1 VERY : muy 2 **~ a nice man!** : ¡qué hombre tan simpático! 3 **~ that** : de tal manera que

suck ['sʌk] vt **1** or ~ **on** : chupar **2** or ~ **up** : sorber (bebidas), aspirar (con una máquina) — **sucker** ['sʌkər] n **1** SHOOT : chupón m **2** FOOL : imbécil mf — **suckle** ['sʌkəl] vt **-led; -ling** : amamantar — **suction** ['sʌkʃən] n : succión f

sudden ['sʌdən] adj **1** : repentino **2 all of a ~** : de repente — **suddenly** ['sʌdənli] adv : de repente

suds ['sʌdz] npl : espuma f (de jabón)

sue ['su:] vt **sued; suing** : demandar (por)

suede ['sweɪd] n : ante m, gamuza f

suet ['su:ət] n : sebo m

suffer ['sʌfər] vi : sufrir — vt **1** : sufrir **2** BEAR : tolerar — **suffering** ['sʌfərɪŋ] n : sufrimiento m

suffice [sə'faɪs] vi **-ficed; -ficing** : bastar — **sufficient** [sə'fɪʃənt] adj : suficiente — **sufficiently** [sə'fɪʃəntli] adv : (lo) suficientemente

suffix ['sʌˌfɪks] n : sufijo m

suffocate ['sʌfəˌkeɪt] v **-cated; -cating** vt : asfixiar — vi : asfixiarse — **suffocation** [sʌfə'keɪʃən] n : asfixia f

suffrage ['sʌfrɪdʒ] n : sufragio m

sugar ['ʃugər] n : azúcar mf — **sugarcane** ['ʃugərˌkeɪn] n : caña f de azúcar — **sugary** ['ʃugəri] adj : azucarado

suggestion [səg'dʒɛstʃən, sə-] n **1** : sugerencia f **2** TRACE : indicio m — **suggest** [səg'dʒɛst, sə-] vt **1** : sugerir **2** INDICATE : indicar

suicide ['su:əˌsaɪd] n **1** : suicidio m (acto) **2** : suicida mf (persona) — **suicidal** [su:ə'saɪdəl] adj : suicida

suit ['su:t] n **1** LAWSUIT : pleito m **2** : traje m (ropa) **3** : palo m (de naipes) — ~ vt **1** ADAPT : adaptar **2** BEFIT : ser apropiado para **3** ~ **s.o.** : convenir a algn (dícese de fechas, etc.), quedar bien a algn (dícese de ropa) — **suitable** ['su:təbəl] adj : apropiado — **suitcase** ['su:tˌkeɪs] n : maleta f, valija f Lat

suite ['swi:t, for 2 also 'su:t] n **1** : suite f (de habitaciones) **2** : juego m (de muebles)

suitor ['su:tər] n : pretendiente m

sulfur ['sʌlfər] n : azufre m

sulk ['sʌlk] vi : enfurruñarse fam — **sulky** ['sʌlki] adj **sulkier; -est** : malhumorado

sullen ['sʌlən] adj : hosco

sultry ['sʌltri] adj **sultrier; -est 1** : bochornoso **2** SENSUAL : sensual

sum ['sʌm] n **1** : suma f — ~ vt **summed; summing** ~ **up** : resumir — **summarize** ['sʌməˌraɪz] v **-rized; -rizing** : resumir — **summary** ['sʌməri] n, pl **-ries** : resumen m

summer ['sʌmər] n : verano m

summit ['sʌmət] n : cumbre f

summon ['sʌmən] vt **1** : llamar (a algn), convocar (una reunión) **2** : citar (en derecho) — **summons** ['sʌmənz] n, pl **summonses** SUBPOENA : citación f

sumptuous ['sʌmptʃʊəs] adj : suntuoso

sun ['sʌn] n : sol m — **sunbathe** ['sʌnˌbeɪð] vi **-bathed; -bathing** : tomar el sol — **sunbeam** ['sʌnˌbi:m] n : rayo m de sol — **sunburn** ['sʌnˌbərn] n : quemadura f de sol

Sunday ['sʌnˌdeɪ, -di] n : domingo m

sundry ['sʌndri] adj : varios, diversos

sunflower ['sʌnˌflaʊər] n : girasol m

sung → **sing**

sunglasses ['sʌnˌɡlæsəz] npl : gafas fpl de sol, lentes mpl de sol

sunk → **sink** — **sunken** ['sʌŋkən] adj : hundido

sunlight ['sʌnˌlaɪt] n : (luz f del) sol m — **sunny** ['sʌni] adj **-nier; -est** : soleado — **sunrise** ['sʌnˌraɪz] n : salida f del sol — **sunset** ['sʌnˌset] n : puesta f del sol — **sunshine** ['sʌnˌʃaɪn] n : sol m, luz f del sol — **suntan** ['sʌnˌtæn] n : bronceado m

super ['su:pər] adj : súper fam

superb [sʊ'pərb] adj : magnífico, espléndido

superficial [ˌsu:pər'fɪʃəl] adj : superficial

superfluous [sʊ'pərfluəs] adj : superfluo

superimpose [ˌsu:pərɪm'po:z] vt **-posed; -posing** : sobreponer

superintendent [ˌsu:pərɪn'tendənt] n **1** : superintendente mf (de policía) **2 building ~** : portero m, -ra f **3** or **school ~** : director m, -tora f (de un colegio)

superior [sʊ'pɪriər] adj : superior — ~ n : superior m — **superiority** [sʊˌpɪri'ɔrəti] n, pl **-ties** : superioridad f

superlative [sʊ'pərlətɪv] adj **1** : superlativo (en gramática) **2** EXCELLENT : excepcional — ~ n : superlativo m

supermarket ['su:pərˌmɑrkət] n : supermercado m

supernatural [ˌsu:pər'nætʃərəl] adj : sobrenatural

superpower ['su:pərˌpaʊər] n : superpotencia f

supersede [ˌsu:pər'si:d] vt **-seded; -seding** : reemplazar, suplantar

supersonic [ˌsu:pər'sɑnɪk] adj : supersónico

superstition [ˌsu:pər'stɪʃən] n : superstición f — **superstitious** [ˌsu:pər'stɪʃəs] adj : supersticioso

supervisor ['su:pərˌvaɪzər] n : supervisor

m, -sora *f* — **supervise** ['suːpərˌvaɪz] *vt* -**vised**; -**vising** : supervisar — **supervision** [ˌsuːpərˈvɪʒən] *n* : supervisión *f* — **supervisory** [ˌsuːpərˈvaɪzəri] *adj* : de supervisor

supper ['sʌpər] *n* : cena *f*, comida *f*

supplant [səˈplænt] *vt* : suplantar

supple ['sʌpəl] *adj* -**pler**; -**plest** : flexible

supplement ['sʌpləmənt] *n* : suplemento *m* — ~ ['sʌpləment] *vt* : complementar — **supplementary** [ˌsʌpləˈmentəri] *adj* : suplementario

supply [səˈplaɪ] *vt* -**plied**; -**plying** 1 : suministrar 2 ~ **with** : proveer de — ~ *n*, *pl* -**plies** 1 : suministro *m*, provisión *f* 2 ~ **and demand** : oferta y demanda 3 **supplies** *npl* PROVISIONS : provisiones *fpl*, víveres *mpl* — **supplier** [səˈplaɪər] *n* : proveedor *m*, -dora *f*

support [səˈpoːrt] *vt* 1 BACK : apoyar 2 : mantener (una familia, etc.) 3 PROP UP : sostener — ~ *n* 1 : apoyo *m* (moral), ayuda *f* (económica) 2 PROP : soporte *m* — **supporter** [səˈpoːrtər] *n* : partidario *m*, -ria *f*

suppose [səˈpoːz] *vt* -**posed**; -**posing** 1 : suponer 2 **be** ~**d to (do sth)** : tener que (hacer algo) — **supposedly** *adv* : supuestamente

suppress [səˈpres] *vt* 1 : reprimir 2 : suprimir (noticias, etc.) — **suppression** [səˈpreʃən] *n* 1 : represión *f* 2 : supresión *f* (de información)

supreme [suˈpriːm] *adj* : supremo — **supremacy** [suˈpreməsi] *n*, *pl* -**cies** : supremacía *f*

sure ['ʃur] *adj* **surer**; -**est** 1 : seguro 2 **make** ~ **that** : asegurarse de que — ~ *adv* 1 OF COURSE : por supuesto, claro 2 **it** ~ **is hot!** : ¡qué calor! — **surely** ['ʃurli] *adv* : seguramente

surfing ['sərfɪŋ] *n* : surf *m*, surfing *m*

surface ['sərfəs] *n* : superficie *f* — ~ *v* -**faced**; -**facing** *vi* : salir a la superficie — *vt* : revestir

surfeit ['sərfət] *n* : exceso *m*

surfing ['sərfɪŋ] *n* : surf *m*, surfing *m*

surge ['sərdʒ] *vi* **surged**; **surging** 1 SWELL : hincharse (dícese del mar) 2 SWARM : moverse en tropel — ~ *n* 1 : oleaje *m* (del mar), oleada *f* (de gente) 2 INCREASE : aumento *m* (súbito)

surgeon ['sərdʒən] *n* : cirujano *m*, -na *f* — **surgery** ['sərdʒəri] *n*, *pl* -**geries** : cirugía *f* — **surgical** ['sərdʒɪkəl] *adj* : quirúrgico

surly ['sərli] *adj* **surlier**; -**est** : hosco, arisco

surmount [sərˈmaunt] *vt* : superar

surname ['sərˌneɪm] *n* : apellido *m*

surpass [sərˈpæs] *vt* : superar

surplus ['sərˌplʌs] *n* : excedente *m*

surprise [səˈpraɪz, sər-] *n* 1 : sorpresa *f* 2 **take by** ~ : sorprender — ~ *vt* -**prised**; -**prising** : sorprender — **surprising** [səˈpraɪzɪŋ, sər-] *adj* : sorprendente

surrender [səˈrendər] *vt* : entregar, rendir — *vi* : rendirse — ~ *n* : rendición *m* (de una ciudad, etc.), entrega *f* (de posesiones)

surrogate ['sərəgət, -ˌgeɪt] *n* : sustituto *m*

surround [səˈraund] *vt* : rodear — **surroundings** [səˈraundɪŋz] *npl* : ambiente *m*

surveillance [sərˈveɪlənts, -ˈveɪljənts, -ˈveɪlənts] *n* : vigilancia *f*

survey [sərˈveɪ] *vt* -**veyed**; -**veying** 1 : medir (un solar) 2 INSPECT : inspeccionar 3 POLL : sondear — ~ ['sərˌveɪ] *n*, *pl* -**veys** 1 INSPECTION : inspección *f* 2 : medición *f* (de un solar) 3 POLL : encuesta *f*, sondeo *m* — **surveyor** [sərˈveɪər] *n* : agrimensor *m*, -sora *f*

survive [sərˈvaɪv] *v* -**vived**; -**viving** *vi* : sobrevivir — *vt* : sobrevivir a — **survival** [sərˈvaɪvəl] *n* : supervivencia *f* — **survivor** [sərˈvaɪvər] *n* : superviviente *mf*

susceptible [səˈseptəbəl] *adj* ~ **to** : propenso a — **susceptibility** [səˌseptəˈbɪləti] *n*, *pl* -**ties** : propensión *f* (a enfermedades, etc.)

suspect ['sʌsˌpekt, səˈspekt] *adj* : sospechoso — ~ ['sʌsˌpekt] *n* : sospechoso *m*, -sa *f* — ~ [səˈspekt] *vt* : sospechar (algo), sospechar de (algn)

suspend [səˈspend] *vt* : suspender — **suspense** [səˈspents] *n* 1 : incertidumbre *m* 2 : suspenso *m* *Lat*, suspense *m* *Spain* (en el cine, etc.) — **suspension** [səˈspentʃən] *n* : suspensión *f*

suspicion [səˈspɪʃən] *n* : sospecha *f* — **suspicious** [səˈspɪʃəs] *adj* 1 QUESTIONABLE : sospechoso 2 DISTRUSTFUL : suspicaz

sustain [səˈsteɪn] *vt* 1 : sostener 2 SUFFER : sufrir

swagger ['swægər] *vi* : pavonearse

swallow[1] ['swɑloː] *v* : tragar — ~ *n* : trago *m*

swallow[2] *n* : golondrina *f* (pájaro)

swam → **swim**

swamp ['swɑmp] *n* : pantano *m*, ciénaga *f* — ~ *vt* : inundar — **swampy** ['swɑmpi] *adj* **swampier**; -**est** : pantanoso, cenagoso

swan ['swɑn] *n* : cisne *f*

swap ['swɑp] *vt* **swapped**; **swapping** 1

: intercambiar 2 ~ **sth for sth** : cambiar algo por algo 3 ~ **sth with s.o.** : cambiar algo a algn — ~ *n* : cambio *m*

swarm ['sworm] *n* : enjambre *m* — ~ *vi* : enjambrar

swat ['swɑt] *vt* **swatted; swatting** : aplastar (un insecto)

sway ['sweɪ] *v* **1** : balanceo *m* **2** INFLUENCE : influjo *m* — ~ *vi* : balancearse — *vt* : influir en

swear ['swær] *v* **swore** ['swor]; **sworn** ['sworn]; **swearing** *vi* **1** : jurar **2** CURSE : decir palabrotas — *vt* : jurar — **swearword** ['swær,word] *n* : palabrota *f*

sweat ['swɛt] *vi* **sweat** *or* **sweated; sweating** : sudar — ~ *n* : sudor *m* — **sweater** ['swɛtər] *n* : suéter *m* — **sweatshirt** ['swɛt,ʃərt] *n* : sudadera *f* — **sweaty** ['swɛti] *adj* **sweatier; -est** : sudado

Swedish ['swi:dɪʃ] *adj* : sueco — ~ *n* : sueco *m* (idioma)

sweep ['swi:p] *v* **swept** ['swɛpt]; **sweeping** *vt* **1** : barrer **2** ~ **aside** : apartar **3** ~ **through** : extenderse por — *vi* : barrer — ~ *n* **1** : barrido *m* **2** : movimiento *m* circular (de la mano, etc.) **3** SCOPE : alcance *m* — **sweeping** ['swi:pɪŋ] *adj* **1** WIDE : amplio **2** EXTENSIVE : extenso — **sweepstakes** ['swi:p,steɪks] *ns & pl* : lotería *f*

sweet ['swi:t] *adj* **1** : dulce **2** PLEASANT : agradable — ~ *n* : dulce *m* — **sweeten** ['swi:tən] *vt* : endulzar — **sweetener** ['swi:tənər] *n* : endulzante *m* — **sweetheart** ['swi:t,hɑrt] *n* **1** : novio *m*, -via *f* **2** (*used as a form of address*) : cariño *m* — **sweetness** ['swi:tnəs] *n* : dulzura *f* — **sweet potato** ['swi:t 'pəˌteɪ̯toʊ] *n* : batata *f*, boniato *m*

swell ['swɛl] *vi* **swelled; swelled** *or* **swollen** ['swoʊlən, 'swʌl-]; **swelling 1** *or* ~ **up** : hincharse **2** INCREASE : aumentar, crecer — ~ *n* **1** : oleaje *m* (del mar) — **swelling** ['swɛlɪŋ] *n* : hinchazón *f*

sweltering ['swɛltərɪŋ] *adj* : sofocante

swept → sweep

swerve ['swərv] *vi* **swerved; swerving** : virar bruscamente

swift ['swɪft] *adj* : rápido — **swiftly** *adv* : rápidamente

swig ['swɪg] *n* : trago *m* — ~ *vi* **swigged; swigging** : beber a tragos

swim ['swɪm] *vi* **swam** ['swæm] **swum** ['swʌm]; **swimming 1** : nadar **2** REEL : dar vueltas — ~ *n* **1** : baño *m* **2 go for a** ~ : ir a nadar — **swimmer** ['swɪmər] *n* : nadador *m*, -dora *f*

swindle ['swɪndəl] *vt* **-dled; -dling** : estafar, timar — ~ *n* : estafa *f*, timo *m fam*

swine ['swaɪn] *ns & pl* : cerdo *m*, -da *f*

swing ['swɪŋ] *v* **swung** ['swʌŋ]; **swinging** *vt* **1** : balancear, hacer oscilar **2** MANAGE : arreglar — *vi* **1** : balancearse, oscilar **2** SWIVEL : girar — ~ *n* **1** : vaivén *m*, balanceo *m* **2** SHIFT : cambio *m* **3** : columpio *m* (para niños) **4 in full** ~ : en pleno proceso

swipe ['swaɪp] *v* **swiped; swiping** *vt* STEAL : birlar *fam*, robar — *vi* ~ **at** : intentar pegar

swirl ['swərl] *vi* : arremolinarse — ~ *n* **1** EDDY : remolino *m* **2** SPIRAL : espiral *f*

swish ['swɪʃ] *vt* : agitar (haciendo un sonido) — *vi* **1** RUSTLE : hacer frufrú **2** ~ **by** : pasar silbando

Swiss ['swɪs] *adj* : suizo

switch ['swɪtʃ] *n* **1** WHIP : vara *f* **2** CHANGE : cambio *m* **3** : interruptor *m*, llave *f* (de la luz, etc.) — ~ *vt* **1** CHANGE : cambiar de **2** EXCHANGE : intercambiar **3** ~ **on** : encender, prender *Lat* **4** ~ **off** : apagar — *vi* **1** : sacudir (la cola, etc.) **2** CHANGE : cambiar **3** SWAP : intercambiarse — **switchboard** ['swɪtʃ,bord] *n* : centralita *f*, conmutador *m Lat*

swivel ['swɪvəl] *vi* **-veled** *or* **-velled; -veling** *or* **-velling** : girar (sobre un pivote)

swollen → swell

swoon ['swu:n] *vi* : desvanecerse

swoop ['swu:p] *vi* ~ **down on** : abatirse sobre — ~ *n* : descenso *m* en picada

sword ['sord] *n* : espada *f*

swordfish ['sord,fɪʃ] *n* : pez *m* espada

swore, sworn → swear

swum → swim

swung → swing

syllable ['sɪləbəl] *n* : sílaba *f*

syllabus ['sɪləbəs] *n*, *pl* **-bi** [-,baɪ] *or* **-buses** : programa *m* (de estudios)

symbol ['sɪmbəl] *n* : símbolo *m* — **symbolic** [sɪm'bɑlɪk] *adj* : simbólico — **symbolism** ['sɪmbəˌlɪzəm] *n* : simbolismo *m* — **symbolize** ['sɪmbəˌlaɪz] *vt* **-ized; -izing** : simbolizar

symmetry ['sɪmətri] *n*, *pl* **-tries** : simetría *f* — **symmetrical** [sə'mɛtrɪkəl] *adj* : simétrico

sympathy ['sɪmpəθi] *n*, *pl* **-thies 1** COMPASSION : compasión *f* **2** UNDERSTANDING : comprensión *f* **3** CONDOLENCES : pésame *m* **4 sympathies** *npl* LOYALTY : simpatías *fpl* — **sympathize** ['sɪmpəˌθaɪz] *vi* **-thized; -thizing 1** ~ **with** PITY : compadecerse de **2** ~

with UNDERSTAND : comprender —
sympathetic [ˌsɪmpə'θeţɪk] *adj* **1** COM-
PASSIONATE : compasivo **2** UNDER-
STANDING : comprensivo
symphony ['sɪmpfəni] *n, pl* **-nies** : sinfonía *f*
symposium [sɪm'poːziəm] *n, pl* **-sia**
[-ziə] *or* **-siums** : simposio *m*
symptom ['sɪmptəm] *n* : síntoma *m* —
symptomatic [sɪmptə'mæţɪk] *adj*
: sintomático
synagogue ['sɪnəˌgag, -ˌgɔg] *n* : sinagoga *f*
synchronize ['sɪŋkrəˌnaɪz, 'sɪn-] *vt*
-nized; -nizing : sincronizar
syndrome ['sɪnˌdroːm] *n* : síndrome *m*
synonym ['sɪnəˌnɪm] *n* : sinónimo *m* —

synonymous [sə'nɑnəməs] *adj* : sinónimo
synopsis [sə'nɑpsɪs] *n, pl* **-opses** [-ˌsiːz]
: sinopsis *f*
syntax ['sɪnˌtæks] *n* : sintaxis *f*
synthesis ['sɪnθəsɪs] *n, pl* **-theses** [-ˌsiːz]
: síntesis *f* — **synthesize** ['sɪnθəˌsaɪz] *vt*
-sized; -sizing : sintetizar — **synthetic** [sɪn'θeţɪk] *adj* : sintético
syphilis ['sɪfələs] *n* : sífilis *f*
Syrian ['sɪriən] *adj* : sirio
syringe [sə'rɪndʒ, 'sɪrɪndʒ] *n* : jeringa *f*,
jeringuilla *f*
syrup ['sərəp, 'sɪrəp] *n* : jarabe *m*
system ['sɪstəm] *n* **1** : sistema *m* **2** BODY
: organismo *m* **3** digestive ~ : apara-
to *m* digestivo — **systematic** [ˌsɪstə-
'mæţɪk] *adj* : sistemático

T

t ['tiː] *n, pl* **t's** *or* **ts** ['tiːz] : t *f*, vigésima
letra del alfabeto inglés
tab ['tæb] *n* **1** TAG : etiqueta *f* **2** FLAP
: lengüeta *f* **3** ACCOUNT : cuenta *f* **4**
keep ~s on : vigilar
table ['teɪbəl] *n* **1** : mesa *f* **2** LIST : tabla *f*
3 ~ **of contents** : índice *m* de mate-
rias — **tablecloth** ['teɪbəlˌklɔθ] *n*
: mantel *m* — **tablespoon** ['teɪbəl-
ˌspuːn] *n* **1** : cuchara *f* grande **2** : cucharada *f* (cantidad)
tablet ['tæblət] *n* **1** PAD : bloc *m* **2** PILL
: pastilla *f* **3** *or* **stone** ~ : lápida *f*
tabloid ['tæˌblɔɪd] *n* : tabloide *m*
taboo [tə'buː, tæ-] *adj* : tabú — ~ *n*
: tabú *m*
tacit ['tæsɪt] *adj* : tácito
taciturn ['tæsɪˌtərn] *adj* : taciturno
tack ['tæk] *vt* **1** : fijar con tachuelas **2** ~
on ADD : añadir — ~ *n* **1** : tachuela *f*
2 change ~ : cambiar de rumbo
tackle ['tækəl] *n* **1** GEAR : aparejo *m* **2**
: placaje *m*, tacle *m* Lat (acción) — ~
vt **-led; -ling 1** : placar, taclear Lat **2**
CONFRONT : abordar
tacky ['tæki] *adj* **tackier; -est 1** : pegajoso **2** GAUDY : de mal gusto
tact ['tækt] *n* : tacto *m* — **tactful**
['tæktfəl] *adj* : diplomático, discreto
tactical ['tæktɪkəl] *adj* : táctico — **tactic**
['tæktɪk] *n* : táctica *f* — **tactics** ['tæk-
tɪks] *ns & pl* : táctica *f*
tactless ['tæktləs] *adj* : indiscreto
tadpole ['tædˌpoːl] *n* : renacuajo *m*
tag[1] ['tæg] *n* LABEL : etiqueta *f* — ~ *v*
tagged; tagging *vt* : etiquetar — *vi*

~ **along with s.o.** : acompañar a algn
tag[2] *vt* : tocar (en varios juegos)
tail ['teɪl] *n* **1** : cola *f* **2** ~**s** *npl* : cruz *f*
(de una moneda) — ~ *vt* FOLLOW
: seguir
tailor ['teɪlər] *n* : sastre *m*, -tra *f* — ~ *vt*
1 : confeccionar (ropa) **2** ADAPT : adaptar
taint ['teɪnt] *vt* : contaminar
take ['teɪk] *v* **took** ['tʊk]; **taken** ['teɪkən];
taking *vt* **1** : tomar **2** BRING : llevar **3**
REMOVE : sacar **4** BEAR : soportar,
aguantar **5** ACCEPT : aceptar **6 I ~ it
that...** : supongo que... **7** ~ **a bath**
: bañarse **8** ~ **a walk** : dar un paseo **9**
~ **back** : retirar (palabras, etc.) **10** ~
in ALTER : achicar **11** ~ **in** GRASP : entender **12** ~ **in** TRICK : engañar **13** ~
off REMOVE : quitar, quitarse (ropa) **14**
~ **on** : asumir (una responsabilidad,
etc.) **15** ~ **out** : sacar **16** ~ **over**
: tomar el poder de **17** ~ **place** : tener
lugar **18** ~ **up** SHORTEN : acortar **19**
~ **up** OCCUPY : ocupar — *vi* **1** : prender (dícese de una vacuna, etc.) **2** ~
off : despegar (dícese de aviones, etc.)
3 ~ **over** : asumir el mando — ~ *n* **1**
PROCEEDS : ingresos *mpl* **2** : toma *f* (en
el cine) — **takeoff** ['teɪkˌɔf] *n* **1**
: despegue *m* (de un avión, etc.) —
takeover ['teɪkˌoːvər] *n* : toma *f* (de
poder, etc.), adquisición *f* (de una empresa)
talcum powder ['tælkəm] *n* : polvos *mpl*
de talco
tale ['teɪl] *n* : cuento *m*

talent ['tælənt] *n* : talento *m* — **talented** ['tæləntəd] *adj* : talentoso

talk ['tɔk] *vi* 1 : hablar 2 ~ **about** : hablar de 3 ~ **to/with** : hablar con — *vt* 1 SPEAK : hablar 2 ~ **over** : hablar de, discutir — ~ *n* 1 CHAT : conversación *f* 2 SPEECH : charla *f* — **talkative** ['tɔkətɪv] *adj* : hablador

tall ['tɔl] *adj* 1 : alto 2 **how ~ are you?** : ¿cuánto mides?

tally ['tæli] *n, pl* **-lies** : cuenta *f* — ~ *v* **-lied; -lying** *vt* RECKON : calcular — *vi* MATCH : concordar, cuadrar

talon ['tælən] *n* : garra *f*

tambourine [tæmbə'riːn] *n* : pandereta *f*

tame ['teɪm] *adj* **tamer; -est** 1 : domesticado 2 DOCILE : manso 3 DULL : insípido, soso — ~ *vt* **tamed; taming** : domar

tamper ['tæmpər] *vi* ~ **with** : forzar (una cerradura), amañar (documentos, etc.)

tampon ['tæm,pɑn] *n* : tampón *m*

tan ['tæn] *v* **tanned; tanning** *vt* : curtir (cuero) — *vi* : broncearse — ~ *n* 1 SUNTAN : bronceado *m* 2 : (color *m*) café *m* con leche

tang ['tæŋ] *n* : sabor *m* fuerte

tangent ['tændʒənt] *n* : tangente *f*

tangerine ['tændʒə,riːn, ,tændʒə'-] *n* : mandarina *f*

tangible ['tændʒəbəl] *adj* : tangible

tangle ['tæŋɡəl] *v* **-gled; -gling** *vt* : enredar — *vi* : enredarse — ~ *n* : enredo *m*

tango ['tæŋɡoː] *n, pl* **-gos** : tango *m*

tank ['tæŋk] *n* 1 : tanque *m*, depósito *m* 2 : tanque *m* (militar) — **tanker** ['tæŋkər] *n* 1 : buque *m* tanque 2 *or* ~ **truck** : camión *m* cisterna

tantalizing ['tæntə,laɪzɪŋ] *adj* : tentador

tantrum ['tæntrəm] *n* **throw a ~** : hacer un berrinche

tap[1] ['tæp] *n* 1 FAUCET : llave *f*, grifo *m* *Spain* — ~ *vt* **tapped; tapping** 1 : sacar (un líquido, etc.), sangrar (un árbol) 2 : intervenir (un teléfono)

tap[2] *vt* **tapped; tapping** STRIKE : tocar, dar un golpecito en — ~ *n* : golpecito *m*, toque *m*

tape ['teɪp] *n* : cinta *f* — ~ *vt* **taped; taping** 1 : pegar con cinta 2 RECORD : grabar — **tape measure** *n* : cinta *f* métrica

taper ['teɪpər] *n* : vela *f* (larga) — ~ *vi* 1 NARROW : estrecharse 2 *or* ~ **off** : disminuir

tapestry ['tæpəstri] *n, pl* **-tries** : tapiz *m*

tar ['tɑr] *n* : alquitrán *m* — ~ *vt* **tarred; tarring** : alquitranar

tarantula [tə'ræntʃələ, -'ræntələ] *n* : tarántula *f*

target ['tɑrɡət] *n* 1 : blanco *m* 2 GOAL : objetivo *m*

tariff ['tærɪf] *n* : tarifa *f*, arancel *m*

tarnish ['tɑrnɪʃ] *vt* 1 : deslustrar 2 : empañar (una reputación, etc.) — *vi* : deslustrarse

tart[1] ['tɑrt] *adj* SOUR : ácido, agrio

tart[2] *n* : pastel *m*

tartan ['tɑrtən] *n* : tartán *m*

task ['tæsk] *n* : tarea *f*

tassel ['tæsəl] *n* : borla *f*

taste ['teɪst] *v* **tasted; tasting** *vt* TRY : probar — *vi* 1 : saber 2 ~ **like** : saber a — ~ *n* 1 FLAVOR : gusto *m*, sabor *m* 2 **have a ~ of** : probar 3 **in good/bad ~** : de buen/mal gusto — **tasteful** ['teɪstfəl] *adj* : de buen gusto — **tasteless** ['teɪstləs] *adj* 1 : sin sabor 2 COARSE : de mal gusto — **tasty** ['teɪsti] *adj* **tastier; -est** : sabroso

tatters ['tætərz] *npl* : harapos *mpl* — **tattered** ['tætərd] *adj* : harapiento

tattle ['tætəl] *vi* **-tled; -tling** ~ **on s.o.** : acusar a algn

tattoo [tæ'tuː] *vt* : tatuar — ~ *n* : tatuaje *m*

taught → **teach**

taunt ['tɔnt] *n* : pulla *f*, burla *f* — ~ *vt* : mofarse de, burlarse de

taut ['tɔt] *adj* : tirante, tenso

tavern ['tævərn] *n* : taberna *f*

tax ['tæks] *vt* 1 : gravar 2 STRAIN : poner a prueba — ~ *n* 1 : impuesto *m* 2 BURDEN : carga *f* — **taxable** ['tæksəbəl] *adj* : imponible — **taxation** [tæk'seɪʃən] *n* : impuestos *mpl* — **tax-exempt** ['tæksɪɡ'zempt, -eɡ-] *adj* : libre de impuestos

taxi ['tæksi] *n, pl* **taxis** : taxi *m* — ~ *vi* **taxied; taxiing** *or* **taxying**; **taxis** *or* **taxies** : rodar por la pista (dícese de un avión)

taxpayer ['tæks,peɪər] *n* : contribuyente *mf*

tea ['tiː] *n* : té *m*

teach ['tiːtʃ] *v* **taught** ['tɔt]; **teaching** *vt* : enseñar, dar clases de (una asignatura) — *vi* : dar clases — **teacher** ['tiːtʃər] *n* : profesor *m*, -sora *f*; maestro *m*, -tra *f* (de niños pequeños) — **teaching** ['tiːtʃɪŋ] *n* : enseñanza *f*

teacup ['tiː,kʌp] *n* : taza *f* de té

team ['tiːm] *n* : equipo *m* — ~ *vi or* ~ **up** : asociarse — **teammate** ['tiːm,meɪt] *n* : compañero *m*, -ra *f* de equipo — **teamwork** ['tiːm,wərk] *n* : trabajo *m* de equipo

teapot ['tiː,pɑt] *n* : tetera *f*

tear[1] ['tær] v **tore** ['tor]; **torn** ['torn]; **tearing** vt 1 : romper, rasgar 2 ~ **apart** : destrozar 3 ~ **down** : derribar 4 ~ **off** or ~ **out** : arrancar 5 ~ **up** : romper (papel, etc.) — vi 1 : romperse, rasgarse 2 RUSH : ir a toda velocidad — ~ n : desgarro m, rasgón m

tear[2] ['tɪr] n : lágrima f — **tearful** ['tɪrfəl] adj : lloroso

tease ['tiːz] vt **teased; teasing** 1 : tomar el pelo a, burlarse de 2 ANNOY : fastidiar

teaspoon ['tiːˌspuːn] n 1 : cucharita f 2 : cucharadita f (cantidad)

technical ['tɛknɪkəl] adj : técnico — **technicality** [ˌtɛknəˈkæləʧi] n, pl -ties : detalle m técnico — **technically** [-kli] adv : técnicamente — **technician** [tɛkˈnɪʃən] n : técnico m, -ca f

technique [tɛkˈniːk] n : técnica f

technological [ˌtɛknəˈlɑdʒɪkəl] adj : tecnológico — **technology** [tɛkˈnɑlədʒi] n, pl -gies : tecnología f

teddy bear ['tɛdi] n : oso m de peluche

tedious ['tiːdiəs] adj : tedioso, aburrido — **tedium** ['tiːdiəm] n : tedio m

tee ['tiː] n : tee m (en deportes)

teem ['tiːm] vi 1 POUR : llover a cántaros 2 be ~**ing with** : estar repleto de

teenage ['tiːnˌeɪdʒ] or **teenaged** [-ˌeɪdʒd] adj : adolescente — **teenager** ['tiːnˌeɪdʒər] n : adolescente mf — **teens** ['tiːnz] npl : adolescencia f

teepee → **tepee**

teeter ['tiːt̬ər] vi : tambalcarse

teeth → **tooth** — **teethe** ['tiːð] vi **teethed; teething** : echar los dientes

telecommunication [ˌtɛləkəˌmjuːnəˈkeɪʃən] n : telecomunicación f

telegram ['tɛləˌgræm] n : telegrama m

telegraph ['tɛləˌgræf] n : telégrafo m — ~ v : telegrafiar

telephone ['tɛləˌfoːn] n : teléfono m — ~ v **-phoned; -phoning** : llamar por teléfono

telescope ['tɛləˌskoːp] n : telescopio m

televise ['tɛləˌvaɪz] vt **-vised; -vising** : televisar — **television** ['tɛləˌvɪʒən] n : televisión f

tell ['tɛl] v **told** ['toːld]; **telling** vt 1 : decir 2 RELATE : contar 3 DISTINGUISH : distinguir 4 ~ **s.o. off** : regañar a algn — vi 1 : decir 2 KNOW : saber 3 SHOW : tener efecto 4 ~ **on s.o.** : acusar a algn — **teller** ['tɛlər] n or **bank** ~ : cajero m, -ra f

temp ['tɛmp] n : empleado m, -da f temporal

temper ['tɛmpər] vt MODERATE : temper-ar — ~ n 1 MOOD : humor m 2 **have a bad** ~ : tener mal genio 3 **lose one's** ~ : perder los estribos — **temperament** ['tɛmpərmənt, -prə-, -pərə-] n : temperamento m — **temperamental** [ˌtɛmpərˈmɛntəl, -prə-, -pərə-] adj : temperamental — **temperate** ['tɛmpərət] adj 1 : moderado 2 ~ **zone** : zona f templada

temperature ['tɛmpərˌʧʊr, -prə-, -pərə-, -tʃər] n 1 : temperatura f 2 **have a** ~ : tener fiebre

tempest ['tɛmpəst] n : tempestad f

temple ['tɛmpəl] n 1 : templo m 2 : sien f (en anatomía)

tempo ['tɛmpoː] n, pl -**pi** [-ˌpiː] or -**pos** 1 : tempo m 2 PACE : ritmo m

temporarily [ˌtɛmpəˈrɛrəli] adv : temporalmente — **temporary** ['tɛmpəˌrɛri] adj : temporal

tempt ['tɛmpt] vt : tentar — **temptation** [tɛmpˈteɪʃən] n : tentación f

ten ['tɛn] adj : diez — ~ n : diez m

tenacity [təˈnæsət̬i] n : tenacidad f — **tenacious** [təˈneɪʃəs] adj : tenaz

tenant ['tɛnənt] n : inquilino m, -na f; arrendatario m, -ria f

tend[1] ['tɛnd] vt MIND : cuidar

tend[2] vi ~ **to** : tender a — **tendency** ['tɛndənsi] n, pl -**cies** : tendencia f

tender[1] ['tɛndər] adj 1 : tierno 2 PAINFUL : dolorido

tender[2] vt : presentar — ~ n 1 : oferta f 2 **legal** ~ : moneda f de curso legal

tenderloin ['tɛndərˌlɔɪn] n : lomo f (de cerdo o vaca)

tenderness ['tɛndərnəs] n : ternura f

tendon ['tɛndən] n : tendón m

tenet ['tɛnət] n : principio m

tennis ['tɛnəs] n : tenis m

tenor ['tɛnər] n : tenor m

tense[1] ['tɛnts] n : tiempo m (de un verbo)

tense[2] v **tensed; tensing** vt : tensar — vi : tensarse — ~ adj **tenser; tensest** : tenso — **tension** ['tɛnʃən] n : tensión f

tent ['tɛnt] n : tienda f de campaña

tentacle ['tɛntɪkəl] n : tentáculo m

tentative ['tɛntət̬ɪv] adj 1 HESITANT : vacilante 2 PROVISIONAL : provisional

tenth ['tɛnθ] adj : décimo — ~ n 1 : décimo m, -ma f (en una serie) 2 : décimo m (en matemáticas)

tenuous ['tɛnjuəs] adj : tenue, endeble

tepid ['tɛpɪd] adj : tibio

term ['tərm] n 1 WORD : término m 2 PERIOD : período m 3 **be on good** ~**s** : tener buenas relaciones 4 **in** ~**s of** : con respecto a — ~ vt : calificar de

terminal ['tərmənəl] *adj* : terminal — ~ *n* **1** : terminal *m* **2** *or* **bus** ~ : terminal *f*

terminate ['tərmə,neɪt] *v* **-nated; -nating** *vi* : terminar(se) — *vt* : poner fin a — **termination** [,tərmə'neɪʃən] *n* : terminación *f*

termite ['tər,maɪt] *n* : termita *f*

terrace ['terəs] *n* : terraza *f*

terrain [tə'reɪn] *n* : terreno *m*

terrestrial [tə'restriəl] *adj* : terrestre

terrible ['terəbəl] *adj* : espantoso, terrible — **terribly** ['terəbli] *adv* : terriblemente

terrier ['teriər] *n* : terrier *mf*

terrific [tə'rɪfɪk] *adj* **1** HUGE : tremendo **2** EXCELLENT : estupendo

terrify ['terə,faɪ] *vt* **-fied; -fying** : aterrar, aterrorizar — **terrifying** ['terə,faɪɪŋ] *adj* : aterrador

territory ['terə,tori] *n*, *pl* **-ries** : territorio *m* — **territorial** [,terə'toriəl] *adj* : territorial

terror ['terər] *n* : terror *m* — **terrorism** ['terər,ɪzəm] *n* : terrorismo *m* — **terrorist** ['terərɪst] *n* : terrorista *mf* — **terrorize** ['terər,aɪz] *vt* **-ized; -izing** : aterrorizar

terse ['tərs] *adj* **terser; tersest** : seco, lacónico

test ['test] *n* **1** TRIAL : prueba *f* **2** EXAM : examen *m*, prueba *f* **3** : análisis *m* (en medicina) — ~ *vt* **1** TRY : probar **2** QUIZ : examinar **3** : analizar (la sangre, etc.), examinar (los ojos, etc.)

testament ['testəmənt] *n* **1** WILL : testamento *m* **2** **the Old/New Testament** : el Antiguo/Nuevo Testamento

testicle ['testɪkəl] *n* : testículo *m*

testify ['testə,faɪ] *v* **-fied; -fying** : testificar

testimony ['testə,moni] *n*, *pl* **-nies** : testimonio *m*

test tube *n* : probeta *f*, tubo *m* de ensayo

tetanus ['tetənəs] *n* : tétano *m*

tether ['teðər] *vt* : atar

text ['tekst] *n* : texto *m* — **textbook** ['tekst,bʊk] *n* : libro *m* de texto

textile ['tek,staɪl, 'tekstəl] *n* : textil *m*

texture ['tekstʃər] *n* : textura *f*

than ['ðæn] *conj & prep* : que, de (con cantidades)

thank ['θæŋk] *vt* **1** : agradecer, dar (las) gracias a **2** ~ **you!** : ¡gracias! — **thankful** ['θæŋkfəl] *adj* : agradecido — **thankfully** ['θæŋkfəli] *adv* **1** : con agradecimiento **2** FORTUNATELY : gracias a Dios — **thanks** ['θæŋks] *npl* **1** : agradecimiento *m* **2** ~**!** : ¡gracias!

Thanksgiving [θæŋks'gɪvɪŋ, 'θæŋks,-] *n* : día *m* de Acción de Gracias

that ['ðæt] *pron*, *pl* **those** ['ðoːz] **1** : ése, ésa, eso **2** (*more distant*) : aquél, aquélla, aquello **3 is ~ you?** : ¿eres tú? **4 like ~** : así **5** ~ **is...** : es decir... : los que... — ~ *conj* : que — ~ *adj*, *pl* **those 1** : ese, esa **2** (*more distant*) : aquel, aquella **3** ~ **one** : ése, ésa — ~ *adv* : tan

thatched ['θætʃt] *adj* : con techo de paja

thaw ['θɔ] *vt* : descongelar (alimentos), derretir (hielo) — *vi* **1** : descongelarse **2** MELT : derretirse — ~ *n* : deshielo *m*

the [ðə, *before vowel sounds usu* ðiː] *art* **1** : el, la, los, las **2** PER : por — ~ *adv* **1** ~ **sooner** ~ **better** : cuanto más pronto, mejor **2 I like this one** ~ **best** : éste es el que más me gusta

theater *or* **theatre** ['θiːətər] *n* : teatro *m* — **theatrical** [θi'ætrɪkəl] *adj* : teatral

theft ['θeft] *n* : robo *m*, hurto *m*

their ['ðer] *adj* : su, sus, de ellos, de ellas — **theirs** ['ðerz] *pron* **1** : (el) suyo, (la) suya, (los) suyos, (las) suyas **2 some friends of** ~ : unos amigos suyos, unos amigos de ellos

them ['ðem] *pron* **1** (*used as direct object*) : los, las **2** (*used as indirect object*) : les, se **3** (*used as object of a preposition*) : ellos, ellas

theme ['θiːm] *n* **1** : tema *m* **2** ESSAY : trabajo *m* (escrito)

themselves [ðəm'selvz, ðem-] *pron* **1** (*used reflexively*) : se **2** (*used emphatically*) : ellos mismos, ellas mismas **3** (*used after a preposition*) : sí (mismos), sí (mismas)

then ['ðen] *adv* **1** : entonces **2** NEXT : luego, después **3** BESIDES : además — ~ *adj* : entonces

thence ['ðents, 'θents] *adv* : de ahí (en adelante)

theology [θi'ɑlədʒi] *n*, *pl* **-gies** : teología *f* — **theological** [,θiːə'lɑdʒɪkəl] *adj* : teológico

theorem ['θiːərəm, 'θɪrəm] *n* : teorema *m* — **theoretical** [,θiːə'retɪkəl] *adj* : teórico — **theory** ['θiːəri, 'θɪri] *n*, *pl* **-ries** : teoría *f*

therapeutic [,θerə'pjuːtɪk] *adj* : terapéutico — **therapist** ['θerəpɪst] *n* : terapeuta *mf* — **therapy** ['θerəpi] *n*, *pl* **-pies** : terapia *f*

there ['ðer] *adv* **1** *or* **over** ~ : allí, allá **2** *or* **right** ~ : ahí **3 in** ~ : ahí (dentro) **4** ~**, it's done!** : ¡listo! **5 up/down** ~ : ahí arriba/abajo who's ~? : ¿quién es? — ~ *pron* **1** ~ **is/are** : hay **2** ~ **are three of us** : somos tres — **thereabouts** *or* **thereabout** [ðærə'bauts, -'baut; 'ðærə,-] *adv or* ~ : por ahí — **thereafter** [ðær-'æftər] *adv* : después — **thereby** [ðær-'bai, 'ðær,bai] *adv* : así — **therefore** ['ðær,for] *adv* : por lo tanto

thermal ['ðərməl] *adj* : térmico

thermometer [ðər'mɑmətər] *n* : termómetro *m*

thermos ['ðərməs] *n* : termo *m*

thermostat ['ðərmə,stæt] *n* : termostato *m*

thesaurus [θɪ'sɔrəs] *n, pl* **-sauri** [-'sɔr,ai] *or* **-sauruses** [-'sɔrəsəz] : diccionario *m* de sinónimos

these → **this**

thesis ['θiːsɪs] *n, pl* **theses** ['θi;siːz] : tesis *f*

they ['ðei] *pron* **1** : ellos, ellas **2 where are** ~? : ¿dónde están? **3 as** ~ **say** : como dicen — **they'd** ['ðeid] (*contraction of* **they had** *or* **they would**) → **have, would** — **they'll** ['ðeil, ðel] (*contraction of* **they shall** *or* **they will**) → **shall, will** — **they're** ['ðeir] (*contraction of* **they are**) → **be** — **they've** ['ðeiv] (*contraction of* **they have**) → **have**

thick ['θɪk] *adj* **1** : grueso **2** DENSE : espeso **3 a** ~ **accent** : un acento marcado **4 it's two inches** ~ : tiene dos pulgadas de grosor — ~ *n* **in the** ~ **of** : en medio de — **thicken** ['θɪkən] *vt* : espesar — *vi* : espesarse — **thicket** ['θɪkət] *n* : matorral *m* — **thickness** ['θɪknəs] *n* : grosor *m*, espesor *m*

thief ['θif] *n, pl* **thieves** ['θiːvz] : ladrón *m*, -drona *f*

thigh ['θai] *n* : muslo *m*

thimble ['θɪmbəl] *n* : dedal *m*

thin ['θɪn] *adj* **thinner; -est 1** : delgado **2** : ralo (dícese del pelo) **3** WATERY : claro, aguado **4** FINE : fino — ~ *v* **thinned; thinning** *vt* DILUTE : diluir — *vi* : ralear (dícese del pelo)

thing ['θɪŋ] *n* **1** : cosa *f* **2 for one** ~ : en primer lugar **3 how are** ~**s?** : ¿qué tal? **4 it's a good** ~ **that...** : menos mal que... **5 the important** ~ **is...** : lo importante es...

think ['θɪŋk] *v* **thought** ['θɔt]; **thinking** *vt* **1** : pensar **2** BELIEVE : creer **3** ~ **up** : idear — *vi* **1** : pensar **2** ~ **about** *or* ~ **of** CONSIDER : pensar en **3** ~ **of** REMEMBER : acordarse de **4 what do you** ~ **of it?** : ¿qué te parece? — **thinker** ['θɪŋkər] *n* : pensador *m*, -dora *f*

third ['θərd] *adj* : tercero — ~ *or* **third-**

-ly [-li] *adv* : en tercer lugar — ~ *n* **1** : tercero *m*, -ra *f* (en una serie) **2** : tercero *m* (en matemáticas) — **Third World** *n* : Tercer Mundo *m*

thirst ['θərst] *n* : sed *f* — **thirsty** ['θərsti] *adj* **thirstier; -est 1** : sediento **2 be** ~ : tener sed

thirteen [θər'tim] *adj* : trece — ~ *n* : trece *m* — **thirteenth** [θər'timθ] *adj* : décimo tercero — ~ *n* **1** : decimotercero *m*, -ra *f* (en una serie) **2** : treceavo *m* (en matemáticas)

thirty ['θərti] *adj* : treinta — ~ *n, pl* **thirties** : treinta *m* — **thirtieth** ['θərtiəθ] *adj* : trigésimo — ~ *n* **1** : trigésimo *m*, -ma *f* (en una serie) **2** : treintavo *m* (en matemáticas)

this ['ðis] *pron, pl* **these** ['ðiːz] **1** : éste, ésta, esto **2 like** ~ : así — ~ *adj, pl* **these 1** : este, esta **2** ~ **one** : éste, ésta **3** ~ **way** : por aquí — ~ *adv* ~ **big** : así de grande

thistle ['θɪsəl] *n* : cardo *m*

thong ['θɔŋ] *n* **1** : correa *f* **2** SANDAL : chancla *f*

thorn ['θɔrn] *n* : espina *f* — **thorny** ['θɔrni] *adj* : espinoso

thorough ['θəro] *adj* **1** : meticuloso **2** COMPLETE : completo — **thoroughly** *adv* **1** : a fondo **2** COMPLETELY : completamente — **thoroughbred** ['θəro-,bred] *adj* : de pura sangre — **thoroughfare** ['θəro,fær] *n* : vía *f* pública

those → **that**

though ['ðoː] *conj* : aunque — ~ *adv* **1** : sin embargo **2 as** ~ : como si

thought ['θɔt] → **think** — ~ *n* **1** : pensamiento *m* **2** IDEA : idea *f* — **thoughtful** ['θɔtfəl] *adj* **1** : pensativo **2** KIND : amable — **thoughtless** ['θɔtləs] *adj* **1** CARELESS : descuidado **2** RUDE : desconsiderado

thousand ['θauzənd] *adj* : mil — ~ *n, pl* **-sands** *or* **-sand** : mil *m* — **thousandth** ['θauzənθ] *adj* : milésimo — ~ *n* **1** : milésimo *m*, -ma *f* (en una serie) **2** : milésimo *m* (en matemáticas)

thrash ['θræʃ] *vt* : dar una paliza a — *vi* *or* ~ **around** : agitarse, revolcarse

thread ['θred] *n* **1** : hilo *m* **2** : rosca *f* (de un tornillo) — ~ *vt* : enhilar (una aguja), ensartar (cuentas) — **threadbare** ['θred,bær] *adj* : raído

threat ['θret] *n* : amenaza *f* — **threaten** ['θretən] *v* : amenazar — **threatening** ['θretənɪŋ] *adj* : amenazador

three ['θri] *adj* : tres — ~ *n* : tres *m* — **three hundred** *adj* : trescientos — ~ *n* : trescientos *m*

threshold ['θreʃˌhoːld, -ˌoːld] *n* : umbral *m*

threw → throw

thrift ['θrɪft] *n* : frugalidad *f* — **thrifty** ['θrɪfti] *adj* **thriftier; -est** : económico, frugal

thrill ['θrɪl] *vt* : emocionar — ~ *n* : emoción *f* — **thriller** ['θrɪlər] *n* : película *f* de suspenso *Spain*, película *f* de suspenso *Lat* — **thrilling** ['θrɪlɪŋ] *adj* : emocionante

thrive ['θraɪv] *vi* **throve** ['θroːv] *or* **thrived; thriven** ['θrɪvən] **1** FLOURISH : florecer **2** PROSPER : prosperar

throat ['θroːt] *n* : garganta *f*

throb ['θrɑb] *vi* **throbbed; throbbing 1** PULSATE : palpitar **2** VIBRATE : vibrar **3** ~ **with pain** : tener un dolor punzante

throes ['θroːz] *npl* **1** PANGS : agonía *f* **2** **in the** ~ **of** : en medio de

throne ['θroːn] *n* : trono *m*

throng ['θrɔŋ] *n* : muchedumbre *f*, multitud *f*

throttle ['θrɑtəl] *vt* **-tled; -tling** : estrangular — ~ *n* : válvula *f* reguladora

through ['θruː] *prep* **1** : por, a través de **2** BETWEEN : entre **3** BECAUSE OF : a causa de **4** DURING : durante **5** → **throughout 6 Monday** ~ **Friday** : de lunes a viernes — ~ *adv* **1** : de un lado a otro (en el espacio), de principio a fin (en el tiempo) **2** COMPLETELY : completamente — ~ *adj* **1 be** ~ : haber terminado **2** ~ **traffic** : tráfico *m* de paso — **throughout** [θruˈaʊt] *prep* : por todo (un lugar), a lo largo de (un período de tiempo)

throw ['θroː] *v* **threw** ['θruː]; **thrown** ['θroːn]; **throwing** *vt* **1** : tirar, lanzar **2** : proyectar (una sombra) **3** CONFUSE : desconcertar **4** ~ **a party** : dar una fiesta **5** ~ **away** *or* ~ **out** : tirar, botar *Lat* — *vi* ~ **up** VOMIT : vomitar — ~ *n* : tiro *m*, lanzamiento *m*

thrush ['θrʌʃ] *n* : tordo *m*, zorzal *m*

thrust ['θrʌst] *vt* **thrust; thrusting 1** : empujar (bruscamente) **2** PLUNGE : clavar **3** ~ **upon** : imponer a — ~ *n* **1** : empujón *m* **2** : estocada *f* (en esgrima)

thud ['θʌd] *n* : ruido *m* sordo

thug ['θʌg] *n* : matón *m*

thumb ['θʌm] *n* : (dedo *m*) pulgar *m* — ~ *vt* *or* ~ **through** : hojear — **thumbnail** ['θʌmˌneɪl] *n* : uña *f* del pulgar — **thumbtack** ['θʌmˌtæk] *n* : tachuela *f*, chinche *f Lat*

thump ['θʌmp] *vt* : golpear — *vi* : latir

con fuerza (dícese del corazón) — ~ *n* : ruido *m* sordo

thunder ['θʌndər] *n* : truenos *mpl* — ~ *vi* : tronar — *vt* SHOUT : bramar — **thunderbolt** ['θʌndərˌboːlt] *n* : rayo *m* — **thunderous** ['θʌndərəs] *adj* : atronador — **thunderstorm** ['θʌndərˌstorm] *n* : tormenta *f* eléctrica

Thursday ['θərzˌdeɪ, -di] *n* : jueves *m*

thus ['ðʌs] *adv* **1** : así **2** THEREFORE : por lo tanto

thwart ['θwɔrt] *vt* : frustrar

thyme ['taɪm, 'θaɪm] *n* : tomillo *m*

thyroid ['θaɪˌrɔɪd] *n* : tiroides *mf*

tiara [tiˈæːrə, -ˈɑr-] *n* : diadema *f*

tic ['tɪk] *n* : tic *m* (nervioso)

tick¹ ['tɪk] *n* : garrapata *f* (insecto)

tick² *n* **1** : tictac *m* (sonido) **2** CHECK : marca *f* — ~ *vi* : hacer tictac — *vt* **1** *or* ~ **off** CHECK : marcar **2** ~ **off** ANNOY : fastidiar

ticket ['tɪkət] *n* **1** : pasaje *m* (de avión), billete *m Spain* (de tren, avión, etc.), boleto *m Lat* (de tren o autobús) **2** : entrada *f* (al teatro, etc.) **3** FINE : multa *f*

tickle ['tɪkəl] *v* **-led; -ling** *vt* **1** : hacer cosquillas a **2** AMUSE : divertir — *vi* : picar — ~ *n* : cosquilleo *m* — **ticklish** ['tɪkəlɪʃ] *adj* **1** : cosquilloso **2** TRICKY : delicado

tidal wave ['taɪdəl] *n* : maremoto *m*

tidbit ['tɪdˌbɪt] *n* MORSEL : golosina *f*

tide ['taɪd] *n* : marea *f* — ~ *vt* **tided; tiding** ~ **over** : ayudar a superar un apuro

tidy ['taɪdi] *adj* **-dier; -est** : ordenado, arreglado — ~ *vt* **-died; -dying** *or* ~ **up** : ordenar, arreglar

tie ['taɪ] *n* **1** : atadura *f*, cordón *m* **2** BOND : lazo *m* **3** : empate *m* (en deportes) **4** NECKTIE : corbata *f* — ~ *v* **tied; tying** *or* **tieing** *vt* **1** : atar, amarrar *Lat* **2** ~ **a knot** : hacer un nudo — *vi* : empatar (en deportes)

tier ['tɪr] *n* : nivel *m*, piso (de un pastel), grada *f* (de un estadio)

tiger ['taɪgər] *n* : tigre *m*

tight ['taɪt] *adj* **1** : apretado **2** SNUG : ajustado, ceñido **3** TAUT : tirante **4** STINGY : agarrado **5** SCARCE : escaso **6 a** ~ **seal** : un cierre hermético **7 a** ~ **spot** : un aprieto — ~ *adv* **closed** ~ : bien cerrado — **tighten** ['taɪtən] *vt* **1** : apretar **2** TENSE : tensar **3** : hacer más estricto (reglas, etc.) — **tightly** ['taɪtli] *adv* : bien, fuerte — **tightrope** ['taɪtˌroːp] *n* : cuerda *f* floja — **tights** ['taɪts] *npl* : leotardo *m*, mallas *fpl*

tile ['taɪl] *n* **1** : azulejo *m*, baldosa *f* (de

piso) 2 *or* roofing ~ : teja *f* — ~ *vt*
tiled; tiling 1 : revestir de azulejos,
embaldosar (un piso) 2 : tejar (un
techo)

till¹ ['tɪl] *prep & conj* → until

till² *vt* : cultivar

till³ *n* : caja *f* (registradora)

tilt ['tɪlt] *n* 1 : inclinación *f* 2 at full ~ : a
toda velocidad — ~ *vt* : inclinar — *vi*
: inclinarse

timber ['tɪmbər] *n* 1 : madera *f* (para
construcción) 2 BEAM : viga *f*

timbre ['tæmbər, 'tɪm-] *n* : timbre *m*

time ['taɪm] *n* 1 : tiempo *m* 2 AGE : época
f 3 : compás *m* (en música) 4 at ~s
: a veces 5 at this ~ : en este momento 6 for the ~ being : por el momento 7 from ~ to ~ : de vez en
cuando 8 have a good ~ : pasarlo
bien 9 many ~s : muchas veces 10
on ~ : a tiempo 11 ~ after ~ : una
y otra vez 12 what ~ is it? : ¿qué
hora es? — ~ *vt* timed; timing
: tomar el tiempo a (algn), cronometrar (una carrera, etc.) — timeless
['taɪmləs] *adj* : eterno — timely ['taɪm-
li] *adj* -lier; -est : oportuno — timer
['taɪmər] *n* : temporizador *m*, avisador
m (de cocina) — times ['taɪmz] *prep* 3
~ 4 is 12 : 3 por 4 son 12 — timetable ['taɪmˌteɪbəl] *n* : horario *m*

timid ['tɪmɪd] *adj* : tímido

tin ['tɪn] *n* 1 : estaño *m* 2 CAN : lata *f*,
bote *m* *Spain* — tinfoil ['tɪnˌfɔɪl] *n*
: papel *m* (de) aluminio

tinge ['tɪndʒ] *vt* tinged; tingeing *or*
tinging ['tɪndʒɪŋ] : matizar — ~ *n* 1
TINT : matiz *m* 2 TOUCH : dejo *m*

tingle ['tɪŋɡəl] *vi* -gled; -gling : sentir
(un) hormigueo — ~ *n* : hormigueo
m

tinker ['tɪŋkər] *vi* ~ with : intentar
arreglar (con pequeños ajustes)

tinkle ['tɪŋkəl] *vi* -kled; -kling : tintinear
— ~ *n* : tintineo *m*

tint ['tɪnt] *n* : tinte *m* — ~ *vt* : teñir

tiny ['taɪni] *adj* -nier; -est : diminuto,
minúsculo

tip¹ ['tɪp] *v* tipped; tipping *vt* 1 TILT : inclinar 2 *or* ~ over : volcar — *vi* : inclinarse

tip² *n* END : punta *f*

tip³ *n* ADVICE : consejo *m* — ~ *vt* ~
off : avisar

tip⁴ *vt* : dar una propina a — ~ *n* GRA-
TUITY : propina *f*

tipsy ['tɪpsi] *adj* -sier; -est : achispado

tiptoe ['tɪpˌtoː] *n* on ~ : de puntillas —
~ *vi* -toed; -toeing : caminar de puntillas

tip-top ['tɪpˌtɑp, -ˌtap] *adj* : excelente

tire¹ ['taɪr] *n* : neumático *m*, llanta *f* *Lat*

tire² *v* tired; tiring *vt* : cansar — *vi*
: cansarse — **tired** ['taɪrd] *adj* 1 ~ of
: cansado de, harto de 2 ~ out : agotado — **tireless** ['taɪrləs] *adj* : incansable — **tiresome** ['taɪrsəm] *adj* : pesado

tissue ['tɪʃuː] *n* 1 : pañuelo *m* de papel 2
: tejido *m* (en biología)

title ['taɪtəl] *n* : título *m* — ~ *vt* -tled;
-tling : titular

to ['tuː] *prep* 1 : a 2 TOWARD : hacia 3 IN
ORDER TO : para 4 UP TO : hasta 5 a
quarter ~ seven : las siete menos
cuarto 6 be nice ~ them : trátalos
bien 7 ten ~ the box : diez por caja 8
the mate ~ this shoe : el compañero de este zapato 9 two ~ four
years old : entre dos y cuatro años de
edad 10 want ~ do : querer hacer —
~ *adv* 1 come ~ : volver en sí 2 ~
and fro : de un lado a otro

toad ['toːd] *n* : sapo *m*

toast ['toːst] *vt* 1 : tostar (pan, etc.) 2
: brindar por (una persona) — ~ *n* 1
: pan *m* tostado, tostadas *fpl* 2 DRINK
: brindis *m* — **toaster** ['toːstər] *n*
: tostador *m*

tobacco [təˈbækoː] *n*, *pl* -cos : tabaco *m*

toboggan [təˈbɑɡən] *n* : tobogán *m*

today [təˈdeɪ] *adv* : hoy — ~ *n* : hoy *m*

toddler ['tɑdlər] *n* : niño *m* pequeño,
niña *f* pequeña (que comienza a caminar)

toe ['toː] *n* : dedo *m* (del pie) — **toenail**
['toːˌneɪl] *n* : uña *f* (del pie)

together [təˈɡɛðər] *adv* 1 : juntos 2 ~
with : junto con

toil ['tɔɪl] *n* : trabajo *m* duro — ~ *vi*
: trabajar duro

toilet ['tɔɪlət] *n* 1 BATHROOM : baño *m*,
servicio *m* 2 : inodoro *m* (instalación)
— **toilet paper** *n* : papel *m* higiénico
— **toiletries** ['tɔɪlətriz] *npl* : artículos
mpl de tocador

token ['toːkən] *n* 1 SIGN : muestra *f* 2 ME-
MENTO : recuerdo *m* 3 : ficha *f* (para un
tren, etc.)

told → tell

tolerable ['tɑlərəbəl] *adj* : tolerable —
tolerance ['tɑlərənts] *n* : tolerancia *f* —
tolerant ['tɑlərənt] *adj* : tolerante —
tolerate ['tɑləˌreɪt] *vt* -ated; -ating
: tolerar

toll¹ ['toːl] *n* 1 : peaje *m* 2 death ~
: número *m* de muertos 3 take a ~ on
: afectar

toll² *vi* RING : tocar, doblar — ~ *n*
: tañido *m*

tomato [təˈmeɪt̬o, -ˈmɑ-] n, pl **-toes** : tomate m

tomb ['tuːm] n : tumba f, sepulcro m — **tombstone** ['tuːmˌstoːn] n : lápida f

tome ['toːm] n : tomo m

tomorrow [təˈmɑro] adv : mañana — ~ n : mañana m

ton ['tʌn] n : tonelada f

tone ['toːn] n : tono m — ~ vt **toned**; **toning** or ~ **down** : atenuar

tongs ['tɑŋz, 'tɔŋz] npl : tenazas fpl

tongue ['tʌŋ] n : lengua f

tonic ['tɑnɪk] n 1 : tónico m 2 or ~ **water** : tónica f

tonight [təˈnaɪt] adv : esta noche — ~ n : esta noche f

tonsil ['tɑntsəl] n : amígdala f

too ['tuː] adv 1 ALSO : también 2 EXCESSIVELY : demasiado

took → **take**

tool ['tuːl] n : herramienta f — **toolbox** ['tuːlˌbɑks] n : caja f de herramientas

toot ['tuːt] vt : sonar (un claxon, etc.) — ~ n 1 WHISTLE : pitido m 2 HONK : bocinazo m

tooth ['tuːθ] n, pl **teeth** ['tiːθ] : diente m — **toothache** ['tuːˌθeɪk] n : dolor m de muelas — **toothbrush** ['tuːθˌbrʌʃ] n : cepillo m de dientes — **toothpaste** ['tuːθˌpeɪst] n : pasta f de dientes, pasta f dentífrica

top[1] ['tɑp] n 1 : parte f superior 2 SUMMIT : cima f, cumbre f 3 COVER : tapa f, cubierta f 4 on ~ of : encima de — ~ vt **topped**; **topping** 1 COVER : rematar (un edificio, etc.), bañar (un pastel, etc.) 2 SURPASS : superar 3 ~ off : llenar — ~ adj 1 : de arriba, superior 2 BEST : mejor 3 a ~ executive : un alto ejecutivo

top[2] ['tɑp] n : trompo m (juguete)

topic ['tɑpɪk] n : tema m — **topical** ['tɑpɪkəl] adj : de interés actual

topmost ['tɑpˌmoːst] adj : más alto

topple ['tɑpəl] v **-pled**; **-pling** vi : caerse — vt 1 OVERTURN : volcar 2 OVERTHROW : derrocar

torch ['tɔrtʃ] n : antorcha f

tore → **tear**[1]

torment ['tɔrˌment] n : tormento m — ~ [tɔrˈment, 'tɔr-] vt : atormentar

torn → **tear**[1]

tornado [tɔrˈneɪdo] n, pl **-does** or **-dos** : tornado m

torpedo [tɔrˈpiːdo] n, pl **-does** : torpedo m — ~ vt : torpedear

torrent ['tɔrənt] n : torrente m

torrid ['tɔrɪd] adj : tórrido

torso ['tɔrˌso] n, pl **-sos** or **-si** [-ˌsiː] : torso m

tortilla [tɔrˈtiːjə] n : tortilla f

tortoise ['tɔrt̬əs] n : tortuga f (terrestre) — **tortoiseshell** ['tɔrt̬əsˌʃel] n : carey m, concha f

tortuous ['tɔrtʃuəs] adj : tortuoso

torture ['tɔrtʃər] n : tortura f — ~ vt **-tured**; **-turing** : torturar

toss ['tɔs, 'tɑs] vt 1 : tirar, lanzar 2 : mezclar (una ensalada) — vi ~ **and turn** : dar vueltas — ~ n : lanzamiento m

tot ['tɑt] n : pequeño m, -ña f

total ['toːt̬əl] adj : total — ~ n : total m — ~ vt **-taled** or **-talled**; **-taling** or **-talling** 1 : ascender a 2 or ~ **up** : totalizar, sumar

totalitarian [toˌtæləˈteriən] adj : totalitario

tote ['toːt] vt **toted**; **toting** : llevar

totter ['tɑt̬ər] vi : tambalearse

touch ['tʌtʃ] vt 1 : tocar 2 MOVE : conmover 3 AFFECT : afectar 4 ~ **up** : retocar — vi : tocarse — ~ n 1 : tacto m (sentido) 2 HINT : toque m 3 BIT : pizca f 4 **keep in** ~ : mantenerse en contacto 5 **lose one's** ~ : perder la habilidad — **touchdown** ['tʌtʃˌdaʊn] n : touchdown m — **touchy** ['tʌtʃi] adj **touchier**; **-est** 1 : delicado 2 **be** ~ **about** : picarse a la mención de

tough ['tʌf] adj 1 : duro 2 STRONG : fuerte 3 STRICT : severo 4 DIFFICULT : difícil — **toughen** ['tʌfən] vt or ~ **up** : endurecer — vi : endurecerse — **toughness** ['tʌfnəs] n : dureza f

tour ['tʊr] n 1 : viaje m (por un país, etc.), visita f (a un museo, etc.) 2 : gira f (de un equipo, etc.) — vi 1 TRAVEL : viajar 2 : hacer una gira (dícese de equipos, etc.) — vt : viajar por, recorrer — **tourist** ['tʊrɪst, 'tɜr-] n : turista mf

tournament ['tɜrnəmənt, 'tʊr-] n : torneo m

tousle ['taʊzəl] vt **-sled**; **-sling** : despeinar

tout ['taʊt] vt : promocionar

tow ['toː] vt : remolcar — ~ n : remolque m

toward ['tɔrd, təˈwɔrd] or **towards** ['tɔrdz, təˈwɔrdz] prep : hacia

towel ['taʊəl] n : toalla f

tower ['taʊər] n : torre f — ~ vi ~ **over** : descollar sobre — **towering** ['taʊərɪŋ] adj : altísimo

town ['taʊn] n 1 VILLAGE : pueblo m 2 CITY : ciudad f — **township** ['taʊnˌʃɪp] n : municipio m

tow truck ['toːˌtrʌk] n : grúa f

toxic ['tɑksɪk] adj : tóxico

V

v ['viː] *n, pl* **v's** *or* **vs** ['viːz] : v *f*, vigésima segunda letra del alfabeto inglés

vacant ['veɪkənt] *adj* **1** AVAILABLE : libre **2** UNOCCUPIED : desocupado **3** : vacante (dícese de un puesto) **4** : ausente (dícese de una mirada) — **vacancy** ['veɪkəntsi] *n, pl* **-cies 1** : (puesto *m*) vacante *f* **2** : habitación *f* libre (en un hotel, etc.)

vacate ['veɪkeɪt] *vt* **-cated; -cating** : desalojar, desocupar

vacation [veɪˈkeɪʃən, və-] *n* : vacaciones *fpl*

vaccination [ˌvæksəˈneɪʃən] *n* : vacunación *f* — **vaccinate** ['væksəˌneɪt] *vt* **-nated; -nating** : vacunar — **vaccine** ['væksiːn, væk-] *n* : vacuna *f*

vacuum ['vækjuːm, -kjəm] *n, pl* **vacuums** *or* **vacua** : vacío *m* — ~ *vt* : pasar la aspiradora por — **vacuum cleaner** *n* : aspiradora *f*

vagina [vəˈdʒaɪnə] *n, pl* **-nae** [-niː, -naɪ] *or* **-nas** : vagina *f*

vagrant ['veɪɡrənt] *n* : vagabundo *m*, -da *f*

vague ['veɪɡ] *adj* **vaguer; -est** : vago, indistinto

vain ['veɪn] *adj* **1** CONCEITED : vanidoso **2 in** ~ : en vano

valentine ['væləntaɪn] *n* : tarjeta *f* del día de San Valentín

valiant ['væljənt] *adj* : valiente, valeroso

valid ['væləd] *adj* : válido — **validate** ['væləˌdeɪt] *vt* **-dated; -dating** : validar — **validity** [vəˈlɪdəti, væ-] *n* : validez *f*

valley ['væli] *n, pl* **-leys** : valle *m*

valor ['vælər] *n* : valor *m*, valentía *f*

value ['væljuː] *n* : valor *m* — ~ *vt* **-ued; -uing** : valorar — **valuable** ['væljuəbəl, 'væljəbəl] *adj* : valioso — **valuables** *npl* : objetos *mpl* de valor

valve ['vælv] *n* : válvula *f*

vampire ['væmˌpaɪr] *n* : vampiro *m*

van ['væn] *n* : furgoneta *f*, camioneta *f*

vandal ['vændəl] *n* : vándalo *m* — **vandalism** ['vændəlˌɪzəm] *n* : vandalismo *m* — **vandalize** ['vændəlˌaɪz] *vt* : destrozar, destruir

vane ['veɪn] *n or* **weather** ~ : veleta *f*

vanguard ['vænˌɡɑrd] *n* : vanguardia *f*

vanilla [vəˈnɪlə, -ˈne-] *n* : vainilla *f*

vanish ['vænɪʃ] *vi* : desaparecer

vanity ['vænəti] *n, pl* **-ties 1** : vanidad *f* **2** *or* ~ **table** : tocador *m*

vantage point ['væntɪdʒ] *n* : posición *f* ventajosa

vapor ['veɪpər] *n* : vapor *m*

variable ['veriəbəl] *adj* : variable — ~ *n* : variable *f* — **variance** ['veriənts] *n* **at** ~ **with** : en desacuerdo con — **variant** ['veriənt] *n* : variante *f* — **variation** [ˌveriˈeɪʃən] *n* : variación *f* — **varied** ['verid] *adj* : variado — **variegated** ['veriəˌɡeɪtəd] *adj* : abigarrado, multicolor — **variety** [vəˈraɪəti] *n, pl* **-ties 1** : variedad *f* **2** ASSORTMENT : surtido *m* **3** SORT : clase *f* — **various** ['veriəs] *adj* : varios, diversos

varnish ['vɑrnɪʃ] *n* : barniz *f* — ~ *vt* : barnizar

vary ['veri] *v* **varied; varying** : variar

vase ['veɪs, 'veɪz, 'vɑz] *n* **1** : jarrón *m* **2** *or* **flower** ~ : florero *m*

vast ['væst] *adj* : vasto, enorme — **vastness** ['væstnəs] *n* : inmensidad *f*

vat ['væt] *n* : cuba *f*

vault[1] ['vɔlt] *vi* LEAP : saltar — ~ *n* : salto *m*

vault[2] *n* **1** DOME : bóveda *f* **2** *or* **bank** ~ : cámara *f* acorazada, bóveda *f* de seguridad *Lat* **3** CRYPT : cripta *f*

VCR [ˌviːˌsiːˈɑr] *(videocassette recorder)* *n* : video *m*

veal ['viːl] *n* : (carne *f* de) ternera *f*

veer ['vɪr] *vi* : virar

vegetable ['vedʒtəbəl, 'vedʒətə-] *adj* : vegetal — ~ *n* **1** : vegetal *m* (planta) **2** ~**s** *npl* : verduras *fpl* — **vegetarian** [ˌvedʒəˈteriən] *n* : vegetariano *mf* — **vegetation** [ˌvedʒəˈteɪʃən] *n* : vegetación *f*

vehemence ['viːəmənts] *n* : vehemencia *f* — **vehement** ['viːəmənt] *adj* : vehemente

vehicle ['viːəkəl, 'viːˌhɪkəl] *n* : vehículo *m*

veil ['veɪl] *n* : velo *m* — ~ *vt* **1** : cubrir con un velo **2** CONCEAL : velar

vein ['veɪn] *n* **1** : vena *f* **2** : veta *f* (de un mineral, etc.)

velocity [vəˈlɑsəti] *n, pl* **-ties** : velocidad *f*

velvet ['vɛlvət] *n* : terciopelo *m* — **velvety** ['vɛlvəti] *adj* : aterciopelado

vending machine ['vendɪŋ-] *vt* : máquina *f* expendedora

vendor ['vɛndər] *n* : vendedor *m*, -dora *f*
veneer [və'nɪr] *n* **1** : chapa *f* **2** FACADE : apariencia *f*
venerable ['vɛnərəbəl] *adj* : venerable — **venerate** ['vɛnə.reɪt] *vt* **-ated; -ating** : venerar — **veneration** [.vɛnə'reɪʃən] *n* : veneración *f*
venereal [və'nɪriəl] *adj* : venéreo
venetian blind [və'ni:ʃən-] *n* : persiana *f* veneciana
Venezuelan [.vɛnə'zweɪlən, -zu'eɪ-] *adj* : venezolano
vengeance ['vɛndʒənts] *n* **1** : venganza *f* **2 take ~ on** : vengarse de — **vengeful** ['vɛndʒfəl] *adj* : vengativo
venison ['vɛnəsən, -zən] *n* : (carne *f* de) venado *m*
venom ['vɛnəm] *n* : veneno *m* — **venomous** ['vɛnəməs] *adj* : venenoso
vent ['vɛnt] *vt* : desahogar — **~** *n* **1** *or* **air ~** : rejilla *f* de ventilación **2** OUTLET : desahogo *m* — **ventilate** ['vɛntəl.eɪt] *vt* **-lated; -lating** : ventilar — **ventilation** [.vɛntəl'eɪʃən] *n* : ventilación *f* — **ventilator** ['vɛntəl.eɪtər] *n* : ventilador *m*
ventriloquist [vɛn'trɪləkwɪst] *n* : ventrílocuo *m*, -cua *f*
venture ['vɛntʃər] *v* **-tured; -turing** *vt* **1** RISK : arriesgar **2** : aventurar (una opinión, etc.) — *vi* : atreverse — **~** *n* *or* **business ~** : empresa *f*
venue ['vɛnju:] *n* : lugar *m*
Venus ['vi:nəs] *n* : Venus *m*
veranda *or* **verandah** [və'rændə] *n* : veranda *f*
verb ['vərb] *n* : verbo *m* — **verbal** ['vərbəl] *adj* : verbal — **verbatim** [vər'beɪtəm] *adv* : palabra por palabra — **~** *adj* : literal — **verbose** [vər'bo:s] *adj* : verboso
verdict ['vərdɪkt] *n* **1** : veredicto *m* **2** OPINION : opinión *f*
verge ['vərdʒ] *n* **1** : borde *m* **2 on the ~ of** : a punto de (hacer algo), al borde de (algo) — **~** *vi* **verged; verging ~ on** : rayar en
verify ['vɛrə.faɪ] *vt* **-fied; -fying** : verificar — **verification** [.vɛrəfə'keɪʃən] *n* : verificación *f*
vermin ['vərmən] *ns & pl* : alimañas *fpl*
vermouth [vər'mu:θ] *n* : vermut *m*
versatile ['vərsətəl] *adj* : versátil — **versatility** [.vərsə'tɪləti] *n* : versatilidad *f*
verse ['vərs] *n* **1** LINE : verso *m* **2** POETRY : poesía *f* **3** : versículo *m* (en la Biblia) — **versed** ['vərst] *adj* **be well ~ in** : ser muy versado en
version ['vərʒən] *n* : versión *f*
versus ['vərsəs] *prep* : versus

vertebra ['vərtəbrə] *n, pl* **-brae** [-.breɪ, -.bri:] *or* **-bras** : vértebra *f*
vertical ['vərtɪkəl] *adj* : vertical — **~** *n* : vertical *f*
vertigo ['vərti.go:] *n, pl* **-goes** *or* **-gos** : vértigo *m*
verve ['vərv] *n* : brío *m*
very ['vɛri] *adv* **1** : muy **2 at the ~ least** : por lo menos **3 the ~ same thing** : la misma cosa **4 ~ much** : mucho **5 ~ well** : muy bien — **~** *adj* **verier; -est 1** PRECISE, SAME : mismo **2** MERE : solo, mero **3 the ~ thing** : justo lo que hacía falta
vessel ['vɛsəl] *n* **1** CONTAINER : recipiente *m* **2** SHIP : nave *f*, buque *m* **3** *or* **blood ~** : vaso *m* sanguíneo
vest ['vɛst] *n* **1** : chaleco *m* **2** *Brit* UNDERSHIRT : camiseta *f*
vestibule ['vɛstə.bju:l] *n* : vestíbulo *m*
vestige ['vɛstɪdʒ] *n* : vestigio *m*
vet ['vɛt] *n* **1 →** veterinarian **2 →** veteran
veteran ['vɛtərən, 'vɛtrən] *n* : veterano *m*, -na *f*
veterinarian [.vɛtərə'nɛriən, .vɛtə'nɛr-] *n* : veterinario *m*, -ria *f* — **veterinary** ['vɛtərə.nɛri] *adj* : veterinario
veto ['vi:to:] *n, pl* **-toes** : veto *m* — **~** *vt* : vetar
vex ['vɛks] *vt* ANNOY : irritar
via ['vaɪə, 'vi:ə] *prep* : por, vía
viable ['vaɪəbəl] *adj* : viable
viaduct ['vaɪə.dʌkt] *n* : viaducto *m*
vial ['vaɪəl] *n* : frasco *m*
vibrant ['vaɪbrənt] *adj* : vibrante — **vibrate** ['vaɪ.breɪt] *vi* **-brated; -brating** : vibrar — **vibration** [vaɪ'breɪʃən] *n* : vibración *f*
vicar ['vɪkər] *n* : vicario *m*, -ria *f*
vicarious [vaɪ'kæriəs, vɪ-] *adj* : indirecto
vice ['vaɪs] *n* : vicio *m*
vice president *n* : vicepresidente *m*, -ta *f*
vice versa [.vaɪsɪ'vərsə, .vaɪs'vər-] *adv* : viceversa
vicinity [və'sɪnəti] *n, pl* **-ties 1** : inmediaciones *fpl* **2 in the ~ of** ABOUT : alrededor de
vicious ['vɪʃəs] *adj* **1** SAVAGE : feroz **2** MALICIOUS : malicioso
victim ['vɪktəm] *n* : víctima *f*
victor ['vɪktər] *n* : vencedor *m*, -dora *f*
victory ['vɪktəri] *n, pl* **-ries** : victoria *f* — **victorious** [vɪk'to:riəs] *adj* : victorioso
video ['vɪdi.o:] *n* : video *m*, vídeo *m Spain* — **~** *adj* : de video — **videocassette** [.vɪdio:kə'sɛt] *n* : videocasete *m* — **videotape** ['vɪdio.teɪp] *n* : video-

cinta f — **~** vt **-taped; -taping** : videograbar

vie ['vaɪ] vi **vied; vying** ['vaɪɪŋ] : competir

Vietnamese [vi̯etnə'miːz, -'miːs] adj : vietnamita

view ['vjuː] n 1 : vista f 2 OPINION : opinión f 3 **come into ~** : aparecer 4 **in ~ of** : en vista de (que) — **~** vt 1 : ver 2 CONSIDER : considerar — **viewer** ['vjuːər] n or **television ~** : televidente mf — **viewpoint** ['vjuːˌpɔɪnt] n : punto m de vista

vigil ['vɪdʒəl] n : vela f — **vigilance** ['vɪdʒələnts] n : vigilancia f — **vigilant** ['vɪdʒələnt] adj : vigilante

vigor or Brit **vigour** ['vɪgər] n : vigor m — **vigorous** ['vɪgərəs] adj 1 : enérgico 2 ROBUST : vigoroso

Viking ['vaɪkɪŋ] n : vikingo m, -ga f

vile ['vaɪl] adj **viler; vilest** 1 : vil 2 REVOLTING : asqueroso 3 TERRIBLE : horrible

villa ['vɪlə] n : casa f de campo

village ['vɪlɪdʒ] n : pueblo m (grande), aldea f (pequeña) — **villager** ['vɪlɪdʒər] n : vecino m, -na f (de un pueblo); aldeano m, -na f (de una aldea)

villain ['vɪlən] n : villano m, -na f

vindicate ['vɪndəˌkeɪt] vt **-cated; -cating** 1 JUSTIFY : justificar

vindictive [vɪn'dɪktɪv] adj : vengativo

vine ['vaɪn] n 1 : enredadera f 2 GRAPEVINE : vid f

vinegar ['vɪnɪgər] n : vinagre m

vineyard ['vɪnjərd] n : viña f, viñedo m

vintage ['vɪntɪdʒ] n 1 : cosecha f (de vino) 2 ERA : época f — **~** adj 1 : añejo (dícese de un vino) 2 CLASSIC : de época

vinyl ['vaɪnəl] n : vinilo m

viola [vi'oːlə] n : viola f

violate ['vaɪəˌleɪt] vt **-lated; -lating** : violar — **violation** [ˌvaɪə'leɪʃən] n : violación f

violence ['vaɪlənts, 'vaɪə-] n : violencia f — **violent** ['vaɪlənt, 'vaɪə-] adj : violento

violet ['vaɪlət, 'vaɪə-] n : violeta f (flor), violeta m (color)

violin [ˌvaɪə'lɪn] n : violín m — **violinist** [ˌvaɪə'lɪnɪst] n : violinista mf — **violoncello** [ˌvaɪələn'tʃeloː, ˌviː-] → **cello**

VIP [ˌviːˌaɪ'piː] n, pl **VIPs** [-'piːz] : VIP mf

viper ['vaɪpər] n : víbora f

virgin ['vərdʒən] n : virgen mf — **~** adj 1 : virgen (dícese de la lana, etc.) 2 CHASTE : virginal — **virginity** [vər'dʒɪnəti] n : virginidad f

virile ['vɪrəl, -ˌaɪl] adj : viril — **virility** [və'rɪləti] n : virilidad f

virtual ['vərtʃʊəl] adj : virtual — **virtually** ['vərtʃʊəli, 'vərtʃəli] adv : prácticamente

virtue ['vərˌtʃuː] n 1 : virtud f 2 **by ~ of** : en virtud de

virtuoso [ˌvərtʃu'oːsoː, -zoː] n, pl **-sos** or **-si** [-ˌsiː, -ˌziː] : virtuoso m, -sa f

virtuous ['vərtʃuəs] adj : virtuoso

virulent ['vɪrələnt, 'vɪrjə-] adj : virulento

virus ['vaɪrəs] n : virus m

visa ['viːzə, -sə] n : visado m, visa f Lat

vis-à-vis [ˌviːzə'viː, -sə-] prep : con respecto a

viscous ['vɪskəs] adj : viscoso

vise ['vaɪs] n : torno m de banco

visible ['vɪzəbəl] adj 1 : visible 2 NOTICEABLE : evidente — **visibility** [ˌvɪzə'bɪləti] n, pl **-ties** : visibilidad f

vision ['vɪʒən] n 1 : visión f 2 **have ~s of** : imaginarse — **visionary** ['vɪʒəˌneri] adj : visionario — **~** n, pl **-ries** : visionario m, -ria f

visit ['vɪzət] vt : visitar — vi 1 : hacer una visita 2 **be ~ing** : estar de visita — **~** n : visita f — **visitor** ['vɪzətər] n 1 : visitante mf 2 GUEST : visita f

visor ['vaɪzər] n : visera f

vista ['vɪstə] n : vista f

visual ['vɪʒuəl] adj : visual — **visualize** ['vɪʒuəˌlaɪz] vt **-ized; -izing** : visualizar

vital ['vaɪtəl] adj 1 : vital 2 CRUCIAL : esencial — **vitality** [vaɪ'tæləti] n, pl **-ties** : vitalidad f, energía f

vitamin ['vaɪtəmən] n : vitamina f

vivacious [və'veɪʃəs, vaɪ-] adj : vivaz, animado

vivid ['vɪvəd] adj : vivo (dícese de colores), vívido (dícese de sueños, etc.)

vocabulary [voˈkæbjəˌleri] n, pl **-laries** : vocabulario m

vocal ['voːkəl] adj 1 : vocal 2 OUTSPOKEN : vociferante — **vocal cords** npl : cuerdas fpl vocales — **vocalist** ['voːkəlɪst] n : cantante mf, vocalista mf

vocation [voˈkeɪʃən] n : vocación f — **vocational** [voˈkeɪʃənəl] adj : profesional

vociferous [voˈsɪfərəs] adj : vociferante, ruidoso

vodka ['vɑdkə] n : vodka m

vogue ['voːg] n 1 : moda f, boga f 2 **be in ~** : estar de moda, estar en boga

voice ['vɔɪs] n : voz f — **~** vt **voiced; voicing** : expresar

void ['vɔɪd] adj 1 INVALID : nulo 2 **~ of** : falto de — **~** n : vacío m — **~** vt : anular

volatile ['vɑlətəl] adj : volátil — **volatility** [ˌvɑlə'tɪləti] n : volatilidad f

volcano [vɑl'keɪnoː] n, pl **-noes** or **-nos** : volcán m — **volcanic** [vɑl'kænɪk] adj : volcánico

volition [voː'lɪʃən] n of one's own ~ : por voluntad propia

volley ['vɑli] n, pl **-leys** 1 : descarga f (de tiros) 2 : torrente m (de insultos, etc.) 3 : volea f (en deportes) — **volleyball** ['vɑliˌbɔl] n : voleibol m

volt ['voːlt] n : voltio m — **voltage** ['voːltɪdʒ] n : voltaje m

voluble ['vɑljəbəl] adj : locuaz

volume ['vɑljəm, -juːm] n : volumen m — **voluminous** [və'luːmənəs] adj : voluminoso

voluntary ['vɑlənˌteri] adj : voluntario — **volunteer** [ˌvɑlən'tɪr] n : voluntario m, -ria f — ~ vt : ofrecer — vi ~ to : ofrecerse a

voluptuous [və'lʌptʃuəs] adj : voluptuoso

vomit ['vɑmət] n : vómito m — ~ v : vomitar

voracious [vɔ'reɪʃəs, və-] adj : voraz

vote ['voːt] n 1 : voto m 2 SUFFRAGE : derecho m al voto — ~ vi **voted; voting** : votar — **voter** ['voːtər] n : votante mf — **voting** ['voːtɪŋ] n : votación f

vouch ['vaʊtʃ] vi ~ for : responder de (algo), responder por (algn) — **voucher** ['vaʊtʃər] n : vale m

vow ['vaʊ] n : voto m — ~ vt : jurar

vowel ['vaʊəl] n : vocal m

voyage ['vɔɪɪdʒ] n : viaje m

vulgar ['vʌlgər] adj 1 COMMON : ordinario 2 CRUDE : grosero, vulgar — **vulgarity** [ˌvʌl'gærəti] n, pl **-ties** : vulgaridad f

vulnerable ['vʌlnərəbəl] adj : vulnerable — **vulnerability** [ˌvʌlnərə'bɪləti] n, pl **-ties** : vulnerabilidad f

vulture ['vʌltʃər] n : buitre m

vying → vie

W

w ['dʌbəlˌjuː] n, pl **w's** or **ws** [-juːz] : w f, vigésima tercera letra del alfabeto inglés

wad ['wɑd] n : taco m (de papel, etc.), fajo m (de billetes)

waddle ['wɑdəl] vi **-dled; -dling** : andar como un pato

wade ['weɪd] v **waded; wading** vi : caminar por el agua — vt or ~ **across** : vadear

wafer ['weɪfər] n : barquillo m

waffle ['wɑfəl] n : gofre m Spain, wafle m Lat

waft ['wɑft, 'wæft] vt : llevar por el aire — vi : flotar

wag ['wæg] v **wagged; wagging** vt : menear — vi : menearse

wage ['weɪdʒ] n or **wages** npl : salario m — ~ vt **waged; waging** ~ **war** : hacer la guerra

wager ['weɪdʒər] n : apuesta f — ~ v : apostar

wagon ['wægən] n 1 CART : carrito m 2 → **station wagon**

waif ['weɪf] n : niño m abandonado

wail ['weɪl] vi : lamentarse — ~ n : lamento m

waist ['weɪst] n : cintura f — **waistline** ['weɪstˌlaɪn] n : cintura f

wait ['weɪt] vi : esperar — vt 1 AWAIT : esperar 2 ~ **tables** : servir a la mesa

— ~ n 1 : espera f 2 **lie in** ~ : estar al acecho — **waiter** ['weɪtər] n : camarero m, mozo m Lat — **waiting room** n : sala f de espera — **waitress** ['weɪtrəs] n : camarera f, moza f Lat

waive ['weɪv] vt **waived; waiving** : renunciar a — **waiver** ['weɪvər] n : renuncia f

wake¹ ['weɪk] vi **woke** ['woːk]; **woken** ['woːkən] or **waked; waking** vi or ~ **up** : despertarse — vt : despertar — ~ n : velatorio m (de un difunto)

wake² n 1 : estela f (de un barco) 2 **in the** ~ **of** : tras, como consecuencia de

waken ['weɪkən] vt : despertar — vi : despertarse

walk ['wɔk] vi 1 : caminar, andar 2 STROLL : pasear 3 **too far to** ~ : demasiado lejos para ir a pie — vt 1 : caminar por 2 : sacar a pasear (a un perro) — ~ n 1 : paseo m 2 PATH : camino m 3 GAIT : andar m — **walker** ['wɔkər] n : paseante mf 2 HIKER : excursionista mf — **walking stick** n : bastón m — **walkout** ['wɔkaʊt] n STRIKE : huelga f — **walk out** vi 1 STRIKE : declararse en huelga 2 LEAVE : salir, irse 3 ~ **on** : abandonar

wall ['wɔl] n : muro m (exterior), pared f (interior), muralla f (de una ciudad)

wallet ['wɑlət] *n* : billetera *f*, cartera *f*
wallflower ['wɔl,flauər] *n* **be a ~**
: comer pavo
wallop ['wɑləp] *vt* : pegar fuerte — **~** *n*
: golpe *m* fuerte
wallow ['wɑlo:] *vi* : revolcarse
wallpaper ['wɔl,peipər] *n* : papel *m* pintado — **~** *vt* : empapelar
walnut ['wɔl,nʌt] *n* : nuez *f*
walrus ['wɔlrəs, 'wɑl-] *n*, *pl* **-rus** *or*
-ruses : morsa *f*
waltz ['wɔlts] *n* : vals *m* — **~** *vi* : valsar
wan ['wɑn] *adj* **wanner; -est** : pálido
wand ['wɑnd] *n* : varita *f* (mágica)
wander ['wɑndər] *vi* **1** : vagar, pasear **2**
STRAY : divagar — *vt* : pasear por —
wanderer ['wɑndərər] *n* : vagabundo
m, **-da** *f* — **wanderlust** ['wɑndər,lʌst] *n*
: pasión *f* por viajar
wane ['wein] *vi* **waned; waning** : menguar — **~** *n* **be on the ~** : estar disminuyendo
want ['wɑnt, 'wɔnt] *vt* **1** DESIRE : querer **2**
NEED : necesitar **3** LACK : carecer de —
~ *n* **1** NEED : necesidad *f* **2** LACK
: falta *f* **3** DESIRE : deseo *m* — **wanting**
['wɑntiŋ, 'wɔn-] *adj* **be ~** : carecer
wanton ['wɑntən, 'wɔn-] *adj* **1** LEWD
: lascivo **2 ~ cruelty** : crueldad *f* despiadada
war ['wɔr] *n* : guerra *f*
ward ['wɔrd] *n* **1** : sala *f* (de un hospital,
etc.) **2** : distrito *m* electoral **3** : pupilo
m, **-la** *f* (de un tutor, etc.) — **~** *vt* **~**
off : protegerse contra — **warden**
['wɔrdən] *n* **1** : guardián *m*, **-diana** *f* **2**
or **game ~** : guardabosque *mf* **3** *or*
prison ~ : alcaide *m*
wardrobe ['wɔrd,ro:b] *n* **1** CLOSET : armario *m* **2** CLOTHES : vestuario *m*
warehouse ['wær,haus] *n* **1** : almacén *m*,
bodega *f* *Lat* — **wares** ['wærz] *npl*
: mercancías *fpl*
warfare ['wɔr,fær] *n* : guerra *f*
warily ['wærəli] *adv* : cautelosamente
warlike ['wær,laik] *adj* : belicoso
warm ['wɔrm] *adj* **1** : caliente **2** LUKEWARM : tibio **3** CARING : cariñoso **4** I
feel ~ : tengo calor **5 ~ clothes**
: ropa *f* de abrigo — **~** *vt* *or* **~ up**
: calentar — *vi* **1** *or* **~ up** : calentarse
2 ~ to : tomar simpatía a (algn),
entusiasmarse con (algo) — **warm-blooded** ['wɔrm'blʌdəd] *adj* : de sangre caliente — **warmhearted** ['wɔrm-
'hɑrtəd] *adj* : cariñoso — **warmly**
['wɔrmli] *adv* **1** : calurosamente **2**
dress ~ : abrigarse — **warmth**
['wɔrmpθ] *n* **1** : calor *m* **2** AFFECTION
: cariño *m*, afecto *m*

warn ['wɔrn] *vt* : advertir, avisar—
warning ['wɔrniŋ] *n* : advertencia *f*,
aviso *m*
warp ['wɔrp] *vt* **1** : alabear (madera,
etc.) **2** DISTORT : deformar — *vi*
: alabearse
warrant ['wɔrənt] *n* **1** : autorización *f* **2**
arrest ~ : orden *f* judicial — **~** *vt*
: justificar — **warranty** ['wɔrənti,
,wɔrən'ti:] *n*, *pl* **-ties** : garantía *f*
warrior ['wɔriər] *n* : guerrero *m*, **-ra** *f*
warship ['wɔr,ʃip] *n* : buque *m* de guerra
wart ['wɔrt] *n* : verruga *f*
wartime ['wɔr,taim] *n* : tiempo *m* de
guerra
wary ['wæri] *adj* **warier; -est** : cauteloso
was → be
wash ['wɔʃ, 'wɑʃ] *vt* **1** : lavar(se) **2**
CARRY : arrastrar **3 ~ away** : llevarse
4 ~ over : bañar — *vi* : lavarse —
~ *n* **1** : lavado *m* **2** LAUNDRY : ropa *f* sucia
— **washable** ['wɔʃəbəl, 'wɑ-] *adj*
: lavable — **washcloth** ['wɔʃ,klɔθ,
'wɑʃ-] *n* : toallita *f* (para lavarse) —
washed-out ['wɔʃ,aut, 'wɑʃt-] *adj* **1**
: desvaído (dícese de colores) **2** EXHAUSTED : agotado — **washer** ['wɔʃər,
'wɑ-] *n* **1** : arandela *f* (de una llave, etc.) **2**
: arandela *f* (de una llave, etc.) —
washing machine *n* : máquina *f* de
lavar, lavadora *f* — **washroom** ['wɔʃ-
,ru:m, 'wɑʃ-, -,rum] *n* : servicios *mpl*
(públicos), baño *m*
wasn't ['wʌzənt] (*contraction of* **was**
not) → **be**
wasp ['wɑsp] *n* : avispa *f*
waste ['weist] *v* **wasted; wasting** *vt* **1**
: desperdiciar, derrochar, malgastar **2**
~ time : perder tiempo — *vi* *or* **~**
away : consumirse — **~** *adj* : de
desecho — **~** *n* **1** : derroche *m*, desperdicio *m* **2** RUBBISH : desechos *mpl* **3**
a ~ of time : una pérdida de tiempo
— **wastebasket** ['weist,bæskət] *n* : papelera *f* — **wasteful** ['weistfəl] *adj*
: derrochador — **wasteland** ['weist-
,lænd, -lənd] *n* : yermo *m*
watch ['wɑtʃ] *vi* **1** : mirar **2** *or* **keep ~**
: velar **3 ~ out!** : ¡ten cuidado!, ¡ojo!
— *vt* **1** : mirar **2** *or* **~ over** : vigilar,
cuidar **3 ~ what you do** : ten cuidado con lo que haces — **~** *n* **1** : reloj *m*
2 SURVEILLANCE : vigilancia *f* **3** LOOKOUT : guardia *mf* — **watchdog** ['wɑtʃ-
,dɔg] *n* : perro *m* guardián — **watchful**
['wɑtʃfəl] *adj* : vigilante — **watchman**
['wɑtʃmən] *n*, *pl* **-men** [-mən, -,men]
: vigilante *m*, guarda *m* — **watchword**
['wɑtʃ,wərd] *n* : santo *m* y seña
water ['wɔtər, 'wɑ-] *n* : agua *f* — **~** *vt* **1**

: regar (el jardín, etc.) **2 ~ down** DI-
LUTE : diluir, aguar — *vi* **1** : lagrimar
(dícese de los ojos) **2 my mouth is
~ing** : se me hace agua la boca —
watercolor ['wɔt̬ər,kʌlər, 'wɑ-] *n* : acuarela *f* — **watercress** ['wɔt̬ər,krɛs,
'wɑ-] *n* : berro *m* — **waterfall** ['wɔt̬ər-
,fɔl, 'wɑ-] *n* : cascada *f*, salto *m* de agua
— **water lily** *n* : nenúfar *m* — **water-
logged** ['wɔt̬ər,lɔgd, 'wɑt̬ər,lɑgd] *adj*
: lleno de agua, empapado — **watermelon** ['wɔt̬ər,mɛlən, 'wɑ-] *n* : sandía *f*
— **waterpower** ['wɔt̬ər,pauər, 'wɑ-] *n*
: energía *f* hidráulica — **waterproof**
['wɔt̬ər,pruf, 'wɑ-] *adj* : impermeable
— **watershed** ['wɔt̬ər,ʃɛd, 'wɑ-] *n* **1**
: cuenca *f* (de un río) **2** : momento *m*
crítico — **waterskiing** ['wɔt̬ər,skiɪŋ,
'wɑ-] *n* : esquí *m* acuático — **watertight** ['wɔt̬ər,taɪt, 'wɑ-] *adj* : hermético
— **waterway** ['wɔt̬ər,weɪ, 'wɑ-] *n* : vía *f*
navegable — **waterworks** ['wɔt̬ər-
,wərks, 'wɑ-] *npl* : central *f* de abastecimiento de agua — **watery** ['wɔt̬əri,
'wɑ-] *adj* **1** : acuoso **2** DILUTED : aguado, diluido **3** WASHED-OUT : desvaído
(dícese de colores)

watt ['wɑt] *n* : vatio *m* — **wattage** ['wɑt-
,ɪdʒ] *n* : vataje *m* f

wave ['weɪv] *v* **waved; waving** *vi* **1**
: saludar con la mano **2** : flotar (dícese
de una bandera) — *vt* **1** SHAKE : agitar
2 CURL : ondular **3** SIGNAL : hacer
señas a (con la mano) — **~** *n* **1** : ola *f*
(de agua) **2** CURL : onda *f* **3** : onda *f* (en
física) **4** : señal *f* (con la mano) **5**
SURGE : oleada *f* — **wavelength**
['weɪv,lɛŋkθ] *n* : longitud *f* de onda

waver ['weɪvər] *vi* : vacilar

wax[1] ['wæks] *vi* : crecer (dícese de la
luna)

wax[2] *n* : cera *f* (para pisos, etc.) — **~** *vt*
: encerar — **waxy** ['wæksi] *adj* **waxier;
-est** : ceroso

way ['weɪ] *n* **1** : camino *m* **2** MEANS
: manera *f*, modo *m* **3 by the ~** : a
propósito, por cierto **4 by ~ of** : vía,
pasando por **5 come a long ~** : hacer
grandes progresos **6 get in the ~**
: meterse en el camino **7 get one's
own ~** : salirse uno con la suya **8
mend one's ~s** : dejar las malas cos-
tumbres **9 out of the ~** REMOTE : remoto, recóndito **10 which ~ did he
go?** : ¿por dónde fue?

we ['wi] *pron* : nosotros, nosotras

weak ['wik] *adj* **1** : débil **2** DILUTED
: aguado **3 a ~ excuse** : una excusa
poco convincente — **weaken** ['wikən]
vt : debilitar — *vi* : debilitarse —

weakling ['wiklɪŋ] *n* : debilucho *m*,
-cha *f* — **weakly** ['wikli] *adv* : débilmente — **~** *adj* **weaklier; -est** : enfermizo — **weakness** ['wiknəs] *n* **1**
: debilidad *f* **2** FLAW : flaqueza *f*, punto
m débil

wealth ['wɛlθ] *n* : riqueza *f* — **wealthy**
['wɛlθi] *adj* **wealthier; -est** : rico

wean ['win] *vt* : destetar

weapon ['wɛpən] *n* : arma *f*

wear ['wær] *v* **wore** ['wor]; **worn** ['worn];
wearing *vt* **1** : llevar (ropa, etc.),
calzar (zapatos) **2** or **~ away** : desgastar **3 ~ oneself out** : agotarse **4
~ out** : gastar — *vi* **1** LAST : durar **2
~ off** : desaparecer **3 ~ out** : gastarse — **~** *n* **1** USE : uso *m* **2** CLOTHING
: ropa *f* **3 be the worse for ~** : estar
deteriorado — **wear and tear** *n* : desgaste *m*

weary ['wɪri] *adj* **-rier; -est** : cansado —
~ *v* **-ried; -rying** *vt* : cansar — *vi*
: cansarse — **weariness** ['wɪrinəs] *n*
: cansancio *m* — **wearisome** ['wɪri-
səm] *adj* : cansado

weasel ['wizəl] *n* : comadreja *f*

weather ['wɛðər] *n* : tiempo *m* — **~** *vt*
1 WEAR : erosionar, desgastar **2** EN-
DURE, OVERCOME : superar — **weath-
er-beaten** ['wɛðər,bit̬ən] *adj* : curtido
— **weatherman** ['wɛðər,mæn] *n, pl*
-men [-mən, -mɛn] : meteorólogo *m*,
-ga *f* — **weather vane** *n* : veleta *f*

weave ['wiv] *v* **wove** ['wov] *or*
weaved; woven ['wovən] *or* **weaved;
weaving** *vt* **1** : tejer (tela) **2** INTERLACE
: entretejer **3 ~ one's way** : abrirse
camino — *vi* : tejer — **~** *n* : tejido *f*
— **weaver** ['wivər] *n* : tejedor *m*, -dora
f

web ['wɛb] *n* **1** : telaraña *f* (de araña) **2**
: membrana *f* interdigital (de aves) **3**
NETWORK : red *f*

wed ['wɛd] *v* **wedded; wedding** *vt*
: casarse con — *vi* : casarse

we'd ['wid] (*contraction of* **we had, we
should,** *or* **we would**) → **have,
should, would**

wedding ['wɛdɪŋ] *n* : boda *f*, casamiento
m

wedge ['wɛdʒ] *n* **1** : cuña *f* **2** PIECE : porción *f*, trozo *m* — **~** *vt* **wedged;
wedging 1** : apretar (con una cuña) **2**
CRAM : meter

Wednesday ['wɛnz,deɪ, -di] *n* : miércoles *m*

wee ['wi] *adj* **1** : pequeñito **2 in the ~
hours** : a las altas horas

weed ['wid] *n* : mala hierba *f* — **~** *vt* **1**
: desherbar **2 ~ out** : eliminar

week ['wiːk] n : semana f — **weekday** ['wiːkˌdeɪ] n : día m laborable — **weekend** ['wiːkˌɛnd] n : fin m de semana — **weekly** ['wiːkli] adv : semanalmente — ~ adj : semanal — ~ n, pl **-lies** : semanario m

weep ['wiːp] v **wept** ['wɛpt]; **weeping** : llorar — **weeping willow** n : sauce m llorón — **weepy** ['wiːpi] adj **weepier**; **-est** : lloroso

weigh ['weɪ] vt 1 : pesar 2 CONSIDER : sopesar 3 ~ **down** : sobrecargar (con una carga), abrumar (con preocupaciones, etc.) — vi : pesar

weight ['weɪt] n 1 : peso m 2 **gain** ~ : engordar 3 **lose** ~ : adelgazar — **weighty** ['weɪti] adj **weightier**; **-est** 1 HEAVY : pesado 2 IMPORTANT : importante, de peso

weird ['wɪrd] adj 1 : misterioso 2 STRANGE : extraño

welcome ['wɛlkəm] vt **-comed**; **-coming** : dar la bienvenida a, recibir — ~ adj 1 : bienvenido 2 you're ~ : de nada — ~ n : bienvenida f, acogida f

weld ['wɛld] v : soldar

welfare ['wɛlˌfær] n 1 WELL-BEING : bienestar m 2 AID : asistencia f social

well¹ ['wɛl] adv **better** ['bɛtər]; **best** ['bɛst] 1 : bien 2 CONSIDERABLY : bastante 3 **as** ~ : también 4 **as** ~ **as** : además de — ~ adj : bien — ~ interj 1 (used to introduce a remark) : bueno 2 (used to express surprise) : ¡vaya!

well² n : pozo m — ~ vi or ~ **up** : brotar, manar

we'll ['wiːl, wɪl] (contraction of **we shall** or **we will**) → **shall, will**

well-being ['wɛlˈbiːɪŋ] n : bienestar m — **well-bred** ['wɛlˈbrɛd] adj : fino, bien educado — **well-done** ['wɛlˈdʌn] adj 1 : bien hecho 2 : bien cocido (dícese de la carne, etc.) — **well-known** ['wɛlˈnom] adj : famoso, bien conocido — **well-meaning** ['wɛlˈmiːnɪŋ] adj : bienintencionado — **well-off** ['wɛlˈɔf] adj : acomodado — **well-rounded** ['wɛlˈraʊndəd] adj : completo — **well-to-do** [ˌwɛltəˈduː] adj : próspero, adinerado

Welsh ['wɛlʃ] adj : galés — ~ n 1 : galés m (idioma) 2 **the** ~ : los galeses

went → **go**

wept → **weep**

were → **be**

we're ['wɪr, 'wər, 'wiːər] (contraction of **we are**) → **be**

weren't ['wərənt, 'wərnt] (contraction of **were not**) → **be**

west ['wɛst] adv : al oeste — ~ adj : oeste, del oeste — ~ n 1 : oeste m 2 **the West** : el Oeste, el Occidente — **westerly** ['wɛstərli] adv & adj : del oeste — **western** ['wɛstərn] adj 1 : del oeste 2 **Western** : occidental — **Westerner** ['wɛstərnər] n : habitante mf del oeste — **westward** ['wɛstwərd] adv & adj : hacia el oeste

wet ['wɛt] adj **wetter**; **wettest** 1 : mojado 2 RAINY : lluvioso 3 ~ **paint** : pintura f fresca — ~ vt **wet** or **wetted**; **wetting** : mojar, humedecer

we've ['wiːv] (contraction of **we have**) → **have**

whack ['hwæk] vt : golpear fuertemente — ~ n : golpe m fuerte

whale ['hweɪl] n, pl **whales** or **whale** : ballena f

wharf ['hwɔrf] n, pl **wharves** ['hwɔrvz] : muelle m, embarcadero m

what ['hwɑt, 'hwʌt] adj (used in questions and exclamations) : qué 2 WHATEVER : cualquier — ~ pron 1 (used in questions) : qué 2 (used in indirect statements) : lo que, que 3 ~ **does it cost?** : ¿cuánto cuesta? 4 ~ **for?** : ¿por qué? 5 ~ **if** : y si — **whatever** [hwɑtˈɛvər, 'hwʌt-] adj 1 : cualquier 2 **there's no chance** ~ : no hay ninguna posibilidad 3 **nothing** ~ : nada en absoluto — ~ pron 1 ANYTHING : lo que 2 (used in questions) : qué 3 ~ **it may be** : sea lo que sea — **whatsoever** [ˌhwɑtsoˈɛvər, 'hwʌt-] adj & pron → **whatever**

wheat ['hwiːt] n : trigo m

wheedle ['hwiːdəl] vt **-dled**; **-dling** : engatusar

wheel ['hwiːl] n 1 : rueda f 2 or **steering** ~ : volante m (de automóviles, etc.), timón m (de barcos) — ~ vt : empujar (algo sobre ruedas) — vi or ~ **around** : darse la vuelta — **wheelbarrow** ['hwiːlˌbærˌoː] n : carretilla f — **wheelchair** ['hwiːlˌtʃær] n : silla f de ruedas

wheeze ['hwiːz] vi **wheezed**; **wheezing** : resollar — ~ n : resuello m

when ['hwɛn] adv : cuándo — ~ conj 1 : cuando 2 **the days** ~ **I clean the house** : los días (en) que limpio la casa — ~ pron : cuándo — **whenever** [hwɛnˈɛvər] adv : cuando sea — ~ conj 1 : cada vez que 2 ~ **you like** : cuando quieras

where ['hwɛr] adv 1 : dónde 2 ~ **are you going?** : ¿adónde vas? — ~ conj

& *pron* : donde — **whereabouts** ['ʰwerəˌbauts] *adv* : (por) dónde — **~ ns** & *pl* : paradero *m* — **wherever** [ʰwer'evər] *adv* 1 : en cualquier parte 2 WHERE : dónde, adónde — **~** *conj* : dondequiera que

whet ['ʰwet] *vt* **whetted; whetting** 1 : afilar 2 **~ the appetite** : estimular el apetito

whether ['ʰweðər] *conj* 1 : si 2 **we doubt ~ he'll show up** : dudamos que aparezca 3 **~ you like it or not** : tanto si quieras como si no

which ['ʰwitʃ] *adj* 1 : qué, cuál 2 **in ~ case** : en cuyo caso — **~** *pron* 1 (*used in questions*) : cuál 2 (*used in relative clauses*) : que, el (la) cual — **whichever** [ʰwitʃ'evər] *adj* : cualquier — **~** *pron* : el (la) que, cualquiera que

whiff ['ʰwif] *n* 1 PUFF : soplo *m* 2 SMELL : olorcillo *m*

while ['ʰwail] *n* 1 : rato *m* 2 **be worth one's ~** : valer la pena 3 **in a ~** : dentro de poco — **~** *conj* 1 : mientras 2 WHEREAS : mientras que 3 ALTHOUGH : aunque — **~** *vt* **whiled; whiling ~ away the time** : matar el tiempo

whim ['ʰwim] *n* : capricho *m*, antojo *m*

whimper ['ʰwimpər] *vi* : lloriquear— **~** *n* : quejido *m*

whimsical ['ʰwimzikəl] *adj* : caprichoso, fantasioso

whine ['ʰwain] *vi* **whined; whining** 1 : gimotear 2 COMPLAIN : quejarse — **~** *n* : quejido *m*, gemido *m*

whip ['ʰwip] *v* **whipped; whipping** *vt* 1 : azotar 2 BEAT : batir (huevos, crema, etc.) 3 **~ up** AROUSE : avivar, despertar — *vi* FLAP : agitarse — **~** *n* : látigo *m*

whir ['ʰwər] *vi* **whirred; whirring** : zumbar— **~** *n* : zumbido *m*

whirl ['ʰwərl] *vi* 1 : dar vueltas, girar 2 *or* **~ about** : arremolinarse — **~** *n* 1 : giro *m* 2 SWIRL : torbellino *m* — **whirlpool** ['ʰwərlˌpuːl] *n* : remolino *m* — **whirlwind** ['ʰwərlˌwind] *n* : torbellino *m*

whisk ['ʰwisk] *vt* 1 : batir 2 **~ away** : llevarse — **~** *n or* **egg ~** : batidor *m*— **whisk broom** *n* : escobilla *f*

whisker ['ʰwiskər] *n* 1 : pelo *m* (de la barba) 2 **~s** *npl* : bigotes *mpl* (de animales)

whiskey *or* **whisky** ['ʰwiski] *n, pl* **-keys** *or* **-kies** : whisky *m*

whisper ['ʰwispər] *vi* : cuchichear, susurrar — *vt* : susurrar — **~** *n* : susurro *m*

whistle ['ʰwisəl] *v* **-tled; -tling** *vi* 1 : silbar, chiflar *Lat* 2 : pitar (dícese de un tren, etc.) — *vt* : silbar — **~** *n* 1 : silbido *m*, chiflido *m* (sonido) 2 : silbato *m*, pito *m* (instrumento)

white ['ʰwait] *adj* **whiter; -est** : blanco — **~** *n* 1 : blanco *m* (color) 2 : clara *f* (de huevos) 3 *or* **~ person** : blanco *m*, -ca *f* — **white-collar** ['ʰwait'kɑlər] *adj* 1 : de oficina 2 **~ worker** : oficinista *mf* — **whiten** ['ʰwaitən] *vt* : blanquear — **whiteness** ['ʰwaitnəs] *n* : blancura *f* — **whitewash** ['ʰwaitˌwɔʃ] *vt* 1 : enjalbegar 2 CONCEAL : encubrir (un escándalo, etc.) — **~** *n* 1 : jalbegue *m*, lechada *f* 2 COVER-UP : encubrimiento *m*

whittle ['ʰwitəl] *vt* **-tled; -tling** 1 : tallar (madera) 2 *or* **~ down** : reducir

whiz *or* **whizz** ['ʰwiz] *vi* **whizzed; whizzing** 1 BUZZ : zumbar 2 **~ by** : pasar muy rápido — **~** *or* **whizz** *n, pl* **whizzes** : zumbido *m* — **whiz kid** *n* : joven *m* prometedor

who ['huː] *pron* 1 (*used in direct and indirect questions*) : quién 2 (*used in relative clauses*) : que, quien — **whodunit** [huːˈdʌnit] *n* : novela *f* policíaca — **whoever** [huːˈevər] *pron* 1 : quienquiera que, quien 2 (*used in questions*) : quién

whole ['hoːl] *adj* 1 : entero 2 INTACT : intacto 3 **a ~ lot** : muchísimo — **~** *n* 1 : todo *m* 2 **as a ~** : en conjunto 3 **on the ~** : en general — **wholehearted** ['hoːlˈhɑrtəd] *adj* : sincero — **wholesale** ['hoːlˌseil] *n* : venta *f* al por mayor — **~** *adj* 1 : al por mayor 2 **~ slaughter** : matanza *f* sistemática — **~** *adv* : al por mayor — **wholesaler** ['hoːlˌseilər] *n* : mayorista *mf*— **wholesome** ['hoːlsəm] *adj* : sano — **whole wheat** *adj* : de trigo integral — **wholly** ['hoːli] *adv* : completamente

whom ['huːm] *pron* 1 (*used in direct questions*) : a quién 2 (*used in indirect questions*) : de quién, con quién, en quién 3 (*used in relative clauses*) : que, a quien

whooping cough *n* : tos *f* ferina

whore ['hor] *n* : puta *f*

whose ['huːz] *adj* 1 (*used in questions*) : de quién 2 (*used in relative clauses*) : cuyo — **~** *pron* : de quién

why ['ʰwai] *adv* : por qué — **~** *n, pl* **whys** : porqué *m* — **~** *conj* : por qué — **~** *interj* (*used to express surprise*) : ¡vaya!, ¡mira!

wick ['wik] *n* : mecha *f*

wicked ['wikəd] *adj* 1 : malo, malvado 2

MISCHIEVOUS : travieso **3** TERRIBLE : terrible, horrible — **wickedness** ['wɪkədnəs] n : maldad f

wicker ['wɪkər] n : mimbre m — ~ adj : de mimbre

wide ['waɪd] adj **wider; widest 1** : ancho **2** VAST : amplio, extenso **3** or ~ **of the mark** : desviado — ~ adv **1** ~ **apart** : muy separados **2 far and** ~ : por todas partes **3** ~ **open** : abierto de par en par — **wide-awake** ['waɪd'weɪk] adj : (completamente) despierto — **widely** ['waɪdli] adv : extensivamente — **widespread** ['waɪd-'sprɛd] adj : extendido

widow ['wɪdoː] n : viuda f — ~ vt : dejar viuda — **widower** ['wɪdowər] n : viudo m

width ['wɪdθ] n : ancho m, anchura f

wield ['wiːld] vt **1** : usar, manejar **2** EXERT : ejercer

wiener ['wiːnər] → **frankfurter**

wife ['waɪf] n, pl **wives** ['waɪvz] : esposa f, mujer f

wig ['wɪg] n : peluca f

wiggle ['wɪgəl] v **-gled; -gling** vt : menear, contonear — vi : menearse — ~ n : meneo m

wigwam ['wɪg,wɑm] n : wigwam m

wild ['waɪld] adj **1** : salvaje **2** DESOLATE : agreste **3** UNRULY : desenfrenado **4** RANDOM : al azar **5** FRANTIC : frenético **6** OUTRAGEOUS : extravagante — ~ adv **1** → **wildly 2 run** ~ : volver al estado silvestre (dícese de las plantas), desmandarse (dícese de los niños) — **wildcat** ['waɪld,kæt] n : gato m montés — **wilderness** ['wɪldərnəs] n : yermo m, desierto m — **wildfire** ['waɪld,faɪr] n **1** : fuego m descontrolado **2 spread like** ~ : propagarse como un reguero de pólvora — **wildflower** ['waɪld-,flaʊər] n : flor f silvestre — **wildlife** ['waɪld,laɪf] n : fauna f — **wildly** ['waɪldli] adv **1** FRANTICALLY : frenéticamente **2** EXTREMELY : locamente

will[1] ['wɪl] v past **would** ['wʊd]; pres sing & pl **will** vi WISH : querer — v aux **1 tomorrow we** ~ **go shopping** : mañana iremos de compras **2 he** ~ **get angry over nothing** : se pone furioso por cualquier cosa **3 I** ~ **go despite them** : iré a pesar de ellos **4 I won't do it** : no lo haré **5 that** ~ **be the mailman** : eso ha de ser el cartero **6 the couch** ~ **hold three people** : en el sofá cabrán tres personas **7 accidents** ~ **happen** : los accidentes ocurrirán **8 you** ~ **do as I say** : harás lo que digo

will[2] n **1** : voluntad f **2** TESTAMENT : testamento m **3 free** ~ : libre albedrío m — **willful** or **wilful** ['wɪlfəl] adj **1** OBSTINATE : terco **2** INTENTIONAL : intencionado — **willing** ['wɪlɪŋ] adj **1** : complaciente **2 be** ~ **to** : estar dispuesto a — **willingly** ['wɪlɪŋli] adv : con gusto — **willingness** ['wɪlɪŋnəs] n : buena voluntad f

willow ['wɪloː] n : sauce m

willpower ['wɪl,paʊər] n : fuerza f de voluntad

wilt ['wɪlt] vi : marchitarse

wily ['waɪli] adj **wilier; -est** : artero, astuto

win ['wɪn] v **won** ['wʌn]; **winning** vi : ganar — vt **1** : ganar, conseguir **2** ~ **over** : ganarse a — ~ n : triunfo m, victoria f

wince ['wɪnts] vi **winced; wincing** : hacer una mueca de dolor — ~ n : mueca f de dolor

winch ['wɪntʃ] n : torno m

wind[1] ['wɪnd] n **1** : viento m **2** BREATH : aliento m **3** FLATULENCE : flatulencia f **4 get** ~ **of** : enterarse de

wind[2] ['waɪnd] v **wound** ['waʊnd]; **winding** vi : serpentear — vt **1** COIL : enrollar **2** ~ **a clock** : dar cuerda a un reloj

windfall ['wɪnd,fɔl] n : beneficio m imprevisto

winding ['waɪndɪŋ] adj : tortuoso

wind instrument n : instrumento m de viento

windmill ['wɪnd,mɪl] n : molino m de viento

window ['wɪn,doː] n : ventana f (de un edificio o una computadora), ventanilla f (de un vehículo), vitrina f (de una tienda) — **windowpane** ['wɪn,doː,peɪn] n : vidrio m — **windowsill** ['wɪn,doː,sɪl] n : repisa f de la ventana

windpipe ['wɪnd,paɪp] n : tráquea f

windshield ['wɪnd,ʃiːld] n **1** : parabrisas m **2** ~ **wiper** : limpiaparabrisas m

window-shop ['wɪndoː,ʃɑp] vi **-shopped; -shopping** : mirar las vitrinas

wind up ['waɪnd,ʌp] vt : terminar, concluir — vi : terminar, acabar — **windup** n : conclusión f

windy ['wɪndi] adj **windier; -est 1** : ventoso **2 it's** ~ : hace viento

wine ['waɪn] n : vino m — **wine cellar** n : bodega f

wing ['wɪŋ] n **1** : ala f **2 under s.o.'s** ~ : bajo el cargo de algn — **winged** ['wɪŋd, 'wɪŋəd] adj : alado

wink ['wɪŋk] vi : guiñar — ~ n **1** : guiño m **2 not sleep a** ~ : no pegar el ojo

winner ['wɪnər] n : ganador m, -dora f —

winning ['wɪnɪŋ] *adj* 1 : ganador 2 CHARMING : encantador — **winnings** ['wɪnɪŋz] *npl* : ganancias *fpl*

winter ['wɪntər] *n* : invierno *m* — ~ *adj* : invernal, de invierno — **wintergreen** ['wɪntər,griːn] *n* : gaultería *f* — **wintertime** ['wɪntər,taɪm] *n* : invierno *m* — **wintry** ['wɪntri] *adj* **wintrier; -est** : invernal, de invierno

wipe ['waɪp] *vt* **wiped; wiping** 1 : limpiar 2 ~ **away** : enjugar (lágrimas), borrar (una memoria) 3 ~ **out** : aniquilar, destruir — ~ *n* : pasada *f* (con un trapo, etc.)

wire ['waɪr] *n* 1 : alambre *m* 2 : cable *m* (eléctrico o telefónico) 3 TELEGRAM : telegrama *m* — ~ *vt* **-wired; wiring** 1 : instalar el cableado en (una casa, etc.) 2 BIND : atar con alambre 3 TELEGRAPH : enviar un telegrama a — **wireless** ['waɪrləs] *adj* : inalámbrico — **wiring** ['waɪrɪŋ] *n* : cableado *m* — **wiry** ['waɪri] *adj* **wirier; -est** 1 : hirsuto, tieso (dícese del pelo) 2 : esbelto y musculoso (dícese del cuerpo)

wisdom ['wɪzdəm] *n* : sabiduría *f* — **wisdom tooth** *n* : muela *f* de juicio

wise ['waɪz] *adj* **wiser; wisest** 1 : sabio 2 SENSIBLE : prudente — **wisecrack** ['waɪz,kræk] *n* : broma *f*, chiste *m* — **wisely** ['waɪzli] *adv* : sabiamente

wish ['wɪʃ] *vt* 1 : desear 2 ~ **s.o. well** : desear lo mejor a algn — *vi* 1 : pedir (como deseo) 2 **as you** ~ : como quieras — ~ *n* 1 : deseo *m* 2 **best** ~**es** : muchos recuerdos — **wishbone** ['wɪʃ,boːn] *n* : espoleta *f* — **wishful** ['wɪʃfəl] *adj* 1 : deseoso 2 ~ **thinking** : ilusiones *fpl*

wishy-washy ['wɪʃi,wɔʃi, -,wɑʃi] *adj* : insípido, soso

wisp ['wɪsp] *n* 1 : mechón *m* (de pelo) 2 : voluta *f* (de humo)

wistful ['wɪstfəl] *adj* : melancólico

wit ['wɪt] *n* 1 CLEVERNESS : ingenio *m* 2 HUMOR : agudeza *f* 3 **at one's** ~**'s end** : desesperado 4 **scared out of one's** ~**s** : muerto de miedo

witch ['wɪtʃ] *n* : bruja *f* — **witchcraft** ['wɪtʃ,kræft] *n* : brujería *f*, hechicería *f*

with ['wɪð, 'wɪθ] *prep* 1 : con 2 **I'm going** ~ **you** : voy contigo 3 **it varies** ~ **the season** : varía según la estación 4 **the girl** ~ **red hair** : la muchacha de pelo rojo 5 ~ **all his work, the business failed** : a pesar de su trabajo, el negocio fracasó

withdraw [wɪð'drɔ, wɪθ-] *v* **-drew** [-'druː]; **-drawn** [-'drɔn]; **-drawing** *vt* : retirar — *vi* : apartarse — **withdraw-al** [wɪð'drɔəl, wɪθ-] *n* 1 : retirada *f* 2 : abandono (de drogas, etc.) — **withdrawn** [wɪð'drɔn, wɪθ-] *adj* : introvertido

wither ['wɪðər] *vi* : marchitarse

withhold [wɪθ'hoːld, wɪð-] *vt* **-held** [-'held]; **-holding** : retener (fondos), negar (permiso, etc.)

within [wɪð'ɪn, wɪθ-] *adv* : dentro — ~ *prep* 1 : dentro de 2 (*in expressions of distance*) : a menos de 3 (*in expressions of time*) : dentro de, en menos de 4 ~ **reach** : al alcance de la mano

without [wɪð'aʊt, wɪθ-] *adv* **do** ~ : pasar sin algo — ~ *prep* : sin

withstand [wɪθ'stænd, wɪð-] *vt* **-stood** [-'stud]; **-standing** 1 BEAR : aguantar 2 RESIST : resistir

witness ['wɪtnəs] *n* 1 : testigo *mf* 2 EVIDENCE : testimonio *m* 3 **bear** ~ : atestiguar — ~ *vt* 1 SEE : ser testigo de 2 : atestiguar (una firma, etc.)

witticism ['wɪtə,sɪzəm] *n* : agudeza *f*, ocurrencia *f*

witty ['wɪti] *adj* **-tier; -est** : ingenioso, ocurrente

wives → **wife**

wizard ['wɪzərd] *n* 1 : mago *m*, brujo *m* 2 **a math** ~ : un genio de matemáticas

wizened ['wɪzənd, 'wiː-] *adj* : arrugado

wobble ['wɑbəl] *vi* **-bled; -bling** 1 : tambalearse 2 : temblar (dícese de la voz, etc.) — **wobbly** ['wɑbəli] *adj* : cojo

woe ['woː] *n* 1 : aflicción *f* 2 ~**s** *npl* TROUBLES : penas *fpl* — **woeful** ['woːfəl] *adj* : triste

woke, woken → **wake**

wolf ['wʊlf] *n*, *pl* **wolves** ['wʊlvz] : lobo *m*, **-ba** *f* — ~ *vt* or ~ **down** : engullir

woman ['wʊmən] *n*, *pl* **women** ['wɪmən] : mujer *f* — **womanly** ['wʊmənli] *adj* : femenino

womb ['wuːm] *n* : útero *m*, matriz *f*

won → **win**

wonder ['wʌndər] *n* 1 MARVEL : maravilla *f* 2 AMAZEMENT : asombro *m* — ~ *v* : preguntarse — **wonderful** ['wʌndərfəl] *adj* : maravilloso, estupendo

won't ['woːnt] (*contraction of* **will not**) → **will**

woo ['wuː] *vt* 1 COURT : cortejar 2 : buscar el apoyo de (clientes, votantes, etc.)

wood ['wʊd] *n* 1 : madera *f* (materia) 2 FIREWOOD : leña *f* 3 or ~**s** *npl* FOREST : bosque *m* — ~ *adj* : de madera — **woodchuck** ['wʊd,tʃʌk] *n* : marmota *f* de América — **wooded** ['wʊdəd] *adj* : arbolado, boscoso — **wooden** ['wʊdən]

['wʊdən] *adj* : de madera — **wood-pecker** ['wʊd‚pɛkər] *n* : pájaro *m* carpintero — **woodshed** ['wʊd‚ʃɛd] *n* : leñera *f* — **woodwind** ['wʊd‚wɪnd] *n* : instrumento *m* de viento de madera — **woodwork** ['wʊd‚wərk] *n* : carpintería *f*

wool ['wʊl] *n* : lana *f* — **woolen** *or* **woollen** ['wʊlən] *adj* : de lana — ~ *n* 1 : lana *f* (tela) 2 ~**s** *npl* : prendas *fpl* de lana — **woolly** ['wʊli] *adj* **-lier; -est** : lanudo

word ['wərd] *n* 1 : palabra *f* 2 NEWS : noticias *fpl* 3 ~**s** *npl* : letra *f* (de una canción, etc.) 4 **have ~s with** : reñir con 5 **just say the ~** : no tienes que decirlo 6 **keep one's ~** : cumplir su palabra — ~ *vt* : expresar — **word processing** *n* : procesamiento *m* de textos — **word processor** *n* : procesador *m* de textos — **wordy** ['wərdi] *adj* **wordier; -est** : prolijo

wore → wear

work ['wərk] *n* 1 LABOR : trabajo *m* 2 EMPLOYMENT : trabajo *m*, empleo *m* 3 : obra *f* (de arte, etc.) 4 ~**s** *npl* FACTORY : fábrica *f* 5 ~**s** *npl* MECHANISM : mecanismo *m* — ~ *v* **worked** ['wərkt] *or* **wrought** ['rɔt]; **working** *vt* 1 : hacer trabajar (a una persona) 2 : manejar, operar (una máquina, etc.) — *vi* 1 : trabajar 2 FUNCTION : funcionar 3 : surtir efecto (dícese de una droga), resultar (dícese de una idea, etc.) — **worked up** *adj* : nervioso — **worker** ['wərkər] *n* : trabajador *m*, -dora *f*; obrero *m*, -ra *f* — **working** ['wərkɪŋ] *adj* 1 : que trabaja (dícese de personas), de trabajo (dícese de la ropa, etc.) 2 **be in ~ order** : funcionar bien — **working class** *n* : clase *f* obrera — **workingman** ['wərkɪŋ‚mæn] *n*, *pl* **-men** [-mən, -‚mɛn] : obrero *m* — **workman** ['wərkmən] *n*, *pl* **-men** [-mən, -‚mɛn] 1 : obrero *m* 2 ARTISAN : artesano *m* — **workmanship** ['wərkmən‚ʃɪp] *n* : artesanía *f*, destreza *f* — **workout** ['wərk‚aʊt] *n* : ejercicios *mpl* (físicos) — **work out** *vt* 1 DEVELOP : elaborar 2 SOLVE : resolver — *vi* 1 TURN OUT : resultar 2 SUCCEED : lograr, salir bien 3 EXERCISE : hacer ejercicio — **workshop** ['wərk‚ʃɑp] *n* : taller *m* — **work up** *vt* 1 EXCITE : ponerse como loco 2 GENERATE : desarrollar

world ['wərld] *n* : mundo *m* 2 **think the ~ of s.o.** : tener a algn en alta estima — ~ *adj* : mundial, del mundo — **worldly** ['wərldli] *adj* : mundano —

worldwide ['wərld‚waɪd] *adv* : en todo el mundo — ~ *adj* : global, mundial

worm ['wərm] *n* 1 : gusano *m*, lombriz *f* 2 ~**s** *npl* : lombrices *fpl* (parásitos)

worn → wear — worn-out ['wɔrn‚aʊt] *adj* 1 USED : gastado 2 TIRED : agotado

worry ['wəri] *v* **-ried; -rying** *vt* : preocupar, inquietar — *vi* : preocuparse, inquietarse — ~ *n*, *pl* **-ries** : preocupación *f* — **worried** ['wərid] *adj* : preocupado — **worrisome** ['wərisəm] *adj* : inquietante

worse ['wərs] *adv* (*comparative of* **bad** *or of* **ill**) : peor — ~ *adj* (*comparative of* **bad** *or of* **ill**) 1 : peor 2 **from bad to ~** : de mal en peor 3 **get ~** : empeorar — ~ *n* 1 **the ~** : el (la) peor, lo peor 2 **take a turn for the ~** : ponerse peor — **worsen** ['wərsən] *v* : empeorar

worship ['wərʃəp] *v* **-shiped** *or* **-shipped; -shiping** *or* **-shipping** *vt* : adorar — *vi* : practicar una religión — ~ *n* : adoración *f*, culto *m* — **worshiper** *or* **worshipper** ['wərʃəpər] *n* : adorador *m*, -dora *f*

worst ['wərst] *adv* (*superlative of* **ill** *or* *of* **bad** *or* **badly**) : peor — ~ *adj* (*superlative of* **bad** *or of* **ill**) : peor — ~ *n* **the ~** : lo peor, el (la) peor

worth ['wərθ] *n* 1 : valor *m* (monetario) 2 MERIT : mérito *m*, valía *f* 3 **ten dollars' ~ of gas** : diez dólares de gasolina — ~ *prep* 1 **it's ~ $ 10** : vale $ 10 2 **it's ~ doing** : vale la pena haccrlo — **worthless** ['wərθləs] *adj* 1 : sin valor 2 USELESS : inútil — **worthwhile** [wərθ'hwaɪl] *adj* : que vale la pena — **worthy** ['wərði] *adj* **-thier; -est** : digno

would ['wʊd] *past of* **will** 1 **he ~ often take his children to the park** : solía llevar a sus hijos al parque 2 **I ~ go if I had the money** : iría yo si tuviera el dinero 3 **I ~ rather go alone** : preferiría ir sola 4 **she ~ have won if she hadn't tripped** : habría ganado si no hubiera tropezado 5 ~ **you kindly help me with this?** : ¿tendría la bondad de ayudarme con esto? — **would-be** ['wʊd‚biː] *adj* **a ~ poet** : un aspirante a poeta — **wouldn't** ['wʊd-ənt] (*contraction of* **would not**) → **would**

wound[1] ['wuːnd] *n* : herida *f* — ~ *vt* : herir

wound[2] ['waʊnd] → **wind**

wove, woven → weave

wrangle ['ræŋgəl] *vi* **-gled; -gling** : reñir — ~ *n* : riña *f*, disputa *f*

wrap ['ræp] vt **wrapped; wrapping 1** : envolver **2 ~ up** FINISH : dar fin a — **~ n 1** : prenda f que envuelve (como un chal) **2** WRAPPER : envoltura f — **wrapper** ['ræpər] n : envoltura f, envoltorio m — **wrapping** ['ræpɪŋ] n : envoltura f, envoltorio m

wrath ['ræθ] n : ira f, cólera f — **wrathful** ['ræθfəl] adj : iracundo

wreath ['riːθ] n, pl **wreaths** ['riːðz, 'riːθs] : corona f (de flores, etc.)

wreck ['rɛk] n **1** WRECKAGE : restos mpl **2** RUIN : ruina f, desastre m **3 be a nervous ~** : tener los nervios destrozados — ~ vt : destrozar (un automóvil), naufragar (un barco) — **wreckage** ['rɛkɪdʒ] n : restos mpl (de un buque naufragado, etc.), ruinas fpl (de un edificio)

wren ['rɛn] n : chochín m

wrench ['rɛntʃ] vt **1** PULL : arrancar (de un tirón) **2** SPRAIN, TWIST : torcerse — ~ n **1** TUG : tirón m, jalón m **2** SPRAIN : torcedura f **3** or **monkey ~** : llave f inglesa

wrestle ['rɛsəl] vi **-tled; -tling** : luchar — **wrestler** ['rɛsələr] n : luchador m, -dora f — **wrestling** ['rɛsəlɪŋ] n : lucha f

wretch ['rɛtʃ] n : desgraciado m, -da f — **wretched** ['rɛtʃəd] adj **1** : miserable **2 ~ weather** : tiempo m espantoso

wriggle ['rɪɡəl] vi **-gled; -gling** : retorcerse, menearse

wring ['rɪŋ] vt **wrung** ['rʌŋ]; **wringing 1** or **~ out** : escurrir (el lavado, etc.) **2**

TWIST : retorcer **3** EXTRACT : arrancar (información, etc.)

wrinkle ['rɪŋkəl] n : arruga f — ~ v **-kled; -kling** vt : arrugar — vi : arrugarse

wrist ['rɪst] n : muñeca f — **wristwatch** ['rɪst,wɑtʃ] n : reloj m de pulsera

writ ['rɪt] n : orden f (judicial)

write ['raɪt] v **wrote** ['roːt]; **written** ['rɪtən]; **writing** : escribir — **write down** vt : apuntar, anotar — **write off** vt CANCEL : cancelar — **writer** ['raɪtər] n : escritor m, -tora f

writhe ['raɪð] vi **writhed; writhing** : retorcerse

writing ['raɪtɪŋ] n : escritura f

wrong ['rɔŋ] n **1** INJUSTICE : injusticia f, mal m **2** : agravio m (en derecho) **3 be in the ~** : haber hecho mal — ~ adj **wronger** ['rɔŋər]; **wrongest** ['rɔŋəst] **1** : malo **2** UNSUITABLE : inadecuado, inapropiado **3** INCORRECT : incorrecto, equivocado **4 be ~** : no tener razón — ~ adv : mal, incorrectamente — ~ vt **wronged; wronging** : ofender, ser injusto con — **wrongful** ['rɔŋfəl] adj **1** UNJUST : injusto **2** UNLAWFUL : ilegal — **wrongly** ['rɔŋli] adv **1** UNJUSTLY : injustamente **2** INCORRECTLY : mal

wrote → write

wrought iron ['rɔt] n : hierro m forjado

wrung → wring

wry ['raɪ] adj **wrier** ['raɪər]; **wriest** ['raɪəst] : irónico, sardónico (dícese del humor)

XYZ

x n, pl **x's** or **xs** ['ɛksəz] : x f, vigésima cuarta letra del alfabeto inglés

xenophobia [ˌzɛnəˈfoːbiə, ˌziː-] n : xenofobia f

Xmas ['krɪsməs] n : Navidad f

X ray ['ɛks,reɪ] n **1** : rayo m X **2** or **~ photograph** : radiografía f — **x-ray** vt : radiografiar

xylophone ['zaɪlə,foːn] n : xilófono m

y ['waɪ] n, pl **y's** or **ys** ['waɪz] : y f, vigésima quinta letra del alfabeto inglés

yacht ['jɑt] n : yate m

yam ['jæm] n **1** : ñame m **2** SWEET POTATO : batata f, boniato m

yank ['jæŋk] vt : tirar de, jalar Lat — ~ n : tirón m, jalón m Lat

Yankee ['jæŋki] n : yanqui mf

yap ['jæp] vi **yapped; yapping** : ladrar — ~ n : ladrido m

yard ['jɑrd] n **1** : yarda f (medida) **2** COURTYARD : patio m **3** : jardín m (de una casa) — **yardstick** ['jɑrd,stɪk] n **1** : vara f (de medir) **2** CRITERION : criterio m

yarn ['jɑrn] n **1** : hilado m **2** TALE : historia f, cuento m

yawn ['jɔn] vi : bostezar — ~ n : bostezo m

year ['jɪr] n **1** : año m **2 she's ten ~s old** : tiene diez años **3 I haven't seen them in ~s** : hace siglos que no los veo — **yearbook** ['jɪr,bʊk] n : anuario m — **yearling** ['jɪrlɪŋ, 'jərlən] n : animal m menor de dos años — **yearly** ['jɪrli] adv **1** : anualmente **2 three**

times ~ : tres veces al año — **~** *adj* : anual

yearn ['jərn] *vi* : anhelar — **yearning** ['jərnɪŋ] *n* : anhelo *m*, ansia *f*

yeast ['jiːst] *n* : levadura *f*

yell ['jɛl] *vi* : gritar, chillar — *vt* : gritar — **~** *n* : grito *m*, chillido *m*

yellow ['jɛloː] *adj* : amarillo — **~** *n* : amarillo *m* — **yellowish** ['jɛloɪʃ] *adj* : amarillento

yelp ['jɛlp] *n* : gañido *m* — **~** *vi* : dar un gañido

yes ['jɛs] *adv* **1** : sí **2 say ~** : decir que sí — **~** *n* : sí *m*

yesterday ['jɛstərˌdeɪ, -di] *adv* : ayer — **~** *n* **1** : ayer *m* **2 the day before ~** : anteayer

yet ['jɛt] *adv* **1** : aún, todavía **2 has he come ~?** : ¿ya ha venido? **3 not ~** : todavía no **4 ~ more problems** : más problemas aún **5** NEVERTHELESS : sin embargo — **~** *conj* : pero

yield ['jiːld] *vt* **1** PRODUCE : producir **2 the right of way** : ceder el paso — *vi* : ceder — **~** *n* : rendimiento *m*, rédito *m* (en finanzas)

yoga ['joːgə] *n* : yoga *m*

yogurt ['joːgərt] *n* : yogur *m*, yogurt *m*

yoke ['joːk] *n* : yugo *m*

yolk ['joːk] *n* : yema *f* (de un huevo)

you ['juː] *pron* **1** (*used as subject—familiar*) : tú; vos (*in some Latin American countries*); ustedes *pl*; vosotros, vosotras *pl* Spain **2** (*used as subject—formal*) : usted, ustedes *pl* **3** (*used as indirect object—familiar*) : te, les *pl* (se before lo, la, los, las), os *pl* Spain **4** (*used as indirect object—formal*) : lo (Spain sometimes le), la; los (Spain sometimes les), las *pl* **5** (*used after a preposition—familiar*) : ti; vos (*in some Latin American countries*); ustedes *pl*; vosotros, vosotras *pl* Spain **6** (*used after a preposition—formal*) : usted, ustedes *pl* **7 with ~** (*familiar*) : contigo; con ustedes *pl*; con vosotros, con vosotras *pl* Spain **8 with ~** (*formal*) : con usted, con ustedes *pl* **9 ~ never know** : nunca se sabe — **you'd** ['juːd, jud] (*contraction of* you had *or* you would) → **have, would** — **you'll** ['juːl, jul] (*contraction of* you shall *or* you will) → **shall, will**

young ['jʌŋ] *adj* **younger** ['jʌŋgər]; **youngest** [-gəst] **1** : joven **2 my ~er brother** : mi hermano menor **3 she is the ~est** : es la más pequeña **4 the ~** : los jóvenes — **~** *npl* : jóvenes *mfpl* (de los humanos), crías *fpl* (de

los animales) — **youngster** ['jʌŋkstər] *n* : chico *m*, -ca *f*; joven *mf*

your ['jʊr, 'jɔr, jər] *adj* **1** (*familiar singular*) : tu **2** (*familiar plural*) su, vuestro Spain **3** (*formal*) : su **4 on ~ left** : a la izquierda

you're ['jʊr, 'jɔr, jər, 'juːr] (*contraction of* you are) → **be**

yours ['jʊrz, 'jɔrz] *pron* **1** (*belonging to one person—familiar*) : (el) tuyo, (la) tuya, (los) tuyos, (las) tuyas **2** (*belonging to more than one person—familiar*) : (el) suyo, (la) suya, (los) suyos, (las) suyas; (el) vuestro, (la) vuestra, (los) vuestros, (las) vuestras Spain **3** (*formal*) : (el) suyo, (la) suya, (los) suyos, (las) suyas

yourself [jər'sɛlf] *pron, pl* **yourselves** [-'sɛlvz] **1** (*used reflexively—familiar*) : te, se *pl*, os *pl* Spain **2** (*used reflexively—formal*) : se **3** (*used for emphasis*) : tú mismo, tú misma; usted mismo, usted misma; ustedes mismos, ustedes mismas *pl*; vosotros mismos, vosotras mismas *pl* Spain

youth ['juːθ] *n, pl* **youths** ['juːðz, 'juːθs] **1** : juventud *f* **2** BOY : joven *m* **3 today's ~** : los jóvenes de hoy — **youthful** ['juːθfəl] *adj* **1** : juvenil, de juventud **2** YOUNG : joven

you've ['juːv] (*contraction of* you have) → **have**

yowl ['jaʊl] *vi* : aullar — **~** *n* : aullido *m*

yucca ['jʌkə] *n* : yuca *f*

Yugoslavian [ˌjuːgoˈslɑviən] *adj* : yugoslavo

yule ['juːl] *n* CHRISTMAS : Navidad *f* — **yuletide** ['juːlˌtaɪd] *n* : Navidades *fpl*

z ['ziː] *n, pl* **z's** *or* **zs** : z *f*, vigésima sexta letra del alfabeto inglés

zany ['zeɪni] *adj* **-nier; -est** : alocado, disparatado

zeal ['ziːl] *n* : fervor *m*, celo *m* — **zealous** ['zɛləs] *adj* : entusiasta

zebra ['ziːbrə] *n* : cebra *f*

zenith ['ziːnəθ] *n* **1** : cenit *m* (en astronomía) **2** PEAK : apogeo *m*

zero ['ziːroː, 'zɪroː] *n, pl* **-ros** : cero *m*

zest ['zɛst] *n* **1** : gusto *m* **2** FLAVOR : sazón *f*

zigzag ['zɪgˌzæg] *n* : zigzag *m* — **~** *vi* **-zagged; -zagging** : zigzaguear

zinc ['zɪŋk] *n* : cinc *m*, zinc *m*

zip ['zɪp] *v* **zipped; zipping** *vt* *or* **~ up** : cerrar la cremallera de, cerrar el cierre de *Lat* — *vi* SPEED : pasarse volando — **zip code** *n* : código *m* postal — **zipper** ['zɪpər] *n* : cremallera *f*, cierre *m* Lat

zodiac [ˈzoːdiˌæk] *n* : zodíaco *m*
zone [ˈzoːn] *n* : zona *f*
zoo [ˈzuː] *n, pl* **zoos** : zoológico *m*, zoo
m — **zoology** [zoˈɑlədʒi, zuː-] *n* : zoología *f*

zoom [ˈzuːm] *vi* : zumbar, ir volando —
~ *n* **1** : zumbido *m* **2** *or* ~ **lens**
: zoom *m*
zucchini [zuˈkiːni] *n, pl* **-ni** *or* **-nis** : calabacín *m*, calabacita *f Lat*

Common Spanish Abbreviations

SPANISH ABBREVIATION AND EXPANSION		ENGLISH EQUIVALENT	
abr.	abril	Apr.	April
A.C., a.C.	antes de Cristo	BC	before Christ
a. de J.C.	antes de Jesucristo	BC	before Christ
admon., admón.	administración	—	administration
a/f	a favor	—	in favor
ago.	agosto	Aug.	August
Apdo.	apartado (de correos)	—	P.O. box
aprox.	aproximadamente	approx.	approximately
Aptdo.	apartado (de correos)	—	P.O. box
Arq.	arquitecto	arch.	architect
A.T.	Antiguo Testamento	O.T.	Old Testament
atte.	atentamente	—	sincerely
atto., atta.	atento, atenta	—	kind, courteous
av., avda.	avenida	ave.	avenue
a/v	a vista	—	on receipt
BID	Banco Interamericano de Desarrollo	IDB	Interamerican Development Bank
Bo	banco	—	bank
BM	Banco Mundial	—	World Bank
c/, C/	calle	st.	street
C	centígrado, Celsius	C	centigrade, Celsius
C.	compañía	Co.	company
CA	corriente alterna	AC	alternating current
cap.	capítulo	ch., chap.	chapter
c/c	cuenta corriente	—	current account, checking account
c.c.	centímetros cúbicos	cu. cm	cubic centimeters
CC	corriente continua	DC	direct current
c/d	con descuento	—	with discount
Cd.	ciudad	—	city
CE	Comunidad Europea	EC	European Community
CEE	Comunidad Económica Europea	EEC	European Economic Community
cf.	confróntese	cf.	compare
cg.	centígramo	cg	centigram
CGT	Confederación General de Trabajadores *o* del Trabajo	—	confederation of workers, workers' union
CI	coeficiente intelectual *o* de inteligencia	IQ	intelligence quotient
Cía.	compañía	Co.	company
cm.	centímetro	cm	centimeter
Cnel.	coronel	Col.	colonel
col.	columna	col.	column
Col. *Mex*	colonia	—	residential area
Com.	comandante	Cmdr.	commander
comp.	compárese	comp.	compare
Cor.	coronel	Col.	colonel
C.P.	código postal	—	zip code

SPANISH ABBREVIATION AND EXPANSION		ENGLISH EQUIVALENT	
CSF, c.s.f.	coste, seguro y flete	c.i.f.	cost, insurance, and freight
cta.	cuenta	ac., acct.	account
cte.	corriente	cur.	current
c/u	cada uno, cada una	ea.	each
CV	caballo de vapor	hp	horsepower
D.	Don	—	—
Da., D.ª	Doña	—	—
d.C.	después de Cristo	AD	anno Domini (in the year of our Lord)
dcha.	derecha	—	right
d. de J.C.	después de Jesucristo	AD	anno Domini (in the year of our lord)
dep.	departamento	dept.	department
DF, D.F.	Distrito Federal	—	Federal District
dic.	diciembre	Dec.	December
dir.	director, directora	dir.	director
dir.	dirección	—	address
Dña.	Doña	—	—
do.	domingo	Sun.	Sunday
dpto.	departamento	dept.	department
Dr.	doctor	Dr.	doctor
Dra.	doctora	Dr.	doctor
dto.	descuento	—	discount
E, E.	Este, este	E	East, east
Ed.	editorial	—	publishing house
Ed., ed.	edición	ed.	edition
edif.	edificio	bldg.	building
edo.	estado	st.	state
EEUU, EE.UU.	Estados Unidos	US, U.S.	United States
ej.	por ejemplo	e.g.	for example
E.M.	esclerosis multiple	MS	multiple sclerosis
ene.	enero	Jan.	January
etc.	etcétera	etc.	et cetera
ext.	extensión	ext.	extension
F	Fahrenheit	F	Fahrenheit
f.a.b.	franco a bordo	f.o.b.	free on board
FC	ferrocarril	RR	railroad
feb.	febrero	Feb.	February
FF AA, FF.AA.	Fuerzas Armadas	—	armed forces
FMI	Fondo Monetario Internacional	IMF	International Monetary Fund
g.	gramo	g., gm, gr.	gram
G.P.	giro postal	M.O.	money order
gr.	gramo	g., gm, gr.	gram
Gral.	general	Gen.	general
h.	hora	hr.	hour
Hnos.	hermanos	Bros.	brothers
I+D, I & D, I y D	investigación y desarrollo	R & D	research and development
i.e.	esto es, es decir	i.e.	that is
incl.	inclusive	incl.	inclusive, inclusively

SPANISH ABBREVIATION AND EXPANSION		ENGLISH EQUIVALENT	
Ing.	ingeniero, ingeniera	eng.	engineer
IPC	índice de precios al consumo	CPI	consumer price index
IVA	impuesto al valor agregado	VAT	value-added tax
izq.	izquierda	l.	left
juev.	jueves	Thurs.	Thursday
jul.	julio	Jul.	July
jun.	junio	Jun.	June
kg.	kilogramo	kg	kilogram
km.	kilómetro	km	kilometer
km/h	kilómetros por hora	kph	kilometers per hour
kv, kV	kilovatio	kw, kW	kilowatt
l.	litro	l, lit.	liter
Lic.	licenciado, licenciada	—	—
Ltda.	limitada	Ltd.	limited
lun.	lunes	Mon.	Monday
m	masculino	m	masculine
m	metro	m	meter
m	minuto	m	minute
mar.	marzo	Mar.	March
mart.	martes	Tues.	Tuesday
mg.	miligramo	mg	milligram
miérc.	miércoles	Wed.	Wednesday
min	minuto	min.	minute
mm.	milímetro	mm	millimeter
M-N, m/n	moneda nacional	—	national currency
Mons.	monseñor	Msgr.	monsignor
Mtra.	maestra	—	teacher
Mtro.	maestro	—	teacher
N, N.	Norte, norte	N, no.	North, north
n/o	nuestro	—	our
n.º	número	no.	number
N. de (la) R.	nota de (la) redacción	—	editor's note
NE	nordeste	NE	northeast
NN.UU.	Naciones Unidas	UN	United Nations
NO	noroeste	NW	northwest
nov.	noviembre	Nov.	November
N.T.	Nuevo Testamento	N.T.	New Testament
ntra., ntro.	nuestra, nuestro	—	our
NU	Naciones Unidas	UN	United Nations
núm.	número	num.	number
O, O.	Oeste, oeste	W	West, west
oct.	octubre	Oct.	October
OEA, O.E.A.	Organización de Estados Americanos	OAS	Organization of American States
OMS	Organización Mundial de la Salud	WHO	World Health Organization
ONG	organización no gubernamental	NGO	non-governmental organization
ONU	Organización de las Naciones Unidas	UN	United Nations
OTAN	Organización del Tratado del Atlántico Norte	NATO	North Atlantic Treaty Organization

SPANISH ABBREVIATION AND EXPANSION		ENGLISH EQUIVALENT	
p.	página	p.	page
P, P.	padre	Fr.	father
pág.	página	pg.	page
pat.	patente	pat.	patent
PCL	pantalla de cristal líquido	LCD	liquid crystal display
P.D.	post data	P.S.	postscript
p. ej.	por ejemplo	e.g.	for example
PNB	Producto Nacional Bruto	GNP	gross national product
p°	paseo	Ave.	avenue
p.p.	porte pagado	ppd.	postpaid
PP, p.p.	por poder, por poderes	p.p.	by proxy
prom.	promedio	av., avg.	average
ptas., pts.	pesetas		
q.e.p.d.	que en paz descanse	R.I.P.	may he/she rest in peace
R, R/	remite	—	sender
RAE	Real Academia Española	—	
ref., ref.ª	referencia	ref.	reference
rep.	república	rep.	republic
r.p.m.	revoluciones por minuto	rpm.	revolutions per minute
rte.	remite, remitente	—	sender
s.	siglo	c., cent.	century
s/	su, sus	—	his, her, your, their
S, S.	Sur, sur	S, so.	South, south
S.	san, santo	St.	saint
S.A.	sociedad anónima	Inc.	incorporated (company)
sáb.	sábado	Sat.	Saturday
s/c	su cuenta	—	your account
SE	sudeste, sureste	SE	southeast
seg.	segundo, segundos	sec.	second, seconds
sep., sept.	septiembre	Sept.	September
s.e.u.o.	salvo error u omisión	—	errors and omissions excepted
Sgto.	sargento	Sgt.	sergeant
S.L.	sociedad limitada	Ltd.	limited (corporation)
S.M.	Su Majestad	HM	His Majesty, Her Majesty
s/n	sin número	—	no (street) number
s.n.m.	sobre el nivel de mar	a.s.l.	above sea level
SO	sudoeste/suroeste	SW	southwest
S.R.C.	se ruega contestación	R.S.V.P.	please reply
ss.	siguientes	—	the following ones
SS, S.S.	Su Santidad	H.H.	His Holiness
Sta.	santa	St.	Saint
Sto.	santo	St.	saint
t, t.	tonelada	t., tn	ton
TAE	tasa anual efectiva	APR	annual percentage rate
tb.	también	—	also
tel., Tel.	teléfono	tel.	telephone
Tm.	tonelada métrica	MT	metric ton
Tn.	tonelada	t., tn	ton
trad.	traducido	tr., trans., transl.	translated
UE	Unión Europea	EU	European Union
Univ.	universidad	Univ., U.	university

SPANISH ABBREVIATION AND EXPANSION		ENGLISH EQUIVALENT	
UPC	unidad procesadora central	CPU	central processing unit
Urb.	urbanización	—	residential area
v	versus	v., vs.	versus
v	verso	v., ver., vs.	verse
v.	véase	vid.	see
Vda.	viuda	—	widow
v.g., v.gr.	verbigracia	e.g.	for example
vier., viern.	viernes	Fri.	Friday
V.M.	Vuestra Majestad	—	Your Majesty
V^oB^o, V.^oB.^o	visto bueno	—	OK, approved
vol., vol.	volumen	vol.	volume
vra., vro.	vuestra, vuestro	—	your

Spanish Numbers

Cardinal Numbers

1	uno	28	veintiocho
2	dos	29	veintinueve
3	tres	30	treinta
4	cuatro	31	treinta y uno
5	cinco	40	cuarenta
6	seis	50	cincuenta
7	siete	60	sesenta
8	ocho	70	setenta
9	nueve	80	ochenta
10	diez	90	noventa
11	once	100	cien
12	doce	101	ciento uno
13	trece	200	doscientos
14	catorce	300	trescientos
15	quince	400	cuatrocientos
16	dieciséis	500	quinientos
17	diecisiete	600	seiscientos
18	dieciocho	700	setecientos
19	diecinueve	800	ochocientos
20	veinte	900	novecientos
21	veintiuno	1,000	mil
22	veintidós	1,001	mil uno
23	veintitrés	2,000	dos mil
24	veinticuatro	100,000	cien mil
25	veinticinco	1,000,000	un millón
26	veintiséis	1,000,000,000	mil millones
27	veintisiete	1,000,000,000,000	un billón

Ordinal Numbers

1st	primero, -ra	17th	decimoséptimo, -ma
2nd	segundo, -da	18th	decimoctavo, -va
3rd	tercero, -ra	19th	decimonoveno, -na; or
4th	cuarto, -ta		decimonono, -na
5th	quinto, -ta	20th	vigésimo, -ma
6th	sexto, -ta	21st	vigésimoprimero,
7th	séptimo, -ta		vigésimaprimera
8th	octavo, -ta	30th	trigésimo, -ma
9th	noveno, -na	40th	cuadragésimo, -ma
10th	décimo, -ma	50th	quincuagésimo, -ma
11th	undécimo, -ca	60th	sexagésimo, -ma
12th	duodécimo, -ma	70th	septuagésimo, -ma
13th	decimotercero, -ra	80th	octogésimo, -ma
14th	decimocuarto, -ta	90th	nonagésimo, -ma
15th	decimoquinto, -ta	100th	centésimo, -ma
16th	decimosexto, -ta	1,000th	milésimo, -ma

English Numbers

Cardinal Numbers

1	one	20	twenty
2	two	21	twenty-one
3	three	30	thirty
4	four	40	forty
5	five	50	fifty
6	six	60	sixty
7	seven	70	seventy
8	eight	80	eighty
9	nine	90	ninety
10	ten	100	one hundred
11	eleven	101	one hundred and one
12	twelve	200	two hundred
13	thirteen	1,000	one thousand
14	fourteen	1,001	one thousand and one
15	fifteen	2,000	two thousand
16	sixteen	100,000	one hundred thousand
17	seventeen	1,000,000	one million
18	eighteen	1,000,000,000	one billion
19	nineteen	1,000,000,000,000	one trillion

Ordinal Numbers

1st	first	16th	sixteenth
2nd	second	17th	seventeenth
3rd	third	18th	eighteenth
4th	fourth	19th	nineteenth
5th	fifth	20th	twentieth
6th	sixth	21st	twenty-first
7th	seventh	30th	thirtieth
8th	eighth	40th	fortieth
9th	ninth	50th	fiftieth
10th	tenth	60th	sixtieth
11th	eleventh	70th	seventieth
12th	twelfth	80th	eightieth
13th	thirteenth	90th	ninetieth
14th	fourteenth	100th	hundredth
15th	fifteenth	1,000th	thousandth